THE APOSTOLIC FATHERS

Ancient Literature *for* New Testament Studies

VOLUME 4

THE APOSTOLIC FATHERS

PAUL FOSTER, EDITOR

CRAIG A. EVANS AND CECILIA WASSÉN, SERIES EDITORS

ADELA YARBRO COLLINS, JOHN J. COLLINS, AND GRANT MACASKILL, CONSULTING EDITORS

NATHAN C. JOHNSON, MANAGING EDITOR

ZONDERVAN ACADEMIC

ZONDERVAN ACADEMIC

The Apostolic Fathers

Published by Zondervan, 3950 Sparks Drive SE, Suite 101, Grand Rapids, MI 49546, USA. Zondervan is a registered trademark of The Zondervan Corporation, L.L.C., a wholly owned subsidiary of HarperCollins Christian Publishing, Inc.

Requests for information should be addressed to customercare@harpercollins.com.

Zondervan titles may be purchased in bulk for educational, business, fundraising, or sales promotional use. For information, please email SpecialMarkets@Zondervan.com.

Library of Congress Cataloging-in-Publication Data

Names: Foster, Paul editor
Title: The Apostolic Fathers / Paul Foster, editor ; Craig A. Evans and Cecilia Wassén, series editors .
Description: Grand Rapids, Michigan : Zondervan Academic, [2025] | Series: Ancient literature for New Testament studies | Includes bibliographical references and index.
Identifiers: LCCN 2025025151 (print) | LCCN 2025025152 (ebook) | ISBN 9780310495635 hardcover | ISBN 9780310495642 ebook
Subjects: LCSH: Apostolic Fathers | Christian literature, Early--Greek authors--History and criticism
Classification: LCC BR60.A65 A64 2025 (print) | LCC BR60.A65 (ebook) | DDC 270.1--dc23/eng/20250820
LC record available at https://lccn.loc.gov/2025025151
LC ebook record available at https://lccn.loc.gov/2025025152

HarperCollins Publishers, Macken House, 39/40 Mayor Street Upper, Dublin 1, D01 C9W8, Ireland (https://www.harpercollins.com)

Cover design: Brian Bobel
Cover art: © Stig Alenas / Shutterstock
Interior design: Kait Lamphere

Printed in the United States of America

25 26 27 28 29 LBC 5 4 3 2 1

CONTENTS

SERIES PREFACE

The several volumes that make up the Ancient Literature for New Testament Studies series provide introductions to the diverse bodies of literatures that are in various ways cognate to biblical literature, especially to the New Testament. These volumes have been written to serve the needs of advanced students who aspire to become New Testament interpreters, as well as the needs of veteran scholars who lack expertise in some of the fields these volumes treat.

The last two generations have witnessed the discovery and publication of a remarkable amount of ancient literature that in various ways is relevant to New Testament interpretation. Scholarly research has made it abundantly clear that much of this material proves to be contextually and exegetically helpful in the interpretation of the writings that make up the New Testament. But the sheer magnitude and diversity of this material have also proven to be intimidating to many students. Indeed, there are many scholars and teachers of biblical literature who are not sure exactly what makes up this literature, how it is relevant, and how it is to be accessed. It is the purpose of Ancient Literature for New Testament Studies to address this challenge.

The editors and contributors believe that if one is to interpret New Testament literature in full context, one must know something of these diverse writings and their relevance for the New Testament. Some of these writings are vital for understanding the literature of the New Testament, some much less so. But all are referred to in scholarly discourse. Thus, intelligent reading of New Testament scholarship more broadly requires familiarity with these writings.

The general editors are grateful to the many contributors and volume editors who have made this important work possible. We are also grateful to our colleagues at Zondervan Academic, and we thank our consulting editors Adela Yarbro Collins, John J. Collins, and Grant Macaskill.

Craig A. Evans
Cecilia Wassén

EDITOR'S PREFACE

The growth and developments in the early Jesus movement in the second century remains opaque. This is especially the case for the first half of that period. The chief exceptions are several of the writings that now constitute the collection of texts known as the Apostolic Fathers. As is frequently noted, this is an artificial and primarily modern collection of texts. These writings stem from several different authors, they were written in various locations, and the concerns and theological understandings they exhibit reveal different perspectives of the faith about which they speak. Yet despite these observable differences, they reveal much about nascent Christianity in the second century and perhaps, in some cases, into the third century. Neither individually nor even collectively do these writing permit a holistic reconstruction of Christianity in the period. Instead, what they provide is a collection of unrivaled snapshots into moments in the emergence and continued development of the Jesus movement at certain points during the second century.

For instance, the text known as 1 Clement reflects the connectedness of certain Christian communities and a shared repository of authoritative texts. This lengthy text written from Rome to the gathering of believers in Corinth challenges some of the recent happenings in Corinth, wherein younger men had displaced long-term leaders. Examples of jealousy and false behavior are drawn from various of the Jewish scriptural writings, as well as Paul's letter known as 1 Corinthians addressed to the same city. The fact that a group of believers in the distant city of Rome felt able to address those fellow believers in Corinth about an internal matter of church order reveals something of the interconnectedness of early Christ believers and their shared committed to certain scriptural texts. Likewise, Polycarp's *To the Philippians* provides advice from a church leader in Smyrna in the Roman province of Asia to a group of believers in the city of Philippi. In this case, it appears that the Philippian Christians had requested Polycarp's guidance, ostensibly on the topic of righteousness. However, as one reads the contents of the letter it becomes apparent that there were some specific issues, such as the presbyter Valens apparently abusing his position by using group funds for his own benefit, as well as young males engaging in practices that were not seen as exemplifying righteousness.

Alongside these cordial interventions stands the seven-letter collection of the writings of Ignatius. Perhaps written in the space of only a few weeks, these texts are remarkable for what they reveal about five early Jesus communities in the Roman province of Asia, as well as the personal concerns of Ignatius expressed to believers in the distant imperial capital of Rome. These letters reflect Ignatius's perception of challenges faced by the communities he addresses. With a directness not found in 1 Clement or Polycarp's *To the Philippians*, Ignatius praises, challenges, and even berates these groups of Christians in relation to their beliefs, their acceptance of teachings contrary to his understanding of the faith, the treatment of leaders in these groups, and the manner in which the Eucharist is understood or practiced without authorization from the *episkopos* or "bishop" of the community. These letters are a tour de force. Yet, for all their uncompromising rhetoric, there are moments of genuine pastoral sensitivity directed toward those communities being addressed. Given that these seven letters were written while Ignatius was being transported to Rome to be executed, they reflect both a confidence of faith but a fragility of existence that was at times part of the experience of the early Christian movement.

These are just three of the better-known texts that constitute what has become a fairly standard collection of eleven texts (with Ignatius's seven letters counted as a single entry) in the corpus of the writings of the Apostolic Fathers. In many ways, it is the intermixing of diversity of views and situations alongside some examples of shared beliefs and similar community structures that best reflects second-century Christianity, especially in the early decades. This was a movement continuing to form its identity, to define its structures, and to articulate its core beliefs. It was a time of energy and anxiety. Despite the paucity of source material, the writings of the Apostolic Fathers provide unparalleled insights into that formative period of the nascent Christian movement.

The purposes of this volume are chiefly twofold. First, to provide readers with greater awareness and access to the writings of the Apostolic Fathers. Paradoxically, the aim is not that readers should focus on what is written in these pages. Rather, it is that they might turn to the writings of the Apostolic Fathers themselves and, in so doing, allow themselves to hear anew words written by ancient believers that, although distant from our own times, are yet surprisingly familiar, reflecting very human concerns coupled with the desire for a deeper faith. The second purpose is to make readers aware of the major scholarly issues that surround these texts. These include the state of the surviving manuscripts for each writing, debates concerning authorship, date and location of each writing, and setting out alternative interpretations of the texts themselves. Additionally, there is discussion of how these writings relate to those writings that would later, in a period after the writing of the Apostolic Fathers, become known as the New Testament. This is undertaken in two ways. First, the contributors look for examples of literary dependence on the Gospels, letters, or other writings that would form the New Testament. Second, they consider how the expression of key beliefs, understanding of the faith, or the structures of early Christian communities both drew on and yet also developed ideas found in New Testament texts.

After the introduction, the volume is arranged in two parts. In the first part the eleven writings that constitute the Apostolic Fathers are discussed individually. There is a common structure to each of these chapters in order to facilitate ease of use. However, this structure is not imposed or followed in a wooden fashion. Rather, the texts themselves dictate where the emphasis is placed since they differ in length, structure, and contents. In the second part, the authors take a more synthetic approach. These essays range across the entire corpus of the writings of the Apostolic Fathers in relation to key topics such as Christology, soteriology, ecclesiology, eschatology, women and gender, ethics and education, martyrdom, and the use of New Testament writings. Here the contributors assemble for readers a comparative understanding of key ideas expressed in the writings of the Apostolic Fathers. In both parts, the various authors, who are leading experts in the field, bring their deep learning and decades of scholarship to bear on these ancient texts. The result is not only a superb overview of these perennially fascinating texts, but in all cases they offer genuinely new and cutting-edge scholarly insights. In this sense the present volume is far more than an introduction or a statement of the current state of research on the Apostolic Fathers. Instead, it represents a truly groundbreaking contribution to the study of these texts, with new insights that advance the field of scholarship in important and highly significant ways. As such, it takes the study of these texts further forward and suggests new ways in which the continuous task of scholarship into early Christianity might progress in the coming decades.

Collaborating with the various contributors to this volume has been a constant joy and privilege. Often, existing friendships and partnerships have been deepened, while at other times new friendships have been formed. This is a reminder that at its best academic scholarship is a joint enterprise, spans the globe, and is enriched by listening to others and being willing to learn from the insights of others. Personally, it has been that process of listening and learning from fellow contributors that has been the most pleasurable aspect of this process. All the value and the strengths of this volume belong to those contributors who have drawn on their own deep scholarly studies to share their insights in such a clear, ordered, and readable manner. It is also right to acknowledge the series editors Craig A. Evans and Cecilia Wassén. The vision for the volumes for the Ancient Literature for New Testament Studies (ALNTS) series was largely due to Craig Evans. Cecilia Wassén has helped at various points in bringing this volume to completion, and for that I am truly grateful. The team at Zondervan has been amazing and remarkable. Various people have been incredibly generous with their time, hospitality, and professionalism. It is only fitting to acknowledge Katya Covrett, now vice president and publisher of Zondervan Academic. Her encouragement and ability to keep the series progressing in a positive and timely manner is a testament to her many skills. Also, the contribution of Christopher Beetham, senior editor at Zondervan Academic, has been truly magnificent. He is the type of copyeditor for which any author can only hope. Being an expert in the area of New Testament studies, he brings deep knowledge of the field to the table as well as an awareness of ancient languages. Coupled with this, he has a keen and accurate eye for detail. This volume is much stronger and has fewer typographical errors due to his careful work.

So, with thanks expressed to contributors, series editors, and the team at Zondervan Academic, all that is left is to thank the readers of this volume. Its success will not be measured by reviews, favorable or otherwise, but by the outcome that you set this volume aside and read the writings of a motley and unlikely assemblage of second-century writers. There were significant differences between these ancient authors, but they shared one common goal. That was that they might encourage those who read their works to grow and remain steadfast in the faith they expressed in Jesus. History, and perhaps even the appearance of this volume, suggests that their desire was achieved. However, at the time they wrote these texts, the authors now known as the Apostolic Fathers faced challenging circumstances and a precarious existence. Perhaps in the end that is the legacy they leave to contemporary readers: that through the uncertainties and vicissitudes of life, remaining firm in one's beliefs, values, and ethical behavior is the best response in an uncertain world.

Paul Foster
School of Divinity, University of Edinburgh
Ascension Day, 2025

CONTRIBUTORS

Brian J. Arnold serves as Senior Pastor of First Baptist Church Paducah in western Kentucky. Before this, he served for eight years at Phoenix Seminary as Professor of Theology and Church History, the last four of which he served as President. He has authored two books, *Justification in the Second Century* (2017) and *Cyprian of Carthage: His Life and Impact* (2017), as well as numerous articles.

Michael F. Bird is Deputy Principal and Lecturer in New Testament at Ridley College in Melbourne, Australia (Australian University of Theology). His publications include *The Cambridge Companion to the Apostolic Fathers* (coeditor, 2021) and *Jesus Among the Gods: Early Christology in the Greco-Roman World* (2022), *A Bird's Eye-View of Luke and Acts* (2023), and *An Anomalous Jew: Paul Among Jews, Greeks, and Romans* (2016). The primary focus of his work has been the New Testament, Christian origins, and Christian theology.

Paul Foster is Professor of New Testament and Early Christianity in the School of Divinity at the University of Edinburgh. His work focuses on the emergence of the Jesus movement in the first two centuries of the common era. His publications include *The Apocryphal Gospels: A Very Short Introduction* (2009), *The Gospel of Peter: Introduction, Critical Edition and Commentary* (2010), and *Colossians* in Black's New Testament Commentaries (2016). He has written extensively on the Apostolic Fathers, including editing *The Writings of the Apostolic Fathers* (2007). He is a series editor of the Oxford Apostolic Fathers, which provides critical editions and commentaries on those texts.

Andrew Gregory is Chaplain at University College, Oxford. He is author of *The Gospel According to the Hebrews and the Gospel of the Ebionites* (2017), *The Reception of Luke and Acts in the Period Before Irenaeus* (2003), and chapters and articles on the New Testament and other early Christian literature. His edited books include *The Reception of the New Testament in the Apostolic Fathers* (2005) and *Trajectories Through the New Testament and the Apostolic Fathers* (2005). He is a series editor of the Oxford Early Christian Gospel Texts and Oxford Apostolic Fathers.

Mark Grundeken is (extracurricular) Professor of New Testament and Early Christian Literature in the Faculty of Theology at the University of Freiburg (Germany), Head of Independent Junior Research Group in the Heisenberg Program of the German Research Foundation (DFG), and Speaker of the Young Academy of the Heidelberg Academy of Sciences and Humanities. His research focuses on the letter to the Ephesians in the context of ancient philosophical discourse; on the Apostolic Fathers, especially the Shepherd of Hermas; and on early Christian commentarial techniques in the first two centuries of the common era. His publications include *Community Building in the Shepherd of Hermas: A Critical Study of Some Key Aspects* (2015), *Der eine Gott, der durch alle ist: Epheser 4,6* *im Kontext antiker Diskurse über Gott und die Welt* (2020), and the edited volume (with Henk Jan de Jonge, John Kloppenborg, and Christopher Tuckett) *The Gospels and Their Receptions: Festschrift Joseph Verheyden* (2022).

Scott Harrower is Lecturer in Early Christianity and Theology at Ridley College, Melbourne, Australia (Australian University of Theology). His work focuses on the development of Christian hagiographical media and theology between 200–1100 CE. His publications include *Trauma and Recovery in Early North African Christianity* (2024). He is the coeditor of the *Cambridge Companion to the Apostolic Fathers* (2019) as well as Baylor University Press's forthcoming *Second-Century Christianity: A Sourcebook.*

Paul Hartog is Professor of Theology at Faith Baptist Theological Seminary. His research primarily focuses on the Apostolic Fathers and second-century Christianity. He is the author of *Polycarp and the New Testament* (2002), *Polycarp's Epistle to the Philippians and the Martyrdom of Polycarp* (2013), and *Calvin on the Death of Christ* (2021). He also served as the editor of *The Contemporary Church and the Early Church* (2009) and *Orthodoxy and Heresy in Early Christian Contexts* (2015).

Clayton N. Jefford is Professor of Scripture at Saint Meinrad Seminary and School of Theology in St. Meinrad, Indiana. Though he teaches New Testament studies in general and Gospels specifically, he is most widely known for research in the Apostolic Fathers. Among his publications are *The Sayings of Jesus in the Teaching of the Twelve Apostles* (1989), *Reading the Apostolic Fathers* (1996; 2012 [2nd ed.]), *The Apostolic Fathers and the New Testament* (2006), and *The Epistle to Diognetus (with the Fragment of Quadratus)* (2013), as well as six other edited volumes. He has also served as coeditor of the online journal *Foundations and Facets Forum* (2013–2021) and President of the North American Patristics Society (2021–2022).

James A. Kelhoffer is Professor of New Testament Studies in the Faculty of Theology at Uppsala University in Sweden. He has written numerous research monographs. His first book *Miracle and Mission* (2000) was a study of the message of the longer ending of Mark. Next came a groundbreaking study titled *The Diet of John the Baptist* (2005), a multifaceted study on the traditions surrounding the locusts and wild-honey tradition in Synoptic and patristic interpretation. Two further influential monographs followed, *Persecution, Persuasion and Power* (2010), studying the value of withstanding persecution as a means of identity formation, and *Conceptions of "Gospel" and Legitimacy in Early Christianity* (2014), which gathered sixteen revised and updated articles on these intertwined topics. Currently he is writing the Hermeneia commentary on Second Clement.

Michael J. Kruger is the Samuel C. Patterson Professor of New Testament and Early Christianity at Reformed Theological Seminary in Charlotte, North Carolina. He has written extensively on the emergence and development of the New Testament canon and also on the transmission of the New Testament text. Some publications include *Christianity at the Crossroads: How the Second Century Shaped the Future of the Church* (2018), *The Question of Canon: Challenging the Status Quo in the New Testament Debate* (2013), *The Early Text of the New Testament* (2012), and *Gospel Fragments* (2009).

David Lincicum is Associate Professor of Christianity and Judaism in Antiquity at the University of Notre Dame. He works at the intersection of early Jewish, early Christian, and New Testament studies. He is the author of *Paul and the Early Jewish Encounter with Deuteronomy* (2010; repr. 2013), which won a Manfred Lautenschlaeger Award for theological promise, and of *The Commentarial Impulse: Interpretation and Actualization in the Pauline Tradition* (2025). He is currently working on an edition, translation, and commentary for the Epistle of Barnabas.

Teresa Morgan is McDonald Agape Professor of New Testament and Early Christianity at Yale University. Her research centers on the history of ideas and mentality across ancient history, the New Testament, and early Christian studies. She has written widely on ancient Greek, Roman, and Christian education (*Literate Education in the Hellenistic and Roman Worlds* [1998]), ancient Mediterranean ethics (*Popular Morality in the Early Roman Empire* [2007]), and Paul and is currently finishing a four-volume study of the history and theology of early Christian faith: *Roman Faith and Christian Faith* (2015), *The New Testament and the Theology of Trust* (2022), *Trust in Atonement* (2024), and *Faith in the Making* (forthcoming).

Carolyn Osiek is Professor Emerita of New Testament from Brite Divinity School, Texas Christian University, and previously Professor of New Testament at Catholic Theological Union, Chicago. Her dissertation topic was *Rich and Poor in the Shepherd of Hermas*, and she continued her interest in the text as author of the Hermeneia commentary on the Shepherd of Hermas. She has also published widely on women and social context in early Christianity, including *Ordained Women in the Early Church: A Documentary History*, with Kevin Madigan (2005), and *A Woman's Place: House Churches in Earliest Christianity*, with Margaret Y. MacDonald and Janet Tulloch (2006).

Clare K. Rothschild is Professor of Scripture Studies at Lewis University (USA) and Professor Extraordinary, Department of Ancient Studies at Stellenbosch University (South Africa). Her main research interests are Luke-Acts, the Muratorian fragment, and the Apostolic Fathers. She spent a year as Humboldt Fellow in Munich researching her book, *Hebrews as Pseudepigraphon* (2009), on the Pauline attribution of this early Christian text. Her current research focuses on the Epistle of Barnabas, on which she is preparing a commentary for the Hermeneia series. She serves as general editor of *Early Christianity* as well as the SBL series Writings from the Greco-Roman World.

Gregory Vall is Professor of Scripture at Notre Dame Seminary, New Orleans. He is the author of *Ecclesial Exegesis: A Synthesis of Ancient and Modern Approaches to Scripture* (2022), and *Learning Christ: Ignatius of Antioch and the Mystery of Redemption* (2013). These two titles indicate his primary areas of scholarly interest and expertise.

William Varner is Professor of Biblical Studies at The Master's University in Santa Clarita, California. He is the author of over twenty books and a hundred journal articles. His interest in the Apostolic Fathers is shown in his commentaries on the Didache and on Second Clement, and in his monograph, *The Apostolic Fathers: An Introduction and Translation* (2023).

Joseph Verheyden is Emeritus Professor of New Testament in the Faculty of Theology and Religious Studies at the University of Leuven. His research interests include the Synoptic Gospels and Acts, early Christian apocrypha, the reception history of the New

Testament in the early church, second-century Christianity, and the spread of Christianity in the Greco-Roman world. Recent publications include several coedited volumes: *The Composition, Theology, and Early Reception of Matthew's Gospel* (2022, with J. Schröter and D. C. Sim); *From Protology to Eschatology: Competing Views on the Origin and the End of the Cosmos in Platonism and Christian Thought* (2022, with G. Roskam and G. Van Riel); *The Synoptic Problem 2022* (2023, with O. Andrejevs et al.); *Procopius the Christian Sophist: Catenist, Compiler, Epitomist* (2024, with D. Zaganas and J.-M. Auwers).

ABBREVIATIONS

ABD	*Anchor Bible Dictionary*. Edited by David Noel Freedman. 6 vols. New York: Doubleday, 1992
AFCS	Apostolic Fathers Commentary Series
AGJU	Arbeiten zur Geschichte des antiken Judentums und des Urchristentums
AIPHOS	*Annuaire de l'Institut de philologie et d'histoire orientales et slaves*
AJEC	Ancient Judaism and Early Christianity
ANRW	*Aufstieg und Niedergang der römischen Welt: Geschichte und Kultur Roms im Spiegel der neueren Forschung*. Part 2, *Principat*. Edited by H. Temporini and W. Haase. Berlin: de Gruyter, 1972–
AThR	*Anglican Theological Review*
BDAG	Danker, Frederick W., Walter Bauer, William F. Arndt, and F. Wilbur Gingrich. *Greek-English Lexicon of the New Testament and Other Early Christian Literature*. 3rd ed. Chicago: University of Chicago Press, 2000
BETL	Bibliotheca Ephemeridum Theologicarum Lovaniensium
BJRL	*Bulletin of the John Rylands University Library of Manchester*
BR	*Biblical Research*
BZNW	Beihefte zur Zeitschrift für die neutestamentliche Wissenschaft
CahRB	Cahiers de la Revue biblique
CahGSEP	Cahiers du Groupe Suisse d'études patristique
CBQ	*Catholic Biblical Quarterly*
ConBNT	Coniectanea Neotestamentica or Coniectanea Biblica: New Testament Series
CRINT	Compendia Rerum Iudaicarum ad Novum Testamentum
CurBR	*Currents in Biblical Research*
ECA	Early Christian Apocrypha
ECL	Early Christianity and Its Literature
ECS	Eastern Christian Studies
ETL	*Ephemerides Theologicae Lovanienses*
fl.	Latin *floruit*, "flourished"
FRLANT	Forschungen zur Religion und Literatur des Alten und Neuen Testaments
GCS	Die griechischen christlichen Schriftsteller der ersten [drei] Jahrhunderte
GTA	Göttinger theologische Arbeiten
GTR	Gender, Theory, and Religion
HDR	Harvard Dissertations in Religion
HNT	Handbuch zum Neuen Testament

HTR	*Harvard Theological Review*
JAAR	*Journal of the American Academy of Religion*
JBL	*Journal of Biblical Literature*
JBRec	*Journal of the Bible and Its Reception*
JECS	*Journal of Early Christian Studies*
JEH	*Journal of Ecclesiastical History*
JRH	*Journal of Religious History*
JSJ	*Journal for the Study of Judaism in the Persian, Hellenistic, and Roman Periods*
JSNT	*Journal for the Study of the New Testament*
JSNTSup	Journal for the Study of the New Testament Supplement Series
JTS	*Journal of Theological Studies*
KAV	Kommentar zu den apostolischen Vätern
LCL	Loeb Classical Library
LNTS	The Library of New Testament Studies
MBT	Münsterische Beiträge zur Theologie
MH	*Museum Helveticum*
Mosc. Ep.	Moscow Epilogue
NIGTC	New International Greek Testament Commentary
NovT	*Novum Testamentum*
NovTSup	Supplements to Novum Testamentum
NT	New Testament
NTTSD	New Testament Tools, Studies, and Documents
OAF	Oxford Apostolic Fathers
OECGT	Oxford Early Christian Gospel Texts
OECS	Oxford Early Christian Studies
OECT	Oxford Early Christian Texts
OT	Old Testament
par(r).	parallel(s)
PGL	*Patristic Greek Lexicon*. Edited by Geoffrey W. H. Lampe. Oxford: Clarendon, 1961
PMS	Patristic Monograph Series
RB	*Revue biblique*
ResQ	*Restoration Quarterly*
SANT	Studien zum Alten und Neuen Testament
SAQ	Sammlung ausgewählter kirchen- und dogmengeschichtlicher Quellenschriften
SBLStBL	Society of Biblical Literature Studies in Biblical Literature
SBLSymS	Society of Biblical Literature Symposium Series
SC	Sources chrétiennes
SEÅ	*Svensk exegetisk årsbok*
SEAug	Studia Ephemeridis Augustinianum
SecCent	*Second Century*
SHAW	Sitzungen der Heidelberger Akademie der Wissenschaften
SNTSMS	Society for New Testament Studies Monograph Series
StBibLit	Studies in Biblical Literature (Lang)
StPatr	Studia Patristica (Peeters)
SVTQ	*St. Vladimir's Theological Quarterly*

TENTS	Texts and Editions for New Testament Study
Them	*Themelios*
ThH	Théologie historique
TP	*Theologie und Philosophie*
TSAJ	Texte und Studien zum antiken Judentum
TSMEMJ	Texts and Studies in Medieval and Early Modern Judaism
TU	Texte und Untersuchungen
TUGAL	Texte und Untersuchungen zur Geschichte der altchristlichen Literatur
TZ	*Theologische Zeitschrift*
USQR	*Union Seminary Quarterly Review*
VC	*Vigiliae Christianae*
VCSup	Vigiliae Christianae Supplements
v.l.	Latin *varia lectio*, variant reading
WBCR	Wiley Blackwell Companions to Religion
WUNT	Wissenschaftliche Untersuchungen zum Neuen Testament
ZAC	*Zeitschrift für Antikes Christentum/Journal of Ancient Christianity*

INTRODUCTION

CHAPTER 1

THE APOSTOLIC FATHERS: AN INTRODUCTION

PAUL FOSTER

1. SECOND-CENTURY CHRISTIANITY

The difference between the early Jesus movement at the beginning of the second century and its strength and status at the end of that century is immense. Around the year 100 CE the movement had spread well beyond the confines of Galilee and Palestine, but the various communities were scattered, marginal, and striving to develop a sense of permanence and identity. However, by the end of the second century, while the Christian movement had become even more dispersed, it had developed a greater sense of being an established and empire-wide community, with a united and global identity. By the year 200 CE, communities of Christ believers existed throughout the entire Roman Empire and even beyond its territorial boundaries. Within communities there was a more developed hierarchical system of leadership. The literary output of the movement sought to compete with the philosophical and intellectual ideas of the period. While subject to sporadic and unpredictable persecution, there was a greater sense of confidence in the movement's status, social importance, and permanence. Moreover, a series of Jewish revolts resulted in "a significant shift in the centre of gravity of Christian geography."[1] This commenced with the first revolt of 66–70 CE that led to the destruction of Jerusalem, followed by a series of revolts at multiple sites late in Trajan's reign (115–117), and a couple of decades later with the Bar Kokhba revolt (132–135). Not only did this series of events result in early Christians leaving or being displaced from Jerusalem and Judea, but many distanced themselves from fellow Judeans. Consequently, they settled elsewhere in the Empire, and thus they organically promulgated the new faith among pagans.

Despite the momentous changes for the Christian movement in this period, the sources documenting the movement's expansion and the development of its internal structures and practices are sparse. This is particularly true for the first half of the second century. Even for those surviving Christian writings traditionally dated to this period, there are questions relating to the correctness of dating them to this period and concerns raised about whether such texts are representative of the movement as a whole. While overly precise dating should be avoided, the tendency to redate such documents to later periods is typically unwarranted. By contrast, issues raised in a single text should perhaps not be understood

1. M. M. Mitchell, "From Jerusalem to the Ends of the Earth," in *Origins to Constantine*, vol. 1 of *The Cambridge History of Christianity*, ed. M. M. Mitchell and F. M. Young (Cambridge: Cambridge University Press, 2006), 296.

as representative of events in the wider movement without further support. Therefore, in many ways the second century is one of the most formative periods in the history of Christianity, but it is also one of the most sparsely documented and least understood. Yet, while the limitation of sources prevents a fully connected and global understanding, the texts that are extant present multiple fascinating windows into this exceptionally important period. They provide evidence of both continuing diversity as well as efforts toward standardization. They reveal many shared beliefs alongside points of highly contested theological debate. Christian communities are sometimes portrayed as existing in relative peace, but at other times as being subject to hostile opposition and even persecution. The contents of these texts show early Christians attempting to interact with highest examples of intellectual, literary, and philosophical thought on the one hand, while on the other engaging in wider culture in terms of folk beliefs and practices. In other words, even with all its shared core commitments and common practices, the early Christian movement was able to encompass diverse behavior and forms of faith. It continued to express itself as popular and accessible to the masses, while striving to situate itself alongside the intellectual elites. While this mix created tensions, such hybridity was probably key to the survival and growth of a movement that could offer different things to various classes of people. The diversity of the movement is reflected in a number of the texts that survive from the first half of the second century and beyond. Chief among those texts is the collection that has become known as the writings of the Apostolic Fathers.

2. WHO AND WHAT ARE THE APOSTOLIC FATHERS?

The term "Apostolic Fathers" has a dual reference. It refers both to a group of individuals who were prominent in the early church about a generation or two after the time of the apostles, as well as initially denoting a set of writings that were written by those same figures. Over the course of time, the contents of that collection of writings have been enlarged. Now the collection of writings is seen typically as containing a maximum of eleven writings, or more correctly ten writings that survive in full or in fragmentary form, and a collection of seven letters by Ignatius, which are typically counted as a single unit among the eleven-item collection.

There is some scholarly dispute concerning the origin of the term "Apostolic Fathers." Often this is traced to a possible antecedent used in Cotelier's first printed edition of a collection of several of the texts included in what is now known as the Apostolic Fathers. Cotelier's first edition contained seven texts: the Epistle of Barnabas, two letters ascribed to Clement, the seven letters of Ignatius (taken as a single entry), Polycarp's *Epistle to the Philippians*, the Martyrdom of Polycarp, and the Shepherd of Hermas, along with several other writings that have not established themselves as part of the typical collection of texts that form the collection. This collection was published under the title *SS. Patrum qui Temporibus Apostolicis Floruerunt Opera*,[2] which is in English translation *Works of the Holy Fathers Who Flourished in the Time of the Apostles*. While some of the texts are attributed to figures who were directly connected with the apostles, such as the Epistle of Barnabas (Acts 4:36; 9:27; 11:22–15:39; Gal 2:1, 9, 13; Col 4:10) and Clement (Phil 4:3), the majority are more correctly ascribed to authors who lived in the decades after the death of the apostles. In this sense, these are the part of the literary record of the early Christian

2. Jean-Baptist Cotelier, *SS. Patrum Qui Temporibus Apostolicis Floruerunt; Barnabae, Clementis, Hermae, Ignatii, Polycarpi; Opera Edita et Inedita, Vera et Suppositicia. Una cum Clementis, Ignatii, Polycarpi Actis atque Martyriis* (Paris: Petri le Petit, 1672).

movement in the period after the composition of many of the writings that were later to be collected to form the New Testament.

While the specific title *Patres Apostolici*, or "Apostolic Fathers," did not originate with Cotelier's first printed edition of several of the texts that have come to form the corpus,[3] a virtually identical form is found in the title of the first English edition of these texts. In 1693, some twenty-one years after Cotelier's volume appeared and undoubtedly dependent on that work, William Wake published the seven texts along with the account of the martyrdom of Ignatius under the title *The Genuine Epistles of the Apostolical Fathers*.[4] This terminology influenced the reprinting of Cotelier's own work with the editor of the 1699 edition, Thomas Ittig, using the title *Patres Apostolici*. However, it has recently been observed that Wake was perhaps not the person who originated the use of the title Apostolic Fathers in relation to these texts. In a splendid piece of recent detective work, David Lincicum examines several copies of Cotelier's volume. He argues that the title "Apostolic(al) Fathers," in Latin *Patres Apostolici*, was due to what he describes as "paratextual attempts to shorten Cotelier's lengthy title, *SS. Patrum Qui Temporibus Apostolicis Floruerunt*."[5] He observes that the book was shipped as unbound gatherings, which were individually bound either by the booksellers or the purchasers of the prebound volumes. This is seen as accounting for the diversity in spine titles. Lincicum surveys around thirty copies of the 1672 edition of Cotelier's work in order to compare the titles on the spines. It is noted that there exists "a certain predominance among British copies of *patres apostolici* and variants . . . the binding of at least one of which can be securely dated to 1674."[6] This phenomenon may not be the sole factor, but it is a further contributory feature in the emergence of the terminology of "Apostolic Fathers" becoming the typical designation for the collection of texts printed in Cotelier's volume and subsequent editions of these texts.

Thus, by the end of the seventeenth century the Latin term *Patres Apostolici*, or in English "Apostolical Fathers," had become an established designation for the set of seven texts that Cotelier first published as a collection. However, this raises both a prior and a posterior question. The prior question concerns how and why Cotelier came to group together the seven texts that he selected. That question pertains to the basis of the emergence of this corpus of seven writings. The posterior question concerns the enlargement of the corpus from Cotelier's core of seven writings of the Apostolic Fathers to the now commonly established collection of eleven texts. It is those two questions that are addressed in the following sections.

3. THE FORMATION OF THE COLLECTION OF THE APOSTOLIC FATHERS

While Cotelier is often credited as the originator of the formation of the collection of writings that would later become known as the Apostolic Fathers, that is incorrect and reifies

3. Bart Ehrman describes the discussion over the origin of the title "Apostolic Fathers" as being "rather pointless." He notes that in the preface, Cotelier twice "refers to his 'Apostolicorum Patrum collectio' (pp. vii and x)" (B. D. Ehrman, ed., *The Apostolic Fathers*, 2 vols., LCL [Cambridge: Harvard University Press, 2003], 1:8).

4. The complete title, reflecting the style of the day, is fulsome and describes the contents: W. Wake, *The Genuine Epistles of the Apostolical Fathers; St. Clement, St. Polycarp, St. Ignatius, St. Barnabas, the Pastor of Hermas; and an Account of the Martyrdoms of St. Ignatius and St. Polycarp Written by Those Who Were Present at Their Sufferings: Being, Together with the Holy Scriptures of the New Testament, A Complete Collection of the Most Primitive Antiquity, for about a Hundred and Fifty Years After Christ* (London: Printed for Ric. Sare at Grays-Inn Gate next Holbourn, 1693).

5. D. Lincicum, "The Paratextual Invention of the term 'Apostolic Fathers,'" *JTS* 66 (2015): 139–148, here 143.

6. Lincicum, "Paratextual Invention," 144.

a modernist perspective on this scholarly endeavor. Initially, nearly all of the writings that constitute the current corpus circulated separately and independently. The probable exception is the case of two of Ignatius's letters sent to Smyrna, presumably together. One was addressed to the community, and the other to Polycarp, whom Ignatius describes as the bishop of that community. It is likely those two letters were dispatched at the same time from Troas (Ign. *Smyrn.* 12.1; *Pol.* 8.1), arrived at the same time, and may have been kept together from that time onward. The next stage of the collection also involves the letters of Ignatius. Writing in response to the Philippians, Polycarp informs them that "we are sending to you the letters of Ignatius that were sent to us by him together with any others that we have in our possession" (Pol. *Phil.* 13.2). Michael Holmes notes that Codex Mediceo-Laurentianus, which is the only surviving Greek manuscript of a collection of Ignatius's letters in the middle recension, presents six letters in the following order: *Smyrnaeans, Polycarp, Ephesians, Magnesians, Philadelphians,* and *Trallians.* Consequently, Holmes draws the following plausible observation: "This sequence is consistent with Polycarp's remark to the Philippians (Pol. *Phil.* 13.2) . . . and may represent the order of the letters in the earliest collection made of them."[7]

Over the next couple of centuries, there are references to several of the texts that would form the Apostolic Fathers collection, or to their authors. Additionally, there are various short citations in the works of several other early Christian writers. In that regard the most significant source of information is to be found in Eusebius's *Ecclesiastical History.* While not including full texts, Eusebius provides extensive descriptions or citations of a number of the writings that form the modern collection of the Apostolic Fathers. Thus, 1 Clement is described as a letter sent in the name of the church in Rome to the Christian community in Corinth (Eusebius, *Hist. eccl.* 3.16.1). Eusebius also attests the existence of a second epistle attributed to Clement. He states, "There is also a second letter ascribed to Clement, but we have not the same knowledge of its recognition as we have of the former, for we do not even know if the primitive writers used it" (3.28.2). Discussing episcopal succession in various sees, Eusebius initially mentions Ignatius as being "famous as the second bishop of Antioch" (3.22.1). Later he is more fulsome as he describes Ignatius as "still a name of note" (3.36.1). In the lengthy section that follows, Eusebius mentions all seven letters of the middle recension, noting that while in Smyrna, Ignatius wrote letters to Ephesus, Magnesia, Tralles, and Rome. Additionally, he cites a lengthy passage from Ignatius's letter to Rome (Ign. *Rom.* 5.1–3). Next it is noted that while at Troas, Ignatius wrote letters to the communities in Philadelphia and Smyrna, and a letter to Polycarp. In this context, Eusebius cites Ignatius, *To the Smyrnaeans* 3.2 (see Eusebius, *Hist. eccl.* 3.36.1–15).

In the same passage, Eusebius mentions Polycarp, "a disciple of the apostles, who was a man of eminence in Asia, having been entrusted with the episcopate of the church of Smyrna by those who had seen and heard the Lord" (Eusebius, *Hist. eccl.* 3.36.1). Significantly, Eusebius is aware that Polycarp, in his letter to the Philippians, refers to the letters of Ignatius. Additionally, Eusebius cites two passages from the letter in their entirety (Pol. *Phil.* 9.1–2; 13.1–2a). In book 4, again Eusebius mentions "a very powerful epistle of Polycarp written to the Philippians," and furthermore he notes that the letter draws on material "from the First Epistle to Peter" (Eusebius, *Hist. eccl.* 4.14.8–9).

Furthermore, Eusebius also reveals knowledge of the text contained in the Apostolic Fathers under the title the Martyrdom of Polycarp. In fact, he provides lengthy excerpts

7. M. W. Holmes, *The Apostolic Fathers: Greek Texts and English Translations*, 3rd ed. (Grand Rapids: Baker, 2007), 177.

from the text (Eusebius, *Hist. eccl.* 4.15.3–45). Thus, Eusebius states, "I consider it most important that his death, a written account of which is still extant, should be recorded in this history" (4.15.1). Eusebius's version of the Martyrdom of Polycarp provides extensive overlap with the text preserved in manuscript sources. There are admittedly several omissions of various sizes, as well as rewording and some additions.[8]

Eusebius is also the key source for several of the fragmentary writings which now form the corpus of the Apostolic Fathers. He mentions Papias in both his *Chronicon* (Eusebius, *Chron.*), and in his *Ecclesiastical History* (3.36.2; 3.39.1–16). In the latter long section, Eusebius provides information about Papias and also cites various sections of his work (3.39.1–16). The briefer references present him as a contemporary of Ignatius and Polycarp. There are two references to Quadratus. First, he is mentioned as a prominent figure who "was renowned along with the daughters of Philip for his prophetical gifts" (3.37.1). Later, in book 4 Eusebius again mentions a figure called Quadratus, although it is not entirely clear that the two people named Quadratus are identical. In that later context, Eusebius mentions the *Apologia* written by Quadratus and cites the sole extant fragment, which is now included in the writings of the Apostolic Fathers (Eusebius, *Hist. eccl.* 4.3.1–2).

Discussing and categorizing early Christian writings into three groups—those that belong to the New Testament, those whose inclusion in the New Testament is disputed, and those that are rejected—Eusebius makes the following comment concerning the final group.

> Among the rejected writings must be reckoned also the Acts of Paul, and the so-called Shepherd, and the Apocalypse of Peter, and in addition to these the extant Epistle of Barnabas, and the so-called Teachings of the Apostles; and besides, as I said, the Apocalypse of John, if it seem proper, which some, as I said, reject, but which others class with the accepted books. (Eusebius, *Hist. eccl.* 3.25.4)

It would appear that here Eusebius shows further knowledge of three of the remaining writings that constitute the modern collection of the Apostolic Fathers. Without citing any portion of the relevant texts, here Eusebius reveals knowledge of the Shepherd of Hermas, the Epistle of Barnabas, and presumably the Didache. The Didache is almost certainly the text referred to as "the Teachings of the Apostles." That text appears to have several related titles in both Greek and Latin tradition, either the Teaching of the (Twelve) Apostles or the longer version, the Teaching of the Lord to the Gentiles by the Twelve Apostles.[9]

Thus, the surviving writings of Eusebius may well reflect knowledge of ten of the eleven texts. The one text Eusebius does not demonstrate knowledge of is the Epistle to Diognetus. Of the ten others, Eusebius reveals high regard for the writings of Clement, Ignatius, Polycarp, Quadratus, and the account of Polycarp's martyrdom. While Eusebius has reservations concerning Papias's chiliastic views (Eusebius, *Hist. eccl.* 3.39.12), overall he is happy to consider him as a contemporary representative of subapostolic Christianity. So while the writings of Clement, Ignatius, Papias, Polycarp, Quadratus, and the Martyrdom of Polycarp did not circulate as a collection, Eusebius considers them to be written by trustworthy followers of the apostles, or in the case of the Martyrdom of Polycarp, about such figures. By contrast, Eusebius is ambivalent about the text known as 2 Clement, since he

---

8. A synoptic comparison in parallel columns is conveniently set out in B. Dehandschutter, *Polycarpiana: Studies on Martyrdom and Persecution in Early Christianity: Collected Essays*, BETL 205 (Leuven: Peeters, 2007); see in particular ch. 1, "An Updated Edition of the Martyrdom of Polycarp," 3–22.

9. Holmes, *Apostolic Fathers*, 334.

cannot be certain of the pedigree of its author. Moreover, he knows of three further texts that are now part of the collection of the writings of the Apostolic Fathers: Shepherd of Hermas, the Epistle of Barnabas, and presumably the Didache. He says little about these texts and does not cite any of their contents. Instead, he simply says that they do not form part of the New Testament. Eusebius's wide-ranging acquaintance with at least ten of the eleven texts that constitute the now standard corpus of the Apostolic Fathers is remarkable, as is his ability to cite extensive passages from some of these texts, which suggests he had access to copies of these writings.

The next window into the association of multiple texts in the corpus comes not from the comments of early Christian writers but from the contents of ancient biblical codices. The fourth-century pandect biblical manuscript Codex Sinaiticus (א 01) includes as its final two texts the Epistle of Barnabas and part of the Shepherd of Hermas (Herm. 1.1–31.6). Presumably, more of the Shepherd of Hermas was originally present, although it is impossible to be certain of the original extent of the version of this text that that was contained in Codex Sinaiticus. The presence of these two texts in a biblical codex perhaps helps to make further sense of Eusebius's comment that these texts should be rejected as belonging to the New Testament (Eusebius, *Hist. eccl.* 3.25.4). Such a comment would appear to be required precisely because some wished to include these writings alongside other New Testament texts, and Codex Sinaiticus bears witness to that phenomenon. Similarly, the fifth-century biblical manuscript Codex Alexandrinus (02 A) contains two texts that are now part of the collection of writings of the Apostolic Fathers. These are 1 and 2 Clement. The text of 1 Clement is extant for 1.1–57.6 and 64.1–65.2 but lacks 57.7–63.4. For 2 Clement the text preserves 1.1–12.5a, but is lacunose for 12.5b–20.5. The titles of these two texts imply that they are attributed to the same author—Clement.[10]

After this manuscript evidence for multiple Apostolic Fathers texts, further evidence is lacking for several centuries, apart from manuscripts that contain collections of the letters of Ignatius of Antioch. Perhaps most notable in this regard are three Syriac manuscripts dating from the sixth to the tenth century, which contain abbreviated forms of three of the letters of Ignatius, *To Polycarp*, *To the Ephesians*, and *To the Romans*.[11] This form of the Ignatian corpus is known as the short recension.

Around the eleventh century onward, two further pieces of significant evidence emerge that are of significance in determining the circulation and collection of multiple texts that would later become known as the Apostolic Fathers. First, from the eleventh to sixteenth centuries twelve Greek manuscripts survive, which contain parts of Polycarp's *To the Philippians* and the Epistle of Barnabas. What is interesting here is that these do not circulate as separate texts, but rather significant portions of both texts have been spliced together to form a new single text circulating as Polycarp's letter. These twelve manuscripts are all genetically related, since they join these two texts in the same manner. The contents comprise Polycarp's *To the Philippians* salutation + 1.1–9.2, with only the three final words of 9.2 lacking (τοῦ θεοῦ ἀναστάντα), immediately followed by text from the Epistle of Barnabas beginning at

10. In the manuscript of Codex Alexandrinus, the title of 1 Clement is given as Κλημεντος προς Κορινθιους Α. Second Clement has no title with the text, but in the table of contents it is listed as Κλημεντος ε[πιστολ]ν β′. See Holmes, *Apostolic Fathers*, 44, 138.

11. It should be noted that toward the end of the short recension of *To the Romans*, the Syriac redactor inserts a passage from *To the Trallians* 4–5. The aim is to heighten the portrait of Ignatius as a calm and resolute martyr. See the discussion in P. Foster, "The Ignatian Problem: The Recensions of a Letter Corpus as a Reflection of Theological Concerns and Developments," in *Texts in Context: Essays on Dating and Contextualising Christian Writings from the Second and Early Third Centuries*, ed. J. Verheyden, J. Schröter, and T. Nicklas, BETL 319 (Leuven: Peeters, 2021), 5–50, here 45.

5.7 (τὸν λαὸν τὸν καινόν) and continuing to the end of that epistle. The earliest surviving manuscript of this arrangement of this conflation of the epistles of Polycarp and Barnabas is the eleventh-century Vaticanus Graecus 859 (V), housed at the Vatican Library.

The second piece of evidence from the eleventh century is of far greater significance for understanding the process of collecting writings that would become known as the Apostolic Fathers and for the shape of modern editions of the corpus. In 1873, Bryennios discovered a medieval codex, which would become known as Codex Hierosolymitanus,[12] usually designated with the siglum H or more fully as H54.[13] A colophon permits the codex's completion to be dated precisely to 11 June 1056. The manuscript was discovered in the monastery of the Holy Sepulchre in Constantinople (modern Istanbul), but was moved by Bryennios to the library of the Greek Patriarchate in Jerusalem for safekeeping. Images of the complete manuscript are available online.[14] The manuscript is written on parchment, with a precise minuscule hand that makes some use of ligatures and abbreviations. The manuscript achieved fame for bringing to light the text of the Didache, which was previously unknown, although its contents had been reused in later Christian texts. An abbreviated list of the contents of Codex Hierosolymitanus is sometimes presented in works on the Apostolic Fathers, implying that it only contained works from that corpus. In fact, the first text in the manuscript is John Chrysostom's *Synopsis of the Testaments*. There then follows the Didache, the Epistle of Barnabas, 1 Clement, 2 Clement, and the long recension of the letters of Ignatius. Not only did Codex Hierosolymitanus herald the discovery of the text of the Didache, which subsequently has typically been included among the writings of the Apostolic Fathers, it is also the Greek manuscript that contains the largest collection of multiple texts that would become part of modern editions of the corpus. Counting the long recension of Ignatius as a single entry, it contains in the same codex five of the eleven writings that would form the standard modern collection.

From the twelfth century onward, multiple manuscripts survive with various combinations of the writings of the Apostolic Fathers. For instance, manuscripts of the conflated version of Polycarp's *To the Philippians* and the Epistle of Barnabas often circulated with the long recension of the Epistles of Ignatius.[15] However, this combination of the version of Polycarp's *To the Philippians* supplemented with the Epistle of Barnabas, alongside the long recension of thirteen Greek letters of Ignatius, does not relate to Polycarp's initial response to the Philippians in sending his own letter along with the letters of Ignatius that he was able to obtain. Rather, this is a much later development that postdates the first phase of the formation of Greek long recension and occurred before the phenomenon is first observed in manuscript Vaticanus 859.[16] Such late medieval manuscripts became part of the basis of the earliest first printed editions of the individual texts that would subsequently be collected to form the Apostolic Fathers collection.

12. The codex has also been designated with the Anglicized form the Jerusalem Codex, or sometimes named after its discoverer as the Bryennios manuscript, or as Codex Constantinopolitanus.

13. Holmes uses the siglum C to designate this manuscript, after the title Codex Constantinopolitanus. See Holmes, *Apostolic Fathers*, 38.

14. "Panagios Taphos 54. John Chrysostom: Synopsis of the Testaments; Apostolic Fathers. 1056 A.D. 120 f. Pg. 16ft.," Library of Congress, www.loc.gov/resource/amedmonastery.00279389694-jo/?sp=1&st=list.

15. For a description of the contents of some of the relevant manuscripts, see J. B. Lightfoot, *The Apostolic Fathers, Part II: S. Ignatius, S. Polycarp. Revised Texts with Introductions, Notes, Dissertations, and Translations*, 2nd ed., 3 vols. (London: Macmillan, 1889–1890), 1:545–51.

16. Lightfoot describes this connection as "late and accidental." While being late, accidental is probably incorrect. The connection appears to have been motivated by knowledge of the relationship between Polycarp and Ignatius as two closely associated figures from the same period (Lightfoot, *Apostolic Fathers, Part II*, 1:547).

4. INDIVIDUAL TEXTS OF THE APOSTOLIC FATHERS IN PRINT

The surviving manuscripts reveal only a limited part of the story of the formation and evolution of the collection of writings that emerged as the typical corpus of the Apostolic Fathers. As has been noted, taking the letters of Ignatius as a single entry, Cotelier's volume contained seven of the eleven texts that would later become the standard corpus of the Apostolic Fathers. Such a volume would not have been possible prior to the seventeenth century. Codex Alexandrinus was brought from Alexandria to Constantinople in 1621 by Cyril Lucaris, after he was translated from the post as Greek Orthodox Patriarch of Alexandria to the role of Ecumenical Patriarch of Constantinople. The protestantizing Cyril was influenced by Calvinism, especially while studying at Geneva. Cyril was an admirer of the Church of England. Moreover, the British government had provided support to Cyril during his struggles with Turkish authorities. In gratitude, Cyril arranged for Codex Alexandrinus to be sent as a gift to James I. However, James died before the gift could be received. In 1627, the codex was finally presented to Charles I. It was this gift of a fifth-century pandect codex that made available the text of 1 and 2 Clement to modern scholarship in western Europe.

The first edition of the extant text of these two writings was published in 1633,[17] and then reissued by Patrick Young, the royal librarian, in 1637.[18] The title page of this volume refers only to the first letter, but after the text of the first letter concludes Young adds the title *Fragmentum Epistolae Secundae ex Eodem Ms* ("fragments of the second epistle from the same manuscript"), although there is no reference to the second text on the title page of Young's editio princeps. Young's edition was less than perfect, and according to Lightfoot the two epistles "were transcribed with tolerable but not strict accuracy."[19] Therefore, over the following two hundred and forty-two years, until the publication of the text of these letters based on the form of text found in Codex Hierosolymitanus, the chief improvement was due to a more accurate transcription and careful attempts to resolve various lacunae.

The history of the publication of the Letters of Ignatius is complicated by the various recensions in which those writings appear. Various forms of the long recension exist, with certain Ignatian letters found only in Latin. In fact, a Latin form of the long recension was first published by Jacques Lefèvre d'Étaples in 1498.[20] The text of the long recension containing thirteen letters, including the expanded versions of the seven letters of the middle recension, was initially published sixty years later.[21] Here, however, the concern is with the publication of the middle recension of what are widely regarded as the seven authentic letters of Ignatius. In 1644 James Ussher published the Latin text of the middle recension.[22] Two years later in 1646, Isaac Voss published the Greek text of six of the seven letters of the middle recension based on the then newly discovered Codex Mediceo-Laurentianus

17. The editio princeps was published as P. Young, ed., *Clementis ad Corinthios Epistola Prior* (Oxford: Iohannes Lichfield, 1633).

18. P. Young, ed., *Clementis ad Corinthios Epistola Prior*, 2nd ed. (Oxford: Iohannes Lichfield, 1637).

19. J. B. Lightfoot, *The Apostolic Fathers, Part I: S. Clement of Rome*, 2nd ed., 2 vols. (London: Macmillan, 1890), 1:118.

20. J. L. d'Étaples, *Theologia Vivificans, Dionysii Coelestis Hierarchia, Ss. Ignatii XV Epistolae, Polycarpi Epistolai* (Paris, 1498). This edition comprised eleven letters in the following order: 1. Trallians, 2. Magnesians, 3. Tarsians, 4. Philippians, 5. Philadelphians, 6. Smyrneans, 7. Polycarp, 8. Antiochians, 9. Hero, 10. Ephesians, 11. Romans.

21. H. Frid, *Του Μακαριου Ιερομαρτυρος Ιγνατιου, Beati Ignatii Opuscula Omnia* (Dilligen: Sebaldus Mair, 1557). This edition contains twelve letters of the long recension: 1. *To Mary Cassobola*, 2. *To the Trallians*, 3. *To the Magnesians*, 4. *To Those in Tarsus*, 5. *To the Philippians*, 6. *To the Philadelphians*, 7. *To the Smyrnaeans*, 8. *To Polycarp*, 9. *To the Antiocheans*, 10. *To Hero*, 11. *To the Ephesians*, 12. *To the Romans*.

22. J. Ussher, ed., *Polycarpi et Ignatii Epistolae* (Oxford: Leonardus Lichfield Academiae Typographus, and Henry Hall, 1644).

57,7.[23] The middle recension of Ignatius's *To the Romans* has a different transmission history. At an early stage it was "incorporated into the Antiochene Acts of Martyrdom of Ignatius, and thus dislocated from the other six."[24] The Greek text of the middle recension of *To the Romans* was first published in 1689 by T. Ruinart.[25]

No complete manuscript of the Greek text of Polycarp's *To the Philippians* survives. The text is fully extant in Latin, and the editio princeps of that version was published by Lefèvre in 1498, along with the Latin long recension of the letters of Ignatius (see above). Of the fourteen chapters that comprise *To the Philippians*, the first nine chapters and the majority of chapter fourteen survive in Greek. The Greek text was first published by Halloix in 1633.[26] However, just over a decade later, "James Ussher published an improved text of the Greek in 1644."[27] Ussher appears to have used copies of the Greek text originally made by Turrianus and Andrew Schott that had been supplied by Voss. In his edition,[28] Ussher corrected the edition of Halloix based on the copies of these two transcriptions.[29]

The first Greek edition of the Martyrdom of Polycarp stems from the work of Ussher. It was published in 1647 as *Appendix Ignatiana*, and the edition followed a single eleventh century manuscript of the Greek text, Codex Baroccianus.[30]

In this same period, the first published edition of the Epistle of Barnabas was prepared by Hugh Menard. It was published in Paris in 1645 under the oversight of Luke D'Achery, following Menard's death. However, prior to this publication another edition of the Epistle of Barnabas had been prepared by Ussher in conjunction with Voss. According to J. Backhouse, the intention was for this edition to be included with Ussher's edition of Polycarp and Ignatius published in 1644 and mentioned above.[31] The printed sheets for that edition, which had been stored ready for binding, were destroyed by fire on Sunday, 6 October 1644.[32] However, a single copy has survived in the Bodleian Library at least since 1674, bound with an unrelated work published in 1658, and preserving the entirety of Ussher's preface and slightly more than the first eight chapters of the text of the epistle.[33]

The history of publication of the text of the Shepherd of Hermas is distinctive and different from other texts among the Apostolic Fathers in several ways. The first edition was printed early in the sixteenth century. In 1513 the Shepherd was edited by Lefèvre and printed in Paris.[34] However, this was an edition of the Latin Vulgate version, which probably came into existence between the end of the second century and the middle of the third century (i.e., 180–250 CE). The Shepherd of Hermas, however, was originally composed in Greek. Manuscripts of the Greek text did not come to light until around the middle of the nineteenth century. The first to come to light was Codex Athos (A),

23. I. Voss, ed., *Epistolæ Genuinæ s. Ignatii, ex Bibl. Florentina. Adduntur s. Ignatii Epistolæ, Quales Vulgo Circumferuntur. Adhaec s. Barnabæ Epistola* (Amsterdam: Ioannem Blaev, 1646).

24. J. B. Lightfoot, ed., *The Apostolic Fathers: Revised Texts with Short Introductions and English Translations*, edited and completed by J. R. Harmer (London: Macmillan, 1891), 101.

25. T. Ruinart, *Acta Primorum Martyrum Sincera et Selecta* (Paris: Franciscus Muguet, 1689).

26. P. Halloix, *Illustrium Ecclesiae Orientalis Scriptorum Vitae et Documenta* (Douai: Bogard, 1633), 525ff.

27. Ehrman, *Apostolic Fathers*, 330.

28. Ussher, *Polycarpi et Ignatii Epistolae*.

29. Lightfoot, *Apostolic Fathers, Part II*, 3:318–19.

30. J. Ussher, ed., *Appendix Ignatiana* (London: Georgii Thomasoni, 1647).

31. J. H. Backhouse, *The Editio Princeps of the Epistle of Barnabas by Archbishop Ussher, as Printed at Oxford A.D. 1642, and Preserved in an Imperfect Form in the Bodleian Library* (Oxford: Clarendon, 1883), vii–viii.

32. The surviving title page contains the date 1642, which suggests the printed pages had been in storage for perhaps around two years.

33. Backhouse, *Editio Princeps of the Epistle of Barnabas*, x.

34. J. Lefèvre, *Libre Trium Vivorum et Trium Spiritualium Virginum* (Paris: Estienne, 1513).

which was discovered in a monastic library on the eponymous Mount Athos in the 1850s. This led to the publication of the editio princeps of a Greek text of the surviving part of the Shepherd of Hermas (Vis. 1.1.1–Sim. 9.30.3 [1.1–107.3]).[35] Thereafter, there appeared further Greek manuscripts, most notably Codex Sinaiticus, which came to the attention of Constantin Tischendorf in the period 1846–1860 with publication of the contents of the codex taking place in 1862.[36] Since this period, various critical editions have been published both individually and in editions of collections of the writings of the Apostolic Fathers. However, the section of Shepherd of Hermas 107.4b–114.5 does not survive in Greek and hence is typically printed in Latin in most critical editions.

Henri Estienne made a transcription of the Epistle to Diognetus in 1586. This transcription was later published by Estienne under the Latinized form of his name, Henricus Stephanus, in 1592. This printed text thus became the editio princeps of the Epistle to Diognetus. However, although this text was available to Cotelier and other seventeenth- and eighteenth-century editors of collections of the texts of the Apostolic Fathers, the first to include it in a collection under that title was K. Hefele in 1839.[37] Presumably one of the reasons for not including it was that it was viewed as a representative of the apologetic tradition that is typically understood as arising chiefly in the second half of the second century. Thus, in all likelihood it was deemed to belong to a subsequent generation of early Christianity after the writings of the other Apostolic Fathers.

The text of the Didache is the most recently discovered new text to be added to the corpus of the Apostolic Fathers. The manuscript containing the text, Codex Hierosolymitanus, was discovered in 1873 by Bryennios, who later published the editio princeps of the Didache in 1883.[38] The reason for this delay of ten years is not fully apparent. While it has been suggested that the delay was due to the fact that Bryennios initially overlooked the presence of this text in the codex and instead was captivated by the discovery of the complete texts for the two writings attributed to Clement in the corpus of the Apostolic Fathers, this seems unlikely. Lightfoot in his 1877 volume, which published the additional portions of 1 and 2 Clement that were found in Codex Hierosolymitanus, also refers to the contents of the codex as including "fol. 76a–80 Διδαχὴ τῶν δώδεκα Ἀποστόλων [Teaching of the Twelve Apostles]."[39] Thus, it appears that Bryennios did recognize the presence of the Didache in the manuscript at an early stage. However, he published the

35. R. Anger and G. Dindofius, eds., *Hermae Pastor: Graece* (Leipzig: Weigel, 1856).

36. C. Tischendorf, *Bibliorum Codex Sinaiticus Petropolitanus* (Leipzig: Giesecke & Devrient, 1862).

37. K. J. Hefele, *Patrum Apostolicorum Opera: Textum ex Editionibus Praestantissimus Repetitum Recognovit, Annotationibus Illustravit, Versionem Latinam Emendatiorem, Prolegomena et Indices* (Tübingen: Henrici Laupp, 1839). Prior to this, Andreas Gallandi had included the Epistle to Diognetus alongside nine of the other texts that form the Apostolic Fathers corpus (the text of the Didache had not been discovered at that stage). However, Gallandi's work, *Bibliotheca Veterum Patrum Antiquorumque Scriptorum Ecclesiasticorum*, was not simply a collection of texts that constituted the Apostolic Fathers. It was a much larger project ranging over fourteen volumes published in Venice between 1765–1781, presenting texts from the second to the eighth century. As such, it is probably incorrect to see it as the first collection of the Apostolic Fathers to contain the Epistle to Diognetus. Rather, as the name states, it is a compendium or ecclesial library of texts attributed to early Christian writers. However, after Hefele's volume the inclusion of the Epistle to Diognetus in the collection of the Apostolic Fathers becomes more standard.

38. P. Bryennios, ed., *Διδαχὴ τῶν δώδεκα ἀποστόλων ἐκ τοῦ ἱεροσολυμιτικοῦ χειρογράφου νῦν πρῶτον ἐκδιδομένη μετὰ προλεγομένων καὶ σημειώσεων ἐν οἷς καὶ τῆς Συνόψεως τῆς Π.Δ., τῆς Ἰωανν. τοῦ Χρυσοστόμου αὐτοῦ χειρογράφου* (Constantinople: Voutyra, 1883). An English translation of the text only can be found in R. D. Hitchcock and F. Brown, eds., *Teaching of the Twelve Apostles: Recently Discovered and Published by Philotheos Bryennios, Metropolitan of Nicomedia* (New York: Scribner, 1884).

39. J. B. Lightfoot, *S. Clement of Rome: An Appendix containing the Newly Recovered Portions, with Introductions, Notes, and Translations* (London: Macmillian, 1877) 224.

edition of First Clement and Second Clement prior to the publication of the Didache. According to an interview conducted with Bryennios, he recollected his discovery in the following ecstatic terms:

> This! This! This! This must be the Διδαχή [the Didache], the book that was lost, that the church mourns over to this day, the foundation of part of the Apostolic Constitutions. Εὕρηκα εὕρηκα εὕρηκα [I have found it, I have found it, I have found it].[40]

A few years later in 1887 the first facsimile images of the manuscript appeared.[41]

The fragments of Papias and the single fragment of Quadratus do not have first printed editions in the same sense as other texts in the Apostolic Fathers corpus. Various of these fragments first appeared in print with the publication of the earliest editions of Eusebius's *Historia ecclesiastica* and editions of several other early Christian writers, such as Irenaeus. Thus, the publication history is more complex, and in the case of the fragments of Papias the collection of possible texts attributed to him (or about him) developed over time as a rolling and contested corpus.[42] However, the earliest attempt at publishing an edition of the fragments of Papias was undertaken by Halloix as part of a more compendious collection of early Christian writers born in the first century.[43] This work has already been mentioned in connection with Polycarp's *To the Philippians*. Therefore, the first edition of a collection of the fragments of Papias appeared in 1633. Consequently, it can be seen that the Greek text of many of the writings that came to be known as the Apostolic Fathers were not available in print until the 1630s or 1640s. It was only two or three decades after this period that Cotelier published the first collection of texts in 1672 that had a recognizable resemblance to modern editions of the Apostolic Fathers. Together the discovery of various manuscripts and the publication of the individual editio princeps of each text became the building blocks for collections and editions of writings of the Apostolic Fathers.

5. COLLECTIONS OF THE WRITINGS OF THE APOSTOLIC FATHERS IN PRINT

As has been noted, the first printed collection of texts that can be described as representing the writings of the Apostolic Fathers was Cotelier's edition published in 1672. It included seven texts that are now typically included in modern editions of the collection. Five of these texts were seen as being genuine writings: the Epistle of Barnabas, 1 Clement, the Shepherd of Hermas, the seven letters of Ignatius in the form of the middle recension, and Polycarp's *To the Philippians*. Alongside this, Cotelier published texts that were either suspected to be inauthentic (2 Clement and the long recension of the Letters of Ignatius) or were not written by the Apostolic Fathers themselves, such as the text describing the death of Polycarp, the so-called Martyrdom of Polycarp. The volume contained ancient-language versions of the text either in Greek or Latin. Thus, for the first time, a collection of texts that represented the core of modern editions of the Apostolic Fathers appeared in print.

Of particular interest for the history of the collection of the writings of the Apostolic Fathers in the English-speaking world is the edition of Wake first published in 1693.

---

40. E. A. Grosvenor, "An Interview with Bishop Bryennios–The Discovery of the Teaching," *Andover Review* 2 (1884) 515–516, here 516.

41. J. R. Harris, *The Teaching of the Apostles: Newly Edited with a Facsimile Text and a Commentary* (Baltimore: Johns Hopkins University, 1887).

42. For a recent, excellent treatment of the surviving fragments and testimonies of Papias, see S. C. Carlson, ed., *Papias of Hierapolis Exposition of Dominical Oracles: The Fragments, Testimonia, and Reception of a Second-Century Commentator*, OECT (Oxford: Oxford University Press, 2021).

43. Halloix, *Illustrium Ecclesiae Orientalis Scriptorum Vitae et Documenta*, 635–49.

Wake was later Archbishop of Canterbury (1716–1737). Wake's volume contains English translations (without original-language texts) of the same seven texts that Cotelier's volume has in common with current standard editions of the Apostolic Fathers. Additionally, and also in common with Cotelier, Wake included the account of the Martyrdom of Ignatius. However, he did not include the extra letters contained in the long recension of the writings of Ignatius. Wake acknowledged that 2 Clement was of lesser reputation in the early church than 1 Clement. However, for Wake this lack of repute was not determinative of the authenticity of the authorship by Clement of the Second Epistle. Thus he states, "It is most probable that it was written by *St. Clement*; and has many excellent things, and worthy of that holy man in it."[44] Hence, for Wake the value of the writings collected in his volume was that, apart from the New Testament, "there is nothing remaining of the truly genuine Christian antiquity more early than these pieces I have put together here."[45]

During the late seventeenth and eighteenth centuries a few further editions of the writings of the Apostolic Fathers appeared. These tended to do one of two things. Some editions reduced the scope of Cotelier's collection, removing the Epistle of Barnabas and the Shepherd of Hermas.[46] Presumably, such volumes did not see these two texts as exhibiting the same degree of fidelity to the apostolic tradition and lineage as writings associated with Clement, Ignatius, and Polycarp. On the other hand, other editions reproduced Cotelier's set of texts.[47]

The next development relating to the size of the corpus of writings of the Apostolic Fathers occurred with the publication of Hefele's 1839 volume, *Patrum Apostolicorum Opera*. Hefele was the first to include the Epistle to Diognetus in a collection of texts under the title *Works of the Apostolic Fathers*.[48] A few decades later, printed editions began to include the fragments of Papias. The first example occurred in the 1875–1877 three-volume edition edited by Gebhardt, Harnack, and Zahn.[49] The editors included nineteen possible fragments from the works of Papias. Just over a decade later, the text of the Didache was included in the Lightfoot and Harmer single volume edition of the Apostolic Fathers that was published in 1891.[50] As Harmer states in the introductory note to that volume, Lightfoot had prepared the text and translation for the edition prior to his death

44. Wake, *Genuine Epistles of the Apostolical Fathers*, part 2, page 1.

45. Wake, *Genuine Epistles of the Apostolical Fathers*, part 1, paragraph 25.

46. T. Ittig, *Bibliotheca Patrum Apostolicorum Græco-Latina, Qua Continentur I. S. Clementis Romani Prior & Posterior ad Corinthios Epistola, II. S. Ignatii Epistolæ Septem Genuinæ, Qvibus ejusdem Interpolatæ & Spuriæ Epistolæ, Nec Non Acta Ignatiani Martyrii Accedunt, III. S. Polycarpi Epistola ad Philippenses, Cui Præter Fragmenta Polycarpi Ecclesiæ Smyrnensis de Polycarpi Martyrio Epistola Integra Adjungitur Præmissa Est Dissertatio de Patribus Apostolicis, Seu Scriptoribus Ecclesiasticis, Qvi Apostolorum Comites & Discipuli Fuisse Perhibentur* (Leipzig: Lipsiae Lanckisch Lipsiae Richter, 1699); J. L. Frey, *Epistolae Sanctorum Patrum Apostolicorum Clementis, Ignatii et Polycarpi atque Duorum Posteriorum Martyria: Omnia Graece et Latine cum Variorum Annotationibus et Praefatione* (Basel: J. K. von Mechel Witwe, 1742).

47. R. Russel, *SS. Patrum Apostolicorum Barnabae: Hermae, Clementis, Ignatii, Polycarpi, Opera Genuina; Una cum Ignatii & Polycarpi Martyriis: Versionibus Antiquis ac Recentioribus, Variantibus Lectionibus, Selectisque Variorum Notis Illustrata: Accesserunt S. Ignatii Epistolae, tum Interpolatae, tum Supposititiae, I–II* (London: Apud Gulielmum Russel, sub Horatii Capite, extra Portam Temple-Bar, 1746).

48. Pratscher attributes the inclusion of the Epistle to Diognetus to Gallandi in his multivolume work *Bibliotheca Veterum Patrum Antiquorumque Scriptorum Ecclesiasticorum*, dated to 1765–1781. In part this is a question of definition. Gallandi's compendious collection was an assembly of a vast array, or a library of early Christian texts. In this collection the Epistle to Diognetus appeared as an early Christian texts, not necessarily as a text grouped with those known as the writings of the Apostolic Fathers. That happened in an unambiguous way only with Hefele's edition in 1839. See W. Pratscher, ed., *The Apostolic Fathers: An Introduction* (Waco, TX: Baylor University Press, 2010), 2–3.

49. O. von Gebhardt, A. von Harnack, and T. Zahn, eds., *Patrum Apostolicorum Opera: Textum ad Fidem Codicum Graecorum et Latinorum Adhibitis Praestantissimus Editionibus*, 3 vols. (Leipzig, 1875–1877).

50. Lightfoot, *Apostolic Fathers*. Harmer edited and completed the work.

in 1889.[51] It was not until the beginning of the twentieth century that the fragment of Quadratus was first included as a member of the collection of the writings of the Apostolic Fathers. This occurred in Funk's edition of 1901.[52]

Several editions of the writings of the Apostolic Fathers have appeared throughout the twentieth and early twenty-first centuries. Not all of these have included the eleven members that now form a standard established corpus of the Apostolic Fathers. However, the more significant scholarly editions that contain original-language texts and modern-language translations tend to contain these eleven members of the corpus or a close approximation to that set of writings. Occasionally some of the fragmentary texts are omitted, or in the case of the fragments of Papias, varying numbers of fragmentary texts are presented. In other instances, the Shepherd of Hermas has been omitted, presumably due to its length. However, over the more than three centuries that have elapsed since the appearance of Cotelier's defining landmark volume, the seven items he included in his collection have remained the firm core of later editions. However, over that time four further items have been added. Thus, as a result of a fresh manuscript discovery, the Didache quickly became established as a fixed member of the corpus in subsequent editions. By contrast, the Epistle to Diognetus, the fragment of Quadratus, and the fragments of Papias had a slower path to inclusion in the collection. Their place was established by a more gradual evolving scholarly consensus that developed from the mid-nineteenth century onward. Currently the corpus is relatively fixed with eleven members. However, fresh manuscript discoveries, or perhaps further changes of scholarly opinion, might alter the size and contents of the collection. The corpus of writings labeled as the Apostolic Fathers has always been and remains a somewhat artificial assemblage of texts of different genres, written at various times and in multiple places by authors with unique perspectives. Yet, despite this diversity, this rolling corpus provides a glimpse into rich streams of Christian faith and practice primarily, but not exclusively, for the period of the first half of the second century.

6. SCHOLARLY RESOURCES FOR THE STUDY OF THE APOSTOLIC FATHERS

For continuing and deeper study of the Apostolic Fathers, a range of resources are necessary and available. The main tools required are editions of the texts in the original languages, a range of detailed commentaries, and for those wishing to gain an overview of the texts as a whole there are several helpful introductory works.

6.1 Recent Original-Language Editions of the Apostolic Fathers

The key resource is an edition of the primary texts that constitute the corpus. Here there are three main alternatives. In order of date of publication, first from 1992 there is the volume edited by Andreas Lindemann and Henning Paulsen, *Die apostolischen Väter*.[53] This edition presents original-language texts with facing German translation. The volume is a revision of the earlier and often reprinted version of Karl Bihlmeyer first published in 1924,[54] but it also integrates Molly Whittaker's Greek and Latin text of the Shepherd of Hermas.[55] This volume may be the natural choice for German speakers.

51. Lightfoot, *Apostolic Fathers*, ix.

52. F. X. Funk, *Die apostolischen Väter*, SAQ 2.1 (Tübingen: Mohr Siebeck, 1901).

53. A. Lindemann and H. Paulsen, eds., *Die apostolischen Väter: Griechisch-deutsche Parallelausgabe* (Tübingen: Mohr Siebeck, 1992).

54. K. Bihlmeyer, *Die apostolischen Väter: Neubearbeitung der Funkschen Ausgabe, Teil I: Didache, Barnabas, Klemens I und II, Ignatius, Polykarp, Papias, Quadratus, Diognetbrief*, SAQ 2.1.1 (Tübingen: Mohr Siebeck, 1924).

55. M. Whittaker, *Die Hirt des Hermas*, 2nd ed., Die grieschische christliche Schriftsteller 48 (Berlin: Akademie, 1967).

Two important English editions of the Apostolic Fathers have been published that contain original-language texts with facing English translation. Bart Ehrman's two-volume edition in the Loeb Classical Library contains all eleven texts that now form the standard collection of the writings of the Apostolic Fathers,[56] although the subtitle to the first volume that simply lists "Polycarp" as an entry has misled some into thinking that the Martyrdom of Polycarp is omitted. That is incorrect. Ehrman's edition is itself an updated edition of the earlier Loeb Classical Library two-volume set edited by Kirsopp Lake and published in 1912–1913.[57] Ehrman provided a new introduction and fresh translations of the texts. However, the Greek (and Latin) text remained unchanged throughout, since Ehrman was not commissioned to work on the original-language text. Instead, he was asked only to update the English-language translation. This remains one of the two key scholarly editions available for English-speaking readers.

The second significant collection of the Apostolic Fathers providing original-language texts with English translations is now in its third edition. This is the single-volume collection of Michael W. Holmes.[58] Again, this is a revision of an earlier edition—namely, the collection that drew on the work of Lightfoot, posthumously completed by Harmer.[59] While the edition of Lightfoot and Harmer was a model of late nineteenth-century erudition, the various revisions made by Holmes have further strengthened the scope, utility, and quality of that original work. The Lightfoot edition lacked the text of the fragment of Quadratus that is present in the third edition of Holmes. Whereas in the Lightfoot edition the Greek texts are continuous with English translations following on subsequent pages, the Holmes edition provides facing English translations. This makes working with the text more straightforward and accessible. There are also new introductions provided for each text, with references to recent scholarly debates and relevant bibliographical entries. However, the most important change involves the revision of original-language texts based on recent manuscript finds or on a reevaluation of the textual evidence. Thus, as Holmes notes, "This third edition, then, while genetically descended from the 1891 Lightfoot-Harmer diglot edition, is in effect a fresh and comprehensive revision."[60] With the whole corpus in a single volume, this is now perhaps the most widely used and consulted edition of the Apostolic Fathers corpus.

6.2 Commentary Series on the Apostolic Fathers

In this section, seven commentary series will be briefly discussed. Four are in-depth, advanced treatments that offer detailed analysis of the texts in their original languages with attention to philological and text-critical matters. The other three series are highly valuable and contain a wealth of insights in their comments. However, they do not contain the same level of concern with the details of original-language text. None of these series as yet provides a complete treatment of all eleven texts that constitute the Apostolic Fathers. Moreover, only one of the popular series is complete in terms of the volumes to be published—although it does not cover all eleven texts. Here more will be said in regard to the four series that offer more in-depth treatments of the text.

The first of the Sources Chrétiennes volumes dealing with the Apostolic Fathers was

56. B. D. Ehrman, ed., *The Apostolic Fathers*, 2 vols., LCL (Cambridge: Harvard University Press, 2003).

57. K. Lake, ed., *The Apostolic Fathers*, 2 vols., LCL (Cambridge: Harvard University Press, 1912–1913).

58. M. W. Holmes, *The Apostolic Fathers: Greek Texts and English Translations*, 3rd ed. (Grand Rapids: Baker, 2007).

59. Lightfoot, *Apostolic Fathers*.

60. Holmes, *Apostolic Fathers*, xii.

published in 1945. This first volume provides an edition of the original-language texts of the letters of Ignatius, Polycarp's *To the Philippians*, and the Martyrdom of Polycarp, with French translations and commentary. This edition by P.-T. Camelot was republished in a revised form in 1998.[61] Since the publication of that volume in 1945, a total of six Sources Chrétiennes volumes have appeared covering eight of the eleven texts in the corpus of the Apostolic Fathers. In addition to the texts covered in Camelot's volume, others have dealt with the Epistle to Diognetus,[62] the Shepherd of Hermas,[63] 1 Clement,[64] the Epistle of Barnabas,[65] and the Didache.[66] The three texts that are yet to receive coverage in the Sources Chrétiennes series are 2 Clement, the fragment of Quadratus, and the fragments of Papias. Due to their fragmentary state, it is perhaps unsurprising that a volume has not been devoted to the latter two sets of textual remains.

Published by Vandenhoeck and Ruprecht, the Kommentar zu den Apostolischen Vätern (KAV) presents technical and highly detailed treatments of individual texts among the corpus of the Apostolic Fathers. These volumes are written in German and provide original texts with German-language translations combined with detailed introductions tackling standard questions pertaining to authorship, date, state of the text, rhetorical and compositional analysis, and an account of the history of research. Currently, seven volumes have appeared covering the following texts: 1 Clement,[67] 2 Clement,[68] the Letter of Polycarp to the Philippians,[69] the Martyrdom of Polycarp,[70] the Didache,[71] the Epistle of Barnabas,[72] and the Shepherd of Hermas.[73] The majority of these are landmark volumes, which are required reading for those conducting detailed research on these texts. Only one, Niederwimmer on the Didache, has been translated in English. The others must be read in German.

The next significant series is a subseries of the Hermeneia commentaries. To date only three volumes have appeared, although others are in preparation. It is in this series that the English-language translation of Niederwimmer's commentary on the Didache appears.[74] The other two volumes are William Schoedel's *Ignatius of Antioch* (1985),[75] and Carolyn Osiek's *Shepherd of Hermas*.[76] The same qualities that exemplify the treatment of biblical texts covered in the series are also to be found in these volumes. There is close analysis of the text in the original languages, detailed interaction with the best secondary literature, and extensive commentary typically provided in verse-by-verse format.

61. P.-T. Camelot, *Ignace d'Antioche–Polycarpe de Smyrne: Lettres. Martyre de Polycarpe*, 2nd ed., SC 10 bis. (Paris: Éditions du Cerf, 1998).

62. H.-I. Marrou, *À Diognète*, SC 33 bis. (Paris: Éditions du Cerf, 1951 [1st ed.]; 1965 [2nd ed.; repr., 2007]).

63. R. Joly, *Le Pasteur*, SC 53 bis. (Paris: Éditions du Cerf, 1958 [1st ed.]; 1968 [2nd ed.; repr., 1997]).

64. A. Jaubert, *Clément de Rome: Épitre aux Corinthiens*, SC 167 bis. (Paris: Éditions du Cerf, 1971 [repr., 2000]).

65. R. A. Kraft and P. Prigent, *Épitre de Barnabé*, SC 172 (Paris: Éditions du Cerf, 1971).

66. W. Rordorf and A. Tuilier, *La Doctrine des douze apôtres (Didachè)*, SC 248 bis. (Paris: Éditions du Cerf, 1978 [1st ed.]; 1998 [2nd ed.]).

67. H. E. Lona, *Der erste Clemensbrief*, KAV 2 (Göttingen: Vandenhoeck & Ruprecht, 1998).

68. W. Pratscher, *Der zweite Clemensbrief*, KAV 3 (Göttingen: Vandenhoeck & Ruprecht, 2007).

69. J. B. Bauer, *Die Polykarpbriefe*, KAV 5 (Göttingen: Vandenhoeck & Ruprecht, 1995).

70. G. Buschmann, *Das Martyrium des Polykarp*, KAV 6 (Göttingen: Vandenhoeck & Ruprecht, 1998).

71. K. Niederwimmer, *Die Didache*, KAV 1 (Göttingen: Vandenhoeck & Ruprecht, 1989).

72. F. R. Prostmeier, *Der Barnabasbrief*, KAV 8 (Göttingen: Vandenhoeck & Ruprecht, 1999).

73. N. Brox, *Der Hirt des Hermas*, KAV 7 (Göttingen: Vandenhoeck & Ruprecht, 1991).

74. K. Niederwimmer, *The Didache: A Commentary*, trans. L. M. Maloney, Hermeneia (Minneapolis: Augsburg Fortress, 1998).

75. W. R. Schoedel, *Ignatius of Antioch: A Commentary*, Hermeneia (Philadelphia: Fortress, 1985).

76. Carolyn Osiek, *Shepherd of Hermas: A Commentary*, Hermeneia (Minneapolis: Augsburg Fortress, 1999).

More recent is the Oxford Apostolic Fathers (OAF) series. Volumes in this series provide extensive introductions covering the gamut of significant issues of manuscript evidence, attestation to the texts in the early church and beyond, discussions of authorship, provenance, date, analysis of genre and literary features, as well as an investigation of the theology and themes of each text. There then follows an edition of the text with facing English translation. Lastly, and building on the previous sections, a detailed commentary on the text in the original language is provided. Thus far, three volumes have appeared in the series, covering five of the eleven texts of the Apostolic Fathers: Christopher Tuckett, *2 Clement* (2012);[77] Paul Hartog, *Polycarp's Epistle to the Philippians and the Martyrdom of Polycarp* (2013);[78] and Clayton Jefford, *The Epistle to Diognetus (with the Fragment of Quadratus)*.[79] Volumes covering all of the remaining texts in the corpus have been commissioned.

Alongside these four series providing in-depth analysis of the texts in their original language are three further important series, which, while not providing the same detailed analysis of the original-language texts, nonetheless are important contributions that, where necessary, discuss textual issues in the Greek or Latin forms of the texts. The German Handbuch zum Neuen Testament series first included volumes dealing with the texts of the Apostolic Fathers in the early 1920s. These earlier volumes include Bauer on the Ignatian letters and Polycarp's letter to the Philippians (1920);[80] Knopf on the Didache and the Letters of Clement (1920);[81] Windisch on the Epistle of Barnabas (1920);[82] and Dibelius on the Shepherd of Hermas (1923).[83] More recently, two newer volumes have appeared. The first is by Paulsen, dealing with the letters of Ignatius and Polycarp's *To the Philippians* (1985).[84] The second is Lindemann's commentary on Clement's letters (1992).[85]

Another important and ambitious series was initiated by Robert Grant in the 1960s, which covers nine of the eleven texts in the corpus. The omissions are the Epistle to Diognetus and the fragment of Quadratus. Grant offers a twofold explanation for the omission of these texts in his introductory volume. He states, "The letter to Diognetus and the solitary fragment of Quadratus belong not to the Apostolic Fathers but to the apologetic literature of the second century after all. They were written not for those within the Christian community but for those outside."[86] If the parameters of the collection were fixed by considerations of genre and audience, Grant's observations would be entirely correct. However, for good or for bad, the collection has developed organically without

77. C. M. Tuckett, *2 Clement: Introduction, Text, and Commentary*, OAF (Oxford: Oxford University Press, 2012).

78. P. Hartog, *Polycarp's Epistle to the Philippians and the Martyrdom of Polycarp: Introduction, Text, and Commentary*, OAF (Oxford: Oxford University Press, 2013).

79. C. N. Jefford, *The Epistle to Diognetus (with the Fragment of Quadratus): Introduction, Text, and Commentary*, OAF (Oxford: Oxford University Press, 2013).

80. W. Bauer, *Die Briefe des Ignatius von Antiochia und der Brief des Polykarp von Smyrna*, HNT Ergänzungsband, Die Apostolischen Väter 2 (Tubingen: Möhr Siebeck, 1920).

81. R. Knopf, *Die Lehre der zwölf Apostel: Die zwei Clemensbriefe*, HNT Ergänzungsband, Die Apostolischen Väter 1 (Tubingen: Möhr Siebeck, 1920).

82. H. Windisch, *Der Barnabasbrief*, HNT Ergänzungsband, Die Apostolischen Väter 3 (Tubingen: Möhr Siebeck, 1920).

83. M. Dibelius, *Der Hirt des Hermas*, HNT Ergänzungsband, Die Apostolischen Väter 4 (Tubingen: Möhr Siebeck, 1923).

84. H. Paulsen, *Die Briefe des Ignatius von Antiochia und der Brief des Polykarp von Smyrna*, 2nd ed., HNT 18 (Tubingen: Möhr Siebeck, 1985).

85. A. Lindemann, *Die Clemensbriefe*, HNT 17 (Tubingen: Möhr Siebeck, 1992), at 277 pages.

86. R. M. Grant, *An Introduction*, vol. 1 of *The Apostolic Fathers: A New Translation and Commentary* (New York: Thomas Nelson, 1965), vi.

strict logic being applied to its contents. In the remaining five volumes of the series, the following texts are treated: volume 2, Grant and Graham cover the letters of Clement (1965);[87] volume 3, Kraft on the Didache and the Epistle of Barnabas (1965);[88] volume 4, Grant on the Letters of Ignatius (1966);[89] volume 5, Schoedel on the Letter of Polycarp, the Martyrdom of Polycarp, and the fragments of Papias (1967);[90] and lastly, volume 6, Snyder on the Shepherd of Hermas (1968).[91] The volumes differ in level of treatment, although the translation remains a focal point. For instance, the volume on the Shepherd of Hermas, no doubt due to the length of the translation, contains minimal commentary and notes. By contrast, there is much more by way of introduction and notes in the volume treating the letters of Ignatius. The volume on the Didache and the Epistle of Barnabas has a valuable introduction, but in the commentary section the Two Ways material in Barnabas 18.1–21.9 is treated in conjunction with the parallel material in Didache 1.1–6.2. While this may save space, it detracts from treating each text as a whole. The first five of these volumes have recently been reissued by Wipf & Stock.[92]

At this stage, a series of mid-length commentaries on the writings of the Apostolic Fathers is being published by Cascade (an imprint of Wipf & Stock), under the series title Apostolic Fathers Commentary Series (AFCS). Thus far, four very helpful volumes have appeared. Each volume offers a fresh translation of the text being analyzed, a set of introductory essays, and a commentary which deals with the final form of the text in a section-by-section format. These commentaries do discuss the text in the original language where necessary, but with accompanying English translations. The first volume in the series is by Wilhite on the Didache (2020).[93] In many ways this is a major contribution to the study of the Didache, with a detailed introduction (pp. 3–98) and a comprehensive commentary (pp. 99–235). This work will be valued alike by specialists and those seeking an initial, detailed introduction to the text. The second entry in the series is by William Varner on 2 Clement.[94] This is equally incisive, but a little shorter in scope. The introduction discusses key topics for orienting readers to the major issues surrounding the text (pp. 3–46). There then follows a helpful commentary (pp. 49–153), with the key Greek terms and phrases discussed. The third volume to be published in the series was Jonathon Lookadoo's excellent discussion of the Epistle of Barnabas (2022).[95] The fourth and most recent volume is the jointly authored treatment by Michael J. Svigel and Caroline P. Buie on the Shepherd of Hermas (2023). In many ways this represents a landmark treatment, with some reference to the Greek text.[96] This has already proven itself to be a significant series of commentaries.

87. R. M. Grant and H. H. Graham, *First and Second Clement*, vol. 2 of *The Apostolic Fathers: A New Translation and Commentary* (New York: Thomas Nelson, 1965).

88. R. A. Kraft, *The Didache and Barnabas*, vol. 3 of *The Apostolic Fathers: A New Translation and Commentary* (New York: Thomas Nelson, 1965).

89. R. M. Grant, *Ignatius of Antioch*, vol. 4 of *The Apostolic Fathers: A New Translation and Commentary* (New York: Thomas Nelson, 1966).

90. W. R. Schoedel, *Polycarp. Martyrdom of Polycarp, Fragments of Papias*, vol. 5 of *The Apostolic Fathers: A New Translation and Commentary* (New York: Thomas Nelson, 1967).

91. G. F. Snyder, *Hermas*, vol. 6 of *The Apostolic Fathers: A New Translation and Commentary* (New York: Thomas Nelson, 1968).

92. These five volumes were republished in 2020.

93. S. J. Wilhite, *The Didache: A Commentary*, AFCS (Eugene, OR: Cascade, 2019).

94. W. Varner, *Second Clement: An Introductory Commentary*, AFCS (Eugene, OR: Cascade, 2021).

95. J. Lookadoo, *The Epistle of Barnabas: A Commentary*, AFCS (Eugene, OR: Cascade, 2022).

96. M. J. Svigel and C. P. Buie, *The Shepherd of Hermas: A New Translation and Commentary*, AFCS (Eugene, OR: Cascade, 2023).

6.3 Introductory Works

Introductory works are of primary value in providing an overview of the various texts contained in the standard collection of the writings of the Apostolic Fathers. Typically they discuss standard introductory questions and highlight key ideas or theological themes, rather than providing detailed commentary on specific texts. Furthermore, the majority of these volumes also provide bibliographical selections of works that are useful for further study of individual texts.

One particularly useful volume in this regard, first published in 1996 (with a second edition in 2012) is Clayton Jefford's *Reading the Apostolic Fathers*. This is a model of balanced perspectives and centrist observations, written by a scholar with expertise across the entire corpus of texts.[97] Two further introductions comprise chapters written by a range of authors with expertise in each of the specific texts that comprise the corpus. Treating them in order of publication date, the first, published in 2007, by Paul Foster (ed.), *The Writings of the Apostolic Fathers*, collects a series of chapters originally published as successive articles in *The Expository Times* from January 2006 to January 2007.[98] The volume contains an introductory essay by Helmut Koester, followed by eleven chapters on each of the writings contained in the corpus.[99] The third significant introductory volume was first published in German in 2009 but subsequently translated into English as Wilhelm Pratscher (ed.), *The Apostolic Fathers: An Introduction* (2010).[100] The volume contains an introduction to the corpus and the contents of various modern editions of the texts, followed by eleven chapters written by different experts on each of the standard texts that constitute the collection, followed by a concluding essay by Jörg Ulrich, "The Apostolic Fathers Yesterday and Today."[101] This is a volume filled with seminal insights and drawing upon a wealth of scholarship, particularly that published originally in German. A number of contributors have authored volumes in the prestigious Kommentar zu den Apostolischen Vätern (KAV) series, and thus the individual essays are a distillation of many of those wider insights.

Those wishing to undertake more detailed work are well served with scholarly resources, including original language texts, introductory works, and commentaries. Not every text in the collection is equally well covered with commentaries, but most have at least one outstanding commentary to guide readers. Additionally, there are various monographs and learned articles. Many of these are referenced elsewhere in this volume, as well as in the bibliographies contained in the works discussed in this overview of scholarly resources on the Apostolic Fathers.

7. THE VALUE OF STUDYING THE APOSTOLIC FATHERS

Individually, each of the writings that constitute the collection of texts contained in modern editions of the Apostolic Fathers casts light on the concerns, practices, and beliefs of the early Jesus movement, primarily in the first half of the second century or thereabouts. These texts address different issues. Some reflect problems that had arisen in relation to community hierarchy and the cohesion of these early groups of believers. Several betray

97. C. N. Jefford, *Reading the Apostolic Fathers: A Student's Introduction*, 2nd ed. (Grand Rapids: Baker Academic, 2012).

98. Individual details will not be provided, but the relevant issues are *The Expository Times* 117.4 (Jan 2006) to 118.4 (Jan 2007).

99. P. Foster, ed., *The Writings of the Apostolic Fathers* (London: T&T Clark, 2007).

100. W. Pratscher, ed., *The Apostolic Fathers: An Introduction* (Waco, TX: Baylor University Press, 2010).

101. J. Ulrich, "The Apostolic Fathers Yesterday and Today," in Pratscher, *Apostolic Fathers*, 255–60.

the tense relationship with Judaism in the early second century.[102] Together as a collection, albeit largely a modern construct, they form a rich repository of information about the inner spiritual life—both corporate and individual—based on a combination of ethics, eschatological hopes, core faith commitments focused on Christ, and a call for perseverance in the face of persecution that was at times feared and at other times became a reality.

While it has been repeatedly acknowledged that the collection is artificial, and in fact somewhat arbitrary, when read together these texts present greater insight into the early Jesus movement than can be gleaned from reading them individually. This is certainly a case where the value of the whole far outweighs the sum of the individual texts. The reason for this is because together they present the diversity of the early Jesus movement and the range of its concerns chiefly during the first half of the second century. Within the collection there are some more natural points of commonality. For instance, 1 Clement and Polycarp's *To the Philippians* both tackle issues of group maintenance and stability, not in the authors' own communities but in relation to other groups of Jesus believers. The letters of Ignatius have a natural connection with the figure of Polycarp and the writings associated with him. Polycarp and his community received two letters from Ignatius, and Polycarp references Ignatius in his own letter to the Philippians. Moreover, the martyrological fervor especially present in Ignatius's letter to the Romans is also to be found in a different and more developed form in the account of the Martyrdom of Polycarp. The Epistle to Diognetus, an example of a Christian apologetic text (at least in its first and largest section), shares the same outward-looking concerns as the small fragment of the Apology of Quadratus. Both these texts attempt to provide a robust and intellectually appealing defense of the Christian faith for those who were not group members. Other commonalities and points of contact could be listed among various of the texts in the collection. What emerges from this comparison is that while the texts are diverse, there is, nonetheless, a great deal of unity amid that difference. Certainly the early Christian movement in the first half of the second century was not monolithic. However, neither was it riven with irreconcilable factionalism. Alongside these differences, there was a network of communication between the disparate groups that produced the texts in the collection. In many ways, it was this combination of local group cohesion and a sense of being part of a larger, translocal movement that simultaneously sustained the larger movement and provided adherents with a sense of identity.

These texts are also of value to contemporary readers in that they show the emergence of structures, roles, and systems of belief that have had a lasting impact on the articulation of Christian faith. Admittedly, alongside these recognizable features one can at times identify elements or ways of expressing belief that did not become part of the lasting legacy of the Christian movement. In this way, one is better able to appreciate the creative attempts, some successful while others not so, to express core beliefs and to shape group structures. For instance, the ecclesial offices advocated by Ignatius and his articulation of eucharistic theology became normative and have remained so for much of subsequent Christianity. The approach to the Jewish Scriptures that read them through a heavy christological lens while perhaps picking up something already present among New Testament authors, takes

---

102. As Holmes observes, "Throughout the postapostolic period, then, we find the emerging Christian movement struggling to define itself vis-à-vis its Jewish roots and, increasingly, vis-à-vis the Greco-Roman culture and society into which it was expanding. Moreover, a central aspect of this struggle involved the tension between continuity and change: how to maintain and propagate the tradition received from Jesus and his followers in the midst of rapidly changing circumstances and in the face of new and often unanticipated challenges" (Holmes, *Apostolic Fathers*, 16).

this even further in several texts such as 1 Clement and the Epistle of Barnabas. From this viewpoint, the Jewish Scriptures were read as *praeparatio evangelica*—that is, as a preparation and precursor to the message of the gospel and as finding their divinely intended fulfilment in the person of Jesus. While this theological perspective is prominent in several of the texts, one must acknowledge with the wisdom of hindsight that it has resulted in consequences for Judaism that cannot be ignored. Furthermore, in many ways the ecclesial structures advocated by Ignatius appear to be harbingers of systems of church governance that would be adopted in later decades. His elevated views of the office of bishop should not be read as a developed notion of monarchical episcopacy, as that was yet to come. However, there is little doubt that his advocacy of monepiscopacy—that is, the appointment and authoritative oversight of a single person in each Christian community—laid the foundations for developments that occurred in subsequent decades and centuries.[103]

Therefore, for those interested not just in the history of the Jesus movement in the second century but also with fundamental questions about the way in which the early Jewish messianic group centered on the person of Jesus transformed itself into a global faith system, the writings of the Apostolic Fathers provide vital evidence. It is possible to gain insight into multiple groups, although still small in size, which were scattered around the Eastern Mediterranean world and in the imperial capital, Rome.[104] These disparate groups and multiple authors do not provide a full understanding of early Christianity in the period of the early second century. However, as a collection, together they provide the surviving evidence from that period. As such they are the bright lights that emerge from that otherwise murky and little documented period of the early Jesus movement.

BIBLIOGRAPHY

Standard Editions of the Greek Text with English Translations

Ehrman, B. D., ed. *The Apostolic Fathers*. 2 vols. LCL. Cambridge: Harvard University Press, 2003.

Holmes, M. W., ed. *The Apostolic Fathers: Greek Texts and English Translations*. 3rd ed. Grand Rapids: Baker Academic, 2007.

Lightfoot, J. B., ed. *The Apostolic Fathers: Revised Texts with Short Introductions and English Translations*. Edited and completed by J. R. Harmer. London: Macmillan, 1891.

Introductory Works and Commentaries

Foster, P., ed. *The Writings of the Apostolic Fathers*. London: T&T Clark, 2007.

Hartog, P. *Polycarp's Epistle to the Philippians and the Martyrdom of Polycarp: Introduction, Text, and Commentary*. OAF. Oxford: Oxford University Press, 2013.

Jefford, C. N. *The Epistle to Diognetus (with the Fragment of Quadratus): Introduction, Text, and Commentary*. OAF. Oxford: Oxford University Press, 2013.

Jefford, C. N. *Reading the Apostolic Fathers: A Student's Introduction*. 2nd ed. Grand Rapids: Baker Academic, 2012.

Lightfoot, J. B. *The Apostolic Fathers, Part I: S. Clement of Rome*. 2nd ed. 2 vols. London: Macmillan, 1890.

Lightfoot, J. B. *The Apostolic Fathers, Part II: S. Ignatius, S. Polycarp. Revised Texts with Introductions, Notes, Dissertations, and Translations*. 2nd. ed. 3 vols. London: Macmillan, 1889–1890.

Niederwimmer, K. *The Didache: A Commentary*. Trans. L. M. Maloney. Hermeneia. Minneapolis: Augsburg Fortress, 1998.

Osiek, C. *Shepherd of Hermas: A Commentary*. Hermeneia. Minneapolis: Augsburg Fortress, 1999.

Pratscher, W., ed. *The Apostolic Fathers: An Introduction*. Waco, TX: Baylor University Press, 2010.

Schoedel, W. R. *Ignatius of Antioch: A Commentary*. Hermeneia. Philadelphia: Fortress, 1985.

Tuckett, C. M. *2 Clement: Introduction, Text, and Commentary*. OAF. Oxford: Oxford University Press, 2012.

---

103. For a seminal discussion of this issue, see F. A. Sullivan, *From Apostles to Bishops: The Development of the Episcopacy in the Early Church* (New York: Newman, 2001).

104. For a detailed study of Christian presence in Rome in this period, see P. Lampe, *From Paul to Valentinus: Christians at Rome in the First Two Centuries* (London: T&T Clark, 2003).

PART 1

THE TEXTS

CHAPTER 2

THE DIDACHE

JOSEPH VERHEYDEN

1. INTRODUCTION

The Didache (Greek for "Teaching"), so called after the first word of the title of the work, is an intriguing document in more than one respect. Its author, precise date of composition, and provenance are unknown, its genre seemingly unique for the period, its structure and contents at times slightly confusing, its sources in part debated and in part still a mystery, its purpose open for discussion, its concept of authority puzzling, its theological interests apparently an amalgam of practical advice and reflections of a more theoretical character, and its relation to Christian tradition a matter of ongoing debate. But that is what "an intriguing document" is all about! In what follows, these various aspects will be addressed in more detail.

1.1 The State of the Text and the Surviving Manuscripts

No complete text of the Didache has been discovered. The text up to 16.8 is preserved in only one manuscript, Codex Hierosolymitanus, dated to 1056, that was first published in 1883. In addition, there have been preserved two very small papyrus fragments among the Oxyrhynchus papyri. The first fragment is part of a miniature codex that may have served as an amulet (P.Oxy. 1782, from the fourth century, with the text of Did. 1.3c–4a and 2.7b–3.2a). The second is a Coptic fragment of 10.3b–12.2a of uneven quality, dating from the fifth century. After the edition of 1883, it was discovered that almost the full text of the Didache had been integrated into book 7 of the Apostolic Constitutions, a fourth-century church order. A paraphrastic Ethiopic translation of Didache 11.3–13.7 and 8.1–2 was discovered in an Ethiopian church order, which gives a good clue about the genre of the original. Loose portions of the work are also met in other church orders, the Latin *Doctrina Apostolorum*, the Greek *Apostolic Church Order*, and its *Epitome*, and in later sources, but none of these can be considered to be direct witnesses of the text, as they may also go back to the teaching on the Two Ways that constitutes the first part of the Didache. A Georgian translation of the work that was published in the early twentieth century proved to be a modern translation. The textual situation with only one (incomplete) manuscript obviously poses problems for deciding on the original version of the text.

1.2 Date and Provenance

The work is generally said to be one of the oldest Christian writings after Paul and (most of) the Gospels. A date around 100 CE, with perhaps a slight preference for a date in the early second century, is widely accepted, even if there is no hard evidence, internal or external, for such an early dating. Syria (Antioch) as the place of origin still remains the majority opinion, with Egypt as runner-up. Internal evidence for one or the other is weak and indirect. The term "fragment" in 9.3 to denote the fragmented bread in the Eucharist may point to liturgical usage in Egypt, but the motif of the wheat growing on the hills in 9.4 would rather direct us away from Egypt, though not necessarily to Syria. The possibility that the author relied on Jewish tradition in the opening chapters (see below) would work for both venues. The external evidence may be stronger, as the work is (fragmentarily) attested in Coptic (see sec. 1.1 above) and is used and cited by a couple of authors working in Egypt from the time of Clement of Alexandria onward (ca. 190 CE). The question is further complicated by the composite nature of the work, which allows for the possibility that parts of it were originally composed in different places and then put together at one of these locations, or elsewhere.

2. SUMMARY OF CONTENT

With about 2,200 words, the Didache is a relatively short document, divided in the editions in sixteen chapters of unequal length. It is short but diversified in topic, tone, and genre. The work is singled out by its double title—a short form ("The Teaching of the Twelve Apostles") and a longer one that looks like a variant in which the status of the apostles and their intended audience is specified ("The Teaching of the Lord through the Twelve Apostles to the Gentiles/Nations"). The apostles are the mouthpiece of the Lord, and they wish to proclaim the gospel among a non-Jewish audience. If the first part of this title refers to a well-known motif—the apostles are missionaries of the Lord and do not preach at their own initiative—the second gives a rather general indication of the intended readership. The relation between the two titles, as well as their authenticity, poses a problem. The longer title does not stand apart but rather looks like the opening phrase of the document. However, this does not have to mean that it was never intended to be a title, nor that the short title was the original one. The short one could also be a later addition, and the longer might just as well have been the title of the opening section. Perhaps one should then even reckon with the possibility that both titles were added afterward.

Scholars have suggested various proposals for structuring the material, but the differences are rather limited and basically have to do with whether particular sections are further subdivided into smaller units. Major breaks are met at 6.3/7.1, 10.7/11.1, and 15.4/16.1, which yields a structure in four main parts.

Structure of the Didache

Titles:	Short and long title
Main Body:	
Did. 1.1–6.3	The way of life and the way of death
Did. 7–10	Instructions on baptism, prayer and fasting, and the Eucharist
Did. 11–15	Church order
Did. 16	Eschatological teaching

Didache 1.1–6.3

The Didache opens mightily with its impressive declaration that "there are two paths, one of life and one of death, and the difference between the two paths is great" (1.1).[1]

1. All translations in this essay of the Apostolic Fathers are from B. D. Ehrman, *The Apostolic Fathers*, 2 vols., LCL (Cambridge: Harvard University Press, 2003).

That statement sets the tone and formulates in a most succinct way the contents of the first six chapters. This is a teaching about how to be saved and how to escape eternal damnation. The section is often referred to as "The Two Ways Tractate," the larger part of which has parallels in other early Christian works, which may point to the relatively free use of a common tradition (see below). If read in light of the next section, which opens with instructions for how to baptize, and of the Didache's interest in what looks like catechetical teaching, one is perhaps entitled also to call this section a baptismal catechesis. The "way of life" part takes the lion's share, covering the first four chapters; the one on death is limited to chapter 5, with the final chapter functioning as a kind of conclusion or perhaps even an epilogue. The "way of life" part (1.2–4.14) can be further divided into seven sections based on form and content. The first, very brief one (1.2), straightforwardly defines the path to life by means of two famous commandments, known also from the teaching of Jesus in the Gospels, that are introduced here without any context or reference to Jesus: the double love command—of God and of one's neighbor—and a negatively formulated version of the golden rule (cf. Matt 7:12).

Didache 1.3–2.1 is commonly called the *sectio evangelica*, and one immediately sees why this title is chosen and how appropriate it is. The better part of the section reads like a freely composed anthology of Jesus sayings, a good number of these echoing or looking quite similar to sayings from the Sermon on the Mount/Plain, especially the sections on retaliation and love for one's enemy (Matt 5:38–42, 43–48; Luke 6:27–30, 32–36). It is conceived as a kind of practical illustration of the love command and is introduced accordingly. Jesus is not mentioned, and the instructions, like the rules in Didache 1.2, are formulated with imperatives and presented as if universally and automatically effective if applied. The golden rule is further illustrated (so 2.1) in 2.2–7 with a quite diversified series of twenty-five mostly short prohibitions (as a rule with οὐ/οὐκ, "not," and the second-person future) forbidding forms of criminal (murder), illegal (practicing magic), and above all immoral behavior (adultery and many other things). In 3.1–6 a second series of prohibitions is added (now with μή, "not" + aorist imperative), partly overlapping with the previous one but somewhat different in tone, as the addressee—taken as an individual—is now five times called "child," and some more explanation is given than in the first series for why one should refrain from any such acts. The same, more comforting tone is kept in 3.7–10 when urging the addressees to be meek and humble in the knowledge "that nothing occurs apart from God" (3.10). A third, much longer series follows in 4.1–11 that once more repeats the address "child" and combines prohibitions with commandments that more directly deal with daily-life situations in the family (4.9–11) and in society (4.1–8), including almsgiving, speaking fair judgment, and choosing the right company. The path-of-life section concludes in 4.12–14 with a kind of summary formula inciting the addressees to avoid ("hate") hypocrisy, not to tamper with God's commandments, and publicly to confess their sins.

The advice regarding "the path of death" contains some overlap with its counterpart (warning against magic, etc.) and shares with it the manner of listing wrongdoings, though instead of (negative) imperatives, now using mere nouns in a first series (5.1) and a combination of a noun and a participle in a second one (5.2), which gives the first more the outlook of a catalogue of vices, whereas the second reads like a list of which kind of people one will meet on that road. The list of 5.1 is long, diverse, and may look slightly chaotic when putting together murder (first) and irreverence (last) with all kinds of everything in between, but the general impression is that the list goes in a descending order and is more or less topically arranged (after murder, sexual issues, idolatry and magic, all sorts of deceit, and a good number of other vices). The second list again partly overlaps with that in 5.1. It gives the same somewhat chaotic impression but has a more outspoken social component, as was the case also in 4.1–11, and concludes with a reference to sin, as in 4.11, when mentioning lawless judges of the poor, "altogether sinful" as the last category of people to meet on this way (5.2).

The first way is quite demanding, but the second one is outrightly frightening. The short concluding passage in 6.1–3 once more stresses the need to stay on the right path (6.1). Yet it then also introduces a sort of mitigating or encouraging note when showing an awareness that reaching perfection in this regard is probably not possible. It does so by assuring the audience that it is a matter of doing one's best (6.2), thereby citing as an example how food laws (and fasting) are to be handled along this line, allowing for some flexibility according to one's capacity, with the notable exception of abstaining from idol food at all cost (6.3).

Didache 7–10

The second, larger section covering chapters 7–10 contains instructions on baptism (7), then on fasting and prayer (8), and finally on the other sacrament, the Eucharist (9–10). Ideally the faithful are baptized in running water (i.e., by submerging the catechumen) and while invoking the Trinity (7.1), but the author again shows his pragmatic side and allows for alternatives if no running water is available (7.2–3a). The Trinitarian formula should of course always be said (7.3b), and so one should also make sure that the candidate and the one baptizing are purified by fasting, specifying the conditions for the former as a one- or two-day fast, ideally together with other candidates (7.4), which not only illustrates the ecclesial aspect of the ritual but probably also the same concern again to make it all bearable.

The note of fasting brings the author to the next topic, combining instructions on fasting with those on praying. The information that is provided is again quite concrete, but is now opposed to what others do, which recalls the way Jesus contrasts his teaching on prayer and fasting in Matthew 6:5–15, 16–18 to that of gentiles (v. 7) and certain unidentified hypocrites (v. 16). The author does not identify the opponents by name but only through the label "hypocrites" and the days they keep fast (8.1). The reference, no doubt, is to contemporary Jewish practice, which tells us something about the origin of (the majority of) the members of the community or communities the author is addressing, as well as about the ongoing appeal of the old religious practice for Christians of Jewish descent. If the first issue is apparently only about the timing, the second is about content (and maybe also attitude related to content). No information is given on how or what the hypocrites pray, but the Christian prayer is cited in full and is none other than a slightly different version of the Lord's Prayer that Jesus taught his disciples (8.2), which is to be prayed three times a day, as the author adds by way of conclusion (8.3).

The instructions on how to celebrate the Eucharist differ in several respects from how Jesus formulates this at the Last Supper according to the Gospels. Thanks is said over the bread and over the cup, but the cup comes first (so also Luke 22:17–20). The thanksgiving over the cup is, with some variation, repeated for the bread, speaking of "the vine of David" (for the cup) and "the life and knowledge" (for the bread) that was made known through Jesus as the child (or servant) of God and ending with a doxology (9.2–3). Yet it is then also largely expanded upon (9.4), and core elements in any of the formulae met in the Gospels or Paul, such as a reference to Jesus's blood or body, the forgiveness of sins (Matt 26:28), the notion of remembrance (Luke 22:19; 1 Cor 11:25), or the parousia, are all lacking.

The longer thanksgiving formula over the bread stresses the unity of the church in the kingdom of God, who is honored with a third concluding doxological formula. The chapter ends on a practical and critical note when stipulating that only those who are baptized can partake in the meal (9.5).

A second, much longer thanksgiving to God follows after the meal. It opens with more or less the same wording (10.2, addressing God as father, Jesus as servant/child, a doxology), but it then goes on to praise God as the Creator, to thank him for sustaining humans with food and drink—materially and spiritually—granting humankind eternal life (10.3), and being powerful (10.4), to ask that he protect and unite the church (10.5, with an allusion to 9.4), and finally also to pray for the coming of the Lord to gather his people (10.6). Again, the chapter concludes on a practical note, indicating that the prophets should be allowed to say thanks, which in this context means being permitted to hold the Eucharist as often as they wish (10.7). In two textual witnesses, there follows one more phrase of thanks for the ointment received from God. This combination of praise, thanksgiving, prayer, and request forcefully combines several key aspects of what such thanksgiving is all about.

Didache 11–15

Chapters 11–15 are commonly considered to be a church order dealing with issues of hierarchy, hospitality, reconciliation in the community and among community members, and church discipline in general. The first item to be addressed is how to handle outsiders. The community should practice hospitality. Visiting teachers are welcomed, but not indiscriminately, for their teaching is to be tested against what is found in the Didache, as it is said almost apodictically (11.1). They can enrich this teaching, but they cannot possibly deviate from it (11.2). In one respect, the rule is clearly formulated, but at the same time it is also frustratingly vague. There is room for variation and even for deepening the teaching, but not a word is said about who is to decide whether this is the case and on which criteria this is to be decided. Furthermore, it is not said what should be done if the teaching poses problems, but that aspect is addressed in what follows.

Two more categories of visitors are mentioned—apostles, meaning missionaries and not the Twelve, and prophets—and here the focus is almost entirely on how to handle these on a practical level. Unfortunately, the Didachist does not say whether and how these two relate to each other or to the teachers previously mentioned. They are treated one after the other, but what is said of the apostles in part also seems to apply to the prophets, and representatives of both groups who transgress the rules are denounced as "false prophets" (11.5, 6 and 11.8–10). Apostles are subject to certain conditions regarding their behavior and the duration of their stay. The latter should be limited to one and at most two days (11.5), the former involves not asking for money (perhaps with the implication that the community is expected to support them) and taking only as much food as is necessary to reach the next stay (11.6). Prophets are likewise to be assessed on the basis of how they handle food and money (11.9, 12), with the complicating factor that they might convince their audience by pretending to speak in the Spirit, and with the interesting nuance that one should consent if the money is meant to serve those in need. However, in their case the situation seems to be slightly more complex. The community is warned not to despise prophetic behavior as such (11.7), but to take into account certain rules for distinguishing true from false. The first of these rules is whether the prophet lives and acts like Jesus (11.8); a second one, derived from it, whether the prophet lives according to what he teaches (11.10); and a third one, slightly puzzling, specifying that a true prophet does not necessarily have to impose his lifestyle on others (11.11). The Didachist's major concern is about how the community should behave or react, probably based on past experiences with the visitors and the visited.

In the next chapter the issue is partly repeated, but the perspective is broadened. The rules about welcoming strangers apply to all sorts of visitors. Passersby should be helped for two days at most (12.2). Those who wish to stay longer should sustain themselves from their own work (12.3). For those who cannot do so, the community is asked to use sound judgment to assess the case (12.4) and dismiss such persons if need be (12.5). The passage echoes real-life situations, hinting at how Christians used to travel, looking for shelter among fellow believers, yet warning against gullibility.

The Didachist once more comes back to the case of the prophets (mentioning other teachers in passing), pointing out that those who deserve it should be provided with the first portion of any food, including meat (13.3), wine and oil (13.6), and money, clothing, and anything else that is available (13.7), and to be considered as if they were high priests (13.3), a strange echo of a Jewish past. A puzzling little phrase specifies that this service is to be upheld toward the poor when no prophets are visiting (13.4). It cannot possibly mean that the poor in the community would be the first victims of such visits, but rather should be read as an exhortation always to share the common goods of the group with those in need.

In the next, short chapter the author addresses the way the Eucharist, emphatically defined as a sacrifice in each of its three verses, should be held on the Lord's Day. Bread is broken and thanks is given, but not before members have confessed their sins and excluding such members who have a grudge toward each other. An unidentified citation of Malachi 1:11, 14, with a pointed reference to "the gentiles," both links Christian ritual to Jewish tradition and stresses once more its sacrificial character.

The second to last chapter touches on several topics, in part repeating with some variation elements that had been mentioned in the previous one. It opens with a short comment on the leadership of the community, which consists of "bishops" and deacons, and this leadership is elected from among respected Christians. Their qualities are first summarized in the phrase "worthy of the Lord" and then illustrated with four qualifications, including gentleness, not being keen on money, true, and "approved" (15.1). It is not further explained why this combination of virtues is selected, three of which are of a more abstract nature, as representing the ideal profile of leaders. However, it is not said who runs the procedure and makes the decision (the community as a whole?), nor whether these figures need to be members of the community or can be called upon from elsewhere. Instead, there follows a somewhat puzzling comment on how these leaders (both types?) should conduct the ministry of teachers and prophets. Together these are the four types of leadership the Didachist promotes, thereby also giving some instructions on how these relate to each other in terms of authority. Then the focus switches to the faithful. They are obviously to honor their (self-chosen?) leaders (15.2), but they should in turn display an exemplary behavior within the group. The instructions in 15.3 echo some of what had been said in chapter 14 about distancing oneself from sinners until they have repented and about how to reprimand one another in peace, and not in anger, as found in the gospel. The true Christian way of life is then summarized most succinctly in 15.4 in three ways: pray, do charity, and always live according to the rules laid down in the gospel. The double reference to the term *gospel*, in the singular, is most noteworthy and recalls at a crucial point the way its authority had been evoked before in 8.2 to introduce the Didache's version of the Lord's Prayer and in 11.3 to instruct readers about how to behave toward prophets and missionaries. If in the case of 15.3 the focus is also on one particular point, the second adopts a far more general perspective, declaring "the gospel" as the source of inspiration for the whole of one's life.

Didache 16

That life is precious, but also under threat in an even more encompassing way than is the case in the previous set of instructions, is made clear in the final chapter. For indeed, the Didache not only instructs about community life, leadership, and Christian behavior in general but also looks forward to the future and the end time, concluding with an impressive evocation of how that scenario will materialize and what it involves. The chapter is replete with allusions to phrases and motifs known from the canonical Gospels, as will be shown below. It opens with a twofold warning to be vigilant. The first one is formulated in general terms, the second one in the negative with a twofold motif of how not to be ready, which is then resumed in the positive in a formulaic phrase as "be prepared" (16.1a). The warning and exhortation are motivated from humans' lack of knowledge about when the end will come (16.1b). The faithful should prepare themselves, readying their soul in the assurance that this will save them when the end has come (16.2). It is a most forceful instigation to live the right life and an impressive way to say what the end is about; the use of the verb "to be perfect" adds to this overall impression.

Familiar characters and images from similar end-time scenarios are called upon to stress the message. False prophets are to be expected. These false prophets receive a special focus after the preceding instructions about how to distinguish such figures, who are described as corrupting faith and turning the faithful into their opposite, fighting each other with all means at a time that lawlessness will reign (16.3–4a). These events announce the arrival of the antichrist masquerading as the son of God, conquering the earth with his false signs and wonders, and bringing chaos to its climax (16.4b). According to the Didache, many will succumb to the test, but those who keep faith will be saved (16.5). The earth and its history will be wrapped up: a sign in heaven, the sound of a trumpet, the resurrection of the dead, and it is all over and gone (16.6), or almost. For then the Lord is to arrive with his holy ones (16.7–8a), but what will happen next has not been preserved, for the manuscript breaks off, a fitting feature for a passage dealing with what is still to come and a fine contrast with the many details of the scenario that had already been made known.

3. INTERPRETATIVE ISSUES

The Didache continues to present readers and scholars with challenges in interpreting this text. Among the many issues it raises, three will be briefly addressed here. First and foremost is the question of the genre and contents of the text, second its sources, and third the way the Didache presents a Christian community.

3.1 Genre and Contents

Probably the best way to define the work is to call it a church order. The fact that we do not possess other examples for the first half of the second century should not be held against this designation. The examples of a somewhat later period mentioned above only strengthen the case for classifying the Didache in this way, in particular because the work had been integrated in such a church order long before it became known to modern scholars and, more generally, because of the similarities in form and content, including the diversity of topics in a seemingly random order. This is true even if one must admit that the eschatological chapter at the end is a bit of an odd element.

3.2 Sources

The Didache does not say a word about its sources, but the specific character of the first five chapters, and the fact that parallels to this section are met in other similar works, has led many scholars to assume that this section may be (part of) an originally independent treatise on the Two Ways, such as there have been found in others in ancient literature. Some have argued that the original version of the treatise stems from Jewish circles, which is in theory not impossible and would characterize the Didache as the work of a Jewish-Christian author or community. Yet the massive presence of Christian motifs and passages that have a parallel in the Gospels (see below) has largely obscured that original form and makes any attempt at reconstructing it very speculative. The text that we have is without any doubt a Christian text. It is equally difficult to say more about the origins of other parts of the work, beyond the general observation that it made use of traditions, rather than written sources, that freely circulated in Christian communities. The lack of parallel material from the same time as the Didache makes it impossible to say how much of this material is specific to this community and what may have been borrowed from others.

3.3 Presentation of Christian Community

As the Didachist sees it, the Christian community is the center of Christian life and praxis. There were at least indirect contacts with other communities through visiting prophets and missionaries, but the author gives the strong impression that such persons are best received with some skepticism and tested in regard to their goals and character. The author also pays due attention to issues of internal leadership and organization. A matter of great interest is the liturgical life of the community, including baptism, prayers, and the Eucharist. The last chapter that is preserved gives a hint on how the community looked toward the future. The community lives by its leaders and by the teaching and inspiration it receives from its visitors. Yet the real authority rests, first and foremost, with "the Lord," which may refer both to God and to Christ, as is occasionally also the case in the Gospels. The name of Jesus is used only in the eucharistic prayers in Didache 9.2–4 and 10.2–3 addressed to the Father and identifying the former as God's child.

If one accepts that the title(s) is (are) authentic, an authority of a higher level, above that of the local leaders, is that of the Twelve. The text claims that it is their teachings that are transmitted and preserved in the Didache and that should rule the life of any Christian community. Whether original or added, this perspective, in which the local leaders are part of a hierarchy that goes well beyond their own position and authority, constitutes a remarkable feature of the work in its current form, and one that is stressed right from the beginning. That the apostles, as one body, teach what the Lord (God or Christ) has taught them is presented as a given and the rule that directs all that follows. The authority of the contents of the work is fixed and undisputed.

4. KEY PASSAGES FOR NEW TESTAMENT STUDIES AND THEIR SIGNIFICANCE

The Didache abounds with verses and also longer passages that have parallels in the New Testament writings, mostly with the Gospels, though there are a couple of instances of a parallel with one of Paul's letters, one instance also with 1 Peter (1.4) and perhaps one with Acts (4.8). One passage is formally introduced as a citation, unlike the others, of which the source remains unknown (1.6). When the Didache was composed, the creation of a canon of the New Testament writings was not yet an issue. Moreover, the Didache shows little interest about indicating its sources. In fact, it contains only one more or less formally introduced mixed citation from the Old Testament (14.3, citing Mal 1:11, 14 as "said by the Lord"). This means the way is wide open to discuss the origin of parallel material that is also met in New Testament writings.

Basically, there are two ways to explain the parallels. Either they could be due to oral tradition, or they could be the product of indirect or direct literary dependence. The rather more singular solution—to regard the Didache as the source of the Gospel of Matthew—is actually a derivative one, since ultimately it also must account for the material through one of these two channels—unless one is prepared to argue that all such material was created by the Didachist. The first option is, in a sense, the easy one and has the significant advantage that it can explain away every difference from known sources as stemming from fluid oral tradition. This works better for gospel stories (and sayings) than for epistolary material, although it cannot be excluded in principle for the latter. On the negative side, however, one must note that it can easily be abused as *the* all-round explanation. The alternative is the more difficult explanation because it is more complex. Nonetheless, when taking this into account it might offer concrete and valuable indications of the author's redaction and handling of the source material. First, literary dependence does not have to mean that the author always had access to the written version, as if it was laying on the table. One can cite from memory and still produce a very reliable version, and one can cite a passage *de visu* and yet make mistakes or changes.

Second, it has often been noted that the text of the Gospels (and the letters) was not yet fixed in those early days in the way this would become the case much later. That is probably true, but there is no reason to assume that it was a complete chaos. The oldest evidence shows that the variations are not significantly more abundant than is the case in medieval manuscripts; the so-called Western text (Codex Bezae and a few others in that line) represent a more idiosyncratic development that would prove to remain the exception. Copying texts, by definition, produces variation—intentionally or not, and certain worries about a particular reading may have inspired scribes and users to intervene and to meddle with the text. However, this cannot be used as a decisive argument to conclude that looking for indicators of literary dependence is a futile exercise.

Third, a work may depend on known or unknown sources. The latter, be they lost ones or preliminary forms of the known ones, is always an option, but sound methodology should begin with testing the evidence against the known sources before calling in unknown entities. Fourth, there is no absolute rule for proving literary dependence when an author does not mention the source. The closest one is able to come to such a rule is to look for traces of redactional intervention in the source that strongly indicate the hand of the original author. For the Gospels, any decision on the matter is closely linked to which solution one favors for explaining the relation between the Gospels. If Matthew is dated after the other Synoptic Gospels, the Didache may be given a middle position in which it depends on these earlier Gospels while being the source of the later one. For the letters, this is more difficult to establish, though perhaps easier for Paul than for any of the others because of the sheer amount of material available with which to compare, taking into account that Paul has been flexible in formulating his views on any topic he has addressed. But the method may work to some degree to distinguish which of two parallel sources has been used.

Fifth, and as the counterpart of the previous point, it is equally difficult to look for traces of redaction by the Didachist. The writing is short, and we know very little about the author, the context, and the purpose of the work to decide which differences from the source as we know it must come from the author's pen and which may reflect oral tradition or the use of an unknown (lost) version of that same source. All this is to warn readers to stay alert and not to rush to conclusions when coming across material that looks very similar to what one finds in the Gospels or in Paul. Nonetheless, these cautions should not be used to rule out in principle that the Didache may well have relied on any of these writings and resort to the notion that the similarities are simply examples of utilizing floating oral traditions. Key factors in the decision are the closeness of the parallel, the degree to which differences can be explained in terms of the author's intentions, and the amount of parallel material that is found in the Didache. The latter is often neglected but is important, for it is the basis to build a cumulative argument and is a methodologically sound approach. One should start from those passages in which parallel material abounds and then work one's way through the rest, always keeping in mind that "hard results" are often out of reach.

The three options mentioned above regard the Didache either as representing a parallel tradition along with our written sources, as the source of part of this written material, or as one of the earliest witnesses of the use of New Testament writings. The choice one makes evidently determines the status one gives to the Didache in assessing the parallel material. Methodologically, it makes good sense first to try and explain the parallels on the hypothesis of literary dependence, the two other options being more evasive or speculative. This is also the approach taken in what follows.

Four times the Didache mentions "the gospel" (8.2; 11.3; 15.3–4). The word is always used in the singular, three times in the absolute and once with the qualification "the Lord in his gospel" (8.3). Each time its authority is duly emphasized, using different verbs—to command (8.2), to decree (11.3), and to learn (from) (15.3–4). In the first occurrence, it introduces the text of the Lord's Prayer, but in the other instances it is referred to in a more general way as the source and norm for how to behave toward apostles and prophets (11.3) and toward each other (15.3), and for how to follow a Christian life of prayer and charity (15.4). This absolute use of the word gives it a most forceful dimension. This is not just "the gospel according to . . . ," but the "Lord's gospel," as all the individual Gospels actually should be considered, and indeed are; only this time this is spelled out as such. However, one should not be misled by the terminology. It does not rule out the possibility that the author was familiar with one or more of our canonical Gospels and relied on gospel traditions instead, as some have tried to argue. It just does not privilege any one Gospel over the others, which, admittedly, works better for those instances that have not one specific passage in view. It certainly does not (implicitly) criticize Gospels that would not contain the information that is referenced (e.g., the Lord's Prayer being missing from two of our canonical Gospels and being preserved in rather different wording in the two others). It rather reflects a use of the word that is not unknown also in later times. Even today, especially in a pastoral and ministerial context, but not just there, one hears phrases such as "the gospel says . . ." There is no reason, then, to conclude that the Didachist did not know any of the Gospels that have come down to us.

It is not possible to study, however briefly, all of the passages that have a parallel in the Gospels. To organize the material, one might opt to distinguish three types of references: (1) passages that are or seem to be considered as explicit citations from something the Lord had said; (2) passages that should probably be taken in the same way but are not explicitly linked to the teaching of Jesus; and (3) shorter, more isolated, passages that sound like they were taken from or inspired by parallels in the Gospels. Not all of this material carries the same weight when it comes to demonstrate that the Didache knew and used some of the canonical Gospels instead of mere tradition. But taken as a whole, the approach has a cumulative impact on two levels—that of using the hypothesis for all such parallel material and that of explaining the Didache's version in terms of its handling this material. If it can be reasonably argued that the Didachist turned to the Gospels in sections with larger chunks of parallel material, this should also be the first way to assess material where this is perhaps less clearly the case, unless there is strong proof of the contrary. And if a reasonable and coherent explanation can be given for why the author altered the source text at one place, this type of explanation based on redactional and compositional factors may also apply to other passages where the evidence is perhaps less profiled.

4.1 Substantial Parallels with Explicit Reference to the Use of a Source

The first group is a rather limited one. It basically consists of the Didache's version of the Lord's Prayer in 8.2 and the little phrase at the end of 9.5, both of which are introduced as material spoken by the Lord.

The Didache passes by the context in which the prayer is found in the Gospels of Matthew and of Luke, but it retains the emphasis that the words of the prayer were instructed by Jesus. The way in which this is said ("you should pray as follows") is closer to Matthew's than to Luke's version. The author does not say why he wished to emphasize this aspect, but it makes good sense in a work that claims to transmit the instructions of the apostles. What the Lord once told them, they have passed on, while recognizing the original source through which they themselves came to know the prayer. Note also the qualification "hypocrites" for those praying in the wrong way, as in Matthew 6:5 (no parallel in Luke).

The Didache's version of the prayer is much closer to Matthew's than to Luke's version as found in modern editions. The variants are limited in number and affect the text only minimally. The singular "in heaven" for Matthew's plural (6:9) is weakly attested also for the Gospel in the so-called Middle Egyptian Coptic version and is most probably not authentic, as Matthew likes to use the plural "heavens" in addressing the Father (just for the Sermon on the Mount, see Matt 5:16, 45; 6:1; 7:11, 21) and made this formulation one of his signature interventions in rewriting his sources. The Didache never uses the plural elsewhere (see 16.6, 8) and may have been tempted to harmonize with the wording in Matthew 6:10 (or mixed up the two); see also the variant "heavenly" in 6:14 (and v. 32) instead of "in the heavens." It also prefers the singular "debt" for Matthew's plural in 6:12, which is not otherwise attested in the textual tradition of the Gospel. There is no difference in meaning, but it creates a nice contrastive parallel with the many "debtors" we are urged to forgive in the second half of the verse. The same reason may be behind the choice for the present indicative of the verb "forgive" instead of the perfect in Matthew's second half of the verse, a variant that in this case is well attested among ancient witnesses (also in Luke): "as we forgive our debtors, so God forgives us." The limited textual basis of the Didache does not allow one to conclude that its author was at the origin of this reading, or that it reflects a scribal choice. In any case, it does away with the potential assumption that we first have to forgive others and only then will be forgiven. Finally, the Didache also knows a version of the formulaic extra or doxology in 6:13 that is itself widely attested,[2] with minor differences, in the Greek textual tradition and in several of the versions. Again, it is not possible firmly to conclude whether the Didachist found it in Matthew's version or whether it was added by a scribe, but there is also no reason to prefer the second option over the first one. The manuscript, in any case, does not indicate that it was a later addition in the Didache. The extra element of the doxology is a remarkable element of the Matthean textual tradition that apparently did not make it into the Lukan tradition, which is in itself quite telling for a text that was so much contaminated. So, all in all, the Didache is closer

2. This "extra" is the textual addition that provides the Matthean version of the Lord's Prayer with a doxological conclusion: "for yours is the kingdom and the power and the glory forever. Amen." This doxology is based on 1 Chr 29:11–13, and the longer text is attested in various New Testament manuscripts.

to Matthew than to Luke, but there is a double caveat: Luke's version has been heavily contaminated by Matthew's in the textual tradition (at least that is how modern editors of the Gospel texts interpret the variants), and our limited evidence for the Didache does not allow for any apodictic conclusions regarding its original text. But perhaps this much can be said: one of the variants is attested solely in the Didache (the singular "debt"), and two others can plausibly be explained as potential changes made by the author for stylistic reasons. One should not rush into any firm conclusions, but Matthew's version is definitely closer to that of the Didache, and its textual tradition is overall less contaminated by Lukan parallels than the other way around. This may perhaps suffice to conclude that the Didache was working from Matthew's version, certainly when taking into account that, as a doubtlessly widely used text already in the earliest communities, the Lord's Prayer may have suffered small variants (see the variant forms of the verb "to forgive" in Luke in comparison with Matthew).

Then there is the format of the prayer. By presenting this prayer as "the" Christian prayer par excellence, the Didachist probably only confirmed what was already common praxis in the communities he is addressing, but it marks the author's interest in positioning himself in that tradition and in pointing out the importance of being connected with Jesus through prayer. Yet, at the same time, the author also adds a little instruction of his own when specifying at the end that one should pray three times a day. However, other instructions, as found in Matthew's Gospel are not mentioned, but these may well be implied in the general reference to the "hypocrites."

The Lord's saying on not giving to the dogs what is holy with which the author closes chapter 9 verbally agrees with the opening words of the isolated saying in Matthew 7:6, a saying which itself is also part of the Sermon on the Mount. One can only guess as to why the second, much longer half on the pearls and swine is missing. Perhaps it is just a concern for brevity, and one should probably not be tempted to speculate about whether this is proof that the author did not know the "full" form with the two parts and was perhaps merely citing tradition. Furthermore, it is probably wise to resist the temptation to connect this form of the saying with any considerations about the social context of the author and the community that is being addressed. The contrast between citing the whole text of the mighty Lord's Prayer and then this semi-proverbial little saying is worth noting and may be taken as an indication that the Didachist did not turn to the Gospels only for crucial material.

4.2 Substantial Parallels without Reference to a Source

Examples of the second group are met at the beginning and again at the end of the work. The first instance may perhaps also be reckoned with the first group, depending on how one reads the longer title of the Didache, "The Teaching of the Lord through the Twelve Apostles to the Gentiles/Nations." If this is taken to refer to the whole of the work, as I think it should, the source and authority behind the teaching on the Two Ways in Didache 1–5 is not specifically identified, and the text can safely be listed within the second group.

Didache 1.3–2.1 contains a significant amount of material that can be paralleled with passages from the Gospels, primarily Matthew's, and in a few instances perhaps also Luke's. The number of points of contact are so extensive that this passage is often referred to as "the gospel section," and moreover scholars who have argued for the existence of a Jewish tractate on the Two Ways behind chapters 1–5 have suggested expunging or cutting out this part from the original source. It should be noted that the Two Ways motif is widely attested throughout the ancient world, Jewish and non-Jewish, both as a motif and in a more developed format that could be called a tractate. The Didache is one of the oldest Christian witnesses to the motif, but is not the very first one, for it is met in a most vivid form already in Matthew 7:13–14. Moreover, the longer title clearly indicates that the author is certainly no longer interested in the Jewish antecedents, if there were any, for the instructions and teaching are meant for the "nations" (gentiles).

There is a way of life and a way of death. The former is qualified in general by the double love commandment from Scripture that is also cited in the Gospels and by the so-called golden rule that is cited in different versions in Matthew 7:12 and Luke 6:31, and also appears here in yet another format (Did. 1.2b). The fact that the latter occurs in Matthew in the immediate vicinity of the Two Ways passage is a strong indication first to turn to this Gospel to explain its presence here. In Scripture the two parts of the double love command are found at different places (Deut 6:5 and Lev 19:18) that are cited together in the three Synoptic Gospels (Matt 22:37–39; Mark 12:30–31; Luke 10:27). This again points to the Gospels as the Didache's major source of inspiration. The second, short command about loving one's neighbor is formulated in identical wording in all witnesses. For the first one, the Didache has opted for a short version that is not as such attested in any of the witnesses just mentioned. It merely says, "Love the God who made you." The reference to the Creator (see also Did 5.2) is missing from Deuteronomy and the Gospels, which instead have a long and diversified, semi-hymnic addition about how one should love God. The choice for this shorter version may have been inspired by the fact that the Gospels differ among each other and that none of them fully agrees with Deuteronomy 6:5. Furthermore, this is potentially strengthened by the concern to produce a more balanced text with two parts of equal length. The two parts are counted, as this is also the case in Mark and, perhaps in a sense even more emphatically, in Matthew (see 22:38). The counting and the order in which the two commands are given leaves no doubt about which of the two is the most important one.

The Didache cites the golden rule in its negative form (Did. 1.2b). This seems to point away from the Gospels as a possible source, but perhaps the distance is less significant than one might think. First, it is not particularly difficult to formulate the negative version on the basis of the positive one. Actually, the opening words ("whatever you do . . . want," in the singular) recall Matthew's version (Matt 7:12, here pl.). One will also note that Matthew 7:12 precedes the Two Ways passage in that Gospel (Matt 7:13–14). Second, Irenaeus at the turn of the end of the second century, Codex Bezae, and a few other later manuscripts are familiar with both the positive and the negative format, the latter of which they attest in a longer version of the text of Acts 15:20 and again at 15:29, from the so-called "Jerusalem Synod," two crucial verses in the attempt to find a compromise or modus vivendi between Jewish and gentile Christians (see also Did. 6.3). The longer text is most probably not original, but it is very old, and it makes good sense as a way to summarize the one principle that holds together the rules on which both parties had agreed. Third, the precise relation between the double love command and the golden rule is not specifically clarified. It is possible to regard the golden rule as a way to concretize the second of the double commandment in general terms, which in a sense it indeed is: this is how one should behave toward others. However, the relation between the golden rule and commandment is slightly more complex. A longer series of concrete actions and attitudes is listed in Didache 1.3–6, but these are all formulated in positive terms and therefore seem to be in tension with the negative formulation of the golden rule in 1.2. However, the list of 1.3–6 is then followed in 2.2–7 with an equally impressive list of negatively formulated commandments, starting with "do not murder" (2.2) and ending with "do not hate anyone" (2.7), followed by a positively formulated commandment that brings the reader back to the list of 1.3–6.

This second list is introduced with a somewhat puzzling phrase declaring it "the second commandment of the teaching" (2.1). This leads one to assume that the Didachist took the double commandment as a first one and the golden rule, in its negative format, as a second one. The list in 1.3–6 illustrates what it means to "love one's neighbor" (and actually, by the same token, also "to love God"); the list of 2.2–7 would then offer the illustration of the golden rule as a "second commandment." The formulation in 2.1 is perhaps a bit unfortunate because it is confusing, but it makes sense when explained as is here suggested. And fourth and last, even if this negative version were not inspired by the one in Matthew (and Luke), it does not have to mean that all the rest of the parallel material in this section cannot have been taken from the Gospels.

If the list in Didache 2.2–7 basically elaborates on that contained in Exodus 20:13–17, the one in 1.3–6 is clearly inspired by material that is met also in the Sermon on the Mount/Plain. Didache 1.3 seems to combine elements from Matthew 5:44, 46–47 and its parallel in Luke 6:28, 32–33. This does not have to mean that the Didachist relied on independent tradition. The textual tradition of Matthew 5:44 shows that bits and pieces from Luke have crept in; so mixing up the two is well attested in later tradition but may have begun much earlier already. Most noteworthy is the addition in the middle of Matthew 5:44 of Luke 6:28a, 27b (in this order), enlarging Matthew's two elements in verse 44 to four, as in Luke 6:27–28. Something similar seems to have happened in Didache 1.3, which counts three elements and opens with a phrase that is nearly identical to Luke 6:28a—a phrase, by the way, that is not ascribed to Q by those holding this hypothesis and that contains a verb ("to bless") that is a favorite of Luke and used only by him in this context.

The second element in Didache 1.3 ("pray for your enemies") combines the verb Matthew and Luke share for their last motif with what is the first motif in both Gospels—to love one's enemies. The third element picks up Matthew's second one about caring for one's persecutors but introduces a third verb, as the one in Matthew had already been used and speaks of "fasting" for persecutors instead of praying. It may seem a rather surprising choice, but there is ample evidence, biblical and Christian, that the two can easily be linked, as shown also by Matthew in 6:5–6 and 6:16–18. Didache 1.3b can also be explained as a shortened and slightly reordered combination of elements from Matthew 5:46a, 47b and its parallel in Luke 6:32a, 33b. It reflects the same approach and the same procedure as in the first part of Didache 1.3, including the question at the end and the reference to "Gentiles," as in Matthew. Didache 1.3 concludes with a form of the love command that resembles the one in Luke 6:27b (as a variant also in Matt 5:44) that was echoed in its opposite form in Matthew 5:43 ("hate your enemy"), which has no parallel in Luke.

Again, the Didache seems to have gone right to the heart of the matter by focusing on these motifs and in a form that closely resembles that of Matthew and Luke, without merely reproducing either of them. If Matthew mentions only two motifs and Luke four, the Didachist gives three; and when Matthew and Luke can play with the order of the passage, then also the Didache must be allowed to do so.

The parallel is above all with Matthew, but Luke has not disappeared and continues in Didache 1.4. The little phrase that opens the passage has a close parallel in 1 Peter 2:11 and looks like an oddity in regard to content in this context. Yet then it reverts back to the Sermon with a phrase that is almost verbally identical to Matthew 5:39, including the detail of turning the right cheek that is often seen as a trace of Matthean redaction, and a qualification ("you will be perfect") that is found only in Matthew 5:48 in this context (note Matthew's addition of the same adjective to Mark's phrasing in Mark 10:21 at Matt 19:21).

The next motif in Didache 1:4 is identical with Matthew 5:41, which has again no parallel in Luke (the verb used for "go with" is found in Matt 4:10 and 5:24 and seems to be a favorite). The next motif, about not objecting to those who want to take your cloak, and its generalizing conclusion, are closer to Luke again (Luke 6:29b–30), who offers a less verbose and also more logical order in regard to structure and phrasing than Matthew and may therefore have been chosen, even if he is not reproduced *ad litteram*.

The opening words in Didache 1.2 show that the author is truly able to get at the essence of the Christian message and to bring this to the reader in its most succinct and acclaimed form. They also are a sign of the author's sense of autonomy in formulating that message in such a way that it allows for concretizing it in a positive and a negative format. It is the kind of opening that sticks! The same is true of Didache 1.3–5a. The Didachist plays with the material but keeps to the essence. Of course, it cannot be a priori excluded that the author relied on tradition instead, but this alternative does not offer any further insight in how the Didachist worked, as the form in which this material circulated in tradition cannot be checked and there is no reason to think he merely copied fixed tradition.

There are two more issues to be addressed. First, the author, quite remarkably, does not seem to care to identify the source and authority behind these rules and instructions, especially if the longer title does not refer only to this opening section. Perhaps the author felt no need to repeat this information right after the title, though it would not have caused any harm to do so. Or perhaps it was on purpose, as it allowed the author to handle this material more freely, as he does, thereby giving himself a role in mediating the teachings of the Lord and the apostles. In any case, this does not argue against dependence on the Gospels, or for influence from tradition. Second, one may have the impression that the author has been cherry-picking. This is indeed the case, but there is no reason to conclude that this is only true on the hypothesis that he was working with the Gospels. The selective approach does not mean that the rest of the Gospel text was unavailable. Many authors would continue do so all through history, and the Didachist has the merit to have picked up the good and important things that are relevant to the message of the text in question.

One meets the same selective but impressive use of parallel material from the Gospel of Matthew in the last chapter (Did. 16). Without going into details, one can safely say that the same approach, hence the same hand, seems to be at work as in the opening chapters. Vivid details from Matthew's eschatological discourse in Matthew 24 are used to picture a vision of the end that is as evocative as its much longer original. Yet this shorter form does not miss anything worth mentioning as far as one can judge from the part of Didache 16 that has survived. This whole (final?) chapter of the work is of a rather different character than what preceded, for it switches from practical advice and instructions on how to organize the community and live a Christian life to a more doctrinal issue, but that is only one side of the issue. The scenario that is detailed serves the purpose of warning and exhorting the members to stay watchful, and in this way it connects this chapter very well with the instructions that precede it. The opening words in Didache 16.1 illustrate this abundantly and in wording that recalls above all Matthew 24:42 (there is a widely attested variant reading "hour" for "day"; see also v. 44) and 24:44 ("be prepared"). The middle part of Didache 16.1 with its combination of "lamps" and "robes" rather seems to echo Luke 12:35, though the first motif is also met in Matthew's parable of the ten virgins (Matt 25:1–13) that reads like a narrativization of Luke 12:35–38 and of the warnings in Matthew 24:42–51 // Luke 12:38–48 and that has the same verb for "extinguish" as in Didache 16.1 (see Matt 25:8). The second motif is made more concrete in Matthew 25:5 where it is said that the foolish maidservants had fallen asleep (the verb "to loose" of Did. 16.1 occurs in Matt 15:32 // Mark 8:3).

4.3 Isolated Parallels

The third group to be distinguished consists of short and isolated phrases for which there are parallels in the Gospels. They are, as a rule, not specifically singled out or earmarked; hence, it is even more difficult in this case than with the previous group to pinpoint the source. In Didache 3.7, in the middle of a long section in which the reader is fatherly addressed as "my child" but that contains no other echoes of parallels with gospel material, one encounters the phrase "but be meek, for the meek will inherit the earth." Matthew 5:5 springs to mind (no parallel in Luke or Mark), but so does Psalm 37:11 (36:11 LXX). Perhaps the former has a slight advantage in that it also consists of two elements—an address/ee and an explanation.

The phrase "yoke of the Lord" in Didache 6.2, in combination with the notion of "perfection," makes good sense against the background of Matthew 11:28–30, a passage that is unique to Matthew. The Trinitarian baptism formula in Didache 7.1 recalls Matthew 28:19 (again, a passage with no parallel in the other Gospels). However, in Didache 7.1 it is part of a much longer and more concrete set of instructions on how to baptize. The reference to the "hypocrites" in 8.1 has been mentioned above. In instructing the readership on how to deal with prophets, the phrase "for every sin will be forgiven, but not this sin" in 11.7 faintly recalls Matthew 12:31. The sin is defined differently from Matthew, for now it is about not testing or condemning a prophet, not about speaking blasphemy. Yet perhaps one can turn to Matthew after all, because of the similarity in structure of the phrase and the mention of the Spirit in Didache 11.8. (Note also the mention of false prophets in Did. 11.8 and Matt 7:15, which precedes the parallel to Matt 12:33 in 7:16–20, though this may be a bridge too far). In similar instructions about behavior toward teachers, one encounters the phrase, "so too a true teacher, like the worker, deserves his food" (Did. 13.2). Matthew uses the motif for the apostles in his mission discourse in 10:10, and together with the fact that the Didache's version is verbally identical, this may be a sufficient parallel in content and partly also in context to argue for dependence, keeping in mind that the motif is of course also known from Paul (cf. 1 Cor 9:9; see also 1 Tim 5:18) and is itself proverbial. The warning in Didache 14.2 not to invite anyone who has a quarrel with his neighbour to take part in the Eucharist looks like a variant on the instruction in Matthew 5:23–24, which is yet another passage without a parallel in Luke or Mark. Noticeably, this in turn would bring us back to the Sermon on the Mount (see the verb "reconcile" and the word "offer/sacrifice").

These "stray parallels" may look weak as evidence for the dependence on the Gospels. The argumentation for this third group relies on its cumulative weight. This is not necessarily a weakness, for cumulative arguments can be fairly solid, and they certainly function as subsidiary evidence in combination with the material of the first two groups. More than for these latter, one can only speculate why the Didachist found it helpful to insert such an echo to the Gospel of Matthew. Maybe there is no rationale, but just the observation that Matthew was constantly on his mind.

5. CONCLUSION

The Didache is best defined as an early church order, most probably devised and composed without any model, which may explain some of its idiosyncrasies. Nothing is known about its author, date, or provenance, but the author seems to have been familiar with the Gospel of Matthew and to have used it quite extensively. The work reflects a great concern with issues related to the organization of the community and its religious life. Baptism and the Eucharist receive due attention, as do matters of leadership and dealing with visiting missionaries. The latter may in part have been inspired by some less fortunate events. The former shows the importance of these two rituals in the life of the Christian community. The opening chapters and the final chapter of the work are singled out in a peculiar way. The Two Ways motif is used elaborately and infused with a lot of material that has a parallel in the Gospel of Matthew. The eschatological scenario likewise reflects the use of gospel material and is not less impressive in emphasizing that Christian life is lived on earth with a strong focus on another life to come. The Didache stands out as a most valuable testimony to Christian community praxis and Christians' hope concerning the afterlife. It also stands out as one of our earliest witnesses to the use of a written Gospel and not just gospel tradition.

BIBLIOGRAPHY

Draper, J. A., ed. *The Didache in Modern Research*. AGJU 37. Leiden: Brill, 1996.

Draper, J. A., and C. N. Jefford, eds. *The Didache: A Missing Piece of the Puzzle in Early Christianity*. ECL 14. Atlanta: SBL Press, 2015.

Garrow, A. J. P. *The Gospel of Matthew's Dependence on the Didache*. LNTS 254. London: T&T Clark, 2004.

Jefford, C. N. *The Sayings of Jesus in the Teaching of the Twelve Apostles*. Supplements to Vigiliae Christianae 11. Leiden: Brill, 1989.

Jefford, C. N., ed. *The Didache in Context: Essays on Its Text, History, and Transmission*. NovTSup 77. Leiden: Brill, 1995.

Milavec, A. *The Didache: Faith, Hope, and Life of the Earliest Christian Communities, 50–70 C.E.* New York: Newman, 2003.

Niederwimmer, K. *The Didache: A Commentary*. Translated by L. M. Maloney. Hermeneia. Minneapolis: Augsburg Fortress, 1998.

Pardee, N. *The Genre and Development of the Didache*. WUNT 2/339. Tübingen: Mohr Siebeck, 2012.

Sandt, H. van de, ed. *Matthew and the Didache: Two Documents from the Same Jewish-Christian Milieu?* Minneapolis: Fortress, 2005.

Tuckett, C. M. "Synoptic Tradition in the Didache." Pages 197–230 in *The New Testament in Early Christianity = La réception des écrits néotestamentaires dans le christianisme primitif*. Edited by J.-M. Sevrin. BETL 86. Leuven: Leuven University Press, 1989.

Verheyden, J. "Didache." Pages 337–62 in *The Reception of Jesus in the First Three Centuries*. Vol. 1 of *From Paul to Josephus: Literary Receptions of Jesus in the First Century CE*. Edited by C. Keith, H. K. Bond, C. Jacobi, and J. Schröter. London: Bloomsbury T&T Clark, 2020.

Wilhite, S. J. *The Didache: A Commentary*. AFCS 1. Eugene, OR: Cascade, 2019.

CHAPTER 3

FIRST CLEMENT

CLARE K. ROTHSCHILD

1. INTRODUCTION

Much like the letters to the Colossians and Ephesians and the letters of Ignatius, 1 Clement translates Pauline theology into later ecclesiastical doctrine. Its purported occasion is the expulsion of older presbyters by younger members of the Corinthian church (1 Clem. 47.6). Although the reader never learns the motivation for the rebellion, the author refers to these younger members as forming a "vile and profane faction stoked by a few reckless and headstrong persons" (1 Clem. 1.1).[1] Similar to 1 Corinthians, 1 Clement exhorts "peace and harmony [ὁμόνοια]" in the face of notional defiance (1 Clem. 63.2) and promotes traditional Jewish-Christian moral ideals (expressed in lists of virtues and vices, household duties, and community rules) and a few central Christian doctrines (i.e., creation by God, resurrection of Jesus, future resurrection of Christians). Source materials utilized by 1 Clement include the Hebrew Bible, sayings of Jesus, and letters of Paul, as well as what seem to be kerygmatic and liturgical materials, including one intercessory prayer. Interpreters have debated whether heretical teachers, even "gnostics," spurred the dispute addressed in the letter. However, the letter contains no polemical remarks against false teaching. Opponents aside, one important feature of this text—aptly compared with Luke-Acts and Ignatius, *To the Romans* 4.3 (cf. 1 Clem. 5)—is that it presents Peter and Paul side by side. However, 1 Clement's purpose for such a presentation seems less to do with representing apostolic succession, let alone monarchical episcopacy (as often supposed, 1 Clem. 44.1–2), and more about demonstrating compatibility of the earliest authorities. The first purpose of this text is to bring about "harmony" (ὁμόνοια) even among current church leaders, connoting the reinstatement of and obedience to older presbyters. Even if the letter's purported situation is invented, no reader can avoid the conclusion that peace is primary.

1.1 The State of the Text and the Surviving Manuscripts

First Clement is arguably the best attested of the Apostolic Fathers, as far as the manuscripts are concerned, although if the various recensions of the letters of Ignatius are taken into account, then there are far more manuscripts of Ignatius's letters. There are, moreover, twelve Greek manuscripts of Polycarp's *To the Philippians*—although they may be interrelated. There are also several Greek manuscripts of Hermas, but some are fragmentary and none is complete. Nevertheless, as Donald Hagner observes, "Of all Greek writings,

1. All citations of 1 Clement in this entry come from B. D. Ehrman, *The Apostolic Fathers, Volume 1*, LCL (Cambridge: Harvard University Press, 2003).

the epistle of Clement stands second only to the NT in the wealth of evidence available for purposes of textual criticism."[2] First Clement survives in two Greek manuscripts—Codex Alexandrinus (A) and Codex Constantinopolitanus (Lake's C) or Hierosolymitanus (Ehrman's H)—and four versions: Latin (L), Syriac (S), and two in Coptic (Co and Co[1]). Comments on each witness are provided next.

Codex A

Codex Alexandrinus is a fifth-century Greek majuscule manuscript that originally contained the whole Bible. It resides in the British Library in London (MS Reg. 1 D VIII, fol. 159a–fol. 168a col. 1) and is the oldest witness to 1 Clement, appearing at the end of the codex after Revelation with 2 Clement. Although the quality of this manuscript is good (most errors seem accidental), it is mutilated, lacking, among other things, the end of 1 Clement (i.e., 57.7–63.4).

Codex C

Codex Constantinopolitanus is a Greek minuscule manuscript containing many of the so-called "Apostolic Fathers," including 1 Clement, 2 Clement, the Letter of Barnabas, the letters of Ignatius, and the Didache. With regard to 1 Clement, the significance of this codex is that it is the only Greek witness to the text's ending. According to a final colophon, Leo the Notary copied this codex in 1056 CE, and Philotheos Bryennios published it in Constantinople in 1875. Today the manuscript resides at the library of the Jerusalem Monastery of the Holy Sepulchre, MS 54, and is therefore sometimes referred to as Codex Hierosolymitanus ("I" [Bryennios; Hilgenfeld] or "C" [Gebhardt; Harnack]). The scribal accuracy of C is superior to A (and independent of A), although C incorporates some deliberate changes, such as assimilating biblical allusions to a known form. The text of 1 Clement begins with a title, "Clement to the Corinthians." Lightfoot includes photographs of the manuscript in his volume on 1 and 2 Clement.[3]

Codex L

The Latin version of 1 Clement is extant in a single manuscript housed at the Seminary at Namur in southern Belgium. The manuscript does not include 2 Clement. Although it was most likely written in the eleventh century, the version it represents may be much older. Since Lactantius seems to have relied on this or a closely related version, it may represent a second- or early third-century translation from North Africa or Rome. This text was made available in 1894 by Dom Morin in Anecdota Maredsolana, vol. 2, as *S. Clementis Romani ad Corinthios versio latina antiquissima*.

Codex S

The Syriac version, like the Latin (above), is extant in only one manuscript. Its date is unknown—perhaps eighth century.[4] It contains the complete NT and currently resides at the University Library, Cambridge (Add. MSS 1700). In this witness, 1 and 2 Clement appear together after the Catholic Epistles. The witness is valuable because it contains the end of 1 Clement missing in A (see above). According to Lightfoot, S often agrees with A,

2. D. A. Hagner, *The Use of the Old and New Testaments in Clement of Rome*, NovTSup 34 (Leiden: Brill, 1973), 13.

3. J. B. Lightfoot, ed., *The Apostolic Fathers, Part I: S. Clement of Rome*, 2nd ed., 2 vols. (London: Macmillan, 1890), 1:425.

4. K. Lake, *The Apostolic Fathers*, vol. 1 (Cambridge: Harvard University Press, 1912), 5.

where A and C differ, even though it is clearly an independent witness. Both texts have a heading and colophon, claiming they are letters from Clement at Rome to the Corinthians. Lightfoot offers a collation of this text in his volume.[5] R. H. Kennett published the text in *The Epistles of St. Clement to the Corinthians in Syriac* (London, 1899).

Co and Co[1]

Two Coptic manuscripts of 1 Clement are extant in manuscripts in the Akhmîmic dialect. The older and better preserved is a fourth-century manuscript from the White Monastery of Shenoute. It is currently housed in the Königliche Bibliothek in Berlin (MS. Orient, fol. 3065). Carl Schmidt published it in *Der erste Clemensbrief in altkoptischer Übersetzung*, TU 32.1 (Leipzig: Hinrichs, 1908). In this witness, 1 Clement is joined to the canonical books, suggesting canonical status.

The second manuscript is fragmentary. Currently housed in Strassburg (Austria), it was most likely written in the seventh century.[6] In 1910, Friedrich Rösch published it as *Bruchstücke des ersten Clemensbriefes* (Strassburg: Schlesier & Schweikhardt, 1910).

Finally, Clement of Alexandria treats 1 Clement as Scripture, citing it often—a point of relevance in connection with MSS A and C. A thorough understanding of genetic relationships between the various witnesses remains a desideratum of textual scholarship on this text. For this reason, Lake describes any critical text as necessarily eclectic.[7] Fortunately, the witnesses vary less than one might expect—passages of extreme doubt are generally rare.

Summation

Two Greek Texts

1. Codex Alexandrinus (5th cent.; lacks 57.7–63.4)
2. Codex Hierosolymitanus (1056 CE)

Attesting its popularity, the work was translated into three languages: Coptic, Latin, and Syriac. The Latin translation may be very early.

Four Versions

1. Latin 11th cent. MS, ed. G. Morin
2. Syriac NT MS (1169 CE), ed. R. H. Kennett (for R. L. Bensly)
3. Coptic 4th cent. MS, ed. C. Schmidt (omits 34.6–42.2)
4. Coptic, fragmentary 5th cent. (?) MS, ed. F. Rösch (1.1–26.2 only)

Final Note

Patrick Young published the first edition in 1633.[8]

---

5. Lightfoot, *Apostolic Fathers, Part I*, 2:5–188.
6. Lake, *Apostolic Fathers*, 6.
7. Lake, *Apostolic Fathers*, 7.
8. The editio princeps was published as P. Young, ed., *Clementis ad Corinthios Epistola Prior* (Oxford: Iohannes Lichfield, 1633). There was a reissued and corrected edition four years later in 1637.

1.2 Authorship and Date of 1 Clement

First Clement claims to be written by the church at Rome, rather than by any individual person. That said, it is unanimously attributed to Clement in its reception history, who served as the third or fourth bishop of Rome in the last decades of the first century (Irenaeus, *Haer.* 3.3.3). Origen thought that Clement was Paul's companion mentioned in Philippians 4:3 (Eusebius, *Hist. eccl.* 3.4.15; Origen, *Comm. John* 6.36). The Shepherd of Hermas (Vis. 2.4.3) mentions a Clement with the duty to write to other churches, although this text was in all likelihood written after 1 Clement. Some scholars connect authorship of 1 Clement with Titus Flavius Clemens of the imperial Flavian family. According to Dio Cassius, in 95 CE Domitian accused T. Flavius Clemens (Domitian's cousin) of treason on the basis of Jewish proclivities. He was put to death, and his wife Domitilla, was banished. That this "Clement" composed our text is unlikely. It is possible, however, that a slave or freedman "Clemens" of the Flavian family—someone who also would have held a position in the Christian community at Rome—may have written it. In short, the attribution of 1 Clement to Clement is not original, and the identity of the Clement to whom the text is attributed (by writers citing it) is unknown.

A question perhaps underemphasized in discussions of the authorship of 1 Clement is why a text originally attributed to the community in Rome (i.e., ἡ ἐκκλησία τοῦ θεοῦ ἡ παροικοῦσα Ῥώμην, "the church of God which sojourns at Rome") acquired a second attribution (i.e., to Clement). This difficulty is discussed at greater length below. On the basis of style, 1 Clement seems to be the product of a single author. That the same author composed 2 Clement is unlikely based upon significant divergences in style, vocabulary, and content. In some measure (also discussed below), the text was most likely intended to carry Paul's authority.

As a letter ostensibly from one church to another, first-person plural references ("we") are frequent and almost always denote the author and/or his Christian congregation. A handful of occurrences of the first-person plural also arise in citations from Scripture. Correspondingly, the addressee is almost always addressed in the second-person plural. An exception to both of these rules arises in the prescribed oath in 1 Clement 54.2, in which the opponent is exhorted to refer to himself in the first-person singular. Sixty-seven of seventy incidences of the first-person singular in this text occur in scriptural citations, usually denoting God but also Rahab, Abraham, or David (i.e., the psalmist). The first-person singular refers to the opponent only in 1 Clement 54—a chapter Grant and Graham characterize as one of the "most important" in the letter.[9] The first-person singular is typical for oath formulae. Yet the evidence may also suggest that the oath is imbued with a scriptural, solemn, or even holy tone.

The epistle is frequently dated to the end of the first century, about 95–96 CE. Eusebius (*Hist. eccl.* 4.23.11) records that Dionysius, bishop of Corinth (fl. ca. 170 CE) wrote to Soter, bishop of Rome, asserting that "the epistle sent by Clement" was still being read in the Christian assembly. If this comment refers to 1 Clement, then it had been written by about 170 CE. Eusebius writes that an epistle of Clement (successor to Anencletus as bishop of the church of the Romans and fellow worker of Paul) was read publicly in churches "both in the days of old and in our own time," suggesting the time of Hegesippus (*Hist. eccl.* 3.16–17). Today these dates are disputed. Polycarp, writing to the Philippians,

9. R. M. Grant and H. H. Graham, *First and Second Clement*, vol. 2 of *The Apostolic Fathers: A New Translation and Commentary* (New York: Thomas Nelson, 1965), 86.

cites 1 Clement extensively; the date of Polycarp's letter is, however, even less certain than 1 Clement's. Toward the end of the second century also, Clement of Alexandria cites 1 Clement frequently (e.g., *Paed.* 1.91.2; *Strom.*), and Irenaeus praises it, summarizing its initial chapters (*Haer.* 3.3.3).

For years the possible allusion to persecution in 1 Clement 1.1 was thought to suggest that the text was written toward the end of the reign of Domitian (81–96 CE). Supporting this hypothesis, 1 Clement 5 refers to the Neronian persecution (i.e., the deaths of Peter and Paul) as in the past. Against this hypothesis, 1 Clement 42 and 44 suggest that the apostolic age is over. First Clement 44 implies that one or more generations of presbyters have died. First Clement 47.6 refers to the church at Corinth as ancient (ἀρχαῖος). These arguments—particularly claims about persecution of Christians under Domitian—have fallen under some scrutiny in recent years. Lake emphasizes the tenuousness of arguments concerning 1 Clement's date:

> We know very little of the alleged persecution in the time of Domitian, and it would not be prudent to decide that the epistle cannot be another ten or fifteen years later. It is safest to say that it must be dated between 75 and 110 A.D.; but within these limits there is a general agreement among critics to regard as most probable the last decade of the first century.[10]

In 1970, W. C. van Unnik argued that the letter known as 1 Clement is "a plea for peace and concord," or περὶ ὁμονοίας, similar to contemporaneous writings composed to quell seditious outbreaks or στάσεις in the cities of the Roman Empire (more below, "Literary Genre"). Agreeing with van Unnik, Laurence L. Welborn in 1984 persuasively argued against the traditional Domitian dating of this letter (i.e., ca. 96 CE) by demonstrating that a standard component of this category of writings is to open with an apology for not yet intervening in the conflict or στάσις. This conventional apology functions as a *captatio benevolentiae* insofar as it expresses empathy with the addressee by suggesting that the sender also *needs* the advice it gives. This point is explicit in 1 Clement 7.1: "We are writing these things, loved ones, not only to admonish you but also to remind ourselves. For we are in the same arena and the same contest is set before us." This rhetorical interpretation of the letter's prescript (1 Clem. 1.1; cf. 3.1–4) invalidates attempts to ascertain from it the letter's historical circumstances. When this evidence is added to recent theories delaying the traditional date of, for example, the Ignatian corpus and the Martyrdom of Polycarp, we observe a surge of "apostolic" teaching during the middle as opposed to the beginning of the second century. Today, scholars no longer regard the year 100 CE as a historical or theological watershed. Increasingly, texts of even the canonical New Testament are persuasively dated to the first half of the second century. A mid-second-century date for 1 Clement is, therefore, likely.

1.3 The Genre and Literary Integrity of 1 Clement

As mentioned above, in 1970 W. C. van Unnik (building on an argument made by W. Wrede) persuasively argued that 1 Clement is "a plea for peace and concord." In fact,

10. K. Lake, *Apostolic Fathers*, 2 vols., LCL (Cambridge: Harvard University Press, 1912–1913], 1:3–7. Andrew Gregory argues that 1 Clement's *terminus post quem* can be extended earlier to 70 CE. See A. F. Gregory, "Disturbing Trajectories: *1 Clement*, the *Shepherd of Hermas* and the Development of Early Roman Christianity," in *Rome in the Bible and the Early Church*, ed. Peter Oakes (Carlisle: Paternoster, 2002), 142–66; A. F. Gregory, "*1 Clement*: An Introduction," in *The Writings of the Apostolic Fathers*, ed. P. Foster (London: T&T Clark, 2007), 29.

1 Clement utilizes the literary model of "a plea for peace" (περὶ ὁμονοίας) among cities from start to finish. Literary parallels with Dio Chrysostom's *Orations* 38–41 are especially close. Additionally, 1 Clement refers to the Christian community as an "association" or "government" (πολίτευμα; cf. Phil 3:20). Its primary exhortation is to the "leaders" or "instigators" (ἀρχηγοί; 1 Clem. 51.1). Its recommendation to the factionalizing individual (or, perhaps, two) is voluntary exile (1 Clem. 54.2). Individual members of the congregation are referred to as "citizens" (οἱ πολιτευόμενοι) of the "city of God" (πολιτεία τοῦ θεοῦ, 1 Clem. 54.4) and are exhorted as an "army" (στρατευσώμεθα), holding offices, including that of prefect, tribune, and centurion that together serve the king and leaders (1 Clem. 37.1–5).

First Clement also, however, extrapolates data from 1 Corinthians, to some extent mapping its own argument on Paul's letter. It probably does so for a number of reasons, not least of which is to promote the acceptance of 1 Clement as genuine and the acceptance of its authority as a result. The most significant way that 1 Clement agrees with 1 Corinthians is perhaps in its argument that the removal of a certain individual has become a community imperative (1 Cor 5:5; 1 Clem. 54.2). The most significant way 1 Clement diverges from 1 Corinthians concerns authorship. First Clement does not claim to be written by an individual (e.g., Paul, or even Clement for that matter), but by the church "sojourning" (so Lake) or "dwelling temporarily" (so Ehrman) in Rome (ἡ ἐκκλησία τοῦ θεοῦ ἡ παροικοῦσα Ῥώμην, 1 Clem. 1.1). This element (i.e., city church writing to city church) conforms to the model of περὶ ὁμονοίας on which the text is based. If, however, one admits 1 Peter as an interpretive guide on this point, then description of the churches of the cities of Rome and Corinth as "sojourning" (παροικοῦσα) may employ the convention nonliterally. "Sojourning" implies being in a city *without* citizenship or with a superior citizenship elsewhere. First Clement's prescript, effectively "those *without* citizenship in Corinth" to "those *without* citizenship in Rome," if figurative, controverts the epistolographic convention of the genre, perhaps even encoding new meaning. It certainly implies two different communities, perhaps two communities centered on different ways of behaving: unified Romans writing to factionalizing Corinthians; or perhaps communities emphasizing different ways of interpreting tradition: righteous Romans writing to ecstatic Corinthians. In any case, we can be certain that early readers were unsatisfied with 1 Clement's original attribution. Canonization may have demanded a *titulus* distinguishable from Paul's letter "to the Corinthians." Whatever the reason, the text acquires the second ascription to "Clement," to whom a substantial amount of second- and third-century pseudepigraphic literature is likewise attributed. In this acquisition, 1 Clement provides the example of the attribution of an attributed text, familiar to the so-called Old Testament Pseudepigrapha and its literature.

These observations may indicate that 1 Clement is a letter between two cities only formally. Functionally, it was neither written from a church in Rome nor delivered to (or even intended for) a church in Corinth. Instead, as a missive from one community of Christians to another, it convincingly maps a new epistolary scenario on an older authoritative one with a similar purpose. In such a case—double attribution notwithstanding—1 Clement would be considered a pseudepigraphon. The elements of the *new* epistolary scenario thus become our only foothold into real authorship, addressee(s), and occasion.

Returning to the question of genre, as Odd Bakke has shown recently, a chief means of persuasion in letters of concord is the historical exemplum, consisting of both proofs by induction and "witnesses" (μάρτυρες).[11] In Dio Chrysostom's letters "concerning harmony" (περὶ ὁμονοίας), the "discord" (στάσις) between the Spartans and Athenians in the Peloponnesian War constitutes such an example. Dio Chrysostom goes back to the famous disagreement between Athens and Sparta as an example to contemporary cities engaged in a dispute. First Clement dubs its examples "signs" (ὑποδείγματα) as opposed to "patterns, models" (παραδείγματα cf. τύπος in 1 Cor 10:6) and concentrates these examples in the *probatio* (Gk. πίστεις) in chapters 4–19 (cf. also 31–32, 43), selectively reprising them in a *peroratio* (ἐπίλογος) in 51.1–58.2. Although many of the exempla of the *peroratio* are repeated from the earlier *probatio* section, the climax of the exempla in the *peroratio* is an allusion not yet brought forward in the text: the golden-calf incident (53.2–5). This new exemplum has important consequences for our understanding of the text's most immediate opponent and purpose. Whereas most recipients of the golden-calf tradition employ it for its negative portrayal of the sin of idolatry committed by the wilderness generation, 1 Clement uses it for its positive portrayal of Moses as leader. Moses is prepared, not just to beg the Lord's forgiveness on behalf of the sinful people, but to die with them should the Lord be unwilling to forgive. Moses thus exemplifies the author's solution to the present στάσις in the church: the leaders of the opponents should be willing to die for the sake of the group.

In terms of the letter's integrity, the question is infrequently addressed. Although cases can be made that the author has used sources—for example that (1) the doxologies and Trinitarian formulae signify the conclusion of letter segments (another instance of 1 Clement following the Pauline epistolary model, as Romans uses doxologies/benedictions to mark the terminations of sections); (2) the digressions were once individual sermons; and (3) the liturgical prayer in 1 Clement 59.1–61.3 is an outside (possibly later) source—no single theory has persuaded a majority. The relentless outpouring of disconnected mandates, prooftexts, and dicta leave modern interpreters wondering how it would be possible to tell whether a source was involved.

2. SUMMARY OF CONTENT

Whereas some regard 1 Clement as long, discursive, and unsusceptible to structural analysis, others discern subtle organizing principles. To be sure, the text reflects knowledge of Greco-Roman rhetoric but is not, therefore, unaffected by Jewish compositional strategies. Like 1 Corinthians, 1 Clement is a deliberative letter, the body of which shares elements in common with ancient speeches. The theme of "harmony" (ὁμόνοια) was a frequent topic of deliberative oratory. As with many early Christian texts, the letter-speech hybrid met a variety of the demands of both genres. Epistolary prescripts and postscripts were often removed in published collections of letters. Such generic hybridism was a popular feature of Christian composition, although it was hardly unique to early Christians.

Rhetorical analyses of 1 Clement tend to skip over what is, to my mind, the first step of such projects; namely, an explanation of what the author determines to be the points in dispute and, in turn, how the reader is being asked to adjudicate these points. In 1 Clement, the point in dispute is clearly deposition of older presbyters by a younger faction (1 Clem. 1.1b; 7.1; 44.1–3; 47.6; 57.1). First Clement's argument is deliberative because, lacking the authority to reestablish them by *fiat*, the author must rather persuade the addressees of the

11. O. M. Bakke, *"Concord and Peace": A Rhetorical Analysis of the Language of the First Letter of Clement with an Emphasis on the Language of Unity and Sedition*, WUNT 2/143 (Tübingen: Mohr Siebeck, 2001), 57–61.

appropriateness of the presbyters' reinstatement. Clearly, the gap between the positions of "church leader" and "heretic" are much closer than they will eventually be. The contents and flow of the argument of 1 Clement can be laid out as follows.

Prescript	
Prologue	Identification of sender and addressee with greeting
1 Clem. 1.1	Explanation of letter's delay
Body	
1 Clem. 1.2–3.4	Purpose of letter to address internal disputes
1 Clem. 4–6	Examples from Jewish Scriptures, contemporary Christians, and pagans illustrating evils of jealousy
1 Clem. 7.1–4	Recitation and expansion of letter's *causa* (7.1), plus four mandates
1 Clem. 7.5–39.9	Arguments from repentance, faith, holiness, humility, cosmology, reverence, resurrection, God's omnipresence, election, and leadership, with digressions interspersed
1 Clem. 40–47	Refutations from disorderly sacrifice, succession, reliability of Scripture, principle of unity, reliability of 1 Corinthians
1 Clem. 48–58	Series of mandates
1 Clem. 59–61	Liturgical prayer
Conclusion	
1 Clem. 62–63	Summation, catalogue of virtues, benediction, doxologies
1 Clem. 64–65	Benediction, doxologies

Prologue

First Clement begins with an epistolary prescript including a *superscriptio*, denoting the name and location of the principal sender ("the church of God . . . in Rome"), an *adscriptio* with the name, location, and further qualification of principal addressees ("the church of God . . . in Corinth"), and a *salutatio*, "May grace and peace be increased among you."

1 Clement 1.1

The author next provides a customary explanation of the letter's delay (cf. Dio Chrysostom, *Or.* 40.2; Aelius Aristides, *Or.* 24.1; [Socrates], *Ep.* 31) and a statement of the letter's *causa* or purpose characterized as "matters causing disputes among you . . ."; a "vile and profane faction that is alien and foreign to God's chosen people," "stoked by a few reckless and headstrong persons," such that the addressees' "venerable and renowned reputation has been slandered."

1 Clement 1.2–3.4

The writer next proceeds with arguments from history seriatim. Four rhetorical questions concerning the high reputation of the church in Corinth commence the list: (1) "For who has ever visited you and not approved your highly virtuous and stable faith?" (2) "And not been astonished by your temperate and gentle piety in Christ?" (3) "And not proclaimed the magnificent character of your hospitality?" (4) "And not uttered a blessing for your perfect and unwavering knowledge?"

Five past behaviors of the addressees (cf. household codes) serve as reminders of correct behavior: "For you used to . . ." (1) "act impartially in all that you did"; (2) "and you walked according to the ordinance of God . . ."; (3) "you instructed your young people to think moderate and respectful thoughts"; (4) "you directed women to accomplish all things with a blameless, respectful, and pure conscience"; and (5) "and you taught them to run their households respectfully." Three characteristics define pre-schismatic behavior: (1) "All of you used to be humble"; (2) "You heeded his words"; and (3) "And his sufferings were before your eyes." Three consequences correspond to past good behavior: (1) "For this reason a deep and rich peace was given to all"; (2) "along with . . . desire for doing good"; and (3) "a full outpouring of the Holy Spirit."

In catchword association with this mention of the Holy Spirit, the author next outlines nine favorable consequences of past Spirit possession: (1) "You used to stretch out your hands"; (2) "Day and night you struggled on behalf of the entire brotherhood"; (3) "You were sincere and innocent and bore no grudges"; (4) "Every faction and schism was loathsome to you"; (5) "You had no regrets when doing good"; (6) "You were prepared for every good deed"; (7) "You were adorned with a highly virtuous and honorable way of life"; (8) "You accomplished all things in reverential awe of him"; and (9) "The commandments and righteous demands of the Lord were inscribed upon the tablets of your heart."

The author next appends a prooftext from Deuteronomy 32:15, which explains gifts of spiritual possession as lapsing into vices and ultimately schism. A catalogue of vices secures the point; the writer lists jealousy, envy, strife, faction, persecution, disorderliness, war, and captivity (1 Clem. 3.2). In 3.3 an initial conclusion is drawn: dishonorable young leaders have risen up against honorable "presbyters" (cf. Isa 3:5), and peace is now "far removed" (cf. Isa 59:14). Three behaviors characterize the congregation: they have (1) abandoned reverential awe of God; (2) become dim-sighted in faith, failing to proceed in the ordinances of his commandments and not living according to what is appropriate; and (3) each one walks according to the desires of his evil heart.

1 Clement 4–6

First Clement 4–6 offers examples from the Jewish Scriptures, contemporary Christians, and pagans to illustrate the evils of jealousy. Examples from the Jewish Scriptures include some famous pairs: Cain and Abel, Jacob and Esau, Moses and Pharaoh, Abraham and Miriam, Dathan and Abiram, David and Saul. Contemporary examples are the athlete-apostles, Peter and Paul (5.1–7)—Paul being the "greatest example of endurance." Other contemporary examples include faithful women ("like Danaids and Dircae"), persecuted as a result of jealousy, jealousy that estranges husbands from wives, violating Genesis 2:23, and jealousy that has overturned great cities and uprooted great nations.

1 Clement 7.1–4

At the beginning of chapter 7 the writer recapitulates and expands upon the letter's purpose. He opens with a brief summary both as an exhortation to the addressee ("for your admonition," νουθετοῦντες) and as self-reminder that both parties participate "in the same contest." Four mandates follow: (1) "Leave behind empty and frivolous thoughts"; (2) "Come to the famous and venerable rule of tradition"; (3) "realize what is good"; and (4) "Gaze intently on the blood of Christ and realize how precious it is . . . for when it was poured out for our salvation, it brought the gracious gift of repentance to the entire world."

1 Clement 7.5–39.9

To support these exhortations, the author commences a series of eleven arguments with accompanying exempla (ch. 8). The first is an argument from *repentance* (#1), for which the exempla are Noah and Jonah. These examples from history prompt a brief thematic exhortation on repentance, utilizing three prooftexts: (1) Ezekiel 33:11; (2) Ezekiel 33 (?); and (3) Isaiah 1:16–20. The prooftexts culminate in a summary statement: "Because he wanted all his loved ones to have a share in repentance, he set it in place by his all-powerful will."

Five mandates follow from the argument on repentance (1 Clem. 9.1–3): we should (1) "obey"; (2) "fall down before him"; (3) "turn to his compassionate ways, leaving behind our pointless toil and strife"; (4) "gaze intently on those who have perfectly served his magnificent glory"; and (5) "consider Enoch."

The writer then argues from *faith* (#2). In a catchword association with the fifth mandate of the previous section, he commences a catalogue of five examples (9.3–12.8), with Enoch (9.3), followed by Noah (9.4), Abraham (10.1–7), Lot (11.1–2), and Rahab (12.1–8).

Three mandates follow from these exemplars of faith (ch. 13). We should (1) "be humble-minded, laying aside all arrogance"; (2) "act in accordance with what is written," backed by prooftexts from Jeremiah 9:23–24; 1 Corinthians 1:31; and 2 Corinthians 10:17; and (3) "especially remember the words the Lord Jesus spoke," with prooftexts from Matthew 5:7; 6:14–15; 7:1–2, 12; and Luke 6:31, 36–38. The writer concludes with the exhortation: "Let us strengthen one another in this commandment and these demands, so that we may forge ahead." Isaiah 66:2 backs this plea.

Next the writer argues from *holiness* (#3, chs. 14–15). The section begins with a rule supporting the letter's overall purpose (against strife): "It is right and holy for us to obey God . . . rather than follow those who instigate a foul jealousy." Then he delineates the consequences of disobedience: "We subject ourselves to real danger if we take part in strife and factions." Bolstering the point, the writer urges the congregation to "treat one another kindly"—an exhortation backed by prooftexts from Proverbs 2:21–22; Psalm 37:9, 38; and Psalm 37:35–37. Chapter 15 follows with another mandate: "Cling to those who keep the peace with piety, not those who wish for peace out of hypocrisy." Supporting this rule are five prooftexts: (1) Isaiah 29:13; Mark 7:6; Matthew 15:8; (2) Psalm 62:4; (3) Psalm 78:36–37; (4) Psalm 31:18; and (5) Psalm 12:4–6.

Fourth, the writer argues from *humility* (#4, chs. 16–19). This section commences with two theological dicta: (1) Christ belongs to the humble-minded; and (2) Jesus came with a humble mind. Two prooftexts are provided: Isaiah 53:1–12 and Psalm 22:6–8. The writer then offers a rhetorical question: "For if the Lord was humble-minded in this way, what shall we ourselves do, who through him have assumed the yoke of his gracious favor?" This question is followed by a list of mandates. The first instruction is to "become imitators also of those who went about in the skins of goats and sheep . . ." (cf. Heb 11:37). Seven exemplars (1 Clem. 17–18) are provided: Elijah, Elisha and Ezekiel, Abraham (prooftext, Gen 18:27), Job (prooftexts, Job 1:1; 14:4–5 [LXX]), Moses (prooftexts, Num 12:7; Heb 3:2; and one unknown source), and David (prooftexts, 1 Sam 13:14; Acts 13:22; Ps 51:1–17).

Humility improves people as witnessed by past exemplars. This fact gives rise to six mandates: (1) "We should forge ahead to the goal of peace"; (2) "We should gaze intently on the Father and Creator of the entire world"; (3) "[We should] cling to his magnificent and superior gifts of peace and acts of kindness"; (4) "We should observe him with understanding"; (5) "We should look upon his patient will with the eyes of our soul"; and (6) "We should realize how he feels no anger toward his entire creation."

The fifth argument (1 Clem. 20) comes from *cosmology* (#5) and features a cosmological poem concluding with a doxology—one of many in 1 Clement. The sixth argument comes from *reverence* (#6, ch. 21). Here the writer issues seven general mandates: (1) "You should take care that his many acts of kindness do not lead to judgment against all of us"; this directive is backed by a prooftext from Proverbs 20:27 ("for somewhere it says"); (2) "We should realize how near he is"; (3) "[We should realize] that none of our thoughts or the disputes we have had is hidden from him"; (4) "We should revere the Lord Jesus Christ"; (5) "We should respect our leaders"; (6) "We should honor the elderly"; and (7) "We should discipline our youth in the reverential fear of God." The last mandate has a clear application to the letter's demand that youthful leadership step down.

From this statement about youth, the author moves to a few family mandates: one mandate for husbands regarding their wives, four mandates for wives themselves, and three mandates for children (1 Clem. 21). The mandate for husbands is: "We should set our wives along the straight path that leads to good." The four mandates for wives are: (1) "Let them display a character of purity"; (2) "Let them exhibit the innocent will of their meekness"; (3) "Let them manifest the gentleness of their tongues"; and (4) "Let them show their love not with partiality, but equally." The three mandates for children are: (1) "Let our children partake of the discipline that is in Christ"; (2) "Let them learn the strength of humility before God and the power of pure love"; (3) "Let them learn how the reverential awe of him is beautiful . . . and how it saves." The section concludes with a premise on which the advice is based. It also functions as a motivation to obey: "For he [God] is the one who explores our understandings and desires. His breath is in us, and when he wishes, he will remove it."

The seventh argument returns to the topic of *faith* (#7; cf. #2 above). The section begins with a theological dictum: "The faith that is in Christ guarantees all these things." It is backed by two prooftexts: Psalm 34:11–17, 19 and Psalm 32:10. According to the writer of 1 Clement, purity of resolve is crucial to faith; thus, any "double-mindedness" must be eradicated. In this vein, the writer offers the following statement of truth: "The beneficent father, compassionate in every way, has pity on those who stand in awe of him; gently and kindly does he bestow his gracious gifts on those who approach him with a pure resolve." Two mandates flow from this truth: (1) "And so, we should not be of two minds"; and (2) "Nor should we entertain wild notions about his superior and glorious gifts." The prooftext for these mandates is a parable of unknown source. The interpretation of the parable is that time is short, for which Isaiah 13:22 (LXX) and Malachi 3:1 provide backing.

The eighth argument is based upon the hope of *resurrection from the dead* (#8) and features four mandates: (1) "We should consider, loved ones, how the Master continuously shows us the future resurrection"; (2) "We should look, loved ones, at the resurrection that happens time after time"—supported by proof from nature: "Day and night reveal to us a resurrection: the night sleeps and the day arises; the day departs and the night arrives"; (3) "We should consider the crops," supported by a prooftext from Mark 4:3; cf. 1 Corinthians 15:36; and (4) "Let us consider the incredible sign that occurs in the eastern climates"—the example of the mythical phoenix. Following the example of the phoenix, the author poses an a fortiori rhetorical question: "Do we then think that it is so great and marvelous that the Creator of all things will raise everyone who has served him in a holy way with the confidence of good faith, when he shows us the magnificence of his promise even through a bird?" The question echoes Matthew 6:26//Luke 12:24 and is backed by prooftexts in Psalms 28:7; 3:5; 26:3; and Job 19:26.

Just before commencing the ninth argument, the writer composes his first digression. It is a collection of mandates, proverbs, and prooftexts (Wis 12:12; Ps 19:1–3) on the theme of God's faithfulness (1 Clem. 27). Building from the digression, the ninth argument (ch. 28) develops the theme of *God's omnipresence* (#9). It commences with a mandate: "Since everything is seen and heard, we should stand in awe, leaving behind depraved desires . . . that we may be protected from the judgments that are to come." The author then turns to the consequences of disobedience formulated as three rhetorical questions: "For where can any of us flee?"; "And what world will welcome any of those who desert him?" A prooftext from Psalm 139:7–8 introduces the final (rhetorical) question: "Where can a person go, or where escape the one who encompasses all things?"

The tenth argument is from *election* (#10). Like many before, it opens with a mandate: "And so we should approach him with devout souls, raising pure and undefiled hands to him and loving our gentle and kind-hearted Father, who made us his own chosen portion." It is backed by prooftexts: Deuteronomy 32:8–9 (cf. Num 18:27; Deut 4:34; 24:2). Eight mandates with prooftexts follow. (1) "Since then we are a holy portion, we should do everything that pertains to holiness, fleeing slander and vile and impure sexual embraces, drunken revelries, rebellions and loathsome passions, foul adultery and loathsome haughtiness"—with prooftexts from Proverbs 3:34; James 4:6; and 1 Peter 5:5; (2) "We should, therefore, cling to those who have been bestowed with God's gracious gift"; (3) "We should be clothed with harmony," with a prooftext from Job 11:2–3 (LXX); (4) "Let our praise be with God and not from ourselves," supported by the theological dictum, "For God hates those who praise themselves"; (5) "Let the testimony of our good behavior be given by others," supported by the theological dictum: "Audacity, insolence, and effrontery belong to those who are cursed by God: gentleness, humility, and meekness to those blessed by God"; (6) "So we should cling to his blessing"; (7) "[We should] discern the paths that lead to it"; and (8) "We should unravel in our minds what has taken place from the beginning," for which Abraham, Isaac, and Jacob offer exempla.

Having summarized his arguments thus far, the writer now pauses to utter a theological dictum with the dual function of a charge (1 Clem. 32): "Whoever will honestly consider each of these matters will recognize the greatness of the gift given by God." Four proofs connected genealogically to Jacob ("from Jacob came the priests and all the Levites," "from him came the Lord Jesus," "from him came the kings, rulers, and leaders in the line of Judah," and "his other scepters enjoyed no small glory either") support this dictum, after which the writer summarizes: "All of these, therefore, were glorified and exalted not through themselves or their deeds or the upright actions they did, but through his own will." He concludes with the correlative statement: "So too we who have been called through his will in Christ Jesus are made upright not through ourselves." This section concludes with a doxology.

Chapters 33–36 present digressions, utilizing rhetorical questions, proverbs, mandates, and other literary forms to express God's omnipotence, holiness, blessings, and the response expected of God's people. Chapter 36 focuses on the role of Jesus as high priest known in the canonical New Testament in the Letter to the Hebrews.

The eleventh and last argument comes from *leadership* (#11). A group of fifteen hortatory statements develop two metaphors. The first metaphor involves war: (1) "And so, brothers, with all eagerness let us do battle as soldiers under his blameless commands"; (2) "Consider those who soldier under our own leaders." The second metaphor—with clear Pauline resonances—involves the human body (cf. 1 Cor 12:21): (3) "Take your own body"; (4) "Let our whole body be healthy in Christ Jesus"; (5) "Let each person be subject to his neighbor"; (6) "Let the one who is strong take care of the weak"; (7) "Let the weak show due respect to the strong"; (8) "Let the wealthy provide what is needed to the poor"; (9) "Let the poor offer thanks to God, since he has given"; (10) "Let the one who is wise show forth wisdom not through words but through good deeds"; (11) "Let the one who is humble not testify to himself but permit another to testify on his behalf"; (12) "Let the one who is pure in the flesh not act arrogantly"; (13) "Let us carefully consider, brothers, the material from which we have been made"; (14) "Let us consider from what kind of tomb and darkness we were led into the world"; and (15) "Since we have all these things from him, we ought to thank him in every way." Chapter 38 concludes with the traditional doxology.

Chapter 39 sums up the historical circumstances as the author sees them: "Those who are ignorant . . . mock and ridicule us." Prooftexts from Job 4:16–18; 15:15; and 4:19–5:5 address five rhetorical questions on the frailty of the human condition.

1 Clement 40–47

Chapters 40–47 offer a series of refutations: from (1) disorderly sacrifice, (2) succession, (3) reliability of Scripture, and (4) the principle of unity. In the first refutation, the writer issues four mandates: (1) "We should do everything the Master has commanded us to perform in an orderly way and at appointed times"; (2) "He commanded that the sacrificial offerings and liturgical rites be performed not in a random or haphazard way"; (3) "He set forth both where and through whom he wished them to be performed"; (4) "Brothers, let each of us be pleasing to God by keeping to our special assignments with a good conscience, not violating the established rule of his ministry, acting in reverence."

The second refutation from succession (chs. 42–43) asks a question: since "the apostles were given the gospel by the Lord Jesus Christ, and Jesus Christ was sent forth from God . . . ," both taking place "in an orderly way according to the will of God" (prooftext, Isa 60:17 [LXX]), "Why should it be so amazing if those who were in Christ and entrusted by God with such a work appointed the leaders mentioned earlier?" (prooftexts, Num 12:7; Heb 3:5). The author then poses two rhetorical questions, using Moses as an example: "What do you think, loved ones? That Moses did not know in advance this would happen? Of course, he knew." "He did this so that there might be no disorderliness in Israel."

In chapter 44 the author then appeals to the example of smooth succession: "So too our apostles knew through our Lord Jesus Christ that strife would arise over the office of the bishop. For this reason . . . they appointed those we have already mentioned." The writer concludes: "Thus we do not think it right to remove from the ministry those who were appointed by them or, afterwards, by other reputable men, with the entire church giving its approval." "Indeed we commit no little sin if we remove from the bishop's office those who offer the gifts in a blameless and holy way." One additional opinion is added: "How fortunate are the presbyters who passed on before. . . . For they have no fear that someone will remove them from the place established for them"; with the added observation: "We see that you have deposed some from the ministry held blamelessly in honor among them even though they had been conducting themselves well."

The third refutation is based on the reliability of Scripture (ch. 45), championing it as a collection in which the upright are never cast out by the unholy and reminding readers that God protected Daniel and his friends in ancient Babylon.

The fourth and final refutation is a series of mandates, prooftexts, and questions based on the principle of unity. The first mandate is, unsurprisingly, to cling to the examples provided in this letter and Scripture. The first prooftext comes from an unknown source, the second, from Psalm 18:25–26. The second mandate, "We should cling to those who are innocent and upright," is followed by five questions: (1) "Why are there conflicts, fits of anger, dissensions, factions and wars among you?" (2) "Do we not have one God, and one Christ, and one gracious Spirit . . . and one calling in Christ?" (note the first iteration of a Trinitarian formula); (3) "Why do we mangle and mutilate the members of Christ?" (4) "[Why do we] create factions in our own body?" (5) "Why do we come to such a pitch of madness as to forget that we are members of one another?" Next, this section appends a statement of authorial opinion: "Your schism has corrupted many and cast many into despondency, many into doubt, and all of us into grief. And your faction persists even now!" (1 Clem. 46.9).

The third mandate is to "take up the epistle of the blessed apostle, Paul." It is followed by a question, "What did he write to you at the beginning of his proclamation of the gospel?" and an answer, "To be sure, he sent you a letter in the Spirit concerning himself and Cephas and Apollos, since you were even then engaged in partisanship." The fourth and final mandate is to "consider who has corrupted you and diminished the respect you had because of your esteemed love of others." The author concludes with a statement concerning the outcome of the addressees' behavior: "It is shameful . . . that the most secure and ancient church of the Corinthians is reported to have created a faction against its presbyters, at the instigation of one or two persons . . . that blasphemies have been uttered against the Lord's name because of your foolishness; and you are exposing yourselves to danger."

1 Clement 48–58

Chapters 48–58 comprise a kind of closing argument in which the author brings to a pitch the barrage of mandates and questions. Chapter 48 offers six mandates: (1) "And so let us dispose of this problem quickly and fall down before the Master and weep, begging him to be merciful and to be reconciled to us, and to restore us to our respected and holy conduct, seen in our love of others," with a prooftext from Psalm 118:19–20; (2) "Let a person be faithful"; (3) "Let him be able to speak forth"; (4) "Let him be wise"; (5) "Let him be pure in deed"; (6) "For the more he appears to be great, the more he should be humble, striving for the good of all."

Chapter 49 features only one mandate, "The one who experiences love in Christ should do what Christ commanded." It is followed by rhetorical questions and a panegyric on love (cf. 1 Cor 13:4–7). Chapter 50 issues two mandates: (1) "Observe, loved ones, how great and amazing love is; there can be no exposition of its perfection"; (2) "And so we should implore and plead for his mercy." Supporting prooftexts come from Isaiah 26:20; Ezekiel 37:12; Psalm 32:1–2; and Romans 4:7–9.

Chapter 51 has two mandates: (1) "And so we should ask to be forgiven"; and (2) "In addition those who became the leaders of the faction and dissension should consider the common ground of hope." At this point, the author inserts another opinion: "For those who conduct themselves with reverential awe and love prefer to undergo torture themselves. . . . They would rather have condemnation fall on themselves than on the unity that has been nobly and justly delivered over to us." He also adds a dictum: "For it is more noble for a person to confess his transgressions than to harden his heart," with prooftexts from Numbers 16:33; Psalm 49:14; and Exodus 14:23 (paraphrase). The applicability of this chapter to the overall purpose of the letter is clear. Those who have displaced the older leaders should repent, admit the error of their ways, and step down, allowing the displaced elders to return to their roles.

Chapter 52 commences with a theological maxim: "The Master is in need of nothing, brothers, and craves nothing from anyone, but to be praised," backed by prooftexts from Psalm 69:30–32; Psalm 50:14–15; and Psalm 51:17. However, Chapter 53 adopts a different strategy—appealing this time to flattery: "For you know the sacred Scriptures, loved ones—and you know them quite well—and you have gazed into the sayings of God." These claims are supported with prooftexts from Exodus 32:7–10, 31–32 and Deut 9:12–14 (paraphrase).

Chapter 54 asks three genuine questions: (1) "Who, therefore, among you is noble?" (2) "[Who is] compassionate?" and (3) "[Who is] filled with love?" The questions are followed by an important mandate to proclaim self-exile: "Let that one say, 'If I am the cause of faction, strife, and schisms, I will depart; I will go wherever you wish and do what is commanded by the congregation. Only allow the flock of Christ to be at peace with the presbyters who have been appointed.'" The expected result of this recommended self-proclamation is: "The one who does this will have made himself eminent in Christ and will be welcomed everywhere." The concluding theological dictum backs the recommendation: "Those who have performed their civic duty to God, without regrets, have done these things and will continue to do them."

Chapter 55 offers five additional paragons of virtue for comparison: "We should bring in examples from the Gentiles as well," exemplified by pagan kings, persecuted Christ followers, and women performing "manly deeds," such as Judith (cf. Jdt 8), and Esther (cf. Esth 7; also 4:16). These illustrations are followed by two new mandates (1 Clem. 56): (1) "We should pray for those caught up in any unlawful act"; and (2) "We should welcome discipline, loved ones; no one should be irritated by it." These recommendations are backed by a theological dictum: "It is good and supremely useful to rebuke one another, for this binds us to the will of God," which is in turn supported by prooftexts in Proverbs 3:12; cf. Job 5:17–26; Psalm 141:5; and Hebrews 12:6.

Chapter 57 lays out three mandates, each incorporating the proposed punishment first noted in chapter 54: (1) "Thus you who laid the foundation of the faction should be subject to the presbyters and accept the discipline that leads to repentance, falling prostrate in your heart"; (2) "Learn to be submissive"; and (3) "Lay aside the arrogant and haughty insolence of your tongue." A theological dictum stems from the second mandate: "For it is better for you to be considered insignificant but reputable in the flock of Christ than to appear prominent while sundered from his hope," backed by a prooftext from Proverbs 1:23–33.

Chapter 58 offers two final mandates: (1) "We should be obedient to his most holy and glorious name, fleeing the dangers foretold by Wisdom, which threaten the disobedient." The consequence of obedience is delineated: "In this way we will dwell with confidence in the most holy name of his magnificence"; and (2) "Take our advice and you will have no regrets. For as God, the Lord Jesus Christ, and the Holy Spirit all live" (the second iteration of a Trinitarian formula), which is followed by a theological dictum: "The one who does the righteous demands and commandments given by God with humility and fervent gentleness, and without regret will be included and held in esteem among the number of those who will be saved through Jesus Christ." The section concludes with a traditional doxology.

1 Clement 59–61

Chapters 59–61 comprise a liturgical invocation opening with a threat: "But if some disobey the words he has spoken through us, they should realize that they entangle themselves in transgression and no little danger." This threat is followed by a statement of the author's innocence: "But we ourselves will be innocent of this sin." Two petitions follow next: (1) "Grant us, O Lord, that we may hope in your name"; and (2) "Open the eyes of our heart" (cf. Eph 1:18). Next the author lists seventeen attributes of God:

1. "The one alone who is the highest"
2. "The holy one who rests among the holy"

3. "The one who humbles the insolence of the proud"
4. "Who destroys the reasonings of the nations"
5. "Who exalts the humble"
6. "Who humiliates the exalted"
7. "The one who enriches and impoverishes"
8. "Who kills and brings to life"
9. "The sole benefactor of spirits"
10. "The God of all flesh"
11. "The one who peers into the places of the abyss"
12. "Who observes the works of humans"
13. "Helps those in danger"
14. "The savior of those who have abandoned hope"
15. "The creator and overseer of every spirit"
16. "The one who multiplies the nations upon the earth"
17. "Who from them all has chosen those who love you through Jesus Christ."

Twelve petitionary imperatives follow the attributes of God: "We ask you, O Master, to . . ."

1. "Be our helper and defender"
2. "Save those of us who are in affliction"
3. "Show mercy to those who are humble"
4. "Raise those who have fallen"
5. "Show yourself to those who are in need"
6. "Heal those who are sick
7. "Set straight those among your people who are going astray"
8. "Feed the hungry"
9. "Ransom our prisoners"
10. "Raise up the weak"
11. "Encourage the despondent"
12. "Let all the nations know you"
    A. "That you alone are God"
    B. "That Jesus Christ is your child"
    C. "And that we are your people and the sheep of your pasture." (cf. Ps 95:7)

Chapter 60 begins with seven attributes of God's character, adding to the seventeen above for a total of twenty-four. The prayer does not follow the usual Greco-Roman sequence of (1) invocation; (2) argument (narrative paradigm or recitation of relevant attributes); and (3) petition(s). Instead, the author bounces back and forth between invocations, arguments, and petitions, perhaps imitating the format of LXX Psalms filtered through Greco-Roman conventions of hymnic prayer:

1. "For you have made plain the eternal structure of the world . . ."
2. "You, O Lord, created the world in which we live."
3. "You are faithful from one generation to the next . . ."
4. "You are wise when you create."
5. "[You are] understanding when you establish what exists."
6. "You are good in what is seen."
7. "[You are] kind to those who trust you."

These statements are followed by ten petitionary requests:

1. "You who are merciful and compassionate, forgive us . . ."
2. "Take into account none of the sins committed by your male slaves and female servants."
3. "But cleanse us with your truth."
4. "Set our steps straight."
5. "Yes, Master, make your face shine on us in peace, for our own good, that we may be protected by your powerful hand and rescued from our every sin by your exalted arm."
6. "And rescue us from those who hate us without cause."
7. "Give harmony and peace both to us and to all those who inhabit the earth."
8. "And allow us to be obedient to your all-powerful and all-virtuous name, and to those who rule and lead us here on earth."
9. "Give to them [leaders], O Lord, health, peace, harmony, and stability."
10. "Make their plan conform with what is good and acceptable before you."

Chapter 61 concludes with a doxology: "You who alone can do these things for us, and do what is more abundantly good, we praise you through the high priest and benefactor of our souls, Jesus Christ, through whom the glory and majesty be yours both now and for all generations and forever. Amen."

1 Clement 62–63

Chapters 62–63 draw the long letter to a conclusion with an epistolary postscript. The writer begins with an epistolary summation: "Brothers, we have written you enough about what is fitting for our worship and what is most profitable for the virtuous life" (62.1), after which he catalogues some of those virtues (v. 2) and then appeals to the addressees with flattery (v. 3). Chapter 63 offers a rule and its anticipated effect. Both directly address the point to be adjudicated in the letter: "It is right for us to bow our necks in submission and assume a position of obedience"; "in this way, by putting a halt to the futile faction, we will truly reach the goal set before us, with no blame attached."

Following the hypothetical statement: "You will make us joyful . . . if you become obedient to what we have written . . . and excise the wanton anger expressed through your jealousy," the writer reports a recent, legal action taken: "We have sent faithful and temperate men who have lived blamelessly among us from youth to old age; these will serve as witnesses between you and us," with an explanation of the reason: "We have done this that you may know that our every concern has been—and is—for you to establish the peace quickly."

1 Clement 64–65

Chapter 64 comprises a benediction, catalogue of virtues, and doxology, and chapter 65 issues a final mandate, "Send back to us quickly our envoys . . . that they may inform us without delay about the peace and harmony that we have prayed and desired for you," a final benediction, "The grace of our Lord Jesus Christ be with you and with all those everywhere who are called by God through him," and a doxology, "Through whom be to him all glory, honor, power, greatness, and the eternal throne, forever and ever. Amen." Emphasis on God's "eternal throne" in this doxology underscores the theme of judgment in the letter.

3. INTERPRETATIVE ISSUES

As noted, the central theme of 1 Clement is "harmony" or "concord" (ὁμόνοια). All of the letter's authoritative exhortations and mandates are delivered in goodwill, intended as the means by which this end is to be accomplished. The evidence in 1 Clement suggests that the opponent's relationship with the proto-orthodox author of 1 Clement is not yet beyond repair. According to the argument of this text, disharmony has negative connotations for the universal church, making the restoration of concord not merely desirable but necessary. The letter exhorts the addressees to reinstall deposed presbyters and imposes voluntary exile on their younger (?) usurpers (1 Clem. 54.1–4; cf. 47.7). Since this recommendation is not expected to garner majority approval (1 Clem. 44.1–6), the author guarantees approval by Christ as a preferable alternative. Both the letter's rhetoric and tone (e.g., repetition of the hortatory subjunctive) suggest that the author neither dislikes the addressees nor possesses the necessary influence to enforce mandates. For this reason, interpreters often emphasize the letter's deliberative or hortatory (Gk.: συμβουλευτικόν) style.

Much like 1 Corinthians, the stated purpose of 1 Clement is to replace the "conflict" (στάσις) with "harmony" (ὁμόνοια) in the church at Corinth. While the correction is directed at Corinth (note that the Roman church evidently shares their struggle, 1 Clem. 7.1), these cities may be not actual/literal but fictional/figurative references (see above). It has been argued that 1 Clement was originally intended as a weapon against the gnostics. To be sure, the text was brandished for this purpose by Clement of Alexandria and Irenaeus.

Although it has been argued that the text's primary purpose was to establish a divine origin of church order, it hardly traces divine succession of a monarchical ecclesial office. Moreover, the phoenix myth in 1 Clement 25, in addition to references to virtuous pagans in 1 Clement 54.1–55.2 (omitted by Clement of Alexandria), implies an openness to pagan traditions uncharacteristic of second-century ecclesial apologetics. A number of elements taken together suggest that the text's overriding purpose, whatever its position on ecclesiology, is the interpretation of Pauline tradition. These elements are: (1) the epistolary genre (particularly when encapsulating a deliberative speech), (2) the address to the church at Corinth, (3) the supplementation of 1 Corinthians 13 with the explicit concept of "harmony" (ὁμόνοια) in 1 Clement 49.5, (4) new views on punishment for schism from 1 Corinthians 5, and (5) application of the "body" concept from 1 Corinthians 6 to "church" in 1 Clement 37.1–5 together. Furthermore, as noted, exempla comprise the evidence in the argument's *probatio*. The golden-calf exemplum, added to the recapitulation of evidence in the closing argument, is both unconventional in its adaptation and positioned as climax among evidence summoned. It stresses not the sin of the Israelites but Moses as moral example par excellence: the answer to the problem of conflict in the community is addressed by this example in particular. If the text is dated to 100–140 CE and not confined literally to the city of Corinth, a few explanations of this unusual application of the golden-calf motif suggest themselves. R. Joseph Hoffman once argued that 1 Clement attacks Marcion. Hoffman acknowledges the following points of connection between the two:

> The stress placed on marriage and family life (1.3); the disquisitions on the nature of God as creator, judge, savior, and father (61.2; 59.3; 27.1; 35.1; 19.2; 18.4; 23.1); the strong anti-docetic tincture of the phrase Ἰησοῦς Χριστὸς ὁ παῖς σου (59.4; 16.3, etc.); the pedagogical use of the OT as a Christian book, together with references to the "commandments" of

Christ and the ordinances of the Lord (τὰ προστάγματα καὶ τὰ δικαιώματα τοῦ κυρίου, 2.8; cf. 3.4); and finally the emphasis on judgment and resurrection (24.1f.; 25.1f.; 27.1, etc.).[12]

Other points of contact with Marcion, not noted by Hoffman, include the following eight observations.

1. First Clement's central concern of "conflict" (στάσις), in particular, "over the office of bishop" (1 Clem. 44.1) may be historically associated with Marcion (Epiphanius, *Pseud.-Tert.* 17; Optatus 4.5).
2. The text's primary recommendation is that an unspecified one or two usurpers accept voluntary exile or even death (1 Clem. 54.2). Marcion's ultimate separation from the church could be construed as his acceptance of such advice for the sake of the larger group. Moreover, according to Eusebius, Marcionites were known for accepting martyrdom willingly—perhaps *more* willingly than the proto-orthodox. Eusebius even reports female Marcionite martyrs (*Hist. eccl.* 3.12; 4.5; 5.16; *Mart. Pal.* 100.10), possibly accounting for the otherwise enigmatic parallels to Judith and Esther in the recapitulation (1 Clem. 55.4–6; cf. the endorsement of female prophecy at 12.8; "Danaids and Dircae" in 6.2 to Peter and Paul's martyrdom in 1 Clem. 5).
3. Possibly citing Ephesians 4:4–6, 1 Clement 46.6 (cf. 16.12) refutes Marcion's hallmark argument against the unity of the first principle. Here we also note 1 Clement's decisive emphasis on God as creator (20.11).
4. More than once, Tertullian refers to Marcion as a *nauclerus* ("pilot"). After a long list of exempla from the Jewish Scriptures of not only behavior that the opponents ought to avoid but also that which they should demonstrate, 1 Clement 20.5–8 surprisingly turns to an extended example from nature featuring the sea, which the author says, must also obey God's ordinances.
5. As a shipowner, Marcion was wealthy. Disapproving references to riches constitutes a minor theme in 1 Clement (2.2; 13.1; 16.10; 38.2; and 59.3). Reflecting on the theme of wealth in 1 Clement, Welborn observes that whoever 1 Clement's opponents are, "money seems to have been involved."[13]
6. Higher respect paid to Paul (over Peter) in 1 Clement 5 coheres with the established Marcionite proclivity for Paul.
7. First Clement 1.1 qualifies its opponents as "aliens" and "strangers." "Alien" is both Marcion's description of the good God and his reference to himself and those Christians accepting his doctrine (i.e., "aliens"; Latin, adj. *alienus*; Greek, adj. ξένος).
8. Many associate 2 Clement—a text with a close relationship to 1 Clement from an early stage—with Marcion. Likewise, Polycarp's *To the Philippians* (adopting a significant quantity of material from 1 Clement) is directed against Marcionism, famously referring to him as the "first-born of Satan" in 7.1 (cf. Irenaeus, *Haer.* 3.3.4). Other "Clementine literature," too, such as the Pseudo-Clementines, openly seeks to combat Marcionism.

12. R. J. Hoffman, *Marcion: On the Restitution of Christianity: An Essay on the Development of Radical Paulinist Theology in the Second Century*, American Academy of Religion Academy Series 46 (Chico, CA: Scholars Press, 1984), 36.

13. L. L. Welborn, "Clement, 1 Epistle of," *ABD* 1:1059.

In addition to these eight points, there is one additional piece of evidence. In *Adversus Marcionem* 2.26.1–4, Tertullian explicitly attributes to Marcion the version of the golden-calf episode contained in 1 Clement. This emphasis on Moses's positive (rather than the Israelites' negative) moral example is, to my knowledge, not attested elsewhere in the vast and complicated reception history of this well-known tradition. Marcion, according to Tertullian, extols Moses as better than God in this passage because, whereas God plans destruction as punishment for the Israelites, Moses opts for forgiveness:

> And it is you, Marcion, who have forced God to do this: for even so long ago God had foreknowledge of you. . . . On that other occasion also God made himself little even in the midst of his fierce anger, when in his wrath against the people because of the consecration of the (golden) calf he demanded of his servant Moses, *Let me alone, and I will wax hot in wrath and destroy them, and I will make thee into a great nation.* On this you are in the habit of insisting that Moses was a better person than his own God—deprecating, yes and even forbidding, his wrath [*unde meliorem soletis affirmare Moysen deo suo, deprecatorem, immo et prohibitorem irae*]: for he [Moses] says, You shall not do this: or else destroy me *along with them.* Greatly to be pitied are you, as well as the Israelites, for not realizing that in the person of Moses there is a prefiguring of Christ, who intercedes with the Father, and offers his own soul for the saving of the people.[14]

On this reading, the golden-calf interpretation in 1 Clement suggests that it was composed—albeit without the vitriol of later attacks—against Marcionites. Moses is the prime exemplar against Marcion because he and probably some of his followers endorse Moses as a self-sacrificial and forgiving leader *superior* to Moses's selfish god. First Clement turns this cherished view of Moses back on the Marcionites by depicting him as a leader who—irrespective of blame—exhibits willingness to abdicate his position and step down. A genuine aim to persuade Marcionites explains why the approach in 1 Clement is congenial, accentuating coherence between its own and the opponent's position and delivering most of its advice on mutually agreeable terms. Furthermore, not every point is debated. For example, 1 Clement extols God as just *and* good, compassionate, and merciful (1 Clem. 33.2–3; 60.1), rather than refuting Marcion's position that Moses's God is just but lacks goodness, compassion, and mercy.

The form with which one could imagine persuading Marcionites would, of course, be a Pauline letter. On reading "the church sojourning in Corinth," Marcionite recipients would have recognized instantly they were being addressed both on their own terms (as Christians favoring Paul and even Paul's first letter to the Corinthians) *and* as a faction. Assuming that 1 Clement signifies a real problem on the ground in Corinth as early as 98 CE, Hoffmann concluded that similarities between 1 Clement and Marcionism did not amount to anything since 1 Clement was written before the emergence of Marcionism. If, however, "church sojourning in Corinth" is a figurative expression and a mid-second century date is plausible (see above), then the configuration of data may suggest that 1 Clement addresses Marcionism. While it is impossible to identify with certainty the purpose of this text, hopefully this hypothetical background offers a sense of its possible role and effect in a second-century context.

14. E. Evans, ed. and trans., *Tertullian: Adversus Marcionem, Books 1 to 3*, OECT (Oxford: Clarendon, 1972), 59.

4. KEY PASSAGES FOR NEW TESTAMENT STUDIES AND THEIR SIGNIFICANCE

Among the corpus of the Apostolic Fathers, 1 Clement reveals knowledge of the greatest range of scriptural writings. Taking into consideration that citation practices in antiquity were different from modern practices (not only punctuation but widespread use of paraphrase), links can be discerned based on basic verbal correspondences. First Clement relies on at least two groups of sources.

4.1 The Jewish Scriptures

The Jewish Scriptures comprise an important source for the author of 1 Clement. Not unlike Hebrews, they are considered a means by which God is thought to speak (1 Clem. 33.5; cf. Heb 1:5, 7, etc.). Among other things, the Scriptures are appreciated as prophesying church order and concord (1 Clem. 42.5, citing Isa 60:17), the central concern of the letter.

Most references to the Jewish Scriptures serve as historical exempla (ὑποδείγματα), comprising central proofs in the argument of this letter that certain usurping presbyters must step down. First Clement contains forty-three such exempla, organized in seven thematic units of seven exempla each (one unit has only a single exemplum, see below) and usually ordered chronologically within the unit. An exemplum is typically one individual person such as Abraham, Moses, or Paul, but it might also be a group such as kings, Christians, or women. Themes include jealousy, repentance, and obedience. As a part of the exemplum, the author may cite or paraphrase biblical passages. In a few cases, mere mention of the name serves to recall an individual's reputation. For example, the topic of the first set is "jealousy" (ζῆλος): the perpetrators (1 Clem 4.1–13) followed by their victims (5.1–6.4). The privileged position of the golden-calf tradition features Moses as an example of self-sacrifice. Chapters 16–18 showcase two units of exempla on the topic of humility. The first, chapter 16 has just one exemplum, Jesus (vv. 1–17). Chapter 17 begins with the exhortation, "become imitators" (μιμηταὶ γενώμεθα; cf. Eph 5:1), after which the writer lists three prophets ordered chronologically, plus four historical figures also arranged chronologically. References to Job in this section and elsewhere signal the theme of humility.[15] The author highlights the golden-calf incident in Exodus in order to set Moses apart as the example par excellence of self-sacrifice. In this section, the author submits that Korah and Pharaoh were punished for selfish hardness of heart—contrasted with Moses, who offered to sacrifice himself on behalf of the Israelites who sinned against God. Moses demonstrated crowning unselfishness when he exclaimed, "Forgive the sin of this people, or cancel me too from the book of the living" (ἢ κἀμὲ ἐξάλειψον ἐκ βίβλου ζώντων, 1 Clem. 53.4). The writer marks each unit of exempla with an explicit reference either just prior to or immediately following the set (5.1; 5.1 and 6.1; 7.5; 16.17; 17.1; 31.1; 53.1 and 55.1). In certain passages the writer discusses the importance of exempla (e.g., 5:1; 6.1; 7.1, 5; 9.2; 13.1; 14.1; 16.17).

Finally, 1 Clement (23.3–4) cites as if scriptural an otherwise unknown passage also cited in 2 Clement 11.2–4.

4.2 New Testament Writings

In addition, 1 Clement cites or alludes to the New Testament and Jesus tradition, citing Romans, 1 Corinthians, Hebrews, and sayings of Jesus that are not attested elsewhere (e.g., 1 Clem. 13; 46). The most extensive references are made to 1 Corinthians—even denoted

15. Cf. Job 1:1 in 1 Clem. 17.3; Job 4:16–18 in 1 Clem. 39.3–4; Job 4:19–5:5 in 1 Clem. 39.5–9; Job 5:17–26 in 1 Clem. 56.6–15; Job 11:2–3 in 1 Clem. 30.4; Job 14:4–5 in 1 Clem. 17.4; Job 15:15 in 1 Clem. 39.5; Job 19:26 in 1 Clem. 26.3; and Job 38:11 in 1 Clem. 20.7.

as Paul's epistle (1 Clem. 47:1)—probably indicating the author's aim to imitate that letter. This accounts for the extensive borrowing or paralleling of material from 1 Corinthians.[16] The letter also appears to be indebted to the Epistle to the Hebrews at several points.[17] This was a letter that was frequently attributed to Paul among later Christian writers.

Moreover, 1 Clement's reliance on 1 Corinthians is fundamental to its purpose. It corresponds to 1 Corinthians in both structural elements—such as prescript, postscript, and occasion—and content, such as allusions, including an allusion to Paul's letter *qua* letter. Both types of agreement demonstrate 1 Clement mapping its new epistolary circumstances on Paul's prior letter (discussed above). Like 1 Corinthians, 1 Clement preserves the Pauline custom of exhorting over commanding, even though by the time of 1 Clement's composition (no earlier than 96 CE) the concept of episcopal authority had moved to the forefront. First Clement's authority is not a product of Pauline *attribution*, but of Pauline *situation*—that is, upbraiding members of the Christian community for creating strife through factionalizing *just as Paul does* in 1 Corinthians. First Clement adopts Paul's position as a primary but not only rhetorical strategy. Specifically, it addresses the question of apostolic succession, appealing to Paul's letters to manage the disagreement. Specific solutions adapted from 1 Corinthians include: (1) submission to present authority; (2) recognition of differences in love; (3) expulsion of community members when necessary; and (4) capitulation to what Paul himself says. The point of inquiry to be adjudicated in 1 Clement is: As Paulinists, will the addressee(s) heed their apostle or not?

5. CONCLUSION

First Clement was composed primarily to combat unknown usurpers to the bishopric in Corinth, though perhaps it also has faction and strife within the church universal in its purview. Even with its long strings of mandates, dicta, questions, and prooftexts, the letter submits to rhetorical analysis. The letter is deliberative, exhorting "harmony" by means of the self-imposed exile of a "younger" generation of leaders. If this letter is genuine, then its deliberative character suggests that the situation "on the ground" in Corinth varies little from the time when Paul wrote 1 Corinthians. A combination of schisms (1 Cor 1:10–17; 3:1–23) and usurpers (1 Cor 5; 2 Cor 10–12) threaten community stability, a problem that deliberation is adopted to address. If, as suggested above, the letter is not "real" but is intended (as other Pauline letters were also used) as a general, circular, or even "catholic" teaching possessing the weight and authority held by 1 Corinthians and that was to be applied to one or more situations elsewhere in the Empire (perhaps in Rome), then no situation "on the ground" in Corinth is implied or can be directly assessed on the basis of 1 Clement. This hypothesis, that 1 Clement constitutes a general letter addressing the Marcionite or another theological and political assault on Christian faith in the western Roman Empire, is worth considering, particularly because it brings a fresh line of thinking with potential to ignite new areas of research.

---

16. For example, 1 Cor 1:31 in 1 Clem. 13.1; 1 Cor 2:9 in 1 Clem. 34.8; 1 Cor 4:10 in 1 Clem. 3.3; 1 Cor 4:14 in 1 Clem. 7.1; 1 Cor 12:4 in 1 Clem. 38.1; 1 Cor 12:8–9 in 1 Clem. 48.5; 1 Cor 12:21–22 in 1 Clem. 37.5; 1 Cor 13:3 in 1 Clem. 55.2; 1 Cor 13:4–7 in 1 Clem. 49.5; 1 Cor 15:20 in 1 Clem. 24.1; 1 Cor 15:23 in 1 Clem. 37.3; 1 Cor 15:35–38 in 1 Clem. 24.5; and 1 Cor 16:15 in 1 Clem. 42.4.

17. Possible places where the author draws upon Hebrews include Heb 1:3–5, 7, 13 in 1 Clem. 36.2–5; Heb 2:17; 3:1 in 1 Clem. 36.1; Heb 3:2, 5 in 1 Clem. 43.1; Heb 3:7; 10:15 in 1 Clem. 13.1; 16.2 (cf. 8.1; 22.1; 45.2); Heb 4:12 in 1 Clem. 21.9; Heb 4:15 in 1 Clem. 36.1; Heb 6:18 in 1 Clem. 27.2; Heb 11 in 1 Clem. 9–11; Heb 11:37 in 1 Clem. 17.1; Heb 12:9 in 1 Clem. 64.

BIBLIOGRAPHY

Bakke, O. M. *"Concord and Peace": A Rhetorical Analysis of the Language of the First Letter of Clement with an Emphasis on the Language of Unity and Sedition*. WUNT 2/143. Tübingen: Mohr Siebeck, 2001.

Breytenbach, C., and L. L. Welborn, eds. *Encounters with Hellenism: Studies on the First Letter of Clement*. AGJU 53. Leiden: Brill, 2003.

Grant, R. M., and H. H. Graham. *First and Second Clement*. Vol. 2 of *The Apostolic Fathers: A New Translation and Commentary*. New York: Thomas Nelson, 1965.

Gregory, A. F. "1 Clement and the Writings that Later Formed the New Testament." Pages 129–57 in *The Reception of the New Testament in the Apostolic Fathers*. Edited by A. F. Gregory and C. M. Tuckett. Oxford: Oxford University Press, 2005.

Hagner, D. A. *The Use of the Old and New Testaments in Clement of Rome*. NovTSup 34. Leiden: Brill, 1973.

Lindemann, A. "Paul's Influence on 'Clement' and Ignatius." Pages 9–24 in *Trajectories Through the New Testament and Apostolic Fathers*. Edited by A. F. Gregory and C. M. Tuckett. Oxford: Oxford University Press, 2005.

Lindemann, A. *Die Clemensbriefe*. HNT 17. Tübingen: Mohr Siebeck, 1992.

Lona, H. E. *Der erste Clemensbrief*. KAV 1. Göttingen: Vandenhoeck and Ruprecht, 1998.

Rothschild, C. K. "*Horror vacui*: Welborn's 'Retrospect on a Challenge to the Consensus on the Date of 1 Clement.'" *BR* 65 (2020): 104–13.

Rothschild, C. K. *New Essays on the Apostolic Fathers*. WUNT 375. Tübingen: Mohr Siebeck, 2017.

Welborn, L. L. "On the Date of 1 Clement." *BR* 29 (1984): 35–54. Repr., pages 197–216 in *Encounters with Hellenism: Studies on the First Letter of Clement*. Edited by C. Breytenbach and L. L. Welborn. AGJU 53. Leiden: Brill, 2003.

Welborn, L. L. "Retrospect on a Challenge to the Consensus on the Date of 1 Clement." *BR* 65 (2020): 95–103.

Welborn, L. L. *The Young and the Old: Generational Conflict in First Clement*. Lanham, MD: Lexington Books/Fortress Academic, 2018.

CHAPTER 4

SECOND CLEMENT

JAMES A. KELHOFFER

1. INTRODUCTION

For several reasons, the name given to the Second Letter of Clement to the Corinthians (hereafter: 2 Clement) could be confusing. It is not a letter, nor even the second of two related writings. Additionally, the work has no obvious connection either to someone named "Clement," or to Christ believers in Corinth. Each of these possible points of confusion merits explanation.

In terms of its genre, 2 Clement lacks the standard epistolary prescript and postscript of a Hellenistic Greek letter.[1] Moreover, although the "two" in 2 Clement suggests that it is a sequel to 1 Clement, the work's markedly different theologies, agendas, and Greek styles indicate that they, in fact, were penned by different authors. Regardless of who wrote 2 Clement, he or she chose to remain anonymous—at least to readers other than the original addressees. As a result, the attribution of 2 Clement to someone named Clement is highly uncertain and probably mistaken. Moreover, although some interpreters hold that 2 Clement was written for believers in Corinth, to which 1 Clement is addressed,[2] the connection is only a hypothesis. Others regard Egypt, Syria, Asia Minor, or Rome as possible, even plausible, settings, although there is no conclusive proof for any of those alternatives, either.[3] Despite these uncertainties, I will, for the sake of convenience, refer to the author as "Clement," leaving as open questions where, and to whom, the work was written.[4]

The upshot of the aforementioned uncertainties about 2 Clement is that nearly all proposals about the writing's author, date, location, addressees, and (possible) opponents are based on *internal evidence*—that is, the fruit of analyzing the text itself. The resultant challenge for interpreters can thus be precarious, since inferences drawn from the text, which are then used to interpret the text, can be based on circular reasoning. Even if one acknowledges that all interpretation ultimately becomes circular, the hermeneutical spiral for understanding 2 Clement is more tightly wound than can be the case for other early Christian sources. Nevertheless, much can be ascertained from the writing, to which we now turn, about the author's theology and rhetorical strategies.

---

1. The question of whether 2 Clement should be categorized as a "homily" will be taken up below (see sec. 1.1).

2. See J. B. Lightfoot, *The Apostolic Fathers, Part I: S. Clement of Rome*, 2nd ed., 2 vols. (London: Macmillan, 1890; repr., Peabody, MA: Hendrickson, 1989), 2:191–210; K. P. Donfried, *The Setting of Second Clement in Early Christianity*, NovTSup 38 (Leiden: Brill, 1974), 1–15; W. Varner, *Second Clement: A Commentary*, AFCS (Eugene, OR: Cascade, 2020), 11–17.

3. W. Pratscher, *Der zweite Clemensbrief*, KAV 3 (Göttingen: Vandenhoeck & Ruprecht, 2007); C. M. Tuckett, *2 Clement: Introduction, Text, and Commentary*, OAF (Oxford: Oxford University Press, 2012), 59–61.

4. Also, for reasons of expedience, I refer to Clement with the pronouns "he/him/his," while recognizing that the person's gender is also unknown.

1.1 Genre: Homily, Hortatory Address, or Something Else?

Is 2 Clement a "homily" (or sermon)? Along with the Book of Hebrews, it is often regarded as among the earliest Christian sermons preserved in written form. Correspondingly, most view Clement as a preacher, whose sermon was written down before, or after, it was delivered.[5] However, this consensus viewpoint is questionable for several reasons.[6]

The main value of establishing a work's genre is to have a benchmark for understanding the work relative to established literary conventions. For the interpretation of 2 Clement, this would indeed be helpful *if* we knew what routines early Christians may have had for preparing, delivering, and disseminating sermons. But very little about the form and content of actual preaching in Christ congregations is revealed in the writings of the New Testament and the Apostolic Fathers. Moreover, the depictions of preaching in the Acts of the Apostles, as well as the proclamation(s) implied in the New Testament Gospels and Paul's letters, have little in common with the form and content of 2 Clement. This lack of evidence has not, however, stopped preconceptions about early Christian preaching and liturgy from spawning tenuous hypotheses about 2 Clement's genre, setting, and occasion.[7] Even a context (i.e., *Sitz im Leben*) of delivering a "homily" would have little explanatory power, for *any* early Christian writing, when read to an assembly of mostly illiterate believers, would have a sermonic function.[8]

As noted above, 2 Clement lacks the epistolary prescript and postscript that one expects to find in a Hellenistic Greek letter, such as Paul's authentic letters, Ephesians, and 1 Clement. Scholars therefore agree that, as is also the case for the Book of Hebrews, 1 John, and the Epistle to Diognetus, the designation "letter" is inaccurate for 2 Clement. Nevertheless, the repeated exhortations to "brothers" (ἀδελφοί) also feature in early Christian letters, including those of Paul, Ignatius, and Polycarp, as well as 1 Clement.[9] This feature has led some to classify 2 Clement as a "hortatory address" or an example of "paraenesis."[10]

1.2 "Testimonia" as a Basis of Argumentation

If it is not persuasive to classify 2 Clement as a homily or a letter, what is it? One need not assume that any work (ancient or modern) completely fits within a single genre. For 2 Clement, a possibility worth considering is whether "testimonia" is an apt designation for much of the writing—in particular, the argumentation from the succession of Scripture quotations in 2 Clement 2–17.

At Qumran, a short writing comprising a single leaf, known as "The Testimonia" (4Q175

5. For example, Lightfoot, *Apostolic Fathers*; A. Lindemann, *Die Clemensbriefe*, HNT 17 (Tübingen: Mohr Siebeck, 1992); E. Baasland, "Der 2. Klemensbrief und frühchristliche Rhetorik: 'Die erste christliche Predigt' im Lichte der neueren Forschung," *ANRW* 27.1:78–157; Pratscher, *Clemensbrief*, 25–27; and Wolfgang Grünstäudl, "Epilog, Ouvertüre oder Intermezzo? Zur ursprünglichen Funktion von 2 Clem 19,1–20,4," *Early Christianity* 4 (2013): 242–60.

6. J. A. Kelhoffer, *The Second Letter of Clement: Thematic and Exegetical Studies* (Tübingen: Mohr Siebeck, forthcoming).

7. E.g., Grünstäudl, "Epilog"; P. Parvis, "2 Clement and the Meaning of the Christian Homily," in *The Writings of the Apostolic Fathers*, ed. P. Foster (London: T&T Clark, 2007), 32–41.

8. On the reading of letters in early Christian assemblies, see, e.g., 1 Thess 5:27, Col 4:16, and Rev 1:3.

9. On uses of the vocative ἀδελφοί in 2 Clement, see 1.1; 4.3; 5.1, 5; 7.1; 8.4; 9.11; 10.1; 11.5; 13.1; 14.1, 3; 16.1. For this usage in early Christian letters, see, e.g., Rom 1:13; 7:1; 8:12; 1 Cor 1:11, 26; 7:24, 29; Gal 1:11; 3:15; 4:12, 28, 31; Jas 1:2, 16, 19; 2 Pet 1:10; Ign. *Eph.* 16.1; *Rom.* 6.2; *Phld.* 3.3; 5.1; Pol. *Phil.* 3.1; 1 Clem. 13.1; 14.1; 37.1; 41.1–2, 4; Barn. 2.10; 3.6. See also Heb 3:1, 12; 10:19; 13:22; 1 John 3:13; Mart. Pol. 4.1; 22.1; Herm. Vis. 2.4.1 (8.1); 3.1.1, 4 (9.1, 4).

10. Donfried, *Setting*, 19–36; Pratscher, *Clemensbrief*, 24. Neither "hortatory address" nor "paraenesis" are genre designations, however.

or 4QTest; 1st c. BCE), quotes and interprets five brief passages from the Hexateuch.[11] The passages are treated in rapid succession and anticipate the appearance in the end times of three figures—a prophet like Moses, a messiah, and a teacher of righteousness.

Another example may be seen in the Letter to the Galatians, where Paul defends the validity of the message that he had proclaimed.[12] Throughout Galatians 3–4, the repeated appeals to Scripture prove that his "gospel" is consistent with the promises made to ancient Israel.[13] Thus, his message is not the opinion of a putative apostle but is faithful to scriptural traditions that both he and his Christ-believing opponents recognized (Gal 1:12–23). Likewise, in Romans 4 and 9–11, Paul quotes numerous Scriptures in order to showcase the validity of the teaching he intends to share with believers in Rome.

Such argumentation also features prominently in the Epistle of Barnabas, a work that highlights the importance of God's "righteous deeds."[14] These are interpreted with recourse to one Scripture citation after another, demarcating those who do, and do not, belong to the covenant people.[15] Yet another example is Justin Martyr's *Dialogue with Trypho*, which quotes much longer parts of the Septuagint in conversation with a (likely fictitious) Jew named Trypho.[16]

It should not be assumed that, as in earlier scholarship (e.g., Rendel Harris), ancient Jews and early Christ-believers used *one common* book of Scripture quotations, or "testimonies." Nor can writings as diverse as 4Q175, Galatians, Barnabas, Justin's *Dialogue with Trypho*, and 2 Clement be herded into a single literary genre. The basso continuo among these works is the method of argumentation—utilizing a series of prooftexts and interpretations to remind the faithful of what God said and its relevance for self-definition, eschatology, or both. In 2 Clement, it is the warnings about the future judgment, and possible eternal punishment, of some Christ-believers that are presented as rooted in Scripture.

1.3 Attestation and Textual Criticism

Why was 2 Clement preserved, and used as Scripture, by some in the early church? The witnesses to the early attestation of 2 Clement are quite sparse. Although it has been suggested that Origen of Alexandria (240s CE) alludes to the writing, the first clear references to it are from Eusebius of Caesarea (early 4th century) and Jerome (late 4th century).[17] The only manuscript preserving the entire Greek text is the eleventh-century Codex Constantinopolitanus.[18] There is also a Syriac translation preserved in a twelfth-century manuscript (University Library, Cambridge, Add. MSS 1700). The earliest Greek witness is Codex Alexandrinus (ca. 450–500 CE), which breaks off in the middle of 2 Clement 12.5.[19]

11. The passages cited are, in the following order, Deut 5:28–29; Deut 18:18–19; Num 24:15–17; Deut 33:8–11; and Josh 6:26.

12. Paul maintains that his version of the good news (τὸ εὐαγγέλιον, Gal 1:11) is not of human origin (κατὰ ἄνθρωπον, 1:11) but came to him through Christ's revelation (δι' ἀποκαλύψεως, 1:12).

13. See Gal 3:6 (cf. Gen 15:6); Gal 3:8 (Gen 12:3; 18:18); Gal 3:10 (Deut 27:26); Gal 3:11 (Hab 2:4); Gal 3:12 (Lev 18:5); Gal 3:13 (Deut 21:23); Gal 3:16 (Gen 13:15; 17:8; 24:7); etc.

14. On God's "righteous deeds" (or "commandments," δικαιώματα) in the Epistle of Barnabas, see, e.g., 1.2, 2.1, and 4.11.

15. See, e.g., Barn. 2.5, 7, 8, 10; 3.1–2, 3–5; 4.3, 4, 5, 7, 8, 11.

16. E.g., Justin, *Dial.* 13.2–9; 14.4–7; 15.2–6; 16.1a, 1b, 5; 17.2a, 2b, 3, 4; 19.2, 3, 6. To these references, scores of additional examples could be given.

17. Eusebius, *Hist. eccl.* 3.38.4; Jerome, *Vir. ill.* 15.

18. In some scholarly literature, Codex Constantinopolitanus (C) is referred to as Codex Hierosolymitanus (H), or the Jerusalem Codex.

19. Another witness to 2 Clement's early reception may be identified in 2 Clem. 19–20, if those verses were composed by a later hand as a revised conclusion to the work (see sec. 1.5).

In terms of reconstructing the original text (i.e., textual criticism), there are the three aforementioned manuscripts for 2 Clement 1.1–12.5a. For the remainder of the work (12.5b–20.5), we have only Constantinopolitanus and the Syriac; when those two witnesses differ in 1.1–12.5a, the Syriac tends to agree with the earliest witness, Alexandrinus. That agreement suggests that the Greek text presupposed by the Syriac was closer to the original than the version of Constantinopolitanus. Thus, when the Syriac and Constantinopolitanus differ in 12.5b–20.5, the Syriac is usually preferred. At times, though, the original text may be uncertain or open to conjecture.

An irony in the preservation of 2 Clement may also be noted. In all three manuscripts, it follows directly after 1 Clement and, as mentioned above, is presented as the author's second letter. Were it not for the fact that some in the early church *thought* that the same subapostolic author wrote both 1 and 2 Clement, it is possible that 2 Clement would not have survived to us today.

Another reason for its preservation could be the fact that, in Codex Alexandrinus and the Syriac manuscript, 1 and 2 Clement are preserved *along with the New Testament*. In Codex Alexandrinus, they appear directly after the New Testament writings.[20] In the Syriac, the order of works is unusual: 1 and 2 Clement appear in between the Catholic Epistles and the Pauline letters. This inclusion in biblical manuscripts suggests that some in the early church regarded 1 and 2 Clement as Scripture, and that they were read as such in some, perhaps many, Christian congregations.

1.4 Date

When was 2 Clement written? The answer is quite uncertain, although most place the work in the second quarter of the second century.[21] If sayings of Jesus quoted do indeed reflect Matthean and Lukan redaction, that means that similarities cannot be accounted for by either oral traditions or pre-Matthean and pre-Lukan written sources. Rather, 2 Clement was written after those Gospels and cites either them or written source(s) based on them. Thus, the work was penned after Matthew and Luke were written, collected, and cited together; and, finally, were used by Clement (see sec. 4, below). Those developments probably would not have been completed before 125 CE.[22]

Prior to Eusebius of Caesarea in the early fourth century, there is no firm basis for establishing the time before which it had been written (i.e., its *terminus ante quem*). Attempts to date the work relative to gnostic sources (however construed) have been, at best, inconclusive and, at times, speculative (see sec. 3.2). Its scriptural citations include material from numerous other sources that the later church excluded from its scriptural canon. Over time, the power of proto-orthodox voices in defining the biblical canon grew. As a result, a work like 2 Clement may have been less likely to be written, and to be preserved, in the third century, which would favor a date in the mid- to late second century. This, however, is only a conjecture. Although Clement's multifaceted canon may fit better with what we know about the second century, an early third-century date for the work is not impossible.

20. In Codex Alexandrinus, 1 and 2 Clement appear directly after the New Testament writings, although the two Clementine writings seem to stem from a later hand than the person who copied those of the New Testament. Although the Clementine writings were not originally *intended* to be in Alexandrinus, their eventual inclusion probably had the *effect* of presenting them as Scripture to subsequent readers of the codex.

21. Pratscher, *Clemensbrief*, 62–64; Tuckett, *2 Clement*, 62–64.

22. The date of 125 CE is only a hypothesis (if also a plausible one) about the time after which (i.e., *terminus post quem*) it was written.

1.5 Literary Integrity

Was 2 Clement 18.2 or 20.5 the work's original conclusion? Nearly all scholars agree that differences in vocabulary and style between 2 Clement 1–18 and 19–20 indicate that the latter two chapters were composed by a later author.[23] However, there is no consensus regarding the origin and purpose of chapters 19–20.[24] One possibility is that 2 Clement 19–20 corrects a central teaching in 2 Clement 1–18 (see sec. 1.2)—namely, the necessity that believers engage in a reciprocal relationship with God, as a consequence of which they can expect remuneration from God and, ultimately, the consummation of their salvation. To accept 19.1–20.5 as authentic would thus alter substantially the work's overall message and theology.

Despite the differences, there are also many similarities between 2 Clement 19–20, on the one hand, and both 1 Clement and 2 Clement 1–18, on the other hand. Those similarities suggest that the compositional strategy driving 2 Clement 19–20 involves the imitation of both Clementine writings in order to make the addition appear authentic. Chapters 19–20 is therefore of interest for its reception of both 1 and 2 Clement and for its shifting of some distinctive theological positions found in 2 Clement 1–18 (e.g., on reciprocity toward God). As a correction of 2 Clement 1–18, the addition of 19–20 may also have contributed to 2 Clement's preservation as an encore to 1 Clement in Codex Alexandrinus and Codex Constantinopolitanus.

2. SUMMARY OF CONTENT

When coming to grips with 2 Clement's structure, one could just as easily speak of its *lack* of structure. Some even regard the work as rambling and repetitive. If a unifying pattern in the work were to be identified, it would probably be the recurring quotations and interpretations of an array of sacred texts. In the approximately ninety verses of 2 Clement 2–17, a scriptural passage is quoted in approximately every fourth or fifth verse. The expositions of those quotations account for much of the remainder of the work. The author could thus be described as a "prooftexter"—that is, as one who grounds exhortations and admonitions through appeals to established traditions. To some modern readers, however, the selection of texts quoted may seem random. Several of the work's interpretations of Scripture can also appear speculative, arbitrary, or even forced (see sec. 4). Thus, the following outline calls attention not so much to the work's structure but rather to its content, argumentation, and *possible* sources.

Introduction

2 Clem. 1.1–2	Christ as the judge of both believers and unbelievers.
2 Clem. 1.3–8	Reciprocity toward a benevolent God—an integral part of redemption.

Prooftexts and Interpretations

2 Clem. 2.1–3	A barren woman (Isa 54:1) and the need for prayer
2 Clem. 2.4–7	The calling to sinners (Matt 9:13) and the need to save others
2 Clem. 3.1–3	Acknowledging Christ (Matt 10:32 // Luke 12:8) and shunning polytheism

23. E.g., R. Knopf, *Die Lehre der zwölf Apostel, die zwei Clemensbriefe*, HNT Ergänzungsband, Die Apostolischen Väter 1 (Tübingen: Mohr Siebeck, 1920); English edition, *A Commentary on the Didache and on 1–2 Clement*, trans. J. N. Cerone, Classic Studies on the Apostolic Fathers 2 (Eugene, OR: Pickwick, 2023).

24. See Pratscher, *Clemensbrief*, 18–21; Grünstäudl, "Epilog."

2 Clem. 3.4–5	Honoring God with one's lips, heart, and mind (Isa 29:13; Matt 15:8)
2 Clem. 4.1–3	Recognizing Jesus as Lord and doing what he says (Matt 7:21)
2 Clem. 4.4–5	The need to fear God, not people (Matt 10:28; 7:23; Luke 13:27)
2 Clem. 5.1–7	Peter's question about lambs among wolves (Matt 10:16 // Luke 10:3)
2 Clem. 6.1–6	Serving either of two masters—God or money (Luke 16:13)
2 Clem. 6.7–9	The righteous deeds of Noah, Job, and Daniel (Ezek 14:13–20)
2 Clem. 7.1–6	Competing in the games, attaining a crown, and punishing dishonest athletes (Isa 66:24).
2 Clem. 8.1–4	A potter's broken vessel and the need for a change in mindset
2 Clem. 8.5–9.5	Guarding what is "small" and keeping the flesh pure (Luke 16:10–12)
2 Clem. 9.6–11	Doing the will of the Father and loving one another (Matt 12:50)
2 Clem. 10.1–11.1	Future delight or the promise of torment; on "teaching evil" to others
2 Clem. 11.2–6	A "prophetic word" on double-mindedness (1 Clem. 23.3–4)
2 Clem. 11.7–12.6	The kingdom's arrival once "the two" have become "one" (Gos. Thom. 22)
2 Clem. 13.1–4	Unbelievers who blaspheme the Lord's name (Isa 52:5); Christians who do not love their enemies (Luke 6:32)
2 Clem. 14.1–2	The "first" church—in the beginning with Christ (Gen 1:27), but now transformed into "a den of robbers" (Jer 7:11)
2 Clem. 14.3–5	The spiritual church revealed in Christ's flesh; receipt of the spirit and guarding one's flesh
2 Clem. 15.1–5	Self-control, redemption, the nearness of God (Isa 65:24), and a promise of reward
2 Clem. 16.1–4	Renouncing pleasures and returning to God through prayer, fasting, and charitable giving (Tob 12:8–9)
2 Clem. 17.1–7	Condemnation and eternal torment, even for Christians who have not kept the Lord's commandments (Isa 66:18, 24)
Original Conclusion to the Work	
2 Clem. 18.1–2	The author's pursuit of righteousness and fear of the coming judgment
Secondary Conclusion[25]	
2 Clem. 19.1–20.2	The reading of an "exhortation"—a summary of the work's central themes
2 Clem. 20.3–4	(Re)interpretation of the teaching on reward and repayment
2 Clem. 20.5	Doxology

2 Clement 1

As mentioned above, the anonymous writing does not begin with an epistolary preface that is characteristic of a Hellenistic Greek letter. Rather, the work's main theme is introduced, which is also how several other early Christian writings begin (e.g., Heb 1:1–2; 1 John 1:1–4; Did. 1.1). Alarmingly, some in the congregation underestimate the importance of Christ as the "judge of the living and the dead" and thereby also the import of

25. The likelihood that 2 Clem. 19–20 is a later addition to the work is discussed above (sec. 1.5).

their salvation.[26] Addressing the hearers as "brothers (and sisters)" (ἀδελφοί), the speaker reflects a familiarity with those who are already part of the Christian assembly. He also expresses deep concern for their standing before Christ on the day of judgment. Merely to identify as a Christ-believer is inadequate; something more is needed, which is laid out in the ensuing chapters.

2 Clement 2–4

To question the standing of those who already identified as Christian may have been unsettling and controversial. Is their redemption not guaranteed on the day of judgment? Clement says no. His stark warning is grounded in a series of Scripture quotations. He therefore does not merely express pastoral concern for his flock's well-being. Rather, he reminds them of authoritative traditions—above all, from the Israelite prophets and sayings of Jesus—that the community has already received and used for understanding their faith. The question, then, is whether they live in accordance with what they are supposed to believe.

The structure of 2 Clement 2–4 is governed by appeals to six quotations—two from Isaiah and four from gospel traditions. A pattern may be seen in the similar structures of 2.1–3 and 2.4–7 that is also in play later in the writing: a quotation (2 Clem. 2.1a; 2.4) is followed by its interpretation (2.1b–3; 2.5–7). In chapter 2, then, there is room for little, if anything, else.

The first source, about a woman who cries out in the pains of childbirth (Isa 54:1 LXX), has no introduction (e.g., "The Lord said . . .") but follows directly on the heels of 2 Clement 1. The second authority is a gospel tradition on Jesus's calling "not the just but sinners" (cf. Matt 9:13b).

Chapter 3 is also structured around two citations. The first is from a gospel tradition and accentuates the need to "acknowledge publicly" (ὁμολογέω) Christ, in order to receive public acknowledgement (again, ὁμολογέω) by Christ to the Father.[27] Another prooftext accuses: "this people honors me with the lips, but their heart is far away from me" (3.5; cf. Isa 29:13a LXX).

The next two sayings are close to their counterparts in Matthew, although a source is not named (2 Clem. 4.1–5). In 4.2, Clement calls to mind Christ's warning, "Not everyone who says to me, 'Lord, Lord,' will be redeemed, but (only) the one who does what is just." The significant verbal overlap with Matthew 7:21 suggests that Clement either modified the Matthean verse or drew on some written source that had already done so. In the light of that overlap, it may be plausibly excluded that Clement relied on a pre-Matthean oral or written tradition.

In 2 Clement 4.5b–c, the end of the quote corresponds closely to the wording of Matthew 7:23.[28] However, Clement's version is much longer and attributes to Jesus something that is not borne in any of the New Testament Gospels: "If you are with me, gathered in my embrace [κόλπος], but do not carry out my commandments, I will cast you aside" (2 Clem. 4.5b). This is the first of several instances where the version, or content, of the Scripture quoted differs from that of other known sources and is a point to which we will return.[29]

---

26. See 2 Clem. 1.1; cf. Rom 2:3–11. Here and elsewhere in this chapter, translations of 2 Clement and other early Christian writings are my own.

27. 2 Clem. 3.2; cf. Matt 10:32//Luke 12:8.

28. Cf. Luke 13:27. We will return to this quotation and its possible sources below (sec. 4).

29. See 2 Clem. 5.2–4 (discussed immediately below), 8.5, and 12.2.

2 Clement 5

What follows is something unique within the writing: rather than teachings based on what the Lord (or Christ) "says" or "said," a dialogue is given. The first part, on being "like lambs amid wolves," has Synoptic parallels.[30] The same is true for the last part, on fearing not a person who could kill you but rather the need to fear God, who could later cast you into fiery Gehenna.[31] What comes in between links the two sayings, which are incorporated into a short dialogue between Jesus and Peter: "But Peter answered him, 'What, then, (happens) if the wolves tear the lambs into pieces?' Jesus said to Peter, 'After the lambs have died, let them not fear the wolves'" (2 Clem. 5.3–4a). This distinctive exchange (5.3–4a) has thus been combined with two 'Synoptic' sayings (5.2, 4b). This combination of sources is to be credited either to Clement himself or, perhaps more likely, to the hand behind his gospel source.[32]

2 Clement 6–8

Several complementary warnings are given in these chapters. Readers of Matthew or Luke would have found the first of those familiar: one cannot serve two masters, and one must serve God rather than "riches."[33] Moreover, there would be no benefit if a person were to gain the whole world but lose their "soul."[34] In a further appeal, Clement alludes to Ezekiel when arguing from the lesser example to the greater: just as Noah, Job, and Daniel could not have redeemed wayward Israelites, a harsh judgment awaits those believers who violate the pledge made at their baptism.[35]

Complementing what Ezekiel had warned about individual responsibility, a Hellenistic metaphor is then given: winners of an athletic competition are crowned, while cheaters are punished and expelled. Clement hopes that "all" will be crowned, or at least come "close" to that honor (7.2–3). As a consequence, some who think that their training is adequate, or that they have already been crowned, may actually be violating the regulations of their spiritual journey.

Following on the heels of Ezekiel's warning and a Hellenistic metaphor, another illustration is given that would have been germane to both Semitic and Greco-Roman milieux: a potter's misshapen clay vessel exemplifies why some may need to examine the adequacy of their loyalty to Christ. If the potter discovers a mistake early on, the clay can be reused to make something useful. But if the mistake comes to light after the clay has been heated (i.e., hardened) in the kiln, it can only be discarded. Christ-believers are therefore urged to "re-evaluate" (μετανοέω) their standing before God.[36] At present, their faith can be reformed, but action must be taken before it is too late.

2 Clement 9

Building on the warnings in 2 Clement 6–8, three reasons are given for guarding the "flesh" (σάρξ): it will be judged; it is "like a temple" that must be protected; and Christ,

---

30. See 2 Clem. 5.2; cf. Matt 10:16//Luke 10:3.

31. 2 Clem. 5.4b; cf. Matt 10:28//Luke 12:4–5.

32. We will return to the question of what gospel source, or sources, Clement may have used, below (see sec. 4).

33. Gk. μαμωνᾶς, 2 Clem. 6.1; cf. Matt 6:24//Luke 16:13.

34. Gk. ψυχή, 2 Clem. 6.2; cf. Matt 16:26//Mark 8:36//Luke 9:25.

35. 2 Clem. 6.8–9; cf. Ezek 14:13–20.

36. In 2 Clement, the terms μετανοέω (8.1, 2c, 3; 9.8; 13.1a, 1b; 15.1; 16.1; 17.1) and μετάνοια (8.2d; 16.4) are usually translated, respectively, as "repent" and "repentance." However, for an argument that, since 2 Clement does not state that they have sinned, what seems to be needed is "a change in mindset," see Kelhoffer, *Second Clement*.

too, came in the flesh (9.1–5). In antiquity, a temple was not just a place of worship but was also a repository of wealth. For Clement, to defile the flesh would debase its value and thereby damage the possibility of its redemption. It is also urged that loving one another, entrusting oneself to God, and returning "eternal praise" to God are necessary in order to be recognized as Christ's "brothers" (9.6–10).

The proof given for that assertion is that Christ's "brothers are those who do [his] Father's will" (9.11). In each of the Synoptic Gospels, the wording of this saying is slightly different.[37] In Clement's version, the first six words exactly match Luke 8:21, but the last five words follow Matthew 12:50. There is no obvious theological reason why Clement (or anyone else) would have combined the two versions. In regard to the early reception of Matthew and Luke, then, when some early Christians read Matthew and Luke, these texts were open to adaptation, including the source quoted in 2 Clement 9.11.

2 Clement 10–11

A contrast is drawn between pursuing pleasure or pursuing virtue, which will, respectively, result in future torment or future delight (10.1–4). The problem of those who "are teaching evil to innocent souls" is also acknowledged (10.5; see sec. 4, below). The faithful are then encouraged to do what is right, which will result in being "just" (δίκαιοι), receiving God's reward, and entering the kingdom (11.1, 5–7). These assurances are supported by a quotation of unknown origin, which assures that those who have withstood tribulation will be rewarded.[38]

2 Clement 12

The faithful are exhorted to "await" the kingdom of God "with love and righteousness," because the time of the kingdom's arrival is unknown (12.1). Clement then attributes to "the Lord Himself" a saying that the kingdom will come "whenever the two will be one, and what is outside corresponds to what is inside, and what is male with the female, neither male nor female" (12.2b). What the saying may have meant in its original context is unclear. Clement's interpretation focuses on the *ethical* conduct expected of believers, who must speak the truth (12.3), produce "good works" (12.4), and "think" (φρονέω, 12.5) about one another without regard to gender. The only parallels to such a saying are the Gospel of Thomas and the so-called Gospel of the Egyptians.[39]

2 Clement 13–14

God's name can be "blasphemed" among "the pagans" (13.2a, quoting Isa 52:5 LXX). The reason for the blaspheming is that believers' behavior is not consistent with their message (2 Clem. 13.2b–4). As a result, the "house" of the Father "has become a den of robbers" (14.1b; Jer 7:11 LXX). What, specifically, they have done wrong is not specified, although it could entail not living in accordance with the conduct commended in 2 Clement 12.3–5.

Clement acknowledges differences among congregations that claim allegiance to God and urges the hearers to "choose" (αἱρετίζω) affiliation with "the church [ἐκκλησία]

37. Matt 12:50//Mark 3:35//Luke 8:21. As is the case for other gospel materials in 2 Clement, there is no indication that material stemming specifically from the Gospel of Mark is quoted.

38. 2 Clem. 11.2–4. The source is also cited in 1 Clem. 23.3–4. See the discussion in sec. 4, below.

39. The version in 2 Clement is apparently independent of the Gospel of Thomas, and there are questions about whether the Gospel of the Egyptians, which Clement of Alexandria claims to quote, was, in fact, a written Gospel. See Tuckett, *2 Clement*, 226–30.

of life."[40] A novel interpretation of Genesis 1:27 demonstrates the standing of that church over its illegitimate alternative: the first "person" (ἄνθρωπος) was, as Genesis tells it, both male and female. But this did not refer to Adam and Eve: the male was Christ, and the "spiritual church" was the female. Clement's reasoning is rooted in chronological priority: the spiritual church must be chosen over her later, degenerate form as a den of robbers.

The assertion that the church existed "in the beginning" (ἄνωθεν, 2 Clem. 14.2b) with Christ is said to be based on what "the books and the apostles" teach, although it is unclear what sources Clement has in mind. This notion of a preexistent church could, rather, be a novelty in early Christian literature, although two deutero-Pauline letters might suggest it (or be open to such an interpretation).[41]

2 Clement 15–16

Following the writing's advice on "self-control" (ἐγκράτεια) is imperative, because this is necessary for "rescuing" (or "redeeming," σῴζω, 15.1) oneself and others. Thus, one must renounce "pleasures" and prepare for the day of judgment (16.3). Signs of that preparation include "charitable giving," fasting, and prayer, which are also commended in Tobit 12:8–9.[42]

2 Clement 17–18

The climax arrives at the end of the work with a series of dire warnings. Lest "any of us should perish," both idolatrous pagans and those who already "know God" must be instructed (17.1). The references to "restoring the weak" and to being "warned by the elders" suggest a purpose for the writing of 2 Clement: the author speaks *as* an elder in order to restore those who waver in their conduct and faith (7.2–3).

Drawing from parts of Isaiah 66, the next verses paint a bleak picture of what awaits those who are not prepared to face the final judgment.[43] Strikingly, some within the congregation are counted among "the unbelievers" (οἱ ἄπιστοι, 2 Clem. 17.5a), since they later regret that they had not believed (πιστεύω, 17.5b) and had not heeded what the elders had said about their "rescue" (or "redemption," σωτηρία, 17.5b). When the fateful day arrives, there will be no opportunity for those who "denied Jesus" to avoid a fate of eternal torment.[44]

By contrast, the righteous (οἱ δίκαιοι), who have endured torments and renounced luxurious pleasures, will be rewarded (17.7). In concluding the work, Clement expresses humility toward, and solidarity with, those to whom he has written. He is subject to his own teaching—aware of his own sinfulness, the temptations he continues to endure, his pursuit of righteousness, and fear of the coming judgment (18.2). He speaks as their fellow athlete in training, not as someone who has already completed the race.[45]

---

40. 2 Clem. 14.1c. It could be debated whether ἐκκλησία should be translated here as "church" or, for example, as "congregation" or "assembly." Against the latter alternatives is the fact that, in 14.1–2, Clement speaks of an ἐκκλησία whose existence was analogous to that of the preexistent Christ and, therefore, of something more than an individual gathering of Christ-believers. Thus, "church" seems to be the preferrable translation in this context.

41. Col 1:15–18; Eph 1:3–5 (esp. 1:4), 22–23a; 2:6; 5:21–32.

42. D. J. Downs, "Redemptive Almsgiving and Economic Stratification in 2 Clement," *JECS* 19 (2011): 493–517.

43. 2 Clem. 7.4–6; cf. Isa 66:18, 24 LXX.

44. 2 Clem. 17.5–6. Some of Clement's listeners may have recalled the earlier warning about a potter's misshapen vessel: the clay could be reworked, but only before it has been heated in the furnace (8.2–3).

45. See above, on the metaphor of an athletic competition in 2 Clem. 7.

2 Clement 19–20

Most interpreters consider the work's final chapters to be a summary of the work composed by a later hand. We will return to this below.

3. INTERPRETATIVE ISSUES

The interpretative issues to be taken up here concern the theology of reciprocity and redemption, and possible "gnostic" opponents. Other issues concerning 2 Clement's preservation with 1 Clement, its date, its original conclusion, the work's genre, and its Scripture quotations and interpretations as "testimonia," were discussed above (see sec. 1).

3.1 Reciprocity and Redemption

Second Clement warns urgently that to receive the gift of salvation comes with ongoing obligations toward God and Christ. Both to give and receive is paramount in 2 Clement. It is problematic to expect to "receive little" from Christ (λαμβάνω, 1.2), and a believer must comprehend what they need to "give" to Christ (δίδωμι, 1.3a) in response to what he has "given" to them (again, δίδωμι, 1.3b). The term used for what they are to give—ἀντιμισθία ("payback")—occurs five times in the work but is very rare in other early Christian literature.[46] Precisely what may have been meant by ἀντιμισθία may not have been obvious to the hearers of 2 Clement 1, but it is spelled out in the remainder of the work. What is clear is that the ἀντι- prefix signals a response to a payment (i.e., a μισθός) received. Within this transactional relationship, Jesus is presented, above all, as savior and judge. Whereas the former role is highlighted early in the writing, the latter comes to the fore more at the end.[47]

Earlier scholarship (e.g., R. Bultmann) had judged 2 Clement harshly for what was perceived as salvation purchased by works (see above, on ἀντιμισθία), and therefore as a corruption of Paul's teaching about faith and grace without works. An alternate explanation interprets the work's soteriology in the light of Hellenistic divine-human patronage: in order for the patronage relationship to be preserved, ongoing reciprocity is required.[48] Both the god and the god's devotees must continually give to, and receive from, one another. Works do not earn a god's (or a human patron's) benevolence, but displays of honor and fidelity cement, and deepen, the patron-client relationship. According to Clement, the necessary response includes "praise" (αἶνος, 1.5) and "fruit" (i.e., deeds; καρπός, 1.3) in keeping with Christ's benevolence. A likely purpose, or occasion, of 2 Clement is therefore to warn that a fitting response to God's gift is required from Christ's true followers.

3.2 Opponents

Did the author of 2 Clement write in response to a particular group of opponents, and, if so, were they "gnostics"? Generations of scholars have agreed that Clement was a (proto-) orthodox author who endeavored to combat heretical and morally lax "gnostics."[49] A key weakness in that view is the uncertainty whether, in the second century, there actually was a defined group whose theology centered on retellings of the biblical creation account,

---

46. See 2 Clem. 1.3, 5; 9.7; 11.6; 15.2; cf. Rom 1:27; 2 Cor 6:13; Theophilus, *Apology to Autolycus* 2.9 (ca. 170s CE).

47. The work's overarching attention to soteriology and orthopraxis largely eclipses christological themes highlighted in other early Christian writings—e.g., on Jesus's birth, family of origin, miracles, death, resurrection, humanity, divinity, or relationship to the Father or the Spirit.

48. See Kelhoffer, *Second Clement*.

49. E.g., Knopf, *Lehre der zwölf Apostel, die zwei Clemensbriefe*; Donfried, *Setting*; Lindemann, *Clemensbriefe*; Pratscher, *Clemensbrief*, 51–55.

combined with the belief that a lesser, demiurgic god created the material world. Recent scholarship has therefore viewed the gnostic hypothesis as uncertain,[50] and even fundamentally called it into question.[51] Those who interpret 2 Clement in the light of strained parallels to allegedly libertine gnostics run the risk of obscuring its important and distinctive message.

Clement did indeed compete for influence with some Christ-believing opponents, who, he laments, were "teaching evil" (10.5). Much of their disagreement may remain unknown to us, for he never specifies what the opponents taught. If one were to hazard a guess based on the writing's soteriological and ethical emphases (see sec. 3.1), the opponents need not have been leaders of a distinct group, or school, among the competing early Jesus movements. In Clement's view, the opponents could have more general deficiencies—insufficient emphasis on reciprocity toward Christ (1.2–3; 9.7–8), overconfidence prior to the day of judgment (6.9; 7.4–5; 8.2), and a lack of commitment to purity and right conduct in keeping with the promises made at one's baptism (5.6; 7.6; 8.6).

4. KEY PASSAGES FOR NEW TESTAMENT STUDIES AND THEIR SIGNIFICANCE

Second Clement bears witness to an intriguing chapter in the history of the New Testament canon. Above (see sec. 2), we saw that the recurring appeals to scriptural authority in 2 Clement 2–17 undergird the author's warnings about the impending judgment that not only unbelievers but also the addressees will face. In regard to those sources, several matters are perennially debated: the number of quotations; whether some allusions to Scripture are intentional; how many of the addressees would likely have grasped those allusions; and whether some verbal overlaps with biblical texts are coincidental, rather than quotations. Most scholars agree, however, that 2 Clement quotes passages that stem from not only the Septuagint (especially the prophets) but also the Gospels of Matthew and Luke. But in some instances, Clement may not be citing those writings directly but rather using one or more sources dependent on those writings. In what follows, we will consider several examples of the work's (possible) use of sources.

In 2 Clement 2.1, the lack of an introduction alerting the audience that a quotation is about to be given suggests that the audience is already familiar with the tradition:

> Rejoice, O infertile woman who does not give birth! Burst into joy and cry out, you who do not bear the pains of childbirth! For the children of the barren woman are more numerous than those of her who has a husband.

Clement's version matches exactly the twenty-three words of Isaiah 54:1 in the Septuagint. The quotation therefore stems either directly from the LXX or from some intermediate (e.g., a catechetical) source that included the verse. Clement even finds a way to include the verb εἶπεν (aorist tense of λέγω) from the source: in Isaiah, the oracle concludes with εἶπεν γὰρ κύριος ("for the Lord has said [it]"), while 2 Clement 2.1b begins with ὃ εἶπεν ("Concerning what he said . . ."), before the oracle is interpreted. If any in the audience were familiar with the context of Isaiah 54, they may not have anticipated the interpretations given: the infertile woman is the church who, previously, was

50. Tuckett, *2 Clement*, 47–57.
51. Kelhoffer, *Second Clement*.

without metaphorical "children"; the crying out refers to prayer; and having many children means that the church has become more numerous than adherents to the synagogue (2.1b–3).

As if the import of the Isaianic oracle were self-evident and settled, another prooftext is cited in 2.4—this time, a gospel tradition:

2 Clement 2.4	Matthew 9:13b
οὐκ ἦλθον καλέσαι δικαίους ἀλλὰ ἁμαρτωλούς. I did not come to call the just but sinners.	οὐ γὰρ ἦλθον καλέσαι δικαίους ἀλλ' ἁμαρτωλούς. For I did not come to call the just but sinners.

The sayings are identical, except for the absence of the conjunction γάρ in 2 Clement 2.4.[52] In the interpretation (2 Clem. 2.5–7), the act of "calling" (καλέω) is taken to mean "delivering" (or "redeeming," σῴζω), and "sinners" (ἁμαρτωλοί) are understood as "those who are perishing" (ἀπόλλυμι). Conspicuously, there is no reference to *Jesus's* ministry to "sinners," a ministry which would set a precedent for outreach by Christ believers. Nor is the source of the quotation specified. Rather, it is introduced as ἑτέρα . . . γραφή, "another [part of] Scripture," which implies that the gospel material (whatever its origin) is placed on a par with the preceding quotation of Isaiah 54:1 LXX.

The next prooftext speaks of when the Lord is inadequately acknowledged: "This people honors me [με τιμᾷ] with the lips, but their heart is far away [πόρρω ἄπεστιν] from me" (2 Clem. 3.5; cf. Isa 29:13a LXX). For the first time in the writing, a specific source is acknowledged—Isaiah, which is fitting since the wording is very close to Isaiah 29:13a LXX.[53] It may not be a coincidence, however, that Matthew 15:8–9 likewise quotes the whole verse (Isa 29:13 LXX), also naming the source as Isaiah. In the one instance where the Matthean version of Isaiah 29:13a differs from the LXX, the *same* difference is also borne in 2 Clement 3.5.[54] This suggests that the quotation from Isaiah in 2 Clement 3.5 may actually be *a quotation of Matthew's quotation from Isaiah*.[55]

A novelty in 2 Clement 4.5 is that the gospel tradition cited not only overlaps with a saying of Matthew and Luke but also *combines* it with another saying that is not preserved in any of the New Testament Gospels:

52. Since the γάρ is not needed in 2 Clem. 2.4, it may have been omitted for stylistic reasons (see Kelhoffer, *Second Clement*). Another possible source is the version of the saying in Mark 2:17, which also lacks γάρ. However, there are no (other) indications in 2 Clement that distinctively Markan (rather than Matthean or Lukan) material is quoted.

53. Thirteen words in Clement's quotation are identical to the LXX, although one possessive pronoun is omitted (αὐτῶν). Additionally, one verbal form differs but has the same meaning (τιμῶσι/τιμᾷ), and another verb is replaced by a synonym (ἀπέχει/ἄπεστιν).

54. The meaning of τιμῶσί με (Isa 29:13a LXX) and με τιμᾷ (Matt 15:8; 2 Clem. 3.5) is the same; both can be translated "honors me."

55. Another possible indication of Clement's use of Matthew's quotation of Isaiah is the very slight difference between ἀπέχει ("it is distant," Isa 29:13 LXX; Matt 15:8) and ἄπεστιν ("it is absent," 2 Clem. 3.5). Although the original text of Matthew reads ἀπέχει, several early witnesses have ἐστίν ("it is," Matt 15:8; D 1424 latt; Cl). As a result, if Clement knew of both the LXX and a copy of Matthew that read ἐστίν, he could have taken the ἀπ- prefix of ἀπέχει (Isa 29:13 LXX) and combined it with ἐστίν (the variant reading of Matt 15:8), yielding ἄπεστιν (2 Clem. 3.5)—a verb that occurs only seven times in the NT and six times elsewhere in the Apostolic Fathers.

Matthew 7:23	Luke 13:27	2 Clement 4.5
[23a] And then I will declare to them,	[27a] And he will say [ἐρεῖ] to you,	[5a] For this reason, if you do these things, the Lord has said,
		[5b] "If you are with me, gathered in my embrace [κόλπος], but do not carry out my commandments, I will cast you aside and will say [ἐρῶ] to you,
		[5c] 'Go away from me!
[23b] "I never knew you.	[27b] "I do not know from where you come.	I do not know from where you come,
Depart from me,	Withdraw from me,	
you who work lawlessness!"	[you] workers of injustice!"	[you] workers of lawlessness!'"

On the whole, the last part of the saying (2 Clem. 4.5c) is closer to the Lukan version than to the saying in Matthew. In 2 Clement 4.5b, moreover, Jesus is also credited with a saying that is preserved in neither of those Gospels nor any other early Christian writing known to us. Clement does not argue *that* the Lord said all this; rather, the reading is *assumed* to be part of the received tradition. What this suggests is that he used some written gospel source in which the Lukan saying had already been attached to another saying.[56] Notably, this combined saying holds the same scriptural weight as the preceding quotations (2.1, 4; 3.2, 5; 4.2).

The only occurrence of εὐαγγέλιον in 2 Clement appeals to what "the Lord says in the gospel" (8.5). This is arguably among the earliest uses of εὐαγγέλιον referring to a *writing*, rather than to oral proclamation.[57] The saying, on guarding something "small" in order to be given something "large" (or great), overlaps somewhat with Luke 16:12 and 16:10 (in that order). However, the differences in wording suggest that some written gospel tradition other than Luke is quoted here.[58]

Later in the work, Clement exhorts the faithful to persist in doing what is right in order to be "just" and enter the kingdom. The exhortation is supported by the work's lengthiest quotation, which promises reward for those who have withstood tribulation (2 Clem. 11.2–4). Clement refers to it as a (single) "prophetic word," although there are several distinct parts to the oracle:

- a woe against the double-minded (11.2b);
- a question about the delay (or lack) of eschatological fulfilment (11.2c–d);
- a rebuke rooted in the phases of a vine's cyclical development—from shedding leaves to the growth of new buds, unripe grapes and ultimately mature grapes (11.3);

56. The saying about Jesus's "embrace" (or "bosom," κόλπος) has a murky history. The only other witness to a saying like 2 Clem. 4.5b is a marginal note in a NT manuscript (MS 1424; 9th or 10th c. CE). Beside the text of Matt 7:23 (*not* Luke 13:27), it is stated in the margin that the following is in the "Jewish" Gospel: "If you are in my embrace [κόλπος] and do not do the will of my Father in heaven, I will shove you away from my embrace [κόλπος]." In circumstances unknown to us, then, the two versions of the "Q" source (Matt 7:23//Luke 13:27) came to be combined with the κόλπος saying.

57. Cf. Did. 8.2; 15.3–4. Apparently, Marcion of Sinope also used εὐαγγέλιον in reference to his own written Gospel.

58. See Tuckett, *2 Clement*, 193–94.

- and an assurance that the Lord's "people," having faced "insurrections [tumults?] and hardships," will be rewarded (11.4).

Those parts may have had a redactional history to which we do not have access. Nor is the source itself known. The only other witness to it is 1 Clement 23.3–4, which gives a slightly shorter version of the same quotation. Both writings accord to the source a kind of canonical authority: in 2 Clement, it is called a "prophetic word," and 1 Clement refers to it as "this [part of] Scripture."[59] Since the version in 1 Clement is shorter, the author of 2 Clement apparently accessed the source independently of 1 Clement.

5. CONCLUSION

The Second Letter of Clement to the Corinthians may have been preserved for reasons other than its actual origin, setting, and purpose: it is not a letter and is not a sequel to 1 Clement. It is not sent (or spoken) by someone named Clement and is not addressed to a problem in Corinth. Nevertheless, the work is intriguing not only for the traditions that it preserves but also for its distinctive message.

Among the interpretive issues we have taken up is the question whether it is helpful to interpret 2 Clement as if it were an early "homily" (or sermon; sec. 1.1). Instead, the recurring quotations of Scripture may more aptly be described as "testimonia," which interpret what the Lord has said and its relevance for defining boundaries as well as eschatological anticipation (sec. 1.2). A central theme in the work is the presentation of redemption within a divine-human relationship, within which mutual, and ongoing, giving and receiving is essential for preserving the relationship until the day of judgment (sec. 3.1). It is unclear, however, whether Clement wrote in opposition to a distinct group of Christians; regardless, it is dubious to label them as heretical "gnostics" and, correspondingly, to label 2 Clement as representative of a (the?) proto-orthodox tradition (sec. 3.2). It may be that the work happened to survive because it was copied along with 1 Clement, and because some Christians regarded both writings as Scripture (sec. 1.3). The use of sayings of Jesus that reflect Matthean and Lukan redaction indicate that 2 Clement was composed after those two Gospels (sec. 1.4). The work originally comprised chapters 1–18; the addition of chapters 19–20 not only summarize the work but also moderate its teaching on reciprocity toward God (sec. 1.5).

In section 4 above, we considered examples of what can be ascertained about one early Christian author's "Bible" based on the sources quoted and interpreted in 2 Clement. To later "orthodox" church fathers, the choice of prooftexts may have seemed random, reckless, and heretical. Even some modern scholars have been puzzled by the eclectic potpourri of scriptural authorities leveraged in the work. But if we are to avoid such anachronisms, it must be granted that Clement's biblical prooftexts made sense to him, and probably also to his audience. For he never argues *that* a Scripture passage should be recognized but assumes a common understanding with his flock. For those Christ-believers, the collection, or collections, of authoritative texts included Septuagintal, post-Matthean, post-Lukan sources, as well as ones whose origin remains unknown to us. His reception of Matthew and Luke reveals that these evangelists' versions were not the final word but could be combined in new ways with other gospel traditions. The voice given to distinctive (or unique) traditions, combined with the apparent silence of Mark's Gospel, the Johannine writings,

59. Cf. 2 Clem. 2.4, referring to a saying of Jesus as "another [part of] Scripture."

the Catholic Epistles, and even Paul's letters,[60] attests to the fact that, without 2 Clement, we would know even less about the murky history of the New Testament canon than what the surviving sources reveal.

BIBLIOGRAPHY

Baasland, E. "Der 2. Klemensbrief und frühchristliche Rhetorik: 'Die erste christliche Predigt' im Lichte der neueren Forschung." *ANRW* 27.1:78–157. Part 2, *Principat*. New York: de Gruyter, 1993.

Donfried, K. P. *The Setting of Second Clement in Early Christianity*. NovTSup 38. Leiden: Brill, 1974.

Downs, D. J. "Redemptive Almsgiving and Economic Stratification in 2 Clement." *JECS* 19 (2011): 493–517.

Foster, P. "The Absence of Paul in *2 Clement*." Pages 61–78 in *The Apostolic Fathers and Paul*. Edited by T. D. Still and D. E. Wilhite. Pauline and Patristic Scholars in Debate 2. London: Bloomsbury, 2017.

Grünstäudl, W. "Epilog, Ouvertüre oder Intermezzo? Zur ursprünglichen Funktion von 2 Clem 19,1–20,4." *Early Christianity* 4 (2013): 242–60.

Kelhoffer, J. A. *The Second Letter of Clement: Thematic and Exegetical Studies*. Tübingen: Mohr Siebeck, forthcoming.

Knopf, R. *Die Lehre der zwölf Apostel, die zwei Clemensbriefe*. HNT Ergänzungsband, Die Apostolischen Väter 1. Tübingen: Mohr Siebeck, 1920. English edition: *A Commentary on the Didache and on 1–2 Clement*. Translated by J. N. Cerone. Classic Studies on the Apostolic Fathers 2. Eugene, OR: Pickwick, 2023.

Lightfoot, J. B. *The Apostolic Fathers, Part I*. Vol. 2. London: Macmillan, 1890. Repr., Peabody, MA: Hendrickson, 1989.

Lindemann, A. *Die Clemensbriefe*. HNT 17. Tübingen: Mohr Siebeck, 1992.

Parvis, P. "2 Clement and the Meaning of the Christian Homily." Pages 32–41 in *The Writings of the Apostolic Fathers*. Edited by P. Foster. London: T&T Clark, 2007.

Pratscher, W. *Der zweite Clemensbrief*. KAV 3. Göttingen: Vandenhoeck & Ruprecht, 2007.

Tuckett, C. M. *2 Clement: Introduction, Text, and Commentary*. OAF. Oxford: Oxford University Press, 2012.

Varner, W. *Second Clement: A Commentary*. AFCS. Eugene, OR: Cascade, 2020.

60. P. Foster, "The Absence of Paul in *2 Clement*," in *The Apostolic Fathers and Paul*, ed. T. D. Still and D. E. Wilhite, Pauline and Patristic Scholars in Debate 2 (London: Bloomsbury, 2017), 61–78, argues persuasively there is no clear-cut use of a Pauline letter in 2 Clement. Nevertheless, when one considers Clement's "free" usage of Matthew and Luke, and the combinations of material from those Gospels with other sayings, it is difficult to rule out the possibility of one or more other NT writings in the work (e.g., Rom 2:3–11, on God's future judgment of both believers and unbelievers).

CHAPTER 5

THE FRAGMENTS OF PAPIAS

WILLIAM VARNER

1. INTRODUCTION

Occasionally when antiquarians get together (I count myself among them), we wonder about and sometimes hope for what the next great manuscript discovery will be. We may long for another significant cache of Jewish literature to be found in the Judean wilderness (like the Dead Sea Scrolls). Or perhaps there will be unearthed another jar containing Coptic manuscripts from Egypt (like the Nag Hammadi papyri). When this discussion takes place, I always offer my personal wish that the long-lost five volumes of Papias's *Exposition of the Sayings of the Lord* (or *Dominical Oracles*) will emerge from the dusty shelves of some Orthodox monastery in Greece or the Middle East. Photius, the ninth-century patriarch of Constantinople, refers to the writings of Papias, as do some other early medieval authors, although we are not sure that these later authors actually had a copy in front of them. Possibly somewhere a copy of Papias's work may have survived the pillages of medieval conquerors and will emerge into the light someday. Frankly, I would settle for the scrap of an ancient papyrus copy. Well, at least one can hope!

1.1 The Text of Papias

No copy of Papias's work, *Exposition of the Sayings of the Lord*, has survived from its writing in the early decades of the second century (perhaps to be dated to the period 100–120 CE, see below). From the quotations that survive and that will be examined, its original language undoubtedly was Greek. The sayings of Papias are preserved primarily in the writings of the second- and fourth-century Christian authors Irenaeus and Eusebius. Other possible citations and references will be examined and debated as to their authenticity and accuracy.

1.2 The Author

The name "Papias" is Phrygian in origin and has often been discovered in inscriptions at Pamukkale (ancient Hierapolis), suggesting that Papias may have been of Phrygian descent himself.[1] We know that he was the spiritual leader of the Christian congregation in Hierapolis (a city near Laodicea and Colossae in Asia Minor) during the early decades of the second century CE. His lifespan, however, reached back to the last quarter of the first century, possibly as early as the destruction of Jerusalem and the temple in 70 CE, a fact not to be overlooked in the following discussion. For years his writing was assigned by many

1. W. R. Schoedel, *Polycarp, Martyrdom of Polycarp, Fragments of Papias*, vol. 5 of *The Apostolic Fathers: A New Translation and Commentary*, ed. R. M. Grant (Camden, NJ: Thomas Nelson, 1967; repr., Eugene, OR: Wipf & Stock, 2020), 91.

writers to a later date (ca. 135 CE), but recently scholars are opting for his composition of the *Exposition* during the first decade of the second century. As argued effectively by Yarbrough, Eusebius's *Chronicon* places in order the apostle John, Papias, Polycarp, along with Ignatius and then assigns the equivalent of the date we know as 100 CE.[2] Eusebius also wrote: "Irenaeus and others record that John, the theologian and apostle, survived until the time of Trajan. After this Papias of Hierapolis and Polycarp, bishop of Smyrna, both of whom had heard him, became well known."[3] An earlier date for his ministry is also suggested because, according to Eusebius, his life overlapped with that of the apostle Philip, who lived in Hierapolis with his daughters.[4] Furthermore, a neglected passage in Eusebius mentions that both Ignatius (died ca. 108 CE) and Papias were famous contemporaries of Polycarp and that the latter was "bishop of the see of Hierapolis" and "to this day is universally remembered" (*Hist. eccl.* 3.36.1).

1.3 Date of Papias

As we shall also see, Irenaeus, who wrote around 180 CE, describes Papias as "an ancient man" and as "a hearer of the Apostle John" (*Haer.* 5.33.4; Eusebius, *Hist. eccl.* 3.39, 1, 13). The adjective that Irenaeus uses to describe Papias is ἀρχαῖος, "ancient" or "of the early period." It is the same word that Luke in Acts 21:16 uses of the Cypriot Mnason as an "early disciple" or "disciple of long standing."[5] Just as Mnason went back to the early days of the Jesus movement in Cyprus and Jerusalem, so Papias went back to the early days of the same movement in the Phrygian region of Western Asia. Efforts to place Papias decades later in the second century are based on a statement by Philip of Side (ca. 430 CE), associating him with Hadrian's rule, but there are very good reasons to conclude that Philip garbled information that he received from Eusebius and confused a Quadratus the prophet with the earlier Quadratus the apologist. Yarbrough argues this point convincingly and concludes that Papias wrote around 101–108 CE, and he is followed in this regard also by such scholars as Robert Gundry.[6]

1.4 Historical Context

The location of Papias's ministry in Hierapolis has led some writers to emphasize his key role as a tradent of Jesus's deeds and logia. Hierapolis, only briefly referred to in Colossians 4:13, was at a crucial crossroads between Laodicea and Colossae. V. Bartlet concurs with Lightfoot that the location of the city in that central Roman province of "Asia" placed him at what could be called the "centre of gravity in the Church" for a century after the death of Paul.[7] While Eusebius called him a "bishop," this may be an anachronistic usage of ἐπίσκοπος. What we know about Papias's *Exposition*, however, certainly implies that he was an informed spiritual leader in the West Asian city of Hierapolis.

2. R. W. Yarbrough, "The Date of Papias: A Reassessment," *JETS* 26.2 (1983): 181–91.

3. Eusebius, *Chron*. Full citations from the Holmes edition of *The Apostolic Fathers* will be marked with his assigned number of the fragment, e.g., 1., as above. Numbers in parentheses, e.g., (1), are the subsections in the Eusebian citations (M. W. Holmes, *The Apostolic Fathers: Greek Texts and English Translations*, 3rd ed. [Grand Rapids: Baker, 2007]).

4. Holmes, *Apostolic Fathers*, 737.

5. BDAG 137. Or "of the earliest time in a given period" (J. Diggle et. al., eds., *The Cambridge Greek Lexicon*, 2 vols. [Cambridge: Cambridge University Press, 2021], 1:224).

6. Yarbrough, "Date of Papias," 182–86; R. H. Gundry, *Mark: A Commentary on His Apology for the Cross* (Grand Rapids: Eerdmans, 1993), 1027–29.

7. V. Bartlet, "Papias's 'Exposition': Its Date and Contents," in *Amicitiae Corolla: A Volume of Essays Presented to James Rendel Harris*, ed. H. G. Wood (London: University of London Press, 1933), 15.

1.5 Genre of the "Exposition"

Eusebius attributes to Papias a work that evidently consisted of five treatises and was entitled "Exposition of the Sayings of the Lord." As was mentioned, some have preferred the last expression translated as "Dominical Oracles."[8] The document may have taken the form of an interpretation of Jesus's sayings, but it could also have been a narrative about Jesus with a prelude on creation and a postlude on apostolic stories following the resurrection. Papias describes his research methods in historiographic terms, particularly emphasizing the importance of eyewitnesses whom he interviewed or those who heard the apostles. Richard Bauckham has thoroughly examined each of the Greek words in this title (λογίων κυριακῶν ἐξήγησις) and affirms the above general observations.

> In view of the lamentably few fragments of Papias's work that survive, any conclusions about its literary genre must be quite tentative. But by investigation of a variety of aspects of his work I have made a cumulative case for the view that it was not a commentary on or exposition of written Gospels, but itself (was) something like a Gospel: an account of the deeds and words of Jesus arranged in the form of a historical narrative.[9]

On the other hand, Stephen Carlson has argued that the overwhelming usage of λογία in both testaments and in the early fathers was in reference to the divine oracles in what Christians later called the Old Testament. Thus, these oracles collected by Papias were more likely messianic oracles fulfilled by Jesus. The meaning of Papias's title has also been understood to convey, in addition to Bauckham's description above, a commentary on Matthew, or a commentary on a sayings source, or even on Revelation.[10] Carlson cites the nineteenth-century J. B. Gregory, who argued that Papias's work was a commentary on messianic promises and prophecies from the Old Testament. These oracles would have been supplemented "with additional material from oral traditions."[11] If Carlson is correct, Papias's *Exposition of Dominical Oracles* would be joined in its christological methodology later by the author of the Epistle of Barnabas, as well as by Justin Martyr's *Dialogue with Trypho*, Melito's *Peri Pascha*, and Eusebius's *Preparation for the Gospel*. In response to Carlson, however, it is possible that Papias was simply building on these "Old Testament" divine "oracles" (λογία) by applying the term to what he viewed as divine oracles coming from Jesus.

While Bauckham and Carlson offer the best genre proposals, Bauckham's well-advised caution above against dogmatism on the genre of *Exposition* should be heeded. As we shall see, there are just too few undoubted "fragments" from which to base a firm decision about its genre. There are too many of Papias's λογία of which we are unaware and that could help solve this problem of its genre.

8. Entire articles have been written on each word of this title. We have preferred the title, *Exposition of Dominical Oracles*. This translation of λογίων κυριακῶν ἐξήγησις, found in fragment 3, is consistent with the definitions found in a number of Greek lexicons and is preferred also by a number of scholars, such as Stephen Carlson. See footnote 10.

9. R. Bauckham, "Did Papias Write History or Exegesis?," *JTS* 65 (2014): 463–88. This was republished in *The Christian World Around the New Testament* (Grand Rapids: Baker Academic, 2017), 143–64. The quotation is taken from p. 164 of this book.

10. S. Carlson, *Papias of Hierapolis, Expositions of Dominical Oracles: The Fragments, Testimonia, and Reception of a Second-Century Christian Commentator*, OECT (Oxford: Oxford University Press, 2021), 34–40.

11. Carlson, *Papias of Hierapolis*, 39. For the Gregory reference, see 36n179.

2. SUMMARY OF CONTENT

The writings of Papias are known to us only in fragments quoted by later Christian authors. The longest and probably the most reliable descriptions of the fragments come from Irenaeus and Eusebius. The number of the actual "fragments of Papias" in most editions range from a dozen to over two dozen, some of which are probably based on oral traditions themselves! Holmes mentions twenty-eight of them, but not in chronological order, and some are doubtful, while others simply repeat information that is found in other fragments.[12] Ehrman more carefully limits the number of quotations to sixteen and attempts to place his fragments in chronological order.[13] In the citing of possible fragments in the rest of this chapter, we will follow Holmes's numbering of them, as well as his translations, unless otherwise noted. It is important to note that the fragments consist of two types of citations. There are the actual "quotations" from *Exposition of Dominical Oracles*, referred to here as genuine "fragments." These will be set apart by indentation. Then there are "testimonies" or *testimonia*, which are not direct quotations but are summaries of what a subsequent writer wrote about Papias, and these will be placed in quotation marks. This distinction between fragments and testimonies is not always clear, especially in writers later than Eusebius.[14]

Not all of the fragments, especially the "testimonies," will be discussed and explained in this chapter. Particular attention will be given to five writers: Irenaeus, Eusebius, Apollinaris, Andrew of Caesarea, and Victorinus. These appear to be witnesses to the direct use of Papias, while most later writers were simply citing Eusebius or passing on what they have heard that Papias wrote.[15] The writers quoted will be cited and discussed in what appears to be their chronological order.

2.1 Papias and Irenaeus

We should allow Papias to describe his own views, or at least at first through the quotations about him from the late second-century church father, Irenaeus.

> 14. The blessing thus foretold undoubtedly belongs to the times of the kingdom, when the righteous will rise from the dead and reign, when creation, too, renewed and freed from bondage, will produce an abundance of food of all kinds "from the dew of heaven and from the fertility of the earth," just as the elders, who saw John the disciple of the Lord, recalled having heard from him how the Lord used to teach about those times and say:
>
>> The days will come when vines will grow, each having ten thousand shoots, and on each shoot ten thousand branches, and on each branch ten thousand twigs, and on each twig ten thousand clusters, and in each cluster ten thousand grapes, and each grape when crushed will yield twenty-five measures of wine. And when one of the saints takes hold of a cluster, another cluster will cry out, "I am better, take me, bless the Lord through me." Similarly a grain of wheat will produce ten thousand heads,

12. Holmes, *Apostolic Fathers*, 732–67.

13. B. D Ehrman, *The Apostolic Fathers*, vol. 1, LCL 24 (Cambridge: Harvard University Press, 2003), 93–119.

14. Carlson has published a comprehensive collection of ninety-eight fragments from Papias and testimonies about him that have been recorded well into the medieval period (*Papias of Hierapolis*, 112–370). He concludes that there are only sixteen, or more accurately thirteen, that are possible "fragments" of his writing.

15. Unlike those four who mention Papias, Victorinus does not "cite" him, but he may have used his writings (S. C. Carlson, "The Fragments of Papias," in *The Cambridge Companion to the Apostolic Fathers*, ed. M. F. Bird and S. Harrower (Cambridge: Cambridge University Press, 2021), 349.

> and every head will have ten thousand grains, and every grain ten pounds of fine flour, white and clean. And the other fruits, seeds, and grass will produce in similar proportions, and all the animals feeding on these fruits produced by the soil will in turn become peaceful and harmonious toward one another, and fully subject to man.
>
> Papias, a man of the early period [or, "an ancient man"], who was a hearer of John and a companion of Polycarp, bears witness to these things in writing in the fourth of his books, for there are five books composed by him. And he goes on to say: "These things are believable to those who believe." "And," he says, "when Judas the traitor did not believe and asked, 'How, then, will such growth be accomplished by the Lord?,' the Lord said, 'Those who live until those times will see.'"
>
> *Irenaeus of Lyons,* Against Heresies *[*Haer.*] 5.33.3–4, written ca. 180–185).*[16]

Earlier comments were made about the meaning of Irenaeus's description of Papias as an "ancient man" or one who went back to the early days of the Christian movement in Phrygia. What is most interesting in this combination of both a fragment and a testimony is what Papias reveals about his own eschatology. The dominical oracle appears to be from Matthew 26:27–29 (the "fruit of the vine"). The comments also seem heavily dependent on Jewish apocalyptic ideas, perhaps specific texts like 2 Baruch 29.5–6 and 1 Enoch 10.19. The number "ten thousand" may be drawn from Genesis 27:28, and there may be a link to the messianic oracle in Genesis 49:12. The peace among animals recalls other apocalyptic texts like Isaiah 11:6–9. If Eusebius's demeaning remark about Papias being a person of little intelligence was made because of Papias's extravagant eschatology and millennial associations (Eusebius, *Hist. eccl.* 3.39.3), we may have a passage here that illustrates some of Papias's hoped for millennial plenty! Jesus's quoted response to Judas was not a rebuke but an encouragement to him to simply believe. If he does, then faith will help him to comprehend these things and to believe what appears to be the unbelievable. Finally, Papias's references to the Old Testament texts mentioned above would support Carlson's earlier suggestion that the *Exposition* was a sort of commentary on messianic prophecies.

2.2 Papias and Eusebius

The following collection of sayings about and by Papias are preserved by Eusebius.

> 3. (1) Five books of Papias are in circulation, which are entitled "Exposition of the Sayings of the Lord" [or "Dominical Oracles"]. Irenaeus also mentions these as the only works written by him, saying something like this: [. . .]. (2) So says Irenaeus. Yet Papias himself, in the preface to his discourses, indicates that he was by no means a hearer or eyewitness of the holy apostles, but shows by the language he uses that he received the matters of the faith from those who had known them:
>
>> (3) I will not hesitate to set down for you, along with my interpretations, everything I carefully learned then from the elders and carefully remembered, guaranteeing their truth. For unlike most people I did not enjoy those who have a great deal to say, but those who teach the truth. Nor did I enjoy those who recall someone else's commandments, but those who remember the commandments given by the Lord to the faith

16. All translations of Papias's fragments and, in turn, the citations from Irenaeus, Eusebius and others are from Holmes, *Apostolic Fathers,* 733–741 (here, 735).

> and proceeding from the truth itself. (4) And if by chance someone who had been a follower of the elders should come my way, I inquired about the words of the elders—what Andrew or Peter said, or Philip, or Thomas or James, or John or Matthew or any other of the Lord's disciples, and whatever Aristion and the elder John, the Lord's disciples, were saying. For I did not think that information from books would profit me as much as information from a living and abiding voice.
>
> (5) Here it is worth noting that he lists the name of John twice. The first he mentions in connection with Peter and James and Matthew and the rest of the apostles, clearly meaning the Evangelist, but he classes the other John with others outside the number of the apostles by changing the wording and putting Aristion before him, and he distinctly calls him "elder." (6) Moreover, by these remarks he confirms the truth of the story told by those who have said that there were two men in Asia who had the same name, and that there are two tombs in Ephesus, each of which even today is said to be John's. It is important to notice this, for it is probably the second, unless one prefers the first, who saw the Revelation that circulates under the name of John. (7) And Papias, of whom we are now speaking, acknowledges that he had received the words of the apostles from those who had followed them, but he says that he was himself a hearer of Aristion and John the Elder. In any event he frequently mentions them by name and includes their traditions in his writings as well. Let these statements of ours not be wasted on the reader.
>
> (8) It is worthwhile to add to the statements of Papias given above other sayings of his, in which he records some other remarkable things as well, which came down to him, as it were, from tradition. (9) That Philip the Apostle resided in Hierapolis with his daughters has already been stated, but now it must be pointed out that Papias, their contemporary, recalls that he heard an amazing story from Philip's daughters. For he reports that in his day a man rose from the dead, and again another amazing story involving Justus, who was surnamed Barsabbas: he drank a deadly poison and yet by the grace of the Lord suffered nothing unpleasant. (10) The Book of Acts records that after the ascension of the Savior the holy apostles put forward this Justus with Matthias and prayed for the choice by lot to fill out their number in place of the traitor Judas; the passage runs as follows: "And they put forward two, Joseph, called Barsabbas, who was surnamed Justus, and Matthias; and they prayed and said. . . ." (11) The same writer has recorded other accounts as having come to him from unwritten tradition, certain strange parables of the Lord and teachings of his and some other statements of a more mythical character. (12) Among other things he says that there will be a period of a thousand years after the resurrection of the dead when the kingdom of Christ will be set up in material form on this earth. These ideas, I suppose, he got through a misunderstanding of the apostolic accounts, not realizing that the things recorded in figurative language were spoken by them mystically. (13) For he certainly appears to be a man of very little intelligence, as one may say judging from his own words. Yet he was the reason that so many ecclesiastical writers after him held the same opinion, on the grounds that he was a man of the early period—like Irenaeus, for example, and anyone else who has expressed similar ideas."[17]

The above "fragment" of Papias (i.e., 3–4) in this quotation from Eusebius deals mainly with events associated with Jesus and the apostles that he had heard about from eyewitnesses to those events. The significance of these remarks will be addressed subsequently.

17. Holmes, *Apostolic Fathers*, 735–39.

We learn also about the eschatological views of Papias and how strongly Eusebius disagreed with those views. The following fragments, also preserved by Eusebius, deal with the issues related to the eyewitness accounts. We also learn about some interesting traditions concerning the origins of the Gospels of Matthew and Mark, as well as 1 John.

> (14) In his writing he also hands on other accounts of the sayings of the Lord belonging to Aristion, who has been mentioned above, and the traditions of John the Elder, to which we refer those interested. For our present purpose we must add to his statements already quoted above a tradition concerning Mark, who wrote the Gospel, which has been set forth in these words:
>
>> (15) And the Elder used to say this: "Mark, having become Peter's interpreter, wrote down accurately everything he remembered, though not in order, of the things either said or done by Christ. For he neither heard the Lord nor followed him, but afterward, as I said, followed Peter, who adapted his teachings as needed but had no intention of giving an ordered account of the Lord's sayings. Consequently, Mark did nothing wrong in writing down some things as he remembered them, for he made it his one concern not to omit anything which he heard or to make any false statement in them."
>
> Such, then, is the account given by Papias with respect to Mark. (16) But with respect to Matthew the following was said:
>
>> So Matthew composed the oracles in the Hebrew language and each person interpreted them as best he could.
>
> (17) The same writer utilized testimonies from the first letter of John and, likewise, from that of Peter. And he has related another account about a woman accused of many sins before the Lord, which the Gospel According to the Hebrews contains. And these things we must take into account, in addition to what has already been stated"
>
> *Eusebius,* Church History *[*Hist. eccl.*] 3.39*[18]

Having seen the surviving fragments of Papias in Irenaeus and Eusebius, it is appropriate to pay closer attention to what he says about Mark and Matthew. Papias delivers his statements about the two Gospel writers as from "the Elder" or "Presbyter," not as simply what he remembered that he had heard. This report from the Elder extends through what he reports about Mark and what he says about Matthew. If what Papias reports is correct, and he can be trusted here to report what he heard from the Elder, then there are important implications for studies in the Synoptic Gospels. The clear implication is that Matthew wrote his Gospel partly to correct what he perceived as Mark's lack of "order."

18. Holmes, *Apostolic Fathers*, 741. Another attestation about the story of the adulterous woman was in fact written by another citizen of Hierapolis, the tenth-century historian, Agapius. "At this time there lived in Hierapolis a prominent teacher and author of many treatises; he wrote five treatises about the Gospel. In one of these treatises, which he wrote concerning the Gospels, he relates that in the book of John the Evangelist there is a report about a woman who was an adulteress. When the people led her before Christ our Lord, he spoke to the Jews who had brought her to him: 'Whoever among you is himself certain that he is innocent of that of which she is accused, let him now bear witness against her.' After he had said this, they gave him no answer and went away" (Holmes, *Apostolic Fathers*, 761 [Papias fragment 23]). This citation is preserved in Arabic, and the city in that language is transliterated as *Manbij.* This city, however, is not the Hierapolis of Phrygia but the Hieropolis of Syria, and the word "Papias" in Arabic appears to be a corruption. See Carlson, *Papias of Hierapolis*, 233nn1 and 2.

Thus Mark wrote first, and Matthew followed. The tradition that Mark and Matthew wrote the Gospels that bear their names is as early and authoritative as one could express. But was this Mark the "John Mark" of the New Testament? According to Eusebius, Papias also knew 1 Peter [see above Papias fragment 3 (17)]. In 1 Peter 5:13 Mark is mentioned as Peter's "son." Papias would have known that fact when he asserts, through the testimony of the Elder, that Mark was Peter's interpreter. Acts 12:11–17 places Peter in John Mark's home after his "escape" from prison. This is the same John Mark, cousin of Barnabas, who accompanied Barnabas and Paul together (Acts 13:13) and later Barnabas alone (Acts 15:36–41). Later epistles attributed to Paul also locate Mark with him (Col 4:10; 2 Tim 4:11; Phlm 24). There is no other Mark with the credentials to qualify him to be the "Mark" mentioned by Papias through his Elder.

Papias describes Mark's role as an "interpreter" who wrote down what he heard Peter preach. He could have followed Peter to Rome and translated the apostle's Aramaic into Greek, the lingua franca of the Roman Empire. Remember that Paul wrote to the Roman church, not in Latin but in Greek, and Clement wrote an epistle from there in Greek. Nearly a century later Emperor Marcus Aurelius wrote his *Meditations* in Greek. On the other hand, the thorough Hellenization of Galilee in the first century makes one wonder if Peter knew Greek well enough to speak it for himself. Perhaps a better approach is to view Mark's role as an "expositor" or "interpreter" rather than as a translator. In this approach, Mark became Peter's interpreter when he wrote his Gospel as an exposition of Peter's oral teachings. The statement of Papias could thus describe Mark as "becoming" (participle γενόμενος) an oral interpreter of Peter before he "wrote" (aorist ἔγραψεν) the Gospel.[19] Peter remembered and related some, but not all, of Jesus's words and deeds, and Mark accurately wrote down in order what he heard Peter teach. The difference between how Matthew conveyed those teachings and actions of Jesus will be seen in the terse but significant verbs that Papias (and his Elder) uses in the above Eusebian report.

This chapter will not depart too far from the subject of Papias to venture further in arguing for the Markan authorship of the second Gospel. Consideration should be given, however, to the unlikelihood of Papias falsely ascribing its writing to someone who was neither a famous apostle nor even one of the original apostles at all, because he was not an eyewitness of Jesus's words and works. He was at most a young helper of apostles, and one should not forget that he had to live with a blemished record, if Luke is to be believed (Acts 13:13; 15:36–39). The value of the Elder's and Peter's roles in being eyewitnesses of Jesus will be addressed later in the chapter.

Papias's description (and the Elder's) of Matthew's composition of Jesus's "oracles" is far more concise but filled with more mystery than Mark's role. "But with respect to Matthew the following was said: So Matthew composed the oracles in the Hebrew language and each person interpreted them as best he could" (Eusebius, *Hist. eccl.* 3.39.16).

It has already been suggested that Papias is passing on the "traditions" not as his own, but as those of the "Elder." The controversial question of the specific identity of this elder, whether the apostle John or another ancient witness, must wait until Mathew's role is better understood. The key to understanding his role is the meaning of the expression "composed the oracles in the Hebrew language [Ἑβραΐδι διαλέκτῳ, *Hebraidi dialektō*]." While there have been a number of suggestions as to the meaning of these words, the predominant view is that Matthew composed this Gospel in the Aramaic or Hebrew language. Then others made attempts to translate it into Greek or possibly other languages. The lack of

19. I am thankful to Gundry for this formulation of the process described by Papias (*Mark*, 1036).

any manuscript trace of an Aramaic or Hebrew Matthew is compounded by the fact that the Gospel of Matthew simply does not bear the marks of what could be called "translation Greek." In addition, Matthew shows knowledge of the LXX where the Hebrew text differs (see, e.g., Matt 12:21; 13:14–15). It is simply not clear what Papias had in mind when he referred to the variety of translations of Matthew. Conceivably the Jewish example of translating the Hebrew canonical texts orally (the *targums*) may lie in the background of Papias's verb "interpreted" (ἡρμήνευσε, *hērmēneuse*). Another idea is that he was trying to account for the existence of Jewish Christian gospels (like the Gospel of the Hebrews) that were rivaling the authority of Matthew's text.

Perhaps another path should be taken rather than seeing Ἑβραΐδι διαλέκτῳ as "the Hebrew" or "the Aramaic" language. While it cannot be the final argument, the lack of an article before "Hebrew language" may at least support the suggestion that Matthew composed his Gospel in "a Hebrew dialect" or style. Recall that Papias and the Elder clearly described Mark's writing of Peter's words as not being in "order." The verb used of Matthew's writing is "arranged" (συνετάξατο, *sunetaxato*). What Matthew did with the "dominical oracles" is precisely not what Mark did; he arranged them in a specific "order." The verb, therefore, conveys not primarily how he wrote down the logia but how he structured them. Mark was an "interpreter" of Peter in that he explained Peter's preaching. Matthew was an "interpreter" of the logia by providing a structure for them that Mark lacked. Thus, we should view Matthew's effort as an *explanation* rather than a *translation*. And the act of the readers mentioned was to explain them rather than translate them, their ability being expository rather than linguistic. Returning to the lack of an article before "Hebrew dialect," the expression should be viewed rather as stylistic. When Ἑβραΐδι διαλέκτῳ or only the word διαλέκτῳ appear in the book of Acts, the article always precedes the word(s) (Acts 1:19; 2:6, 8; 21:40; 22:2; 26:14). Furthermore, a rather general description of "each person" handling the words as they were able fits better an attempt at interpreting a Gospel in a lingua franca rather than translating it into Greek. In "a Hebrew dialect" then means in a Hebraic way of presenting the messiahship of Jesus, something that all readers of Matthew will agree is certainly present in the book. One thinks of the many Old Testament texts that Matthew cites, his presenting Jesus as the Son of David and Messiah, and the tracing of that Messiah's royal genealogy at its beginning as just a few of the Gospel's "Hebraic" characteristics.[20]

Regarding Papias's description of Mark and Matthew, we may summarize a few points as follows:

1. Papias wrote his *Exposition* before 110 CE.
2. Papias quoted what the "Elder" told him that he witnessed rather than passing on general tradition.
3. Matthew arranged his "Gospel" with a corrective eye back to Mark's lack of order.
4. The contrast between Mark and Matthew has to do with style and not with the language form.
5. The "Elder John," whoever he might be specifically, ascribes a Gospel to the apostle Matthew and another Gospel to Peter as the source of Mark's material.

20. Gundry's treatment of Papias on Mathew is helpful in the above, but his extending these ideas to describing Matthew's midrashic style by inventing events in his early chapters must give one pause (R. H. Gundry, *Matthew: A Commentary on His Handbook for a Mixed Church Under Persecution*, 2nd ed. (Grand Rapids: Eerdmans, 1995), 620.

6. As we noted that the obscure character of Mark would be an unlikely character to credit with a Gospel, so Matthew would probably not be the first choice to assign authorship of an apocryphal work. Such Christian and Jewish apocryphal texts in antiquity usually were "authored" by a well-known character so as to enhance their prestige.

While Irenaeus and Eusebius are our primary sources for the Papian logia, only a few more isolated traditions confidently traced to Papias are preserved in later writers. Some of them even border on the bizarre to the modern reader.

2.3 Papias and Apollinaris

For example, while Acts 1:18 contains a rather gory description of the end of Judas, Papias's elaboration preserved by Apollinaris of Laodicea is one in which we could probably be spared the details!

> 18. From Apollinaris: Judas did not die by hanging but lived on, having been cut down before he choked to death. Indeed, the Acts of the Apostles makes this clear: "Falling headlong, he burst open in the middle and his intestines spilled out" [Acts 1:18]. Papias, the disciple of John, recounts this more clearly in the fourth book of the *Exposition of the Sayings of the Lord*, as follows:
>
>> Judas was a terrible, walking example of ungodliness in this world, his flesh so bloated that he was not able to pass through a place where a wagon passes easily, not even his bloated head by itself. For his eyelids, they say, were so swollen that he could not see the light at all, and his eyes could not be seen, even by a doctor using an optical instrument, so far had they sunk below the outer surface. His genitals appeared more loathsome and larger than anyone else's, and when he relieved himself there passed through it pus and worms from every part of his body, much to his shame. After much agony and punishment, they say, he finally died in his own place, and because of the stench the area is deserted and uninhabitable even now; in fact, to this day no one can pass that place unless they hold their nose, so great was the discharge from his body and so far did it spread over the ground.[21]

While it is attractive to view this fragment as from the Apollinaris who was the second-century bishop of Hierapolis, the city of Papias, it is beyond reasonable doubt that it is from the fourth-century Apollinaris of Laodicea. Eusebius informs us that the latter wrote many commentaries, which are now lost (*Hist. eccl.* 4.27.1). In citing Papias, Apollinaris, like many a commentator, was attempting to harmonize the two accounts of Judas's suicide in Matthew 27:3–10 and Acts 1:16–20. The attempt at suicide was unsuccessful (Matthew), and Judas survived to face another terrible day (Acts). It is possible that Judas's bloating and vision may be connected to passages such as Psalm 109:18 and to the guilty wife's experience in Numbers 5:21–27. The rather grotesque details of Judas's plight may also reflect such passages as Herod Agrippa's experience in Acts 12:23 and be related to the influence of the demonic alluded to in John 13:25–27 ("Satan entered into him"). Carlson calls attention to the fact that the work of Apollinaris is lost and the above is preserved in "textually divergent catenae" that do not agree on how much is actually attributed to

21. Holmes, *Apostolic Fathers*, 755–57.

Papias. "Most scholars today take the maximalist position attributing the entire lurid account of the death of Judas in grisly detail, but in my view only the first sentence can safely be assigned to Papias."[22] Indication in the passage of the lateness of these later details is corroborated by an *argumentum ex silentio*—namely, the silence of earlier readers of Papias, such as Eusebius, about any indication that Judas died in this gruesome way.

This last observation about the doubt expressed concerning some of the fragments containing the actual words written by Papias points out the difficulty of dogmatism about some of the items assigned to him, when none of them survive independently apart from citations by later writers. This personal opinion is not meant to discourage any confidence in Papian studies, but only to counsel that careful and critical attention be given to what are genuine "fragments" and what are "testimonies."

2.4 Papias and Andrew of Caesarea

Although our concern has primarily been about how Papias pronounced on matters concerning Jesus and the canonical Gospels, a few of the "fragments" actually convey his views on some Old Testament passages and one important New Testament book. Fragment 11 preserved by Andrew of Caesarea (6th c. CE), for example, relates the story about the fall of the angels to whom God entrusted the governing of the world, while fragment 24 deals with the fall of Satan.

> 11. But Papias says, word for word:
>
> "Some of them"—obviously meaning those which once were holy—"he assigned to rule over the orderly arrangement of the earth, and commissioned them to rule well." And next he says: "But as it turned out, their administration came to nothing. And the great dragon, the ancient serpent, who is called the Devil and Satan, was cast out; the deceiver of the whole world was cast down to the earth along with his angels."[23]

> 24. And Papias spoke in the following manner in his treatises: "Heaven did not endure his earthly intentions, because it is impossible for light to communicate with darkness. He fell to earth, here to live; and when mankind came here, where he was, he did not permit them to live in natural passions; on the contrary, he led them astray into many evils. But Michael and his legions, who are guardians of the world, were helping mankind, as Daniel learned; they gave laws and made the prophets wise. And all this was war against the dragon, who was setting stumbling blocks for men. Then their battle extended into heaven, to Christ himself. Yet Christ came; and the law, which was impossible for anyone else, he fulfilled in his body, according to the apostle. He defeated sin and condemned Satan, and through his death he spread abroad his righteousness over all. As this occurred, the victory of Michael and his legions, the guardians of mankind, become complete, and the dragon could resist no more, because the death of Christ exposed him to ridicule and threw him to earth, concerning which Christ said: 'I was seeing Satan fallen from heaven like a lightning bolt.'
>
> In this sense the teacher understood not his first fall, but the second, which was through the cross; and this did not consist of a spatial fall, as at first, but rather judgment and expectation of a mighty punishment."[24]

22. Carlson, "Fragments of Papias," 342. Carlson also attributes this approach to Bartlet's insightful article, "Papias's 'Exposition,'" 36–39.

23. Holmes, *Apostolic Fathers*, 749.

24. Holmes, *Apostolic Fathers*, 763.

Papias here supports the traditional teaching found in Judaism that angels were appointed over the various divisions of nature at creation and that some of these angels fell away from their divinely appointed spheres. This theme can also be seen in such New Testament passages as Jude 6 and reflected in such texts as Ephesians 2:2. "Papias' comment may have been made in connection with Matthew 25:41, which breathes something of the same atmosphere as Jude 6 and Revelation 12:7–8."[25]

Carlson suggests another way of looking at the second fragment that deserves further consideration. He writes, "Given the brevity of the quotation, it is difficult to conceive in what context it was made, but the focus on the angels does not look so much like Papias commenting on the text of Revelation, but rather on a Septuagint form of Deut. 32:8 ('God set the borders of the nations according to the angels of God'), known to Justin, *Dial.* 131.1."[26] These varying ideas also point up the obvious fact that a greater surviving context of Papias' work could possibly clarify some of his views.

An often overlooked reference to Papias by Andrew of Caesarea is when he is somehow associated with the New Testament word "God-breathed" (θεόπνευστος, *theopneustos*) in regard to the Apocalypse.

> 10. Regarding, however, the divine inspiration [τοῦ θεοπνεύστου] of the book [i.e., the Apocalypse] we think it superfluous to speak at length, since the blessed Gregory (I mean the Theologian) and Cyril, and men of an older generation as well, namely Papias, Irenaeus, Methodius, and Hippolytus, bear witness to its genuineness.
>
> *Andrew of Caesarea, 563–637 [CE],* Preface to the Apocalypse[27]

The first time the word θεόπνευστος appears in surviving Greek literature is when it is applied to the "Old Testament" Scripture in 2 Timothy 3:16. Occasionally a modern writer will argue that Papias also used this word in referring to the Apocalypse.[28] However, such an assertion does not recognize that the actual "fragments" or "quotations" from *Exposition of Dominical Oracles* should be distinguished from the "testimonies," which are not quotations but observations that a subsequent writer wrote about what Papias said or believed. Andrew of Caesarea is not stating in this "testimony" that Papias earlier used the word θεόπνευστος, but that he gave witness to the "genuineness" (ἀξιόπιστον, *axiopiston*) of the Apocalypse. It was Andrew, not Papias, that used the adjective θεόπνευστος to describe the last book in the New Testament. This is an important example of distinguishing between an author's "quotation" from Papias and an author's offering a "testimony" about him.

2.5 Papias and Victorinus

Because ancient writers often were not concerned about careful attribution in the way that modern academics are in their citations, we should not be surprised that there may very well exist in the tradition some "anonymous" or unaccredited uses of Papias. The conclusion of this chapter will mention some "reliques from the Elders" that possibly could

25. Schoedel, *Polycarp*, 113.

26. Carlson, "Fragments of Papias," 344. Carlson also cites Enrico Norelli's work, *Papia*, 407, as suggesting this approach to the passage.

27. Holmes, *Apostolic Fathers*, 749.

28. See, e.g., J. R. Edwards, *From Christ to Christianity: How the Jesus Movement Became the Church in Less Than a Century* (Grand Rapids: Baker Academic, 2021), 78. Edwards was probably influenced by Lampe (*PGL* 630), who attributed θεόπνευστος to Papias.

also be traced back to him. As another possible example, the third-century Victorinus of Pettau wrote a commentary on Revelation, in which he had the following to say about Revelation 4:4: "Mark, Peter's interpreter who remembered what he taught in his office wrote down but not in order, and he began with the word of prophecy announced by Isaiah."[29] The expression "but not in order" about how Mark wrote Peter's words is paralleled in Eusebius's quotation from Papias mentioned earlier. Since Victorinus predated Eusebius, this is probably genuine evidence that he used Papias.[30] This also raises the possibility that Victorinus may have used Papias elsewhere since we know of the latter's fondness for the Apocalypse. Because of examples like this, we may also reflect on how many other unattributed fragments may possibly have survived in the first millennium of Christian writers.

3. INTERPRETATIVE ISSUES

The extant fragments of Papias's literary work raise a number of interpretative and exegetical issues for modern scholars. The following three topics are perhaps the most prominent in the scholarly literature.

3.1 Papias, Presbyters, and Apostles in Eusebius

Papias claims to draw his information from "the presbyters" about the things Jesus's disciples had said or were saying. For Eusebius as well as for Papias, "presbyters" and "apostles" were probably used interchangeably, with the word "apostle" never actually appearing in the latter's surviving fragments. Eusebius tried to draw a distinction between the two, especially when either John the apostle or John the presbyter is named as a contemporary of Papias. It should not be automatically assumed that two different Johns are mentioned, since both times the name occurs it refers to a "disciple of the Lord," and both times it is found in close association with the word "presbyter." More about this, however, will be explored.

Eusebius described Papias as a "man of very little intelligence" (*Hist. eccl.* 3.39.13). This verdict is perhaps a bit unfair based on such limited data, and it was probably motivated because of Papias's rather fulsome depictions of eschatological millennial plenty. Eusebius made it clear that he did not believe that they could be traced back to the elders/apostles, who, in his opinion, spoke figuratively about these future events. It is true that Papias seems to have been fascinated by eschatological hopes, especially when they involved some extravagant and bizarre projections of certain features of the present life into the future.

3.2 Papias and "John"

One more topic that Irenaeus and Eusebius raised must be addressed. They both refer to a man or men with the name "John." Do these references refer to two men—namely "John the Apostle" and another man referred to simply as "John the Elder"? This not an easy question to answer. The reader is asked to look back to Papias fragment 14 in a quotation from Irenaeus (see above, sec. 2.1) and Papias fragment 3 in a quotation from Eusebius at (3)–(5) (see above, sec. 2.2), which fragments are summarized as follows. Irenaeus mentions "John the disciple of the Lord" and states that "Papias was a hearer of John." He does not mention the "Elder John," and since there is no further descriptor we may assume that his "John" was the son of Zebedee, known also as the "apostle John." Eusebius, however,

29. Victorinus is not included in the fragments presented by Holmes or by Ehrman.

30. Carlson, "Fragments of Papias," 349.

records Papias as saying that he "inquired" (ἀνέκρινον, *anekrinon*) from his informants about what those seven original apostles, including John, "spoke" (aorist εἶπεν, *eipen*) and what the elders heard. He then adds that he would also listen to what "Aristion and the elder John, the Lord's disciples, were saying [present λέγουσιν, *legousin*]." Eusebius concludes that Papias classes that second John "with others outside the number of the apostles by changing the wording and putting Aristion before him, and he distinctly calls him 'elder.'" He then adds that there were memorials to two Johns in Ephesus, which supports his assertion that John the Apostle and John the Elder were two different men.

Scholars have intensely debated and disagreed about the identity of "John the Elder." Sometimes advocates of two different men will argue that John the Apostle was not the "beloved disciple" in the Gospel but that it rather was John the Elder. Also, many advocates of the two Johns will argue that the John in the Apocalypse and/or the author of the Johannine Epistles was John the Elder. To illustrate how difficult it is to decide this question, the following major New Testament scholars hold that the two Johns mentioned in Eusebius were one and the same—that is, John the son of Zebedee, author of the Gospel: F. F. Bruce; Robert Gundry.[31] On the other hand, the following major New Testament scholars hold that the two "Johns" in Eusebius are different people: Martin Hengel; Richard Bauckham.[32]

In a chapter like this, we cannot list all the reasons that these and many other writers have argued the identity or nonidentity of the two Johns.[33] In suggesting my own perspective, I remind the reader that while Irenaeus and Eusebius approach this issue from different conclusions, it is interesting that neither of them offer the idea that John the Elder was the author of the Gospel. Furthermore, some writers have noted that Eusebius's dislike of the chiliasm of Papias probably motivated him to divide the two Johns and possibly assign the writing of the Apocalypse to John the Elder, thus diminishing the apostolic authority of that book.

In light of all the above arguments and counterarguments, I affirm the validity of Eusebius's point that the grammar of the passage in Papias does support the suggestion that the two Johns were different men. The apostle John was among those seven disciples/apostles who "said" (εἶπεν) things in the past. Afterward Aristion and John the Elder, when he had contact with them, were "saying" (λέγουσιν) these things in his own hearing, although he had not heard directly what the earlier named seven apostles "said." A straightforward reading of Papias's account of the Johns does imply some distinction between the apostles (including John the son of Zebedee) and the last two individuals (Aristion and Elder John). The second John was then called "the Elder" (Aristion was not) to distinguish him from the apostle, who had just been named. It is preferred, therefore, to conclude that Aristion and the Elder/Presbyter John were regarded by Papias as personal "disciples" of Jesus but who were not among the Twelve. Later tradition often distinguished between the two Johns. The fourth century *Apostolic Constitutions*, as only one example, records that John the Elder was ordained by John the Evangelist (7.46).

---

31. F. F. Bruce, "St. John at Ephesus," *BJRL* 60 (1978): 339–61; Gundry, *Matthew*, 599–609.

32. M. Hengel, *The Johannine Question*, trans. J. Bowden (London, SCM, 1989); R. Bauckham, *Jesus and the Eyewitnesses: The Gospels as Eyewitness Testimony*, 2nd ed. (Grand Rapids: Eerdmans, 2017), 358–411, 550–89.

33. In addition to the work by Bauckham just mentioned (*Jesus and the Eyewitnesses*), see his *The Testimony of the Beloved Disciple* (Grand Rapids: Baker Academic, 2007), 70–72. In addition to the authors mentioned in note 31, an essay by Lorne Zelyck raises some problems with Bauckham's and Hengel's arguments and defends the traditional authorship of the Gospel: L. Zelyck, "Irenaeus and the Authorship of the Fourth Gospel," in *The Origins of John's Gospel*, ed. S. E. Porter and H. T. Ong (Leiden: Brill, 2016), 239–58.

This distinction between the two Johns, however, does not require that John the Elder was the "beloved disciple," the brother of James and son of Zebedee. Neither does it necessarily imply that he was the author of the Apocalypse, although the argument that he was, in my opinion, is stronger than the argument that he authored the Fourth Gospel. In concluding the discussion of this fascinating issue raised by Papias, I suggest that serious attention be given to the idea that "Elder John" is "the Elder" who identifies himself that way as the author of the second and third epistles in the New Testament traditionally attributed to "John" (2 John 1; 3 John 1). A later patristic advocate of this division of the three letters between John the Apostle and John the Elder was Jerome (*Vir. ill.* 9.5). While recognizing that tradition is not infallible, a strong tradition also assigns the authorship of Revelation and 1 John to the apostle John. It also seems possible that John the Elder may have been the third party responsible for the final form of the Gospel of John (John 21:24), while utilizing the testimony from that "other" John who was Jesus's "beloved disciple." Of course, none of the above points can conclusively be drawn from the evidence in Papias, but the points also would not really be offered if we had no knowledge of what Papias wrote about "John" and the "Elder John."

3.3 Papias's Interpretation of Genesis 1–3

Anastasius of Sinai (7th c. CE) relates how Papias interpreted Genesis 1 as referring to Christ and the church, and the account of paradise in Genesis 2–3 as referring to the church of Christ (Papias fragments 12 and 13).[34] It is unclear if these fragments, especially from Anastasius, are also from *Exposition of Dominical Oracles*, or from another unknown volume, or simply passed down as "Sayings of Papias"!

We have mentioned that there are at least ninety authors that possibly reference Papias through the early Middle Ages. We can be very doubtful that the later writers actually had a copy of his *Exposition* in their possession; it is more likely that they are simply citing what Eusebius had previously written about him. As we look back, authors like Irenaeus, Eusebius, Apollinaris, Andrew, and Victorinus probably provide the most reliable of the "fragments" of Papias where we can look for information on what he originally wrote.[35]

4. KEY PASSAGES FOR NEW TESTAMENT STUDIES AND THEIR SIGNIFICANCE

Now that we have examined the main Papias traditions through these later authors, what can we say about the further value of the scattered remains of this apostolic father? Of particular interest in this regard is the high regard that Papias placed on eyewitnesses who saw and heard Jesus. How valuable is this evidence? Past scholarship has not always held Papias in great esteem, and Eusebius's comment about his intellectual ability ("a man of very little intelligence") may have contributed to some modern pessimism about the value of his reports. It should again be kept in mind, however, that Eusebius's comments probably reflected his dislike of Papias's chiliasm. Whatever be his personal theological beliefs, we should also look at what he said about the eyewitnesses in valuing the fragments that have come down to us. What he wrote about the origins of the Gospels of Matthew and Mark also may have great value. It is in these last areas that Papias may have the greatest value for us today.

The contemporary scholar Richard Bauckham has made a significant effort to rehabilitate Papias for modern scholarship. What follows draws on his significant analysis of the

34. Holmes, *Apostolic Fathers*, 749–51.
35. See Carlson, "Fragments of Papias," 337–49.

surviving fragments of this bishop of Hierapolis. Papias's work is important because he speaks about the methods he used to gather information about Jesus's words and actions. He states that his inquiries were focused on the actual statements of Jesus and the early eyewitnesses. It is important to recognize that the "elders," and possibly some of Jesus's disciples, were still living at the time of Papias's inquiries when he was a young man. While most of the apostles had died, at least Aristion and John the Elder were still teaching. While Aristion cannot be identified, Papias considered him a personal disciple of Jesus. If Papias was born between 50 and 70 CE and wrote his work around 110 CE, he would have been able to hear from some of the eyewitnesses of the apostles even while they were still alive. This provides an alternative to some views of higher-critical scholarship since the Gospels were being written near the time that Papias was gathering his information.

Papias states that he preferred a "living and abiding voice" rather than information in books. It should be noted that he had nothing against books since he was actually writing a book! Consulting oral, eyewitness sources was considered the best way of gathering authoritative information. The emphasis in Papias is not on the chain of transmission of an idea but on the reliability of the witness who conveys the ideas. The "living" voice that Papias sought was not the voice of a lengthy oral tradition, but the literal voice of a living eyewitness, reporting information firsthand. Papias gathered his information from disciples of living elders who had known the first-generation disciples. But he also gathered information from disciples of some of the still living, first-generation disciples. Much of the reason for receiving reports from secondary sources was due to Papias's location in Hierapolis, not in the same location as the primary sources. It is also easy to forget that the prologue of Luke's Gospel (1:1–4) refers to the same priority of eyewitness testimony. Interview with an eyewitness was recognized as the best way to obtain reliable information to be passed down.[36]

We can learn from Papias that although he did not know the apostles, he heard from these "elders" by way of those who heard them. But he did know Aristion and John the Elder, although we cannot be certain that this John is the apostle John. Papias connects us with two generations of Christians about whom far too little is known. The impression left is that Papias can vouch for what was being said about Jesus, since he heard from those who had heard their voices. The presence of the eyewitnesses was both a guarantee of the reliability of Jesus's sayings and deeds and an authentication of those who were writing things about Jesus.[37]

5. CONCLUSION

The contributions of Papias remind us that the written Gospels represent only a part of the material from Jesus that was circulating at the turn of the first century. The author of the Gospel of John stated that Jesus did much more than he has recorded (John 20:30; 21:25), and it is safe to assume that he also said much more than what was recorded in the Gospels (see, e.g., Acts 20:35). Furthermore, after the composition of our canonical Gospels, oral traditions continued to circulate and even influence the written text. These oral traditions were highly valued in a sociocultural setting that regarded memory as much more valuable than is customary today. Papias's preference for the "living" voice should not be viewed as his privileging of orality over writing. He claims to distinguish between "those who teach the truth" and "those who have a great deal to say." It is only the sources that Papias already

36. The paragraph is a summary of R. Bauckham's ideas in *Jesus and the Eyewitnesses*, 12–38.

37. Bauckham, *Jesus and the Eyewitnesses*, 30.

considered authoritative because of their connection to Jesus that he treasured for their orality.[38] This close connection to Jesus enables them to provide a more accurate picture of Jesus's teaching than what books can provide. Regarding Papias's preference for "the living and abiding voice" over written sources, Carlson observes: "This should not be interpreted as a skepticism to the written word *per se*, but rather as an invocation of the common ancient trope that the best instruction comes from a personal teacher."[39] The isolation of these sources is one of Papias's most valuable contributions toward a reconstruction of the Gospel narratives.

Finally, Papias is a witness to a period of time in an important region of the early Christian movement in which the literature that would someday be the "New Testament" was viewed as authoritative sources for life and doctrine. He was thus an early Christian leader who provides evidence for an early recognition of several books later included in an authoritative canon. If some readers are hesitant about the reliability of Papias due to Eusebius's earlier mentioned remark about his intelligence, remember that Jerome later commented on the elegant style of the *Exposition* and expressed his own inability to translate adequately this work into Latin.[40] In addition to Bauckham, many modern writers also testify to Papias's great value. "The information he passes on from 'the elder' about Gospel origins has a permanent place among the *instrumenta studiorum* of both Church and academy."[41] "What is clear is that Papias is an invaluable witness to Christian views about eschatology and the origin of the Gospels—especially that of Mark—in decades immediately following the composition of the Gospels."[42]

I now return to the opening observation in this chapter about my personal "wish" that someday Papias's five volumes of *Exposition of Dominical Oracles* would be found and published so we can see all that he originally wrote. Even if my wish is not granted, the fragments of Papias that have been recovered from later writers have certainly enhanced our understanding of the earliest days of the Christian movement. This also results, in this writer's opinion, in a better understanding of the founder of that movement.

ADDENDUM: THE "RELIQUES FROM THE ELDERS"

Lightfoot includes in his edition of the Apostolic Fathers what he calls "Reliques from the Elders" that are not expressly attributed to Papias. Holmes included a selection of five of Lightfoot's "reliques" that may also, without attribution, come originally from Papias.[43] Yet because current scholarship does not suggest the reliability of these anonymous quotations as being from Papias, they have not been included in this discussion.

BIBLIOGRAPHY

Bartlet, V. "Papias's 'Exposition': Its Date and Contents." Pages 15–44 in *Amicitiae Corolla: A Volume of Essays Presented to James Rendel Harris*. Edited by H. G. Wood. London: University of London Press, 1933.

Bauckham, R. B. "Papias on the Eyewitnesses." Pages 12–38 in *Jesus and the Eyewitnesses: The Gospels as Eyewitness Testimony*. 2nd ed. Grand Rapids: Eerdmans, 2017.

---

38. A. F. Walls, "Papias and Oral Tradition," *VC* 21 (1967): 137–40.

39. Carlson, "Fragments of Papias," 346. See also S. C. Carlson, "Papias's Appeal to the 'Living and Lasting Voice' over Books," in *Rise of the Early Christian Intellectual*, ed. L. O. Ayers and C. Ward, Arbeiten zur Kirchengeschichte 139 (Berlin: de Gruyter, 2019).

40. Jerome, *Epist.* 71.5.

41. C. Hill, "Papias of Hierapolis," in *The Writings of the Apostolic Fathers*, ed. P. Foster (London: T&T Clark, 2007), 42–51, here 51.

42. Carlson, "Fragments of Papias," 350.

43. Holmes, *Apostolic Fathers*, 769–73.

Carlson, S. C. "The Fragments of Papias." Pages 332–50 in *The Cambridge Companion to the Apostolic Fathers*. Edited by M. F. Bird and S. D. Harrower. Cambridge: Cambridge University Press, 2021.

Carlson, S. C. *Papias of Hierapolis, Expositions of Dominical Oracles: The Fragments, Testimonia, and Reception of a Second-Century Christian Commentator*. OECT Oxford: Oxford University Press, 2021.

Gundry, R. H. *Mark: A Commentary on His Apology for the Cross*. Grand Rapids: Eerdmans, 1999.

Gundry, R. H. *Matthew: A Commentary on His Handbook for a Mixed Church Under Persecution*. 2nd ed. Grand Rapids: Eerdmans, 1991.

Hill, C. "Papias of Hierapolis." Pages 42–51 in *The Writings of the Apostolic Fathers*. Edited by P. Foster. London: T&T Clark, 2007.

Norelli, E. *Papia di Hierapolis: Esposizione degli oracoli del Signore: I frammenti*. Letture cristiane del primo millennio 36. Milan: Paoline, 2005.

Schoedel, W. R. "Papias." *ABD* 5:140–142.

Schoedel, W. R. *Polycarp, Martyrdom of Polycarp, Fragments of Papias*. Vol. 5 of *The Apostolic Fathers: A New Translation and Commentary*. Edited by R. M. Grant. Camden, NJ: Thomas Nelson, 1967. Repr., Eugene, OR: Wipf & Stock, 2020.

Varner, W. C. "Fragments of Papias." Pages 225–34 in *The Apostolic Fathers: Introduction and Translation*. London: T&T Clark, 2023.

Walls, A. F. "Papias and Oral Tradition." *VC* 21 (1967): 137–40.

Yarbrough, R. W. "The Date of Papias: A Reassessment." *JETS* 26.2 (1983): 181–91.

CHAPTER 6

THE APOLOGY OF QUADRATUS

ANDREW GREGORY

1. INTRODUCTION

The one surviving fragment of Quadratus is preserved as a quotation in the early fourth-century *Ecclesiastical History* by Eusebius of Caesarea.[1] Recent discussions of the fragment tend to consider it among or alongside the writings of either the Apostolic Fathers (as in this volume),[2] or the Apologists.[3] Comparisons with texts in either corpus, or from early Christian literature more widely, may be helpful in establishing a broad context in which to discuss it. In what follows, I will consider what we may conclude about Quadratus on the basis of the fragment that survives, giving due attention to the literary context in which Eusebius has placed it and its likely original context in the early second century CE. The short length of the fragment, and of Eusebius's introductory and concluding remarks, allows us to quote them in full later, in section 2 below.

Eusebius also refers to the same Quadratus in an earlier work, the *Chronicle*, in a section preserved in a Latin translation by Jerome.[4] Eusebius's evidence in these two books,

1. For a recent and authoritative introduction to the study of Eusebius, see Aaron P. Johnson, *Eusebius*, Understanding Classics (London: I. B. Tauris, 2014). Still valuable are the introduction and extensive notes found in the second volume of H. J. Lawlor and I. E. L. Oulton, trans. and eds., *Eusebius, Bishop of Caesarea, The Ecclesiastical History and the Martyrs of Palestine*, 2 vols. (London: SPCK, 1927). The most recent English translation of *Ecclesiastical History* is J. M. Schott, *Eusebius of Caesarea: The History of the Church* (Oakland, CA: University of California Press, 2019), who also offers a useful introduction. In the present chapter, all English translations of the *Ecclesiastical History* are taken from Schott. For Greek text with facing commentary, see the two-volume edition in the Loeb Classical Library. The first volume, which includes books 1–5, comes with an English translation by Kirsopp Lake (Cambridge: Harvard University Press, 1926). The second, which contains books 6–10, reprints the English translation by Oulton (Cambridge: Harvard University Press, 1932).

2. E.g., the recent discussions by P. Foster, "The Apology of Quadratus," in *The Writings of the Apostolic Fathers*, ed. P. Foster (London: T&T Clark, 2007), 52–62; and by W. Pratscher, "Quadratus," in *The Apostolic Fathers: An Introduction*, ed. W. Pratscher (Waco, TX: Baylor University Press, 2010), 181–95. The text of the fragment is included in C. N. Jefford, ed., *The Epistle to Diognetus (with the fragment of Quadratus): Introduction, Text and Commentary*, OAF (Oxford: Oxford University Press, 2013), and in the recent editions of the Apostolic Fathers by B. Ehrman, ed., *The Apostolic Fathers*, 2 vols., LCL (Cambridge: Harvard University Press, 2003), and by M. Holmes, ed., *The Apostolic Fathers: Greek Texts and English Translations*, 3rd ed. (Grand Rapids: Baker Academic, 2007).

3. E.g., D. H. Williams, *Defending and Defining the Faith: An Introduction to Early Christian Apologetic Literature* (Oxford: Oxford University Press, 2020); R. M. Grant, *Greek Apologists of the Second Century* (Philadelphia: Westminster, 1988). The text is also included in the influential editions of Otto and Goodspeed, which have played an important role in shaping how many authors understand which texts are considered to be apologies.

4. R. Helm, ed., with U. Treu, *Die Chronik des Hieronymus*, vol. 7 of *Eusebius Werke*, 3rd ed., GCS 47 (Berlin: Akademie, 1984). Eusebius likely began this work in 308 CE and completed it after 311 CE. See J. Corke-Webster, *Eusebius and Empire: Constructing Church and Rome in the Ecclesiastical History* (Cambridge: Cambridge University Press, 2019), 40n105, citing R. Burgess, "The Dates and Editions of Eusebius' *Chronici Canones* and *Historia Ecclesiastica*," *JTS* 48.2 (1997): 471–504.

critically assessed, is the only reliable basis for any conclusions that historians may reach about Quadratus or his work. Some later testimony of Jerome, which goes beyond what Eusebius records, is almost certainly dependent on Eusebius and is unlikely to reflect any evidence that did not come from Jerome's reading of references in Eusebius that we shall now discuss.

1.1 Authorship, Date, and Place of Composition

In his *Chronicle*, Eusebius mentions Quadratus, the author of an apology, and places him in his account of the 226th Olympiad. This dates the event that he records to 124–125 CE, the ninth year of the reign of the Emperor Hadrian. Eusebius notes a visit of Hadrian to Eleusis (near Athens), states that Hadrian gave gifts to the Athenians, refers to Quadratus as a "student" or "disciple of the apostles [*discipulus apostolorum*]," and associates him with Aristides of Athens. Both men, he says, "composed books on behalf of the Christian religion to give to Hadrian" (*Chronicle*, 226th Olympiad).[5] Eusebius frames the account in such a way that may suggest that this took place in Athens, but he does not say so explicitly.[6] Thus he allows his readers to infer that the gift of these books was comparable to the emperor's gifts to the Athenians, which could suggest an elevated view of the importance of the authors that may have been much less evident to their non-Christian contemporaries than it may have been to later Christian readers of Eusebius's work. I shall return below to questions about the likelihood of the emperor or other educated pagans reading Christian texts. For now, the key point to note is that while Eusebius associates Quadratus with Aristides the Athenian, he does not explicitly associate Quadratus with Athens. Even if Hadrian was presented with a copy of Quadratus's work while at Athens, Quadratus may have lived elsewhere and could have traveled to Athens (or sent his treatise there) in order for the Emperor to be given a copy.[7]

There may also be some ambiguity about what Eusebius means by his reference in his *Chronicle* to Quadratus as a "student" or "disciple of the apostles." One possibility is that he presents Quadratus as someone who had learned directly from the apostles and had a personal acquaintance with them. If so, Eusebius's testimony about Quadratus may be

---

5. Helm, *Die Chronik*, 199. The Syriac version of Aristides's apology, published in 1891, has Aristides address the Emperor Antoninus Pius (full name: Caesar Titus Hadrian Antoninus Augustus Pius), who succeeded Hadrian (full name: Caesar Hadrian Trajan Augustus). If the later date is correct, it is possible that Quadratus should also be dated to the time of Antoninus Pius, since Eusebius associates him with Aristides. Against this, Eusebius does not claim to have had direct access to the work of Aristides, whereas he does claim access to the work of Quadratus and to quote verbatim from it, so he is likely to have known to which emperor it was addressed. Eusebius's testimony seems more likely to be correct than the Syriac version of Aristides, where such a mistake might easily have been made.

6. Helm, *Die Chronik*, 199, gives the text of Jerome's Latin translation as follows: "Hadrianus sacris Eleusinae initiatus multa Atheniensibus dona largitur Quadratus discipulus apostolorum et Aristides Atheniensis noster philosophus libros pro XPiana religione Hadriano dedere compositos." This may be translated: "After he was initiated in the sacred rites of Eleusis, Hadrian gave many gifts to the Athenians. Quadratus the disciple of the apostles and Aristides of Athens, our philosopher, gave to Hadrian books that they had composed in defense of the Christian way of life."

7. As David Evans observes, the online Oxford resource Lexicon of Greek Personal Names (or LGPN, www.lgpn.ox.ac.uk) records more individuals named Quadratus in central Greece than it does elsewhere. See D. Evans, "Christian Identity Formation in the Second Century: The Two Quadratuses of Athens," *Early Christianity* 10 (2019): 184–200, here 185n4. This would certainly be consistent with Quadratus being an Athenian, but Evans may claim too much when he suggests that it supports "the likelihood that Quadratus the apologist wrote from Athens." The evidence from central Greece (including Athens) for a relatively large number of individuals known to have been named Quadratus shows that the name may have been relatively common there, but it need not increase the likelihood that any one individual named Quadratus was from Athens or elsewhere in central Greece.

compared to his claim that Polycarp, whom Eusebius dates to the reign of Emperor Trajan, was a "pupil" or "student of the apostles [τῶν ἀποστόλων ὁμιλητής, *tōn apostolōn homilētēs*]," and had been made bishop by the eyewitnesses and ministers of the Lord (*Hist. eccl.* 3.36.1; cf. Luke 1:2). This would require Quadratus to have been a very considerable age at the time of Hadrian, even if he had been very young when he had met any of Jesus's apostles—which is not impossible, but perhaps not very likely. The Martyrdom of Polycarp has its eponymous protagonist claim that he had served Christ for eighty-six years, and, as Markus Bockmuehl observes, recent studies suggest that at any one time about 5 percent of the population of imperial Rome was aged sixty or over.[8] Quadratus, like Polycarp, may have been among that 5 percent. Another possibility is that Eusebius wishes to emphasize that Quadratus stood in a tradition rooted in the teaching of the apostles and therefore derived his authority from theirs, even if he himself had not met them. This does not require Quadratus to have been writing his *Apology* at an advanced age, and on that basis seems more likely. It is also a plausible and straightforward reading of Eusebius's text.

In Eusebius's later *Ecclesiastical History*, when he refers to Quadratus as the author of a work addressed to Hadrian, he again associates him with Aristides and repeats his claim (made earlier in the *Chronicle*) that both men each addressed an apology to Hadrian (*Hist. eccl.* 4.3.1–3). Eusebius's reference to Quadratus addressing the emperor is the first thing that he includes in his account in the *Ecclesiastical History* of the principate of Hadrian. This may suggest an earlier date than that given in the *Chronicle*, since Hadrian succeeded Trajan in 117 CE, and Eusebius goes on to refer to events in the third year of his reign (*Hist. eccl.* 4.4). However, he seems less concerned to give an absolute date than to emphasize the early date at which Quadratus wrote, as may be seen in the way in which he introduces the text (*Hist. eccl.* 4.3.2, on which, see further below). Interestingly, here he associates neither Quadratus nor Aristides with Athens, and he names Quadratus without any form of introduction. This may suggest that this Quadratus is known already to readers of Eusebius's narrative, which may mean that he is the same Quadratus as Eusebius had recently introduced as someone famous at the time of Polycarp, Papias, and Ignatius and who "was another of the luminaries during this period, who word has it was granted the prophetic gift along with the daughters of Philipp" and was among others who "held the first position in the apostolic succession" (*Hist. eccl.* 3.37.1, referring back to 3.36.1). The association with the daughters of Philip could (but need not) locate this Quadratus the prophet in Asia Minor (as might the links between Quadratus and Ammia of Philadelphia, *Hist. eccl.* 5.17.3–4). The reference to the place of Quadratus the prophet among those who "held the first position in the apostolic succession" is consistent with Eusebius's wish to locate Quadratus the apologist at an early date and may suggest that his reference in the *Chronicle* to Quadratus as a "student" or "disciple of the apostles" should be understood to mean that he was their worthy successor rather than a pupil who had sat at their feet, even if that claim is difficult to reconcile with the reign of Trajan. The identification of Quadratus the apologist with Quadratus the prophet is therefore plausible, but (as we shall see) sheds little light on the interpretation of the one surviving fragment of the apology.

Much less plausible is any association of Quadratus the early apologist with Quadratus the later bishop of Athens, whom Eusebius dates to the reign of Marcus Aurelius (*Hist. eccl.* 4.23.3), although Jerome appears to have conflated the two (*Vir. ill.* 39). As noted above,

8. M. Bockmuehl, "New Testament *Wirkungsgeschichte* and the Early Christian Appeal to Living Memory," in *Memory in the Bible and Antiquity*, ed. S. C. Barton, L. T. Stuckenbruck, and B. G. Wold, WUNT 212 (Tübingen: Mohr Siebeck, 2007), 341–368, on 354.

the name Quadratus was relatively common in central Greece, and there is little reason to associate these two figures in the narrative of Eusebius's *Ecclesiastical History*; he makes no link between Quadratus the apologist and Athens, and when he introduces Quadratus, bishop of Athens, he does so as if for the first time. Identifying the two figures requires us to reject what Eusebius says about the date when Quadratus the bishop was appointed to that office, and there seems no good reason to do so. Nor is there any reason to move Quadratus the apologist to a later date, since that also requires us to reject the broad outline of Eusebius's chronology without good reason and might be at variance with the internal evidence of the fragment and its reference to survivors who "even lasted into our times."[9]

It is important to be clear about what we may or may not conclude from Quadratus's own words that some of those whom Jesus healed or raised from the dead survived to his own time. It need not mean that they were still alive when Quadratus composed his text, but a straightforward literal reading of this temporal reference does entail a claim that the author's "own time" was early enough that people who had direct contact with Jesus were still alive within the lifetime of people whose lives overlapped with that of Quadratus, even if they were not still alive while Hadrian was emperor.[10] This is why Eusebius notes that the author "shows that he wrote in the ancient past when he recounts this in his own words" (*Hist. eccl.* 4.3.2). It is easier to understand the rhetorical force of this chronological claim if it refers to someone who was a successor to the apostles rather than someone taught directly by them, for anyone who had direct personal acquaintance with any of the apostles and was still active in the reign of Hadrian must have lived to a very considerable age.

It is also possible that Eusebius's references to Quadratus's "understanding" and "apostolic correctness" (*Hist. eccl.* 4.3.1) may be associated with his reference to his early date. Eusebius is keen to establish Quadratus's credentials as a reliable, early, and orthodox authority, even if we have to accept Eusebius's word for his intellect and apostolic correctness rather than discern it for ourselves. As we shall note below, Eusebius presents Quadratus the prophet (who was likely Quadratus the apologist) alongside other early authors of whom he approved, including Polycarp, Papias, and Ignatius, and he wants us to perceive Quadratus in the same way.

The text's interest in Jesus as a wonder-worker does not help us to date it, since this was an important topic in Christian discourse from at least the time that the first Gospels were written through to the early fourth century, when Eusebius finished work on his *Ecclesiastical History* (and also after that date).

1.2 Genre and Purpose

Eusebius refers to Quadratus's work as "a discourse" and "an *Apology* on behalf of our mode of piety" (*Hist. eccl.* 4.3.1) and compares it to the work of Aristides that he describes as "an *Apology* on behalf of the faith" (*Hist. eccl.* 4.3.3). The word that Schott translates as "*Apology*" is the Greek noun ἀπολογία (*apologia*), which is sometimes translated as "defence." Scholars use the term *apologetic literature* to refer to texts written to articulate

9. For further discussion of Eusebius's references to these individuals named Quadratus, and a note of how other scholars have variously understood them as one, two, or three individuals, see Evans, "Christian Identity Formation," 185–88.

10. As Foster, "Quadratus," 57, observes, "The verbal aspect of the entire description implies that such survivors from the time of Jesus had died by the time of the composition of the apology. However, there were people among the current generation of Christians who could remember those who claimed to have received dominical healing. Such a conclusion is suggested by the phrasing Quadratus uses. This states that those healed 'were always present,' employing the imperfect tense to imply a continual state in the past."

and defend Christian claims, often by setting out to rebut claims made either by pagan or Jewish opponents of Christianity, or by authors who might see themselves as Christians but whom the authors of apologetic texts identify as heretics whose views lie outside the scope of those that they consider acceptable for other Christians to hold.[11] This broad understanding of apologetic literature allows it to be applied to a wide range of texts, which may otherwise differ in form and in structure, and is important in the present context because (as we shall discuss below) it gives room to see the fragment of Quadratus as engaged in polemic, either with pagans or Jews or other Christians.[12]

1.3 Intended Audience

In his *Chronicle*, Eusebius states that Quadratus (like Aristides) composed a book to give to Hadrian, and in the narrative of his *Ecclesiastical History* he provides an occasion when Quadratus might have done so (*Hist. eccl.* 4.3.1). We have no good reason to dispute that Quadratus addressed his text in the way that Eusebius said he did, but this need not mean that he actually expected the emperor or one of his officials to read or respond to his text. Justin Martyr addressed his *First Apology* to the emperor Antoninus Pius (and to his sons Verissimus and Lucius, and to the Roman senate, and to all the Roman people), but we do not know if he expected that the emperor or his officials (let alone the Roman senate and people) would ever see or hear it. The aggressive and insulting tone that he adopts when directly addressing the emperor suggests that he was not writing for his stated addressees but for other Christians who would be more receptive to his arguments, and who might learn from them more about the reasons for the faith that they professed.[13] We do not have enough of Quadratus's text to comment on the tone in which he addressed the emperor, or whether or how he referred to imperial administration, including the requirements of the imperial cult, but we cannot assume that his primary audience was pagan rather than Christian. The fact that other early Christian literature was likely written for internal consumption[14] would suggest that so was Quadratus's *Apology*.

It might be argued that it only makes sense for Quadratus to address the emperor if Eusebius's evildoers were Roman officials, as otherwise Hadrian would have little interest in them, and less reason to intervene. Such a hypothesis would assume that Quadratus really did direct his address to the emperor, and that he had some expectation of a favorable response. If so, the fragment of Quadratus might be read in the light of the correspondence between Pliny and Trajan about Christians in Bithynia, or in the light of the *Rescript* of Hadrian (Eusebius, *Chron.*, 226th Olympiad;[15] Eusebius, *Hist. eccl.* 4.9.1–3, Justin,

11. For further discussion of early Christian apologies and apologetics, see Williams, *Defending and Defining the Faith*; F. M. Young, "Greek Apologists of the Second Century," in *Apologetics in the Roman Empire: Pagans, Jews and Christians*, ed. M. Edwards, M. Goodman, and S. Price, with C. Rowland (Oxford: Oxford University Press, 1999), 81–104; R. A. Norris, "The Apologists," in *The Cambridge History of Early Christian Literature*, ed. F. Young, L. Ayres, and A. Louth (Cambridge: Cambridge University Press, 2004), 36–44; Grant, *Greek Apologists*.

12. I use the term *pagan* for polytheists in the Roman Empire, for want of a better term, and without the perjorative or polemical connotations that it can often carry today (as it also did in the past). For discussion of the issues involved, see A. Cameron, *The Last Pagans of Rome* (Oxford: Oxford University Press, 2011), 14–32, esp. 25–28, and C. P. Jones, *Between Pagan and Christian* (Cambridge: Harvard University Press, 2014), 6–8.

13. P. L. Buck, "Justin Martyr's Apologies: Their Number, Destination and Form," *JTS* 54.1 (2003): 45–59, on 51–55; A. Gregory, "Among the Apologists? Reading Acts with Justin Martyr," in *Engaging Early Christian History: Reading Acts in the Second Century*, ed. R. R. Dupertuis and T. Penner, BibleWorld (Durham: Acumen, 2013), 169–86, on 182–84; Williams, *Defending and Defining the Faith*, 141–44.

14. Gregory, "Among the Apologists," 182–84; Williams, *Defending and Defining the Faith*, 11–12, 33–36, 78–80.

15. Helm, *Die Chronik*, 199.

1 Apol. 68, Melito, fragment 1.10, likely from his *Apology* to which Eusebius refers at *Hist. eccl.* 4.13.8).[16] In the former it is a Roman governor and not a Christian apologist who raises the treatment of Christians with the emperor, so the parallel is only partial, but the emperor takes notice and responds to the issues that Pliny raises. The same appears to be the case in the latter, although the *Rescript* survives only as quoted by Christian authors, who do not preserve the letter of the Roman official Serenius Granianus, to which the *Rescript* (addressed to Minicius Fundanus, whom it names as the successor of Serenius Granianus) appears to reply. Minicius Fundanus was proconsul of Asia in 122–123 CE,[17] just before the date of Hadrian's visit to Eleusis and Athens, so if Quadratus were aware of the *Rescript* it may have emboldened him to appeal directly to that emperor in defense of Christians.

However, even if Quadratus were familiar with the *Rescript*, it need not mean that he really did intend his work for the emperor or for other Roman officials. If his address to the emperor was a literary or rhetorical device, and his text intended for use by Christians living under the empire, knowledge of the *Rescript* might still have encouraged him to write in this way. It would emphasize to Christians who might fear persecution that there was no imperial directive that they be sought out and put on trial, since that decision had been made prior to and independently of any argument or appeal that Quadratus might make. The suggestion that Eusebius's evildoers must have been Roman officials assumes that Quadratus really wrote to the emperor, but does not prove that he did. On balance, it is much more likely that he wrote for an audience of other Christians.

2. SUMMARY OF CONTENT

The brevity of Eusebius's quotation, and of the comments with which he prefaces and follows it, allow us to quote them in full. They are as follows:

Text of the Fragment of Quadratus (Eusebius, *Hist. eccl.* 4.3.1–3)

Τραϊανοῦ δὲ ἐφ' ὅλοις ἔτεσιν εἴκοσι τὴν ἀρχὴν μησὶν ἓξ δέουσιν κρατήσαντος, Αἴλιος Ἀδριανὸς διαδέχεται τὴν ἡγεμονίαν. τούτῳ Κοδρᾶτος λόγον προσφωνήσας ἀναδίδωσιν, ἀπολογίαν συντάξας ὑπὲρ τῆς καθ' ἡμᾶς θεοσεβείας, ὅτι δή τινες πονηροὶ ἄνδρες τοὺς ἡμετέρους ἐνοχλεῖν ἐπειρῶντο· εἰς ἔτι δὲ φέρεται παρὰ πλείστοις τῶν ἀδελφῶν, ἀτὰρ καὶ παρ' ἡμῖν τὸ σύγγραμμα· ἐξ οὗ κατιδεῖν ἔστιν λαμπρὰ τεκμήρια τῆς τε τοῦ ἀνδρὸς διανοίας καὶ τῆς ἀποστολικῆς ὀρθοτομίας. ὁ δ' αὐτὸς τὴν καθ' ἑαυτὸν ἀρχαιότητα παραφαίνει δι' ὧν ἱστορεῖ ταῦτα ἰδίαις φωναῖς·

Τοῦ δὲ σωτῆρος ἡμῶν τὰ ἔργα ἀεὶ παρῆν ἀληθῆ γὰρ ἦν, οἱ θεραπευθέντες, οἱ ἀναστάντες ἐκ νεκρῶν, οἳ οὐκ ὤφθησαν μόνον θεραπευόμενοι καὶ ἀνιστάμενοι, ἀλλὰ καὶ ἀεὶ παρόντες, οὐδὲ ἐπιδημοῦντος μόνον τοῦ σωτῆρος, ἀλλὰ καὶ ἀπαλλαγέντος ἦσαν ἐπὶ χρόνον ἱκανόν, ὥστε καὶ εἰς τοὺς ἡμετέρους χρόνους τινὲς αὐτῶν ἀφίκοντο.

τοιοῦτος μὲν οὗτος: καὶ Ἀριστείδης δέ, πιστὸς ἀνὴρ τῆς καθ' ἡμᾶς ὁρμώμενος εὐσεβείας, τῷ Κοδράτῳ παραπλησίως ὑπὲρ τῆς πίστεως ἀπολογίαν ἐπιφωνήσας Ἀδριανῷ καταλέλοιπεν: σῴζεται δέ γε εἰς δεῦρο παρὰ πλείστοις καὶ ἡ τούτου γραφή.[18]

16. For further discussion, see Williams, *Defending and Defining the Faith*, 152–54; D. Minns, "The *Rescript* of Hadrian," in *Justin Martyr and His Worlds*, S. Parvis and P. Foster (Minneapolis: Fortress, 2007), 38–49; and P. Keresztes, "The Imperial Roman Government and the Christian Church I: From Nero to the Severi," *ANRW* 23.1:247–315, on 287–92.

17. H. H. Scullard, "Minicius Fundanus, Gaius," in *Oxford Classical Dictionary*, 4th ed., ed. S. Hornblower, A. Spawforth, and E. Eidinow (Oxford: Oxford University Press, 2012), 958.

18. Text from E. Schwartz, T. Mommsen, and F. Winkelmann, eds., *Die Kirchengeschichte*, vol. 2 of *Eusebius Werke*, 2nd ed., 3 vols., GCS 6.1–3 (Berlin: Akademie, 1999), 1:302–4.

Translation of the Fragment of Quadratus

When Trajan had ruled for twenty full years less six months, Aelius Hadrianus received the imperium. To him Quadratus addressed and delivered a discourse, composing an *Apology* on behalf of our mode of piety, because certain wicked men were trying to harass our people. It is still current among many of the brothers, and we indeed have the work. From it one can see clear evidence of the man's understanding and apostolic correctness. He shows that he wrote in the ancient past when he recounts this in his own words:

> But the deeds of our Savior were always present, for they were true. Those who had been healed, those raised from the dead—they could be observed not only after they were healed or raised, they were always present, for they did not live only at the time of the Savior, but even after he departed they lived long enough that some of them even lasted into our own times.

Such was this man. But Aristides, too, a faithful man motivated by our form of piety, like Quadratus has left behind an *Apology* on behalf of the faith addressed to Hadrian. This man's writing, too, is preserved up to the present among many.[19]

3. INTERPRETATIVE ISSUES

3.1 Dealing with Fragments

The most significant issue that we encounter in interpreting this text is how to deal with a short fragment or excerpt that is shorn from its original literary context and known to us only as it appears in a quotation in another text.

In this case, there is at least no doubt about where the quotation begins and ends. Eusebius makes this clear since he introduces his source with an explicit attribution formula ("He shows that he wrote in the ancient past when he recounts this in his own words"), and he follows it with a reference to what he has just quoted ("Such was this man") before continuing with his own account. Nor is there any specific reason to question the wording of Eusebius's quotation, even if ancient authors sometimes adapted or paraphrased their sources, and we have no source with which to compare the text that Eusebius presents. Eusebius claims to have had direct access to Quadratus's work (presumably in the library of Pamphilius),[20] and to use his own words. This suggests that we may have a reasonable degree of confidence that Eusebius does present accurately the wording of his source, since Inowlocki has shown that, in other places where Eusebius's claims to quote verbatim may be tested, he appears generally to reproduce faithfully the wording of the text that he cites.[21]

Yet, as Inowlocki has also shown, even if Eusebius is faithful in reproducing the wording of direct quotations, he can quote them out of context or in a way that serves his own purpose rather than the purpose of the author whom he cites.[22] Since Eusebius's dating

19. Translation from Schott, *Eusebius of Caesarea*, 178.

20. A. J. Carriker, *The Library of Eusebius of Caesarea*, VCS 67 (Leiden: Brill, 2003), 189, 255.

21. S. Inowlocki, *Eusebius and the Jewish Authors: His Citation Technique in an Apologetic Context*, AJEC 64 (Leiden: Brill, 2006), 221–22; see also 68–70, 190–92. Her key findings are summarized by C. J. Berglund, *Origen's References to Heracleon: A Quotation-Analytical Study of the Earliest Known Commentary on John*, WUNT 450 (Tübingen: Mohr Siebeck, 2020), 91, although he omits some of the minor qualifications that Inowlocki includes in her own presentation of the results of her research.

22. Inowlocki, *Eusebius and the Jewish Authors*, 190, 289–93, summarized by Berglund, *Origen's References to Heracleon*, 91. See also C. Concannon, *Assembling Early Christianity: Trade, Networks and the Letters of Dionysios of Corinth* (Cambridge: Cambridge University Press, 2017), 9–19, who discusses the methodological problems with reference to the way in which Eusebius draws on fragments and summaries of the otherwise lost letters of Bishop Dionysius of Corinth.

of Quadratus to the time of Hadrian is difficult (although not impossible) to reconcile with his claim that people whom Jesus had healed or raised from the dead were still alive in Quadratus's lifetime, we might ask if Eusebius has in any way distorted the meaning of his source to make the claim that he does. As he presents it, Eusebius's quotation indicates that Quadratus claimed to have been aware of reports of the outworking of Jesus's wonder-working power made by people whose lifetimes overlapped with people from an earlier generation who had lived during the ministry of Jesus. Yet the brevity of Eusebius's quotation means that we cannot know if Quadratus addressed the question of whether any of his sources had themselves met any of these beneficiaries of Jesus's power, or if they knew of them only at secondhand. The question becomes more pressing if we also ask how likely it was that anyone living outside Galilee or Judea might have met anyone whom Jesus was said to have healed or raised during his ministry in those areas. It is certainly true that we cannot exclude the possibility that some of those whom Jesus cured were among those who embarked on an itinerant ministry and traveled to Asia Minor or Greece or elsewhere as Paul, Peter, and others did, and that this is how Quadratus's source or sources were aware of them. Yet although this is possible, and consistent with what Eusebius quotes from Quadratus, what seems to make sense in passing in a literary context becomes more problematic when we ask about how this rhetorical claim (if such it is) may or may not correspond to lived realities outside the narrative world that Eusebius constructs in his *Ecclesiastical History*.

There may also be better ways to make sense of Quadratus's testimony. It is not necessarily the case that those who testified to surviving beneficiaries of Jesus's power would have had to meet any of them face to face. Another explanation could be that they had heard of them through oral reports, transmitted by witnesses they considered reliable. Such reports would travel more easily from Galilee or Judea to Greece or Asia Minor or elsewhere than would those people whom Jesus was said to have healed or to have raised, and Eusebius does elsewhere associate Quadratus with Papias (*Hist. eccl.* 3.37.1, referring back to 3.36.1). Thus, it is possible that he understands him as someone who presents information drawn from a living and remaining voice, which is how Papias describes the way in which he himself preferred to work (*Hist. eccl.* 3.39.3–4). Another possibility is that either Quadratus or his source must have assumed that those whom Jesus had healed or raised lived on for some time, for their belief about the nature of Jesus's wonder-working power, recorded in traditions that were collected in written Gospels, demanded that it must be so. We shall return to this issue below in our discussion of how this text might shed light on the role of eyewitness testimony or collective memory among early followers of Jesus.

A further question arises because of the starting point from which Eusebius chooses to begin his quotation from Quadratus. The fact that it begins with a "but" makes it difficult or impossible to be confident about the context from which the quotation was excerpted, even if the general thrust of the passage that Eusebius quotes seems clear. As we can see, Quadratus is making a claim about Jesus's power: when he healed people or raised them from the dead, they were truly alive. They did not momentarily appear when healed or raised, but continued to live for some time, even after Jesus had died and within living memory of Quadratus and his audience. Much less clear, however, is the identity of others responsible for the works with which Jesus's words were contrasted. They may have been rival wonder-workers, in which case Quadratus appears to present Jesus as superior to them. Or it is possible that they were opponents of Christianity, who challenged or questioned Christian claims about Jesus as a wonder-worker, perhaps by comparing him to other wonder-workers, in which case Quadratus may be responding to their critique.

We shall return to this question in our discussion below of Quadratus's portrayal of Jesus as a healer and as someone who raised the dead. For now, we note that Eusebius's decision to begin his quotation at a "but" both suggests a contrast with what preceded the excerpt that he cites and deprives us of its original literary context in Quadratus's text. We cannot read the excerpt except in the way that Eusebius has framed it, so his wider narrative rather than that of Quadratus is the primary literary context with which we have to work as we try to interpret this single isolated fragment or extract from Quadratus.

3.2 Jesus as Healer and Raiser of the Dead

The title that Quadratus uses for his subject (presumably Jesus) is "Saviour," and he presents him as someone whose works included healing the sick and raising the dead. The short length of the citation means that we do not know if Quadratus always or usually referred to Jesus in this way, or if he deliberately used "Saviour" when he refers to Jesus's power to heal the sick and raise the dead, but used other titles (e.g., "Lord" or "Christ") at other points in his text.

The term "Saviour" appears often in the LXX where it was almost always applied to God as the deliverer of his people and the one who bestowed benefits on them (e.g., Deut 32:15, Pss 24:5 [23:5 LXX]; 25:5 [24:5 LXX]; 27:9 [26:9 LXX]; Isa 12:2; 17:10; cf. 43:3; 60:16). However, it was also used widely in the Greco-Roman world,[23] and took on particular prominence in the imperial cult in reference to the emperor,[24] so its frequent use in Christian texts from the late first century and early second century onward may take on a polemical tone and reflect Christian claims that salvation comes from God or Christ, not from the emperor. It is used five times of Jesus in the Pastoral Epistles, where it also used five times of God (2 Tim 1:10; Titus 1:3, 4; 2:13; 3:6; cf. 1 Tim 1:1; 2:3; 4:10; Titus 2:10; 3:4), and five times in 2 Peter (2 Pet 1:1, 11; 2:20; 3:2, 18), but much less frequently elsewhere in the New Testament (Luke 2:11; John 4:42; Acts 5:31; 13:23; Eph 5:23; Phil 3:20, 1 John 4:14). However, it is used of Jesus in a range of noncanonical authors and texts that may be dated to the second century. These include: 2 Clement 20.5; Diognetus 9.6; Martyrdom of Polycarp 19.2; Ignatius, *To the Ephesians* 1.1; *To the Magnesians* salutation; *To the Philadelphians* 9.2; *To the Smyrnaeans* 7.1; *To Polycarp* salutation; P.Oxy. 840 (3x); Epistle to the Apostles 3, 5, 6, 8, 10, 12, etc.; Gospel of Peter 13; Gospel of the Egyptians as found in Clement of Alexandria, *Stromateis* 3.63; *Excerpta ex Theodoto* 67; Gospel of Truth 16.38; Wisdom of Jesus Christ 91.5, 10, 24; 92.5; 94.4; etc.; Secret Book of John 20.8; 77.5; Gospel of Philip 112.3; Acts of Thomas 39; 42; 48 etc. According to Irenaeus (*Haer.* 1.1.3), Valentinians preferred to call Jesus "saviour" rather than "Lord."[25] Its frequent use in these other second-century texts suggests that it was a natural term for Quadratus to use. I consider below the question of whether its potentially polemical, anti-imperial connotations might have any bearing on the audience for whom Quadratus composed his work.

As Grant observes, Eusebius refers at different points to miracles as evidence for the

23. A. D. Nock, "Soter and Euergetes," in *Essays on Religion and the Ancient World*, ed. Z. Stewart, 2 vols. (Oxford: Oxford University Press, 1972), 2:720–35; A. D. Nock, *Early Gentile Christianity and Its Hellenistic Background* (New York: Harper & Row, 1964), 35–42.

24. D. Cuss, *Imperial Cult and Honorary Terms in the New Testament*, Paradosis 23 (Fribourg: Fribourg University Press, 1974), 67–69; D. L. Jones, "Christianity and the Roman Imperial Cult," *ANRW* 23.2:1023–54, on 1028 (Claudius), 1029 (Nero), 1032 (Vespasian), 1037 (Hadrian). See also *TDNT* 7:1010–12.

25. A. F. Gregory, ed., *The Gospel According to the Hebrews and the Gospel of the Ebionites*, OECGT (Oxford: Oxford University Press, 2017), 89–90.

outworking of "the merciful and gracious help of our Saviour."[26] This is one of the themes to which Eusebius draws attention in his preface to his *Ecclesiastical History*, as a guide for readers and hearers of his work (*Hist. eccl.* 1.1, here at 1.1.2). Thus it is possible that he quoted this passage from Quadratus not only because it gave him material for his account of Christianity in the early second century but also because of his own interest in miracles.[27] It need not mean that Jesus's miracles were a central concern of Quadratus's text, although they were certainly prominent in a wide range of New Testament and other early Christian literature. This can be seen in canonical and noncanonical Gospels, the Acts of the Apostles and noncanonical Acts, and the Pseudo-Clementines, which variously present Jesus or his followers as wonder-workers who healed the sick and raised the dead. Thus we would have no reason to be surprised if it were a topic of interest for Quadratus, even if we cannot tell how much space he devoted to it.

In his introduction to his quotation, Eusebius tells his readers explicitly, albeit in only vague and general terms, the circumstances that led Quadratus to write when and as he did. Quadratus, he states, composed an apology or "defence" of the Christian faith, in response to "some evildoers" who were attempting to trouble "our people" (i.e., fellow Christians "like us," as opposed to evildoers "like them" from whom we distance ourselves). As Pratscher observes, Eusebius uses the verb "to trouble" and related nouns often.[28] This may make it more likely that this is his own preferred language here, rather than a verb that Quadratus may have used. This may also suggest that the equally vague reference to "some wicked men" is also Eusebius's phraseology and not taken from Quadratus.

Given the vague nature of Eusebius's statement, and our ignorance of the extent and content of the rest of Quadratus's text, it is difficult to know whether the evildoers to whom Eusebius refers may be taken as the same people with whom Jesus appears to be contrasted in the fragment. That would seem unlikely if they were Roman officials.[29] It might seem

26. R. M. Grant, *Eusebius as Church Historian* (Oxford: Clarendon, 1980), 142, 147–53.

27. Recent discussions of the place of miracles in fourth-century Christianity include H. A. Drake, *A Century of Miracles: Christians, Pagans, Jews and the Supernatural, 312–410* (Oxford: Oxford University Press, 2017), and R. A. Greer, *The Fear of Freedom: A Study of Miracles in the Roman Imperial Church* (University Park: Penn State University Press, 1989). L. Jefferson, *Christ the Miracle Worker in Early Christian Art* (Minneapolis: Fortress, 2014) notes the preponderance in fourth-century Christian visual art of depictions of Christ as miracle-worker. On the place of miracles in second-century debates, see H. Remus, *Pagan-Christian Conflict over Miracle in the Second Century*, PMS 10 (Cambridge: Philadelphia Patristic Foundation, 1983). Recent studies focusing on NT portrayals of miracles and Jesus as miracle-worker include E. Eve, *The Healer from Nazareth: Jesus' Miracles in Historical Context* (London: SPCK, 2009), G. H. Twelftree, *Jesus the Miracle Worker: A Historical and Theological Study* (Downers Grove, IL: IVP Academic, 1999), and H. Remus, *Jesus as Healer* (Cambridge: Cambridge University Press, 1997). J. Carleton Paget, "Miracles in Early Christianity," in *The Cambridge Companion to Miracles*, ed. G. H. Twelftree (Cambridge: Cambridge University Press, 2011), 131–48, offers an incisive discussion of the place of miracles in Christian texts after the death of Jesus, while R. Garland, "Miracles in the Greek and Roman World," in Twelftree, *Cambridge Companion to Miracles*, 75–94, focuses on their wider context. H. C. Kee considers a wide range of early Christian and other ancient literature in *Miracle in the Early Christian World: A Study in Sociohistorical Method* (New Haven: Yale University Press, 1983), as well as in *Medicine, Miracle and Magic in New Testament Times*, SNTSMS 55 (Cambridge: Cambridge University Press, 1986). R. MacMullen gives miracles a prominent place in his account of the spread of early Christianity in his *Christianizing the Roman Empire A.D. 100–400* (New Haven: Yale University Press, 1984), as does E. Gibbons in *The History of the Decline and Fall of the Roman Empire*, 6 vols. (London: Strahan & Cadell, 1776–1789).

28. Pratscher, "Quadratus," 185. As examples he gives *Hist. eccl.* 4.13.6; 7.13; 9.1.5.

29. Another possibility is that the evildoers were not Roman officials but other people who associated Christians with Jews who had recently been involved in an uprising in the final years of Trajan (*Hist. eccl.* 4.2.1–5), and that Quadratus wanted to differentiate Christians from these Jewish rebels, to whose rebellion Eusebius refers shortly before introducing Quadratus. If so, Quadratus's reference to Jesus's miracles might be part of a strategy in which he identifies contemporary Christians alongside Jesus and his life-giving works, in

more likely that Eusebius's evildoers were Quadratus's implied rivals to Jesus if a major concern of the text were some sort of debate or controversy about wonder-working or the basis on which Jesus was said to heal the sick and raise the dead, but less so if the topic was not central to the text. It is not clear whether or how Eusebius's reference to evildoers may cast light on the contrast that Quadratus appears to draw between the lasting works effected by Jesus and the less-lasting results that his opponents or rivals achieved. Assuming that such rival wonder-workers are implied and that they should be identified or somehow associated with Eusebius's evildoers, we may note at least three options as to who those rival wonder-workers were.

The first is that Quadratus contrasts Christian claims about Jesus' healing and raising of the dead with similar claims that were made for pagan gods or demons or heroes, possibly in response to claims that they, too, could do what Jesus did and that this diminished Christian claims about Jesus. Justin Martyr could compare the claim that Jesus healed the sick and raised the dead with similar claims advanced on behalf of Asclepius (*1 Apol.* 56), so it is possible that pagan opponents made similar comparisons, but in ways intended to discredit Christian claims about Jesus. If so, Quadratus may be responding to such attacks. Celsus, a second-century pagan opponent of Christianity, claimed that Jesus was a magician, and Christian authors including Justin (*1 Apol.* 30, *Dial.* 69.6–7), Tertullian (*Apol.* 21.17), and Origen (*Cels.* 1.28, 68; 2.32, 44, 49; 8.41; etc.) responded to such charges, so it is possible that Quadratus was also involved in similar debates.

A second possibility is that Quadratus contrasts Christian claims about Jesus with those made for Jewish rivals, or in response to Jewish accusations that Jesus was a magician. Origen suggests that Celsus's Jewish opponent of Christianity (who may be Celsus's own literary creation) attributed Jesus's miracles to magic (*Cels.* 1.68; 2.44). The canonical Gospels do not record any accusation that Jesus was a magician, but the Synoptic Gospels record Jesus's Jewish opponents as attributing his wonder-working power to demonic possession (Mark 3:22–27 // Matt 12:22–29 // Luke 11:14–23; Matt 9:32–34; 10:25), and the Fourth Gospel has Jesus's Jewish opponents refer to him as demon-possessed (John 7:20; 8:48; 10:20). Quadratus could have been responding to similar claims made by or attributed to Jewish opponents, albeit in a way that may be indistinguishable from how he would have responded to similar charges attributed to pagan opponents.

A third option is that Quadratus is comparing the efficacy of Jesus's miracles with inferior miracles attributed to rivals who identify themselves as followers of Jesus but whom Quadratus and other proto-orthodox Christians consider heretics. Justin notes how Simon Magus and Meander were held up as rival wonder-workers to Jesus (*1 Apol.* 56), so Quadratus could have been responding to similar claims made by others whose claims to be Christians he rejected. According to Irenaeus, miracles attributed to the Carpocratians (and perhaps others whom he also labels "gnostics") were in fact not only performed through magic but were no more than "illusory visions that cease immediately and do not last even for one moment" (*Haer.* 2.32.3). Thus, Irenaeus compares those who perform them to Simon the magician, and not to Jesus, in a way that is similar to the argument that

---

contrast to the violence and sedition of Jewish insurgents and their false king. So Evans, "Christian Identity," 190–96. Less likely is the suggestion these evildoers might be Jews who took part in the Bar Kokhba rebellion and persecuted Christians who did not join them in their rebellion against Rome. So A. Galimberti, "Hadrian, Eleusis, and the Beginning of Christian Apologetics," in *Hadrian and the Christians*, ed. M. Rizzi, Millenium Studies 30 (Berlin: de Gruyter, 2010), 71–83. However, as Evans notes ("Christian Identity," 193n28), the Bar Kokhba rebellion took place in 131–132 CE, so this argument may be entertained only if Quadratus is dated later than is usually thought.

Quadratus may have made if he, too, were engaged in debate—not with pagans or Jews but with others who also claimed to follow Jesus.

A lack of evidence makes it difficult to adjudicate between these three options. We cannot even be entirely confident that Quadratus's emphasis on Jesus's wonder-working power is necessarily presented in contrast to that of some rival or rivals, let alone that such rivals should be identified or associated with the evildoers to whom Eusebius refers. Firm conclusions are difficult to reach, since the excerpt that Eusebius presents is so short, and we have no other access to what Quadratus wrote.

That being so, it may be prudent simply to note the christological interest of the fragment, expressed by reference to Jesus's healing of the sick and raising the dead, and to interpret it without reference to Eusebius's remark about the evildoers, whose troublemaking prompted Quadratus to compose his apology. If we do so, the focus of the interpreter, like that of the fragment, will be on Christian claims about Jesus's wonder-working powers and the benefits that he brings to those in need of healing or new life. This leaves the issue of the identity of Eusebius's evildoers as an unresolved question about how Eusebius frames the fragment. All that we may note is that Eusebius places the evildoers outside the Christian tradition in which he stands and in which he includes Quadratus as a distinguished and early predecessor, whom he is pleased to commend to others.

3.3 Eyewitness Testimony and Collective Memory

A third issue that the fragment may raise is the matter of how unwritten testimony is transmitted over time, and related questions about memory and tradition.

Strictly speaking, the fragment of Quadratus says little directly or explicitly about memory or tradition. However, we may infer from it that people who were alive during Quadratus's lifetime had either encountered people whom Jesus was said to have healed or restored to life, or that they had heard about such people. This suggests that testimony about such beneficiaries of Jesus's wonder-working had survived the beneficiaries themselves, and therefore raises the question of how such claims are transmitted over time, especially when there is no evidence for any form of written record. In addition, Eusebius's testimony to Quadratus in his *Chronicle* claims that he was a "disciple of the apostles." The fragment of Quadratus is itself too short to cast any particular light on this topic, and Eusebius's claims about Quadratus are too elliptical to do the same. Nevertheless, they point to the importance of claims about memory and tradition in early Christian literature as reflected both in the New Testament and in other texts. It seems hardly accidental that Eusebius's reference to Quadratus as a "student" or "disciple" [Latin *discipulus*] of the apostles" is similar to Eusebius's reference to Polycarp as a "pupil" or "student [Greek ὁμιλητής] of the apostles" (*Hist. eccl.* 3.36.1), especially if we identify Quadratus the apologist with Quadratus the prophet who was among the many "who held the first position in the apostolic succession" (*Hist. eccl.* 3.37.1). Taken together, such references show at least that Eusebius wished to present Quadratus as someone who was an early and orthodox defender of the Christian faith, who based his work on the teaching of the apostles, and that Eusebius believed that links between those who encountered Jesus for themselves and those who were taught by or overlapped with them, ensured the reliable transmission of Christian teaching.

4. KEY PASSAGES FOR NEW TESTAMENT STUDIES AND THEIR SIGNIFICANCE

As noted above, it seems likely that Quadratus contrasted the wonders performed by Jesus with what he took to be inferior or counterfeit wonders performed by rivals, and/or responded to accusations that Jesus's wonders were illusory or fleeting. If so, he may have been responding to some form of accusation raised against Jesus that was itself a response to Christian claims about his wonder-working power. This may be compared to passages in the Fourth Gospel in which Jesus's opponents say that he was demon-possessed (John 7:20; 8:48, 52; 10:20) and to passages in the Synoptic Gospels where his healings and exorcisms lead opponents to claim that Jesus himself has a demon or casts out demons by the rule of the demons, or is to be identified with Beelzebul, the prince of demons (Mark 3:22–27 // Matt 12:22–29 // Luke 11:14–23; Matt 9:32–34, 10:25). The charge that Jesus is demon-possessed is not identical to the charge that he is a magician, as Celsus and others seem to have claimed, but it reflects a similar type of polemic in which an opponent does not dispute what Jesus did but denies that he did so in the name or power of God.

The fragment is too short to shed much light on the particular gospel passages noted above. However, it helps to anchor the New Testament in a world in which such debates focused mainly on questions about *how* wonder-workers accomplished what they did, rather than *whether* they did so, as do other second-century texts that reflect disputes about how Jesus was understood to have healed the sick or raised the dead. Thus, the author of the fragment appears to take and to present at face value claims that Jesus healed people (cf. Mark 1:29–34 // Matt 8:14–18 // Luke 4:38–41, etc.), as well as claims that Jesus raised people from the dead (cf. Mark 5:35–43 // Matt 9:23–25; Luke 7:11–17; John 11:38–44). We cannot tell, however, if he was claiming that any of the people "who lasted into our own times" are to be identified with those referred to in any of these specific passages from the Gospels, or if the author refers more generally to the healing or raising of other people as part of the many other things that Jesus was said to have done (John 21:25). It is possible that he appeals to his readers to believe in Jesus's miraculous power because some of them may have encountered those whom Jesus healed; more likely he assumes that both he and those for whom he writes will accept claims about what Jesus did because of who they believed that Jesus was, in the context of their belief that it was possible for the sick to be cured and the dead to be raised from the grave.

The fragment may also be compared with passages in the New Testament that refer to the transmission of tradition at more than one remove, or over more than one generation. One example may be 1 Corinthians 15:1–8, since there Paul refers to tradition that he had received and that he in turn handed on (1 Cor 15:3). Another example may be Luke 1:1–4, where Luke refers to what was handed on "to us" by those who were "eyewitnesses and servants of the word" and that he put into written form for Theophilus (Luke 1:2 NRSV). In the case of Paul, the period of oral transmission was likely quite short, whereas it was likely longer for Luke, especially if his work is to be dated closer to 100 CE than to 64 CE. In both cases the content of the tradition was conveyed at least twice before it reached the recipients to whom Paul and Luke wrote. In the case of Quadratus, his claims about those whom Jesus had healed also likely went through at least two stages of transmission, first from those who handed on what they knew of the people whom Jesus had healed or raised to those who, second, conveyed those reports to Quadratus, who in turn committed them to writing.

5. CONCLUSION

Although very short, the one surviving fragment from the apology of Quadratus sheds light on two issues in the study of the New Testament, as noted in section 4 above. Its relevance to debates about early wonder-working and to the workings of collective memory and the transmission of tradition show that these were issues that remained live in the second century and beyond. This in turn demonstrates how texts later than the New Testament may shed light on those earlier texts as well as on the development of Christianity in the period when they were written. Also of interest is the way in which Eusebius used the fragment to point to links between early followers of Jesus and those whom he considers their legitimate successors, in the same tradition in which he himself claims to stand.

BIBLIOGRAPHY

Bardy, G. "Sur l'apologiste Quadratus." *AIPHOS* 9 (1949): 75–86.

Carleton Paget, J. "Miracles in Early Christianity." Pages 131–48 in *The Cambridge Companion to Miracles*. Edited by G. H. Twelftree. Cambridge: Cambridge University Press, 2011.

Drake, H. A. *A Century of Miracles: Christians, Pagans, Jews and the Supernatural, 312–410*. Oxford: Oxford University Press, 2017.

Evans, D. A. "Christian Identity Formation in the Second Century: The Two Quadratuses of Athens." *Early Christianity* 10 (2019): 184–200.

Foster, P. "The Apology of Quadratus." Pages 52–62 in *The Writings of the Apostolic Fathers*. Edited by P. Foster. London: T&T Clark, 2007.

Grant, R. M. *Greek Apologists of the Second Century*. Philadelphia: Westminster, 1988.

Grant, R. M. "Quadratus, the First Christian Apologist." Pages 177–83 in *A Tribute to Arthur Vööbus: Studies in Early Christian Literature and Its Environment, Primarily in the Syrian East*. Edited by R. H. Fischer. Chicago: Lutheran School of Theology at Chicago, 1977.

Jefford, C., ed. *The Epistle to Diognetus (with the Fragment of Quadratus): Introduction, Text and Commentary*. OAF. Oxford: Oxford University Press, 2013.

Kee, H. C. *Medicine, Miracle and Magic in New Testament Times*. SNTSMS 55. Cambridge: Cambridge University Press, 1986.

Norris, R. A. "The Apologists." Pages 36–44 in *The Cambridge History of Early Christian Literature*. Edited by F. Young, L. Ayres, and A. Louth. Cambridge: Cambridge University Press, 2004.

Pratscher, W. "Quadratus." Pages 181–95 in *The Apostolic Fathers: An Introduction*. Edited by W. Pratscher. Waco, TX: Baylor University Press, 2010.

Remus, H. *Pagan-Christian Conflict over Miracle in the Second Century*. PMS 10. Cambridge: Philadelphia Patristic Foundation, 1983.

Williams, D. H. *Defending and Defining the Faith: An Introduction to Early Christian Apologetic Literature*. Oxford: Oxford University Press, 2020.

Young, F. M. "Greek Apologists of the Second Century." Pages 81–104 in *Apologetics in the Roman Empire: Pagans, Jews and Christians*. Edited by M. Edwards, M. Goodman, and S. Price, with C. Rowland. Oxford: Oxford University Press, 1999.

CHAPTER 7

THE SHEPHERD OF HERMAS

MARK GRUNDEKEN

1. INTRODUCTION

The Shepherd of Hermas (henceforth "Hermas") offers a lengthy sequence of visions the author Hermas says he received and their detailed explanations by various revelatory agents, especially Woman Church and the Shepherd (whence the title of the work).[1] Although Hermas did not become part of the biblical canon, it is part of one of the most important manuscripts of the Christian Bible: the fourth-century Codex Sinaiticus.[2] Hermas's revelations aim at the change and renewal (μετάνοια, *metanoia*) of the Christian community with its sinful members. In this regard, Hermas mentions more or less every sin one could possibly imagine. He is primarily concerned with practical matters like patronage: he calls on his addressees to provide support for the needy. To modern readers, Hermas offers valuable insights into many aspects of early Christian community life in Rome around the beginning of the second century.[3] One of these aspects is church hierarchy. Hermas reflects a presbyterial form of church leadership (not a monarchical episcopacy) in early second-century Rome. For those interested in early Christianity, Hermas is one of the central texts to study.

1.1. Surviving Manuscripts and Reception of the Text

Originally written in Greek, the complete work has come down to us only in Latin and Ethiopic. The two Latin versions, the (so-called) Vulgata (L^1, around 200 CE) and Palatina (L^2, 4th or 5th c. CE), are attested in several medieval manuscripts. The Ethiopic version (E, 4th c. CE) is attested in four manuscripts dating from the fourteenth to the sixteenth century.[4] There are also Coptic, Middle Persian, and Georgian versions. All Greek

1. The text of Hermas is cited from the edition of M. Leutzsch, "Hirt des Hermas," in *Papiasfragmente, Hirt des Hermas*, ed. U. H. J. Körtner and M. Leutzsch, Schriften des Urchristentums 3 (Darmstadt: Wissenschaftliche Buchgesellschaft, 1998), 105–497. References are given in the traditional way, which divides the work into three parts (Visions 1–5, Mandates 1–12, and Similitudes 1–10), rather than the more recent one, which divides it into 114 chapters. The translations are mine. Other critical editions of Hermas that are based on all four main Greek manuscripts are those by B. D. Ehrman, ed., "The Shepherd of Hermas," in *The Apostolic Fathers*, vol. 2, LCL 25 (Cambridge: Harvard University Press, 2003), 161–473, and M. W. Holmes, ed., "The Shepherd of Hermas," in *The Apostolic Fathers: Greek Texts and English Translations*, 3rd ed. (Grand Rapids: Baker Academic, 2007), 442–685.

2. See Codex Sinaiticus, https://codexsinaiticus.org/en/.

3. See, e.g., M. Grundeken, *Community Building in the Shepherd of Hermas: A Critical Study of Some Key Aspects*, VCSup 131 (Leiden: Brill, 2015).

4. For the Vulgata, see C. Tornau and P. Cecconi, eds., *The Shepherd of Hermas in Latin: Critical Edition of the Oldest Translation Vulgata*, TUGAL 173 (Berlin: de Gruyter, 2014). For the Palatina, see A. Vezzoni, ed., *Il Pastore di Erma: Versione Palatina*, Il Nuovo Melograno 13 (Florence: Le Lettere, 1994). For the recent discovery of a fourth Ethiopic manuscript of Hermas, see T. Erho, "A Fourth Ethiopic Witness to the Shepherd of Hermas," in *Caught in Translation: Studies on Versions of Late-Antique Christian Literature*, ed. M. Toca and D. Batovici, Texts and Studies in Eastern Christianity 17 (Leiden: Brill, 2020), 241–66.

manuscripts are incomplete or fragmentary. Of the largest Greek manuscripts, Codex Athos (A, 15th c. CE) contains Visions 1.1.1–Similitudes 9.30.2; Codex Sinaiticus (א, 4th c. CE), Visions 1.1.1–Mandates 4.3.6; Papyrus Michigan 129 (M, 3rd c. CE) Similitudes 2.8–9.5.1; and Papyrus Bodmer 38 (Bo, 4th or 5th c. CE) Visions 1–3. The Greek text of Similitudes 9.30–33 and 10 is attested only partially in more than twenty Greek papyri or parchment fragments stemming from various scrolls and codices. Since the dating of Papyrus Iandanae 1.4 (I, Mand. 11.19–24; 12.1.2–3) to the early second century is controversial, the earliest safely dated witness to the Greek text is Papyrus Michigan 130 (M^2, second half of the 2nd c. CE), a fragment from a scroll with the text of Mandates 2.6–3.1. Recent new editions of the Latin and Ethiopic versions show the necessity of a new critical edition of Hermas, preferably on the basis of a family tree of all textual witnesses (*stemma codicum et versionum*).

Hermas is attested from the early church all through the Middle Ages. Its long reception history shows a wide spectrum of assessments, varying from high esteem to outright rejection. On one side of the spectrum stands, for instance, Pseudo-Cyprian, who cites the work as "divine Scripture": (*scriptura divina*; *Adv. Aleat.* 2). On the other side there is, for example, Tertullian, who designates it as "apocryphal and false" (*apocrypha et falsa*; *Pud.* 10.12). The editio princeps of Hermas (in Latin) was published in 1513 by Lefèvre. The Greek text was rediscovered when Constantine Simonides found Codex Athos around 1855. This discovery (which, because of the questionable reputation of its finder, aroused much suspicion and controversy among scholars), together with Constantine Tischendorf's 1862 facsimile edition of the Codex Sinaiticus, formed the starting point of modern research on Hermas.

1.2 Authorship and Provenance

The author calls himself "Hermas."[5] There is no reason to think that this is a pseudonym, because the author does not pay special attention to the name, which was not uncommon in his day. It cannot be proven that he is the Hermas mentioned by Paul in Romans 16:14 (cf. Origen, *Comm. Rom.* 10.31) or the brother of bishop Pius of Rome (cf. Muratorian Fragment, lines 73–77). Hermas presents himself, among other things, as a visionary (passim), freedman (Vis. 1.1.1–2), *pater familias* with wife and children (Vis. 1.3.1–2; 2.2.2–3; 2.3.1; Sim. 7.3), and failed (small) businessman (Vis. 2.3.1; 3.6.7). Judging by the level of his Greek, he is probably to be situated in the lower social classes with limited education. It is reasonable to presume that the same applies to the community to which he belonged. The author remains otherwise unknown.

The most likely place of composition is Rome. There are various references to this city and its surrounding areas (esp. Vis. 1.1.1–3; 2.1.1; 2.4.1, 3; 4.1.2). Several other indications are in line with this localization: the Latin loanwords (e.g., Vis. 3.1.4; Sim. 5.1.1–2), described vegetation (e.g., deciduous trees, Sim. 3; a willow tree, Sim. 8), and viticulture, especially the typical *arbustum* (Sim. 2). The only geographical reference that does not fit in with this picture, the reference to Arcadia (Sim. 9.1.4), can be sufficiently explained as a bucolic topos (cf., e.g., Vergil, *Ecl.* 10).

1.3. Date and Compositional Stages

The date of composition lies probably somewhere between the end of the first and the middle of the second century. That is not to say that the text was composed over a longer

5. Vis. 1.1.4; 1.2.2–4; 1.4.3; 2.2.2; 2.3.1; 3.1.6; 3.8.11; 4.1.4, 7.

period of time.[6] The *terminus post quem* may lie sometime after the reign of Emperor Nero, because the author seems to imply that severe violence against Christians belongs to the past (esp. Vis. 3.1.9–3.2.1). It should be noted, however, that the assaults mentioned cannot be convincingly linked to any particular emperor. The fact that for the church in Rome a presbyterial form of leadership is envisioned (esp. Vis. 2.4.3) does not prove an early date, because it is unknown whether a monarchical structure existed there before the middle of the second century (cf. perhaps the episcopate of Anicetus). The *terminus ante quem* lies sometime before the late second century, because Hermas was known to Irenaeus in Gaul, Clement in Alexandria, and Tertullian in Carthage. Other external evidence is not conclusive. Origen's assumption that Hermas was Paul's acquaintance probably has the intention to upgrade the authority of Hermas by connecting it with the apostolic age. By contrast, the remark in the Muratorian Fragment that Hermas wrote his work (*pastorem*) "recently in our times" (*nuperrime temporibus nostris*, line 74), when Hermas's brother Pius was *episcopus* in Rome (lines 74–77; i.e., according to Eusebius, *Hist. eccl.* 4.11.6, around the middle of the 2nd c. CE), can be seen as an attempt to downgrade Hermas as a "recent" work (cf. lines 77–80). On the basis of the available evidence, an exact date of composition cannot be determined.

The original unity of Hermas is disputed. An internal argument against its unity is the fact that Visions 1–4 do not refer to the other parts of Hermas, whereas Visions 5.5–6 and Similitudes 9.1.1–3 imply a tripartite work consisting of Visions, Mandates, and Similitudes.[7] An external argument against the unity relates to the manuscript evidence: Papyrus Bodmer 38 (Bo) may have contained only Visions 1–4, and Papyrus Michigan 130 (M^2) only Visions 5–Similitudes 10, but this remains uncertain. A strong argument in favor of the literary integrity of Hermas, however, is the fact that the external evidence for its original unity (Clement of Alexandria, who at the end of the 2nd c. CE quotes from all three parts of Hermas) is older and more secure than the evidence for the work's composition in successive stages and/or from various components (M, dated around 250 CE).[8] Another issue is whether Hermas was composed by one or more authors. Concerning this problem, it should be noted that theories of multiple authorship create more problems than they solve and have so far always remained a minority position.

1.4 Intended Destination and Genre

It is widely assumed that Hermas originated in a Jewish-Christian context, but this cannot be proven. Jewish themes like Torah observance (e.g., dietary laws, Sabbath rest, and circumcision) are not addressed. In fact, it is stated that Christians have their own law (Sim. 1.5–7). Jesus is not presented as fulfillment of the Scriptures. Overall, any literary dependence on the Hebrew Bible or Septuagint is uncertain. There are affinities between Hermas and Jewish traditions (e.g., Sim. 9.15.4), but these are no conclusive evidence of a Jewish-Christian background. Allusions to Jewish traditions do not necessarily point at

6. Cf., e.g., J. Muddiman, "The Church in Ephesians, 2 Clement, and the Shepherd of Hermas," in *Trajectories Through the New Testament and the Apostolic Fathers*, ed. A. F. Gregory and C. M. Tuckett (Oxford: Oxford University Press, 2005), 107–21, 117, who argues that the theory of a composition over a longer period of time "does not seem to do justice to the urgency that the author feels (see Vis. 2.4.3) to send his message abroad."

7. Cf. D. Hellholm, *Das Visionenbuch des Hermas als Apokalypse: Formgeschichtliche und texttheoretische Studien zu einer literarischen Gattung, Teil 1: Methodologische Formüberlegungen und makrostrukturelle Textanalyse*, ConBNT 13 (Lund: Gleerup, 1980), 11–13.

8. Cf., e.g., P. Henne, *L'unité du Pasteur d'Hermas: Tradition et redaction*, CahRB 31 (Paris: Gabalda, 1992), 18–21.

an interest in Judaism. Moreover, Jewish material may have been borrowed from Christian (oral or written) sources. Furthermore, some of the Jewish traditions have been reinterpreted (e.g., in Sim. 9.17.1–2, the "twelve tribes [φυλαί, *phylai*]" are said to be the world's "twelve peoples [ἔθνη, *ethnē*]"). Besides, some of the alleged Jewish traditions are not specifically Jewish at all (cf., e.g., the Two Ways teaching in Mand. 6.1 with that in Hesiod, *Op.* 286–92 and Xenophon, *Mem.* 2.1.21–34). Finally, the focus of the author is not on the Jewish roots of the church but on its present state and future hope. In this regard, the core message of Hermas could be summarized as follows: at present, the church is a *corpus mixtum* (see esp. Vis. 3 and Sim. 9, where the church is portrayed as a "tower" built of useful and, for the greater part, useless "stones"), but with a transformation (μετάνοια) of its members it will soon (cf. Vis. 3.8.9; Sim. 8.8.3, 5; 9.5.1; 9.12.3; 9.18.3; 10.4.4) be a perfect community (e.g., Vis. 3.2.6; Sim. 9.9.7; 9.13.5; 9.18.3–4). The author intends to build up a church of transformed believers.

Hermas is an apocalyptic writing. It shares several general characteristics with contemporary apocalypses: revelations (among others, about the imminent end of time characterized by affliction [θλῖψις, *thlipsis*]), raptures, visionary experiences, exchanges between heavenly and human beings, a narrative framework, and a paraenetic orientation (in reaction to an [assumed] crisis of the church). Moreover, it reflects several motifs that recur regularly in early Christian apocalyptic writings: a proclamation of the reign of God connected with a call to change (μετάνοια; e.g., Sim. 9.12, 20, 31), a universal missionary perspective (e.g., Sim. 9.17), a developed angelology (e.g., Vis. 2.2.7; 5.2; Mand. 5.1.7; 6.2; Sim. 5.4.4; 5.5.3; 7.1, 3; 8.1.2; 8.3.3; 9.1.3; 9.14.3; 9.24.4; 9.25.2; 9.27.3; 9.31.3), a two-age paradigm (e.g., Vis. 4.3.5; Sim. 1, 3–4), an expectation of the parousia (though not of Jesus Christ but of God, Sim. 5.5.3), an anticipation of the final judgment (esp. Vis. 3.9.5 [κρίσις, *krisis*]; cf., e.g., Sim. 8.11.3; 9.18), and the hope of eternal life (esp. Vis. 2.3.2–3; 4.3.5; Sim. 5.6–7).

2. SUMMARY OF CONTENT

The work consists of three parts: five Visions (Vis.), twelve Mandates (Mand.), and ten Similitudes (Sim.). The Visions are the smallest part of the work (about one-fifth), the Mandates are a bit larger (also about one-fifth), and the Similitudes form the largest part (about three-fifths). On the one hand, the division into three parts does not really reflect the structure of the work, because visionary, paraenetic, and parabolic material is found in all three parts. On the other hand, the multiple use of the terms "vision" (ὅρασις, *horasis*/ ὅραμα, *horama*), "mandate" (ἐντολή, *entolē*), and "parable" (παραβολή, *parabolē*) as internal cross-references (apart from the headings) indicates that the work is meant to have a tripartite structure. Yet, there is also a bipartite structure: the figure of Woman Church appears only in Visions 1–4, whereas the Shepherd appears only in Visions 5–Similitudes 10. The text of Hermas can be divided as follows:

Opening Scene	
Vis. 1.1	Hermas's Remembrance and Vision of His Former Matron Rhoda
Main Body	
Vis. 1.2–Vis. 4	Revelations by Woman Church (and Others)
Vis. 5–Sim. 9	Revelations by the Shepherd
Closing Scene	
Sim. 10	Hermas's Encounter with the Angel, the Shepherd's Chief

2.1 Visions

In the first vision, Hermas narrates how one day in Rome he began to admire the beauty of his former (slave) owner, Rhoda (1.1.1–2). After this short introduction, he gives a lengthy and detailed description of the visions he says he has seen (up to the end of Hermas). To begin with, Hermas describes a vision of Rhoda speaking from heaven and accusing him of having sinned against her because of his sinful thoughts about her (vv. 3–9). As a result, he asks himself if he can still be saved (1.2.1). He then describes a vision in which an elderly lady appears, who explains to him why God is angry with him and his family, and that all are in need of change (μετάνοια, 1.2.2–1.3.2). She then reads to him from a book (cf. 1.2.2), after which she disappears (1.3.3–1.4.3).

Following this, Hermas says he received a second vision. Hermas sees the elderly lady again. She gives him a booklet and asks him to copy it and to pass on her message to God's elect. After Hermas has copied it, it is suddenly taken away (2.1.1–4). Later on, Hermas receives a revelation of its meaning: all who truly change (μετανοεῖν, *metanoein*) will be forgiven (2.2.1–2.3.4). Hermas receives another revelation by a handsome young man, who tells him that the elderly woman is the church (2.4.1). Subsequently, he sees a new vision of the elderly lady, who tells him that she wants to add something to the book and that Hermas is to make two copies of it. Hermas is to read his transcript to the presbyters, who are the leaders of the church in Rome, while Clement is to send his copy to the communities outside the city, and Grapte is to use her copy to instruct the widows and orphans (vv. 2–3).

The third vision continues with the same interlocutor. Hermas sees again a vision of the elderly lady; they agree where and when she will reappear to him (3.1.1–3). At the agreed time and place, Hermas sees an ivory couch; he is all alone (vv. 4–5). Then the elderly lady appears, and Hermas asks her to show him the promised vision (3.1.6–3.2.3). She shows him a tower that is being built of various stones and explains it to him as an image of the church and its members (3.2.4–3.8.9; cf. Sim. 9). She commands him (3.8.10–11) to communicate her message (3.9.1–10) to all believers. She then disappears (3.10.1–2). Hermas tells his audience that each time he had seen Woman Church, she seemed to be younger (vv. 3–5). Woman Church appears again in a vision and tells Hermas that every prayer requires humility and that he needs to fast (v. 6). After one day of fasting, Hermas sees a vision of a young man, who explains to him the three stages of the woman's rejuvenation in the sense of the renewal of the church (3.10.7–3.13.4).

There is a change of mode of revelation in the fourth vision. At this point, Hermas hears a (heavenly) voice, which tells him not to be double-minded (4.1.1–4). Hermas sees a cloud of dust and a scary beast (vv. 5–10). Hermas then sees a vision of Woman Church as a bride, who explains to him the beast named Thegri as an image of the coming great affliction (θλῖψις, 4.2.1–4.3.7).

The fifth and final vision in the sequence is in some ways more tightly linked to the commandments that follow than it is to the preceding visions. Here a new figure appears, the Shepherd, who is key throughout the remainder of the work. This Shepherd-Angel tells Hermas that he will recapitulate the visions he saw earlier and will dictate commandments and similitudes to him. The following Mandates and Similitudes are thus presented as Hermas's transcript of the Shepherd's words.

2.2. Mandates

In the first mandate, the Shepherd calls for (monotheistic) faith (πίστις, *pistis*, 1.1–2), fear or reverence (φόβος, *phobos*), and self-control (ἐγκράτεια, *enkrateia*, v. 2). He promises

Hermas that if he keeps this commandment, does away with evil, and puts on every virtue of righteousness, he will live to God (v. 2). A further explanation of this mandate will be offered in Mandates 6–8.

In the second mandate, the Shepherd calls for (above all) simplicity (ἁπλότης, *haplotēs*) and innocence (ἀκακία, *akakia*). He states that one should neither speak evil nor listen to those who speak evil, because by believing in evil speaking one shares in it (2.2–3). He then calls for dignity (σεμνότης, *semnotēs*, v. 4). Hermas is called on to support the needy, without bothering whether the recipient is indeed in need or merely pretends to be so; the one who receives is accountable to God (vv. 4–6). The Shepherd admonishes Hermas to keep this commandment, so that his and his household's change (μετάνοια) will turn out to be simple and innocent (v. 7).

In the third mandate, the Shepherd calls for (above all) truthfulness (ἀλήθεια, *alētheia*). Everyone receives from God a spirit free from lies, since liars are defrauders of the Lord (3.1–2). When Hermas hears this, he starts weeping. The Shepherd asks him why he weeps. Hermas answers that he does not know whether he can be saved, because he has told so many lies (v. 3). The Shepherd replies that Hermas's thought is correct, because as a servant of God he should have walked in truthfulness, without an evil conscience and without sadness (v. 4). Hermas should keep these words, so that his former lies in his business affairs become trustworthy. Everyone who keeps this commandment and abstains from lying will live to God (v. 5).

In the fourth mandate, the Shepherd calls for chastity (ἁγνεία, *hagneia*, 4.1.1–3; 4.3.2; 4.4.3–4). At this point, he explains to Hermas rules concerning marriage and divorce, which are said to apply to both husband and wife (4.1.8, 10). Divorce in case of (known) adultery or other filthy things is required (vv. 4–6, 9); (direct) remarriage is not allowed, because one is to give one's partner *one* chance to change. If the partner repents, then one is to take him or her back (vv. 6–10). It is emphasized that this is not an excuse to sin but an exhortation to sin no more (v. 11). The Shepherd explains to Hermas that "change" (μετάνοια) is "understanding" (σύνεσις, *synesis*, 4.2). He then explains that baptism brings forgiveness (ἄφεσις, *aphesis*) of one's previous sins and that those who have already been baptized have (only) *one* chance to change (μετάνοια, 4.3). Finally, the Shepherd says that remarriage after the death of one's partner is allowed, but that it is better to remain single (4.4.1–2).

In the fifth mandate, the Shepherd calls for patience (μακροθυμία, *makrothymia*) and warns against quick temper (ὀξυχολία, *oxycholia*). When Hermas is patient, the Holy Spirit that dwells in him will be pure, not obscured by an evil spirit (5.1.1–2). But when quick temper enters, the Holy Spirit will try to flee from the impure place, because it is vexed by the evil spirit. The Lord lives in patience; the devil in quick temper (vv. 3–4). The Shepherd clarifies this with a simile: just as a little bit of wormwood spoils a whole jar of honey, quick temper defiles patience in such a way that one's intercession is useless to God (vv. 5–6). Hermas asks the Shepherd to explain to him the working of quick temper, so that he can be on his guard against it. The Shepherd replies that Hermas, his household, and all should keep away from it (v. 7) and then explains its working and how it leads God's servants who are not full of faith and are double-minded astray from righteousness (5.2). The Holy Spirit does not want to be in a vessel with evil spirits and therefore leaves such a person (vv. 5–7). If Hermas masters this commandment, he will also be able to keep the Shepherd's next commandments; this applies not only to Hermas, but to everyone (v. 8).

In the sixth to the eighth mandate, the Shepherd gives Hermas a further explanation of Mandates 1. In Mandates 6, he first states that there are two kinds of faith, fear, and self-control (6.1.1) and clarifies this with a Two Ways paraenesis (vv. 2–5). He then explains to

Hermas that there are two kinds of faith: one should believe what is righteous, but not what is evil. There are two angels with every person: one of righteousness and one of evil (6.2). In Mandates 7, the Shepherd explains to Hermas that fear works in two ways: one should fear the Lord, but not the devil. Finally, in Mandates 8 the Shepherd explains to Hermas that self-control, too, has two aspects: one should refrain from evil, but not from good things.

In the ninth mandate, the Shepherd exhorts Hermas and the readers and hearers to do away with double-mindedness (διψυχία, *dipsychia*). One should ask the Lord God without doubting. If one does so, one will receive what one asks for, but if one doubts, one will not obtain anything (9.1–8). If one does not receive what one asks for right away, this may be due to some temptation or transgression (v. 7). Double-mindedness even uproots those who are very faithful and strong, because it is the daughter of the devil (v. 9). Therefore, Hermas and all other believers should keep away from double-mindedness, which is an earthly spirit from the devil, and put on faith, which is from above, from the Lord (vv. 10–12).

In the tenth mandate, the Shepherd tells Hermas and the readers and hearers to do away with sadness (λύπη, *lypē*) and to put on joyfulness (ἱλαρότης, *hilarotēs*). When the Shepherd says that sadness is a sister of double-mindedness and quick temper (10.1.1), Hermas responds that he does not understand this, to which the Shepherd replies that sadness is more evil than all other spirits, wipes out the Holy Spirit, and again saves us (vv. 2–3). Hermas asks for an explanation (v. 3). The Shepherd first explains, using a simile (v. 5), that only those who fear God, inquire after divinity and truth, and do not occupy themselves with earthly concerns, have full understanding (vv. 4–6). He then explains that both double-mindedness and quick temper sadden the Holy Spirit, but have different effects on the person involved: double-mindedness causes failure, failure sadness (because one did not succeed), and such sadness wipes out the Holy Spirit (10.2.2, 4); quick temper causes bitterness, bitterness sadness (because one acted wickedly), but such sadness makes someone to change his life (μετανοεῖν) and therefore brings salvation (vv. 3–4). In any case, one should avoid sadness, because it may cause the indwelling Holy Spirit to leave (vv. 5–6). Instead, one should put on joyfulness (10.3.1). A sad person always does evil, because that person saddens the Holy Spirit and acts wickedly by not praying or confessing to the Lord. Moreover, the intercession of a sad person has no power to ascend to God's altar (v. 2). The Shepherd explains this to Hermas by using a simile (v. 3). The mandate ends with the familiar promise that Hermas and all believers who keep the commandment will live to God (v. 4).

The eleventh mandate differs from the others, because here the Shepherd shows Hermas a vision. It is a vision of men sitting on a bench and another man sitting on a chair. The Shepherd explains that the group represents believers and the other person a false prophet (ψευδοπροφήτης, *pseudoprophētēs*) who corrupts the double-minded, but not the faithful (11.1–6). He then explains how true and false prophets can be distinguished (vv. 7–14), illustrating this with several similes (vv. 15–21).

In the twelfth and final mandate, the Shepherd explains to Hermas that there are two kinds of desire (ἐπιθυμία, *epithymia*): one should desire good, but not evil things (12.1.1–12.3.1). Having given the twelve commandments, the Shepherd emphasizes that all who endeavor to keep them will be able to do so (12.3.2–12.6.5), which he illustrates (again) with a simile (12.5.3–4).

2.3 Similitudes

At this point in the text there follows a series of ten parables of image-laden comparisons. In the first similitude, the Shepherd tells Hermas a parable, which contrasts the earthly "foreign land" with the heavenly "homeland."

In the second similitude, Hermas sees an *arbustum* (a vineyard where vines grow on elm trees). The Shepherd appears to him and interprets the elm and vine as a symbol for the mutual relation between the rich and poor. This is a call for patronage.

In a vision narrated in the third similitude, the Shepherd shows Hermas trees without leaves (winter trees) and interprets these as a symbol for the indistinguishability of the righteous and sinners in this world.

In the fourth similitude, the Shepherd shows Hermas budding as well as withered trees (summer trees) and interprets these as a symbol for the distinguishability of the righteous and sinners in the world to come.

In the fifth similitude, the Shepherd appears to Hermas and tells him how to fast in the right way (5.1). He then narrates a parable of a vineyard (5.2) and interprets it first with regard to fasting (serving charity, 5.3). When Hermas asks for further explanation (5.4), the Shepherd interprets the parable allegorically (5.5), christologically (5.6), and finally soteriologically (5.7).

In the sixth similitude, the Shepherd appears to Hermas and tells him not to be double-minded about his commandments (6.1.1–4). The Shepherd then shows Hermas a vision of two shepherds and interprets the one as the angel of luxury and deceit, leading his flock to death and destruction, and the other as the angel of punishment, leading his flock to a righteous life (6.1.5–6.5.7).

In the seventh similitude, the Shepherd appears to Hermas and explains to him why he is being afflicted by the angel of punishment. It is because of the sins of his household members, who need to change (μετανοεῖν) and cleanse (καθαρίζειν, *katharizein*) themselves.

In the eighth similitude, the Shepherd shows Hermas a vision of a great willow tree and an angel of the Lord cutting branches from it, giving them to the people gathered in the shade of the tree, and later on collecting them again. The sticks look different, and the people are categorized on the basis of their sticks. Only some groups of people are allowed into the "tower" (8.1.1–8.2.4). The angel instructs the Shepherd to check the sticks of the people carefully and then disappears (8.2.5). The Shepherd and Hermas gather and plant the sticks, and the Shepherd says to Hermas that they will wait to see which of them will revive (vv. 6–9). The Shepherd then explains the vision allegorically (8.3). After a few days, the Shepherd and Hermas return to the place and call the people to pull out their sticks and to present them to them. They categorize the people on the basis of their sticks (8.4–5). The Shepherd then explains to Hermas that the different groups of sticks/people stand for different groups of believers (8.6–10). At the end, the Shepherd commands Hermas to go and tell everyone to change (μετανοεῖν), so that they may live to God (8.11).

In the ninth similitude, the Shepherd appears to Hermas and tells him that he needs to learn more accurately from him what Woman Church had shown him (9.1.1–3). The visions in Similitudes 9 are indeed more or less an elaboration of the vision of the tower in Visions 3. The Shepherd takes Hermas away to Arcadia and shows him a vision in which twelve mountains, each in a different appearance, surround a big plain (Sim. 9.1.4–10). In the middle of the plain, Hermas sees a large white rock with a door, twelve women standing around it (9.2), and six men and a multitude of men who are building, together with the women, a tower on the rock, using different stones (9.3–4). When the building project is paused, Hermas asks the Shepherd for the meaning of all these things, but the Shepherd replies that they will come back later (9.5.1–5). After a few days, the Shepherd and Hermas return to the place, and Hermas sees a vision of a tall man (the lord of the tower, who is the Son of God, cf. 9.12.8), whose height exceeds that of the tower, accompanied by a multitude of people, including those involved in the building project. The man inspects the tower and commands his workers to remove the useless stones from the tower. He orders the Shepherd to clean the stones and put those who fit in with the rest into the tower. He then leaves (9.5.6–9.7.3). The Shepherd explains to Hermas that they will come back to clean the stones and see whether the cleansed stones will fit into the tower (9.7.4–6).

After two days, the Shepherd and Hermas return, and the Shepherd commands Hermas and others to cleanse the tower. Once the tower has been cleansed, it looks like a monolith (9.7.7–9.10.4). Hermas asks the Shepherd to explain to him all the things he had seen, but the Shepherd replies that he will do so later on. He leaves Hermas alone with the women (vv. 5–6). Hermas spends the night with the women as brother and sisters (9.7.7–9.11.7; cf. the opening scene of Hermas). The Shepherd returns and explains to Hermas the things he saw as a symbol of the change (μετάνοια) of the members of the church (9.11.8–9.31.2). The Shepherd exhorts the readers and hearers to change themselves while the tower is still being built (9.31.3–9.32.5). He reassures him that all things written above have been revealed by him (cf. Vis. 5), the angel of change (μετάνοια), and that all who change shall be able to live to God (9.33.1). Finally, the Shepherd explains to Hermas a detail of the vision of the tower, about which Hermas had forgotten to ask (vv. 2–3).

In the tenth and final similitude, the angel (probably Michael, cf. Sim. 8.3.3), who had handed Hermas over to the Shepherd (cf. Vis. 5), appears to Hermas together with the Shepherd (Sim. 10.1.1). The angel tells Hermas to keep the Shepherd's commandments (10.1.2–3) and to pass on the urgent message of change (esp. 10.2.2–3; 10.4.2). The women will stay with Hermas to help him and his household to keep the commandments (10.3.1–3, 5). Hermas is handed over again to the Shepherd (vv. 4–5). The angel addresses himself to the readers and hearers: all should change themselves now, before it is too late; the building of the tower will soon be finished (10.4.4). The angel, the Shepherd, and the women leave, but the angel guarantees Hermas that he (the angel) will send the Shepherd and the women back to his (Hermas's) house (v. 5).

This rich, yet multifaceted text seeks to teach readers many things. However, its overarching theme is a call to change the church (by the personal change [μετάνοια] of its members) in light of the eschaton.

3. INTERPRETATIVE ISSUES

There are numerous interpretative issues surrounding Hermas. This section will discuss two highly controversial issues and the major stands taken on them in the course of the scholarly debate. We are referring to Hermas's call to "change" (μετάνοια) and his views on the resurrection of Jesus and that of the believers in life after death.

3.1 Hermas's Call to "Change" (Μετάνοια)

The key theme of Hermas is the perfection of the church—that is, the process of making the church perfect. In this connection, the terms for "change" (μετάνοια; μετανοεῖν; and derivatives) play a central part; it is used more than 150 times. The meaning of this concept and the reason why it is highlighted belong to the most debated scholarly issues of the work.

One question concerns the meaning of μετάνοια in Hermas. A major issue here is whether it involves ritualized or institutionalized forms of "penitence." This is partly due to the Latin rendering *paenitentia* (e.g., in the parts of Hermas that have only come down to us in Latin). Moreover, in several passages, μετάνοια relates to "torturing" (βασανίσαι, *basanisai*), "humbling" (ταπεινοφρονῆσαι, *tapeinophronēsai*), and "distressing" (θλιβῆναι, *thlibēnai*) one's "soul" (ψυχή, *psychē*; esp. Mand. 4.2.2; Sim. 7.4). One position is that institutionalized forms of penitence are meant.[9] Another position is that it concerns penitential acts like fasting (e.g., Vis. 3.10.6).[10] A third position is that a change of one's inner attitude is implied.[11] An elaborate and quite appropriate definition of μετάνοια in Hermas published decades ago in French remained largely unnoticed.[12] Recently, an attempt has been made to retain an adapted version of this definition, concluding that μετάνοια means one's personal transformation (see, e.g., Vis. 3.13.4; Mand. 4.2.2; Sim. 9.14.3) in the sense of a change of attitude, behavior, feeling, heart, soul, and mind, aiming at moral renewal by regretting one's old self and beginning a new life.[13] A ritual or institutional aspect cannot be ascertained.

Another question is what the author is reacting to. One position is that he polemicizes against more rigorous views on the subject (cf., e.g., Heb 6:4–6; 10:26; 12:17).[14] Another position is that the author is, in fact, a rigorist himself who stresses that baptized believers have *only one* other chance.[15] A third position brings in the idea of a double message with pastoral concerns;[16] the author warns the unbaptized that they have only one chance to change their life and to receive forgiveness, after which they should sin no more (esp. Mand. 4.3.2), and he assures baptized believers who have sinned that they do have another chance, but not more than one (v. 6), after which they must not sin anymore (v. 7). Taking into account Mandates 4.3, this last position seems to be the most plausible one. Here it is said that baptized believers who have sinned have "one chance to change" (μίαν μετάνοιαν, *mian metanoian*, v. 6). It is emphasized that this is not an "excuse" (ἀφορμή, *aphormē*) for those who want to be baptized: they do not have "[μετάνοια] of sins," but "[ἄφεσις] of their previous sins" (v. 3; cf. v. 1). For the author, the problem is that there are baptized believers who sin. Overall, the work portrays the church as a mixed community. Its objective, articulated in its call to μετάνοια, is to improve the church in view of the eschaton.[17]

3.2 Hermas's Understanding of Resurrection

Christology is clearly not something that interests the author much, but the question whether he reckons with Jesus's resurrection is hotly debated. As Jesus's resurrection is

9. See, e.g., K. Rahner, "The Penitential Teaching of the Shepherd of Hermas," in *Theological Investigations* 15 (1982): 57–113, 108: "intervention by the Church in the penance of a sinner."

10. See, e.g., M. Dibelius, *Der Hirt des Hermas*, HNT Ergänzungsband: Die Apostolischen Väter 4 (Tübingen: Mohr Siebeck, 1923), 510–13; R. Joly, *Hermas: Le Pasteur*, SC 53 (Paris: Cerf, 1958), 22–30; N. Brox, *Der Hirt des Hermas*, KAV 7 (Göttingen: Vandenhoeck & Ruprecht, 1991), 209, 476–85; and C. Osiek, *Shepherd of Hermas: A Commentary*, Hermeneia (Minneapolis: Augsburg Fortress, 1999), 114, 192.

11. See esp. W. C. van Unnik, "Zur Bedeutung von Ταπεινοῦν τὴν ψυχήν bei den Apostolischen Vätern," in *ZNW* 44 (1952–1953): 250–55, who argues that the passages just mentioned refer to one's inner self.

12. See J. Paramelle and P. Adnès, "Hermas," in *Dictionnaire de spiritualité, ascétique et mystique, doctrine et histoire*, vol. 7.1 (Paris: Beauchesne, 1969), 316–34, 328, unfortunately with hardly any references to the text of Herm.

13. See Grundeken, *Community Building in the Shepherd of Hermas*, 140.

14. See, e.g., I. Goldhahn-Müller, *Die Grenze der Gemeinde: Studien zum Problem der Zweiten Buße im Neuen Testament unter Berücksichtigung der Entwicklung im 2. Jh. bis Tertullian*, GTA 39 (Göttingen: Vandenhoeck & Ruprecht, 1989), 286; A. Schneider, *"Propter sanctam ecclesiam suam": Die Kirche als Geschöpf, Frau und Bau im Bußunterricht des Pastor Hermae*, SEAug 67 (Rome: Institutum Patristicum Augustinianum, 1999), 73–74; and V. Blomkvist, "The Teaching on Baptism in the Shepherd of Hermas," in *Ablution, Initiation, and Baptism: Late Antiquity, Early Judaism, and Early Christianity = Waschungen, Initiation und Taufe: Spätantike, Frühes Judentum und Frühes Christentum*, ed. D. Hellholm, T. Vegge, Ø. Norderval, and C. Hellholm, 3 vols., BZNW 176.1–3 (Berlin: de Gruyter, 2011), 2:849–70, see 867.

15. See, e.g., Brox, *Hirt des Hermas*, 479.

16. See, e.g., B. Poschmann, *Paenitentia secunda: Die kirchliche Buße im ältesten Christentum bis Cyprian und Origenes: Eine dogmengeschichtliche Untersuchung*, Theophaneia 1 (Bonn: Hanstein, 1940), 165–66.

17. See, e.g., Grundeken, *Community Building in the Shepherd of Hermas*, 128–40.

widely considered the basis of any early Christian teaching, it is often assumed that Jesus's resurrection must be thought to be implied in the theology of Hermas. The problem, however, is that resurrection terminology is absent, even where one would expect it to occur. The key passage is Similitudes 5.6–7.[18] Here it is stated that "God made the preexistent Holy Spirit [. . .] to dwell in the flesh that he chose" (Sim. 5.6.5). The "flesh" (σάρξ, *sarx*) refers to Jesus as a human being with an earthly life (vv. 5–6), despite the fact that the name "Jesus" and the title "Christ" do not occur in Hermas. As a reaction to his exemplary conduct (vv. 5–7), God chose him as "partner" (κοινωνός, *koinōnos*) of the Holy Spirit (v. 6) and gave him "some dwelling place" (τόπον τινὰ κατασκηνώσεως, *topon tina kataskēnōseōs*, v. 7), lest he would "lose the reward for [his] service" (v. 7). It is added that all flesh in which the Holy Spirit dwells and that is found uncorrupted will receive a reward (v. 7). It is concluded that if Hermas lives an irreproachable life (5.7.1–2, 4), his flesh, which is not to be regarded as "perishable" (φθαρτή, *phthartē*, v. 2), will be justified by God (v. 1), so that he will be saved (v. 3) and live to God (v. 4).

Interpretations of this passage vary and remain intrinsically inconsistent. One position is that resurrection is implied.[19] The problem with this view is that the passage uses no resurrection terminology.[20] Another position is that an angelic afterlife is envisioned.[21] There are two problems with this idea. First, any trace of angel Christology is lacking in Hermas. The great and glorious angel (see esp. Vis. 5.2; Mand. 5.1.7; Sim. 5.4.4; 7.1, 3; 8.1.2; 9.1.3) is not (directly or indirectly) identified as Jesus,[22] but as Michael (Sim. 8.3.3). The author differentiates the Son of God from the angels (cf., e.g., Sim. 5.6.2, 4, 7; 9.6.1; 9.7.1; 9.12.6–8). Second, the references to some kind of fellowship with the angels (Vis. 2.2.7; Sim. 9.24.4; 9.25.2; 9.27.3) do not imply that the dead become angels,[23] but that they are in some way accompanied by angels.[24] In fact, Rhoda, who says to Hermas "from heaven" (ἐκ τοῦ οὐρανοῦ, *ek tou ouranou*, Vis. 1.1.4) that she has been "taken up" (ἀνελήμφθην, *anelēmphthēn*, v. 5), is not depicted as an angelic figure (Vis. 1.1.3–9). A third position postulates an ascension of the soul to heaven.[25] But body-soul dualism does not occur in Hermas.[26] and it is not the immortality of the soul but of the flesh that is spoken of. A fourth position argues that a not further specified immortality[27] or a form of continued

18. P. Henne, *La christologie chez Clément de Rome et dans le Pasteur d'Hermas*, Paradosis 33 (Fribourg: Éditions Universitaires, 1992), 172–83, and B. G. Bucur, "The Son of God and the Angelomorphic Holy Spirit: A Rereading of the Shepherd's Christology," *ZNW* 98 (2007): 120–42, 135–38, reject a christological reading of Sim. 5.6.4–8. Note, however, its cross-references to the parable of the vineyard in 5.2 and to its explanation in 5.5.

19. See, e.g., Joly, *Hermas*, 241n3; T. H. C. van Eijk, *La résurrection des morts chez les Pères apostoliques*, ThH 25 (Paris: Beauchesne, 1974), 87, 93–95; C. E. Hill, *Regnum Caelorum: Patterns of Future Hope in Early Christianity*, OECS (Oxford: Clarendon, 1992), 82; Osiek, *Shepherd of Hermas*, 181; and C. Setzer, *Resurrection of the Body in Early Judaism and Early Christianity: Doctrine, Community, and Self-Definition* (Leiden: Brill, 2004), 74.

20. With, e.g., Brox, *Hirt des Hermas*, 509n10.

21. Cf., e.g., H. Moxnes, "God and His Angel in the Shepherd of Hermas," *Studia Theologica* 28 (1974): 49–56, who sees God's Son in Hermas as the "Angel of the Lord."

22. *Pace* Dibelius, *Hirt des Hermas*, 575–76, and E. Muller, "A Distinctive Feature of Early Roman Angelomorphic Christology," in *Ascetica, Liturgica, Orientalia, Critica et Philologica, First Two Centuries*, ed. J. Baun et al., Studia Patristica 45 (Leuven: Peeters, 2010), 285–86.

23. *Pace* K. Lake, *The Apostolic Fathers*, vol. 2, LCL 25 (repr., Cambridge: Harvard University Press, 1976), 21n2, 315n1.

24. See, e.g., Hill, *Regnum Caelorum*, 87; Osiek, *Shepherd of Hermas*, 55, 248–50.

25. See, e.g., L. Pernveden, *The Concept of the Church in the Shepherd of Hermas*, Studia Theologica Lundensia 27 (Lund: Gleerup, 1966), 273.

26. See, e.g., Brox, *Hirt des Hermas*, 326.

27. See esp. K. Lake, *Landmarks in the History of Early Christianity* (London: Macmillan, 1920), 111.

existence[28] is meant. This idea stays closest to the language and imagery of Hermas and is therefore to be preferred. This interpretation of Similitudes 5.6–7 has major christological and soteriological consequences: Jesus is not the risen one but God's adopted and exalted Son, and true (renewed) believers will be granted eternal life. How the adoptionist Christology (Sim. 5.6.6–7) fits in with the implied preexistence of the Son of God (Sim. 9.12.2) remains unclear.[29] A humiliation-exaltation Christology is not implied (cf. Sim. 5.6.1 with Phil 2:6–11).

4. KEY PASSAGES FOR NEW TESTAMENT STUDIES AND THEIR SIGNIFICANCE

Hermas contains no quotations from and no unequivocal allusions to New Testament passages. There is just one quotation from an Old Testament pseudepigraphal book, Eldad and Modad (Vis. 2.3.4). In the following overview, some passages relevant for the study of traditions and writings transmitted in the New Testament are listed thematically. The list of passages mentioned here is not exhaustive.

4.1 Apocalypticism

Hermas presents his work at several points as a written revelation with a heavenly origin (esp. Vis. 1.2.2; 2.1.3–4; 2.2.1–2.3.4; 2.4; 5.5–7; Sim. 9.1.1; 10.1.1), as does the author of Revelation (esp. Rev 1:9–20; 2:1, 8, 12, 18; 3:1, 7, 14). Raptures as that of Hermas in Visions 1.1.3, 2.1.1, and Similitudes 9.1.4 are familiar in revelatory literature (cf., e.g., Luke 4:5, 9 par.; 2 Cor 12:2; Rev 17:3; 21:10). Changes of appearance as those of Woman Church (esp. Vis. 3.10–13) and the Shepherd (esp. Vis. 5.4; Mand. 12.4.1) parallel Jesus's transfiguration in Mark 9:2 and parallels, but only distantly. The (heavenly) "sound of a voice" (ἦχος φωνῆς, *ēchos phōnēs*) answering Hermas in Visions 4.1.4 sounds familiar (cf., e.g., Mark 1:11 parr.; John 12:28; Rev 6:6; 19:1; 21:3). In the description of the vision of the monster Thegri (Vis. 4.1.6), the image which combines a cloud of dust (κονιορτός, *koniortos*), darkness ("the sun shines out a little," μικρὸν ἐξέλαμψεν ὁ ἥλιος, *mikron exelampsen ho hēlios*), and locusts (ἀκρίδες, *akrides*), evokes Revelation 9:2–3 (καπνός, *kapnos*, "smoke"; ἐσκοτώθη ὁ ἥλιος, *eskotōthē ho hēlios*, "the sun was darkened"; ἀκρίδες, *akrides*, "locusts"). The use of θυσιαστήριον, *thysiastērion*, in Mandates 10.3.2–3 (cf. Sim. 8.2.5) for the heavenly altar is a further point of agreement between Hermas and Revelation (cf., e.g., Rev 6:9; 8:3, 5; 9:13; 14:18; 16:7).

4.2 Baptism

In Hermas, baptism is regarded as the initiation rite that leads to incorporation into the church (esp. Sim. 9.31.1, where the "seal," *sigillum*, refers to baptism). The concept resembles that in, for instance, 1 Corinthans 12:13 ("we were all baptized into one body," εἰς ἓν σῶμα ἐβαπτίσθημεν, *eis hen sōma ebaptisthēmen*), but the terminology differs. The reference in Visions 3.7.3 to those who heard the word and wanted to be baptized in the name of the Lord (presumably Jesus, see esp. Sim. 9.12.4–5, 8; 9.13.2–3, 7; 9.16.3–4; cf., e.g., Acts 2:38; 10:48; 19:5) reminds us of several New Testament passages about catechumens (cf., e.g., Mark 4:14–20 parr.; Acts 2:37–38; 10:44–48; 19:5). The baptismal statement in Visions 3.3.5 that "your life was saved [ἐσώθη, *esōthē*] and will be saved [σωθήσεται, *sōthēsetai*] through water [διὰ ὕδατος, *dia hydatos*]" calls to mind 1 Peter 3:20–21 (cf. esp.

28. See esp. Grundeken, *Community Building in the Shepherd of Hermas*, 63–68.

29. Cf., e.g., J. C. Wilson, *Toward a Reassessment of the Shepherd of Hermas: Its Date and Its Pneumatology* (Lewiston, NY: Mellen, 1993), 132–34, who tries to reconcile the christological inconsistencies.

διεσώθησαν δι᾽ ὕδατος . . . σῴζει βάπτισμα, *diesōthēsan di hydatos . . . sōzei baptisma*, "were saved through water . . . baptism saves"). The connection made in Mandates 4.3.6 (cf. v. 1) between calling (κλῆσις, *klēsis*) and baptism is analogous to that in Ephesians 4:1, 4–5. The way in which Similitudes 9.16 speaks of death and life in relation to baptism resembles that in Romans 6:1–11. Yet, unlike Paul, Hermas does not use this language to describe the process of being baptized into Jesus Christ's death associated with the belief that one will live to God, but to contrast the pre-baptismal with the post-baptismal state. The description (in Sim. 9.16) of how deceased Christian preachers convert and baptize deceased pre-Christian righteous ones, parallels the motif of the *descensus ad inferos* ("descent into hell"; cf. Christ's role in esp. 1 Pet 3:19–21; 4:6) and in some way also the notion of baptism for the deceased mentioned by Paul (1 Cor 15:29).

4.3 Christology

In Hermas, the name "Jesus" and the title "Christ" do not occur, perhaps because the author wants to emphasize that Jesus is the *Son of God*, God's adopted and exalted *Son*. However, he does mention many other familiar christological designations and images. For instance (ordered on the basis of first occurrence): "Son (of God)" (Vis. 2.2.8, etc.; cf., e.g., Mark 12:6–7 parr.; Rom 1:3–4); "Lord" (Vis. 3.7.3, etc.; cf., e.g., Acts 10:36; Rom 1:3; 10:9; 1 Cor 12:3; Phil 2:11); "slave" (esp. Sim. 5.5.2; cf., e.g., Phil 2:7); mediator of God's law or commandments (esp. Sim. 5.5.3; 5.6.3; cf., e.g., John 10:18); the one who cleansed the people's sins (esp. Sim. 5.6.2–3; cf., e.g., Eph 5:26; Titus 2:14; Heb 1:3); God's heir (esp. Sim. 5.6.4; cf., e.g., Mark 12:7 parr.; Heb 1:2); the one who was indwelt by God's Holy Spirit (esp. Sim. 5.6.5–6; cf., e.g., Mark 1:10; 15:37; Luke 4:1; Acts 2:33); God's chosen one (esp. Sim. 5.6.5; cf., e.g., 1 Pet 2:4, 6); the one who was rewarded by God (esp. Sim. 5.6.5–7; cf., e.g., Phil 2:8–9) for being trustworthy (πιστός, *pistos*, Sim. 5.2.2; cf., e.g., Heb 2:17; 3:2, 6; Rev 1:5; 3:14; 19:11) and undefiled (ἀμίαντος, *amiantos*; cf., e.g., Heb 7:26); God's adopted Son (esp. Sim. 5.6.6; cf., e.g., Rom 1:3–4); the one who was exalted (esp. Sim. 5.6.7; cf., e.g., Phil 2:9; Acts 2:33; 3:13; Heb 8:1–2); the one whose sudden arrival is expected (esp. Sim. 9.7.6; cf., e.g., 1 Thess 5:2; 2 Pet 3:10; Rev 3:3); the "rock" (πέτρα, *petra*, esp. Sim. 9.12.1; cf. esp. 1 Cor 10:4; cf. also Rom 9:33; 1 Pet 2:8) that sustains as fundament the church (θεμέλιος, *themelios*, esp. Sim. 9.4.2; cf. 9.3.1; 9.14.4–6; cf. esp. 1 Cor 3:11) and the whole cosmos/creation (Sim. 9.2.1; 9.14.5; cf. esp. Heb 1:3); the "gate" (πύλη, *pylē*, esp. Sim. 9.12.1, 6; cf. esp. 1 Clem. 48.2–4; cf. θύρα, *thyra*, in John 10:7, 9), through which those who are to be saved will enter into the kingdom of God (Sim. 9.12.3) and which is the only "entrance" (εἴσοδος, *eisodos*) to God (v. 6; cf. προσαγωγή, *prosagōgē*, in Eph 2:18); and the preexistent one (esp. Sim. 9.12.2; cf., e.g., Col 1:15, 17; Rev 3:14).

4.4 Church "Offices"

Almost all titles used in Hermas for those who serve the community are found in (among others) the Pauline Letters, often in similar constellations (ordered alphabetically on the basis of the Greek terms): "apostles" (ἀπόστολοι, *apostoloi*, Vis. 3.5.1; Sim. 9.15.4; 9.16.5; 9.17.1; 9.25.2; cf., e.g., 1 Cor 12:28–29; Gal 1:17, 19); "deacons" (διάκονοι, *diakonoi*, Vis. 3.5.1; Sim. 9.15.4; 9.26.2; cf., e.g., Rom 16:1; Phil 1:1); "teachers" (διδάσκαλοι, *didaskaloi*, Vis. 3.5.1; Sim. 9.15.4; 9.16.5; 9.25.2; cf., e.g., 1 Cor 12:28–29); "overseers" (ἐπίσκοποι, *episkopoi*, Vis. 3.5.1; Sim. 9.27.2; cf., e.g., Phil 1:1); "presbyters" (πρεσβύτεροι, *presbyteroi*, Vis. 2.4.2–3; perhaps 3.1.8; cf., e.g., 1 Tim 5:17; Titus 1:5; cf. the singular in 2 John 1; 3 John 1); "prophets" (προφῆται, *prophētai*, Sim. 9.15.4; cf., e.g., 1 Cor 12:28–29); "presiders" ("presbyters who preside over the church," πρεσβύτεροι οἱ προϊστάμενοι τῆς ἐκκλησίας, *presbyteroi hoi proistamenoi tēs ekklēsias*, Vis. 2.4.3; cf. 1 Tim 5:17, where a similar combination of πρεσβύτεροι, *presbyteroi*, and προΐστημι, *proistēmi*, is used; for προϊστάμενοι, *proistamenoi*, cf., e.g., Rom 12:8; 1 Thess 5:12). An exception is the title "church leaders" (προηγούμενοι τῆς ἐκκλησίας, *proēgoumenoi tēs ekklēsias*, Vis. 2.2.6; 3.9.7), which is, however, used in other, non-Pauline New Testament writings (cf. ἡγούμενοι, *hēgoumenoi*, in Acts 15:22; Heb 13:7, 17, 24).

The author envisions a presbyterial form of church leadership in Rome in his time (see esp. Vis. 2.4.3). Hermas's former matron Rhoda (Vis. 1.1) may have been the hostess of a house-church community, like Mary, the mother of John Mark (Acts 12:12), Lydia (16:14–15, 40), and Nympha (Col 4:15), but this remains uncertain. The remark in Visions 2.4.3 that "Grapte should admonish [νουθετήσει, *nouthetēsei*] the widows and orphans" probably refers to her teaching (because the "admonishment" is supposed to take place on the basis of the booklet given to her by Hermas). Similarly, Titus 2:3–4 hints at instruction by (elderly) women. The (implicit) association of church leadership with shepherding in Similitudes 9.31.6 has tradition-historical connections with several New Testament passages (cf., e.g., Matt 10:5–6; John 21:15–17; Acts 20:28; Eph 4:11), especially with 1 Peter 5:2–4, because of the combination of "(acting as) shepherds" (cf. ποιμένες, *poimenes*, with ποιμάνατε, *poimanate*, in 1 Pet 5:2), "flock" (ποίμνιον, *poimnion*, as in 1 Pet 5:2–3), and "master of the flock" or "chief shepherd" (being above the shepherds; cf. δεσπότης τοῦ ποιμνίου, *despotēs tou poimniou*, in Sim. 9.31.6, with ἀρχιποίμην, *archipoimēn*, in 1 Pet 5:4).

4.5 Ecclesiology

The personification of the church as a woman (esp. Vis. 2.4.1; cf. 1.2.2–4.3.7) is found also in several New Testament writings (cf., e.g., Eph 5:25–33; 1 Pet 5:13; 2 John 1, 5, 13). More in particular, the depiction of the church as a bride in Visions 4.2.1–2 evokes some of the New Testament bridal images of the church (cf. 2 Cor 11:2; Eph 5:25–33). The unusual designation of the Christian assembly as "synagogue" (συναγωγή, *synagōgē*, Mand. 11.9, 13–14) occurs in the New Testament only in two later writings (Heb 10:25; Jas 2:2). The author further designates the church as "the house of God" (ὁ οἶκος τοῦ θεοῦ, *ho oikos tou theou*, Sim. 9.13.9; 9.14.1), as several later New Testament writings do (cf., e.g., 1 Tim 3:15; Heb 3:6; 10:21; 1 Pet 4:17; cf. also, e.g., Eph 2:19). The image of the church (ἐκκλησία, *ekklēsia*, i.e., the tower, which is the church, see esp. Sim. 9.13.1) built on a rock (πέτρα, *petra*, esp. Sim. 9.3.1; 9.4.2; 9.14.4) compares with Matthew 16:18, but in Hermas the rock is the Son of God (see Sim. 9.12.1).

Several appellations used for church members also occur in New Testament writings (ordered alphabetically on the basis of the Greek terms): "the holy ones" (οἱ ἅγιοι, *hoi hagioi*, Vis. 1.1.9, etc.; cf., e.g., Acts 9:13, 32; Rom 1:7; 12:13; 15:25; 1 Cor 1:2; 6:1–2; 2 Cor 1:1; Eph 2:19; 3:8; Phil 1:1; 4:22; Col 1:4; 1 Tim 5:10; Phlm 5, 7; Heb 6:10); "the righteous" (οἱ δίκαιοι, *hoi dikaioi*, Vis. 1.4.2, etc.; cf., e.g., Matt 5:45; 13:43, 49; 25:37, 46; Luke 1:17; 14:14; Acts 24:15; Rom 5:19; 1 Tim 1:9; 1 Pet 3:12; 4:18; Rev 22:11); "the slaves of God" (οἱ δοῦλοι τοῦ θεοῦ, *hoi douloi tou theou*, Vis. 1.2.4, etc.; cf., e.g., 1 Pet 2:16; Rev 1:1; 7:3; 19:5; 22:3, 6); "the elect" (οἱ ἐκλεκτοί, *hoi eklektoi*, Vis. 1.3.4, etc.; cf., e.g., Mark 13:20, 22, 27; Luke 18:7; Rom 8:33; Col 3:12; 2 Tim 2:10; Titus 1:1; 1 Pet 1:1; 2:9; 2 John 13; Rev 17:14).

4.6 Eschatology

In Visions 3.7.2, there is the motif of an eschatological fire as place of punishment for unrepentant apostates and sinners (cf., e.g., Matt 5:22; Mark 9:43, 48; Luke 3:9, 17 par.;

2 Pet 3:7; Jude 7, 23; Rev 14:10; 17:16; 18:8; 19:20; 20:10, 14–15; 21:8). In Similitudes 4.4, this motif interrelates with the image of trees (δένδρα, *dendra*, representing unrepentant sinners and unbelievers) that do not bear fruit (ἄκαρποι, *akarpoi*) and are burnt (κατακαυθήσονται, *katakauthēsontai*), which resembles the imagery used in Matthew 3:10 and 7:19. Besides, the designation of the apostates in Visions 3.7.2 as those who "definitely apostatized [ἀποστάντες, *apostantes*] from the living God [τοῦ θεοῦ τοῦ ζῶντος, *tou theou tou zōntos*]" (cf. Vis. 2.3.2: τὸ μὴ ἀποστῆναί σε ἀπὸ θεοῦ ζῶντος, *to mē apostēnai se apo theou zōntos*) is very similar to Hebrews 3:12 (ἀποστῆναι ἀπὸ θεοῦ ζῶντος, *apostēnai apo theou zōntos*; cf. also the use of καρδία, *kardia*, in both verses). The use of συντέλεια, *synteleia* ("consummation") for the end of the age in Visions 3.8.9 and Similitudes 9.12.3 is familiar also (cf., e.g., Matt 13:39–40, 49; 24:3; 28:20; Heb 9:26). The "coming great tribulation [θλῖψις, *thlipsis*]" (esp. Vis. 4.1.1; 4.2.5; 4.3.6) refers to an impending eschatological event, but its exact meaning remains unclear (cf. Mark 13:19, 24; Rev 7:14).

The idea in Similitudes 1 that for believers the present world is a "foreign land" and their "homeland" the world to come, reminds one of various New Testament passages, such as Philippians 3:20, which states that "our citizenship [πολίτευμα, *politeuma*] is in heaven." Hermas's wording ("your city [πόλις, *polis*] is far away from this city [πόλις]," v. 1; for πόλις, see vv. 1–3, 5–6, 9) differs, but the idea is similar. In 1 Peter, the addressees are called "strangers" (παρεπίδημοι, *parepidēmoi*, 1:1; 2:11) and "aliens" (πάροικοι, *paroikoi*, 2:11) who sojourn in a foreign land (παροικία, *paroikia*, 1:17). According to Hebrews 11:13–16, believers are "foreigners [ξένοι, *xenoi*] and strangers [παρεπίδημοι, *parepidēmoi*] on earth" (v. 13) who "seek a homeland [πατρίδα, *patrida*, v. 14]"—namely, the "heavenly" one (ἐπουρανίου, *epouraniou*, v. 16); God has prepared a πόλις for them (v. 16). And Hebrews 13:14 states: "For we do not have a lasting city [πόλις] here, but are looking for the one that is to come [τὴν μέλλουσαν, *tēn mellousan*]" (for the latter phrase, cf. Sim. 1.1: "your city [πόλις], in which you are going to [μέλλετε, *mellete*] dwell"). In this context, Hermas's message that believers should not focus on earthly matters sounds like that of Colossians 3:2, which admonishes its readers that one should "think of the things above [τὰ ἄνω, *ta anō*], not the things on earth [τὰ ἐπὶ τῆς γῆς, *ta epi tēs gēs*]," though in Hermas the contrast is not between this-worldly and otherworldly things, but between materialism and charity (see esp. v. 8).

4.7 Eucharist or the Lord's Supper

There are striking similarities between Visions 3.9 and Paul's critique on the celebration of the Lord's Supper in 1 Corinthians 11:17–34: Paul blames the Corinthians for "taking" their own meal (προλαμβάνει, *prolambanei*, v. 21) rather than dividing it equally among the participants; Hermas reproaches the haves with their "taking" food for themselves (μεταλαμβάνετε, *metalambanete*, v. 2) rather than sharing it with the have-nots. Paul and Hermas both warn their addressees that their behavior leads to "illness" (cf. ἀσθενεῖς, *astheneis*, in 1 Cor 11:30 with ἀσθένειαν, *astheneian*, in Vis. 3.9.3). Both relate the illness of the community members to (God's) "judgment" (cf. κρίμα, *krima*, in 1 Cor 11:29, 34; ἐκρινόμεθα, *ekrinometha*, in v. 31; and κρινόμενοι, *krinomenoi*, as well as κατακριθῶμεν, *katakrithōmen*, in v. 32, with κρίσις, *krisis*, in Vis. 3.9.5). Both speak of "chastisement" (cf. παιδευόμεθα, *paideuometha*, in 1 Cor 11:32, with παιδεύειν, *paideuein*, παιδείαν, *paideian*, and παιδεύετε, *paideuete*, in Vis. 3.9.10). Finally, both use the unusual combination of μὴ ἔχοντες, *mē echontes*, and πεινάω, *peinaō*, and derivatives (in the NT only in 1 Cor 11:21–22; in Herm. only in Vis. 3.9.3, 5). It does not follow that Hermas knew Paul's letter, but the agreements mentioned show that, when dealing with the same subject matter, both authors can use the same language. Furthermore, there is a tradition-historical connection between the use of πρωτοκαθεδρίται, *prōtokathedritai*, in Visions 3.9.7 (cf. 3.1.8; Mand. 11.12) and πρωτοκαθεδρία, *prōtokathedria*, in the Synoptics (esp. Mark 12:39 par.; cf. Luke 11:43 par.): Hermas criticizes church leaders for their desire to occupy the first seats (for being πρωτοκαθεδρίται), presumably at the (eucharistic) community meals. Similarly, the Synoptics criticize Pharisees and scribes for their desire to have "the first seats [πρωτοκαθεδρίας] in the synagogues and the first seats [πρωτοκλισίας, *prōtoklisias*] at meals."

4.8 Fasting

In the Visions, fasting (νηστεία, *nēsteia*) is (part of) the preparation for receiving a revelation (Vis. 2.2.1; 3.1.2; 3.10.7; cf., e.g., Luke 4:2 par.; Acts 13:2). Accordingly, it is seen as an act of humility (ταπεινοφροσύνη, *tapeinophrosynē*, Vis. 3.10.6), which may shed light on Philippians 4:12 (ταπεινοῦσθαι . . . πεινᾶν, *tapeinousthai . . . peinan*; cf., e.g., Isa 58:3, 5 LXX). In the Similitudes, fasting as merely an act of piety (Sim. 5.1.1–2) is criticized, because what counts is the ethical disposition and behavior of the one who fasts; fasting has to serve social purposes (Sim. 5.1, 3; cf., e.g., Isa 58:1–12; Barn. 3). Again, there is a connection with Philippians 4, as it is stated in Similitudes 5.3.8 (cf. 5.1.3, 5) that with such a fast "your sacrifice [θυσία, *thysia*] will be acceptable [δεκτή, *dektē*] to God" (cf. θυσίαν δεκτήν, *thysian dektēn*, in Phil 4:18). "Dining" on the "words of the Lord" (in prayer), when fasting (Sim. 9.11.8), is a biblical motif also (cf., e.g., Deut 8:3 LXX and its quotation in Matt 4:4). The association of food and God's word(s) or law (Sim. 5.5.3; 9.11.8) also occurs in the New Testament, but differently (cf., e.g., apart from Matt 4:4, John 6:31–58; Rev 10:9–10).

4.9 (Holy) Kiss

It seems that Similitudes 9.11.4 alludes to the "holy kiss," as several early (e.g., Rom 16:16; 1 Cor 16:20; 2 Cor 13:12; 1 Thess 5:26) and later (e.g., 1 Pet 5:14) New Testament writings do. By contrast, the kiss in Similitudes 9.6.2 is a welcoming kiss of honor (cf. the kiss as a greeting, e.g., in Mark 14:45; Luke 7:45; 15:20).

4.10 Marriage

Hermas shares with Paul (esp. 1 Cor 7:1, 8, 27, 38) a preference for celibacy. Both highlight problems like sexual immorality (Mand. 4.1.1, 5; 8.3; cf. 1 Cor 6:18; 7:2; 10:8), adultery (Mand. 4.1.4, 6, 9; 8.3; cf. Rom 2:22; 13:9), and divorce (Mand. 4.1.4–10; cf. 1 Cor 7:10–16). Both allow but do not encourage remarriage after the death of one's partner (Mand. 4.4.1–2; cf. 1 Cor 7:39–40). However, they differ in opinion on several points. According to Hermas, divorce is mandatory if one knows that one's partner has committed adultery and the partner does not change their behavior (Mand. 4.1.4–6, 9). Moreover, reconciliation is mandatory if the adulterous partner mends their ways (vv. 7–8). For this reason, remarriage is not allowed, because one is to give the partner *one* chance to change (vv. 6, 8, 10). Another difference with Paul is that Hermas is one of the earliest Christian witnesses to the practice that later became known as "spiritual marriage," a relationship of two partners abstaining from sexual intercourse (Vis. 2.2.3; Sim. 9.11.3; cf. Vis. 1.1.1). Besides, Mand. 4.1.6, which states, "But if he divorces the woman and marries another, he himself also commits adultery," is very similar to the Synoptic tradition found in Mark 10:11–12 parr. and Matthew 19:9, but literary dependence cannot be proven.

4.11 Parable of the Vineyard

The parable of the vineyard in Similitudes 5.2 depicts the same setting (an ἀμπελών, *ampelōn*) as do several New Testament parables, especially Mark 12:1–12 parr., but differs from its biblical counterparts through its plot and happy ending (cf., e.g., Matt 13:24–30, 36–43; 20:1–16; Mark 13:34; cf. also Luke 12:42–46; 19:12–13, 15–24, 26 par.).

4.12 Pneumatology

The Holy Spirit's indwelling in believers (e.g., Mand. 5.1.2: τὸ πνεῦμα τὸ ἅγιον τὸ κατοικοῦν ἐν σοί, *to pneuma to hagion to katoikoun en soi*; cf., e.g., Mand. 5.2.5; Sim. 5.6.5, 7; 5.7.1) is familiar Pauline language (cf., e.g., Rom 8:9; 1 Cor 3:16; 6:19). The call to "the renewal of your spirits" in Visions 3.8.9 (cf. 3.12.2–3; 3.13.2; Sim. 8.6.3; 9.14.3) resembles exhortations in several New Testament passages (cf., e.g., Rom 12:2; Eph 4:23). Finally, in discussing the topic of the discernment of spirits, Mandates 9.11 distinguishes between what comes "from above" (ἄνωθεν, *anōthen*) and what is "earthly" (ἐπίγειον, *epigeion*) and "from the devil" (παρὰ τοῦ διαβόλου, *para tou diabolou*). A similar distinction is made in James 3:15 (ἄνωθεν, *anōthen*; ἐπίγειος, *epigeios*; and δαιμονιώδης, *daimoniōdēs*). One finds the same distinctions in Mandates 11 (see ἄνωθεν in vv. 5, 8, 20–21; ἐπίγειος in vv. 6, 11–12, 14, 17, 19; διάβολος in vv. 3, 17), with the combination in verse 8 of ἄνωθεν and the uncommon word πραΰς, *praus* ("meek" or "gentle"; cf. πραΰτης, *prautēs*, in Jas 3:13). The passages in Hermas, however, deal with the discernment of spirits, whereas James 3:13–17 treats the way in which wisdom from above should find expression in human behavior.

4.13 Prophecy

Hermas (esp. Mand. 11) is an important witness to the continuing practice of prophecy and to the ongoing search for criteria to discern (true) prophets (προφῆται, *prophētai*) from false prophets (ψευδοπροφῆται, *pseudoprophētai*) in second-century Christian communities (cf., e.g., Matt 7:15–23; Acts 13:6; 16:16; 21:9; 1 Cor 12–14; 2 Pet 2:1; 1 John 4:1–6; Rev 2:20; Did. 11; Justin, *Dial.* 82; Irenaeus, *Haer.* 1.13.3–4). The "humility" of the true prophet (Mand. 11.8) stands in contrast to the "self-importance," for instance, of the magician Simon in Acts 8:9.

4.14 Salvation

The language concerning believers being "inscribed into the books of life" (ἐγγραφήσονται εἰς τὰς βίβλους τῆς ζωῆς, *engraphēsontai eis tas biblous tēs zōēs*, Vis. 1.3.2; cf. ἐγγραφήσῃ, *engraphēsē*, in Mand. 8.6 with, e.g., Luke 10:20; Heb 12:23) is reminiscent of the tradition underlying Revelation 20:15, which speaks of someone not being found "written in the book of life" (ἐν τῇ βίβλῳ τῆς ζωῆς γεγραμμένος, *en tē biblō tēs zōēs gegrammenos*; cf., e.g., Rev 3:5; 13:8; 17:8; 20:12; and Phil 4:3). The expression "to live to God" (ζῆν τῷ θεῷ, *zēn tō theō*), very frequent in Hermas (Mand. 1.2, etc.), resembles certain Pauline phrases (cf., e.g., Rom 6:10–11; Gal 2:19). The warning in Visions 4.2.6, leveled at the disobedient, that "it were better for them not to have been born" (αἱρετώτερον ἦν αὐτοῖς τὸ μὴ γεννηθῆναι, *hairetōteron ēn autois to mē gennēthēnai*) recalls Mark 14:21 parr., but the wording and context differ. The idea expressed in Similitudes 8.9.1 that there is no salvation (cf. σωθῆναι, *sōthēnai*, in v. 4) for believers (πιστοί, *pistoi*) who have faith (πίστις, *pistis*) but "without doing the works of faith" (μὴ ἐργαζόμενοι δὲ τὰ ἔργα τῆς πίστεως, *mē ergazomenoi de ta erga tēs pisteōs*) is strongly reminiscent of James 2:14–26 (πίστις, *pistis*, and ἔργα, *erga*; cf. σῶσαι, *sōsai*, in v. 14). The idiom of "entering" into the kingdom of God (Sim. 9.12.3–5, 8; 9.15.2–3; 9.16.2–4; 9.20.2–3; 9.31.2) is known from the Gospels and Acts (esp. Mark 9:47; 10:15 par.; 10:23–25 parr.; John 3:5; Acts 14:22).

4.15 Sins and Forgiveness

The image of the "healing" (ἴασις, *iasis*, and other terms) of sins (Vis. 1.1.9, etc.) calls to mind several New Testament passages (e.g., Mark 2:16–17; Jas 5:16; 1 Pet 2:24), but is attested in pagan literature as well (e.g., Arrian, *Anab.* 7.29.2, ἴασις ἁμαρτίας, *iasis hamartias*); consequently, it cannot be traced back to biblical tradition with certainty (cf., e.g., Deut 30:3 LXX). Hermas takes his own stance between those who hold that there is forgiveness of sins after baptism (cf., e.g., 1 John 1:6–2:2, esp. v. 9) and those who think that there is not (cf., e.g., Heb 6:4–6; 10:26; 12:17, where the possibility of a second μετάνοια, *metanoia*, is denied). On the one hand, he warns new and future believers by telling them that they "have no change [μετάνοια] of sins, but have obtained forgiveness [ἄφεσις, *aphesis*] of their previous sins" (Mand. 4.3.3; see also v. 1; cf., e.g., Mark 1:4; Acts 2:38); on the other hand, he reassures baptized believers who have sinned that they do have another chance of change, but not more than one (μίαν μετάνοιαν, *mian metanoian*, v. 6; cf. esp. Vis. 2.2.4–5). According to Similitudes 6.2.3–4 (cf. 8.6.2–4), blasphemy (βλασφημία, *blasphēmia*) against the name of the Lord is a deadly, unforgivable sin (cf. 1 John 5:16–17), for which there is no chance of μετάνοια. This resembles the remark in Mark 3:28–29 parr. that blaspheming (βλασφημήσῃ, *blasphēmēsē*) against the Holy Spirit is an eternal sin for which there is no forgiveness (ἄφεσις).

4.16 Suffering

Violence against Christians is mentioned both in Hermas and several writings of the New Testament. Visions 3.2.1, for instance, speaks of believers who have endured "whips" (μάστιγας, *mastigas*; cf., e.g., Matt 10:17; 23:34; Acts 22:24–25), "prisons" (φυλακάς, *phylakas*; cf., e.g., Luke 21:12; 22:33; Acts 5:19, 22, 25; 8:3; 12:4–6, 10, 17; 16:23–24, 27, 37, 40; 22:4; 26:10; 2 Cor 11:23; Rev 2:10), "severe torments" (θλίψεις, *thlipseis*; cf., e.g., Matt 24:9; Mark 4:17; Acts 11:19; 20:23; 2 Thess 1:4, 6; Rev 2:10), "crosses" (σταυρούς, *staurous*; cf., e.g., Matt 23:34; Mark 8:34 parr.; Luke 14:27 par.), and "wild animals" (θηρία, *thēria*; cf. 1 Clem. 6.2). The word θλῖψις and others refer several times to affliction or violence menacing believers, who as a result may be tempted to apostatize (see, e.g., Vis. 2.2.7–8; 2.3.4; 3.2.1 [cf. 3.1.9]; 3.6.5; Sim. 8.3.7; 9.21.3). The same themes occur in various New Testament writings (cf., e.g., Matt 24:9–10; Mark 4:17; Acts 14:22; Eph 3:13; 1 Thess 3:3–4; 2 Thess 1:4–6; Rev 2:10). Visions 4.3.4 offers the image of (suffering) believers being "tested" (δοκιμάζεσθε, *dokimazesthe*) as "gold is tested by fire" (τὸ χρυσίον δοκιμάζεται διὰ τοῦ πυρός, *to chrysion dokimazetai dia tou pyros*). A pendant of this image occurs in 1 Peter 1:7 (χρυσίου [...] διὰ πυρὸς δὲ δοκιμαζομένου, *chrysiou* [...] *dia pyros de dokimazomenou*; cf. further, e.g., 1 Cor 3:12–15; Rev 3:18). Similitudes 8.3.6 speaks of "those who have suffered for the law" (οἱ ὑπὲρ τοῦ νόμου παθόντες, *hoi hyper tou nomou pathontes*) as those who "have fought with the devil [μετὰ τοῦ διαβόλου, *meta tou diabolou*] and conquered him," and "have been crowned" (ἐστεφανωμένοι, *estephanōmenoi*). Similar imagery occurs in Revelation 2:10 (see esp. the combination of πάσχειν, *paschein*, διάβολος, *diabolos*, and στέφανον, *stephanon*; cf. also Jas 1:12). The phrase "they have suffered [ἔπαθον, *epathon*] for the name [διὰ τὸ ὄνομα, *dia to onoma*] of the Son of God" in Similitudes 9.28.3 (cf., e.g., Vis. 3.1.9; 3.5.2; Sim. 9.28.5–6) bears likeness to, among others, 1 Peter 4:12–19 (see esp. παθήμασιν, *pathēmasin*, in v. 13, πάσχω, *paschō*, and derivatives, in vv. 15, 19, and ἐν ὀνόματι Χριστοῦ, *en onomati Christou*, in v. 14). The language in Similitudes 9.28.4 concerning believers "being brought under authority" (ἐπ᾽ ἐξουσίαν ἀχθέντες, *exousian achthentes*) for interrogation has several features in common with Luke 12:11: "When they bring you [εἰσφέρωσιν, *eispherōsin*] [...] before the authorities (ἐπὶ [...] τὰς ἐξουσίας, *epi*

[. . .] *tas exousias*]." For those who did not stand the test, Similitudes 8.6.4 uses the phrase "they [i.e., apostates, betrayers, and blasphemers (βλασφημήσαντες, *blasphēmēsantes*)] were ashamed of the name of the Lord that was called over them" (ἐπαισχυνθέντες τὸ ὄνομα τοῦ κυρίου τὸ ἐπικληθὲν ἐπ' αὐτούς, *epaischynthentes to onoma tou kyriou to epiklēthen ep autous*). The phraseology has several elements in common with that of James 2:7 (see esp. βλασφημοῦσιν, *blasphēmousin*, ὄνομα, *onoma*, and τὸ ἐπικληθὲν ἐφ' ὑμᾶς, *to epiklēthen eph hymas*), but the contents are different.

4.17 Theology

God is called the Creator of all (e.g., Vis. 1.1.6; 1.3.4; Mand. 1.1; Sim. 5.5.2; 7.4; cf., e.g., Eph 3:9; Rev 4:11). Visions 1.1.6 says that God "created the things that are from what is not" (κτίσας ἐκ τοῦ μὴ ὄντος τὰ ὄντα, *ktisas ek tou mē ontos ta onta*) just like Romans 4:17 (God καλοῦντος τὰ μὴ ὄντα ὡς ὄντα, *kalountos ta mē onta hōs onta*). This seems to refer to the idea of a creation out of nothing (without articulating this doctrine explicitly). God is also called the "Great King" (Vis. 3.9.8; cf. Matt 5:35). He is the one to rely on: the phrase "you have thrown your sorrow upon God" (τὴν μέριμνάν σου ἐπὶ τὸν θεὸν ἐπέριψας, *tēn merimnan sou epi ton theon eperipsas*) in Visions 4.2.4 (cf. v. 5 and 3.11.3) has much in common with 1 Peter 5:7 (πᾶσαν τὴν μέριμναν ὑμῶν ἐπιρίψαντες ἐπ' αὐτόν, *pasan tēn merimnan hymōn epiripsantes ep auton*; cf. Ps 54:23 LXX). Furthermore, God (the Lord) is called "knower of the heart" (καρδιογνώστης, *kardiognōstēs*, Mand. 4.3.4), an unusual expression that occurs in Greek literature for the first time in Christian writings (cf. Acts 1:24; 15:8; cf. also, e.g., Luke 16:15). The imperative in Mandates 12.6.3, "fear [φοβήθητε, *phobēthēte*] the Lord who can do everything [τὸν πάντα δυνάμενον, *ton panta dynamenon*; cf., e.g., Mark 10:27; 14:36], save and destroy [σῶσαι καὶ ἀπολέσαι, *sōsai kai apolesai*]," telescopes elements from Matthew 10:28 (φοβεῖσθε, *phobeisthe*, τὸν δυνάμενον, *ton dynamenon*, and ἀπολέσαι, *apolesai*) and James 4:12 (ὁ δυνάμενος σῶσαι καὶ ἀπολέσαι, *ho dynamenos sōsai kai apolesai*; cf. Sim. 9.23.4). The words in which Hermas says that God "wants all to live" (θέλει πάντας ζῆν, *thelei pantas zēn*, Sim. 8.2.9) are related to those used in 1 Timothy 2:4. Similitudes 9.23.4 has: if God does not bear grudges (μνησικακεῖ, *mnēsikakei*) against repentant sinners, how could man bear grudges (μνησικακεῖ, *mnēsikakei*) against man, "as if he were able to destroy and to save him [ὡς δυνάμενος ἀπολέσαι ἢ σῶσαι αὐτόν, *hōs dynamenos apolesai ē sōsai auton*]." This argument *a maiore ad minus* shares certain elements with the parable of Matthew 18:23–35 (the unforgiving servant) and the words of James 4:12 (cf. esp. ὁ δυνάμενος σῶσαι καὶ ἀπολέσαι, *ho dynamenos sōsai kai apolesai*).

4.18 Two Ways

The Two Ways paraenetic teaching in Mandates 6.1.2–5 (cf. Vis. 3.2.9; 3.7.1; Sim. 8.9.1) parallels that of Matthew 7:13–14, but a striking difference is that in Hermas the right way is the easier and the wrong way the harder one. On this point, Hermas agrees with Barnabas 20.1. Visions 3.7.1 mentions believers who "leave their true road [τὴν ὁδὸν [. . .] τὴν ἀληθινήν, *tēn hodon* [. . .] *tēn alēthinēn*]," because they "think it is possible to find a better road [βελτίονα ὁδόν, *beltiona hodon*] but go astray [πλανῶνται, *planōntai*] and struggle, while wandering on the roads that are no roads [ἐν ταῖς ἀνοδίαις, *en tais anodiais*]." All this reminds one of several New Testament passages: 2 Peter 2:2, for instance, warns the addressees of false teachers, through whom "the way of truth [ἡ ὁδὸς τῆς ἀληθείας, *hē hodos tēs alētheias*] will be blasphemed"; verse 15 speaks of those who, "leaving (the) straight road [εὐθεῖαν ὁδόν, *eutheian hodon*], have gone astray [ἐπλανήθησαν, *eplanēthēsan*], following the road [τῇ ὁδῷ, *tē hodō*] of Balaam son of Beor"; and James 5:19–20 uses such phrases as "if someone among you would err from the truth [πλανηθῇ ἀπὸ (v.l. τῆς ὁδοῦ) τῆς ἀληθείας, *planēthē apo* (v.l. *tēs hodou*) *tēs alētheias*]" and "the one who turns a sinner back from his wrong way [ἐκ πλάνης ὁδοῦ αὐτοῦ, *ek planēs hodou autou*]." The use of "road" (ὁδός) for the Christian "way" recurs in Acts (see, e.g., 19:9, 23; 22:4; 24:14; cf., e.g., John 14:6). The contrast in Visions 3.7.1 between the "true road" and the (alleged) "better road," as well as the use of ἀνοδία (cf. Mand. 6.1.3) connects this passage with that on the Two Ways (Mand. 6.1).

4.19 Unity of the Church

For the unity of the church, Hermas uses imagery and terminology comparable to those in Ephesians 4:1–5: in Similitudes 9.13.5 (cf. v. 7) he speaks of the church as a "monolith" built of stones—that is, believers (οἱ πιστεύσαντες, *hoi pisteusantes*; cf. πίστις, *pistis*, in Eph 4:5), united by "one spirit" (ἓν πνεῦμα, *hen pneuma*, as in Eph 4:4 [cf. v. 3]) in "one body" (ἓν σῶμα, *hen sōma*, as in Eph 4:4). In Similitudes 9.17.3–4, the church is called a "monochrome," built of stones. These stand for baptized believers, who have "heard" and "believed" (πιστεύσαντα, *pisteusanta*; cf. Eph 4:5), have been "called" (ἐκλήθησαν, *eklēthēsan*; cf. Eph 4:1, 4) in the name of the Son of God, have received the seal (of baptism; cf. βάπτισμα, *baptisma*, in Eph 4:5), and have (among other things) "one faith" (μία πίστις, *mia pistis*, as in Eph 4:5). In Similitudes 9.18.3–4, Hermas says that the "church of God" is becoming "one body [ἓν σῶμα as in Eph 4:4], one thought, one mind, one faith [μία πίστις, as in Eph 4:5], one love [ἀγάπη, *agapē*; cf. Eph 4:2]." In these passages, becoming "one body" is not used in a baptismal (cf. 1 Cor 12:13) or eucharistic (cf. 1 Cor 10:17) sense, but in an ecclesiological sense (regarding the unity of the church).

4.20 Virtues and Vices

Hermas includes several catalogues of virtues and vices (e.g., Vis. 3.8.3–5, 7–8; Mand. 5.2.4; 6.2.3–5; 8.3, 5, 9–10; Sim. 9.15.2–3), as do many New Testament writings (cf., e.g., Mark 7:21–22; 1 Cor 5:10–11; 6:9–10; Gal 5:19–23; Eph 4:31–32; Phil 4:8; 2 Tim 3:2–5; Jas 3:17; 2 Pet 1:5–7). A virtue often mentioned is "simplicity" (ἁπλότης, *haplotēs*, Vis. 1.2.4, etc.; see also *simplicitas* in Sim. 9.31.4; cf. e.g., Luke 11:34 par.; Rom 12:8; 2 Cor 1:12; 8:2; 9:11, 13; 11:3; Eph 6:5; Col 3:22). In Visions 3.6.3, the description of the cracked stones combines two motifs found in the New Testament; these stones stand for people "bearing grudges against one another" (cf. Vis. 2.3.1, etc.; cf., e.g., Matt 5:23; Mark 11:25) and "not being at peace among one another" (cf., e.g., Mark 9:50; Rom 12:18; 1 Thess 5:13). In this regard, God is set as an example for humans (esp. Vis. 3.5.1; Mand. 9.3; Sim. 9.23.4), implying the idea of *imitatio Dei* (cf., e.g., Eph 5:1). Mandates 2.7 uses the notion of "(being) pure and undefiled" (καθαρὰ καὶ [. . .] ἀμίαντος, *kathara kai* [. . .] *amiantos*), the attitude which must support the charity toward the needy, in the same way as James 1:27 (καθαρὰ καὶ ἀμίαντος). The combination of αὐτάρκεια, *autarkeia* ("self-sufficiency") and πᾶν ἔργον δίκαιον, *pan ergon dikaion* ("every righteous work") in Mandates 6.2.3 is also found in 2 Corinthians 9:8–9 (see esp. αὐτάρκεια, πᾶν ἔργον, and δικαιοσύνη, *dikaiosynē*). The virtue of "self-control" (ἐγκράτεια, *enkrateia*) is discussed extensively in Mandates 8. The term is used in the general sense of abstinence from evil (esp. Mand. 8; see also, e.g., Vis. 2.3.2; 3.8.7; Mand. 6.1.1; Sim. 9.15.2); elsewhere, it denotes, more strictly, abstaining from evil deeds and desires (Vis. 1.2.4; 3.8.4; see also, e.g., Sim. 5.1.5) and leaning toward "every virtue of righteousness" (πᾶσαν ἀρετὴν δικαιοσύνης, *pasan aretēn dikaiosynēs*, Mand. 1.2). The virtues of ἐγκράτεια and δικαιοσύνη are also combined in Acts 24:25 (see also 1 Cor 9:25; Gal 5:23; Titus 1:8;

2 Pet 1:6; for sexual abstinence, cf. 1 Cor 7:9). The vice "double-mindedness" (διψυχία, *dipsychia*) is discussed elaborately in Mandates 9. The earliest instances of διψυχία and related terms occur in Christian writings (διψυχία, Vis. 2.2.4, etc.; διψυχέω, *dipsycheō*, v. 7, etc.; δίψυχος, *dipsychos*, 3.4.3, etc.; cf., e.g., Jas 1:8; 4:8). In Mandates 9, it is used in the sense of feeling insecure whether God will answer one's prayer of petition. In verse 6, the antonym of διψυχοῦντες, *dipsychountes*, is ἀδιστάκτως αἰτοῦνται, *adistaktōs aitountai* ("to ask unhesitatingly" or "without doubting"; see also Mand. 9.2, 4; cf. Sim. 2.5, 7; 8.10.3; 9.24.2; 9.29.2). Furthermore, in Similitudes 5.4.4 it is stressed that "God gives without doubt [ἀδιστάκτως, v.l. ἀδιαλείπτως, *adialeiptōs*] to all who ask him" (cf. Sim. 9.29.2). Hermas's message that one should not be double-minded, but confident that God will give what one prays for, agrees with James 1:5–8 (cf. also, e.g., Matt 7:7–11; Mark 11:23–24; John 14:13–14; 15:7; Jas 4:8), but literary dependence of Hermas on any passage in the New Testament cannot be proven. Mandates 10.2, 4 expresses the idea that the vices of "double-mindedness" (διψυχία) and "quick temper" (ὀξυχολία, *oxycholia*) "sadden" (λυπέω, *lypeō*, and derivatives) "the Holy Spirit" (τὸ πνεῦμα τὸ ἅγιον, *to pneuma to hagion*); something similar is said in Ephesians 4:30, where the phrase "do not sadden [μὴ λυπεῖτε, *mē lypeite*] the Holy Spirit [τὸ πνεῦμα τὸ ἅγιον] of God" is followed by a catalogue of vices (v. 31 [and virtues, v. 32]) including "bitterness" (πικρία, *pikria*; cf. πικρανθῇ, *pikranthē*, in Mand. 10.2.3) and various forms of anger (θυμός, *thymos*, ὀργή, *orgē*, κραυγή, *kraugē*; cf. ὀξυχολία in Hermas). The phrase "for they were like-minded" (τὰ γὰρ αὐτὰ ἐφρόνουν, *ta gar auta ephronoun*) in Similitudes 9.13.7 (cf. 9.29.2) resembles idiom current in Paul (τὸ αὐτὸ φρονεῖν, *to auto phronein*; see Rom 12:16; 15:5; 2 Cor 13:11; Phil 2:2; 4:2; cf., e.g., 3:15). Similitudes 9.29.1–3 says that those of childlike innocence will live in the kingdom of God; this compares with Mark 10:14–15 parr., though Hermas uses "infant," νήπιος/νηπιότης, *nēpios/nēpiotēs*, rather than "child," παιδίον, *paidion* (for the combination of νήπια, *nēpia*, and [οὐδεμία] κακία, [*oudemia*] *kakia*, in Sim. 9.29.1, cf. esp. 1 Cor 14:20: τῇ κακίᾳ νηπιάζετε, *tē kakia nēpiazete*).

Finally, Hermas often uses the image of "clothing" oneself with virtues. Visions 4.1.8, for instance, says that Hermas takes courage when "clothed [. . .] in the faith of the Lord" (ἐνδυσάμενος [. . .] τὴν πίστιν τοῦ κυρίου, *endysamenos* [. . .] *tēn pistin tou kyriou*; see also, e.g., Mand. 9.7, 10; Sim. 6.1.2; cf. Mand. 11.4). This parallels especially 1 Thessalonians 5:8 (ἐνδυσάμενοι θώρακα πίστεως, *endysamenoi thōraka pisteōs*, "having put on the breastplate of faith"; cf. Eph 6:11, 16). The phrase "clothed with every virtue of righteousness" (ἐνδυσάμενοι πᾶσαν ἀρετὴν δικαιοσύνης, *endysamenoi pasan aretēn dikaiosynēs*) in Similitudes 6.1.4 (cf. Mand. 1.2) is reminiscent of Ephesians 6:14 (ἐνδυσάμενοι τὸν θώρακα τῆς δικαιοσύνης, *endysamenoi ton thōraka tēs dikaiosynēs*, "having put on the breastplate of righteousness"). Similarly, the call in Mandates 12.2 to "put on [ἔνδυσαι, *endysai*] the desire of righteousness [δικαιοσύνης, *dikaiosynēs*]" and, "after arming oneself [καθοπλισάμενος, *kathoplisamenos*] with the fear of the Lord" (v. 4), to fight against evil and deadly desire (vv. 1–3), the daughter of the devil (διάβολος, *diabolos*, v. 2), recalls that of Ephesians 6:10–17 to "put on [ἐνδύσασθε, *endysasthe*] God's armor [πανοπλίαν, *panoplian*]" (v. 11; cf. v. 13) and "to put on [ἐνδυσάμενοι, *endysamenoi*] the breastplate of righteousness [δικαιοσύνης]" (v. 14) in order to stand against the wiles of the devil (διάβολος, v. 11). The language Mandates 12.2.5 uses for being a slave of (δουλεύω, *douleuō*), and submitting to (ὑποτάσσομαι, *hypotassomai*), the right desire (ἐπιθυμία, *epithymia*) and for mastering (κατακυριεύω, *katakyrieuō*) and submitting to (ὑποτάσσω, *hypotassō*) evil desire, corresponds, for instance, to the phraseology in Titus 3:3, where one of the vices listed is to be a slave (δουλεύω) of all kinds of desires (ἐπιθυμία) and pleasures.

4.21 Wealth

Similitudes 9.20.2 (cf. v. 3) says that "the rich [. . .] will enter the kingdom of God with difficulty" (οἱ δὲ πλούσιοι [. . .] δυσκόλως εἰσελεύσονται εἰς τὴν βασιλείαν τοῦ θεοῦ, *hoi de plousioi* [. . .] *dyskolōs eiseleusontai eis tēn basileian tou theou*). Similar statements occur in Mark 10:23 parr.: δυσκόλως [. . .] εἰς τὴν βασιλείαν τοῦ θεοῦ εἰσελεύσονται (for πλούσιος, *plousios*, see v. 25). The connection made in Similitudes 9.20.1 between the "rich" (πλούσιοι) and "thistles" (ἄκανθαι, *akanthai*) has its parallel in Mark 4:18–19 parr. (ἀκάνθας [. . .] πλούτου, *akanthas* [. . .] *ploutou*).

The preceding overview makes clear that Hermas shows agreements with *all* of the New Testament writings. In recent scholarship, (new) attempts have been made to prove that the author knew at least some of the writings that later formed the New Testament.[30] It is true that some of the parallels are indeed remarkable. There is, however, no convincing evidence for any literary dependence of Hermas on any writing included in the New Testament. There are neither direct citations (with an explicit reference) nor any agreements in passages of some length (e.g., a whole verse). Moreover, several of the parallels are genre bound. To sum up, the agreements between Hermas and the New Testament literature can best be explained by supposing that the author uses terminology and concepts that were familiar in the circles to which he belonged and that found their way into his and other early Christian writings.

5. CONCLUSION

Hermas remains a mysterious writing. Its central message seems to be the call for the change and renewal (μετάνοια) of the (members of the) church. However, much is shrouded in uncertainty. This applies to such fundamental issues as the background and identity of its author, its date, its compositional stages, and its intended readership. Uncertainty is also caused by the fact that portions of the Greek text are (still) missing. It is puzzling that there are so many terminological and conceptual similarities between Hermas and the New Testament writings, but no explicit quotations or unequivocal allusions. The work did not become part of the biblical canon, yet its relatively large amount of surviving manuscripts, its inclusion in Codex Sinaiticus, its early translation into Latin, and the fact that it is attested from the early church throughout the Middle Ages indicate that it was held in high regard in early and later Christian circles. Due to its length and repetitive style, it is now often considered a somewhat tedious work. Its theological ideas are often regarded as rather unclear and inconsistent. Despite all the unsolved problems, uncertainties, and modern objections, it cannot be denied that Hermas is a key source for the study of early Christianity.

BIBLIOGRAPHY

Brox, N. *Der Hirt des Hermas*. KAV 7. Göttingen: Vandenhoeck & Ruprecht, 1991.

Dibelius, M. *Der Hirt des Hermas*. HNT Ergänzungsband, Die Apostolischen Väter 4. Tübingen: Mohr Siebeck, 1923.

30. See, e.g., J. Verheyden, "The Shepherd of Hermas and the Writings that Later Formed the New Testament," in *The Reception of the New Testament in the Apostolic Fathers*, ed. A. F. Gregory and C. M. Tuckett (Oxford: Oxford University Press, 2005), 293–329, and J. E. Soyars, *The Shepherd of Hermas and the Pauline Legacy*, NovTSup 176 (Leiden: Brill, 2019).

Grundeken, M. *Community Building in the Shepherd of Hermas: A Critical Study of Some Key Aspects*. VCSup 131. Leiden: Brill, 2015.

Henne, P. *L'unité du Pasteur d'Hermas: Tradition et rédaction*. CahRB 31. Paris: Gabalda, 1992.

Joly, R. *Hermas: Le Pasteur*. SC 53. Paris: Cerf, 1958.

Leutzsch, M. "Hirt des Hermas." Pages 105–497 in *Papiasfragmente, Hirt des Hermas*. Edited by U. H. J. Körtner and M. Leutzsch. Schriften des Urchristentums 3. Darmstadt: Wissenschaftliche Buchgesellschaft, 1998.

Maier, H. O. "Hermas' *The Shepherd*." Pages 867–70 in vol. 11 of *Encyclopedia of the Bible and Its Reception*. Edited by D. C. Allison et al. Berlin: de Gruyter, 2015.

Osiek, C. *Shepherd of Hermas: A Commentary*. Hermeneia. Minneapolis: Augsburg Fortress, 1999.

Snyder, G. F. *The Shepherd of Hermas*. Vol. 6 of *The Apostolic Fathers: A New Translation and Commentary*. Camden, NJ: Thomas Nelson, 1969.

Soyars, J. E. *The Shepherd of Hermas and the Pauline Legacy*. NovTSup 176. Leiden: Brill, 2019.

Verheyden, J. "Dreams, Visions and the World-to-Come According to the Shepherd of Hermas." Pages 215–34 in *Dreams, Visions, Imaginations: Jewish, Christian and Gnostic Views of the World to Come*. Edited by J. Schröter, T. Nicklas, and A. Puig i Tàrrech. BZNW 247. Berlin: de Gruyter, 2021.

Verheyden, J. "The Shepherd of Hermas and the Writings that Later Formed the New Testament." Pages 293–329 in *The Reception of the New Testament in the Apostolic Fathers*. Edited by A. F. Gregory and C. M. Tuckett. Oxford: Oxford University Press, 2005.

CHAPTER 8

THE EPISTLE OF BARNABAS

DAVID LINCICUM

1. INTRODUCTION

The so-called Epistle of Barnabas is an epistolary tract that addresses itself to a community of Christians and urges them to have "perfect knowledge" in addition to their faith. That knowledge seems to consist, judging from the rest of the epistle, in an allegorical understanding of the texts that will become the Christian Old Testament, and in an ethical admonition drawn from the Two Ways tradition of early Jewish and Christian paraenetical discourse. The epistle offers us our first sustained example of Christian figural interpretation of Scripture and belongs as an early exemplar to the tradition of *adversus Judaeos* literature that sought to distance early Christianity from early Judaism by argumentatively "proving" that Scripture points clearly to Jesus and to other early Christian points of belief.[1]

The Epistle of Barnabas is ascribed to Barnabas in our earliest full manuscript, Codex Sinaiticus (ΒΑΡΝΑΒΑ ΕΠΙΣΤΟΛΗ), and early Christian tradition consistently connects the text with Barnabas. Clement of Alexandria cites it regularly as an authoritative writing of the apostle Barnabas (e.g., *Strom.* 2.6.31.2–3), while Origen refers to what is written "in the Catholic Epistle of Barnabas" (ἐν τῇ Βαρνάβα καθολικῇ ἐπιστολῇ; *Cels.* 1.63). Eusebius, however, evinces doubts about its authorship and places it among the spurious books as the "Epistle of Barnabas" (Βαρναβᾶ ἐπιστολή; *Hist. eccl.* 3.25.4; but cf. 6.13.6–7 and 6.14.1 where Eusebius classes Barnabas as among the "disputed" texts). The text itself is formally anonymous, unless it originally bore a title that made the link to Barnabas clear. The only plausible candidate for the intended ascription is the Barnabas who is depicted in the New Testament as Paul's traveling companion, a Levite from Cyprus (Acts 4:36). It is difficult to imagine a Jewish author penning Barnabas, not least a Levite; we must, therefore, treat the authorial claim as an attempt to secure the authority of an apostolic voice for the text.

1. For surveys of the broader *adversus Judaeos* tradition, see A. L. Williams, *Adversus Judaeos: A Bird's-Eye View of Christian Apologiae until the Renaissance* (Cambridge: Cambridge University Press, 1935); M. Simon, *Verus Israel: A Study of the Relations Between Christians and Jews in the Roman Empire AD 135–425*, trans. H. McKeating (London: Littman Library of Jewish Civilization, 1986 [orig. 1964]); H. Schreckenberg, *Die christlichen Adversus-Judaeos-Texte und ihr literarisches und historisches Umfeld*, 3 vols. (Frankfurt am Main: Peter Lang, 1982–1994); S. Krauss, *The Jewish-Christian Controversy from the Earliest Times to 1789, Volume 1: History*, ed. W. Horbury, TSAJ 56 (Tübingen: Mohr Siebeck, 1996); O. Limor and G. G. Stroumsa, ed., *Contra Iudaeos: Ancient and Medieval Polemics Between Christians and Jews*, TSMEMJ 10 (Tübingen: Mohr Siebeck, 1996); A. Külzer, *Disputationes graecae contra Iudaeos: Untersuchungen zur byzantinischen antijüdischen Dialogliteratur und ihrem Judenbild*, Byzantinisches Archiv 19 (Leipzig: Teubner, 1999); S. Morlet, O. Munnich, and B. Pouderon, eds., *Les dialogues adversus Iudaeos: Permanences et mutations d'une tradition polémique*, Collection des Études Augustiniennes, Série Antiquité 196 (Paris: Institut d'Études Augustiniennes, 2013).

Clement of Alexandria's citations form a *terminus ante quem* for the composition of the letter. The destruction of the temple in 70 CE, which Barnabas mentions explicitly in 16.2–4, supplies the *terminus post quem*.[2] Most scholars have dated the text between 70 CE and the outbreak of the Bar Kokhba revolt in 132 CE, when hopes for the rebuilding of the temple seem to have come to a forced end, although some outlying positions exist.[3] Internally, two major passages have been at the center of discussions of the date of the text. In 4.4–5, the author cites two Danielic texts:

> And so also says the prophet: "Ten kingdoms will reign over the earth, and after them a little king will arise, who will subdue three of the kings with a single blow" [cf. Dan 7:24]. Similarly, Daniel says, concerning the same one: "And I saw the fourth beast, wicked and powerful and more dangerous than all the beasts of the earth, and how ten horns sprang up from it, and from these a little offshoot of a horn, and how it subdued three of the large horns with a single blow" [cf. Dan 7:7–8].[4]

Barnabas cites the material to prove that "the final stumbling block has drawn near," and so seems to take the statements as referring to contemporary circumstances. Identifying the "little horn" with Vespasian, after the "year of the four emperors," allows one to place at least this tradition in the mid-70s. Others have identified the tenth kingdom with the Flavian dynasty, which would yield a date in the late 90s. Some have used this as a firm basis on which to date the whole epistle,[5] but the epistle seems to have incorporated sources, and this may only reflect a date for one source rather than the text as a whole.[6] The other passage is 16.3–4, in which Barnabas references apparently contemporary hopes that the Jewish temple will be rebuilt. The historical referent is far from clear, but may reflect a softening of imperial posture toward the Jews in the reign of Nerva, who repealed the punitive tax known as the *fiscus judaicus* instituted by the Flavians, or arose from Hadrian's plans to rebuild Jerusalem as Aelia Capitolina in 130–132 CE, before the Bar Kokhba revolt broke out.[7] The precise date is difficult to fix with certainty, but the epistle seems to reflect conditions in the first half of the second century.

The provenance of the letter has most often been seen as Alexandria, in light of shared

---

2. In this essay, I use the term "Barnabas" interchangeably for the author and the composition.

3. Recently C. K. Rothschild has suggested that Barnabas may have been composed in Caracalla's reign (198–217 CE), though she does not clarify how to square this with Clement's knowledge of the letter; see Rothschild, "Ethiopianising the Devil: ὁ μέλας in Barnabas 4," *NTS* 65 (2019): 223–45, here 240–44.

4. In this essay, unless otherwise noted, translations of Barnabas follow those of M. W. Holmes, "The Epistle of Barnabas," in *The Apostolic Fathers: Greek Texts and English Translations*, 3rd ed. (Grand Rapids: Baker Academic, 2007), 370–441.

5. For a date in the 70s, see J. A. T. Robinson, *Redating the New Testament* (London: SCM, 1976), 313–319. For the 90s, note A. L. Williams, "The Date of the Epistle of Barnabas," *JTS* 34 (1933): 337–46.

6. For helpful discussions of dating, see J. Carleton Paget, *The Epistle of Barnabas: Outlook and Background*, WUNT 2/64 (Tübingen: Mohr Siebeck, 1994), 9–30; F. R. Prostmeier, *Der Barnabasbrief*, KAV 8 (Göttingen: Vandenhoeck and Ruprecht, 1999), 111–19. The most obvious source is the so-called Two Ways section of chs. 18–21, but scholars have argued for distinctive sources as well; see P. Prigent, *Les Testimonia dans le christianisme primitif: L'Epître de Barnabé 1–16 et ses sources* (Paris: Gabalda, 1961); R. A. Kraft, "The Epistle of Barnabas, its Quotations and their Sources" (PhD diss., Harvard University, 1961), available online at http://ccat.sas.upenn.edu/rak/publics/barn/barndiss01.htm; K. Wengst, *Tradition und Theologie des Barnabasbriefes*, Arbeiten zur Kirchengeschichte 42 (Berlin: de Gruyter, 1971).

7. See the discussion in W. Horbury, *Jewish War under Trajan and Hadrian* (Cambridge: Cambridge University Press, 2014), 298–302; cf. R. Hvalvik, *The Struggle for Scripture and Covenant: The Purpose of the Epistle of Barnabas and Jewish-Christian Competition in the Second Century*, WUNT 2/82 (Tübingen: Mohr Siebeck, 1996), 17–34; Prostmeier, *Barnabasbrief*, 111–19.

exegetical traditions with the Letter of Aristeas and Philo of Alexandria, the early reception by Clement and Origen there (though note that Origen wrote *Contra Celsum* from Caesarea, not Alexandria), and some incidental details in the text that cohere with an Alexandrian origin. Exegetical traditions circulate, however, and allegorical readings are found in Josephus, Melito, Justin Martyr, and other non-Alexandrian authors. The argument from early reception becomes a bit tenuous when one considers that the Shepherd of Hermas, composed in Rome, also had an early Alexandrian reception. Some dissenters from Alexandrian provenance have therefore pointed to other locations, such as Syria-Palestine or Asia Minor, as possible places of composition, where we also find active contact between Jewish and Christian communities.[8] Most points of interpretation of the epistle are not materially affected by the precise provenance one specifies.

More consequential is a reconstruction of the situation envisaged by the letter. The audience is clearly comprised of Christ-followers, and the text assumes a close relationship between author and audience. The author refers to them as "sons and daughters" (1.1) or "brothers" (2.10; 3.6; 6.10), whom he longs to see (1.3). He refers to them as "children of joy" (7.1), "children of love" (9.7), "children of love and peace" (21.9), or simply "children" (15.4). He protests that he is not a teacher (1.8; 4.9) but uses didactic language throughout (5.6; 6.9; 9.7; 14.4; 16.2, 7, 8). The major thrust of the author's rhetoric is clearly to demonstrate that faithful interpretation of Scripture is not found in the literal observation of food laws, circumcision, and so forth, but rather in an allegorical understanding that points to Jesus and other Christian themes throughout. Although the author never mentions Jews and Christians, he operates with a binary "us versus them" mentality, sometimes using the term "Israel" to refer to "them." Does this indicate a situation in which members of a community are actually contemplating a (re)turn to the synagogue? Or is the author simply invoking Judaism as a mere foil for the construction of his audience's Christian identity? Or does perhaps the polemic amount to a veiled critique of another Christian group? We will return to these questions below.

Barnabas survives in full in two Greek manuscripts, both rediscovered in the nineteenth-century: Codex Sinaiticus, in a hand assigned to Scribe A (fols. 334r–340v), and Codex Hierosolymitanus (fols. 39r–51v), which also contains the sole complete manuscript of the Didache. Previously, it was known through a deficient Greek text that only included Barnabas 5.7–21.9 following directly from Polycarp, *To the Philippians* 1.1–9.2: the eleventh- or twelfth-century Codex Vaticanus gr. 859 and twelve manuscripts descended from it. There are two fragmentary papyri: A papyrus assignable to the fourth century contains a fragmentary text of 9.1a–6 (PSI 7.757), with affinities to the textual tradition represented by the Vatican manuscript family, and a soon-to-be published papyrus from Oxyrhynchus (inv. 106/51(a)) containing 6.17–7.6. A Latin translation of 1.1–17.2, possibly made as early as the third century, is preserved in a single manuscript, Codex Petropolitanus Bibl. Publ. Q. v. I. 39, fols. 8–20. There is also extant a single excerpt in Syriac containing 19.1, 2, 8, and 20.1 (Codex Cantabrigiensis Univ. Add. 2033, fol. 61v), a quotation of 6.11–13 and 6.17–18 in a fourth-century Coptic work, P.Berl. 20915, probably made "on the fly" rather than indicating a complete lost translation into Coptic, and a lost Armenian translation noted in the codicil to Codex Vaticanus gr. 859. Although early modern scholars were aware of the epistle's existence, it was not until the Latin manuscript came to light and

8. For Syria-Palestine, see P. Prigent and R. A. Kraft, *Épître de Barnabé*, SC 172 (Paris: Cerf, 1971), 23–24; for Asia Minor, see K. Wengst, *Didache (Apostellehre), Barnabasbrief, Zweiter Klemensbrief, Schrift an Diognet* (Munich: Kösel, 1984), 115–18.

could be used to fill the lacuna in the mutilated Greek tradition that the editio princeps was published in the 1640s.[9]

2. SUMMARY OF CONTENT

The Epistle of Barnabas falls into two major sections. After an epistolary introduction (1.1–5) and an announcement of its themes (1.6–8), the bulk of the treatise offers an allegorical treatment of major institutions or events in Israel's history (chs. 2–16). After a brief transitional section (ch. 17), the work concludes with the Two Ways section of ethical discourse and an epistolary closing (18–21).

Outline of the Epistle of Barnabas

1.1–5	Epistolary introduction
1.6–2.3	Thematic introduction
2.4–16.10	Scriptural gnosis
2.4–10	True sacrifice
3.1–6	True fasting
4.1–14	The last days
5.1–6.7	Prophetic prediction of the Lord's suffering
6.8–19	The land of promise
7.1–11	Day of atonement
8.1–7	The red heifer
9.1–9	True circumcision
10.1–12	The meaning of kashruth
11.1–11	Baptism in Scripture
12.1–11	The cross in Scripture
13.1–14.9	The true covenant
15.1–9	The true Sabbath
16.1–10	The true temple
17	Transitional section
18–20	Two Ways
21	Conclusion

Epistolary Introduction (1.1–5)

Barnabas begins with an epistolary opening that expresses good wishes for his recipients, styled as "sons and daughters" (cf. Joel 2:28), and offers a *captatio benevolentiae* in which the author recounts a good visit with the congregation and resolves, "If I care enough about you to share something of what I have received, I will be rewarded for having ministered to such spirits," and so offers the brief letter (κατὰ μικρόν, *kata mikron*, "briefly") to add "perfect knowledge" (τελείαν . . . γνῶσιν, *teleian . . . gnōsin*) to the audience's faith. If the letter is originally pseudepigraphal, these epistolary elements add to the construction of verisimilitude—that is, a "reality effect" that mimics authentic epistolary exchanges. Gnosis or "knowledge" is one of the central concerns of the treatise. The term and its cognates occur regularly (1.7; 2.3; 5.3; 6.9; 18.1; 19.1), and in the introduction to the Two

9. For the early publication of Barnabas, see the learned discussion in J.-L. Quantin, "L'orthodoxie, la censure et la gloire: La difficile édition princeps de l'Épître de Barnabé, de Rome à Amsterdam (1549–1646)," in *«Editiones Principes» delle Opere dei Padri Greci e Latini*, ed. M. Cortesi (Florence: Edizioni del Galluzzo, 2006), 103–62.

Ways section, the author writes, "Now let us move on to another knowledge and teaching [ἑτέραν γνῶσιν καὶ διδαχήν, *heteran gnōsin kai didachēn*]," which indicates that the body of the letter is conceived as gnosis. The content of gnosis seems at least in part to be connected to proper scriptural interpretation and the closely connected theme of revelation (3.6; 6.7; 7.1).

Thematic Introduction (1.6–2.3)

The author signals, as though programmatically, in 1.6 three dogmas of the Lord: the hope of life, righteousness, and a glad and rejoicing love, but the themes do not seem to structure the discussion that follows. More significant is the characterization in 1.7 of Scripture as a prophetic witness: "The Master has made known to us through the prophets things past and things present, and has given us a foretaste of things to come." Prophecy seems to be the dominant construal of Scripture in Barnabas. In addition to the prophets themselves, the psalmist prophesies (e.g., Barn. 5.13; Pss 22:20 [21:21 LXX]; 119:120 [118:120 LXX]; cf. Barn. 6.4, 6), David prophesies (Barn. 12.10; Ps 110:1 [109:1 LXX]), Moses, "the other prophet" (Barn. 6.8: ὁ ἄλλος προφήτης, *ho allos prophētēs*; cf. 12.8) prophesies, and in fact the "Lord" continues to prophesy in the community (16.9). Even Levitical instruction about the Day of Atonement is cast as the words of the prophet (7.4).[10] The author invokes the apocalyptic trope that "the days are evil and the one who is at work is in power" and frames that as motivation for seeking out the "righteous requirements of the Lord," an overture to subjects he will go on to address in the main body of the work.

Scriptural Gnosis (2.4–17.2)

From chapter 2 onward, the author turns to a series of expositions of themes and figures from Scripture, arguing that in one way or another they prefigure or find their fullest meaning in Christ and Christian themes. Barnabas 2.4–10 takes up the anti-cultic rhetoric of Israel's prophets, and woodenly insists on the claim that God "needs neither sacrifices nor whole burnt offerings nor general offerings" (2.4), but rather sacrifice is a matter of interior disposition toward God. Similarly, relying on Isaiah 58, Barnabas urges that true fasting is a matter of proper ethical conduct toward the poor and oppressed rather than a commandment to be literally observed (Barn. 3.1–6). An analogous case is made with regard to the Sabbath in 15.1–9.

Likewise, the prophetic Scriptures point ahead to the suffering of Jesus (5.1–6.7). Inheriting the land of promise, as gnosis teaches, is a parable concerning the Lord: just as Adam was formed of earth, so "a human is earth suffering" and the land signifies Jesus (6.8–10). Yom Kippur (Lev 16) also supplies a "type" (τύπος, *typos*) of Jesus, the two goats providing an image of the two comings of the Messiah: first, fulfilling the type of Isaac (Barn. 7.3) by dying on the altar, and second returning crowned in glory (7.8–10). But the type is somewhat imprecisely worked out, and the scarlet wool is also taken to be a symbol of the suffering necessary for any who want to see Jesus and gain his kingdom (7.11). Interestingly, the scarlet thread is a detail that does not derive from the biblical text but seems to come from Jewish tradition, of which Barnabas somehow has knowledge.[11] So also

10. See explicit references to the prophet(s) at Barn. 2.4; 4.4; 5.6, 11; 6.2, 4, 6, 7, 8, 10, 13, 14; 7.4; 9.1; 11.3, 4, 6, 9; 12.1, 4, 8; 14.2, 7, 8, 9.

11. See N. Ayali-Darshan, "The Origin and Meaning of the Crimson Thread in the Mishnaic Scapegoat Ritual in Light of an Ancient Syro-Anatolian Custom," *JSJ* 44 (2013): 530–52, for the contention that the scarlet thread, which also appears in Tertullian, *Adv. Jud.* 14.9 (cf. *Marc.* 3.7.7) and in m. Yoma 6:7 is a

the rite of the red heifer (Num 19), Barnabas says, is "plainly" (ἐν ἁπλότητι, *en haplotēti*) about Jesus: the calf is Jesus, the priests who slaughter it are those who executed him, and the children who sprinkle are the ones who announced the gospel (Barn. 8.2–3). All the scriptural rites are "clear to us but to them are quite obscure, because they did not listen to the voice of the Lord" (8.7). The tractate thus draws a fairly direct line between the death of Jesus and the final loss of the covenant with the Jewish people, a trope that will recur in later *adversus Judaeos* tradition.

Circumcision refers not to a physical operation in the flesh, but to the circumcision of the heart and ears—that is, the creation of an ability to receive and welcome the Christian proclamation (9.1–9). When Abraham instituted circumcision, he was looking forward to Jesus because he had been taught about the three letters: namely, the number of servants, 318, which is written by means of three Greek letters: IHT. By playing with some gematria-like number symbolism, these are taken to stand for Jesus (Ἰη[σοῦς]) and the cross, which the Greek letter tau is said to resemble.[12] Levitical kashruth legislation (esp. Lev 11) is also understood ethically, in a tradition that recalls similar treatments in the Letter of Aristeas 139–57 and Philo of Alexandria, *Special Laws* 4.100–125. The chapter seems to be an untidy mix of previous tradition: three precepts are mentioned (Barn. 10.1), followed by the exposition of three types of animal: pigs, unclean birds, and unclean sea creatures (10.1–5). But then the author discusses the hare, the hyena, and the weasel, together with some venturesome biological suggestions (10.6–8),[13] before returning to the threefold discussion with which the chapter began. But the commands, which Moses delivered so well (10.11), never should have been taken literally; rather, Barnabas suggests, "we explain them as the Lord intended" (10.12: λαλοῦμεν ὡς ἠθέλησεν ὁ κύριος, *laloumen hōs ēthelēsen ho kyrios*). Baptism (ch. 11) and the cross (ch. 12) are also cryptically described in advance in Scripture. Barnabas seems to presuppose something like the New Testament's views on baptism as the moment of forgiveness and new creation, which allows baptism to function as an identity marker over against Jewish symbols.[14] As Barnabas writes, "While we descend into the water laden with sins and dirt, we rise up bearing fruit in our heart and with fear and hope in Jesus in our spirits" (11.11). The author finds the cross prefigured in Moses stretching out his hands in prayer during battle (Exod 17:8–13) and in his fashioning of a bronze serpent when the Israelites were bitten by serpents (Num 21:4–8). He also finds in Joshua (in Greek: Ἰησοῦς, *Iēsous*, "Jesus") a type (Barn. 12.10) of the one who was not the son of a human but rather the son of God.

In chapters 13–14, Barnabas returns to the status of the covenant and argues that the "former people" (13.1) lost their covenant, and it has now come to "us." In arguments that recall Paul's line of thought in Romans 9:10–13, Barnabas contends that God foreshadowed the choice of a new people by having the patriarchs of Genesis bless their younger son: "Observe

Syro-Anatolian custom that was borrowed by Israel in the Second Temple period (note also Lev 14:1–7; cf. m. Men. 3:6).

12. R. Hvalvik, "Barnabas 9:7–9 and the Author's Supposed Use of Gematria," *NTS* 33 (1987): 276–82.

13. For an attempt to puzzle out the hare, see C. K. Rothschild, "Down the Rabbit Hole with Barnabas: Rewriting Moses in Barnabas 10," *NTS* 64 (2018): 410–34. On the hyena, see M. Pendergraft, "'Thou Shalt Not Eat the Hyena': A Note on "Barnabas" Epistle 10.7," *VC* 46 (1992): 75–79. The ancient Christian nature-allegory text known as the *Physiologus* takes up Barnabas's discussion of the weasel (sec. 21 Sbordone) and hyena (sec. 24 Sbordone).

14. So D.-A. Koch, "Taufinterpretationen bei Ignatius und im Barnabasbrief: Christologische und soteriologische Deutungen," in *Ablution, Initiation, and Baptism: Late Antiquity, Early Judaism, and Early Christianity = Waschungen, Initiation und Taufe: Spätantike, Frühes Judentum und Frühes Christentum*, ed. D. Hellholm, T. Vegge, Ø. Norderval, and C. Hellholm, 3 vols., BZNW 176.1–3 (Berlin: de Gruyter, 2011), 2:817–48.

how by these means he has ordained that this people should be first, and heir of the covenant" (Barn. 13.6). Chapter 14 goes on to pinpoint the moment of the loss of the covenant: at the golden-calf incident, when Moses smashed the stone tablets. If the first people lost the covenant on Sinai, the "new people" (5.7) received it when "the Lord himself gave it to us, so that we might become the people of inheritance, by suffering for us" (14.4). Jesus himself inherits the covenant (14.5) and then in turn establishes the covenant with the new people.

As with other aspects of Israel's traditions, so the Sabbath is also understood allegorically. Taking the Sabbath to refer to the structure of history (more on this below), Barnabas takes it to signify that "true rest" will only be achieved at the return of the Son, when "he will destroy the time of the lawless one and will judge the ungodly and will change the sun and the moon and the stars" (15.5). This cosmic cataclysm will mark the end of normal history and the inauguration of a new age, in which those who have sanctified themselves will participate. The seven-day structure of history leads to an expressed hope for an "eighth day," "which is the beginning of another world" (ὅ ἐστιν ἄλλου κόσμου ἀρχήν, *ho estin allou kosmou archēn*). This is connected by Barnabas, somewhat awkwardly, to the celebration on the eighth day—that is, Sunday, "the day on which Jesus both arose from the dead and, after appearing again, ascended into heaven" (15.9). Barnabas thus marks an early witness to the liturgical shift away from Sabbath to the "Lord's day."[15]

The temple was not an actual building ("as though it were God's house") but signified the true dwelling of God in human hearts that believe and so form a spiritual temple (ch. 16). Barnabas clearly knows the temple's destruction (16.2), and similarly to his critique of Jewish sacrifice, he cites prophetic texts to demonstrate that God never wanted a physical temple (cf. Isa 40:12; 66:1). As we have seen, the reference to plans for rebuilding the temple in 16.3–4 is obscure: do "the very servants of their enemies" who will rebuild the temple refer to the Romans, as a Hadrianic project might indicate? Regardless, the destruction of the physical temple was by God's design, as proved through an Enochic citation (16.5; cf. 1 En. 89.56, 66), and the community of believers is in fact being built as the true temple of God, "a spiritual temple that is being built for the Lord" (Barn. 16.10).

This long section on scriptural gnosis concludes briefly, with the author expressing his hope that he has explained things clearly, but also signaling the limits of what he has attempted to interpret in light of his audience's limited capacity to understand (ch. 17).

The Two Ways (18–21)

Chapters 18–21 contain the Two Ways tradition (lacking in the Latin version). This closely parallels material also found in Didache 1–6 and in the Latin *Doctrina apostolorum*.[16] Since the discovery and publication of the Didache in 1883, scholars have debated the relationship between Barnabas 18–21 and Didache 1–6. Some early scholarship tended to argue for the priority of Barnabas's version, but more recently a relatively secure scholarly consensus has emerged that they both rely on a common Jewish source.[17] The name "Two Ways" refers to the binary choice that introduces the material: "There are two ways of

15. See R. J. Bauckham, "Sabbath and Sunday in the Post-Apostolic Church," in *From Sabbath to Lord's Day: A Biblical, Historical, and Theological Investigation*, ed. D. A. Carson (Grand Rapids: Zondervan, 1982), 251–98.

16. For both these texts, see W. Rordorf and A. Tuilier, *La Doctrine des Douze Apôtres (Didachè)*, 2nd ed., SC 248 (Paris: Cerf, 1998). For translations of a larger number of Two Ways texts, see A. Stewart-Sykes, ed., *On the Two Ways: Life or Death, Light or Darkness: Foundational Texts in the Tradition*, Popular Patristics Series 41 (Yonkers, NY: St Vladimir's Seminary Press, 2011).

17. See discussion in part 1 of H. van de Sandt and D. Flusser, *The Didache: Its Jewish Sources and Its Place in Early Judaism and Christianity*, CRINT III/5 (Assen: Van Gorcum; Minneapolis: Fortress, 2002).

teaching and power, one of light and one of darkness, and there is a great difference between these two ways" (Barn. 18.1). The ethical instruction is strikingly Jewish in character, coming as it does after a long tirade against Judaism. But rather than being a secondary addition to the epistle,[18] it seems to pick up and solidify an ethical dualism that runs throughout the treatise, and so can rightly be described as an integral part of the epistle in its final form, even if it incorporates a preexisting source.[19] If it might be possible to understand the thoroughgoing allegorization of the law in the preceding chapters as leading to a kind of ethical lawlessness, Barnabas wants to foreclose on that option by including substantial ethical teaching. The way of light comes first (ch. 19) and is longer than the section on the way of darkness (ch. 20). Many of the commands are in fact scriptural in nature, and the audience is urged, "You must not forsake the Lord's commandments" (19.2). A staccato piling up of imperatives (though imperatives interspersed with many imperatival formulations as future indicatives in a Septuagintal fashion) recalls the tradition of ethical instruction in wisdom literature, and many of the instructions turn on proper reverence toward God and merciful conduct toward one's neighbor. The "way of the black one" includes a list of prohibited behavior: "idolatry, audacity, arrogance of power, hypocrisy, duplicity, adultery, murder, robbery, pride, transgression, deceit, malice, stubbornness, sorcery, magic art, greed, lack of fear of God" (20.1b), as well as descriptive characterizations of those who do wicked actions.

A brief conclusion underscores the necessity of doing the "righteous requirements of the Lord" (τὰ δικαιώματα τοῦ κυρίου, *ta dikaiōmata tou kyriou*, in 21.1, recalling the nearly identical phrase in 2.1) and says that the one who does them will be glorified in the kingdom of God, while the one who fails to do so will perish together with their works. The audience is urged to treat one another well, to "be good lawgivers to one another" (21.4), and the author asks that they remember him before giving his farewell and concluding wish: "May the Lord of glory and all grace be with your spirit."

3. INTERPRETATIVE ISSUES

3.1 Anti-Jewish Polemic and the Status of the Covenant

Since at least Adolf von Harnack, scholars have debated whether texts in the *adversus Judaeos* tradition reflect an actual social reality on the ground, in which Jews and Christians were engaged in close contact, leading to competition and conflict, or whether they arise from merely internal Christian discourses of self-formation, and so reflect a "symbolic Judaism" that functions as nothing more than a foil for Christian reasoning.[20] The same debate has played out with Barnabas.

That the epistle reflects an anti-Jewish rhetoric is evident.[21] This is most pronounced in chapters 4 and 13–14. The author alleges that at the golden-calf episode (Exod 32), Israel lost the covenant: as Moses shattered the stone tablets, "their covenant was shattered, in order that the covenant of the beloved Jesus might be sealed in our heart" (Barn. 4.8; cf. 14.3). In fact, the covenant was offered but never formally received: "They were not

18. As suggested by E. Goodspeed, "The Didache, Barnabas, and the Doctrina," *AThR* 27 (1945): 228–47.

19. See J. N. Rhodes, "The Two Ways Tradition in the Epistle of Barnabas: Revisiting an Old Question," *CBQ* 73 (2011): 797–816; J. C. H. Smith, "The *Epistle of Barnabas* and the Two Ways of Teaching Authority," *VC* 68 (2014): 465–497.

20. Note the overview in G. Stroumsa, "From Anti-Judaism to Antisemitism in Early Christianity?," in Limor and Stroumsa, *Contra Iǒudaeos*, 1–26. For the term "symbolic Judaism," see M. S. Taylor, *Anti-Judaism and Early Christian Identity: A Critique of the Scholarly Consensus* (Leiden: Brill, 1995); for nuancing of this view, see J. Carleton Paget, "Anti-Judaism and Early Christian Identity," *ZAC* 1.2 (1997): 195–225.

21. Interestingly, in antiquity the epistle seems to have been appreciated more for its allegory than its anti-Judaism; see F. R. Prostmeier, "Antijudaismus im Rahmen christlicher Hermeneutik: zum Streit über christliche Identität in der Alten Kirche. Notizen zum Barnabasbrief," *ZAC* 6 (2002): 38–58.

worthy to receive it because of their sins" (14.1). Christ's coming enabled him to "complete the full measure of the sins of those who persecuted his prophets to death" (5.11) and to forge a "new people" (5.7). Israel's attempts to obey the law resulted from an interpretative wooden literalness that failed to perceive the figurative or typological nature of the law. This problematic view leads to disparaging or startling statements. For example, circumcision should not have been taken literally—pagan nations understood it that way (9.6)—but Israel disobeyed "because an evil angel 'enlightened' them" (9.4b). This is a surprising statement, to say the least, because it seems to subvert a commandment that the Pentateuch clearly presents as divine in origin and to ascribe it to an evil angel, perhaps to the devil.[22] Or again, Barnabas muses, "Let us see whether this people or the former people is the heir, and whether the covenant is for us or for them" (13.1). The question is answered through demonstrating that the Christians are the heir by pointing to the reversal of the right of primogeniture in the patriarchal accounts, in which the older serves the younger child.

As mentioned above, Barnabas does not explicitly mention Jews or Christians but carries on by way of an exegetical discourse about Israel that opens out into a discussion of "them" and "us." Some scholars have suggested that Barnabas's claims that Israel lost the covenant should not be understood as directed outwardly in polemics, but rather functions inwardly for the Christian community as an instance of the Deuteronomic rhetorical tradition (a "christianized deuteronomism").[23] That is, Barnabas tells a story about the failures of Israel and their subsequent loss of the covenant that is designed to motivate his own audience to persevere and avoid a similar fate. But Barnabas's rhetoric is so pronounced that many scholars sense a genuine anxiety that members of his audience could turn or return to Judaism, or perhaps to a Judaizing Christianity, and so the heated negative characterizations of Israel are intended to address not simply a past people but rather to target a contemporary group or community.[24] Perhaps the clearest indication of this occurs in 3.6, where we see a concern to dissuade an audience from a course of action, "in order that we might not shipwreck ourselves as those who have come over [ἐπήλυτοι, *epēlytoi*; v.l. προσήλυτοι, *prosēlytoi*—that is, "those who have come over" or, in the variant reading, "proselytes"] to their law." Relatedly, it seems genuinely to be the case that for Barnabas there was a single covenant, offered to Israel but suspended until it could be restored in Christ, which would cohere well with a view that sees the text addressing a contemporary option that he hopes to close off.[25]

Recently, Clare Rothschild has made the case, which deserves fuller consideration than can be offered here, that Barnabas should be conceived as an allegorical letter to critique a group of literal-minded Christians, and so the Jews implied by the letter are only ciphers for Christians who make the exegetical errors that Barnabas attacks.[26]

22. See J. Carleton Paget, "Barnabas 9:4: A Peculiar Verse on Circumcision," *VC* 45 (1991): 242–54; and I. T. Soon, "Satan and Circumcision: The Devil as the ἄγγελος πονηρός in Barn 9:4," *VC* 76 (2022): 60–72.

23. J. N. Rhodes, *The Epistle of Barnabas and the Deuteronomic Tradition: Polemics, Paraenesis, and the Legacy of the Golden-Calf Incident*, WUNT 2/188 (Tübingen: Mohr Siebeck, 2004).

24. Carleton Paget, *Epistle of Barnabas*; idem, "Barnabas and the Outsiders: Jews and Their World in the *Epistle of Barnabas*," in *Early Christian Communities Between Ideal and Reality*, ed. M. Grundeken and J. Verheyden, WUNT 342 (Tübingen: Mohr Siebeck, 2015), 177–202; idem, "The Epistle of Barnabas, Jews and Christians," in *Jews and Christians—Parting Ways in the First Two Centuries CE? Reflections on the Gains and Losses of a Model*, ed. J. Schröter, B. Edsall, and J. Verheyden, BZNW 253 (Berlin: de Gruyter, 2021), 217–47; Hvalvik, *Struggle for Scripture and Covenant*; W. Horbury, "Jewish-Christian Relations in Barnabas and Justin Martyr," in *Jews and Christians in Contact and Controversy* (Edinburgh: T&T Clark, 1998), 127–61.

25. For the difficult text at 4.6b, which seems to be corrupt, see J. N. Rhodes, "'Barnabas' 4.6b: The Exegetical Implications of a Textual Problem," *VC* 58.4 (2004): 365–92.

26. C. K. Rothschild, "Soteriology and the Allegorical Construction of Opponents in the Epistle of Barnabas," in *Sōtēria: Salvation in Early Christianity and Antiquity*, ed. D. S. du Toit, C. Gerber, and C. Zimmermann, NovTSup 175 (Leiden: Brill, 2019), 561–76.

3.2 Apocalyptic Theology

Barnabas offers a striking example of a text in relative proximity to the New Testament that retains a strong emphasis on apocalyptic theology. Like Paul (e.g., Gal 1:3–4), Barnabas operates with a two-age schema. In 4.1 he refers to "the present age" (τοῦ νῦν καιροῦ, *tou nyn kairou*), which he contrasts to the "age that is to come" (τὸν μέλλοντα, *ton mellonta*), in which Barnabas conceives of his community living in the "last days" (4.9). The last days are "dark and evil days" (8.6), in which the "evil ruler" (4.13), Satan, is at work. Satan is problematically characterized as "the black one" (4:10; 20.1).[27] But Jesus "redeems our hearts from darkness" (14.5, 6). There will be a final judgment without partiality according to works (4.12; cf. 5.7), and believers should therefore not live "as though they were already justified" (4.10: ὡς ἤδη δεδικαιωμένοι, *hōs ēdē dedikaiōmenoi*; cf. 1 Cor 4:8?). In fact, the resurrection of Christ functions as a proof of a general resurrection to come (5.6).[28]

God's work in the last days is a "second creation" that repristinates the first, in an Urzeit–Endzeit paradigm: "Behold, I make the last things as the first" (6.13), an apocryphal saying that also occurs in the *Dialogue of Jason and Papiscus*.[29] Operating with a Sabbath structure of history, Barnabas suggests that the world age has six thousand years followed by a millennium of bliss (15.4–5).[30] Like 2 Peter 3:8, Barnabas seems to rely on the psalmist's conception that "a thousand years in your sight are like the day of yesterday that passed and a watch in the night" (Ps 90:4 [89:4 LXX] NETS). The Sabbath-structure of history is an idea that recurs in later Jewish tradition as well (e.g., b. Sanh. 97a). In that final age, lawlessness will cease to exist, and all things will be made new by the Lord (Barn. 15.7). The ethical task of the present moment is to live in light of the ultimate fate of all things. The cosmic powers each reign over one of the two ways: "light-giving angels of God" are stationed over the way of life, but angels of Satan over the way of death—that is, the ruler of the present era of lawlessness (18.1–2). But ultimately, the last judgment will vanquish all evil: "The day is near when everything will perish together with the Evil One. The Lord, and his reward, is near" (21.3).

Barnabas does not shy away from a future-oriented eschatology, or evince anxiety at the delay of the parousia, but retains a lively and vivid apocalyptic imagination in service of his ethical admonitions to the community.

3.3 Use of Scripture

Clearly one of Barnabas's major concerns is the interpretation of the Jewish Greek Scriptures (i.e., what we refer to as the Septuagint), and this is a concern that the text shares with much of the New Testament. Barnabas's particular purposes involve allegorizing various scriptural events and institutions, or looking for "types" of Jesus, and this hermeneutic

27. See Rothschild, "Ethiopianising the Devil," although the argument is not entirely convincing.

28. On Barnabas's emphasis on the futurity of salvation, see M. Vinzent, "Ertragen und Ausharren: Die Lebenslehre des Barnabasbriefes," *ZNW* 86 (1995): 74–93.

29. It occurs in the recently rediscovered fragments of the *Dialogue*; see H. Tolley, "The Jewish-Christian Dialogue *Jason and Papiscus* in Light of the Sinaiticus Fragment," *HTR* 114.1 (2021): 1–26, here 24–25. For the text, see A. Resch, *Agrapha: Aussercanonische Schriftfragmente gesammelt und untersucht*, 2nd ed. (Leipzig: Hinrichs, 1906), 167–68; F. R. Prostmeier, *Der Barnabasbrief*, KAV 8 (Göttingen: Vandenhoeck & Ruprecht, 1999), 275–76. Also, note the very fragmentary papyrus, PSI XI 1200 bis that seems to contain similar text; see A. Carlini, "Amicus Plato . . .: A proposito di PSI XI 1200, Gorg. 447B ss.," in *Miscellanea Papyrologica*, ed. R. Pintaudi (Florence: Edizioni Gonnelli, 1980), 41–45.

30. For discussion, see E. Ferguson, "Was Barnabas a Chiliast? An Example of Hellenistic Number Symbolism in Barnabas and Clement of Alexandria," in *Catechesis, Baptism, Eschatology, and Martyrdom*, vol. 2 of *The Early Church at Work and Worship* (Cambridge: Clarke, 2014), 200–212. Ferguson disputes that Barnabas should be thought of as a chiliast.

is also occasionally attested within the New Testament (e.g., 1 Cor 10:1–13; Gal 4:21–31; Heb 8:5). Barnabas cites most often from the prophets (roughly 34 times), the Pentateuch (20 times) and the Psalms (11 times), and these texts are also central to the selection we find in the New Testament. There is also a relatively large number of unknown or nonstandard citations (cf. 2.10; 4.3–5; 6.13; 7.8; 11.9–10; 12.1; 16.3, 5, 6). Beyond broad patterns, there are almost twenty citations common to Barnabas and the New Testament.[31] While many of these derive from common tradition, or perhaps Barnabas's use of testimonia collections, some of them show evidence of being transmitted to Barnabas via the New Testament, though he employs them for his own purposes. In general, Barnabas operates with an interpretative posture that subsumes the historical or original or literal meaning of a scriptural text entirely to his present argument. On the one hand, it is a "high" view of Scripture that sees in it an infinite fund of meaning, but on the other, it requires a startlingly bleak picture of the history of salvation in the period that stretched from the golden-calf episode until the death of Jesus, which, on Barnabas's rendering, is simply a negative parenthesis in God's salvific intentions toward the world.

Consideration of a couple of the citations that are shared with the New Testament is instructive.[32]

Zech 13:7	Matt 26:31//Mark 14:27	Barn. 5.12
πατάξατε τοὺς ποιμένας καὶ ἐκσπάσατε τὰ πρόβατα,	Πατάξω τὸν ποιμένα, καὶ διασκορπισθήσονται τὰ πρόβατα τῆς ποίμνης· (Matt) Πατάξω τὸν ποιμένα, καὶ τὰ πρόβατα διασκορπισθήσονται· (Mark)	Λέγει γὰρ ὁ θεὸς τὴν πληγὴν τῆς σαρκὸς αὐτοῦ ἐξ αὐτῶν· «Ὅταν πατάξωσιν τὸν ποιμένα αὐτῶν, τότε ἀπολεῖται τὰ πρόβατα τῆς ποίμνης.»
"Strike the shepherds and draw out the sheep."	"I will strike the shepherd, and the sheep of the fold will be scattered" (Matt) "I will strike the shepherd, and the sheep will be scattered" (Mark)	"For God speaks of the blow to his flesh from them, 'When they strike their shepherd, then the sheep of the fold will be destroyed.'"

Like Matthew and Mark, Barnabas cites Zechariah as a sort of explanatory prooftext about the death of Jesus, though Barnabas uses it particularly to emphasize the "full measure of the sins of those who persecuted his prophets to death" (Barn. 5.11). But although the tradition is applied to Jesus in all three texts, Barnabas does not seem to be textually dependent on the form found in the Synoptic tradition. He shares the singular "shepherd" (τὸν ποιμένα, *ton poimena*), but uses a different form of the verb πατάσσω, *patassō*, and speaks of the sheep being "destroyed" (ἀπολεῖται, *apoleitai*) rather than "scattered" (διασκορπισθήσονται, *diaskorpisthēsontai*). Barnabas seems to see the destruction of

31. See M. J. J. Menken, "Old Testament Quotations in the *Epistle of Barnabas* with Parallels in the New Testament," in *Textual History and the Reception of Scripture in Early Christianity*, ed. J. de Vries and M. Karrer (Atlanta: Society of Biblical Literature, 2013), 295–321. More broadly, see Wengst, *Tradition und Theologie*; F. R. Prostmeier, *Epistola Barnabae / Barnabasbrief: Eingeleitet, kritisch ediert und übersetzt*, FC 72 (Freiburg: Herder, 2018), 1–157, here 51–54.

32. In this table and those below, I have produced my own, relatively literal translations to call attention to the points of similarity and difference.

Israel, the presumed referent of "the sheep," as foreshadowed in Zechariah already and described as the consequence of their killing Jesus. Needless to say, this is quite distinct from the Synoptic tradition.

Another instance demonstrates how Barnabas and the Fourth Gospel both reflect on a common image, but do so in distinctive ways. In John 3, the evangelist invokes Moses's "lifting up" of the serpent in the wilderness as a sign for the exaltation of the Son of Man on the cross. Barnabas, for his part, retells the event in 12.5–7 in order to demonstrate "that he must suffer, and that the very one whom they will think they have destroyed shall give life" (12.5). His telling of the event is independent of the Fourth Gospel's, although it shares with Justin Martyr a contrast between Moses's commanding that no image of God shall be made and Moses making of the snake (Justin, *Dial.* 94; cf. *1 Apol.* 60).[33]

Num 21:8–9 LXX	John 3:14–15	Barn. 12.7
καὶ εἶπεν κύριος πρὸς Μωυσῆν Ποίησον σεαυτῷ ὄφιν καὶ θὲς αὐτὸν ἐπὶ σημείου, καὶ ἔσται ἐὰν δάκῃ ὄφις ἄνθρωπον, πᾶς ὁ δεδηγμένος ἰδὼν αὐτὸν ζήσεται. καὶ ἐποίησεν Μωυσῆς ὄφιν χαλκοῦν καὶ ἔστησεν αὐτὸν ἐπὶ σημείου, καὶ ἐγένετο ὅταν ἔδακνεν ὄφις ἄνθρωπον, καὶ ἐπέβλεψεν ἐπὶ τὸν ὄφιν τὸν χαλκοῦν καὶ ἔζη.	καὶ καθὼς Μωϋσῆς ὕψωσεν τὸν ὄφιν ἐν τῇ ἐρήμῳ, οὕτως ὑψωθῆναι δεῖ τὸν υἱὸν τοῦ ἀνθρώπου, ἵνα πᾶς ὁ πιστεύων ἐν αὐτῷ ἔχῃ ζωὴν αἰώνιον	Εἶπεν δὲ Μωϋσῆς πρὸς αὐτούς· «Ὅταν», φησίν, «δηχθῇ τις ὑμῶν, ἐλθέτω ἐπὶ τὸν ὄφιν τὸν ἐπὶ τοῦ ξύλου ἐπικείμενον καὶ ἐλπισάτω πιστεύσας ὅτι αὐτὸς ὢν νεκρὸς δύναται ζωοποιῆσαι, καὶ παραχρῆμα σωθήσεται»—καὶ οὕτως ἐποίουν.
"And the Lord said to Moses, 'Make for yourself a snake and place it as a sign, and it will be that if a snake should bite a person, everyone who is bitten, if they look at it, will live.' And Moses made a bronze snake and stood it up as a sign, and it happened that whenever a snake bit a person, and they looked at the bronze snake, that person would live."	"And just as Moses lifted up the snake in the desert, in this way is it necessary for the Son of Man to be lifted up, in order that everyone who believes in him should have eternal life."	"And Moses said to them, 'Whenever', he says, 'one of you should be bitten, let that person come to the snake fixed upon the wood and let that one hope, believing that it, though dead, is able to make alive, and immediately that one will be saved.'—and this is what they would do."

4. KEY PASSAGES FOR NEW TESTAMENT STUDIES AND THEIR SIGNIFICANCE

There are no unambiguous citations of the New Testament in Barnabas, although a few places preserve plausible citations and others interesting parallels.[34] We will here consider only a few of the most suggestive instances.

4.1 Synoptic Tradition

Perhaps the closest verbatim agreement with the New Testament occurs in Barnabas 4.14, in which Barnabas pulls together the threads of his exhortation to be vigilant in

33. Justin and Barnabas have probably relied on a common source; see O. Skarsaune, *The Proof from Prophecy: A Study in Justin Martyr's Proof-Text Tradition: Text-Type, Provenance, Theological Profile*, NovTSup 56 (Leiden: Brill, 1987).

34. These have been well analyzed by James Carleton Paget, to whom I am indebted in this discussion; see J. Carleton Paget, "The *Epistle of Barnabas* and the Writings that Later Formed the New Testament," in *The Reception of the New Testament in the Apostolic Fathers*, ed. A. F. Gregory and C. M. Tuckett (Oxford: Oxford University Press, 2005), 229–49.

maintaining the covenant, lest his hearers lose it the way Israel did. Barnabas then urges, "Let us be on guard lest we should be found to be, as it is written, 'many called, but few chosen.'"

Matt 22:14	Barn. 4.14
πολλοὶ γάρ εἰσιν κλητοὶ ὀλίγοι δὲ ἐκλεκτοί.	ὡς γέγραπται, πολλοὶ κλητοί, ὀλίγοι δὲ ἐκλεκτοὶ
"For many are called, but few are chosen."	"As it is written, 'many are called, but few are chosen."

Notable here is that this logion is introduced with the citation formula ὡς γέγραπται, *hōs gegraptai* ("as it is written"), which points to a written source. Is that source the Gospel of Matthew itself, or simply Synoptic tradition? How one answers that question will be determined in part by broader sensibilities about determining literary knowledge of the Gospels in the second century.[35] Both Barnabas and the Gospel of Matthew use the logion to underline a call to vigilance, and in both texts—the parable of the wedding banquet in Matthew and the discussion of the covenant in Barnabas—the question of a prior group rejected in favor of a subsequent group is featured. The verbal equivalence is exact enough that it is reasonable to assume that Barnabas has either read the Gospel of Matthew or has derived this from a written collection of material composed by someone who had.

A second place where we find proximity to Synoptic tradition occurs in Barnabas 5.9. There, Barnabas writes of Jesus, "When he chose his own apostles who were destined to preach his gospel (who were sinful beyond all measure in order that he might demonstrate that he did not come to call the righteous, but sinners), then he revealed himself to be God's Son." Barnabas plays up the tradition of sinful apostles—though later Christian critics will seize on this and use it in their critiques (see Origen, *Cels.* 1.63)—in order to highlight the grace of Jesus. The wording is once again largely verbatim:

Matt 9:13	Barn. 5.9
οὐ γὰρ ἦλθον καλέσαι δικαίους ἀλλὰ ἁμαρτωλούς.	Ὅτε δὲ τοὺς ἰδίους ἀποστόλους τοὺς μέλλοντας κηρύσσειν τὸ εὐαγγέλιον αὐτοῦ ἐξελέξατο, ὄντας ὑπὲρ πᾶσαν ἁμαρτίαν ἀνομωτέρους, ἵνα δείξῃ ὅτι οὐκ ἦλθεν καλέσαι δικαίους, ἀλλὰ ἁμαρτωλούς, τότε ἐφανέρωσεν ἑαυτὸν εἶναι υἱὸν θεοῦ.
"For I did not come to call the righteous, but sinners."	"And when he chose his own apostles who were about to proclaim his gospel (even though they were lawless beyond all sin) in order that he might demonstrate that he did not come to call the righteous, but sinners, then he showed himself to be Son of God."

Here again we can ask whether this implies literary knowledge of Matthew or simply knowledge of Synoptic tradition. This logion also occurs in Mark 2:17 (οὐκ ἦλθον καλέσαι

35. Cf. W.-D. Köhler, *Die Rezeption des Mattäusevangeliums in der Zeit vor Irenäus*, WUNT 2/24 (Tübingen: Mohr Siebeck, 1987), 109–23, and P. F. Beatrice, "Une citation de l'Évangile de Matthieu dans l'Épître de Barnabé," in *The New Testament in Early Christianity = La réception des écrits néotestamentaires dans le christianisme primitif*, ed. J.-M. Sevrin, BETL 86 (Leuven: Leuven University Press, 1989), 231–45, with H. Koester, "Der Barnabasbrief," in *Synoptische Überlieferung bei den apostolischen Vätern* (Berlin: Akademie, 1957), 124–58.

δικαίους ἀλλὰ ἁμαρτωλούς, *ouk ēlthon kalesai dikaious alla hamartōlous,* "I did not come to call the righteous, but sinners") and Luke 5:32 (οὐκ ἐλήλυθα καλέσαι δικαίους ἀλλὰ ἁμαρτωλοὺς εἰς μετάνοιαν, *ouk elēlutha kalesai dikaious alla hamartōlous eis metanoian,* "I have not come to call the righteous, but sinners to repentance"). The Matthean and Markan versions are virtually identical, apart from Matthew's οὐ γάρ, *ou gar,* and Mark's οὐκ, *ouk,* and in both Gospels Jesus can be characterized as "teaching Israel and performing extraordinary wonders and signs" and as preaching (Barn 5.8), so determining whether this is particularly Matthean seems to be difficult, although it is not unreasonable to consider that the Matthean text in Barnabas 4.14 might slightly incline an interpreter toward seeing Matthean influence here.

4.2 Pauline Tradition

Barnabas's relationship to Pauline tradition is likely in some broad sense, but whether he had direct knowledge of Paul's letters is difficult to say. He is certainly not someone who could be considered part of a Pauline school and uses key theologoumena such as the cross or "flesh" in ways distinctive from Paul. One can point to certain stylistic commonalities: for example, Barnabas has a penchant for φανερόω + ἐν σαρκί, *phaneroō + en sarki* ("revealed" + "in the flesh," 5.6, 9; 6.7, 9, 14; 12.10), which is reminiscent of the tradition cited at 1 Timothy 3:16: ὅς ἐφανερώθη ἐν σαρκί, *hos ephanerōthē en sarki,* "who was revealed in the flesh."[36] But in one instance, Barnabas betrays particularly close verbal similarity to Romans 4:

Gen 15:6; 17:4–5	Rom 4:3, 11	Barn. 13.7
καὶ ἐπίστευσεν Αβραμ τῷ θεῷ, καὶ ἐλογίσθη αὐτῷ εἰς δικαιοσύνην. Καὶ ἐγὼ ἰδοὺ ἡ διαθήκη μου μετὰ σοῦ, καὶ ἔσῃ πατὴρ πλήθους ἐθνῶν. καὶ οὐ κληθήσεται ἔτι τὸ ὄνομά σου Αβραμ, ἀλλ' ἔσται τὸ ὄνομά σου Αβρααμ, ὅτι πατέρα πολλῶν ἐθνῶν τέθεικά σε.	τί γὰρ ἡ γραφὴ λέγει; Ἐπίστευσεν δὲ Ἀβραὰμ τῷ θεῷ, καὶ ἐλογίσθη αὐτῷ εἰς δικαιοσύνην. καὶ σημεῖον ἔλαβεν περιτομῆς, σφραγῖδα τῆς δικαιοσύνης τῆς πίστεως τῆς ἐν τῇ ἀκροβυστίᾳ, εἰς τὸ εἶναι αὐτὸν πατέρα πάντων τῶν πιστευόντων δι' ἀκροβυστίας, εἰς τὸ λογισθῆναι αὐτοῖς δικαιοσύνην	Τί οὖν λέγει τῷ Ἀβραάμ, ὅτε μόνος πιστεύσας ἐτέθη εἰς δικαιοσύνην; «Ἰδού, τέθεικά σε, Ἀβραάμ, πατέρα ἐθνῶν τῶν πιστευόντων δι' ἀκροβυστίας τῷ θεῷ.»
"And Abram believed God, and it was reckoned to him as righteousness." "And as for me, behold, my covenant is with you, and you will be father of a multitude of nations. And no longer will your name be Abram, but your name shall be Abraham, because I have appointed you to be father of many nations."	"For what does Scripture say? 'Abraham believed God, and it was reckoned to him as righteousness.' And he received the sign of circumcision, a seal of the righteousness of faith while he was still uncircumcised, so that he would be father of all who believe through uncircumcision, in order that righteousness should be reckoned to them."	"What then does he say to Abraham, when, he alone having believed, he was appointed to righteousness? 'Behold, I have appointed you, Abraham, father of nations who believe in God through uncircumcision.'"

36. Carleton Paget, "*Epistle of Barnabas* and the Writings," 238.

Here Barnabas first seems simply to be citing the same traditions from Genesis as Paul does. He first alludes to Genesis 15:6, though uses ἐτέθη, *etethē* ("appointed") where Paul has ἐλογίσθη, *elogisthē* ("reckoned"). But then Barnabas goes on to cite Genesis 17:4–5 in a way that incorporates Paul's interpretative additions to Genesis 17:5 in Romans 4:11, particularly in the shift from Genesis's "father of many nations" to Barnabas's "father of the gentiles who believe without being circumcised [lit.: through the foreskin]." The interpretation contained in Romans 4:11 seems clearly to have been taken up by Barnabas, even if the latter simply presents itself as offering an interpretation of Genesis. The influence of Paul is therefore clear, but one cannot judge with certainty whether Barnabas had direct recourse to Romans or whether the Pauline tradition was mediated to Barnabas by an intermediate written source such as a testimony collection.

4.3 Hebrews

Many interpreters have suggested commonalities between Hebrews and Barnabas, and at least one ancient author ascribed the authorship of Hebrews to Barnabas.[37] But even so, as James Carleton Paget writes, "It is very difficult to see any clear evidence of even an allusion to Hebrews. Yet, in terms of theological atmosphere and general tendencies, there is a greater proximity than perhaps is the case with any other NT book."[38] One might compare some suggestive similarities: Barnabas 5.6 with Hebrews 2:14; Barnabas 6.17–19 with Hebrews 2:5–9; Barnabas 7.4 with Hebrews 9:12–13, 19, and 10:4; and Barnabas 5.1 with Hebrews 12:24. Both texts evince an interest in the Day of Atonement as a means of understanding Jesus's death,[39] in the covenant,[40] and in the concept of "rest."[41] Determining any concrete relationship between the two texts is difficult, but they share an interest in common themes and exegetical traditions.

4.4 Christology

At one point, Barnabas criticizes the view that Jesus might be the son of man or the son of David, the former title important to all the New Testament Gospels, the latter for the Synoptics in particular. In 12.8–10, Barnabas develops a contrast between Jesus (i.e., the Septuagint's rendering of Joshua) the son of Nun, and Jesus the Son of God.[42] He wants to distinguish the two and, although committed to the view that Jesus was "in the flesh" (ἐν σαρκί, *en sarki*), Barnabas nevertheless emphasizes the fundamental difference between the two: "Observe again that it is Jesus, not a son of man but the Son of God [οὐχι υἱὸς ἀνθρώπου ἀλλὰ υἱὸς τοῦ θεοῦ, *ouchi huios anthrōpou alla huios tou theou*]."[43] Rather than

37. See E. A. de Boer, "Tertullian on "Barnabas' Letter to the Hebrews" in De pudicitia 20.1–5," *VC* 68 (2014): 243–63.

38. Carleton Paget, "*Epistle of Barnabas* and the Writings," 245.

39. D. S. Ben Ezra, "Fasting with Jews, Thinking with Scapegoats: Some Remarks on Yom Kippur in Early Judaism and Christianity, in Particular 4Q541, *Barnabas* 7, Matthew 27 and Acts 27," in *The Day of Atonement: Its Interpretations in Early Jewish and Christian Traditions*, ed. T. Hieke and T. Nicklas, Themes in Biblical Narrative 15 (Leiden: Brill, 2012), 165–87.

40. K. Backhaus, "Das Bundesmotiv in der frühkirchlichen Schwellenzeit: Hebräerbrief, Barnabasbrief, Dialogus cum Tryphone," in *Der sprechende Gott: Gesammelte Studien zum Hebräerbrief*, WUNT 240 (Tübingen: Mohr Siebeck, 2009), 155–73.

41. Carleton Paget, "*Epistle of Barnabas* and the Writings," 246–48.

42. This recalls Hebrews; see R. Ounsworth, *Joshua Typology in the New Testament*, WUNT 2/328 (Tübingen: Mohr Siebeck, 2012).

43. Holmes translates, "a son of a man," but I omit the indefinite article. To prove the assertion, Barnabas cites a nonstandard text of Exod 17:14: "Take a book in your hands and write what the Lord says, that in the last days the Son of God will cut off by its roots all the house of Amalek."

a straightforward critique of the title, derived from Daniel 7, that we find in the New Testament, this seems to be a focused contrast to highlight the divinity of Jesus, though it skirts worryingly close to certain forms of docetism as a bare assertion.

Immediately after this, Barnabas goes on to write against an unnamed group of opponents who "say that the Messiah is the son of David." To refute this assertion, Barnabas cites Psalm 110:1 [109:1 LXX] (the same text cited in Mark 12:35–37 parr.) and a variant text of Isaiah 45:1, "The Lord said to the Messiah my Lord . . ." (κυρίῳ, *kyriō*, rather than to Κύρῳ, *Kyrō*, that is, to Cyrus). He concludes, "Observe how David calls him 'Lord,' and does not call him 'son'" (Barn. 12.11). Barnabas seems to evince an anxiety about Jewish messianic conceptions that might not endorse the divinity of the Messiah, and so he denies a title that the Gospels seem at most to qualify.[44] While it is not clear that Barnabas knows the text of Ps 110 [109 LXX] directly through the Synoptic usage of it, and so cannot be seen to oppose the Christology of the Synoptics in particular, the text demonstrates a worry that is cognate to Barnabas's general unease with Jewish tradition.

5. CONCLUSION

The Epistle of Barnabas is a fascinating text. It comprises our earliest sustained treatment of Jewish Scripture after the New Testament. The allegorical method it employs allows the author to simultaneously assert the deep meaning of Scripture, while also denying it practical significance as valid law. The treatise shows evidence of a sometimes clumsy incorporation of previous sources, but for all that still maintains an overall point of view. The author wants to urge his audience—whether an actual audience composed of a discrete community who received this letter, or the broader reading public that would consume a pseudepigraphal composition—to guard themselves zealously and hold fast in their confession of and allegiance to Jesus. If they turn to the traditions of Jewish praxis, they are making a retrograde move, since the old law and the old people have been set aside. The polemical rhetoric that undergirds this pastoral appeal means that the text reads in an unfriendly manner today, and more than one reader has expressed relief that the possibly scriptural status it bore for authors like Clement and Origen or (maybe) the compiler of Codex Sinaiticus did not in the end prevail.

It nevertheless supplies the interpreter of the New Testament with a fascinating glimpse of the transformation of trajectories from the earliest period of the Jesus movement into the second century amid the ongoing task of Christian self-definition against both Jewish and pagan "others." Barnabas wants to press those defining lines into greater clarity, and so contributes in some small way to the moving of the early church away from its Jewish roots. At the same time, it attests a striking proximity to that from which it wants to move away: Barnabas knows Jewish exegetical traditions and recommends an approach to the ethical life that seems to derive relatively directly from Jewish tradition with the so-called Two Ways section. It therefore remains an important witness to a period of both proximity and struggle, a window onto the process of becoming two peoples divided by a common Scripture read in disparate ways.

44. For such Jewish or Jewish-Christian messianic conceptions, note Ps.-Clem., *Hom.* 18.13; Justin, *Dial.* 49.1. For discussion, see J. C. Edwards, *The Gospel According to the Epistle of Barnabas*, WUNT 2/503 (Tübingen: Mohr Siebeck, 2019), 63–65.

BIBLIOGRAPHY

Carleton Paget, J. "The *Epistle of Barnabas* and the Writings that Later Formed the New Testament." Pages 229–49 in *The Reception of the New Testament in the Apostolic Fathers*. Edited by A. F. Gregory and C. M. Tuckett. Oxford: Oxford University Press, 2005.

Carleton Paget, J. *The Epistle of Barnabas: Outlook and Background*. WUNT 2/64. Tübingen, Mohr Siebeck, 1994.

Carleton Paget, J. "Paul and the Epistle of Barnabas." Pages 79–100 in *The Apostolic Fathers and Paul*. Edited by T. D. Still and D. E. Wilhite. Pauline and Patristic Scholars in Debate 2. London: Bloomsbury, 2017.

Ehrman, B. D. "Epistle of Barnabas." Pages 1–83 in *The Apostolic Fathers*. Vol. 2. LCL 25. Cambridge: Harvard University Press, 2003.

Holmes, M. W. "The Epistle of Barnabas." Pages 370–441 in *The Apostolic Fathers: Greek Texts and English Translations*. 3rd ed. Grand Rapids: Baker Academic, 2007.

Horbury, W. "Jewish-Christian Relations in Barnabas and Justin Martyr." Pages 127–61 in *Jews and Christians in Contact and Controversy*. Edinburgh: T&T Clark, 1998.

Hvalvik, R. *The Struggle for Scripture and Covenant: The Purpose of the Epistle of Barnabas and Jewish-Christian Competition in the Second Century*. WUNT 2/82. Tübingen: Mohr Siebeck, 1996.

Prigent, P., and R. A. Kraft. *Épître de Barnabé*. SC 172. Paris: Cerf, 1971.

Prostmeier, F. R. *Der Barnabasbrief*. KAV 8. Göttingen: Vandenhoeck and Ruprecht, 1999.

Rhodes, J. N. *The Epistle of Barnabas and the Deuteronomic Tradition: Polemics, Paraenesis, and the Legacy of the Golden-Calf Incident*. WUNT 2/188. Tübingen: Mohr Siebeck, 2004.

Rothschild, C. K. "Epistle of Barnabas and Secession through Allegory." Pages 191–212 in *New Essays on the Apostolic Fathers*. WUNT 1/375. Tübingen: Mohr Siebeck, 2017.

Wengst, K. *Didache (Apostellehre), Barnabasbrief, Zweiter Klemensbrief, Schrift an Diognet*. Munich: Kösel, 1984.

CHAPTER 9

THE LETTERS OF IGNATIUS OF ANTIOCH

PAUL FOSTER

1. INTRODUCTION

Nearly every aspect surrounding Ignatius, a prominent Christian figure in the community of Christ-followers at Antioch, and the letters he wrote has been a source of controversy. There is debate concerning the number of letters he wrote, their date, their authenticity, and the number of groups of opponents described in the letters. These epistles have been at the forefront of various church controversies. Moreover, there have been differences of opinion concerning whether Ignatius was a bishop or deacon, the psychological state of the author, and the value of the letters for understanding the development of theology. These issues and many more are all topics where there are contested and highly polarized views. However, despite such disputed issues, these writings continue to have a magnetic attraction for all who seek to understand the nascent early Jesus movement in the second century. At one level, this is perhaps somewhat surprising, especially given that the letters reflect the views of one individual writing in extreme circumstances, with the period of composition of the letters being compressed into a narrow time period of perhaps only several weeks. Yet for all their limitations, if these letters are what they purport to be—the writings of the bishop of Antioch penned while being transported to Rome for execution—then they are truly remarkable. For despite the circumstances in which they were written, the letters provide insights into the structures of several churches in the Roman province of Asia, and they reveal information concerning various issues confronting those Christian communities in the first part of the second century. Moreover, these letters show both strong points of continuity with the expression of certain ideas contained in the New Testament, while also, on the other hand, revealing clear patterns of development in relation to other issues, such as the structure of leadership in some early Jesus communities. Consequently, no other surviving literary source potentially provides the same level of insight into the early Christian movement in the second century that is to be found in these letters.[1]

1.1 The Letter Collections

One of the significant features surrounding the epistles of Ignatius are the various forms and contents of letter collections that exist in surviving manuscripts. Typically, scholars describe three forms of these collections, but in reality that is an oversimplification.

1. As will be discussed, there are difficulties establishing the form of the text of the letters of Ignatius. Unless otherwise indicated, this discussion is based on the text found in M. W. Holmes, *The Apostolic Fathers: Greek Texts and English Translations*, 3rd ed. (Grand Rapids: Baker Academic, 2007), 166–271. Biblical translations are my own.

However, as a starting point it is helpful to describe that standard categorization, before explaining why it does not fully account for the data. The term "recension" is used to describe these divergent collections.

Short recension	Contains three letters of Ignatius, *To Polycarp, To the Ephesians,* and *To the Romans,* but in a shorter form than exists in the other two recensions. This recension survives in Syriac in three manuscripts. One manuscript dating to the sixth century contains only *To Polycarp.* The other two manuscripts dating between the seventh and ninth centuries both contain three letters, *To Polycarp, To the Ephesians,* and *To the Romans.* However, within the shorter form of *To the Romans,* there is embedded a passage that in the two other recensions is found in *To the Trallians.*
Middle recension	This recension is defined as comprising seven letters, *To the Ephesians, To the Magnesians, To the Trallians, To the Romans, To the Philadelphians, To the Smyrnaeans,* and *To Polycarp.* These letters are in a form that is shorter than their counterparts in the so-called long recension (see below), but longer than the three letters that survive in the short recension (see above). The manuscript evidence is complex. There is one major Greek manuscript that attests this form at least in part. The eleventh-century Codex Mediceo-Laurentianus preserves six letters of the middle recension in the order *Smyrnaeans, Polycarp, Ephesians, Magnesians, Philadelphians, Trallians.* However, alongside this it preserves three further letters (from the long recension), *Mary to Ignatius, Ignatius to Mary, Tarsians* (a fragment). *To the Romans* appears to have circulated separately, and in the middle recension is preserved in four Greek manuscripts dating between the tenth and thirteenth centuries. However, the middle recension is supported by two Latin manuscripts (one now lost) discovered in England and published by Ussher in 1644. There is also an Armenian and Arabic version of the middle recension, probably translated from Syriac. Only three sets of fragments of the middle recension in Syriac exist.
Long recension	This recension contains the seven letters of the middle recension but in longer form, and it also combines a further six letters with these seven letters—*Mary of Cassobola to Ignatius, Ignatius to Mary of Cassobola, Tarsians, Philippians, Antiochenes, Hero,* and in some manuscripts a *Prayer of Hero* written in Greek. Additionally, there exist a further set of four letters only in Latin, which appears to be the language of composition. These are two letters to John the elder, one to Mary the Christ-bearer, and one from Mary the Christ-bearer to Ignatius. There are more than ten Greek manuscripts that contain some or all of the thirteen letters in their long form that comprise the long recension. The Latin versional manuscripts of the long recension are even more numerous.

The long recension is not a unified development of the letter collection.[2] The expanded forms of the seven letters of the middle recension and the six additional Greek letters may reflect the work of a single author or group of editors. Due to the discernible theological tendencies of the long recension, this is most likely to have been the work of ultra-Arians in the second half of the fourth century. However, the four Latin letters appear to be a much later development.

1.2 Authenticity and Authorship

As suggested above, the long recension can be seen as a development of an earlier form of the letter collection. The four Latin letters obviously reflect a much later period with the heightened devotion to the Virgin Mary. The six additional Greek letters and the expansions of the seven letters of the middle recension appear to arise from ultra-Arian concerns of the second half of the fourth century (perhaps after 360 CE). Therefore, the long recension is fairly straightforwardly recognized as being the product of later theological concerns.

Therefore, this leads one to consider whether the short or the middle recension is more likely to be the original form of the Ignatian collection. Given the fact that the tendency to expand a more primitive form into the long recension has been observed, it might initially appear plausible that the same development occurred with the short recension being expanded into the middle recension. This view has recently resurfaced and has been articulated at length.[3] There are, however, a number of factors that count against the short recension being regarded as the earliest form of the letters of Ignatius. Assessing the internal evidence, two factors are significant. First, the short forms of the three letters of the short recension appear to strip away local concerns addressed to the named churches. This is an attempt to universalize the contents. Second, the portion of text found toward the end of shorter version of *To the Romans* that parallels material in *To the Trallians* (Ign. *Trall.* 4–5) is more readily seen as due to intentional editing of material drawn from two letters. It is less likely that this material was extracted from the short form of *To the Romans* and used as the basis for *To the Trallians* found in the middle recension.

External evidence is also significant. The earliest attestation of the short recension comes from the earliest surviving manuscript dating to the sixth century. However, the attestation of the middle recension comes from the beginning of the fourth century. Eusebius in his monumental work *Historia ecclesiastica* mentions seven letters of Ignatius by name, not just three (*Hist. eccl.* 3.36.5–6, 10). Also, he cites a couple of passages from Ignatius's letters. One of which is from *To the Smyrnaeans.* This reveals that by the fourth century the contents of this letter, not part of the short recension, were known. He also cites the entirety of *To the Romans* 5 (*Hist. eccl.* 3.36.7–9). This text is almost identical in both the short and middle recensions, so it is difficult to see this evidence as decisive for Eusebius knowing one form of the text over the other. However, given that the citation from *To the Smyrnaeans* is drawn from the middle recension, it is more plausible to expect that the middle recension was the form of text from which the citation from *To the Romans* was drawn.

---

2. For more discussion of the theological perspectives of the different recensions see P. Foster, "The Ignatian Problem: The Recensions of a Letter Corpus as a Reflection of Theological Concerns and Developments," in *Texts in Context: Essays on Dating and Contextualising Christian Writings from the Second and Early Third Centuries*, ed. J. Verheyden, J. Schröter, and T. Nicklas, BETL 319 (Leuven: Peeters, 2021), 5–50.

3. See M. Vinzent, *Writing the History of Early Christianity: From Reception to Retrospection* (Cambridge: Cambridge University Press, 2019), 266–464. So far, Vinzent's arguments have not gained any widespread support.

Therefore, since the earliest attestation of the short recension is more than two hundred years later than that of the middle recension, because the short recension bears the hallmarks of being an abbreviated text, and due to Eusebius's knowledge of the seven letters of the middle recension, it is much more likely that the middle recension represents the earliest recoverable for the Ignatian letter collection.

While that is almost certainly the case, doubts have been raised concerning whether this collection of texts can authentically be attributed to Ignatius as the author. The challenges against authorship by Ignatius have been raised in two ways. First, there are scholars who suggest that only certain of the letters stem from Ignatius, while the others were added later in the second century. Second, other scholars have suggested that none of the seven letters of the middle recension was written by Ignatius. Representative of the first group, Josep Rius-Camps argues that only four of the letters of the middle recension are genuine, the others being added at a later stage.[4] Alternatively, Robert Joly is an example of those who reject Ignatius's authorship of all of the seven letters of the middle recension.[5] Some of the reasons for rejecting Ignatius's authorship of the letters have been due to either perceived anomalies between terms or concepts used in these writings and a date in the early part of the second century, or because the letters are thought to reflect ideas or theological conflicts of a later period. For instance, Reinhard Hübner observed similarities in the theological language used by the letters of Ignatius and Noetus, and thus proposed that they were responding to the same christological issue in the province of Asia in the period 160–180 CE.[6] Hübner's doctoral student, Thomas Lechner, sought to find additional support for such a dating of the Ignatian letters. He concluded that the letters were pseudepigraphical and were written in the period between 165–175 CE.[7] While such theories have gained some support primarily in German-language scholarship, the majority of scholars have not found the proposed literary or contextual links sufficiently strong. Consequently, there has not been widespread acceptance of these proposals.

1.3 Ignatius's Opponents

In several of his letters, it is apparent that Ignatius is responding strongly against certain views and groups of people. Only in his letter to the Romans, a community that Ignatius has not yet visited and perhaps about which he has little knowledge, is there no condemnation of divergent beliefs or concerns with false teachers. Additionally, in his personal letter to Polycarp there is little specific information concerning opponents or their teachings. The situation is different in the other five letters of the middle recension. In those letters there is a more detailed description of alternative types of teachings being promoted, and the rhetoric against such teachers is more extensive and strident. Notwithstanding this, reconstructing the precise nature of the forms of teaching that

4. For Rius-Camps it is only the four letters written from Smyrna—Ephesians, Magnesians, Trallians, and Romans—that are genuine. The other three, purportedly sent from Troas, he argues were composed by the bishop of Philadelphia to enhance his authority. See J. Rius-Camps, *The Four Authentic Letters of Ignatius, the Martyr: A Critical Study Based in Anomalies Contained in the Textus Receptus*, Orientalia Christiana Analecta 213 (Rome: Pontificium Institutum Orientalium Studiorum, 1980).

5. R. Joly, *Le dossier d'Ignace d'Antioche*, Université libre Bruxelles, Faculté de philosophie et lettres 69 (Brussels: Éditions de l'Université de Bruxelles, 1979).

6. R. Hübner, "Thesen zur Echtheit und Datierung der sieben Briefe des Ignatius von Antiochien," *ZAC* 1 (1997): 44–72.

7. For more on this discussion, see P. Foster, "The Epistle of Ignatius of Antioch," in *The Writings of the Apostolic Fathers* (London: T&T Clark, 2007), 84–89; and Jonathan Lookadoo, "The Date and Authenticity of the Ignatian Letters: An Outline of Recent Discussions," *CurBR* 19 (2020): 88–114.

Ignatius opposes and the identity of those responsible for such instruction remain points of scholarly debate.

In *To the Ephesians*, Ignatius describes some people who "carry about the name maliciously and deceitfully," and he calls such individuals "rabid," or "mad dogs" (Ign. *Eph.* 7.1). The corrective he offers is in the form of one of his semi-creedal statements where he affirms Jesus is both flesh and spirit, born and unborn, along with other binary pairings (7.2). However, Ignatius tells the Ephesians that it is to their credit that they did not give such teachers a hearing. He states that the false teachers "passed your way with evil doctrine, but you did not allow them to sow it among you" (9.1).

There appear to be certain resonances between this rhetoric and that found in *To the Trallians*. The Trallian community is warned against "every strange plant, which is heresy" (Ign. *Trall.* 6.1). Furthermore, it is also told that people pretending to be trustworthy are actually administering "a deadly drug with honeyed wine" (6.2). Again, Ignatius utilizes a semi-creedal statement in the letter as a corrective to such false teaching (9.1–2). Then he continues by describing in greater details the nature of the false teaching. He asserts that those whom he characterizes as "atheists," or "unbelievers," teach that Jesus "suffered in appearance only" (10.1). In contrast to this, he describes the cross on which Jesus suffered as being the means by which the Trallians were called to be members of Christ (11.2). The false teachers appear to have gained more traction in Tralles than they did in Ephesus.

The comments addressed to believers in Smyrna are noticeably similar. Again, Ignatius uses a semi-creedal statement to say among other things that Christ was "truly nailed in the flesh for us under Pontius Pilate" (Ign. *Smyrn.* 1.1b–2a). He reinforces this point in a more fulsome manner in a context where he explicitly identifies the opponents as asserting the following about Jesus: "He truly suffered just as he truly raised himself—not, as certain unbelievers say, that he suffered in appearance only" (2.1). Concerning these opponents, Ignatius informs the Smyrnaeans, "I am guarding you in advance against wild beasts in human form—people whom you must not only not welcome but, if possible, not even meet" (4.1). This is not the end of Ignatius's description of these opponents. He states that "they do not believe in the blood of Christ" (6.1). Moreover, he states that such false teachings have led the opponents into ethical indifference displayed by a lack of compassion toward widows, orphans, and prisoners. Consequently, Ignatius concludes that such teaching has resulted in the opponents having removed themselves from common eucharistic worship, since they "refuse to acknowledge that the eucharist is the flesh of our Saviour Jesus Christ" (6.2).

Across these three letters there is a remarkably consistent picture. These traveling teachers have passed through Ephesus, but they did not receive a very positive response in that city. They appear to have made more impact in Tralles, and they might likely be on their way to Smyrna according to Ignatius. The areas that Ignatius identifies as being defective in their teachings include denying the reality of Christ having suffered in the flesh and refusing to partake of the Eucharist, because those who hold to the same understanding as Ignatius acknowledge the Eucharist to be a demonstration that Jesus actually suffered in the flesh, dying for the sins of those who believe (Ign. *Smyrn.* 6.2).

The concerns around deviant teaching are different in the letters addressed to believers in Magnesia and Philadelphia. In those two letters, and only in those two letters, Ignatius addresses further forms of practice or teaching to which he objects, using terms such as Ἰουδαϊσμός (*Ioudaismos*, "Judaism"), or ἰουδαΐζω (*ioudaizō*, "to Judaize"). Thus, the believers at Magnesia are told that if they "continue to live in accordance with Judaism," it will nullify the grace they have received (Ign. *Magn.* 8.1). Even more stridently, he informs them that "it is utterly absurd to profess Jesus Christ and to practise Judaism" (10.3). In this context, Ignatius claims that the historic prophets actually lived in accordance with Christ (8.2). In this way he declares them proleptically to be believers in Christ. Thus, he finds it incongruous that any in the Christ community in Magnesia would willingly embrace living according to Jewish practice. In exasperated tones he declares, "For Christianity did not believe in Judaism, but Judaism in Christianity" (10.3). While the language might be different, the tone and the sentiment appear to be similar to those of Paul when addressing the Galatians: "Having begun in the Spirit, are you now being perfected by the flesh?" (Gal 3:3). The issue being addressed in Magnesia is not necessarily a perspective that has been brought into the community from outside. Rather, Ignatius seems to address and dismiss an internal tendency among some of the community to take up a Jewish mode of living that observes certain of its religious customs.

While the comments about "Judaism" are concentrated to one section of *To the Magnesians*, the statements concerning Judaism are more diffuse in *To the Philadelphians*. Yet, despite Ignatius's comments being scattered throughout the letter, the sentiments are largely unified. While some of the perspectives expressed when addressing the Philadelphians use similar rhetoric to that found in *To the Magnesians*, a close reading reveals that the underlying problem is not identical, even if both situations are said to represent a tendency to adopt Ἰουδαϊσμός.[8] Some of the rhetorical strategies, however, are similar. In particular, once again he claims the prophets as examples of faithful believers who "anticipated the gospel in their preaching and set their hope on him and waited for him" (Ign. *Phld.* 5.2). However, in contrast to the sentiments in *Magnesians*, Ignatius does not identify any specific practices characteristic of Judaism, nor does he suggest that the Philadelphians might be engaging in Sabbath observance or other Jewish practices. Instead, what is described is the acquisition of knowledge from Jewish sources. Thus Ignatius, in his uncompromising style writes,

> But if anyone expounds Judaism to you, do not listen to him. For it is better to hear about Christianity from a man who is circumcised than about Judaism from one who is not. But if either of them fails to speak about Jesus Christ, I look on them as tombstones and graves of the dead, upon which only the names of people are inscribed. (Ign. *Phld.* 6.1)[9]

In stark opposition to his positive comments concerning the historic prophets, his statements concerning contemporary Judaism are condemnatory. He views Judaism of his own day as being spiritually necrotising. Addressing believers in Philadelphia, the problem is not that of adopting Jewish practices, but rather receiving a form of teaching that is characterized as expounding Judaism. Therefore, the key issue for Ignatius is that such perspectives or forms of teaching appear to negate certain of his own christological affirmations. For this reason, he views the instruction based on Judaism, which is circulating in Philadelphia, as being the antithesis of reliance on Christ-centred teaching. Consequently, he expresses his views in the following terms:

> For I heard some people say, "If I do not find it in the archives, I do not believe it in the gospel." And when I said to them, "It is written," they answered me, "That is precisely the

8. E.g., for the use of the terminology Ἰουδαϊσμός, see Ign. *Magn.* 8.1; 10.3 [twice]; Ign. *Phld.* 6.1 [twice].

9. Ἐὰν δέ τις Ἰουδαϊσμὸν ἑρμηνεύῃ ὑμῖν, μὴ ἀκούετε αὐτοῦ. ἄμεινον γάρ ἐστιν παρὰ ἀνδρὸς περιτομὴν ἔχοντος Χριστιανισμὸν ἀκούειν ἢ παρὰ ἀκροβύστου Ἰουδαϊσμόν. ἐὰν δὲ ἀμφότεροι περὶ Ἰησοῦ Χριστοῦ μὴ λαλῶσιν, οὗτοι ἐμοὶ στῆλαί εἰσιν καὶ τάφοι νεκρῶν, ἐφ᾽ οἷς γέγραπται μόνον ὀνόματα ἀνθρώπων (Ign. *Phld.* 6.1).

> question." But for me, the "archives" are Jesus Christ, the unalterable archives are his cross and death and his resurrection and the faith that comes through him; by these things I want, through your prayers, to be justified. (Ign. *Phld.* 8.1).

Here, Ignatius states that the opinions he reports are views that he heard expressed while he was in Philadelphia. Those promulgating this alternative hermeneutic appear to demand that interpretations expressed about "the gospel" must be supported by statements found "in the archives," *en tois archeiois*, ἐν τοῖς ἀρχείοις. The term ἀρχεῖον, *archeion*, is not standard terminology among early Christian writers, and even here Ignatius reports it as being the formulation used by those whom he opposes. The nonstandard nature of the terminology has led to a variety of suggestions concerning the referent of the term in this context.[10] However, the consensus is that the expression ἐν τοῖς ἀρχείοις was employed by certain members of the Christian community in Philadelphia to refer to the Jewish Scriptures.

Therefore, the issues to which Ignatius responds in his two letters that use the term Ἰουδαϊσμός suggest that the situations in Magnesia and Philadelphia were different, and that there was no single group responsible for the teachings that Ignatius rejected in these two locations. By contrast, the teaching circulating in Ephesus, Tralles, and Smyrna, which asserted that the human form of Jesus was only some kind of appearance, veiling the thoroughgoing divinity, is more unified. This leads to the conclusion that there was more than one issue to which Ignatius was responding in his letters.

Thus, rather than a single unified set of opponents, many have detected two groups—a docetic group that impacted Ephesus, Tralles, and Smyrna, as well as a group of Jewish opponents troubling the communities in Magnesia and Philadelphia. While a good case can be made for a group of traveling docetic teachers, it is more difficult to see the "Jewish" issues in Magnesia and Philadelphia as being identical and stemming from a unified group of Jewish teachers. Rather, the problems in Magnesia and Philadelphia are best not lumped together. Hence, Ignatius may have been responding to three different types of problems, although for convenience he uses the label "Judaism" to describe the tendency to adopt Jewish practices in Magnesia, as well as to describe the tendency to be guided by a Jewish hermeneutic in reading the Scriptures in Philadelphia.

2. SUMMARY OF CONTENT

The contents of the seven letters of the middle recension differ substantially, although there are certain topics that overlap in several letters. The most helpful way to discuss the content of the epistolary writings of Ignatius is to tackle them individually in the order they are set out in Eusebius's *Historia ecclesiastica* (*Hist. eccl.* 3.36.5). It is this order, which has become the standard order for presenting the letters in editions of the texts, which will be the order for the following discussing of the contents of the individual letters.

2.1 *To the Ephesians*

The letter to the Ephesian community is the longest of the seven Ignatian letters of the middle recension. The route taken by Ignatius did not pass through Ephesus; rather, several representatives of the community traveled to Smyrna to meet Ignatius. Ignatius commends these representatives for hurrying to visit him (Ign. *Eph.* 1.2). Among this group

10. For a summary of the major options, see W. R. Schoedel, "Ignatius and the Archives," *HTR* 71 (1978): 97–106, here 97–98.

of leaders or officeholders from the Ephesian congregation were Onesimus, named as the bishop of the Ephesian community, Burrhus a deacon, as well as the named but untitled Crocus, Euplus, and Fronto. While Ephesus is closer to Smyrna than the other cities that sent delegations to visit Ignatius in Smyrna, the size of the delegation in comparison with those from other cities might suggest the Christian community in Ephesus was larger and better resourced than the groups based in Magnesia and Tralles.

Ignatius's knowledge of the situation among believers in Ephesus was derived from the information provided to him by the delegates from that city who visited him in Smyrna. That is not to imply that such information was incorrect. However, it came from the perspective of those in positions of leadership. Therefore, to some extent the topics addressed in the letter are shaped by those reports as well as reflecting several of Ignatius's own concerns. The structure and contents of the letter may be represented in the following form.

Structure

Salutation:	Greetings, praise for the work of the Father and Jesus Christ among them
Eph. 1–2	Thanks for the visit, praise of the bishop and other delegates
Eph. 3–6	Instruction to obey the bishop
Eph. 7–9	Warnings against false teachers
Eph. 10–12	Eschatological teaching and Ignatius's impending fate
Eph. 13–15	Exhortation to frequent meeting, unity, actions that align with faith
Eph. 16–17	Further warnings about false teaching
Eph. 18–19	Jesus's humble death, reality of incarnation, mystery of Mary's conception
Eph. 20–21	Promise of a second letter and farewell greetings

Salutation. The opening takes the form of a greeting in which Ignatius introduces himself, names his addressees, and then lavishes praise on the recipients primarily because of the status they possess through union with God and Christ. Here, in that third element, the Ephesians are told that they have been blessed "with greatness through the fulness of God the Father, predestined before the ages . . . and elect through genuine suffering by the will of God the Father and of Jesus Christ our God" (Ign. *Eph.* salut.).

Chapters 1–2. Ignatius expresses thanks for the visit from the delegation from the Ephesian community while he was in Smyrna (*Eph.* 1–2). He states that when those in Ephesus heard of his transportation to Rome "in chains for the sake of our shared name and hope," "you hurried to visit me" (1.2). There are five named visitors in the group from Ephesus: Onesimus the bishop, Burrhus a deacon, and Crocus, Euplus, and Fronto, whose precise roles are not mentioned. Ignatius describes Onesimus as the "bishop" or "overseer" (ἐπίσκοπος, *episkopos*), and depicts him as a divine blessing to the Ephesian community (1.3). This comment reflects a larger concern that Ignatius discusses on several occasions in various letters—namely, that of the status and role of the *episkopos* in each community. However, the fact that the name of the Ephesian bishop and Philemon's runaway slave is the same is likely coincidental. As Schoedel notes, "The name Onesimus is a relatively common one, especially (but not exclusively) for slaves."[11]

Chapters 3–6. Here the role of the bishop and the necessity of the community's

11. W. R. Schoedel, *Ignatius of Antioch*, Hermeneia (Philadelphia: Fortress, 1985), 43–44.

obedience to its episcopal leader is discussed. This is an idea that recurs in many of the letters, and it should be seen as one of Ignatius's key contributions to early Christian thought and the development of ideas about ecclesiological leadership structures. In presenting these instructions to the Ephesians, Ignatius adopts a diffident tone: "I am not instructing you as though I were someone important" (Ign. *Eph.* 3.1). However, he grounds his understanding of the basis of episcopal leadership on the pattern of Christ's own ontological link with God.

Next, Ignatius turns to a musical metaphor to extend his argument that the unity that he advocates for the Ephesian community can only be achieved under the appropriate leadership structure of the church. In this context, Ignatius makes his first reference to the "presbyterium," or "council of presbyters" (πρεσβυτέριον, *presbyterion*) as a leadership group functioning alongside the bishop. He articulates the relationship by describing this "council of presbyters" as being "attuned to the bishop as strings of a lyre" (Ign. *Eph.* 4.1). The wider Ephesian community is then addressed by telling them to join the chorus. For, according to Ignatius, by their singing in harmonious union with the bishop and presbyters the Father is able to acknowledge them as "members of his son" and as having "a share in God" (4.2).

Chapters 7–9. Ignatius provides some of the most transparent statements concerning the nature of what he considers to be the false christological teaching circulating among the Ephesians. Without directly naming these opponents, Ignatius describes people who "carry about the name maliciously and deceitfully," who are characterized as "wild beasts" and as "mad dogs that bite by stealth," and he warns the recipients of the letter to protect themselves from such people because "their bite is hard to heal" (Ign. *Eph.* 7.1). The accusation that such people bear the name of Christ in a deceitful and malicious manner suggests, at least from Ignatius's perspective, that while such individuals claim to be followers of Christ the reality is different. Ignatius describes this carrying of the name of Christ as not only deceitful but also malicious. This suggests that in Ignatius's eyes their purpose is destructive and harmful in that they seek to destabilize the beliefs of true believers. Having described such people as "rabid" or "mad dogs," Ignatius moves to an epidemiological image. These are individuals who spread the mortifying effects of their poisonous teachings among the unsuspecting.

In response, Ignatius presents the first of five semi-creedal statements found in his letters that formulate the correct understanding of the nature of Christ.

> There is only one physician who is both flesh and spirit, born and unborn, God in man, true life in death, both from Mary and from God, first subject to suffering and then beyond it, Jesus Christ our Lord. (Ign. *Eph.* 7.2)

As will become apparent at other points in the letters of Ignatius, these affirmations are made in response to those who teach the divinity of Christ to the exclusion of his humanity and reject the idea that this divine Christ could experience the reality of suffering. Here, Ignatius's theological response to the false teaching is simply to assert both components of a series of what might appear to be antithetical and binary pairings: Jesus is both flesh and spirit, born and unborn, from Mary and from God, suffering and beyond suffering. Ignatius does not explain how these apparently contradictory affirmations might simultaneously hold true. He simply states that both elements equally represent the nature of Christ. Overall the pairings tend to state the human aspect prior to the exalted or divine aspect. This is likely intentional, since it was the human side of Jesus's existence that was rejected by the alternative teachers. Schoedel states that Ignatius "emphasized the historical side in opposition to what he regarded as the heart of the false teaching of the opponents—namely, Docetism."[12]

Chapters 10–12. Ignatius discusses the behavior required of believers and of himself toward nonbelieving humanity. There is a particular concern in regard to the conduct Ignatius sees himself required to display in the face of his impending execution. Ignatius commands the Ephesians to pray for humanity in the hope that they will repent and become faithful to God (Ign. *Eph.* 10.1). This reflects a theme that does not surface with great frequency in the letters—namely, Ignatius's missionary or conversionist ideology.

Ignatius commends the Ephesians for their historic links with the apostles, describing them as "the highway of those who are being killed for God's sake." In this context he describes the Ephesians as "fellow initiates of Paul" and prays for himself that "I may be found in his footsteps when I reach God" (Ign. *Eph.* 12.2). Here Ignatius seems to know and also to exploit the tradition of Paul's meeting with the Ephesian elders prior to his visit to Jerusalem, which Paul anticipated would be his last meeting with representatives from that community (Acts 20:38). Even more clearly, Ignatius connects his impending fate in Rome with the execution of Paul in the same city.

Chapters 13–19. This section opens with the injunction to meet frequently, which Ignatius understands as a key way of giving thanks and glory to God. This is reflective of the importance of corporate worship in early Christian communities. Moreover, such unity of faith is perceived as instrumental in negating the work of Satan, to which is attributed the role of creating discord and disunity. Ignatius promotes ὁμόνοια, *homonoia* ("unity," or "harmony") and εἰρήνη, *eirēnē* ("peace") as the chief behavioral qualities required to guard against division in the community. Again, a cosmic view of the significance of such actions is presented.

Two major, but related ideas emerge in chapters 14–15. First, Ignatius returns to his favorite pairing of faith and love, which he describes as being respectively the beginning and end of life. Second, building on the assertion that actions verify spoken claims, Ignatius states "it is better to be silent and be real than to talk and not be real" (Ign. *Eph.* 14.1). This is another, fairly transparent attempt to defend the actions and status of the verbally reticent bishop Onesimus by lauding the virtue of silence (cf. 6.1).

Further, Ignatius issues another direct warning against accepting false teaching (Ign. *Eph.* 16) and then follows a series of statements that seem to be rebuttals of the alternative teaching that Ignatius views as being pernicious (17–19). Ignatius describes the people who propagate the teaching he rejects as "those who adulterously corrupt households" (16.1). This is obviously a metaphor, since he makes the comparative analogy that if those who physically corrupt households by adultery are worthy of death, then these teachers who are corrupting "faith in God, for which Jesus was crucified" are worthy of a far worse fate. Ignatius spells out the punishment: "Such a person, having polluted himself, will go to the unquenchable fire, as will also the one who listens to him" (16.2).

Ignatius informs his readers that the false teaching has cosmic origins, and its purpose is to deceive and rob believers of eternal life. In contrast with the false teaching he states:

> For our God, Jesus the Christ, was conceived by Mary according to the plan of God, both from the seed of David and of the Holy Spirit. He was born and was baptized in order that by suffering he might cleanse the water. (Ign. *Eph.* 18.2)

12. Schoedel, *Ignatius of Antioch*, 61.

Unabashedly, Ignatius declares Jesus to be "our God." Alongside this, Christ's conception by Mary also affirms the full humanity of the one described as "our God." Ignatius does not explain how both aspects can be simultaneous true; rather, he simply states that both are correct and that the human conception was fully in accord with the divine plan. For Ignatius, Christ's sufferings have salvific effect. Moreover, he sees this salvation being imparted through the cleansing water of baptism that removes the state of death associated with sin. The link between the death of Christ and baptism is signaled in the New Testament, both in the Gospels when Jesus asks his disciples in reference to his impending death whether they are able "to be baptised with the baptism with which I am baptised" (Mark 10:38). Similarly, in Paul's letters baptism is associated with the experience of dying (Rom 6:4).

The description of the three mysteries in *To the Ephesians* 19 is both striking and at the same time somewhat elusive in its meaning. Ignatius introduces this section by stating that the three mysteries are the virginity of Mary, her giving birth to Jesus, and the death of Jesus. Then in mystic tones, Ignatius describes these elements as "three mysteries of a cry which were done in the silence of God" (Ign. *Eph.* 19.1). The paradox is that the three mysteries which cry out can only be heard in the silence of God. It is probable that he is undercutting the opponents' claim to possess a deeper, more mystical understanding of the divine plan.

Chapters 20–21. In his concluding remarks (Ign. *Eph.* 20–21), a number of important themes in this letter coalesce. There is reference to the "divine plan," the humanity of Jesus, the virtues of faith and love occur in combination, and there is an affirmation of the sufferings and resurrection of Jesus. Ignatius promises the Ephesians a fuller explanation in an intended second letter, "especially if the Lord reveals anything to me." The historical record does not preserve any trace of a proposed second letter being written. It is likely the case that it was never written. Ignatius also instructs the Ephesians to gather in the name of Jesus, to recognize him as Son of Man and Son of God, and to obey both the bishop and the council of the presbyters. Ignatius also commends the importance of continuing to "break one bread" together. In this context, he describes this eucharistic meal as "the medicine of immortality, the antidote we take in order not to die but to live forever in Jesus Christ" (20.2). There is no doubt that Ignatius attributes life-giving power to the eucharistic elements. The final greetings and closing requests reveal details of a loose network of communities of Jesus believers, and they are also a poignant reminder of the immediate fate that awaited Ignatius.

Summary. Ignatius's letter to the Ephesians is an occasional letter, written in circumstances that are personally dire for its author. Yet, despite these limitations, it provides rich insights into the situation of the Christian community in Ephesus. That community is characterized as facing divisions occasioned by those promoting alternative understandings of Christology and ecclesiology, and potentially by a bishop accused of a tendency toward silence rather than direct rebuttal of these opposing teachers. He instructs the recipients to remain loyal to Onesimus and to the presbyters, to receive the Eucharist that is offered under the bishop's oversight, and to understand that they receive eternal life only through recognizing that Jesus was truly human, born of Mary, and that he underwent the reality of suffering on the cross. It is holding to these things, Ignatius tells his Ephesian readers, that guarantees both their faith and salvation. The boldness and confidence he expresses is breathtaking, and yet alongside this it is possible to see a figure who is genuinely concerned about his own resolve in the face of his impending fate.

2.2 *To the Magnesians*

Ignatius addresses this letter to "the church at Magnesia on the Maeander." The town is located a little over twenty kilometers from the coast, about the same distance southeast of Ephesus, and approximately sixty kilometers south southeast of Smyrna. The delegation sent from Magnesia to Smyrna to meet Ignatius is only slightly smaller in size than that sent from Ephesus. A party of four people is described, with each person's office in the church being described: Damas the bishop, Bassus and Apollonius as presbyters, and Zotion a deacon.

Structure

Salutation:	Greetings, praise for the work of the Father and Jesus Christ among them
Magn. 1	Praise of Magnesians and prayer for union of flesh and spirit
Magn. 2–7	Thanks for the delegation, community life, obedience to the bishop
Magn. 8–10	Relationship between Christianity and Judaism
Magn. 11	Reason for writing and core beliefs about Christ
Magn. 12–13	Praise of Magnesians and call for obedience to the bishop
Magn. 14–15	Request for prayer and farewell greetings

Salutation. The opening greeting is of the same form as that in *To the Ephesians*, although it is neither as lengthy nor as lavish in its praise. The author identifies himself to the recipients as "Ignatius, the one also called Theophorus," where the alternative name means something like the "God-carrier." The basis for using the additional name is not entirely clear. Ignatius uses the name Theophorus in addition to his own name consistently in all seven letters, even though the basis for this additional appellative cannot be determined with any certainty. Ignatius tells the community that they are "blessed in the grace of God the Father in Christ Jesus our Saviour" (Ign. *Magn.* salut.).

Chapters 1–2. Ignatius writes to the whole community, thanking them for the delegation they sent to meet with him in Smyrna. Ignatius draws attention to his "chains," saying that although being bound this incarceration provided the ability to "sing the praises of the churches." He states that his prayer for all the churches "is a union of flesh and spirit that comes from Jesus Christ." The reference to flesh and spirit here is most readily understood as being a petition that the earthly behavior of the Magnesian believers should align with their spiritual status that derives from Christ. No doubt Ignatius's call for endurance of abuse is shaped by his own circumstances and the fate awaiting him at the conclusion of his transportation to Rome.

Some of the details of the church structure and situation become more apparent in the next section. Here Ignatius thanks the Magnesians for the delegation they sent to meet him in Smyrna. The group of visitors from Magnesia comprised Damas the bishop, presbyters Bassus and Apollonius, and the deacon Zotion. Here one sees representatives of the threefold structure of church leadership that Ignatius supports. The bishop Damas is described as "worthy of God" (ἀξιόθεος, *axiotheos*), the presbyters as simply "worthy" (ἄξιος, *axios*), but the most fulsome praise is reserved for the deacon Zotion, with whom Ignatius identifies. Ignatius describes Zotion as "my fellow servant," and requests that he might "enjoy his company, because he is subject to the bishop, as to the grace of God, and to the presbytery as to the law of Jesus Christ" (Ign. *Magn.* 2.1). This self-identification as a fellow deacon does not call into question the status of Ignatius as bishop of Antioch (cf. Ign. *Rom.* 2.2). Rather, it is the qualities of service and subservience exhibited by Zotion that lead Ignatius to make such a comparison.

Chapters 3–7. Having lauded the example of the deacon Zotion, Ignatius turns from this specific case to expand his discussion to considering the way the community should relate to Damas the bishop. The first concern Ignatius expresses relates to the youthful (νεωτερικός, *neōterikos*) state of the bishop. Here Ignatius acknowledges that while Damas's age is not an issue for the presbyters, nonetheless there are some in the community who seek to take advantage of the bishop's youth. For Ignatius, the bishop represents, or perhaps better, is the image of God's oversight of all believers.

Ignatius refers to certain individuals who are "only called Christians" yet who are characterized by calling a person "bishop but doing everything without regard for him" (Ign. *Magn.* 4.1). In this regard, Ignatius singles out one practice that such people adopt—namely, they meet together in a manner that Ignatius considers as being invalid. Surely by this he envisages meetings that are not sanctioned with the authority of the bishop, or the carrying out of liturgical rites in such meetings without the bishop's permission. Here, given Ignatius's comments elsewhere, he may be describing the celebration of the Eucharist without direct episcopal permission (cf. Ign. *Smyrn.* 8.1).

In some ways the next section (Ign. *Magn.* 5) interrupts the flow of the discussion about the status of bishops and the basis for episcopal authority. It is, however, occasioned by the distinction in the previous section between so-called Christians and actual Christians. For Ignatius, emulating Christ's suffering is the guarantee that new life is present in an individual. Having finished this digression, Ignatius returns to the topic of the function of the bishop, and the theological basis for the leadership roles in Christian communities.

Ignatius first forges a connection with the addressees by informing them that through meeting the delegates they have sent, he has developed, through faith, a deep love for the congregation. This is the basis from which Ignatius exhorts the community. The first instruction is to "do everything in godly harmony" (Ign. *Magn.* 6.1). However, the concord that the congregation is called to display is, according to Ignatius, only achievable by maintaining the correct form of community governance. In a carefully constructed and hierarchical description, Ignatius sets out his understanding of leadership roles accompanied with a typological comparison that provides a theological underpinning for the structure being advocated. Thus he writes about

> the bishop presiding in the place of God and the presbyters in the place of the council of the apostles and the deacons, who are especially dear to me, since they have been entrusted with the ministry of Jesus Christ, who before the ages was with the Father and appeared at the end of time. (Ign. *Magn.* 6.1)

On the basis of correct leadership structure, Ignatius calls on the Magnesians to reject all divisions.

Chapters 8–11. A theme surfaces that is found elsewhere only in the letter to the Philadelphians (Ign. *Phld.* 6.1–2). The topic that occupies Ignatius is his warning against those who advocate living according to Jewish practices while professing to be Christian. The rejection of Jewish practices has led to a scholarly debate as to whether in his letter corpus Ignatius was responding to two different types of false teaching, docetism and Judaizing tendencies, or whether there was one group that promoted a docetic Christology while advocating Jewish practices. That these topics are more or less treated distinctly in separate letters appears to suggest that there were at least two (if not three) different problems, and that they occurred in different geographical contexts.

The theme of this section can perhaps be summed up in Ignatius's own statement that "it is utterly absurd to profess Jesus Christ and to practice Judaism" (Ign. *Magn.* 10.3).

Ignatius claims that the prophets lived in accordance with Christ and were persecuted because of this, and this leads him into a set of theological affirmations. In this regard he states that the prophets taught belief in one God, but a God who was revealed in his Son, Jesus Christ.

In the following section, Ignatius identifies one practice that the former Jews had abandoned when they received the new hope. He states that they are characterized by "no longer keeping the sabbath but living in accordance with the Lord's day" (Ign. *Magn.* 9.1). The term "the Lord's day" is found only once in the New Testament (Rev 1:10). However, it occurs with increased frequency during the second century as a way of designating Sunday as the day of weekly commemoration of the resurrection.[13] It is likely that Ignatius had singled out observance of the Sabbath, because this is one of the ongoing practices of those he refutes for continuing the practice of Judaism.

Ignatius moves from describing the prophets as being believers in Jesus to issuing a set of injunctions to the recipients of the letter in Magnesia. As a further corrective, Ignatius presents another semi-creedal statement that articulates his understanding of some of the core tenets of belief in Christ. Thus he informs them

> to be fully convinced about the birth and the suffering and the resurrection that took place during the time of the governorship of Pontus Pilate. (Ign. *Magn.* 11.1)

While this affirmation is the type of statement issued in response to the challenge of docetic tendencies in several of the other letters, here it seems to function as a standard formulation which states the reality of the incarnation, passion, and the resurrection as well as locating this in a fixed historical context. Ignatius assures the recipients of the truth of these claims and prays that they might not be turned aside from this understanding.

Chapters 12–13. Again, in this short section, Ignatius returns to the major topic of the letter—the need to be under the authority of the bishop and leadership of the church. Ignatius first forges a bond of solidarity with the Magnesians. He states that being in chains makes him less than them, since they are at liberty.

Having presented this warm commendation, Ignatius reprises his central point of the letter, although in some respects his reasoning is presented in reverse order. Earlier he first mentioned the three roles of bishop, presbyters, and deacons, with each immediately followed by their heavenly typological equivalent (Ign. *Magn.* 6.1). Here he begins with the call to be "grounded in the precepts of the of the Lord and the apostles." The call for such subjection to these celestial authorities becomes the basis in this discussion of the earthly obedience to the bishop. Unity must be realized by community members both on earth by being subject to leaders and in heaven through the spiritual obedience modeled by Christ and the apostles.

Chapters 14–15. The letter is drawn to a close with a set of requests and greetings. He asks for the prayers of the Magnesians that he might reach God. For Ignatius this means faithfully undergoing execution as a Christian in Rome. He then has an extended request for prayer on behalf of the church in Syria. From what is apparent in other letters, when Ignatius left Syria there was a degree of turmoil or disharmony in the church. Ignatius, however, tells the Magnesians that their fervent prayers have the capacity to refresh the church in Syria.

13. D. A. Carson, *From Sabbath to Lord's Day: A Biblical, Historical and Theological Investigation* (Grand Rapids: Zondervan, 1982).

Summary. In Ignatius's *To the Magnesians*, two central topics emerge. The one that predominates is that the community should be obedient to and exercise unity under its appointed leaders. The second topic that concerns Ignatius in this letter is a tendency, presumably reported to him, that some in the community continue to adopt Jewish practices and perhaps disdain being labeled primarily as Christians (Ign. *Magn.* 10.1). On the whole, the polemic contained in this letter is not as fierce as that found in several of the other letters. Rather, the purpose is to advocate and establish the form of ecclesial polity that Ignatius not only viewed as preferable but as being fundamentally correct, since it mirrored the relationships between the Father, Christ, and the apostles that existed in the heavenly sphere.

2.3 *To the Trallians*

The city of Tralles (modern Aydin) is approximately 160 kilometers southeast of Smyrna. The trip to visit Ignatius while he was in Smyrna would have been a significant undertaking. It may be the factor of distance that accounts for Polybius the bishop being the only person named as visiting Ignatius from Tralles.

Structure

Salutation:	Greetings
Trall. 1	Praise of Trallians, thanks for the visit from Polybius
Trall. 2–3	Need for obedience to the bishop, respect for deacons and presbyters
Trall. 4–5	Union with God, approaching sufferings
Trall. 6–8	Threat of false teaching, security by adhering to the bishop
Trall. 9–11	Reality of Christ's incarnation
Trall. 12–13	Farewell greetings, final prayers for group unity and love

Salutation. The opening greeting employs the standard self-identification of the writer of the letter using the double name "Ignatius, also called Theophorus" (Ign. *Trall.* salut). The recipients are first described in terms of their relationship to God "being loved by God the Father of Jesus Christ." This compressed formula expresses several of Ignatius's core theological beliefs. In particular, he asserts that fellow believers have experienced divine love, and that God is most fully defined through the paternal relationship to Jesus. The recipients are identified as a community or a church of holy ones who are geographically located in Tralles in Asia. Ignatius concludes his salutation by stating that his greeting comes "in the fulness of God in the apostolic manner." Here, Ignatius is not claiming apostolic status for himself. Rather, he is drawing attention to the fact that the form of his greeting aligns with the greeting that the apostles gave in their letters.

Chapter 1. The immediate circumstances that led to the composition of this letter are disclosed in part in this section. There is a description of the character of the faith of the Trallians: "You have a disposition that is blameless and unwavering in patient endurance, not from habit but by nature" (Ign. *Trall.* 1.1). Ignatius then describes how this characterization has been made known to him by Polybius, bishop of Tralles, who visited Ignatius in Smyrna. Unlike the five-person delegation from Ephesus (Ign. *Eph.* 2.1) or the four-person party from Magnesia (Ign. *Magn.* 2.1), the Trallians were represented only by their bishop. Ignatius affirms in a positive manner the benefit of this visit: "And so he rejoiced with me, one bound in Christ Jesus, so that I saw in him your whole community" (Ign. *Trall.* 1.1). This leads Ignatius to express praise for the entire group on the basis of Polybius's positive report. In particular, Ignatius singles out the fact that Polybius communicated that the

Trallians were "imitators of God" (1.2). Ignatius sees imitation of God, or of Christ, as one of the significant marks of a faithful Christian community.

Chapters 2–3. Ignatius turns to a topic that dominates many of his letters—namely, obedience to the bishop and maintenance of the threefold pattern of leadership in the form of a bishop, a council of presbyters, and deacons. The opening statement is an affirmation that being subject to the bishop transcends mere obedience of human authority patterns. Instead, according to Ignatius, it is a demonstration of obedience to Christ. This leads Ignatius to reiterate his point concerning obedience to church leaders. In a typical rhetorical move, Ignatius tells the Trallians that they are already doing what he requires them to do when he states, "continue your practice." What they are to continue doing is acting only with the consent of the bishop and being subservient to the presbyters.

Next, Ignatius turns to the role of deacons. The following comments provide some insight into the duties associated with deacons. It is stated that "they are not merely deacons of food and drink" (Ign. *Trall.* 2.3). Although Ignatius notes their role is greater than this, in this context he affirms the view that distribution of food and drink were central responsibilities (cf. Acts 6:1–2). It is uncertain if by this stage the distribution of food and drink was part of providing for the poor, or if it was the more stylized distribution of the eucharistic bread and wine (Justin, *1 Apol.* 65.5).[14] The view that the "food and drink" in question were the eucharistic elements is perhaps supported by the fact that, prior to the reference, Ignatius also describes them as "deacons of the mysteries of Jesus Christ," which seems to align with Ignatius's wider understanding of the mystical power of the bread and wine (cf. Ign. *Eph.* 20.2). The prevailing issue in this section appears to be that the deacons are leaving themselves open to complaints, αὐτοὺς φυλάσσεσθαι τὰ ἐγκλήματα, *autous phylassesthai ta enklēmata*, "they must guard against criticism" (Ign. *Trall.* 2.3, my trans.). While the context of this comment would presumably be well understood to the original recipients of the letter, it is somewhat opaque for modern readers. Schoedel suggests that the deacons might have been showing favoritism in the distribution of food.[15]

Balancing this concern about the deacons, Ignatius continues to promote the significance of the diaconal role. He states, "Let everybody respect the deacons as Jesus Christ" (Ign. *Trall.* 3.1). Thus, Ignatius calls both for respect of deacons and better conduct on their part. Ignatius commends the demeanor of Polybius as exemplifying power through gentleness. Ignatius continues by stating that "even the godless respect him" (3.2). It is unclear whether the term "godless" is a characterization of unbelievers or of those whose teachings are opposed by Ignatius. If it is the latter, then perhaps the community at Tralles is more harmonious under the leadership of Polybius than it is described by Ignatius.

Chapters 4–5. The letter continues by describing both the spiritual knowledge possessed by Ignatius, while also portraying his weakness and desire to avoid boasting. Ignatius states of himself that "I have many thoughts in God" (πολλὰ φρονῶ ἐν θεῷ, *polla phronō en theō*, Ign. *Trall.* 4.1). This statement has been understood as meaning that Ignatius claims to "have many deep thoughts in union with God."[16] Initially Ignatius does not explain the content of the deep knowledge. Instead, his concern is not to succumb to those who would flatter him on account of his impending execution. Here one gains insight into the inner

14. For a discussion of Justin's depiction of deacons as those responsible for the bread and wine of the Eucharist, see P. Foster, "Deacons (Διάκονοι) and Διακονία in the Writings of Justin and Irenaeus," in *Deacons and Diakonia in Early Christianity: The First Two Centuries*, ed. B. J. Koet, E. Murphy, and E. Ryökäs, WUNT 2/479 (Tübingen: Mohr Siebeck, 2018), 215–26, here 215–19.

15. Schoedel, *Ignatius of Antioch*, 141.

16. Holmes, *Apostolic Fathers*, 217.

turmoil that death is causing Ignatius. He appears to be saying that his fast-approaching death has brought him into deeper union with God, and thereby he has attained a fuller knowledge of spiritual matters. Yet he recognizes a danger in this. Both the flattery of others and a self-inflated ego can result in an attitude of superiority and self-sufficiency.

Chapters 6–7. Much of the discussion to this point has been preparatory and functioned to construct a sense of shared identity between Ignatius and the Trallians to whom he writes. The letter now presents a sustained attack against docetic teachings in chapters 6–11, with only a slight but related digression dealing with appropriate ethical conduct in chapter 8.

The opening exhortation primarily uses the twin metaphors of food and drink to portray the contrast between the true teaching that Ignatius and Polybius present, and the alternative teaching offered by those with a docetic Christology. Ignatius continues his vivid portrayal of the mixing of true teaching with the false teachers' own opinions by stating that what they offer is a deadly drug combined with honeyed wine. Here the "honeyed wine" might be the residue of correct teaching about Christ that is retained in their instruction. Therefore, for Ignatius the consequence of accepting this alternative teaching is dire, since it leads to ultimate death and removes people from salvation.

As a protective against this fatal teaching, Ignatius offers various pieces of advice which are primarily based on maintaining allegiance to ecclesial leadership. The Trallians are encouraged to be on guard against such teachers, and to avoid any feelings of pride. Here the pride in question may refer back to the earlier warning against being enamored with possessing heavenly knowledge (Ign. *Trall.* 5.1–2). For Ignatius the remedy is to "cling inseparably to Jesus Christ and to the bishop and to the commandments of the apostles" (7.1).

Chapter 8. In some ways what follows in chapter 8 is an interlude, but this slight digression functions as a platform on which to construct the second stage of his argument against those he considers to be promoting a false teaching (Ign. *Trall.* 9–11). Ignatius commences the argument in this section with a strategy found elsewhere (cf. Ign. *Eph.* 3.2; *Magn.* 11; *Smyrn.* 4.1)—namely, saying that the problem he has just described does not exist among the Trallians. Rather, he tells them, "I am guarding you in advance because you are very dear to me, and I foresee the snares of the devil" (Ign. *Trall.* 8.1).

Momentarily, as Ignatius continues, his focus shifts. He turns away from the topic of false teaching. Instead, he exhorts the Trallians not to hold a grudge against a neighbor. The reason Ignatius gives for this instruction is to prevent nonbelievers having any basis for criticizing the Christian community. Again, in the context, Ignatius affirms the conduct of the majority of the Trallian believers: "lest the godly majority be blasphemed on account of a few foolish people" (Ign. *Trall.* 8.2). This perspective is supported by a fairly free citation of a scriptural passage from Isaiah (Isa 52:5 LXX). It is likely that Ignatius commends this quietistic and non-dissentious behavior in the presence of nonbelievers both to win their approval and as a way to avoid any possible basis for persecution.

Chapters 9–11. Having slightly interrupted his main argument, Ignatius returns fully to rebuffing the teachings of those he opposes. Whereas initially he had criticized his opponents for not being subordinate to appropriate church leadership, here he confronts their teachings directly. In particular, from Ignatius's stance, the fundamental defects relate to their views concerning the incarnation of Jesus and the reality of his sufferings. Having mentioned Jesus Christ, Ignatius describes him as the one

> who was of the family of David, who was from Mary, who was truly born, both ate and drank, truly was persecuted under Pontius Pilate, truly was crucified and died while those in heaven

and on earth and under the earth looked on. Who also was truly raised from the dead, his Father having raised him. (Ign. *Trall.* 9.1–2)

Before discussing the contents of the various statements, it is striking to note how often Ignatius uses the term "truly" (ἀληθῶς, *alēthōs*). He states that Christ was "truly born," "truly persecuted," "truly crucified," and "truly raised." It is not possible to know if the statement was traditional and incorporated (perhaps with modification), or whether it is entirely due to Ignatius's handiwork. Since no trace of it can be found prior to Ignatius, at the very least in this form the contents must be attributed to Ignatius.

The major area of disagreement with the opponents concerns the reality of the passion of Jesus. In response, Ignatius affirms that Jesus underwent physical suffering and death. He locates in time both the persecution and crucifixion of Jesus as occurring when Pilate was governor in Judea. Not only is the reference to Pilate traditional and repeated elsewhere in Ignatius's letters (cf. Ign. *Magn.* 11.1; *Smyrn.* 1.2), it responds to any notion that the death of Christ was only a mythological account of redemption or that it happened in appearance only. For Ignatius the events of suffering and crucifixion are closely linked, and not just in regard to the resurrection of Jesus alone. Elsewhere, Ignatius sees the suffering of Jesus as the basis for the resurrection of believers (Ign. *Rom.* 6.3). However, in line with ideas expressed in the letters of Paul (cf. 1 Cor 6:14; 15:15; 2 Cor 4:14), Ignatius affirms that Jesus was raised by his Father.

It is difficult to discern exactly where the list of traditional or semi-creedal affirmations stop and where Ignatius returns more fully to his own ideas. Perhaps the transition occurs after mentioning the resurrection of Jesus. In what follows, Ignatius intensifies the rhetoric against those promoting docetic ideas. He labels them as both "atheists" (ἄθεοι, *atheoi*), and as "unbelievers" (ἄπιστοι, *apistoi*). The basis of this assessment according to Ignatius is that these teachers say that Jesus "suffered in appearance" (τὸ δοκεῖν πεπονθέναι αὐτόν, *to dokein peponthenai auton*, Ign. *Trall.* 10.1). The term "docetism" used to characterize the belief system of the alternative teaching is derived from the Greek verb δοκέω, *dokeō*, meaning "to seem" or "to appear." According to Ignatius, their key claim was that the humanity and the sufferings of Jesus only have the semblance of being real. However, for Ignatius the reality of the suffering and death of Christ is the basis and model for his own death. For by this act of following Jesus, Ignatius understands that he is now following the path of true discipleship. In turn, this underscores and establishes the truth of his theological beliefs.

Ignatius turns from refutation of the teachings of the docetic teachers to a series of exhortation directed toward the Trallians. They are told to flee from such people. Then using various horticultural metaphors, he informs his readers of the deadly danger that these teachers pose. They are described as "wicked offshoots that bear deadly fruit" (Ign. *Trall.* 11.1). In this context Ignatius tells the Trallians that if they so much as taste this fruit death will result. Those who have dissociated themselves by denying the reality of the sufferings of Christ demonstrate that they are not joined to God. Ignatius's final assessment of the docetic teachers is not conciliatory at any level. They are a fatal poison, and they are unbelievers with no connection to God.

Chapters 12–13. In this final section of the letter Ignatius offers greetings, requests prayer be offered to support him as he faces death, and he reprises the major theme of unity under correctly constituted church leadership. Many of the sentiments expressed in chapter 12 are repeated in chapter 13, albeit in different words.

Ignatius again draws attention to the fact that he is in chains, stating that he bears those bonds for the sake of Jesus. In this way, he uses his incarceration to validate the reliability of the instructions he provides to the Trallians. He states that his intercession on behalf of the community is that they "persevere in your unanimity and in prayer for one another" (Ign. *Trall.* 12.2). Ignatius commands the Trallians to listen to him in love, yet in this context there is a warning articulated: "so that I may not by virtue of having written to you become a witness against you" (12.3). Ignatius then returns to the theme of mutual love. He requests that the Trallians also express their love for him by praying that he would endure his impending death in the correct manner.

In chapter 13, Ignatius requests prayers for the church in Syria (Ign. *Magn.* 14.1), again stating that he is not worthy to be called a member of that group. He concludes by bidding the Trallians farewell, while commanding them to be obedient to the bishop and the presbyters with an undivided heart.

Summary. The letter to the Trallians centers on several key concerns. The three most prominent are, first, that the Christian communities should be united under the leadership of the bishop, presbyters, and deacons. Second, they should not entertain teaching that denies the reality of the incarnation, suffering, and death of Jesus. Third, they should uphold Ignatius in prayer so he may fulfill what he sees as his destiny to die because of his faith in Christ. The skill of the letter is the way in which these three themes are interwoven, so that each element reinforces and is mutually dependent on the other elements.

2.4 *To the Romans*

Ignatius's letter *To the Romans* is noticeably different from his other letters in terms of its content and also to some degree in terms of its structure. In regard to content, there is no defense of the threefold pattern of ministry, there is no polemic against teachings opposed by Ignatius, and there is no strong articulation of a theology of the Eucharist. Notwithstanding this, some familiar themes emerge. In passing, Ignatius states some of his core christological understandings, and he discusses the nature of discipleship. However, these topics only appear in relation to his overarching concern—namely, his understanding of martyrdom and his fear that the Roman Christians will intervene in some way to obtain his release. In essence, this is a letter with fundamentally only one item of concern—the impending death of Ignatius in Rome.

Structure

Salutation	
1.1–3.3	Plea not to intervene to prevent Ignatius's death
4.1–5.3	Sacrificial nature of Ignatius's death
6.1–8.1	Death as eschatological transformation
8.2–10.3	Final petition, prayer request, and letter details

Salutation. The salutation that opens the letter to the Romans is the longest greeting contained in all of Ignatius's letters. The primary reason for this is probably due to the fact that Ignatius had no previous personal contact with the Christian community in Rome.

Ignatius does not appear to know of any individual holding the position of bishop in Rome, and this might be an indication that a different leadership structure prevailed in the Roman churches around the beginning of the second century.[17] Therefore, he states that it is the church as a whole that "presides," or exercises authority in the region of Rome. His

17. P. Lampe, *Christians at Rome in the First Two Centuries: From Paul to Valentinus* (London: Continuum, 2006).

second use of the term "presides" (or "sit in a place of honor," προκάθημαι, *prokathēmai*) in the salutation defines the nature of this precedence. That role of presiding over the territory of Rome is to be exemplified by love (προκαθημένη τῆς ἀγάπης, *prokathēmenē tēs agapēs*). Thus, Ignatius states, the Roman church is characterized by a preeminence in love. It is that love to which he will appeal when he requests them not to interfere in his death.

Chapters 1–3. The central concern of this section is summed up in Ignatius's own words, "I am afraid of your love, in that it might do me wrong" (Ign. *Rom.* 1.2). Here, the concern is that a misguided sense of love might lead to an intervention that gains release for Ignatius. While acknowledging that they might consider such an action would stem from love, Ignatius explains that such a course would be entirely wrong. He tells them that they would do him a wrong and would be acting in line with what they want, rather than what he or God desires. Ignatius perhaps reveals a little of the harsh realities of his transportation and his mental state when he declares that "it is difficult for me to reach God" (1.2). Precisely how Ignatius envisages that the Roman believers would have secured his release is difficult to know. However, some sources seem to speak of ransoms being paid (1 Clem. 55.2). Furthermore, others have speculated about the presence of influential imperial figures among early believers in Rome.[18]

Ignatius implores the Romans to allow him to be poured out as a libation or offering (σπονδισθῆναι, *spondisthēnai*) to God on the altar (Ign. *Rom.* 2.2). This image may resonate with the similar sentiments that Paul expresses as he faces his own death: "for I am already being poured out as a drink offering [σπένδομαι, *spendomai*]," (2 Tim 4:6; cf. Phil 2:17). The journey to the west from the east (εἰς δύσιν ἀπὸ ἀνατολῆς, *eis dysin apo anatolēs*) mirrors the journey of Paul to his death in Rome and also forms the basis for the image of setting from the world and rising to God in the final statement of this paragraph (τὸ δῦναι ἀπὸ κόσμου πρὸς θεόν ἵνα εἰς αὐτὸν ἀνατείλω, *to dynai apo kosmou pros theon hina eis auton anateilō*, Ign. *Rom.* 2.2). This play on words is possible because Greek uses the same semantic groups to designate the west and the setting of the sun, and for east and the rising of the sun. Hence, Ignatius states that although in relation to his physical life there will be an end or a setting in the west, spiritually this actually is the means through which he will rise to God. Thus, the orientation of his journey becomes a metaphor for his hope of resurrection. In this way, the location of Rome takes on symbolic meaning for Ignatius. It is where he will both end his earthly life but attain true life as he becomes, as he describes it, a genuine word of God.

Ignatius says what he requires from the Christians in Rome is their prayers that he might have "strength both outwardly and inwardly" (Ign. *Rom.* 3.2). Ignatius states that he strives for an inward disposition that makes him have the assurance that such a fate is best for him and enables him to become a true disciple. This perspective is reinforced by his comment that he does not desire to "merely be called a Christian but actually prove to be one" (Ign. *Rom.* 3.2). By dying a Christlike death, Ignatius expresses the hope to experience a Christlike transformation.

Chapters 4–5. In this section Ignatius reflects on his impending death, using sacrificial imagery. At times the language used to portray his fate is florid and perhaps reveals something of Ignatius's state of mind and also how he rationalized the torments he expected to face in theological terms. After assuring the Roman community that his death was a free choice and that he was dying for God, Ignatius yet again pleads with them not to intervene to prevent his death. He envisages his fate as that of being eaten by wild beasts. Then in what

18. For a careful and balanced discussion of these possibilities, see Schoedel, *Ignatius of Antioch*, 168–69.

is perhaps at least superficially a disturbing image, he states, "I am God's wheat, and I am being ground by the death of the wild beast, so that I may prove to be pure bread" (Ign. *Rom.* 4.1). The image is likely indebted to instructions concerning the pure offering to be placed on the altar in the temple. Thus the Levites were instructed to be engaged in the "the purifying of all things . . . both for the bread of the presence and the fine flour" that was to sit on tables of gold in the temple (1 Chr. 23:28–29; for "fine flour," see Lev 2:1–7; Num 7:13–79).

In what follows, the realities of the treatment Ignatius received during his transportation become more apparent. It appears that he had traveled both "by land and sea," that he was chained perhaps for the entirety of the journey, and that he was guarded by a company of ten Roman soldiers. Alongside these details one gets a sense of the brutal treatment to which he was subjected. In regard to the soldiers, whom he describes as "ten leopards," he states they "only get worse when they are well treated" (Ign. *Rom.* 5.1). The imagery here perhaps anticipates Ignatius's fate in Rome. He states that during the course of his journey to Rome that he is already "fighting with wild beasts," and he represents his tormentors as leopards (cf. 1 Cor 15:32). It is not unrealistic to suppose that the soldiers extorted money from the local Christian communities in exchange for access to Ignatius and for permission to write letters. Perhaps having recognized Ignatius as a source of financial gain, they may have physically assaulted him to gain more money as a price for stopping such behavior. While presumably the ten soldiers were in charge of more than one prisoner, perhaps they recognized the monetary opportunity that Ignatius presented. In response to this, Ignatius interprets such brutal treatment as a means to attain his goal; "because of their mistreatment I am becoming more of a disciple" (Ign. *Rom.* 5.1).

Chapters 6.1–8.1. In this following section, Ignatius expands on his final statement that his death is the means by which he will reach Christ. He develops that idea in a new way, and in doing so he articulates an understanding of death as an eschatological transformation. In his catalogue of torments, the final element in the list is "cruel tortures of the devil" (Ign. *Rom.* 5.3). This hints at something that is more explicit in this new section of the letter. That is that Ignatius's impending fate is seen as having a cosmic dimension. It is not simply the punishment carried out by state authorities. Rather, for Ignatius, it is part of a larger cosmic conflict. In this vein he speaks of the machination of the "ruler of this age" working against him (7.1), and he employs eschatological imagery of the birth pains being upon him (6.1). Thus, at a deeper level, Ignatius portrays himself as engaged in a battle against demonic forces, and the earthly dimension of his fate is only part of the larger conflict in which he is engaged.

Ignatius inverts the understanding of life and death. He beseeches the Roman Christians, "Do not keep me from living, do not desire my death" (Ign. *Rom.* 6.2). What he is actually asking is that they will not intervene to prevent his death, in the desire to preserve his earthly life. Here he instructs them to "allow me to become an imitator of the sufferings of my God" (6.3). Two things are particularly striking in this context. First, for Ignatius the purest form of divine imitation is through suffering. Second, he refers to "the sufferings of my God" and not to the sufferings of Christ. At one level this is not surprising, since he so frequently and readily refers to Christ as God (cf. Ign. *Eph.* 15.3; 18.2; *Trall.* 7.1; *Smyrn.* 1.1; *Pol.* 8.3).

The address continues with Ignatius imploring the Roman believers not to prevent his death. The phrase that is often translated as "do not let envy dwell among you" (Ign. *Rom.* 7.2),[19] probably has a stronger sense than expressing a tendency toward envy. The Greek

19. Holmes, *Apostolic Fathers*, 233.

term βασκανία, *baskania*, expresses something of the worldview of the day, which saw actions potentially controlled by malevolent forces. Here, in line with earlier references to the "ruler of this age" (7.1), Ignatius seems to refer to a "bewitchment" or "demonic misdirection," which would lead the Romans to prevent his death.[20] Ignatius then tells the Romans that it is possible that he might waiver in his own resolve, but they should be guided by the written instructions in the letter and not listen to him if he weakens in his resolve when he arrives in Rome. Ignatius then launches into some highly florid rhetoric concerning his desire for death. To modern ears this can sound obsessive. However, apart from strengthening his own resolve, it also expresses a key theological conviction that earthly physical life is of little value and that true existence is attained when one is joined with Christ in the life to come. In many ways, although expressed in different terms, Ignatius's statements match those of Paul when writing to believers in Philippi (Phil 1:21–23). Here Ignatius writes:

> For though I am still alive, I am passionately in love with death as I write to you. My passionate love has been crucified and there is no fire of material longing in me, but only water living and speaking in me, saying within me, "Come to the Father." (Ign. *Rom.* 7.2)

Thus for Ignatius, his impending death casts into sharper focus the contrast between the lack of value of material longings and the ultimate worth of spiritual union with God. The image of "water living and speaking in me" is striking, although not fully obvious.

Ignatius concludes this section with two statements. The first summarizes the fervent declarations he has just made. In a more straightforward manner, Ignatius declares, "I no longer want to live according to human standards" (Ign. *Rom.* 8.1). This simple statement encapsulates much of what has just been mentioned. The reason for these ardent rejections of physical life become apparent in the second statement: "And this will be, if you want it. Want it, that you might also be wanted" (8.1). Here Ignatius implores the Roman believers to align their desires with his own. The Greek verb θέλω, *thelō* ("I want" or "I desire") is used four times in these two statements. Here Ignatius continues to express his concern that those in Rome will intervene to prevent his execution in a well-meaning but ultimately misguided understanding of what Ignatius sees as his own divinely intended fate.

Chapters 8.2–10.3. Ignatius again requests that the Roman believers take him at his word. Using a striking metaphor, Ignatius informs the recipients of the letter that the truth of his words will be made apparent through Jesus Christ, who is described as "the unlying mouth by whom the Father has spoken truly" (Ign. *Rom.* 8.2). It is doubtful that this imagery has any direct connection with the Logos Christology of the Johannine prologue (John 1:1, 14).[21] Rather, this seems to be an image of Ignatius's own making, which aligns the veracity of his statement with divine truth. The thing Ignatius requests from those in Rome is their prayers. Specifically, he asks that they would pray that he would remain steadfast and thus attain to his goal that he might die in Rome, and therefore be united with Christ. For the second time in quick succession, Ignatius states that this request is in accordance with the mind of God. His impending sufferings are what the believers in Rome must desire if they are to align themselves with the will of God. Any attempted

---

20. Schoedel comes to the same decision concerning the sense of the term (*Ignatius of Antioch*, 184).

21. While direct dependence on specific passages is unlikely, Vall is probably correct that the "Johannine principle of the Son's revelation of the Father is central to Ignatius's theology" (G. Vall, *Learning Christ: Ignatius of Antioch and the Mystery of Redemption* [Washington, DC: Catholic University of America Press, 2013], 170).

interference or intervention is seen by Ignatius as a rejection of what is divinely intended for him.

Next, Ignatius turns to his immediate circumstances. He informs the Roman believers that he is writing from Smyrna, "through the Ephesians" (Ign. *Rom.* 10.1). It appears that the Ephesians have supplied a letter carrier to take Ignatius's epistle to those in Rome so that it might arrive ahead of him. The specific reference to Crocus suggests that he has been designated with that task, or perhaps that he is the leader of a group going on before Ignatius to Rome. Crocus is also mentioned when Ignatius writes to the Ephesians (Ign. *Eph.* 2.1). Along with Burrhus, he is one of the two people whom Ignatius requested to remain with him. Presumably the intention was to notify believers in Rome that a fellow Christ-believer was being transported to the city for execution. Perhaps such information not only permitted them to prepare for the arrival of Ignatius but perhaps to be on guard in case there was an accompanying rise in hostility against members of the Christ movement in the imperial capital. Ignatius asks the Romans to let the Syrian delegation know that his arrival is imminent. Here, Ignatius appears to anticipate that by the time his letter from Smyrna arrived in Rome, he would be close to arriving in the city. This is the only letter that is dated, albeit without a year, "the ninth day before the calends of September" (Ign. *Rom.* 10.3).[22] The reference to the date is intended to provide more certainty to the recipients of the approximate date of Ignatius's arrival.[23] The final greeting Ignatius provides is ominous and recalls the fate that awaits him: "farewell to the end" (10.3).

Summary. Ignatius's *To the Romans* is unlike any other letter in the corpus. Ignatius had not visited the city before writing or met delegates from that location. His concerns are not with resolving issues of Christology or promoting loyalty to the bishop and leadership structure of local churches. Instead, this letter reminds readers of the reason why Ignatius is on his journey through the Roman province of Asia. This most remarkable letter develops an outlook, or better, a theology that revolves around being put to death for the sake of Christian beliefs. At times the imagery appears morbid, praying for the pleasure of being devoured by wild beasts (Ign. *Rom.* 5.2), or that he might be ground as pure wheat in their mouths (4.1). Yet, alongside these macabre sentiments are statements of simple trust and pure faith. Ignatius's self-denial and true discipleship appear to be real: "I am learning to desire nothing" (4.3), and, "I am becoming more of a disciple" (5.1, 3). Ignatius also presents a life-inverting theology, whereby intervening to save his life will result in his death, but allowing him to die will result in him reaching God and thus receiving true life (6.2). While such rhetoric might be seen by some as repellent, for Ignatius and those who would be subject to similar fates the belief in an eschatological reversal that would lead to true life was a means of sustaining a steadfast resolve even if that required the loss of physical life. For this reason, Ignatius's reflections as contained in this letter have proved a rich repository for those undergoing persecution in subsequent eras and in other places.

2.5 *To the Philadelphians*

Ignatius's letter *To the Philadelphians* is among a group of three letters written from Troas, after Ignatius had left Smyrna. A number of concerns emerge in the letter. First, Ignatius encourages the community to be united around the bishop and to be on guard against divisive teaching. Second, there is an extended refutation of "Judaism," which is

22. The calends were the first day of a given month. Due to inclusive counting that date equated to the 24th of August, although the specific year is unknown.

23. Schoedel, *Ignatius of Antioch*, 191.

combined with a self-defense of Ignatius's behavior while in Philadelphia. Lastly, the letter closing provides some insight into Ignatius's onward journey from Smyrna to Troas.

Structure

Salutation	
1.1–2	Value of the bishop and his ministry
2.1–5.2	Warnings against divisions and false teachers
6.1–9.2	Threat of adopting Jewish teachings
10.1–11.2	Personal requests and final greetings

Salutation. The salutation is one of the longest, surpassed only by that addressed to the believers in Rome. A number of features are apparent. Ignatius praises the Philadelphians for their steadfastness in belief and for their internal harmony. He also speaks of them as recipients of eternal joy. Yet he adds the caveat that this joy is made certain by maintaining unity with the leaders in the church since, from Ignatius's perspective, they have been appointed in accordance with Christ's will and their ministry is established through the work of the Spirit. Several of these comments foreshadow topics that will be discussed more fully in the body of the letter.

Chapter 1. First, Ignatius turns to the figure of the bishop in the Philadelphian community. It is striking that the bishop is not named. This stands in contrast to Ignatius's practice in the letters addressed to Ephesus, Magnesia, and Tralles, where Onesimus, Damas, and Polybius are named as bishops of those communities. It appears that Ignatius had not traveled through those three cities, so naming the bishop might have been a way of demonstrating knowledge of the Christian communities in those places. In fact, in his letter to Smyrna, Ignatius does not name Polycarp, although in the accompanying letter to Polycarp the recipient is explicitly named as bishop of Smyrna.

One significant characteristic that Ignatius praises in the bishop of Philadelphia is his silence: "He accomplishes more through silence than others do by talking" (Ign. *Phld.* 1.1). The unnamed episcopal figure does not appear to have been drawn into quick responses to people engaged in speculative teachings. He is praised for forbearance. It is noteworthy that Ignatius recognizes and praises such a quality when it was not necessarily one that Ignatius possessed.

Chapters 2–4. Despite this laudatory assessment of the character of the bishop, Ignatius warns the community about the dangers of divisions and false teachings. On the one hand, Ignatius writes that he found no division among the Philadelphian community. In fact, he declares, "I found that there had been a purification" (Ign. *Phld.* 3.1). This leads one to ask why such a purification or filtering out of such elements had been required. It may be the case that Ignatius's statement that he found no division is made for rhetorical effect. Ignatius uses two metaphors to describe those accused of false teaching and promoting division. Although seemingly trustworthy they are wolves, and they are evil plants not cultivated by Christ. Ignatius argues that acceptance of such teaching jeopardizes believers from running "in God's race" (2.2). In even more absolute terms, Ignatius informs the Philadelphians that those who follow individuals who divide the community (εἴ τις σχίζοντι ἀκολουθεῖ, *ei tis schizonti akolouthei*, "if anyone follows" a "schismatic" or "divider") they will themselves not inherit the kingdom of God. Thus Ignatius raises the stakes in order to dissuade the Philadelphians from considering engaging with such teachings.

As a measure of authenticity, or true faith, Ignatius encourages his addressees to "participate in one eucharist" (Ign. *Phld.* 4.1). For Ignatius, this is a fundamental marker of unity under the legitimate leadership of the bishop, the council of presbyters, and the deacons of the community.

Chapter 5. Apart from warning against false teachers, Ignatius also presents the Philadelphians with what he views as the remedy against such a tendency. Both in the face of his impending death and as a safeguard against false teaching, Ignatius counsels refuge both in the gospel, which he equates with the flesh of Jesus, and also in the apostles, who are presented as being represented in some contemporary sense as the council of presbyters. Exactly how these equivalencies work is not fully explained. However, holding to the truth of the gospel and to apostolic teaching is for Ignatius the chief way not to be drawn toward false instruction.

Chapters 6–9. While mentioning false teaching in general terms, to this point in the letter Ignatius has said little concerning its content or specific focus. That changes in what follows, with Ignatius describing in part the nature of the false teaching and alluding to his response to it while he was in Philadelphia. Ignatius's opening comment in this section is, "But if anyone expounds Judaism to you, do not listen to him" (Ign. *Phld.* 6.1). Here Ignatius discloses what he understands to be at the heart of the false teaching in Philadelphia. In this context, Ignatius does not fully explain what he means by Judaism or the practice of expounding it. However, his further comments offer some insight into what Ignatius believes is happening in Philadelphia. He raises what appears to be the theoretical possibility of hearing about Christianity from a person who was circumcised (presumably a Jew). He states that such a possibility is preferable to what is presumably the root problem, which is hearing about Judaism from somebody who is not circumcised. Therefore, the basic problem, according to Ignatius, is that some uncircumcised people in the Philadelphian community were promoting Jewish teachings. Ignatius sees this form of teaching as contradicting a full and correct understanding of Christ.

Next, Ignatius recalls his time at Philadelphia while he was being transported onward initially to Smyrna. In many ways it appears not to have been a happy visit on either side. Ignatius declares that he has a clear conscience in regard to his behavior. The very fact he has to issue such a statement is telling. It has been suggested that making this statement to the recipients of the letter who may have been more favorable to Ignatius reveals that even they considered his conduct to have been too extreme.[24] Moreover, Ignatius refutes the apparent claim that he had been "put up" to attacking these Judaizing teachers. Instead, Ignatius declares the source of his knowledge as being the Holy Spirit: "I did not learn this from any human being. No, the Spirit itself was preaching" (Ign. *Phld.* 7.2). Ignatius's presence in Philadelphia appears to have been a disruptive influence. It may be the case that he had been accused of dividing the community and creating disunity.

Unlike the situation in Magnesia, the issue does not appear to be primarily that of embracing Jewish practices; in fact, the teachers in Philadelphia appear to have been uncircumcised. Thus, rather than praxis, the problem appears to be pedagogical. Those accused of being false teachers are promoting a hermeneutic that takes their reading of the Jewish Scriptures as the lens through which they formed christological interpretations. The words Ignatius attributes to his opponents are that they claimed, "If I do not find it in the archives, I do not believe it in the gospel" (Ign. *Phld.* 8.2). In this context, the term "the archives" appears to be a designation for the Jewish Scriptures. Ignatius portrays those he opposes as diminishing the understanding of Christ due to a narrow or overly literal

24. Thus Schoedel observes that "[Ignatius's] sensitivity on this point suggests that even his friends felt that he had gone too far" (*Ignatius of Antioch*, 204).

reading of the Scriptures. According to Ignatius, the point at which he disagreed with his opponents was both their interpretation of "the archives" and also what constitutes a legitimate reading of these texts. Hence he states, "But for me the archives are Jesus Christ, the unalterable archives are his cross and death and his resurrection" (8.2). Rather than reading the Scriptures in order to justify the claims about Christ in the gospel, Ignatius reverses the approach and says if one accepts what he teaches about Christ, then it becomes clear that the same things are written in the archives, or the Jewish Scriptures. Hence, the dispute revolves around competing hermeneutical priorities, or interpretative starting points.

Chapter 9. Here, Ignatius rounds out this argument. The claim that the priests were good but the high priest is better is a claim based on identifying Jesus as the high priest. Ignatius makes this equation by seeing that the high priest alone could enter the Holy of Holies, and that Jesus alone is the door through which the patriarchs, prophets, apostles, and the church gain access to the Father. Thus, Ignatius argues that the gospel is the fundamental interpretative key since it describes Christ's coming, suffering, and resurrection. Drawing these strands together, he ends the argument where he commenced it, with the prophets. Ignatius states that "the beloved prophets preached in anticipation of him, but the gospel is the imperishable finished work" (Ign. *Phld.* 9.2). Ignatius claims that one needs first to accept the truth of the gospel and its witness to Christ. Then, it is argued, one will recognize that the "archives," or Scriptures, confirm those gospel perspectives, as even the prophets had recognized.

Chapters 10–11. The letter is closed with a request that Ignatius's coworkers be given respect, and a final personal greeting. Ignatius informs the Philadelphians that their prayers on behalf of the church in Antioch have been answered. Further, Ignatius tells the Philadelphians that the church in Antioch is now at peace. What precisely might have been the circumstances prior to this return to peace have been widely discussed. This has often been seen as a cessation of external persecution, of which Ignatius is a victim being transported to Rome for execution.[25] However, others suggest that the problem was internal disharmony in the Antiochene church that Ignatius had not been able to resolve prior to his departure. Some have even suggested that Ignatius, with his uncompromising views, may have been part of the source of the problem in Antioch and that the return to harmonious relations was partially due to Ignatius himself no longer being present as a polarizing figure. The reality is that the letter reveals nothing more than a return to a peaceable state. In response to this restored state of affairs, Ignatius requests that the Philadelphian congregation send a deacon to Antioch to extend congratulations.

Next, Ignatius turns his attention to two fellow travelers and supporters. The first is Philo, a deacon from Cilicia. He is described as a person who assists Ignatius in the word of God. The second is a person called Rhaius Agathopus, described as a chosen man from Syria. These two figures appear to have had a mixed reception from believers in Philadelphia. A further description is provided in regard to Rhaius Agathopus. Ignatius describes him as "a chosen man who followed me from Syria, having renounced this life" (Ign. *Phld.* 11.1). First, it appears that Rhaius Agathopus had accompanied Ignatius throughout his entire journey from Antioch. Second, it is unclear how he became a chosen or selected person to accompany Ignatius. Third, both the language of "following" Ignatius and as being one who had "renounced his life" might suggest that the same fate awaited him in Rome as Ignatius was to endure. If that is the case, then it is possible that either he, or the church

25. See J. B. Lightfoot, *The Apostolic Fathers, Part II: S. Ignatius, S. Polycarp. Revised Texts with Introductions, Notes, Dissertations, and Translations*, 2nd ed., 3 vols. (London: Macmillan, 1889–1890), 2:277.

in Syria, had volunteered him to accompany Ignatius. Alternatively, he might have been arrested by the authorities as a fellow Christ believer in Antioch. If the latter were true, it might lend support to the notion that the church in Antioch was enjoying peace after a time of persecution. In the end, there is simply insufficient evidence to reconstruct the situation in the church at Antioch, which led to the arrest and transportation of Ignatius.

Summary. It is apparent that Ignatius's visit to Philadelphia was painful, and his presence divided the community. He requests that the Philadelphians honor his fellow travelers and coworkers, who appear to have been recipients of the same hostility that was directed to Ignatius. This letter represents just one side of a brief yet complex interaction. It is not possible to know what impact this letter had on the recipients after its arrival. However, its preservation might suggest a favorable and transformative impact.

2.6 *To the Smyrnaeans*

Like *To the Philadelphians*, Ignatius's *To the Smyrnaeans* is among a group of three letters written from Troas. Again he draws attention to the dangers of false teachers, linking bad beliefs to bad ethical practices. Ignatius commands obedience to the bishop, before thanking the Smyrnaeans for their care displayed toward him. The letter concludes by sharing news about his traveling companions and the changed circumstances in Antioch, alongside a set of final greetings.

Structure

Salutation	
1.1–3.3	Affirmation of belief in the humanity of Christ
4.1–7.2	False teachers and their bad example
8.1–9.1	Encouragement to hold to the authority of the bishop
9.2–10.2	Thanks for the care received in Smyrna
11.1–3	Situation in Antioch
12.1–13.2	Final requests and closing greetings

Salutation. The salutation is fairly succinct. However, several features are noteworthy. Within the opening greeting, Ignatius twice draws attention to the spiritual gifts possessed within the community. He tells the recipients that they are "endowed with every spiritual gift" and also that they are "not lacking in any spiritual gift." This suggests that such a giftedness was something Ignatius saw as a characteristic of the Smyrnaean believers. Another aspect of the greeting is that Ignatius affirms that the believers in Smyrna are "filled with faith and love." The dyad of "faith and love" is central in the thought of Ignatius, and later in the letter he will return to the combination of virtues when he declares, "faith and love are everything; nothing is preferable to them" (Ign. *Smyrn.* 6.1).

Chapters 1–3. The first topic to be addressed is an affirmation of the humanity of Christ. This is perhaps the longest and most sustained discussion of the incarnation, although Ignatius presents this topic from various perspectives and will return to it when speaking of the nature of the false teaching that is to be avoided.

The opening declaration is striking. Ignatius says, "I glorify Jesus Christ, the God who made you wise" (Ign. *Smyrn.* 1.1). This is one of the clearest examples among the several statements where Ignatius explicitly declares Jesus to be God.[26] So while the focus of

26. For other examples, see Ign. *Trall.* 7.1, or where he describes Jesus Christ as "our God," see Ign. *Eph.* 15.3; 18.2; Ign. *Rom.* inscript; 3.3; Ign. *Pol.* 8.3.

the ensuing discussion falls on the humanity of Jesus, it is clear that Ignatius holds the divinity of Christ as a central belief. While one should not reify this into the language of fourth and fifth century creeds, it is nonetheless apparent that without fully explaining the mechanism or how the two are held together, Ignatius affirms Christ to be both God and human. It is interesting to observe that this belief can be recognized in the thought of a Christian writer at least as early as the first part of the second century.

Ignatius commends the "unshakable faith" of the Smyrnaeans, and then makes the striking claim that their faith could be described as "having been nailed to the cross of the Lord Jesus Christ both in body and spirit" (Ign. *Smyrn.* 1.1). Precisely what Ignatius means by this statement is open to debate. Perhaps, if the reference to body and spirit denotes the modes of Jesus' existence, then this is a further affirmation that the faith of the Smyrnaean community was based both on the reality of the human sufferings of Christ and his resurrection as entailing an ongoing and other-worldly existence.

Next, it appears that Ignatius draws a series of three traditional statements or semi-creedal affirmations each one containing the adverb "truly" (ἀληθῶς). Initially, he states "our Lord truly being from family of David according to the flesh; Son of God according to will and power" (Ign. *Smyrn.* 1.1). The importance of affirming the reality of the sufferings of Christ becomes the focus of Ignatius' argument when he states that "for he suffered all these things for our sakes, in order that we might be saved" (Ign. *Smyrn.* 2.1). Therefore, Ignatius sees Christ's sufferings as beneficial for believers, and he defines that benefit in soteriological terms.

Chapters 4–7. Ignatius informs the Smyrnaeans that some false teachers are "wild beasts in human form" and that one should not even meet or welcome them (Ign. *Smyrn.* 4.1). It is difficult to determine whether this is a warning given in advance of the arrival of such teachers in Smyrna, or whether it is given after the event and is an attempt to have the Smyrnaeans cease any contact with such individuals. Despite this protective warning, Ignatius displays some degree of pastoral sensitivity toward those whom the Smyrnaeans are not to receive. He sees such false teachers to be in need of repentance, and he calls on the recipients of the letter to pray on behalf of such individuals, noting that Christ has the power to bring them back to a proper understanding of faith.

Next Ignatius links his own impending fate to the reality of Christ's incarnation. It is striking that the rhetorical question, "Why, moreover, have I surrendered myself to death?" (Ign. *Smyrn.* 4.2), appears to imply a certain level of volunteerism in Ignatius's impending execution. Perhaps this reflects the reality that he could escape his fate either by denying his faith or by asking the Roman believers to intervene on his behalf. For Ignatius, if Christ did not truly undergo suffering and crucifixion, then his own impending execution would lose much of its force, especially in regard to permitting Ignatius to be more fully united with Christ.

Ignatius continues his rebuttal of the false teachers by inverting the consequences of their declarations. While they can be seen as denying the reality of the sufferings and death of Christ, the consequence for them is that they will be denied by Christ (Ign. *Smyrn.* 5.1). In strident tones, he calls such people unbelievers, refuses to dignify them by remembering their names, and again links belief in the reality of the suffering of Christ with the ability to participate in resurrection life.

Ignatius then accuses the false teachers of not only promoting wrong doctrines; he argues further that their ethics are suspect. Ignatius states that such individuals do not show compassion for various marginalized groups: widows, orphans, the oppressed, prisoners or the released, or those in need of physical sustenance (Ign. *Smyrn.* 6.2). The list is reminiscent of the words of Jesus in Matthew 25:35–36. However, the similarity is most likely stereotypical of wider Christian teachings on social responsibilities. Apart from defective ethics, Ignatius also states that the ecclesial practices of his opponents are deficient, as demonstrated by a refusal to participate in the Eucharist or in communal prayer.

Ignatius concludes this section of the letter by outlining more of the consequences for those who hold such docetic forms of teaching. Due to denying the reality of Christ suffering in the flesh, Ignatius first says these teachers will perish. No doubt this refers to them not participating in Christ's risen life. He accuses them of not loving, again alluding to his previous description of the teachers as being ethically deficient.

Chapters 8.1–9.1. At this juncture Ignatius turns to another of his prominent topics in his letters—namely, ecclesial structure and loyalty to the bishop. Ignatius commands those in Smyrna to avoid divisions, to be subject to the threefold ecclesial hierarchy of bishop, council of presbyters, and deacons, and not to engage in any religious practices without the permission of the bishop. Thus Ignatius is a strong advocate for a structured and hierarchical form of church governance. From this perspective, Ignatius is able to state his underpinning theory of his ecclesiology: "Whenever the bishop appears, there let the congregation be; just as wherever Jesus Christ is, there is the catholic church" (Ign. *Smyrn.* 8.2). It is perhaps unsurprising that the phrase ἡ καθολικὴ ἐκκλησία, *hē katholikē ekklēsia*, "the catholic church," has occasioned much debate concerning the sense in which this phrase is used. Some have taken it as limited to being a geographical referent denoting the spread of various individual churches, while others have seen in this phrase a strong development reflecting the catholicity of the church in a theological sense.[27] Ignatius appears to intend more by this phrase than Paul does when he refers to "all the churches" (cf. 1 Cor 4:17; 7:17; 11:16; 14:33). Rather than simply denoting the geographical spread of individual churches, Ignatius implies that in the office of bishop, in a way analogous to the presence of Christ in believing communities, it is possible to recognize the presence of the authentic church. Ignatius polarizes the consequences for those who either accept or refuse the authority of the bishop, stating that this aligns either with service of God or service of the devil. As Ignatius presents the matter, the stakes could be no higher, and the consequences of that decision determine one's eternal fate.

Chapters 9.2–10.2. At this point there is a sudden change in tone, and the rhetoric becomes far less heated. Ignatius thanks the Smyrnaeans for the support they have already provided. He recalls that they refreshed him, and that both while he was with them and even when he was absent they expressed love for him. Ignatius tells the Smyrnaeans that because of their actions they themselves will be rewarded by God and refreshed by Christ. However, there is a caveat to receiving this reward. Ignatius reminds them that enjoying the future state of dwelling in the divine presence is conditional on steadfastness in this life: "If you endure everything for his sake, you will reach him" (Ign. *Smyrn.* 9.2).

Chapter 11.1–3. Moving into this closing section, alongside more standard themes and remarks, Ignatius inserts a reflection on some recent news he had received. Toward the end of his letter to the Philadelphians, he informed that community of the positive news of a return to peace in the church in Antioch (Ign. *Phld.* 10.1). He shares that same news with the Smyrnaeans, but in a fuller manner and with a more explicit set of instructions. Ignatius tells those in Smyrna that in order to perfect their work they must send a delegate to congratulate the church in Antioch, "because they are at peace and have regained their proper stature and their corporate life has been restored to its proper state" (Ign. *Smyrn.* 11.2).

27. For a more extensive discussion of Ignatius's ecclesiology, see sec. 3.4 below.

Chapters 12.1–13.2. Having supplied this recent news on the situation in Antioch, Ignatius returns to closing greetings and final requests. He sends greetings from his present location of Troas. He states he is writing through Burrhus, who is presumably acting as a scribe for Ignatius. Presumably, the costs of Burrhus's travel expenses have been met by the communities in Ephesus and Smyrna. Ignatius sees Burrhus as exemplary in his kindness and the tasks he has carried: "He is a model of service to God" (Ign. *Smyrn.* 12.1).

At this juncture, Ignatius proceeds to issue his final greetings. These reflect more than a set of names. This prosopographical data provides some insight into the composition of the church in Smyrna in the early part of the second century. Ignatius sends greetings to "households of my brothers with their wives and children, and the virgins who are called widows" (Ign. *Smyrn.* 13.1). This suggests that the larger Smyrnaean community of believers, at least in part, comprised households of believing families. These were typically led by a *paterfamilias* who could be described as a "brother" by fellow believers. Such influential males might have been the members of the community from which the council of presbyters was formed. Alongside these "brothers," Ignatius refers to their wives and children, who also were part of the community of believers in Smyrna. Ignatius then refers to "the virgins who are called widows" (13.1). The most plausible explanation concerning this obscure phrase is that the provision for widows described in certain Pauline writings (e.g., 1 Tim 5:3–16) had been enlarged to include other women, perhaps of advanced age, who had not married and hence had no support from relatives.[28]

Ignatius bids the Smyrnaeans "farewell in the power of the Father," which perhaps both reinforces his authority and reflects his belief that his own actions and fate were in accord with the divine will. There then follow more greetings. First, Ignatius sends greetings from the deacon Philo, who is also in Troas, to the Smyrnaeans. Next, Ignatius specifically greets "the household of Gavia." She is designated along with her household. This may suggest that she was a person of some standing. Alce, another woman, is sent greetings. She is also mentioned in the personal letter to Polycarp (Ign. *Pol.* 8.3), and there is a person of the same name mentioned in Martyrdom of Polycarp 17.2.[29] Lastly, Ignatius then concludes the list by greeting two men, "the incomparable Daphnus, and Eutecnus," prior to greeting everybody individually but without naming them. Ignatius concludes by issuing a second farewell, which this time is expressed "in the grace of God," in comparison to the previous one "in the power of the Father."

2.7 *To Polycarp*

This is the only letter among the seven letters of the middle recension addressed to an individual. Yet, while the letter contains some personal comments addressed to Polycarp, these are intended to be "overheard" by the community and thus among other things Ignatius mentions in this letter are intended to bolster the authority of Polycarp and his position of leadership.

---

28. T. Zahn, *Ignatius von Antiochien* (Gotha: Perthes, 1873), 334–38.

29. The text in question reads, "So he incited Nicetes, the father of Herod and brother of Alce, to appeal to the magistrate not to hand over his body, 'or else,' he said, 'they may abandon the crucified one and begin to worship this man.' All this was done at the instigation and insistence of the Jews, who even watched when we were about to take the body from the fire. They did not know that we will never be able either to abandon the Christ who suffered for the salvation of the whole world of those who are saved, the blameless on behalf of sinners, or to worship anyone else" (Mart. Pol. 17.2).

Structure

Salutation	
1.1	Approval of Polycarp
1.2–5.2	Instruction for the bishop
6.1–2	Call for obedience to the bishop
7.1–3	Request for a delegation to be sent to Antioch
8.1–3	Travel itinerary, final requests, and closing greetings

Salutation. The salutation has the traditional elements of conveying the identity of sender and recipient, and also of extending greetings to the one addressed. However, it goes beyond the merely conventional. The sender identifies himself both by name, Ignatius, but also with the descriptive nomenclature of "God bearer" (θεοφόρος, *theophoros*). The recipient is likewise identified as Polycarp, but that is qualified with the expansive phrase "bishop of the church of the Smyrnaeans." Ignatius qualifies the description of Polycarp as bishop of the Smyrnaeans by saying that the secondary recipients are those who are "overseen by God the Father and the Lord Jesus Christ." Here the term ἐπισκοπημένῳ, *episkopēmenō*, "overseen," is a verbal form related to the noun ἐπίσκοπος, *episkopos*, "bishop." Thus Ignatius asserts that Polycarp is a representative of the true divine oversight experienced by the community of believers in Smyrna.

Chapters 1.1. Ignatius continues his praise of Polycarp. The qualities that are lauded are Polycarp's godly mind and the fact that his mind is "grounded . . . upon an immovable rock" (Ign. *Pol.* 1.1). Hence Polycarp is depicted as a pious leader who has a stable and secure faith. During his brief visit to Smyrna, Ignatius felt much affinity with Polycarp. Hence he praises him in an abundant manner and acknowledges that their mutual fellowship brought him immense joy.

Chapters 1.2–5.2. Ignatius reflects on the role and responsibilities of a bishop. Initially, he provides some guiding instructions that are to characterize the type of episcopal oversight that Polycarp is to exercise. Using an athletic image, Ignatius describes Polycarp as engaged in a race. However, this is a spiritual race that consists of encouraging all people in order that they might be saved. It is striking that the first task that Ignatius urges upon Polycarp is to ensure the salvation of others. Whether this is seen as an evangelistic enterprise or the maintenance of the commitment of the community of faith would be perhaps to create an unnecessary dichotomy. Presumable Ignatius expected Polycarp to carry out both of these tasks.

Another activity that Ignatius lists as befitting for a bishop is constancy in prayer (Ign. *Pol.* 1.3). The focus of prayer is stated as being the request for increased understanding. Ignatius recommends a pastorally open communication style with believers in the community. Thus Polycarp is to "speak to people individually, in accordance with God's example" (Ign. *Pol.* 1.3). Here the role of supporting and encouraging community members comes to the fore. Ignatius continues his advice to Polycarp, but slightly alters the tone. Rather than continuing with positive actions, he instructs Polycarp concerning something he should not do—namely, not to show partiality to "good disciples." There is no suggestion that Polycarp is engaged in this negative behavior. It may simply be an encouragement or reminder to continue ministering to more problematic group members.

In chapter 3, the circumstances that confront Polycarp are made more explicit with the instruction, "Do not let those who appear to be trustworthy yet who teach strange doctrines baffle you" (Ign. *Pol.* 3.1). Here, no details of the nature of the "strange doctrines" are provided, although some of the affirmations that follow a little later appear to be given as intentional rebuttals of the ideas promulgated by such teachers. However, prior to that, Ignatius's first response is to encourage Polycarp to be resolute. The injunction to "stand firm" and the simile that Polycarp should be "like an anvil struck with a hammer" (Ign. *Pol.* 3.1) suggest that Ignatius desires Polycarp to be implacable in his reaction to these teachers. By nature, Ignatius comes across as more direct and confrontational in his leadership style, whereas Polycarp adopted a more conciliatory and gentle approach. There are hints in the letter addressed to the congregation in Smyrna that the response to the false teachers has not been as robust as Ignatius might have expected ("avoid such people and do not speak about them either privately or publicly," Ign. *Smyrn.* 7.2).[30]

Next, we see the strongest hint that Ignatius considered Polycarp not to have been sufficiently robust in tackling these false teachers. He commands Polycarp to "be more diligent than you are" (Ign. *Pol.* 3.2). Thus, alongside the positive welcome Ignatius received from Polycarp and the genuine warmth that appears to have existed between them, nonetheless Ignatius exhorts Polycarp to engage in a more sustained response to the false teachers. The additional instruction to "understand the times" creates an air of urgency concerning the necessity of Polycarp's response. It is certainly correct to see an eschatological aspect in this temporal reference. It is likely that Ignatius viewed his own fate as linked with the end of the age (cf. "these are the last times," Ign. *Eph.* 11.1).

Ignatius next turns to some concrete advice concerning matters to which Polycarp should be attentive in the leadership and administration of the community. There is a strong concern for the marginalized in the group, but this is also combined with some practical advice to guard against the exploitation of generosity. Administratively, Polycarp is to retain oversight of the affairs of the church and is to seek God's consent for his actions—presumably by prayer, but perhaps also by words of prophecy. The second piece of administrative advice concerns the frequency of community gatherings. Ignatius does not specify how often such meetings should take place, only that such meetings should "be held more frequently" (Ign. *Pol.* 4.2). Precisely which meetings are in view is unclear, since it might be assumed that the practice of meeting on the first day of every week was already established.[31] If this were an already established practice in Smyrna, then presumably Ignatius is speaking about additional meetings. Additionally, Polycarp is instructed to "seek out everyone by name" (Ign. *Pol.* 4.2). This command to include all community members is no doubt intended to produce group cohesion and loyalty to the bishop. The third topic of advice concerns the treatment of slaves who are part of the community. Ignatius commands that they be treated with equal respect as other members. Balanced alongside this, Polycarp is instructed to prevent slaves from becoming conceited.

Ignatius instructs Polycarp to assist the believers in Smyrna to turn away from "evil practices" (Ign. *Pol.* 5.1). His advice to Polycarp is to deliver a homily (ὁμιλία, *homilia*) concerning avoidance of evil. Polycarp is to provide instructions about marital relations. It is striking that Ignatius first provides instructions that are to be given to "the sisters." The female marriage partners are to be told "to be content with their husbands spiritually and physically" (Ign. *Pol.* 5.1). The latter aspect conveys ideas of sexual fidelity, while the former might be part of a larger concern about not being swept up with the spiritual teachings of those described as false teachers. The reciprocal responsibility upon male marriage

30. Further comments on this issue can be found in Schoedel, *Ignatius of Antioch*, 266.

31. That appears to be the practice implied in the Didache: "Every Lord's day gather together and break bread . . ." (Did. 14.1). However, it is difficult to ascertain how widespread this practice was around the beginning of the second century.

partners is that they should show love toward their wives. The language here appears to cite the teaching on this topic contained in Ephesians 5:25. Ignatius concludes this set of instructions for Polycarp concerning how he is to regulate the community with an overarching principle. He concludes by stating, "Let all things be done for the honour of God" (Ign. *Pol.* 5.2). This is not a mere "catchall" to regulate other social matters in the group. Rather, it is the standard by which to test all behavior and actions.

Chapter 6. Here Ignatius moves from instructions given to Polycarp to instructions for community members. The material in this section demonstrates that the letter was not intended as a piece of private correspondence for Polycarp alone but was also intended to be heard and received by the entire community of believers in Smyrna. The pressing issue for Ignatius is that community members should heed the instructions and teachings of their bishop, Polycarp.

Chapter 7. Here Ignatius commences the conclusion of the letter with some final requests being made to the Smyrnaeans, or to Polycarp in particular. While Syria is mentioned in all seven of Ignatius's letters, it is only in the three letters sent from Troas that one finds a specific reference to Antioch (Ign. *Phld.* 10.1; Ign. *Smyrn.* 11.1; Ign. *Pol.* 7.1). In both the letters to the Philadelphians and to Polycarp, Ignatius mentions that he has received news that "the church of Antioch in Syria is at peace." Such news is described as being a source of great encouragement to Ignatius.

In light of the news of the restoration of peace in Antioch, Ignatius requests that Polycarp convene a council in Smyrna. It is unclear whether that would have been just the leaders or the entire community. This detail suggests some kind of collective decision-making process rather than that Polycarp could make unilateral decisions. Ignatius calls on those assembled to send a delegate to Antioch. It is not entirely clear what Ignatius expected this courier to do.

Chapter 8. Ignatius commences this final section of the letter with an updated detail concerning his travel itinerary. He states that his route takes him by boat in a northwesterly direction across the Aegean Sea from Troas to Neapolis. Ignatius notes two implications, one theological and other practical. Rather than attribute this unexpectedly hasty progression as due to the wishes of the Roman soldiers or as a result of procuring passage, Ignatius states that this happened "as the divine will commands" (Ign. *Pol.* 8.1). The practical implication is that this meant that Ignatius had not been able to write to all the churches—presumably those he had visited or those that had sent delegates to meet him—in the Roman province of Asia. Consequently, Ignatius tasks Polycarp with the responsibility of writing to the remaining churches, requesting that they also send messengers, or failing that, letters, to the church in Antioch. Here one sees the importance of communication networks between early Christ-believing communities around the first quarter of the second century. Presumably this was a way of sustaining and encouraging these small groups of believers and helping them to view themselves as part of a larger movement.

Finally, in a poignant moment, Ignatius takes his leave of the Smyrnaeans, commending them to "our God Jesus Christ" (Ign. *Pol.* 8.3). Thus, the poignancy of the final words is linked with Ignatius's christological belief that Jesus is himself "our God," thereby asserting the divinity of Christ. He also prays for those in Smyrna that they would "continue," or "remain" (διαμένω, *diamenō*) in Christ.

Summary. At this point, with his correspondence from Troas interrupted by the onward journey toward Rome, knowledge of Ignatius from his own pen disappears. It is uncertain why no further letters were written (or perhaps did not survive) from later points on the journey. Did this reflect a less-developed network of Christian communities at places along the later stages of the journey (although surely not in Philippi)? Or did his custody become more severe and limiting, or was the remainder of the journey undertaken mainly via sea routes? It is not possible to answer these questions, as intriguing as they may be. However, other sources, including Polycarp himself, continued to write about Ignatius. Some of the later sources may not provide the most reliable information, but they speak with a unified voice of Ignatius meeting his end, or as he would have preferred to say, "attaining to God," in Rome.

3. INTERPRETATIVE ISSUES

In studying the history of the development of Christian theological ideas, the writings of Ignatius have been of great importance for understanding early developments around doctrinal thought and ecclesiological structures. The significance of these ideas has also been entwined with debates concerning the authenticity, or otherwise, of the seven letters of the middle recension outlined earlier. Leaving those continuing debates aside, here several of the key theological commitments articulated in the letter of Ignatius will be discussed.

3.1 God

Ignatius offers no examination of the ontological nature of God. Instead, God is taken to be a present and real entity in Ignatius's thought. The Greek term θεός, *theos*, occurs approximately 177 times in the seven letters.[32] God is a frequent presence in all of the letters of Ignatius. All of the opening salutations contain references to God, and those addressed to the Philadelphians and Smyrnaeans describe the recipients as being "the church of God the Father" (Ign. *Phld.* inscript; Ign. *Smyrn.* salut.). This formulation also contains reference to God as "Father" (πατήρ, *patēr*). Although not used with the same frequency as the term "God," the description of God as Father is commonplace throughout the letters and is often found in the expression "God the Father." When not used in combination with the term θεός, it is often employed as a designation of the filial relationship that Jesus is described as possessing with God.

There are a couple of striking occurrences of the use of the description of God as Father. Using the image of the building of God the Father, in the construction process Jesus is described as a hoisting machine or crane (μηχανή, *mēchanē*), and the Holy Spirit as the rope (Ign. *Eph.* 9.1). To designate this as a Trinitarian formula is perhaps to exceed the bounds of what is actually said. However, the threefold reference to the Father, Jesus, and the Spirit working together is suggestive of shared participation in the divine economy. Perhaps a stronger example that leans in the direction of a Trinitarian affirmation is when Ignatius tells the Magnesians that all their actions should be carried out "in faith and love, in the Son and the Father and in the Spirit" (Ign. *Magn.* 13.1). Here, unlike the previous example, there is not just a designation of a common purpose but a statement that together Father, Son, and Spirit constitute the space or domain in which believers find their own sense of being.

In passing, Ignatius refers to several attributes of God or describes ways in which believers are to relate to or derive their own sense of identity from the deity. The Ephesians are to be worthy of God (Ign. *Eph.* 2.1), and to live in harmony with the mind of God (3.2). Ignatius is not always explicit concerning how believers have access to the divine will,

32. Without taking into account variant readings, the Greek term θεός occurs with the following frequencies across the seven letters: Ign. *Eph.* 43x; Ign. *Magn.* 23x; Ign. *Trall.* 13x; Ign. *Rom.* 26x; Ign. *Phld.* 23x; Ign. *Smyrn.* 25x; Ign. *Pol.* 24x.

or mind. However, it appears this is primarily through union with Christ, often assisted with a few helpful reminders from Ignatius or through the oversight of leaders. In a passage that might be formed at least in part of inherited traditions, Ignatius refers to "the silence of God" (19.1). This might be the closest Ignatius comes to describe the inner state of divine ontology. If that is correct, it designates a place of serenity that is uninterrupted by external forces. Unsurprisingly, God is described as belonging to a different realm. Here Ignatius refers to two types of coinage and speaks of "the one of God and the other of the world" (Ign. *Magn.* 5.2). This suggests that those who belong to God, like the deity, are not part of the material world.

God is frequently mentioned throughout the letters, and on other occasions is assumed to be behind the circumstances described. The fact that Ignatius does not need to describe or argue for the nature of God reveals that he and his readers presumably had many shared understandings concerning God. Moreover, many of these were derived from understandings contained in Jewish writings and traditions. Perhaps Ignatius's most significant innovation concerns those references where Jesus is described as "our" or "my God." Those cases will be discussed in the following section dealing with Ignatius's understanding of Christ.

3.2 Jesus Christ

From a doctrinal perspective, Ignatius's comments concerning Jesus are some of the most significant and hotly contested aspects of his theology. There are several occasions when Ignatius describes Jesus as "our God" (Ign. *Eph.*, inscript; 15.3; 18.2; Ign. *Rom.* inscript; 3.3; Ign. *Pol.* 8.3), or as "my God" (Ign. *Rom.* 6.3; Ign. *Phld.* 6.3). These occurrences are striking, although some have considered the use of the possessive pronouns "our" and "my" as in some sense weakening the sense of absolute or unqualified divinity. However, elsewhere in an apparently unqualified manner that does not explicitly name Jesus, Ignatius refers to the event "when God appeared in human form to bring the newness of eternal life" (Ign. *Eph.* 19.3). While the teaching of the wider passage is somewhat exotic, the statement cited here is a reference to the incarnation of Christ, which Ignatius describes as θεοῦ ἀνθρωπίνως φανερουμένου, *theou anthrōpinōs phaneroumenou*—that is, a manifestation or an appearance of God in human form. For Ignatius this divine manifestation, which is disclosed in Christ's incarnation or fleshly existence, is a transformative event. As Lookadoo has noted, "Jesus's appearance in the flesh brought about the beginning of the downfall of everything evil in creation."[33] Ignatius's way of speaking about the divinity of Jesus is not equivalent to, or spoken in the same register as, the creeds of the fourth and fifth centuries. There was much theological reflection, debate, and dissent that would occur prior to the formulation of such statements.

Alongside the strong affirmations of divinity, Ignatius also speaks of the reality of the humanity of Christ. One of the chief motivations for this is as part of his multifaceted rebuttal of teachers who promoted docetic christological perspectives. On one occasion Ignatius's language seems imprecise when he declares that a person blasphemes if that individual does not confess that the Lord "was clothed in the flesh" (Ign. *Smyrn.* 5.2). This might appear to suggest that the human form simply veiled the inner reality. However, Ignatius derives rhetorical value from the clothing metaphor. He is able to turn it back on his opponents and state that their denial of the reality of Christ's humanity reveals that they are not recipients of life but are, in fact, "clothed in a corpse" (Ign. *Smyrn.* 5.2).

33. Jonathon Lookadoo, *The High Priest and the Temple: Metaphorical Depictions of Jesus in the Letters of Ignatius of Antioch*, WUNT 2/473 (Tübingen: Mohr Siebeck, 2018), 283.

Earlier in the same letter, Ignatius had been more direct about the incarnation, especially emphasizing that Christ remained in the flesh at the point of his death and beyond. Thus Ignatius writes that Christ was "truly nailed in the flesh for us" (1.2), and in a declarative statement Ignatius further states, "For I know and believe that he was in the flesh even after the resurrection" (3.1). Based on these texts, Vall comments that Ignatius "places a strong accent on the historical reality and physical humanity of Christ, explicitly mentioning Jesus' 'flesh' (σάρξ) in connection with the incarnation, the passion, and the resurrection."[34] However, perhaps the most common way in which Ignatius affirms the humanity of Jesus is simply to assert it alongside declarations of his divinity. A classic example occurs in one of the semi-creedal statements, where Ignatius writes, "There is only one physician, who is both flesh and spirit, born and unborn, God in man, true life in death, both from Mary and from God, first subject to suffering and then beyond it, Jesus Christ our Lord" (Ign. *Eph.* 7.2). The pairings such as flesh and spirit, born and unborn, from Mary and from God, and subject to suffering then beyond suffering present binary perspectives, which in some cases appear mutually exclusive and in others at least create tension. Nonetheless, Ignatius simply declares both realities to be true. However, he does not attempt to explain the basis on which one might reason that such apparently contradictory affirmations can be held together. Yet Ignatius relentlessly declares the humanity and the divinity of Christ. While such theological perspectives are used in his polemical responses, they do not primarily emerge in an argumentative context. Rather, such statements reflect cherished beliefs that emerge from a deeply held piety. They show how Ignatius understands Jesus to be the Savior who brings true life and the promise of resurrection.

3.3 Holy Spirit

Whereas Ignatius devotes much space and detailed reflection to describing his christological beliefs and also presents several references to God, his statements concerning the Holy Spirit are far more limited and do not form the subject of extended theological reflection. In fact, Ignatius only employs the term "Holy Spirit" on three occasions. First, it occurs in his famous tripartite construction in the metaphor of believers being stones of the temple in the building of God the Father, which is constructed by the crane which is the cross of Christ, and "using as a rope the Holy Spirit" (Ign. *Eph.* 9.1). One might be excused for thinking Ignatius became a little carried away with the metaphor, to the point that the final element communicates little understanding of the nature or role of the Spirit.[35] From this passage it appears that Ignatius has a broadly trinitarian outlook, but this does not include a developed understanding of the Spirit.

The second reference to the Holy Spirit occurs in one of Ignatius's semi-creedal statements, where it is stated that Jesus was conceived "both from the seed of David and of the Holy Spirit" (Ign. *Eph.* 18.2). This is probably not a citation of Romans 1:3–4. Rather, the similar outlook suggests that this formulation might have been in wider circulation, and hence taken over by Ignatius. Thus, while Ignatius is happy to affirm the dual nature of Jesus's ancestry, he has not here offered any deeper understanding of the Spirit.

The final reference to the Holy Spirit is made in reference in the threefold leadership of the community at Philadelphia. Ignatius states that these leaders are appointed through

34. Vall, *Learning Christ*, 185.

35. It is notable that in the body of Schoedel's discussion of this passage he devotes no space to Ignatius's reference to the Holy Spirit (apart from in his translation of the passage). However, in a footnote he states, "the spirit as the third member of the trinity plays only a minor role in Ignatius" (Schoedel, *Ignatius of Antioch*, 66).

the mind of Christ and that they are "securely established by his Holy Spirit" (Ign. *Phld.* salut.). This brief comment reveals that, for Ignatius, the Spirit is in some kind of proximate relationship with Jesus for it is "his Holy Spirit." It is difficult to specify precisely what the pronoun denotes in this brief formulation, although some kind of possessive relationship appears to be intended. This could either denote Jesus's own spirit (cf. Acts 16:8), or perhaps the Spirit is viewed as an entity that Jesus can impart to provide security to the Philadelphian community leaders (cf. John 14:26; 15:26; 16:13–14).

Alongside these explicit references to "the Holy Spirit," Ignatius also speaks of the prophets, describing them in relation to Christ as "his disciples in the spirit" (Ign. *Magn.* 9.2). Presumably here the references to the Spirit are made to reinforce Ignatius's understanding that when the Spirit came upon the prophets they were given divine perception to know that their message proleptically spoke about Jesus, and consequently they could be viewed as disciples. Also, in the letter to the Magnesians, as part of his prayer for that community, Ignatius employs a tripartite formula, asking that they might prosper "in the Son, in the Father and in the Spirit" (Ign. *Magn.* 13.1). Again, little is communicated about the role of the Spirit or the relation to the other two members of this formula.

While Ignatius does not show a significantly developed pneumatology in his letters, nonetheless a few features are apparent. In a natural way, on a couple of occasions, Ignatius can employ a threefold formula of Father, Son, and Spirit. Since this formulation requires no explanation or justification, it appears that it was already widely accepted and adopted. Without any detailed explanation, Ignatius believes that the Spirit comes to believers both from the Father and from Jesus. Ignatius presents himself as one who is guided by the Spirit, and he states the Spirit protects him from deception. Moreover, the same Spirit also provides security and protection for leaders in the believing communities in Asia.

3.4 Ecclesiology

Without doubt, in the history of interpretation of the letters of Ignatius, one factor that made them controversial was the perspectives they contained on the nature of the church and the structure of its leadership hierarchy. For some readers, especially in the post-Reformation period, the views contained in the letters were an example of a deviation from the pristine teachings of the New Testament, and thus a representation of early Catholicism, or alternatively an indication that the letters were late fabrications written in the name of the early second-century figure Ignatius. On the other side of the debate, others took the letters as a justification for sixteenth- and seventeenth-century ecclesial structures. Hence the perspectives in the letters were seen as a demonstration that those who adopted other forms of church leadership were innovators who did not hold to the ancient traditions of the church and could be seen as deviants and even heretics. Therefore, the uses to which the letters were put in ecclesial debates were anything but irenic. Instead, the letters became loaded with the freight of later theological controversies and debates. While it is perhaps impossible to strip away all the theological baggage that the letters attracted in the post-Reformation era, the aim here is to be attentive to what the letters actually say about the nature of the church and the forms of leadership advocated by Ignatius.

Ignatius uses the term ἐκκλησία, *ekklēsia*, on thirty-eight occasions in his writings, and there is no letter in which he does not use the term.[36] Thus, Ignatius's understanding of

36. Ign. *Eph.* inscript; 5.1, 2; 8.1; 17.1; 21.2; Ign. *Magn.* inscript; 1.2; 14.1 [twice]; 15.1; Ign. *Trall.* inscript; 2.3; 3.1; 12.1; 13.1; Ign. *Rom.* inscript; 4.1; 9.1, 3; Ign. *Phld.* inscript; 3.2; 5.1; 9.1; 10.1 [twice], 2; Ign. *Smyrn.* inscript; 1.2; 8.1, 2; 11.1, 2; Ign. *Pol.* inscript; 5.1; 7.1; 8.1 [twice].

the nature of ἐκκλησία is a central concern and topic of discussion in his letters. The term ἐκκλησία occurs in the introductions of all seven letters. As such, it functions as a marker of group identity. This use aligns with the pattern found in several of Paul's letters (1 Cor 1:2; 2 Cor 1:1; 1 Thess 1:1), although on at least one occasion Paul speaks of multiple churches in a region to which a letter is addressed (Gal 1:2). Also similar to examples of Paul's use, Ignatius on occasion refers to the group addressed as "the church of God" (Ign. *Phld.* inscript; Ign. *Smyrn.* salut.), prior to mentioning the geographical location. Thus, Ignatius provides a double designation, both belonging to God and located in a specific place. In several of the letters the reference of belonging to God is dropped, and Ignatius refers to the group by geographical location alone. These descriptions often are accompanied with other designations that are either theological in nature or serve to disambiguate the location. For example, Ignatius states that his letter addressed to the Ephesians is sent "to the church worthy of blessing which is in Ephesus of Asia" (Ign. *Eph.* salut.), or he can provide greater geographical precision, such as "to the church which is in Magnesia on the Maeander" (Ign. *Magn.* salut.).

While the description of the church as a single, translocal entity is not as frequent in the letters of Ignatius, the concept of the universal ἐκκλησία is still recognizable in his writings. Some of the clearest statements in this regard are found in the letter to the Smyrnaeans. Continuing on from one of his semi-creedal statements, Ignatius describes Christ's redemptive activity "for his holy and faithful people, whether among Jews or among Gentiles, in the one body of his church" (Ign. *Smyrn.* 1.2). Here the church is conceived as a single entity constituted and unified through becoming recipients of the benefits of the suffering and resurrection of Jesus.

This same train of thought is found elsewhere in the letter, particularly in a passage that has attracted multiple and contested interpretations. Discussing the function of a bishop as one around whom the local congregation is to gather, Ignatius makes the analogous statement, ὥσπερ ὅπου ἂν ᾖ Χριστὸς Ἰησοῦς, ἐκεῖ ἡ καθολικὴ ἐκκλησία, *hōsper hopou an ē Christos Iēsous, ekei ē katholikē ekklēsia* (Ign. *Smyrn.* 8.2). It is the meaning of the penultimate word, καθολική, that has occasioned a range of interpretive suggestions. The basic comparative meaning of the clause is clear: "where Jesus Christ is, there is the [καθολική] church." The term καθολική carries the idea of something being universal or general. Alongside this, it evolved as a technical term for the catholicity of the church, or as a way of naming all believers as belonging to the catholic church. Given Reformation debates and their repercussions, such terminology, although found only here in the writings of Ignatius, not only occasioned discussion but was at times overloaded with theological perspectives derived from later periods. At the very least, the adjective καθολική enlarges the horizon of the scope of the term ἐκκλησία beyond a specific geographical context or a specified collection of local churches. However, for Lightfoot the adjective is a means for denoting geographical extension. Hence, he states, "In its earliest usages therefore, as a fluctuating epithet of ἐκκλησία, 'catholic' means 'universal,' as opposed to 'individual,' 'particular.'"[37] Others have seen the term encapsulating much more than this, with Zizioulas perhaps somewhat idiosyncratically excluding any suggestion that the term is a reference to geographical scope, arguing that the term means "whole," rather than "universal."[38] This logic

37. Lightfoot, *Apostolic Fathers, Part II*, 2:311.

38. J. D. Zizioulas, *Eucharist, Bishop, Church: The Unity of the Church in the Divine Eucharist and the Bishop During the First Three Centuries*, trans. E. Theokritoff (Brookline, MA: Holy Cross Orthodox Press, 2001), 107–20.

is not entirely clear. Despite Lightfoot's wish to limit the use of καθολική in this context to a universal geographical sense, it does appear that Ignatius's view of the translocal church encapsulates more than geographical extent. While the term καθολική may primarily designate geographical scope beyond the local level, in the context where the term is used it functions as a way of designating the uniformity of local practice that conforms to the behavior of dispersed communities correctly gathered around the bishop and conducting permissible baptisms or agape meals. However, this designation had certainly not yet emerged as a technical term, nor did it depict hierarchical structures that are operative across the boundaries of local communities.

Inextricably linked to Ignatius's understanding of the nature of the church is the pattern of leadership he advocates as the proper structure in each local community. As is well-known, Ignatius promoted a three-tiered hierarchy for church leadership. From his perspective, every correctly constituted community of believers that administered baptism and Eucharist could only legitimately do so if it had the requisite leadership structure. That structure comprised a single ἐπίσκοπος *episkopos* (an "overseer," or "bishop"), supported by a group of πρεσβύτεροι, *presbyteroi* ("elders," or "presbyters") that together formed a presbyterial council (πρεσβυτέριον, *presbyterion*), and assisted by various διάκονοι, *diakonoi* ("deacons," or "ministers"). Ignatius does not devote equal space to describing the functions of each of these roles. Rather, his focus falls on the status and role of the figure of the ἐπίσκοπος.

The interest in the episcopal role and the concern that each local church should be constituted under the leadership of a bishop is not explained on the basis of an authoritarian perspective. Rather, several slightly different but mutually reinforcing theological explanations are provided as to why this threefold pattern of roles under the leadership of the bishop was both correct and divinely instituted. The term ἐπίσκοπος is found in each of the seven letters, although only once in the letter to the Romans (an observation that is worthy of further consideration). In total, Ignatius uses the term ἐπίσκοπος on fifty-six occasions.[39] However, only once does Ignatius refer to himself as an ἐπίσκοπος, and even then in a circuitous manner describing his impending death: "God has judged the bishop from Syria worthy to be found in the west, having summoned him from the east" (Ign. *Rom.* 2.2). However, Ignatius speaks of bishops in those five cities to which he writes: Onesimus in Ephesus, Demas in Magnesia, Polybius in Tralles, Polycarp in Smyrna, and an unnamed bishop in Philadelphia (Ign. *Phld.* 1.1). By contrast, Ignatius does not show awareness of a bishop in Rome. There could be several reasons for this. There might be a bishop in Rome, but Ignatius is unaware of this person. Alternatively, the form of church leadership with a single episcopal leader may have originated in the east in Syria or Asia and still be unknown in Rome in the first quarter of the second century.

With reference to the bishops in Asia, on several occasions Ignatius instructs the community to which a particular letter is addressed to do nothing without the permission of the bishop (Ign. *Magn.* 4.1; 7.1; Ign. *Trall.* 2.2; 7.2; Ign. *Phld.* 7.2; Ign. *Smyrn.* 8.1). Specifically this appears to be in relation to conducting baptisms or religious meals without the bishop's permission: "It is not permissible either to baptize or to hold a love feast without the bishop" (Ign. *Smyrn.* 8.2). It is incumbent on community members to give the

39. Ign. *Eph.* 1.3 [twice]; 2.2; 3.2; 4.1 [twice]; 5.1, 2, 3; 6.1 [twice]; 20.2; Ign. *Magn.* 2.1 [twice]; 3.1 [twice], 2; 4.1; 6.1, 2; 7.1; 13.1, 2; 15.1; Ign. *Trall.* 1.1; 2.1, 2; 3.1, 2; 7.1, 2; 12.2; 13.2; Ign. *Rom.* 2.2; Ign. *Phld.* inscript; 1.1; 3.2; 4.1; 7.1, 2; 8.1; 10.2; Ign. *Smyrn.* 8.1 [three times], 2 [twice]; 9.1 [three times]; 12.2; Ign. *Pol.* inscript; 5.2 [twice]; 6.1 [twice].

bishop respect (Ign. *Magn.* 3.1; Ign. *Trall.* 3.1). For example, in relation to the youthful Damas, bishop of Magnesia, the community is not to exploit his youthful appearance but instead to "defer to him who is wise in God; yet not really to him, but to the Father of Jesus Christ, the bishop of all" (Ign. *Magn.* 3.1). Two things are striking here. First, Ignatius views those holding episcopal office as being gifted with wisdom. Second, he views bishops as ultimately exercising a representative function, since it is God who is the overseer or bishop of all. Ignatius understands the episcopal leadership to be a universal and divinely ordained pattern, not simply a local preference: "The bishops appointed throughout the world are in the mind of Christ" (Ign. *Eph.* 3.2).

Ignatius employs some memorable comparisons to illustrate the high status that he attributes to the role of bishops. He informs the Ephesians that "we must regard the bishop as the Lord himself" (Ign. *Eph.* 6.1). Within a local gathering of believers, Ignatius states that "the bishop [is] presiding in the place of God" (Ign. *Magn.* 6.1). Group members must be obedient to their bishop, as such deference is seen as signifying the possession of a pure conscience (Ign. *Trall.* 7.2). Many of Ignatius's images of leadership roles within the communities of believers that he addresses refer concurrently to the three offices of the bishop, a council of presbyters, and a group of deacons.

Presbyters are referred to in two slightly different ways in Ignatius's letters. First, Ignatius describes them as a group, using the collective term πρεσβυτέριον ("council of presbyters," or "presbyterate"). This term is a favorite of Ignatius, but it is not found among the other writers included in the collection of writings of the Apostolic Fathers. Therefore, when Ignatius speaks collectively of the council of presbyters by using the term πρεσβυτέριον, this is nearly always done in connection with a reference to the bishop. Ignatius portrays the council of presbyters as part of the bishop's inner leadership group, and the comparison which likens them to the apostles suggests that Ignatius sees them in a supportive, yet subservient role.

Ignatius uses the term πρεσβύτερος on nine occasions, all of which occur in the plural.[40] On one occasion he preserves the language of "a council" by saying the presbyters stand in the place of the council of the apostles (καὶ τῶν πρεσβυτέρων εἰς τόπον συνεδρίου τῶν ἀποστόλων, *kai tōn presbyterōn eis topon synedriou tōn apostolōn*, Ign. *Magn.* 6.1). Ignatius does not explain the function of the presbyters, apart from saying they are the group gathered around the bishop. However, Ignatius does state that without presbyters no group can describe itself as a church: "They should respect . . . the presbyters as God's council and as the band of the apostles. Without these no group can be called a church" (Ign. *Trall.* 3.1).

Deacons are the third recognized leadership group in believing communities. Deacons are mentioned in six of the seven letters. The exception is the letter to the Romans, where Ignatius appears to have little knowledge of the leadership structures in that city, or perhaps leadership is not a topic of interest when sending his preemptive letter to the believers in Rome. Ignatius seems to hold deacons in high regard and in some way to identify with them. He refers to the deacon Zotion as "my fellow servant" (Ign. *Magn.* 2.1). Similarly, writing to the Philadelphians, he describes the deacons collectively as "my fellow servants" (τοῖς συνδούλοις μου, *tois syndoulois mou*, Ign. *Phld.* 4.1; cf. Ign. *Smyrn.* 12.2). The reason for this warmth and familiarity is not fully apparent. Perhaps Ignatius had served as a deacon at some stage prior to becoming bishop of Antioch. Alternatively, perhaps he saw his impending death as some kind of diaconal service, or maybe he had benefited from the service of specific deacons, such a Philo and Rhaius Agathopus who had accompanied

40. Ign. *Magn.* 2.1; 3.1; 6.1; 7.1; Ign. *Trall.* 3.1; 12.2; Ign. *Phld.* inscript; 10.2; Ign. *Pol.* 6.1.

Ignatius on at least part of his journey (Ign. *Phld.* 11.1; Ign. *Smyrn.* 10.1). It might even be the case that Rhaius Agathopus had determined to accompany Ignatius even to the point of execution, since he is described as "a chosen man who followed me from Syria, having renounced this life" (Ign. *Phld.* 11.1). Ignatius does provide a little information about the role of deacons. Describing the role of deacons to the Trallians, Ignatius states,

> Furthermore, it is necessary that those who are deacons of the mysteries of Jesus Christ please everyone in every respect. For they are not merely deacons of food and drink but ministers of God's church. Therefore they must avoid criticism as though it were fire. (Ign. *Trall.* 2.3)

Schoedel sees the reference to food and drink as a reference to their main task being the distribution of provisions to the poor in line with their original function (Acts 6:1–6).[41] However, for Ignatius their function is larger than this; they are ministers of the church and administer the mysteries of Jesus Christ. For Ignatius, deacons were integral to the threefold pattern he advocated. They carried out a number of practical as well as spiritual duties, if it is even correct to distinguish those as two separate categories.

Ignatius's contribution to ecclesiology is profound. He is the first known advocate of the threefold pattern of church leadership that subsequently became the form of hierarchy in many church traditions. His description of the church both as local communities and also as a translocal unified institution can find antecedents in the letters of Paul. However, his use of the descriptive phrase ἡ καθολικὴ ἐκκλησία, while yet not a technical term, nonetheless was to become a standard way of describing the church as a universal entity, which was united in belief and structure beyond local boundaries. Ignatius is, without doubt, one of the most influential figures in the development of ecclesial self-understanding and practices in the early centuries of the church and beyond.

3.5 The Eucharist

Ignatius's understanding of the Eucharist is closely linked to his ecclesiology. The link arises from his claim that the only legitimate Eucharist is that which is conducted with episcopal authorization. Thus Ignatius declares, "Only that Eucharist which is under the authority of the bishop (or whomever he himself designates) is to be considered valid" (Ign. *Smyrn.* 8.1b). It is notable that Ignatius does not state that the bishop must preside at every eucharistic celebration, but rather that those events must take place under his authority or with his delegated permission. In the wider context of this statement, Ignatius suggests that certain people "do not believe in the blood of Christ" (Ign. *Smyrn.* 6.1), thus making themselves liable to judgment. Furthermore, it appears that certain opponents who hold docetic beliefs have abstained from the Eucharist. For Ignatius, refusal to participate in the Eucharist was not merely a rejection of the bishop's authority, but it reflected deviant beliefs concerning the reality and redemptive nature of Christ's death.[42]

In this context, as a polemical response to those holding the beliefs that Ignatius opposes, he makes his strongest and most direct claim, affirming the Eucharist as "the flesh of our Saviour Jesus Christ" (Ign. *Smyrn.* 6.2). While this statement is certainly compatible with later understandings of the real presence of Christ in the Eucharist, and hence with a more developed notion of transubstantiation, it would nevertheless be unhelpful to take

41. Schoedel, *Ignatius of Antioch*, 141.

42. For more on this, see H. Löhr, "The Epistles of Ignatius of Antioch," in *The Apostolic Fathers: An Introduction*, ed. W. Pratscher (Waco, TX: Baylor University Press, 2010), 91–115, esp. 108–9.

this statement out of its charged polemical context. In other passages, Ignatius perhaps does not go as far in equating the Eucharist with the flesh of Christ. For instance, writing to the Philadelphians, the community is instructed to unite in partaking of one Eucharist. The rational for this instruction is "for there is one flesh of our Lord Jesus Christ, and one cup that leads to unity through his blood; there is one altar, just as there is one bishop, together with the council of presbyters and the deacons, my fellow servants" (Ign. *Phld.* 4.1). Here the Eucharist, like Christ's blood, and like church-leadership structures, should lead to unity rather than division. Ignatius does not provide a thoroughgoing theology of the Eucharist. However, what emerges is his strong and repeated belief that only a Eucharist held under the authority of the bishop or his delegate is legitimate. Furthermore, Ignatius presses the comparison between the eucharistic elements and the flesh and blood of Christ.[43]

3.6 Eschatology

Ignatius's writings appear to reflect a fairly standard Christian eschatological outlook. There is a belief in a future resurrection, with a final judgment at the end of the current age, and for believers the hope of partaking in a glorified state in the divine presence. Alongside this, Ignatius views some aspects of the eschatological future as already inaugurated, both through the resurrection of Jesus and in the transformed lives of believers. In his fullest eschatological statement, he writes:

> These are the last times. Therefore let us be reverent; let us fear the patience of God, lest it become a judgment against us. For let us either fear the wrath to come or love the grace that is present, one of the two; only let us be found in Christ Jesus, which leads to true life. (Ign. *Eph.* 11.1)

A number of features pertaining to his eschatological thought are apparent in this passage. First, due to the perspective that the contemporary period constitutes the last times, Ignatius suggests this should create a certain attitudinal and behavioral pattern among believers. They should adopt a reverent lifestyle. Second, according to Ignatius, if there is not a display of behavior commensurate with the patient forbearance of God, then individuals will render themselves liable to a judgment against them.[44] Third, Ignatius provides two motivations for commitment to Christ, one of which is negative and the other positive. On the negative side he warns of future judgment as a reason to embrace participation in Christ with the behaviors that requires. More positively, he describes the experience of grace in the present. Thus, he sees Christian life as intrinsically being the better form of existence for living in the current age. However, if that should provide insufficient motivation, he reminds addressees of future judgment and wrath to come. Hence, Ignatius appears to hold a binary view of the future fates of humanity.

While Ignatius does not describe his view of eschatology as fully elsewhere, he does make other comments that reinforce the perspective set out when writing to the Ephesians. Without expressing a timeframe, Ignatius informs those in Smyrna that only humans will face future judgment, but "even the heavenly beings and the glory of angels and rulers, both visible and invisible, are subject to judgment if they do not believe in the blood of Christ"

43. See further C. N. Jefford, *Reading the Apostolic Fathers: A Student's Introduction*, 2nd ed. (Grand Rapids: Baker Academic, 2012), 56.

44. For more on this, see Löhr, "Epistles of Ignatius of Antioch," 111–13.

(Ign. *Smyrn.* 6.1). Here the concern appears to be with those who deny the reality of the sufferings of Christ. However, the argument presented that such individuals will come to judgment is based on the claim that heavenly beings also receive judgment. Furthermore, in the same letter, Ignatius views the current age as an interim period where humans can make a decision that determines one's future fate: "It is reasonable for us to come to our senses while we still have time to repent and turn to God" (Ign. *Smyrn.* 9.1). Writing to the Magnesians, Ignatius restates his belief that the incarnation of Christ commenced the eschatological age: "Jesus Christ, who before the ages was with the Father and appeared at the end of time" (Ign. *Magn.* 6.1). The Trallians are informed that in the future they will rise and be with Christ (Ign. *Trall.* salut.). This is described more fully in the body of the letter, when Ignatius states, "In the same way his Father will likewise also raise up in Christ Jesus us who believe in him" (Ign. *Trall.* 9.2). Ignatius uses the hope of life in the age to come as a motivating factor when encouraging Polycarp to be faithful to his ministry: "Be sober, as God's athlete; the prize is incorruptibility and eternal life" (Ign. *Pol.* 2.3).

Eschatology is not a major topic in the writings of Ignatius, and his views align with wider Christian thinking on the topic, especially as found in the letters of Paul. Ignatius affirms that humanity is living in the last times and views that age as commencing with the appearance of Christ in bodily form. The future return of Christ is presented by Ignatius as a motivation for correct ethical behavior in the current period, with believers being encouraged to put aside shameful practices and to adopt a lifestyle that is reverent and morally upright. In all these aspects, Ignatius appear to hold to fairly traditional Christian views, and there is little innovation in his thought in relation to his eschatological perspectives.

4. KEY PASSAGES FOR NEW TESTAMENT STUDIES AND THEIR SIGNIFICANCE

It is helpful to remember the reality of the physical circumstances endured by Ignatius at the time of writing his seven letters. He describes himself as being transported to Rome while chained to guards (Ign. *Rom.* 5.1). Therefore, it is unlikely that Ignatius had any direct access to scriptural manuscripts while being transported. Consequently, perhaps one should not ask which writings Ignatius knew that would later become the New Testament. He may well have known of various texts that are not cited or utilized in his surviving letters. Instead, it is preferable to inquire about those scriptural writings that are used or appear to be used in the letters of Ignatius. It is helpful to first consider what Jewish scriptural texts are potentially cited in Ignatius's writings.

There is only one marked citation in the seven letters of the middle recension. Ignatius illustrates his point that opposition to the bishop is disobedience toward God with the following statement: "For it is written, 'God opposes the arrogant'" (γέγραπται γάρ· Ὑπερηφάνοις ὁ θεὸς ἀντιτάσσεται, *gegraptai gar hyperēphanois ho theos antitassetai*, Ign. *Eph.* 5.3). This appears to be a citation of the first half of Proverbs 3:34, "The Lord opposes the arrogant" (κύριος ὑπερηφάνοις ἀντιτάσσεται, *kyrios hyperēphanois antitassetai*). There are some notable differences. First, "God" replaces "Lord," and second the subject ("God") is placed after the dative plural noun ("the arrogant ones"). How are these differences to be explained? Did Ignatius modify the text of Proverbs 3:34 LXX due to faulty memory, or is he dependent on a different Greek version? There is also another possibility that requires consideration. Several other early Christian texts that may be prior to Ignatius also cite this text (Jas 4:6; 1 Pet 5:5; 1 Clem. 30.2).[45] Therefore, a further possibility is that it

45. W. R. Inge, "Ignatius," in *The New Testament in the Apostolic Fathers*, ed. A Committee of the Oxford Society of Historical Theology (Oxford: Clarendon Press, 1905), 63, 76.

might be the case that this scriptural text is known to Ignatius through mediated and prior Christian use of this citation.

Aside from this text that in some form originated from the Greek translation of Proverbs, Ignatius also show awareness of several texts drawn from writings that would later become part of the New Testament. Ignatius has much to say about Jesus, but most of what he says does not find a close literary parallel with texts seen in the four Gospels of the New Testament. There is no plausible example of Ignatius's use of the Gospel of Mark or the Gospel of John. Some have seen a parallel between *To the Smyrnaeans* 3.2a and Luke 24:39. For comparative purposes the texts may be set out as follows:

Ign. *Smyrn.* 3.2a	**Luke 24:39**
καὶ ὅτε πρὸς τοὺς περὶ Πέτρον ἦλθεν, ἔφη αὐτοῖς· Λάβετε, ψηλαφήσατέ με καὶ ἴδετε ὅτι οὐκ εἰμι δαιμόνιον ἀσώματον. "And when he came to Peter and those with him, he said to them: 'Take hold of me; touch me and see that I am not a disembodied demon.'"	ἴδετε τὰς χεῖράς μου καὶ τοὺς πόδας μου ὅτι ἐγώ εἰμι αὐτός· ψηλαφήσατέ με καὶ ἴδετε, ὅτι πνεῦμα σάρκα καὶ ὀστέα οὐκ ἔχει καθὼς ἐμὲ θεωρεῖτε ἔχοντα. "See My hands and My feet, that it is I Myself; touch Me and see, for a spirit does not have flesh and bones as you see that I have."

Here there is a string of five Greek words in common, as well as a negative particle. The similarity of this phase "touch me and see that" must be weighed alongside the divergence in the other elements. When Lightfoot commented on *To the Smyrnaeans* 3.2–3, he stated, "The reference is plainly to the same incident which is related in Luke xxiv. 36 sq. . . . The words in which it is told are different."[46] Therefore, while one might see elements of a common tradition behind Luke 24:39 and *To the Smyrnaeans* 3.2a, there is insufficient evidence arising from this single example that permits the conclusion that Ignatius was likely to have known the Gospel of Luke.

When it comes to the case of the Gospel of Matthew, there is much stronger evidence available, which in fact makes it likely that Ignatius knew and drew on this text at several places in his letters. One of the difficulties with showing that an author knew a specific Gospel is that the Synoptic Gospels themselves have a high level of verbatim agreement between themselves in certain passages. Therefore, in order to demonstrate knowledge of a specific Gospel, the argument is enhanced if the later author reproduces material that is unique to a specific Gospel. This in fact happens with Ignatius when he describes the baptism of Jesus. Ignatius states that Jesus was baptized by John "in order that all righteousness might be filled by him" (ἵνα πληρωθῇ πᾶσα δικαιοσύνη ὑπ' αὐτοῦ, *hina plērōthē pasa dikaiosynē hyp autou*; Ign. *Smyrn.* 1.1). In the Gospel of Matthew, Jesus convinces John to permit him to undergo baptism by saying, "For thus it is fitting for us to fulfill all righteousness" (οὕτως γὰρ πρέπον ἐστὶν ἡμῖν πληρῶσαι πᾶσαν δικαιοσύνην, *houtōs gar prepon estin hemin plērōsai pasan dikaiosynēn*; Matt 3:15). The significance of this agreement is not based solely on the three shared words (which differ in grammatical forms). Rather, the detail of "fulfilling all righteousness" is unique to Matthew. Moreover, the term "righteousness" is favored Matthean vocabulary. Among the Synoptic Gospels, Matthew use the term seven times (Matt 3:15; 5:6, 10, 20; 6:1, 33; 21:32). Therefore, given that Ignatius is describing the baptism of Jesus by John, and that he describes it using a redactional detail

46. Lightfoot, *Apostolic Fathers, Part II*, 2:294.

found only in Matthew that is also a favorite term of the author but occurs nowhere else in the letters of Ignatius, this provides strong evidence for Ignatius's knowledge of the phraseology from the Gospel of Matthew.

Having established Ignatius's likely knowledge of Matthew, other phrases in his letters appear to draw on the first Gospel. On two occasions he states that those he describes as false teachers are not plants of the Father (οὗτοι γὰρ οὔκ εἰσιν φυτεία πατρός, *houtoi gar ouk eisin phyteia patros*, Ign. *Trall.* 11.1; διὰ τὸ μὴ εἶναι αὐτοὺς φυτείαν πατρός, *dia to mē einai autous phyteian patros*, Ign. *Phld.* 3.1). This description appears to draw on a metaphor found in Matthew 15:13, which is a saying of Jesus found in the Gospel of Matthew among the canonical Gospels. The saying in Matthew states, "Every plant which my heavenly Father did not plant will be uprooted" (πᾶσα φυτεία ἣν οὐκ ἐφύτευσεν ὁ πατήρ μου ὁ οὐράνιος ἐκριζωθήσεται, *pasa phyteia hēn ouk ephyteusen ho patēr mou ho ouranios ekrizōthēsetai*, Matt 15:13). A further example with greater verbal correspondence occurs when Ignatius states, "Be as shrewd as a snake in all circumstances, yet always innocent as a dove" (φρόνιμος γίνου ὡς ὁ ὄφις ἐν ἅπασιν καὶ ἀκέραιος εἰς ἀεὶ ὡς ἡ περιστερά, *phronimos ginou hōs ho ophis en hapasin kai akeraios eis aei hōs hē peristera*, Ign. *Pol.* 2.2). An almost identical idea is expressed in the Gospel of Matthew, albeit using the plural forms "snakes" and "doves."[47] Matthew states "therefore be as shrewd as snakes and as innocent of as doves" (γίνεσθε οὖν φρόνιμοι ὡς οἱ ὄφεις καὶ ἀκέραιοι ὡς αἱ περιστεραί, *ginesthe oun phronimoi hōs oi opheis kai akeraioi hōs ai peristerai*, Matt 10:16b). This might actually be viewed as the strongest single piece of evidence for Ignatius's knowledge and use of the Gospel of Matthew. There is, however, a complicating factor. While the saying in Matthew 10:16b is unique among the four Gospels that would come to be part of the New Testament, this saying is also found in the Gospel of Thomas, both among the Greek fragments (P.Oxy. 655, lines 47–49) and in the Coptic version (saying 39c). Therefore, it is possible to argue that this saying was a free-floating tradition that came independently to Matthew, the Gospel of Thomas, and Ignatius. Alternatively, a strong case can be made for the dependence of the Gospel of Thomas on the Gospel of Matthew.[48] On that basis it is more likely that Ignatius derived this saying directly from Matthew and not as a piece of independent tradition.

The cumulative weight of evidence from these three cases builds a compelling case for the view that Ignatius knew material unique to the Gospel of Matthew and was therefore familiar with this text in a written form. By contrast, the evidence for knowledge of the other three Gospels that came to be part of the New Testament is far less persuasive, and hence the case for Ignatius's possible knowledge of Mark, Luke, or John is not equally compelling.

When it comes to establishing Ignatius's knowledge of at least some of Paul's letters, there is more direct and explicit evidence available. Writing to the Ephesians, Ignatius mentions Paul by name and also his letter writing: "You are fellow initiates of Paul . . . who in every letter remembers you in Christ Jesus" (Ign. *Eph.* 12.2). Apart from the fascinating reference to Paul and his letters (cf. Ign. *Rom.* 4.3), it is striking that Ignatius states that Paul remembers the Ephesians in every letter. This is a statement that will be discussed further below.

---

47. It is worth noting that the reading in Codex Sinaiticus for Matt 10:16b gives a the singular for "snake" (ὁ ὄφις), but not for doves.

48. S. J. Gathercole, *The Composition of the Gospel of Thomas: Original Language and Influences*, SNTSMS 151 (Cambridge: Cambridge University Press, 2012), esp. 168–84.

Without any doubt among the writings that would later form the New Testament, 1 Corinthians is a text that is quoted most frequently and explicitly. Ignatius tells the Ephesians, "Do not be led astray; those who corrupt households will not inherit the kingdom of God" (βασιλείαν θεοῦ οὐ κληρονομήσουσιν, *basileian theou ou klēronomēsousin*, Ign. *Eph.* 16.1). While not containing the same vice list, the language of "not inheriting the kingdom of God" is a close match of Paul's phrasing (οὐχ ἅρπαγες βασιλείαν θεοῦ κληρονομήσουσιν, *ouch harpages basileian theou klēronomēsousin*, 1 Cor 6:10). A potentially stronger case is Ignatius's statement in the same letter that "the cross" "is a stumbling block to unbelievers but salvation and eternal life to us. Where is the wise? Where is the debater? Where is the boasting of those who are thought to be intelligent?" (Ign. *Eph.* 18.1). The language is strongly similar to 1 Corinthians 1:18, 20, although the slight complicating issue is that the second half is itself a citation of Isaiah 33:18 LXX. However, in both Paul and Ignatius that citation from Isaiah is deployed as a commentary on the cross. Ignatius tells the Magnesians to "throw out the bad yeast that has become old" (Ign. *Magn.* 10.2). Paul writes to the Corinthians, "Cleanse out the old leaven" (1 Cor 5:7). Again, Pauline language from 1 Corinthians is discernible in Ignatius's letters, even though the verbal correspondence is not perfect. Similarly, Ignatius's phrase "but not by this have I been made righteous" (ἀλλ' οὐ παρὰ τοῦτο δεδικαίωμαι, *all ou para touto dedikaiōmai*, Ign. *Rom.* 5.1), mirrors Paul's comment, although there is more divergence in the Greek than is apparent in the English translation (ἀλλ' οὐκ ἐν τούτῳ δεδικαίωμαι, *all ouk en toutō dedikaiōmai*, 1 Cor 4:4).

Further examples could be added, but sufficient examples have been provided to draw a meaningful conclusion. Ignatius certainly knew the text of 1 Corinthians and saw it as a source of authoritative teaching. However, the portions of text he draws on are not exact citations. It would in fact be strange if these uses of 1 Corinthians were exact (maybe even suspicious), given his circumstances. As one being transported under guard for execution in Rome, it is unlikely that Ignatius was traveling with literary texts in his possession. In fact, the inexact form of the material drawn from 1 Corinthians supports that observation and adds weight to the conclusion that it is Ignatius drawing on elements of that letter from memory. In the longer recension of Ignatius's letters, there are several citations from New Testament writing that are more exact in terms of their literary parallels. Although not typically stated as an argument in favor of the authenticity of the middle recension of the letters of Ignatius, it should be recognized that if the letters were literary forgeries, as in the case of the long recension, one might expect a much higher level of verbatim agreement than one actually finds. Therefore, the imprecise nature of these citations of material from 1 Corinthians actually attests to the genuineness of Ignatius as author of the letters. Notwithstanding this, when one considers the range of material that Ignatius draws upon from that letter, it must be assumed that he had great familiarity with its contents (perhaps he knew significant portions from memory), and he may have known the letter for several years, if not decades.

Apart from 1 Corinthians, it appears that Ignatius knew several other letters that name Paul as their author. The opening of Ignatius's letter to the Ephesians (Ign. *Eph.* salut.) appears to draw on key phrases from the New Testament letter to the Ephesians (Eph 1:3–14). Lightfoot stated that "this opening contains several obvious reminiscences of Ephes. I.3 sq.... the acquaintance of Ignatius with that epistle [Ephesians] appears from other passages besides this exordium."[49] One of the most striking other examples is when Ignatius commands "brothers" in the name of Christ "to love partners as the Lord loves the church"

49. Lightfoot, *Apostolic Fathers, Part II*, 2:23.

(Ign. *Pol.* 5.1). This recalls the language of Ephesians, "love your wives just as Christ loved the church" (Eph 5:25). Although not with the same frequency as the use of 1 Corinthians, the evidence suggests that Ignatius was familiar with Ephesians. A strong case can also be made for Ignatius's knowledge and use of 1 and 2 Timothy in his letters. In particular, the material in 1 Timothy 1:3–5 finds parallels at various places in Ignatius's letters (Ign. *Eph.* 14.1; 20.1; Ign. *Magn.* 8.1).[50] Some have suggested that Ignatius also used Romans. However, the case is weaker. Perhaps the most suggestive example is Ignatius's comment that the Lord was "from the family of David according to flesh, son of God according to will and power" (Ign. *Smyrn.* 1.1). This is somewhat similar to Paul's statement in Romans 1:3–4: "Concerning his Son, who was born from the seed of David according to flesh, yet was declared Son of God in power according to the spirit of holiness." Ignatius's declaration occurs in one of his semi-creedal statements. This may suggest that he received this as a preformed tradition, rather than drawing directly and reworking this from Romans 1:3–4.

Drawing these threads together, there is a strong case for viewing Ignatius as knowing and using the Gospel of Matthew at various points in his letters. Ignatius knows of Paul by name and also knows that he was a writer of letters. There are four letters where the evidence is sufficiently strong to suggest that Ignatius is consciously using those epistles, although it is unlikely that he had copies in front of him during his journey. Therefore, he appears to have memorized or internalized parts of 1 Corinthians, Ephesians, and 1 and 2 Timothy. In writing to the Ephesians, Ignatius states that Paul remembers them in all his letters. That is simply not the case. Therefore, several commentators have seen this as mere hyperbole.[51] There is, however, another possibility—namely, that Ignatius was correct in regard to the evidence he knew. Only in four of the Pauline letters are the Ephesians explicitly mentioned. The references are 1 Corinthians 15:32; 16:8; Ephesians 1:1;[52] 1 Timothy 1:3; 2 Timothy 1:18; 4:12. Strikingly, these are the four letters that Ignatius can be shown to have drawn upon with a high degree of certainty.[53]

Ignatius's use of the writings that would later form the New Testament is limited, but also highly instructive. While there are only five texts that can reasonably be identified, it is noteworthy that they span a Gospel text and four of Paul's letters. Thus, they incorporate texts from the two earliest subcollections of New Testament writings. While there might appear to be a paucity of texts used, when one takes into account Ignatius's physical circumstances it is remarkable that he is able to draw on material from this range of writings apparently from memory. That fact possibly says something about the status of those writings for Ignatius. It would overstretch the evidence to say that these texts are viewed as scriptural in a sense akin to the texts included among the Jewish Scriptures. However, at the very least, these five texts were viewed by Ignatius as authoritative and of value for communicating practical and ethical instructions to communities of Jesus believers. In this sense, they had already become texts of importance and of authoritative status among Christ-believing groups.

5. CONCLUSION

The letters of Ignatius are perhaps the best-known writings among the collection of texts that constitute the Apostolic Fathers. Unlike the other entries in that collection, this is

50. A fuller discussion of other passages that might drawn from 1 and 2 Timothy can be found in Foster, "Epistles of Ignatius of Antioch and the Writings," 170–72.

51. Lightfoot, *Apostolic Fathers, Part II*, 2:65.

52. There is a significant textual variant here.

53. Foster, "Epistles of Ignatius of Antioch and the Writings," 172.

not a single textual entity but a subcollection of seven letters that form a corpus in their own right. These letters reveal a remarkable yet controversial individual who did not shy away from polemical debate. However, rather than remembering Ignatius solely for his fiery rebuttals of those with whom he disagreed, it is important to reflect on his deep piety and Christian faith as he was confronted with the immediacy of his impending execution. While some have wanted to psychoanalyze Ignatius, representing him as unstable or with a manic death wish, that is probably an instance of imposing somewhat unhelpful modern categories on a figure who had been sentenced to death in the Roman arena.

Whatever one might make of Ignatius's personal state of mind, his seven letters have left a remarkable and important theological legacy. Perhaps written in the space of only a few weeks, they provide an unrivaled insight into the nature of various churches in the Roman province of Asia in the early decades of the second century. Theologically, they reflect both continuity with early Christian writings such as the letters of Paul, but also portray marked developments in theological beliefs and the understanding of church structures. Without these seven hurriedly written letters, any understanding of the Christian movement in that period would be greatly impoverished. While one should resist the tendency to project the perspectives contained in these letters onto other Christian communities in different locations, what they offer in regard to understanding the context to which they were addressed is invaluable, and in turn they reveal much about early developments in beliefs and practices among certain communities of Christ believers.

BIBLIOGRAPHY

Brent, A. *Ignatius of Antioch: A Martyr Bishop and the Origin of Episcopacy*. London: T&T Clark, 2007.

Corwin, V. *St. Ignatius and Christianity in Antioch*. New Haven: Yale University Press, 1960.

Foster, P. "The Epistle of Ignatius of Antioch." Pages 81–107 in *The Writings of the Apostolic Fathers*. Edited by P. Foster. London: T&T Clark, 2007.

Foster, P. "The Ignatian Problem: The Recensions of a Letter Corpus as a Reflection of Theological Concerns and Developments." Pages 5–50 in *Texts in Context: Essays on Dating and Contextualising Christian Writings from the Second and Early Third Centuries*. Edited by J. Verheyden, J. Schröter, and T. Nicklas. BETL 319. Leuven: Peeters, 2021.

Grant, R. M. *Ignatius of Antioch*. Vol. 4 of *The Apostolic Fathers: A Translation and Commentary*. Camden, NJ: Thomas Nelson, 1966.

Joly, R. *Le dossier d'Ignace d'Antioche*. Université libre Bruxelles, Faculté de philosophie et lettres 69. Brussels: Éditions de l'Université de Bruxelles, 1979.

Lechner, T. *Ignatius adversus Valentinianos? Chronologische und theologiegeschichtliche Studien zu den Briefen des Ignatius von Antiochien*. VCSup 47. Leiden: Brill, 1999.

Lightfoot, J. B. *The Apostolic Fathers: Clement, Ignatius, and Polycarp: Revised Texts with Introductions, Notes, Dissertations, and Translations*. 2nd ed. 2 vols. in 5 parts. London: Macmillan, 1889–1891.

Löhr, H. "The Epistles of Ignatius of Antioch." Pages 91–115 in *The Apostolic Fathers: An Introduction*. Edited by W. Pratscher. Waco, TX: Baylor University Press, 2010.

Lookadoo, J. *The Christology of Ignatius of Antioch*. Studies in Early Christology. Eugene, OR: Cascade, 2023.

Lotz, J.-P. *Ignatius and Concord: The Background and Use of the Language of Concord in the Letters of Ignatius of Antioch*. Patristic Studies 8. New York: Peter Lang, 2007.

MacDiarmid, F. *The Memory of Ignatius of Antioch: The Martyr as a Locus of Christian Identity, Remembering and Remembered*. WUNT 2.581 (Tübingen: Mohr Siebeck, 2022).

Maier, H. O. *The Social Setting of the Ministry as Reflected in the Writings of Hermas, Clement, and Ignatius*. Studies in Religion 1. Waterloo: Wilfrid Laurier University Press, 1991.

Rius-Camps, J. *The Four Authentic Letters of Ignatius, the Martyr: A Critical Study Based in Anomalies Contained in the Textus Receptus*. Orientalia Christiana Analecta 213. Rome: Pontificium Institutum Orientalium Studiorum, 1980.

Schoedel, W. R. *Ignatius of Antioch*. Hermeneia. Philadelphia: Fortress, 1985.

Trevett, C. *A Study of Ignatius of Antioch in Syria and Asia*. Studies in the Bible and Early Christianity 29. Lewiston: Edwin Mellen, 1992.

Vall, G. *Learning Christ: Ignatius of Antioch and the Mystery of Redemption*. Washington, DC: Catholic University of America Press, 2013.

CHAPTER 10

POLYCARP'S *EPISTLE TO THE PHILIPPIANS*

PAUL FOSTER

1. INTRODUCTION

The epistle of Polycarp addressed to the Philippians is the sole surviving writing that most scholars attribute to this long-standing and influential second-century bishop. Despite this meagre literary preservation, it could be argued that Polycarp, bishop of Smyrna, is in fact the most significant Christian figure of the second century. Polycarp's importance does not arise solely from his lengthy period in office as leader of the Christian community at Smyrna, which perhaps spans five decades (ca. 110–156 CE). Rather, it is due to the fact that he can be viewed as the central Christian figure of that century, connecting the ideas and prominent Christian figures from the beginning to the end of the second century. In fact, according to Eusebius, Polycarp's connections reach back into the first century. Eusebius claimed that Polycarp was instructed by several of the apostles and that he had met several other people who knew Jesus (Eusebius, *Hist. eccl.* 4.14.3). Furthermore, apparently near the beginning of his time in office, he extended hospitability to Ignatius when he stopped in Smyrna during his transportation to Rome for execution. Later in his life, Polycarp visited Rome to meet with Anicetus, the bishop of Rome, to discuss the varying practices relating to the date for the celebration of Easter. It is further recorded that during the visit to Rome he also met Marcion. That encounter was less amiable than his meeting with Anicetus. Eusebius records that when Marcion asked Polycarp if he knew who he was, the curt reply was, "I know the firstborn of Satan" (Eusebius, *Hist. eccl.* 4.14.7). Whether true or not, it is certainly a good anecdote.

Not long after the visit to Rome, Polycarp returned to his home city. During a period of violence directed against Christians, Polycarp was executed for refusing to swear an oath to the genius of Caesar (Mart. Pol. 10.1). However, his death did not mark the end of his influence on second-century Christianity. Irenaeus, author of the most significant theological work of the second century, *Adversus haereses*, records his personal acquaintance with Polycarp and the impression he made (Irenaeus, *Haer.* 3.3.4). Thus Polycarp was a towering figure of early Christianity in the second century. His influence, either in person or through shaping the thought of his successors, created an indelible impression that was incredibly formative for the structure of mainstream Christian thought and theology.

Despite this impact, the sole writing usually attributed to him has evoked mixed reactions. Polycarp's *To the Philippians* is a short, occasional piece of correspondence. It is no propositional treatise or work of systematic theology. Perhaps this has generated some of the negative reactions. Its authenticity has been denied, its literary integrity questioned, and its theological value impugned. This is hardly a ringing endorsement for this piece of early Christian literature. However, such an assessment is one-sided and in part results from judging the quality of the work by the norms and values of later scholarship. When Polycarp's *To the Philippians* is read in its own context and on its own terms, a different picture emerges. This conciliatory and pastorally sensitive piece of correspondence portrays much about the character of the author, the beliefs he held, and the relationships between early Christian communities at the start of the second century. As such, it provides an unrivaled and invaluable insight into the early Jesus movement, and it permits a much fuller understanding of Polycarp of Smyrna, the person who is arguably the central figure of Christianity in the second century.

1.1 The State of the Text and the Surviving Manuscripts

Several studies mention the poor state of preservation of the text of Polycarp's *To the Philippians*. For instance, Holmes's assessment is as follows: "The text of the letter has been poorly preserved. Nine late Greek manuscripts are extant, all incomplete and all derived from the same defective source, in which 9.2 (through καὶ δι᾽ ὑμᾶς ὑπό) is immediately followed by the likewise incomplete text of The Epistle of Barnabas, beginning in 5.7 (τὸν λαὸν τὸν καινόν)."[1] There are in fact more than nine Greek manuscripts. It is correct, however, that none is complete, since they all break at *To the Philippians* 9.2. In addition, there are several Latin manuscripts that preserve the complete text. Furthermore, Eusebius has preserved in Greek the entirety of chapter 9 and most of chapter 13 (apart from the final statement). This means that the majority of the text is available in the original Greek, and the section where the Greek is not extant, 10–12 and 13.2b–14.1, is available in its early Latin translation. This means that the entire content of the letter is available to modern readers in a form presumably close to the original form written by Polycarp. This is a markedly different situation from other early Christian texts such as P.Egerton 2 or P.Oxy. 1224, where only fragmentary remains of these noncanonical gospel texts are extant. Hence, while the text is not perfectly preserved in its original Greek, its content is available in full.

The surviving Greek manuscripts may be listed as follows. The content of each comprises Polycarp's *To the Philippians* salutation + 1.1–9.2, with only the three final words of 9.2 lacking (τοῦ θεοῦ ἀναστάντα, *tou theou anastanta*).

1. *Vaticanus* 859 [v]. 11th century. Vatican Library. Conflated Epistles of Polycarp and Barnabas on folios 195–211.
2. *Ottobonianus* 348 [o]. 15th–16th century. Vatican Library. Conflated Epistles of Polycarp and Barnabas on folios 63–84.
3. *Florentinus Laur.* vii. 21 [f]. 16th century. Laurentian Library at Florence. A direct copy of *Ottobonianus* 348 [o].
4. *Parisiensis Graec.* 937 [p]. 16th century. Formerly catalogued as *Colbert.* 4443. La Bibliothèque nationale de France in Paris. A direct copy of [f].
5. Casanatensis G. v. 14 [c]. 15th–16th century.
6. *Salmasianus* [s]. 17th century. A transcription of [c] made by Claudius Salmasius and used by Voss and Ussher for their editions of the Greek text. Now lost (or unidentified).
7. *Neapolitanus* ii. A. 17 [n]. 16th century. Paper MS. National Library (Bibliotheca Borbonica) in Naples.

1. M. W. Holmes, ed., *The Apostolic Fathers: Greek Texts and English Translations*, 3rd ed. (Grand Rapids: Baker Academic, 2007), 277.

8. Vaticanus Reginensis gr. Pii II.11 ("Theatinus") [t]. 15th–16th century.
9. *Barberinus* 7 [b]. Barberini Library in Rome. 16th century. A direct copy of [t].
10. *Andros Hagios* 64 [a]. 16th–17th century. Paper MS. Zoodochos Pigi monastery in Andros.
11. *Vaticani graeci* 1655 [d]. 16th century.
12. *Vaticani graeci* 1909 [r]. 16th century. Folios 70–75.

Additionally, there are at least thirteen Latin manuscripts of *To the Philippians*.[2] There are widely varying opinions concerning the quality of the Latin translation. Parvis provides the most balanced assessment, saying of the Latin that "the text is often periphrastic. The translator seems at times not to understand what he is translating, and unusual words elude him. On the whole, however, the Latin renders the general sense fairly well and can at least serve as a check on the Greek."[3] Together with the surviving, though incomplete, Greek manuscripts, they form the primary textual witnesses for the letter. The twelve Greek manuscripts have been arranged into three groups based on the proximity of their textual affinities. This arrangement carried out by Prostmeier was a revision of the two-group arrangement present by Lightfoot and replicated by Holmes.[4] Prostmeier's three groups are as follows:

v o / f p / n t[b] c[s] a d r

1.2 Polycarp as Author of the Letter

Prior to the Reformation there is no surviving evidence that attests an attempt to question the authorship of *To the Philippians* as being written by anybody else apart from Polycarp of Smyrna. Lightfoot notes the following as the earliest example of calling into question Polycarp's authorship of the letter: "The Magdeburg Centuriators (II. p. 173 sq) were the first to throw any doubt upon it."[5] A few centuries later, in a fairly idiosyncratic argument Cotterill argued that the letter in its entirety was composed by the seventh-century monk, Antiochus Palaestinensis.[6] This theory was almost immediately refuted,[7] and appears not to have gained any support. Overall, it has been rare for scholars to completely reject all of the contents of the letter as having no connection with Polycarp as author. Rather, the more common strategy has been to bring forward various theories of additions or interpolations. The aim of these has primarily been to show that some or all of the references to Ignatius and his letters do not derive from the hand of Polycarp.

2. In addition to the Latin manuscripts listed by Lightfoot and Holmes, T. B. Sailors notes the following manuscripts: "Brussels, Koninklijke Bibliotheek/Bibliothèque royale, MSS 1034 and 905, *olim* Bibliothèque royale des ducs de Bourgogne MSS 703 and 20132 (copies of b); Charleville-Mézières, Bibliothèque municipale, MS 173; and Arras, Bibliothèque municipale, MS 281, *olim* 51." See T. B. Sailors, "Review of M. W. Holmes, *The Apostolic Fathers: Greek Texts and English Translations*, 3rd ed.," in *Bryn Mawr Classical Review* (2009), https://bmcr.brynmawr.edu/2009/2009.07.08/.

3. P. Parvis, "Polycarp, *To the Philippians*," in *From Thomas to Tertullian: Christian Literary Receptions of Jesus in the Second and Third Centuries CE*, vol. 2 of *The Reception of Jesus in the First Three Centuries*, ed. C. Keith, H. K. Bond, C. Jacobi, and J. Schröter (London: T&T Clark, 2020), 59–72, here 61.

4. F. R. Prostmeier, "Zur handschriftlichen Überlieferung des Polykarp- und des Barnabasbriefes: Zwei nicht beachtete Deszendenten des Cod. Vat. Gr. 859," *VC* 48 (1994): 48–64.

5. J. B. Lightfoot, *The Apostolic Fathers, Part II: S. Ignatius, S. Polycarp. Revised Texts with Introductions, Notes, Dissertations, and Translations*, 2nd ed., 3 vols. (London: Macmillan, 1889–1890), 1:578.

6. J. M. Cotterill, "The Epistle of Polycarp to the Philippians and the Homilies of Antiochus Palaestinensis," *Journal of Philology* 19 (1891): 241–85.

7. C. Taylor, "St. Polycarp to the Philippians," *Journal of Philology* 20 (1891): 65–110.

Thus *To the Philippians* has become caught up in the larger and fiercer debate surrounding the authenticity of the letters of Ignatius.

1.3 The Literary Integrity of *To the Philippians*

There has been detailed examination of the letter to attempt to ascertain whether it is likely to have originated as a single unified composition. When the issue is discussed, the form of the letter that is being examined is the fourteen-chapter version of the letter found in the Latin textual tradition. Given the lateness of the surviving manuscripts, the incomplete nature of the Greek manuscripts, perceived internal contradictions, and the sense that the statement at the end of chapter 13 (which survives only in Latin) has an ideological motivation to authenticate the Ignatian writings, some scholars have found a sufficient basis for doubting the literary integrity of the fourteen-chapter form of the letter.

Moreover, certain post-Reformation Protestants found the letter to be of mixed value in supporting their ecclesiological views. From their perspective on the positive side, the letter seems to reflect a form of church leadership based on presbyters and deacons, rather than the threefold structure with a presiding bishop, a council of presbyters, and deacons. The latter leadership structure is attested in the letters of Ignatius. However, Polycarp's letter is potentially the earliest document that supports the authenticity of the letters of Ignatius: "We are sending to you the letters of Ignatius that were sent to us by him together with any others we have in our possession" (Pol. *Phil.* 13.2).[8] Thus, around the middle of the seventeenth century, J. Daillé resolved this tension by judging chapter 13 to be a later interpolation.[9] Approximately two centuries later, Albrecht Ritschl developed a more detailed interpolation theory. He saw chapters 3, 9, 11, and 13 as being later additions that attempted to create connections between the letter and the leading early figures of Paul and Ignatius.[10] A very fulsome discussion and rebuttal of these early theories was put forward by Lightfoot.[11] While his response might not have totally suppressed opposing views, it certainly made them less fashionable.

Nearly fifty years after this, P. N. Harrison presented a new challenge to the literary integrity of Polycarp's *To the Philippians*. While some aspects are connected with early theories, he developed his views along new lines. In essence, Harrison's theory states that the material in the Latin fourteen-chapter version of the letter all derives from Polycarp. However, it represents two letters composed several decades apart, which at some stage had been conjoined and presented as a single unified composition. Harrison's theory has proved widely influential. However, it has not been universally accepted, and several counterarguments have been leveled against this idea. The influence of this theory can be seen in the publication of a major commentary of the text that isolates two letters along the lines proposed by Harrison and then offers commentary in turn on each of these letters.[12] Harrison stated the essence of his thesis in the following words: "Polycarp wrote to the Philippians at different times two letters, which were copied out at an early date on to the same papyrus roll, and so fused into one."[13]

---

8. Unless otherwise noted, all translations of the Apostolic Fathers are from Holmes, *Apostolic Fathers*.

9. J. Daillé, *De scriptis quo sub Dionys. Areop. et Ignatii Antioch* (Geneva, 1666), 427.

10. A. Ritschl, *Entstehung der altkatholischen Kirche*, 2nd ed. (Bonn, 1857), 584.

11. Lightfoot, *Apostolic Fathers, Part II*, 1:578–603.

12. J. B. Bauer, *Polykarpbriefe*, KAV 5 (Göttingen: Vandenhoeck & Ruprecht, 1995).

13. P. N. Harrison, *Polycarp's Two Epistles to the Philippians* (Cambridge: Cambridge University Press, 1936), 15.

Harrison's ideas have shaped much subsequent scholarship on *To the Philippians*. Several scholars have adopted his ideas and analyzed the letter in light of the hypothesis that it is a literary synthesis of two earlier letters.[14] There has been debate concerning the likelihood of two letters being spliced together in the way that Harrison's theory requires. Those in favor of the theory have suggested similar examples such as 2 Corinthians, Romans 16, or Justin's *Second Apology* being a compilation of fragments. The difficulty is that all these supposed examples of composite documents are challenged. Perhaps even more strange is that the most obvious example is not discussed. The surviving Greek manuscript evidence for Polycarp's *To the Philippians* shows that at a later stage it was itself preserved from the beginning to 9.2 and then joined with Barnabas, commencing at Barnabas 5.2 onward. So the formation of composite documents was possible in antiquity, since the *To the Philippians* was itself spliced with another document, forming a larger composite text.

Notwithstanding this, many scholars are of the opinion that the tension between *To the Philippians* 9.1–2 and 13.2 is not so strong as to require a composite document theory to resolve it. There is no need to invoke some kind of Schrödinger's Cat explanation, employing uncertainty to explain two simultaneous states of existence for Ignatius—dead and alive.[15] It does appear to be the case in 9.2 that Polycarp knows of (or at the very least assumes) the death of Ignatius. By contrast, 13.2 appears to request information concerning the circumstances of the execution of Ignatius. Therefore, 13.2 does not necessarily suggest that Polycarp is ignorant of the death of Ignatius. It is possible that he knows the basic fact that Ignatius had been killed, or that sufficient time had elapsed to assume the execution had taken place. Yet, beyond that he was requesting further information. Hence, it is probably best to read the letter as a unified composition. That said, Harrison's theory is certainly not impossible. Moreover, it should be recognized as being an affirmation of Polycarp's composition of all of the material that is contained in *To the Philippians*. As such, it should not be read as a radical rejection of the historical value of the epistle. Instead, Harrison himself was reacting against those more radical voices who rejected the authenticity of the letter—not so much as an end in itself but to discredit the authenticity of the Ignatian letter collection.

2. SUMMARY OF CONTENT

Polycarp's *To the Philippians*, as it stands, was written in response to a piece of correspondence he received from the community in Philippi. Toward the end of Polycarp's letter he states that both the Philippians and Ignatius had written to him (presumably separately), requesting that a now no longer surviving letter from the Philippians should not remain in Smyrna with Polycarp but that it should be sent on to Syria: "Both you and Ignatius have written to me that if anyone is travelling to Syria, he should also take along your letter" (Pol. *Phil.* 13.2). This would appear to be in order that Syrian believers, perhaps chiefly in Antioch, might have news of Ignatius's journey to Rome. Also, Polycarp further outlines that he is fulfilling a further request from the Philippians—namely, that he send to them "the letters of Ignatius that were sent to us by him together with any others that we have in our possession" (13.2). Furthermore, Polycarp addresses the broad topic of "righteousness," which he states he is doing at the request of the Philippians (3.1). However, the topics addressed in the return letter of Polycarp to the Philippians cover a range of issues beyond

14. E.g., see Parvis, "Polycarp, *To the Philippians*," 59–72.

15. E. Schrödinger, "Die gegenwärtige Situation in der Quantenmechanik," *Naturwissenschaften* 23.48 (1935): 807–12.

those mentioned in these requests. It might be the case that the letter carrier made Polycarp aware of certain issues in the Philippian community, and thus in response Polycarp took the opportunity to discuss a wider range of issues than the reply to the letter from Philippi strictly required.

In terms of its structure, the letter exhibits the classic form of an ancient letter with its introductory greetings, its specific contents in the central body, and its closing requests and final good wishes for the recipients. However, the topics covered in the body of the letter provide insights into some of the specific issues in Philippi and a view of how networks of early Christian communities communicated with each other and promoted a standard of common belief and behavior. There have been various attempts to represent the structure of the letter by those who view it as a single document,[16] and most of these are in broad agreement.

Letter Opening	
Salutation:	Identity of senders, wishes for mercy and peace from God
Phil. 1	Rejoicing because of the actions and faith of the Philippians
Main Body	
Phil. 2	Serve God who raised Jesus and shows mercy to all people
Phil. 3	Life of righteousness and the teachings of Paul
Phil. 4–6	Practical instructions for righteous living
Phil. 7–8	Warnings against false teaching
Phil. 8–10	The example of Christ and of those who died for their faith
Phil. 11	The case of Valens and his wife
Phil. 12	Rely on the Scriptures and be built up in faith
Letter Closing	
Phil. 13	Sharing of letters and information
Phil. 14	Commendation of Crescens and farewell

To the Philippians, Salutation

The letter opens in a manner that is fairly standard in Greco-Roman epistles of the period, with the identity of the sender and the intended recipients clearly stated. In this case both identities reflect collective groups. The collective group of senders, "Polycarp and the presbyters with him," might be a mere formality since the letter was probably Polycarp's own composition, although possibly written with the aid of an amanuensis. By contrast, the recipients' identity suggests that the letter was to be read in a communal setting of the gathered community of believers in Christ who resided in Philippi. In his introduction, Polycarp does not mention his own title or status among the leadership group of the Christian community at Smyrna. He mentions the "presbyters with him," which for some suggests that Polycarp was a member of this collective leadership group. Alternatively, the authority exhibited in authoring the letter, with the name "Polycarp" being the first word in the epistle, may suggest a more senior role. Polycarp does not give himself a title in this context or elsewhere in the letter. Unlike the letters of Ignatius, which use the formulation "Polycarp, bishop of the church of the Smyrnaeans" (Ign. *Pol.* salut.), the term "bishop," ἐπίσκοπος, *episkopos*, is not found in Polycarp's letter to the Philippians. It is not possible to tell whether this absence of the term shows that the church at Smyrna had a two-level

16. For a discussion of whether the letter is a single composition, a combination of two letters, or has been interpolated at various places see sec. 1.3 above.

leadership structure of presbyters and deacons (perhaps even with a senior presbyter), or had the threefold structure beloved of Ignatius with a bishop, a council of presbyters, and various deacons (with the self-effacing Polycarp not using his title). However, one can conclude that there was significant fluidity in leadership structures in Christian communities in this period.

Whereas in Greco-Roman letters the identity statements are followed by greetings, in this letter, and many Christian letters, the author requests that abundant divine gifts might be received by the recipients. Here Polycarp wishes the Philippians to receive "mercy and peace." This may be a stereotypical Christian set of qualities that one might desire the recipients to receive. However, the hope for peace might also relate to the concerns about false teaching (Pol. *Phil.* 7) and the upheaval caused by the case of Valens (11). Regardless of whether the desire for the Philippians to possess a greater degree of mercy and peace is general in nature or related to some specific set of circumstances in the life of the group, Polycarp sees both those qualities as having a heavenly dual origin. The mercy and peace originate from "God Almighty and Jesus Christ our Saviour." In this context, the relationship between "God Almighty" and "Christ our Saviour" is not explained. Polycarp expects his readers to understand this colocation as part of the faith commitment he shares with the recipients. Similarly, the designation of Jesus Christ as "Saviour" receives no explanation since it is a core element of the shared faith of the letter sender and the recipients. Instead, the hope for an abundance of mercy and peace being granted from God and Christ is an implicit prayer based on a shared identity established through a common faith in Christ the Savior and the almighty God.

To the Philippians 1

In this section, Polycarp identifies two major reasons to rejoice in the faith and fidelity of the believers at Philippi. First, he expresses joy because of their support and hospitality extended to those about to be put to death for their faith. Second, he also rejoices because of their own endurance in their long-standing faith.

In relation to the first reason, Polycarp recalls that the Philippians had "helped on their way those confined by chains" (Pol. *Phil.* 1.1). While no individuals are named at this point, later in the letter specific individuals are identified (9.1). Polycarp states that he rejoices with the Philippians because they had welcomed those destined for execution. The common basis of rejoicing presumably arises from the fact that the church in Smyrna had also welcomed at least Ignatius and perhaps others who were being transported for execution. Polycarp comments on the harsh reality endured by such individuals when he notes that they were "confined by chains" (1.1) However, he immediately reverses the impact of dehumanizing shackles. Instead, they are viewed as tokens of heavenly status, being described as "the diadems of those who are truly chosen by God and our Lord" (1.1). One wonders if here Polycarp's imagery, although not identical, is indebted to Ignatius. When writing to the Ephesians from Smyrna, Ignatius likewise informs them that the chains he carries with him are "my spiritual pearls" (Ign. *Eph.* 11.2). Admittedly, although Polycarp does not use the identical expression, the idea of viewing the chains as a glorious spiritual blessing is shared.

The second basis for rejoicing arises from the Philippians' continuance in their "firmly rooted faith, renowned from the earliest times" (Pol. *Phil.* 1.2). Here Polycarp alludes to the apostolic foundation of the Christian community in Philippi. This is a point made explicitly later in the letter (3.2; 11.3). However, Polycarp primarily rejoices over the Philippians because their faith endures rather than their historical foundation.

He describes their contemporary faith as being of a type that "bears fruit to our Lord Jesus Christ." This reference to Jesus leads Polycarp to make a confessional, or semi-creedal series of statements about Christ, "who endured for our sins, facing even death, whom God raised up, having loosed the birth pangs of Hades" (1.2). Here Polycarp, without describing the exact mechanism, views the sufferings of Christ as being vicarious in relation to the sins of believers. He affirms the reality of Christ's death. He proclaims a divine vindication of Jesus enacted through God raising him. Lastly, these events are seen as destabilizing the power of Hades. The wording of these last two elements forms a partial parallel with a statement from Peter's Pentecost speech in Acts, "whom God raised up, putting an end to the birth pangs of death" (Acts 2:24).[17] If, as might be a possibility, Polycarp is drawing on the tradition contained in Acts 2:24 (whether directly or indirectly), then his statement that God "loosed the birth pangs of Hades" is a way of declaring the divine destruction of the power of death. Such a sentiment is particularly appropriate in the wider context where Polycarp has already described those who will face physical death for their confession of faith in Jesus.

From these creedal sentiments, Polycarp moves to more concrete reasons for rejoicing in the faithfulness of the Philippian believers. He notes that while the Philippians have not physically seen Christ, they "believe in him with an inexpressible and glorious joy" (Pol. *Phil.* 1.3). This sentiment concerning believing in Christ, whom they have not seen, is a compressed form of the affirmation of faithfulness given in 1 Peter 1:8. The pastiche of scriptural texts being used to praise the Philippians continues in the following statement. Here Polycarp clearly and closely draws on material from Paul's letter to the Ephesians (Eph 2:5, 8–9). This further note of praise of the Philippians relates to their knowledge that their salvation is based on grace rather than works, and that it is determined by the will of God through Jesus Christ.

It is difficult to tell whether Polycarp intentionally selected these scriptural texts, perhaps especially the Pauline elements, because of the Philippians' foundation by Paul and thus their possible familiarity with these texts. Alternatively, it could be the case that language of these texts had so permeated Polycarp's speech and preaching that while he was still dependent on these writings, it was in a less conscious manner. What, however, is fully apparent is that the basis for praising the "firmly rooted faith" of the Philippians is expressed in terms of the lofty doxological expressions drawn from texts with which they themselves were already familiar.

To the Philippians 2

On the basis of their belief in Christ and the knowledge of their own salvation, Polycarp encourages the Philippians to ready themselves for action through the reverential service of God. Three examples of worthy service are outlined. Two of these are negative in that they involve not participating in certain behaviors. The third action is positive, since it describes an attitude that the Philippians are commended to adopt. The two patterns of behavior that are to be avoided are "vain empty talk" (τὴν κενὴν ματαιολογίαν, *tēn kenēn mataiologian*) and "the error of the many" (Pol *Phil.* 2.1). At this point Polycarp provided no further context or explanation to understand whether these were general exhortations to avoid negative behavior or whether specific concerns stood behind these admonitions. If it is the latter, then some have inferred that Polycarp is warning the Philippians to guard against the type of docetic teachings about which Ignatius so vehemently writes.

17. In fact, several Western witnesses to the text of Acts read "Hades" here rather than "death."

This is not impossible. However, if this is the case, then Polycarp is more opaque at this point in describing this teaching he opposes (cf. 7.1). The positive behavior that is to be the hallmark of the Philippians' service of God is their belief in the resurrection and heavenly enthronement of Christ. Reference to Christ being glorified and having a throne at the right hand of God leads Polycarp to reflect on coming eschatological judgment. He reminds the Philippians of Christ's return and his coming role as judge of the living and the dead (cf. Matt 25:31–46). Polycarp presents the key determinative criterion for judgment as being disobedience to Christ. Those who disobey, Polycarp states, will be the ones held responsible by God for the blood of Christ. In this pithy section, Polycarp presents a clear link between the practice of correct behavior in the present and the eschatological consequences on judgment day. Both present behavior and eschatological judgment are fundamentally portrayed as related to christological beliefs.

The following statements both build on the instructions just given but also anticipate some of the themes and topics that will emerge in the letter. Polycarp assures the Philippians that the God who raised Jesus will also raise them. This, however, is stated as being dependent on following the commandments. It is not clear whether the pronouns in the references "his will," "his commandments," and the subject of the clause "loving the things he loved," refer to God or to Jesus (Pol *Phil.* 2.2). The latter clause suggests that perhaps Jesus is the subject. However, Polycarp is not precise in his designation of the subject and probably sees little separation between the will and commandments of God, or of Jesus. Having provided some general ethical imperatives, Polycarp seems to move to more specific behaviors. The Philippians are told to avoid "unrighteousness, greed, love of money, slander and false testimony" (2.2). The theme of righteousness is the topic on which the Philippians have sought guidance from Polycarp (3.1). Later in the letter the specific problem of greed and love of money will be discussed in reference to the case of Valens and his wife (11.1–4). Having listed a set of behaviors to be avoided, Polycarp then moves into a series of statements that recall the teachings of Jesus, and which also have resonance with ethical teachings found more widely in the New Testament. The first two elements of the instruction about non-retaliation, "not repaying evil for evil or insult for insult," appear to be lifted from 1 Peter 3:9. Polycarp enlarges this instruction with two additional elements: "or blow for blow or curse for curse." Although perhaps not in as a direct a manner, these elements may draw on earlier traditions (cf. Matt 5:38–39).

The material in *To the Philippians* 2.3 is largely a catena of citations drawn from traditions contained in the Sermon on the Mount or the Sermon on the Plain. Polycarp marks this material as originating with Jesus by use of the introductory phrase "remembering what the Lord said as he taught." The phrase "do not judge, so that you may not be judged" matches the wording of Jesus's use of this formulation in Matthew 7:1 (cf. Luke 6:37 for a slightly different form of wording). He concludes by linking poverty and persecution to possession of God's kingdom.

To the Philippians 3

Having concluded the previous section by recalling the beatitude that speaks of those persecuted for the sake of righteousness, Polycarp discloses to the recipients of the letter that this was not a random statement or a piece of generalized hortatory encouragement. Rather, he states that the topic of righteousness has been addressed because the Philippian believers have requested that he instruct them on this topic (Pol. *Phil.* 3.1). Presumably that request was either included in the letter the Philippians had written to Polycarp (13.1) or had been communicated by the letter bearers.

At this juncture, for the first time in the letter, Polycarp refers to the apostle Paul. In deferential tones, Polycarp states that neither he nor anybody else can display the same level of wisdom as Paul. However, the point of the reference to Paul is not simply in order that Polycarp might portray himself as unqualified to address the topic of righteousness in comparison with the instructions given by the one he calls "the blessed and glorious Paul" (Pol. *Phil.* 3.2). Rather, the purpose appears twofold. First, Polycarp reminds the Philippians that they already possess the resources that instruct about truth and build up the community. These resources are the recollection of Paul's teachings while he was present with the Philippians and the study of the correspondence from Paul that will edify them in their faith.

The reference to multiple letters written by Paul to the Philippians is a cause of curiosity. Since subsequent history preserves only one letter of Paul to the Philippians, this comment is at odds with the situation of surviving texts. How is this discrepancy to be explained? There are several possible explanations. Perhaps the most obvious is either Polycarp knew of more letters of Paul addressed to the Philippians than the single letter that survived,[18] or alternatively this is either a misunderstanding on his part or even a case of authorial hyperbole to make his point. The latter explanation is probably the most likely. Polycarp emphasizes Paul's presence and his correspondence to reassure the Philippians that they already possess the full and necessary instructions to equip them with knowledge of the truth and the pattern for a righteous life.

The second reason Paul appears to have been mentioned is so Polycarp might draw on a significant Pauline idea. The triad of "faith, hope, and love" is a Pauline formulation (1 Cor 13:13; 1 Thess 1:3; 5:8), which appears to have been well-known not only to Polycarp but also to his contemporary Ignatius (Ign. *Phld.* 11.2), although more frequently in the reduced form of reference to faith and love (cf. Ign. *Eph.* 1.1; 9.1; 14.1–2; 20.1; *Magn.* 1.1–2; 5.2; 13.1; *Trall.* 8.1; *Rom.* salut.; *Smyrn.* salut.; 1.1; 6.1; 13.2; *Pol.* 6.2). Polycarp presents the virtues of faith, hope, and love as the cornerstone of true belief and righteous living. He states that whoever possesses "these has fulfilled the commandment of righteousness" (Pol. *Phil.* 3.3). Moreover, specifically in regard to love, which Polycarp has stated must be expressed toward God and Christ as well as toward one's neighbors (cf. Matt 22:34–40), it is stated that such love is a guard against sin. Here Polycarp presents his understanding that love focused on God and Christ and on the well-being of others functions to remove one from the realm of sin. Perhaps Polycarp reasons that sin is a self-seeking attitude, whereas love exemplifies an outlook which is focused away from oneself.

To the Philippians 4

Polycarp turns from commenting on righteousness in a generalized manner to considering some of the practical actions that reflect righteous living. Presumably at least some of the examples chosen are selected because they address concrete difficulties or concerns in the Philippian community. That is certainly the case in regard to Polycarp's opening statement in this section: "But the love of money is the beginning of all troubles" (Pol. *Phil.* 4.1). This may well be a loose paraphrase of "the love of money is the root of all kinds of evil" (1 Tim 6:10). The purpose in raising this topic as an example of righteous behavior

18. Taking this statement as support for the various partition theories for Paul's letter to the Philippians appears very flimsy. The train of thought would be that Polycarp was correct in his statement that Paul wrote multiple letters to the Philippians. These in turn were then merged to form the single composition that later generations know as Paul's letter to the Philippians. For an accessible example of partition theory, see F. W. Beare, *A Commentary on the Epistle to the Philippians*, BNTC (London: A&C Black, 1959).

will become apparent later in the letter when Polycarp discusses the case of Valens. The former presbyter Valens is said to have failed in his office in regard to financial conduct. In contrast to his behavior, the Philippians are commanded to "avoid the love of money, and be pure and truthful. Avoid every kind of evil" (Pol. *Phil.* 11.1). Admittedly, in 4.1 Polycarp's initial reference to the love of money is not linked directly to the specific case of Valens but is presented as an example of unrighteous behavior. Polycarp coordinated the command against love of money with an existential rational for the perspective—"we brought nothing into the world and cannot take anything out" (4.1). This is a Pauline statement (1 Tim 6:7) that is also closely linked with the love of money saying (1 Tim 6:10). The pastiche of statements from Paul continues with the instruction, "Let us arm ourselves with the weapons of righteousness" (cf. 2 Cor 6:7). The sentence concludes with the somewhat ambiguous instruction "to follow the commandment of the Lord," without specifying which command is in view. It is likely that this looks back to 3.3 where Polycarp made reference to "the commandment of righteousness." This in turn is said to be fulfilled through love of God and Christ on one hand, and love of neighbor on the other. Moreover, the language of "command" (ἐντολή, *entolē*) recalls the question addressed to Jesus concerning the greatest command. In this context, the answer given concerns love of God, but to this is adjoined the command to love one's neighbor. Hence it is likely that the somewhat opaque reference to "the command of the Lord" is denoting Jesus's twin commands to love God and one's neighbor. This not only aligns with the gospel perspective on the greatest command, but it fits the flow of Polycarp's argument in 3.3.

The address to "instruct your wives" makes the instructions in 4.2 read like part of a household code, although the foregoing commandments were not specifically addressed to husbands or masters (cf. Col 3:18–19, where the addressees are more explicit). Here the wives are not addressed directly. Instead, Polycarp provides a set of instructions that the husbands are to communicate to their wives. While these instructions have various elements that infuse them with the perspectives of the beliefs of the community, overall these are standard injunctions to maintain purity, fidelity, and chastity. The more specifically Christian elements revolve around continuing in the faith they have received and instructing children in a godly manner. Apart from these elements, the values are chiefly those of the prevailing Greco-Roman society.

By contrast, the interest in widows and the instructions to be given to them reflects the role of widows in the early Jesus movement and the undertaking to provide for members of this group who might otherwise be destitute. The first two instructions to be communicated to widows are that they "must think soberly about the faith and pray unceasingly for everyone" (Pol. *Phil.* 4.3). These twin instructions encapsulate the positive aspect of the contribution of widows to the believing community. Accompanying this is a fuller set of prohibitions. Widows are to refrain from various kinds of negative speech, such as "malicious talk, slander, false testimony." Next Polycarp provides an additional warning against love of money (here to be addressed specifically to widows). He concludes with an all-encompassing warning to stay away from "any kind of evil" (4.3). Polycarp concludes this set of instructions to be given to widows by providing a theological basis. He states that widows are "God's altar, and that all sacrifices are carefully inspected and nothing escapes him." With this daring imagery, Polycarp employs sacrificial metaphors to compare the widows with the altar of offering. It is likely that the comparison is predicated on the notion that the prayers of the saints are like incense before the altar of God (cf. Rev 5:8; 8:3–4; 11:1). Finally, the widows are to be reminded that all actions are known by God, and this is set forth as a further motivation to maintain godly behavior.

To the Philippians 5–6

The letter moves forward from direct instructions concerning the behavior of widows in the previous section, first to a general exhortation and then to specific instruction to office-holders in the community. However, Polycarp recalls the list of inappropriate behavior that concluded with "love of money, and any kind of evil" (Pol. *Phil.* 4.3) when he states that "God is not mocked" and that believers should instead live in a righteous manner characterized by conformity to "his commandment and glory" (5.1). It is not coincidental that this list of vices moves to a climax, with reference to love of money being represented as an action that mocks God. The chilling reminder that "God is not mocked" (cf. Gal 6:7) warns readers of consequences and punishment for those who disregard the call to a form of righteous living that aligns with the commandments of God and is a reflection of the essence of the glorious being of the deity.

From this general exhortation, Polycarp turns attention to the specific leadership group of deacons. The instructions directed to deacons are framed in reference to the theme of righteousness, which is the topic on which Polycarp's instruction has been sought (Pol. *Phil.* 3.1). The overarching principle that guides the requisite behavior of deacons is that they "must be blameless in the presence of his righteousness" (5.2). The idea expresses the perspective that believers now exist at some level in the divine sphere. Therefore, the behavior of deacons must be appropriate for those who are in the presence of the God of righteousness. Polycarp expands on the reason for righteous behavior by reminding deacons that they are "servants of God and Christ" and are not subjected to human masters. From this general advice, a contrasting set of vices and virtues are listed for deacons. Three behaviors are listed that they are to avoid: slander, insincerity, and love of money. Again, avarice, or love of money forms the climax of the list of negative behaviors. The contrasting set of three positive virtues are self-control, compassion, and diligence. While the first two elements are stereotypical of Greco-Roman virtue-ethics, diligence is less common. It may have been selected and placed in the final position because it was a behavior that was particularly appropriate for the role of deacons. The motivation for aligning conduct with this positive set of behaviors is centered on the example of Christ. The deacons are told that such actions are "in accordance with the truth of the Lord, who became servant of all" (5.2). Holmes draws attention to a wordplay that is more obvious in Greek than in English. He states, "In Gk the word-play between deacons (*diakonoi*) and servant (*diakonos*) is very clear."[19] Finally, in the address to deacons, an eschatological motivation is provided for adopting correct behavior. Pleasing God in the present state of existence is said to guarantee entry into the coming age through resurrection. Moreover, such correct behavior is viewed as demonstrating that the deacons are "citizens worthy of him." The language of citizenship may intentionally recall Paul's own statement in his letter to the Philippians (Phil 3:20), where heavenly citizenship is linked with the eschatological return of Christ. Polycarp concludes his brief address to deacons by subtly shifting from behavioral requirements to mentioning the necessity of constancy in faith or belief. The content of the belief requirement is not stipulated, but from the immediately foregoing statements it is obviously christological in focus.

The next group to be addressed by Polycarp is not a specific leadership group like the deacons addressed in the previous paragraph, or the presbyters who will be addressed in the following section. Rather, the focus is on the "younger men" in the community, with a fleeting reference also to "virgins," παρθένους, *parthenous*, or young women at the end of

19. Holmes, *Apostolic Fathers*, 287.

the paragraph. Here the focus is not on financial ethics but instead on sexual purity. The instruction provided draws heavily on Pauline teaching and is formulated as an abbreviated version of 1 Corinthians 6:9–10, which reduces the longer list of Pauline vices to just a selection of those that relate to sexual behavior. Similarly Polycarp recalls the same sanction as Paul for those who do not adhere to the group's sexual ethics. Specifically, such people will not "inherit the kingdom of God" (Pol. *Phil.* 5.3). The address to younger men is, at one level, similar to the address in 1 John to the young men (1 John 2:13–17). In that context, there might be some reference to sexual continence with the exhortation to avoid "the lust of the flesh and the lust of the eyes" (1 John 2:16), but equally there may be a concern with the young men in the Johannine community forming a subgroup attracted to the docetic form of teaching that is being opposed.

Polycarp concludes this section with two further injunctions. The first is again addressed to the young men, who are to be obedient to the leadership of the presbyters and deacons. Lastly, the παρθένους, or young women, are to maintain their purity and to preserve a blameless conscience. The latter presumably arises from more than sexual purity.

In *To the Philippians* 6, Polycarp returns to providing instructions for the leadership groups in the community before issuing general guidance applicable to all believers. Again adopting a pattern of lists of positive and negative behavior, Polycarp addresses the senior leadership group of presbyters. They are told that their behavior must exhibit compassion and mercy, that they must correct those who deviate from the faith, and that special concern must be directed to the marginal—the sick, widows, orphans, and the poor. Moreover, as an overarching principle governing behavior, presbyters are to ensure that all their actions are honorable before God and the people. At one level, the teaching is fairly standard in terms of the values instilled in leaders in the early Jesus movement (cf. 1 Tim 3:2–7; Titus 1:7–9, where hospitality is a key virtue). However, the focus on the powerless and marginal was perhaps a quality that differentiated the early Jesus movement from other associations in the Greco-Roman world. Polycarp then lists vices to be avoided with a particular reference to "staying far away from all love of money" (Pol. *Phil.* 6.1). As will become apparent later in the letter but was obviously well-known to the initial recipients of the letter, Valens, the former presbyter, had failed in the office of presbyter and been removed from the role because of some form of financial greed or corruption (11.1). Here, however, the need to avoid the "love of money" is raised in a generalized manner, with no reference to a specific case. Polycarp also elaborates on the need for presbyters to adopt a moderated approach in dealing with accusations against individuals and any sanctions against wrongdoers. They are neither "to believe things spoken against anyone," nor to be "harsh in judgment" (6.1). In regard to the last point, Polycarp deploys a common Pauline idea of universal sinfulness (cf. Rom 3:23), although there is no obvious use of a specific Pauline text.

As the discussion continues, there appears to be a shift from a specific focus on instruction to presbyters toward a set of exhortations that apply to all members of the Philippian community. Expanding on the statement that "all are in debt with respect to sin" (Pol. *Phil.* 6.1), Polycarp states that all who have asked for divine forgiveness must be willing to forgive others. Again, an eschatological motivation is supplied to encourage the Philippians to practice forgiveness. Not only are their actions seen by "the Lord and God," they are also reminded that they will stand before Christ's judgment seat to account for those actions. From here Polycarp widens the perspective of his instruction. The coming judgment should motivate all believers to adopt an attitude of "fear and all reverence" (6.2). Although Polycarp states that the call to "fear and reverence" was commanded by the Lord and the apostles who preached the gospel, no specific scriptural text appears to underscore this claim.

Use of the term "gospel" leads Polycarp to echo another important early Christian claim—namely, that the prophets preached Christ prior to his coming (cf. Ign. *Magn.* 8.2; 9.2; *Phld.* 5.2; 9.2; *Smyrn.* 7.2; Justin, *1 Apol.* 23). Having made this theological claim, Polycarp offers what at first might appear to be a general statement to do good and to "avoid those who tempt others to sin" (Pol. *Phil.* 6.3). As he continues his train of thought, however, it becomes obvious that something more concrete is in view. He continues this section by warning against "false brothers, and those who bear the name of the Lord hypocritically, who lead foolish people astray" (6.3). The specific concerns that called forth this admonition become clearer in the following chapter 7.

To the Philippians 7

Polycarp, utilizing a stark statement drawn from 1 John, informs his readers that everyone "who does not confess that Jesus Christ has come in the flesh is antichrist" (Pol. *Phil.* 7.1; see 1 John 4:2–3; cf. 2 John 7). The concerns that Polycarp addresses in this section reflect the temporal and socioreligious setting of the letter. While there is an obvious resonance with the concerns addressed in the Johannine letters, taken as a whole this section expresses sentiments perhaps even more closely aligned with those found in several of Ignatius's letters. Given that Ignatius is named in Polycarp's letter and that Ignatius addresses similar issues in his letter to Polycarp, it is perhaps unsurprising that several of the same concerns are tackled by both authors.

In a highly compressed form, Polycarp summarizes the nature of the false teaching by listing four of its characteristics (Pol. *Phil.* 7.1). According to Polycarp, it entails a denial of Jesus Christ having come in the flesh, it does not acknowledge the testimony of the cross, it engages a hermeneutic that twists the sayings of Jesus, and it claims that there is neither resurrection nor judgment. If the younger men addressed earlier in the letter (at 5.3) were attracted to this teaching and practiced a freer sexual ethic because of the belief that there would be no future judgment, then it appears that a further problem the teaching was causing was failure to obey the presbyters and deacons. Each of these aspects, to a greater or lesser degree, is present in Ignatius's critique of his docetic opponents as described in his letters *To the Ephesians*, *To the Trallians*, and *To the Smyrnaeans*. For instance, in *To the Trallians*, Ignatius accuses his opponents of saying that Christ did not truly suffer since he did not actually come in the flesh: "But as some, who are atheists—that is unbelievers—say, that he only appeared to suffer, it is they who are the appearance [δοκεῖν, *dokein*]" (Ign. *Trall.* 10.1). The critique is presented in a more fulsome manner when addressing believers in Smyrna:

> For what good does it do me if someone praises me but blasphemes my Lord by not confessing that he was clothed in flesh? Anyone who does not acknowledge this thereby denies him completely and is clothed in a corpse. Given that they are unbelievers, it did not seem worthwhile to me to record their names. Indeed, far be it from me even to remember them, until such time as they change their mind regarding the passion, which is our resurrection. (Ign. *Smyrn.* 5.2–3)

According to Ignatius these false teachers do not affirm the incarnation, and they reject belief in the sufferings and resurrection of Christ. Those whom Polycarp critiques here, admittedly in briefer compass, appear to hold very similar beliefs. Whereas Ignatius labels these people as "unbelievers" or even "atheists," Polycarp states that their views come from the devil and they themselves are "the firstborn of Satan" (Pol. *Phil.* 7.1). Later in the letter

Polycarp advises a pastorally sensitive approach when dealing with Valens and his wife, who have been involved in some kind of financial embezzlement. However, there is no tolerance to be shown to those who promulgate teachings that deny the incarnation, passion, and resurrection of Christ.

Having briefly described the beliefs of these deviant teachers who are accused of leading people into sin, Polycarp next instructs the Philippian community as to how to respond. They are to leave behind this populist view and the associated teachings. The fact that it is described as the "speculation of the crowd" suggests a certain numerical strength among the group who adhered to this form of teaching. The remedy is presented as a return to the original teaching that the Philippians received and a rejection of recent innovation. Here there is a reminder of their apostolic foundation. At a practical level, Polycarp counsels discipline in regard to prayer and fasting. This may suggest that such spiritual disciplines and practices were not characteristic of the teaching being opposed. This possibility is further reinforced by the injunction that the Philippians should pray that they are not led into temptation, coupled with the traditional recognition of the weakness of the flesh. The citation of the saying, "the spirit is indeed willing, but the flesh is weak" (Matt 26:41), is a saying of Jesus made while he was in Gethsemane. The selection of a dominical saying that exemplified the torment of the human Jesus as part of his passion might not be coincidental. The saying may well have been chosen not only because it makes the point that spiritual perseverance is required in the face of intense trials, but because it also undercuts the teachings of the alternative teachers by showing Jesus's own conflict and turmoil in the face of his impending sufferings.

To the Philippians 8–10

The opening statement is transitional as it continues to undercut the teachings of those whom Polycarp opposes, while anticipating what follows (Pol. *Phil.* 8.2–10.3) where the suffering of martyrs and of Christ is to be the model that underpins righteous living. In contrast with those who deny the reality of Christ's sufferings on the cross (7.1), Polycarp issues a twofold response. First, he asserts the representative nature of Christ's death, stating that the sinless Jesus bore the sins of believers "in his own body on the tree." Second, expanding on the image of the body on the tree, Polycarp affirms the reality of Jesus's physical suffering and its function in imparting life to his followers: "He endured all things, in order that we might live in him" (8.1). Such suffering, according to Polycarp, becomes the model for the life of discipleship, and hence he informs the readers of the letter that "we should suffer for the sake of his name . . . for this is the example he set for us in his own person" (8.2).

Polycarp, having encouraged the Philippians to be willing to follow the example of the sufferings of Christ, also draws on the more recent sufferings of other figures as models of righteous suffering. He reminds the Philippians that they have seen firsthand such righteous endurance from "not only blessed Ignatius and Zosimus and Rufus" but also "in others from your congregation and in Paul himself and the rest of the apostles" (Pol. *Phil.* 9.1). While the references to Paul and the other apostles draw on historical examples, the other figures are mentioned to draw attention to those who have displayed righteous endurance that can be recalled in the recent living memory of the Philippians. The story of Ignatius and his connection with Polycarp is well-known. Polycarp's letter implies that, after departing from Smyrna, Ignatius's onward journey took him through Philippi. The other two named individuals, "Zosimus and Rufus," are unknown. They are classed as believers destined for martyrdom. It is unclear whether they traveled with Ignatius or in a separate group. Perhaps the former is unlikely since Ignatius does not name them. Presumably Zosimus and Rufus were not members of the Philippian group, since in the following comment Polycarp contrasts these three named figures with others "from your congregation" who suffered a similar fate.

The reference to Paul and the other apostles forms a slight tension in Polycarp's logic, since he commences this section by telling the Philippians that they have seen these examples of heroic suffering with "your own eyes." Here the rhetoric of the passage and the desire to remind the Philippians of their Pauline foundations move the train of thought forward to contemplation not only of contemporary righteous suffering, but also of historic examples. The reference to "the rest of the apostles" is vague. Perhaps the story of the death of Peter was in circulation. However, it is impossible to know which accounts of the righteous sufferings of apostles were in circulation and known to the Philippians at this stage, nor indeed whom the Philippians would have classed as apostles. While Polycarp does not need to clarify these issues for his first readers, later readers cannot determine the specific references.

What follows, although presented in stylized language, makes it clear that Polycarp names certain figures because they suffered death for the sake of their faith. He describes these people as having "not run in vain" and as being "in the place due to them with the Lord." Moreover, he links their fate with that of Jesus, stating in reference to Christ that it was him "with whom they also suffered" (Pol. *Phil.* 9.2). Here the teaching of those whom Polycarp opposes may still be in view. The sufferings even to death of these believers is of value because they follow the example of the death and sufferings of Christ. In this process they themselves become Christlike examples to the Philippians.

Ignatius makes this point far more stridently when he protests the value of his own fate: "If . . . he [Jesus] suffered in appearance only . . . , why am I in chains? And why do I want to fight with wild beasts? If that is the case, I die for no reason; what is more I am telling lies about the Lord" (Ign. *Trall.* 10.1). According to Ignatius, and apparently in agreement with Polycarp, the teachings of the docetic opponents not only deviated in their christological affirmations but resulted in undermining the basis on which contemporary believers suffered for their faith. According to both Ignatius and Polycarp, such endurance of sufferings made sense because it was the ultimate way believers were united with the Lord—through replicating his righteous endurance even to the point of surrendering one's life for the faith.

In many ways, Polycarp's teachings on righteousness reach a climax at this point in the letter. While he affirms certain ethical types of behavior, many of which would have been held in common with the prevailing Greco-Roman culture, the distinctive Christian act of righteousness that Polycarp sees as being conjoined with faith is a willingness to "exercise unlimited endurance" by following the example of those who had died for their faith and thus exemplified and replicated the sufferings of Christ.

From the beginning of chapter 10 (with the exception of the majority of ch. 13), the remainder of the epistle survives in Latin, not in Greek. The discussion in chapter 10 flows naturally from that in chapter 9. Hence there is little reason to doubt the integrity of the material in this section of the letter. The topic of following exemplary behavior continues. Polycarp returns to the example of Jesus, though it is not possible to link every behavior Polycarp identifies to an antecedent in the recorded accounts of the ministry and sufferings of Jesus. However, for the purpose of the argument of the letter, each desired characteristic is said to be based on "the example of the Lord" (*domini exemplar*). Inner group ethics come to the fore. The Philippians are exhorted to exemplify the following group behaviors:

"loving the family of believers, cherishing one another, united in the truth, giving way to one another in the gentleness of the Lord, despising no one" (Pol. *Phil.* 10). The language of "family" replicates the ideas of fictive kinship found throughout the New Testament and other early Christian writings. The general perspective of Christian writers is that joining a Christ group creates a new familial reality, where former physical ties are supplanted by relational links within the association of believers. Cohesion, or "unity," is lauded as a key goal to maintain group stability.

Alongside this, the Philippians are encouraged to adopt a deferential attitude based on the gentleness promoted by Jesus (perhaps grounded in texts such as Matt 5:5). Similarly, the exhortation to do good and to extend charity echoes the teachings of Jesus without citing any particular scriptural texts (again these ideas may be based on various saying attributed to Jesus; cf. Matt 5:16; 6:1–4, 31–33; 7:12; 1 Pet 2:12; 5:5). There is also a perspective of this pattern of behavior that is outward looking. Polycarp informs the Philippians that by adopting such a high standard of inner-group ethics, those around them will see their behavior as unimpeachable, and even those who are not group members will be impressed by the way the Philippian group conducts itself.

Failure to practice this standard of behavior can, however, have negative consequences. Polycarp warns against acting in a way that allows the group to be reproached: "Woe to the one through whom the name of the Lord is blasphemed" (Pol. *Phil.* 10.3). The exact source of this statement is difficult to determine, since a very similar statement in found in Paul's writings (cf. Rom 2:24), yet which in turn is based on Isaiah 52:2 LXX. Furthermore, Ignatius also cites a form of this saying (Ign. *Trall.* 8.2). Since *To the Trallians* was composed in and dispatched from Polycarp's home city of Smyrna, it is possible that this saying is derived from Ignatius and not directly from the scriptural texts. Since the text survives in Latin, rather than the original Greek, it is difficult to identify secure indications of the likely source. The implication Polycarp derives from this text is that all believers should adopt the self-control by which he says the Philippians live. This is surely a piece of exaggerated rhetorical encouragement intended to produce the behavior in that group that is already being praised. If the whole group was fully practicing self-control, it would be unlikely that Polycarp would need to encourage it. Moreover, the letter has already suggested that the "younger men" were engaging in a freer form of sexual behavior, which, according to Polycarp, required correction (Pol. *Phil.* 5.3).

To the Philippians 11

Polycarp next comes to the point in his letter where he addresses one of the pressing community concerns in the Philippian group of believers. The recipients of the letter will already have heard the repeated refrain in the letter to avoid the love of money (Pol. *Phil.* 2.2; 4.1, 3; 5.2; 6.1). The reason for repeating this admonition would have been clear to the Philippians as they heard Polycarp's letter read to them. However, for subsequent readers, it is not until this point in the letter that the reason for the financial admonition becomes apparent. The warning is not general or theoretical in nature. Rather, it stems from the financial misdemeanor of one of the leaders of the community. Here Polycarp identifies by name the former presbyter, Valens. While the precise details of the monetary offense are not described, the misdemeanor is made to represent a more significant failing. Polycarp says of Valens that "he fails to understand the office entrusted to him" (11.1). Here, what was presumably some type of embezzlement is seen as symptomatic of a spiritual failure to understand that the value of the leadership role surpassed any financial comparison and that presbyters are to be exemplars of "irreproachable standard of conduct among the Gentiles" (10.2) that had just been outlined. Thus, one sees a clear portrayal of early Christian self-understanding. They class themselves neither as Jews or gentiles but as a distinctive third way committed to faith in Christ and consequently expected to hold to an ethical standard that transcends that of unbelieving neighbors.

For Polycarp, the most significant problem with Valens's financial offense is that it nullifies the group's claim that they live by a higher ethical standard. Moreover, Valens's actions betray his hypocrisy as one who preaches self-control, but is unable to govern himself (*qui autem non potest se in his gubernare*, Pol. *Phil.* 11.2). It is quite likely the Greek text advocated maintenance of ἐγκράτεια, *enkrateia*, "self-control." This was one of the cardinal virtues advocated by several philosophers in their discussions of virtue ethics. The fact that Valens failed in this regard may have been seen as calling into question the Christian belief system, since it did not produce the highest standards of ethical conduct. For this reason, Polycarp compares love of money to the pollution of idolatry, and—perhaps drawing on traditional Jewish perspectives that idolatry was a stereotypical gentile sin—he advances the conclusion that those guilty of avarice "will be judged as one of the Gentiles, who are ignorant of the Lord's judgment" (11.2). The complaint is that the actions of Valens weaken the Christian claim that their life in Christ enables them to live a more virtuous life.

The mention of "the Lord's judgment" leads Polycarp to cite a Pauline text that likewise is applied to a group with suspect ethical conduct, to motivate them to live up to the standards that align with their calling. Polycarp cites Paul's teaching that "the saints will judge the world" (cf. ἢ οὐκ οἴδατε ὅτι οἱ ἅγιοι τὸν κόσμον κρινοῦσιν, *ē ouk oidate hoti hoi hagioi ton kosmon krinousin*, 1 Cor 6:2). Since Polycarp attributes this saying to Paul, the Greek text underlying the Latin can be reconstructed with a high degree of confidence at this point.

Polycarp's next comment that he had "not observed or heard of any such thing among you, in whose midst the blessed Paul laboured, and who are praised in the beginning of his letter" (Pol. *Phil.* 11.3) does not seem to mean that he was questioning the Philippians' knowledge of the immediately preceding comment that believers are to judge the world. Rather, it appears to hark back to the statement before that. Hence, he states his confidence that "no one in Philippi has ever gone so far in love of money as to be numbered with idolatrous Gentiles."[20] By contrast, he reminds the Philippians of their Pauline pedigree. Next, in a somewhat hyperbolic statement, he says that Paul boasts about the Philippians among all believing communities. Then in a moment of self-humility, he further comments by drawing attention to the fact that his own community was founded after that of the Philippians. Therefore, Polycarp's recalling the apostolic foundation of the group in Philippi is intended to provide solace in the face of the circumstances that confront them.

Pastoral concerns continue to come to the fore, not only for the community but also for Valens and his unnamed wife. Polycarp expresses sincere grief for the second time (cf. Pol. *Phil.* 11.1), and he expresses his desire that the Lord might grant them true repentance. It appears that Polycarp has to counsel the Philippians to moderate the response directed towards Valens and his wife. They are to be treated not "as enemies, but as sick and straying members" (11.4; cf. the advice Ignatius gave to Polycarp, Ign. *Pol.* 2.1). It appears that the community's response might have been disproportionate and purely punitive. Polycarp therefore seeks a change of approach where the goal is restorative rather than retributive. He informs the Philippians that such a merciful approach will not only benefit Valens and

20. H. O. Maier, "Purity and Danger in Polycarp's Epistle to the Philippians: The Sin of Valens in Social Perspective," *JECS* 1 (1993): 229–43, here 239–40.

his wife but will generate greater community cohesion. The display of mercy, according to Polycarp, provides its own reward.

To the Philippians 12

Polycarp moves from this specific case to abstract some general principles. He praises the Philippians for their knowledge of Scripture. Then, in what is presumably slightly mocking humility, Polycarp states there is nothing hidden from them although it might be from him. Next he reverses that statement by citing some very clear scriptural guidance that should have been as equally transparent to the Philippians as it was to him. This implies that obvious Christian behavior has become hidden from the Philippians. He then presents a short catena of two Pauline texts, both drawn from Ephesians. These texts are "be angry but do not sin" (Eph 4:25; itself drawn from Ps 4:4 [4:5 LXX]), and the second text is really a continuation of the first, "do not let the sun set on your anger" (Eph 4:26). To these texts, Polycarp adds his own beatitude: "Blessed is the one who remembers this." He then gives his assessment of the Philippians, saying he actually believes that they do know these teachings. However, their outrage at Valens has meant they have forgotten to be merciful and forgiving.

In doxological tones, Polycarp launches into a prayer on behalf of the Philippians. Nearly every phrase has an antecedent in the early Christian epistolary tradition. While many of the phrases may be ultimately dependent on epistolary texts, they may have embedded themselves in the sociolect of early Christian discourse. Thus, either indirectly from Scripture, or from the common language of prayer, Polycarp is able to draw on this repository of Christian language without directly consulting the texts from where the phrases originated. Possible parallels are suggested in the table below:

Phrase in Pol. *Phil.* 12.2–3	Potential Parallels in Early Christian Epistles
the God and Father of our Lord Jesus Christ	Cf. Rom 15:6; 2 Cor 1:3; Eph 1:3; 1 Pet 1:3
and the eternal high priest himself, the Son of God Jesus Christ	Cf. "a great high priest who has passed through the heavens, Jesus, the Son of God" (Heb 4:14)
build you up in faith and truth	Loose connection with Col 2:7
and in all gentleness and in all freedom from anger	Eph 4:25–26
and forbearance and steadfastness and patient endurance and purity	Cf. Col 1:23, a loose association of ideas
and may he give to you a share and a place among his saints	"what are the riches of the glory of his inheritance in the saints" (Eph 1:18); "who has qualified you to share in the inheritance of the saints in light" (Col 1:12)
and to all those under heaven	"in all creation under heaven" (Col 1:23)
believe in our Lord and God, Jesus Christ	Cf. Ign. *Rom.* 3.3; Ign. *Pol.* 8.3, "our God Jesus Christ"
in his Father who raised him from the dead.	"God the Father who raised him from the dead" (Gal 1:1); "God who raised him from the dead" (Col 2:12); cf. Rom 4:24; 7:4; 8:1; 1 Pet 1:21; Ign. *Trall.* 9.2

(continued)

Phrase in Pol. *Phil.* 12.2–3	Potential Parallels in Early Christian Epistles
Pray for all the saints	Cf. Eph 6:18
Pray also for kings and magistrates and rulers	"supplications, prayers, intercessions, and thanksgivings be made for all people, for kings and all who are in high positions" (1 Tim 2:1–2)
and for those who persecute and hate you	"bless those who persecute you" (Rom 12:14); cf. Matt 5:44, "Love your enemies and pray for those who persecute you"
and for the enemies of the cross	"enemies of the cross" (Phil 3:18)
so that your fruit may be evident among all people	"the fruit that increases to your credit" (Phil 4:17)
so that you may be perfect in him	"that you may be perfect" (Jas 1:4); cf. Matt 5:48; Ign. *Eph.* 15.2; *Phld.* 1.2; *Smyrn.* 4.2; 11.3; *Pol.* 1.3

As Berding observes, "The prayer of 12.2 is a pastiche of early Christian expressions, *all* of which are found in similar form somewhere in the NT, but none of which can be definitively connected with any particular text."[21] This observation should be extended in two ways. First it should also include 12.3, and second it should be extended beyond the New Testament to incorporate other early Christian writers, such as the letters of Ignatius. By citing apostolic sources, Polycarp aims to form apostolic Christians.

To the Philippians 13

With this doxological tone and the prayer requests, Polycarp has perhaps signaled that the letter was moving to its conclusion. In *To the Philippians* 13 this is even more apparent with the brief comments on practical arrangements. These arrangements chiefly concern the circulation of various letters. The discussion provides insight into the wider structure of early Christian communities. Rather than functioning as discrete and isolated groups, early Christian groups gained a sense of belonging to a larger global movement through communication networks. This was achieved in several ways. Travelers between communities could relate news among the disparate groups. The potential danger was that this could lead to reliance on the perspectives of an individual who might be idiosyncratic in their views and not representative of the leadership of the community from where the news originated. The main alternative method was through the circulation of letters that were sent from community leaders. These were typically conveyed by letter bearers, and so there was also the possibility of inquiring after further explanation or details.

Polycarp informs the Philippians that he has received instructions from both the Philippians and Ignatius that a letter sent from the Philippians should be conveyed westward to Syria. The contents are unknown. Presumably the letter related to Ignatius's circumstances when he had reached Philippi during his transportation to Rome (cf. Ign. *Smyrn.* 11.3; Ign. *Pol.* 7.2). This request seems to provide evidence that Polycarp's letter (or at least this section of it) was written while Ignatius's journey was still in progress, or very shortly after his arrival in Rome. Polycarp informs the Philippians that he intends to send the letter on to Syria, either carrying it himself or using a representative. By land the

21. K. Berding, *Polycarp and Paul: An Analysis of Their Literary and Theological Relationship in Light of Polycarp's Use of Biblical and Extrabibical Literature*, VCSup 62 (Leiden: Brill, 2002), 120.

journey from Smyrna to Antioch was a little over a thousand kilometers, so the promise to convey the letter was a significant undertaking. Polycarp also responds positively to a second request from the Philippians. They sought copies of Ignatius's letters. Polycarp promises to forward to them "the letters of Ignatius that were sent to us by him together with any others that we have in our possession" (Pol. *Phil.* 13.2). The first category, "letters sent to us," presumably comprises the letter addressed to the community in Smyrna as well as the personal letter addressed to Polycarp. The contents of the second category, "any others that we have in our possession," are more difficult to determine. On the one hand, from the statements made in his letters, Ignatius wrote four letters from Smyrna (cf. Ign. *Eph.* 21.1; *Magn.* 15.1; *Trall.* 12.1; *Rom.* 10.1). By contrast, the other three letters, *To the Philadelphians*, *To the Smyrnaeans*, and *To Polycarp*, were written from Troas (cf. Ign. *Phld.* 11.2; *Smyrn.* 12.1; *Pol.* 8.1).[22] It is possible that the Smyrnaean church retained copies of the four letters that were sent while Ignatius was with them, along with the two they received. Alternatively, the Greek manuscript tradition of the middle recension reveals a separate textual history for *To the Romans*, whereas the six other letters are preserved as a collection (along with other letters in the long recension) in the order *Smyrnaeans*, *Polycarp*, *Ephesians*, *Magnesians*, *Philadelphians*, *Trallians*. If this six-letter collection has any connection with the group of letters sent by Polycarp to the Philippians, it might reveal that he was able to obtain copies of letters sent by Ignatius to those communities relatively proximate to Smyrna, but he could not obtain a copy of the letter sent to the more distant location of Rome. If the latter is the case, then Polycarp might both be the originator of the collection of the initial corpus of Ignatian letters as well as being responsible for the divided textual history for *To the Romans* and the other six authentic letters of Ignatius. It is also noteworthy that the two letters sent to Smyrna stand first in this six-letter collection, as attested in Codex Mediceo-Laurentianus.

Furthermore, Polycarp assesses Ignatius's letters as having great value in instructing Christ believers. Not only does he inform the Philippians that they will benefit from reading the letters, but he also identifies what he perceives to be the major themes of the epistles. He states, "They deal with faith and patient endurance and every kind of spiritual growth that has to do with our Lord" (Pol. *Phil.* 13.2). It is striking that Polycarp's perspective on the thematic emphases of the letters is so different from modern assessments. Typically, recent commentators have drawn attention to the prominence of ideas around Christology, ecclesiology, the Eucharist, and the rebuttal of false teachings. However, Polycarp identified a set of positive themes. The difference is likely a reflection of a change of concerns when modern audiences read the Ignatian letters.

The final comment in *To the Philippians* 13 is a request to the Philippians from Polycarp asking that they might supply him with more information concerning Ignatius's fate: "Let us know what certain information you have learned about Ignatius himself and those with him" (Pol. *Phil.* 13.2). For those who see the current form of the letter as a composite, or even as inauthentic, this is a key piece of evidence. Those who judge the letter inauthentic typically see the request as an authenticating device, which indicates that the letter wishes to present itself as being written while Ignatius was still alive and thus to be placed securely during the lifetime of Polycarp. Those who see the current text of the letter as formed from two epistles written by Polycarp understand this section as stemming from a short note

22. Hartog wrongly assigns *To the Philadelphians* to Smyrna. See P. Hartog, ed., *Polycarp's Epistle to the Philippians and the Martyrdom of Polycarp: Introduction, Text, and Commentary*, OAF (Oxford: Oxford University Press, 2013), 158.

written when the final fate of Ignatius was unknown. By contrast, the reference to Ignatius in *To the Philippians* 9 is seen as coming from a later letter when the execution of Ignatius had taken place and was widely known. According to the composite or two-letter theory, when writing the second letter Polycarp shows that he is aware that Ignatius and the fellow martyrs are already "in the place due to them with the Lord, with whom they also suffered" (Pol. *Phil.* 9.2). While the two-letter theory is possible, the tension between 9.1–2 and 13.2 is not as great as sometimes suggested. It is possible that in chapter 9 Polycarp could write as if the looming execution of Ignatius had already taken place (and it may have done so), whereas in 13.2 he inquires after the specific circumstances surrounding the death of Ignatius. What the request does reveal is the genuine concern Polycarp has for Ignatius and the bond of respect and admiration expressed toward those willing to sacrifice their life rather than compromise faith in Christ. Perhaps it is in light of this outlook that Polycarp identifies the most important themes in the letter of Ignatius as "faith," "patient endurance," and "spiritual growth."

To the Philippians 14

The closing section comprises two elements: a word of support for Crescens and his unnamed sister. Like the wife of Valens, the female person remains unidentified by personal name, instead only being identified by relationship to a male figure. The role of Crescens is not specified with great clarity. He is associated with the letter that Polycarp is about to conclude and send. It appears the commendation of Crescens is required because he will soon be with the Philippians. This may suggest that he was to act as the letter carrier. Whether he had a more involved role as the amanuensis of the letter is difficult to determine, although it is not impossible.

As has been noted, the word of commendation, at least as it is preserved in the Latin text, is somewhat overloaded with temporal references: *quem in praesenti commendavi vobis, et nunc commendo* (Pol. *Phil.* 14.1). Literally this could be translated as "whom in the present I have commended to you, and now I commend." The reason for this emphatic double note of commendation is difficult to discern. Polycarp states of Crescens that "his conduct while with us has been blameless" (14.1). This suggests two things. The qualification "while with us" suggests that Crescens was not a member of the Smyrnaean community and that he had only spent a short period of time with Polycarp and the Christ group in Smyrna. It might be the case that he carried the letter from Philippi to Smyrna and was about to return with Polycarp's correspondence. More cryptic is the assurance that "his conduct . . . has been blameless." Perhaps Crescens had not been blameless in behavior in the past while in Philippi, and Polycarp now writes to assure the Philippians that his conduct has reverted to the standard required. If Crescens were a young man entrusted with the delivery of the letter, it is not impossible that his actions in some way aligned with those failings in the younger men that Polycarp addressed in 5.3. Interestingly, in that context Polycarp commands the young men to be "blameless" (ἄμεμπτοι, *amemptoi*). Here Crescens is commended for being "blameless" (*inculpabiliter*). Perhaps the correspondence is coincidental. Nonetheless, it is intriguing. Polycarp, however, assures the Philippians that when Crescens comes to them, presumably carrying the letter from Smyrna, that his behavior will remain blameless.

Even less can be said about Polycarp's comment concerning the sister of Crescens: "And you will consider his sister to be commended when she comes to you." While it is obvious that she is not with the Philippian group when Polycarp was writing, it is not obvious that she was in Smyrna with Crescens, although that is possible. It appears that she is known to the Philippians, yet she required a commendation to guarantee her acceptance when she arrives in Philippi at some point in the future. There is obviously much more behind these comments than can be determined from the partial and opaque commendations.

The letter closes with a warm christologically infused sentiment: "Farewell in the Lord Jesus Christ in grace, you and all those with you. Amen." The centrality of "grace" (Latin, *gratia*) as a divinely imparted gift is a key idea in the early Christian movement, able to be traced back as early as the writings of Paul.[23] Alongside the farewell being issued "in grace," it is also issued "in the Lord Jesus Christ." It perhaps otiose to debate whether the farewell itself is issued in the name of the Lord Jesus Christ to draw attention to the fact that Christ is the source of grace or, alternatively, whether it is intended to communicate the shared status of Polycarp and the Philippian recipients as having their identity defined through the status of being in Christ. The farewell language is both evocative and pregnant. Hence it is not inappropriate to legitimately see a plurality of meaning here. Consequently, Polycarp's wish for the Philippians is that they progress positively and productively in the future by being recipients of grace. He issues this wish in the name of Christ who is the source of that grace, while drawing attention to the common status of sender and recipients as those who define their identity through being in Christ. Therefore, Polycarp reminds the Philippians that they are recipients of divine grace. Perhaps this element is intended to underscore the fact that as recipients of God's free gift, they are to exhibit generosity in all their dealings. He extends this christological farewell to incorporate not only the immediate recipients of the letter but also the wider, but loosely defined group that incorporates those who are with them. Finally, in stereotypical terms, Polycarp closes this prayerful farewell greeting with "amen," thus signaling the end of the letter.

3. INTERPRETATIVE ISSUES

For many, Polycarp's *To the Philippians* has at best minimal theological value. Thus, in dismissive tones, Thomas Torrance damned it as being "a little disappointing to the student of historical theology."[24] A couple of decades earlier, an even more damning assessment was made in German scholarship. Martin Dibelius impugned the writing as "a completely unoriginal, very insignificant but well-intended letter."[25] While it is the case that in no sense can Polycarp's letter be characterized as a work of systematic theology, such assessments appear to judge the theological value by the norms of a later period and do not adequately recognize the significant theological contributions the letter makes in a particular context addressing specific pastoral questions.

Righteousness is the principal topic that Polycarp identifies as the central concern of the letter. This, however, is the theme that occupies his thought in response to the pressing invitation from the Philippians that he should address them on that topic (Pol. *Phil.* 3.1). For Polycarp, righteousness is a shorthand way of denoting a set of ethical behaviors that align with believers' faith in Christ. Polycarp states that the fullest expression of righteousness comes through loving Christ and loving neighbor. These twin actions reveal that a person "has fulfilled the commandment of righteousness" (3.3). Although Polycarp repeatedly draws on Pauline writings, his understanding of righteousness (at least as it can be seen in *To the Philippians*) does not seem to reflect Pauline ideas of a status given to

---

23. For a seminal treatment, see J. M. G. Barclay, *Paul and the Gift* (Grand Rapids: Eerdmans, 2015).

24. T. F. Torrance, *The Doctrine of Grace in the Apostolic Fathers* (London: Oliver and Boyd, 1948), 91.

25. M. Dibelius, *Geschichte des urchristlichen Literarur* (Berlin: de Gruyter, 1926), 119, as translated by B. Dehandschutter, "Polycarp's Epistle to the Philippians: An Early Example of Reception," *BETL* 86 (1989): 275–91, here 275.

believers (Rom 4:1–25; 5:18–21). Rather, it appears more closely aligned with the understanding of righteousness found in the Gospel of Matthew where one's ethical conduct or righteousness must surpass the standard of societal norms (cf. Matt 5:20) and must align with the requirements of the kingdom (Matt 6:33).

Polycarp also reveals his thought on many other theological ideas. While he offers no sustained presentation of his understanding of Jesus, his Christology emerges through various statements in the letter. He sees divine actions and blessings as having a dual origin. Thus, in his salutation, "mercy and peace" are both said to come from "God Almighty and Jesus Christ our Saviour" (Pol. *Phil.* salut.). It is well-known that Ignatius affirms Jesus as God (cf. Ign. *Eph.* 18.2; Ign. *Smyr.* 1.1), and Polycarp may have agreed with Ignatius's perspective. It is, however, debatable whether Polycarp explicitly makes a similar declaration in his letter to the Philippians. Admittedly, at one point he may refer to those who "believe in our Lord and God Jesus Christ and in his Father who raised him from the dead" (Pol. *Phil.* 12.2). Yet in this case there are a number of textual issues. First, the reading is preserved only in the Latin version, with the key phrase reading *qui credituri sunt in dominum nostrum et deum Iesum Christum*. However, the tradition is divided in regard to the omission or inclusion of the key words *et deum*, "and God."[26] Therefore, it is probably safest not to utilize this phrase as conclusive proof that Polycarp referred to Jesus as God. Notwithstanding this caveat, Polycarp joins with other early Christians in addressing Jesus as Lord and attributing to Christ actions and prerogatives typically indicative of divine status.

Polycarp's writings present God as a constant presence, informing the status of believers and shaping their actions. Thus, the Philippian believers are identified as a community in relationship to God: "the church of God that dwells at Philippi" (Pol. *Phil.* salut.). However, the primary way that God is understood is in relation to Christ. Thus Polycarp has a Christocentric understanding of the identity of God. In particular, God is designated as "Father of our Lord Jesus Christ" (12.2). This filial relationship is central to how Polycarp understands the link between God and Christ. Perhaps an even more prominent way of Polycarp's representing this relationship is by presenting God as the one "who raised up our Lord Jesus Christ from the dead and gave him glory" (2.1). Thus Polycarp understands the actions of God and Christ operating together in a way that reveals a unity of purpose. That unity is predicated on the filial relationship and the divine action of restoring Christ to life. However, Polycarp does not provide a reflection on the ontological basis of the relationship. To expect him to do so would be perhaps to require him to think in categories that emerged in the fourth and fifth centuries, not in the early second century.

Eschatology is also prominent in the letter, although there is a lack of fervor arising from an expectation of an imminent return of Christ. This does not mean that Polycarp's eschatology has become realized in nature. His eschatological outlook is still oriented toward the future, albeit there is no sense that the return of Christ will happen in the immediate future. Primarily for Polycarp the certainty of Christ's return is a motivation for righteous ethical conduct in the present. Furthermore, the return of Christ is the basis of future hope for believers. Polycarp closely links right behavior, belief in Christ, resurrection, and future blessing. He states,

---

26. In regard to the key phrase *et deum*, the Latin witnesses are divided concerning its inclusion (L^{rmpf}) or its omission (L^{ovbct}). None of these manuscripts is typically dated earlier than the ninth century, and some are dated as late as the fifteenth or sixteenth century.

> If we please him in this present world, we will receive the world to come as well, inasmuch as he has promised that he will raise us from the dead and that if we prove to be citizens worthy of him, we shall also reign together with him—if, that is, we continue to believe. (Pol. *Phil.* 5.2b)

Thus, for Polycarp, the eschaton results both in a transformed state of existence and a transformed status when believers will reign with Christ in his kingdom.

Possible insight into ecclesial structures is tantalizing but uncertain on the basis of statements in Polycarp's letter. While Ignatius considered the term ἐπίσκοπος, *episkopos* ("bishop") as the most apt way to describe Polycarp's role among his own community—"to Polycarp, bishop of the church of the Smyrnaeans" (Ign. *Pol.* salut.)—Polycarp nowhere uses this title in relation to himself or anyone else. What this implies is debatable. What Polycarp does say about community leadership is that the presbyters stand with the deacons as the leaders of the Philippian community (Pol. *Phil.* 5.3). While Polycarp does not describe significant factors that distinguish the two roles, he does attribute a greater range of roles to the presbyters than to the deacons. At least explicitly, Polycarp only describes two leadership offices. It might be the case that this structure was operative in the Philippian group and perhaps the group at Smyrna. Alternatively, Polycarp may have found it unnecessary to mention his own role as ἐπίσκοπος, "bishop." Hence, it is possible that the group at Smyrna adopted a threefold pattern of leadership as described at length in Ignatius's letters.

4. KEY PASSAGES FOR NEW TESTAMENT STUDIES AND THEIR SIGNIFICANCE

More than any other writing contained among the corpus of the Apostolic Fathers, Polycarp's *To the Philippians* reveals knowledge of the greatest range of those writings that were later to become the New Testament. In particular, Polycarp draws on various letters of Paul. He names Paul on four occasions in his own letter (Pol. *Phil.* 3.2; 9.1; 11.2, 3), and in one of those instances he reveals his knowledge that Paul had written to the Philippians. What is interesting about that comment is that Polycarp refers to multiple letters to the Philippians: "When he was absent he wrote you letters" (3.2). Whether the plural is hyperbole, or whether Paul wrote additional letters apart from the one we now possess is impossible to determine.

Typically, Polycarp does not provide verbatim citations, but in many of the examples the language is close enough to reveal knowledge of the passage in a form that might be intentionally modified or abbreviated, and perhaps recalled from memory. An example of the use of material from Romans provides a guide to the way in which Polycarp utilizes Pauline material. The example below is probably the strongest cases showing dependence on Romans.

Pol. *Phil.* 6.2	**Rom 14:10, 12**
καὶ πάντας δεῖ παραστῆναι τῷ βήματι τοῦ Χριστοῦ καὶ ἕκαστον ὑπὲρ αὑτοῦ λόγον δοῦναι.	πάντες γὰρ παραστησόμεθα τῷ βήματι τοῦ θεοῦ, . . . ἄρα [οὖν] ἕκαστος ἡμῶν περὶ ἑαυτοῦ λόγον δώσει [τῷ θεῷ].
"We must all appear at the judgment-seat of Christ, and must every one give an account of himself."	"For we shall all stand before the judgment seat of God. . . . So then each one of us shall give account of himself to God."

This example is neither an exact citation, nor a vague allusion. There is verbal correspondence, the use of different forms of the same verb, and a commonality in word order. Yet there are also some changes, such as the switch in genitive referent from τῷ βήματι τοῦ θεοῦ in Romans 14:10 to τῷ βήματι τοῦ Χριστοῦ in *To the Philippians* 6.2. There might also be a minor conflation of Pauline texts, since Paul refers to τοῦ βήματος τοῦ Χριστοῦ elsewhere in his writings (2 Cor 5:10).[27]

In relation to the Pauline writings, Polycarp appears to have known eight of Paul's letters: Romans, 1 Corinthians, Galatians, Ephesians, Philippians, 2 Thessalonians, 1 and 2 Timothy, quite possibly a ninth, 2 Corinthians, and even a tenth, Colossians (although at times some of the phrases are also paralleled in Ephesians, thus further complicating the determination). Polycarp's *To the Philippians* is, therefore, one of the most important pieces of evidence reflecting knowledge of an early and reasonably extensive collection of the letters of Paul. Beyond this, Polycarp also appears to know 1 Peter (Pol. *Phil.* 1.3//1 Pet 1:8), although Polycarp presents the ideas from 1 Peter 1:8 in a shorter and selective form. There are other parallels that are not quite as strong between 1 Peter and Polycarp's *To the Philippians*. Polycarp's knowledge of 1 John is demonstrable in one passage.

Pol. *Phil.* 7.1	1 John 4:2b–3a; 3:8
"For everyone 'who does not confess that Jesus Christ has come in the flesh, is antichrist'; and whoever does not acknowledge the testimony of the cross 'is of the devil.'"	"Every spirit which confesses that Jesus Christ has come in the flesh is of God, and every spirit that does not confess Jesus is not from God; and this is the antichrist." "The one who practices sin is of the devil."

While this does not constitute a direct citation, the language Polycarp uses is reminiscent of the way the polemical accusations are formulated in 1 John.

Polycarp's knowledge of Acts is often defended. This depends on one passage in Polycarp's letter. Polycarp describes Jesus as the one "whom God raised up, having loosed the pains of Hades" (Pol. *Phil.* 1.2c). In similar terms, reporting Peter's Pentecost speech, the author of Acts has Peter state that Jesus was the one "whom God raised up having loosed the pains of death" (Acts 2:24). The key phrases that occurs in Acts 2:24 is "pains of death," which in both contexts is combined with a reference to the resurrection of Christ. The phrase, however, is not uncommon in the Jewish Scriptures.[28]

Citation practice in antiquity was different from modern practices. Typically links have to be detected on the basis of verbal correspondence. Given the usually loose way of citing material, it is striking that Polycarp actually names specific Pauline correspondence with the Philippians. Moreover, Polycarp reveals knowledge of at least eight (and possibly ten) Pauline letters, two further letters in the New Testament, and perhaps even the Acts of the Apostles. While there is no clear use of material drawn from the Gospels, this perhaps is unsurprising given the nature of the content of Polycarp's letter. What is particularly

27. For a fuller discussion of this passage, see P. Foster, "The Text of the New Testament in the Apostolic Fathers," in *The Early Text of the New Testament*, ed. C. E. Hill and M. J. Kruger (Oxford: Oxford University Press, 2012), 282–301.

28. This expression occurs on a number of occasions in the Jewish Scriptures, e.g., 2 Sam 22:6; Ps 116:3 [114:3 LXX]. The related phrase "pains of Hades" occurs in Ps 18:5 [17:6 LXX]. To further complicate matters, among Greek witnesses there is a variant reading of Acts 2:24 found in D (Codex Bezae) that reads "pains of Hades" rather than the variant "pains of death" found in the majority of manuscripts.

noteworthy is the highly significant evidence Polycarp provides for an early and reasonably extensive collection of the letters of Paul.

5. CONCLUSION

Polycarp may not have left the same literary output as some contemporary figures, such as Ignatius. His rhetoric might not be equally aflame with passion and anger. His theological affirmations might not be as daring and as innovative. Yet, in many ways he may be more representative, and hence more revealing of the nature of the Christ movement in the second or third decade of the second century. He occupies a central place in understanding the Jesus movement in this period, not just temporally but more importantly ecclesially and pastorally. He was a conciliatory figure, available to communities beyond Smyrna who consulted him for his pastoral leadership. As such, Polycarp's oft maligned *To the Philippians* may be one of the most important documents available to those who wish to understand the structures and the beliefs of the nascent Jesus movement in that period.

BIBLIOGRAPHY

Bauer, J. B. *Polykarpbriefe.* KAV 5. Göttingen: Vandenhoeck & Ruprecht, 1995.

Berding, K. *Polycarp and Paul: An Analysis of Their Literary and Theological Relationship in Light of Polycarp's Use of Biblical and Extrabibical Literature.* VCSup 62. Leiden: Brill, 2002.

Foster, P. "Polycarp's Teaching: The Reception and Development of Theology." Pages 279–313 in *Studies on the Intersection of Text, Paratext, and Reception: A Festschrift in Honor of Charles E. Hill.* Edited by G. R. Lanier and J. Nicholas Reid. TENT 15. Leiden: Brill, 2021.

Foster, P. "The Text of the New Testament in the Apostolic Fathers." Pages 92–118 in *The Cambridge Companion to the Apostolic Fathers.* Edited by M. Bird and S. Harrower. Cambridge: Cambridge University Press, 2021.

Foster, P. "The Text of the New Testament in the Apostolic Fathers." Pages 282–301 in *The Early Text of the New Testament.* Edited by C. E. Hill and M. J. Kruger. Oxford: Oxford University Press, 2012.

Harrison, P. N. *Polycarp's Two Epistles to the Philippians.* Cambridge: Cambridge University Press, 1936.

Hartog, P., ed. *Polycarp's Epistle to the Philippians and the Martyrdom of Polycarp: Introduction, Text, and Commentary.* OAF. Oxford: Oxford University Press, 2013.

Lightfoot, J. B. *The Apostolic Fathers, Part II: S. Ignatius, S. Polycarp. Revised Texts with Introductions, Notes, Dissertations, and Translations.* 2nd. ed. 3 vols. London: Macmillan, 1889–1890.

Parvis, P. "Polycarp, *To the Philippians.*" Pages 59–72 in *From Thomas to Tertullian—Christian Literary Receptions of Jesus in the Second and Third Centuries CE.* Volume 2 of *The Reception of Jesus in the First Three Centuries.* Edited by C. Keith, H. K. Bond, C. Jacobi, and J. Schröter. London: T&T Clark, 2020.

Prostmeier, F. R. "Zur handschriftlichen Überlieferung des Polykarp- und des Barnabasbriefes: Zwei nicht beachtete Deszendenten des Cod. Vat. Gr. 859." *VC* 48 (1994): 48–64.

Schoedel, W. R. *Polycarp, Martyrdom of Polycarp, Fragments of Papias.* Vol. 5 of *The Apostolic Fathers: A Translation and Commentary.* Edited by R. M. Grant. New York: Thomas Nelson, 1967.

CHAPTER 11

THE MARTYRDOM OF POLYCARP

SCOTT HARROWER

1. INTRODUCTION

The purpose of this essay is to introduce, describe, and assess the scholarly debates around the Martyrdom of Polycarp, with a special focus on how it relates to the documents of the New Testament as well as groups such as Johannine and Pauline circles.[1]

1.1 Polycarp

Born in the late first century, Polycarp was the bishop of Smyrna in the first half of the second century. His prominent status in second-century Christianity was made possible by his long term in leadership from approximately 110 to 155 CE. Polycarp's long life and influence were a bridge between Jesus's first followers on the one hand, and successive generations of Christians on the other. Evidence of Polycarp's central status across Mediterranean Christianity includes the ongoing reception and preservation of the Martyrdom of Polycarp, his extant correspondence *To the Philippians*, as well other works attributed to him, including a Didaskalia,[2] and references to him by contemporaries such as Ignatius and Tertullian.[3] Ignatius, for example, writes about "loving Polycarp,"[4] the "Bishop of the Smyrnaeans," who "refreshed" him during his time in Smyrna.[5]

Polycarp's reputation was cemented and promoted by the Martyrdom's vivid description of his virtues during his final days, arrest, and execution, and of his postmortem influence. During its gripping narrative, the Martyrdom promotes Polycarp's exemplary Christlike behavior and faith in the context of horrendous religious persecution.[6] Polycarp's faithful-

1. I am thankful to Rebecca Muir and Andrew Malone (Ridley College, Australia) and Jonathon Lookadoo (Presbyterian University and Theological Seminary, Republic of Korea) for their insightful suggestions that improved this essay. All biblical references are from the NIV.

2. J. B. Lightfoot, *The Apostolic Fathers, Part II: S. Ignatius, S. Polycarp. Revised Texts with Introductions, Notes, Dissertations, and Translations*, 2nd ed., 3 vols. (London: Macmillan, 1889–1890), 1:447, 351n1, cited in P. Hartog, "Polycarp's Epistle to the Philippians and the Martyrdom of Polycarp," in *The Cambridge Companion to the Apostolic Fathers*, ed. M. Bird and S. Harrower (Cambridge: Cambridge University Press, 2021), 226; B. Dehandschutter, "Polycarpiana: Notes on the Hagiographic 'Dossier' of a Saint," in *Studies on Martyrdom and Persecution in Early Christianity: Collected Essays*, ed. J. Leemans (Leuven: Leuven University Press, 2007).

3. Ign. *Magn.* 15; Ign. *Eph.* 21.1; Tertullian, *Praescr.* 32.2, all cited in Éric Rebillard, *Greek and Latin Narratives About the Ancient Martyrs* (Oxford: Oxford University Press, 2017), 81.

4. Ign. *Eph.* 21.1, in R. Brannan, *The Apostolic Fathers: A New Translation* (Bellingham, WA: Lexham Press, 2017), 82.

5. Ign. *Magn.* 15, in Brannan, *Apostolic Fathers*, 89. Throughout this work, the version of Mart. Pol. upon which I draw is "The Martyrdom of Saint Polycarp—Bishop of Smyrna," in Brannan, *Apostolic Fathers*, 263–76.

6. "The *Martyrdom of Polycarp* presents the narrative of Polycarp's death in order to recast him as an imitator of Christ. That is, it provides a narratological mirroring of details, his persona, and the villains to match the

ness to God's will, paralleling Christ's own faithfulness to God, was theologically interpreted. The purposes and nature of his death were understood in the context of both divine and human events; it was the death of an exemplary man, yet God ultimately directed and endorsed it.[7] The main portion of the work was likely composed in Smyrna, with a pan-Mediterranean audience in mind (20.1).[8] Its primary context for use was within liturgical settings.[9] The Martyrdom of Polycarp had a crucial influence in the development of the concept of Christian martyrdom and became a template for early Christian martyrdom accounts from the second century onward.[10]

The story was composed as a response to the fundamentally human interest of the Christians in Philomelium, who simply wanted to know what became of Polycarp.[11] This human and existential dimension of the composers and recipient community should not be overlooked among the scholarly discussions that attend the work. Parvis writes:

> If we read between the lines, we can see a community which is all too human: where some step forward in bravado and catapult others into the centre of a horrific and deadly entertainment; where the community can remember some members with loving pride and brush aside even the names of others.[12]

Above all, for scholars today the story serves as a vista into early Christianity, revealing local views on important themes such as the demarcations of Christian identity, as well as how to suffer and die "according to the gospel" (Mart. Pol. 1.1; 19.1). Because the Martyrdom makes use of earlier Christian beliefs and practices, it offers a snapshot of the second-century social and religious development by later generations of Christians. Of particular interest in this essay is how religious traditions that predated Polycarp's life and ministries shaped the contours and content of the work. In what follows, we reckon with the text, its attendant interpretative issues, theological themes, and use of earlier Christian traditions in a complex manner.

1.2 Genre: A Letter Understood as Hagiographical Media

Lightfoot classified the Martyrdom's genre as an epistle, or letter.[13] However, the kind of epistle it is, its intended effects on readers, as well as its interest in exemplary persons as role models for the audience add up to it being classified as an epistle that belongs to the genre of hagiographical media.

Before proceeding with this argument, it is important to place the discussion of Martyrdom's genre in the context of long-term scholarly research into martyr texts. Awareness of these debates, especially the bias and assumptions that various genre

---

Gospel narratives" (S. J. Wilhite, "'That We Too Might Be Imitators of Him': The Martyrdom of Polycarp as *Imitatio Christi*," *Churchman* 129.4 [2015]: 319).

7. Theological interpretation is the generative origin of martyrdom traditions such as Mart. Pol. See G. Buschmann, *Das Martyrium des Polykarp übersetzt und erklärt*, KAV 6 (Gottingen: Vandenhoeck & Ruprecht, 1998), 180.

8. J. B. Lightfoot, *The Apostolic Fathers* (Grand Rapids: Baker, 1974), 103.

9. Buschmann, *Das Martyrium des Polykarp*, 48.

10. B. Dehandschutter, "Le Martyre de Polycarpe et le développement de la conception du martyre au deuxième siècle," in *Polycarpiana: Studies on Martyrdom and Persecution in Early Christianity: Collected Essays*, ed. J. Leemans (Leuven: Leuven University Press, 2007).

11. Dehandschutter, "Le Martyre de Polycarpe," 94.

12. S. Parvis, "The Martyrdom of Polycarp," in *The Writings of the Apostolic Fathers*, ed. P. Foster (London: T&T Clark, 2007), 145.

13. Lightfoot, *Apostolic Fathers*, 103.

ascriptions carry with them, will enable a constructive engagement with more recent work on the work's genre.

The genre of the Martyrdom of Polycarp has been variously described. A long-standing tradition in the scholarly study of martyr texts, such as the Martyrdom of Polycarp, had been to classify the genre of martyr accounts as belonging to either the *acta* or *passio* genres. The distinction held that the *acta* "genre was concerned with the report or proceedings of a trial during which Christians were condemned to die."[14] On the other hand, *passio* "described the sufferings, tortures, and execution of the martyrs in greater depth."[15] The perceived historical reliability of the *acta* was assumed to be higher than *passio* texts because *acta* were mostly written up as legal proceedings against Christians who would subsequently be martyred.[16] Passion texts, such as the *Passion of Perpetua and Felicity*, "dealt more with stylized narratives and legends and were deemed less trustworthy."[17] According to this distinction, the Martyrdom of Polycarp would be a *passio*, because it is a highly stylized document that far exceeds a record of Polycarp's arrest, trial, and death. The entailment of this genre distinction would be that the work is therefore not a reliable account of what occurred, and hence not representative of events that may have taken place in late second-century Christianity in Smyrna. However, because Martyrdom goes into great details about the factuality of its account (i.e., 21), giving it a *passio* genre designation—and then interpreting it on this basis—seems artificial to the text's own features.[18]

Moreover, the genre distinction between *acta* and *passio* martyr texts—together with its assumptions regarding the historical/ahistorical merits of the document—has been challenged and mostly dismissed, because most martyr accounts combine features of both genres, as does the Martyrdom of Polycarp.[19] Further problematizing the *passio*/*acta* distinction is that there is good reason for scholarly doubt about whether *acta* before 260 BCE are based on actual trial records or the memory of those who attended the trial; this problematizes the assumption that they are more historically based than *passio* accounts. Because the clear distinction between the *passio* relative to the *acta* cannot be applied to the Martyrdom of Polycarp,[20] a new approach to the genre of the work is required.

A more fruitful way forward with the question of the work's genre begins with the plain recognition that it is a letter between two communities. In terms of it being a letter, Martyrdom includes the features evident in other early Christian texts, namely "a prologue that frames the work in terms of tradition and innovation; third-person, sequential narrative prose with occasional first-person insertions; topographic and ekphrastic digressions; and, significantly, embedded speeches imputed to the narrative's historical actors."[21] Once this letter or epistle framework is in place, the key question is what kind of relationship the author or composer[22] is trying to establish and "exploit" with their audience.[23] Attention

14. C. R. Moss, "Current Trends in the Study of Early Christian Martyrdom," *Bulletin for the Study of Religion* 41.3 (2012): 22.

15. Moss, "Current Trends," 22.

16. L. S. Cobb, *Divine Deliverance: Pain and Painlessness in Early Christian Martyr Texts* (Oakland, CA: University of California Press, 2017), 40.

17. Moss, "Current Trends," 22.

18. Moss, "Current Trends," 22.

19. Moss, "Current Trends," 22.

20. Rebillard, *Greek and Latin Narratives*, 15–21.

21. C. M. Bay, "Exemplarity, Exegesis, & Ethnography: Abraham in Pseudo-Hegesippus as a Test Case for Biblical Reception in Christian Late Antiquity," *JBRec* 8.1 (2021): 37.

22. In this work I will use author(s) and composer(s) interchangeably, and I will assume that such authorship is communal, as I argue later in the work.

23. Cobb, *Divine Deliverance*, 41.

to what the author or composers are doing with reference to the recipient community (at Philomelium) via the Martyrdom of Polycarp—and by what techniques they do it—is key for seeing the genre of the text for what it is.

The intention of the work was to move the minds, emotions, and lives of the story's hearers. "Our understanding of . . . Christian martyr texts," writes Cobb, "is richer when we ask what an author gains from the genre rather than simply identifying the genre."[24] The author of the Martyrdom establishes a sense of intimacy with the audience, and thus can make full use of the "psychological aspects of the genre to good effect."[25] Primary among these psychological tools is the rhetorical technique of *ekphrasis*. *Ekphrasis* is a phenomenon whereby speech is communicated to the audience in such a way that it works "an immediate impact on the mind of the listener, sparking mental images of the subjects it 'placed before the eyes.'"[26] That is, "by activating the images already stored in the listener's mind, the speaker creates a feeling *like* that of a direct perception, a simulacrum of perception itself. It is the *act of seeing* that is imitated, not the object itself, by the creation of a *phantasia* that is like the result of direct perception."[27] The persuasive use of *ekphrasis* in martyrdom literature and its reception was well-known by Christians in the third and fourth centuries. For example, Augustine wrote that when martyr stories were read aloud in church, "I go and watch the martyrs; when the passions of the martyrs are read, I am a spectator, watching them."[28] He further described the audience's passionate involvement as they were addressed by a public reading and commentary on the *Martyrdom of Cyprian*: "We were listening with our ears, attending to it with our minds; we could see him contending, in a way we were afraid for him in his peril, but we trusted God to help him."[29]

In the Martyrdom of Polycarp, such visualizing of the martyrs revolves around Polycarp's exemplarity, and for that reason the work's genre is best understood as hagiography, or better as hagiographical media, as we shall see below.

1.3 Genre and Exemplarity

In Martyrdom of Polycarp 17.3, the celebration-worthiness of Polycarp, together with that of the others who died around the same time, is promoted as the example that the letter writers and recipients should emulate. Polycarp and the other martyrs were "martyrs and disciples of the Lord because of their unsurpassable affection towards their own king and teacher. May we also become both their partners and be fellow disciples." The attributes of Polycarp and the others in the document are clearly exemplary and provide an ideal that can be imitated by other Christians. "Exemplarity," writes Carson Bay, "refers to the ethical and evaluative discourse, typified by the Romans, wherein great figures and deeds from the past come to represent ideal examples [exempla] and norms for the present."[30] In the case of the Martyrdom of Polycarp, an exemplary character is used to persuade the Philomelian church about God's involvement in their lives as they also follow Christ and Polycarp's

24. Cobb, *Divine Deliverance*, 41.

25. Cobb, *Divine Deliverance*, 41.

26. M. Motia, "Three Ways to Imitate Paul in Late Antiquity: Ekstasis, Ekphrasis, Epektasis," *HTR* 114.1 (2021): 107.

27. E. Scarry, *Dreaming by the Book* (New York: Farrar, Straus, and Giroux, 1999), 6, emphases original, cited in Motia, "Three Ways to Imitate Paul," 108.

28. Augustine, *Serm.* III/8, cited in Cobb, *Divine Deliverance*, 8.

29. Augustine, *Serm.* 313A.3, cited in Cobb, *Divine Deliverance*, 4.

30. Bay, "Exemplarity," 36.

examples of suffering rightly according to God's will (17.3).[31] Such intense participation impressed on the audience the need for—and benefits of—adopting Polycarp's beliefs and conduct. A story revolving around an exemplary figure has traditionally been designated as a hagiography, and such a designation has been helpfully applied to the Martyrdom of Polycarp. Paul Hartog, among other scholars, claims that "the narrative is not a report of the *bruta facta* but a theologized work of hagiographical edification intended to form communal character."[32] A hagiography can be transformative because when the audience is transported into the story, they can experience life "outside of social norms" and begin to adopt the realities the stories propose;[33] in addition, the story itself can become a medium for communing with Christ.[34]

In the case of the Martyrdom of Polycarp, however, we need to expand the genre designation beyond saying it is a hagiography.[35] Because the work itself informs readers that the meaning, representation, and power of the text occurs within a broader field of diverse media that includes Polycarp's bones and annual celebrations around his relics, the Martyrdom is best acknowledged as a *letter that functions as hagiographic media*.[36] This genre designation helps understand the Martyrdom as what it intends to be, which is persuasive pedagogical literature that revolves around an exemplary figure. It is carefully crafted to "reshape the historical events and recollection of Polycarp's death for pedagogical purposes."[37]

2. SUMMARY OF CONTENT

2.1 Structure of the Text

Understanding the structure is important for appreciating the flow of the account. The structure of the Martyrdom is comprised of twenty chapters, as well as a number of endings due to its manuscript history.[38] Following chapter 20, there are a number of preserved epilogues, because two of the nine instances of the Martyrdom (BHG 1556–1557) do not belong to the majority of the textual lineage and therefore vary in terms of the text as well as the epilogue.[39] With the exception of these two significant variants, the work is found within "collections containing various readings for saints' days in February, and all belong to the same family (labelled g)."[40] Outside of the text family g, the first of these variants

31. "Exemplarity, ethnography, and exegesis are three forms of cultural practice well known to the ancient Mediterranean world. The use of role models, the 'writing' of peoples, and the interpretation of authoritative writings (i.e. 'Scriptures') were ways in which many authors of Greco-Roman and Judeo-Christian antiquity situated themselves and others within history" (Bay, "Exemplarity," 35).

32. Hartog, "Polycarp's Epistle to the Philippians and the Martyrdom of Polycarp," 239.

33. N. O. Hoel, "Hues of Martyrdom: Monastic and Lay Asceticism in Two Homilies of Gregory the Great on the Gospels," *The Downside Review* 138.1 (2020): 6.

34. C. R. Moss, *The Other Christs: Imitating Jesus in Ancient Christian Ideologies of Martyrdom* (Oxford: Oxford University Press, 2010), 46.

35. The use of the term *hagiography* has been problematized recently by the "new wave hagiographers"; see M. A. Rondolino, "Some Foundational Considerations on Taxonomy: A Case for Hagiography," *Religions* 10.10 (2019): 1–9.

36. On the new wave in hagiography and hagiology, see the essays in M. A. Rondolino, ed., *Religions Journal Special Issue: Comparative Hagiology: Issues in Theory and Method* (Basel: MDPI, 2020), and M. A. Rondolino, *Cross-Cultural Perspectives on Hagiographical Strategies: A Comparative Study of the "Standard Lives" of St. Francis and Milarepa*, Sanctity in Global Perspective (Oxford: Routledge, 2017). For the notion of hagiographic media, see A. T. Hollander, "Hagiography Unbound: A Theory of Making and Using Holy Media," *JAAR* 89.1 (2021): 72–102.

37. For Wilhite, this reshaping is "in order to communicate *imitatio Christi* motifs" (Wilhite, "That We Too Might Be Imitators of Him," 319).

38. Lightfoot, *Apostolic Fathers*, 103.

39. Rebillard, *Greek and Latin Narratives*, 82–83.

40. Parvis, "Martyrdom of Polycarp," 134n126. Rebillard, *Greek and Latin Narratives*, 83.

is the twelfth century "Moscow" or M manuscript, which contains some textual variants yet is most notable for its unique and much longer ending.[41] The second manuscript is a twelfth century manuscript, Konstantia 28 or K, which also has a unique epilogue and "seems to occupy an intermediary position" between M and the majority tradition.[42] These epilogues may equally be later additions or disregarded original endings of the work. They may have been ignored because their record of the "history of transmission" "might have been of no interest to later copyists" of the Martyrdom.[43] In the structural description that follows, I will include discussion of the majority as well as the Moscow endings of the text.

Letter Opening	Greetings from the sending church of Smyrna to the Philomelians
Mart. Pol. 1	Purpose statement: Polycarp's martyrdom described to demonstrate what a "martyrdom according to the gospel" entails
Mart. Pol. 2	Martyrdoms according to God's will are virtuous
Mart. Pol. 3	Germanicus, exemplary martyr
Mart. Pol. 4	Counterexample to Germanicus: Quintus, example of vice
Mart. Pol. 5	Polycarp's passion and martyrdom begins
Mart. Pol. 6	The authorities search for Polycarp, a "sharer with Christ"
Mart. Pol. 7	God's will is done as Polycarp allows himself to be arrested
Mart. Pol. 8	Polycarp remains steadfast in faith as he is transferred to the stadium
Mart. Pol. 9	A heavenly voice encourages Polycarp, who is interrogated
Mart. Pol. 10	Polycarp states he is a Christian despite pressure to venerate Caesar
Mart. Pol. 11	The proconsul threatens Polycarp with temporary, not eternal, torments
Mart. Pol. 12	The stadium's crowd decries Polycarp and demands he be burnt alive
Mart. Pol. 13	The crowd speeds the preparation of a pyre, as Polycarp rests in God
Mart. Pol. 14	Polycarp adores and praises God for the gift of martyrdom
Mart. Pol. 15	The pyre is set alight, yet Polycarp is not consumed by fire
Mart. Pol. 16	Polycarp is slain, a dove exits the pyre as blood overwhelms the fire
Mart. Pol. 17	Christians are denied Polycarp's body, for fear of them worshiping him
Mart. Pol. 18	Polycarp's bones are taken and honored by Christians after his body is burnt
Mart. Pol. 19	Polycarp's martyrdom was exemplary, he enjoys a postmortem life with God
Mart. Pol. 20	Plea to circulate the Martyrdom so that God may be glorified
Mart. Pol. 21	Dates of Polycarp's arrest and death
Mart. Pol. 22	Farewell by Pionius, the copyist who had a vision of postmortem Polycarp
Mart. Pol. 23	Moscow ending: Irenaeus the source of Mart. Pol. and other stories of Polycarp, the copyists in a long chain of transmission

41. Rebillard, *Greek and Latin Narratives*, 83.
42. Rebillard, *Greek and Latin Narratives*, 83.
43. Rebillard, *Greek and Latin Narratives*, 83.

2.2 Working through the Structure

The Martyrdom of Polycarp opens with a theological description of the Smyrnaean composers of the work and its Philomelian recipient audience. One "church of God" writes to another "church of God." Christian identity comes to the fore immediately: both churches are temporary residents in their locales, and belong to the wider "holy and catholic church which resides in every place." The author or composer then anticipates ongoing divine action as the living context for the aforementioned worldwide church: "mercy, peace and love of God the Father and our Lord Jesus Christ be multiplied." Placing the churches and the story to follow in the context of divine love, peace, and mercy will reframe what is otherwise a brutal and horrific story. Rather than allowing this story to generate religious problems and struggles to do with an apparent lack of God's care for Polycarp and the other martyrs mentioned in the text, placing God at the opening of the text allows for a Christian theological retelling of events. Such a retelling will accent God's will and ongoing activity in and through the passion and martyrdom of Polycarp and thereby will encourage the readers to experience and interpret their own suffering in a similar theologically driven manner.

Martyrdom of Polycarp 1

The epistle's purpose is given in this section. The martyrdom stories that will follow, especially Polycarp's, are offered as demonstrations of what "a martyrdom in accordance with the gospel" entails (1.1). What this gospel-consistent martyrdom includes is unpacked as other-person focused love modeled on Jesus's own: "For he waited to be betrayed as also the Lord . . . looking out for . . . the concerns of our neighbours. For true and steadfast love is not only to desire oneself to be saved, but all the brothers as well" (1.2). The intention behind bringing this kind of martyrdom to the attention of the church in Philomelium is that they also may follow the example set forth by Polycarp and the other Smyrnaean martyrs: that "we also might be imitators of him [Polycarp] not only looking out for our own concerns but also the concerns of our neighbours" (1.2). In the account, the term "martyr" is used to refer to Polycarp and others who suffered around the same time. The usage of this term is one of the earliest in Christianity, which in turn shaped its definition: "The least ambiguous use of the term *martyr* as a blood witness and as an imitation (μίμησις) of Christ can be found in the account of Polycarp's martyrdom (*Mart. Pol.* 14.2, ca. 165/170) and in the *Letter of the Churches of Lyons and Vienne* 1.170, ca. 177."[44] Hence, "*martyr* became unequivocally associated with volitional self-sacrifice for Christ (cf. 1 Clem. 5.4, μαρτυρήσας)."[45] Importantly, the honorific designation—martyr—transforms the character of the deceased and involves them on the winning, divine side of a cosmic battle against Satan: "Martyrdom transformed the most savage stigma of their alleged deviance, their public humiliation, degradation and execution as criminals and enemies of mankind, into an opportunity to share Christ's passion and partake directly in the struggle with Satan."[46] Christian identity is once again reinforced for the recipients of the Martyrdom of Polycarp,

---

44. T. J. Heffernan, *The Passion of Perpetua and Felicity* (New York: Oxford University Press, 2012), 145. He immediately adds: "By the end of the second century, it appears that the terms *martyr* and *martyrdom* had become so aligned with the idea of death for the faith that their application to those who had not shed their blood was roundly rejected. See *Ltr Chr Lyons & Vienn* 5.22–4, Tert. *Cor.* 2; Hipp. *Dan.* 2.36.6; and Cypr. *Ep.* 5.2 and his *Laps.* 3–4. Such witnesses were to be called *confessores* (ὁμόλογοι)" (145).

45. Heffernan, *Passion of Perpetua and Felicity*, 145.

46. G. Phillips, "Deviance, Persecution and the Roman Creation of Christianity," *Journal of Historical Sociology* 29.2 (2016): 266.

who understood themselves on the side of the martyr in the story, and against the martyr's enemies: "Martyrdom had a specific meaning for all Christians that marked their group identity out from that of their persecutors."[47]

Martyrdom of Polycarp 2

In this section, martyrdoms according to God's will are described as virtuous: they are approved as "blessed and noble" for the reason that they have occurred "according to the will of God" (Mart. Pol. 2.1). The composer attributes the martyrs' deaths to the will of God because God is the sole ruler over all that eventuates (2.1). In a similar way to God having his great-making properties such as sovereign power, the martyrs have their own admirable virtues: their "nobility, patience and love for the Master" (2.2). The endurance of the martyrs is evidenced by their lack of pain even when the scourging of their bodies is so severe that it affects onlookers. At bottom, the bodies of the martyrs are battlefields on which they warred against the schemes and temptations of the devil. The perseverance they display is more than merely human grit: the martyrs receive their Christ-enabled rewards during the passion of martyrdom. The rewards include the fact that martyrs are not alone during their affliction: "The Lord was standing beside them speaking with them" as they "purchased eternal life," in the wake of the works of Christ and an illumination of the heart that allowed them to see the previously inconceivable good future that awaited them (2.2). Finally, during this process the martyrs experience a form of transhumanism in which they become angels (2.3). The work's description of the martyrs' rewards counterbalances the horrors the narrative describes.

Martyrdom of Polycarp 3

Having described the virtues and cosmic conflict in which martyrs find themselves, Germanicus is introduced as a Christian who embodies exemplary martyrdom. By means of his own perseverance and steadfastness in the face of the proconsul's persuasive efforts, as well as in the arena as he is mauled to death, Germanicus encourages his fellow martyrs to persevere and not give into fear (3.1). However, this positive outcome angers the crowd, which shouts in rage, "Away with the atheists!" as it demands that Polycarp be found out (3.2).

The accusation of atheism may have been the foundational and most serious accusation against Christians.[48] In the Martyrdom, atheism is expressed as Polycarp's refusal to acknowledge and participate in any worship associated with any gods other than his own. Somewhat surprisingly, atheism was a designation that Christians were happy to acknowledge, both for themselves as well as for their enemies. Christians were atheists with respect to Roman religion, and in turn the opponents of Christianity were atheists in that they denied the revelation of God in the Lord Jesus Christ and in the Holy Spirit.[49]

---

47. Phillips, "Deviance," 266. Phillips also writes that "persecution similarly marked out the distinct boundaries of Christian theology, ensuring its ultimate commitment to monotheism (and thereby halting the drift to henotheism) and shaping its scriptures" (266).

48. Keresztes writes that "the most basic and important charge was 'atheism'" (P. Keresztes, "The Emperor Hadrian's Rescript to Minucius Fundanus," *Phoenix* 21.2 [1967]: 124). Keresztes makes his case in part by drawing on Eusebius's description of mass violence against Christians in Lyon (Lugdunum), as well as from the Mart. Pol. itself. See also C. R. Moss, "Infant Exposure and the Rhetoric of Cannibalism, Incest, and Martyrdom in the Early Church," *JECS* 29.3 (2021): 344–46.

49. T. Whitmarsh, "'Away with the Atheists!' Christianity and Militant Atheism in the Early Empire," in *Christianity in the Second Century*, ed. J. Carleton Paget and J. Lieu (Cambridge: Cambridge University Press, 2017), 285.

Martyrdom of Polycarp 4

Because he was a "coward," Quintus is a vivid counterexample and foil to the exemplary Germanicus and the martyrs of chapter 2. He serves as a warning to readers because his vices (pride and cowardice) prevent him from attaining eternal life via martyrdom, as well as experiencing Christ and his mercies on the way to becoming suprahuman in the course of temporary suffering (2.2–3). Therefore, Quintus is a tragic figure because of what he fails to achieve and receive. More seriously still, he is a dangerous figure because he had encouraged other Christians to volunteer for martyrdom irrespective of whether God had called them to such a fate. For this reason, the text warns listeners that "the gospel does not so teach" that people voluntarily offer themselves up for martyrdom. The double emphasis on Quintus's place of origin, in describing him as a "Phrygian, recently having come from Phrygia" seems deliberate given that geographical details have not been provided for Germanicus or the unnamed martyrs, or Polycarp so far. The significance of this for understanding the theology of the work has been emphasized and seen as decisive for some scholars. For example, Dehandschutter argued that the overall theology of the Martyrdom is decidedly set against a form of "pre-Montanism."[50] However, given Polycarp's prophetic activity and the dynamic actions of God in the text, such purported resistance to a pre-Montanist theology is not clearly evident.

Martyrdom of Polycarp 5

Polycarp's passion and martyrdom begins as Polycarp hears about the search for him, and though he is unperturbed by it, he is encouraged to flee to the countryside. Away from the city, though he is in the company of other Christians, Polycarp's attention is on God as he prays for the universal church both day and night (Mart. Pol. 5.1). Polycarp's piety is at the forefront of how he is depicted, clearly establishing him as a Christian of virtue and communion with God: these befit a legitimate martyr (5.1–3). Underscoring Polycarp's character is the claim that these devotional practices have not been brought on by the calamity at hand, but rather his prayerfulness was "his custom" (5.1). The contrast with Quintus could not be clearer: Polycarp has not volunteered for martyrdom, yet when faced with persecution's specter he does not waver in his faith.

Unsurprisingly, in the context of prayer Polycarp is given a glimpse of his fate when he "fell into a trance," in which he saw "his pillow being consumed by fire" (5.2). Based on this insight, he is able to foretell that "I must be burned alive" (5.2). However, this burning will not take place in the manner the audience probably expects at this point in the narrative.

Martyrdom of Polycarp 6

The authorities search for Polycarp, who upon his arrest begins the path to accomplish God's will for him, which was to become a "sharer with Christ" (6.2). Such lofty destiny is a contrast to the "punishment of Judas himself" that awaits those who gave away Polycarp's location under torture (2.1).

Martyrdom of Polycarp 7

God's will is the focus of the scenes presented in chapter 7. Though he could have escaped, Polycarp allows himself to be arrested because his apprehension was the means by which "the will of God be done" (7.1). Polycarp continues to act surprisingly: he calmly acts as a hospitable host toward those who have come to arrest him as if he were "a rebel" (7.2).

---

50. Dehandschutter, "Le Martyre de Polycarpe," 96–97.

The armed authorities are surprised that such a well-disposed old man would demand such furious attention (7.2). Having granted Polycarp's request to be allowed an hour to pray before their departure, they regretfully have to bring that time to a close after two hours (7.3). Once again, the captors are bewildered, both by the goodness of Polycarp and his actions, as well as the order to arrest this kind of person in the first place (7.3).

Martyrdom of Polycarp 8

Polycarp is steadfast in faith as he is transferred to the stadium. He is first seated on a donkey and enters the city on "a great Sabbath" (8.1). After being relocated to a carriage, Polycarp is harassed by the persuasive efforts and rough treatment of the police chief in particular (8.2). The story's hearers presumably could not help but wince when the elderly Polycarp is finally ejected from the carriage with such disregard that his leg is harmed (8.3). However, pity is quickly overwhelmed by a sense of dread when it is revealed that the stadium's chaotic clambering could be heard from a distance (8.3).

Martyrdom of Polycarp 9

Though it has previously been stated that "no one could be heard" due to the commotion within the stadium, "there was a voice from heaven" that spoke to Polycarp: "Be strong, Polycarp, and be a man!" (9.1). The divine voice is only audible to Christians, consistent with the theme that only the Christians in the story are privy to unique experiences of God and communication with him in the course of their sufferings.

The crowd's uproar is once again sparked off when Polycarp enters the stadium and it hears that he had been arrested (Mart. Pol. 9.1). As such, the crowd's clamoring brackets the divine encouragement Polycarp received—this raises the tension in the narrative and raises the prospect that the crowd may overwhelm Polycarp and God's will. A more formal process of identification and interrogation begins as the proconsul asks Polycarp to identify himself and then attempts to persuade Polycarp to "recant." A number of persuasive tactics are employed, the proconsul saying, "Have respect for your age." The interrogation continues with other similar exhortations. The content of recanting as well as the requirement for freedom from a horrific death are laid before Polycarp: "Swear by the fortune of Caesar, repent, say 'Away with the atheists!'" (9.2). Without hesitation, and "with a serious face," Polycarp turns the accusation onto the crowd: "Away with the atheists!" Polycarp's determination to face his trial "with a serious face," possibly echoes the decisive moment in Jesus's passion when—in light of his own passion predictions—"as the time approached for him to be taken up to heaven, Jesus resolutely set out for Jerusalem" (Luke 9:51).[51] Polycarp had also made his own passion prediction (Mart. Pol. 5.2), knew he had to suffer, and the ongoing references to the stadium reinforce this fact; Polycarp's suffering is framed by Jesus's passion narratives.

Because it is preceded by Polycarp directing his gaze toward heaven, his cry, "Away with the atheists!" is a condemnation and a judgment on the "lawless" anti-Christ mobs. The judgment that awaits the crowd has already been described as "the fire which is eternal and never quenched" (Mart. Pol. 2.3). Loyalty to Christ comes to the fore, as the proconsul presses Polycarp to "revile Christ" in exchange to his freedom (9.3). Polycarp's reason for why he will not revile Christ—and by extension why he could not venerate nor show any

51. In light of Jesus's own passion predictions, Luke 9:51 points out that "Jesus is now conscious that he must suffer, and 'Jerusalem' becomes a symbol of this fact" (I. H. Marshall, *The Gospel of Luke: A Commentary on the Greek Text*, NIGTC [Grand Rapids: Eerdmans, 1978], 401).

allegiance to Caesar—is given as "eighty-six years I have served him [Christ] and he has done me no wrong. How could I blaspheme my king who saved me?" (9.3).

Polycarp makes the point that he is not an anti-authoritarian, quasi-Cynic or an anarchist. Rather, he respects the proconsul and has "been taught to render honour, as fitting, to rulers and authorities under God, if it does not hurt us" (10.2). Therefore, for Polycarp, honoring Caesar and other authorities such as the proconsul was not problematic per se; rather, the issue is that the degree of honor required for the Caesar would displace the primary honor and allegiance given to the Christian God. It would "hurt" the Christians to honor Caesar in a way that would undermine acknowledging the honor and rulership of God. Reviling Christ would also hurt them. The use of the word "hurt" is important here: Polycarp has already stated that Christ has done him "no wrong" and moreover has saved him, so how could he possibly bring about the hurt involved in denying Christ—either implicitly or explicitly?

Martyrdom of Polycarp 10

Despite acknowledging the limited obedience and honor that Polycarp can offer the authorities (in line with Rom 13:1–6 and 1 Pet 2:13–17), the battle of wills between himself and the proconsul continues. The proconsul persists with the demand that Polycarp "swear by the fortune of Caesar" (Mart. Pol. 10.1). Polycarp then claims that it is his identity that impedes him from honoring Caesar in the way demanded of him: "You pretend to be ignorant of who I am, listen plainly, I am a Christian." This identity claim, "I am a Christian," was widespread in early Christian martyr accounts and functions as a defining claim because it indicates the impossibility of a Christian doing things that are contrary to their Christian nature. For example, in the diary portion of the *Passion of Perpetua and Felicity* (ca. 203 CE), Perpetua responds to her father's demand that she "change her mind," with "see this vase lying there. . . . Can it be called by any other name than what it is? . . . So it is the same with me: I cannot be called anything but what I am, a Christian."[52] Shortly thereafter, having been brought before the procurator Hilarianus and asked to "make the sacrifice for the health of the emperors" (*Passion of Perpetua* 6.3), Perpetua states "I will not," and the reason given is, "I am a Christian" (6.4). For Perpetua, "the name 'Christian' now identifies her most profound sense of self."[53] The same sense of a Christian self is likely true for Polycarp, as the Martyrdom of Polycarp is a likely source for the *Passion of Perpetua and Felicity*.[54] Importantly, a "subtle Christological point" is made by the designation Christian: it is a recognition that they have "now become one with the body of Christ that Paul proclaimed (Gal 2.20; Col 1.24)."[55] The negative side of the christologically generated identity and unity that Christians experienced was that it could invite a death sentence. Identifying oneself as Christian was, "since Trajan's rescript to Pliny (112 CE), . . . a necessary first step in the legal proceedings that could lead to their deaths. There is ample evidence that a declaration of creedal affiliation and, in particular, an acknowledgement that one was Christian, could provoke a capital charge."[56] In other words, by claiming to be a Christian, Polycarp initiates the events that would condemn him to death (Mart. Pol. 12.1) and that fulfill his words that he would be "burned alive" (5.2).

A moment of humor to do with persuasion follows: in the face of attempts to persuade

52. *Passion of Perpetua*, 3.1–2, in Rebillard, *Greek and Latin Narratives*, 307.
53. Heffernan, *Passion of Perpetua and Felicity*, 153.
54. Heffernan, *Passion of Perpetua and Felicity*, 139.
55. Heffernan, *Passion of Perpetua and Felicity*, 153.
56. Heffernan, *Passion of Perpetua and Felicity*, 157. Heffernan cites Justin Martyr, *1 Apol.* 4.4, as evidence.

him to deny the Christian faith and show allegiance to Caesar, Polycarp offers to teach the proconsul about the Christian faith. The implication is that the proconsul would likely become a Christian too. The proconsul deflects the question by telling Polycarp to "persuade the people" instead. Somewhat surprisingly, Polycarp insults the crowd as a mob undeserving of persuasion (Mart. Pol. 10.2).

Martyrdom of Polycarp 11

The proconsul threatens Polycarp with "beasts," stating that "unless you repent," "I will throw you to them." This is no empty threat, as Germanicus had very recently been killed by a beast (Mart. Pol. 3.1). Polycarp makes fun of the proconsul's use of "repent": Polycarp makes the point that repenting should lead away from bad things and toward good things; this would not be the case if Polycarp repented of his faith, because the fate of "the ungodly" is "the fire of the coming judgement and eternal punishment" (11.2). After being threatened with fire, Polycarp bids the proconsul to carry out his plans.

Martyrdom of Polycarp 12

The significance of Polycarp's claim to be a Christian becomes evident as the proconsul's herald is sent "into the middle of the stadium to proclaim three times: 'Polycarp has confessed himself to be a Christian'" (Mart. Pol. 12.1). By this proclamation, the crowd is stirred into a frenzy, their "rage" being a chaotic contrast to Polycarp's demeanor, who was "filled with courage and joy, and his face was full of grace . . . he did not collapse" (12.2). The "grace of Christ" may be behind this supernatural affect, as may the promise that martyrs become angels (2.3), in which case Polycarp is beginning to undergo a supernatural transfiguration of his own.

On hearing the herald's news, the stadium's crowd gives an answer to the question that has bubbled away under the surface of the document so far: Why is Polycarp such a high-profile target for the authorities? "This is the teacher of Asia, the father of the Christians, the destroyer of our gods, who teaches many not to offer sacrifice or worship" (Mart. Pol. 12.2). Hearing that he is to be burned alive, Polycarp turns "to those faithful ones with him" and reiterates the fate he had "prophetically" foreseen in the trance: "I must be burned alive" (12.3). This fulfillment serves to confirm the narrative's underlying theology that God is in control even of the minutiae of the events that are taking place, despite the frightening rage of the crowd and the temporal power of Polycarp's enemies.

Martyrdom of Polycarp 13

Eager to speed Polycarp's demise, the crowd is rapidly involved in the preparation of a pyre. The rush is contrasted with the measured description of Polycarp as he undresses: he was in full possession of his faculties and accepted his fate. The high regard in which he was held by the Christian community is revealed in the detail that he was not used to removing his own shoes, as others volunteered to do this for him so that they might take the opportunity to come into contact with his body (Mart. Pol. 13.2). Polycarp's virtues are given the reason behind the urge to touch him: "For he had been adorned with every good thing because of his way of life, even before his martyrdom" (13.2). Polycarp's strengths are apparently magnified by his refusal to be nailed in place within the pyre. However, it is quickly apparent that it is the strength of another person—Christ—who will allow him to die stoically in the flames: "He who allows me to endure the fire will allow me to remain in the fire" (13.3). The identity of the greater one has been mentioned earlier in the text: it is "the Lord," "standing beside [and] speaking with them" (2.2).

Martyrdom of Polycarp 14

Polycarp is bound "just like a choice ram . . . for sacrifice," a bound victim, "a whole burnt offering, made ready and acceptable to God" (Mart. Pol. 14.1). The theological significance of Polycarp's martyrdom occurring on a "great Sabbath" (8.1; 21.1) becomes clear: he is being sacrificed by the will of God for the good of others. This interpretation of Polycarp's death is precisely what the introduction to the work has claimed: like the Lord Jesus Christ, Polycarp embodied "true and steadfast love," which is "not only to desire oneself to be saved but all the brothers as well" (1.2). Echoes of Johannine Christology—in which dying for one's friends is an expression of love for them and for Christ—run throughout this section.[57] Polycarp is not only the victim in the scene but appears to lift up a high-priestly prayer of his own. He honors God and then thanks him for the vocation he has received according to God's will and that will result in a great reward for Polycarp. Martyrdom is both a vocation and a gift. Polycarp will "receive a share among the number of the martyrs in the cup of Christ, to the resurrection of life eternal, both soul and body, in the immortality of the Holy Spirit" (14.2). By means of this explication, Polycarp expands on earlier promises of the eternal life that awaits the martyrs. His statement is also an important vista into second-century Smyrnaean soteriology and eschatology, as well as into the likely sources for these beliefs. A christological segment rounds out Polycarp's prayer to God. In this, Polycarp's own "high-priestly prayer" is placed in a secondary relation to Christ, who is described as "the eternal and heavenly high priest," through whom Polycarp has access to God (14.3).

Martyrdom of Polycarp 15

The pyre is set alight, and the fire roars to life. However, the Christian witnesses "beheld a miracle" (Mart. Pol. 15.1): Polycarp is surrounded by fire rather than burnt by it. His body resembles elements which hold their form in heat—a loaf in an oven or metals in the furnace (15.2). Not only is he not consumed by fire, but a special aroma is also generated: "an intense fragrance, like the scent of incense or . . . precious spice" (15.2).

Martyrdom of Polycarp 16

Because Polycarp was not burned by the flames, he is slain with a dagger. A miracle occurs immediately: "A dove came out." Strikingly, another miracle immediately follows the first: a gushing flow of blood overwhelms the fire (Mart. Pol. 16.1). These miracles suggest divine endorsement of Polycarp's martyrdom. The result is that the crowd "was astonished that there was such a difference between the unbelievers and the elect" (16.1). Polycarp is presented as a prime example of those who are elect (16.2).

Martyrdom of Polycarp 17

The devil impedes the Christian community's desire to collect Polycarp's body, primarily by manipulating the local authorities into refusing the request. Their proposed rationale is that perhaps Polycarp would become an object of worship, perhaps even displacing "the crucified one" in Christian devotion (Mart. Pol. 17.2). The perceived potential for supplanting Christ causes the document's editors to make the comment that Christ could never be deposed because only he "suffered for the salvation of the whole world of those who are saved, the blameless for the sinful . . . the Son of God" (17.2–3). The commentor immediately makes the caveat that the worship of Christ does

57. Moss, *Other Christs*, 46–51.

not require relegating the martyrs to an unimportant status: "We love the martyrs as disciples and imitators of the Lord . . . because of their unsurpassable affection towards their own king and teacher" (17.3). This high regard for the martyrs is aspirational and has a profound influence on other believers: "May we also become both their partners and be fellow disciples" (17.3). This catena likely echoes Paul's charge that the Corinthian Christians imitate him as he imitated the Lord: "Follow my example, as I follow the example of Christ" (1 Cor 11:1).

Martyrdom of Polycarp 18

Polycarp is finally burned as a way of ending the conflict over who has access to the body. The narrator employs the "we" voice to include themselves in the party that finally collects Polycarp's bones and takes them away to a suitable place. It will be at this unnamed location that the narrator tells the audience that they hope to celebrate the one-year anniversary of Polycarp's martyrdom. The purpose of this celebration is recalling the memory of "those who have already competed" as well as "of those who are about to compete; both those in training and those in preparation" (Mart. Pol. 18.3). This statement informs how the Martyrdom is to be understood too: it serves both as a memory of Polycarp's honorable martyrdom "according to the gospel" (19.1), as well as being for the edification and encouragement of those who will experience similar ordeals.

Martyrdom of Polycarp 19

As if to underline the points made immediately above about the importance and ongoing helpfulness of Polycarp the martyr, the exemplary nature of Polycarp's martyrdom is christologically rooted as "in accordance with the gospel of Christ," and as such it is a "martyrdom all desire to imitate" (Mart. Pol. 19.1). Though he is a powerful role model, Polycarp does not merely belong to the realm of memory through relics and martyr stories: he is vitally alive with God and his Christ in the present (19.2).

Martyrdom of Polycarp 20

The author begins to close the epistle by stating that the story they have just told serves as a sufficient account of what took place, and hence they have fulfilled their responsibility to respond to the Philomelian church's request for news about Polycarp. Interestingly, the author states that what has been "explained in summary" comes by way of Marcion.

A counter-request is then placed upon the readers that they may circulate the epistle to other Christians in order that God may be glorified by considering what he accomplished through his elect. A doxology develops the goal of glorifying God: "And to him who is able to bring us all in his grace and gift, to his heavenly kingdom, by his one and only child, Jesus Christ, be glory, honour, power and majesty forever" (Mart. Pol. 20.2). Greetings follow, particularly from Evarestus, "who wrote this" (20.2).

Martyrdom of Polycarp 21

Dates of Polycarp's arrest and death are provided. His martyrdom was "on the second day of the first part of the month of Xanthicus, the seventh day before the calends of March, a great Sabbath." The time is given as approximately two o'clock in the afternoon. The arrest by Herod took place within the high priesthood of Philip of Tralles and during the proconsulate of Statius Quadratus—yet these were subject to the rule of Christ. A doxology to Jesus Christ follows, somewhat mirroring the doxology to God in 20.2, "to whom be glory, honor, majesty, and an eternal throne from generation to generation" (21.1).

Martyrdom of Polycarp 22

A farewell is offered, in which the logic of martyrdom is described as a way of life according to God's electing will, the word of Christ, and the example of Polycarp: to "walk in the word of Jesus Christ in accordance with the gospel . . . for salvation, that of his [God's] holy elect, just as the blessed Polycarp was martyred. . . . May it be granted to us to be found in his footsteps in the kingdom of Christ" (Mart. Pol. 22.1). This christologically oriented view of martyrdom is framed by reference to the Father and the Spirit (22.1).

Though the story of Polycarp's martyrdom is over, he is prominent in this (often final) portion of the Martyrdom. Polycarp's influence on the propagation of his martyrdom continued after his death. First, his disciple Irenaeus was the source of Gaius's version of the story. Second, as an extension of Polycarp's life beyond the grave (19.2), he directed Pionius to a copy of the work via a "vision." Pionius then expresses his hope that just as he collected the worn-out pages of Socrates's text, so may he be collected into the Lord Jesus Christ's kingdom, whom he honors in the context of the Father and the Spirit once again (22.3). This threefold, non-oppositional adoration of the Father, Son, and Spirit suggests an implicit, pragmatically oriented Trinitarianism in the second-century Smyrnaean church.[58]

Martyrdom of Polycarp 23

This is the "Moscow ending, the 'longer final coda.'"[59] It fits coherently with the earlier part of the work, as Polycarp is the central focus of the action, as is Irenaeus, who is the source of much of what is known of Polycarp the person and the Martyrdom of Polycarp itself. Gaius, mentioned in 22.2, serves as an organic link between Polycarp and Irenaeus. He is Polycarp's disciple as well as Irenaeus's fellow townsman in Rome for a time. The author writes that Irenaeus was in Rome at the time of Polycarp's martyrdom, and while there Irenaeus battled against heresy as well as passed on to others the "received . . . ecclesiastical and catholic rule from the holy one" (23.3).[60]

Irenaeus also related to Gaius the story of when Polycarp was approached by Marcion for approval, while they also were both in Rome. Polycarp not only refused to recognize Marcion as a fellow Christian but rather stated: "I recognize you, the firstborn of Satan" (Mart. Pol. 23.4). The strength of the relationship between Irenaeus and Polycarp is suggested by the fact that when Polycarp was martyred far away from Irenaeus, he heard "a trumpet blast, saying 'Polycarp has been martyred.'" A history of transmission follows, as does a doxology that closely parallels the one ending the previous section (22.3).

3. INTERPRETATIVE ISSUES

3.1 Why the Interpretation of the Martyrdom of Polycarp Matters to Scholars Today

Given the range of debated points and speculative solutions to do with the text of the Martyrdom of Polycarp, one might be tempted to wonder why researchers, students, and even everyday Christians would bother with a text such as the Martyrdom. Though a number of reasons could be adduced, I will restrict myself to the primary one. The key reason

58. Naturally, the doxologies noted above are "not as succinct as polished Trinitarian declarations would become" (Hartog, "Polycarp's Epistle to the Philippians and the Martyrdom of Polycarp," 240).

59. Parvis, "Martyrdom of Polycarp," 134n126.

60. This "ecclesiastical and catholic rule" may be Irenaeus's well-known "rule of faith," for which he claimed a universally binding rule in catholic churches. The rule begins with the statement that "for the Church, though dispersed throughout the whole world, even to the ends of the earth, has received from the apostles and their disciples this faith . . ." (Irenaeus, *Haer.* 1.2, cited in J. Stevenson, *A New Eusebius: Documents Illustrating the History of the Church to AD 337* [London: SPCK, 1987], 111).

the work matters is that if it does describe real events and conveys them according to how early Christians understood them, then readers have access to how the reception of Jesus's teaching by the first generation of Christians was deployed for belief and practice and then subsequently passed on to Christians in the late second century, such as Irenaeus. If the Martyrdom is authentic in terms of the events and theologies it describes, then one can say that scholars then have evidence of authentic transmission of belief between the followers of St. John and St. Paul in the late first century and early second century on the one hand, to late second-century figures such as Irenaeus and Justin Martyr on the other.

> It is not too strong to say that the whole notion of an unbroken doctrinal tradition accessible to us now . . . depends on what we can securely say about Polycarp. If the Apostolic Fathers are generally thought of as the bridge between New Testament times and the emergence of the great Christian writers of the latter half of the second century such as Justin Martyr and Irenaeus, it is Polycarp who holds that bridge together, since he is uniquely claimed to have spanned the whole period with his own life, knowing the apostles in his youth, and Irenaeus in his old age.[61]

3.2 Polycarp: His Connections to Pauline and Johannine Influences

The question of how Polycarp relates to other early Christians, including Jesus's disciples and their first-generation followers, has stimulated research into who Polycarp the person was; the results of one's research on this matter will shape how the Martyrdom is viewed. Scholars have access to the ways in which Polycarp was remembered and interpreted by various early Christian communities, including in the Martyrdom itself,[62] each of which provides a unique impression of Polycarp.[63] This does not mean that we have no access to Polycarp's mind or the impact that he made on his contemporaries. For example, Polycarp's *To the Philippians*, securely attributed to Polycarp and dated to 110–120 CE, provides important insights into Polycarp's use of Pauline theology and practices.[64] Perhaps what is most significant for this present work is that Polycarp is related to both Paul as well as John and their disciples, such as Irenaeus. Hence a study of portrayals of Polycarp is an important part of the study of how canonical works may have influenced him and played both implicit as well as explicit roles in his surviving works and works like the Martyrdom. In other words, how Polycarp's exemplary martyrdom is related to sources such as John and Paul is an important aspect of the question of what the role of the New Testament is in the Apostolic Fathers, including the Martyrdom of Polycarp.

An important strand of tradition associated Polycarp with John, based on the account of Irenaeus. The best known and studied sources to do with Polycarp's life and martyrdom include Irenaeus's second-century references in *Adversus haereses*, which portray Polycarp as the orthodox defender of legitimate Christianity.[65] The fourth-century historian Eusebius of Caesarea includes a shortened version of the Martyrdom of Polycarp in his

---

61. Parvis, "Martyrdom of Polycarp," 126.

62. Buschmann, *Das Martyrium des Polykarp*, 38.

63. Dehandschutter, "Polycarpiana," 260.

64. The reasons for attributing *To the Philippians* to Polycarp are covered in P. Hartog, *Polycarp's Epistle to the Philippians and the Martyrdom of Polycarp: Introduction, Text, and Commentary*, OAF (Oxford: Oxford University Press, 2013), 40–45.

65. *Haer.* 3.3.4. Jerome presents Polycarp as a defender of orthodoxy who argued against the teachings of Marcion and Valentinus (*Vir. ill.* 17). On the polemical use of Polycarp for the sake of Christian orthodoxy, see J. Hoover, "False Lives, False Martyrs: 'Pseudo-Pionius' and the Redating of the Martyrdom of Polycarp," *VC* 67 (2013): 471–98, esp. 490–96.

Historia ecclesiastica, after introducing Polycarp's visit to Rome to discuss the proper date of Easter with Pope Anicetus—as told by Irenaeus.[66]

In these works, Polycarp was related to key personal sources of ancient Christian literature. Irenaeus, for example, presents Polycarp as an important link between the earliest Jesus traditions and their reception by early Christian communities because of his relationships with members of the first generation of Jesus's disciples, especially John.[67] For Irenaeus, the importance of Polycarp also lay in the fact that he knew other Christians of his own generation who were also acquainted with Jesus's heirs and teachings, such as Florinus.[68] There may also be a non-Irenaean source, or sources, that emphasizes Polycarp's relationship and affinity with Paul rather than John.[69] This connection with Pauline thought and ministries would make sense, given how heavily Polycarp's *To the Philippians* draws on Paul, a dependence that is very stark relative to the ten other works in the Apostolic Fathers collection.[70]

Polycarp may also be related to others beside Paul, John, and Florinus,[71] for example the Synoptic Gospels and Hebrews. The current state of scholarship requires open-mindedness about what sources may be at work as frameworks and sources for depictions of Polycarp and his martyrdom, because further work needs to be carried out on a third- or fourth-century *Vita Policarpi*,[72] and a *Life of Polycarp* written by the year 400 CE,[73] as well as the Harris Fragments.[74] Three later, likely sixth-century receptions of earlier traditions about Polycarp speak to his ongoing influence as well as the pliability of his character.[75] The significance of the theological and exegetical schools upon Polycarp the person, as well as the Martyrdom of Polycarp's writers and composers, is especially felt in the debates about the historical and/or theological nature of the text, to which we turn next.

3.3 The Factual, Historical Nature of the Incidents Described in the Martyrdom of Polycarp

The author of the Martyrdom of Polycarp and later redactors include details about the time and date on which Polycarp was martyred, as well as under whose reign as well as high priesthood it took place (Mart. Pol. 21.1). These indicate an appreciation for the factuality of the event, suggesting that the story is not a folk tale. On the other hand, immediately

66. Eusebius, *Hist. eccl.* 4.14–15.

67. Hartog points out that Irenaeus links Polycarp with John in *Haer.* 3.3.4 and 5.33.4, as do Irenaeus's "Letter to Victor" and "Letter to Florinus" as preserved in Eusebius's *Hist. eccl.* 5.24.11–17 and 5.20.4–8 respectively (Hartog, "Polycarp's Epistle to the Philippians and the Martyrdom of Polycarp," 226).

68. Hartog, "Polycarp's Epistle to the Philippians and the Martyrdom of Polycarp," 226–27.

69. J. Lookadoo, "Categories, Relationships and Imitation in the Household Codes of 1 Clement, Ignatius and Polycarp: A Comparison with Household Codes in the Pauline Corpus," *Neotestamentica* 53.1 (2019): 47.

70. P. Foster, "The Text of the New Testament in the Apostolic Fathers," in *The Cambridge Companion to the Apostolic Fathers*, ed. M. Bird and S. Harrower (Cambridge: Cambridge University Press, 2021), 117; Lookadoo, "Categories."

71. Hartog, *Polycarp's Epistle to the Philippians and the Martyrdom of Polycarp*, 5. Dehandschutter, "Polycarpiana," 259n252. See also A. Stewart-Sykes, *The Life of Polycarp. An Anonymous Vita from Third-Century Smyrna*, Early Christian Studies 4 (Sydney: St. Pauls, 2002).

72. Hartog, *Polycarp's Epistle to the Philippians and the Martyrdom of Polycarp*, 5.

73. Rebillard, *Greek and Latin Narratives*, 85–86.

74. Rebillard, *Greek and Latin Narratives*, 82–83. Rebillard is noncommittal when it comes to Weidmann's speculation about these channeling a third-century source, believing these fragments and the history of reception they reflect require further study in order to come to surer conclusions (Rebillard, *Greek and Latin Narratives*, 82; F. W. Weidmann, *Polycarp and John: The Harris Fragments and Their Challenge to the Literary Traditions* [Notre Dame: University of Notre Dame Press, 1999]).

75. Rebillard, *Greek and Latin Narratives*, 81. Dehandschutter, "Polycarpiana," 259–60, 264. On Polycarp's "hagiographical dossier," see Rebillard, *Greek and Latin Narratives*, 81.

after pointing out the historical markers for the events described in the work, the author adds that all that occurred took place during the larger context of the more impressive reign of Christ (21.1). Because the facts of history and their theological context are found together in the document, there is a stark range of scholarly opinion on the historicity of the account, as well as the usefulness of the Martyrdom itself for indicating its historical setting and factuality.

Ironically, by preserving much of Polycarp's martyrdom in his own abridged account of it, Eusebius of Caesarea provided purported evidence that has been deployed by some modern scholars in order to undermine the Martyrdom's historicity. How one explains the shortened version of the text in Eusebius's account, versus the longer extant manuscripts of the Martyrdom, is decisive for—and probably reflects preconceptions about—the historical veracity of the events described in the work. Recent study has moved away from a merely source-critical investigation of the text, critiquing the arbitrary and speculative nature of such an approach to the Martyrdom.[76] Most importantly, the differences between the Martyrdom and Eusebius's account of Polycarp's martyrdom can be reasonably put down to Eusebius mostly summarizing the story, as he did with other events.[77] Hence, "Eusebius does not provide a testimony of an independent and earlier version of MPol."[78] This means that the work as we have it from non-Eusebian sources no longer needs to be treated as an artificial elaboration of earlier events and is thus open to being researched on its own internal literary terms and merits.[79] This literary approach is enriched by the fact that the Martyrdom can be securely placed and hence studied within the second-century context.

Historically, Lightfoot argued that there was significant second-century external evidence for the existence of the document from Irenaeus, Polycrates, the *Letter of the Galician Churches*, and Lucian's *Peregrinus Proteus*.[80] Sara Parvis, on the other hand, complements Lightfoot's approach by turning to the internal evidence within the Martyrdom of Polycarp. Parvis ranks it as a reliable second-century text and thus a genuine reflection of the events described, albeit through the theological perspective of the Christian authors. To her mind, the Martyrdom is plausible as a genuine second-century reflection of events, because other rival theories fail to be convincing, and additionally the text has all the hallmarks of a second-century document.[81] Consequently, the internal evidence within the text accurately locates the action and actors it describes, and hence she writes that its historical merits are the strongest among the best-known post-apostolic works.[82] Though Candida Moss has been highly skeptical of the work of Parvis and others who share her conclusions,[83] recent scholarship has pointed out the reasonability of the historical case for a second-century composition, and factuality of, the Martyrdom.[84] This is not to say that it is not shaped by theological concerns and ideas in contradistinction to Roman and Jewish piety—it is, and profoundly so.[85] Such an approach also does not mean ignoring important

76. Parvis makes some excellent points in this regard ("Martyrdom of Polycarp," 135–36).

77. Rebillard, *Greek and Latin Narratives*, 82.

78. Rebillard, *Greek and Latin Narratives*, 82.

79. G. Buschmann, *Martyrium Polycarpi—Eine formkritische Studie: Ein Beitrag zur Frage nach der Entstehung der Gattung Märtyrerakte*, BZNW 70 (Berlin: de Gruyter, 1994), 196–98.

80. Lightfoot, *Apostolic Fathers*, 103.

81. Parvis, "Martyrdom of Polycarp," 126, 145–46.

82. Parvis, "Martyrdom of Polycarp," 126, 145–46.

83. C. R. Moss, "On the Dating of Polycarp: Rethinking the Place of the Martyrdom of Polycarp in the History of Christianity," *Early Christianity* 1.4 (2010); Moss, *Other Christs*, 196–97.

84. Hartog, "Polycarp's Epistle to the Philippians and the Martyrdom of Polycarp," 239–40.

85. Hartog, "Polycarp's Epistle to the Philippians and the Martyrdom of Polycarp," 240–41.

issues in the text; for example, the miraculous events of chapter 16 must be reckoned with as either intrinsic to the supernatural worldview that permeates the document, or as per Lightfoot, a "later interpolation."[86] These questions to do with historicity naturally require a discussion of the work's theology, to which we turn next.

3.4 Theology

As the doxologies at multiple points in the Martyrdom of Polycarp show (20.2; 22.1; 22.3), the structure and contents of the work are set in a unique theological matrix. Polycarp's exemplary martyrdom is interpreted within the worship of the Lord Jesus Christ, God the Father, and the Holy Spirit. The Martyrdom's theology expressed the Smyrnaean church's liturgy as well as the framework for their lived religion.[87]

Because the Martyrdom is highly theological literature, it is important to note both the role(s) that God plays in it and to be aware of the canonical paradigms for divine action on which such theologies draw. Furthermore, the kind of God that God is in the work also seems to draw on uniquely Christian interpretations of divinity in the wake of the life of Christ and the reception of the Spirit at Pentecost. This explains why God is understood in a triadic manner. He is God the Father, who is adored together with his Son, the Lord Jesus Christ, as well as the Holy Spirit. Doxologies are offered to Christ as much as they are to God. The theological dimensions are important for noticing what kind of pressures the work places on its readers and hearers, because the divine action evident in the story is presumed to be the same kind of divine action one can expect in the present audience's worship and Christian vocations.[88] The theological dimensions of martyr texts are the primary reason why they are "religious texts that articulated the continued presence of God among the faithful; through *ekphrasis*, they brought the miraculous deeds of God into the present."[89]

3.5 Dating of Polycarp's Death and Martyrdom of Polycarp's Composition

Taken at face value, and even accounting for some internal contradictions, the details of Martyrdom of Polycarp 21 suggest the date 156–157 CE for Polycarp's demise.[90] Hartog concludes that "a placement between 155–161 seems most plausible."[91] The claim that the Martyrdom is a later work, possibly from the mid-third century,[92] can be dismissed for the reason that the details of the account as well as the style, manner, and aims in composition reflect a mid-second-century date rather than a later one.[93]

86. Lightfoot, *Apostolic Fathers*, 103.

87. Hartog, "Polycarp's Epistle to the Philippians and the Martyrdom of Polycarp," 240.

88. I am adapting this from Rowe's use of theological "pressures" in biblical texts that coerce theological judgments from their listeners. See C. K. Rowe, "Biblical Pressure and Trinitarian Hermeneutics," *Pro Ecclesia* 11.3 (2002): 295–312.

89. Cobb, *Divine Deliverance*, 9. "Christians heard martyr stories within the context of Christian worship and thus their theological meaning must not be underestimated: these stories verified, commented on, and provided further testimony of Christian beliefs. . . . Not only did martyr texts need to be rhetorically effective; they also had to be religiously instructive . . . we must keep in mind the liturgical contexts in which they functioned for earliest Christianity" (Cobb, *Divine Deliverance*, 9).

90. Hartog, "Polycarp's Epistle to the Philippians and the Martyrdom of Polycarp," 241.

91. Hartog, "Polycarp's Epistle to the Philippians and the Martyrdom of Polycarp," 241.

92. Moss, *Other Christs*, 197.

93. "Phillip of Tralles and Statius Quadratus fit nowhere else; the Justin parallels fit nowhere better; the ghetto mentality fits nowhere later so well. The Gospel parallels seem too forced to be invented; the proconsul's actions seem too unusual for polemic. The level of narrative artistry concerning such a recent atrocity may give us pause, but it is an effective means of distancing the narrator from the horror of what is being described" (Parvis, "Martyrdom of Polycarp," 145).

Any claim about the dating of the work's composition needs to account for when the narrative was first composed and then to what degree it was edited later into the form(s) of it that we have today. In terms of its original composition, the author of the Martyrdom claims to be a witness to the martyrdom of Polycarp and hopes to celebrate the "birthday" of Polycarp's martyrdom (18.3). The fact that the author writes that they hope to celebrate Polycarp's birthday in the future could be taken to imply that the document was written within a year of Polycarp's death. Some scholars therefore have argued that the work was composed between 156–160 CE.[94] Lightfoot, for example, concluded that the Martyrdom of Polycarp was "written shortly after the martyrdom itself, which happened A.D. 155 or 156."[95] On the other end of the spectrum on this issue, Moss writes that such an early view of composition is ideologically biased and is only plausible if one takes the Martyrdom of Polycarp to be the first instance of a number of terms that will become technical ones in later Christianity, such as καθολικὴ ἐκκλησία, *katholikē ekklēsia* (preface; 8.1; 16.2; 19.2; relatedly 5.1; 23.2).[96] Moss concludes that though there was a "historical Polycarp who died in Smyrna in the middle of the second century," due to the Martyrdom of Polycarp's use of canonical sources and technical terms, while at the same time leaving no literary footprint until the Decian persecution, the "extant form" of the work "can be dated no earlier than the middle part of the third century and the persecution of Decius."[97] Moss's claims have been refuted by a number of scholars, resulting in a broad consensus that the document's composition took place in the second century.[98]

The question of how many stages of redaction were involved in producing the Martyrdom we have today has received focused scholarly attention.[99] Based on the internal evidence within the document itself, the Martyrdom's literary style and theological purview suggest that it was primarily composed by one author.[100] There may have been later addenda, redactions, and omissions. These changes, however, can be identified in short sections of the story, and do not necessarily warrant the speculative theories that have dominated scholarship on this question. Theories on the history of the "original" materials and later stages of change to the narrative have proven unsuccessful for exalting the features of the document more convincingly than primarily single-author theories, and they struggle at the methodological level. The corporate nature of the document (prologue; 20), however, suggests that its composition may well have been composed as a group effort. An important caveat to note with respect to communal composition is that this does not necessarily mean the work was redacted over multiple generations and hence barely reflects the original source material.[101] However, given the variation that exists within the manuscript tradition, we can agree with Zimbalist that the Martyrdom of Polycarp is best interpreted as comparative hagiographic media, and as such nuance interpretations of it by means of comparative work between diverse manuscript families.[102]

---

94. Dehandschutter, "Le Martyre de Polycarpe," 94.

95. Lightfoot, *Apostolic Fathers*, 103.

96. Moss, "On the Dating of Polycarp," 558.

97. Moss, *Other Christs*, 197.

98. Hartog, "Polycarp's Epistle to the Philippians and the Martyrdom of Polycarp," 237–38.

99. The best-known recent example in this long tradition of scholarship is O. Zweirlein, *Die Urfassungen der Martyria Polycarpi et Pionii und das Corpus Polycarpianum*, Untersuchungen zur antiken Literatur und Geschichte 116 (Berlin: de Gruyter, 2014).

100. Dehandschutter, "Le Martyre de Polycarpe," 94.

101. P. Hartog, "The *Martyrdom of Polycarp* as Communal, Moral Formation," *Science et Esprit* 67.3 (2015): 437–41.

102. B. Zimbalist, "Comparative Hagiology and/as Manuscript Studies: Method and Materiality," *Religions* 10.10 (2019): 2–6.

3.6 "Martyrdom in Accordance with the Gospel"

The Martyrdom of Polycarp frames the death of Polycarp within the larger purposes of God, and it is this theological frame that explains what the document means when it says that Polycarp's death was exemplary because it was "martyrdom in accordance with the gospel." A theocentric perspective on the story's events—including the nature of Polycarp's exemplarity—opens the body of the document: "Nearly all the things that happened previously happened in order that the Lord might demonstrate to us again a martyrdom in accordance with the gospel" (1.1). In other words, God wants to demonstrate what he evaluates positively in terms of martyrdom. At the close of the story, the author repeats that Polycarp's martyrdom was one that "all desire to imitate; it happened in accordance with the gospel of Christ" (19.1). Clues to unpacking what "in accordance with the gospel (of Christ)" means are found immediately after 1.1. The composer writes that the martyr behaved like Christ did in terms of allowing himself to suffer for the good of others, at great cost to himself: "For he [Polycarp] waited to be betrayed as also the Lord, in order that we also might be imitators of him not only looking out for our own concerns but also the concerns of our neighbours. For true and steadfast love is not only to desire oneself to be saved, but all the brothers as well" (1.2).[103]

The Martyrdom's twin ideas of sacrificial suffering for the good of others and of enduring the full extent of the trial *as Christ did* are likely a reflection of Polycarp's own beliefs: "We should persevere unceasingly in . . . Jesus Christ, who bore our sins in his own body on the tree, who committed no sin, and no deceit was found in his mouth, but because of us, in order that we might live in him, endured all things" (Pol. *Phil.* 8.1).[104] Polycarp cemented the notion of the imitation of Christ's virtues in the next line: "Therefore let us be imitators of his endurance, and if we should suffer because of his name, we should glorify him. For this is the example he set for us in himself, and this we have believed" (Pol. *Phil.* 8.2).[105]

The second reference to martyrdom "in accordance with the gospel of Christ" (Mart. Pol. 19.1) is also unpacked with reference to Polycarp's virtues: his "endurance," rejoicing in the context of righteousness, and glorifying God the Father, all of which Jesus does in the course of his ministry (Luke 4:1–13; 10:21; 22:39–46; John 12:27–28). Clearly, then, Jesus's virtues are models for Polycarp's behavior, which in turn are promoted for the moral formation of the Smyrnaeans and Philomelians.[106] Wilhite rightly argues that the Martyrdom's central aim is to present "the death of Polycarp so as to invite the reader towards *imitatio Christi* motifs."[107] What these virtues are more precisely is unpacked by means of how Polycarp models what Jesus himself modeled, as we shall see below. By pointing out that Polycarp was able to embody Jesus's virtues, the work is essentially offering the Smyrnaean and Philomelian churches a more contemporary and locally flavored version of Paul's call to "follow my example, as I follow the example of Christ" (1 Cor 11:1).

3.7 Parallels Between Jesus and Polycarp

Martyrdom accounts are able to promote the imitation of Christ to a greater degree than other Christian hagiographical literature because they can describe the Christlikeness

103. Cf. Dehandschutter, "Le Martyre de Polycarpe," 95.
104. Brannan, *Apostolic Fathers*, 127.
105. Brannan, *The Apostolic Fathers*, 127.
106. Hartog, "*Martyrdom of Polycarp* as Communal, Moral Formation," 447–48.
107. Wilhite, "That We Too Might Be Imitators of Him," 319, 329–32.

of the protagonist in their death as well as their life.[108] The parallels between the final hours of Jesus and Polycarp appear to reinforce the impression that Polycarp's conduct in both his life and death was exemplary because he embodied the same virtues as Christ did in his passion.[109]

There are many parallels to events within Jesus's own passion as well as Jesus's own behavior during the passion. However, the most important concept that generates these story-level parallels is Jesus's teaching on the nature of love in John 13–15, especially when he said:

> My command is this: Love each other as I have loved you. Greater love has no one than this: to lay down one's life for one's friends. You are my friends if you do what I command. I no longer call you servants, because a servant does not know his master's business. Instead, I have called you friends, for everything that I learned from my Father I have made known to you." (John 15:12–15)

Moss writes that "in John, the command to love is redefined in terms of imitation, discipleship and self-sacrifice."[110] John's "readers must love imitatively, following the example of Jesus, by laying down their lives for his or her friends (cf. 1 John 3:16). It is as a consequence of their act of love that they will be recognized by others as disciples (John 13:35) and by Jesus as friends (15:14)."[111] Though the bulk of the parallels are found in Martyrdom of Polycarp 5–7,[112] the parallels between specific events in Jesus's passion and Polycarp's, as well as parallels in terms of virtue, occur throughout the narrative.

Event parallels between Jesus's and Polycarp's passions include that the passions of Jesus and Polycarp take place according to the sovereign will of God (John 12:49; 14:31; Mart. Pol. 2.1); Jesus and Polycarp are both betrayed (Matt 26:48; Mart. Pol. 1.2); there is intense prayer before their arrests (Matt 26:36–44; Mart. Pol. 5.1–2; 7.2–3); Jesus was arrested under the rule of a "Herod," so is Polycarp (Luke 23:7–11; Mart. Pol. 6.2); Jesus's Last Supper—which included Judas—is paralleled by Polycarp's hosting a final meal that included those who would bring about his downfall (Matt 26:21–23; Mart. Pol. 7.2); Jesus was betrayed by Judas, an insider of the discipleship group, so Polycarp is betrayed by a "Judas" (Matt 26:49; Mart. Pol. 6.2); as Jesus was arrested by armed soldiers as an outlaw, so is Polycarp (Matt 26:47, 55; Mart. Pol. 7.1); both Jesus and Polycarp are arrested at night (Matt 26:31, 34; Mart. Pol. 7.1); both Jesus and Polycarp were led to their destinies on donkeys (Matt 21:7; John 12:14–15; Mart. Pol. 8.1); their deaths have sacrificial overtones connected with Passover (Luke 22:15; John 19:14; Mart. Pol. 21.1); both Romans and Jews are involved in the deaths of Jesus and Polycarp (Luke 22:52–23:24; Mart. Pol. 6.2; 8.2; 9.2–11.1; 13.1–2); both Jesus and Polycarp are given opportunities by the authorities to avoid condemnation (Matt 27:11–24; cf. Mart. Pol. 9.2–10.1); both Jesus and Polycarp's bodies are pierced by stabbing (John 19:34; Mart. Pol. 16.1); an unusual form of blood follows the death of both Jesus and Polycarp (John 19:34; Mart. Pol. 16.1); the death of both Jesus and Polycarp are shortly followed by symbolism to do with the future presence of the Holy Spirit among the disciples (Luke 24:49; John 20:22; Mart. Pol. 16.1); distrust

108. F. de Azevedo Ramos, "O martírio de São Policarpo de Esmirna como imitação da Paixão de Jesus Cristo," *Lumen Veritatis* 10.38 (2017): 18.

109. Dehandschutter, "Le Martyre de Polycarpe," 95.

110. Moss, *Other Christs*, 50.

111. Moss, *Other Christs*, 50.

112. Dehandschutter, "Le Martyre de Polycarpe," 95.

and dispute surround the fate of both Jesus's and Polycarp's corpses (Matt 27:58–66; Mart. Pol. 17.1–18.2); a centurion is at the center of confusing events around the deaths of both men (Matt 27:54; Mart. Pol. 18.1).

Virtue parallels between Jesus and Polycarp include a consistently virtuous life: both men are righteous (Matt 3:15; Luke 23:47; Mart. Pol. 17.1); prayerfulness: Jesus and Polycarp are unwavering in appropriate prayer before their capture (Matt 26:36–44; Mart. Pol. 5.1–2; 7.2–3); supernatural knowledge: Jesus and Polycarp are aware of the betrayal before it occurs (Matt 26:23–24; John 13:18–19; Mart. Pol. 1.2); faithfulness to God's will: prior to his passion, Jesus explicitly gave himself over to the will of God, Polycarp does the same (Luke 22:42; Mart. Pol. 7.1); radical hospitality: both Jesus and Polycarp generously host a meal for friends and enemies alike (Matt 26:20–30; Mart. Pol. 7.2); predicting their own deaths: both Jesus and Polycarp predict they would die (Matt 16:21–28; Mart. Pol. 5.2; 12.3); trusting in God's vindication rather than human vindication: neither Jesus nor Polycarp makes the case for their righteousness before the crowd (Luke 22:69; John 16:16; Mart. Pol. 10.2); actually dying as an expression of love for God and for others (John 10:18; 15:12–13; Mart. Pol. 17.3); endurance: both Jesus and Polycarp endure and complete a great trial (John 19:28–30; Mart. Pol. 19.2).

Both event as well as virtue parallels appear to be deliberate rather than merely superficial similarities.[113] It is reasonable to expect that the event parallels between Christ and Polycarp in the narrative were generated by early Christians who were trying to understand and promote Polycarp's death in light of Jesus's behavior.[114] However, the parallels between Polycarp's virtues and Jesus's virtues appear to be the most significant ones for the author's concept of the imitation of Christ (Mart. Pol. 17.3; 19.1).

Focusing on virtue over events, Dehandschutter concludes that the parallels are intended to promote a single virtue—namely, obedience to God: "demonstrating that Polycarp's attitude is in harmony with the will of God and in accordance with the gospel."[115] To his mind, the parallels between the events of Jesus's passion and Polycarp's passion are quite limited and superficial,[116] and not the focus of imitation.[117] Obedience to the will of God is the virtue that both Jesus and Polycarp embody and hence is the virtue of interest for readers of the account. Dehandschutter's reasoning is that the will of God is decisive for the narrative, as argued by the fact that martyrdom is not for those who volunteer to do so but only for those chosen and enabled by God for it. Hence, true martyrdom is a martyrdom that is perfectly conformed to the electing and enabling will of God. The link between the will of God and martyrdom in accordance with the gospel is that when it conforms to the will of God, martyrdom parallels the gospel message of Jesus's own perfect conformity to God's will. For Dehandschutter, God's will is "the sole point of connection between the death of Christ and that of the martyrs; there is no other common ground for their deaths other than the will of God."[118] Dehandschutter's view is helpful for focusing

113. Dehandschutter, "Le Martyre de Polycarpe," 95–96.

114. Dehandschutter, "Le Martyre de Polycarpe," 95–96.

115. My translation of the claim that in the Mart. Pol. "ne veut pas imiter la passion, mais démontrer que l'attitude de Polycarpe est en harmonie avec la volonté de Dieu et conforme à l'évangile" (Dehandschutter, "Le Martyre de Polycarpe," 98).

116. Dehandschutter, "Le Martyre de Polycarpe," 96.

117. Dehandschutter, "Le Martyre de Polycarpe," 98.

118. Dehandschutter, "Le Martyre de Polycarpe," 99. This is my own translation of "La seule relation entre la passion du Christ et celle des martyrs ne peut être que leur origine commune: la volonté de Dieu." Dehandschutter, "Le Martyre de Polycarpe," 99.

on virtues rather than events; however, unfortunately it leaves aside other important virtues in the narrative.

A more productive approach is to recognize that obedience to the will of God—a key christological virtue—is indeed at the forefront of "martyrdom according to the gospel" yet is not the only virtue in mind. This emphasis is coherent with the portrayal of other characters in the narrative; for example, Germanicus, in terms of faithful trust in, and submission to, the will of God rather than to the will of human beings (Mart. Pol. 3.1–4.1).[119] A focus on the importance of the virtues paralleled in Jesus and Polycarp also coheres with the Martyrdom's own claim that the respective achievements of Jesus's and Polycarp's deaths are so different that they *cannot be strictly paralleled*.[120]

Importantly, a focus on virtues rather than events explains the lack of precision between the parallels between Jesus and Polycarp—a precision that has confounded interpreters. If the focus is on virtue parallels, this accounts for the fact that Polycarp is not crucified (13.3), a dissimilarity that undermines the argument for strong parallels between Jesus's and Polycarp's death.[121] Whereas Jesus is nailed to the cross, Polycarp is not held stationary by force as he faces his death. Rather, he is unbound. This fact has generated related issues—for example, Moss claims that the lack of restraints on Polycarp at his death means that relative to Jesus, "Polycarp appears to outperform" him.[122] However, Polycarp is not competing with Jesus. This has been made clear by the contrast between worshiping the Son of God and not Polycarp (Mart. Pol. 17.3), as well as the contrasting presentation of Polycarp as a martyr who is to be imitated (19.1), whereas the Lord Jesus Christ is blessed as "Saviour," "Shipmaster," and "Shepherd of the catholic church throughout the world" (Mart. Pol. 19.2). This contrast does not detract from Polycarp's martyrdom; the reverse is true. Polycarp had successfully embodied Jesus's own obedience to God ("Father, if you are willing, take this cup from me; yet not my will, but yours be done," Luke 22:42). His achievement was to demonstrate what it looks like to imitate Jesus's committed self-giving for the sake of others, as Polycarp wrote to the Philippians: be "self-controlled in all things . . . walk according to the truth of the Lord, who became a servant of all" (Pol. *Phil.* 5.2).[123]

The purpose of the Martyrdom of Polycarp was to promote Polycarp's exemplary imitation of Christ's virtues and obedience to God; the author's expectation was that hearers would be so moved by Polycarp's own example that they would act as Polycarp did in extreme circumstances, which secondarily reflect events in Jesus's passion as depicted in the canonical Gospels. An investigation of the canonical sources for Martyrdom of Polycarp's depiction of the imitation of Christ will further consolidate the case that Jesus's virtues were the model and criteria for "martyrdom according to the gospel."

4. KEY PASSAGES FOR NEW TESTAMENT STUDIES AND THEIR SIGNIFICANCE

Scholarly opinion on the role of canonical texts in Martyrdom of Polycarp is diverse. On the one hand, Foster's careful research suggests that in the work there is "little or no use of the

119. Dehandschutter, "Le Martyre de Polycarpe," 97.

120. Dehandschutter, "Le Martyre de Polycarpe," 99.

121. Holmes, "Martyrdom of Polycarp," 424. "The juncture at which Polycarp refuses to be nailed to the stake and is instead bound (13.3) can and has been understood as a break in the *imitatio Christi* motif" (C. R. Moss, "Nailing Down and Tying Up: Lessons in Intertextual Impossibility from the Martyrdom of Polycarp," *VC* 67.2 (2013): 128.

122. Moss, "Nailing Down and Tying Up," 129n128.

123. Dehandschutter left open the possibility that Mart. Pol.'s composers knew and were influenced by Ignatius's famous line "allow me to be an imitator of the suffering of my God," in Ign. *Rom.* 6.3 (cited from Brannan, *Apostolic Fathers*, 100). See Dehandschutter, "Le Martyre de Polycarpe," 95.

New Testament."[124] On the other hand, a number of scholars agree that Martyrdom draws on some larger ideas from several traditions that would be enshrined in the New Testament canon, such as Johannine and Pauline ones, rather than the direct use of texts. On this (more dominant) view, the Martyrdom works within the parameters sketched by canonical New Testament texts; these schools of thought provide the design and the framework for creating the exemplary story but not its details. That is, meta-beliefs, such as Christlike obedience to God and self-giving, shape the portrayal of Polycarp, yet mostly without direct allusion. We may use an analogy of how an artist conceives, designs, and completes their work in order to understand how the authors or composers of the Martyrdom employed texts aligned with the final form of the New Testament canon in their work.[125] On this analogy, canonical gospel traditions and the Pauline circles are to the composers of the Martyrdom what schools of influence (e.g., impressionism) are to artists. These influences provide larger conceptual vistas within which the work is produced, and hence it is "saturated with scriptural and cultural intertexts."[126] Scholars need to be open to indirect and unconstrained relationships between canonical texts and receptions of these in works such as the Martyrdom of Polycarp, in which the details of these intertexts and allusions may be variegated as well as difficult to identify with certainty.[127] For this reason, other than in a few cases, the use of relationship between final-form canonical texts and the Martyrdom is more often indirect than direct. A closer investigation of the work's use of Pauline and Johannine traditions—which is consistent with the two schools of thought with which Polycarp has been historically related—reveals some candidates for a strong relationship between the Martyrdom of Polycarp and what would later become canonical texts.

4.1 The Martyrdom of Polycarp and the Pauline School

In a sense, a Pauline influence upon the Martyrdom of Polycarp is unsurprising, given that Polycarp belonged to a Pauline school of worship and mission.[128] Polycarp himself was indebted to Pauline ways of thinking in terms of Christian love, Christlikeness, and house codes, as Lookadoo points out: in Polycarp's *To the Philippians*, Ignatius's *To Polycarp*, and 1 Clement,

> the importance of love in the household, as well as the way in which Christ can be viewed as a theological ground for right behaviour, indicate that the authors were working with ways of thinking that are ultimately indebted to Paul himself and are variously found in Ephesians, Colossians, 1 Timothy and Titus.[129]

124. Foster, "Text of the New Testament in the Apostolic Fathers," 95.

125. This analogy is not merely a thought experiment. As an artist myself, having exhibited works in galleries such as the National Gallery of Victoria, I can attest that this analogy reflects how many artists work in relation to schools of influence as well as local and personal factors.

126. Moss, "Nailing Down and Tying Up," 119.

127. "Deeply embedded in these treatments of intertextuality in the Martyrdom of Polycarp are three assumptions: first, that the intertexts are pure—the author utilized single texts or traditions directly and with respect for their integrity—and that deviation from a pure intertext is either the independent innovation of the author in keeping with the genre of the martyrdom account or the hallmark of historicity; second, that intertextual forms can be used as a gauge for canonicity and thus for dating; and third, that intertextuality is at odds with authenticity. Each of these assumptions is tied to a scholarly agenda preoccupied with canonical texts" (Moss, "Nailing Down and Tying Up," 127).

128. C. Jefford, "Missing Pauline Tradition in the Apostolic Fathers? Didache, Shepherd of Hermas, Papias, the Martyrdom of Polycarp, and the Epistle to Diognetus," in *The Apostolic Fathers and Paul*, ed. T. D. Still and D. E. Wilhite (Oxford: Bloomsbury T&T Clark, 2016), 52.

129. Lookadoo, "Categories," 47.

Somewhat surprisingly, the Pauline school exercises a very select influence over the composition of the Martyrdom. It is a lesser influence relative to that of Gospels materials. Paul Hartog is correct to point out that in it, "very few biblical texts appear,"[130] yet at the same time the circles and schools from which the New Testament texts will emerge exercise a determinative conceptual influence on the Martyrdom: "The *Mart. Pol.* sketches parallels with the passion of Jesus, draws from Pauline reflections of self-donation, and echoes of the martyrdom of Stephen and the martyr reflections of Revelation."[131]

Holmes restricts their use of Paul to a mostly allusive and broader conceptual use of the apostle.[132] Jefford argues that Martyrdom of Polycarp 1.2 ("not only looking out for our own concerns but also the concerns of our neighbours") is a "virtual quotation" of Philippians 2:4 "not looking to your own interests but each of you to the interests of the others." Martyrdom of Polycarp 2.3 ("they looked above to the good things which are preserved for those who have endured, which neither ear has heard, nor eye has seen, nor has it entered into the human heart, but it was shown by the Lord to them") is another such quotation from a source that Paul quotes in 1 Corinthians 2:9 ("However, as it is written: 'What no eye has seen, what no ear has heard, and what no human mind has conceived'—the things God has prepared for those who love him").[133] Foster, however, points out that material drawn on by both 1 Corinthians 2:9 and Martyrdom of Polycarp could be independent material that is similarly drawn upon by 2 Clement 11.7 and 14.5, and therefore is not a Pauline source for the Martyrdom but rather "a different branch of early Christian tradition."[134]

Within the context of this larger Pauline influence, and in a way analogous to an artist primarily filling in the details of their work according to their unique interests, experience, personality, and ability, the author(s) of Martyrdom of Polycarp develop the details of the story with a priority on the martyrdom itself. This explains why there are only a few near-direct or allusive uses of Paul in the work. The same logic applies to the work's use of Petrine sources.[135] A more profitable route for exploring the particular use of New Testament aligned works in the Martyrdom is to notice how Gospel texts and motifs influence the narrative and are present in the final form(s) of the work.[136]

4.2 The Martyrdom of Polycarp and the Gospels

Whereas Pauline works provide little in terms of the detail for the story, the Gospels are drawn on strongly and in some detail in the Martyrdom of Polycarp. They have a stronger influence than Pauline texts. This was covered above in sections 3.6 ("Martyrdom

130. Hartog, "Polycarp's Epistle to the Philippians and the Martyrdom of Polycarp," 242.

131. Hartog, "Polycarp's Epistle to the Philippians and the Martyrdom of Polycarp," 242.

132. M. Holmes, "The Martyrdom of Polycarp and the New Testament Passion Narrative," in *Trajectories Through the New Testament and the Apostolic Fathers*, ed. A. F. Gregory and C. M. Tuckett (Oxford: Oxford University Press, 2005), 428.

133. Jefford, "Missing Pauline Tradition in the Apostolic Fathers?," 54.

134. P. Foster, "The Absence of Paul in 2 Clement," in Still and Wilhite, *Apostolic Fathers and Paul*, 69. See J. Kozlowski "The Participle κολαφιζόμενοι in *Martyrium Polycarpi* 2.4 and 2 Cor 12:1–10," *VC* 72.5 (2018): 506–12, for his argument that Mart. Pol. 2.4 may be indebted to 2 Cor 12:1–10.

135. By means of deploying the sojourning/exiled motif applied to churches in Mart. Pol.'s prologue, a Petrine connection may be revealed (cf. 1 Pet 1:1, 17; 2:11). However, the sojourning motif was also shared by other second-century documents, such as Polycarp's own epistle *To the Philippians*, the anonymous *Letter from Vienna and Lyons*, and 1 Clement. Such a shared use makes the origin of the concept, and a definite shared meaning, hard to identify with certainty. See C. K. Rothschild, "The Reception of Paul in 1 Clement," in Still and Wilhite, *Apostolic Fathers and Paul*, 103–6.

136. Hartog, "Polycarp's Epistle to the Philippians and the Martyrdom of Polycarp," 243.

according to the Gospel") and 3.7 above ("Parallels between Jesus and Polycarp"), with special attention given to the conceptual importance of the Johannine love command as the generating theology for imitation and sacrifice as the expressions of the love that Jesus requires of his friends and followers (John 15). In addition, there are virtue and event parallels between the Gospels and the Martyrdom, also demonstrated above. We can conclude with Parvis that the composers had an "obvious love of and knowledge of the Gospels."[137]

Finally, the importance of Matthew 10:23 needs to be noted for Martyrdom's restriction of martyrdom to the elect. Matthew 10:23 reads: "When you are persecuted in one place, flee to another," and may be interpreted as promoting fleeing from persecution rather than volunteering for martyrdom. It may be that the story and reflection on Quintus are written under the text's influence, warning that "we do not praise those who hand themselves over because the gospel does not so teach" (4.1).[138] In sum, it is best to acknowledge that the Martyrdom of Polycarp is "sketching" an impression of Christlike obedience to God, within a largely Pauline and Johannine "conceptual" framework. In addition, gospel narrative materials provide the details of the events and virtues in view.

5. CONCLUSION

The Martyrdom of Polycarp is an epistle that functioned as hagiographic media from the mid-second century onward. The letter vividly drew its audience into the action it narrated, situating them as witnesses to God's dramatic works in the context of violence against Christians. It focused on Polycarp's last days and death as an exemplary Christian martyr; its intention was to promote Polycarp's embodiment of the virtues that Christ displayed during his own passion. Current scholarship suggests that drawing from Synoptic Gospel sources, the author(s) set up a number of event and virtue parallels between Jesus and Polycarp's final days. In addition, theological ideals and religious practices drawn largely from Johannine and Pauline circles probably stand behind the other-person focused love that Polycarp provides as a template for imitation by subsequent Christians.

BIBLIOGRAPHY

Buschmann, G. *Das Martyrium des Polykarp übersetzt und erklärt.* KAV 6. Gottingen: Vandenhoeck & Ruprecht, 1998.

Cobb, L. S. *Divine Deliverance: Pain and Painlessness in Early Christian Martyr Texts.* Oakland, CA: University of California Press, 2017.

Dehandschutter, B. "Le Martyre de Polycarpe et le développement de la conception du martyre au deuxième siècle." Pages 93–104 in *Polycarpiana: Studies on Martyrdom and Persecution in Early Christianity: Collected Essays.* Edited by J. Leemans. Leuven: Leuven University Press, 2007.

Dehandschutter, B. "Polycarpiana: Notes on the Hagiographic 'Dossier' of a Saint." Pages 259–70 in *Polycarpiana: Studies on Martyrdom and Persecution in Early Christianity: Collected Essays.* Edited by J. Leemans. Leuven: Leuven University Press, 2007.

Foster, P. "The Text of the New Testament in the Apostolic Fathers." Pages 92–118 in *The Cambridge Companion to the Apostolic Fathers.* Edited by M. Bird and S. Harrower. Cambridge: Cambridge University Press, 2021.

Hartog, P. "Polycarp's Epistle to the Philippians and the Martyrdom of Polycarp." Pages 226–47 in *The Cambridge Companion to the Apostolic Fathers.* Edited by M. Bird and S. Harrower. Cambridge: Cambridge University Press, 2021.

Hartog, P. *Polycarp's Epistle to the Philippians and the Martyrdom of Polycarp: Introduction, Text, and Commentary.* OAF. Oxford: Oxford University Press, 2013.

Hollander, A. T. "Hagiography Unbound: A Theory of Making and Using Holy Media." *JAAR* 89.1 (2021): 72–102.

137. Parvis, "Martyrdom of Polycarp," 145.

138. Moss, "Nailing Down and Tying Up," 125.

Kozlowski, J. "The Participle κολαφιζόμενοι in *Martyrium Polycarpi* 2.4 and 2 Cor 12:1–10." *VC* 72.5 (2018): 506–12.

Lookadoo, J. "Categories, Relationships and Imitation in the Household Codes of 1 Clement, Ignatius and Polycarp: A Comparison with Household Codes in the Pauline Corpus." *Neotestamentica* 53.1 (2019): 31–52.

Moss, C. R. *The Other Christs: Imitating Jesus in Ancient Christian Ideologies of Martyrdom*. Oxford: Oxford University Press, 2010.

Parvis, S. "The Martyrdom of Polycarp." Pages 126–46 in *The Writings of the Apostolic Fathers*. Edited by P. Foster. London: T&T Clark, 2007.

Rebillard, Éric. *Greek and Latin Narratives About the Ancient Martyrs*. Oxford: Oxford University Press, 2017.

Schoedel, W. R. *Polycarp, Martyrdom of Polycarp, Fragments of Papias*. Vol. 5 of *The Apostolic Fathers: A Translation and Commentary*. New York: Thomas Nelson, 1967.

Zweirlein, O. *Die Urfassungen der Martyria Polycarpi et Pionii und das Corpus Polycarpianum*. Untersuchungen zur antiken Literatur und Geschichte 116. Berlin: de Gruyter, 2014.

CHAPTER 12

THE EPISTLE TO DIOGNETUS

MICHAEL F. BIRD

1. INTRODUCTION

The Epistle to Diognetus is a second-century apologetic-protreptic treatise with a homiletical addition spliced on at the end and is ordinarily dated to ca. 150–200 CE.[1] We know next to nothing about the author, the recipient named "Diognetus," the transmission history of the text, or its circulation in the early church. Diognetus is never once mentioned by authors of the patristic and medieval periods, so we are completely in the dark as to its provenance and preservation. What we do know is that a manuscript containing Diognetus was allegedly discovered in a fishmonger's shop in Constantinople in 1436. The manuscript, known as Codex Argentoratensis Graecus 9, was dated to the 13th/14th centuries, and Diognetus was located within it at the end of a series of works by Justin Martyr. The manuscript was eventually taken to France and was first published in 1592 by Henri Estienne (aka Henricus Stephanus). Because of the text's late discovery, a few have wondered whether Diognetus is in fact a Renaissance forgery, but virtually all researchers support its authenticity. Sadly, the codex containing Diognetus was destroyed in the nineteenth century. The manuscript was stored in the Strasbourg library and was incinerated by a fire during the Franco-Prussian war of 1870. The Greek text is now preserved only in transcriptions made by several scholars.[2]

For a long time, Diognetus was wrongly categorized. First, it was initially attributed to Justin Martyr, even though the literary style does not comport with Justin's. Second, Diognetus is not an actual epistle; it is an apologetic-protreptic treatise with an epistolary opening and a homiletical appendix. Third, the text's precise genre and contents means it belongs more properly among the second-century apologists than with the Apostolic Fathers.[3] It was the Italian patristics scholar Andrea Gallandi (1709–1779) who first included Diognetus in his 1765 edition of the Apostolic Fathers on the conjecture that

1. For recent translations, see K. Wengst, *Didache (Apostellehre), Barnabasbrief, Zweiter Clemensbrief, Schrift an Diognet*, Schriften des Urchristentums 2 (München: Kösel, 1984), 312–41; B. D. Ehrman, *The Apostolic Fathers*, 2 vols., LCL (Cambridge: Harvard University Press, 2003), 2:121–60; M. W. Holmes, *The Apostolic Fathers: Greek Texts and English Translations*, 3rd ed. (Grand Rapids: Baker Academic, 2007), 686–720; R. Brannan, *The Apostolic Fathers: A New Translation* (Bellingham, WA: Lexham, 2017), 277–89. Translations in this essay are from Holmes, those with "MFB" are by the author.

2. L. B. Radford, *The Epistle to Diognetus* (London: SPCK, 1908), 7–10; H. I. Marrou, *A Diognète: Introduction, edition critique, traduction et commentaire*, 2nd ed., SC 33.2 (Paris: Cerf, 1997), 5–10, 33–37; C. N. Jefford, *The Epistle to Diognetus (with the Fragment of Quadratus): Introduction, Text, and Commentary*, OAF (Oxford: Oxford University Press, 2013), 7–8.

3. K. Lake, *The Apostolic Fathers*, 2 vols., LCL 25 (Cambridge: Harvard University Press, 1913), 2:348; R. M. Grant, *Greek Apologists of the Second Century* (Philadelphia: Westminster, 1988), 178–79.

it was written by Paul's companion Apollos.[4] Gallandi's authorial conjecture never found support in subsequent scholarship, but the inclusion of Diognetus among the Apostolic Fathers became something of an accepted custom for the Apostolic Fathers' collection ever since.[5]

It is unfortunate that Diognetus was forgotten and lost in church history, because it is one of the high points of Christian literary and theological achievements. Diognetus is an exemplar of second-century Christian critiques of Greco-Roman religion and contains a creative synthesis of Pauline and Johannine motifs. It offers a sublime exposition of the vocation of Christians as the soul of the world, a vigorous presentation of Christian theism and the Son's incarnation, a powerful account of the atonement, a moving emphasis on God's mercy, and a concerted exhortation toward the imitation of God. Diognetus, says Clayton Jefford, offers "a fascinating view into how early Christian authors were able to harness biblical features for their rhetorical agendas and, in this particular case, to create a text whose style offers a simple beauty that is easily appreciated."[6]

As already mentioned, the text of Diognetus was attested exclusively in a single manuscript, Codex Argentoratensis Graecus 9, which was destroyed by a fire in Strasbourg in 1870. The text is otherwise preserved in transcriptions made by B. Haus (*Codex Misc. Tübingen M.b. 27* [1580]), Henricus Stephanus (*Codex Graecus Voss.* Q. 30 [1586]), and a commentary by Prudentius of Saint Maur (1742). The editio princeps or first critical edition of the book was published by Estienne (1592).[7]

The text of Diognetus is anonymous as there is nothing that names the author, or even hints at the author's identity. The fact that Codex Argentoratensis Graecus 9 located Diognetus among a collection of writings attributed to Justin Martyr meant that Diognetus was initially identified as belonging with writings attributed to Justin.[8] However, it was soon recognized that the author's style is markedly different from Justin's, and hence the theory of authorship by Justin was soon abandoned. Other proposed authors have included Aristides, Tatian, Melito of Sardis, Theophilus of Antioch, Pantanaeus of Alexandria, and Hippolytus of Rome.[9] The best educated guesses are the apologist Quadratus[10] and bishop Polycarp of Smyrna.[11] However, it is hard to avoid the conclusion that these proposals are mostly conjecture, as we simply do not know who the author might have been! Taking a sober perspective, all we know for certain is that the author is a Greek speaker, educated, and erudite, a teacher of Christianity in an ostensibly hostile context, theologically shaped by Paul's letters and John's Gospel, perhaps familiar with the Epistle of Barnabas and Preaching of Peter, and who trades in Christian anti-pagan tropes and *contra Iudaeos* rhetoric.

Dating Diognetus is equally dubious due to a lack of patristic mention and quotation, as well as a paucity of manuscript attestation. It is more likely than not that, given the resonance of Diognetus 1–10 with second-century apologetic works, as well as the similarity of

4. Holmes, *Apostolic Fathers*, 5.
5. Lake, *Apostolic Fathers*, 2:348.
6. Jefford, *Diognetus*, 12–13.
7. Cf. Holmes, *Apostolic Fathers*, 689–90; Jefford, *Diognetus*, 5–8.
8. See Marrou, *Diognète*, 12–13, 24–25.
9. Cf. Jefford, *Diognetus*, 15–29.
10. P. Andriessen, "The Authorship of the *Epistula ad Diognetum*," *VC* 1 (1947): 129–36.
11. P. F. Beatrice, "Der Presbyter des Irenäus, Polykarp von Smyrna und der Brief an Diognet," in *Pléroma: Salus Carnis: Homenaje a Antonio Orbe, S.J.*, ed. E. Romero-Pose (Santiago de Compostella, 1990), 179–202; C. E. Hill, *From the Lost Teaching of Polycarp: Identifying Irenaeus' Apostolic Presbyter and the Author of Ad Diognetum*, WUNT 186 (Tübingen: Mohr Siebeck, 2006), 128–65.

Diognetus 11–12 with second-century homiletical writings, that a date in the mid- to late second century is reasonable.[12]

The addressee of the letter is just as mysterious as the anonymous author. The name of the addressee, Diognetus (Διόγνητος, *Diognētos*), was common in antiquity and is attested in various texts, inscriptions, and papyri.[13] Scholars have tried to identify the addressee with one of the many figures named Diognetus in antiquity. First, the emperor Marcus Aurelius had a tutor named Diognetus, whom Aurelius admired for his freedom from superstition and for ingraining in him a love of philosophy and Greek disciplines (Marcus Aurelius, *Med.* 1.6). Second, the Alexandrian procurator Tiberius Claudius Diogenes is known from papyri dated between 197 and 203 CE, and he is even called "the most excellent Diognetus" in one papyrus, which resembles the opening address in Diognetus 1.1.[14] Third, an inscription in Smyrna dated 150–210 CE mentions a grandfather and grandson both called Diognetus, who occupied socially prominent positions in the province of Asia.[15] One can plausibly imagine the document being addressed to one of the aforementioned figures. However, the problem is that there is little evidence to establish or falsify the options. Of course, Diognetus might even be an entirely fictitious entity, symbolic for pagan inquirers of Christianity. All the more plausible given that "Diognetus" means literally "heir/child of Dios/Zeus."[16] What we can say, from a literary standpoint, is that the implied reader is an educated pagan interested in learning about Christianity who perhaps shares some affinity with the author in Greek philosophy. Otherwise, we do well to remember that apologetic literature was often composed for internal consumption by sectarian groups. Therefore, Christian readers might be primary, and a pagan recipient, whether real or imagined, would be secondary to fortifying a Christian group's identity in a hostile socioreligious setting.

There are questions about the textual integrity of Diognetus, as transcribers noticed gaps in the text between 7.6 and 7.7 and again at 10.8. The original copyist of Codex Argentoratensis Graecus 9 noted the lacunae with marginalia. In addition, the final two chapters, Diognetus 11–12, stand apart from Diognetus 1–10 as a homiletical composition, which assumes a Christian rather than pagan audience. The final two chapters are different with their explicit quotation of 1 Corinthians 8:1, an allegorical interpretation of Genesis 2:9, a protocanonical affirmation of Law, Prophets, and Gospels, and a texture that is catechetical rather than apologetic. Accordingly, Diognetus 11–12 is reckoned to be a later addition.[17] A minority of scholars regard these chapters as original to the work,[18] or perhaps a separate work by the same author.[19] Diognetus 11–12 was perhaps appended

12. Jefford (*Diognetus*, 28) comments: "Following the bulk of contemporary scholarship, the text is most likely to be attributed to some moment during the 2nd century, with a preference for the latter decades of that period."

13. BDAG 250.

14. Marrou, *Diognète*, 254–56, 267–68.

15. Hill, *Lost Teaching of Polycarp*, 160–65.

16. H. E. Lona, *An Diognet: Übersetzt und erklärt*, Kommentar zu frühchristlichen Apologeten 8 (Freiburg: Herder, 2001), 73–74; Jefford, *Diognetus*, 25.

17. See discussion of their unity and integrity in R. H. Connolly, "Ad Diognetum xi–xii," *JTS* 36 (1936): 2–15; Meecham, *Diognetus*, 64–68; Lona, *Diognet*, 47–48; Jefford, *Diognetus*, 43–51.

18. Andriessen, "Authorship," 135–36; Marrou, *Diognète*, 219–27; Hill, *Lost Teaching of Polycarp*, 106–27, 167; esp. M. Rizzi, *La questione dell'unità dell' "Ad Diognetum"*, SPM 16 (Milan: Università Cattolica del Sacro Cuore, 1989).

19. T. J. Lang, *Mystery and Making of a Christian Historical Consciousness: From Paul to the Second Century*, BZNW 219 (Berlin: de Gruyter, 2017), 149.

to represent the type of instruction that a pagan convert to Christianity like "Diognetus" would require in order to mature in the faith.

2. SUMMARY OF CONTENT

Concerning the contents of Diognetus, it commences with a prologue (Diogn. 1.1–2), which sets out the three questions that are addressed in the document: (1) What god do the Christians believe in and worship? (2) What is the nature of their love for each other?; and (3) Why has this new people and their peculiar way of life suddenly emerged? Then, Diognetus provides a dual critique of pagan idol worship as well as the Jerusalem cultus and the ceremonial laws of the Jews (Diogn. 2–4). The author proceeds to an encomium to Christians for their exemplary way of life and positive influence upon the world (Diogn. 5–6).[20] Diognetus 7 is a transitional section that presents a discourse on God's providence and the sending of God's Word to save the world. Next, Diognetus 8–9 comprises an exposition of God's purposes, revelation, and the sending of God's beloved child to save the powerless and the unrighteous. Then, in Diognetus 10, it is claimed that faith leads to knowledge, which leads in turn to love, and love is an imitation of God's very goodness. The homily in Diognetus 11–12 is probably not original to the work, perhaps even written by a different author, but is nonetheless attached here. The homily includes an exposition of the incarnation of the Logos and the two trees planted in the garden of Eden from Genesis 2:9. The structure of Diognetus can be stratified as follows:

Treatise Opening	
1.1–2	Prologue
Main Body	
2.1–10	The folly of pagan idolatry
3.1–4.6	The folly of Jewish cultus and ceremonial laws
5.1–6.10	Encomium to the Christian *genos*
7.1–9	The heavenly Word in the world
8.1–11	The Christian God and his Child
9.1–6	The Christian God's power to salvation
10.1–8	The knowledge, love, and imitation of God
Homily	
11.1–12.9	A homily on the "epiphany of the Word"[21]

Prologue (1.1–2)

The prologue begins with mention of its addressee, the "most excellent Diognetus." The name "Diognetus" means "son of Dios," and "Dios" is a Greek name for "Zeus." It was a popular name in antiquity and is attested in several texts and inscriptions. Much like "most excellent Theophilus" in Acts 1:1, there is debate as to whether the addressee is a historical figure or a symbolic character. Diognetus is regarded as an inquirer of Christianity, and he has three questions about Christians: (1) What God do they believe in and worship to the point that they disregard the world, despise death, and discard Greek deities and Jewish superstitions?; (2) What is the motivation for their deep affection for each other?; and

20. The critique of pagan worship, Jewish worship, and describing Christians as a "new people" is probably modeled on Preaching of Peter §2 and comprises something of an extended commentary on that text.

21. Grant, *Greek Apologists*, 178.

(3) Why has this new group (*genos*)[22] of Christians and their peculiar way of life suddenly appeared now rather than earlier? The author in turn welcomes Diognetus's interest and asks God to empower him to speak and Diognetus to listen, so that the hearer benefits and the speaker has no regrets about what he has said.

The Folly of Pagan Idolatry (2.1–10)

The first major section of Diognetus engages in a critique of idol worship. The argument is fashioned in the tradition of Jewish[23] and Christian[24] polemics against idol worship and visible representations of deity. The Jewish Scriptures prescribed an aniconic monolatry that expressly forbade the worship of idols (Exod 20:4; 34:17; Lev 19:4; 26:1; Deut 4:15–26; 5:8). Jewish authors considered sacrificing to idols to be apostasy and a form of defection to Hellenism (1 Macc 1:43). Christian authors typically regarded idolatry as something from which people should be converted (1 Thess 1:9; 2 Clem. 17.1) and irreconcilable with the practice of Christian faith (1 Cor 5:10–11; 6:9; 2 Cor 6:16; Gal 5:20; 1 Pet 4:3; 1 John 5:21; Aristides, *Apol.* 15). The aim of this section is to demonstrate the absurdity of idol worship and the bravery of Christians for opposing it to the point of persecution.

Thus, the author begins by inviting Diognetus to cleanse his mind of presumptions and prejudices, to cast aside the customs of his native religion, and to become a new person after hearing this new message (Diogn. 2.1a). Diognetus is then challenged to see the true nature of the idols which he is accustomed to worship. The author argues that stone idols are no different from the stone pavement that one walks upon; bronze idols are no better than the bronze utensils forged for everyday use; wooden idols are susceptible to rot; silver idols need someone to guard them to stop them from being pilfered; iron idols can be corroded by rust; and pottery idols can be used as chamber pots. Thus, one problem with idols is that they are perishable (cf. Wis 14:8). Not only that, the various makers of these idols—sculptors, silversmiths, and craftsman—could have turned their materials into any number of items for human usage, of which an idol is only one (cf. Isa 44:9–20). Idols have several other deficiencies: they are deaf, blind, soulless, emotionless, immobile, and subject to decay. Furthermore, the worship of idols and calling them gods is dehumanizing because people become the very things that idols represent. In other words, the problem with paganism is that people become what they worship (2.1b–5).

Christians are hated because they do not accept the lie that these idols are real gods (Diogn. 2.6). Yet the author turns the tables on pagans by arguing that they are the ones who despise idols. The fact that people lock up their gold and silver idols and yet leave the iron and pottery idols unprotected is proof that they do not value them as deities but as precious metals. In addition, the sacrifices of blood and fat offered to idols would be insulting to them if they were conscious. Alternatively, if idols are inanimate objects, then sacrificing animals to them exposes them as frauds (2.5–8).[25] No human being would be willing to undergo such a test because they possess consciousness and a capacity for reasoning (2.9).

The author ends the section by noting that many things could be said about Christians, who are distinct for not being slaves to idols, but if the preceding arguments are unpersuasive then further disputation is probably pointless on this matter (2.10).

22. Cf. BDAG 194: "group, nation, people."

23. Isa 40:19–20; 44:9–20; Jer 10:1–6; Wis 14:8–12, 27–31; 15:15–19; Philo, *Spec. Leg.* 1.26.

24. Rom 1:23–25; 1 Cor 10:1–22; Justin, *1 Apol.* 9; Aristides, *Apol.* 13; Athenagoras, *Leg.* 15; 18; 26–27; Theophilus, *Autol.* 1.10; Preaching of Peter §2.

25. This part of the argument has a high probability of being dependent upon Preaching of Peter §2.

The Folly of Jewish Cultus and Ceremonial Laws (3.1–4.6)

In the next phase of the argument, the author resources and rehearses Christian *contra Iudaeos* arguments to establish the newness and superiority of Christian piety vis-à-vis the Jewish mode of worship. Much like Preaching of Peter §2, the argument shifts from a critique of idol worship to a critique of Jewish observances. Much like Barnabas 2.4–3.6, the author of Diognetus consecutively critiques the Jerusalem cultus (3.1–5) and then Jewish ceremonial observances (4.1–6). While the argument contains rhetorical verve and addresses a context riddled with sectarian strife, to anyone with an ounce of canonical sensibilities, who appreciates the Jewish heritage of the Christian church, the arguments mustered appear needlessly derisive, shallow, and tendentious.

The author imagines Diognetus wondering why Christians do not worship in the manner of the Jews (Diogn. 3.1). The author recognizes that the Jews rightly share his allergy to idol worship and his commitment to monotheism. Even so, he equates the Jerusalem cultus with idol worship since the Jerusalem cultus makes the same kind of sacrificial offerings to God that idolaters offer to their idols (3.2). The author does not attack the Jerusalem cultus per se, as if it were a mistake or offering false worship; rather, he attacks as folly the notion that God somehow *needs* the sacrifices offered to him (3.3).[26] Ancient Greek philosophers, as well as Jews and Christians, had championed the idea of divine aseity—that is, God does not have needs that must be satisfied by humans, whether by their piety, temples, or sacrifices (Plato, *Euthyphr.* 12E–15E; 2 Macc 14:35; 3 Macc 2:9; Josephus, *Ant.* 8.111; 1 Clem. 52.1; Barn. 2.4; Preaching of Peter §2; Justin, *1 Apol.* 13.1).

The argument made by the author, that the God of heaven and earth who meets human needs himself needs nothing (Diogn. 3.4), is very similar to Acts 17:24–25: "The God who made the world and everything in it, he who is Lord of heaven and earth, does not live in shrines made by human hands, nor is he served by human hands, as though he needed anything, since he himself gives to all mortals life and breath and all things" (NRSV). The author of Diognetus takes the same argument about pagan sacrifices and shrines but applies it mutatis mutandis to the Jerusalem temple and its sacrificial cultus. The author of Barnabas argued similarly by appealing to Isaiah 1:11–13, Jeremiah 7:22–23, Zechariah 8:17, and Psalm 51:17 (50:19 LXX) about God's rejection of sacrificial worship if done with a wrong spirit or without love toward others (Barn. 2.4–10). The sacrificial cultus was done away with, Barnabas argued, "in order that the new law of our Lord Jesus Christ, which is free from the yoke of compulsion, might have its offering, one not made by humans" (Barn. 2.6). Similar, too, is Justin who argued:

> We who worship the Creator of this world; we who say, as we have been taught, that he does not need blood, and libations, and incense; we who praise him, to the best of our ability, by a word of prayer and thanksgiving for everything we eat; we who have learnt that this is the only honour worthy of him—not to destroy by fire what has been brought about by him for sustenance but to use it for ourselves and for those in need and, in accordance with reason,

26. It was possible in Christian discourse to shift from rejecting idols to casting aspersions on the Jerusalem temple for its man-made nature. Whereas the Jewish Scriptures dismissed idols as something made "by human hands" (Deut 4:28; 2 Kgs 19:18; Ps 115:4; 135:15; Isa 37:19; Wis 13:10; 14:8; Jdt 8:18; Bel 5), Christian authors disparaged the temple as something made "by human hands" because of its inability to contain all of God's cosmic presence, its inferiority compared to the heavenly temple, and its redundancy in the new dispensation of Christ and the Spirit (Mark 14:58; Acts 7:48; 2 Cor 5:1; Heb 9:11, 24). Philo, for all his concern about preserving the holiness and grandeur of the temple (*Embassy* 295; *Spec. Laws* 1.123), rejects the worship of God in houses "of stone and timber" (*Cher.* 99–100).

> to send processions and hymns in gratitude to him for our creation, and for all the provisions for well-being—of qualities of produce and of changes of seasons. (*1 Apol.* 13.1)

The author equates Greek and Jewish sacrificial worship because the Greek makes offerings to objects unable to receive them, while the Jews make offerings to a God who does not need them (Diogn. 3.5). In Diognetus 3.1–5 we find a mixture of anti-Jewish polemic combined with the idea that Christian worship, true worship as the author understands it, is neither iconic nor cultic, but immaterial and intellectual.

The topic changes to Jewish ceremonies (i.e., rituals, food laws, and calendar), effectively "Jewish boundary markers," analogous to Paul's version of "works of the law."[27] The author is scathing about these practices and assumes that Diognetus already regards them as ridiculous and unworthy of discussion. He labels the Sabbath as a "superstition," circumcision as "pride," and associates the observance of fasting and new moons with "hypocrisy" (Diogn. 4.1). The author rehearses distinctly Roman, anti-Jewish tropes about Jewish distinctives (e.g., Cicero, *Flac.* 28.67; Josephus, *C. Ap.* 1.205–11; Tacitus, *Hist.* 5.8.3; 5.13.1; *Ann.* 2.85.4; Suetonius, *Tib.* 36) and is comparable in his argumentation to other Christian authors who faulted the Jews for (mis)observance of their ancestral laws (e.g., Barn. 3.1–6; Justin, *Dial.* 21–24). The argument is that it is not unlawful to accept or eat the things that God has created for human consumption (Diogn. 4.2); it is not impious to declare that God allows us to do good on the Sabbath (4.3); it is ridiculous to take "pride in the mutilation of the flesh as a sign of election" or even the grounds of divine love (4.4); and dividing the year into times of feasting and fasting is not a mark of godliness, as it is arbitrary and indicates ignorance (4.5).

The preceding remarks justify Christian separation from Jews as they are typified by absurdity, deception, pedantry, and pretentiousness. The mystery of the Christian religion must not be learned from humans like the Jews, but from a divine source (Diogn. 4.6). Although the author appears to echo Paul in some ways (e.g., Gal 4:10; Phil 3:2; Col 2:16),[28] he goes far beyond Paul's attempt to negotiate elements of the Torah for his gentile assemblies. Paul, it must be remembered, affirmed the value of circumcision (Rom 3:1) and imputed its significance to gentile Christ believers (Rom 2:25–29; Phil 3:3), while also treating the observance of days as a matter of individual conscience (Rom 14:5–6). The author can be faulted for failing to grapple with the fact that, even if Jewish ceremonies are not appropriate for Christ-believing gentiles, they were originally instituted by God for the nation of Israel. L. W. Barnard is correct that "the writer's attitude towards Judaism in Chs i–x is more extreme than that found in the New Testament and other second century Apologists."[29] The author has affinities with Marcion to the degree that "faith" is antithetical to Jewish practices,[30] is akin to orthodox anti-Marcionite responses insofar as the deficiency of the old dispensation is not the God of the Jews but the Jewish people (e.g., Tertullian, *Marc.* 3.6), and is somewhat analogous also with Manichaeanism

27. M. Bockmuehl, *Jewish Law in Gentiles Churches: Halakhah and the Beginning of Christian Public Ethics* (Edinburgh: T&T Clark, 2000), 217n134; M. J. Thomas, *Paul's "Works of the Law" in the Perspective of Second-Century Reception* (Downers Grove, IL: InterVarsity Press, 2020), 153.

28. Cf. M. F. Bird, "The Reception of Paul in the *Epistle to Diognetus*," in *Paul and the Second Century: The Legacy of Paul's Life, Letters, and Teaching*, ed. M. F. Bird and J. R. Dodson, LNTS 412 (London: T&T Clark, 2011), 75–77.

29. L. W. Barnard, "The Enigma of the Epistle to Diognetus," in *Studies in the Apostolic Fathers and Their Backgrounds* (Oxford: Oxford University Press, 1966), 172.

30. Bird ("Reception," 88) says the author stands at "a point between proto-orthodoxy and Marcion," while Thomas (*Paul's "Works of the Law"*, 157) sees the author leaving "an open door for Marcion's advance."

with its derogatory attitude toward Jewish ceremonies (e.g., Augustine, *Faust.* 6.1). This argumentative step, disingenuous as it might appear now, would have been expedient if one were commending Christianity to pagan intellectuals after the Jewish revolts in Cyprus and Cyrenaica (115–117 CE) and the Bar Kochba revolt (132–135 CE) in a setting such as mid-to-late second-century Alexandria.[31]

Encomium to the Christian *Genos* (5.1–6.10)

The author of Diognetus reaches something of a rhetorical crescendo in the praise of Christians for their ethnographical diversity, quiet piety, ethics, love for others, and endurance despite persecution (Diogn. 5.1–17). He praises them as the "soul" of the world, since much like a soul they are religiously invisible, hated, loving, unifying, immortal, and punished (6.1–10). The author constructs here a powerful piece of epideictic rhetoric by praising Christians for their distinctiveness, innocence, and the exemplarity of their lives in a hostile world. In a world that was often cruel as it was merciless, Christians represented a different way of being human that enticed as much as it offended observers.

The author begins with the observation that Christians look and live just like everyone else in their native environs (Diogn. 5.1). They do not have their own cities, language, or weird habits (5.2). Their teaching was not contrived by human reflection, nor is it something peddled for profit (5.3). Whereas Christians abide in cities and follow the same customs as everyone else, they demonstrate the peculiar nature of their citizenship in other ways (5.4). This leads to a series of contrasts where the author says that although Christians are ordinary citizens, they are foreigners by ethos, even in their homeland (5.5). For, while they marry and beget children, they do not engage in infanticide or share their wives (5.6–7). The author next packs together in 5.8–16 a tight series of allusions to Pauline texts where the distinctive character of Christians is accented.[32] We see that in Christian opposition to the "flesh" (Rom 8:12–13); Christian possession of a heavenly citizenship (Phil 3:20); responding to curses with blessings (Rom 12:14; 1 Cor 4:12); and the whole section is framed like Paul's own catalogue of hardships encountered in his missionary journeys (2 Cor 6:3–10). The author describes Christians as inhabiting the flesh without living according to the flesh (Diogn. 5.8). They dwell on earth, yet possess a citizenship in heaven (5.9). They obey the local laws, yet transcend them in their individual conduct (5.10). They love everyone, but are persecuted by everyone (5.11). They are unknown, but condemned; sentenced to death, yet made alive (5.12). They are poor, but make many rich; in need, yet abounding (5.13). They are dishonored and slandered yet glorified and justified (5.14). They respond to curses with blessings and to insults with respect (5.15). Christians are unique as they abound in good deeds and rejoice even amid their punishments (5.16). In addition, although they are assaulted by Jews and persecuted by Greeks, in each case, it is a hatred without reason (5.17). In effect, the author identifies with the "the paradoxical experience of Paul that God's power shows itself precisely in suffering and hardship, and this integration is where the attraction to Christians takes root."[33]

31. T. Nicklas, "*Epistula ad Diognetum* (Diognetus): The Christian 'New Genos' and Its Construction of the Others," in *Sensitivity Towards Outsiders: Exploring the Dynamic Relationship between Mission and Ethics in the New Testament and Early Christianity*, ed. J. Kok, T. Nicklas, D. T. Roth, and C. M. Hays, WUNT 2/364 (Tübingen: Mohr Siebeck, 2014), 501–2.

32. Bird, "Reception of Paul," 77–78.

33. R. Noormann, "Himmelsbürger auf Erden: Anmerkungen zum Weltverhältnis und zum 'Paulinismus' des Auctor ad Diognetum," in *Die Weltlichkeit des Glaubens in der Alten Kirche*, ed. B. Aland, C. Schäublin, D. Wyrwa, FS U. Wickert, BZNW 85 (Berlin: de Gruyter, 1997), 228 ("die paradox Erfahrung des Paulus, daß die Kraft Gotte sich gerade in Leiden und Bedrängnis erweist, zu integrieren und eben darin die Anziehungskraft der Christen wurzeln zu lassen").

Deploying the soul-world analogy (e.g., Plato, *Tim.* 31b–36e; *Phaedr.* 245C–250C), Christians are likened to the world as a soul is to the body (Diogn. 6.1). Just as the soul is dispersed across the body, so too are Christians dispersed across the cities of the world (6.2). Just as the soul dwells in the body but does not belong to the body, so too are Christians in the world but not of the world (6.3). Just as the soul is invisible, so too is the Christian religion practiced out of sight (6.4). Just as the flesh wages war on the soul and makes it suffer, so too does the world hate Christians and make them suffer (6.5). Just as the soul loves the flesh that hates it, so too do Christians love those who hate them (6.6). Just as the soul is confined to the body yet holds the body together, so too are Christians imprisoned even while they hold the world together (6.7). Just as the immortal soul dwells in a mortal tent, so too Christian live among the perishable waiting for an imperishable future (6.8). Just as the soul, when deprived of bodily appetites gets better, so too do Christians abound when they are punished (6.9). God has ordered the world with Christians in this place, it is a noble vocation, and thus it is not fitting for them to refuse it (6.10).

The Heavenly Word in the World (7.1–9)

The next phase of the argument introduces the heavenly Word whom God sends into the world for its salvation (Diogn. 7.1–9), which in turn prepares the way for the discourse concerning God's child (8.1–11) and God's salvation (9.1–6). The author puts forward a type of Logos Christology, whereby "the one whom God sends is that very power through whom all things were created and ordered (7.2), that was set into motion as a king dispatches a son in royalty (7.4), received the divine plan for salvation and revealed it among people (8.9–11), and was offered as a ransom for the unworthy (9.2)."[34]

Much like Paul's words in 1 Corinthians 2:13, the author asserts that Christian teaching is a divine mystery. Harking back to Diognetus 4.6 and 5.3 about the "mystery" of the inability of Christian religion to be humanly devised, the author adds that the Christian revelation is not an "earthly discovery," nor a "mortal idea," nor an "administration of human mysteries" (7.1). Rather, the omnipotent Creator established among humans the true, holy, incomprehensible "Word." This "Word" has affinity with Johannine thought (John 1:1–18), even if it is mediated to the author via other channels (e.g., Justin Martyr). Importantly, the Word is distinguished from various intermediary figures, including subordinate beings, angels, authorities, and heavenly figures. More precisely, the Word is not an intermediary; he participates in the Creator-creation distinction as the "Designer and Creator of the universe," the one "by whom" God created the heavens, enclosed its limits, and who commands heavenly objects like the moon and stars. The author later describes God as the "Master and Creator" (8.7), but here attributes the same demiurgical role to the Word. The notion of God as demiurge who acts in creation through the Word/Son is a common motif in second-century writings. Athenagoras referred to God as the "Creator of the universe" who "created all things by the Logos" (*Leg.* 6.2). Irenaeus described the "uncreated God—the Father planning everything well and giving his commands, the Son carrying these into execution and performing the work of creating, and the Spirit nourishing and increasing what is made" (*Haer.* 4.38.3). The Word has special authority as God's instrument to order the celestial and earthly realms (Diogn. 7.2).

The motivation and manner of the sending of the Word is then described (Diogn. 7.3–5). The Word was not sent to "rule by tyranny, fear, and terror"; instead, he comes "in gentleness and meekness." The next assertions are quite remarkable because, first, they

34. Jefford, *Diognetus*, 228.

introduce the motif of sonship, with God sending the Word as a king might send a son. Then, second, the Son unites in himself both God and humanity because the Son comes "as God" in the manner that a son of king "is a king." Additionally, he is sent to humans "as a human." If one takes the differentiation of the Word from intermediaries and combines it with the depiction of the Son coming "as God" and "as a human," then we have christological concepts that broadly correlate with later creedal formulas of the Son's dual consubstantiality in deity and humanity—that is, *vere deus et vere homo* ("true God and true man"). The Word/Son comes, as well, to save by persuasion not compulsion, calling rather than persecuting, loving rather than judging.

The ending of this section in Diognetus 7.6–9 is confused because, just after denying that the Son was sent to judge, he adds in 7.6 that he will be sent as a judge, and his future coming will be hard for anyone to endure (possibly alluding to Mal 3:2). There is a lacuna in the manuscript at this point, and some eschatological teaching has probably been lost to us. The author next returns to valorizing Christians for their courage, for even as they are thrown to wild beasts, they refuse to deny their Lord, rendering them as "unconquered" (μὴ νικωμένους, *mē nikōmenous*, 7.7). In fact, the more they are punished, the more they multiply. Christian endurance in the face of persecution is such that they do not appear to be human endeavors, but proofs of God's power in them and God's presence among them.

The Christian God and His Child (8.1–11)

The author shifts toward God's hiddenness and inscrutability, which was amplified rather than solved by ancient philosophy, to convey that God is only truly known in the revelation of "faith" (Diogn. 8.1–6). God is the kind master of creation who is good and who intends good (8.7–8). God's plan is communicated to his Son, and in turn, through him, people participate in God's generosity (8.9–11). Astoundingly the author believes that there is no *praeparatio evangelica* ("preparation for the gospel") in Greek philosophy, Israel's sacred history and Scriptures, or even in nature. There is no knowledge of God in Athens, Jerusalem, or the wilderness. God is found exclusively in the faith of the Christian dispensation where God's goodness and salvation are revealed.

The author rhetorically asks whether any person had knowledge of God before "he came," presumably referring to the sending of the Word (Diogn. 8.1). The whole industry of philosophy is a sham, as it identified God with physical elements, like water and fire; and fire, the author quips, is what the philosophers are destined for! At best, philosophers deify nature, at worst they are no better than magicians engaged in deceit (8.2–4). In a faint echo of John's Gospel (John 1:18), the author says that no one has either seen or known God, but he has still revealed himself through "faith" (πίστις, *pistis*). This "faith" is a synecdoche for the entire Christian dispensation (Diogn. 8.5–6; cf. Gal 3:23–24). God, as "Master and Creator of the universe," made and arranged all things. The author does not say that the creation exhibits divine attributes, but he believes that God is uniquely kind, tender, good, and always will be so (Diogn. 8.7–8). Next, the author declares that God has a "great and marvelous plan," which is communicated to his "child alone." The "plan" (βουλή, *boulē*) pertains to deliverance and was kept in "mystery" (μυστήριον, *mystērion* [trans. MFB]), to the point that it seemed as if God was unconcerned with humanity by not revealing it to them. But the plan was revealed through his "beloved child" to give people knowledge of things "from the beginning" and to "share in his benefactions and to see and understand things that none of us would have expected" (8.9–11 [trans. MFB]). Notably, the beloved child is not the content of revelation as much as its conduit. The author certainly knows that the child is, in some sense, both divine and human (7.4) and is the instrument of redemption (9.2–5), but here he majors on the motif of the beloved child as mediating knowledge of the hidden God.

The Christian God's Power to Salvation (9.1–6)

The material in Diognetus 9.1 functions as a transitional passage that marks a shift in the argument from the divine plan to divine salvation. This is achieved by dividing history into two periodic parts: "season of unrighteousness" and "season of righteousness." It is claimed that God's latent act to deal with sins was not on account of procrastination, but patience. God met human righteousness with his goodness, mercy, and power in an act whereby he gave up his Son as a ransom to cover over sins and to justify the unrighteous (9.2–4). The author lauds, in almost Puritan praise, "the sweet exchange," with the Son hiding sin in himself in order to justify sinners. God reveals in the economy of redemption the Savior's power to save the powerless, which in turn makes God worthy of a number of descriptors from nurse to counselor (9.5–6). This chapter is so pervaded by Pauline soteriology and its associated language that, as Brian Arnold rightly notes, it provides "the clearest teachings on the atonement and justification in the ante-Nicene church."[35] Indeed, it would be no exaggeration to say that such a passage represents something of a midpoint between Paul and Protestantism.[36]

The saving plan narrated in Diognetus 8.9–11 is now carried out through God's "child," so that those "unworthy of life" and unable to "to enter the kingdom" might be "made worthy" and enter the kingdom by "Gods' power." The plight presupposed by this solution is that God permitted people to dwell in a "season of unrighteousness" characterized by sinful desires and fulfilling their unrighteousness. God's delay in acting was not because of a delight in sin, but to prepare for the coming season of righteousness that would make people properly righteous. The delay is really a manifestation of God's goodness, power, kindness, and love (9.1–2a). The author assures readers that God is not motivated by hatred or a grudge, but only by patience and mercy. The proof is that "he took upon himself our sins" by "giving up his own Son as a ransom for us." It is hard not to hear an echo of the Aqedah tradition of Abraham not sparing Isaac (Gen 22) via Roman 8:32, as well as the Suffering Servant tradition (Isa 52–53) via Matthew 20:28 (cf. Titus 2:14; Barn. 19.10). The nature of the "for" (ὑπέρ, *hyper*) in "for us" is neither representative nor moral exemplar, but substitutionary in the sense of trading places: "the holy one for the lawless, the guiltless for the guilty, the just for the unjust, the incorruptible for the corruptible, the immortal for the mortal." The Son's own "righteousness," his obedience to the marvelous plan, is a covering for sins. It is "in" the Son alone that the lawless and ungodly are justified (Diogn. 9.2b–4). The author praises this event as a "sweet exchange" (γλυκείας ἀνταλλαγῆς, *glykeias antallagēs*) summed up as "the sinfulness of many hidden in one righteous person while the righteousness of one should justify many" (9.5). This is a possible allusion to Romans 5:18–19 combined with a Pauline notion of interchange in Christ, since this exchange takes place "in" the Son of God. Importantly, the justification (δικαιόω, *dikaioō*) is unlikely to be in a strictly forensic sense, since it is parallel with being "made worthy" (ἀξιόω, *axioō*) and "obtain[ing] life" (τυχεῖν ζωῆς, *tychein zōēs*). The main theme, as Arnold notes, is: "Where sinful humanity is weak and prone to decay, he [the

35. B. J. Arnold, *Justification in the Second Century* (Waco, TX: Baylor University Press, 2018), 94; cf. B. D. Crowe, "Oh Sweet Exchange! The Soteriological Significance of the Incarnation in the Epistle to Diognetus," *ZNW* 102 (2011): 96–109.

36. Bird, "Reception," 87.

Son] is strong and incorruptible. Where humanity is full of impurity and wickedness, He is full of innocence and righteousness. The Son is everything sinful people are not and yet must become."[37]

The Knowledge, Love, and Imitation of God (10.1–8)

Coming to a conclusion, the author argues for the necessity of knowledge of the Father as the condition for love of God (Diogn. 10.1–2), and love as the condition for the imitation of God (10.3–4a). He then explains what the imitation of God's goodness looks like in practice (10.4b–6). Thereafter, the author contends that such a perspective will enable Diognetus to love and admire Christians even as they are persecuted for their faith (10.7–8).

If Diognetus wishes to attain "faith," then he requires "full knowledge of the Father" (Diogn. 10.1). This knowledge is propositional and is conveyed in a sentence-long summary of the story of creation and salvation, a miniaturized *regula fidei* ("rule of faith"), similar to summaries found in Irenaeus (*Haer.* 1.10.1; 3.4.2; 4.33.7; *Apud.* 6) and Tertullian (*Praescr.* 13; *Prax.* 2). The summary, somewhat Johannine in idiom and theme, begins with God's love for humanity, for whom he made the world,[38] to whom he imparted cognitive functionality and the divine image, then sent to them "his one and only Son," and promised the "kingdom in heaven" to those who "loved him" (Diogn. 10.2). Knowledge of such a story will fill Diognetus with joy and compel him to love the one who first loved him. Next, the natural outworking of love for God is to be "an imitator of his goodness" (10.3–4a).

The imitation of God(s) was a well-known trope in philosophical literature (e.g., Plato, *Theaet.* 176; Philo, *Virt.* 168) and found its way into Christian exhortation (e.g., Eph 5:1; Ign. *Eph.* 1.1; *Trall.* 1.2; Ps.-Clem. 1.26), with some tacit connections to the Hebrew Scriptures (e.g., Lev 19:2). For the author, imitation of the divine is not a remote aspiration but something genuinely possible "if God is willing" (Diogn. 10.4b). God is great in the sense of his beneficence, and few people can imitate this aspect of the divine character (10.5). Yet one who takes up a neighbor's burden, who helps those in need, becomes a god to that person by their benefaction and so imitates God's own goodness (10.6).

If Diognetus accepts this paradigm of knowledge, love, and imitation, then he will know that "God lives in heaven." In addition, he will be fit to declare the "mysteries of God"—that is, God's purposes unveiled in the Son. Moreover, he will love and admire Christians even when they are punished, and he will condemn the deceit and error of the world. Then, as a Christian convert, Diognetus would understand "the true life in heaven" and also learn to despise the death of the body, as opposed to the "real death" of "eternal fire" for those who deserve it (10.7). The author hopes Diognetus admires those who endure the "transitory fire" of persecution, and do so for "righteousness' sake," which is tantamount to God's saving plan (cf. Matt 3:15). At this point, the argument breaks off abruptly.

A Homily on the "Epiphany of the Word" (11.1–12.9)

The homily provides a short exhortation or catechesis for an ideal pagan convert by describing the Word as an agent of revelation, utilizing a blend of Pauline and Johannine language, reiterating the significance of grace, featuring an allegorical interpretation of the

37. Arnold, *Justification*, 94.

38. Cf. 4 Ezra 6.53–59, where God made the world for Israel, while in Herm. Vis. 2.4.1, God made the world for the church.

two trees in Eden, all for the neophyte to attain true knowledge. The homily begins and ends with reference to the Word (Diogn. 11.2; 12.9) and divides into two parts consisting of the "Word of Grace" (11.1–8) and "Knowledge of the Word" (12.1–9).

In the first part, the author of the homily adopts the first person and insists that his instruction is not about "strange things" or "irrational speculation." He roots himself in earlier tradition as one who tries to "minister in a worthy manner the teachings that have been handed down." He self-describes as a "disciple of the apostles," much like postapostolic elders (cf. Irenaeus, *Haer.* 3.3.4; 4.27.1), and "a teacher of the Gentiles," just like Paul (cf. 1 Tim 2:7). The reader, it is hoped, will be among those who are "becoming disciples of the truth" (Diogn. 11.1). Anyone who is rightly instructed will come to love the Word and learn the things that the Word made known to the disciples. The Word himself explained to the disciples the "mysteries of the Father" (11.2). Then, echoing 1 Timothy 3:16, the Word was sent so that he might appear in the world, be shamed by the Jewish people, be preached by the apostles, and be believed in by the gentiles (11.3). The Word is an eternal deity, "the Eternal One," known as a "Son," who enriches the church and multiplies grace to the saints (11.5). This "grace" is something of a generous impartation of understanding to enable the faithful to grasp God's comprehensive purposes (11.5). When this understanding is effective, it leads to a kind of protocanonical consciousness, so that "the reverence of the law is praised in song, and the grace of prophets is recognized, and the faith of the gospels is established, and the tradition of the apostles is preserved" (11.6). If this grace is grasped rather than grieved, then the reader will understand what the Word says, who he says it through, whenever he wishes to declare it (11.7). The author professes that he is merely sharing what he himself has been led to speak by "the will of the commanding Word" and out of a "love for the things that have been revealed to us" (11.8).

The second part begins with an exhortation to listen to the truths just expounded, as this will enable the reader to know the good things that God grants to those who love him and enable them to bear all kinds of fruit (Diogn. 12.1). The author then shifts to an allegorical interpretation of the tree of life and tree of the knowledge of good and evil in Genesis 2:9. Adopting a revisionist approach, he comments that it is not the tree of knowledge that kills but the act of disobedience (Diogn. 12.2). God, according to the Scriptures, planted trees of knowledge and life in the garden, because life comes from knowledge. The problem was not with the tree of knowledge per se, but with the primeval couple who did not use it "purely" as they were deceived by the serpent (12.3–4). The allegory is proved by the apostle Paul's words from 1 Corinthians 8:1 that "knowledge puffs up, but love builds up." Paul's words are taken to prove that knowledge leads to life and life leads to fruitfulness (12.5–6). The author exhorts the reader to have a heart full of knowledge and to make room in his life for the "true Word" (trans. MFB). This advice is its own tree, so that, if cultivated, it will lead to a harvest of fruit that God desires and which the serpent cannot infect (12.7–8a).

Next is an abrupt change of topic, with the author promising that in this fruitful dispensation, "Eve is not corrupted; instead, a virgin is trusted," which is perhaps a metaphor for the church. The style is poetic and almost creedal as the author concludes by mentioning the manifestation of salvation, the instruction of the apostles, an enigmatic reference to the "Passover of the Lord," which could be either the Eucharist or hope for his parousia. The Word is then personified as rejoicing as he teaches the saints and as the vehicle from whom the Father is glorified. The text of Diognetus ends with a concluding doxology: "To him be glory forever. Amen" (12.8b–9).

3. INTERPRETATIVE ISSUES

3.1 Theological Value and Significant Themes

Concerning God, the letter is driven to explain what God Christians believe in and worship (Diogn. 1.1). Diognetus amplifies Jewish tradition that God is not to be worshiped as objects crafted with human hands (2.2–9) and rejects associations of God with physical elements like fire and water (8.2). The rejection of Jewish cultic worship is due to divine aseity, where God does not have needs to be met by sacrificial offerings (3.4–5). God is celebrated as "Master and Creator" (8.7), "omnipotent Creator" (7.2), who made "heaven and earth" (3.4), akin to a "king" (7.4), who rules over the universe (10.7), sovereign over heavenly subordinates indicative of a "monarchical monotheism,"[39] combined with a strong sense of divine providence (7.2). Importantly, God's character is loving as opposed to tyrannical (7.4; 10.2). God is described as patient with people in their unrighteousness, and he is especially good by setting forth salvation (8.7–8; 9.1–2, 6). Imitation of God is imitation of divine benevolence (10.4–7). God is invisible and unknowable and therefore becomes self-revealing, as he wants people to have proper "knowledge" through faith and the Word (8.1, 5–6, 11; 10.1–3; cf. 11.2; 12.1–7). At one climactic point, God is described with an array of titles: "nurse, father, teacher, counsellor, healer, mind, light, honor, glory, strength, and life" (9.6). In sum, God is described as an absolute cosmic monarch with an unusual kindness and benevolence toward humanity.

The christological dimensions have several prominent features. To begin with, the name "Jesus" and the title "Christ" are never once used.[40] There is no extant knowledge of the Jesus tradition, though there is clear familiarity with the Johannine Logos tradition (even if indirectly). God's chief agent is not angelic beings, but the "holy, incomprehensible Word from heaven," the "Designer and Creator of the universe" (Diogn. 7.2), who is "sent" (7.2, 4–5, 10.2; cf. 11.3), for a time of loving and not judging (7.6), described also as a "son" who is a "king" like his father (7.4), "his only-begotten Son" (τὸν υἱὸν αὐτοῦ τὸν μονογενῆ, *ton huion autou ton monogenē*, 10.2 [MFB]), who comes "as God" and "as a human" (7.4). As such, the coming of the Son is also the coming of God (8.1). As God's "beloved child" (ἀγαπητοῦ παιδός, *agapētou paidos*), he receives the divine plan for salvation and transmits it to the church (8.9–11), rendering the child both the bearer and content of God's plan (9.1). In such a plan, God puts forward the Son as a "ransom" (9.2). Justification is found "in the Son of God alone," demonstrating the "Saviour's power to save even the powerless" (9.4, 6). The Son will be sent again, next time in judgment (7.6).

The homily expresses a Logos Christology, where the "Word" is revealed to and through the disciples and even in the church (11.2–3, 7–8; 12.6). The Word is the "Eternal One," with origins "from the beginning," who is reckoned as a Son (11.4–5), and the Father is glorified through the Word (12.9). The Christology of Diognetus is similar to the Logos Christology of Justin, except that it has an almost exclusive focus on the Word as revealer and redeemer, even if combined with a divine Christology that—from our perspective—moves a step closer toward the formulas of Nicaea and Constantinople.

The Son as "Savior" reveals a specific mode of "salvation" (Diogn. 9.6; 12.9). God's kindness and love (9.1, 2, 6; 10.2–4, 7) is such that humanity, although powerless to save themselves (9.1, 6), can be saved from the ignorance of idolatry and philosophy (2.1–10;

39. T. Ludwig, "Monotheism," in *The Encyclopedia of Religion*, ed. L. Jones, 2nd ed., 15 vols. (Detroit: MacMillan, 2005), 9:6159.

40. Of course, the fact that the label "Christians" is used throughout surely implies the designation "Christ" after whom they are so named (1.1; 2.6–7, 10; 3.1; 4.6; 5.1; 6.1–9).

8.2–4), an inability to enter the kingdom (9.1), the "season of unrighteousness" where humans were captive to their wicked impulses (9.1–2), their sins, lawlessness, impiety (9.3–4), the fear of death (10.7), condemnation and death (9.2), and the "real death" of "eternal fire" (8.2; 10.7). God' solution is "a great and marvelous plan" from the beginning that was secretive and utterly unexpected (8.9–11; 9.1). In this plan, salvation is by God's power (9.1–2), through "faith" in the "Son of God alone," who brings "knowledge" of the Father (8.6, 10–11; 9.4, 6; 10.1, 3). Salvation is liberative with redemption (9.2), forensic with justification (5.14; 9.4–5), ethnographically transformative as one becomes part of the new *genos* of Christians (1.1; 5.1–17). To be saved means that one enters the "season of righteousness" where one is "made worthy" of God, enabled to enter the kingdom of God (9.1), is able to love God, and to imitate God (10.3–4). Salvation means citizenship in heaven (5.9) and waiting for an imperishable life in heaven (5.12, 16; 6.8; 10.2, 7). The closest the author gets to describing anything like a mechanism of salvation or a model of atonement is 9.2–6:

> He himself experienced our sin, he himself gave his own son, a ransom on our behalf, the Holy for the lawless, the innocent for the guilty, the righteous for the unrighteous, the incorruptible for the corruptible, the immortal for the mortal. For what else than that one's righteousness could cover up our sin? In who else than in the Son of God alone could our lawlessness and ungodliness possibly be justified? Oh, the sweet exchange! Oh, the fathomless creation! Oh, the unexpected benefits that the lawlessness of many should be concealed in the one righteous, and righteousness of the one should justify many lawless.[41]

The language deployed here is that of substitution,[42] with connotations of sacrifice in the mention of "ransom" and "covering" (cf. Exod 30:16; Ps 32:1; Isa 44:22–23; Jas 5:20). In addition, there is a clear *iustificatio impii* ("justification of the ungodly"), with the Son's own righteousness as a covering over the lawless. The author poetically expands on Paul's articulation of the justification of the ungodly and presents an array of images to demonstrate the forensic and Christocentric nature of justification.[43] Furthermore, in the homily, salvation is also achieved by the new Eve (Diogn. 12.8–9), faith is instrumental (11.3), there is new birth (11.4), knowledge and fruitfulness (11.2, 5, 7–8; 12.1–4, 8), and the salvific ministry of the church is arguably described as the "Passover of the Lord," where the apostolic message is celebrated and attested (12.9).

The best descriptor for salvation in Diognetus would be "to share in his benefactions," in the sense of sharing the benefits of faith in the Son (8.11 [MFB]). At the risk of anachronism, one could venture to say that much here resonates with theological motifs defined as *sola gratia*, *sola fide*, and *solus Christus*.

The only mention of the "church" is in the homily, where the church stands in organic union with the Son and promulgates the instruction of the apostles (Diogn. 11.5–6). Similarly, there is mention of the "saints" who are born anew, experience grace, and are instructed by the Word (11.4–5; 12.9). Even while the homily eulogizes the Word, its focus is on the apostolicity of the church and its teaching rather than on its christological foundation. In the main body, the author much prefers to speak of "Christians" (1.1; 2.6–7, 10;

41. Brannan, *Apostolic Fathers*, 285–86.

42. Cf. Lona, *Diognet*, 267; Crowe, "Oh Sweet Exchange!," 104–7; Arnold, *Justification*, 96–99. Contra Meecham, *Diognetus*, 130, who sees an exchange of states rather than of persons, which flounders on the observation that it is persons in the states of unrighteousness and righteousness respectively that are rectified.

43. Bird, "Reception," 87.

3.1; 4.6; 5.1; 6.1–9) who are believers, knowers, lovers, and imitators of God. The claim that Christians are a "new race" (1.1) resonates with Aristides, who called Christians a "third race" beside Jews and Greeks,[44] perhaps derivative of the apostle Paul who divided the world into Jews, Greeks, and the church of God (1 Cor 10:32). The innovative element in Diognetus is that while the Christian *genos* is ostensibly similar to others in their dwellings, dialect, diet, and dress, yet they are separate on account of their worship and way of life (Diogn. 5.1–7). In other words, the author envisages something that would be either mystifying or mortifying to outsiders— namely, that it was possible to severe the link between people, *polis* ("city"), *politeuma* ("citizenship), *pietas* ("piety"), and *pantheon* ("precinct of various temples and deities"), to be a new kind of people under a new deity. In which case, one's worship redefined one's citizenship, acting as a transcultural and transethnographic marker, demonstrating a universalizing function that can compete against other universalizing identities such as Greek-ness and Roman-ness. This creates a conflict of identities and loyalties for Christians, for while they are perhaps Syrian, Thracian, Greek, or Roman citizens, they are first and foremost "citizens of heaven" (5.5, 9).[45]

Finally, the author rehearses the *contra Iudaeos* tradition by equating the Jerusalem cultus as no better than idol worship since God does not need sacrifices (Diogn. 3.1–6), and its mode of *Gesetzeskritik* "ridicules the Torah as superstitious" (4.1–6).[46] The homily sanitizes the Torah through allegorical interpretation and coordinating the Torah with the Prophets, Gospels, and apostolic tradition (11.6; 12.3–5). The author assumes that Judaism and Christianity have parted ways, although it far exceeds the intra-Jewish polemic of the New Testament.

4. KEY PASSAGES FOR NEW TESTAMENT STUDIES AND THEIR SIGNIFICANCE

Diognetus contains a number of echoes and allusions to the New Testament, principally Paul's letters and John's Gospel.[47] One interesting facet is that the author critiques the Jerusalem temple cultus in Diognetus 3.1–5 even though the temple had been destroyed as much as a century earlier. The implication is that the critique of the temple cultus in the book of Hebrews likewise does not require the temple to be currently operating at the time the author was writing. Otherwise, significant texts for New Testament study include the following.

John 3:16–17 has the famous line, "For God so loved the world that he gave his only Son . . . God did not send the Son into the world to condemn the world, but in order that the world might be saved through him." Such language and sentiment are arguably rehearsed in Diognetus with "when he [God] sent him [Son] he did so as one loving, not judging" (Diogn. 7.5) and "for God loved humanity . . . to them he sent his one and only Son" (10.2).[48] Passages such as this indicate that Diognetus riffs on Johannine tradition in its expression of the incarnation. Diognetus thus buttresses the affirmation of Jesus's preexistence, divine sonship, and sending for the purpose of salvation, a rehearsal of much of the Johannine tradition.

---

44. Aristides, *Apol.* 2.2; 16.4; cf. Preaching of Peter §2; Tertullian, *Nat.* 1.8, 20.

45. Cf. D. K. Buell, *Why This New Race? Ethnic Reasoning in Early Christianity* (New York: Columbia University Press, 2005), 29–33.

46. D. Lincicum, "Against the Law: The *Epistle of Barnabas* and Torah Polemic in Early Christianity," in *Law and Lawlessness in Early Judaism and Early Christianity*, ed, D. Lincicum, R. Sheridan, and C. M. Stang, WUNT 420 (Tübingen: Mohr-Siebeck, 2020), 105–21, at 114.

47. Cf. e.g., Bird, "Reception"; C. E. Hill, *Johannine Corpus in the Early Church* (Oxford: Oxford University Press, 2006), 361–66; Jefford, *Diognetus*, 72–93.

48. Cf. Hill, *Johannine Corpus*, 363–64.

Paul's mention of "citizenship in heaven" in Philippians 3:20 is alluded to in Diognetus 5.9: "They live on earth, but their citizenship is in heaven." In one sense, Christians are heavenly colonists in the cities of the Greco-Roman world; but in another sense they are sojourners waiting for a "kingdom in heaven" and attaining "true life in heaven" (10.2, 7). The notion of Christians as heavenly citizens in Diognetus stands very much between Paul's ecclesiology and Augustine's *City of God* with its representation of the church as sojourners among the city of men.

Paul's catalogue of hardships in 2 Corinthians 6:3–10 is mirrored in Diognetus 5.10–17 where Christian distinctiveness leads to persecution and deprivation. Apart from some shared language, there is a shared function, as the unjust treatment that Christians endure demonstrates their virtuous character, fails to impede their mission, and functions as a badge of their fidelity to God. By superseding expectations of what citizens would normally be able to endure, and acting without aggravation or animosity, Christians demonstrate the superiority of their way of life. This builds on the author's case for Christians as a new *genos* with a new and distinctive way of life that defies socioreligious norms of the Greco-Roman world.

The exhortation about imitating God, specifically imitating God's goodness by active benevolence toward one's neighbors found in Diognetus 10.4, 6, is potentially resourced from Ephesians 5:1. In Ephesians 5, believers are urged to live and act as beloved children by becoming "imitators of God." What is more, both Ephesians 5.1–2 and Diognetus 10.3–6 share the motif of love as the proof of imitating the divine. The idea of imitating the god was known to Platonic, Stoic, and Pythagorean philosophers, as well as to Philo. However, as Michael Heintz states, "Unlike the moral theorists of the Hellenistic world, who viewed moral growth as the product of self-disciplined effort and as the achievement and property of the virtuous person, the *Epistle* emphasizes human incapacity and powerlessness apart from God's intervention in his *logos*. The imitation of God is understood and expressed in terms of the divine plan revealed in that *logos*."[49]

In Romans 5:18–19, Paul's comparison of Adam's disobedience unto condemnation for all and Christ's act of righteousness to justify many seems to be programmatic for Diognetus 9.3–5, where the "sinfulness of many should be hidden in one righteous person, while the righteousness of one should justify many sinners."[50] There may not be a federal theology operating in Diognetus, as there is no reference to Adam's solidarity with humanity, but as Brandon Crowe observes, "The author's focus on the Son's righteousness may be an example of an early Christian interpretation of Rom 5."[51] The author of Diognetus here expands on Paul's theme of the justification of the ungodly and deploys language to demonstrate the forensic and Christocentric nature of justification. Viewed this way, Diognetus arguably stands as a middle point between Paul and the Protestant tradition.

Finally, we might note that the only explicit citation of a New Testament text is 1 Corinthians 8:1, in Diognetus 12.6: "Knowledge puffs up, but love builds up." Paul's maxim about the potential haughtiness of knowledge without love is transformed into a salvific paradigm whereby knowledge and life are interdependent. Paul's words are taken to prove the noetic path to life and the vitalizing power of knowledge. For the author, knowledge of God is necessary because ignorance leads to disobedience.[52]

---

49. Cf. M. Heintz, "*Mimesis Theou* in the Epistle to Diognetus," *JECS* 12 (2004): 118.

50. Meecham, *Diognetus*, 130; Lona, *Diognet*, 53, 273; Crowe, "Oh Sweet Exchange!," 108–9; Bird, "Reception," 87.

51. Crowe, "Oh Sweet Exchange!," 109.

52. Bird, "Reception," 74–75.

5. CONCLUSION

Notwithstanding the mystery of origins, authorship, and addressee, Diognetus is a powerful piece of Christian apologetic literature. It defines the Christian *genos* over and against Greco-Roman religious practices and Judaism, identifies Christians as having a positive role in the world as its life-giving soul, offers moving testimony to God's purposes and love, narrates a robust account of the incarnation with Jesus as divine and human, majors on the motif of divine love, offers a poignant image of justification resulting from a "sweet exchange," and exhorts readers to the imitation of God. Even the homiletical appendix includes a memorable account of the Word bringing knowledge of God's love. There is an amazing synthesis of Pauline and Johannine language and themes. It is quite a shame that this document had been lost and forgotten for most of church history. One can only imagine its reception among Athanasius, Augustine, Abelard, and Aquinas. Despite its tendentious dismissal of Judaism, the glaring absence of the Old Testament, and an unfortunate pneumatic disinterest, the author's core convictions about God, Son, and salvation are among the most sublime expositions of Christian faith in the entire gamut of second-century Christian writings.

BIBLIOGRAPHY

Bird, M. F. "The Reception of Paul in the *Epistle to Diognetus*." Pages 70–90 in *Paul in the Second Century*. Edited by M. F. Bird and J. R. Dodson. LNTS 412. London: T&T Clark, 2011.

Bird, M. F., and K. MacKerras. "The Epistle to Diognetus and the Fragment of Quadratus." Pages 309–11 in *The Cambridge Companion to the Apostolic Fathers*. Edited by M. Bird and S. Harrower. Cambridge: Cambridge University Press, 2021.

Crowe, B. D. "'Oh Sweet Exchange! The Soteriological Significance of the Incarnation in the Epistle to Diognetus." *ZNW* 102 (2011): 96–109.

Foster, P. "The Epistle to Diognetus." Pages 147–56 in *The Writings of the Apostolic Fathers*. Edited by P. Foster. London: T&T Clark, 2007.

Hill, C. E. *From the Lost Teaching of Polycarp: Identifying Irenaeus' Apostolic Presbyter and the Author of Ad Diognetum*. WUNT 186. Tübingen: Mohr Siebeck, 2006.

Jefford, C. N. *The Epistle to Diognetus (with the Fragment of Quadratus): Introduction, Text, and Commentary*. OAF. Oxford: Oxford University Press, 2013.

Lona, H. E. *An Diognet: Übersetzt und erklärt*. Kommentar zu frühchristlichen Apologeten 8. Freiburg: Herder, 2001.

Marrou, H. I. *À Diognète: Introduction, edition critique, traduction et commentaire*. 2nd ed. SC 33.2. Paris: Cerf, 1997.

Meecham, H. G. *The Epistle to Diognetus*. Manchester: Manchester University Press, 1949.

PART 2

THEOLOGICAL THEMES

CHAPTER 13

CHRISTOLOGICAL PERSPECTIVES IN THE APOSTOLIC FATHERS

PAUL FOSTER

1. INTRODUCTION

It is no exaggeration to say that virtually every text contained in the corpus of the Apostolic Fathers is a christological writing. Admittedly, the degree of christological emphasis varies between the writings. However, ultimately, every text in the collection emerges from a context where both the author and the addressees share an interest in, or a commitment to, Jesus. In some texts that commitment is taken as a given. It is a shared basis of belief, and it is from this position of common faith that other themes or topics in the writing are discussed. At other times it is christological perspectives or beliefs themselves that are contested. When that is the case, the author typically devotes more space to the presentation of christological understandings, while dismissing and denigrating the opposing views.

The texts that constitute the typical collection of writings in the corpus of the Apostolic Fathers differ in terms of genre, contents, quality of preservation, and the purpose of writing. They do not articulate the same formulations to express their beliefs about the significance of Jesus. In part, such variety may be due to regional differences and depend on community preferences. Some expressions appear novel, if not at times simply odd. Others are immediately recognizable, perhaps building on ideas contained in the New Testament or developing formulations that were to become embedded in the theological vocabulary of subsequent generations. There is, therefore, a rich tapestry of christological ideas, images, language, expressions, and understandings. The second century, the period when most of the texts found in the Apostolic Fathers were written, was a period of innovation and clarification. This development and crystallization of ideas can be seen in the formulations of christological affirmations.[1] Yet, despite this diversity, there remain aspects of Christology that appear to be unifying elements across texts. The commonality in calling Jesus "Lord" is a regular and typical feature. Furthermore, several texts assume a basic christological narrative. This narrative declares Jesus's unique filial relationship to God the Father, describes Christ's death as an act of obedience with saving significance, and proclaims a

1. In regard to the NT, James Dunn notes that "the NT documents cover an intense period of innovation and/or development in what we now call 'christology'" (J. D. G. Dunn, *Christology in the Making: A New Testament Inquiry into the Origins of the Doctrine of the Incarnation*, 2nd ed. [Grand Rapids: Eerdmans, 1989], xii). That period of innovation did not conclude with the NT but continued into the period of the Apostolic Fathers and beyond.

vindication that overturns death and thus demonstrates that Jesus was more than a mere human figure. Not every writing in the corpus deploys all of these elements, especially those that are fragmentary. However, they do share much in common even when their modes of expression differ.

The purpose of this essay is twofold. The first is to discuss the christological perspectives of each text that is part of the Apostolic Fathers collection. Obviously, the discussion of the christological views of, for instance, the single fragment that survives of the Apology of Quadratus is of a different order from the analysis of the christological statements and perspectives articulated in the seven authentic letters of Ignatius of Antioch. Second, a comparative analysis will then follow. Here, both the differences in christological expressions and the similarities in understandings of the significance of Jesus will be explored. There is no agenda at work here, just the desire to accurately map out the lines of divergence and convergence. In the process it is hoped that the formative vibrancy of the period, as a time of rich theological reflection, might be better appreciated.

The method for describing an author's Christology has been developed in regard to the writings that came to form the New Testament. A classic aspect of the method has been a so-called titular approach.[2] This method primarily looks at the titles used to describe Jesus, based on the understanding that the elevated titles that writers apply to Jesus indicate the status attributed to him and reflect beliefs about his identity. This approach can only take interpreters so far. Consequently, an overemphasis on a titular approach has been critiqued. The writings of early Christianity convey christological beliefs in multifaceted ways and do not confine their christological perspectives merely to a set of preferred titles.[3] Rather, narratives, primitive creedal statements, theological debates, and visionary experiences of the risen Christ all form part of the rich tapestry of early Christian christological expression. Moreover, the acts of devotion and the practice of the worship of the risen Jesus reflect christological commitments as a key part of the praxis of early believers.[4] Such features are present to varied extent in the writings of the Apostolic Fathers. Therefore, a multidimensional approach is required to map the christological perspectives of the various texts that were subsequently assembled and collectively known as the Apostolic Fathers.

2. CHRISTOLOGY IN THE INDIVIDUAL WRITINGS OF THE APOSTOLIC FATHERS

In this section, the eleven texts that typically constitute the collection of writings are discussed individually. The sequence follows the arrangement in the collection edited by Michael Holmes.[5] That sequence is based on the order of texts contained in the edition edited by Lightfoot and Harmer,[6] with further texts having been subsequently added to the collection.

2. Some of the best-known examples of this titular approach to NT Christology include O. Cullmann, *The Christology of the New Testament* (London: SCM, 1959), and F. Hahn, *The Titles of Jesus in Christology* (London: Lutterworth, 1969).

3. On this point, see C. M. Tuckett, *Christology and the New Testament: Jesus and His Earliest Followers* (Edinburgh: Edinburgh University Press, 2001), 11.

4. In regard to devotion to Jesus as an indicator of christological understandings, see L. W. Hurtado, *Lord Jesus Christ: Devotion to Jesus in Earliest Christianity* (Grand Rapids: Eerdmans, 2003).

5. M. W. Holmes, ed., *The Apostolic Fathers: Greek Texts and English Translations*, 3rd ed. (Grand Rapids: Baker Academic, 2007). Unless otherwise noted, all translations of the Apostolic Fathers in this essay are from Holmes.

6. J. B. Lightfoot, ed., *The Apostolic Fathers: Revised Texts with Short Introductions and English Translations*, edited and completed by J. R. Harmer (London: Macmillan, 1891).

2.1 First Clement

The First Letter of Clement to the Corinthians is not primarily concerned with christological matters. The chief concern is of an ecclesial nature. The letter makes clear that the long-term leaders had been displaced (1 Clem. 57.1). From the perspective of the author of the letter, their legitimate authority had been usurped, and younger, ambitious men had taken their place (1 Clem. 3.3). This had caused disunity among the believers in Corinth.

Given 1 Clement's focus on resolving the difference of opinions concerning ecclesial matters, it is perhaps not surprising that statements about Christology are typically made in passing and without further justification. This suggests a largely shared and uncontested understanding of christological commitments both within the Corinthian context and also between the community in Rome and that in Corinth. That apparent agreement on christological perspectives is striking, and at the very least reflects the fact that the author of 1 Clement did not perceive any christological differences between himself and his addressees in Corinth that required debate or clarification.

The author uses a number of fulsome phrases to refer to Jesus. In line with Pauline terminology, on several occasions a combination of names and titles is employed in the naming formula "Lord Jesus Christ," which occurs ten times throughout the letter.[7] Given the author's knowledge of at least some of Paul's letters, including certainly Romans and 1 Corinthians, this phrase appears to be inherited from earlier Christian tradition and use. That, however, does not negate its significance. The letter repeatedly speaks of blessing or status coming to believers "through our Lord Jesus Christ." Thus "those who are called and sanctified by the will of God" receive both the calling and sanctification "through our Lord Jesus Christ" (1 Clem. salut.). Immediately following this, using a slightly truncated christological formula, the agency of Jesus is again asserted: "May grace and peace from almighty God through Jesus Christ be yours in abundance." Here, not only is Christ the agent through whom the divine blessings are bestowed on believers, but more significantly Jesus is portrayed as being inextricably linked with the salvific actions of God that result in status, blessing, and holiness being imparted to believers. Similarly, the author reminds the Corinthians that they have been able to take refuge in God's "compassionate mercies through our Lord Jesus Christ" (1 Clem. 20.11), and that the apostles were given foreknowledge of the strife that would arise over leadership roles "through our Lord Jesus Christ" (1 Clem. 44.1).

The letter does little to explain the relationship between Jesus and God beyond the descriptions familiar from the writings that would later become the New Testament. The additional metaphors it offers are rich in imagery but lacking in theological precision. For instance, Jesus's filial relationship with God is affirmed. Hence, with the confirmation of a scriptural text the letter states, "But of his son the Master spoke thus, 'You are my son, today I have begotten you. Ask of me and I will give you the Gentiles for your inheritance, and the ends of the earth for your possession'" (1 Clem. 36.4). The first part of the citation is shared with Hebrews 1:5a (which itself is a citation of Ps 2:7b LXX), and the second part continues the citation of Psalm 2 (Ps 2:8 LXX).[8] In this context, God is referred to as

7. See 1 Clem. salut.; 20.11; 21.6; 24.1; 42.2, 3; 44.1; 58.2; 64.1; 65.2.

8. There is a rich and yet complex citation pattern here. While the continuation of the citation drawing on Ps 2:8 LXX might initially suggest that the text is being drawn exclusively from Psalm 2 and not from Heb 1:5b, the following verse 1 Clem. 36.5 also cites Ps 110:1 LXX, which is likewise cited in the same context in Hebrews (Heb 1:13). In fact, as Lindemann notes, "The similarity of 1 Clem 36.2–5 to Hebrews 1:3–5, 7, 13 is so great that the use of Hebrews by 1 Clem must still be considered possible" (A. Lindemann, "The First Epistle of Clement," in *The Apostolic Fathers: An Introduction*, ed. W. Pratscher [Waco, TX: Baylor University Press, 2010], 47–69, here 59).

"the master" (ὁ δεσπότης, *ho despotēs*), a term infrequent in the New Testament writings[9] and never used in a formulation of the father-son relationship between God and Jesus in the New Testament. Therefore, while varying the terminology, 1 Clement affirms the widespread christological concept of Jesus being God's Son.

Another idea repeated in the letter revolves around Jesus's role as a teacher. In 1 Clement 13.1–4 a series of exhortations is introduced with the command, "Let us remember the words of the Lord Jesus, which he spoke as he taught gentleness and patience" (1 Clem. 13.1b). There then follows a pastiche of gospel-like sayings.[10] A similar formula is used later in the letter to again highlight the teachings given by Jesus: "Remember the words of Jesus our Lord" (1 Clem. 46.7).

One of the most prominent christological ideas in the letter concerns the sacrificial and redemptive death of Jesus. At various points the letter describes the blood of Jesus as efficacious for salvation. One of the fullest statements exhorts the Corinthians to regard the blood of Christ with a sense of wonder and veneration: "Let us fix our eyes on the blood of Christ and understand how precious it is to the Father, because being poured out for our salvation, it won for the whole world the grace of repentance" (1 Clem. 7.4). It would be misleading to read these statements in support of certain modern ideas regarding atonement. However, taking the statements on their own terms, it is striking that Christ's blood is declared to be precious to the Father. Here the author is surely picking up on ideas of the obedience to God involved in the death of Jesus. In line with wider concepts of sacrifice both in Judaism and in Greco-Roman cults, the blood of Christ is said to be poured out for salvation. Thus, the blood of Christ is considered the means of salvation for believers. Moreover, the author celebrates the plenary power of this salvation, stating the grace of repentance that it brings is for the whole world. Elsewhere it is made clear that the blood of the Lord brings repentance "to all who believe and hope in God" (1 Clem. 12.7). Hence the author appears to affirm both poles of the debate concerning the scope of salvation. On the one hand, it is "for the whole world," while, on the other hand, it is limited to "all who believe." Furthermore, it is stressed that the death of Christ is representative and in the stead of believers: "Because of the love that he had for us, Jesus Christ our Lord, in accordance with God's will, gave his blood for us, and his flesh for our flesh, and his life for our lives" (1 Clem. 49.6).

Therefore, in 1 Clement one finds a developed christological reflection on the redemptive nature of Christ's death. That death is carried out in obedience to God and hence is precious to God, is the means by which believers receive salvation and redemption, and is a vicarious exchange of the flesh and life of Jesus in place of the flesh and life of believers. It is on this basis that salvation is also given an ecclesial dimension with the exhortation, "Let the whole body be saved in Christ Jesus" (1 Clem. 38.1). In this context, the corporate dimension of salvation is affirmed alongside a clear directive for individual believers to live in harmony and mutual subjection "so that the whole body may be saved" (1 Clem. 37.5). Here 1 Clement brings a shared perspective on salvation to bear on the issue of the disunity

---

9. In the NT, the term δεσπότης is used as a designation for God in the following passages: Luke 2:29; Acts 4:24; 2 Tim 2:21; 2 Pet 2:1; and Rev 6:10. It is used once to refer to "our only Master and Lord, Jesus Christ" (Jude 4).

10. In regard to these sayings, Holmes lists the likely points of contact with gospel traditions and makes the following observation: "Cf. Matt. 5:7; 6:14; 7:1–2, 12; Luke 6:31, 36–38. Because of the differences between these citations and the canonical texts, it is widely thought that Clement is here (and in 46.8 as well) dependent on a collection of sayings independent of (and possibly earlier than) Matthew and Luke" (Holmes, *Apostolic Fathers*, 61, 63).

arising from leadership struggles. It is argued that the key concern should be the salvation of all members in Christ, rather than individual desire to claim positions of prominence.

The letter provides little sustained reflection on the incarnation, or first coming of Christ. However, some fleeting statements and subtle hints indicate alignment with wider views in the period. Having just described the humility of Jacob (1 Clem. 31.4), it is stated that "from Jacob come all the priests and Levites who minister at the altar of God; from him comes the Lord Jesus according to the flesh" (1 Clem. 32.2). The phrase "according to the flesh" suggests that the author understands the Lord Jesus also to possess a non-fleshly line of descent. Thus, some type of incarnational idea stands behind this statement. While the author at no point speaks clearly of a prior existence of Christ, one statement aligns with some kind of *praeparatio evangelica*: among figures from the Jewish Scriptures, Elijah, Elisha, Ezekiel, the prophets, and others of renown are said to have engaged in "preaching the coming of Christ" (1 Clem. 17.1). This indicates some knowledge of Christ among the prophets prior to his coming. Hence, there are only brief statements and ideas expressed in regard to the incarnation or prior existence of Christ.

By contrast, the author provides fuller statements concerning the vindication, exaltation, and future return of Christ. The Corinthian believers are commanded to be "fully assured by the resurrection of our Lord Jesus Christ" (1 Clem. 42.3). In fact, the discussion presents a lengthy discourse concerning the resurrection and its plausibility. Initially it is stated in stereotypical language that God "made the Lord Jesus Christ the first fruit when he raised him from the dead" (24.1). This is presented as the prime reason why believers should be assured of their own future resurrection. Next follows a series of exemplary proofs that are intended to persuade readers of the veracity of the resurrection, including the departing and rising of the sun (24.3), seeds that although dead spring to life (24.4), and an extended discussion of the rebirth of the phoenix (25.1–26.1). However, apart from the scriptural citation, "Sit at my right hand" (36.5), there is little discussion of Christ's location after the resurrection. By contrast, there is, however, a clear expectation of his future return. Again, drawing on Scripture, it is affirmed that the Lord "will come quickly and not delay; and the Lord will come suddenly into his temple, even the Holy One whom you expect" (1 Clem. 23.5; cf. Isa 13:22 LXX; Mal 3:1 LXX). Again, with scriptural warrant, the letter declares, "Behold, the Lord comes, and his reward is with him, to pay each one according to his work" (1 Clem. 34.3; cf. Isa 40:10; 62:11 LXX). Also in his own words, the author speaks of a time when those who were perfected in grace from the time of Adam "will be revealed when the kingdom of Christ visits us" (1 Clem. 50.3). While there is no sense of imminence, there is nonetheless a belief in the certainty of Christ's future return.[11] This eschatological hope is predicated on Christ's own resurrection, which itself is the basis for belief in the resurrection of believers. There is also an articulation of the ideas of Christ's future return at which his kingdom will be established.

Despite the fact that the central concern of the letter is focused on the pressing issue of community disharmony and not on christological matters, there are many key affirmations about Jesus and an obvious shared understanding of his significance for believers both in Rome and Corinth. In terms of the form of designation, the letter frequently uses the formula "Lord Jesus Christ," or shorter forms "Lord Jesus," "Jesus Christ," "Christ Jesus,"

11. Lindemann detects a similar orientation in the author's eschatology. He states, "The strictly future-oriented eschatology implies that the world God created is nearly immortal—the end times are no longer hoped for concretely, but rather are basically conceived abstractly and in any case not near the goal of history" (Lindemann, "First Epistle of Clement," 63).

and even once the unusual combination "Lord Christ Jesus" (1 Clem. 16.2). Christ's death, described as "the shedding of blood," is seen as redemptive and soteriological. Moreover, the author declares it to be representative in that Jesus gave his life in place of the life of believers. The teachings of the earthly Jesus are of paramount importance in providing ethical guidance to contemporary believers. Furthermore, the one who came first in the flesh will come again in the future to establish the kingdom. None of this is contested or a point of debate in the letter. The author states these matters as part of an appeal to the shared understanding of the significance of Jesus and in the hope that those common beliefs will help rectify the dissension over leadership roles in the Corinthian community.

2.2 Second Clement

The text known as the Second Epistle of Clement is neither a letter nor written by the same author as 1 Clement. Rather, the majority view is that the text is a sermon with paraenetic aims. That is, it seeks to gently remind readers of moral behaviors to be either practiced or avoided, addressed to an audience that shares the author's belief commitments.[12] However, this classification as a homily or sermon has been strongly critiqued.[13] Despite the attribution of the title, the author is unknown. Given the differences between 1 Clement and 2 Clement in content, style, and articulation of theological beliefs, common authorship is difficult to sustain. This then leads one to expect some differences in christological outlook between the two documents.

In 2 Clement, the fulsome title "Lord Jesus Christ" is never used. The author employs the binomial form "Jesus Christ" on three occasions (2 Clem. 1.1, 2; 17.6). The term "Lord," κύριος, *kyrios*, is used twenty times.[14] However, not all of these designations refer to Jesus. This is most obvious when the term occurs twice in a context where a saying of Jesus is recalled: "Now the Lord [κύριος] says, 'No servant can serve two masters [κυρίοις]'" (2 Clem. 6.2). Here, the second occurrence of the term in the plural obviously refers to earthly lords or masters. There are other cases where the referent is not quite as obvious. The term κύριος is used four times in 2 Clement 4. In this context the author employs a version of a saying of Jesus related to a Q saying (Matt 7:21//Luke 6:46) where Jesus refers to himself as Lord.[15] However, all four occurrences of κύριος here probably designate God, rather than Jesus. In the first place, the phrase in the preceding verse (2 Clem. 3.5), "in Isaiah he also says," likely denotes God and not the preexistent Christ. If so, then in the following clause, "let us, therefore, not merely call him Lord" (2 Clem. 4.1), the pronoun "him" still likely refers to God. Moreover, in 2 Clement 4.4 the audience is reminded that it "must not fear humans but God." Then, following this explicit reference to God, the

12. On the classification of 2 Clement both as a sermon and as a piece of paraenetic writing, see C. M. Tuckett, ed., *2 Clement: Introduction, Text, and Commentary*, OAF (Oxford: Oxford University Press, 2012), 19–23, 24–26.

13. J. A. Kelhoffer, "If Second Clement Really Were a 'Sermon,' How Would We Know, and Why Would We Care? Prolegomena to Analyses of the Writing's Genre and Community," in *Early Christian Communities Between Ideal and Reality*, ed. M. Grundeken and J. Verheyden (Tübingen: Mohr Siebeck, 2015), 83–108. See also Varner, who describes the writing as "a hortatory address delivered in a particular *Sitz im Leben*, namely a Christian congregational setting" (W. Varner, *Second Clement: An Introductory Commentary*, AFCS [Eugene, OR: Cascade, 2020], 21).

14. These twenty occasions are 2 Clem. 4.1, 2 (twice), 5; 5.2; 6.1 (twice); 8.2, 4, 5; 9.5, 11; 12.2; 13.2; 14.1, 5; 15.4; 17.3 (twice), 4.

15. The version of the saying in 2 Clem. 4.2 agrees exactly with the opening seven words of Matt 7:21, Οὐ πᾶς ὁ λέγων μοι· κύριε κύριε, *ou pas ho legōn moi kyrie kyrie*, "Not everybody who calls me, 'Lord, Lord.'" Therefore, it is perhaps more likely that the author of 2 Clement drew on the Gospel of Matthew in some way rather than an earlier form of the saying.

author states, "For this reason, if you do these things, the Lord has said . . ." (4.5), which appears to use the term κύριος to denote God. The matter is not straightforward, because in the following section where another saying is introduced with the formula, "for the Lord says" (5.2), it is clear from what follows that Jesus is designated by the term κύριος. Therefore, the author is flexible in applying κύριος terminology either to God or, more frequently, to Jesus. The fact that the author does not exercise caution in reserving the term "Lord" for God but uses it interchangeably also as a referent for Jesus might reflect a common divine status.

This confusion of the use of the term "Lord" in the references in citation formulae is most clearly seen in 2 Clement 13. First, a passage is cited from Isaiah 52:5 LXX, which in its original context was spoken by Yahweh. In 2 Clement 13.2 it is introduced with the somewhat ambiguous formula, "for the Lord says." By contrast, in 13.4 a second citation occurs. This is based on material drawn from the Lukan Sermon on the Plain (Luke 6:32, 35). In the Lukan context, the material was spoken by Jesus. However, here the author introduces it with, "God says" (2 Clem. 13.4). At one level this could be attributed to confusion on the part of the author. Moreover, it would be difficult to claim on the basis of this citation formula that the author is describing Jesus as God. Rather, it appears that for the author of 2 Clement the voice of Scripture, cited from the Old Testament or the New Testament, can be attributed either to God or to Jesus in whatever way best suits the argument being made.[16] Alongside this, the term κύριος exhibits the same flexibility. More typically it refers to Jesus in this text, but when the author wishes to switch the referent to God there is no strong signal that this has happened.

Apart from titles, the content of christological references communicates greater insights into the author's beliefs about Jesus. In the opening of the text, the author presents Jesus as "judge of the living and the dead" (2 Clem. 1.1). No doubt Christ's role as judge is intended to be motivational and hence serves the paraenetic purpose of the letter in reminding readers of the ethical standard of life to which they have been called. However, the description of Jesus as judge is prefaced by the statement, "Think of Jesus Christ as we do of God" (2 Clem. 1.1). This clause is not the focus of the statement; instead, the emphasis is the juridical role of Christ.[17] The fact that the preamble is incidental is itself striking, since the author probably understands the exhortation to think about Jesus in the same way as one thinks about God as uncontroversial. However, the author's meaning is not fully explained. At the very least, the statement attributes to Jesus the same role as eschatological judge that would typically have been understood as the prerogative of God. This does not prove the author's belief in any claim of ontological likeness. Such categories were yet to be developed. However, it does seem to show that for the author, Jesus fulfills some of the same functions as God, in particular being the one who delivers eschatological judgment.

Another key aspect of the author's christological beliefs is the understanding of the role of Jesus as Savior of humanity. Christ's sufferings are said to be on behalf of humans, when it is recalled "how much suffering Jesus Christ endured for our sake" (2 Clem. 1.2).

16. Tuckett asks the following questions in relation to the citation formula "God says" in 2 Clem. 13.4: "Is it a reflection of a (relatively naïve) equation between Jesus and God (cf. 1.1)? Or has the Jesus tradition become encapsulated in written form such that it is acquiring the status of scripture, so that what is said there can be regarded as akin to the words of the (Jewish) scripture and hence seen as part of 'the oracles of God' (cf. v. 3) and be taken as something that 'God says' (cf. present tense!)? Perhaps the latter is more likely (though certainty is not possible)" (Tuckett, *2 Clement*, 243).

17. This point is also observed by Holt Graham when he writes, "The opening verse is of course a Christological statement (Lightfoot, p. 211), but that is not its function." R. M. Grant and H. H. Graham, *First and Second Clement*, vol. 2 of *The Apostolic Fathers*, ed. R. M. Grant (New York: Thomas Nelson, 1965), 112.

Once again, the purpose of this statement is not an exposition of soteriology, but it is stated in order to motivate loyal obedience. Throughout the opening chapter, as the text is now divided, further comments of a soteriological nature are made. The author notes both that Christ "saved us when we were perishing" (2 Clem. 1.4) and also in a similar vein that "he saved us when we had no hope of salvation" (1.7). Here the text expresses a central tenet of Christian faith—namely, that Jesus is the one who brings salvation to those who were undeserving and who, apart from his mercy and compassion (1.7), had no likelihood of receiving salvation. In a daring way, the author uses the language of creation to describe the re-creation of those addressed in this text: "He called us when we did not exist, and out of nothing he willed us into being" (1.8). For the author, existence without the salvation made possible through Christ is equivalent to nonexistence. In the process, the text expresses an idea of what might be described as salvation ex nihilo. Jesus's role as an agent of salvation is made more explicit in the final doxology, where he is described as the one sent by God as "the saviour and founder of immortality," τὸν σωτῆρα καὶ ἀρχηγὸν τῆς ἀφθαρσίας, *ton sōtēra kai archēgon tēs aphtharsias* (2 Clem. 20.5). Hence, one of the key christological affirmations is that Jesus is the Savior who through his passion, which is seen as an unmerited act of mercy, brings salvation to believers that results in the gift of immortality. It is that notion of incorruptibility that probably stands behind the existential language of being called out of nonexistence into an authentic state of being.

One of the most important christological statements in the text communicates something of the author's understanding of the incarnation. In the context of 2 Clement 9, the author is primarily articulating his understanding of the anthropological state. The main argument is that humans are called in the flesh and that they will be raised and judged in the flesh. Here there is a rebuttal of the notion that "this flesh is not judged" (2 Clem. 9.1). However, the language of "flesh" leads to the following christological aside: "There is one Christ, the Lord who saved us, who was first spirit, but became flesh" (9.5).[18] This aside states or implies several ideas. First, it declares the oneness of Christ's being. Second, it affirms that it is Christ who saves believers. Third, there is a sequence in the modes of being that Christ experienced. Fourth, the prior mode of existence was as a spirit. Fifth, subsequent to existence as a spirit Christ became flesh. Therefore, in this statement it is possible to recognize much of the classic understanding of the incarnation, wherein the preexistent Christ assumes human flesh without rupturing continuity of being. Thus, the author draws on belief in the incarnation to inform readers that future rewards will be received in the flesh. Thus, Tuckett helpfully summarizes the point of the author's argument in the following manner: "Hence the condition of the flesh is nothing transitory, but will last into resurrection existence as well."[19]

The text expresses several other important christological commitments. The author cites the gospel tradition, "Whoever acknowledges me before men, I will acknowledge before my Father" (2 Clem. 3.2). Although expressed in the words of a gospel citation (Matt 10:32//Luke 12:8), this is one of the author's most explicit statements concerning Jesus's filial relationship to God as his Father. A second is like it. In 2 Clement 9.11, it is recalled that "the Lord," who in this context is Jesus, stated that his true siblings are "those who do the will of my Father" (Matt 12:50//Mark 3:35//Luke 8:21). Thus 2 Clement affirms the

18. There is a significant textual problem here. The opening of this statement as it occurs in the three Greek manuscripts (A C S) is εἷς Χριστός, *heis Christos*, "there is one Christ," yet on the basis of Syriac fragments of the text some have favored the emendation εἰ Χριστός, *ei Christos*, "if Christ." For the latter, see Holmes, *Apostolic Fathers*, 148–49. For a fuller discussion of the variant, see Tuckett, *2 Clement*, 205.

19. Tuckett, *2 Clement*, 206.

widespread, early Christian conviction that Jesus is the Son of God. This is articulated not through explicit use of that terminology but by describing God as the Father of Jesus.

Although not explicitly described as a teacher, Jesus's pedagogical role is of paramount importance and undergirds the paraenetic instructions given to readers. Thus, the author's instructions are frequently given authority by an appeal to Jesus, who is the community's ultimate teacher. Thus the addressees are told, "Let us turn away from life as transient residents in this world . . . and let us not be afraid to depart from this world" (2 Clem. 5.1). This exhortation is reinforced in the following verse, being predicated on dominical teaching: "For as the Lord says . . ." (5.2). Such use of sayings of Jesus as the ultimate basis of Christian teaching is found at various points (cf. 6.1; 8.5). There are also repeated references to the commands of the Lord or the commands of Jesus (17.3, 6).

The author also presents an eschatological dimension to his Christology. This is not only expressed through an affirmation of Christ's role at the final judgment (1.1), but more prominently by portraying Jesus as the one who will return to bring the future kingdom and eternal life (5.5; 12.2).

The author also reflects on the role of Jesus in relation to the church. In this regard, the text describes a preexistent status for the church by telling those addressed that they belong to "the first church, the spiritual one, which was created before the sun and moon" (14.1). Then Christ's relationship to the church is expounded. In fairly typical terms it is stated that "the living church is the body of Christ" (14.2). Next, predicated explicitly on the creation of humanity as male and female, the author states, "The male is Christ; the female is the church" (14.2). It is tempting to suspect that, perhaps at some stages removed, the thought of Ephesians 5:25 lies behind this image: "Husbands love your wives, as Christ loved the church," with Christ implicitly equated with the male husband and the church portrayed as the female wife.[20] The author links the earthly existence of the church to the incarnation: "The church, being spiritual, was revealed in the flesh of Christ" (2 Clem. 14.3). Here the preexistent church of 14.1 is described as being made manifest through the incarnation. In this way the author's perspectives on Christology and ecclesiology are inextricably linked.[21]

One area where the author's thought is not fully developed is in relation to pneumatology. As a consequence of the author's ecclesial perspectives, it is stated that "the flesh is the church, and the Spirit is Christ." If somebody abuses the church, this person "will not receive the Spirit, which is Christ" (2 Clem. 14.4). This "Spirit" is then identified as the "Holy Spirit": "So great is the life and immortality that this flesh is able to receive, if the Holy Spirit is closely joined with it" (14.5). As Tuckett notes, "There is a virtual equation made between Christ and Spirit."[22] By later doctrinal norms this could be seen as an example of confusing the persons of the Trinity. It would, however, be unfair to level this accusation against the author of 2 Clement, who was writing at a stage before such theological precision had been developed. Here the author's belief in the continued presence of Christ with believers is articulated through describing an equivalence with believers possessing the Holy Spirit, being closely joined with the flesh. From the author's perspective, therein this enables them to receive life and immortality.

20. Varner observes this connection but describes the way in which the author of 2 Clement extends the idea. He writes, "While Clement may have been aware of these Pauline themes, he takes the discussion in a more imaginative direction than this. He sees the church as the continuation of the preexistent bride of the Lord. He sees Christ and the church as the great realities of which the male and the female (14.2) are shadows" (Varner, *Second Clement*, 118).

21. Further on this point, see Grant and Graham, *First and Second Clement*, 125–26.

22. Tuckett, *2 Clement*, 258.

While 2 Clement is no treatise on Christology, many key ideas about Christ are expressed, albeit in passing and in an ad hoc manner. Paramount to the author's teaching in this letter is the description of Christ as Savior, future judge, and the ultimate teacher of Christian ethical behavior. The author has a clear belief in the preexistence of Christ and a developed understanding of incarnation. His ecclesiology is inseparably linked to an understanding of the role of Christ in revealing the church that existed beforehand to humanity. The author appears to closely equate Christ and the Spirit in ways that reflect an underdeveloped pneumatology from the perspective of later centuries. Most striking is the range of christological beliefs and affirmations stated without justification. These beliefs are assumed to be the shared and uncontroversial perspectives of both author and audience.

2.3 The Letters of Ignatius

Among the Apostolic Fathers, only one author addresses Christology as a central topic and in an overt manner.[23] The christological perspectives of Ignatius are presented as a corrective and as an explicit response to what he views as false understandings of the identity and nature of Jesus. Some of his statements have developed beyond the ideas expressed in many of the other writings among the Apostolic Fathers. This more fully developed theology has led some to dismiss the literary corpus that has survived in his name as being a later, inauthentic set of writings, penned in the second half of the second century with the name of Ignatius attached. Certainly, the conceptual distance that appears to separate the writings of Ignatius from the writings of his supposed near contemporaries has been one of the key reasons for also advocating a temporal separation. Consequently, the date of the Ignatian letters has been pushed late into the second century by some modern scholars.[24] This, however, is not the only possible explanation for the developed, innovative, and one might even say, daring, christological affirmations that are to be found in the middle recension of the letters of Ignatius. As an author addressing what are perceived as deficiencies in the christological conceptions of his opponents, Ignatius was forced to formulate his own ideas about Christ in ways that unambiguously combated those views. Thus, his christological statements of necessity exhibit greater precision, his ideas are pressed more fully to their logical conclusion, and his formulations seek to avoid ambiguity.

The seven letters of the middle recension are addressed to six different communities, five in Asia Minor and one in Rome. The letter sent to Rome is markedly different from the other six. Addressing believers in the imperial capital, Ignatius betrays little knowledge of circumstances in that location, and his primary concern is to ensure that believers in Rome will not intervene to prevent his martyrdom (Ign. *Rom.* 1.1–3.3). To be sure, there is material in that letter that is christological in nature, but it arises from a different set of circumstances. However, some of the innovative christological affirmations made in the more polemically focused writings are carried over into his letter to the Romans. Thus, they can be viewed as fundamental expressions of his core christological convictions.

By contrast, the remaining letters appear to respond to opponents whose views Ignatius contests. While there has been debate concerning the number of groups of opponents, it is certainly the case that Ignatius responds to two broad types of problems—a tendency to

23. Schoedel states that "the special mark of Ignatius' theology is the centrality afforded the incarnation and crucifixion of Jesus Christ" (W. R. Schoedel, *Ignatius of Antioch*, Hermeneia [Philadelphia: Fortress, 1985], 84–85).

24. In particular, see R. M. Hübner, "Thesen zur Echtheit und Datierung der Sieben Briefe des Ignatius von Antiochien," *ZAC* 1 (1997): 44–72.

adopt a form of Jewish Christianity, as well as an expression of what for the convenience of shorthand can be labeled as a docetic Christology. The former tendency is addressed primarily in Ignatius's letters to the Magnesians and the Philadelphians. By contrast, docetic views are combated in his letters to the Ephesians, the Trallians, the Smyrnaeans, and to a lesser extent in the letter addressed to Polycarp, the leader of the Christian community in Smyrna. Furthermore, Ignatius's letters include five semi-creedal statements (Ign. *Eph.* 7.2; 18.2; *Magn.* 11.1; *Trall.* 9.1–2; *Smyrn.* 1.1–2).[25] These statements are succinct, yet pregnant with elevated theological affirmations. While they undoubtedly serve Ignatius's polemical purpose, he moves beyond mere polemics to a spontaneous outburst of praise and doxological reflection on the nature and soteriological significance of Christ.

It is instructive to begin by considering the way Ignatius names Jesus and the titles employed to describe him. Ignatius does not use the threefold form "Lord Jesus Christ" with great frequency (only on six occasions, Ign. *Phld.* 1.1; 4.1; 9.2; 11.2; *Smyrn.* 1.1; *Pol.* salut.). It is striking, however, that it occurs typically near the beginning or ending of his letters, or with a concentration in the letter to the community in Philadelphia. By contrast, the two-part form "Jesus Christ" is extremely frequent throughout the seven letters (111 times, although only three times in the letter addressed to Polycarp). Ignatius also uses the form "Christ Jesus," but with a far lower frequency; it occurs twelve or thirteen times across five letters.[26] When using this order, the word Χριστός, *Christos*, appears to be given greater weight as a title connoting the messiahship of Jesus. It is also natural for Ignatius to speak of Jesus as "Lord" without connection to the terms "Jesus" or "Christ." However, Ignatius does not employ this designation with the same frequency as several of the other writings in the corpus of the Apostolic Fathers. It occurs in six of the seven letters (not being found in Ignatius's *To the Romans*), and including the tripartite form "Lord Jesus Christ," it occurs a total of thirty-one times.[27]

Beyond the mere use of names and titles, one of the most notable features of the Christology of Ignatius is the way he identifies Jesus as God. Without hesitation or feeling the necessity of explanation, Ignatius can speak of the Ephesians having been chosen "by the will of the Father and of Jesus Christ our God" (Ign. *Eph.* salut.). Likewise, in the same letter, describing the incarnation, Ignatius states "our God, Jesus the Christ, was conceived by Mary according to God's plan" (18.1). Here a number of important christological ideas are present. The decision to use the article to refer to Jesus as "the Christ," ὁ Χριστός, appears to be an explicit choice to emphasize the titular aspect of the term and thereby to identify Jesus as Messiah. While some of the material in this semi-creedal statement may well be traditional, the designation of "our God" as "Jesus the Christ" appears to be characteristic of the Christology of Ignatius and an example of the daring and unabashed way in which he speaks of Jesus as divine.[28] Ignatius uses this understanding to describe the manner in which believers have the divine presence dwelling within them. Thus he informs the Ephesians that they are the Lord's temples, and consequently they should behave in a morally appropriate manner in order that Jesus "may be in us as our God" (15.3). This language is not a careless turn of phrase. Rather, it is intentional, and it forms part of Ignatius's

25. C. N. Jefford, *Reading the Apostolic Fathers: A Student's Introduction*, 2nd ed. (Grand Rapids: Baker Academic, 2012), 55.

26. The form "Christ Jesus" is found in Ign. *Eph.* 1.1; 10.3; 11.1; 12.2; [18.2]; *Magn.* salut.; 8.2; *Trall.* 1.1; 9.2; *Rom.* 1.1; *Phld.* 10.1, 2; 11.2.

27. Ign. *Eph.* 6.1; 7.2; 10.3; 15.3; 17.1, 2; 19.1; 20.2; 21.1; *Magn.* 7.1; 13.1; *Trall.* 8.1; 10.1; *Rom.* 4.2; *Phld.* salut.; 1.1; 4.1; 8.1; 9.2; 11.1, 2; *Smyrn.* 1.1; 4.2; 5.2; 10.1; *Pol.* salut.; 1.2; 4.1; 5.1, 2; 8.3.

28. See Schoedel, *Ignatius of Antioch*, 84–85.

considered argument both as a rebuttal of the christological claims of his opponents and as an admonition to believers in Ephesus to behave in a morally appropriate manner.

At times Ignatius can speak of the key christological moment of the passion as an event that has God as its subject. In this vein, he speaks unreservedly concerning "the suffering of my God" (Ign. *Rom.*6.3). A favorite designation of Jesus is referring to him as "our God." This occurs six times (Ign. *Eph.* salut.; 15.3; 18.2; *Rom.* salut.; 3.3; *Pol.* 8.3). It is notable that while Ignatius uses various formulations that designate Jesus as God, he does not do so in the two letters that are addressed to communities facing Judaizing tendencies—that is, addressing the Magnesians and the Philadelphians. It might be the case that this is an intentional choice. Alternatively, he may reserve references to Jesus being God to demonstrate to those with docetic proclivities that he is not denying the divine aspect of the nature of Jesus. Rather, he holds that to be true alongside the affirmation that Jesus is fully human. Moreover, he sees both the human and the divine aspects of Christ as fully experiencing incarnation and suffering. Hence when referring to Jesus as the "one physician," this is in the context of holding in tension categories that appear to be mutually exclusive, "both flesh and spirit, born and unborn, God in humanity, true life in death, both of Mary and God, subject to suffering yet incapable of suffering" (Ign. *Eph.* 7.2). Ignatius does not explain how these apparently contradictory descriptions can be held together; instead, he simply affirms them simultaneously as part of his core theological conviction that Jesus was both divine and human. It would be overreaching to see this as an early example of a developed form of a two-natures Christology, similar to that expressed later in fourth-century conciliar statements. Nonetheless, there is an obvious duality in this representation and understanding of the being of Christ. Hence, it is not inappropriate to see this as in some sense an antecedent to later expressions of Christology. However, it must be stated that there was much theological ground to be covered before this affirmation of two sets of apparently contradictory categories could develop into a more ontologically reasoned account of the nature of the person of Christ.[29]

Alongside the innovative and bold affirmation of Jesus as God, Ignatius also employs more traditional modes of expressing the relationship between Jesus and the deity. Using typical christological language, Ignatius describes Jesus as God's Son, and God as the Father of Jesus in a unique manner. Thus, writing to the Magnesians, he describes Jesus as the mechanism of divine revelation, and in the same clause he emphasizes his filial relationship to God: "There is one God who revealed himself through Jesus Christ his Son, who is the Word who came forth from the silence, who in every respect pleased the one who sent him" (Ign. *Magn.* 8.2). The proximity of the dual descriptions of Jesus as Son of God and the means of divine revelation is not coincidental. Ignatius expects readers to understand that precisely because of the intimacy of the filial relationship to God, Jesus was uniquely equipped to reveal God to humanity. Here there is an intentional contrast between the silent realm from which the Son comes forth and his identification as the Word who gives voice to the otherwise unknowable mysteries of God.[30]

In several of his semi-creedal statements, Ignatius utilizes the description "son of God" alongside an affirmation of the humanity of Jesus. Thus Jesus is described in the following terms as the one "who was a descendent of David, who is son of man and Son of God" (Ign. *Eph.* 20.2). The title "son of man," while common in the Synoptic Gospels, occurs nowhere

29. For the history of these later developments, see J. N. D. Kelly, *Early Christian Doctrines*, 5th ed. (London: Continuum, 2000).

30. On this point, see Schoedel, *Ignatius of Antioch*, 120.

else in Ignatius's writings. However, in this context he employs it to emphasize the humanity of Christ,[31] not in contrast to, but alongside his divinity, which is expressed by the parallel expression "son of God." Ignatius also employs the term "son" as a reference to Jesus in contexts where he discusses ecclesiology. Thus, the Ephesians are reminded that they are "members of his [God's] son" (Ign. *Eph.* 4.2),[32] and those addressed in Rome are described as "the church that has found mercy in the majesty of the father most high and Jesus Christ" (Ign. *Rom.* salut.). Later in the same context, the believers in Rome are greeted "in the name of Jesus Christ, son of the father" (Ign. *Rom.* salut.). Thus, for Ignatius, believers exist as the church through their relationship to Jesus, and this can be described as being members of the Son of God. When Ignatius occasionally employs a Trinitarian formulation, he does so using the terms "son" and "father." Thus he prays for the Magnesians that they "may prosper, physically and spiritually, in faith and love, in the son and the father and in the spirit" (Ign. *Magn.* 13.1).[33] While the order of the three elements might recall the Pauline sequence of Lord Jesus Christ, God, and the Holy Spirit in 2 Corinthians 13:14, the fact that Ignatius uses the term "son" rather the name Jesus Christ may suggest that he is influenced by the Matthean baptismal formulation (Matt 28:19).

In actuality the affirmation of Jesus's real human existence is the central concern in his response to the docetic opponents. Thus, Ignatius declares the reality of both the human descent and lineage of Jesus, "conceived by Mary . . . from the seed of David" (Ign. *Eph.* 18.2; cf. *Trall.* 9.1; *Smyrn.* 1.1). In terms of the reality of the incarnation, both asserting that Jesus had a human birth and affirming his Davidic pedigree are the twin ways in which Ignatius refutes any notions that the birth and conception of Jesus were anything other than in accord with human existence.

Similarly, and perhaps even more explicitly, Ignatius asserts the reality of the death of Jesus. For Ignatius, there is no divine intervention or protection from the harsh reality of suffering and death. The sufferings of Christ are understood to have a purifying and redemptive power. Thus he states of Jesus, "He was born and baptized in order that by his sufferings he might cleanse the water" (Ign. *Eph.* 18.2). Thus, Jesus is portrayed as in solidarity with the experience of believers by undergoing birth and baptism. Yet more than this, the sufferings of Jesus cleanse the waters of baptism, making them efficacious for those who are subsequently baptized. The details of Ignatius's understanding are not clarified. However, he appears to see the sufferings and death of Jesus as having soteriological significance insofar as the baptismal waters had been purified, presumably for the washing away of sins. This sentiment is expressed without reference to baptism in *To the Trallians.* In reference to the cross as an instrument of suffering, Ignatius states that the sufferings of Jesus permit believers to become united with him: "the same cross by which he, through his sufferings, calls you who are members" (Ign. *Trall.* 11.2). Thus, the sufferings are seen as enabling union with Christ, which is another way of expressing the salvation of believers.

31. Grant observes this point when he states, "Ignatius is obviously employing the enigmatic expression [son of man] used in the Gospels by Jesus, not in the context of late Jewish apocalyptic thought—where 'Son of man' often means a divine being—but in a context like Psalm 8:4 or Ezekiel, where it means 'man' (so also Barn. 12:10)" (R. M. Grant, *Ignatius of Antioch*, vol. 4 of *The Apostolic Fathers*, ed. R. M. Grant [New York: Thomas Nelson, 1965], 52).

32. While it might not be possible to find a direct link with any single passage in the Pauline writing, the image is resonant with Paul's ideas, and given Ignatius's knowledge of 1 Corinthians the expression could be drawn from a passage such as 1 Cor 12:12–27.

33. The more image-laden references to God the father, Jesus Christ, and the Holy Spirit in Ign. *Eph.* 9.1 do not use the term "son." This is because the three designations are dispersed and Ignatius is more concerned to develop the crane metaphor than to use a standard Trinitarian formula.

Moreover, from Ignatius's perspective, the passion is integral to the message of the gospel: "The gospel possesses something distinctive, the coming of the Savior, our Lord Jesus Christ, his suffering, and the resurrection" (Ign. *Phld.* 9.2). Consequently, Ignatius speaks of a concatenation of events—of the coming or incarnation along with the passion and resurrection of Jesus—and these together have soteriological impact since they demonstrate the arrival of the Savior.

In several of his letters, Ignatius engages in fierce debate with his perceived opponents. A chief issue is the divergence in christological views between himself and those whom he accuses of holding that Christ only came in the appearance or semblance of human flesh. In order to combat this position, Ignatius repeatedly affirms the reality of the incarnation and also the painful suffering and death of Jesus. Yet alongside this, Ignatius unreservedly describes the divine aspect of Christ. He not only adopts the typical early Christian formula of referring to Jesus as the Son of God, but even more daringly declares him to be God. While Ignatius frequently refers to Jesus as "our God," on one occasion he uses this identification in a more absolute manner without the possessive pronoun, when he tells the believers in Smyrna that "I glorify Jesus Christ, the God who made you wise" (Ign. *Smyrn.* 1.1). This direct description goes beyond even the most explicit affirmations of the divine status of Jesus found in the New Testament (cf. John 20:28; Titus 2:13). This absolute statement made by Ignatius appears to rebut any idea that he distinguished between the types of divinity possessed by Christ and the father.[34] While Ignatius does not explicitly describe Jesus as Savior with great frequency (Ign. *Eph.* 1.1; *Magn.* salut.; *Phld.* 9.2; *Smyrn.* 6.2), he does speak in other ways of believers having received a new status and as having been given the "medicine of immortality" (Ign. *Eph.* 20.2).

Therefore, the writings of Ignatius are more explicitly christological than any of the other writings in the corpus of the Apostolic Fathers. For some, this development in christological thought can only be explained by suggesting a date late in the second century for the composition of these letters. That supposition is unnecessary. The christological perspectives expressed as part of his wider theological thought are the product of the polemical context in which he wrote. In combating those with whom he disagreed, Ignatius expressed his Christology in ways that were a direct rebuttal of the views he opposed and with a desire to avoid ambiguity. This led him to repeatedly affirm Jesus as truly human, suffering and dying without avoidance of pain. Moreover, Ignatius declared Jesus to be "our God" as a way of explicitly stating the true divinity of Christ. Therefore, the highly charged letters of Ignatius, more than any other writings in the corpus of the Apostolic Fathers, are christological texts from beginning to end. As such, they are of prime importance in the study of the development of doctrinal theology.

2.4 The Letter of Polycarp to the Philippians

Like many of the other writings that constitute the corpus of the Apostolic Fathers, Polycarp's *To the Philippians* makes the author's christological perspectives known through discussion of other issues. The letter is a pastoral epistle, with the primary purpose of addressing various ecclesial problems that had arisen in the community of Christ believers in Philippi. Chief among these problems was the financial misdemeanor of Valens,

---

34. See P. Foster, "The Ignatian Problem: The Recensions of a Letter Corpus as a Reflection of Theological Concerns and Developments," in *Texts in Context: Essays on Dating and Contextualising Christian Writings from the Second and Early Third Centuries*, ed. J. Verheyden, J. Schröter, and T. Nicklas, BETL 319 (Leuven: Peeters, 2021), 5–50, here 16.

a former presbyter, and his wife (Pol. *Phil.* 11.1–4). Additionally, there appears to have been a problem with younger members of the community not maintaining pure behavior. Thus, the primary concerns of the letter are dealt with by discussing the topic of "righteousness" on which Polycarp has been invited to address the Philippians (3.1). Specifically, the need for instruction on this topic arose from deficits in behavior within the community. By contrast, there is little suggestion there was a misunderstanding in relation to christological beliefs. The one probable exception to this is the set of statements that denounce those who do not affirm the humanity of Jesus and the reality of his sufferings and resurrection, and also reject the future judgment (7.1). Apart from this exception, what Polycarp states in relation to the identity and significance of Christ may function as the ultimate basis for the ethical conduct he seeks to instill, but it is largely incidental to the central purpose of the letter.

Polycarp employs a number of designations to refer to Jesus. On five occasions he uses the threefold appellation, "Lord Jesus Christ" (Pol. *Phil.* 1.1, 2; 2.1; 12.2; 14.1). It is notable that this expanded form is prominent near the beginning and end of the letter.[35] In the body of the letter, shorter designations are typically based on various combinations of the three elements of the longer appellation.[36] The most frequent title that Polycarp uses is κύριος, which occurs on twenty-six occasions.[37] When it is used in combination with other christological titles, the referent is clearly Jesus. When used in isolation, the context often makes it clear whether or not Jesus is the designee. For example, a reference to the Lord is sometimes followed by a saying or deed attributed to this figure, which in the Gospels are spoken or performed by Jesus (2.3; 5.2; 7.2). Similarly, references to the coming of the Lord (6.3) are most naturally understood as denoting the arrival of Christ as foretold by the prophets. Sometimes two figures appear to be denoted in expressions such as "those who are truly chosen by God and our Lord" (1.1) and "we are in the full view of the eyes of the Lord and God" (6.2). These are unambiguous references to Jesus. While other examples are less decisive, the case can be made that in this letter all instances of κύριος refer to Jesus and not to God. For instance, the statement that Ignatius's letters provide instruction concerning "every kind of spiritual growth that has to do with our Lord" (13.2) must surely be a reference to spiritual development for those in Christ. The discussion of blaspheming the Lord's name (10.2, 3), and the example of the Lord and his gentleness (10.1) again most plausibly refer to Jesus. Perhaps the most ambiguous use is when discussing the fate of Valens and the fate of individuals who love money, "who are ignorant of the Lord's judgments," *qui ignorant iudicium domini* (11.2).[38] While the context might not be decisive, the fact that elsewhere in the letter Polycarp uses the term κύριος lends weight to the supposition that here also Jesus is in view. Thus it appears that in *To the Philippians*, Polycarp uses the title κύριος to designate Jesus, and nowhere to refer to God.

In common with many early Christian texts, Polycarp speaks freely and without qualification about the relationship between Jesus and God by using filial language. This can either be expressed by describing God as "Father of our Lord Jesus Christ" (Pol. *Phil.* 12.2),

35. P. Foster, "Polycarp's Teachings: The Reception and Development of Theology," in *Studies on the Intersection of Text, Paratext, and Reception: A Festschrift in Honor of Charles E. Hill*, ed. G. R. Lanier and J. N. Reid, TENT 15 (Leiden: Brill, 2021), 279–313, here 291.

36. Polycarp can speak of "Jesus Christ" (Pol. *Phil.* 1.3; 7.1; 12.2) or "Christ Jesus" (8.1) in a way where both expressions appear to be broadly equivalent. The term "Christ" is used singly on several occasions.

37. Pol. *Phil.* 1.1 [twice], 2; 2.1, 3; 4.1, 3; 5.2; 6.2 [twice], 3 [twice]; 7.1, 2; 9.2; 10.1 [twice], 2, 3; 11.2, 3, 4; 12.2 [twice]; 13.2; 14.1.

38. While this section of the letter survives only in Latin, it is highly plausible that the Greek behind the Latin *domini* was a genitive form of κύριος.

or alternatively and in the same breath inverting the relationship by referring to "the Son of God, Jesus Christ" (12.2). This passage concludes with a statement whereby Polycarp appears to unambiguously declare Jesus not simply to be the Son of God, but actually to be divine: "Believe in our Lord and God Jesus Christ and in his Father who raised him from the dead" (12.2). However, much caution is required here. As has been noted elsewhere,

> Textual problems abound. First, this phrase occurs in a portion of the letter that is only preserved in the Latin version, and is not extant in the surviving Greek manuscript evidence. The relevant portion of the Latin printed text reads, *qui credituri sunt in dominum nostrum et deum Iesum Christum*. Yet in regard to the key phrase *et deum*, the Latin witnesses are divided concerning its inclusion (L^{rmpf}) or its omission (L^{ovbct}). None of these manuscripts is typically dated earlier than the ninth century, and some as late as the fifteenth or sixteenth century.[39]

Given the difficulties here, it is impossible to state with certainty whether Polycarp himself described Jesus as "our Lord and God," or whether a later pious scribe elaborated the christological sentiment by providing an unambiguous affirmation of the deity of Christ.

More certain, and aligned with the perspectives of other writings in the corpus, Polycarp clearly describes Jesus as "Savior" in his opening greeting (Pol. *Phil.* salut.) and affirms the soteriological significance of Jesus. The declaration that Christ is the source of salvation is affirmed through the use of Pauline phraseology drawn from Ephesians 2:5, 8: "By grace you have been saved, not because of works, but by the will of God through Jesus Christ" (Pol. *Phil.* 1.3). While the phrasing is drawn from Ephesians, Polycarp makes it his own both by reformulating the words in a condensed form and by deploying them to have a rhetorical function in his own argument. Thus, although Polycarp provides no sustained reflection on the crucifixion or any other event as a mechanism of salvation, his statements align with wider christological affirmations of the period in declaring Christ to be both the Savior and the means through which believers receive salvation.

Potentially the most revealing statement of Polycarp's Christology emerges in a polemical context where he cites material drawn from the Johannine epistolary tradition (Pol. *Phil.* 7.1; see 1 John 4:2–3; cf. 2 John 7). In this context, Polycarp's perspectives appear to align with those of Ignatius in rejecting opponents promulgating a docetic Christology. Polycarp charges these teachers with other offenses in addition to the denial of the true humanity of Jesus. He states they reject the testimony of the cross, apparently because they deny that Christ underwent and experienced the reality of human pain and suffering. Furthermore, they are accused of being people who "twist the sayings of the Lord" (Pol. *Phil.* 7.1). This appears to refer to a type of interpretative exegesis that supported the christological beliefs being taught. Lastly, they are charged with rejecting resurrection and future judgment. Perhaps this accorded with a denial of continuity of existence for the human body. Polycarp provides no further details. However, what he describes maps onto the type of teaching that Ignatius also opposed and is suggestive of a widespread set of docetic-type teachings circulating in the areas around Ephesus and Smyrna during the early part of the second century.[40] This form of Christology is strongly rejected. While not

39. See Foster, "Polycarp's Teachings," 294.

40. Hartog correctly notes that "we cannot be certain whether Polycarp was condemning opponents already in the Philippian church or whether he was warning of possible threats. The general nature of the caution may perhaps argue for the latter, and the materials may even reflect opposition in Smyrna rather than Philippi" (P. Hartog, ed., *Polycarp's Epistle to the Philippians and the Martyrdom of Polycarp: Introduction, Text, and Commentary*, OAF (Oxford: Oxford University Press, 2013), 131.

articulating his own Christology to any great extent, in opposition to these views Polycarp holds to the reality of Christ having come in the flesh—that is, the incarnation. He affirms that Jesus underwent pain and suffering on the cross in actuality, not only in appearance. Moreover, rather than divine intervention removing Jesus from suffering, Polycarp instead affirms a divine vindication through resurrection. Lastly, the affirmation of future judgment may reinforce the idea stated earlier in the letter that Christ will come again "as judge of the living and the dead" (Pol. *Phil.* 2.1). Thus Polycarp represents the early stream of christological thought that centers on the sequence of incarnation, passion, resurrection, and Jesus's return as eschatological judge. As the argument continues, it becomes clear that Polycarp regards adherence to false teaching as one of the fundamental causes of ethical failings in community life.[41]

Therefore, in Polycarp's *To the Philippians,* while Christology is not the main purpose of the writing, one does find a series of statements that align with perspectives in other writings of the period. Polycarp employs the fulsome designation "Lord Jesus Christ" as well as shorter variations. He speaks naturally of the father-son relationship between Jesus and God and devotes no space to justifying that representation. This also reflects that this was a commonplace understanding. He greets the Philippians in the name of Jesus who is designated as Savior, and he expects them to share his belief that salvation has come through Jesus without needing to explain the process by which that happened. Polycarp's Christology, as expressed in the epistle, reflects standard Christian beliefs of the time concerning Jesus, and this is largely presented without the need for justification. Rather, he simply assumes that what he says in relation to Jesus reflects the shared faith held by himself and the Philippian believers.

2.5 The Martyrdom of Polycarp

The Martyrdom of Polycarp is primarily a narrative text that relates events surrounding the death of the eponymous title character, Polycarp. It is an early example of Christian martyrological literature, and as such—regardless of judgments concerning the historicity of the account—it is instrumental in the development of many ideas concerning Christian voluntary death. While there is no sustained reflection on the identity of Christ, several important christological statements are formulated with special reference to the martyrological context. In particular, the death of Christ becomes exemplary and is to be imitated by followers being put to death for their faith. This mimesis of Christ extends beyond mere imitation. The remembrance of the passion shapes how the narrative of Polycarp's martyrdom is told. This is not only in relation to superficial details, such as the arresting officer "coincidentally" being named Herod (Mart. Pol. 6.2), but in much deeper ways, with the refusal to escape arrest and the demeanor of calmness being an imitation of the portrayal of the death of Jesus as depicted in the gospel accounts.

The tripartite appellation "Lord Jesus Christ" occurs three times in the Martyrdom of Polycarp (Mart. Pol. salut.; 19.2; 22.3).[42] In common with Polycarp's *To the Philippians,*

41. Again, see Hartog, *Polycarp's Epistle to the Philippians and the Martyrdom of Polycarp,* 131.

42. It should be noted that the occurrence of the title "Lord Jesus Christ" in 22.3 occurs in the two forms of the additional material at the end of the text—both the shorter form and the so-called Moscow ending. The shorter ending is found in four Greek manuscripts dating from the tenth to the twelfth centuries (codices bpha). The longer form is found in Codex Mosquensis, dating to the thirteenth century. For a fuller discussion of the manuscript tradition, see B. Dehandschutter, *Polycarpiana: Studies on Martyrdom and Persecution in Early Christianity: Collected Essays,* ed. J. Leemans (Leuven: Peeters, 2007), see esp., "An Updated Edition of the Martyrdom of Polycarp," 3–22.

this three-part form is found at the beginning and near the end of the text. In line with classic Christian usage, it is employed as part of an opening greeting, where the author prays that the recipients of the text may be endued with "mercy, peace, and love" coming from a dual origin: "from God the Father and our Lord Jesus Christ" (Mart. Pol. salut.). This aligns with a common Christian perspective that blessings believers receive are bestowed by the common purpose of the Father and of Christ. The text uses a number of shorter forms, with a particular preference for the form "Jesus Christ," which occurs five times in the latter part of the text (Mart. Pol. 14.3; 20.2; 21.1; 22.1 [twice]), but never the form "Christ Jesus." The designation Jesus Christ often occurs in the context of other christological affirmations. For instance, it is found in the following context: "through the eternal and heavenly high priest, Jesus Christ, your beloved Son" (Mart. Pol. 14.3). It is difficult to resist the supposition that this high-priestly Christology finds its ultimate origin in Hebrews (cf. "a great high priest who has passed through the heavens, Jesus, the son of God," Heb 4:14). However, this perspective may have been mediated to the author through other means, since similar language is found in other texts (1 Clem. 36.1; 61.3; 64.1; Pol. *Phil.* 12.2). Similarly, the name Jesus Christ is used in conjunction with a reference to royal status: "while Jesus Christ was reigning as king forever" (Mart. Pol. 21.1).

The depiction of God as parent and Christ as child is affirmed repeatedly throughout the narrative, and often in close connection with the name form, Jesus Christ. In this vein, the text addresses God as "Father of your beloved and blessed Son Jesus Christ" (Mart. Pol. 14.1), and as has already been seen alongside the designation of Jesus Christ as high priest, in the prayer addressed to God he is described again as "your beloved Son" (14.3). Similarly, in a statement that takes on doxological overtones addressed to God, it is stated that God will bring the faithful into his eternal kingdom "through his child, the only begotten Jesus Christ" (20.2). The description of God's child as τοῦ μονογενοῦς Ἰησοῦ Χριστοῦ, *tou monogenous Iēsou Christou*, would appear to draw on Johannine ideas concerning the "unique" or "only begotten Son" (John 3:16, 18; 1 John 4:9).

A christological theme that is communicated strongly in the text is the portrayal of Christ as the one who suffers in faithful obedience to God, especially during his passion. Such a portrayal of Jesus serves an exemplary function, both by forming the ideological basis for righteous suffering and providing the pattern that is to be emulated by followers who are themselves put to death. From this perspective, Polycarp's own death is presented as itself being a revelation from Jesus, "in order that the Lord might show us once again a martyrdom that is in accord with the gospel" (Mart. Pol. 1.1). In this sense, Polycarp's martyrdom is judged authentic (unlike the failed attempt of Quintus, 4.1), because it was patterned on Christ's example of righteous suffering and death. Here the author stresses that Polycarp was betrayed, just as was the Lord (1.2). This creates a stark contrast with the example of Quintus, who came forward voluntarily and who, from the perspective of the author, was seeking the glorification of martyrdom rather than following the pattern of Christ's obedient suffering. For this reason, the text is able to portray Polycarp's impending death as the means by which he reached "his appointed destiny of being made a sharer with Christ" (6.2). The idea of becoming a partaker or sharer in the death of Christ has been traced in scholarly discussion, but it finds its ultimate antecedents in Paul's ideas about sharing in the sufferings of Christ.[43] The notion of Polycarp's death exemplifying "the pattern of the gospel" is taken up again toward the end of the account (19.1). In that context

43. Hartog, *Polycarp's Epistle to the Philippians and the Martyrdom of Polycarp*, 289. The most pertinent Pauline texts are Rom 8:17; 2 Cor 1:7, 9; 4:10; Phil 1:6; 3:10; Col 1:24.

it is stated that not only was he a prominent martyr (μάρτυς ἔξοχος, *martys exochos*),[44] but that he himself become an example to emulate since his death is aligned with "the pattern of the gospel of Christ" (19.1).

There is also a soteriological dimension to the text's Christology. Not only is Jesus directly called "the Savior of our souls" (Mart. Pol. 19.2), elsewhere the means of salvation is described. The text explicitly states that salvation is achieved through Christ's sufferings, the scope of this saving act is described, and moreover that it is a representative act, with Jesus suffering on behalf of sinners: "Christ who suffered for the salvation of the whole world of those who are saved, the blameless on behalf of sinners" (17.2). It is probably unwise to read this statement as providing strong support for any modern theories regarding the scope of Christ's salvific work. The author employs the unusual locution "the whole world of those who are saved" (τὸν ὑπὲρ τῆς τοῦ παντὸς κόσμου τῶν σῳζομένων, *ton hyper tēs tou pantos kosmou tōn sōzomenōn*, 17.2). It feels as though the author corrected his first sentiment—namely, that Christ suffered on behalf of the whole world, and glosses that universalistic outlook with the qualification "of those who are saved."[45] Regardless of the precise interpretation of this statement, the text presents Christ as savior and understands salvation to have been made possible through his faithful sufferings and death.

One of the author's literary techniques is to create a sequence of christological affirmations. Some of these are recognizably traditional, others are innovative or less common. In this respect, one example of the use of the tripartite name stands at the head of a string of christological descriptions: "our Lord Jesus Christ, the saviour of our souls and helmsman of our bodies and shepherd of the catholic church throughout the world" (Mart. Pol. 19.2). The exact sense intended by the third characterization, "helmsman of our bodies," is not totally clear. This nautical image obviously depicts Christ as one who directs the body of believers. In that sense, it is probably intended to convey some aspect of providence and protective oversight. The fourth image is much clearer. Here the relationship between the author's Christology and ecclesiology finds its most transparent articulation. Christ is portrayed in a pastoral role, shepherding and protecting the universal church in every location in which it is found. The universal, or catholic church (ἡ καθολικὴ ἐκκλησία, *hē katholikē ekklēsia*), is a favorite designation in the Martyrdom of Polycarp (salut.; 8.1; 16.2; 19.2; cf. 23.1). Elsewhere among the writings of the Apostolic Fathers it is used only once by Ignatius (Ign. *Smyrn.* 8.20), interestingly while addressing Polycarp's own community. From a christological perspective, Christ is the one providing pastoral care to the universal church throughout the world.

There is also an explicitly Trinitarian formulation contained in the so-called Moscow ending: "that the Lord Jesus Christ might also gather me together with his chosen ones into his heavenly kingdom; to whom be the glory with the Father and the Son and the Holy Spirit for ever and ever. Amen" (Mart. Pol. 23.2). Strictly speaking, the reference to "the Son" in the closing formula is unnecessary. The phrase "to whom be the glory" refers back to the Lord Jesus Christ, who is the Son. However, the formula is not attempting to be logically correct, but rather to provide a standard closing to this note. Regardless of the sense, the Moscow ending is only found in one manuscript (Codex Mosquensis, 13th c.) and is obviously a later addition to the text.

44. There is a textual variant here. In place of the description of Polycarp as a "prominent [ἔξοχος] martyr," the adjective is replaced with a superlative form (ἐξοχώτατος), thereby characterizing him in even more elevated terms as the "most prominent martyr."

45. Hartog, *Polycarp's Epistle to the Philippians and the Martyrdom of Polycarp*, 319.

The Christology expressed in the Martyrdom of Polycarp plays a subordinate function to the larger aims of the text. The purpose is to provide an inspiring narrative of the death of Polycarp, while serving the didactic purpose of instructing readers about the correct understanding and disposition toward martyrdom. Notwithstanding the subservient role of the christological statements (since martyrdom is an expression of ultimate faith in Christ), such christological beliefs underpin the ideology of the text. Above all, Christ is presented as the exemplary faithful sufferer, who when betrayed went to his death in faithful obedience to God. This pattern then is presented as a model for those confronted with the prospect of martyrdom. The death of Christ is also presented as salvific and representative for all who find salvation through him (Mart. Pol. 17.2). In terms of titles and designation, on the whole the author uses traditional terminology. However, on a few occasions nonstandard images are employed, such as the nautical depiction of Christ as the "helmsman of our bodies" (19.2). In the end, the essential contribution is the presentation of the sufferings of Christ as both a pattern and having a mimetic function for those who might be called to emulate his death.

2.6 The Didache

Speaking of the Christology of the Didache is, at a fundamental level, a misnomer. The reason for this is the simple fact that the word "Christ" is absent (or virtually absent) from the text.[46] This absence might not be immediately obvious to readers of translations of the Greek text. There are two reasons for this. First, the closing line of a eucharistic prayer contains the phrase "through Jesus Christ" (διὰ Ἰησοῦ Χριστοῦ, *dia Iēsou Christou*, Did. 9.4). However, this is a variant reading found in Codex Hierosolymitanus (H54), but not in texts that have the Didache embedded within them. If the phrase is original to the Didache, then it occurs in a liturgical prayer that the author is citing without making any significant theological point. However, it may not have been part of the original form of the text. Second, among a series of warnings against itinerant apostles and prophets, the addressees are told that any such figure who settles among them but is unwilling to work, instead demanding financial support from the community, "is trading on Christ" (12.5). In this context, the Greek text does not employ the term Christ (Χριστός), but instead it coins a neologism "Christ-trader" in the phrase χριστέμπορός, *christemporos*.

Even more widely, the text contains only limited references to Jesus, often employing other terminology and titles. In the so-called Two Ways section there is no reference to Jesus by name. The term Lord (κύριος, *kyrios*) is used in the singular on several occasions in this section (Did. 4.1 [twice], 12, 13; 6.2). Kraft notes that among these examples, "the tradition probably had Jesus in mind in such (ambiguous) passages as 4.1; 6.2 . . . , but that the examples in 4.12–13 are much more ambiguous."[47] Yet, despite the relative lack of direct references to Jesus, the Two Ways tractate is sprinkled with sayings attributed to Jesus in the Gospels—in particular, material drawn from either the Matthean Sermon on the Mount, the Lukan Sermon on the Plain, or some tradition standing behind these two traditions, such as the Q document.

The remainder of the text (Did. 7.1–16.8) contains more frequent and explicit references to Jesus, using a range of terms. Yet even here there is no significant reflection on the

46. This point is made by Jonathan Draper when he states, "The use of the word 'Christology' to describe the Did's understanding of the person and work of Jesus is in itself misleading, since the word 'Christ' does not occur in the writing" (J. A. Draper, "The Didache," in Pratscher, *Apostolic Fathers*, 15).

47. R. A. Kraft, *The Didache and Barnabas*, vol. 3 of *The Apostolic Fathers: A New Translation and Commentary*, ed. R. M. Grant (New York: Thomas Nelson, 1965), 70.

status of Jesus. Instead, it is assumed readers will understand the references, which tend to occur in the prayer or liturgical contexts. Hence in reference to baptism, those being addressed are told to baptize in the threefold name of "the Father and the Son and the Holy Spirit" (Did 7.1, 3). This is probably best understood as a familiar formula rather than being some type of incipient Trinitarian theology. The instruction to recite three times a day the form of the Lord's Prayer that occurs in the Didache begins, "Pray . . . just as the Lord commanded in his gospel" (8.2).

Alongside the ritual of baptism, the text devotes significant space to teaching pertaining to the liturgy of the Eucharist. In relation to the cup, thanks is given to the Father "for the holy vine of David your servant, which you have made known to us through Jesus your servant" (9.2). Here the "holy vine of David your servant" is not equated with "Jesus your servant." Instead, the former is said to be revealed by the latter. Moreover, the contents of the cup are not spoken of in terms of being the blood of Jesus, and there is no stated connection with the death of Jesus. Similarly, the bread is not described as the body of Christ, but "this broken bread was scattered upon the mountains and then was gathered and became one" (9.4). Here, typical links between the Eucharist, the death of Jesus, and the salvific significance of that death are not referenced. However, the text is clear that only those "who have been baptized into the name of the Lord" may partake of the eucharistic meal.

Throughout this section Jesus is repeatedly described as the Father's servant or child (παῖς, *pais*, see 9.2, 3; 10.3). However, the author never defines or explains in what sense Jesus is the servant of God. Toward the end of this section, the injunction, "Remember your church, Lord" (10.5),[48] appears to employ the term "Lord" to designate God rather than Jesus. Similarly, the use of the Aramaic plaintive cry "Maranatha" (meaning "Our Lord, come") is apparently to be directed to the "God of David," which is the subject that precedes it earlier in the verse (10.6). This is in distinction to its use in 1 Corinthians 16:22, where Paul uses the term Maranatha in close connection with references to the Lord Jesus (1 Cor 16:23) and Jesus Christ (1 Cor 16:24) as a way of expressing expectation of the future parousia of Jesus.[49]

By contrast, in the section dealing with teachers and itinerant apostles and prophets (Did. 11.1–13.12), references to the Lord appear to denote Jesus more uniformly. Thus the author instructs that teachers who contribute "to righteousness and the knowledge of the Lord" are to be welcomed "as you would the Lord" (11.1). Since the welcome is to be like a greeting extended to the Lord, it is natural to take this as referring to Jesus. This section repeats the instruction to welcome traveling figures of esteem "as the Lord" (11.4). Traveling prophets can be tested for their authenticity by determining if such an individual "exhibits the Lord's ways" (11.4). Similarly, everyone who comes to the community "in the name of the Lord is to be welcomed" (12.1). However, the community is encouraged to practice discernment in testing the motives of such itinerant figures. If such individuals are more interested in accruing money or food for themselves, they can be judged to be false in their claims. It appears that the community has been abused by those who claim to be teachers or prophets. Such people are named "Christ-traders" (12.1), and the community is instructed to be wary of these individuals.

The remainder of the text is a miscellany of instructions and teachings. It can speak

48. Thus without feeling any need to justify the observation, Niederwimmer simply notes that "the *Didache* does not pray for Israel or Jerusalem, but for the church of God" (K. Niederwimmer, *The Didache*, Hermeneia [Minneapolis: Fortress, 1998], 159).

49. See A. C. Thiselton, *The First Epistle to the Corinthians*, NIGTC (Grand Rapids: Eerdmans, 2000), 1349.

of the "Lord's day"[50] on which the community gathers and breaks bread. This aligns with early Christian practice in naming Sundays after the Lord. However, in this context there is no explanation that this relates to the resurrection of Jesus. Later in this section a quotation from Malachi 1:11, 14 is introduced with the formula "the Lord said," which would appear to refer to God rather than to Jesus. In calling addressees to follow the gospel, the author instructs them to do everything as they "find it in the gospel of the Lord" (Did. 15.1). Given the similar expression in Didache 8.2 when instructing them to recite the Lord's Prayer as commanded by the Lord in his gospel, it appears that this use of Lord in connection with the gospel is a way of designating the gospel of Jesus. Similarly, the two examples of κύριος terminology in the final eschatological chapter (16.1, 8) are clear references to the parousia. Here one sees the expression of an expectation of the future return of Jesus.

The Didache does not contain extensive references to Jesus. Where such references do occur, there is little sustained reflection on Jesus's significance. A term such as "Lord," κύριος, can be used to designate either God or Jesus, and several occurrences are ambiguous. This may well reflect the complex and multistage composition of this text. In many ways, among the texts in the collection of the writings of the Apostolic Fathers, the Didache contains less relevant material for discussing the topic of Christology than the other writings. While this might be seen as frustrating, at another level it is fascinating. It leads one to ponder the identity of this community and what it understood the significance of Jesus to be in relation to its practices. While that is a perennially fascinating question, due to a paucity of evidence it is, at least at this stage, unanswerable.

2.7 The Epistle of Barnabas

The Epistle of Barnabas is a masterclass in early Christian typological exegesis. This form of exegesis is prominent in the New Testament in the Epistle to the Hebrews, especially in its presentation of Jesus as the great high priest who is both superior to the Levitical priests and is the ultimate and final fulfillment of the priestly role by being both priest and sacrificial victim. In this way the author of Hebrews appropriates the infrastructure of the Jewish cult and interprets in such a way to legitimate the christological perspectives contained in that text. The Epistle of Barnabas takes this typological exegesis to a higher level, through a more thoroughgoing rereading of multiple Jewish biblical and extrabiblical traditions. This reading strategy serves primarily to legitimate key claims made about the identity and salvific significance of Jesus. However, before considering the typological Christology of Barnabas, first consideration will be given to the christological titles and terms employed.

In common with many writings among the Apostolic Fathers, the term "Lord," κύριος, is a favored way to refer to Jesus. In terms of raw numbers, the term itself occurs 107 times in Barnabas. However, the author uses the designation "Lord" to refer both to Jesus and to God. On many occasions the intended referent is clear. However, at other times such clarity is lacking. Moreover, it appears to be the case that in some ambiguous instances the author quickly shifts between using κύριος to designate God and then Jesus. While "Lord" is the most frequent designation for Jesus, "the same title also is freely used for God—a fact which makes precise interpretation difficult in many passages."[51]

---

50. The expression κατὰ κυριακὴν δὲ κυρίου, *kata kyriakēn de kyriou*, is unusual and tautologous, as it literally means "on the Lord's day of the Lord."

51. Kraft, *Didache and Barnabas*, 36.

The three-part title "Lord Jesus Christ" is used only once, but it is used in reference to a key theological claim in the epistle. It is asserted that the Jewish sacrificial system has been abolished "in order that the new law of our Lord Jesus Christ, which is free from the yoke of compulsion, one not made by humans, might have its offering, one not made by human hands" (Barn. 2.6). Here the author does more than claim that the new covenant perfectly fulfills the requirements of the old order. Rather, the previous system of offering was fundamentally flawed both because it required compulsion and it utilized sacrifices performed by humans. In a similar vein, responding to those who assert the old covenant remains in force, Barnabas radically refutes that conviction. For Barnabas it was not the death of Jesus that annulled the validity of the Mosaic covenant. Rather, its validity ended when Moses came down the mountain and saw the golden calf and shattered the stone tablets (Exod 32:1–20). In this way, the author makes the provocative claim that the Mosaic covenant failed almost at the moment it began. Nonetheless, he still finds purpose in the alleged failure of the Mosaic covenant, stating this happened "in order that the covenant of the beloved Jesus might be sealed in our heart, in hope inspired by faith in him" (Barn. 4.8).[52]

The discussion of covenant is a recurrent topic in the epistle. In fact, the author weaponizes the notion of covenant failure against the Jews to make his point that Christians are the true recipients of the divine promises. The lengthy discussion in Barnabas 13–14 comes to a climax by revisiting the story of the golden calf, to show that the original recipients were unworthy. By contrast, it is asserted concerning the Mosaic covenant that "the Lord himself gave it to us, so that we might become the people of inheritance, by suffering for us" (14.4). Here there is not a distinction drawn between the former covenant and the new covenant. Instead, there is an even more radical claim: the Sinai covenant and its promises are inherited by the followers of Jesus. Next the author presents his understanding of the purpose of the coming of Jesus.

> And he was made manifest in order that they might fill up the measure of their sins and we might receive the covenant through the Lord Jesus who inherited it, who was prepared for this purpose, in order that by appearing in person and redeeming from darkness our hearts, which had already been paid over to death and given over to the lawlessness of error, he might establish a covenant in us by his word. (Barn. 14.5)

Here it is stated that Jesus was made manifest to establish stark binary fates. First, the sins of the Jews that were revealed on Sinai are filled up through their rejection of Christ. Second, believers in Christ inherit the covenant that is established through his word. Here the author intertwines the idea of Christians being the inheritors of the covenant with a strong anti-Jewish rhetoric that blames them for their covenant failure. Within this scheme, Jesus is the one whose redemptive actions ensure that the covenant blessings are received by his followers, who are claimed to have always been the intended recipients of the divine blessings.[53]

In this text, Jesus's identity as Son of God is repeatedly affirmed. In relation to judgment on the Jewish people, "the Son of God came in the flesh . . . so that he might complete

52. Hvalvik recognizes the rhetorical power of this example. He states, "When Barnabas so strongly focuses on the golden calf episode, he touches a very sore point in the history of the Jews. This was an episode which also in the eyes of later generations was seen as the sin *par excellence*" (R. Hvalvik, *The Struggle for Scripture and Covenant*, WUNT 2/82 [Tübingen: Mohr Siebeck, 1996], 155).

53. In relation to the author's perspective on the people of Israel, Kraft states, "They never really received the covenant (4:7 f. = 14.1 ff.), but it was reserved for the 'new people'" (*Didache and Barnabas*, 33).

the full measure of the sins of those who persecuted his prophets to death" (Barn. 5.11). The prophets are identified as belonging to "the Son of God"—that is, as being prophets of Christ. In the context of the letter the prophets are claimed to have spoken in reference to Christ, and they are in some sense portrayed as proto-Christians.[54] The Son of God is given a future eschatological role, being "destined to judge the living and the dead," and as Son of God he was the only one qualified to suffer on behalf of his people (7.2). Exploiting the play on the Greek form of the name Joshua, which is Jesus, the author interprets statements made in relation to Joshua as pertaining to Jesus: "Observe again that it is Jesus, not a son of man but the son of God, and revealed in the flesh by a symbol" (12.10). Again, the author uses the idea of prefigurement to suggest that the coming of the Son of God as Jesus in the flesh was anticipated in the person of "Jesus son of Nun," to whom Moses prophetically gave that name, so that "the people might hear that the Father was revealing everything about his son Jesus" (12.9). Thus, one of the author's key christological claims is that the testimony of Scripture is prophetic, and its whole witness speaks about the coming of Jesus, who is the Son of God.

The author operates with a strong incarnational theology that is linked with his understanding of the salvific significance of Jesus. Thus the author writes, "If he had not come in the flesh, people could have in no way been saved by looking at him" (Barn. 5.10). Prior to the moment of incarnation, the author speaks of the preexistence of Christ as being present at the foundation of the world (5.5). For this reason the author argues that in the period between the creation and incarnation, people were told to "set your hope on Jesus, who is about to be revealed to you in the flesh" (6.10). Thus the author's understanding of incarnation is tightly linked to his belief in the preexistence of the Son of God and the idea that there had been a prophetic disclosure of the future coming of Jesus in the flesh. Alongside this, the rejection of the title "son of David" (12.10–11) is perhaps motivated by twin concerns. First, the author wishes to further cut links with Judaism by rejecting the notion that Jesus was merely a Jewish Messiah. Second, by emphasizing that David addresses Jesus as Lord, the text may also seek to assert the existence of Jesus prior to David, thus reinforcing ideas of his preexistence and role in creation.[55]

The most prominent feature of the Christology of Barnabas is framing its understanding of Christ is terms of a typological exegesis that interprets the Jewish Scriptures as primarily being about Jesus. Consequently, Jesus is seen as being present and active in creation (Barn. 5.5, 10; 6.12). He is the one Moses foresaw would bring the covenant to its intended recipients (4.8; 12.5; 14.3–5). The testimony of the prophets is understood as speaking about Jesus (5.6; 6.10; 12.1). In many ways the majority of the epistle is a treatise written to claim that the covenant, the prophecies, and Scriptures of Jewish tradition were always about Christ and mediated by him for the benefit of his people. The author's ideas about the incarnation, the passion, and salvation coalesce into a unified understanding. Thus the purpose of the incarnation was to achieve salvation for those who believe in Jesus (5.10). Furthermore, the death of Jesus and his sufferings took place "so that we might be cleansed by the forgiveness of sins" (5.2). The wounds of Jesus are life-giving and vicarious, since "the Son of God could not suffer except for our sake" (7.2).[56]

---

54. This is most notable in Barn. 12.1, where the cited prophecy is said to be "a reference about the cross and about the one who was destined to be crucified."

55. F. R. Prostmeier, "The Epistle of Barnabas," in Pratscher, *Apostolic Fathers*, 27–45, here 37.

56. Prostmeier makes a similar observation when he states, "Salvation in Barn is grace that works through the suffering of the cross and remains tied to the cross of Christ (Barn 7.11)" (Prostmeier, "Epistle of Barnabas," 38).

The Epistle of Barnabas is not a christological treatise. However, the entire exegetical exercise it undertakes is predicated on the belief that Jesus is the Son of God who was alongside the Father at creation, is attested by the entire witness of the prophetic Scriptures, assumes human flesh and suffers for his people, and will return to judge the living and the dead. Without a commitment to those core christological convictions, the purpose of the epistle—with its appropriation of Jewish scriptural traditions—would be unnecessary. Therefore, the christological perspective of the author is the whole premise on which the argument of the epistle is constructed.

2.8 Shepherd of Hermas

The Shepherd of Hermas is a long and complex text. Its key thematic concerns do not include Christology, but focus more centrally on the topics of repentance and ecclesiology. The composite nature of the text leads to the observation that christological titles are used in different ways in the different sections of the text, and this may reflect divergent understandings concerning Jesus across the text. Thus it has been noted by David Hellholm that "the Christology in PH [Pastor Hermae] is distinguished on the one hand by the connection with the pneumatology and on the other hand by a shift in emphasis among the three parts."[57] In a similar vein, Clayton Jefford observes that "the text of the Shepherd does not reveal a consistent understanding of Christology."[58] Apart from a lack of consistency, the text is simply not primarily interested in Christology. There is little reference to the life and deeds of Jesus, and unlike several of the other texts among the Apostolic Fathers there is little affirmation of the soteriological significance of Jesus, or indeed of the way in which his sufferings and passion mediate salvation to humanity. Notwithstanding these limitations, the text has its own ways of speaking about Christ.

The selection of titles or appellations to refer to Jesus is significant, particularly the nonuse of certain terms. This pattern has been clearly summarized by Osiek:

> The name Jesus never occurs in *Hermas*, and the title Christ appears only three times in very dubious manuscript variants, though there are a number of references to "the name," either of God or of the Son. The omission of the personal name or title is puzzling, and may occur because of reverential avoidance.[59]

Moreover, while there are numerous uses of the title "Lord" (κύριος), the majority appear to refer to God rather than to Jesus. While some occurrences are ambiguous, others clearly denote God as Lord rather than Jesus; for example, "The Lord has sworn by his son" (Herm. Vis. 2.2.8), or "The Lord took his son and glorious angels as counsellors" (Herm. Sim. 5.6.4). Examples of the reverse phenomenon, where "Lord" designates Jesus, are more difficult to locate. When Hermas speaks of "those who have suffered for the name of the Lord" (Herm. Vis. 3.5.2), one is inclined to understand this as a reference to Jesus, given the fact that the formula "the name of the Lord" is such a stereotypical reference to the name of Jesus in early Christian writings.[60] The designation of Jesus by the term Lord may pertain to other examples where suffering or persecution is referenced: "Whenever

57. D. Hellholm, "The Shepherd of Hermas," in Pratscher, *Apostolic Fathers*, 228.

58. Clayton N. Jefford, *Reading the Apostolic Fathers: A Student's Introduction*, 2nd ed. (Grand Rapids: Baker Academic, 2012), 151.

59. C. Osiek, *The Shepherd of Hermas*, Hermeneia (Fortress: Minneapolis, 1999), 34.

60. As Osiek comments, "The name for which they have suffered is that of 'the Lord,' that is, here, Christ" (Osiek, *Shepherd of Hermas*, 71).

persecution comes, they deny their Lord because of riches and their business affairs" (Herm. Vis. 3.6.5). Hence, in line with other Christian perspectives on wealth, the author claims that the rich are inclined to prefer preservation of possessions over fidelity to Christ.

The titles "son" or "son of God" occur several times in the work, but not uniformly throughout. With the exception of the occurrence in Visions 2.2.8 mentioned above, the other forty-eight examples are all in the Similitudes section.[61] The parable of the great tree that overshadows the earth is equated with the law of God, of which the author says, "This law is the son of God, who has been proclaimed to the ends of the earth" (Herm. Sim. 8.3.2). The Son of God is described as having a primary role in creation. Thus, "The son of God is far older than all his creation, with the result that he was the Father's counsellor in creation" (Herm. Sim. 9.12.2). Here the Son is understood to be prior to the created order and instrumental in it being brought into existence. However, the author does not attribute eternal existence to the Son. The Son's role as a counselor may reflect a form of wisdom Christology, with the Son having a role in the providential plans of God. The Son is also attributed a role in the soteriological purposes of God. Thus the Son is described as the door that provides access to the divine presence. This is most fully explained when the text states, "The door is the son of God; there is only one entrance to the Lord. No one, therefore, will go in to him in any other way than through his son" (Herm. Sim. 9.12.6). In this section, the Son is described both as the ancient rock and the newly revealed door, which is provided "in order that those who are going to be saved may enter the kingdom of God through it" (Herm. Sim. 9.12.3). Hence, the Son is the access point and means by which believers receive salvation in God's kingdom. This same sentiment is echoed a little earlier in the text, when it is explained that "the Lord wants those who were called through his Son to be saved" (Herm. Sim. 8.11.1). Therefore, the Similitudes section conveys a clear link between its Christology and its soteriology. It is stated that salvation is achieved through the Son, where the Son serves as a door or entrance point into the kingdom of God.

Another complicated aspect of the christological perspectives in this text is the lack of clear differentiation between Christology and pneumatology. In what has been described as "one of the most frustrating statements in the book,"[62] the angel of repentance states, "I want to explain to you what the holy spirit that spoke with you in the form of the church revealed to you; for that spirit is the son of God" (Herm. Sim. 9.1.1). At one level there appears to be a straight equation between the spirit and the Son, or, to employ later and anachronistic assessments, a confusion of the persons of the Trinity. Such a conclusion is not only foreign to the thought-world of Hermas, but it also lacks a sensitivity to the visionary and image-laden form of communication undertaken in the text. Rather than seeking to provide an analytic understanding of the roles of Son and spirit, it offers a visionary sense of the commonality of purpose and coworking that is shared by the Son and the spirit. The text speaks of the spirit as a son, while appearing to speak of another son: "The son is the holy spirit and the slave is the son of God" (Herm. Sim. 5.5.2). In this context, the spirit is said to be prior to the one called "the son of God." The "holy spirit" is said to have "created the whole creation" and was permitted "to live in the flesh that he wished." It then appears that God gave this flesh in which the spirit dwelt, and it was given an existence of its own: "The conduct of this flesh pleased the Lord . . . so he took the son and the glorious angels as counsellors, in order that this flesh also, having served the spirit

61. This is noted by Hellholm ("Shepherd of Hermas," 228).

62. Osiek, *Shepherd of Hermas*, 35.

blamelessly, might have some place to live" (Herm. Sim. 5.5.4–6). What is being communicated here is complicated and replete with ambiguities. Osiek is a helpful interpreter when she states, "The easiest way to understand these verses is to see them as teaching a pneumatic adoptionist Christology: the pre-existent Holy Spirit by coming to dwell in the historical person of Jesus constituted him as holy."[63] It probably is difficult to align this with the depiction elsewhere in the composite text of the Son of God, who is not the spirit, being far older than creation and counseling God in the act of creation (Herm. Sim. 9.12.2). However, it may be erroneous to try and seek consistency across separate sections of this complex text.

The Christology of the Shepherd of Hermas is striking and in many ways unique. It makes no use of the name Jesus, or the title Christ.[64] The title Lord is typically, but not exclusively, reserved to speak of God. The Son of God is a prominent figure in the Similitudes section of the text, but it is not always entirely clear what is being stated in regard to this figure. The Son of God has a significant role in creation alongside God and is prior to creation. Furthermore, the Son of God is the entrance or door to God's kingdom and thus the means of salvation for those who have been chosen by God. The relation of this Son of God to the Holy Spirit (also described as God's Son) is complex and not readily resolvable into distinguishable attributes and roles. This theological conundrum did not seem to perturb ancient readers to the degree it might modern readers. Perhaps the reason for this is that ancient readers appreciated the genre of the text as communicating visionary and polysemous ideas about the relationship between the divine and the church. Therefore, they responded to the call for believers to forgo double-mindedness, and instead to live a life of genuine repentance that was an expression of an ethical existence.

2.9 The Epistle to Diognetus

The Epistle to Diognetus covers considerable ground before it refers to its christological commitments. It first presents the Christian faith as a rational and superior form of worship in comparison with both pagan religion and Judaism. It then introduces the one who is sent by God (Diogn. 7.2) as the mode of revelation. Then follows a rapid sequence of christological affirmations. It is striking that nowhere in the writing are the terms "Jesus" or "Christ" used. Even the term "Lord" is used sparingly. Its two occurrences are used without significant reflection (7.7; 12.9). Some assessments of the Christology of Diognetus have seen it as underdeveloped at best. Thus Meecham suggests,

> The Christology is simple and unscholastic. It is plainly of the "pneumatic" type. The Son is a heavenly being who descended, being "sent" to appear to men. No precise definition of the relation of the Son to the Father is attempted.[65]

This is perhaps an overly negative assessment, and it fails to state that during this period, while Christ's filial relationship to the Father is frequently affirmed, there is little concern to probe the ontological basis of this relationship.

A Logos Christology is present in both the apologetic section (Diogn. 1.1–10.8), where it is only fleetingly referenced (7.2), and far more prominently in the appended

63. Osiek, *Shepherd of Hermas*, 179.

64. For further on this, see Hellholm, "Shepherd of Hermas," 228–30.

65. H. G. Meecham, *The Epistle to Diognetus: The Greek Text with Introduction, Translation, and Notes* (Manchester: Manchester University Press, 1949), 26.

homily (11.1–12.9). Keeping the two parts separate in order to apprehend the christological thought contained in each composition permits a deeper appreciation of what is being affirmed in these sections. The first section contains two obvious breaks at Diognetus 7.6 and 10.8, with the now lost exemplar having contained a marginal note at both of these points drawing attention to an interruption in the text. The former break in particular disrupts a section where the author was in full flow of christological thought.[66]

In the apologetic section, the christological material is introduced through a description of humanity's inability to comprehend the divine and concomitantly its need to receive revelation of "the truth and the holy, incomprehensible word from heaven" (Diogn. 7.2). In this context there is little to suggest that "the word," ὁ λόγος, *ho logos*, is personified or intended to convey a Logos theology. Neither is there any sense that "the word" has any agency. Therefore, resisting the temptation to read the interpretation of this passage through the theological lens of the appended homily, this use of *ho logos* does not resonate strongly with Johannine concepts.[67] Taken on its own terms the text affirms that God's truth and word are not revealed by sending "some subordinate, or angel, or ruler, or one who manages earthly matters" (7.2). Instead, the heavenly truths that God discloses are to be revealed by a different type of figure described as "the Designer and Creator of the universe himself"[68] (Diogn. 7.2). The Greek behind this translation, αὐτὸν τὸν τεχνίτην καὶ δημιουργὸν τῶν ὅλων, *auton ton technitēn kai dēmiourgon tōn holōn*, is interesting. First, the term τεχνίτην designates some type of craftsperson, responsible for planning and conceptualizing the shape of the object to be made. In the New Testament it is used to describe humans who have artisanal skills (such as craftspeople who worked in conjunction with Demetrius the silversmith, Acts 19:24, 38; or more generally those trained in any craft, Rev 18:22). Alternatively, the term can be used of God, as the one who planned or designed the heavenly city (Heb 11:10). Within that context in Hebrews, God is described with the two terms τεχνίτης and δημιουργός (*dēmiourgos*), and the phrase is typically translated along the lines of "designer and builder." However, the term δημιουργός, "demiurge," takes on a technical sense in much Greek philosophical and Nag Hammadi literature. In the context of Diognetus 7.2, the author might be seeking to capitalize on the tradition and nontechnical usage that appears in Hebrews 11:10. At the same time, he might be appealing to the implied non-Christian readership by introducing a term that was familiar as a designation of the highest intermediary in closest proximity to the ultimate deity and therefore able to reveal divine intentions to humans. Under the influence of Middle Platonic ideas, which may have shaped the thought-world of the author of Diognetus, the demiurge had developed in status from the original Platonic understanding of an artisan who fashioned the universe (Plato, *Tim.* 28a). Instead, the figure was conceived as a second god, who was the means by which the thought of God was revealed. In Nag Hammadi literature, the demiurge functions as an agent of the Supreme God. While the demiurge in some sense knows the mind of God (although at times can act antithetically to the purpose of God), this figure fundamentally protects the Supreme God from the taint associated with the materiality of creation and the earth. Therefore, it appears that the author of Diognetus has sought to utilize a term that would resonate with philosophically minded readers, and

66. See C. N. Jefford, ed., *The Epistle to Diognetus (with the Fragment of Quadratus): Introduction, Text, and Commentary*, OAP (Oxford: Oxford University Press, 2012), 178, 184.

67. This point is also made by Jefford, *Epistle to Diognetus*, 62.

68. This is Holmes's translation (Holmes, *Apostolic Fathers*, 705).

then he commences redefining the role of this figure in line with more standard christological ideas.

Having described this figure as exercising a key role in creation, the author reverts to describing the idea that this figure was sent by God "as a king might send his son who is a king" (Diogn. 7.4). Here both royal status and equality with God are affirmed. This is further described in the first part of the phrase: "He sent him as God; he sent him as a human to humans" (7.4). The precise force of the comparative term "as" is debated.[69] At the very least it designates a representative function and the conferring of a divine status, but it may imply more than this. Alongside this, the author describes the Son being sent as a human. It might be tempting to read into these statements some kind of two-natures Christology. That would be a case of reading later understandings into the text, and it would not allow the author to speak in his own terms. There is no formula of "fully human and fully divine." Instead, there is a genuine desire to show that God's Son fully represents God and comes among humanity as a human. The important point that the author wishes to communicate is that in sending his Son, God bridges the otherwise unbridgeable gap between the heavenly and the earthly. This was an issue discussed in the wider religious thought-world of antiquity. Referring to this figure as the Son of God or as God's child is one of the author's favorite christological designations. Consequently, the divine plan was communicated and revealed in a unique way to his child (8.9, 11). In fact, this child is understood to be involved in formulating the divine plan (9.1). Thus, the providential, divine purpose is devised both by God and his child.

Salvation is achieved through this Son of God. The divine salvation brought by the Son is presented as an act of persuasion, "not compulsion, since compulsion is no attribute of God" (Diogn. 7.4). Hence, the Son acts in full accord with the divine character. Echoing the ransom saying of Mark 10:45, God acts through his Son as the agent of salvation who bears human sin. Hence it is stated of God that "in his mercy he took upon himself our sin; he himself gave up his own Son as a ransom for us, the holy one for the lawless, the guiltless for the guilty, the just for the unjust, the incorruptible for the corruptible, the immortal for the mortal" (Diogn. 9.2). From this perspective, God acts to deal with the consequences of sin, but the agent of salvation is the son who stands in the stead of humanity. While this idea of ransom is drawn from Markan theology, the author of Diognetus makes it his own and extends the representative understanding of the role of the son. It is the righteousness of the son that "covered our sins" (9.3), and it was otherwise impossible for humans "to be justified, except in the son of God alone" (9.4). This theological reflection on the mechanism of salvation erupts into a moment of unalloyed doxological praise: "O the sweet exchange, O the incomprehensible work of God, O the unexpected blessings, that the sinfulness of many should be hidden in one righteous person, while the righteousness of one should justify many sinners!" (9.5). This doxological moment captures a number of the author's key christological and soteriological beliefs. The son of God is the one righteous person, and his righteousness is the means by which the transgressions of "many" can be removed. According to the author this vicarious exchange was unexpected and incomprehensible apart from the divine revelation brought about through the sending of the son. This passage leads the author to use for the only time in this writing the title "saviour" to designate the son: "having now revealed the saviour's power to save even the powerless" (9.6). Thus, the son of God is both a revelatory and a redemptive figure, he is sent and he saves, and

69. See the discussion in Meecham, *Epistle to Diognetus*, 121.

through the work of ransom and release from sin the providential plan formulated by God and his son is made known to humanity. In a likely use of Johannine phraseology, it is declared that God sent his only begotten son, τὸν υἱὸν αὐτοῦ τὸν μονογενῆ, *ton huion autou ton monogenē*, to enable participation in the heavenly kingdom.

Thus, for the author, the son is integral in the creation of the world and instrumental in the formulation of the foreordained plan of salvation. The son mediated this providential plan and is moreover the agent by which it is instigated, since the son is sent as God but comes as a human. The plan involves rescue of humanity from its sinfulness. This is achieved through the son's actions representative and vicarious actions, as they create the sweet exchange that leads to salvation. In a broken sentence before a lacuna in the text, it is also affirmed that the son will be sent again "as judge," and at that time nobody will be able to "endure his coming" (Diogn. 7.6).[70] Presumably if the text had survived, at that point more would have been stated in regard to the author's eschatological outlook.

The short, appended homily contains some christological perspectives that are related to the apologetic section, but that also bear the hallmarks of a different outlook. Primarily any Logos Christology that was incipient in the former section is more developed and reflects the theology of the Johannine prologue more explicitly. There is less sense of the Logos being sent; instead, agency is more self-determined. Hence, "the Word appeared and revealed" right teaching to the disciples (Diogn. 11.2). Those addressed must "understand what the Word has to say," and the author communicates a message provided "by the will of the commanding Word" (11.7–8). In the closing doxology, there are two references to the Logos. The Logos continues a teaching role: "The Word rejoices as he teaches the saints." Furthermore, the logos is the medium through which the Father receives glory: "the Word through whom the Father is glorified" (12.9). Thus, at this point, the glorification of the Father is presumably drawing on another important Johannine idea (cf. John 13:31–32; 14:13; 17:1, 4–5).

The homily makes a reference to the son of the Eternal one (Diogn. 11.5). It is through the son that "the church is enriched and grace is unfolded and multiplied to the saints." This links the Christology and the ecclesiology of the author, though the idea is not developed beyond the content of this single comment. In the end, the christological statements contained in the homily are largely based on a reflection on Johannine Logos Christology (cf. John 1). The word has an ongoing role in teaching believers, enriching the corporate life of the church, and bringing glory to the Father. It appears that the author of this sermon was well-versed in the Fourth Gospel. Consequently, this informed the christological perspectives of this section of the text.

2.10 The Fragment of Quadratus

All that remains of the apologia that Quadratus addressed to the emperor Hadrian is a single fragment of the larger writing, which is preserved as a citation in Eusebius's *Ecclesiastical History* (*Hist. eccl.* 4.3.1–2). Despite the paucity of the remains of the larger writing, every clause of the brief fragment reflects the christological perspectives of Quadratus.[71]

The preamble or narrative introduction supplied by Eusebius is largely descriptive about

70. Jefford notes that at this point in the text "anticipation of the Lord's 'return' is at work" (*Epistle to Diognetus*, 232).

71. For a fuller discussion of the introductory issues surrounding this fragment, see P. Foster, "The Apology of Quadratus," *ExpTim* 117 (2006): 353–58; reprinted in P. Foster, ed., *The Writings of the Apostolic Fathers* (London: T&T Clark, 2007), 52–62.

the time and circumstances in which Quadratus composed the apologia. If it contains any christological idea it is simply this: Eusebius names adherents of the movement Quadratus was defending as Christians. Thus, believers are named after their founder. However, that detail comes from the pen of the fourth-century Christian writer Eusebius, and not from Quadratus.

The single citation from the fragment provides a much richer seam of christological thought. The only title used is "saviour," which occurs twice. Quadratus refers to "the works of our saviour" in the opening line of the cited text, and again later he speaks of the time "while the saviour was living." Both of these references reveal that, for Quadratus, his understanding of the significance of Jesus is related to the fact that he is viewed as the one who brings salvation to believers. While this short snippet of text does not explicitly explain how that salvation is achieved or actualized for believers, the description of the Savior's works does include acts of supernatural deliverance. Individuals are described as having been healed or raised from the dead. This reflects the belief that healings and death-negating works are to be attributed to Jesus. From Quadratus's perspective, some of the recipients of such healings or resurrections continued to have testimonial function within early communities of believers. Quadratus does not say that any of these individuals were alive when he composed his apologia, but rather that "some of them survived to our own time." This suggests that among the contemporaries of Quadratus there were individuals who had contact with and heard the testimonies of those who claimed to have been healed or raised from the dead by Jesus. Thus Quadratus presents as one of his arguments for the veracity of the Christian faith the testimony of those who had been healed or raised to life by Jesus. While firsthand testimony no longer existed in his own day, there were contemporaries who had heard such firsthand testimony themselves.

In a circuitous way, the fragment also references the death of Jesus. It mentions that those recipients of the Savior's works were present during Jesus's lifetime, and also "even after he had gone they were alive for a long time." However, the portion of text cited by Eusebius does not discuss any significance in relation to the death of Jesus, nor does it explicitly reference a belief in his resurrection. However, the mere fact that Quadratus composed an apologetic writing in defense of Christianity, and Eusebius's remark that this writing provides "clear proof of his intellect and apostolic orthodoxy," leads to the supposition that he held standard Christian beliefs about the soteriological significance of the death of Jesus and potentially affirmed belief in Jesus's resurrection from the dead in his writing.

Quadratus's christological affirmations that can be explicitly gleaned from the single surviving cited fragment of his work are these. First, he declares Jesus to be the "saviour," and moreover that salvation is received within the community of believers since Jesus is known as "our saviour." Second, Quadratus states that during his earthly life Jesus performed miraculous healings and raised people who had died. This latter detail is one of the few statements in the writings of the Apostolic Fathers about the actions of the historical Jesus.[72]

72. For Grant, this statement of the reality of the earthly deeds of Jesus is understood as a counter to early gnostic ideas that focused on the cosmic identity of the Christ rather than the physical activities of Jesus (R. M. Grant, "Quadratus, the First Christian Apologist," in *A Tribute to Arthur Vööbus: Studies in Early Christian Literature and Its Environment, Primarily in the Syrian East*, ed. R. H. Fischer (Chicago: Lutheran School of Theology at Chicago, 1977), 177–83, here 181. If, however, the work was addressed to Hadrian as a defense of the Christian faith, it might be less likely that it was used as a vehicle to attack a proto-gnostic faction in the movement.

2.11 The Fragments of Papias

What is known of the writings of Papias is mediated through a selection of fragments of his works preserved in the writings of later authors, as well as through comments about his life, beliefs, and works.[73] Scholars have mined these fragments primarily for the information they relate concerning the composition of the Gospels, variation in the form of certain gospel stories such as the death of Judas or the woman caught in adultery, and the chain of Christian tradition through early figures in the movement. It is rare for any comments to be made on the christological perspectives of the writings. A methodological problem also accompanies the discussion of Papias's own theological beliefs. Not only are such beliefs mediated through the comments of others, but even the fragments grouped as belonging to Papias are of mixed value. Holmes presents twenty-eight fragments in the section on Papias.[74] While a number of these are citations of text attributed to Papias, others are scholarly conjectures concerning material that should be attributed to Papias (sometimes because they are parallels to citations elsewhere attributed to Papias), and others are statements concerning Papias and thus do not record his own statements. By contrast, Carlson classifies only sixteen traditions as fragments of Papias's now-lost writings.[75] This means extreme caution must be exercised when attributing any theological view to Papias. One position seems more certain than most, due to it being attributed directly to him and having multiple attestations—namely, Papias held to the view that the kingdom of Christ would be set up on earth for a period of one thousand years (see frags. 3.12; 7.7, 27). This idea does have christological significance. However, most of the other potential christological views held by Papias that are mentioned in the fragments of his writings occur only in passing.

Papias's major work was titled *Exposition of the Sayings of the Lord*, λόγια κυριακῶν ἐξηγήσεως, *logia kyriakōn exēgēseōs* (frags 3.1; 6.1; 15.1; 16.1; 18.3; 28; and in Latin, *Explanatio Sermonum Domini*, 7.1). The term κυριακός, *kyriakos*, is an adjective of quality or origin, describing the nature and source of the sayings. Therefore, the title Papias presumably gave to his own literary work outlines the contents of the writing. It is a compendium of sayings attributed to Jesus, designated as Lord, which are explained or exegeted for readers. Hence, Papias understands Jesus to be a figure who presented important instruction in the forms of sayings or oracles. This material apparently requires further explanation to draw out the full meaning. Several other references to the sayings of the Lord are made in connection with Papias. Eusebius records that Papias "passes along other accounts of sayings of the Lord belonging to Aristion" (frag 3.14; source Eusebius, *Hist. eccl.* 3.39.3). Furthermore, Papias is recorded as saying that Mark wrote down "the things either said or done by Christ" based on Peter's nonchronological presentation "of the Lord's sayings" (frag. 3.15). Hence, Papias is remembered as a collector and transmitter of sayings of Jesus. Papias himself describes Mark as recording Peter's account of such sayings. Presumably these saying were valued because of the status of the one who spoke them and because they had continuing value for the instruction of believers. Papias also speaks of the way in which he prized oral communication from those who had known Jesus and hence

73. For a full discussion of these fragments and testimonies, see S. C. Carlson, ed., *Papias of Hierapolis Exposition of Dominical Oracles: The Fragments, Testimonia, and Reception of a Second-Century Commentator*, OECT (Oxford: Oxford University Press, 2021).

74. Holmes, "Fragments of Papias," in Holmes, *Apostolic Fathers*, 722–73. He includes a further five fragments listed as the "Traditions of the Elders," which are drawn from the writings of Irenaeus but may have come to him through Papias (727).

75. Carlson, *Papias of Hierapolis*, 111–29.

could "remember the commandments given by the Lord to the faith and proceeding from the truth" (frag. 3.3). In this context, the words of Jesus are labeled as commandments concerning the faith.

Papias uses the title "Lord," κύριος, in various ways in fragments that claim to cite material penned by him. Twice he refers to the disciples of the Lord (frag. 3.4). It is stated by Papias that Justus was protected from the adverse consequences of poison by "the grace of the Lord" (frag. 3.9). The title "Christ" is also used on several occasions. Papias is described as holding a chiliastic view in the form that "after the resurrection of the dead there will be a thousand-year period when the kingdom of Christ will be set up in material form on this earth" (frag. 3.12; cf. 7.1; 27). This reference to the thousand-year reign is described as being "among other things he says," but it is difficult to know whether this is a direct citation of his teaching or a summary presented in Eusebius's own words. Papias's five-volume work is also said to state that "Justus drank the poison of a snake in the name of Christ" (frag. 5.6). Philip of Side says the following was recorded in Papias's work: "As for those who were raised from the dead by Christ, he states that they survived until the time of Hadrian" (frag. 5.8). This appears to be a misattributed and slighted mangled version of the surviving fragment of the apologia written by Quadratus.

The remaining fragments in the collection are a mixture of traditions concerning Papias and retellings of much of the material contained in Eusebius's earlier comments about Papias. Overall, the material presents only a few possible insights into Papias's christological beliefs. The little that can be determined may be summarized as follows. Papias valued highly the words of Jesus. He sought to ascertain these words from the first hearers and disciples of Jesus. Moreover, he recorded this gathered teaching in his five-volume work *Exposition of the Sayings of the Lord*. He believed that Christ would return after the dead were raised, and at that point he would reign on earth for a period of a thousand years. Beyond this, little can be said with certainty due to the fragmentary survival of his writings, since this material exists as citations where Papias's own words are often difficult to separate from the larger literary frame in which they now appear.

3. OVERARCHING THEMES

Whereas the treatment of individual texts has attempted to map both the prominent and particular features of the individual texts that constitute the Apostolic Fathers, this section draws out common patterns in the use of titles and the expression of christological beliefs. This does not mean the features discussed in this section are common in every text found among the corpus, only that they are shared by several of the texts among the Apostolic Fathers.

3.1 Common Christological Titles

The three-membered title "Lord Jesus Christ" is found in several of the writings that comprise the Apostolic Fathers.[76] Furthermore, either singly or doubly, at least one of those three terms is found in every text among the Apostolic Fathers, with the exception of the fragment of Quadratus. Due to its brevity, nothing should be inferred from this.

While at one level this is suggestive of a common christological perspective, there are significant differences between several of the texts. Most notably, the longest text in the

76. The tripartite title "Lord Jesus Christ" is found ten times in 1 Clement, six times in the letters of Ignatius, five times in Polycarp's *To the Philippians*, four times in the Martyrdom of Polycarp, and once in Barnabas. That is a total of twenty-six occasions across the entire corpus.

collection, the Shepherd of Hermas, never uses the name "Jesus" or the title "Christ." The same is true of the Epistle to Diognetus. The Epistle of Barnabas uses the term "Christ" on just one occasion in the three-part formula, "Lord Jesus Christ" (Barn. 2.6), although the name Jesus is prominent. Similarly, the Didache only has a single, though textually contested, use of "Christ" (Did. 9.4). The remaining texts in the corpus use the name "Jesus" and the title "Christ" freely, with Ignatius having a particular penchant for the form "Jesus Christ."

Many of the texts find varied ways to describe the salvific significance of Jesus. However, the actual term "saviour" is not used with great frequency.[77] On one occasion, it appears that God, rather than Jesus, is addressed as "saviour" (1 Clem. 59.3). Typically, Jesus is portrayed as a salvific figure who brings eternal life or immortality to his followers (2 Clem. 20.5), and in particular he is presented as one who rescues souls that would otherwise be lost (Mart. Pol. 19.2).

Jesus is also designated by reference to his filial relationship with God. Thus, he is often simply described as "son" (cf. Barn. 6.12). More fully, several of the authors employ the phrase "son of God" to depict the close and unique relationship that Jesus enjoys with God. Barnabas uses this title to speak of the incarnation of Jesus: "The son of God came in the flesh" (Barn. 5.11). The same phrase is employed to describe the eschatological role that Jesus will undertake as judge: "the son of God, who is Lord and is destined to judge the living and the dead" (Barn. 7.2). The title is also prominent in the Similitudes section of the Shepherd of Hermas, with frequent use of the phrase "the name of the son of God" (eleven times).[78] Believers are said to bear and receive the name of the Son of God (Herm. Sim. 9.13.3, 7; 9.14.5; 9.15.5; 9.16.3). Also, among such believers are some who have suffered for that name (9.28.2, 3). The name itself is said to be incomprehensible and also functions as the means by which the world is sustained (9.14.5). Moreover, the apostles and teachers are said to have preached the name of the Son of God (9.16.5). Thus, for Hermas the Son of God and his name are key christological categories. However, at times this image-rich text collapses categories and appears to identify the Holy Spirit as the Son of God (Herm. 9.1.1). Diognetus uses the title "son of God" only once, but it occurs in a theologically significant passage that speaks of the rectification of people previously alienated from God: "In whom was it possible for us, the lawless and the ungodly, to be justified, except in the son of God alone?" (Diogn. 9.4). So while only being employed on one occasion, for Diognetus the christological title "son of God" refers to the ability of the one so designated to bring about forgiveness and salvation. Ignatius only uses this title twice (Ign. *Eph.* 20.2; *Smyrn.* 1.1). On both occasions it is set in contrast with the human nature of Jesus and his physical descent. Thus, whereas the humanity of Jesus derives from Davidic descent, his identity as "son of God" comes about "with respect to the divine will and power" (Ign. *Smyrn.* 1.1). In his letter to the Philippians, Polycarp presents the most explicit identification of Jesus as the divine Son. This is achieved by placing the name in apposition with the title in a concatenation of christological affirmations: "Now may the God and Father of our Lord Jesus Christ, and the eternal high priest himself, the son of God, Jesus Christ build you up" (Pol. *Phil.* 12.2).[79]

77. It occurs on a total of twelve occasions: four times in the letters of Ignatius, twice in Quadratus, and once in each of 1 Clement, 2 Clement, Polycarp's *To the Philippians*, the Martyrdom of Polycarp, Diognetus, and the fragments of Papias.

78. Herm. Sim. 9.13.3, 7; 9.14.5 [twice]; 9.15.2; 9.16.3, 5, 7; 9.17.4; 9.28.2, 3.

79. This affirmation is in part of the letter that only survives in Latin: *Deus autem et pater domini nostri Iesu Christi et ipse sempiternus pontifex, dei filius Iesus Christus* (Pol. *Phil.* 12.2). As has been mentioned earlier, there are several textual difficulties in this passage.

Whereas the title "son of God," which is taken over from the New Testament, continues to be used freely in several of the writings of the Apostolic Fathers, the dominical self-designation "Son of Man" is rare. In the writings that constitute the New Testament, the title "Son of Man" occurs frequently across all four Gospels, typically on the lips of Jesus (but cf. John 12:34). Outside of the Gospels its use is infrequent, occurring once in Acts (Acts 7:56) and twice in Revelation (Rev 1:13; 14:14). The use in Hebrews is as a designation for humans (Heb 2:6). It appears that the post-Easter Jesus movement did not regularly use the self-designation "Son of Man" as a common way of referring to Jesus. Presumably it was somewhat ambiguous and perhaps did not convey a sufficiently elevated sense of Jesus's identity. This lack of use in the Apostolic Fathers is therefore typical of the pattern in early Christian literature outside of the Gospels. Ignatius contains the only example of precise use of the title with the article before the first reference to "son" (τῷ υἱῷ ἀνθρώπου, *tō huiō anthrōpou*) when he states that Jesus Christ is the one "who is the son of man and son of God" (Ign. *Eph.* 20.2). Here it occurs in a typical construction of Ignatius where he simultaneously affirms both the human and divine nature of Jesus. A second closely related example occurs in Barnabas, but without the article before the term "son": "Observe again that it is Jesus, not a son of man but the son of God" (οὐχὶ υἱὸς ἀνθρώπου ἀλλὰ υἱὸς τοῦ θεοῦ, *ouchi huios anthrōpou alla huios tou theou*, Barn. 12.10). What is striking about this example is not the lack of the article but the statement that Jesus is "not a son of man." Here the phrase is not being used in a titular sense, but to declare that rather than being a mere human, Jesus is in fact "son" of God.[80] It would, however, be too much to see this as a rejection of the title "Son of Man" as contained in the Gospels.[81]

Consequently, it may be correctly observed that several of the most common christological titles in early Christian literature are also frequently found throughout the writings of the Apostolic Fathers. However, while this is not unexpected, it must be noted that the pattern is observed across the whole corpus and is not necessarily reflective of the individual writings. Several of the writings have their own preferences for ways of referring to Jesus, and some also appear to have reasons for avoiding certain of the more common ways of designation.

3.2 Actions Attributed to Jesus

Many actions and activities are attributed to Jesus throughout the writings of the Apostolic Fathers. However, some of the most frequent relate to a role in creation, references to the birth or humanity of Jesus, reflection on his death and its soteriological significance, and a presentation of the idea that Jesus is presently with the Father and will return to inaugurate the final judgment.

In regard to creation, Barnabas asks (and answers) the rhetorical question as to how the one "to whom God said at the foundation of the world, 'Let us make humankind according to our image and likeness'" (Barn. 5.5), could also suffer on behalf of humanity. The question presents the following christological perspectives. Jesus is understood to be preexistent, present at creation, and an agent of creation in whose image humanity was formed. In another context, Barnabas cites the statement from the creation story (Gen 1:26), along with several other phrases from the Genesis account. In regard to these citations, Barnabas states, "These things he said to the son" (Barn. 6.12).

80. Further on this point, see Kraft, *Didache and Barnabas*, 121–22.

81. This issue is discussed more fully in F. R. Prostmeier, *Der Barnabasbrief*, KAV 8 (Göttingen: Vandenhoeck & Ruprecht, 1999), 432–36.

The agency of Jesus in creation is also a key feature in parts of the Shepherd of Hermas. Probably the key contribution of Hermas is to enlarge and extend ideas of the preexistence of the Son. Where Barnabas emphasizes that the Son was with the Father at creation, Hermas extends the existence of the Son beyond the beginning of creation. Thus, according to Hermas, the Son is a primary agent in creation—"He was the Father's counsellor in creation," and more than this "the son of God is far older than all his creation" (Herm. Sim. 9.12.2).[82] In a complex passage drawing on philosophical ideas, Diognetus speaks of "the omnipotent creator of all, the invisible God" sending one "by whom he created the heavens" and the rest of the created realm (Diogn. 7.2). This figure is described as τὸν τεχνίτην καὶ δημιουργὸν τῶν ὅλων, which is typically translated along the lines of "the Designer and Creator of all" (Diogn. 7.2). However, as discussed previously, the term δημιουργός, "demiurge," may have a more specific sense as an intermediary being functioning to bring about the existence of the physical realm on behalf of the high God, who is kept distant from the taint of materiality. At this point the author's reflections on the role of this figure in relation to creation move away from more typical christological ideas and draw on creation myths from wider traditions. However, across a variety of texts in the corpus of the Apostolic Fathers, many attribute a role in creation to a preexistent son-of-God figure. These reflections ultimately may be dependent on the Johannine prologue for their own christological understandings of the role of the Son in creation.

Ignatius is the writer among the Apostolic Fathers who most fully reflects upon the incarnation, since he sees it as key to his affirmation of the humanity of Jesus. In fact, Ignatius often employs references to the birth of Jesus in relation to other events that demonstrate his humanity. Thus, addressing believers in Magnesia, he instructs them "to be fully convinced about the birth and the suffering and the resurrection that took place during the governorship of Pontius Pilate. These things were truly and most assuredly done by Jesus Christ" (Ign. *Magn.* 11.1). For Ignatius, the birth of Jesus is more than a mere historical event. As the first stage of Jesus's human existence, it is thus a demonstration of the fleshly existence of Christ. He then weaponizes this incarnational event to rebut the christological views he attributes to his opponents. Contrary to the reality of the birth of Jesus, these opponents are accused of denying him any meaningful human existence. Ignatius presents an interconnected system of theological commitments. Hence, the incarnation of Christ is viewed as being providentially ordered by God. Ignatius states, "Our God, Jesus the Christ, was conceived by Mary according to God's plan" (Ign. *Eph.* 18.2). However, from Ignatius's perspective, that incarnational event is inextricably linked to its redemptive effect for humanity: "He was born and baptized in order that by suffering he might cleanse the water" (18.2). Thus, as Schoedel observes, Ignatius's Christology is "dominated by the idea of the incarnation."[83]

For the author of Barnabas, the incarnation is also a central aspect of his thought. As part of his anti-Jewish rhetoric, he writes that "the son of God came in the flesh for this reason, so that he might complete the full measure of the sins of those who persecuted his prophets to death" (Barn. 5.11). Hence, according to Barnabas, the guilt associated with the murder of prophets finds its continuation and consummation in the actions of those to whom responsibility for the death of Jesus is attributed. While the negative consequence of

82. The concept of preexistence is used on several occasions in Hermas, but the author is not consistent in the way the idea is expressed, nor is the concept reserved exclusively for speaking of the Son. As Osiek notes, "The preexistence of the Son is clearly stated in v. 2, but he is in good company: previously the church and the great angel are also said to be preexistent" (Osiek, *Shepherd of Hermas*, 179).

83. W. R. Schoedel, *Ignatius of Antioch*, Hermeneia (Philadelphia: Fortress, 1985), 20.

the incarnation is to increase the guilt of one group, Barnabas also sees the incarnation as having soteriological effect for others. Thus he states, "The Lord endured the deliverance of his flesh to corruption, so that we might be cleansed by the forgiveness of sins" (Barn. 5.1). For Hvalvik, these verses provide two key answers to the question of why Christ dies for sins.[84] Yet behind this stands the assumption that the incarnation was necessary in order to facilitate both the redemptive and condemnatory activity that took place in the flesh. By contrast, in 2 Clement the incarnation is mentioned only briefly: "The Lord who saved us became flesh (even though he was originally spirit), and in that state called us" (2 Clem. 9.5). Without further explanation, Christ's salvific role is linked with the incarnation.[85]

The author who comes closest to Ignatius's perspective on the incarnation is his associate Polycarp. However, this is only mentioned in one passage. Polycarp states, "Everyone who does not confess that Jesus Christ has come in the flesh is antichrist; and whoever does not acknowledge the testimony of the cross is of the devil" (Pol. *Phil.* 7.1). This sentiment and some of the phraseology sound so much like Ignatius that it is tempting to think that Polycarp acquired this theological outlook from his fellow church leader. As Hartog notes, "The 'cross' is emphasized in Ignatius' writings . . . , including polemical passages aimed at the docetists (Ign. *Smyrn.* 1.1–2)."[86] The idea of influence from Ignatius might be further suggested by the two-part designation "Jesus Christ." This is Ignatius's favored christological designation (111 times). By contrast, Polycarp prefers the tripartite form "Lord Jesus Christ," or some variant of it (Pol. *Phil.* 1.1, 2; 2.1; 12.2, 2 [twice]; 14.1). The two-part form "Jesus Christ" is much less common (Pol. *Phil.* salut.; 1.3; 7.1; cf. "son of God, Jesus Christ," 12.2). Along with influence from Ignatius, the language is also reminiscent of 2 John 7. So perhaps here is an example of a combination of the language of 2 John and the Christology of Ignatius mediated by Polycarp. Regardless of the origin, the point of Polycarp's deployment of this incarnational statement appears to be as a direct counter to those who deny the reality of Christ's existence in human flesh.

The suffering and death of Christ is discussed in several of the writings that comprise the Apostolic Fathers. In many of these texts, the sufferings of Christ are viewed as representative—that is, Jesus is portrayed as suffering in the place of sinful humans who deserve the death he underwent. For instance, the author of 1 Clement draws out this representative role by citing Isaiah 53 when he describes Christ as "the one who bears our sins and suffers pain for our sake" (1 Clem. 16.4). In 2 Clement there is only one clear reference to the sufferings of Jesus. Toward the beginning of the text, the author reminds his audience of "how much suffering Jesus Christ endured for our sake" (2 Clem. 1.2). Here the representative aspect of the sufferings of Jesus is again present, since his pain was "endured for our sake." However, the author does not clarify what such sufferings achieve for believers, nor why they need something to be done for their sake. In fact, elsewhere in the letter the author seems to place responsibility for salvation on those being addressed. In this regard, those addressed are implored to repent immediately and to "wipe off from ourselves our former sins and be saved" (2 Clem 13.1). Thus, salvation appears to be something that believers still need to achieve, or perhaps to renew and continue to attain with acts of repentance and the self-purging of sin.[87]

84. Hvalvik, *Struggle for Scripture and Covenant*, 178.

85. For more on this verse, see Tuckett, *2 Clement*, 206.

86. Hartog, *Polycarp's Epistle to the Philippians and the Martyrdom of Polycarp*, 128.

87. Tuckett, *2 Clement*, 240–41.

The author of Barnabas links together several major christological ideas to illustrate how they form the divine plan to enact human salvation (Barn. 5.1–14). In common with 1 Clement 16, Barnabas draws on Isaiah 53 as a christological prooftext to establish both that Christ suffered because of human sin and that his suffering brings about healing of salvation for believers (Barn. 5.2; cf. Isa 53:5). The author then presents a detailed disquisition on the reasons "the Lord of the whole world . . . submitted to suffer at the hands of humans" (Barn. 5.5). The incarnation is inextricably linked to the necessity of suffering in human form to effect salvation: "If he had not come in the flesh, people could in no way have been saved by looking at him" (5.10). While expressing the idea in his own way, the author of Barnabas reveals much commonality in theological thought with the letters of Ignatius and 1 Clement. Thus he understands the sufferings of Christ to be representative and in the place of sinful humans. Moreover, by undergoing suffering and death on the cross, Christ made salvation possible for those who look upon him through the eyes of faith.

By contrast, the Martyrdom of Polycarp does not develop christological themes to any great extent. Nonetheless, it does briefly describe Christ as the one "who suffered for the salvation of the whole world of those who are saved" (Mart. Pol. 17.2). While this passage opens the debate concerning the extent of the efficacy of salvation,[88] the key point is that Christ's sufferings were endured to bring about salvation.

Diognetus described Christ's sufferings as representative and as effecting salvation in a passage that transitions into an outpouring of lyrical doxology. In that moment of praise, the author lauds the plan of salvation: "O the sweet exchange, O the incomprehensible work of God, O the unexpected blessings, that the sinfulness of the many should be hidden in one righteous person, while the righteousness of one should justify many sinners!" (Diogn. 9.5). The language of "exchange" clearly betokens the idea of Christ's role as a substitute on behalf of humanity. Yet this is a twofold exchange. Human sins are hidden in Christ, while former sinners receive his righteousness. In Pauline terms, the deserved recompense for unrighteousness, or its "wages," should have received "punishment and death" (Diogn. 9.2; cf. Rom 3:23). Instead, God acted mercifully toward humanity and "gave up his own son as a ransom for us" (Diogn. 9.2). Thus, while only by implication is it understood that the deserved punishment and death of the unrighteous is shifted onto the Son, this is what is intended by the ransom language. Consequently, the natural benefits that accrue to the Son through the filial relationship with God are shared with believers. Diognetus states this sharing of divine blessings explicitly: "through his beloved child" believers "share in his benefits" (8.11).[89] Therefore, the understanding of salvation in Diognetus is fundamentally christological. Salvation is enabled by the sweet exchange to which Christ subjects himself. That exchange is a two-way process. The Son of God takes human sins upon himself in order that humans might in exchange receive divine benefactions that are possessed by the Son. This transformation in the status of formerly sinful humanity is described as a

---

88. This passage, in combination with Mart. Pol. 22.1, has been seen as providing support for the view of limited atonement. Thus Jarvis Williams concludes his discussion by observing in relation to the Martyrdom of Polycarp that "we can infer that this text affirms that Jesus' death was only for the holy elect, which results in the salvation *only* of the holy elect" (J. J. Williams, *For Whom Did Christ Die? The Extent of the Atonement in Paul's Theology*, Paternoster Biblical Monographs [Milton Keynes: Paternoster, 2014]).

89. Meecham finds the origin of these ideas in Pauline thought. He states, "The essential points in these sections (the divine design for long kept secret—the possible charge against God of neglect of man—the revelation through the son of the plan prepared from the beginning—the consequent blessings contrary to all man's expectations) are drawn from Paul's teachings, and there is some similarity of language also. See especially Rom. xvi, 25f.; 1 Cor. ii, 7–10; Eph. iii, 4f.; Col. i, 26f." (Meecham, *Epistle to Diognetus*, 126).

revelation of "the saviour's power to save even the powerless" (9.6). Therefore, Diognetus, utilizing its own imagery and metaphor of the sweet exchange, presents the classic understanding of salvation. Fundamentally it is a christological act that is part of the divine plan. The Son takes upon himself the sufferings and death deserved by sinners. Through faith, former sinners receive a share in divine blessings.

Christ is also described in several of the texts among the Apostolic Fathers as having an eschatological role. Believers are reassured that he will return to gather them to himself in his heavenly kingdom and that at his return he will act as the judge of humanity. The term "parousia," παρουσία, *parousia*, is used four times in the Apostolic Fathers (Ign. *Phld.* 9.2; Herm. Sim. 5.5.3; Diogn. 7.6, 9). However, only two of these examples use it as a technical term to designate the future return of Christ (Herm. Sim. 5.5.3; Diogn. 7.6). In the other two, it designates the first coming of Christ (Ign. *Phld.* 9.2),[90] or is used in a general sense to refer to the presence of God (Diogn. 7.9). Thus, in Hermas the intervening period without the physical presence of Christ is described in the following terms: "The absence of the master is the time remaining until his coming [παρουσίαν]" (Herm. 5.5.3). Just prior to a lacuna in the text, Diognetus contrasts the first time God sent his Son in a nonjuridical role with the time when the Son will be sent again, "for he will send him as judge, and who will endure his coming [παρουσίαν]?" (Diogn. 7.6). These two texts present typical Christian hopes for the return of Christ, employing the technical term παρουσία.

In other places, future hope for the coming of Christ or a gathering into the kingdom is expressed without parousia terminology. For instance, the Didache in a eucharistic prayer addressed to God presents the intercession, "May your church be gathered together from the ends of the earth into your kingdom" (Did. 9.4). While this event is probably conceived as belonging to some final consummation, there are not clear links with the actions of Christ. So this eschatological hope is not obviously Christocentric. Related to this view of end-time events, 1 Clement presents the resurrection of Christ as an example of the future promised resurrection (1 Clem. 24.1). However, in this context, the author is more concerned to demonstrate the plausibility and veracity of resurrection by deploying the example of the phoenix, rather than to portray Christ's role in eschatological events.

A final assize is an element found in several of the texts contained in the Apostolic Fathers. For instance, 1 Clement speaks of believers being "shielded by his [God's] mercy from the coming judgments" (1 Clem. 28.1). While future judgment is in view, it is not linked with Christ's return or role as judge. By contrast, in 2 Clement the link between Christ and future judgment is more prominent. The opening exhortation encourages those addressed to regard Jesus in the same way they regard God—namely, "as judge of the living and the dead" (2 Clem. 1.1). While the judgment of the living and the dead is self-evidently an eschatological event, this is made explicit at other places in the text. Speaking of the eschatological future, the author refutes the idea "that this flesh is not judged and does not rise again" (9.1). More fully, the author reminds the recipients that they "know the day of judgment is already coming" (16.3) and that the standard by which people will be judged is according to their obedience to or perversion of "the commandments of Jesus Christ" (17.6).

Polycarp has a more descriptive account of both the exalted and future role of Christ. First, he links the resurrection and exaltation by describing God as "the one who raised

90. Schoedel states that "Christ's 'coming' (παρουσία is used here for the first time of the 'first coming' of Christ and thus reflects the shift from eschatological to incarnational categories in Ignatius and elsewhere)" (*Ignatius of Antioch*, 210).

our Lord Jesus Christ from the dead and gave him glory and a throne at his right hand" (Pol. *Phil.* 2.1). In this enthroned state, Polycarp declares that all things, earthly and heavenly, have been subjugated to Christ. Moreover, it is from this exalted state that Christ will return as the one "who is coming as judge of the living and the dead" (2.1). Polycarp uses this modified form of 1 Peter 4:5 (cf. Acts 10:42) to bolster his exhortation for ethical behavior in the present. Thus, the expectation of the future return and judgment of Christ should encourage the Philippians to follow his commandments and to avoid unrighteous practices in their current situation (Pol. *Phil.* 2.2).[91] Barnabas has an almost identical statement, declaring that "the son of God" is "Lord and is about to judge the living and the dead" (Barn. 7.12). There is a sense of immediacy in this statement concerning Christ's future role as judge, which reveals that the fervency of parousia expectations had not fully abated when the epistle was written.

Other texts in the corpus also have prominent eschatological concerns. In many ways the Shepherd of Hermas is a thoroughgoing apocalyptic text, and several of its visions concern future promises that believers will receive.[92] However, the function of the Son of God in that future age is not a concern. By contrast, Papias is noted for holding a chiliastic position. Thus Eusebius states of Papias, "He says that after the resurrection of the dead there will be a period of a thousand years when the kingdom of Christ will be set up in material form on the earth" (Eusebius, *Hist. eccl.* 3.39.12). Papias is described as having a major concern not with the juridical role of Christ, but rather with his monarchical role as king during the thousand-year reign on earth. However, caution is required. Papias's eschatological concerns are reported secondhand and by those who wish to present the elements of his thought with which they disagreed.

While not as prominent as some of the other christological roles attributed to Jesus, eschatology is a repeated theme in several of the writings in the collection of the Apostolic Fathers. In particular, the most common elements are the presentation of Christ as the eschatological judge who exercises a juridical function over both the living and the dead. The statement that he will come "to judge the living and the dead" is formulaic and finds its antecedent in earlier writings (Acts 10:42; 2 Tim 4:1; 1 Pet 4:5). However, this eschatological role has been reinscribed in several of the writings of the Apostolic Fathers as a key christological belief that provides final justice and vindication for believers. The other prominent motif is that believers will join with Christ in his heavenly kingdom. This idea is used both as a promise of future hope and a motivation for maintaining correct ethical behavior. In these ways, the function is similar to several other early Christian texts.

4. CONCLUSION

Unsurprisingly, christological concerns are prominent in many of the writings of the Apostolic Fathers, and their rhetoric and contents are predicated on an understanding of Jesus in his relation to God. There are, however, some striking exceptions. The Didache has few references to Jesus and only one use of the term Christ (Did. 9.4), although there has been some dispute about its textual originality. Notwithstanding this, in relation to baptismal and eucharistic prayers, reference to the Son of God, or to Jesus, occurs as an element in common with other early Christian tradition. Other texts, such as the single

---

91. Schoedel suggests that the resurrection of believers "is contingent on doing God's will which includes (a) the avoidance of vices and (b) the willingness to suffer for righteousness' sake in showing mercy to others" (W. R. Schoedel, *Polycarp, Martyrdom of Polycarp, Fragments of Papias*, vol. 5 of *The Apostolic Fathers: A Translation and Commentary*, ed. R. M. Grant [New York: Thomas Nelson, 1965], 11).

92. N. Brox, *Der Hirt des Hermas*, KAV 7 (Göttingen: Vandenhoeck & Ruprecht, 1991), 179.

surviving fragment of Quadratus, can only supply limited evidence. However, despite the slender evidential base, the fragment that survives has a strong christological focus. Despite the christological diversity across the corpus, recurrent and frequent elements span various texts. Titles such as Son of God, Lord Jesus Christ, or shorter forms are widespread. No doubt this commonality reflects wider Christian sociolect, showing connections between individual communities and a repository of shared tradition. The same is true of many actions attributed to Christ, although because these require more complex explanation than the deployment of a title, there is more diversity of expression. Multiple texts exhibit a christological understanding that the Son of God played a role in creation, became fully human, and experienced sufferings with representative and soteriological functions. Moreover, in several of the texts, belief in the resurrection of Christ leads to reflection on both his heavenly role and his expected return when there will be a judgment of the living and the dead.

In this way all the texts are christological at one level or another. In fact, it would be surprising if that were not the case. However, alongside these christological commitments, christological divisions can be seen. This is most obviously the case with the letters of Ignatius where the author confronts those who hold different positions from the author's own. Some of these issues appear also to be in the background to Polycarp's *To the Philippians*,[93] although not as obviously as in Ignatius's writings. By contrast, the Didache has a relative lack of interest in christological themes, and the spirituality it advocates appears to be dependent on ethical living in obedience to the way of God. This diverse evidence leads to the conclusion that, in the period in which these texts were written, christological formulations were not uniformly monolithic. However, the converse is not true. Neither were they unrestrained and entirely free. There was a significant degree of commonality in thought and expression. In the majority of the texts, Jesus is the central figure of worship and devotion. Perhaps this is in part why these texts have survived, and others have not. Concomitantly, these common perspectives may have proved most useful for Christian worship and practice. In the end, the centrality of Christology is the most distinctive feature of the nascent religious movement even in its diverse forms. Any attempt to express the beliefs of the movement required explanation of the identity and significance of Jesus. For most of the authors, employing titles (e.g., Lord, the Christ, the Son of God) or descriptions (e.g., the one intimately involved in creation; incarnate as a human; serving, suffering, saving, and redeeming humanity, then raised to reign at God's right hand, before returning as judge and to gather his elect), were ways in which these distinctive christological beliefs were expressed. Devotion to Jesus in worship led to intellectual reflection on his identity and significance. Many of these core affirmations became central within later christological statements and formulations.[94] The one who was the focus of worship in these nascent communities also became the locus of intellectual thought as expressed in many of its early writings. In this way, the christological thought prominent among many of the texts contained in the corpus of the Apostolic Fathers was in fact the outworking of a prior devotion to the one named and worshiped as the Lord Jesus Christ.[95]

---

93. See Hartog, *Polycarp's Epistle to the Philippians and the Martyrdom of Polycarp*, 131.

94. Gregory Vall makes this point specifically in relation to Ignatius when he writes, "It is remarkable in this regard how many of these formulations anticipate later Christological reflection and even dogma" (G. Vall, *Learning Christ: Ignatius of Antioch and the Mystery of Redemption* [Washington, DC: Catholic University of America Press, 2013], 16).

95. The relationship between Christ devotion and christological thought is a major topic of research in its own right. On this issue, see L. W. Hurtado, *How on Earth Did Jesus Become a God? Historical Questions About Earliest Devotion to Jesus* (Grand Rapids: Eerdmans, 2005).

BIBLIOGRAPHY

Bauer, J. B. *Polykarpbriefe*. KAV 5. Göttingen: Vandenhoeck & Ruprecht, 1995.

Brox, N. *Der Hirt des Hermas*. KAV 7. Göttingen: Vandenhoeck & Ruprecht, 1991.

Foster, P. *The Writings of the Apostolic Fathers*. London: T&T Clark, 2007.

Hartog, P., ed. *Polycarp's Epistle to the Philippians and the Martyrdom of Polycarp: Introduction, Text, and Commentary*. OAF. Oxford: Oxford University Press, 2013.

Jefford, C. N. *The Epistle to Diognetus (with the Fragment of Quadratus): Introduction, Text, and Commentary*. OAF. Oxford: Oxford University Press, 2013.

Jefford, C. N. *Reading the Apostolic Fathers: A Student's Introduction*. 2nd ed. Grand Rapids: Baker Academic, 2012.

Kraft, R. A. *The Didache and Barnabas*. Vol. 3 of *The Apostolic Fathers: A New Translation and Commentary*. Edited by R. M. Grant. New York: Thomas Nelson, 1965.

Meecham, H. G. *The Epistle to Diognetus*. Manchester: Manchester University Press, 1949.

Niederwimmer, K. *The Didache*. Hermeneia. Minneapolis: Fortress, 1998.

Osiek, C. *Shepherd of Hermas: A Commentary*. Hermeneia. Minneapolis: Augsburg Fortress, 1999.

Pratscher, W., ed. *The Apostolic Fathers: An Introduction*. Waco, TX: Baylor University Press, 2010.

Schoedel, W. R. *Ignatius of Antioch*. Hermeneia. Philadelphia: Fortress, 1985.

Tuckett, C. M., ed. *2 Clement: Introduction, Text, and Commentary*. OAF. Oxford: Oxford University Press, 2012.

Varner, W. *Second Clement: An Introductory Commentary*. AFCS. Eugene, OR: Cascade, 2020.

CHAPTER 14

SOTERIOLOGY IN THE APOSTOLIC FATHERS

BRIAN J. ARNOLD

1. INTRODUCTION

The creeds of the early church identify salvation as the purpose of the incarnation. Take, for instance, the Nicene Creed, which states, "who for us men and for our salvation came down and was incarnate." Or consider Irenaeus's version of the *regula fidei*, which confesses faith "in one Christ Jesus, the Son of God, who became incarnate for our salvation" (*Haer.* 1.10). Salvation was at the forefront of the thinking and writing of patristic authors, especially as the church was gaining new adherents, and they promised salvation to all those who would come. This concern for salvation can be traced back into the earliest documents of the church, both in the books that came to constitute the New Testament and in the writings of the second century known to us as the Apostolic Fathers. How these authors conceived of salvation has garnered no shortage of interest and debate, not least of all because there is no accord between them, but also because Christian doctrine was in its most nascent form.

The greatest challenge, then, is that soteriology was never handled in a systematic or protracted way. No writer in the Apostolic Fathers, or in the second century for that matter, offers a complete theory of salvation that indicates shared assumptions with their original audience. It is left to us to pick up the scattered fragments in their writings and piece together a mosaic of salvation, but we must be humble enough to recognize that the pieces of this mosaic can be used, and have been used, to construct different pictures.[1] Complicating the matter further is the need to compare the mosaic of the Apostolic Fathers with the New Testament to see what resemblance there is.

The most important comparison in this regard is the relationship between the Apostolic Fathers and Paul, about which there has been a flurry of scholarship in the last half century, much of it in response to two particular misconceptions that have had outsized influence over the topic of Paul and the early church. The first is the "Pauline captivity" narrative put forward by F. C. Baur and then advanced and nuanced by Walter Bauer, which suggests that the proto-orthodox did not use Paul because he was used by gnostics.[2] This theory

1. Consider even my recent work, B. J. Arnold, *Justification in the Second Century* (Waco, TX: Baylor University Press, 2018), and M. J. Thomas's book *Paul's "Works of the Law" in the Perspective of Second Century Reception*, WUNT 468 (Tübingen: Mohr Siebeck, 2018). I argue that a Pauline view of justification by faith was present in the second century, even if it was subtle and not the dominant view, and Thomas argues that the fathers he examined had a view more akin to the so-called New Perspective on Paul—that is, they differentiated getting into the faith and staying in the faith. I will return to this discussion in my conclusion.

2. See F. C. Baur, *The Church History of the First Three Centuries*, trans. A. Menzies, 3rd ed., 2 vols., Theological Translation Fund Library (London: Williams and Norgate, 1878–79), and W. Bauer, *Orthodoxy and Heresy in Earliest Christianity* (Philadelphia: Fortress, 1971). For good responses, see P. Hartog, ed.,

grossly overstated the absence of Paul and his writings in the early church, and fortunately has been corrected.[3] The second is the notion that the Apostolic Fathers immediately abandoned Paul's doctrine of salvation. T. F. Torrance argued this position in his book *The Doctrine of Grace in the Apostolic Fathers*, and this view still holds sway in scholarship on this question.[4] Due to Torrance's prominence, he serves as an important interlocutor throughout this essay. Contrary to Torrance, the Apostolic Fathers used Paul often and, at times, appealed to his doctrine of salvation by grace through faith.

2. SOTERIOLOGIES IN THE INDIVIDUAL WRITINGS OF THE APOSTOLIC FATHERS

This chapter summarizes the soteriology of each writing/author in the Apostolic Fathers in order to demonstrate that there is no single unifying soteriology.[5] To be sure, these documents share many overlapping themes and exhibit varying degrees of correspondence to the New Testament, but it is best to speak of soteriologies if we are talking about the Apostolic Fathers as a whole. For this reason, it is important to survey each author's soteriology in its own right. The primary focus in each section is on the interplay between faith and works, as this is the most crucial aspect of soteriology in these texts. Does faith alone save? Are works required for salvation? Or is it some combination of faith and works that achieves salvation? I try to resolve this tension within each work, and at times demonstrate how it relates to the soteriology of the New Testament. Other doctrines that mattered for salvation, such as polemics against Judaism, baptism, and almsgiving, are also explored along the way. Only after examining each work individually do I offer concluding remarks that try to synthesize the soteriologies of the Apostolic Fathers.[6]

2.1 First Clement

The purpose of First Clement was to quell factions that had flared up once again in the Corinthian church (1 Clem. 1; 46–47).[7] Clement identified jealousy as the root cause of these factions, and his response to this crisis forms the structure of the letter. Thus, he

Orthodoxy and Heresy in Early Christian Contexts: Reconsidering the Bauer Thesis (Cambridge: James Clarke, 2015), and in particular Hartog's essay titled, "Walter Bauer and the Apostolic Fathers" (34–59), in which he calls for "apostolic normativity" (56) against "Bauer's tenuous reconstructions" (59). See also B. L. White, *Remembering Paul: Ancient and Modern Contests over the Image of the Apostle* (Oxford: Oxford University Press, 2014), esp. 21–33, 43–49.

3. See A. Lindemann, *Paulus im ältesten Christentum: Das Bild des Apostels und die Rezeption der paulinischen Theologie in der frühchristlichen Literatur bis Marcion*, BHT 58 (Tübingen: Mohr Siebeck, 1979); D. N. Penny, "The Pseudo-Pauline Letters of the First Two Centuries" (PhD diss., Emory, 1980); D. K. Rensberger, "As the Apostle Teaches: The Development of the Use of Paul's Letters in Second-Century Christianity" (PhD diss., Yale University, 1981); M. F. Bird and J. Dodson, eds., *Paul and the Second Century*, LNTS 412 (New York: T&T Clark, 2011); T. D. Still and D. E. Wilhite, eds., *The Apostolic Fathers and Paul* (New York: T&T Clark, 2017); A. F. Gregory and C. M. Tuckett, eds., *Trajectories Through the New Testament and the Apostolic Fathers* (Oxford: Oxford University Press, 2005).

4. T. F. Torrance, *The Doctrine of Grace in the Apostolic Fathers* (Grand Rapids: Eerdmans, 1959).

5. Because of space constraints, I do not examine the fragments of Quadratus or Papias here, nor was there space for the Martyrdom of Polycarp, which contains little by way of soteriology.

6. So as not to privilege one text above another, I simply follow the order of the Apostolic Fathers provided by M. W. Holmes, *The Apostolic: Greek Texts and English Translations*, 3rd ed. (Grand Rapids: Baker Academic, 2007). Also, unless otherwise noted, all translations come from him.

7. This section is adapted from my chapter on 1 Clement in *Justification in the Second Century*, 18–35. On 1 Clement and its purpose, see, e.g., W. C. van Unnik, "Studies on the So-Called First Epistle of Clement: The Literary Genre," in *Encounters with Hellenism: Studies on the First Letter of Clement*, ed. C. Breytenbach and L. L. Welborn, trans. L. L. Welborn, AGJU 53 (Leiden: Brill, 2004), 115–81, as well as B. E. Bowe, *A Church in Crisis: Ecclesiology and Paraenesis in Clement of Rome*, HDR 23 (Minneapolis: Fortress, 1988), 61–74, for a helpful discussion of van Unnik's work.

wrote a parenetic letter that placed a heavy emphasis on behaviors that needed to change in order to bring about unity in the church. However, his call for good works is tempered with one of the strongest statements on justification by faith among the Apostolic Fathers, found in 1 Clement 32. Clement holds faith and works in tension, not in confusion, in much the same way that many modern interpreters would hold Paul and James together.

Clement spends a large portion of the letter giving examples, both ancient and recent, of jealousy and its detrimental consequences. On the negative side, he cites the familiar stories of Cain and Abel, Jacob and Esau, Joseph and his brothers, and several more from the Old Testament as warnings to the fractured congregation. For Clement, jealousy is out of place for Christians, which is why he calls them to repentance by inciting them to "fix [their] eyes on the blood of Christ and understand how precious it is to his Father, because, being poured out for [their] salvation, it won for the whole world the grace of repentance" (1 Clem. 7.4). Clement then shifts in chapter 9 to positive examples of men and women who "perfectly served his magnificent glory" (9.2). Illustrations of Noah, Abraham, Lot, Rahab, and others abound as those who lived obedient lives, culminating in the quintessential example, Jesus Christ (16.1–17). Interjected into his long section on right behavior is the plea for humility. He spends an exorbitant amount of time on morality in order to shame those who had caused the faction, as well as to exhort those who remained in the church to live in harmony with Scripture. Right living, in accord with the faith they profess, is the antidote to fracture, which is the abrupt shift Clement makes.

In 1 Clement 32.3–4, Clement pauses from his moral exhortation to make a strong declaration of justification by faith, which forms the heart of his soteriology:

> All, therefore, were glorified and magnified, not through themselves or their own works or the righteous actions that they did, but through his will. And so we, having been called through his will in Christ Jesus, are not justified through ourselves or through our own wisdom or understanding or piety, or works that we have done in holiness of heart, but through faith [διὰ τῆς πίστεως, *dia tēs pisteōs*], by which the Almighty God has justified all who have existed from the beginning; to whom be the glory for ever and ever. Amen.

Several important facets of Clement's soteriology stand out in this passage. First, those glorified—presumably saved—are glorified by God's will. Second, works do not play into the initial act of salvation, as people are neither saved through their own works nor through righteous actions. Third, the saved are those who are called through the will of Christ Jesus, perhaps an early reference to monergism. Fourth, they are not saved through wisdom, piety, or works done in holiness of heart. Fifth, Christians are justified by faith alone. Nothing else contributes to salvation in this passage, and he claims that even those in the previous time were justified by faith.

The idea that even those in previous times were saved through faith is made explicit when Clement speaks of Abraham. In the previous chapter, Clement recalls the story of Abraham, saying, "Let us call to mind again the things which happened from the beginning. Why was our Father Abraham blessed with grace? Was it not because he attained righteousness and truth through faith?" (1 Clem. 31.1–2). Once more he uses the prepositional phrase "through faith" (διὰ πίστεως) in order to demonstrate that "righteousness" (δικαιοσύνη, *dikaiosynē*) comes only through "faith" (πίστις). He also mentions Abraham's faith in 10.1, where he acknowledges that Abraham "was found faithful when he became obedient to the words of God." Abraham proved himself to be full of faith through his works of obedience. Works, in Clement, serve to evidence faith, not to garner salvation.

For Clement, as for Paul, Abraham serves as the prototype of justification of those in former times, confirming that God has always saved his people through faith.

The challenge is that Clement makes other comments that appear, at first glance, to teach the exact opposite position. In 1 Clement 30.3, Clement exhorts the Corinthians to clothe themselves in harmony and to keep away from gossip and slander, "because we are justified by works, and not by words" (ἔργοις δικαιούμενοι καὶ μὴ λόγοις, *ergois dikaioumenoi kai mē logois*). This seems to negate what he says just two chapters later that one is justified through faith. This verse forms the basis of Torrance's critique:

> And so Clement can say that we are "justified by works, not by words" ἔργοις δικαιούμενοι μὴ λόγοις, and insists that we are not justified by πίστις alone but by πίστις and εὐσέβεια, by πίστις and φιλοξενία, by πίστις and ἀληθεία. *This means that Clement is well on the way to the legalism of later times*, as is evidenced also by his almost liturgical use of δικαιώματα and προστάγματα.[8]

For Torrance, this sentence (30.3) repudiates the New Testament vision of salvation and puts the church on a trajectory toward works righteousness. When specifically addressing justification in chapter 32, Torrance writes, "There can be no doubt that this is Pauline language, but it cannot be understood in a Pauline fashion."[9] He acknowledges that Clement refers to justification in a Pauline manner, but then denies that Clement meant something similar to Paul. Instead of reading Clement in his context, Torrance seeks to pierce through Clement's language "to look for other meanings in his use of traditional language."[10]

The two best solutions to the apparent contradiction are that Clement either pulled together indicative and imperative language in Paul, or that he was holding Paul and James in tension, whether intentionally or not. Regarding the indicative/imperative distinction, this solution seems plausible when one considers the opening verse of chapter 33. In response to the declaration that one is saved through faith, he says, "What then shall we do, brothers? Shall we idly abstain from doing good, and forsake love?" He answers insistently: "May the Master never allow this to happen." Immediately after claiming that justification is by faith alone, he asks what the reader should do in response, much like Paul does in Romans 6 after expounding justification by faith in Romans 3–5.[11] Good works, then, are the appropriate response to the work of God in salvation, not the foundation for justification. The indicative, one is justified by faith, grounds the imperative, one is justified by works.

J. B. Lightfoot offers a second way to solve the apparent discrepancy.[12] The solution is to see 1 Clement as a practical guide for bridging the gap between Paul and

8. Torrance, *Doctrine of Grace*, 49. Emphasis added.

9. Torrance, *Doctrine of Grace*, 50.

10. Torrance, *Doctrine of Grace*, 50.

11. A. Lindemann says of 1 Clem. 33.1, "'Clement' is here using the style of diatribe, as Paul had done in the transition from Rom. 5 to Rom. 6" ("Paul's Influence on 'Clement' and Ignatius," in Gregory and Tuckett, *Trajectories*, 13–14). However, Lindemann continues, "But, unlike Paul, 'Clement' does not put his argument in *Christological* but rather in *theological* terms" (14). On the comparison of Clement's argument of works and justification to Paul in Rom 5–6, see R. Knopf, *Die apostolischen Väter* (Tübingen: Mohr Siebeck, 1920), 98, and H. Räisänen, "'Righteousness by Works': An Early Catholic Doctrine? Thoughts on 1 Clement," in *Jesus, Paul, and Torah: Collected Essays*, trans. D. E. Orton, JSNTSup 43 (Sheffield: Sheffield Academic, 1992), 213.

12. J. B. Lightfoot, *The Apostolic Fathers, Part I: S. Clement of Rome*, 2nd ed., 2 vols. (London: Macmillan, 1890), 1:96. Lightfoot is probably correct in assuming Clement's reconciliation of the two apostles was "coincidentally affirmed."

James.[13] Justification has two distinct vantage points, one before conversion and one after. Paul viewed justification from the side of pre-conversion and argued that people are justified on the basis of faith alone. James, on the other hand, was looking back on salvation and making an argument that justification is not a reality if works are absent. In a similar fashion, Clement contends in 1 Clement 32.3–4, along with Paul, that a person is justified through faith. In 1 Clement 30.3 Clement takes up the mantle of James to argue that words are not sufficient in themselves—they must be accompanied by works, such as the works he had been advocating through his many examples.[14] Seen in this context, Clement was not a harbinger of works righteousness in the early church.[15]

Other soteriological themes buttress the aforementioned. For Clement, salvation begins with God's election (1 Clem. 59.2), is accomplished through the blood of Christ, which opens up an opportunity for repentance (7.4), is then appropriated by faith (32.4), and finally is demonstrated by works (30.3). But at the core is his balance of justification by faith and works, which function harmoniously in his thought. Clement flanks his doctrine of justification by faith, which comes across clearest in chapter 32, with clarion calls to obedience and works in chapters 30 and 33, without which a person cannot be secure in his justification. Soteriology, we might say, is the suture that pulls together the wounded flesh of the church, reminding them of their justification by faith alone, which is demonstrated by good works.

2.2 Second Clement

Second Clement is a sermon, not an epistle, and it is unlikely that Clement authored it.[16] As an early sermon, it gives a unique insight into how soteriological themes were expressed in the preaching of the early church. The author takes Isaiah 54 as his text and preaches on the necessity of genuine, heartfelt repentance and righteousness, without which salvation is impossible. The sermon is intended for Christians, which explains the emphasis on continual repentance and obedience for an audience who already considered themselves to be in the faith.[17] Belief in the person of Christ, that he is God, and the work of Christ, that he suffered for our sake, forms the basis of salvation that necessarily issues forth in righteous works and holiness, without which there will be no final salvation.

The sermon begins with one of the highest christological claims in the entire corpus of the Apostolic Fathers: "Brothers and sisters, we ought to think of Jesus Christ as we do of

13. Dale Allison has one of the more comprehensive discussions of how scholars have tried to understand the relationship between Paul and James. See his *A Critical and Exegetical Commentary on the Epistle of James*, ICC (London: Bloomsbury, 2013), 426–28.

14. Pace Carey Newman, who maintains that "it is clear that Clement embraced 'justification by faith' as the way to obtain salvation. . . . It is also clear that Clement understood good works as the means to maintain salvation" (C. Newman, "Righteousness," in *Dictionary of the Later New Testament and Its Developments*, ed. R. P. Martin and P. H. Davids [Downers Grove, IL: InterVarsity Press], 1057).

15. Räisänen brings out a point that commentators on Clement and Paul would do well to remember: "If all Pauline statements were measured with equally strict yardsticks as those used on poor Clement's, we should read much more often of the apostle's latent, or not quite subdued, synergism or the like" ("'Righteousness by Works,'" 213).

16. W. Pratscher, "The Second Epistle of Clement," in *The Apostolic Fathers: An Introduction*, ed. W. Pratscher (Waco, TX: Baylor University Press, 2010), 74, confirms that this is the scholarly consensus. Christopher Tuckett cautions that we do not know enough to claim that this is a sermon. He differentiates sermon from homily, which he says is a "detailed interpretation of a specific scriptural text," and says that this could be a sermon, but is likely not a homily (C. M. Tuckett, *2 Clement: Introduction, Text, and Commentary*, OAF [Oxford: Oxford University Press, 2012], 22).

17. One evidence for this is the frequent use of the hortatory subjunctive. The author encourages his listener to join him in faith, repentance, and obedience.

God, as judge of the living and the dead" (2 Clem. 1.1). Not only is Jesus considered God, but he is cast as the eschatological judge, which sets the tone for the rest of the sermon that obedience and repentance are necessary. Jesus is also seen as the one who suffered for our sake (παθεῖν ἕνεκα ἡμῶν, *pathein heneka hēmōn*, 1.2) and who "saved us when we were perishing" (ἀπολλυμένους ἡμᾶς ἔσωσεν, *apollymenous hēmas esōsen*, 1.4). The author even speaks to the incarnation in 9.5, saying, "Christ, the Lord who saved us, became flesh (even though he was originally spirit)," lending support to the idea that Gnosticism lurks in the background.[18] As Tuckett acknowledges, "For the most part the focus is on the 'salvation' achieved by God/Christ in the coming of Christ himself,"[19] at least in the first half of the sermon.[20]

But it is the ethical considerations that drive the sermon. The author is concerned that some might profess faith in Jesus but not live in accordance with his commands. In 2 Clement 4.1 he writes, "Let us, therefore, not merely call him Lord, for this will not save us," and then quotes Matthew 7:21 that not everyone who calls Jesus "Lord" will be saved. He goes on, "Let us acknowledge him in our actions by loving one another." Love fulfills the command of Christ, and it is the actions that prove the confession. Salvation, then, is both past and future—confessing Christ in the past and living righteously in the future. If one verse summarizes soteriology in 2 Clement and pulls these themes together, it is 15.3: "Let us, therefore, in righteousness and holiness remain true to the things we have believed." What was believed is attested by righteousness and holiness.

Tuckett rightly identifies the timing of salvation as the "notorious crux" of soteriology in 2 Clement. Did God save in the past (2 Clem. 1.4, 7; 2.7; 3.3; 9.5)? Or is salvation a future reality that depends on righteousness in the present and future (8.2; 13.1; 14.1; 15.1; 17.2; 19.3)?[21] Salvation actually has three time dimensions for Clement. Salvation is a past reality based on belief in Jesus Christ, confirmed with present righteousness, with the fear of future judgment.[22] We do not need to attribute this tension to theological confusion or lack of precision. Tuckett notes, "In the absence of other indications to the contrary, one has to assume that the author at least thought that he could hold together statements about salvation as past *and* future without any embarrassment."[23] The author holds in tension salvation as a past, present, and future reality, that requires both faith and works, depending on which vantage point of salvation is being viewed.[24]

---

18. Pratscher argues that the scholarly consensus is that gnostics were the main opponents in the sermon ("Second Epistle of Clement," 85–86). Pace Torrance's suggestion that "the tendency is to lay all the emphasis on knowledge" (*Doctrine of Grace*, 127).

19. Tuckett, *2 Clement*, 76. There are places where the "author firmly insists that Christians have already been 'saved' (cf. 1.4, 7; 2.7; 3.3; 9.2, 5)" (56).

20. Tuckett writes, "Despite what is said earlier (e.g. in 1.4, 7) about salvation as something already achieved, it seems that at least 'final' salvation is still future and not guaranteed even for the Christian" (*2 Clement*, 295).

21. Tuckett, *2 Clement*, 70. Donfried takes a different view altogether, arguing that the author is laying out an opponent's view in 1.4–8 when talking about salvation in the past, only to correct it throughout the remainder of the sermon. However clever this theory may be, it is wanting because the author speaks of past salvation throughout the letter. We might just as easily flip Donfried's analysis. Perhaps the author is laying out salvation as a past reality early on so that he is not misunderstood in a sermon that relies heavily on Christian ethics. He does not want the reader to believe that salvation depends entirely on works, even if works do play an important role in future salvation. See Tuckett, *2 Clement*, 70, and his discussion of K. Donfried, "The Theology of Second Clement," *HTR* 66 (1973): 487–501.

22. Pace Torrance, who argued that "Σωτηρία has a fundamentally future bearing" (*Doctrine of Grace*, 128).

23. Tuckett, *2 Clement*, 70, emphasis original.

24. The apostle Paul does this in the NT: Rom 6:17–22, Gal 4:8–10, Eph 2:11–22, and Col 1:21–23. See W. Varner, *2 Clement: An Introductory Commentary*, AFCS (Eugene, OR: Cascade, 2020), 41.

Tuckett provides an excellent summary of how grace and works function together in 2 Clement:

> Thus the behaviour now demanded of the hearers as the necessary prerequisite for future salvation is not (only) put in terms of obedience to ethical demands which may have existed for ever: rather, it is the appropriate response to grace which has already been given to the hearers in the salvation achieved through Christ. The response is the ἀντιμισθία (1.3, 5; 9.7; 15.2) which Christians must make in response to the gracious and loving God's prior act of salvation. Any act of future salvation, and demands for ethical behaviour in order (in some sense) to "earn" such salvation, takes place within the broader context of the grace of salvation which has already been achieved through the action of Christ.[25]

The call to repay God (ἀντιμισθία, *antimisthia*) is a key feature of 2 Clement's soteriology. Four times throughout the sermon, the preacher speaks of repaying God for what has been received (2 Clem. 1.3, 5; 9.7; 15.2). The example in 9.7 is most telling because he provides an actual succinct response to how we repay God: "While we still have time to be healed, let us place ourselves in the hands of God the physician, and pay him what is due. What is that? Sincere, heartfelt repentance." Clearly this text teaches that healing from future sin is necessary, and we must do our part to pay God his due, which is "sincere, heartfelt repentance" (τὸ μετανοῆσαι ἐξ εἰλικρινοῦς καρδίας, *to metanoēsai ex eilikrinous kardias*). One repays God with genuine repentance.

Repentance is a major theme of 2 Clement and forms much of the structure of the sermon, especially the second half, which has three calls for repentance (2 Clem. 8; 13; 16).[26] Repentance has both qualitative and quantitative characteristics. Qualitatively, repentance must be sincere and heartfelt (8.2; 17.1). God knows the heart, and repentance must be genuine to take effect. Quantitatively, repentance is ongoing and must be sought immediately and for as long as we are alive (5.5; 6.6; 13.1).[27] We may not be too bold to suggest that 2 Clement is a precursor, at least in spirit, of Martin Luther's first thesis: "When our Lord and Master Jesus Christ said, 'Repent' (Mt 4.17), he willed the entire life of believers to be one of repentance."[28]

What is more, the author cites his own need for continual repentance and states that he has not yet escaped temptation (2 Clem. 18.2). He presumes himself to be in the faith, which is why he shuns the works of the devil and pursues righteousness, but he also fears future judgment, and this fear propels him forward in faithful obedience. In other words, the preacher preaches to himself, while also exhorting his hearer, to escape temptation and pursue righteousness. Repentance includes the works of righteousness, most clearly noted in 19.3: "Let us, therefore, practice righteousness [πράξωμεν . . . δικαιοσύνην, *praxōmen . . .*

25. Tuckett, *2 Clement*, 70–71. Tuckett likens 2 Clement to the covenantal nomism found in E. P. Sanders's seminal work *Paul and Palestinian Judaism: A Comparison of Patterns of Religion* (Philadelphia: Fortress, 1977), suggesting that for the writer of 2 Clement, God has graciously saved by grace but good works are necessary for final salvation. It is similar to the approach Matthew Thomas takes on the second-century fathers in *Paul's "Works of the Law"*, though Thomas does not appeal to 2 Clement in his book.

26. For a helpful overview of the structure, see Pratscher, "Second Epistle of Clement," 73–74.

27. Torrance is not wrong here: "Even after baptism [Christians] are represented as heavy sinners, necessitating endless repentance" (*Doctrine of Grace*, 129). Torrance also seems correct in his previous sentence that "clearly, Christians are still liable to damnation." Sincere repentance provides healing from future sins.

28. Kurt Aland, ed., *Martin Luther's 95 Theses: With the Pertinent Documents from the History of the Reformation* (St. Louis: Concordia, 1967), 50.

dikaiosynēn], so that we may be saved in the end" (cf. 2 Clem. 6.9; 8.4). Without righteousness practiced through repentance, one has no hope of final salvation.

Two other facets of soteriology in 2 Clement deserve brief mention—baptism and redemptive almsgiving. Baptism must be kept "pure and undefiled" (2 Clem. 6.9), and the seal left unbroken (7.6). Yet, even for those who threaten to defile their baptism, the prescription remains consistent: "While we are yet on earth, let us repent" (8.1). Almsgiving is better than both prayer and fasting, for it covers a multitude of sins (16.4; cf. 1 Pet 4:8). David Downs puts this verse in the context of 2 Clement 1.2–5 where "salvation is made available through Christ's suffering," and then highlights the "theme of unmerited salvation made possible through Jesus Christ" in 2 Clement 1.6–8 that "is punctuated with a declaration of salvation on the basis of God's mercy and compassion."[29] Yet somehow in 2 Clement "cruciform love shown by believers has the power to atone for the sins of those who demonstrate such love."[30] Both are true in 2 Clement.

The preacher disdains lighthearted, inauthentic repentance. Salvation, achieved by Christ and appropriated through belief, is contingent on continual repentance and righteous living, which proves the genuineness of faith. Words of repentance are cheap; works of repentance are convincing. His final exhortation is significant: "Let us have faith, brothers and sisters! We are competing in the contest of a living God" (2 Clem. 20.2). The exhortation is to have faith and to compete in the contest—both themes that saturate the sermon.

2.3 The Letters of Ignatius

We glimpse Ignatius through seven authentic letters he wrote on his way to Rome to face the lions in the Colosseum.[31] Fighting churches, lack of authority, and pending martyrdom all play into Ignatius's theology and specifically his soteriology. Certainly, there was strife between Jews and gentiles, just as there were serious questions about authority structures in the church. But looming above all these issues in the church was Ignatius's psychological wrestling with death and his ultimate goal—to attain Christ by whatever means necessary, even if through the mouths of lions. Salvation for Ignatius was bound up in faith, love, prayer, and martyrdom.

Ignatius's polemic against the Jews is an important backdrop for his soteriology. There are two things in play for Ignatius as he regards Judaism—first, there was Judaism of the Old Testament, which had prepared the way for Christianity, and second, there were Judaizers who tried to mix former Jewish practices with their new Christian faith. He is far more favorable to the former than to the latter, even though he sometimes speaks of Judaism in general when he seems to be referring to Judaizers in particular (e.g., Ign. *Phld.* 6.1).

Of the seven letters, only two contain significant interactions against Judaizers—*To the Philadelphians* and *To the Magnesians*.[32] Ignatius solemnly charges them, "If anyone expounds Judaism to you, do not listen to him" (Ign. *Phld.* 6.1). Judaism, for Ignatius,

29. D. J. Downs, *Alms: Charity, Reward, and Atonement in Early Christianity* (Waco, TX: Baylor University Press, 2016), 199–200.

30. Downs, *Alms*, 201.

31. I have condensed this section from my chapter on Ignatius in *Justification in the Second Century*, 36–76.

32. William Schoedel identifies the opponents of Ignatius in these letters as "Judaizing Christians," saying, "*Phd.* 5–9 has many affinities with *Mag.* 8–10. Both passages are concerned with the problem of Judaizing Christians" (*A Commentary on the Letters of Ignatius of Antioch*, Hermeneia [Philadelphia: Fortress, 1985], 200). Michael Goulder detects an element of Judaizing in more than just Ign. *Phld.* and Ign. *Magn.*; he thinks, for instance, that Ignatius's praise of the church in Ephesus (that no αἵρεσις, *hairesis*, resides there) refers to their freedom from Judaizing (M. Goulder, "Ignatius' 'Docetists,'" *VC* 53 [1999]: 17).

was now antithetical to Christianity—the two faiths stood as polar opposites to one another. Christians could not dabble in Judaism, and Jews could not retain their Judaism and assent to Christianity. These faiths may share a common heritage but only insofar as Judaism recognized Christianity as the anticipated hope of the Jews. For Ignatius, the ways were parted. "It is utterly absurd," said Ignatius, "to profess Jesus Christ and to Judaize" (Ign. *Magn.* 10).[33]

Despite his complaints against Judaism, Ignatius acknowledges that Christianity sprang out of Judaism even though he says, "Christianity did not believe in Judaism, but Judaism in Christianity" (Ign. *Magn.* 10.3). Ignatius spoke favorably of the prophets, who spoke beforehand of Christ (Ign. *Phld.* 5.2; cf. 9.2; *Magn.* 8.2). The prophets link Judaism in the Old Testament and Christianity in the New Testament.

> And we also love the prophets, because they anticipated the gospel in their preaching and set their hope on him and waited for him; because they also believed in him, they were saved, since they belong to the unity centered in Jesus Christ, saints worthy of love and admiration, approved by Jesus Christ and included in the gospel of our shared hope. (Ign. *Phld.* 5.2)

They foresaw the coming of Jesus Christ and they "set their hope on him," "believed in him," and "they were saved" because "they belonged to the unity centered in Jesus Christ." It was their "anticipation of the gospel"—namely, the coming and work of Jesus, and their faith in this Christ—that secured their salvation and made them "saints worthy of love."[34] Together the faithful Jews of old and the Christians of late have a "shared hope" in the gospel and in this way have shared a common faith.

Ignatius also had positive constructions of soteriology. If one phrase encapsulates Ignatius's view of salvation, it could very well be "faith and love." To the Smyrnaeans he writes, "Faith and love are everything" (Ign. *Smyrn.* 6.1). Faith and love form the basis for Christianity as far as Ignatius is concerned, and nothing is preferable to them (Ign. *Magn.* 1). Everything could be summed up in these two things—faith in Jesus Christ and love for both him and others. This he makes plain in *To the Ephesians* 14.1: "None of these things escapes your notice, if you have perfect faith and love toward Jesus Christ. For these are the beginning and the end of life: faith is the beginning and love is the end, and the two, when they exist in unity, are God. Everything else that contributes to excellence follows from them." Faith is the beginning (ἀρχή, *archē*), and love is the end (τέλος, *telos*). Of the sixty-four occurrences of "love" in Ignatius, sixteen are joined together with "faith."[35] Faith and love were even allegorized in the elements of the Eucharist—faith corresponded to the body, and love to the blood (Ign. *Trall.* 8.1). Faith and love are nearly always tied to the message of the gospel for Ignatius.

---

33. Holmes's translation of this phrase as "utterly absurd" captures the tone of Ignatius well (*Apostolic Fathers*, 209). Adam Becker and Annette Reed comment that this phrase in Ign. *Magn.* 10.3 often serves "as the representative example for those who claim that 'Jew' and 'Christian' became clear-cut and mutually exclusive religious identities in the first century CE. However, counter-examples abound, both from this period and well beyond" (A. H. Becker and A. Y. Reed, *The Ways That Never Parted: Jews and Christians in Late Antiquity and the Early Middle Ages* [Tübingen: Mohr Siebeck, 2003], 2n6). Counterexamples may abound, but they do not lessen *Ignatius's* belief that the two were indeed "clear-cut and mutually exclusive." Space does not allow for a deeper discussion on the so-called "parting of the ways."

34. C. T. Brown helpfully writes, "Ignatius' εὐαγγέλιον is specifically defined by the salvific παθός and ἀνάστασις of Jesus. For Ignatius, Jesus is the content of the εὐαγγέλιον" (*The Gospel and Ignatius of Antioch*, StBibLit 12 [New York: Peter Lang, 2000], 79). Torrance adds, "It is quite clear that salvation has as much to do with the death of Christ as with the Incarnation" (*Doctrine of Grace*, 60).

35. Schoedel, *Ignatius*, 24.

One important text on justification comes in *To the Philadelphians* 8.2:

> But for me, the "archives" are Jesus Christ, the inviolable archives are his cross and death and his resurrection and the faith that comes through him; by these things I want, through your prayers, to be justified.

The crux of the gospel message is present in this verse, not to mention that this statement comes in the broader context of an Ignatian reference to the gospel, as this verse comes sandwiched between three important uses of εὐαγγέλιον, *euangelion* (Ign. *Phld.* 8.2; 9.2 [twice]). The focus is on faith in the death and resurrection of Jesus Christ by which he wants to be justified. Charles Thomas Brown observes, "In *Phld.* 8.2 as in *Phld.* 5.1, Ignatius connects his own ultimate goal (in 8.2 to be justified, and in 5.1 the 'lot in which I attain mercy') with the εὐαγγέλιον (as well as the prayer of the Philadelphian church). It is the present faith in the past events of Jesus' life, death and resurrection that is the locus of justification for Ignatius."[36]

Soteriology was personally urgent for Ignatius. His execution was days or weeks away at the time of writing, and above all else he wanted to attain Christ. His bloodlust for death, as seen in statements like "I am passionately in love with death" (Ign. *Rom.* 7), must be kept in the perspective of his claim that the Spirit revealed his impending martyrdom, such that any release from death would have meant his failure to follow the Spirit in faith.[37] In this sense, his personal martyrdom is connected to his salvation, but not in a way that binds all others to martyrdom for salvation.

2.4 Polycarp, *To the Philippians*

The letter of Polycarp to the Philippians gives the most straightforward, and most avowedly Pauline, statement on salvation by grace found in the Apostolic Fathers.[38] In *To the Philippians* 1.3, Polycarp plainly states, "By grace you have been saved, not because of works, but by the will of God through Jesus Christ." Salvation is by God's will and election (Pol. *Phil.* 1.1, 3), through the person and work of Christ (8.1), and it is on the basis of grace, not works (1.3; 3.1–2), though works do play into final salvation (2.2; 5.2). His stated purpose for the letter is to instruct them in righteousness (3.1), which those in Philippi invited him to write. Even Torrance admits that with Polycarp's letter "we have the most venerable of the Apostolic Fathers, and perhaps the chief depository of the primitive Gospel tradition," although he accuses Polycarp of lacking originality in his theology.[39]

36. Brown, *Gospel and Ignatius of Antioch*, 18.

37. See M. Haykin, "'Come to the Father': Ignatius of Antioch and His Calling to Be a Martyr," *Them* 32 (2007): 26–39.

38. Many scholars observe that we need to keep Paul, his letters, and his theology separate. See, e.g., Lindemann, *Paulus im ältesten Christentum*, 221–32. In Polycarp, we have the image of Paul mentioned (a man "blessed and glorious"), and he is referred to as a letter writer ("when he was absent he wrote you a letter"). Finally, Paul's theology is displayed, as I explore in this section, albeit briefly. Paul Hartog has a helpful discussion of Polycarp's use of Paul that summarizes the major scholarly opinions on this matter. See P. Hartog, *Polycarp's Epistle to the Philippians and the Martyrdom of Polycarp: Introduction, Text, and Commentary* (Oxford: Oxford University Press, 2013), 65–68.

39. Torrance, *Doctrine of Grace*, 90–91. Boudewijn Dehandschutter warns that the brevity and occasional nature of the letter means that it "cannot serve as a summary of important theological themes that were current in the first half of the second century" ("The Epistle of Polycarp," in Pratscher, *Apostolic Fathers*, 127). He unironically goes on to argue that the letter can provide a helpful window into early ecclesiology. I think it best to be temperate in all our conclusions of doctrine in the Apostolic Fathers given the snapshots we see. I say more about this in the conclusion.

Regarding Paul and his letters, Polycarp says, "If you study them carefully, you will be able to build yourselves up in the faith that has been given to you, which is the mother of us all, while hope follows and love for God and Christ and for our neighbor leads the way" (Pol. *Phil.* 3.1–3). Two important things stand out in his statement about faith. First, faith itself is a gift that is given, presumably by God. A strong connection exists between Ephesians 2:8–9 and both *To the Philippians* 3.2 and 1.3. In 1.3, he uses the exact phrase "by grace you have been saved" (χάριτί ἐστε σεσωσμένοι, *chariti este sesōsmenoi*), and 3.2 has at least a conceptual link between "a gift from God" (θεοῦ τὸ δῶρον, *theou to dōron*) and "the faith that has been given to you" (τὴν δοθεῖσαν ὑμῖν πίστιν, *tēn dotheisan hymin pistin*). Second, he calls faith the "mother of us all," because it is faith that gives birth to believers, and then he adds hope and love, following the pattern in 1 Corinthians 13:13. Faith (πίστις, *pistis*, Pol. *Phil.* 1.2; 3.2; 4.2; 9.2; 10.1; 12.2; 13.2) is foundational to Polycarp's soteriology; it is a gift that is given on the basis of grace. Grace, though appearing only twice (1.3; 14), bookends the epistle and gives helpful context for the moral exhortations that fill most of the letter.

Halfway through the letter, Polycarp gives the grounding of Christian belief.[40] "Let us, therefore, hold steadfastly and unceasingly to our righteousness, who is Christ Jesus, who bore our sins in his own body upon the tree, who committed no sin, and no deceit was found in his mouth; instead, for our sakes he endured all things, in order that we might live in him" (Pol. *Phil.* 8.1; cf. 1 Pet 2:22). He affirms the impeccability of Christ ("who committed no sins") and substitutionary atonement (Jesus "bore our sins in his own body . . . for our sakes"). Of great significance, Polycarp calls Christ Jesus "our hope and the guarantee of our righteousness" (τῇ ἐλπίδι ἡμῶν καὶ τῷ ἀρραβῶνι τῆς δικαιοσύνης, *tē elpidi hēmōn kai tō arrabōni tēs dikaiosynēs*).[41] This leaves a pressing question: How does Christ as the guarantee of righteousness relate to individual righteousness throughout the letter?

This question of righteousness is at the center of the debate about Polycarp's soteriology. Many commentators argue that he emphasizes individual righteousness for salvation, but this is unlikely given the following points.[42] First, the occasion of the letter was for Polycarp to instruct the Philippians on righteousness (Pol. *Phil.* 3.1), so the reader should expect a strong dose of ethics. Second, as noted, he begins the letter with a quotation from Ephesians 2:8–9 to emphasize that salvation is by grace through faith, not works, lest he be misunderstood when describing how to live out their faith. Third, he places a heavy emphasis on Christ's atoning work for sinners, with the expectation that the believer would "live in him" (Pol. *Phil.* 8.1). Fourth, Polycarp uses conditional language, similar to Paul (e.g., Col 1:23), so that a person does not presume on inactive faith. Those who do not continue in obedience should not expect to be saved (2.2; 5.2).[43] Fifth, he urges his reader to "obey the teaching about righteousness" (πειθαρχεῖν τῷ λόγῳ τῆς δικαιοσύνης,

40. Polycarp's exalted Christology comes mostly in response to docetism—Jesus Christ came in the flesh, suffered in the flesh, and rose again in the flesh: "Jesus Christ, who endured for our sins, facing even death, whom God raised up, having loosed the birth pangs of Hades" (Pol. *Phil.* 1.2).

41. Surprisingly, Polycarp rarely, if ever, mentions the Holy Spirit (perhaps 5.3). However, he speaks of Christ as the τῷ ἀρραβῶνι τῆς δικαιοσύνης, though Paul calls the Spirit the ἀρραβών in Eph 1:14, an epistle which Polycarp clearly used often.

42. See Hartog's summary of Torrance, Schoedel, and Bovon-Thurneysen on this issue (*Polycarp's Epistle to the Philippians and the Martyrdom of Polycarp*, 133).

43. Marcion could be lurking in the background of Polycarp's conditional language. What was the church to do with those who professed faith but then either denied it, altered it, or abandoned it through unrighteousness? See C. E. Hill, *From the Lost Teaching of Polycarp: Identifying Irenaeus' Apostolic Presbyter and the Author of Ad Diognetum*, WUNT 186 (Tübingen: Mohr Siebeck, 2006), 83.

peitharchein tō logō tēs dikaiosynēs, 9.1) and encourages them not to run in vain, "but with faith and righteousness" (ἀλλ' ἐν πίστει καὶ δικαιοσύνῃ, *all' en pistei kai dikaiosynē*, 9.2), again giving faith priority in this expression, though no doubt touting the importance of both. Sixth, Polycarp offers a litany of ways that believers can demonstrate their "firm and immovable faith" (10.1; cf. 2, 4), such as loving the family of believers, cherishing one another, and giving charity that can deliver one from death, which could be yet another example of redemptive almsgiving (10.1–2). The necessity of righteousness for final salvation is present, but it does not negate, supplant, or stand at odds with the place of faith.

Berding and Hartog offer good insights into why Polycarp puts so much emphasis on personal righteousness. Although Berding sees no attempt to correlate faith and works in Polycarp, he does note that the driving force in the letter is ethical.[44] He writes, "It seems that one of the keys to understanding Polycarp is not that he is driven simply by an ethical impulse, but that he wants to describe a *true* Christian," for those who are truly chosen (Pol. *Phil.* 1.1) and show true repentance (11.4).[45] Likewise, Hartog states, "Based upon the pledge of Christ's atoning work, the believer lives an ethical life of righteousness."[46] In short, Polycarp is writing to describe the Christian life far more than he is talking about how one becomes a Christian. Even still, along with Diognetus (examined below), Polycarp's *To the Philippians* resonates closest to the apostle Paul's teaching on salvation.[47]

2.5 Didache

"There are two ways, one of life, and one of death, and there is a great difference between these two ways." Thus starts the Didache, or the Teaching of the Twelve Apostles, a church manual that was highly regarded in the early church.[48] In addition to the Two Ways material (Did. 1–5), the Didache focuses on liturgy, such as instructions for baptism and the Eucharist, the right days for fasting, a Matthean formula for prayer, and directives on food (Did. 6–10). This is followed by discussion of church offices, including a section on teachers, rules governing legitimate prophets, bishops and deacons, and the Lord's Day (Did. 11–15). It finishes off with a brief eschatological section (Did. 16).[49] The goal was to teach baptizands how to live as Christians on the way of life, to give instructions for the sacred practices of baptism and the Eucharist, and to initiate the reader into community life.

Soteriology is not the focus of the work since it assumes a person has been saved and is entering into the communion of saints. Neither does the author take much time to address how one came into salvation, though a few statements sprinkled throughout point back to the foundation of their faith and speak to salvation as it relates to behavior expected of

---

44. K. Berding, *Polycarp and Paul: An Analysis of Their Literary and Theological Relationship in Light of Polycarp's Use of Biblical and Extra-Biblical Literature*, VCSup 62 (Leiden: Brill, 2002), 171.

45. Berding, *Polycarp and Paul*, 174.

46. Hartog, *Polycarp's Epistle to the Philippians and the Martyrdom of Polycarp*, 133.

47. Hill, *From the Lost Teaching of Polycarp*, argues for Polycarp's authorship of Diognetus. Hill shows many parallels and even stylistic overlaps. He briefly overlays their theology on Christ's atoning death, seen in Pol. *Phil.* 1.2 and 8.1 with Diogn. 9.2–5 (p. 139), though I think he misses the conceptual connection of salvation by faith espoused in both writings.

48. See E. L. Gallagher and J. D. Meade, *The Biblical Canon Lists from Early Christianity: Texts and Analysis* (Oxford: Oxford University Press, 2017), 266. Eusebius, for instance, has the Didache listed as part of the *antilegomenon* (*Hist. eccl.* 3.25.4).

49. Scholars take multiple approaches to structure. I prefer K. Niederwimmer's approach that identifies these four main sections (*The Didache*, Hermeneia [Minneapolis: Fortress, 1998], 1). See also C. K. Rothschild, who divides the book into six sections (*New Essays on the Apostolic Fathers*, WUNT 375 [Tübingen: Mohr Siebeck, 2017], 178–79).

the Christian.[50] Charles Guth distinguishes between the basis of salvation and how one becomes a Christian and notes that the latter is more difficult to pin down.[51] Regarding the basis of salvation, Guth highlights five christological statements in chapters 9–10 that establish salvation and its benefits as being "through Jesus" (διὰ Ἰησοῦ, *dia Iēsou*; Did. 9.2, 3, 4; 10.2, 3).[52] "Life and knowledge," "eternal life," and "knowledge and faith and immortality" are all listed as that which comes "through Jesus," though this is never explicitly tied to faith or belief.

How one becomes a Christian is not as easy to decipher, though repentance and faith both play a role. Prior to taking the Eucharist, the individual is to have a moment of introspection to examine his holiness. "If anyone is holy, let him come; if anyone is not, let him repent" (Did. 10.6). Whether this refers to initial repentance or continual repentance is not entirely clear.[53] That said, 9.5 prohibits the Eucharist from those who are unbaptized, so this injunction must be for baptized followers of Jesus who are warned to repent from present sin.

In the closing chapter, the Didachist mentions the importance of faith, saying, "Those who endure in their faith will be saved by the accursed one himself" (Did. 16.5). Endurance in faith through the "fiery test" is necessary for final salvation, which squares with Jesus's apocalyptic teaching in Matthew 24:13. But the reverse is also true—failure to endure means one will not be saved. We can reasonably deduce that the object of their faith is Christ, the accursed one (cf. Gal 3:13), but that this faith must be lived out in obedience to the list of commands provided in the first section of the Didache.

How, then, do works fit into the author's soteriology? Several times throughout the work, he makes subtle remarks about salvation that tend toward works righteousness, as in Didache 16.2: "Gather together frequently, seeking the things that benefit your souls, for all the time you have believed [πίστεως, *pisteōs*] will be of no use to you if you are not found perfect in the last time." He connects the foundation of salvation, belief, with the need for perfection. Faith and perfection work hand in hand to result in final salvation, and belief, no matter the duration, cannot overcome a lack of perfection.[54] The Didachist, who drew liberally from the Gospel of Matthew, could just be echoing Jesus's words in Matthew 5:48: "You therefore must be perfect, as your heavenly Father is perfect" (ESV). Nevertheless, the Christian ethic and the call for perfection come after faith. There is no hint that works play into salvation or "getting in" to the faith, but Christians are expected to uphold the highest level of holiness.

The other verse that rings of works righteousness comes from Didache 4.6: "If you earn something by working with your hands, you shall give a ransom for your sins." The idea is that a person is able to atone for her sins through almsgiving, which is probably in the Didachist's mind in 1.5–6 as well. David Downs argues that the atonement here is for specific sins and not sins in the abstract.[55] Yet, what redemptive almsgiving accomplishes and how it accomplishes it is murky, as he does not expound further. Within the immediate context of 4.5–8, this verse is about sharing perishable things with those in need so that

50. See S. J. Wilhite, *The Didache: A Commentary*, AFCS (Eugene, OR: Cascade, 2019), 70, who says that only "hints" of soteriology exist and that no "soteriological formulas appear nor do clear soteriological categories emerge."

51. C. J. Guth, "The Relationship of Faith and Works in the Soteriologies of the Apostolic Fathers" (PhD diss., University of Aberdeen, 1994), 217.

52. Guth, "Relationship of Faith and Works," 202–17.

53. Niederwimmer calls 10.6 "one of the most difficult *cruces interpretum* in the Didache" (*Didache*, 161).

54. This verse should be read next to 6.2, which has a more permissive ethic. See Wilhite, *Didache*, 225.

55. Downs, *Alms*, 236.

they might become sharers in the imperishable. Within the broader context of the Two Ways material in chapters 1–6, this quick statement on redemptive almsgiving seems standard, as it appears similarly in the Two Ways section of the Epistle of Barnabas.[56] The point here, as it pertains to soteriology, is that nothing too definitive can be stated.

Some have argued that the entire Two Ways tradition is an exposition of works righteousness. Torrance, who holds this view, writes, "There can be no Christian explanation of the unevangelical nomism that runs through the whole writing," even referring to the moral standards as "legalism."[57] This diagnosis is too strong. How might one reconcile the Two Ways material and the call for perfection with the notion that salvation is based on belief in the person of Christ? Quite simply, it is to remember that the intent of the letter was to instruct new Christians about how to live and not on how to become converts, and so it is not surprising that he gives robust ethical commands.

Downs's comment about redemptive almsgiving in the Didache applies to soteriology throughout this work: "Since the *Didache* is not a theological, and certainly not a soteriological, treatise, it should not be criticized for not offering a 'theology of the cross.'"[58] Nor should it be criticized for introducing works righteousness. The Didache yields less about soteriology than the other works examined in this chapter because the purpose of the book is to provide a church manual to Christians. Faith in Christ, though understated, is present, but the emphasis of his soteriology is living in the way of life.

2.6 The Epistle of Barnabas

For Barnabas, hope is the grounding of salvation, and salvation is the grounding of works, but full confidence in one's salvation cannot be established in this life. Barnabas is notoriously challenging on this point because he seems to speak in multiple directions. However, like 1 Clement, he holds hope and works in tension. The priority he gives to hope, love, and less frequently, faith, in a Pauline fashion, and the emphasis on works that flow from a new heart, in the manner of James through the Two Ways tradition, brings cohesion to his thought, especially in his polemic against Judaism. This stands in contradistinction from scholars like Torrance who demurs that "justification and righteousness in [Barnabas] are not understood in a Pauline sense."[59]

Barnabas's soteriology is bound together with the purpose of the work. He is preoccupied with the relationship between Christianity and Judaism.[60] To be sure, discussion of the Jewish Scriptures takes up a large portion of the epistle, but the question still remains *why* the author was driving this point home. Barnabas gives two statements that could be taken as the purpose behind his writing. In 1.5, he writes "so that along with your faith you might have perfect knowledge as well," signaling his desire to add depth of understanding for his audience.[61] Then, in 17.1, he narrows his purview to salvation, writing, "I hope,

56. Scholars generally agree that the Didache and Barnabas were using a mutual source for their Two Ways material. See J. S. Kloppenborg, "The Transformation of Moral Exhortation in Didache 1–5," in *Didache in Context: Essays on Its Text, History, and Transmission*, ed. C. Jefford, NovTSup 77 (Leiden: Brill, 1995), 88–109.

57. Torrance, *Doctrine of Grace*, 37.

58. Downs, *Alms*, 246.

59. Torrance, *Doctrine of Grace*, 106.

60. Holmes suggests that the main aim of Barnabas is to answer these two questions: "How ought Christians to interpret the Jewish scriptures, and what is the nature of the relationship between Christianity and Judaism?" (*Apostolic Fathers*, 370).

61. We must firmly reject any notion that Barnabas has gnosticism in mind. For one thing, Barnabas has a high view of the OT, the Jewish law, and God the Father. Perfect knowledge here has to do with the completion of Christian knowledge. James Carleton Paget explores the concept of γνῶσις (*gnōsis*, "knowledge") in Barnabas, leaning on the work of H. Windisch, "Der Barnabasbrief," in HNT Ergänzungsband, Die

in accordance with my desire, that I have not omitted anything of the matters relating to salvation," a statement that summarizes the book up to this point, offered before he launches into his Two Ways material, which also has a soteriological, and eschatological, focus. Thus, Barnabas's polemic against Judaism—namely, his understanding of the covenant and his interpretation of circumcision and the Sabbath—as well as his positive teaching on Christianity—namely, his explanation of the person and work of Christ and the centrality of hope in Christ—are stitched together to teach about salvation.[62] In short, both the polemic against Judaism and his positive instruction in Christian doctrine are soteriological, much like we saw in Ignatius.

Barnabas is in part a polemic against Jews and their view of salvation, which the author links to their poor reading of Scripture. We might summarize his polemic under two main arguments: (1) the Jews sinned and lost the covenant, and (2) the Jews interpreted the Bible wrongly. First, Barnabas is explicit that Jews not only lost the covenant but that they were not worthy to receive it because of their sins (Barn. 14.1). Chapter 4 is critical to the argument of the entire epistle, for it is there that he argues that the Jews lost the covenant when Moses descended Mount Sinai, caught them worshiping the golden calf, and smashed the tablets to pieces, forever severing them from the covenant. Second, the Jews interpreted the Bible incorrectly, most notably in their understanding of the law. Barnabas touches on every significant Jewish practice, highlighting distinctives like sacrifices (Barn. 2), circumcision (Barn. 9), food laws (Barn. 10), Sabbath keeping (Barn. 15), and the temple (Barn. 16), in order to demonstrate the superiority of Christian interpretation of these identity markers through the use of allegory, and to make the bigger point that these practices are truly fulfilled through the heart (e.g., Barn. 16.7).[63] The point comes down to this: the Jews missed salvation because they did not see that the Scriptures pointed to Jesus. They failed to see that true, godward religion comes from the heart. James Carleton Paget cuts to the core of the matter that for Barnabas, "Judaism, with its law, was a temporary phenomenon; Christianity is a permanent fixture."[64]

The second theme is the relationship between Christ's work, faith/hope, and salvation. We can organize Barnabas's teaching on salvation into three categories: (1) salvation comes from Jesus Christ and his death on the cross; (2) hope and belief are the ground for salvation; (3) righteous works are necessary for the one who believes. For Barnabas salvation is ultimately tied to the person and work of Christ. He holds a high Christology, presenting Jesus as the Son of God no less than four times (e.g., Barn. 12.10), and frequently speaks to the significance of the cross, casting the atonement in terms of substitution (5.1, 5, 6; 7.5).

Salvation is attained through hope in Christ, which is evident in two particular texts. In Barnabas 6 salvation is renewal that is received through forgiveness of sins for those who hope in Jesus. Thus in 6.9 he states, "But now learn what knowledge has to say: set your

---

Apostolischen Väter 3 (Tübingen: Mohr Siebeck, 1920), who identifies two types of knowledge in Barnabas, essentially an exegetical γνῶσις (2–16) and an ethical γνῶσις (18–20). While these categories may be too neat in that there is certainly crossover between them, it may help explain the two instances of γνῶσις in Barn. 1.5 and 18.1. See J. Carleton Paget, *The Epistle of Barnabas*, WUNT (Tübingen: Mohr Siebeck, 1994), 46–49.

62. See F. R. Prostmeier, "The Epistle of Barnabas," in *The Apostolic Fathers: An Introduction*, ed. W. Pratscher (Waco, TX: Baylor University Press, 2010), 34, who suggests that "the occasion of Barn is a dispute over the soteriological meaning of the Christ event" and goes on to argue that the purpose is to give exegetical proof for this.

63. Barnabas's lack of consistency and his apparent willingness to use whatever method seems best in the moment has led Thomas to state humorously, "Indeed, one may be forgiven for thinking of *Barnabas'* methodology as a version of 'throw everything at the wall and see what sticks,' as it is challenging to place all of the reasons for why these works are to be rejected into consistent categories" (Thomas, *Paul's "Works of the Law"*, 77–78).

64. Carleton Paget, "Paul and the Epistle of Barnabas," 368.

hope upon Jesus, who is about to be revealed to you in the flesh." What then of those who hope in Jesus? "Since he renewed us by the forgiveness of sins, he made us people of another type, so that we should have the soul of children, as if he were creating us all over again" (6.11). Hope leads to forgiveness, which leads to the new-creation idea, which in turn makes a person's heart the dwelling place of God (6.15).

Barnabas 16 is the clearest and most extended development of his soteriology:

> Before we believed in God, our heart's dwelling place was corrupt and weak, truly a temple built by human hands, because it was full of idolatry and was the home of demons, for we did whatever was contrary to God. "But it will be built in the name of the Lord." So pay attention, in order that the Lord's temple may be built gloriously. How? Learn! By receiving the forgiveness of sins and setting our hope on the Name, we became new, created again from the beginning. Consequently God truly dwells in our dwelling place—that is, in us. How? The word of his faith, the call of his promise, the wisdom of his righteous requirements, the commandments of his teaching, he himself prophesying in us, he himself dwelling in us; opening to us who had been in bondage to death the door of the temple, which is the mouth, and granting to us repentance, he leads us into the incorruptible temple. For those who long to be saved look not to the human speaker but to the one who dwells and speaks in that person. (Barn. 16.7–10)

The initial place he orients salvation is in belief—belief leads to forgiveness of sins, which is received, and to the setting of our hope on the name, by which he certainly means Jesus. At this moment, the person becomes a new creation (cf. 2 Cor 5:17). As a consequence of belief, forgiveness, and the setting one's hope in the name of Jesus, God comes to dwell within the heart. The author then even lays out how this happens, which serves as his *ordo salutis*—faith, the call, wisdom of following his righteous requirements, obeying his teaching, and his indwelling presence, which frees from bondage, grants repentance, and leads to the incorruptible temple. Salvation is an act of God to which one responds with hope and repentance, and then out of which one lives in faithful obedience.

Barnabas makes several comments throughout the epistle that seem incongruent with his emphasis on hope in Jesus. Two particular statements stick out in this regard. First, Barnabas speaks of justification as something that has only eschatological potential and is not a current reality. "Do not withdraw within yourselves and live alone, as though you were already justified, but gather together and seek out together the common good" (Barn. 4.10). By this he simply means that justification must not be used as an excuse to rest and not seek the good, which he goes on to say a few verses later: "Let us never fall asleep in our sins, as if being 'called' were an excuse to rest, lest the evil ruler gain power over us and thrust us out of the kingdom of the Lord" (Barn. 4.13). Those who fall asleep or use their justification as a footstool for rest will be overtaken by Satan (a prominent figure in Barnabas's theology).

The second text relates to redemptive almsgiving. Amid the Two Ways material, Barnabas writes:

> Remember the day of judgment night and day, and you shall seek out on a daily basis the presence of the saints, either laboring in word and going out to encourage, and endeavoring to save a soul by the word, or work with your hands for a ransom for your sins. You shall not hesitate to give, nor shall you grumble when giving, but you will know who is the good paymaster of the reward. (Barn. 19.10–11)

Downs recognizes that passages such as this have been used to suggest that early Christians compromised the New Testament teaching of grace (and here he singles out Torrance). Downs, however, does not see this as a move away from grace in Barnabas. "*Barnabas*," he writes, "appears to represent an attempt to encourage 'covenant fidelity and eschatological perseverance' among those who already identify as followers of Jesus."[65] And again, "It is striking how regularly God's gracious initiative is emphasized elsewhere in *Barnabas*."[66]

Neither of these passages are out of step with Barnabas's soteriology of hope in Jesus as the ground for salvation. Besides, Barnabas even encourages his readers with these words: "To the best of our ability, let us cultivate the fear of God and strive to keep his commandments, so that we may rejoice in his righteous requirements" (Barn. 4.11). "To the best of our ability" implies that Barnabas did not hold to a rigid idea of perfectionism or that entire obedience is possible, and the hope is to rejoice in the righteous requirements, not to see them as earning merit of any kind. Works are no more antithetical to Barnabas's soteriology of hope than they are in Paul (Rom 6:1).

At the beginning of the epistle, the author lays out three basic doctrines of the Lord: "the hope of life, which is the beginning and end of our faith; and righteousness, which is the beginning and end of judgment; and a glad and rejoicing love, which is the testimony of works of righteousness" (Barn. 1.6). We might see these as a pyramid, with each phrase adding a layer onto a necessary layer beneath it.[67] Hope in Christ is the foundation of his soteriology, which is the beginning and end of faith. Built onto that foundation is righteousness, which is the beginning and end of judgment. The final layer is glad and rejoicing love, which is the testimony of works of righteousness. Two observations are in order for this final layer. First, the works of righteousness refer to love, not to specific acts that earn favor. Second, it is a testimony of works of righteousness (ἔργων δικαιοσύνης μαρτυρία, *ergōn dikaiosynēs martyria*), which means these works testify to love; they are not meant to merit salvation. Inverting this pyramid misconstrues soteriology in Barnabas.

2.7 Shepherd of Hermas

Adolf von Harnack may not have been exaggerating when he stated, "We have in the Shepherd the most important document for the Church Christianity of the age,"[68] given that the Shepherd was widely read and nearly canonized.[69] Even those who did not consider it Scripture, still praised the merits of the book and encouraged believers to read it.[70] Thus, the vision of soteriology in this work had far-reaching implications on the budding theology of the church. The problem is that the theology is difficult to trace. Torrance begins his assessment of the Shepherd with these words: "It is probably more true of the Author of the *Shepherd* than of the other apostolic Fathers that disciplined thinking in

65. Downs, *Alms*, 240–41.

66. Downs, *Alms*, 241.

67. Guth states, "There may be a hint of a chronological ordering here: hope initiating one into the faith, righteous living as the conduct of appropriate faith, in the end love as the result of a righteous life" ("Relationship of Faith and Works," 256).

68. Adolf von Harnack, *History of Dogma*, vol. 1, trans. Neil Buchanan (Boston: Little, Brown, and Company, 1901), 218.

69. Gallagher and Meade, *Biblical Canon Lists*, 249.

70. See Eusebius, for instance, who spoke of its popularity, noting, "For this reason we know that it has been used in public in churches, and I have found it quoted by some of the most ancient writers" (*Hist. eccl.* 3.3.5–6; cf. 3.25.4).

the realm of theology is conspicuously lacking."[71] This assessment is certainly true of his soteriology, which is quite muddled, although several important themes surface throughout, such as election, righteousness, repentance, double-mindedness, and its opposite, wholeheartedness.

The Shepherd is a pastoral admonition written to a church that had grown lax, which unfolds in three major sections: Visions, Mandates, and Similitudes or Parables. Those within the tower, one of his visions for the church, had become slack in their devotion to Christ, as seen through their disobedience to his law. Those who had believed now practiced works of lawlessness, even while still professing faith in Christ, which led to the gravest charge of double-mindedness.[72] The only solution is wholehearted repentance, but repentance is offered only once. The centerpiece of soteriology in the Shepherd of Hermas, then, is the extension of a one-time repentance after baptism and the command to pursue righteousness, which he envisions the reader can do.

Baptism serves as initiation into the faith and thus into the church. It is water upon which the church is built and through which salvation comes: "Hear, then, why the tower is built upon the water: it is because your life was saved and will be saved through water" (Herm. Vis. 3.3.5).[73] Baptism secures forgiveness of sins (Herm. Mand. 4.3.1), and those without it, though they believe, do not yet have forgiveness (Herm. Mand. 4.3.3). It is the seal of those who go into the water dead, but who come up alive so that they might enter into the kingdom of God (Herm. Sim. 9.16.4). Some draw near to the waters of baptism but return to their evil desires because the purity of truth is too much for them (Herm. Vis. 3.7.3).

What, though, comes of this person who has sinned after receiving the seal of baptism? This question lies at the heart of soteriology in this work, and it is something for which the Shepherd is known. After baptism a person has only one chance for repentance. This comes across, for instance, in Mandates 4.3.6: "But I am warning you . . . if, after this great and holy call, anyone is tempted by the devil and sins, that person has one opportunity for repentance. But if that one sins repeatedly and repents, it is of no use for such a person, for that person will scarcely live." Or again, "There is only one repentance for God's servants" (Herm. Mand. 4.1.8), "for the one who has received forgiveness of sins ought never to sin again" (Herm. Mand. 4.2.2).

The Shepherd defines repentance in Mandates 4.2.2, which is worth citing in full since repentance occurs so frequently throughout the work: "To repent . . . is great understanding. For those who have sinned understand that they have done evil in the Lord's presence, and the act that they committed enters their heart, and they repent and no longer do evil, but do good lavishly, and they humble their own soul and torment it, because they sinned. You see, therefore, that repentance is great understanding" (Herm. Mand. 4.2.2).[74]

71. Torrance, *Doctrine of Grace*, 111. Cf. L. W. Barnard: "Hermas is no theologian and what theology there is in his book is confused" (*Studies in the Apostolic Fathers and Their Background* [New York: Schocken, 1966], 163).

72. The word "double-minded" (διψυχία, *dipsychia*) occurs fifty-five times in all its forms. See C. Osiek, *The Shepherd of Hermas*, Hermeneia (Minneapolis: Fortress, 1999), 30. The origin of this word, whether or not James coined it, is a matter of debate (see Jas 1:8). See, for instance, O. J. F. Seitz, "Relationship of the Shepherd of Hermas to the Epistle of James," *JBL* (1944): 131–40.

73. My numbering follows that of Molly Whittaker, *Der Hirt des Hermas*, GCS 48, Apostolischen Väter 1 (Berlin: Akademie, 1967) and as given in Holmes (though Holmes includes both numbering options).

74. The words μετάνοια, *metanoia*, μετανοεῖν, *metanoein*, and ἐπιστρέφειν, *epistrephein*, occur ninety-eight times prior to the addendum, with a total of 141 uses, including the addendum. See D. Hellholm, "The Shepherd of Hermas," in Pratscher, *Apostolic Fathers*, 225. Osiek's count is higher. She records 156 occurrences of repentance throughout the work (Osiek, *Shepherd of Hermas*, 28n218).

Repentance includes the recognition of evil, the pledge to do good, and the tormenting of the soul, although he does not go into detail about what this means. Also, the author highlights the need for wholehearted repentance (Herm. Vis. 3.13.4; Mand. 9.2; Sim. 9.33.3).

Since forgiveness is limited to one post-baptismal sin, the Shepherd prescribes the strictest ethical standards because future salvation depends on present righteousness. Those who "practice righteousness" (οἱ ἐργαζόμενοι τὴν δικαιοσύνην, *hoi ergazomenoi tēn dikaiosynēn*) are blessed and will not be destroyed (Herm. Vis. 2.3.3). He even goes so far as to say that obedience cures sin (Herm. Sim. 10.2.4). In Visions 12.3.1 the Shepherd gives as close of a summary of salvation as we find in the work, which puts an accent on works: "Practice righteousness and virtue, truth and fear of the Lord, faith and gentleness, and whatever good things are like these. By practicing these you will be an acceptable servant of God and will live to him; indeed, all who serve the good desire will live to God" (cf. Herm. Sim. 5.1.5).

All that has been said about the Shepherd's soteriology is curious based on the author's strong view of election and the priority of faith. He writes, "God's elect will live because those chosen by God for eternal life will be spotless and pure" (Herm. Vis. 4.3.5). He is hopeful that the elect will persevere unto eternal life because God has chosen them and instilled in them righteousness (στάξαντος τὴς δικαιοσύνην, *staxantos tēs dikaiosynēn*) in order that they might be justified and sanctified (Herm. Vis. 3.9.1).[75] However, justification hinges on the righteousness of the person, which throughout is within the capacity of the individual. Torrance proffers that the Shepherd anticipates a "Pelagian doctrine of man," who is able to pull himself up by the proverbial moral bootstraps in order to walk in righteousness.[76] While there is merit to his assessment based on the entire work, it does not account for the role that faith plays in the Shepherd's theology.

Faith occurs infrequently throughout the Shepherd, but when it does appear we gain insight into the priority of faith in salvation and sanctification. The Shepherd begins the first mandate, "First of all, believe that God is one" (Herm. Mand. 1.1), asserting the monotheistic nature of Christianity, and this is followed by the admonition to "believe in him, therefore, and fear him, and fearing him, exercise self-control" (Herm. Mand. 1.2). Those who observe the dual command to have faith and fear will put on every virtue of righteousness, for "faith and fear (= reverence) form the appropriate relationship of human persons to God."[77] Faith, which the elect exercise, forms the basis of the ethical commands that follow. When personifying seven virtues as women who uphold the tower—that is, the church—the first woman is Faith. "The first of them, the woman with the strong hands, is called Faith; through her God's elect are saved" (Herm. Vis. 3.8.3).[78] The elect are saved by faith, instilled with righteousness, and the hope is that "the righteous aim at righteous things" (Herm. Vis. 1.1.8). Those who do not persevere in righteousness, despite the anticipation that they will persevere, presumably lose their salvation, though this is not entirely clear.

One question that naturally surfaces when examining soteriology in the Shepherd is its relationship to the apostle Paul. It seems unlikely that the Shepherd, if indeed he was writing from Rome (Herm. Vis. 1.1.1), did not know of Paul, his letters, or his legacy. Theories range from heavy dependence on Paul to no knowledge of the apostle. Eva Aleith, who

75. Guth, "Relationship of Faith and Works," 286–87.
76. Torrance, *Doctrine of Grace*, 121.
77. Osiek, *Shepherd of Hermas*, 104.
78. Virtues were commonly personified in feminine forms in the Greco-Roman world. See Osiek, *Shepherd of Hermas*, 77.

believes there is no connection to Paul, argues that seeds of later Catholic theology were sown into the Shepherd. She writes, "The *Shepherd* of Hermas, *in which Pauline influence is no longer felt*, shows where the path that the Roman communal theology embarked upon in *1 Clement* and pursued further in *2 Clement* leads. The uniquely catholic stance on justification by works, the emphasis on commandments, and the idea of merit take its place."[79] Likewise, Siegfried Shulz read back into early Christianity the Protestant/Catholic debate. He saw "no evidence of an examination of Paul or even a positive influence" and argued that salvation was through works, not faith, and the Shepherd had a "legalistic religion ('Gesetzreligion')."[80] Other scholars like B. F. Westcott surmised that Paul's "'great truth,' namely the prioritization of faith over works," was present in the Shepherd.[81] Jonathan Soyars has recently written a comprehensive study on Paul's legacy in the Shepherd where he acknowledges that "the emerging Pauline legacy was complex and convoluted."[82] In my estimation, Aleith and Shulz go too far on one side, as does Westcott on the other. Faith is certainly present and given priority in salvation, but the emphasis on works is significant. Paul may be in the background of the Shepherd's theology, but not in terms of justification by faith that expiates sins past, present, and future.[83]

Salvation frames the Shepherd. The book opens with the question: "How can I be saved?" (Herm. Vis. 1.2.1; cf. Mand. 3.3; Sim. 5.7.3), and it ends with final exhortations to walk in belief and obedience (Herm. Sim. 9.33.1). In between is a serious call to righteousness, not the double-mindedness that plagued so many in the church. The elect, by faith, ought to live out the righteousness instilled in them through the sealing of baptism. For those who stumble into sin, there is a single chance for repentance, so long as repentance is sought with the whole heart.

2.8 The Epistle to Diognetus

Unlike most other works in the Apostolic Fathers, which are parenetic letters written to exhort Christians in the faith, Diognetus fits better with the apologetic literature of the latter half of the second century, even earning the accolade of "the pearl of early Christian apologetics" from Avery Cardinal Dulles.[84] The anonymous author seeks to answer three questions Diognetus had raised concerning Christianity. First, what God do they believe in that makes them disregard the world and despise death, neither considering the Greek gods nor Jewish superstitions? Second, what is the nature of their love for one another? Third, why has this new race or way of life come into the world now and not before? In chapter 9, he sets out to respond to the charge of novelty, claiming that the religion is actually quite

79. J. Soyars gives an excellent overview of this conundrum in his recent work *The Shepherd of Hermas and the Pauline Legacy*, NovTSup 176 (Leiden: Brill, 2019), 70, and here he is citing E. Aleith, *Paulusverständnis in der alten Kirche*, BZNW 18 (Berlin: A. Töpelmann, 1937), 3. Translation is from Soyars, as is the emphasis.

80. S. Shulz, *Die Mitte der Schrift: Der Frühkatholizismus im Neuen Testament als Herausforderung an den Protestantismus* (Stuttgart: Kreuz, 1976), 358, as cited in Soyars, *Shepherd of Hermas and the Pauline Legacy*, 75. Lindemann held that the Shepherd likely used Paul unconsciously, and thus was not using his letters or his theology directly (*Paulus im ältesten Christentum*, 290). See Soyars, *Shepherd of Hermas and the Pauline Legacy*, 78.

81. Soyars, *Shepherd of Hermas and the Pauline Legacy*, 64, citing B. F. Westcott, *A General Survey of the History of the Canon of the New Testament*, 1st ed. (Cambridge: Macmillan, 1885), 224–25. Westcott also sees the priority of faith in Herm. Vis. 3.8.3 as significant.

82. Soyars, *Shepherd of Hermas and the Pauline Legacy*, 59.

83. Instead of Paul's doctrine of justification, we see influence in areas such as the command to put off vice and put on virtue (Herm. Sim. 6.1.4). See Soyars, *Shepherd of Hermas and the Pauline Legacy*, 137n153.

84. A. C. Dulles, *A History of Apologetics* (Eugene, OR: Wipf & Stock, 1999), 35. This section is adapted from Arnold, *Justification in the Second Century*, 77–103.

ancient. This chapter also most clearly lays out his soteriology with the twin doctrines of atonement and justification.

> So then, having already planned everything in his mind together with his child, he permitted us, during the former time, to be carried away by undisciplined impulses as we desired, led astray by pleasures and lusts, not at all because he took delight in our sins, but because he was patient; not because he approved of that former season of unrighteousness, but because he was creating the present season of righteousness, in order that we who in the former time were convicted by our own deeds as unworthy of life might now by the goodness of God be [considered] worthy,[85] and, having clearly demonstrated our inability to enter the kingdom of God on our own, might be enabled to do so by God's power. But when our unrighteousness was fulfilled, and it had been made perfectly clear that its wages—punishment and death—were to be expected, then the season arrived during which God had decided to reveal at last his goodness and power (oh, the surpassing kindness and love of God!). (Diogn. 9.1–2a)

In Diognetus 9.1–2, the author unravels God's plan to permit all mankind to be carried away by undisciplined passions and to be led astray by pleasures and lusts (cf. Rom 5). All of this was in the previous time, however, and it was not as though God delighted in sins during that time, lest he give the impression that God is either evil or indifferent. Rather, it was because of God's forbearance that he allowed these things to take place—he never approved of unrighteousness in the former season. God allowed people to walk in their passions because he was creating the present season of righteousness (cf. Rom 3:25–26). The former time was meant to bring about the conviction of their own deeds in order that people might recognize that they were unworthy of life. Although they are unable to obtain life through their own merit, they are now considered worthy because of God's goodness. The author moves from plight to solution.

> He did not hate us, or reject us, or bear a grudge against us; instead he was patient; and forbearing; in his mercy he took upon himself our sins; he himself gave up his own Son as a ransom for us, the holy one for the lawless, the guiltless for the guilty, the just for the unjust, the incorruptible for the corruptible, the immortal for the mortal. For what else but his righteousness could have covered our sins? In whom was it possible for us, the lawless and ungodly, to be justified, except in the Son of God alone? O the sweet exchange, O the incomprehensible work of God, O the unexpected blessings, that the sinfulness of many should be hidden in one righteous person, while the righteousness of one should justify many sinners! Having demonstrated, therefore, in the former time the powerlessness of our nature to obtain life, and having now revealed the Savior's power to save even the powerless, he willed that for both these reasons we should believe in his goodness and regard him as nurse, father, teacher, counselor, healer, mind, light, honor, glory, strength, and life, and not be anxious about food and clothing. (Diogn. 9.2b–6)

In Diognetus 9.2b–5 we have possibly the strongest teaching on the atonement and justification in the ante-Nicene church. For the author, the atonement answers why

---

85. Holmes has "made worthy" here for the verb ἀξιόω, *axioō* (*Apostolic Fathers*, 709), but the sense is better conveyed by "considered worthy." See H. G. Meecham, *The Epistle to Diognetus: The Greek Text with Introduction, Translation and Notes* (Manchester: Manchester University Press, 1949), 85. Meecham has the following note on this verb: "In verbs in -οω derived from adj. of *moral* meaning the factitive sense is modified = 'to regard as,' rather than 'to make'" (128, emphasis original).

God waited so long to intervene. God was overlooking people's sin because it was always his plan to redeem mankind through the work of his Son on the cross.[86] He uses two important terms for the atonement—ransom (λύτρον, *lytron*) and exchange (ἀνταλλαγή, *antallagē*)—and both of these terms have a substitutionary bent for him.[87] God "himself gave up his own son as a *ransom* on our behalf, the holy for the lawless, the innocent for the wicked, the righteous for the unrighteous, the incorruptible for the corruptible, the immortal for the mortal" (Diogn. 9.2; emphasis added). Where sinful humanity is weak and prone to decay, he is strong and incorruptible. Where humanity is full of impurity and wickedness, he is full of innocence and righteousness. The Son is everything sinful people are not and yet must become.[88]

The atonement is also viewed as an exchange. The author makes his argument in the form of a doxology: "O the sweet *exchange*, O the inscrutable work of God, O the unexpected benefits of God, that the lawlessness of many might be hidden in one righteous man, while the righteousness of one might justify many lawless men" (Diogn. 9.5; emphasis added). God placed the punishment that was due the many on the one righteous man while simultaneously giving his righteousness to those who did not deserve it. God sent his innocent Son to stand in the stead of the guilty. Crowe is right that the "climactic proclamation" in 9.5, "O sweet exchange," could very well be "a summary of the epistle's soteriological perspective."[89]

The other significant doctrine explained is justification.[90] In Diognetus 9.3–4 he interposes two rhetorical questions: "For what else was able to cover our sins except the righteousness of that one?" And, "In whom was it possible for us, the lawless and ungodly, to be justified except in the Son of God alone?" The questions are meant to be answered "nothing" and "no one" respectively. There was no hope apart from the sinless Son dying in the place of the sinful people. His righteousness was necessary to cover over sin, and in covering sin, he justified the lawless and the ungodly.[91] The emphasis is on the Son's perfect righteousness as the grounds for justification (Diogn. 9.3), for if he had not lived a life free from sin, then he could not have given his righteousness to sinners.[92] The possibility of imputation comes especially from 9.5 where the author states that while the sinfulness of many was hidden in the one righteous person, the righteousness of the one justified many sinners. Sin was imputed to Christ via his substitutionary atonement, and his righteousness was imputed to sinners for their justification (cf. 2 Cor 5:21). How is this justification obtained? He answers, "And he revealed (himself) through faith, which is the only means

---

86. Cf. Rom 5. Michael Haykin suggests the author is especially dependent on Paul when discussing the atonement. He writes, "What is highlighted in this dialectic [on this act of substitution] are the twin soteriological themes of the Son's utter sinlessness and humanity's radical depravity, a dialectic that recalls the rich Pauline theology of salvation as found in passages like Romans 5:6–10" (M. Haykin, *Rediscovering the Church Fathers: Who They Were and How They Shaped the Church* [Wheaton, IL: Crossway, 2011], 60). See also B. Crowe, "Oh Sweet Exchange: The Soteriological Significance of the Incarnation in the *Epistle to Diognetus*," *ZNW* 102 (2011): 96–109, who writes, "Given the Pauline resonances in Diogn. 9, the author's focus on the Son's righteousness may be an example of an early Christian interpretation of Rom. 5" (109).

87. It is better to see "ransom" here in light of Mark 10:45 and not later ideas of the so-called "ransom theory" of the atonement. See Arnold, *Justification in the Second Century*, 99.

88. Arnold, *Justification in the Second Century*, 94.

89. Crowe, "Oh Sweet Exchange," 97.

90. Seven times throughout Diogn. 9 the author uses some variation of the δικ- word group (five nouns; one adjective; one infinitive).

91. Perhaps the author is thinking in Jewish terms here of atonement as a covering over (כפר, *k-ph-r*) of sins. It may be that Rom 4:7 is in the background where the blessed person is the one whose sins are covered (ἐπικαλύπτω, *epikalyptō*).

92. For a discussion on imputation in Diognetus, see Arnold, *Justification in the Second Century*, 101–2.

by which one is permitted to see God" (Diogn. 8.6). Seeing God, in this case, is a metonymy used for eternal life. Thus, it is faith in the Son of God that justifies.[93]

Diognetus is the closest to the apostle Paul's soteriology in the Apostolic Fathers. Atonement is vicarious, and justification is by faith in the Son, whose righteousness atones for sin. What makes this work unique is that it was written as an apology for someone outside of the faith. The other works examined in this chapter were written to believers to encourage them to press on in good works. Diognetus explains the essence of and entrance into the Christian faith, which makes the focus on vicarious atonement and justification by faith even more significant.

3. SOME COMMON THEMES

The goal of this chapter was to summarize soteriology in the Apostolic Fathers. As stated at the beginning, and demonstrated above, we cannot speak of a singular soteriology in this corpus. Each author has a specific emphasis that comes across in his doctrine of salvation, and so we must speak of soteriologies in the Apostolic Fathers. However, this does not mean that these writings lack any coherence between them or that there are not similar strands of thought that we can trace. Before offering some concluding points of synthesis to show these areas of commonality, a helpful reminder is in order. Even for the most prolific writer in this corpus, Ignatius of Antioch, we still have only a snapshot of his doctrine. Their writings are mostly occasional and predominantly meant to give pastoral advice about how to live the Christian life, so we must be careful not to overburden the evidence. That said, a few themes come across frequently in their writings about salvation.

3.1 Faith and Works

The relationship between faith and works in the Apostolic Fathers is the most difficult soteriological path to track, which makes avoiding the ditches on either side essential. To the one side is the ditch that sees the Apostolic Fathers as harbingers of works righteousness. This is the ditch in which most interpreters, including Torrance, find themselves. On the other side of the road is the ditch that sees these writers as paragons of Pauline soteriology of salvation by faith apart from works. The evidence we have seen should demonstrate that both ditches are too simplistic.[94] It may be better to see faith and works on a spectrum, with some authors placing more emphasis on faith (Pol. *Phil.* and Diogn.), others placing more emphasis on works (Herm. and Did.), and most falling somewhere in between. Even on this spectrum it is important to recognize the role that faith plays in each of these writings. Faith is often laid as the foundation of salvation upon which works are

93. On this verse, Michael Bird says, "[Diognetus] echoes the Pauline pneumatic epistemology about the mode of attaining knowledge of God" (M. F. Bird, "The Reception of Paul in the *Epistle to Diognetus*," in Bird and Dodson, *Paul and the Second Century*, 85). But he goes on to agree more or less with Meecham, who says the "place of 'faith' in the work of justification is doubtless present to his mind, though not explicitly stated" (Meecham, *Diognetus*, 130). For Bird, "The Pauline formulation of righteousness by faith (διά/ἐκ πίστεως) does not loom at all" ("Reception of Paul," 87). Though he does highlight the centrality of faith throughout the epistle (8.6; 9.6; 10.1), he is bothered that there is not an explicit claim to justification by faith. The author of Diognetus places all the pieces of this puzzle down in front of the reader, even showing how they link together. There should be no consternation that he did not link them together since the picture itself is so obvious, especially given the content of chapter 9. See Arnold, *Justification in the Second Century*, 102n88.

94. I think Thomas is on to something in suggesting that some of the second-century fathers argued that faith is the initiation into the faith, but then works are necessary to staying in (*Paul's "Works of the Law"*). However, I also think that there are fathers who hold that faith is necessary for entrance into the Christian faith, but then argue that good works demonstrate genuine faith, as I argue in *Justification in the Second Century*. We must be careful not to suggest a one-size-fits-all approach to faith and works in the fathers.

built. While faith and works both play an important role, so often the assumption is that works are more prominent than faith. Quite frankly, the Apostolic Fathers have not been read generously in this regard.

The problem is methodological. Guth detects the methodological flaw Torrance repeatedly makes in his work, and he believes this error is egregious in Torrance's assessment of Barnabas, which we can take as an example. Guth's critique strikes at the core of the problem of Torrance's reading of the Apostolic Fathers, which applies to many other scholars who think that those after the apostles strayed from their teaching on salvation:

> In evaluating Torrance's interpretation of Barnabas, we might start by addressing a methodological assumption Torrance brought to Barnabas—and all the Apostolic Fathers. After suggesting that Barnabas might be regarded as having a sound doctrine of grace on the basis of a significant number of passages, Torrance went on to find that other ideas and concepts give "the true coloring" and demonstrate that Barnabas' thought was "quite incompatible with the New Testament standpoint." The question we might ask of Torrance is why the "other ideas" give the true coloring to Barnabas' statements about the work of Christ, and not the reverse. In other words, it may be possible that Barnabas' understanding of Christ's death and the effects it achieved ought to be regarded as casting the true color on Barnabas' other ideas.[95]

Why interpret faith through the lens of works, instead of reading works through the lens of faith? Torrance skews the data away from the New Testament as though there is a complete abandonment of Paul's doctrines of faith, grace, and justification, simply because authors in this corpus regularly highlight the need for good works. This approach is to read both Paul and the Apostolic Fathers one-sidedly and on opposite sides of one another, instead of seeing much of the balance that each author, including Paul, brings between faith and works.[96]

We have also noted two approaches in particular that provide this balance. First, the emphasis on salvation by faith, the necessity of good works, and perseverance appear in Paul as well. This especially comes across in Paul's use of both the indicative and the imperative, as well as the conditional language he employs. Those saved by faith must persevere in good works. Second, these authors, whether consciously or unconsciously, reconciled Paul and James, most notably 1 Clement. Robert Eno makes the sweeping claim that the fathers in general "supplemented Paul with James."[97]

The authors we examined almost all place faith in Jesus, repentance from sins, and at times baptism, at the front side of salvation, which they also based on God's grace and election. After this initiation into the faith, they are commanded to live a life of faithful obedience. For some of these writers, those failing to live a life of righteousness will not experience final salvation (2 Clem., Pol. *Phil.*, Did.). For 1 Clement, Diognetus, and Ignatius, works do not seem to condition final salvation. And for the Shepherd, works are absolutely necessary such that two post-baptismal sins would result in damnation.

---

95. Guth, "Relationship of Faith and Works," 272. The very same could be said of Torrance's critique of 1 Clement noted above.

96. Jaroslav Pelikan gives a very important reminder: "To condemn the doctrine of grace in the apostolic fathers, for example, for not being sufficiently Pauline greatly oversimplifies the development both within the first century and between it and the second" (J. Pelikan, *Development of Christian Doctrine: Some Historical Prolegomena* [New Haven: Yale University, 1969], 65).

97. R. Eno, "Some Patristic Views on the Relationship of Faith and Works in Justification," *Recherches augustiniennes* 19 (1984): 4.

Nevertheless, faith and works are placed in balance, with faith being the requirement for initiation and works being necessary for the life of the true believer.

3.2 Judaism

Barnabas and Ignatius both juxtapose their positive view of salvation against their negative view of Judaism. Ignatius could speak positively about Judaism and its prophets, but he still warned not to listen to those who expounded Judaism (Ign. *Phld.* 6.1) and those who "profess Jesus Christ and . . . Judaize" (Ign. *Magn.* 10). For Barnabas, Jews had lost the covenant (Barn. 4; 14.1). They had misread Scripture on sacrifices (2), circumcision (9), food laws (10), Sabbath keeping (15), and the temple (16), and they missed that Jesus is the hermeneutical key to unlocking their Scriptures. Christianity was forming an identity distinct from Judaism, particularly in the way Christians understood salvation.

3.3 Baptism

It is too early to speak of sacraments in the Apostolic Fathers, but the emphasis on baptism is worth noting. The Didache gives the rites of baptism but does not delve into its soteriological meaning (Did. 7). Whether baptism is necessary for salvation, or what baptism is precisely doing, is left untouched. In 2 Clement, baptism must be an unbroken seal (2 Clem. 7.6), and the reader is instructed to keep their baptism pure and undefiled (6.9). Ignatius takes Paul's metaphor of spiritual armor and says, "Let your baptism serve as a shield, faith as a helmet, love as a spear, endurance as armor" (Ign. *Pol.* 6.2). The Shepherd teaches baptismal regeneration, saying, "Your life was saved and will be saved through water" (Herm. Vis. 3.3.5), and of the repentance attached to it "when we descended into the water and received forgiveness of our previous sins" (Herm. Mand. 4.3.1). For the Apostolic Fathers, the significance of baptism was taking shape and would continue to become more prominent in the centuries that followed.

3.4 Redemptive Almsgiving

Redemptive almsgiving would come to answer the question of atonement for sins committed after baptism, though in each instance in the Apostolic Fathers it is said nearly in passing. Redemptive almsgiving appears in 2 Clement, Didache, Polycarp's *To the Philippians*, and Barnabas. In 2 Clement, "Almsgiving is better than both prayer and fasting, for it covers a multitude of sins" (2 Clem. 16.4). The Didachist gives a veiled reference: "If you earn something by working with your hands, you shall give a ransom for your sins" (Did. 4.6). Barnabas suggests that you "work with your hands for a ransom for your sins" (Barn. 19.10). And for Polycarp, "giving charity . . . can deliver one from death" (Pol. *Phil.* 10.2). Although the doctrine is never developed in these writings, the seeds were planted for how to deal with post-baptismal sin that would blossom as time went on.

4. CONCLUSION

Soteriology mattered a great deal to the Apostolic Fathers. How one is saved—namely, the relationship between faith and works, the role of the person and work of Jesus Christ, the need for repentance and baptism, the divergence of Christianity and Judaism, the call for perseverance, and the ethic for Christian living—permeates their writings. However, none of these ideas receive enough attention to give a definitive statement on their soteriology individually, let alone when they are considered collectively. Our conclusions must be measured. So while there are many points of intersection in their thought, we must be content to speak of soteriologies in the Apostolic Fathers.

BIBLIOGRAPHY

Arnold, B. J. *Justification in the Second Century.* Waco, TX: Baylor University Press, 2018.

Brown, C. T. *The Gospel and Ignatius of Antioch.* StBibLit 12. New York: Lang, 2000.

Brox, N. *Der Hirt des Hermas.* KAV 7. Göttingen: Vandenhoeck & Ruprecht, 1991.

Downs, D. J. *Alms: Charity, Reward, and Atonement in Early Christianity.* Waco, TX: Baylor University Press, 2016.

Foster, P., ed. *The Writings of the Apostolic Fathers.* London: T&T Clark, 2007.

Guth, C. "The Relationship of Faith and Works in the Soteriologies of the Apostolic Fathers." PhD diss., University of Aberdeen, 1994.

Hartog, P., ed. *Polycarp's Epistle to the Philippians and the Martyrdom of Polycarp: Introduction, Text, and Commentary.* OAF. Oxford: Oxford University Press, 2013.

Jefford, C. N. *Reading the Apostolic Fathers: A Student's Introduction.* 2nd ed. Grand Rapids: Baker Academic, 2012.

Meecham, G. *The Epistle to Diognetus: The Greek Text with Introduction, Translation and Notes.* Manchester: Manchester University Press, 1949.

Osiek, C. *The Shepherd of Hermas.* Hermeneia. Minneapolis: Fortress, 1999.

Pratscher, W., ed. *The Apostolic Fathers: An Introduction.* Waco, TX: Baylor University Press, 2010.

Soyars, J. *The Shepherd of Hermas and the Pauline Legacy.* NovTSup 176. Leiden: Brill, 2019.

Thomas, M. J. *Paul's "Works of the Law" in the Perspective of Second Century Reception.* WUNT 468. Tübingen: Mohr Siebeck, 2018.

Torrance, T. F. *The Doctrine of Grace in the Apostolic Fathers.* Grand Rapids: Eerdmans, 1959.

Tuckett, C. M., ed. *2 Clement: Introduction, Text, and Commentary.* OAF. Oxford: Oxford University Press, 2012.

Wilhite, S. *The Didache: A Commentary.* AFCS. Eugene, OR: Cascade, 2019.

CHAPTER 15

ECCLESIOLOGY IN THE APOSTOLIC FATHERS

GREGORY VALL

1. INTRODUCTION

The authors responsible for the corpus of the Apostolic Fathers gave serious thought to the nature of the church, local and universal, and its place within the divine economy. This includes its relationship to the person and event of Jesus Christ, its relationship to biblical Israel and Judaism, its leadership structure, and its communal and liturgical life. These authors developed their understanding of the church in creative and interesting ways by drawing on biblical and nonbiblical source materials, and sometimes by coining new terms and concepts. Early Christian ecclesiology is never neatly separable from other aspects of theology, such as Christology, the moral life, and eschatology. In order to penetrate below its surface, therefore, it will be necessary to examine it as an integral aspect of each author's comprehensive vision of Christian existence and in relation to each author's pastoral and literary purpose. In this fashion, the present chapter will consider the ecclesiology of the Didache, 1 Clement, the letters of Ignatius of Antioch, and 2 Clement (which is possibly the order in which they were written). A brief conclusion will identify two broad tendencies in these texts and on this basis relate them to several of the remaining texts in the corpus of the Apostolic Fathers.

2. THE DIDACHE

The Didache is a manual of ecclesial life intended for the guidance of one or more local churches, possibly in Syria, in the late first century CE. The author-compiler, whom scholars refer to as the Didachist, evidently drew upon a number of Jewish and early Christian sources without attempting to homogenize them stylistically or subordinate them to an explicit line of argumentation. The book is thus characterized by abrupt transitions, changes in genre, and thematic tensions. This is not to say that the Didache is entirely lacking in coherence, however. The Didachist's pastoral purpose unifies the work at the deeper level of what might be called ecclesial vision. From its memorable opening line to its apocalyptic conclusion, the Didache gradually unfolds a vision of the Christian mystery as "the way of life" (Did. 1.2)—that is, the "life and knowledge" that the Father has revealed "through Jesus [his] servant" (9.3). This way of life can be lived out only within the ecclesial community, local and universal, which is being gathered "from the ends of the earth into [God's] kingdom" (9.4).[1]

1. Translations of ancient texts throughout this chapter are by the author. Those from the Apostolic Fathers are based on the Greek text in M. W. Holmes, ed., *The Apostolic Fathers: Greek Texts and English Translations*, 3rd ed. (Grand Rapids: Baker Academic, 2007).

This is not exclusively or even primarily the vision of the Didachist himself but one that he has found in his sources. Still, through the selection, reworking, and arrangement of materials, he has put his stamp on the book and has taken responsibility for its contents. This can be seen, for example, in the non-slavish and "somewhat indirect" manner by which he appears to have drawn on the Gospel of Matthew, perhaps quoting it from memory, in crafting what is, after all, "a new literary production."[2] Hermeneutically, then, we must not treat the Didache "as a fragmented collage of materials only" but "as a coherent systematic unity as well."[3]

2.1 Ecclesial Life and the Two Ways

Didache 1–6 present a version of the Two Ways tractate, a tradition found in several early Christian texts.[4] Throughout this section the author addresses the reader in the second-person singular (except in Did. 1.3), emphasizing individual moral accountability. His doctrine is neither individualistic nor merely moralistic, however. The "way of life" is animated by participation in divine love (ἀγάπη, *agapē*), which is available within the ecclesial community. The long sequences of moral injunctions that characterize this section of the Didache serve to unfold the implications of the two love commandments and the golden rule (1.2–3a), which comprise the quintessence of the gospel. The Didachist exhorts his readers to "love those who hate you," whereby they can become "perfect" (τέλειος, *teleios*)—that is, reach the goal of mature humanity for which they have been created (1.3b–4). That this love fulfills and transcends the Pentateuchal command to "love your neighbor as yourself" is evident in this instruction: "You must not hate any human being. Rather, some you shall reprove, some you shall pray for, and some you shall love more than your own soul" (Did. 2.7).

Ecclesial life as the proper context for Christian morality comes into view here, as it also does in the exhortation to "remember night and day the one who speaks the word of God to you" and to "honor him as you would the Lord" (Did. 4.1), a statement that anticipates the author's urgent concern with teachers, apostles, prophets, overseers, and deacons later in the book (6.1; 11.1–12; 13.1–7; 15.1–2). Similarly, the command to "confess your transgressions in church, so that you may not come to prayer with an evil conscience" (4.14), will be echoed later in the book in a specifically eucharistic context (14.1). Though the Didachist supplies us with scant Christology, he recognizes that authentic teaching about the Lord Jesus is vital to the life and unity of the church: "For wherever the lordship [of Jesus] is spoken, there the Lord is" (4.1). The Christian ought to "seek out each day the personal presence of the saints, so to be refreshed by their words" (4.2). The early Christian ethos of holding worldly goods in common and considering nothing one's own (Acts 4:32) is here grounded in the greater and more fundamental fact that Christians share in a life that is "immortal" (Did. 4.8).

The Didachist rounds out his presentation of the Two Ways by exhorting the individual Christian: "If you can bear the whole yoke of the Lord, you will be perfect [τέλειος]; but if you cannot, do what you can" (Did. 6.2). There are two Matthean echoes here. First, the

2. C. M. Tuckett, "The *Didache* and the Writings That Later Formed the New Testament," in *The Reception of the New Testament in the Apostolic Fathers*, ed. A. F. Gregory and C. M. Tuckett (Oxford: Oxford University Press, 2005), 127.

3. H. van de Sandt and D. Flusser, *The Didache: Its Jewish Sources and Its Place in Early Judaism and Christianity*, CRINT III/5 (Assen: Van Gorcum; Minneapolis: Fortress, 2002), 31.

4. K. Niederwimmer, *The Didache: A Commentary*, Hermeneia (Minneapolis: Fortress, 1998), 30–41; Sandt and Flusser, *Didache*, 55–80.

"yoke" of the Lord Jesus is his teaching, viewed as the new law given by the new Moses (Matt 11:29).[5] Second, the presentation of "perfection" as a radical mode of discipleship that perhaps not everyone will be able to attain is also found in Matthew's account of the rich young man: "If you want to be perfect [τέλειος] . . ." (19:21). Beyond this, the reference to individual perfection in Didache 6.2 serves as a structural and thematic hinge within the book. It harkens back to the perfection achieved by those who love their persecutors, spoken of at the beginning of the Two Ways (Did. 1.4), while it looks ahead to the prayer that petitions the Lord Jesus to "perfect" (τελειῶσαι, *teleiōsai*) the church in his love (10.5) and to the final warning that being "perfected" (τελειωθῆτε, *teleiōthēte*) is the sine qua non of eschatological salvation (16.2). While the apparent contradiction between the concession in 6.2 and the warning in 16.2 is not easily resolved, it is clear in any case that the Didachist views both the life of the individual Christian and the life of the church teleologically, for the Christian and the church share the single goal of being perfected in Christ's love.

2.2 The Church's Liturgical Life

We may now turn to the second major section of the Didache (chs. 7–10), which deals with the church's liturgical life and forms the heart of the author's ecclesial vision. Here the second-person-singular grammatical forms that dominated chapters 1–6 give way to second-person-plural forms (except in Did. 7.2–4). In other words, at this point the Didachist ceases to address his readers as individuals and begins to address them as church, and he continues to do so throughout the remainder of the book. The liturgical part of the book begins, as is fitting, with an instruction concerning baptism (7.1–4). Here we learn that the doctrine of the Two Ways is to serve as pre-baptismal instruction (7.1), and we begin to glimpse the unity of the church's life. Christian morality and Christian worship are inseparable. The Trinitarian formula of baptism (7.1; contrast 9.5), which corresponds verbatim to Matthew 28:19, sets the stage for four consecutive prayers addressed to the Father, the first and last of which also refer to the holiness of God's name (Did. 8.2; 9.2, 3; 10.2).

Next, the Didachist instructs his readers not to fast on Mondays and Thursdays, as was the custom in Judaism, but to distinguish themselves from "the hypocrites" by fasting on Wednesdays and Fridays (Did. 8.1). Imitating the Gospel of Matthew, the author employs the word ὑποκριταί, *hypokritai*, as a demeaning label for non-Christian Jews. He might rather have distinguished between "Jews" and "Christians" (cf. Did. 12.4) but chose not to, perhaps because he was not ready to accept the implication that Jewish Christians are no longer Jews. The Didachist and the churches he addresses were evidently deeply rooted in Judaism, but they struggled to understand and articulate the church's relationship to the older religion. They recognized, on the one hand, that a significant degree of continuity with Judaism was essential to their identity as Christians and, on the other hand, that a decisive parting of the ways was taking place and had in a sense already taken place.[6] This fundamental ecclesiological issue surfaces repeatedly in the corpus of the Apostolic Fathers and is handled in a variety of ways.

The remainder of the second major section of the Didache (8.2–10.7) is dominated by a series of formal prayers, which contain much of the book's ecclesiology. First, the author instructs his readers to pray "as the Lord commanded in his gospel" and gives them a form of the Our Father (or Lord's Prayer) that is nearly identical to Matthew's (Did. 8.2b;

5. For "yoke" as a way to refer to the Mosaic law, see Acts 15:10; Gal 5:1; Barn. 2.6; and m. 'Abot 3:5.
6. Niederwimmer, *Didache*, 132.

cf. Matt 6:9–13). This most basic of Christian prayers is both thoroughly Jewish and strikingly new.[7] Once again, the Didachist is concerned to preserve continuity with the church's Jewish roots while at the same time instructing his people to live in a way that distinguishes them from "the hypocrites" (Did. 8.2a; cf. Matt 6:5). Like non-Christian Jews, they are to pray "three times a day" (Did. 8.3; cf. Dan 6:10, 13), but instead of traditional Jewish prayers they are to use the distinctive prayer that the Lord Jesus taught them.[8] The individual Christian's thrice-daily recitation of the Lord's Prayer, presumably in private (Matt 6:6), extends piety to the home and sanctifies the whole week. In both contexts, at home and in church, Christians call upon God as "our Father" (Did. 8.2; 9.2, 3).

The remaining prayers belong to the church's communal life and eucharistic liturgy (Did. 9.1–10.6). The verb εὐχαριστεῖν, *eucharistein*, here still refers to actual prayers of thanksgiving, while the noun εὐχαριστία, *eucharistia*, patently refers to the sacred meal itself (9.5). It seems that the churches addressed in the Didache did not use the institution narrative as a eucharistic prayer.

In the prayer over the eucharistic cup, the church thanks the Father "for the holy vine of David your servant, which you have made known through Jesus your servant" (Did. 9.1). Vine or vineyard is a traditional symbol of the people of Israel (Isa 5:1–7; Jer 2:21; Ps 80:9–17), but the qualifiers "holy" and "of David" modulate this image in the direction of the "expectation of the renewal of Israel through the restoration of the house of David in the last days."[9] After the catastrophic end of the Judean monarchy in 586 BCE and the evanescent governorship of the Davidic scion Zerubbabel two generations later, the royal line slipped below the surface of political history, but remained a life-giving mystery that would one day be revealed ("made known") in and through the Son of David. The parallelism between "David your servant" and "Jesus your servant" in Didache 9.1 links Jesus's identity as Davidic Messiah to his role as the suffering righteous servant of Isaiah 53, who atones for sins and makes known "the holy vine of David."[10] The vine thus signifies three interrelated realities simultaneously: the church's prehistory in Israel, Jesus himself (cf. John 15:1–8), and the church's sacramental life.

In similar fashion, the prayer over the "fragment of bread" (κλάσμα, *klasma*) renders thanks to the Father "for the life and knowledge which you have made known through Jesus your servant" (Did. 9.3). The sacramental signification of the fragment is then expounded: "Just as this fragment was once scattered on the mountains and then gathered into one, let your church be gathered from the ends of the earth into your kingdom" (9.4). Given the salvation-historical overtones of the eucharistic prayers up to this point, we should perhaps interpret this statement as a pregnant analogy. The eucharistic bread preexisted, so to speak, in the grains of wheat that were grown on the hillsides and were then harvested, threshed, milled, and baked into a single loaf. The loaf signifies Christ, and the grains are his Israelite ancestors. This "one loaf" is broken in the "breaking of the bread," which apparently precedes the prayers of thanksgiving (Did. 14.1; cf. Acts 2:42; Ign. *Eph.* 20.2), signifying that Christ was broken in the passion in order to feed his people in the Eucharist. Now, as the eucharistic prayers are offered, each member of the congregation takes his or her κλάσμα in hand. Consuming the eucharistic elements effects

7. U. Luz, *Matthew 1–7: A Commentary*, trans. W. C. Linss, Continental Commentaries (Minneapolis: Augsburg, 1989), 374.

8. Niederwimmer, *Didache*, 138.

9. J. A. Draper, "The Didache," in *The Apostolic Fathers: An Introduction*, ed. W. Pratscher (Waco, TX: Baylor University Press, 2010), 16.

10. Draper, "Didache," 16.

"a communion in the body of Christ" (1 Cor 10:16)—that is, a becoming one with Christ and being united with one another. This communion, moreover, signifies the eschatological gathering of the universal church into God's kingdom.

The longish prayer at the conclusion of the eucharistic meal, which is loosely modeled on the traditional Jewish prayer after meals,[11] comprises four short movements (Did. 10.1–6). In the first of these (10.2), the congregation addresses God as "holy Father" (cf. John 17:11) and thanks him for "your holy name, which you have made to dwell in our hearts." This is the vivifying gift of revelation by which one knows God intimately as Father and calls upon him with trust and affection. It is, in other words, "the knowledge and faith and immortality that you have made known to us through Jesus your servant." The second movement (Did. 10.3–4) places this supreme gift of redemption in its relation to the more foundational gift of creation, while also relating it to the Eucharist itself: "You have created all things for the sake of your name, and you have given food and drink to human beings for their joy [cf. Acts 14:17], but upon us you have bestowed spiritual food and drink [cf. 1 Cor 10:3–4] and eternal life through your servant."

In the third movement (Did. 10.5), which sums up the ecclesiology of the Didache, Jesus Christ is directly addressed for the first time: "Remember your church, O Lord, to deliver her from all evil and to perfect her in your love, and gather from the four winds her who has been sanctified, into your kingdom, which you have prepared for her." There is a striking emphasis here on the necessity for the church to *become* truly holy—delivered from evil, perfected in Christ's love, and sanctified. The church is by no means identified with the kingdom of God. She is on a pilgrim journey, and the kingdom of God is her eschatological goal. Some later texts in the corpus of Apostolic Fathers will speak of the church's preexistence (2 Clem. 14.1–2; Herm. Vis. 2.4.1), but the Didache speaks only of the preexistence of the kingdom of God.

The fourth movement (Did. 10.6) is a series of exclamations. The first of these—"Let grace come and this world pass away!" (cf. 1 Cor 7:31; 1 John 2:17)—might have sounded like a denigration of physical reality had not the prayer already thanked God for the blessings of creation and placed them in their proper relation to the even greater gift of redemption (Did. 10.3). The second exclamation recalls the church's Israelite roots while looking ahead to the eschaton: "Hosanna to the God of David!" The third exclamation issues an invitation to the eschatological banquet, of which the Eucharist is the foretaste—an invitation conditional on holiness: "If anyone is holy, let him come! If anyone is not, let him repent!" The eucharistic liturgy and the entire series of prayers concludes with another invocation of Jesus Christ as "Lord," this time in Aramaic (*mar*), summoning him to "come" in the parousia: "Maranatha! Amen" (cf. 1 Cor 16:22).

Now that the Didachist has explicitly instructed his addressees to use these carefully worded eucharistic prayers, it is surprising to find an exception clause appended to this section: "But permit the prophets to give thanks [εὐχαριστεῖν] as they wish" (Did. 10.7). This statement raises the whole question of ecclesiastical authority and thereby segues into the third and final major section of the Didache.

2.3 Church Order and an Apocalyptic Exhortation

In Didache 11–16 the author deals with various matters of church order before concluding his work with an apocalyptic exhortation. First, he instructs the churches on how to deal with itinerant teachers, apostles, and prophets (Did. 11.1–12). He gives them two

11. Niederwimmer, *Didache*, 155–56; Sandt and Flusser, *Didache*, 311–18.

basic criteria by which to judge them: Do they teach the truth? If so, do they live by the truth that they teach? With respect to the first criterion, he points to two presumably complementary standards by which they can know the truth—namely, the Didache itself (11.1) and "the rule of the gospel" (11.3). With respect to the second criterion, the Didachist attempts, with limited success, to balance two overriding concerns. On the one hand, he wants to protect the churches from being taken advantage of financially, and so he lays down rather strict rules by which they can identify "false prophets" (11.4–6, 8–10, 12). On the other hand, he has great respect for true prophecy and recognizes grave spiritual peril in attempting to discern who truly speaks by the Holy Spirit and who does not. In this regard he reminds his readers of the Lord's teaching about the unforgiveable sin (11.7; cf. Matt 12:31) and of the fact that "the ancient prophets" of Israel sometimes acted out strange symbolic gestures (Did. 11.11b). What exactly the Didachist means by "acting out a cosmic mystery of the church" (11.11a) is unfortunately unclear.[12]

Having laid down these basic principles, the author next deals with a series of related issues. A non-teacher who wishes to join the community and eat at its table must have a trade or otherwise be gainfully employed (Did. 12.1–4). "If he is not willing to do this, he is a Christ-dealer" and should be shunned (12.5). Prophets and teachers who have proved themselves true, on the other hand, deserve their board. In fact, the other members of the church ought to give them the "firstfruits" of all their goods (13.1–7). Here the Didachist applies a precept of the Mosaic law to the life of the local church (cf. Deut 26:1–4). He even goes so far as to say that the community's prophets are in effect their "high priests" (13.3).

This consideration next prompts the author to describe the Lord's Day Eucharist as the community's "sacrifice" (θυσία, *thysia*), a term that occurs often in the Septuagint. If they confess their sins and resolve their differences prior to the breaking of the bread, their sacrifice will be "pure" (Did. 14.1–2). This subsection concludes with a skillfully reworked quote from the prophet Malachi (Mal 1:11, 14): "In every place and time a pure sacrifice is to be offered to me, for I am a great king, says the Lord, and my name is marvelous among the nations" (Did. 14.3). Here the Didachist's vision for ecclesial life extends far beyond the limited perspective of the local church and the present moment. The eucharistic sacrifice unites the church of all times and places. And while the Didachist's ecclesiology remains deeply rooted in Jewish Christianity, he celebrates the marvelous truth that, through Jesus Christ, God's name is known and worshiped also among the gentiles.

Penultimately, the author reminds the local churches that, when all is said and done, they are not dependent on itinerant prophets and teachers: "Elect for yourselves overseers and deacons [ἐπισκόπους καὶ διακόνους, *episkopous kai diakonous*] worthy of the Lord, men [ἄνδρας, *andras*] who are meek, not enamored with money, true, and approved; for they too perform the ministry of the prophets and teachers" (Did. 15.1). The Didachist's agenda was not to *replace* itinerant prophets and teachers with the twofold local hierarchy of ἐπίσκοποι and διάκονοι, which had been present in at least some churches for decades,[13] but to provide the local churches with stable and honorable leadership *alongside* the charismatics (15.2). In any case, the Didache shows no signs of development in the direction of monepiscopacy or the threefold hierarchy of overseer (bishop), presbyters, and deacons.

The Didachist concludes his work with a brief exhortation to persevere in the faith and an apocalyptic warning (Did. 16.1–8). His dynamic and teleological view of Christian existence receives its strongest expression here: "Gather often, seeking what is good for

12. For a plausible interpretation, see Niederwimmer, *Didache*, 180–82.

13. Cf. Phil 1:1; Sandt and Flusser, *Didache*, 336–38.

your souls; for your whole time in the faith will not benefit you unless you are perfected in the last time" (16.2). Remaining "in the faith" is the central theme of the apocalypse. The last days will be characterized by an abundance of false prophets (16.3), and the antichrist figure is described here as "the one who leads the world astray" (ὁ κοσμοπλανής, *ho kosmoplanēs*, 16.4; cf. 2 John 7). Humanity will pass through a fiery trial, and many will fall away from Christ and perish. "But those who persevere in their faith will be saved" (Did. 16.5; cf. Matt 10:22; 24:13). The book ends with a brief account of the parousia, which has been sewn together from prophetic phrases that were already part of the Christian tradition: "The Lord will come, and all his holy ones with him. Then the world will see the Lord coming on the clouds of heaven."[14]

3. FIRST CLEMENT

3.1 Epistolary Purpose

The long epistle sent by the church at Rome to the church at Corinth in the late first century is both an occasional text and a comprehensive vision of ecclesial life. The author, whom ancient tradition plausibly identifies as Clement of Rome, addresses a crisis in the Corinthian community that he describes as an "odious and unholy insurrection" (1 Clem. 1.1). At the instigation of "one or two persons," the Corinthian Christians have deposed "some" of their presbyters, whom Clement considers to have been validly installed and of blameless and proven character (44.3–6; 47.6), apparently in favor of the very upstarts who initiated the rebellion (16.1; 51.1). This insurrection, moreover, seems to have further exacerbated a general state of discord within the community (3.2–3; 14.1–2; 46.5; 54.2). Clement contextualizes this crisis at the beginning of the epistle (chs. 1–3) and deals with it forthrightly toward the end (chs. 44–65). The intervening chapters, however, contain only a handful of mostly oblique references to the situation in Corinth (14.1–3; 15.1; 16.1; 20.4; 21.5–6). Long stretches of the epistle are given over to generalized paraenesis, moral exempla, and doctrinal excurses. In writing very broadly "concerning those things that pertain to our religion and are most beneficial for a virtuous life," Clement has "touched on every topic" (62.1–2).

Irenaeus of Lyons notes that 1 Clement has a twofold purpose: to effect a peaceful reconciliation among the Corinthians and to renew their faith by reminding them of certain fundamental elements of the apostolic tradition (Irenaeus, *Haer.* 3.3.3). Clement himself indicates how these two dimensions of his epistolary purpose merge into a single goal. His doctrinal and moral instruction is meant to warn his readers against insidious doubts about "the coming resurrection" and final judgment, and to persuade them to give up their "futile insurrection" and submit to the rightful "leaders of *our* souls," so that "*we* may attain the goal that is set before *us* in truth" (1 Clem. 23.2–24.1; 63.1). This striking use of first-person-plural pronouns indicates that Clement's epistle is also intended for Christian readers far beyond Corinth and for situations other than the immediate one (cf. 7.1). Clement's sense of urgency, moreover, reflects his recognition that what transpires in a single local church impacts the whole body of Christ (46.7–9). Throughout the epistle Clement expresses an overriding pastoral concern that the full number of those "throughout the world" who have been chosen by God through Jesus Christ may attain eternal salvation (2.4; 35.3–4; 58.2; 59.2). This is the "goal" (σκοπός, *skopos*) to which he refers (63.1; cf. 19.2; 51.1).

---

14. Did. 16.7–8; cf. Dan 7:13; Zech 14:5b; Matt 24:30; 1 Thess 3:13; Rev 1:7.

3.2 The Divine Plan and Ecclesiology

In service of this pastoral purpose, Clement invites his readers to consider "the renowned and venerable rule of our tradition" (1 Clem. 7.2), while he "unrolls" for them, as from a scroll, the biblical account of salvation history "from the beginning" (31.1). The unifying concept of Clement's theology is "the will [θέλημα, *thelēma*] of God," which he mentions explicitly over twenty times. This term and its synonyms (βούλημα, *boulēma*, βούλησις, *boulēsis*, and βουλή, *boulē*) often refer to the single plan of God that encompasses the orders of creation and redemption. "The Father and Creator of the entire world" founded the earth "on the firm foundation of his will" (19.2; 33.3). He sent Jesus Christ into the world, and Jesus in turn sent forth his apostles with the gospel. "Both events happened in an orderly fashion by the will of God" (42.1–2). "By the will of God" Jesus Christ gave his blood, flesh, and life for us (49.6). Likewise, "through his will" those who have been "called in Christ Jesus" are justified by faith, just as were the holy ones of Israel in the Old Testament (32.3–4). And "quickly and suddenly the will of God will be brought to its ultimate goal" (τελειωθήσεται, *teleiōthēsetai*) with the second coming (23.5). The divine plan thus extends from creation to parousia, with the Christ event as its centerpiece. "When he wills and as he wills, he will do all things; and nothing decreed by him will pass away" (27.5). It is thus within this broad conception of the divine will that we must look for Clement's ecclesiology.

Though Clement uses the term ἐκκλησία, *ekklēsia*, only four times (1 Clem. salut. [twice]; 44.3; 47.6), the life of the church is near the center of his concerns, and references to the church, local and universal, fill his epistle. For example, he makes use of biblical metaphors such as "flock of Christ" (16.1; 44.3; 54.2; 57.2; cf. 59.4) and "body" and "members" of Christ (37.5; 38.1; 46.7). His descriptions of life within the church under athletic and military metaphors combine biblical and nonbiblical elements (6.2; 7.1; 37.1–4). Likewise, the idea that ecclesial life is a kind of πολιτεία, *politeia*, or "citizenship" (2.8; 3.4; 6.1; 21.1) has a multifaceted background in the Greco-Roman world, Hellenistic Judaism, and the New Testament.[15] But while this citizenship with its rights and responsibilities is of divine institution—note the phrase ἡ πολιτεία τοῦ θεοῦ, *hē politeia tou theou* (54.4)—Clement would agree with Paul that "our citizenship is in heaven" (Phil 3:20). The church merely "sojourns" in places such as Rome and Corinth (1 Clem. salut.; cf. 1 Pet 1:1, 17; 2:11) while it awaits "the visitation of the kingdom of Christ" (1 Clem. 50.3; cf. 42.3). Always on his guard against an overrealized eschatology, Clement never simply identifies the present church with the kingdom of God.

Arguably, Clement's most theologically significant way of speaking of the church is as the chosen people of God. This idea depends on two themes that are prominent throughout the epistle—namely, the unity of the human race and the mystery of divine "election" (ἐκλογή, *eklogē*). The former is rooted in the order of creation (which Clement thematizes more explicitly and extensively than any other writer in the first hundred years of Christianity), while the latter belongs to the order of redemption. God fashioned man, male and female, to be "the impress of his own image," the "most outstanding and greatest" of his creatures (1 Clem. 33.4–5). Because Adam is "our father" (6.3), we share his singular nature and exalted dignity, but we also share his origin in "matter" and the "dark tomb" of the earth (38.3). As such, humanity appears made for greatness but susceptible to destructive forces.

15. C. Spicq, *Theological Lexicon of the New Testament*, 3 vols. (Peabody, MA: Hendrickson, 1994), 3:124–33.

3.3 Primal Envy and Prefigurations of the Church

Echoing Wisdom 2:24, Clement identifies "envy" (ζῆλος, *zēlos*, or φθόνος, *phthonos*) as the primal sin "through which death entered the world" (1 Clem. 3.4; cf. 9.1). Unlike the author of Wisdom, however, Clement is uninterested in "the envy of the devil" and has nothing to say about the disobedience of Adam and Eve or its effect on the human race. He focuses rather on the fratricidal envy of Cain (4.1–7), the narration of which begins a chronological catalogue of examples of how envy invariably leads to the persecution of a brother or sister, or to rebellion against those whom God has placed in positions of authority (1 Clem. 4–6). The point is clear. By rising up against its presbyters, the once exemplary church of the Corinthians has recapitulated the primal sin of envy, with disastrous consequences (3.1–4). The church, local and universal, is a "brotherhood" (ἀδελφότης, *adelphotēs*, 2.4; cf. 1 Pet 2:17; 5:9), and envy is as poison to its system.

To counter the deleterious effects of envy—above all, "death," that is, eternal damnation—God established "the grace of repentance . . . by his almighty will" (1 Clem. 7–8). It was the precious blood of Christ, "poured out for our salvation," that brought this grace into effect "for the entire world" (7.1). Long before the Christ event, however, God had already "granted an opportunity for repentance to those in every generation who were willing to turn to him" (7.2). Even the Ninevites, to whom Jonah preached repentance, "received salvation, though they were not God's own" (7.7). The universal grace of repentance does not, however, negate the mystery of election. At precisely this point in the epistle Clement begins to unfold the special role of Israel, to whom God has spoken directly and profoundly through a long series of inspired prophets (8.1). To the Ninevites he gave a simple ultimatum—repent, or else!—but to Israel he has disclosed the very intention of his heart: "I do not will the death of the sinner so much as repentance" (8.2). For the Ninevites it sufficed to fast and sit in sackcloth and ashes, but for Israel God has laid out a whole spiritual program of purification and reform (8.3–4).

Next, Clement sets forth a series of five exemplars of faith and hospitality from the Old Testament: Enoch, Noah, Abraham, Lot, and Rahab the harlot (1 Clem. 9–12). Abraham is the central and dominant figure here, in part because he was justified by faith and "through obedience" offered an acceptable sacrifice to God (10.6–7), but also because it was through him and his descendants that a blessing would come to all humanity (10.3).

Clement treats his biblical exemplars in canonical order and for the most part gives Old Testament narratives an *ad litteram* interpretation. They are not mere anecdotes but integral pieces in a single plan of redemption that unfolds in human history. Nevertheless, because this is the *divine* will and therefore "majestic and glorious" (1 Clem. 9.1), it is no mundane history but one in which Old Testament persons and events may also prefigure the greater realities of the new order. Twice in these chapters Clement, without abandoning the literal sense, also gestures toward ecclesiological prefigurations. First, he tells us that Noah "proclaimed regeneration [παλιγγενεσίαν, *palingenesian*] to the world, and through him the Lord saved the living creatures who entered the ark in unanimity [ἐν ὁμονοίᾳ, *en homonoia*]" (9.4). Because the term παλιγγενεσία is redolent of the messianic age (Matt 19:28) and of spiritual regeneration through baptism (Titus 3:5; cf. 1 Pet 1:23), while ὁμόνοια is the sine qua non of a healthy church (1 Clem. 30.3; 34.7; 49.5; 50.5; 60.4)—and thus the very quality that Clement wishes to be restored in Corinth (63.2; 65.1)—it is evident that he intends a typological interpretation here. The ark is a type of the church, and the creatures who enter the ark "in unanimity" prefigure those who will be saved.

Clement is more explicit in his typological exegesis of the story of Rahab the harlot, a woman in whom there was "not only faith but prophecy" (1 Clem. 12.8). The scarlet cloth that she hangs from her house signifies that "redemption is to come through the blood of the Lord" (12.7). The fact that only those whom she gathers under her roof "will be saved," while "those who are found outside the house will perish," suggests that both she and her house are types of the church (12.6).[16]

3.4 Israel, Christ, and the Church

Clement adopts a more directly salvation-historical approach later in the epistle when he explains the founding of the church as a chosen people (1 Clem. 29–32). What he says is nonetheless extraordinary for the continuity it posits between Old Testament Israel and the Christian people. "Our Father made *us* an elect portion for himself," Clement declares (29.1), and then immediately adds that this took place primordially, when God "dispersed the children of Adam" and "his people Jacob became the Lord's own portion, Israel his allotted inheritance" (29.2, quoting Deut 32:8–9). Next, Clement develops this thought with a pastiche of biblical motifs: "Behold, the Lord takes for himself a nation from the midst of the nations, just as a man takes his firstfruits from the threshing floor, and from that nation will come forth the holy of holies" (29.3). In other words, Israel is a kind of firstfruits of humanity, but out of this firstfruits is to come something or someone who is supremely holy, supremely set apart for the purposes of God. Before answering the obvious question—Who or what is this "holy of holies" that is to come forth from Israel?—Clement sums up the virtues of Abraham, Isaac, and Jacob and then notes that Jacob was given "the twelvefold scepter [δωδεκάσκηπτρον, *dōdekaskēptron*] of Israel" (31.2–4).

The otherwise unattested word δωδεκάσκηπτρον, which Clement may have coined, hints that a mystery of divinely instituted authority has come into the world through the patriarch Jacob and the tribal structure of Israel. Clement continues:

> From him came all the priests and Levites who minister at the altar of God.
> From him came the Lord Jesus according to the flesh.
> From him came kings and princes and governors by way of Judah. (1 Clem. 32.2a)

Here as elsewhere (e.g., 1 Clem. 40–44), Clement gives special prominence to liturgical worship in the life of the people of God, whether ancient Israel or the church. The arresting manner by which he splices a reference to Christ's human origins (echoing Rom 9:5) between statements about the tribes of Levi and Judah respectively suggests that Jesus Christ is both priest and king. Earlier in the epistle Clement identified Christ as "the majestic scepter [σκῆπτρον, *skēptron*] of God" and then demonstrated, by quoting Isaiah 53 and Psalm 22, how Jesus paradoxically exercised his royal authority in humility and suffering (1 Clem. 16.1–17). Later he will identify Christ as the church's singular high priest (36.1; 40.5; 41.2; 61.3; 64.1). This effectively answers the question about who the "holy of holies" is.

Jesus Christ is the linchpin in Clement's ecclesiology. He is *the* Elect One, not only because he came forth from the elect people (1 Clem. 29.3; 32.2), but because God has chosen *him* in particular, and "through him" has chosen "us" to be "a people especially his own" (64.1; cf. 50.7). Here Clement uses the phrase λαὸς περιούσιος, *laos periousios*, which is the Septuagint's standard rendering of Hebrew *ʿam segullah* ("a people of special

16. For the development of these two classic types in patristic tradition, see J. Daniélou, *From Shadows to Reality, or Sacramentum Futuri: Studies in the Biblical Typology of the Fathers* (London: Burns & Oates, 1960), 69–112 (Noah) and 244–60 (Rahab).

possession"), a phrase which is used in passages concerned with God's unique election of Israel "from among all peoples on the face of the earth" (Deut 7:6). The Greek form of this phrase gained the status of a technical term in early Christian literature, indicating that the church is in some sense the new Israel (cf. Titus 2:14). For Clement, however, this does not mean that the church has *replaced* Israel—an idea found nowhere in his epistle—but that Israel has come to its fullest realization and perfect distillation in Jesus Christ.

Since the Christ event, the people of God, while remaining centered in Israel, has opened outward to include the gentiles. Clement's prayer addresses God as "you who multiply nations upon earth and from all of them have elected those who love you through Jesus Christ your beloved servant" (1 Clem. 59.3). It is the person and event of Jesus Christ that connects the church to the faithful Israelites of old, so that even gentile Christians can refer to the latter as "our ancestors" (30.7; 60.4; 62.2; cf. 4.8; 31.2). Furthermore, all members of the people of God, whether living before or since the Christ event, have in common that "Almighty God has justified them through faith" (32.4; cf. 10.6).

3.5 Office and Rank in the Church

When Clement finally comes around to addressing the crisis in Corinth more or less directly, he takes up the issue of "office" (τόπος, *topos*) and "rank" (τάγμα, *tagma*) in the church (1 Clem. 40–44). By means of analogy with Old Testament Israel, Clement identifies three offices and four ranks within the church.

> To the *high priest* exclusive rituals have been given,
> and to the *priests* their own office has been assigned,
> and upon *Levites* their own ministries have been imposed;
> the *lay person* has been bound by lay precepts. (1 Clem. 40.5)

At first glance one might suppose that Clement here bears early witness to the threefold hierarchy of the local church. Does not the Old Testament trio of high priest, priests, and Levites prefigure the Christian hierarchy of bishop (singular), presbyters, and deacons respectively? No, that supposition would be only two-thirds correct. As noted above, Clement elsewhere identifies Jesus Christ as the church's sole high priest (1 Clem. 36.1; 61:3; 64:1). Under the new covenant, no one *on earth* occupies this office or bears this title.[17]

Indeed, nowhere in his epistle does Clement refer to the monepiscopacy, whether at Rome, Corinth, or anywhere else. He speaks of two, not three, offices in the local church on earth: "overseers" (ἐπίσκοποι, always plural) and "deacons" (διάκονοι), just as we find in other first-century texts.[18] This is especially clear in 1 Clement 42.4–5, where Clement grounds this twofold structure on apostolic precedent and a somewhat specious prophetic prooftext. He sometimes refers to the overseers as "elders" (πρεσβύτεροι, *presbyteroi*), especially in the case of the deposed Corinthian leaders, who seem to have been men of venerable age (3.3; 44.3–5). This virtual interchangeability of the terms πρεσβύτεροι and ἐπίσκοποι is also found in the New Testament (Acts 20:17, 28; Titus 1:5–7), but when the monepiscopacy and the threefold hierarchy of the local church finally emerge in the letters of Ignatius of Antioch (early second century), these terms will refer to two distinct offices:

---

17. Cf. Ign. *Phld.* 9.1; Pol. *Phil.* 12.2; Mart. Pol. 14.3. Exceptional in this regard is Did. 13.3.

18. Phil 1:1; Did. 15.1; cf. 1 Tim 3:1–13. See A. Lindemann, *Die Clemensbriefe*, HNT 17 (Tübingen: Mohr Siebeck, 1992), 127–28.

that of the "bishop" (ἐπίσκοπος, singular) and that of the "presbyters" (πρεσβύτεροι) who are under his authority, with the deacons representing a third rank (e.g., Ign. *Magn.* 2.1).

Finally, with regard to 1 Clement 40.5, we should not overlook the significance of Clement's reference to "the lay person" (ὁ λαϊκὸς ἄνθρωπος, *ho laikos anthrōpos*), the earliest known use of this term in a Christian text. The laity are by definition those who hold no ecclesial office and therefore by default occupy the lowest rank within the church. Context indicates, however, that Clement mentions and *names* the laity precisely in order to indicate that the church is not limited to the clergy and that lay persons have a place and role within the eucharistic community. Immediately after mentioning the laity Clement writes, "Let each of you, brethren, give thanks [εὐχαριστείτω, *eucharisteitō*] to God in his own rank [ἐν τῷ ἰδίῳ τάγματι, *en tō idiō tagmati*], having a good conscience" (41.1). The use of the term λαϊκός was to pass from Clement of Rome to Clement of Alexandria and then to later writers,[19] thus opening within ecclesial tradition a space for later reflection on the particular dignity and importance of the lay state and lay apostolate.[20]

It is striking and surely significant that Clement's discussion of office and rank within the church says nothing about administrative authority as such. This is not to deny that the overseers had administrative responsibilities, but simply to point out that Clement's focus in chapters 40–44 is almost entirely on liturgical worship. Jesus Christ, who occupies the highest office and rank, is "the high priest *of our offerings*" (1 Clem. 36.1) and thus presides from heaven over all of the church's "cultic services" (λειτουργίαι, *leitourgiai*, 40.5; cf. 41.2). The Corinthian presbyters, who occupied the second rank, were deposed from the office of overseers despite the fact that they "offered the gifts blamelessly and with devotion" (44.4). Since Clement compares the deacons, at the third rank, to the Old Testament Levites, their "ministries" (διακονίαι, *diakoniai*) presumably include liturgical functions in support of the overseers (40.5). And as we have seen, Christians of all ranks, including the laity, participate in "giving thanks" to God (41.1).

3.6 Questions of Apostolic Legitimacy and Roman Primacy

At the heart of Clement's argument against the regime change that has taken place in the Corinthian church is his attempt to ground the offices of overseer and deacon in the Christ event and apostolic practice (1 Clem. 42.1–4; 44.1–3). While he does not directly cite any of the books of the later New Testament canon here, his argument does find strong resonances among those writings. The tight linkage that he posits between God's sending of the Lord Jesus and the latter's sending of the apostles (42.1–2) is also found in dominical logia (Matt 10:40; John 17:18; 20:21) and is akin to Paul's thought as well (Rom 8:3; 1 Cor 1:17; Gal 4:4). The related idea that Christ entrusted his gospel to the apostles so that others might receive it reliably through them (1 Clem. 42.1–3) is likewise attested (Heb 2:3; cf. Jude 3). And the claim that the apostles appointed the "firstfruits" of their own ministry as "overseers and deacons" in each of the local churches (1 Clem. 42.4) finds support in several passages taken cumulatively (Acts 14:23; 1 Cor 16:15–16; Phil 1:1; 1 Pet 5:1–3). In this way Clement plausibly demonstrates that the offices themselves are of divine origin and that at least the first generation of appointees to those offices possessed a kind of apostolic legitimacy.

Still, the presbyters deposed by the Corinthians, though they had served a long time (1 Clem. 44.3), appear not to have been appointed directly by the apostles. Clement finds

19. BDAG 581b.

20. E.g., Vatican Council II, *Lumen Gentium*, nos. 30–38.

it necessary, therefore, to take his argument one crucial step further. Because the apostles had received "perfect foreknowledge" from the Lord Jesus "that there would be strife over the title of overseer," not only did they appoint a first generation of overseers and deacons, Clement claims, but they made provision for the valid appointment of future generations of local church leaders as well (44.1–3). Exactly what sort of provision Clement has in mind here is notoriously difficult to determine, due to this passage's formal ambiguity, which is further exacerbated by a text-critical problem.[21]

When the merits of the various rival interpretations have been weighed, the least problematic is probably the Apostolic Delegates View, according to which "the apostles"—presumably Clement has Peter and Paul especially in mind, given their connections to both Rome and Corinth (cf. 1 Clem. 5.1–7; 47.1–4)—in view of their own impending deaths, designated "other approved men" (ἕτεροι δεδοκιμασμένοι ἄνδρες, *heteroi dedokimasmenoi andres*) to assume regional authority and appoint the next generation of presbyters and deacons for the local churches (44.2).[22] This is precisely the responsibility that the Pastoral Epistles say Paul gave to Titus on Crete and to Timothy in the province of Asia (Titus 1:5; 2 Tim 2:2). It is even possible that Apollos was one such delegate and had a role in appointing the Corinthian presbyters who were later deposed. Note that Clement describes him precisely as "a man approved" (ἀνδρὶ δεδοκιμασμένῳ, *andri dedokimasmenō*) by the apostles Peter and Paul (1 Clem. 47.4). According to this interpretation, when Clement says that the Corinthian presbyters had been appointed "with the approval of the whole church" (1 Clem. 44.3), he means the universal church.

While it is true that Clement's doctrine of ecclesiastical appointments amounts to "a kind of apostolic succession,"[23] one must guard against anachronism here. Though Irenaeus draws explicitly on 1 Clement 44 in formulating his classic doctrine of apostolic succession and adopts Clement's use of the technical term διαδέχομαι, *diadechomai* ("to succeed to"), the bishop of Lyons posits a *monepiscopal* succession in Rome and elsewhere (Irenaeus, *Haer.* 3.3.3), whereas Clement does nothing of the sort.

We must exercise even greater caution when it comes to claims that Clement's epistle bears early witness to Roman primacy and the Petrine ministry.[24] At most one can speak of an implicit, inchoate, and de facto exercise in this regard.[25] Clement never speaks in the first-person singular or identifies himself by name or title. He writes only in the name of the Roman church. From the epistle's opening lines, he appears to go out of his way to place the Roman and Corinthian churches "side by side, on equal footing."[26] He speaks authoritatively, to be sure, and even suggests that the Roman church has written the epistle "through the Holy Spirit" (1 Clem. 63.2), but nowhere does he suggest that this spiritual authority is a function of the de jure primacy of one church over all others. Instead he appeals repeatedly to the authority of Scripture and tradition (7.2; 13.1–4; 43.1; 45.2–3; 47.1–3; 53.1–2) and prays that the Corinthian usurpers would "yield not to us but to

21. See Holmes, *Apostolic Fathers*, 103–5.

22. W. Moriarty, "1 Clement's View of Ministerial Appointments in the Early Church," *VC* 66 (2012): 115–38.

23. Moriarty, "1 Clement's View," 127.

24. E.g., J. Quasten, *The Beginnings of Patristic Literature: From the Apostles Creed to Irenaeus*, vol. 1 of *Patrology* (Utrecht-Antwerp: Spectrum, 1950), 46–47.

25. J. Fullenbach, *Ecclesiastical Office and the Primacy of Rome: An Evaluation of Recent Theological Discussion of First Clement* (Washington, DC: Catholic University of America Press, 1980), 137–44.

26. B. E. Bowe, *A Church in Crisis: Ecclesiology and Paraenesis in Clement of Rome*, HDR 23 (Minneapolis: Fortress, 1988), 36.

the will of God" (56.1).[27] The epistle is in places a rather strongly worded "admonition" (νουθέτησις, *nouthetēsis*), but it is the sort of admonition that the Corinthian church might have been expected to give to the Roman church had the shoe been on the other foot (7.1; 56.2). At the same time, however, Clement and the Roman church certainly rose to the occasion and produced an extraordinary document, which was to gain wide distribution and a positive reception. As a result, the Christians of Rome, who had long had the reputation of being "filled with all knowledge and able to admonish one another" (Rom 15:14), would soon be known as the church that had "taught others" (Ign. *Rom.* 3.1).

4. THE LETTERS OF IGNATIUS OF ANTIOCH

More than any other part of the corpus of the Apostolic Fathers, the seven letters written by Ignatius of Antioch on his way to martyrdom in Rome in the early second century left a permanent mark on the church's emerging sense of her own identity. His groundbreaking ecclesiology features the earliest recorded use of the terms "Christianity" and "the catholic church" (both of which he likely coined) and the first occurrences of the adjective "apostolic" in a Christian context (Ign. *Magn.* 10.1–3; *Smyrn.* 8.2; *Trall.* salut.). Ignatius treats "the gospel" as the church's rule of faith and is the first Christian author to apply the terms "heterodoxy" and "heresy" to doctrines that diverge from this rule.[28] His rich teaching on the Eucharist is closely linked to his ecclesiology, and his letters contain five of the six references to the Virgin Mary in the Apostolic Fathers.[29]

The letters of Ignatius also provide the earliest unambiguous testimony to the monepiscopacy and the threefold hierarchy of the local church. The New Testament, 1 Clement, and the Didache speak of plural "overseers" (ἐπίσκοποι) in the local church and sometimes use this term interchangeably with "elders" (πρεσβύτεροι).[30] Ignatius, on the other hand, consistently refers to a single "bishop" (ἐπίσκοπος) in each local church, and under the bishop's authority he affirms a body of "presbyters" (πρεσβύτεροι, or πρεσβυτέριον, *presbyterion*), which constitute a "bishop's council" (συνέδριον τοῦ ἐπισκόπου, *synedrion tou episkopou*), as well as a number of "deacons" (διάκονοι).[31] According to Ignatius, this threefold hierarchy is the sine qua non for any local Christian community that would be called a "church" (ἐκκλησία, *Trall.* 3.1). As the universal church forms "one body" with Christ as its head (*Smyr.* 1.2), so the local church with its bishop, presbyters, and deacons has "its own bodily integrity" (τὸ ἴδιον σωματεῖον, *to idion sōmateion*, 11.2).

In order to get at the heart of Ignatius's ecclesiology as directly as possible, we shall consider how he might answer four closely related questions: (1) What is the relationship between the Christ event and the origin of the church? (2) What is the relationship between Judaism and Christianity? (3) How does Jesus Christ remain present to his church subsequent to his resurrection? (4) And what is meant by "the catholic church"?[32]

---

27. A. Gregory, "*1 Clement*: An Introduction," in *The Writings of the Apostolic Fathers*, ed. P. Foster (London: T&T Clark, 2007), 27–28.

28. For εὐαγγέλιον ("gospel"), see Ign. *Phld.* 5.1–2; 8.2–9.2; *Smyr.* 5.1; 7.2–8.1. Ignatius uses the noun ἑτεροδοξία ("opinion contrary to the faith") in *Magn.* 8.1 and the verb ἑτεροδοξεῖν ("to hold or spread opinions contrary to the faith") in *Smyr.* 6.2. In the NT the term αἵρεσις usually means "sect, party, faction" (Acts 5:17; 15:5; 24:5, 14; 26:5; 28:22; 1 Cor 11:19; Gal 5:20), but in Ignatius's letters it means "heresy"—i.e., a false doctrine held by a factious group (Ign. *Eph.* 6.2; *Trall.* 6.1; cf. 2 Pet 2:1).

29. Ign. *Eph.* 7.2; 18.2; 19.1; *Trall.* 9.1; *Smyrn.* 1.1; cf. Diogn. 12.8.

30. Acts 20:17, 28; Phil 1:1; 1 Clem. 42.4–5; 44.4–5; Did. 15.1.

31. Ign. *Magn.* 2.1; 6.1; 13.1; *Trall.* 2.2–3; 7.2; *Phld.* salut.; 4.1; 7.1; 8.1; *Smyrn.* 8.1; 12.2; *Pol.* 6.1.

32. For a more detailed treatment of these topics and pertinent bibliography, see G. Vall, *Learning Christ: Ignatius of Antioch and the Mystery of Redemption* (Washington, DC: Catholic University of America Press, 2013), 200–55 and 301–58.

4.1 The Christ Event and the Origin of the Church

According to Luke's presentation of Peter's Pentecost speech, when Jesus Christ was raised from the dead and exalted to God's right hand, "he received the promised Holy Spirit from the Father and poured [him] out" upon his disciples, thus vivifying the church (Acts 2:32–33). Likewise, the Fourth Gospel teaches that Jesus's death and glorification were necessary antecedents to the gift of the Spirit (John 7:39; 16:7; 20:22). Paul for his part presents God's "sending forth" of the Son and his "sending forth" of the Spirit as two distinct but closely related events (Gal 4:4–6). Here we shall consider four passages from the Ignatian letters that similarly link the Christ event to the origin of the church. These four passages also contain some of Ignatius's most interesting ecclesiological symbols.

The first passage, *To the Ephesians* 17, condenses the entire paschal mystery—from the anointing at Bethany to the risen Lord's appearance to the apostles in the cenacle—into a single sentence: "To this end the Lord received myrrh upon his head: that he might breathe imperishability into the church" (Ign. *Eph.* 17.1; cf. Matt 26:8; John 20:22; Gen 2:7). In other words, by accepting the anointing as a prophetic anticipation of his death and burial (Matt 26:12), Jesus consented to the passion, and he did this in order to impart the Spirit to his church as a permanent endowment and inhering principle of imperishable life. Ignatius refers to this endowment as "the gift that the Lord has truly sent" (Ign. *Eph.* 17.2).

The second passage, *To the Smyrnaeans* 1, is an anti-docetic confessional summary of the Christ event, accenting its historical particularity. It includes Jesus's descent from David, birth from the Virgin, baptism by John, crucifixion under Pontius Pilate, and resurrection from the dead. Toward the end of this summary, Ignatius seamlessly transitions from the Christ event to the origin of the church by weaving ecclesiological symbols into his account of the paschal mystery: "We are his fruit, the fruit of his divinely blessed passion, [which he suffered] so that through his resurrection he might raise a standard for the ages, for his holy and faithful ones, whether from the Jews or the gentiles, in the one body of his church" (Ign. *Smyrn.* 1.2). By describing Christians as the "fruit" of Christ's passion, Ignatius presents the cross as a tree of life. He quickly shifts to a new symbol, however, and the cross becomes the messianic battle standard (see Isa 11:12; 49:22; 62:10), which the risen Christ raises aloft in order to gather to himself the members of his mystical body, both Jew and gentile. The upshot of this passage is that Christ's death and resurrection engenders the church.

A similar collocation of symbols is found in the third passage, *To the Trallians* 11. Ignatius describes the docetists as "malignant offshoots that bear deadly fruit," implying by the word "offshoots" that they are (or were) nominal members of the church, but he immediately denies that they are a true "planting of the Father" (Ign. *Trall.* 11.1; cf. Matt 15:13). "For if they were," he continues, "they would appear as branches of the cross, and their fruit would be imperishable. Through [the cross], by his passion, he summons you who are his members. A head cannot be born separately, apart from its members, whereas God promises union, which is himself" (Ign. *Trall.* 11.2). Here Ignatius uses imagery of organic processes to indicate the intimate union between Jesus Christ and his church, but it is crucial to note that this union is brought about by a salvation-historical event—namely, the paschal mystery. The docetists have no share in this union precisely because they have abandoned the concrete, historical, flesh-and-blood reality of the passion, supposing that Christ only "seemed to suffer" (9.1–10.1). Once again, Ignatius indicates that it is by means of the cross that Christ summons the members of his body. And just as a baby's head, when it comes forth from the womb, is followed immediately by its members, so Christ the head comes forth from the tomb in his resurrection and, so to speak, brings with him the members of his body (cf. Rom 6:4, 8; Col 2:20; 3:1). Through its union with Christ, the church participates in the eternal union that "is" God—that is, the union of "Jesus and the Father" (Ign. *Magn.* 1.2). This is not accomplished by means of a primordial quasi-syzygy of Christ and church (cf. 2 Clem. 14.2), but by the saving event of the cross.

In the fourth passage, *To the Ephesians* 9.1, Ignatius again creatively develops an ecclesiological symbol from Scripture: "You are as temple stones prepared beforehand for the edifice of God the Father, borne up to the heights by means of the crane of Jesus Christ, which is the cross, making use of the Holy Spirit as a cable. Your faith is your upward guide, and love is the way that bears you up to God." Ignatius depicts the church as a temple tower, for which each Christian has been prepared as a building stone (cf. 1 Pet 2:5). But instead of focusing on how each stone takes its appointed or deserved place in the structure (cf. Herm. Vis. 3.2.4–9; 3.5.1–3.7.6), Ignatius's extended metaphor is concerned with the upward movement by which the Christian is "borne up to the heights." The temple rests on the earth but evidently reaches to heaven, suggesting that the Christian life is essentially a matter of ascent to God. This ascent is a work of God in which all three persons of the Trinity are involved. And as in the previous two passages, here too the cross of Christ plays the decisive role. It is the crane—literally, the "machine" (μηχανή, *mēchanē*)—by which the believer is hoisted upward. This is no fanciful or magical view of the cross, however. Ignatius recognizes that the cross has its effect in the Christian life by the grace of the Holy Spirit, which is operative through the virtues of faith and love. Ignatius has a sublime conception of the church, but it is firmly grounded in the events of salvation history and the concrete reality of ecclesial existence.

4.2 Judaism and Christianity

If the paschal mystery and outpouring of the Holy Spirit is the salvation-historical cause of the church, does this mean that the church did not in any sense preexist the Christ event? What is the relationship between Israel and the church, and between Judaism and the gospel? Ignatius addresses these matters in his letters to the churches of Magnesia and Philadelphia, where Judaizing factions were observing the Sabbath and absenting themselves from the bishop's eucharistic celebration on the Lord's Day. Ignatius's pastoral response to this crisis represents a significant moment in "the parting of the ways" between the two religions.

The term Ἰουδαϊσμός, *Ioudaismos* ("Judaism") had been in use for centuries by the time of Ignatius (e.g., 2 Macc 2:21; Gal 1:13–14), but in order to place the faith and practice of Jesus's followers in clear juxtaposition to Judaism, for the sake of both comparison and contrast, a semantic counterpart was needed. Ignatius—who was bishop of the local church at Antioch, where "the disciples were first called Christians" (Acts 11:26)—appears to have coined the term Χριστιανισμός, *Christianismos* ("Christianism," or "Christianity") to serve as such a counterpart. This coinage provided the conceptual clarity needed to recognize in the new faith something that belongs to the same genus as Judaism but can be specifically distinguished from it. Ignatius could now display both the continuity and the discontinuity between Judaism and Christianity (Ign. *Magn.* 10.1–3; *Phld.* 5:2–6.1).

Although Ignatius does not accent the continuity between the people of Israel and the Christian people as strongly as Clement of Rome does, he readily acknowledges that there were "saints" among the biblical Israelites and that they "belong to the unity of Jesus Christ" (Ign. *Phld.* 5.2). Foremost among these Old Testament saints are the prophets, who "lived according to Christ Jesus" and were "inspired by his grace"; they "believed in him" and "were saved" (Ign. *Magn.* 8.2; *Phld.* 5.2). Ignatius stops short of calling them "Christians" or members of "the church," reserving these terms for reference to the period subsequent to the Christ event. The prophetic oracles anticipated the gospel, but the gospel itself is "the perfection of imperishability" (5.2; 9.2). Ignatius never abandons the salvation-historical framework, in which the Christ event is the decisive turning point. Jesus Christ is Israel's true "high priest" and the unique "door of the Father," through whom "Abraham, Isaac, and Jacob and the prophets and the apostles and the church, all these, enter into the unity of God" (9.1; cf. Herm. Sim. 9.12.6). There is, then, one historical people of God, from Abraham to the present time, with the patriarchs and prophets preceding the Christ event, and the apostles and the church following it. Jesus Christ is the source of all grace, but "his grace" seems to flow both backward and forward in time from the paschal mystery (Ign. *Magn.* 8.2; cf. Barn. 5.6).

Where does this leave the institutions and observances of Judaism? Unlike the author of the Epistle to Diognetus, Ignatius does not ridicule circumcision, Sabbath, food laws, animal sacrifice, or the festival calendar as "superstition" and "folly" (Diogn. 1.1; 3.1–4.6), for he accepts on the authority of Scripture that they were divinely instituted. Nor does he argue that the precepts of the Mosaic law were never intended to be carried out literally but were only meant to be interpreted allegorically, as does the Epistle of Barnabas (7.3–10.12). Because they come from God and belong to his overarching plan of redemption, the institutions and observances of Judaism are inherently "good" (Ign. *Phld.* 9.1–2). But because they belong to the period of preparation and prefigurement, they are now like "bad yeast, which has grown old and sour"; Christians must set them aside and "turn to the new yeast, that is, to Jesus Christ" (Ign. *Magn.* 10.2). Now that Christ has come, it is "incongruous" to continue the practices of Judaism (10.3). "Those who once conducted their lives in accord with ancient practices have come to a newness of hope" (9.1).

Ignatius considered this principle to have special applicability to the controversy concerning Sabbath and Lord's Day. The former is the heart and soul of Judaism, while the latter is the sum and substance of Christianity. They therefore correspond to the two great eras of the historical economy of redemption, which is recapitulated each week in the passage from Saturday to Sunday. Those who continue to observe the Sabbath make as it were a public confession that they have not yet received the grace of Christ and that they still "live according to Judaism," whereas those who "live according to the Lord's Day" confess that the new life has "dawned" and that they now participate in the "mystery" of Christ's death and resurrection (Ign. *Magn.* 8.1; 9.1).

4.3 The Ongoing Presence of Christ to His Church

Ignatius of Antioch famously states that "wherever Christ Jesus is, there is the catholic church" (Ign. *Smyrn.* 8.2). Before we can determine exactly what he means by "catholic" here, however, we must pose a more basic question. Since Ignatius places such extraordinary emphasis on the concrete historical particularity of the Christ event and views this past event as the cause of the church, how exactly does he understand Jesus Christ to remain present to his church in all subsequent times and throughout the world? A simple answer would be, through the grace of the Holy Spirit. As noted above, Ignatius understands this gift to be a permanent endowment and inhering principle of life for the church. That is the sense of the words, "that he might breathe imperishability into the church" (Ign. *Eph.* 17.1). But in what concrete and tangible ways is this gift available to the members of the church? Without pretending to be exhaustive, we can identify three elements of ecclesial life that Ignatius considers vital.

First, there is the rule of faith, comprising "the gospel" and "the apostles" (Ign. *Phld.* 5.1). The gospel, whether orally or in writing, is "the truth about Jesus Christ" in verbal form (Ign. *Eph.* 6.2): who he is, what he did, and what he taught. Its importance for Ignatius is evident on every page of every letter. Without rejecting the authority of the law and the prophets, Ignatius ascribes "a distinct advantage" to the gospel, inasmuch as it directly proclaims the person and event of Jesus Christ (Ign. *Phld.* 9.2; cf. 5.2; 8.2; *Smyrn.* 5.1; 7.2). Christians are "confirmed in the ordinances of the Lord and of the apostles" (Ign. *Magn.* 13.1). The apostles were chosen by the Lord Jesus, not simply as individuals, but as a "college" (Ign. *Trall.* 3.1). They were gathered "around Peter" when the risen Lord appeared to them in the cenacle, where "they touched him and believed, being mingled with his flesh and spirit" (Ign. *Smyrn.* 3.2). They went forth into the world, and the Lord extended his own activity through them (Ign. *Magn.* 7.1). In martyrdom they "scorned death and were found to be beyond death" (Ign. *Smyrn.* 3.2). The apostles now form a heavenly "council" (Ign. *Magn.* 6.1), but they remain with the church on earth by means of their example and their writings (Ign. *Eph.* 12.2). Ignatius commends the Ephesians because they "have always lived in accord with the apostles" (11.2), and he assures the Trallians that his own teaching and example bear "the apostolic stamp" (Ign. *Trall.* salut.).

Second, the Lord Jesus is present to his church in the Eucharist. Unlike the docetists, Ignatius "confess[es] the Eucharist to be the flesh of our Savior Jesus Christ, that which suffered for our sins and which the Father in his kindness raised" (Ign. *Smyrn.* 7.1). The "one Eucharist" convened by the local church's "one bishop" is the sign and cause of ecclesial unity, "for there is one flesh of our Lord Jesus Christ, one cup for unity in his blood, and one altar" (Ign. *Phld.* 4.1). This reference to the eucharistic table as an "altar" (within a statement in which none of the other terms is metaphorical) indicates that the Eucharist is not only a fellowship meal but a sacrifice, a communal act of worship (cf. Did. 14.1–3). Moreover, the Eucharist makes the person and event of Christ *soteriologically* present. If Jesus is the "one healer," the Eucharist is "the medicine of immortality" that he administers (Ign. *Eph.* 7.2; 20.2).

Third, the local bishop, in union with the presbyters and deacons, makes Jesus Christ present to the church. Ignatius views the bishop as an essential link between heaven and earth. Jesus Christ is "the mindset of the Father," and "the bishops ordained throughout the earth are in the mindset of Jesus Christ" (Ign. *Eph.* 3.2). If the members of the local church are "mingled with" their bishop "just as the [universal] church is with Jesus Christ and as Jesus Christ is with the Father," their communal life will be "harmonious in unity" (5.1). As the Lord Jesus is "the master of the house," so the bishop is the chief steward whom he "sends to dispense the goods of the house on his behalf." One must therefore "look upon the bishop as upon the Lord himself" (6.1). No ecclesial rite may be performed "apart from the bishop and the presbyters," for "the bishop presides in the place of God and the presbyters in the place of the council of the apostles" (Ign. *Trall.* 2.1; *Magn.* 7.1; 6.1). A celebration of the Eucharist is "considered valid" only if the bishop, or someone authorized by him, presides (Ign. *Smyrn.* 8.1).

4.4 The Catholic Church

Although Ignatius's ecclesiology is focused mostly on the local church, he also shows a keen awareness of "the church according to its wholeness" (the literal meaning of ἡ καθολικὴ ἐκκλησία, *hē katholikē ekklēsia*). The catholic church extends "to the ends of the earth," and into it "peoples of every language have been gathered" (Ign. *Eph.* 3.2; *Magn.* 10.3). Its universal extension is not only geographical and cultural, however, but also temporal. As we have seen, the risen Christ raises his standard "for the ages" (εἰς τοὺς αἰῶνας, *eis tous aiōnas*) in order to gather "his holy and faithful ones, whether from the Jews or the gentiles, in the one body of his church" (Ign. *Smyrn.* 1.2).

The passage in which Ignatius actually uses the phrase "the catholic church" makes both a clear distinction and a strong correlation between the universal church and the local church: "Wherever the bishop appears, there let the multitude be; just as, wherever Christ Jesus is, there is the catholic church" (Ign. *Smyrn.* 8.2).[33] Having answered the question as to how the risen Christ remains present to his church, we can now understand what Ignatius means by this statement. Jesus Christ "is" wherever Christians "live in accord with the truth" of the gospel and "no heresy resides" (*Eph.* 6.2), wherever they "live in accord with the apostles" (11.2), wherever they "observe one Eucharist" under "one bishop, together with presbytery and deacons" (Ign. *Phld.* 4.1). The catholic church is realized in each such local church, even as it comprises all of them together.

Ignatius's use of the phrase "the catholic church" thus anticipates important aspects of its later use. Other aspects, however, are missing. While Ignatius is convinced that "the bishops ordained to the ends of the earth are in the mindset of Jesus Christ" (Ign. *Eph.* 3.2), he offers no doctrine of apostolic succession. And though he associates the apostles Peter and Paul with the church of Rome and notes that the Roman Christians "have taught others" (Ign. *Rom.* 3.1; 4.3), his letter to that church does not, as is sometimes supposed, lend support to the doctrine of Roman primacy, to say nothing of the Petrine office. At most, Ignatius's assertion that the Roman church "presides in the place of the region of the Romans" (Ign. *Rom.* salut.) might concede regional jurisdiction to their shepherds, presumably on a par with Ignatius's own regional authority as "bishop of Syria" (2.2). Moreover, Ignatius's surprising failure to greet, or even mention, the bishop of Rome might suggest that he himself was uncertain whether the monepiscopacy had taken hold in Italy.

5. SECOND CLEMENT

The second-century document known as 2 Clement is a sermon, apparently composed and delivered by one of the presbyters of a gentile-Christian congregation, possibly in Egypt.[34] We can sketch in broad strokes the ecclesial situation that the sermon was written to address and the theological outlook embodied in the presbyter's response to this situation. While most aspects of his theology are relatively straightforward, his ecclesiology is complex. Chapter 14 in particular, which deals with the preexistence of the church and its relationship to Christ, is one of the more difficult passages in the corpus of the Apostolic Fathers. Complicating matters further are indicators throughout the sermon that it "was written in an environment of incipient Gnosticism."[35] In accord with a basic hermeneutical principle, therefore, we shall begin with what is tolerably clear before proceeding to what is more obscure.

5.1 Response to a Pastoral Problem

Certain members of the local church, it seems, held that "this flesh" would neither rise again nor face judgment (2 Clem. 9.1) and thus felt free to lead lives of carnal indulgence

33. In early Christianity, "the multitude" (τὸ πλῆθος or similar) is a technical term for the local church, especially in cultic assembly (1 Clem. 54.2; Ign. *Magn.* 6.1; *Trall.* 1.1; 8.2; Herm. Mand. 11.9). See BDAG 825–26.

34. W. Pratscher, "The Second Epistle of Clement," in Pratscher, *Apostolic Fathers*, 74, 87–88.

35. K. P. Donfried, *The Setting of Second Clement in Early Christianity*, NovTSup 38 (Leiden: Brill, 1974), 112.

and, what is worse, to spread their "evil teaching" to "innocent souls" (10.5). The pastoral problem that the presbyter faced was thus both doctrinal and moral, and it posed a threat to the entire Christian community. In addressing this crisis, he is particularly concerned with sins that strike at the heart of ecclesial life, such as adultery, detraction, envy, and the love of money (4.3; 6.1–4). He reminds his hearers that they were "in this flesh" when they were "called" by the Lord Jesus and assures them that they will likewise "come in the flesh" to final judgment (9.2, 4). They must therefore "repent with a whole heart of the evil deeds that [they] have done in the flesh" (8.2) and henceforth "guard the flesh as the temple of God" (9.3; cf. Ign. *Phld.* 7.2).

This concern with the flesh is no mere moralism. The presbyter places it within a soteriological and eschatological framework. When the gentiles were "called" by the Lord Jesus, he "granted [them] light," made them sons and daughters of God, and "saved" them (2 Clem. 1.4; cf. 9.2). They have been delivered not only from immoral actions but from the spiritual darkness of "worshiping stones and pieces of wood," from "a whole way of life" that was "nothing other than death" (1.6). Through Jesus Christ they have come to know "the Father of truth" (3.1). Since baptism is what sets one on the course to "eternal life," to "keep the flesh pure" is also to keep the "seal" of baptism "spotless" (8.6; cf. 7.6). Accordingly, the presbyter warns his congregation that, if they do not "keep their baptism pure and undefiled," they will not "enter the kingdom of God" (6.9). From the sermon's opening sentence to its closing doxology, he places before his listeners the fearful prospect of final judgment and "eternal punishment," while also reminding them of the "great and wonderful promise" according to which those who live "devoutly and righteously" will—after a brief sojourn "in this world of the flesh"—attain "repose in the coming kingdom" and everlasting happiness "with the ancestors above."[36] The author maintains this focus on the last things throughout the sermon, presumably because the false teachers have so radicalized the idea of realized eschatology that they have all but eliminated future eschatology.

It is probably fair to say that the author of 2 Clement has swung the pendulum too far in the opposite direction.[37] He articulates no clear doctrine of grace, conveys no robust sense of life "in Christ," and makes no reference to the indwelling of the Holy Spirit. Instead, he places an extraordinary emphasis on the necessity of good "works" and "doing righteousness."[38] In this respect the presbyter's understanding of Christian existence lacks the depth and richness of the Pauline, Johannine, and Ignatian conceptions. It would be inaccurate, however, to conclude that he entirely eliminates the "already" in favor of the "not yet." On the contrary, he begins the sermon by reminding the congregation that they must not "think small thoughts" about what Jesus Christ has already done for them, lest they also develop a contracted vision of eschatological hope (2 Clem. 1.1–8). Likewise, he deliberately uses the verb σῴζειν, *sōzein* ("to save") to refer both to what has already occurred and to what must yet take place.[39]

5.2 The Person and Mission of Jesus Christ

Next, we shall consider the presbyter's understanding of the person and mission of Christ. Jesus Christ is the preexistent Son of "the only invisible God, the Father of truth,"

36. 2 Clem. 1.1; 5.4–6; 6.7; 19.4; 20.4–5. Cf. 4.5; 6.1–7.6; 8.3–9.6; 10.3–12.6; 14.1–15.5; 16.3; 17.4–18.2; 19.3; 20.2.

37. Donfried, *Setting of Second Clement*, 180.

38. 2 Clem. 4.2–3; 5.6; 6.9; 11.1, 6–7; 12.1, 4; 13.3; 15.3; 16.3; 17.4, 7; 18.2; 19.2–3; 20.3–4.

39. "Already": 2 Clem. 1.4, 7; 2.7; 3.3; 9.1, 5. "Not yet": 4.1–2; 8.2; 14.1; 15.2; 17.2; 19.1, 3.

who "sent [him] forth to us" (2 Clem. 20.5). Though "he was spirit at first, he became flesh" (9.5), and by way of the incarnation he became the revealer, the one "through whom we have come to know the Father of truth" (3.1). Christ's revelatory role is intimately linked, moreover, to his soteriological role. The one through whom the Father "manifested the truth and the heavenly life" is the same one whom he sent to be our "savior" and the "author of imperishability" (20.5). He "came" in the flesh to "call" and "save" sinners (2.7; cf. 1.2–8; 2.4; 3.3; 5.1; 9.5). The presbyter also stresses the fact that Jesus Christ has issued "commandments" (ἐντολαί, *entolai*, or ἐντάλματα, *entalmata*), which the baptized Christian must obey if he or she is to avoid "eternal punishment" and "receive eternal life" (3.4; 4.5; 6.7; 8.4; 17.1–7). Accordingly, on "the day of his manifestation" Christ himself will appear in "his glory and might," reigning as king of the world and "judge of the living and the dead" (1.1; 17.4–5).

Jesus Christ's role as lawgiver and judge must, in turn, be understood in close connection to his role as revealer and savior. The commandments that Jesus Christ has issued are not merely so many ethical requirements, a code to regulate behavior. They are, rather, integral to his manifestation of "the truth and the heavenly life," a truth and life in which he, as "savior" and "author of imperishability," enables his followers to share (2 Clem. 20.5). To receive this revelation is to know "the will of the Father," and to "do" his will is to "live" (10.1). It is also to be "received" by God "as sons [and daughters]" and thus to share in the Lord Jesus's filial relationship to the Father. "For the Lord said, 'My brothers [and sisters] are those who do the will of my Father'" (9.10–11). These statements fit together and make sense only if we grant that Christ's commandments are part and parcel of his revelation of God and that the one who knows and does these commandments in some manner participates in God's own righteous character.

We might say, then, that the author of 2 Clement responds to the incipient gnosticism of the false teachers, not by downplaying the significance of knowledge but by disclosing the unity of truth and love. He asks what it means to possess "knowledge" (γνῶσις, *gnōsis*) of God, and he answers that it means "not to deny the one through whom we know him" but to confess him "by doing what he says and not disobeying his commandments" (2 Clem. 3.1, 4). In other words, true knowledge of God is that which is received from Jesus Christ, the revealer of the Father, and is lived out in concrete acts of obedience to his will. Presumably, then, the author's opponents claim to have "knowledge" of God and are willing to call Jesus "Lord"—they may even claim that they have already been "gathered into [Jesus's] bosom"—but none of this will save them, declares the presbyter, if they neglect his commandments and fail to "do righteousness" (4.1, 4). In fact, not even adherence to Christ's commandments will suffice unless they are performed with love. Like the New Testament writers, the author of 2 Clement appreciates that the sum and substance of the Lord's commandments is to "love one another" (4.3; 9.6; cf. 13.4).

Strikingly, the author of 2 Clement says nothing specific about the life of Jesus. He refers to the Son's incarnation and mission, but only in schematic terms: "sent forth . . . became flesh . . . came and called us . . . saved many" (2 Clem. 20.5; 9.5; 2.7). He does not mention any discrete event of Christ's public ministry and makes only a single vague reference to his passion: "How many sufferings he endured on our behalf" (1.2). Unlike 1 Clement or the letters of Ignatius, the sermon also lacks any indicator of the historical context of the Christ event—no reference to Israelite or Davidic ancestry, the Virgin Mary, John the Baptist, Pontius Pilate, Herod the tetrarch, or Peter and Paul. And although Christ's glorious exaltation is implicit in the judgment scene (17.4–5), the sermon never so much as mentions his resurrection from the dead.

When Paul was faced with the denial of the general resurrection by certain members of the church at Corinth, it seemed obvious to him that they needed to be reminded of the fundamental fact and supreme importance of Christ's own resurrection (1 Cor 15:1–24). Likewise, when Polycarp dealt with those who held that there is "neither resurrection nor judgment," he referred to Christ's resurrection five times in a letter that is scarcely half the length of 2 Clement (Pol. *Phil.* 7.1; see also 1.2; 2.1–2; 9.2; 12.2; cf. 5.2). But when the author of our sermon penned his response to the same false doctrine, it apparently did not occur to him to mention Jesus's resurrection. The sum effect of these omissions is that, despite the presbyter's pointed references to Christ's human "flesh" (2 Clem. 9.5; 14.3), the saving event itself seems to lose its grounding and cohesion.

5.3 Two Ecclesiological Passages

We are now in a position to examine the two explicitly ecclesiological passages in 2 Clement. The first of these is in 2.1–3, where the presbyter quotes and comments upon Isaiah 54:1. For present purposes, we may focus on the beginning and end of the quotation: "Rejoice, you barren one, who do not give birth . . . for many more are the children of the desolate one than of her who has the husband." The presbyter claims that the prophet "spoke of us," and then he proceeds to explain that "our church was barren before children were given to her," adding that "our people seemed to be deserted by God, but now, having believed, have become more numerous than those who seem to have God" (2 Clem. 2.1b, 3b; cf. Gal 4:26–28; Justin, *1 Apol.* 53). Presumably, by "our church" the author means the universal community of Christians—as opposed to the Jews, whom he disparagingly refers to as "those who seem to have God"—and by "our people" he means the gentiles.[40]

Evidently the author views the church as predominantly gentile. His somewhat wooden exegesis of Isaiah 54:1 leads to the strange idea that the church existed prior to the incarnation but was without "children." (What sort of church has no members?) The double problem of a barren church and a deserted people is resolved when Jesus Christ comes to call the latter out of their pagan darkness and to give them to the former to be her children. This approach seems to disconnect the church from Israel and its history and to dismiss the Jewish people as inauthentic, a people who only "seem to have God." This conception is strikingly different from what we found in the Didache, 1 Clement, or even the Ignatian corpus, each of which saw the church as in some sense preexisting in biblical Israel. The author of 2 Clement quotes "the books" (i.e., the Septuagint) alongside "the apostles" (i.e., the nascent New Testament plus one or more noncanonical sources) as authoritative Scripture (14.2), but he shows little or no interest in the narrative of salvation history that connects these two groups of texts.

We turn now to the dense and difficult chapter 14, where the presbyter gives an extended teaching on the church and relates it to what he has already said about Christ and salvation. Here some scholars detect the influence of the Platonic doctrine of the eternal forms in the author's concept of "the first church" and in his use of the terms "the original" (τὸ αὐθεντικόν, *to authentikon*) and "the copy" (τὸ ἀντιτυπόν, *to antitypon*).[41] They also find a striking affinity to the syzygies of Valentinian Gnosticism in its presentation of the preexistent union of Christ and the church as male and female principles respectively.[42] It is

40. Donfried, *Setting of Second Clement*, 199.

41. Donfried, *Setting of Second Clement*, 163n3; W. Varner, *Second Clement: An Introductory Commentary*, AFCS (Eugene, OR: Cascade, 2020), 121.

42. Donfried, *Setting of Second Clement*, 164. But see the cautious and nuanced discussion of both points in Lindemann, *Clemensbriefe*, 240–43.

difficult to determine in this regard whether the presbyter is fighting in enemy territory or on common ground. Back in chapter 12 he quoted an agraphon with strong gnostic overtones—"when the two will be one, and the outside as the inside, and the male with the female, neither male nor female"—but he gave it a moralizing and "most ungnostic" interpretation.[43] Here in chapter 14, however, his strategy seems to be to utilize Platonic and gnostic ideas in order to outflank his foes. At the same time, he claims to base his teaching on "the books and the apostles" (2 Clem. 14.2), and Genesis 1 and Ephesians 5 do indeed appear to play key roles in his presentation.

We shall try to tease out the presbyter's argument, statement by statement. First, he informs the congregation that "if we do the will of God our Father, we shall belong to the first church, the spiritual one created before sun and moon" (2 Clem. 14.1a). Here the church preexists not only the incarnation, as in chapter 2, but the creation of the heavenly bodies on the fourth day and the creation of humanity on the sixth day (Gen 1:14–19, 26–28). Again we seem to have the idea of a primordial church without members. Or does the author wish simply to affirm that the church was in God's mind when he created the world and that the world was in some sense created *for the sake of* the church (cf. Herm. Vis. 2.4.1)? He does not in any case appear to deify the church, for he states explicitly that she has been "created" by God.

Next, the presbyter warns that those who "do not do the will of the Lord" will fall under the condemnation of a biblical word that is both prophetic and dominical: "My house has become a lair of bandits" (2 Clem. 14.1b; cf. Jer 7:11; Mark 11:17). But whereas Jeremiah and the Lord Jesus spoke this way about the Jerusalem temple, the presbyter applies this saying to the church, or perhaps to a portion of the church. In so doing, he points to the perennial danger of the church being corrupted from within, which is a significant concern of his throughout the sermon.[44] Therefore, he exhorts his congregation to take refuge in the spiritual church: "Let us, then, choose to belong to the church of life, so that we may be saved" (2 Clem. 14.1c). This statement, in which ecclesiology and soteriology meet, suggests that his listeners have present access to the preexistent "first church," and that this church is the source (or instrument) of that "life" that leads to salvation. This is about as close to a doctrine of grace as one finds in 2 Clement, but it is not exactly realized eschatology. Perhaps it can be described as realized protology.

Turning to the church's relationship to Christ, the presbyter reminds his congregation that "the living church is the body of Christ" (2 Clem. 14.2a). In Ephesians and Colossians this metaphor has as its complement the affirmation that Christ is the "head" of the church,[45] but the author of 2 Clement has something else in mind. He quotes Genesis 1:27 in a condensed form, which facilitates an implicit literal interpretation according to which the first human was androgynous. This literal interpretation serves, in turn, as the basis for an explicit allegorical reading according to which the union of male and female principles (in the androgynous first human) signifies the primordial union of Christ and the church: "The Scripture says, 'God made the human being male and female'; the male is Christ, the female the church" (2 Clem. 14.2b). This interpretation is likely modeled on the allegorical exegesis of Genesis 2:24 in Ephesians 5:31–32, according to which the spousal union of Adam and Eve signifies the union of Christ and his church.[46] But spousal union and

43. Donfried, *Setting of Second Clement*, 154.

44. 2 Clem. 4.5; 6.9; 7.4–6; 10.5; 13.1–4; 17.5–6; 19.2.

45. Eph 1:22–23; 4:15–16; 5:23; Col 1:18; 2:19.

46. R. M. Grant and H. H. Graham, *First and Second Clement*, vol. 2 of *The Apostolic Fathers: A New Translation and Commentary*, ed. R. M. Grant (New York: Thomas Nelson, 1965), 126.

quasi-syzygy are not the same thing.[47] According to the former concept, it was through his self-offering on the cross that Christ sanctified the church and "presented her to himself" as his bride (Eph 5:25–27), whereas according to the latter concept, God "made" Christ and the church as a primordial and undifferentiated unity of male and female principles.

Next, the presbyter tersely notes that "the church is not now [νῦν, *nyn*], but from the beginning [ἄνωθεν, *anōthen*]" (2 Clem. 14.2c). He cannot, of course, mean that the church does not exist at the present time. He wishes to say, rather, that it does not belong to "this age" (6.3) and did not originate in the flux of human interactions. Despite appearances, the church is not a novelty. To say that it is "from the beginning" thus reinforces his earlier statement that it was "created before sun and moon" (14.1). His formulation recalls, and was perhaps influenced by, Paul's contrast between "the present [νῦν] Jerusalem" and "the Jerusalem above [ἄνω, *anō*]" (Gal 4:25–26).[48] The argument in Galatians, however, is concerned with a complex set of overlapping relationships—between old covenant and new covenant, Israel and the church, the "present evil age" and the "new creation" (1:4; 6:15)—and at its culmination Paul declares the faithful members of the church (who are "neither Jew nor Greek") to be "the Israel of God" (6:16; cf. 3:28).[49] The presbyter's view is less complex. He has brushed aside the Jewish people (2 Clem. 2.3) and nowhere alludes to the history of God's covenants with them, setting the stage for an elegantly simple account of the church's recent appearance in time.

He explains: "For [she] was spiritual, as [was] also our Jesus, but [he] was manifested at the end of days in order to save us. But the church, though spiritual, was manifested in the flesh of Christ" (2 Clem. 14.2b–3a).[50] Just as Christ and the church were united in a primordial spiritual quasi-syzygy, so now they have been manifested together in a single incarnation! The author does not pause to explain how this manifestation of the church played out in the events of Christ's earthly life but hastens on to the moral and spiritual implications for his listeners: "If any of us guards [the church] in the flesh and does not corrupt her, he will receive her back in the Holy Spirit. For this flesh is the antitype of the Spirit. No one, then, who corrupts the antitype will receive the original" (14.3b). Individual Christians possess the mystical presence of the church in their flesh—the same flesh in which they were called and in which they will come to judgment—and thus must "guard the flesh as the temple of God" (9.3–4). They will "receive her back" in the resurrection, unless they have corrupted her in this life (14.3b). Here the author contradicts the false doctrine of his opponents, who denied that "this flesh" would rise and be judged (9.1).

Up to this point in the sermon, the words "spirit" and "spiritual" have been used only to refer to the preincarnate state of Christ or the church (2 Clem. 9.5; 14.1–3a). Beginning with the reference to "the Holy Spirit" in 14.3b, however, the author will use the term "the (Holy) Spirit" six times in the remainder of the chapter (14.3b–5), always with reference to the eschatological reality in which the believer *will* participate. However, this eschatological Spirit is also the protological "original" (αὐθεντικόν, *authentikon*), and "this flesh"—the flesh in which the baptized believer now lives—is the "copy" (ἀντιτυπόν, *antitypon*) by which he or she already in some sense participates in the reality of the church.

---

47. The term "quasi-syzygy" reflects the present author's recognition that 2 Clem. 14.2 by no means presupposes a full-fledged theogonic-cosmogonic myth of emanations.

48. Grant and Graham, *First and Second Clement*, 126.

49. On the phrase τὸν Ἰσραὴλ τοῦ θεοῦ in Gal 6:16, see C. S. Keener, *Galatians: A Commentary* (Grand Rapids: Baker Academic, 2019), 578–82.

50. On the translation of this passage, see Lindemann, *Clemensbriefe*, 242.

Here the presbyter adds a surprising qualification: "But if we say that the flesh is the church and the Spirit is Christ, then he who has abused the flesh has abused the church. Such a one will not participate in the Spirit, which is Christ" (2 Clem. 14.4). This emphatic identification of the eschatological Spirit with Christ himself (cf. 1 Cor 15:45; 2 Cor 3:17; Herm. Sim. 9.1.1) suggests the following schematic summary. The preincarnate Christ and the "first church" are both essentially "spiritual" and form a primordial male-female quasi-syzygy. Without ceasing to be spiritual, they enter the human realm together through the incarnation, in which Christ "was manifested in order to save us" and the church "was manifested in the flesh of Christ." After his earthly life, apparently, Jesus Christ *becomes* "the Holy Spirit," in whom those Christians who have "guarded" the flesh (that is, guarded the church) will participate eschatologically. The author never informs us whether this involves a resurrection and glorification of Christ's human flesh, but he does make it quite clear that for faithful members of the church the blessed afterlife is by no means an escape from the flesh. Rather, they receive their eschatological reward precisely through the resurrection of the flesh: "This flesh is able to receive so great a life and incorruptibility when the Holy Spirit is joined to it, that one can neither express nor declare what the Lord has prepared for his chosen ones" (2 Clem. 14.5).

5.4 A Skeleton of the Divine Economy

The author of 2 Clement preserves a skeleton of the divine economy, which for all intents and purposes he reduces to three events: creation, incarnation, and final judgment. At the beginning of the first of these events, Christ (the male principle) and the church (the female principle) existed as a wholly "spiritual" quasi-syzygy. This quasi-syzygy is the primordial or "original" reality (τὸ αὐθεντικόν, *to authentikon*). Between the first event and the second event, nothing of ecclesiological significance happened apparently. Although the presbyter quotes from the Old Testament several times, he ascribes no ecclesial role or identity to the people of Israel. Indeed, the church was "barren," and the quasi-syzygy of Christ and the church remained in its spiritual state until the second event, when Christ "became flesh" and the church "was manifested in the flesh of Christ" (2 Clem. 2.1; 9.5; 14.3). Henceforth, in some unexplained way, baptized Christians have come to possess "the antitype of the Spirit" in their own flesh, which they must keep pure if they are to "take possession of the original" and "participate in the Holy Spirit" (14.3). These pregnant expressions suggest that what Christians possess in this life is both derivative of the protological reality and at the same time anticipatory of the eschatological reality, which the author here refers to as "the Holy Spirit" but elsewhere calls "the kingdom of God" (5.5; 6.9; 9.6; 12.1–6). This is so because the eschatological reality *is* the protological reality, now made available to human beings through Christ's action as "savior" and "author of imperishability" (20.5).

6. CONCLUSION

The New Testament authors, broadly speaking, understand three realities to be deeply interconnected by the historical threads of the divine economy and the action of the Holy Spirit: the people of Israel, the person and event of Jesus Christ, and the apostolic church. The Christ event is the long-awaited climax to Israel's story, the fulfillment of God's promises, and the event by which Israel has been reborn as the church—leaving the church of Jews and gentiles in an adversarial relationship with non-Christian Judaism. All the greatness and the peril of Christian theology, not least ecclesiology, is nascent in this seminal perspective.

In this regard, two broad tendencies are discernable in the texts we have examined above. The first is present in the Didache (albeit inchoately), 1 Clement, and the letters of Ignatius, all of which maintain the traditional perspective by affirming the historical particularity and deep interconnections of Israel, Christ, and church. Clement and Ignatius complement each other nicely in their respective emphases. Even today we have much to learn from the former's accent on the continuity between Israel and the church, while the latter, with his better grasp of Paul, is right to glory unapologetically in the "newness" (καινότης, *kainotēs*) of Christianity.[51] This term indicates both the qualitative superiority of the grace of Jesus Christ (as compared to the law of Moses) and the fact that it was caused by an event that occurred recently in time. Because Jesus Christ is true God and true man (Ign. *Eph.* 7.2; 20.2), the Christ event has a real locus in history, while it is also a "mystery" that transcends mere chronology (Ign. *Magn.* 9.1). The unity of the one people of God, from the patriarchs to the present, is both historical and suprahistorical (Ign. *Phld.* 9.1). The "newness of eternal life" (Ign. *Eph.* 19.3) does not therefore render Christianity a mere novelty.

The second tendency is present in 2 Clement. The author of this sermon shows little interest in the historical particularity of the life of Christ or his Israelite origins, and he reduces the divine economy to a quasi-historical schema. He cites "the prophetic word" (2 Clem. 11.2) often enough and thus must have some knowledge of Old Testament history, but he seems not to discern any real salvation-historical continuity between the people of Israel and the church. Israel's role in the divine economy is reduced, for all intents and purposes, to prophetic authorship of "the books" (14.2). However, the presbyter would not have us think that the church has come into existence only very recently, or for that matter at any point in human history (14.2). Therefore, he posits a "first church" that "was created before sun and moon" (14.1). He wishes to connect the church very closely to Christ but does not avail himself of any specific historical-theological traditions about the life of Christ or the link between the paschal mystery and the origin of the church. Instead, he posits a protological union of Christ and church (as male and female principles in a single androgynous being), a twofold incarnation (in which the church is manifest in the flesh of Christ), a soteriology according to which the believer who guards the church in the flesh "will receive her back in the Holy Spirit," and an eschatological identification of Christ and the Holy Spirit (14.1–5). There seems to be a real danger here of collapsing Christ, church, and Spirit into a single undifferentiated reality.

Aspects of this second tendency may be found in three other texts in the corpus of the Apostolic Fathers. The Shepherd of Hermas, though it has deep roots in Jewish Christianity, appears largely unconcerned with the historical particularity of either biblical Israel or Jesus of Nazareth, and some of its christological formulations do not clearly distinguish between the Son of God and the Holy Spirit.[52] The Epistle of Barnabas, though keen to find nonliteral references to Christ and the church in the Septuagint, is equally eager to dissociate the people, history, and religion of Israel from Jesus Christ and his church. The author sees salvation history as beginning with the Christ event, and he refuses to call Jesus "Son of David."[53] Most radically, the Epistle to Diognetus (Diogn. 1.1–10.8) rejects Judaism completely and contains only the faintest echoes of the Old Testament, so that

51. Ign. *Eph.* 19.2–3; 20.1; *Magn.* 9.1; 10.2; cf. Rom 6:4; 7:6; 1 Cor 5:7; 11:25; 2 Cor 3:6; 5:17; Gal 6:15; Eph 2:15; 4:24; Col 3:10.

52. C. Osiek, *Shepherd of Hermas: A Commentary*, Hermeneia (Minneapolis: Fortress, 1999), 34–36. E.g., Herm. Sim. 9.1.1.

53. F. R. Prostmeier, "The Epistle of Barnabas," in Pratscher, *Apostolic Fathers*, 37. See Barn. 12.10–11.

the author's burden is to explain why Christianity has appeared "now and not previously" (1.1).[54] Although the second tendency appeared to receive a fatal blow in the rejection of Marcionism, it has never completely disappeared from Christianity.

In most respects, however, it is the first tendency and especially the ecclesiology of Ignatius of Antioch that triumphed in the second century, and the church of Smyrna seems to have played a significant role in this regard. During his pivotal stopover in Smyrna, Ignatius met with bishops, presbyters, and deacons from four churches and composed four of his surviving seven letters. Two of the remaining three letters, which were written from Troas sometime later, were addressed to the Smyrnaeans and their bishop Polycarp. While Polycarp's one surviving letter evidences some reticence on his part to embrace certain of Ignatius's bolder ideas, we probably have Polycarp to thank for the survival and dissemination of the Ignatian corpus (Pol. *Phil.* 13.2). Over the course of his long episcopal tenure, moreover, Polycarp seems to have grown into the Ignatian vision of the monepiscopacy. In the Martyrdom of Polycarp, the Smyrnaean church honors "the most amazing Polycarp, who in our own times became an apostolic and prophetic teacher, bishop of the catholic church in Smyrna" (Mart. Pol. 16.2). Although this account was written some forty years after Ignatius's letters, it is the next earliest text to use the terms "Christianity" (10.1), "apostolic" (16.2), and "catholic church" (salut.; 8.1; 16.2; 19.2), and the next earliest unambiguous witness to the monepiscopacy. Finally, it is possible that the elderly Polycarp contributed to the influence that Ignatius's letters would have on later patristic theology by calling them to the attention of a young man named Irenaeus.[55]

BIBLIOGRAPHY

Bowe, B. E. *A Church in Crisis: Ecclesiology and Paraenesis in Clement of Rome*. HDR 23. Minneapolis: Fortress, 1988.

Daniélou, J. *From Shadows to Reality, or Sacramentum Futuri: Studies in the Biblical Typology of the Fathers*. London: Burns & Oates, 1960.

Donfried, K. P. *The Setting of Second Clement in Early Christianity*. NovTSup 38. Leiden: Brill, 1974.

Fullenbach, J. *Ecclesiastical Office and the Primacy of Rome: An Evaluation of Recent Theological Discussion of First Clement*. Washington, DC: Catholic University of America Press, 1980.

Grant, R. M., and H. H. Graham. *First and Second Clement*. Vol. 2 of *The Apostolic Fathers: A New Translation and Commentary*. Edited by R. M. Grant. New York: Nelson, 1965.

Gregory, A. F., and C. M. Tuckett. *The Reception of the New Testament in the Apostolic Fathers*. Oxford: Oxford University Press, 2005.

Lindemann, A. *Die Clemensbriefe*. HNT 17. Tübingen: Mohr Siebeck, 1992.

Moriarty, W. "1 Clement's View of Ministerial Appointments in the Early Church." *VC* 66 (2012): 115–38.

Niederwimmer, K. *The Didache: A Commentary*. Hermeneia. Minneapolis: Fortress, 1998.

Osiek, C. *Shepherd of Hermas: A Commentary*. Hermeneia. Minneapolis: Fortress, 1999.

Pratscher, W., ed. *The Apostolic Fathers: An Introduction*. Waco, TX: Baylor University Press, 2010.

Sandt, H. van de, and D. Flusser. *The Didache: Its Jewish Sources and Its Place in Early Judaism and Christianity*. CRINT III/5. Assen: Van Gorcum; Minneapolis: Fortress, 2002.

Vall, G. *Learning Christ: Ignatius of Antioch and the Mystery of Redemption*. Washington, DC: Catholic University of America Press, 2013.

Varner, W. *Second Clement: An Introductory Commentary*. AFCS. Eugene, OR: Cascade, 2020.

54. H. E. Lona, "Diognetus," in Pratscher, *Apostolic Fathers*, 203–4.

55. For an example of Ignatius's influence on Irenaeus, see Vall, *Learning Christ*, 205.

CHAPTER 16

ESCHATOLOGY IN THE APOSTOLIC FATHERS

CLAYTON N. JEFFORD

1. INTRODUCTION

While beliefs regarding human mortality, end of time, and final destiny of civilization are often traced throughout New Testament literature, the same is less true with respect to the Apostolic Fathers.[1] Inherent within this corpus is the problem of varied perspectives drawn from diverse geographical regions of the Mediterranean world (from Italy to Asia Minor to Egypt), probably derived from a broad range of years during which remote customs from mixed ethnic situations arose (from the mid-first to early-third centuries). So too, little of the literature speaks directly to a particular author's view of eschatology. When such matters arise, they are either indirectly referenced or offered in limited fashion. This has led to a range of scholarly debates with respect to aspects of each text and its authors/editors, leading to uncertain conclusions in result.

The following survey seeks to define distinct visions of eschatology at work among texts where such studies are available. The sequence of presentation reflects the likely sociohistorical origins of each source rather than any particular impact of its contribution to the topic. By design, specific characteristics of authors within their context of literary production will be identified, leading then to four basic comments about the collection as a whole. One recognizes that such perspectives echo the selected ideas of authors chosen for inclusion within the corpus—a slightly haphazard blend of writers who often had little in common historically—and ignore the views of other ecclesiastical writers who influenced primitive messianic views during the same period yet are not preserved within the collection. What remains is an assortment of approaches that arise throughout the Apostolic Fathers, surely representative of the historical period though clearly not exhaustive in scope for the times.

2. ESCHATOLOGY IN THE INDIVIDUAL WRITINGS OF THE APOSTOLIC FATHERS

2.1 Didache

Perhaps the most vexing tradition to ponder is that of the Didache.[2] Consideration of eschatology in the work is complicated by lack of evidence for the earliest form of the tradition. The most complete witness appears with the late fourth-century Apostolic

1. Three significant older exceptions appear in the studies of A. P. O'Hagan, *Material Re-Creation in the Apostolic Fathers*, TUGAL 100 (Berlin: Akademie, 1968), T. H. C. van Eijk, *La resurrection des morts chez les Pères Apostoliques*, ThH 25 (Paris: Beauchesne, 1974), and H. Lohmann, *Drohung und Verheißung*, BZNW 55 (Berlin: de Gruyter, 1989). See also T. Aono, *Die Entwicklung des paulinischen Gerichtsgedankens bei den Apostolischen Vätern*, EH 23/137 (Bern: Lang, 1979).

2. So too, Lohmann begins his own survey with the Didache (Lohmann, *Drohung und Verheißung*, 29–51).

Constitutions VII, followed by Codex Hierosolymitanus 54, internally dated to 1056 CE. Previous to this, evidence for the writing centers largely on the Two Ways teaching of chapters 1–6 and the closing chapter (ch. 16). This latter material is most intriguing since it is roughly akin to a mini-apocalypse reminiscent of Revelation in the New Testament (cf. the so-called War Scroll [1QM] of the Dead Sea Scrolls), and thus is perhaps designed to function, as does that material for the Christian canon, as a form of visionary experience of the future.

The tradition's call to be watchful for the end times (Did. 16.1) and to beware of "false prophets and corruptors" (οἱ ψευδοπροφῆται καὶ οἱ φθορεῖς, *hoi pseudoprophētai kai hoi phthoreis*, 16.3) initiates an apocalyptic cry reminiscent of the Synoptic Gospels, especially Matthew 24.[3] At the same time, images of a "world deceiver" (κοσμοπλανής, *kosmoplanēs*, 16.4) and signs of the last days foreseen in fire, opening of the heavens, trumpet blast, resurrection of the dead, and the Lord coming on the clouds with his holy ones (16.6–7) reflect imagery known elsewhere from 1 Thessalonians 3:13 and 4:16.[4] Such descriptions feel comfortable in the light of biblical visualizations generally, but stand awkwardly within the Didache, where scholars traditionally have seen limited concern for expression of eschatological views in contrast to the primary didactic and ecclesiological orientation of the work.[5]

A focus on eschatological elements within the Didache arose with the early dissertation of George Eldon Ladd, who argued such materials play a crucial role within the tradition.[6] Ladd recognized a foundational layer of such concerns beneath the ecclesiastical directives that at first glance appear to dominate the writing. For example, evidence of such thought may be seen in the ancient prayer of Didache 9.3–4 over the "broken bread" (κλάσμα, *klasma*). Here the Father is petitioned, "May you collect together your assembly/church from the ends of the earth into your kingdom" (οὕτω συναχθήτω σου ἡ ἐκκλησία ἀπὸ τῶν περάτων τῆς γῆς εἰς τὴν σὴν βασιλείαν, *houtō synachthētō sou hē ekklēsia apo tōn peratōn tēs gēs eis tēn sēn basileian*). Such sentiment undoubtedly derives from some of the earliest of messianic expectations, and from Ladd's perspective one might argue that concern for the parousia is clearly still alive within the community.[7] Dependence on Jewish apocalyptic

---

3. See esp. here J. S. Kloppenborg, "Didache 16 6–8 and Special Matthaean Tradition," *ZNW* 70 (1979): 54–67; V. Balabanski, *Eschatology in the Making*, SNTSMS 97 (Cambridge: Cambridge University Press, 1997).

4. This particular image of when "the Lord will come" (ἥξει ὁ κύριος; Did. 16.8) is particularly problematic given that its usage in 1 Thess 3:13 derives from Zech 14:5. In Zechariah the reference clearly is to the God of Israel, indicated by the phrase "Lord my God" (יהוה אלהי; LXX κύριος ὁ θεός μου), while Paul's own allusion is to "our Lord Jesus" (τοῦ κυρίου ἡμῶν Ἰησοῦ). Neither phrase is replicated exactly by the Didache, thus having engendered scholarly debate about what the Didache tradition may have meant by use of this expression: the so-called "Day of Yahweh" of Hebrew Scripture or the return of the risen Christ anticipated by much early messianic literature. It is entirely possible that the former meaning was the original intention of the tradition based on its quotation of Zechariah (which otherwise is an uncommon characteristic of the Didache), while the latter interpretation ultimately was assumed by subsequent interpreters of the tradition. The situation remains unresolved.

5. One might consider the views of Helen Rhee here, though. She finds that the eschatological orientation of the Didache, particularly with respect to 16.3–8, serves "as a warning to its Jewish Christian community to reinforce righteous living expected in this present age for the retribution at the end of time." This seems both a key element and typical motif of later patristic documents of the Apostolic Fathers. See H. Rhee, "Wealth, Poverty, and Eschatology: Pre-Constantine Christian Social Thought and the Hope for the World to Come," in *Reading Patristic Texts on Social Ethics*, ed. J. Leemans, B. J. Matz, and J. Verstraeten, CSEC (Washington, DC: Catholic University of America Press, 2011), 66–67.

6. G. E. Ladd, "The Eschatology of the Didache" (PhD diss., Harvard University, 1949).

7. Though as Lohmann (*Drohung und Verheißung*, 2–3) correctly notes, Ladd waves away any particularly systematic reconstruction of how such tendencies work within the tradition, focusing primarily on eschatology as a special concern of the editor.

traditions seems especially evident in the contours of the Didache, even those ostensibly prefigured in the works of the apostle Paul (compare the Thessalonian correspondence).[8]

Even more recently, the pivotal study of Shawn Wilhite investigates this likelihood further, tracing basic connections between Two Ways traditions and end-time concerns within Hellenistic and Jewish sources.[9] Wilhite suggests within a Mediterranean context that teachings in Didache tradition reflect basic assumptions about eschatological awareness and communal orientation that came to form the core of the work's evolution. Though views such as these push against certain customary approaches to Didache tradition, much here suggests that the writing's attempts to "organize" the structure of liturgical practices serves as bedrock for ideological assumptions that incorporate an eschatological view of the world.

The perspective of Wilhite is broadly supported elsewhere by Marcello Del Verme, who again links eschatology with ethics as essential to the nature of the work.[10] Del Verme assesses chapter 16 to be properly an apocalypse reflective of a "specific worldview" readily defined as eschatological in scope. He warns that such materials should not be considered in isolation—as too often they are—but must be viewed as intrinsically "ideological" with respect to a unique religious movement within late Judaism. His identification of a restricted Enochic-Essene tradition here remains a matter of debate,[11] but broad concerns for a messianic, apocalyptic drive behind the Didache support Wilhite's own views fittingly. For Del Verme, the tradition echoes customs adapted for use in the ancient Syrian church.

Here then is where the ancient practice of the Didache is vital. For certain, the tradition likely arose within a Matthean context, and thus suggests sensitivity to that Gospel's eschatological assumptions. To that end, the author may simply *accept* the views of the Evangelist without any compunction to repeat the Gospel's own materials. If chapter 16 is from a later hand, however, this may reflect a secondary attempt to establish the work's "catechetical" and "conserving" foci within what ultimately was recrafted into an accent on the end times, indicative of an epoch (whose context is now lost) during which the materials were added. The customary view, which imagines a practical application of apocalyptic ideas within an early Christian community, is favored by scholars in one form or another to date. But a revisionist view that argues the addition of eschatological elements in order to reenvisage the context of nascent Christianity within the text (one thinks of the Pastorals, for instance) deserves further consideration.

Either way, without specific focus on chapter 16, the Didache presents itself as practical teaching that favors ethical living as the essential core of a Christian "way" of instruction.[12] While eschatological fragments are scattered throughout, it is difficult to determine the extent to which specific passages rely on earlier sources without further insight

8. See also J. A. Draper, "The Two Ways and Eschatological Hope: A Contested Terrain in Galatians 5 and the *Didache*," *Neot* 45 (2020): 221–51.

9. S. J. Wilhite, *"One of Life and One of Death": Apocalypticism and the Didache's Two Ways*, Gorgias Studies in Early Christianity and Patristics 70 (Piscataway, NJ: Gorgias, 2019). Wilhite's dissertation research, published here, is from The Southern Baptist Theological Seminary in Louisville, KY (2017).

10. See M. Del Verme, *Didache and Judaism* (London: T&T Clark, 2004), 221–62.

11. Del Verme (*Didache and Judaism*, 261) sees the category of "Enochism" as his historical locus.

12. This so-called "eschatology-ethic" link is clearly prevalent in the Didache and remains a constant throughout most of the Apostolic Fathers. See A. Agnoletto, "Motivi etico-escatologici nella Didaché," in *Convivium Dominicum* (Catania: Università di Catania, 1959), 259–76. Contrary to the conclusions both of Agnoletto and Del Verme, though, this does *not* mean its presence in this particular tradition is necessarily ancient, given the broad influence of eschatological thought and apocalyptic language throughout early patristic literature.

into editorial purpose. One questions whether editorial consciousness at work portrays early messianic orientation as defined by a specific community or, instead, later attempts to reconstruct primitive beliefs through the agency of an eschatological framework. Any consideration of the writing as a reflection of primeval eschatology assumes chapter 16 to be original to the tradition, an argument with roots in research of late nineteenth-century scholarship.[13] One might imagine, however, that the link of these closing materials to the remainder of the work actually is secondary to the tradition, an addition of the late second to third centuries.[14] If so, the eschatological orientation of the tradition may be superfluous to how one understands the roots of messianic tradition preserved in the Didache. In this latter instance, without data on the tradition's secondary reorientation, no firm footing exists to identify the aim of the tradition's "reappropriation" within early patristic literature, leaving any views of the eschatological nature of the Didache tenuous.[15]

2.2 Epistle of Barnabas

How one understands the eschatological vision in Barnabas is partly dependent on what decision is made about the circumstances of the writing's composition. On the surface, the tractate (or more likely homily) is a refutation of contemporary readings of Jewish history as a foil to explicit messianic views of the ancient world. Yet specific details of this setting remain a debate among scholars. Thus, one might envisage the author's fear of a late first-century Jewish reawakening, during which the Jerusalem temple would be rebuilt and thus stifle development of the Christian movement. This is the traditional scholarly perspective.[16] Otherwise, the exact opposite situation may be at work whereby the text is later (during the Bar Kokhba revolt) when Hadrian proposed to build a temple to Jupiter in Jerusalem to crush Jewish hopes for holy renaissance.[17] Evidence from the homily may be applied to either view, with implications that differ in nuance for the issues involved.

One may begin with the issue of whether the author (or subsequent editors) of the tractate relied on a particular source for the work's basic eschatological perspective. The answer remains unclear. Robert Kraft proposed that just such a foundation may lie behind both Barnabas 4 and its parallel in Didache 16, passages that include a call for watchfulness, a quest for salvation, warnings against lawlessness and error/deceit, the victory of the risen Christ, signs in heaven, and coming of a world deceiver. The source-critical question at work is too complex to explore here, but undoubtedly both Barnabas and the Didache share some eschatological trajectory.[18] Kraft acknowledges, "Pseudo-Barnabas knew such

13. The singular exception here might be the brief Latin form of the tradition preserved in the third century (?) *De doctrina apostolorum*, a rendering of the Two Ways tradition without chapter 16.

14. Lohmann ultimately finds the eschatology of the Didache to be concentrated in three main ways: 1) rule of God as focus of hope and prayer (8.2; 9.4; 10.5–6); 2) retribution of the last judgment as a directive for ethics; and 3) end-time events as the foundation of instruction and motivation for community assembly. He sees no chiliasm in this process, but more of a community-oriented movement at work (Lohmann, *Drohung und Verheißung*, 50–51). His conclusions are solid, in my opinion, though this three-pronged orientation within ecclesiastical tradition may be seen either as early or later in the evolution of the tradition. Perhaps one might believe it to be both.

15. For further consideration, see J. A. Draper, "Eschatology in the Didache," in *Eschatology of the New Testament and Some Related Documents*, ed. J. G. van der Watt, WUNT 2/315 (Tübingen: Mohr Siebeck, 2011), 567–82.

16. See the considerations of J. Carleton Paget, *The Epistle of Barnabas*, WUNT 2/64 (Tübingen: Mohr Siebeck, 1994).

17. This more recent, intriguing view is argued by J. N. Rhodes, *The Epistle of Barnabas and the Deuteronomic Tradition*, WUNT 2/188 (Tübingen: Mohr Siebeck, 2004).

18. For detailed analysis of proposed sources and authorial redaction in this chapter, see Aono, *Entwicklung*, 218–22, and Lohmann, *Drohung und Verheißung*, 204–12.

apocalyptic material—and much more—but he has admittedly refrained from dealing with 'things future' as such (17:2). But he cannot hide the widespread influence that the apocalyptic has had on his tradition."[19] Indeed, orientation toward concerns for the future dominates the author's foundational teachings about salvation history. Yet it is an anxiety rooted in Jewish prophecy. By way of illustration, in the midst of the homily's warning the author breaks from parallels to the Didache with quotations taken from Daniel 7:24 and 7:7–8, the prediction of the ten kingdoms to arise and the powerful fourth beast that will subdue the earth (Barn. 4.4–5). Foreboding for the future is at work, yet a sense of urgency integral to the passage also speaks to worries for the present. Prophetic warnings are not introduced simply as academic fare but as immediately relevant elements in the lives of the hearers. In this sense, Barnabas depicts a future orientation whose goal is to motivate believers within their circumstances. Its aims are not to speak to events to come but to how listeners recognize implications for the present.

This focus on a source of teachings raises the question of when the tradition may have circulated, as well as the extent to which the author of Barnabas (and the Didache) may have employed it. Such a source could be among the oldest materials in use, though this need not mean it was necessarily incorporated into Barnabas at its beginning. Instead, the focus on future events reflected in chapter 4 may derive from any of numerous similar usages among early Christian literature. The matter simply remains unknown. Indeed, as James Rhodes suggests, if such a source was applied as late as the reign of Hadrian, it would offer a specific chronological moment in which one might see how concerns for future events were at play within the evolution of the second-century ecclesiastical context.[20]

Regardless of whether Barnabas has drawn this orientation from some specific source, James Carleton Paget properly notes that the author as a rule has a "penchant for eschatological modes of thinking," seen in concerns for the age to come (Barn. 2.1; 4.1, 3, 9; 16.5), the call to walk carefully in faith (19.6; 21.7b), the need to anticipate "the immanent holy age" (8.6; 10.11b; 21.1, 3), the Lord's forthcoming judgment (4.12; 5.7; 7.2; 15.5), and concern to prepare for a "day of recompense" (11.8; 19.10–11; 20.1).[21] Such a broad array of traits defines the homily as driven by images of the imminent day of the Lord, at least in its explicit presentation. Yet whether this speaks to a specific location remains undefined. Hence, Pierre Prigent sees such an orientation as a marker that defies Alexandrian origins for the text.[22] But wide-ranging eschatological concerns at work here can scarcely be applied to any specific region within early Christian development. As readily argued from the literature, such trends populated the ancient Mediterranean world.

---

19. R. A. Kraft, *Barnabas and the Didache*, vol. 3 of *The Apostolic Fathers: A New Translation and Commentary*, ed. R. M. Grant (New York: Thomas Nelson, 1965), 14 (more generally, pp. 7–16). This connection is particularly intriguing given that Barnabas features Two Ways materials in 18–20 in parallel to Didache 1–5, but does not otherwise conclude the writing as does Didache 16 with these same apocalyptic passages. The appearance of the "lawless one" is widespread in the thought of the author (see 4.9; 15.5; 18.2; cf. 2 Clem. 6.4).

20. Rhodes, *Epistle of Barnabas*, 71–87, which features his discussion of the Jerusalem temple in ch. 16.

21. Carleton Paget, *Epistle of Barnabas*, 33. Carleton Paget is highly dependent here on two secondary observations. The first derives from A. Hermanns, "Le Pseudo-Barnabé: Est-il millénariste?," *ETL* 35 (1959): 848–76. Hermanns identifies "the sabbath" in the mind of the author with the "eighth day of the new world," so that the new millennium will become God's eighth day of creation. To this end, Hermanns does not see the text as chiliastic in scope, since the new era will be a completely new creation, but this remains unclear (see too J. W. Mealy, *After the Thousand Years*, JSNTSup 70 [Sheffield: Sheffield Academic, 1992], 48n2). The second perspective is that of Chester, who identifies a variety of broader eschatological elements at work within the writing. See A. Chester, "The Parting of the Ways: Eschatology and Messianic Hope," in *Jews and Christians*, ed. J. D. G. Dunn, WUNT 66 (Tübingen: Mohr Siebeck, 1992), 239–313.

22. P. Prigent, *Épître de Barnabé*, SC 172 (Paris: du Cerf, 1971), 20–22.

As a second point of reference, the author's "penchant" for future alarms is admirably illustrated in the so-called scapegoat passage of chapter 7 in which the text taps into rabbinic interpretations of Leviticus 16 as a means to unite the two goats of the ancient Jewish atonement ritual with the figure of Christ.[23] These goats—attractive and well-matched (καλοὺς καὶ ὁμοίους, *kalous kai homoious*, Barn. 7.6)—represent a dual image of Christ, who suffered the passion of the Gospels, on the one hand, and yet is to be made visible at his return upon the clouds, on the other.[24] Carleton Paget indicates correctly that such a messianic twist finds parallel in the contemporary visions of Justin Martyr (*Dial.* 40.4–5) and Tertullian (*Marc.* 3.7–8), which suggests that this line of exegetical interpretation—understood within the light of rabbinic tradition—reflects pervasive use of scriptural sources as a foundation for early Christian eschatological views. This should not be a surprise given the author's use of the book of Daniel in Barnabas 4. Yet the ready witness of such parallels adds evidence to support that Barnabas stems from a slightly later provenance than scholars often assume.

Perhaps the most obvious illustration of eschatological awareness in Barnabas is detected in the author's discussion of the seven days of creation and their seeming anticipation of the end times.[25] A form of millenarian thought likely is at work as the six days are accepted to be the six thousand years of history (Barn. 15.4) followed by the seventh day in which God rested from the labors of creation. But the author is confusing in this regard, since the ultimate claim to be made is that it is not the seventh day (= the Sabbath) that should be celebrated as an anticipation of the end-times (such as has been observed by Jewish tradition), but a new eighth day (or Sunday) "that will initiate another new world" (ὅ ἐστιν ἄλλου κόσμου ἀρχήν, *ho estin allou kosmou archēn*, 15.8). Thus, Christians celebrate this new day, the eighth of creation, as that when Jesus was raised from the dead and ascended into the heavens. Indeed, the prophet Isaiah is invoked in this effort for his preservation of God's comment that "I cannot stand your new moons and sabbaths" (Isa 1:13), a clear condemnation of the Jewish festival system, at least as the author sees the situation. In this regard Barnabas does not offer faultless logic for this depiction of an eighth day in distinction from the seventh day of rest depicted by the creation account of Genesis. Yet there is no doubt that for the author what is celebrated as ritual worship by Jews focuses on a defective understanding of history and Scripture. It is, instead, toward a true messianic vision that believers must turn for elucidation of how God has endeavored to work within the creation and consummation of the world.

In the final analysis, Barnabas gives clear indication of a millenarian perspective with its orientation toward future eschatology and apocalyptic awareness. At the same time, however, there are implications for the present within the author's vision, seen especially in a tendency to assume an "'appropriation' of the Jewish hope in the repossession of the land."[26] Whether this acquisition of a promised land is material in form or spiritual only is unclear,[27] but in either case the ultimate focus is concern for the future of Christian existence. In this respect, the believing community is a "new creation" conceived within the borders of

23. Lohmann (*Drohung und Verheißung*, 220–24) sees this chapter as a key to the author's perspective to the extent that "the way into the kingdom of Christ is necessarily connected to distress and suffering" (224).

24. See Carleton Paget, *Epistle of Barnabas*, 136–40.

25. See here especially O'Hagan, *Material Re-Creation*, 44–67; generally, see W. Rordorf, *Sunday*, trans. A. A. K. Graham (London: SCM, 1968).

26. See Barnabas 6 for this theme. Carleton Paget, *Epistle of Barnabas*, 134n159.

27. See here O'Hagan, *Material Re-Creation*, 45–50.

the end-times at work within the present.[28] The author's vision is preoccupied with a reorientation of salvation history from an exclusively Jewish theology to a messianic slant. The impetus for this transition resides in the witness of the crucified Christ and his anticipated return, but also by necessity in a disavowal of Jewish ritual and liturgical worship. Here the homily borrows from Jewish Scripture and rabbinic speculation, and in due course its eschatological pedigree resides within a framework of futuristic visions that derive from Jewish foundations.[29]

To be sure, no uniform system of perspective may be reconstructed from the various eschatological statements scattered throughout the work, though comments about the final end of the world clearly indicate an apocalyptic eschatology. As Lohmann indicates, this should not be seen in the narrow sense of a particular vision but as the reflection of a more broadly held tradition.[30]

2.3 First Clement

Though this is recognized as one of the more prominent texts of the Apostolic Fathers, on the surface one might think there is little in 1 Clement to suggest anything of exceptional value with respect to eschatology as envisaged by the early church in Rome who served as its author. The letter leans toward matters of formal organization and unity, albeit formulated within dimensions of a cosmic framework defined by Hellenistic (specifically Stoic) elements as the background for how one might recognize Roman views of ecclesiology.[31] This conclusion seems warranted from a quick review of Horacio Lona's massive 1998 commentary, in which during almost seven hundred pages little focus on eschatology arises as an essential aspect of Christian faith either on behalf of the author (Rome) or the immediate audience (Corinth).[32]

Yet all this having been said, there is good reason to imagine that the author's Hellenistic orientation about cosmic categories related to the "church" (ἐκκλησία, *ekklēsia*) exposes a form of realized eschatology throughout the author's thought.[33] One imagines

28. B. E. Daley, *The Hope of the Early Church* (Cambridge: Cambridge University Press, 1991), 11.

29. Thus the conclusion of Lohmann, *Drohung und Verheißung*, 201–2, in agreement with van Eijk and Aono.

30. Lohmann, *Drohung und Verheißung*, 243. As for the concept of a vision, Aono is convinced that the details, terminology, and general movement of this perspective reflect similar tendencies found in the apostle Paul's letters (*Entwicklung*, 292–97). Daley (*Hope of the Early Church*, 11) does not necessarily see Christian chiliasm at work here, but observes this to be "the first usage by a Christian writer of the traditional pagan conception of history as a 'week' of ages," which might argue for a blend of traditional Jewish elements (via Paul) and Hellenistic tendencies. In this respect, it is perhaps all the more curious then that C. E. Hill (*Regnum Caelorum: Patterns of Millennial Thought in Early Christianity*, 2nd ed. [Grand Rapids: Eerdmans, 2001]) does not treat Barnabas in his review of chiliasm within the Apostolic Fathers.

31. On this perspective, consider again O'Hagan, *Material Re-Creation*, 94–103. O'Hagan argues "the basic scheme to which Clement clings is the Jewish one in which the day of the Lord is the hinge upon which the door of history finally shuts" (94). In support, he offers five elements that typify Jewish influence here: interim state for the righteous dead; resurrection of the body; coming kingdom; final act of human history set out as the judgment to come; and the notion of the promise (see Abraham as "friend" in ch. 10). O'Hagan concludes, "The judgement to come lies at the very centre of Clement's conception of the last things" (103). This analysis may be correct, but it is exceedingly complex given the subtle nature of the writing.

32. See H. E. Lona, *Der erste Clemensbrief*, KAV 2 (Göttingen: Vandenhoeck & Ruprecht, 1998). Admittedly, Lona does give a brief excursus on the topic of eschatology (especially as related to ch. 23), in which he reviews the earlier position of O. Knoch (*Eigenart und Bedeutung der Eschatologie im theologischen Aufriss des ersten Clemensbriefes*, Theophaneia 17 [Bonn: Hanstein, 1964]) generally. He is convinced that Knoch has made the issue something more than the materials might support and, as he says, "assigns a meaning to the text, that when closely considered, is not supportive" (294–97; quotation on 297). In contrast to this view, see the detailed (if brief) discussion of Hill, *Regnum Caelorum*, 78–84.

33. In this respect, see Knoch, *Eigenart und Bedeutung*. In support of Knoch's thesis is B. Weiss, "Amt und

this in 1 Clement 21, for example, where the Corinthians are told, "Let us be ashamed" (ἐντραπῶμεν, *entrapōmen*) before Christ so as to honor leaders and old men, instruct youth with awe for God, guide women in moderation, and teach children through Christ to receive holiness "in pure thought" (ἐν καθαρᾷ διανοίᾳ, 1 Clem. 21.6–8). Indeed, while righteous people suffer many problems, the Lord will deliver them in due time. As for sinners, the author turns toward Jewish sources, specifically Psalm 32:10 (31:10 LXX): "Sinners have many troubles, but mercy encircles those who hope on the Lord" (1 Clem. 22.8). Something of a realized perspective clearly is at work here, providing a framework by which the teachings of Christ may be envisaged as fulfilled in the present, portrayed here quite explicitly in the moral direction that guides the actions of the community of faith.[34]

At the same time, however, there is a distinctly future orientation to such concerns, clearly demonstrated in 1 Clement 34, whereby the author calls for gathering in harmony in order to share in the Lord's "great and wonderful promises" (1 Clem. 34.7). A conclusion to this observation appears with yet another quotation of Isaiah 64:4 (64:3 LXX), offered in the light of Paul's own citation in 1 Corinthians 2:9, which notes, "Eye has not seen and ear has not heard . . . what [the Lord] has prepared for those who are patient" (1 Clem. 34.8).[35] As Clare Rothschild observes in this case, though the purpose of "enduring for the sake of an eschatological reward is the same in both letters," a preference for future recompense appears to direct the mind of 1 Clement rather than that of "present incentive."[36] Thus, while 1 Clement knows the apostle's sway on the church at Corinth, as well as the very epistle of 1 Corinthians itself, it does not mean the author writes as a slave to Paul's perspective. Instead, Psalms is reinterpreted as a keystone of the argument without intrusion by the apostle's own interpretation. In the final analysis, 1 Clement appears to entertain both future objectives and present practicalities at work within the experience of the church as it shares with the Spirit of Christ in its daily living.[37] There is a clear transition in perspective reflective of how the nascent origins of messianic faith evolved into the second-century "church." To this end, one might agree with Berdo Weiss that, while 1 Clement certainly falls within a Pauline school of thought, the nature of eschatology for the early church was in decline and in some sense reoriented through its formation of ecclesiology.[38]

One final passage is worth consideration here, and that is the famous allusion to the rising phoenix of Arabia preserved in 1 Clement 25. This striking image is the denouement of a section that seeks to illustrate the future resurrection of believers as foreshadowed by Christ himself having been raised from the tomb. Two examples of "resurrection" (ἀνάστασις, *anastasis*) are provided in chapter 24—rising of the sun, growth of sown seeds—which serve as precursors for the phoenix image that follows. The crux lies in chapter 26: if God as creator has offered both common imagery (sun/moon, rising seeds) and fantastic mythic history (phoenix), then surely the promise of future resurrection must be

Eschatologie im 1. Clemensbrief," *TP* 50 (1975): 70–83.

34. Lohmann (*Drohung und Verheißung*, 63–64) sees this as well in 5.4, 7; 7.6–7; and 9.1 as the question relates to the martyrdoms of Peter and Paul, the need for repentance and atonement during the times of Noah and Jonah, and the righteousness of Enoch.

35. See the discussion of this same usage in 2 Clem. 11.7 given in sec. 2.7 below.

36. C. K. Rothschild, *New Essays on the Apostolic Fathers*, WUNT 375 (Tübingen: Mohr Siebeck, 2017), 49. Rothschild characterizes this orientation as a reflection of "second century circumstances," which may be true but is by no means a definitive rationale by which to date the context of 1 Clement.

37. For more on Clement's view of heaven, Christology, and assurances of salvation, see Aono, *Entwicklung*, 87–101.

38. Weiss, "Amt und Eschatologie," 81–83.

respected. In support (as seen above), the reader is directed toward Scripture with allusions to Psalm 3:5 (3:6 LXX, "you will raise me up," 1 Clem. 26.2) and Job 19:26 ("you will raise my flesh," 1 Clem. 26.3). With respect to eschatology, once more one detects an implicit dependence on promises for the future as motivators for moral living. Yet here the imagery included is, on the one hand, common and, on the other, extraordinary—typical of daily life and unique to fictional fable. There is no doubt that the author looks toward the future yet in unison sees the power of that promise at work in the lives of the faithful (= institution of the church) in the present.[39]

In the final analysis, Lohmann identifies three themes worth attention here: promise of the resurrection, anticipation of the parousia, and severe torment of retribution. As he states, "Thoughts of otherworldly places, interpretation of the immanent God as omniscient, and singular aspects of a doctrine of retribution characterize the eschatology of 1 Clement as distinctly Hellenistic. Apocalypticism is only partially available."[40] Though 1 Clement clearly derives from specific Jewish contexts and an institutional consciousness of tradition, any apocalyptic considerations in this process actually have been abandoned in favor of an emergent ecclesiology that values promises of eternal rewards for righteous lifestyle. This may have been the general movement of early Christianity at the turn of the century. Yet, as Weiss notes, there may be a specific rationale for its presence in this instance. Rome's focus on cosmic eschatology may be in reaction to revolt in Corinth that, insisting on the present alone without respect for the eternal divine plan, inexorably risked the status of presbyters and any hierarchy of order.[41] Such a specific event may thus have been the catalyst for the church's movement from Jewish apocalyptic concerns to more Greek principles of history.[42] One can hardly doubt this reflects the face of an emergent church whose eschatological foundation eventually turned from the former orientation to the latter perspective.

2.4 Ignatius of Antioch

Any conclusions drawn from the letters of Ignatius about his views on eschatology must be tempered with the recognition that what remains from him was written during forced passage to Rome. Under such conditions one might expect comments that otherwise he

---

39. Lohmann (*Drohung und Verheißung*, 70) correctly sees this as part of an even larger structure based on the theme of resurrection, thus: 1 Clem. 24.1–2 = future resurrection at an appointed time; 24.3 = first evidence from nature (day and night); 24.4–5 = second evidence from nature (seeds and fruit); 25.1–5 = third evidence from nature (the phoenix); 26.1–3 = support of Scripture; 27.2–7 = guarantee of divine promises based on God's omnipotence; and 28.1 = ethical response based on divine proximity.

40. Lohmann, *Drohung und Verheißung*, 85–87 (quotation on 87).

41. Weiss, "Amt und Eschatologie," 81–83 (in agreement is Aono, *Entwicklung*, 101: "In order to properly understand the theology and special tone of Clement, one ultimately must confront the problem of Clement's opponents before achieving a final decision"). Weiss does not think the opponents in Corinth were aware of this connection.

42. Weiss ("Amt und Eschatologie," 83) observes the specific concern of Rome not to relapse back into Jewish thought here. Weiss somewhat reflects the views of Knoch (*Eigenart und Bedeutung*, 448), who finds that the Christian situation of 1 Clement represents a synthesis of exploited Hellenistic synagogue tradition, reflections of cosmic theology, and Hellenistic ethics according to the place, time, and circumstances of the situation. One questions whether this does not ultimately become true of the second-century church in general. By way of tangential comment, see also O'Hagan (*Material Re-Creation*, 103), who concludes that, although a certain Jewish "land" tradition may be at work in the background, the orientation of 1 Clement "shares in the theory of world ages and would seem to regard the final judgement not merely as a moral, but also as a cosmic punishment and purification." Such perspective clearly pushes the Roman situation beyond its likely original Jewish roots.

may not have expressed during his normal pastoral activity.[43] Still, such stresses also reveal the unique essence of his theological perspective and orientation.

Though there is limited context to offer insight into the bishop's views, key comments from his letters are illustrative.[44] William Schoedel identifies these texts as "beginning and end" thought, seen in remarks at Ignatius, *To the Ephesians* 14.1–2, *To the Magnesians* 6.1 and 13.1, and *To the Romans* 1–2.[45] Here is Ignatius in reflection on the bonds between faith and love related to the totality of Christian lifestyle, principally found in two strands of thought related both to the community and his own personal situation.

In his letter to Ephesus, the bishop expounds on qualities that serve as natural parameters for daily existence by those who wish to live an honorable life in Christ. As he observes in 14.1–2, perfected faith and love in Jesus Christ

> are the beginning and end of life. The beginning is faith; the end is love. The two existing as one are God. . . . [As] the tree is recognized by its fruit, thus those proclaiming to be in Christ are known through their activities. For the issue [ἔργον, *ergon*] is not what is asserted now, but being found in the power of faith at the end. (Ign. *Eph.* 14.1–2)

Evidently Ignatius relies less on imagery of end-time speculation in this declaration than on the practical application of realized eschatology as summary of a faith-filled life. This is striking as he is taken to his presumptive death in Rome, circumstances under which one expects the bishop to turn toward apocalyptic imagery at the end.[46] Instead, the Ignatian focus reflects a practical orientation with respect to the inner life of faith, similar in many respects to what appears in the perspectives of the Didache and Diognetus (see sec. 2.10 below). In a true Pauline sense, what is important about life in Christ for Ignatius is to imitate the divine order of the world in general. His eschatology finds its roots and blossom in the guise of total faith.

At the same time, Ignatius recognizes that Jesus Christ as "the new man" (τὸν καινὸν ἄνθρωπον, *ton kainon anthrōpon*) ushers in the final eschatological age through his presence (Ign. *Eph.* 20.1). Therefore, in a Pauline sense, those who are seen as the "body of Christ" (σῶμα Χριστοῦ, *sōma Christou*) necessarily become a part of that age.

> The last days are now. Thus we must be deferential; we must be in trepidation about God's patience so that it not condemn us. Either we fear the wrath to come or love the grace that is here now: one or the other. (Ign. *Eph.* 11.1)

Faith leads to avoidance of the "wrath to come"; participation in Christ's death means to

43. As Lohmann (*Drohung und Verheißung*, 135) observes, the situation of the letters is "extremely complicated" (*höchst kompliziert*).

44. One might consider further the works of E. Fudge, "The Eschatology of Ignatius of Antioch: Christocentric and Historical," *JETS* 15 (1972): 231–37; O'Hagan, *Material Re-Creation*, 104–8; Hill, *Regnum Caelorum*, 84–90.

45. W. R. Schoedel, *Ignatius of Antioch*, Hermeneia (Philadelphia: Fortress, 1985), 28. Though of less importance in this instance, the status of the letter to Rome is now in question, with its origins perhaps to be derived from a later pseudo-Ignatian setting. See C. R. Moss, "Riddle Wrapped in an Enigma: Pauline Reception in the Antiochene Acts of Ignatius," in *Intertextuality in the Second Century*, ed. D. J. Bingham and C. N. Jefford, BAC 11 (Leiden: Brill, 2016), 87–97.

46. While Schoedel rejects any presumption about "mythological prototypes" in this regard, the background for such speculation is certainly present. Consider H. Paulsen, *Studien zur Theologie des Ignatius von Antiochien*, Forschungen zur Kirchen- und Dogmengeschichte 29 (Göttingen: Vandenhoeck & Ruprecht, 1978), 93n91.

escape the future death of eternity (Ign. *Pol.* 3.2).[47] In this respect, Ignatius finds Christian faith to be a reality lived in anticipation of the future. Though the reality of evil leads to constant struggle, the divine promise is ultimate.[48]

Supplementary to this sentimentality is what Ignatius offers to the Magnesians as he writes concerning the role and function of ecclesial offices within each community. In *To the Magnesians* 6.1, for example, he observes that deacons reflect the "service of Jesus Christ, who before the ages was with the Father and appeared at the end." This vision of an eternal Christ—he who existed before time and later appears at the conclusion of all things—offers a pattern familiar among Christian authors of the second century.[49] As a source consideration, Ignatius likely reflects wording from 1 Peter ("while having been foreknown before the foundation of the world, he has been revealed in the end times through you," 1 Pet 1:20). A similar perspective appears in Hebrews.[50]

Ultimately this vision assumes ecclesiastical language as recognition of Christ's presence at the center of time, the Son sent from the Father who thereby returned to be seated in glory, an understanding that may be prefigured in Ignatius's comments in *To the Magnesians* 7.2 ("who came from one Father, both being with and returning to the One"). The scriptural origins of this concept are readily traced to Pauline and Johannine literature. Thus, it is not surprising that reflections of the theme arise repeatedly throughout Ignatian thought, since both the traditions and imagery of Paul and the Fourth Gospel are often utilized by the bishop within his writings. His vision of the end-times seems modestly patterned on those earlier perspectives.

Most important is the way in which Ignatius attaches the sentiment of "love and faith" expressed in *To the Ephesians* 14.1–2 with the bracketing of history from *To the Magnesians* 6.1 in his later expression at *To the Magnesians* 13.1. Here he anticipates, in reflection of the Lord's teaching and apostolic tradition, that the Magnesians will "prosper in all ways, by flesh and spirit, *in faith and love*, in the Son and Father and in the Spirit, *in the beginning and at the end*" together with the bishops, presbyters, and deacons. Indeed, the very gathering of the "eschatological assembly of the chosen people" marks the advent of the messianic age. Central to such assemblies is the breaking of bread by the community, an acceptance of the "medicine of immortality" (φάρμακον ἀθανασίας, *pharmakon athanasias*) by those who share in the death of Christ.[51] As the bishop observes, gathering in faith beyond hereditary religious customs means there is no reason to associate with practitioners of Judaism or to live as a Jew. "It is futile to speak of Jesus Christ yet live as a Jew" (Ign. *Magn.* 10.3). For those who do so, the power of the former age is still at work—and they are doomed to destruction along with it.[52]

---

47. Jesus Christ is the "ultimate goal" for Ignatius and the rationale for anticipated martyrdom. Lohmann (*Drohung und Verheißung*, 174–75) correctly observes that this element stands as central to the bishop's eschatology.

48. Fudge, "Eschatology," 235–36.

49. See, e.g., Herm. Sim. 9.12.2–3; Irenaeus, *Haer.* 1.10.3. Schoedel (*Ignatius*, 114nn10–11) observes that this line of thought continued in "credal contexts," even when later applied to images of Christ's parousia.

50. Fudge ("Eschatology," 233) refers to this as "a doctrine of foreordination: what happens to and for God's people is according to His will and known in advance by God." See especially Ign. *Eph.* salut.; Ign. *Rom.* salut., Ign. *Pol.* 2.3; 8.1. As he observes, "God's ordained will is particularly carried out in Jesus Christ" (so Ign. *Eph.* 20.1; *Phld.* 5.2).

51. Ign. *Eph.* 20.2. See Daley, *Hope of the Early Church*, 12–13.

52. O'Hagan, *Material Re-Creation*, 106–7. Hill (*Regnum Caelorum*, 85) correctly observes that Ignatius rarely uses the commonly employed phrase "kingdom of God" in his letters (only at Ign. *Eph.* 16.1; *Phld.* 3.3), by which he derives that the bishop tends to think less about the community "inheritance" of such an age and more about his own acquisition of that reality. Lohmann (*Drohung und Verheißung*, 144–67) more exactingly sees

Thus is seen the Ignatian insistence that Christian lifestyles, defined by faith and love, reflect in some practical and existential sense the reality of Christ's eternal role from the beginning of time and salvific function within the church during the present day. In a genuine reflection of the Pauline insistence that believers are in effect the "body of Christ," Ignatius likewise accepts the eschatological premise that the manifestation of the eternal Christ is inherent in the temporal functions of those who act in the divine Spirit. In a word, the Ignatian vision clearly accepts a "realized" capacity with respect to his theological understanding that God's anticipated kingdom is immanent in its display in history. In many ways one might see Hellenistic overtones to the cosmic perspective of Ignatian thought here, though O'Hagan cautions that the bishop "cannot be viewed as a complete break-away from the Jewish tradition in which eschatological re-creation of material things had a part."[53] The streams of spiritual imagery versus material considerations are basically indistinguishable within these letters. Undoubtedly both serve their role for the bishop.

2.5 Polycarp, *To the Philippians*

In many respects the bishop of Smyrna's concerns for love and faith closely mirror those of Ignatius, though the eschatological framework of "beginning and end" speculation first identified by Schoedel as the context for those themes is less evident. Instead, Polycarp focuses more on "righteousness" as the ultimate goal of personal faith.[54] According to the issues his letter to the Philippians addresses, this is principally expressed in unity that believing communities must maintain. In this respect the trait of endurance serves as critical for what the bishop meant in his understanding of a person of faith.

What is particularly important about endurance is its orientation toward eschatological consciousness presumably inherent in the thought processes of Polycarp. The question that arises in result is the extent to which the bishop envisaged "the eschaton as having already entered into history in Christ,"[55] versus his expectation that eschatological reward was exclusively future in some ultimate sense. In various ways the former view seems evident in the joy that Polycarp finds in the manifestation of the "Lord Jesus Christ" within the Philippian community (Pol. *Phil.* 1.1.), an observation argued by Annegreth Bovon-Thurneysen.[56] Bovon-Thurneysen acknowledges that even a quick examination of this short letter indicates a clear eschatological consciousness for which evidence appears at numerous junctures. At 2.1, for example, the bishop recalls the cosmic enthronement of

---

the fate of the community as a stream of expectation that stands apart from Ignatius's own hopes for personal reward.

53. O'Hagan, *Material Re-Creation*, 108. This observation raises the question of whether Ignatius thinks of an ultimate "resurrection of the flesh" as he writes. O'Hagan offers uncertainty on this question (pp. 107–8), citing Ign. *Trall.* 9.2, *Smyrn.* 2, *Eph.* 11.2, and *Pol.* 7.1 as evidence to be considered. Hill (*Regnum Caelorum*, 89–90), though, points toward the bishop's insistence on rising up "by means of his bonds" (Ign. *Eph.* 11.2) as an indication that he does not necessarily view corporeal resurrection as the ultimate goal but as "attainment of God" in some spiritual sense as the reward for faithfulness (see Ign. *Rom.* 4.1–3). As Hill concludes, one might derive from a reading of Ign. *Magn.* 9.2 that Ignatius expects to find "the saints of former times in heaven" (p. 90).

54. The theme of "righteousness" (δικαιοσύνη, *dikaiosynē*) permeates this short letter, making its appearance at Pol. *Phil.* 2.3; 3.1, 3; 4.1; 5.2; 8.1; 9.1–2. As Hartog indicates, Polycarp's view of righteousness resembles that found elsewhere in Matthew and 1 Clement. See P. Hartog, ed., *Polycarp's Epistle to the Philippians and Martyrdom of Polycarp*, OAF (Oxford: Oxford University Press, 2013), 51–53 (special support for this conclusion appears in n272).

55. So P. Hartog, *Polycarp and the New Testament*, WUNT 2/134 (Tübingen: Mohr Siebeck, 2002), 13.

56. A. Bovon-Thurneysen, "Ethik und Eschatologie im Philipperbrief des Polykarp von Smyrna," *TZ* 29 (1973): 241–56.

the resurrected Christ "who will come as judge of the living and the dead,"[57] while in 6.2 he reminds the Philippians that "it is necessary for everyone to appear at the witness stand of Christ." Presumably this observation is designed to impact the ethical lifestyle of his audience in some practical sense rather than simply to serve as a promise of future events. Similarly in his rebuff of the presbyter Valens at 11.2, Polycarp recalls that those who love money "will be judged as though one of the nations" (*tanquam inter gentes iudicabitur*), thus to indicate their lot is not with the community of the faithful in the final judgment. As Bovon-Thurneysen correctly indicates, such references to the future activities of a divine decree are brought to bear on the need for the faith community to live within the prospects of Christian ethical mindfulness. In the final analysis, then, the motif of eschatological expectation must be seen as subordinate to the ethical teaching of love of God and neighbor, with the anticipated function of Christ's judgment made subsidiary to moral concerns.[58] She concludes in summary that an important shift has been made away from the basic perspective of the New Testament (see also sec. 2.7 below on 2 Clement), whose general assumption is that eschatology holds primacy of place, while ethical concerns only follow such considerations.[59]

While this may indeed be true, at the same time such readings of Polycarp's language must not be used to dismiss his clear anticipation of future resurrection and divine judgment for Christ's faithful ones (Pol. *Phil.* 5.2; 12.2). He is noticeably directed by concerns for the future. One might agree with Schoedel here that there is no suggestion Polycarp assumed the church was in essence living in the final days of history, a view that itself is often derived from the theological trajectory of Luke-Acts.[60] Indeed, Polycarp is instead clearly oriented around Matthean tradition at the core, a perspective that seems largely comfortable with the church's need to recognize that an undefined period of time remains before the end of history. His views of gospel teaching derive largely from that source, and his hermeneutical lens for how to interpret that trajectory is typical of Matthew.[61] Thus, in agreement with Hartog's notation that "in regard to Polycarp's knowledge of Acts, certain weak similarities are completely inconclusive,"[62] there appears to be no strong evidence for a decidedly "Lukan" vision at work within the bishop's writing.

At the same time, however, there must be concern for the sources from which the bishop drew his eschatological conclusions. Scholars traditionally point to the influence of Jewish perspectives in this regard, offering Old Testament parallels as indicators of the context within which Polycarp and other Christian leaders of the second century drew

57. She notes that this basic confession of early Christian thought follows the earlier observations of Oscar Cullmann, *Les premières confessions de foi chrétiennes*, 2nd ed. (Paris: Universitaires de France, 1948), 31 (Bovon-Thurneysen, "Ethik und Eschatologie," 243n6).

58. Bovon-Thurneysen, "Ethik und Eschatologie," 248–50.

59. Bovon-Thurneysen, "Ethik und Eschatologie," 256.

60. W. R. Schoedel, "Polycarp of Smyrna and Ignatius of Antioch," *ANRW* 27.1:284. One thinks immediately of the comment attributed to Jesus that "the kingdom of God has drawn near to [you]" (Luke 10:11). So too, in Acts 2 it seems that the author understands the sequence of events at the day of Pentecost to reflect the church's embodiment of what God originally intended for humanity at creation. Thus, one might see the sequence of the believers' ability to understand diverse languages through the Spirit, to respond in faith through baptismal waters, and to share as one community without need as a reversal of events found in Gen 1–11 (tower of Babel, great flood, garden of Eden).

61. See W.-D. Koehler, *Die Rezeption des Matthäusevangeliums in der Zeit vor Irenäus*, WUNT 2/24 (Tübingen: Mohr Siebeck, 1987), 97–110, and Hartog, *Polycarp and the New Testament*, 180–90. While Hartog admits that Luke's concern for the poor may have shaped Polycarp's response to the situation of Valens (182) as he interpreted Matthew, this suggestion offers little else in support of the bishop's employment of Lukan tradition.

62. Hartog, *Polycarp and the New Testament*, 185.

their conclusions on the matter.[63] Simultaneously, Lohmann has challenged such suppositions, offering instead an argument for the influence of Hellenistic designs both here and throughout the Apostolic Fathers generally.[64] Admittedly, throughout this literature there is certainly a dilution of the cosmic orientation of eschatology previously witnessed in biblical texts, and (as observed above) a tendency toward morality as the logical result of eschatological concerns. Yet as Schoedel observes, "The view that God brings the world into existence and will bring it to an end continued to function in the theology of the church as an element that contrasted more or less sharply with the general insistence of the philosophers on the eternity of the world. The attenuation of such beliefs does not amount to their abandonment."[65] In result, it seems unnecessary to think Polycarp has thus abandoned basic Jewish principles in this regard.

By way of illustration, intermixed with such Jewish principles are materials that suggest the bishop's use of contemporary messianic tradition. To return to *To the Philippians* 2, Lohmann finds within these materials a creedal fragment (*Credo-Stücken*) broadly perceived within biblical and extracanonical sources.[66] According to this creed, the very Christ whom God raised from the dead will likewise raise those who turn from error and believe in divine deliverance for the obedient. The exaltation of Jesus Christ initiates "the raising of the dead, universal rule, and judicial office," basic functions broadly associated with God's own power elsewhere but ultimately assigned to the "chosen one" as viewed throughout ancient Christendom.[67] The nature of faithful obedience is specified in *To the Philippians* 2.2–3, featuring a list of virtues and vices commonly seen elsewhere in the literature together with logia paralleled in Matthew 5:3, 10, and 7:2 and identified as "what the Lord said as he taught" (Pol. *Phil.* 2.3). It is clear that Polycarp holds a cosmological perspective that incorporates both scriptural foundations and contemporary views of Christ's role in salvation. The teachings of Jesus known from the Gospels figure prominently in this equation and are not unique to the bishop.

What results from this consideration is that Polycarp largely makes theological observations that are couched within eschatological justifications. These views are principally shaped by concerns for the future, but they are distinctly oriented toward what the ultimate goal of Christ's vision for the future might mean for a life of devotion to be lived by the bishop's faith community. This is *not* to argue that Polycarp believed that he and his followers were living in the last days. Instead, this is to acknowledge that future ends have immediate relevance for actions and morals, an assumption about the indicative of the future as an imperative for the present. These views are *not* exclusive to the bishop himself, but they appear as characteristic of contemporary messianic thought patterns. As with the perspective of the apostle Paul in whose tradition the bishop clearly stands, those who are truly faithful—like Christ—ultimately will serve as co-judges of righteousness. For the community to live otherwise is to indicate a rejection of the gospel's core teachings about the divine will. Polycarp thus seems to stand within a solid trajectory of ancient Christian creeds and teaching typical of the late first- and second-century church that has merged eschatological concerns into the framework of contemporary living.

63. See here the comments of Schoedel, "Polycarp of Smyrna and Ignatius of Antioch," 284–85.
64. Lohmann, *Drohung und Verheißung*, 177–94.
65. Schoedel, "Polycarp of Smyrna and Ignatius of Antioch," 285.
66. Lohmann, *Drohung und Verheißung*, 183–84.
67. Cf. Acts 10:42; 2 Tim 4:1; 1 Pet 4:5; 2 Clem. 1.1; Barn. 7.2.

2.6 Papias of Hierapolis

Unlike other authors of the Apostolic Fathers, one must evaluate the eschatological perspective of the bishop Papias through only a few fragments of his writings preserved by others, as well as what various sources offer about him and his views. For ease of reference, I follow the collected fragments published by Bart Ehrman as the most easily accessible and to date the most complete assemblage of references available at the time of writing.[68]

One might begin with what Papias himself preserves with respect to eschatological orientation. In fragment 1, both Irenaeus and Eusebius of Caesarea attest to an ancient teaching that in the future kingdom of divine promise the dead shall rise to rule, creation will be renewed, and the soil will produce in abundance, illustrated by vines with ten thousand boughs, with ten thousand branches, with ten thousand shoots, with ten thousand clusters, with ten thousand grapes, each to produce twenty-five measures of wine. So too, grains and all other vegetation will be as abundant.[69] This image is traced via Papias to his master John (of Fourth Gospel tradition), and through him to the Lord. Descriptions of profuse harvests and those responsible for them are readily traced throughout Jewish literature, and with respect to the promised glory of the kingdom to the teachings of Jesus from the Gospels and Revelation.[70] Illustrations of profundity are replete within early Christian tradition, so it is predictable that Papias should preserve similar motifs about the future kingdom. There is no particular reason to suspect the bishop has drawn this particular image from Gospel sources, however, particularly with a tradition such as 2 Baruch widely available.[71]

Elsewhere, he is reported to have observed with respect to the witness of Revelation, "He appointed some of them (he clearly means the holy angels of old) to rule over the administration of the earth, and he ordered them to rule it well."[72] Suggestive here is recognition by Papias of the extent to which God has control over the regions of the earth throughout history, though later he acknowledges that not all those who were appointed were successful in their tasks. With this reference one observes that Papias, at least from the limited materials he himself is said to have preserved, accepts that the authority of God is at work, not only as a promise of the time that is to come but most certainly (through divine agency) throughout contemporary history. The former is derived from the teachings of the Lord, while the latter results from Papias's own observations.

More to the point however is what tradition has preserved about Papias himself. The most poignant of these recollections is recorded by Eusebius, who states the bishop's belief "that after the resurrection of the dead there will be a thousand-year period, during which the Kingdom of Christ will exist tangibly, here on this earth."[73] In its essence, here is confirmation that—at least in the mind of Eusebius—Papias was an ardent chiliast in perspective, undoubtedly reflective of a strand of thought found throughout Asia Minor in the early second century. Given the bishop's relationship with Johannine tradition, such

68. B. D. Ehrman, ed., *Epistle of Barnabas, Papias and Quadratus, Epistle to Diognetus, the Shepherd of Hermas*, vol. 2 of *The Apostolic Fathers*, LCL 25 (Cambridge: Harvard University Press, 2003), 86–119. One might compare the listing of sources provided by M. A. Shanks, *Papias and the New Testament* (Eugene, OR: Pickwick, 2013).

69. Irenaeus, *Haer.* 5.33.3–4; Eusebius, *Hist. eccl.* 3.39.1.

70. For the latter, consider Matt 13:3–9; 20:1–16; 21:28–32; 26:29; Mark 12:1–9; Luke 13:6–9; John 15; Rev 14:18.

71. So C. E. Hill, "The Fragments of Papias," in *The Writings of the Apostolic Fathers*, ed. P. Foster (London: T&T Clark, 2007), 49–50; in agreement is Shanks, *Papias and the New Testament*, 106–13.

72. Papias, frag. 9 (Ehrman, *Apostolic Fathers*, 111); from Andreas of Caesarea, *On the Apocalypse* 34.

73. Papias, frag. 3 (Ehrman, *Apostolic Fathers*, 101); from Eusebius, *Hist. eccl.* 3.31.11–12.

understanding may find its foundation in opinions on texts like Revelation, as observed with fragment 9 from Andreas's *On the Apocalypse* 34, as well as in his preface from the same work.[74] Jerome similarly records that "he is said to have propagated the Jewish tradition of the millennium, adopted by Irenaeus, Apollinaris, and others, who say that the Lord will rule in the flesh, with his saints, after the resurrection."[75] The link to "Jewish tradition" suggests greatly that, unlike Ignatius of Antioch, Papias was firmly rooted in exegetical techniques linked in part with certain speculation found throughout the synagogue. In this respect, one finds a critical key to how he and others in their day viewed the circumstances of the church with respect to their situation in history. This may reflect the apostle Paul's own missionary activity seen in his Thessalonian and Corinthian letters, which indicates the apostle's conviction at the time of the imminent return of Christ. Papias seems not to have advanced much beyond that persuasion,[76] however, even if the same can hardly be said for his predecessor.

Supplementary evidence of Papias's conviction comes from Anastasius of Sinai, who offers that the bishop, among others, "understood the entire six days of creation to refer to Christ and the church" and that he "understood the stories about Paradise in a spiritual way, as referring to the church of Christ."[77] The symbolic link drawn between the garden of Eden and the institutional church became a commonplace element of second-century exegetical technique, seen elsewhere in the Apostolic Fathers, for example, in Diognetus 11–12. Such imagery, together with Papias's somewhat consistent concern for the nature of the promised afterlife for believers,[78] further supports the conviction of belief for his chiliastic orientation among Christian authors of his day.

In the final analysis, one might agree largely with Hill, who speculates that what Papias preserves in terms of early messianic eschatology reflects "significant contact with Jewish apocalyptic ideas" among believers in Asia Minor in his day.[79] He rightly questions whether such views do not derive from intertestamental literature and oral traditions within Judaism in comparison with logia of Jesus of Nazareth that the bishop could actually validate. Hill states that "Papias' millennial traditions in particular would seem to signify the presence in Asia Minor in his day of Jewish converts who carried over eschatological ideas from nationalistic apocalypses and perhaps from the synagogues."[80] One might indeed imagine this to be true at a practical level, and to the extent this may be one might also visualize links with the situation confronted by Rome in its discussion with Corinth (see

74. Papias, frag. 8 (Ehrman, *Apostolic Fathers*, 108–10); from Andreas of Caesarea, *On the Apocalypse* preface.

75. Papias, frag. 5 (Ehrman, *Apostolic Fathers*, 108–9); from Jerome, *Vir. ill.* 18.

76. About which Philip of Side (*Ecclesiastical History*) reports: "Papias was also mistaken about the future millennium; Irenaeus got his ideas from him" (Ehrman, *Apostolic Fathers*, 113–14 [Papias, frag. 12]).

77. Papias, frags. 10 and 11 (Ehrman, *Apostolic Fathers*, 112–13), from Anastasius of Sinai, *Contemplations on the Hexameron* 1, 7, respectively.

78. Seen, e.g., in the comments about overabundant vines discussed above and the nature of kingdom food, thus attested by Maximus the Confessor concerning "the pleasures of food in the resurrection" (*On the Ecclesiastical Hierarchy* 7) and by Photius (*Bibliotheca*) in relationship to how "the kingdom of heaven involved the enjoyment of foods palpable to the senses" (Ehrman, *Apostolic Fathers*, 100, 117 [Papias, frags. 7, 14] respectively).

79. So Hill, "Papias," 49–51 (quotation on 49).

80. Hill, "Papias," 50. Ulrich Körtner speaks further to this idea in his discussion of chiliasm in the teachings of Papias and the extent to which Asia Minor experienced the influence of wandering prophets into the age of Montanism. He sees such tendencies as the foundation for similar speculation among supporters in later ecclesiastical history. See U. H. J. Körtner and M. Leutzsch, *Papiasfragmente/Hirt des Hermas*, SU 3 (Darmstadt: Wissenschaftliche Buchgesellschaft, 1998), 42–43.

sec. 2.3 above on 1 Clement) as suggested by Weiss, though no certainty is warranted in this regard.

2.7 Second Clement

While it is virtually impossible to be certain with respect to either the date or provenance of 2 Clement, scholars seem convinced this "likely" homily depicts a second-century mindset. One might expect, therefore, to find the author's views of eschatology to be more developed than many other writings within the Apostolic Fathers. In many ways this seems true.

As a basis for reflection, one observes the comments of Christopher Tuckett, who notes without hesitation that "the writer works with a theological scheme that is dominated by a future eschatology." He observes "proper ethical behaviour in the present is continually buttressed by the threat of future judgement and condemnation for those who fail to do what they should do in the present."[81] In this respect the tenor of 2 Clement parallels what appears in Polycarp's letter to Philippi in which the future is envisaged as incentive for the present: indicative-imperative.[82] Yet certain passages within the homily do not provide such clear signs of this "future" focus. A few examples will suffice to illustrate the tenuous nature of the writer's convictions.

In 2 Clement 6 the author insists that those who follow "the will of Christ" will find rest, while those who do not heed his commandments cannot be saved "from eternal judgment" (2 Clem. 6.7).[83] Thereafter one reads there is no guarantee of entry into God's kingdom "if we do not keep [our] baptism pure and unblemished" (6.9). To this is added a further question of who may be found as our "advocate" if our acts not be judged as "holy and righteous"? This concluding comment clearly recalls the opening verse of the homily, in which the audience is charged to think of Jesus Christ as God, judge of the living and the dead. In this respect there is little question about whether the eschatology of 2 Clement is existential in tone—a type of realized insight. What guides the author's rhetoric is expectation of the future, the promise of which must be seen as stimulus for expectations in the present. Here, then, seems to be a clear parallel with Polycarp as mentioned above.[84]

Further, in 2 Clement 9, explanations are given in response to the conviction that Christ, Savior of the world, did indeed come in the flesh.[85] As seen in 9.5, one hears, "If Christ . . . became flesh and called us thus, consequently also we ourselves will receive the reward in this flesh." Thereafter in verse 6, the author enjoins, "Let us thus love one another so that we all may enter into the kingdom of God." Such teaching might appear to muddy the waters about the homily's future eschatology, since the instructional, indicative-imperative tone seen to operate in chapter 6 might be imagined here to reflect a realized view once more. Based on the confession that in the past the historical Jesus came not simply as spirit but in the flesh, the reward offered to all who live in the Lord's name should be available to them "in this flesh" (ἐν ταύτῃ τῇ σαρκί, *en tautē tē sarki*, v. 5) even now. The question in

81. C. M. Tuckett, *2 Clement*, OAC (Oxford: Oxford University Press, 2012), 74.

82. Hill (*Regnum Caelorum*, 99–101) likewise supports this view of a future orientation, observing that "since the author is trying to embolden his hearers to face the prospect of leaving this world, the 'rest of the coming kingdom' would appear to be a prize that awaits the godly immediately at death (rest is also an eschatological reward in 6.7)" (100).

83. Though not reviewed here, similar ideas about "rest" resonate in ch. 5 with respect to Christians as "transients" in the world. As Lohmann (*Drohung und Verheißung*, 98–101) observes, rest in the kingdom to come and eternal life carries significant ethical implications according to 5.5–6.

84. See further, Lohmann, *Drohung und Verheißung*, 101–7.

85. This is clearly a conscious, anti-docetic conviction.

result is whether the promise of the "kingdom of God" seen in verse 6 stands simply as an expectation of the future or, instead, may be experienced in the present as "the reward" to be given in the flesh. The latter interpretation might carry sufficient weight to adjust the argument in favor of a realized vision once more, though this remains unclear.[86]

With a turn toward chapter 11, further evidence may be marshaled to demonstrate the author's eschatological position. In verses 5–7 one encounters the charge, "Let us remain hopeful in order also to obtain the reward . . . thus if we act in righteousness before God, we will enter into his kingdom and receive the promises that ear has not heard nor eye seen nor human heart achieved." Such a promise offers two possible options. On the surface, one might envisage the author to offer consolation for the present in the light of hoped for rewards in the future. Tuckett correctly observes that the conclusion of verse 7 about the unheard and unseen promises echoes a saying widespread in ancient literature. The basis for this observation is Isaiah 64:4 (64:3 LXX), but ready parallels found in 1 Corinthians 2:9, 1 Clement 34.8, Gospel of Thomas 17, and Liber antiquitatum biblicarum 26.13 render conclusions about the author's source tradition unclear.[87] In each instance there is clear witness to recognition of the promises within the present age. For Isaiah, the reference is to that which had been experienced in the past, while for the apostle Paul it is for those who witness in the Spirit at present. To imagine that 2 Clement preserves this perspective is not likewise required, though such expectation is not to be dismissed.

A final example within the homily derives from 2 Clement 17.3–7, where one reads that "all who believe the same will be assembled in life" based on the Lord's promise, "I come to assemble all nations, peoples, and languages" (Isa 66:18). This expectation of future events clearly is anticipated in Isaiah and is reconfirmed by the notation in 2 Clement 17.6 that the Lord "speaks of that day of judgment" when the unrighteous will see their fault and the righteous will receive their reward. While it remains unclear whether the author understands "that day" to be some cosmic, otherworldly moment or, more with Isaiah, a historical event in the life of Israel, the intention is undoubtedly directed toward some future occasion whose anticipation is considered to be both promise and directive for the present.[88]

In the final analysis, 2 Clement appears to straddle two worlds of understanding with respect to eschatology. On the surface, the wording of the author may be taken as clear reference to future events whose import harbors dire implications for the present—a typical early Christian understanding of the Lord's intervention into history drawn from early Jewish literature. At the same time, however, much of what the author suggests might also be read through the Pauline recognition that "life in Christ" means some form of transformation that each believer experiences in contemporary times and through which

86. O'Hagan (*Material Re-Creation*, 70–71) notes that 2 Clem. 6 (together with ch. 8) raises the importance of "resurrection of the flesh" for the author. As he notes, the use of "flesh" (σάρξ, *sarx*) in 9.1–6 "without moral overtones is rare in early Christian writings. It emphasizes, therefore, resurrection's materiality." O'Hagan offers 17.4 as further support for this view and argues 2 Clement, like the Didache, likely "belonged to that traditional [Jewish] school which saw the eschatological kingdom of God as an earthly thing." Whether this is true remains unclear, but it does suggest further linkage between the author's views of present expectations based on future hopes, which O'Hagan argues "belonged to the tradition of hopes in national and earthly restoration."

87. Tuckett, *2 Clement*, 218–19.

88. One might consider various literary parallels to descriptions of the so-called day of judgment found in 2 Clem. 17 with texts like 2 Pet 3:10; Justin, *1 Apol.* 60; Sib. Or. 3.86–87, 5.375–88; Herm. Vis. 4.3.3. See O'Hagan, *Material Re-Creation*, 72–75. O'Hagan offers that the formal assembly of Christians in moments of worship is viewed by the author as "a parallel" that "seems to make these present earthly meetings an image of the eschatological one to come" (74).

the promises of the future spoken by ancient Israel's prophets may be encountered in the present.[89] Where the homilist resides in this equation is perhaps not as easily recognized as Tuckett suggests. Instead, 2 Clement is perhaps better understood to be positioned in early Christian thought between future expectations and existential realities whose parameters are not easily determined.[90]

2.8 Shepherd of Hermas

Perhaps the most immediately obvious text among the Apostolic Fathers that might serve as an indicator of eschatological concerns is the Shepherd of Hermas. Within this extensive tractate, the reader is drawn especially to Visions 4 in which the narrator, Hermas himself, encounters a great creature as he travels along the Campanian Way. This "huge beast," with flaming mouth and porcelain head of black, red, gold, and white, approaches our hero but eventually reclines in docility, and the narrator manages to pass by unmolested. Shortly thereafter a young woman dressed in bridal garments explains to Hermas that he was able to escape because he was not "double-minded" or "hesitant" (δίψυχος, *dipsychos*), and thus the Lord had sent an angel to seal the creature's mouth. He is told then "that this beast is an omen of the great tribulation to come" (Vis. 4.2.5) and that he must preach this message not to be double-minded to all believers, so that in the coming day of judgment they also may escape the ordeal of destruction's flames. As the woman explains, the colors of the beast's head have significance: black reflects the world in its present age; red is the color of blood and fire by which destruction comes; gold symbolizes those who are tested and found worthy to escape through that fire; and white signals the age of eternal life to come in which those who are purified will live forever with God (4.3.2–5).

The imagery at work in this passage has received extensive attention by commentators over the decades,[91] most especially because of the obvious connections to the beast of Revelation that it evokes for even the hastiest reader (cf. Rev 11:7–19:20 passim). There is little else in Shepherd of Hermas to suggest the author has clear awareness of Revelation as a source to consult in production of the work, but thematic parallels suggest awareness of common apocalyptic and eschatological language trajectories that permeated nascent Christian writings.[92]

The presence of vibrant apocalyptic imagery in Visions 4 seeks answers to whether this theme actually indicates eschatological consciousness by the author and, as a related concern, whether its presence should be read as indicative of the entirety of the text as now known or, instead, as a trope specific to one of the work's specific sources and therefore only tangential to our concerns. Let us address these topics in order.

As to an indicator of "eschatological consciousness," a curious note appears in Visions

89. Lohmann (*Drohung und Verheißung*, 132) finds a general theme of retribution at work in 2 Clement that is seen both in the mechanistic events of history and also in the final judgment.

90. As might be expected, O'Hagan (*Material Re-Creation*, 86–87) concludes his review of 2 Clement with the view that the author sees "earthly renewal" and "material restoration" as the central pillar of eschatology. This might be supported by Adolf von Harnack's idea of Satan bound in chains in 2 Clem. 20.4, found in the text as "an unrighteous spirit." His opinion was that the author imagined the devil already constrained with a chain in the present age (see Rev 20:1–3), thus to suggest the thousand-year reign of Christ already underway. Hill (*Regnum Caelorum*, 100–101) concludes his discussion of 2 Clement with a note on this interpretation and concludes such a perspective to be "incongruous" with respect to the remainder of the letter.

91. See, e.g., the excellent surveys of N. Brox, *Der Hirt des Hermas*, KAV 7 (Göttingen: Vandenhoeck & Ruprecht, 1991), 160–80, and C. Osiek, *Shepherd of Hermas*, Hermeneia (Minneapolis: Fortress, 1999), 89–97.

92. In this respect, references to suffering, vindication of the righteous, the colors black, red, gold, and white, etc. all find ready parallel in Revelation, 2 Thessalonians, and 2 Peter, a broad array of texts reflective of eschatological concerns in early messianic literature.

4.3.6 wherein the woman in white says to Hermas that he must always speak to the holy ones about the coming tribulation, "and if you are willing, it will be nothing—remember the things already written." Osiek finds this to be "problematic in an apocalyptic framework in which the end-time struggle will be harrowing even for believers," noting a "hopeful tone" typical of the entire writing that otherwise seeks a change of heart rather than simply fear. She finds "prophetic critique and apocalyptic determinism" to be linked beyond any concern for history here.[93] In some respects this aligns with the remarks of Norbert Brox, who recognizes this language to be "stylized apocalyptically" (*apokalyptisch stilisiert*) and, with reference to what Christians might expect from the promises of a future eon, in fact to be based on a promise that originally "simply constituted a good omen" (*sie ursprünglich wohl einfach das gute Omen darstellte*).[94] Thus, the apocalyptic orientation of Visions 4 in the end may be confusing for how one should fathom the whole of the Shepherd of Hermas in its essence.

Brox offers three observations about the eschatological nature of Shepherd of Hermas *en bloc* that seem apt on the surface. First, he sees eschatology in the text as instrumental—the author preaching a message of urgency—that offers an ultimate deadline for repentance to the audience. Further, he finds it both pastoral and educational in its function, offering only limited imagery concerning eternal judgment and the future, though such imagery is indeed foundational. One thinks here of phrases such as "living to God" in Mandates 1.2, and salvation through baptism in Similitudes 9.16 versus ultimate death through perverse choice of lifestyle as suggested in Mandates 6.2. Such passages are typical of how the author views a call to ethical lifestyle set within a larger framework of eschatological resolve. In a sense, the turn toward repentance is the "eschatological destiny" (*eschatologische Schicksal*) of the well-intentioned person as the author understands the situation. Finally, expectation of the parousia is a natural element of the eschatological vision of the text, though its problematic delay seems often to be subjugated to a focus on repentance and "metanoia" (μετάνοια, *metanoia*). Both parousia and repentance must logically be read together here.[95]

Such remarks lead then to the second question of whether eschatology and apocalyptic language derives from a narrow field of interpretation alone. In some genuine sense, the only true apocalyptic imagery of Shepherd of Hermas is evident in this particular section. The presence of the great beast dominates this descriptive moment, but otherwise there is little else of substance to be found elsewhere in the text. At the same time, however, what *is* evident throughout Shepherd of Hermas is an awareness of eschatology in which the essential importance of the present moment for those who believe is defined by the proximity of that parousia expected in the near future. Of course, while this "near future" is patently symbolic in spirit, for the author's message it is most genuine in present reality.

What remains for the listener is an understanding that time and history (as they are assumed within Shepherd of Hermas) are only relevant to the extent they fulfill the cosmic mysteries of salvation. Time itself is essentially empty or meaningless. Its primary function relates to the way in which penitence or metanoia are possible. History likewise serves as a vehicle for time's active functionality. In this respect one might accept the shepherd himself as an apocalyptic image who appears throughout the work as the interpreter both of what the narrator sees and experiences, as well as of what listeners may expect to encounter in their own faith experiences. As Osiek has said previously, the Shepherd of Hermas is

93. Osiek, *Shepherd of Hermas*, 97.

94. Brox, *Hirt des Hermas*, 179.

95. Brox, *Hirt des Hermas*, 505–12.

"largely apocalyptic paraenesis" in a form similar to that found in the letters of Revelation 2–3.[96] The purpose of apocalyptic imagery in this narrative, then, is for faith instruction. Otherwise, this training is predominantly oriented toward eschatology, primarily as it may be understood through the work's views on ecclesiology.

With emphasis on Osiek's observation that Shepherd of Hermas "can be legitimately categorized as apocalyptic literature by its function," Helen Rhee further observes that the problem is wealth that ties the rich person to the present world in the eyes of the author: eschatological salvation and worldly affluence are simply incompatible.[97] To that end, while Shepherd of Hermas indicates numerous times that the rich are integral to the community—in the construction of the tower that is the eternal church (Sim. 9) and as the supportive tree for the community of faith (Sim. 8)—only true transformation away from such earthly ties may enable such people to experience the promise of another, heavenly existence. The reason, of course, is one's focus on double-mindedness, as observed above,[98] a state in which a believer is neither dead nor alive. The goal must instead be to acquire "heavenly riches" through the purity of almsgiving or other acts of service. Only in this manner may ethics, driven by eschatological considerations, overcome certain death.[99]

With respect to the function of Visions 4 itself, one questions whether the introductory visions of Shepherd of Hermas derive from some source tradition behind the work or, instead, are solely from the imagination of the author. Thus, one asks if apocalypticism is original to the design of the text or secondary to its eschatological orientation. No doubt an eschatological emphasis permeates the entirety of the work, though the same cannot be said of apocalyptic imagery as with Visions 4. This passage stands as a virtual outlier. Thus, one might best presume the opening visions to derive from a source whose origins lie within apocalyptic traditions that the author/editor of Shepherd found useful to incorporate into construction of the text as now known.[100] As with many other writings in our collection discussed above, the ultimate aims of the work's eschatology include instruction and direction of ethical lifestyle. What drives this process is expectation of the parousia, a theme that gives urgency to the author's message yet seems in the long run not to be an immediate threat. This observation is offered without clear understanding of the original audience to be addressed, many of whom may indeed have found expectation of the parousia to be an urgent matter, though the matter of their wealth remains undefined. Regardless, the preservation of the Shepherd in later collections of biblical writings (including the Vulgate, Codex Sinaiticus, and Codex Athous) suggests this message of urgency was preserved

96. C. Osiek, "The Genre and Function of the Shepherd of Hermas," in *Early Christian Apocalypticism: Genre and Social Setting*, ed. A. Y. Collins, Semeia 36 (Decatur, GA: Society of Biblical Literature, 1986), 115.

97. Rhee, "Wealth, Poverty, and Eschatology," 78, in reference to Osiek, "Genre and Function," 113–21.

98. This theme appears in one form or another over forty times in Hermas, as well as occasionally throughout the broader collection: Did. 4.4 (par. Barn. 19:5); 1 Clem. 11.2; 23.2–3; 2 Clem. 11.2, 5; 19.2.

99. Rhee, "Wealth, Poverty, and Eschatology," 78–81. Undoubtedly the author envisages that the church is living in the last days, to be concluded with a final tribulation and last judgment. Whether this future "reward" is seen by the author to be an earthly experience or something beyond remains unclear. Hill (*Regnum Caelorum*, 92–99) argues for the former, though this is not certain from the text itself. What *does* seem clear, however, are Hill's final remarks on the topic: "That we have in Hermas (a) a non-chiliastic view of future history, (b) a notion that the dead in Christ go immediately to the presence of the Lord in heaven . . . and (c) the doctrines of the future resurrection of the body and the great judgment taken for granted speaks powerfully for the validity of the eschatological patterning suggested to us by Irenaeus" (99).

100. O'Hagan (*Material Re-Creation*, 113) correctly notes that Shepherd of Hermas derives its "apocalyptic mood" from "every available tradition," with focus on the symbols of Jewish apocalyptic. Such may apply here it seems. To this end, O'Hagan finds such imagery widely scattered throughout the text, having drawn from such sources as Zechariah, Tobit, 4 Ezra, 1 Enoch, and 2 Baruch (113–32).

despite the late application of the text as ethical instruction—much as with the case of Revelation itself. In this respect, the utility of eschatological themes typically may be seen to transcend their initial value for those who served as the original audience.

2.9 Martyrdom of Polycarp

Eschatology in martyrologies is undoubtedly less about the figure under review than about those who designed the recollection of the event itself. This is indisputably true with respect to Polycarp's fatal end.

Language strewn within the Martyrdom of Polycarp offers much from the perspective of the editor(s). From the beginning, Polycarp's death is portrayed in parallel with that of Jesus in the Gospels (so Mar. Pol. 1.1; 19.1), thus to prejudice the account from the outset with respect to how the New Testament evangelists viewed both the ministry of Jesus and their own community struggles in the light of some eschatological interpretation of history. Such Gospel views are not uniform in perspective, nor can they be surveyed sufficiently here to be of value. Yet, however the Gospels were viewed by the editor(s), they are foundational for the text's reconstruction of Polycarp's death. Whether this says anything about the editor(s)' view of eschatology, though, remains obscure.[101]

From the perspective of Hartog, eschatology within the Martyrdom plays a "subordinate role."[102] Indeed, it is seen primarily in only scattered background allusions. Nevertheless, these are very important. In Martyrdom of Polycarp 2.3, for example, the editor(s) speak of the fortitude of early martyrs generally, observing that "they are redeemed from eternal punishment on behalf of one hour" of pain. In this way they escape the ultimate fire that awaits sinners and receive whatever good may come to those who endure as they are changed from human form into angels.[103] Within this setting the editor(s) portray the youthful Germanicus as one who actually pursued death by the wild beasts, "wishing quickly to be released from [his accusers'] unrighteous and unlawful life" (Mart. Pol. 3.1) in a type of eschatological topos that envisages the believer as an outsider or stranger within the natural world. This same motif reappears once more in the likely contemporary case of Diognetus, as seen below.[104]

With reference to Polycarp himself, one hears how he was destined to share in Christ's own lot versus those who would receive the punishment of Judas (Mart. Pol. 6.2). This imagery is reflected further at his trial, in which he speaks of the temporary fire that will consume him for one quick moment, while to his judges he presages a harsher result: "For you are oblivious to the fire of the judgment to come and eternal retribution earmarked for the ungodly" (11.2). Finally, the editor(s) observe how, through his suffering and death, the bishop was indeed "crowned with the crown/wreath of immortality" (17.1 and 19.2) as anticipated for the fate of all faithful martyrs. Such "reward consciousness" already is

101. Indeed, within their extensive studies neither O'Hagan, *Material Re-Creation*, Lohmann, *Drohung und Verheißung*, Aono, *Entwicklung*, nor Hill, *Regnum Caelorum*, finds it necessary to offer any comment on this particular work.

102. Hartog, *Polycarp's Epistle to the Philippians and the Martyrdom of Polycarp*, 215; so too, G. Buschmann, *Das Martyrium des Polykarp*, KAV 6 (Göttingen: Vandenhoeck & Ruprecht, 1998), 60.

103. Buschmann (*Martyrium*, 111) sees this perspective as indicative of a Two Ways view—life versus death—that permeates early Christian teaching (see secs. 2.1 and 2.2 above).

104. See sec. 2.10 on Diognetus below. Buschmann (*Martyrium*, 69) finds this "stranger in this world" motif to serve a paraenetic function within martyrological literature in general, but also gives reference to a contemporary non-martyrological parallel in 2 Clem. 5.1. In many respects, then, one might argue the theme to be typical of late second-century literature of the church as it portrays itself as "outside" the boundaries of Roman power and hegemony.

present in Polycarp's prayer in chapter 14, in which he asks for a place among the number of the martyrs and "resurrection to eternal life" (14.2).[105] These touchstones suggest quite conspicuously the foundational vision of eschatology viewed by the authors, a perspective that served as a backdrop for the depiction of Polycarp's death, yet also functioned as a template for how future martyrologies would quite often be understood.

In many respects the Martyrdom may reflect a conscious redefinition of eschatological emphasis within the second-century church at a time when its "catholic" leadership faced various theological challenges both from nonorthodox outsiders and others within its immediate ranks. Whether one should see this imagery as truly reflective of the bishop remains unclear; or at the other extreme, whether its presence anticipates a reaction to the challenge of Montanism here also is uncertain.[106] But without question, this was a historical period in which nascent Christian doctrines found themselves in competition inside a boiling cauldron of ecclesiastical aspirations. As appreciated elsewhere, the motif of eschatology and expectations of the future served largely as the anvil on which a lifestyle of patient endurance was forged.[107] Hence, in the Martyrdom visions of future reward function to justify the endurance of those who suffer (presumably with validation) within the world. Otherwise in the Martyrdom, no particular details are specified.

2.10 Epistle to Diognetus

The last text to be considered offers little immediate assistance with respect to explicit eschatological considerations. It is assumed here that Diognetus represents the contributions of at least two hands, the first of which served to fashion chapters 1–10, while the latter contributed the closing materials of chapters 11–12. Neither editor is readily known, though if one might agree with Charles Hill that at least the initial chapters are to be associated with Polycarp in one fashion or another, it would be conceivable to consider close connections between that figure and his writings.[108] As to the final two chapters, it is quite possible this material stems from as late as the writings of Clement of Alexandria, though this is hardly proven and, should this in fact be the situation, lies mostly beyond the boundaries of this study.

As observed in the discussion of the Martyrdom above, the specific topos of the Christian as "stranger" or "foreigner" (ξένος, *xenos*) dominates the discussion of Diognetus 5.1–6.10 and thus, in some sense, the orientation of the entire work. This passage seeks to distinguish the various ways in which believers in Christ exist as citizens of another world

105. Buschmann (*Martyrium*, 283–84) speaks to how this "imaginative, more individualistic eschatology" reflects Luke 2:29–32 and indicates a transitional moment from Second Temple imagery to language of resurrection and incorruptibility found throughout the Apostolic Fathers.

106. See the discussion of Buschmann, *Martyrium*, 56–58.

107. As Daley (*Hope of the Early Church*, 14) observes with respect to this tractate, "It makes skillful use of the eschatological horizon that will become commonplace in martyr-acts" involving "apocalyptic imagery of the Jewish and Christian apocrypha . . . applied directly to the faith and the sufferings of the individual martyr."

108. See sec. 2.5 above. In that particular section, argument is made for a "beginning and end" orientation to Polycarp's eschatological views, with all other elements included within that vision. It is not so clear that such holds true for Diognetus, though, which raises the question of whether Polycarp has shifted position here or possibly is not the inspiration for these materials at all. For Hill's hypothesis, see C. E. Hill, *From the Lost Teaching of Polycarp* (Tübingen: Mohr Siebeck, 2006). My own views and a substantial survey of diverse opinions may be found in C. N. Jefford, *The Epistle to Diognetus*, OAF (Oxford: Oxford University Press, 2013), 15–29. The more recent review by Enrico Norelli rejects Hill's position but favors an Alexandrian setting (following H. E. Lona); see E. Norelli, "Ramener l'*A Diognète* en Asie Mineure? Une discussion de la these de Charles E. Hill," in *A Diognète*, ed. G. Aragione, E. Norelli, and F. G. Nuvolone, CahGSEP 1 (Prahins: Éditions du Zèbre, 2012), 91–117.

who necessarily reside in present society for only a temporary period. Though not easily identified at first glance, they exist as an essential component of a thriving social order—as the soul within the body (Diogn. 6.1–10). In certain respects, this is clearly a metaphorical image. Yet in other ways the author seeks to establish the impression that the very nature of those who live in faith, a lifestyle whose peculiarities might be viewed by outsiders as unique or idiosyncratic characteristics of a "third race," is existentially the life force that keeps civil society and directives in place. This imagery is typical of Middle Platonic thought during the second century, a philosophical revival whose tendrils likely overlap from Diognetus into the perspectives of the Martyrdom of Polycarp and perhaps even into the Shepherd of Hermas and 2 Clement. To this end, what may be said about the eschatology of Diognetus finds its foundation here.[109] Its bearings are in essence more internal in scope rather than (as seen in the majority of texts reviewed above) external in orientation. The call of the author for each "person to become an imitator of God" (Diogn. 10.4) taps into mimetic ritual typical of contemporary literature, which is rooted in Hellenistic foundations whose full expansion appears within later monastic traditions.[110]

But Diognetus does not construct such imaginings out of nothing, since the author clearly depends on Pauline imagery for this discussion. As Rudolf Brändle argues, the focus of Diognetus 5.5–10 concerning the role of Christians with respect to familial relationships—husbands, wives, and households—shows likely dependence on Paul's observations in 1 Corinthians about marriage and one's "concern for the times" (1 Cor 7:26). Most important are the words with which the apostle concludes his comments in this discussion:

> The appointed time has grown very short. From now on, let those who have wives live as though they had none, and those who mourn as though they were not mourning, and those who rejoice as though they were not rejoicing, and those who buy as though they had no goods, and those who deal with the world as though they had no dealings with it. For the present form of this world is passing away. (1 Cor 7:29–31 CEB)

As Brändle notes, Diognetus envisages an "eschatological horizon" at work within the unique perspective of the Christian, a view that supersedes mere concern for the temporal moment. At the same time, this horizon does not betray "imminent apocalyptic distress" (*unmittelbar bevorstehender apokalyptischer Bedrängnisse*) on the part of the believer, so much as a reality that has been divinely decreed "for the benefit of the world" (*zum Nutzen der Welt*). Instead, Diognetus offers an eschatological framework by which to understand the role of faith inside the confines of a hostile culture within the Roman Empire. In this way the author offers a platform for living that finds its grounding within an implicit assumption about eschatology and a divine plan for history.[111]

109. O'Hagan (*Material Re-Creation*, 108–10) acknowledges the clear Hellenistic tendencies here, but does not find "Christianity's Jewish background entirely obliterated" (109). For example, he detects typical Semitic "two aeons" theology still at work, together with recognition of the final age of the divine kingdom brought to earth through the incarnation. Nevertheless, all apocalyptic imagery is now absent, together with any sort of creedal language concerning resurrection, divine judgment, etc. apart from Diogn. 7.6 ("for he will send him as judge, and who will stand firm at his coming?"), which concludes with a textual lacuna. O'Hagan determines that Diognetus offers "Christianity that has freed itself from practically all apocalyptic tension, and that shows itself innocent of the earthly notions of Jewish tradition. Material re-creation of the universe is not opposed by the Epistle to Diognetus; it is merely passed over" (110).

110. See M. Heintz, "Μιμητὴς θεοῦ in the *Epistle to Diognetus*," *JECS* 12 (2004): 107–19.

111. R. Brändle, "*Ad Diognetum*: Eine Wiederaufnahme paulinischer und johanneischer Theologie am Ausgang des zweiten Jahrhunderts," in Aragione, Norelli, and Nuvolone, *À Diognète*, 40–52 (here

This then serves as the eschatological foundation of Diognetus, a recognition that lives of faith reflect transformative values performed within civic culture and are essential to its ultimate maintenance. This tenet ultimately comes to serve as a framework for later Christian ethics and the manner in which the church functions within society—as a constant voice of moral reason and order. The substance of such considerations finds grounding within a specific eschatological orientation that ascertains divine guidance as the explanation for human activity within the temporal world and its transient values. To that end, Diognetus might be considered a prototype of later ecclesial, eschatological attitudes in many respects.

3. SOME COMMON THEMES

A survey of eschatological themes within the Apostolic Fathers provides several motifs worthy of consideration. Some of these have been widely recognized by scholarship throughout the years, while others—being somewhat more subtle in nature—derive from direct reflection on individual tractates and authorial intentions. The resulting configurations produce a tapestry of images that often adjust themselves like a muddled kaleidoscope in constant transition, which undoubtedly offers an appropriate reflection of the ancient patristic landscape. In summation, it appears the outline of eschatological perspectives within the collection reflects a movement from nascent, messianic convictions freely attributed to Jewish foundations toward more settled, institutional perspectives that have incorporated Hellenistic tendencies focused on the value of "church as a collective" with respect to theology and ethical patterns.

3.1 Jewish Roots

The Apostolic Fathers as a corpus feature ancient Jewish traditions reflective of eschatological orientations, apocalyptic tracts, and oral teachings arising within the late Persian (intertestamental) period. Such tendencies are apparent in works such as the Didache, Barnabas, 1 Clement, Polycarp, Shepherd of Hermas, and fragments of Papias, which from the outset give indication of the broad influence of such trajectories. Simultaneously, though opposed to the influence of Judaism as a culture generally, even comments by Ignatius and the Martyrdom of Polycarp indicate how broad an impact Jewish principles had on the early patristic landscape. On the other end of this evolution are texts like Diognetus and 2 Clement, which offer little to no sign of Jewish eschatological or apocalyptic thought, preferring instead a definitive, philosophically oriented image of the institutional church constructed within the boundaries of what was seen within the second century as a more socially acceptable, Greek and Roman matrix of images and cultural identities. This is ultimately echoed in the voice of the author of Diognetus, who advocates for a believer's need to assume some mimetic tradition of discipleship rather than promises of future reward—to a great extent akin to what appears later in the literature of Clement of Alexandria and beyond.

The roots of this tradition as adopted by the Apostolic Fathers can hardly be determined with specificity, though hints of motifs from 4 Ezra, 1 Enoch, 2 Baruch, and Odes of Solomon are evident in writings such as 1 Clement and Shepherd of Hermas, and likely even stood behind and against the perspectives of Ignatius as he developed his own

---

esp. 48–51). Brändle is particularly dependent on the views of Rolf Noorman; see R. Noorman, "Himmelsbürger auf Erden," in *Die Weltlichkeit des Glaubens in der Alten Kirche*, ed. D. Wyrwa, BZNW 85 (Berlin: de Gruyter, 1997), 199–229.

awareness of eschatological meaning.[112] Most prevalent here are themes such as "two city" (earthly and heavenly) orientation, reclamation of the earth, reward and punishment in an afterlife, hope within history of a meaningful future, and motivations for personal piety and self-sacrifice that are supported by numerous Jewish authors outside the canon.[113] At the same time, of course, authors of Hebrew Scripture such as Second Isaiah, Ezekiel, Daniel, Malachi, and Zechariah (and others) conveyed parallel ideas speedily embraced by the Didache, 1 Clement, Barnabas, etc. The extent to which New Testament writers tapped into this same trove of literature (both canonical and noncanonical) necessarily suggests that both corpora of texts relied on Jewish works and motifs for their ideas. Eschatological teachings on the lips of Jesus in the Gospels, Paul's use of end-time imagery in his letters to the churches at Thessalonica and Corinth, dependence on oral traditions by Jude, and apocalyptic imagery in Revelation all provide evidence of this trend. The problem for research into the Apostolic Fathers is identifying the extent to which its own authors drew from a comparative cache of eschatological literature rather than from the New Testament authors directly. The answer to this question must vary from text to text, author to author, but in either case, clearly Jewish motifs lie at the foundation of relevant eschatological questions.

3.2 Regional Versus Universal

It is hardly possible to determine with certainty the varieties and nature of eschatological perspectives among the writings of the Apostolic Fathers as they reflect geographical trends. This is necessarily true given that certain texts (e.g., Didache, Shepherd of Hermas, Diognetus) remain without positive origins of location, date, or authorship, and certain regions are overrepresented (Rome, Syria), while others are largely neglected (Greece, Palestine, Spain). Nevertheless, some features worthy of comment appear within the corpus.

From the outset, to the extent that 1–2 Clement and Shepherd of Hermas can be associated with the region of Rome,[114] parallel eschatological considerations arise throughout the literature. The sources of these motifs remain unclear, perhaps a reflection of a Hellenistic cosmic framework (so 1 Clement) intermingled with Jewish apocalyptic imagery (so Shepherd of Hermas). Yet in each case scholars tend to recognize a future orientation designed to speak to growth of the ecclesial community at large. In other words, themes that portray impending concerns typically apply those to contemporary problems. Clearly this alignment offers a unifying element among texts that otherwise are not so plainly linked in any precise sense. Thus, eschatology and related imagery serve to unify literary tracts where other concerns, such as liturgy, Christology, etc., are not always so evident.

In a turn toward Egypt at the other end of the Mediterranean world, the primary tractate is Barnabas, though some classify the Didache here, as well as the last chapters of Diognetus. As with Shepherd of Hermas above, in the case of Barnabas 4 (and Did. 16) an eschatological source may serve as the apocalyptic setting for limited eschatological concerns. The ensuing perspective about end-time imagery echoes potential millenarian ideas

112. Thus, Hill (*Regnum Caelorum*, 88n41) notes the contrast between the bishop's views of his own death as a new birth (via faith, existentially?) in contrast to the views of 4 Ezra 4.41–42.

113. This is not to say that similar ideas did not arise within Hellenistic literature, but that the preponderance of such themes is to be found in such Jewish literature.

114. This is a broad assumption, since a good argument may certainly be made that 2 Clement has its roots in Greece.

suggestive of a broader regional setting.[115] Much like Roman concerns, Barnabas draws from diverse imagery (often biblical) to establish context for the local community. In many respects the Didache works similarly, though Diognetus turns to such imaginings only in the closing materials, primarily with dependence on Genesis, as the author offers apostolic, ecclesiastical traditions that echo garden metaphors drawn from Eden. In this respect the eschatological framework of Egyptian tradition runs from one extreme (Barnabas) to the other (Diogn. 11–12).

The primary region for consideration is that of Asia Minor and Syria, from which the vast majority of writings in the corpus derive.[116] Imagery varies widely here, from apocalyptic in the Didache and Papias to reflections on future expectations as the motivation for ecclesiastical life in Ignatius, Polycarp, and Martyrdom of Polycarp. Intermingled with such works are various New Testament passages from the Gospels, Paul, and Revelation consistent with our collected works. Without doubt the context for such thought is Jewish tradition that spans broadly across the region, but the influence of such sources is vast and diverse, beyond the scope of the present study.

All that may be said ultimately is that eschatological concerns—whether broad or more specific—run throughout the corpus and, as such, indicate a movement widespread throughout the late first and second centuries of Christianity. The focus of this eschatology varies from region to region, but its broad roots clearly have wide influence within theological speculation.

3.3 Realized Versus Future

A central concern of scholarship has been the degree to which early authors held either a future or realized eschatology. While such speculation seems worthy, its conclusions are hardly definitive. For example, scholars traditionally have divided over whether texts like Barnabas, 1–2 Clement, the Didache, Martyrdom of Polycarp, Polycarp, and Shepherd of Hermas fall within one camp or the other. The determination swings broadly dependent on the partiality of the interpreter, and the final answer may be that their concerns reflect both ends of the spectrum. On the other hand, one might argue with approval that individuals such as Ignatius and the author of Diognetus support a realized perspective, while someone such as Papias clearly stands in a future camp. In reality, such distinctions are not easily determined with assurance and may represent academic factors not necessarily justified. Suffice it to say that the Apostolic Fathers in whole reflect both views of eschatology, the parameters of the argument remaining ill-defined.

3.4 From Personal Piety to Corporate Concern

As with issues of realized-future eschatology, distinctions between personal (= individual) and corporate (= ecclesial) orientation may be similarly opaque. Nevertheless, the matter deserves comment to the extent one might argue whether authors write from within their own perspective or as representatives of a community or institutional vision. Such trends help to define the nature of messianic eschatology as believing communities evolved in the late first and second centuries into the later "great church" of the fourth and fifth centuries.

---

115. See, e.g., the so-called Demotic Chronicle, the messianic lamb of Plutarch's *De proverbiis Alexandrinorum*, "The Oracle of the Potter (to King Amenophis)," Apocalypse of Peter, Coptic Apocalypse of Elijah, and "Vision of Nefer-rohu."

116. Likely, the Didache, Diogn. 1–10, Ignatius, Papias, Polycarp, and Martyrdom of Polycarp.

Scholarship is very much convinced that Ignatius, Papias, and Diognetus present personal views of eschatology not necessarily associated with larger public positions. Each author—at least as known from literary evidence—speaks to specific audiences about individual situations without claim to any particular ecclesiastical standing. By the same token, Polycarp may also reflect a unique perspective though, like Ignatius, his eschatological imagery likely draws from creedal formulas as he speaks to issues of righteousness and personal responsibility.

With respect to corporate or ecclesiastical perspectives, the remaining texts seem to be clear representatives. The author(s) of Barnabas, 1 Clement, and Martyrdom of Polycarp visibly speak from a community position, marshaling their standing within the institution as the basis for their views. Of course, no particular office is ever claimed in this regard, but clearly some authority of leadership is assumed in every instance. More problematic are 2 Clement, Shepherd of Hermas, and the Didache. To the extent that one associates 2 Clement with 1 Clement, one might make an argument once more for ecclesiastical foundations and a broader eschatological position based on the institutional authority of the writer. This may be further justified by the well-developed imagery of the author, suggestive of a later date and perspective. The Shepherd of Hermas is not as clear, since the work appears to derive from the voice of prophecy, again dependent on sources, but directed as a challenge to the institutional leadership itself. In the case of the Didache, the work may reflect both positions, having originally been more individual and pious in scope, though with time having developed into a broader institutional statement on eschatological perspective.

4. CONCLUSION

A summary examination of the Apostolic Fathers suggests the widespread presence of eschatological thought throughout the entirety of the corpus—from Italy to Egypt, from the late first century to the early third, from the letters to the homilies to the historical tractates. In many instances the patterns are distinct, while in others they are more subdued. Yet in every case there is something of the motif to be found.

Consistent within the collection is the influence of intertestamental and contemporary Jewish thought. In certain settings, inspiration derives from biblical sources—especially Genesis, Isaiah, Ezekiel, Daniel, Zechariah, Malachi—or nonbiblical or oral traditions (Didache, Papias, Polycarp, Barnabas, 1 Clement, Shepherd of Hermas). In other instances, interaction within or against the synagogue and its adherents (Ignatius, Barnabas, Martyrdom of Polycarp) occurs, but always the impact of Jewish eschatology is noticeably evident.

This is not to say that Hellenistic motifs are absent, since they quite clearly are at work.[117] But the influence of Greek (and Roman) thought, intermingled with varieties of contemporary culture (often within the Hellenistic synagogues themselves), tends to shift authors gradually away from individual concerns for eschatological imagery (Papias, Ignatius) and toward institutional, ecclesial considerations (Polycarp, 1 Clement, Shepherd of Hermas, Diognetus). To this end, a transference toward stark, apocalyptic motifs as seen in prophecies of the future attributed to Jesus in the Gospels, Paul's end-time imagery offered to

117. Lohmann (*Drohung und Verheißung*, 243–50) concludes his study with the observation that eschatology within the corpus reflects the very process of Hellenization. As such, he notes that in essence "there is little to be gained here other than that the final salvation derived from communion with God or Christ brings unimaginable joy; otherwise, one encounters only eternal calamity, worm and fire, condemnation or ruin" (250).

the Thessalonians, or predictions about the conclusion of history preserved in Revelation (Didache, Papias, Shepherd of Hermas, Martyrdom of Polycarp) becomes the dominant interpretation of the divine plan for the church within the late Roman world. This permeates specific theologies (Barnabas, 2 Clement, Diognetus), liturgical practices (Didache), roles and offices (Ignatius, Shepherd of Hermas), creeds and ethics (1–2 Clement, Shepherd of Hermas, Polycarp, Diognetus), and accounts of apostolic lineage (Diognetus, Papias, Ignatius). Most critically, the outline of an eschatological explanation for the movement of history and the believing community's role within that guided narrative runs rampant throughout the Apostolic Fathers, helping to identify the collection as typical of messianic thought during the period and establishing it as formative for trends that develop later within the institutional narrative of the church's self-identity. It is a conviction defined by messianic faith (Ignatius). Though in many ways perhaps regional among differing authors, the movement is universal in scope and thus, apparently, typical of the Christian mindset during the period.

Finally, it remains unclear to what extent the corpus bears an existential versus future emphasis within this focus. In nearly every case, usages might be construed in either path, though apart from a few departures (Papias, a source behind Barnabas [or even Barnabas itself], and the Didache) the emphasis is not millenarian in scope. Most notably, though, consistent focus remains about how interpretations of the end of history and the church's role in that process must direct the ethical and moral lifestyle of believers. To this end, the motif remains both personal in its piety and corporate in its implications for the institution.

BIBLIOGRAPHY

Balabanski, V. *Eschatology in the Making: Mark, Matthew and the Didache*. SNTSMS 97. Cambridge: Cambridge University Press, 1997.

Bovon-Thurneysen, A. "Ethik und Eschatologie im Philipperbrief des Polykarp von Smyrna." *TZ* 29 (1973): 241–56.

Chester, A. "The Parting of the Ways: Eschatology and Messianic Hope." Pages 239–313 in *Jews and Christians: The Parting of the Ways A.D. 70–135*. Edited by J. D. G. Dunn. WUNT 66. Tübingen: Mohr Siebeck, 1992.

Daley, B. E. *The Hope of the Early Church: A Handbook of Patristic Eschatology*. Cambridge: Cambridge University Press, 1991.

Draper, J. A. "Eschatology in the Didache." Pages 567–82 in *Eschatology of the New Testament and Some Related Documents*. Edited by Jan G. van der Watt. WUNT 2/315. Tübingen: Mohr Siebeck, 2011.

Fudge, E. "The Eschatology of Ignatius of Antioch: Christocentric and Historical." *JETS* 15 (1972): 231–37.

Hermanns, A. "Le Pseudo-Barnabé: Est-il millénariste?" *ETL* 35 (1959): 848–76.

Hill, C. E. *Regnum Caelorum: Patterns of Millennial Thought in Early Christianity*. 2nd ed. Grand Rapids: Eerdmans, 2001.

Jefford, C. N. *The Epistle to Diognetus (with the Fragment of Quadratus): Introduction, Text, and Commentary*. OAF. Oxford: Oxford University Press, 2013.

Knoch, O. *Eigenart und Bedeutung der Eschatologie im theologischen Aufriss des ersten Clemensbriefes: Eine auslegungsgeschichtliche Untersuchung*. Theophaneia 17. Bonn: Hanstein, 1964.

Lohmann, H. *Drohung und Verheißung: Exegetische Untersuchungen zur Eschatologie bei den Apostolischen Vätern*. BZNW 55. Berlin: de Gruyter, 1989.

O'Hagan, A. P. *Material Re-Creation in the Apostolic Fathers*. TUGAL 100. Berlin: Akademie, 1968.

Rhee, H. "Wealth, Poverty, and Eschatology: Pre-Constantine Christian Social Thought and the Hope for the World to Come." Pages 64–84 in *Reading Patristic Texts on Social Ethics: Issues and Challenges for Twenty-First Century Christian Social Thought*. Edited by J. Leemans, B. J. Matz, and J. Verstraeten. CUA Studies in Early Christianity. Washington, DC: Catholic University of America Press, 2011.

Wilhite, S. J. *"One of Life and One of Death": Apocalypticism and the Didache's Two Ways*. Gorgias Studies in Early Christianity and Patristics 70. Piscataway, NJ: Gorgias, 2019.

CHAPTER 17

WOMEN AND GENDER IN THE APOSTOLIC FATHERS

CAROLYN OSIEK

1. INTRODUCTION

What are known today as the Apostolic Fathers is a miscellaneous collection of early Christian texts, some contemporary with the latest New Testament writings, some immediately following, and some later in the second century. Together, these texts witness to the life of Christian communities over several generations, "not an authoritative collection of books, but a convenient one."[1] Interpreted carefully, they give hints of social life and relationships around their origins. In this collection, there are references to biblical women (1 Clement, Barnabas, Diognetus, Papias), probably historical women (Ignatius, Hermas), and mythological and allegorical female figures (1 Clement, Hermas). There are also images of masculinity (Martyrdom of Polycarp, Hermas), issues of family ethics and practice (Didache, Hermas), and gender metaphor (2 Clement, Hermas).

Like other literature of their age, these texts reflect the ideas, attitudes, and behaviors of the people of their time and place with regard to sex and gender. While today notions of "gender" vary widely, this chapter will understand gender as a socially constructed distinction in human thinking and behavior, based on physiology, and will attempt to render it as understood in the time period in which the relevant literature was written.

It will come as no surprise to scholars of Mediterranean antiquity that the thinking and the language of this literature is patriarchal and androcentric. Masculine language for God prevails, though with some surprising exceptions, and male experience is considered the norm, as is masculine address, both singular and plural, whether or not women are present in a mixed group. Sometimes the male composition of the intended audience is reinforced, as in the address "men, brothers" (ἄνδρες ἀδελφοί, *andres adelphoi*) in canonical Acts and 1 Clement. The grammatical convention of masculine plural for mixed groups should be kept in mind, so that it need not always be assumed that only males compose the group; for example, the διάκονοι, *diakonoi* ("ministers," later "deacons") of Ignatius, *To the Trallians* 2.3, or Polycarp, *To the Philippians* 5.2, may include females, remembering Phoebe of Romans 16:1. The presence of women is ambiguous, though there are exceptions; for example, 2 Clement 19.1; 20.2; Barnabas 1.1; and Didache 4.9–10, where gender distinctions are made both in addressing brothers and sisters, sons and daughters, and in treatment of slaves. One wonders if in such unusual cases there were particular factors in the creation of the texts that warranted these exceptions.

1. B. D. Ehrman, *The Apostolic Fathers*, 2 vols., LCL (Cambridge: Harvard University Press, 2003), 1:13.

Gender stereotypes generally prevail, contrasting feminine weakness with masculine heroism and strength. There are instances in the literature in which women show unexpected "masculine" strength. The example of heroic women whose strength confounds shameful male weakness or takeoffs on male ineffectiveness are a known literary theme; for example, Aristophanes, *Ecclesiazusae* (*Women of the Assembly*), and Plutarch, *Mulierem virtutes* (*Virtues of Women*). They are the exceptions that prove the rule.

2. FIRST CLEMENT

Perhaps the best known of the texts in the Apostolic Fathers collection, 1 Clement contains some interesting features from the perspective of this chapter. It purports to be the letter of the Roman Christian community to the comparable group in Corinth, presenting a case against what appears to be a recent coup of younger members against an older governing group there.

The communication is explicitly from one group of males to another. The three envoys sent to Corinth from Rome are specifically ἄνδρες ("males") who are trustworthy and known locally from their youth (1 Clem. 63.3). They are named at 65.1: Claudius Ephebus and Valerius Bito, two names that strongly suggest that they are freedmen, along with Fortunatus, likely the slave of one of them. If so, it is surprising that he is even named, and it may be an indication, like Paul's letter to Philemon, of recognition of the personhood of slaves as a regular practice in these communities. Four times, the recipients of the letter are addressed as ἄνδρες ἀδελφοί ("males, brothers"), envisioning an audience in which only men are considered (14.1; 37.1; 43.4; 62.1; compare the same address in Acts 1:16; 2:29, and twelve more times there). These men are encouraged to protect their women and keep them in line with traditional feminine behavior. Thus the recipients are praised for respecting the elderly, teaching the young proper behavior, and instructing wives to love their husbands, run their households well, and live discretely under the norm of submission (ὑποταγή, *hypotagē*, 1 Clem. 1.3). Likewise later, in something of a modified household code, all should honor the elderly, discipline youth and children, and teach their wives to be virtuous, careful in speech, showing no partiality (21.6–8; cf. Titus 2:1–9). Among the many biblical comparisons are Lot and his wife (Gen 19). Lot is put forth as an example of φιλοξενία, *philoxenia* ("hospitality") and εὐσέβεια, *eusebeia* ("piety"), while his wife, of course, exemplifies the δίψυχοι, *dipsychoi* ("double-minded") (1 Clem. 11.1–2).

The expectation of submission of wives to husbands, using the language of ὑποταγή ("submission"), was by this time endemic to any consideration of household management (see the classic NT texts at Col 3:18; Eph 5:22–24, with reciprocal love on the part of husbands). In 1 Clement 1.3, the text in point comes at the end of a line of praise for the Corinthian recipients for doing everything traditionally; the author will, of course, go on later to point out what they are *not* doing as they should. The literary form is not the household code, in which reciprocal duties are enunciated. Here, there is no counterpart requirement that husbands love their wives. On the contrary, the love command is also an expectation of wives toward their husbands. There is nothing surprising about the picture given here. What does come as a surprise, however, is that 1 Clement 1.3 is the last time in the Christian literature of this period that the language of submission is applied to wives. It simply goes out of use in this context. It continues in mutual submission to one another (38.1; 57.2; 63.1) after the manner of Ephesians 5:21, and will appear applied to slaves in Didache 4.11. But more broadly, submission will now be applied to appropriate deference to church leaders, already, for example, in 1 Clement 57.2; 61.1. The private and domestic has become public and communal.

For the rest, there are passing references to biblical women in narrative contexts in which they would be expected to appear: besides Lot's wife (1 Clem. 11.2), there is Miriam (4.11). There are also more extended positive, even heroic, depictions of three women, after the literary tradition of praising valiant women, such as will be done in the next generation by Plutarch's *Mulierem virtutes*. The story of Rahab of Jericho, who saved her family by hiding and thus saving the Israelite spies, is recited narratively, based on Joshua 2:1–22. In the previous chapter, Lot served as an example of hospitality and piety (11.1), and then Rahab is offered as an example of faith and hospitality at 12.1 (for her faith, see also Heb 11:31). Ironically, while here and in Hebrews Rahab is extolled for her faith, in the ongoing diatribe of James about faith and works, she becomes a heroine of works (Jas 2:25).

Rahab is not only held up as an example of faith and hospitality. The author weaves further meaning from the scarlet cord that she is told to hang in the window in order to save her family from destruction at the hands of the invading Israelites. The color of the cord becomes a sign of blood, the blood of the Lord through which redemption can come to those who believe and hope in God. Never mind that in hanging the scarlet cord, she followed the directions given her: because of her action, Rahab not only exercised faith, but also prophecy (1 Clem. 12.7–8).

Judith and Esther get briefer attention but are also brought forth as examples of heroism, even the performance of manliness (ἀνδρεία, *andreia*, 1 Clem. 55.3), in keeping with the literary tradition that extols the heroism of women to confound the cowardice of men. In the context of many, including many women, who have risked their lives or endangered them, the "blessed" Judith (ἡ μακαρία, *hē makaria*) put herself in danger by going out to the enemy camp, and as a result the enemy leader, Holofernes, was handed over into the hands of a female (θηλεία, *thēleia*, 55.4–5), a shameful death for a military leader. Likewise, Esther placed herself in danger in order to rescue her people, and she saved them—not by her risky appearance in court as in the original story but rather by her fasting and humility by which she begged God for their deliverance (55.6). This idea leads into the beginning of the next theme, an appeal to humility for all (56.1).

These three biblical women, Rahab, Judith, and Esther, are integrated into contexts of exemplary behavior, from heroism to humility. More puzzling is the reference to women persecuted like the Danaids and Dircae (1 Clem. 6.2). The mythical Dircae was killed by being dragged by a bull. This scene is depicted with surprising frequency in Roman domestic art of the period, as evidenced on the walls of domestic settings in Pompeii. The usual interpretation of the reference in 1 Clement is as an allusion to the known cases of reenactment of mythical deaths as public executions, and even of Nero's creative ways of executing Christians after the fire of 64 CE, according to Suetonius (*Nero* 11.12), though Suetonius makes no explicit reference to an execution in the manner of that of Dircae. It is disputed whether the artistic depictions on house walls are meant to recall the amphitheater spectacle or simply the mythical story itself.[2]

The reference to the Danaids is less clear. According to the myths, as punishment for killing their husbands on their wedding night, they were condemned perpetually to carry

2. Cf. E. M. Coleman, "Fatal Charades: Roman Executions Staged as Mythological Enactments," *JRS* 80 (1990): 65–66; D. L. Balch, "Violence in Pompeian/Roman Domestic Art as a Visual Context for the Pauline and Deutero-Pauline Letters," in *Early Christianity in Pompeian Light: People, Texts, Situations*, ed. B. Longenecker (Minneapolis: Fortress, 2016), 129–32, and D. L. Balch, "Greek Tragedy, Pompeian Amphitheater Art, and Christian Martyrs in Nero's Gardens (1 Clem. 6.2 and Tacitus, *Ann.* 15.44)," in *The Social Worlds of Ancient Jews and Christians: Essays in Honor of L. Michael White*, ed. J. Gunderson, G. A. Keddie, and D. Boin, NovTSup 189 (Leiden: Brill, 2022), 225–55.

water jars to fill a bottomless container, "a scenario plainly lacking in spectacular appeal."[3] The appearance of women carrying water jars would immediately suggest the Danaids to a mythologically educated audience, but as Colemen points out, the mythological symbolism did not always have to correspond directly to the manner of execution. The difficulty of interpretation has led to theories of textual corruption, but no extant manuscript supports this.

3. SECOND CLEMENT

Unlike 1 Clement, 2 Clement has no female biblical heroines to propose. Probably not a letter at all but a sermon, it uses the usual male address of "brothers" (ἀδελφοί) frequently throughout. An allusion to a well-attested Gospel saying attributed to Jesus—that those who do the will of the Father/God are brother, sister, and mother to Jesus (Matt 12:50; Mark 3:35; Luke 8:21)—omits sister and mother (2 Clem. 9.11). On the contrary, close to the end, in 19.1 and 20.2, both brothers and sisters are explicitly addressed (ἀδελφοὶ καὶ ἀδελφαί, *adelphoi kai adelphai*), along with other changes in the text, signaling a conclusion perhaps written by someone else (suggested also by allusions there to having heard the word, and the reader now speaking to the recipients [19.1]).

Donfried sees the text of 2 Clement consisting of three distinct sections, based on genre analysis: a theological opener (2 Clem. 1–2), a long section devoted to ethical exhortation (3–14), and an eschatological reflection (15–18), followed by a conclusion (19–20). The text very early sets the tone with a metaphor of motherhood by quoting Isaiah 54:1, a beatitude for the childless woman in reversal of the usual priority on childbearing (2 Clem. 2.1). The author immediately begins the process of extended allegory on a group of biblical texts that will continue through most of the composition. The commentary on Isaiah 54:1 continues through 2 Clement 2.3 and sustains the image of childbearing and labor. The exhortation for the infertile to rejoice refers to "us"—that is, the church, which should not be worn down like a woman in labor.

For the most part, the entire text is a passionate appeal to repentance and conversion of life in conventional terms. That is why it comes as a total surprise that in 2 Clement 12, as exhortation to await the kingdom of God by living rightly, the author includes a passage about the overcoming of difference between male and female as the prerequisite for the arrival of the kingdom: "When the two will be one, and the outside like the inside, and the male with the female, neither male nor female." A very similar passage is known from Gospel of Thomas 22,[4] and a citation attributed by Clement of Alexandria to an unknown Gospel of the Egyptians (Clement of Alexandria, *Strom.* 3.13).[5] Scholars cite various New Testament texts as possible background, among them John 17:20–23; Romans 12:4–5; and Ephesians 2:14–18, all about unity and overcoming differences. Certainly, though, the

3. Coleman, "Fatal Charades," 66.

4. "Jesus saw infants being suckled. He said to his disciples, 'These infants being suckled are like those who enter the kingdom.' They said to him, 'Shall we then, as children, enter the kingdom?' Jesus said to them, 'When you make the two one, and when you make the inside like the outside and the outside like the inside, and the above like the below, and when you make the male and the female one and the same, so that the male not be male nor the female; and when you fashion eyes in the place of an eye, and a hand in place of a hand, and a foot in place of a foot, and a likeness in place of a likeness; then will you enter the kingdom'" (Gos. Thom. 22, trans. T. Lambdin, "Gospel of Thomas," www.marquette.edu/maqom/Gospel%20of%20Thomas%20Lambdin.pdf).

5. "When Salome asked when she would know the answer to her question the Lord replied, 'When you trample underfoot the [garment] of shame, and when the two become one and the male is one with the female, and there is no more male and female'" ("Clement of Alexandria," Christian Churches of God, trans. John Ferguson, www.ccg.org/weblibs/study-papers/b3.html).

most immediately relevant New Testament passage is Galatians 3:28, where "there is no longer male and female, for all of you are one in Christ Jesus" (NRSV). Various interpretations are offered to this passage from Galatians, from community harmony to restoration of an original androgyne human being.[6] It may hint at a certain fluidity in gender roles, though more likely, in certain gnostic circles, at transcendence of earthly passions like sexual desire.

This may be the milieu in which the saying arose and was then used in 2 Clement. It is mysterious, then, that it should appear in this sermon that otherwise shows almost no trace of gnosticizing and that has been argued by Donfried to be actively "degnosticizing."[7] Perhaps the saying was popular in the author's circle, or its proponents were challenging the author's approach, and he moved to reinterpret it according to his purpose. The author completely demystifies the saying by moving it into the realm of ethics and relational behavior: the two are one when we speak truth to each other and have the same spirit (2 Clem. 12.3). The inside is like the outside when a person's soul is just as manifest as the body, through his or her good deeds (12.4). The male and female together, neither male nor female, means regarding one another as brother and sister, not sexual objects (12.5).

The text enters into a glimpse of gendered transcendental ecclesiology in chapter 14. Doing the will of God means belonging to the preexistent spiritual church,[8] which is now the living church, the body of Christ. The creation of humanity as male and female in Genesis 1:27 (2 Clem. 14.1–2) is interpreted in gendered terms: the male is Christ, the female is the church. The spiritual church appeared as the flesh of Christ, the mirror image of the Spirit. Therefore, anyone who abuses or corrupts the flesh does the same to the Spirit (14.3–4). Again, an idea that could lead in a gnosticizing direction is brought down to ethical admonitions that affirm fleshly realities.

Lying behind this passage are familiar New Testament passages like 1 Corinthians 12:12–27, Romans 12:1–8, Colossians 3:18, and Ephesians 1:22–23. Undoubtedly, though, a primary source for the gendering of Christ and church is Ephesians 5:22–33 and whatever earlier traditions may lie behind it, a passage and a paradigm that remain both inspiration and obstacle in contemporary ecclesiology.[9] The association of male with spirit and Christ, in complement to the association of female with flesh and church in a quasi-marital relationship, not only echoes traditional philosophy of gender subordination but cements it by elevating it to the transcendental spiritual realm. It is then embedded in the very nature of the understanding of the human-divine relationship that casts not only women but men as well into the subordinate role of the church. Despite the gender-inclusive nature of incorporation in the church, however, the metaphor is a handy way to legitimate gender subordination.

The author of 2 Clement does not emphasize the hierarchical gendered relationship implied in the Christ-church paradigm. On the contrary, he turns it to his purpose of encouragement to right living for all. Nevertheless, the use of this extended symbolism continues the complex nature of the metaphor in early Christianity.

---

6. Options discussed in W. A. Meeks, "The Image of the Androgyne: Some Uses of a Symbol in Early Christianity," in *In Search of the Early Christians: Selected Essays*, ed. A. R. Hilton and H. G. Snyder (New Haven: Yale University Press, 2002), 3–54.

7. K. P. Donfried, "The Theology of Second Clement," *HTR* 66 (1973): 491–97.

8. For the preexistence of the church, see Herm. Vis. 2.4; Osiek, *Shepherd*, 58–59.

9. See C. Osiek, "The Bride of Christ (Ephesians 5:22–33): A Problematic Wedding," *BTB* 32.1 (2002): 29–39, reprinted in *Sacred Marriages: The Divine-Human Sexual Metaphor from Sumer to Early Christianity*, ed. M. Nissinen and R. Uro (Winona Lake, IN: Eisenbrauns, 2008), 371–92.

4. IGNATIUS AND POLYCARP

The manuscript history of the Ignatian letters is complicated. This chapter assumes the "middle recension" of seven letters. The correspondence of Ignatius with Mary of Cassobola is now recognized as spurious.

The worldview of Ignatius of Antioch as revealed in his letters is pervasively patriarchal. God is a father with ultimate authority, imaged in the bishop. It is debated to what extent the three-tiered hierarchical model of ministry, led by a single bishop with his presbyters and deacons, was already in place in the churches he visited, and to what extent Ignatius was a leading proponent of such a structure, introducing and reinforcing it as he went. Indeed, the seemingly well-developed clerical hierarchy assumed in the letters is an argument for later rather than earlier dating. However that may be, the bishop in his view is to be revered as the Lord himself (Ign. *Eph.* 6.1), standing in the place of God to the community, with the presbyters representing the council of the apostles, and the deacons as a type of Jesus Christ (Ign. *Magn.* 6.1, 13).[10] Whereas Pauline Ephesians 5:22–33 and 2 Clement 14.2 imprint male dominance by equating the male person and husband with Christ, Ignatius expands that analogy from Christ to God: it is now directly the authority of God represented in the bishop. The sphere of male dominance is expanded from the family to the public context of the church. Yet, surprisingly, there are passages that grant equal regard to men and women where it is not expected.

The language of submission is now directed to the community as their proper response to the authority of the bishop. Instructions to wives elsewhere in the Ignatian letters convey a message of love and fidelity, but not of wifely submission (Ign. *Pol.* 5.1). Marriage should take place with the consent of the bishop (5.2), which probably does not yet mean a "church" ceremony, since it will be many centuries before that is evident. Wives are to be taught to love their husbands and raise their children to fear God. Rather than language of submission directed at wives as in earlier texts, while the reciprocal duty of husbands is to love their wives (the Pauline Eph 5:25–33), here there is no language of submission but rather of love as the duty of wives as well as husbands (see also Pol. *Phil.* 4.2).

Beyond the three-tiered hierarchical structure that Ignatius promotes, we learn something with regard to the presumed social organization of these communities, particularly about their services to the needy. Throughout biblical literature, stereotyped but in general probably reflecting actual situations, concern is expressed for the plight of widows and their children when left behind without resources on the death of husbands and fathers (e.g., Deut 10:18; 14:29; 16:11; Wis 2:10; Sir 35:14; Jas 1:27; also Herm. Vis. 2.4.3; Mand. 8.10). The widow and orphan are the classic image of social helplessness, and one of the contemptuous remarks about the heterodox is that they do not care for widow and orphan (Ign. *Smyrn.* 6.2; Barn. 20.2). Already in Luke's depiction of the first years of the church in Jerusalem, widows are the objects of food distribution and of other kinds of assistance (Acts 6:1; 9:36–39). At the same time, there are indications of an order of widows, somewhat similar to female deacons, who must be carefully vetted and are then something of a service group within the community, especially to offer hospitality and personal presence.[11]

First Timothy 5:3–16 seems to vacillate between the two images of the role of widows

10. Later churches of the third and fourth centuries that have deaconesses among their church leaders will pick up this analogy and add deaconesses as a type of the Holy Spirit (*Didascalia* 9, Apos. Con. 2.26.6).

11. Later this order of widows will function with seeming authority as part of local church councils and as ordained substitutes for deaconesses, who instruct women, baptize, and belong to the clergy (*Testamentum Domini*, esp. 1.19, 23, 34; 40.1–2); see K. Madigan and C. Osiek, eds., *Ordained Women in the Early Church: A Documentary History* (Baltimore: John Hopkins University Press, 2005), 156–60.

in the church. In verses 3–8, the qualification is to have no resources from family, and thus to be truly needy. In verses 9–10, however, emphasis has shifted to other qualifications: there is an age minimum and elements of behavior necessary to be "enrolled" on some official list. Such a widow can be no younger than sixty, married only once; she has successfully raised her children and has shown hospitality. Needing assistance is not a factor. The age of sixty was advanced and could preclude many otherwise potential enrollees who had already died. Younger widows are not to be enrolled but rather should remarry, since they are likely not to conform to the behavioral expectations of those so enrolled. Of course, remarriage would preclude their being enrolled later under the rubric of being once married, so there does not seem to be a long-term plan here. The reference to gossip reflects networks of oral communication among women that normally exclude men but are important social media for the ongoing formation of community identity (1 Tim 5:13).

In similar contexts, widows are mentioned twice in the Ignatian letters, probably in the two different ways discussed above. In Ignatius, *To Polycarp* 4.1 comes an ordinary admonishment to Polycarp not to neglect widows, for after God, they are his responsibility. This is a consideration of widows in the more traditional sense, as those in need of regular church assistance. At Smyrna, however, Ignatius sends greetings to his "brothers," along with their wives and children, and then to another kind of widow group: the virgins who are called widows (τὰς παρθένους τὰς λεγομένας χήρας, *tas parthenous tas legomenas chēras*, Ign. *Smyrn.* 13). The practice of celibacy in early Christian circles is attested early. Already Paul in 1 Corinthians 7 gives his opinion on a custom that has arisen in the Corinthian communities. In view of eschatological expectations, he expresses himself cautiously in favor of remaining single for those not already married, as long as they can remain so in peace, without struggle (1 Cor 7:8–9, 25–35). The final point of the strange eunuch saying in Matthew seems to point in the same direction, though not without ambiguity (Matt 19:12). Ignatius in his letter to Polycarp recognizes such a practice, taking it for granted, only commenting on the need not to boast about it (Ign. *Pol.* 5.2). Justin in Rome a few years later witnesses to the practice of celibacy there by those who so choose (*1 Apol.* 1.15, 29). In the Ignatian context, why virgins who are called widows? Why are they not just called by what they are? Perhaps it is because communities at this time were used to groups of widows for the sake of distribution and care, but the grouping together of virgins is new in the community of Smyrna and elsewhere. The title "widows" connoted not only recipients of charity but a group that could be called upon for various services. A group of virgins called by that name, however, is recognized in Philippi by Polycarp (Pol. *Phil.* 5.3).

Immediately after the greeting to the virgins called widows, Ignatius names several people to whom he expresses his gratitude. A deacon named Philo is with him, having come with Ignatius from Cilicia (Ign. *Phld.* 11.1); presumably he is known to the Smyrnaeans. Two women are then named: Tavia and Alce, then two men, Daphnos and Euteknos. Tavia is mistress of a household, all of whose members are greeted by Ignatius. Along with earlier women householders such as Lydia (Acts 16:14–15), Nympha (Col 4:15), and perhaps Chloe (1 Cor 1:11) and Phoebe (Rom 16:1–2), Tavia is hostess and leader of a local community that meets in her house. About the other woman in the verse, Alce, Ignatius simply says that hers is a name dear to him. Nothing else is known about her involvement in the circle of Ignatius, but she may have a continuing family relationship. In Martyrdom of Polycarp 17.2, after Polycarp's death, Nicetas, identified as father of Herod and brother of Alce, petitioned the magistrate not to hand over Polycarp's body to his followers. The naming of the relationship with an otherwise unexplained woman named Alce must presume knowledge of her and her family relationships among the earliest readers of the martyrdom account.

In the context of general moral instruction, Ignatius exhorts Polycarp and his flock to proper treatment of the enslaved, deliberately specifying both male and female slaves in a mutual admonition against arrogance: "Do not be arrogant to male slaves or female slaves" (Ign. *Pol.* 4.3). The slaveholder should not treat the enslaved arrogantly, but neither should the enslaved become arrogant but rather should serve all the more readily and not rely on church funds to buy their freedom. The mention of this possibility suggests a known practice of using church funds for this purpose, which would have been high motivation for conversion on the part of the enslaved. Similar exhortations toward respectful treatment of slaves and servile dedication to service, with no suggestion of the advantage of manumission, were frequent, especially in the so-called household codes (Eph 6:5–9; Col 3:22–4:1; 1 Tim 6:1–2; Did. 4.10–11).[12] The gender distinction deliberately made here, when by grammatical custom the masculine plural is expected to include both sexes, implicitly raises the question that hovers in Christian paraenesis for slaveholding households: that of presumed sexual availability of the enslaved to their slaveholders and the lack of any specific prohibition of sexual abuse of the enslaved in early Christian teaching.[13] One kind of arrogant treatment was sexual abuse; indeed, the Greek word ὑβρίζειν, *hybrizein*, generally meaning to treat outrageously, can also refer to rape. This is not the word used here in Ignatius, *To Polycarp* 4.3; rather it is ὑπερφαίνομαι, *hyperphainomai*, generally to superimpose, but the same question could be suggested: the ambiguous position of especially, but not exclusively, female slaves with regard to sexual availability.

Polycarp's letter to the Philippians faithfully reflects the memory of Paul and draws on other Pauline letters to exhort the recipients to fidelity to the Pauline legacy. In the process, he alludes to Hagar and Sarah, without naming them, as earthly and heavenly Jerusalem (Gal 4:26; Pol. *Phil.* 3.3): faith is our mother, leading to hope and love. In the course of general paraenesis, he quotes the terms for unacceptable sexual behavior from 1 Corinthians 6:9 (Pol. *Phil.* 5.3), but without further comment.

The Ignatius-Polycarp correspondence portrays the two hero-martyrs as examples of manliness, as expected in gender roles of heroic figures: strong yet wise, gracious, and in control. The Martyrdom of Polycarp 9.1 relates a heavenly voice that only Polycarp's community hears, to strengthen him as he enters the stadium for his final combat: "Be strong, Polycarp, and act like a man" (ἀνδρίζου, *andrizou*).[14] These writings reflect a time in which fidelity to the immediate past is of prime importance, yet many structures and understandings have changed.

5. THE DIDACHE

The opening part of the Didache is an extended teaching on the Two Ways, the way of life (Did. 1–4) and the way of death (5). Within the first, the way of life, the first chapter emphasizes love and positive action. The second chapter turns to those actions to avoid: murder, adultery, pederasty, *porneia*,[15] theft, magic, sorcery, and, rather surprisingly, abortion and infanticide (Did. 2.2), one of the earliest Christian sources to specify this

12. Paul's admonition to the enslaved to be satisfied with their status (1 Cor 7:21–24) contains an ambiguity in v. 21 that continues to be debated: either relish the status you have or take advantage of a chance for freedom. Translators are faced with the need to decide one way or the other.

13. See J. A. Glancy, "Slavery and Sexual Availability," in *The Oxford Handbook of New Testament, Gender, and Sexuality*, ed. B. H. Dunning (Oxford: Oxford University Press, 2019), 627–44, and further bibliography there.

14. For comment on this term, see below on Herm. Vis. 1.4.3.

15. An indefinite and often-used word for any kind of sexual irregularity short of adultery, referring to both incest and prostitution in 1 Cor 5–6, then indefinite again at 7:2.

prohibition, along with Barnabas 19.5, where much of the same paraenesis occurs. It is not clear whether the prohibition against killing a child already born includes in the minds of the authors the common practice of exposure or abandonment of unwanted newborns, since many so exposed were taken up by others.[16] Later, Tertullian among others will critique abortion, abandonment, and infanticide and claim that Christians raise all their children (*Apol.* 9).

While abortion and infanticide are not, strictly speaking, issues of gender, across cultures the decisions, moral issues, and blame weigh almost exclusively on women.

As part of the instruction on the Two Ways, the issue of appropriate control of children and slaves is raised (Did. 4.9–11; also Barn. 19.5–7). In both cases, as in Ignatius, *Polycarp* 4.3, male and female children and slaves are verbally differentiated, υἱός, *huios* ("son") from θυγάτηρ, *thygatēr* ("daughter") and δοῦλος, *doulos* ("male slave") from παιδίσκη, *paidiskē* ("handmaid"). The male householder to whom the instruction is addressed is admonished not to remove his hand from son or daughter, but from their youth to teach them the fear of God, presumably including by corporal punishment (similar to Prov 23:13–14). Ephesians 6:2–4 had already admonished fathers to raise their children in παιδεία, *paideia*, and νουθεσία, *nouthesia*, "discipline" and "admonishment." The disciplining of boys with physical punishment runs deep in the literature of παιδεία.[17] Physical discipline of girls does not. Perhaps that is why here the sexes are differentiated, intended for different treatment. The differentiation of gender expectations was great: the boy was expected to form courageous character and physical resistance so as to possess virile strength, while the girl was expected to acquire a gentle character so as to be shaped into shy and silent docility. Of course, the literature is full of contrary examples, women who proved to be more "virile" than men.[18]

In a similar way, male and female slaves are sorted out. In neither case should the slaveholder command out of πικρία, *pikria*, "bitterness," lest the slave, who hopes in the same God, be discouraged. The language of submission, now abandoned for wives to husbands, lingers in the servile relationship: slaves of both sexes are to submit (ὑποτάσσειν, *hypotassein*) to their masters with deference.

As already noted above, canonical Ephesians and Colossians, mirrored in 2 Clement, enhanced the symbolism of male authority by equating husband with Christ (Eph 5:22–33; Col 3:18; cf. 2 Clem. 14.2), and Ignatius raised the level of symbolic authority by equating the bishop with God the Father (Ign. *Eph.* 6.1; *Magn.* 6.1). In a similar way, while canonical Ephesians 6:5–8 and Colossians 3:24–25 enjoin slaves to obey their master as Christ, the Didache escalates that analogy. The master is now a type (τύπος, *typos*) of God (Did. 4.11).

---

16. On rejection of a newborn and chances of survival in the hands of others, see B. Rawson, *Children and Childhood in Roman Italy* (Oxford: Oxford University Press, 2003), 95–119; J. Boswell, *The Kindness of Strangers: The Abandonment of Children in Western Europe from Late Antiquity to the Renaissance* (New York: Pantheon, 1988). On the Roman practice of abandonment of children and Jewish and Christian critique, see C. Osiek and D. L. Balch, *Families in the New Testament World: Households and House Churches* (Louisville: Westminster John Knox, 1997), 65–66, 163–64; C. Osiek and M. Y. MacDonald, with J. H. Tulloch, *A Woman's Place: House Churches in Earliest Christianity* (Minneapolis: Augsburg Fortress, 2006), 51–53; Rawson, *Children*, 114–19. The Apoc. Pet. 8 has special punishment in hell for those who procure abortion or practice infanticide. Other early Christian voices include Athenagoras, *Leg.* 35; Diogn. 5.6; Minucius Felix 30.1.

17. Discussion and examples in Rawson, *Children*, 175–77; M. Y. MacDonald, *The Power of Children: The Construction of Christian Families in the Greco-Roman World* (Waco, TX: Baylor University Press, 2014), 75–81; Osiek and Balch, *Families*, 163–67.

18. Besides well-known examples like Aristophanes, *Ecclesiazousae* and *Lysistrata*; Plutarch, *Mulierum virtutes*, also Blandina in *The Martyrs of Lyon and Vienne*; Perpetua; Judith (1 Clem. 55.4–5).

The section on visiting teacher-prophets (Did. 11–13) assumes grammatically that they are all males, and the analogy with high priests reinforces that assumption (Did. 13.3). Since the grammatical masculine plural is used for mixed groups, it cannot be said with certainty that all such itinerants envisioned in the text are male, though a lone traveling female prophet is unlikely. Given known earlier missionary couples, however (e.g., Prisca and Aquila, Andronicus and Junia) that possibility should be kept in mind. The ἐπίσκοποι, *episkopoi*, and διάκονοι, *diakonoi* ("overseers" and "ministers") who are to replace them are ἄνδρες, *andres* ("males"; Did. 15.1).

6. THE EPISTLE OF BARNABAS

The opening line of the letter is unusual in its gender inclusivity: the greeting is to sons and daughters (see also Barn. 19.5; cf. Did. 4.9). Those who offer the sin offering are ἄνδρες ("males"), as could be expected (Barn. 8.1–2).

Barnabas's idiocentric and sustained insistence is that the Mosaic law was never meant to be followed literally but rather spiritually. It takes up the food prohibitions of Leviticus 11 as allegories of avoidance of certain practices and certain kinds of people: pigs are those who only recognize God when hungry; eels, octopus, and cuttlefish are lowlifes who do not live in the open, etc. In this context, the hare is the allegory of the pederast (παιδοφθόρος, *paidophthoros*, Barn. 10.6). Departing now from the forbidden meats in Leviticus 11, gender fluidity also comes under attack: the hyena, which reputedly changes sexes every year, is likened to the adulterer and the φθορεύς, *phthoreus*, "corrupter" (10.7). The weasel, said to conceive through the mouth, is an allegory for oral sex, either by men or women (Barn. 10.8).

In its teaching on the way of light and the way of death (Barn. 19–20), there are many literary parallels with the similar section of the Didache (Did. 1–4), presumably the earlier document. Thus, there are the same prohibitions on *porneia* (see note 15 above), adultery, and pederasty (Barn. 19.4), abortion and infanticide (19.5), and abuse of slaves (19.7), as well as the same admonition with regard to discipline of sons and daughters (19.5). In the description of the way of darkness, one proof of belonging in that camp is the usual citation of neglect of widows and orphans. Again, infanticide is condemned, along with corrupters of what God has made, a possible reference to gender inconsistency (20.1–2).

Beyond paraenetic passages, the author continues with his biblical allegory. Among many other stories interpreted, previously infertile Rebecca appears as mother of two nations, one of which will dominate the other (Gen 25:21–23). We should understand, says the author, who is Isaac here and who is Rebecca, and which nation proves stronger than the other (Barn. 13.2–3). In his supersessionist interpretation, the answer is clear and does not need to be stated.

7. THE LETTER TO DIOGNETUS

This beautifully written anonymous apology argues that Christians live everywhere and in normal ways (Diogn. 5.1–2), yet it creates a worldview in which they are as soul to the body of the world (Diogn. 6). In that capacity, they live as resident aliens, and so can be at home anywhere (5.5), yet they live within certain boundaries that others do not share. Among those boundaries, they marry and have children but do not practice exposure of children. They share meals but not sex (5.6–7).[19]

There is an enigmatic reference to Eve toward the end of the text. The final chapter is a

19. There is a play on words here: they hold the table κοινήν, *koinēn*, but not κοίτην, *koitēn*.

meditation on the two trees of the garden of Eden, the tree of life and the tree of knowledge of good and evil (Gen 1:9). It is not the tree of knowledge that kills, the author argues, but its misuse through the disobedience of those there at the beginning (not of the woman alone, who is not blamed). Proper knowledge is essential to know the truth, and picking its fruit is safe from the serpent, who cannot reach it. Then Eve is not corrupted, ἀλλὰ παρθένος πιστεύεται, *alla parthenos pisteuetai*, literally, "but a virgin is believed or trusted" (Diogn. 12.8). In the next lines, the final ones of the document, salvation is known, and redemption moves forward. But is this biblical Eve, not otherwise called a virgin, or an image of the heart of the one who seeks true knowledge (12.7)? In many especially gnostic creation myths, the restoration of the primeval androgyne undoes the error of separation and restores the human image to its virginal state.[20] This is perhaps what is intended here.

8. THE FRAGMENTS OF PAPIAS

Two allusions in the fragments are of interest, both from Eusebius's careful compilations. The first is a reference to a story of Jesus and a woman accused before the Lord of many sins, attributed to Papias by Eusebius, who also adds that the same story was found in the Gospel of the Hebrews, an apocryphal collection existing only in a few citations (Eusebius *Hist. eccl.* 3.39.17). Many interpreters have assumed that it is more or less the same as John 7:53–8:11. If so, it is strange that Eusebius relates the story only to the Gospel of the Hebrews, and not to canonical John. Luke 7:36–50 is also a possibly related story. There was more than one story circulating about Jesus and a sinful woman. Not enough is known about this one to say what might be its relationship to the others.[21]

The other is about Philip the evangelist, specified as one of the seven (Acts 6:5), and his four prophetic daughters.[22] They first appear in Acts 21:9 in Caesarea, in an enhanced prophetic context. While the four women do not speak, the next verse brings the prophet Agabus into their house to perform his symbolic action to warn Paul of coming trouble in Jerusalem (Acts 21:10–11). Nothing else is heard about them until the later tradition. Despite the identification of this Philip as one of the seven, or the evangelist, the later traditions confuse him with Philip the apostle. The daughters, too, suffer changing fates. At Eusebius's *Historia ecclesiastica* 3.30.1, quoting Clement of Alexandria (*Strom.* 3.52–53) in defense of marriage, the daughters are all married off to husbands. When quoting Polycrates, Eusebius is not sure how many daughters there were; two remained unmarried into old age and were buried with their father at Hierapolis, while one other was buried in Ephesus (*Hist. eccl.* 3.31.3). When he quotes Gaius, all four daughters are back, and all buried in Hierapolis (*Hist. eccl.* 3.31.4). When Eusebius draws on Papias, it is Philip the apostle living with all four daughters at Hierapolis, where Papias visited them and learned of a wonderful story from them about the resuscitation of a dead person in their own time, as well as another story about Justus Barsabas (*Hist. eccl.* 3.39.8–10).

Whatever the real story, Papias must have been there at some time. Later, by the early fifth century, an impressive martyrion, a square building with an interior octagon, was built on an imposing hill just outside the city of Hierapolis, honoring Philip and his

20. See Meeks, "Myth of the Androgyne," esp. 15–18 and 43n102, 46n117, and 48n131.

21. See discussion in Michael W. Holmes, *Apostolic Fathers: Greek Texts and English Translations*, 3rd ed. (Grand Rapids: Baker Academic, 2007), 724–27; W. Pratscher, ed., *The Apostolic Fathers: An Introduction*, trans. E. G. Wolfe (Waco, TX: Baylor University Press, 2010), 161.

22. Among other women prophets in the tradition: Miriam, Deborah, Huldah, and Noadiah in the OT; Anna (Luke 2:36–39); "Jezebel" (Rev 2:20–23); Ammia (Eusebius, *Hist. eccl.* 5.17.2–4); the daughters of Job in T. Job; Priscilla and Maximilla in Montanist sources.

daughters. A monumental staircase led up to it from the city below. It had obviously become an important place of pilgrimage. Papias was part of the story.

9. THE SHEPHERD OF HERMAS

The Shepherd of Hermas is the most complex and extensive document of the Apostolic Fathers collection to consider from the perspective of gender. Feminine characters comprise both presumably historical and clearly mythological figures and some who cross over from one to the other. Questions of both female and male gender behavior appear, and the overall intentions of the author in this regard are not clear. There is also a discussion of policies about marriage and divorce in the Mandates.

It is customary to reference sections of Shepherd of Hermas by part of the work (Visions, Mandates or Commandments, and Similitudes or Parables, citing chapter and smaller section). The critical edition of Molly Whittaker in 1956 introduced a new sequential system of numbering straight through the whole work. Unfortunately, since then, commentators have had to choose one or the other, or to include both. The former option is used here, and in what follows the traditional system of numbering the Shepherd will be employed, in line with the rest of the essays in this volume.

Theories of composition for this long document abound, though most recent commentators have favored single authorship. For this study, a basic historical foundation is assumed: that a freedman named Hermas, living with a wife and children in Rome or somewhere in the close environs, began with oral accounts of visions, probably in the late first century or early second century CE. These accounts were eventually put in writing over a period of many years by a single author, beginning with the Visions, then adding the Mandates and later doubling back on some of the themes from the Visions in an expanded version, the Similitudes. Some later editing by other editors is possible. How these visions were received in their immediate environment is unknown. The author specifies early in the Visions that he sees himself delegated to proclaim them in the community assembly, while Clement sends copies to other churches, and Grapte presents the message to the widows and orphans (Herm. Vis. 2.4.3). Whatever the original reception, the multiplicity of early manuscripts of the work evidences widespread popularity in the first Christian centuries.[23] The composition, either in parts or as a whole, found ready reception in communities searching for ongoing ways to understand Christian life.

9.1 Probable Historical Female Characters

Female characters who are likely to be historical include Rhoda (Herm. Vis. 1.1.1), Hermas's unnamed wife with probably adult children of unspecified sex (Vis. 1.3; 2.2–3), and Grapte, the woman delegated to instruct the gathering of widows and orphans (Vis. 2.4.3). Rhoda dominates the opening scene. In the first eight words of the text, Hermas has identified himself as an abandoned baby raised into slavery in Rome by an unnamed slaveholder and sold at an unspecified age to a woman named Rhoda.[24] Then after many years, he encountered her again. Since he now has his own household (Vis. 1.3), it must mean here

23. For alternate theories of authorship, see Osiek, *Shepherd*, 9–10; M. Grundeken, *Community Building in the Shepherd of Hermas: A Critical Study of Some Key Aspects*, VCSup 131 (Leiden: Brill, 2015), 11–16; for manuscript history, see Osiek, *Shepherd*, 1–3; J. Lookadoo, *The Shepherd of Hermas: A Literary, Historical, and Theological Handbook* (London: T&T Clark, 2021), 19–33.

24. On the common practice of abandonment of unwanted newborns, see Boswell, *Kindness*; Osiek, *Shepherd*, 42. While the historical reliability of such details in Shepherd of Hermas is often questioned, there is no foreseeable rhetorical advantage to inventing servile origins.

that either Rhoda or probably yet another owner manumitted him,[25] all in unspecified past time. For the rest of Visions 1, however, Rhoda escapes to the quasi-mythological realm. Hermas sees her bathing in the Tiber, a motif that evokes a mythological scenario. He admires her beauty and is later accused by her in a dream of sinful intention toward her (Vis. 1.1.4–8).[26] His protestations of innocence in the face of the accusation launch the following visions.

In the opening scene with Rhoda, Hermas expresses a secret wish to have such a wife, with her beauty and character. Marriages of freedmen with a former mistress were not unknown, though more frequently documented in the inscriptions is the other way, a female slave manumitted *matrimonii causa* for marriage with a former male slaveholder. We soon discover, however, that Hermas already has a wife and children, in fact, a household (οἶκος, *oikos*).[27] Hermas's wife first appears in the reproaches given by Woman Church (Herm. Vis. 1.3; 2.2–3). When Hermas first sees her, he protests his innocence of the secret inappropriate desire for Rhoda of which he has been accused. That accusation is quickly dropped in favor of another, that Hermas as head of his household has badly neglected his authority and responsibility as *paterfamilias* to control their behavior. Their transgressions remain unspecified, only that they have acted lawlessly and sinned against the Lord. A hint of possible explanation lies in the added comment that Hermas himself has suffered setbacks because of ordinary business affairs (Vis. 1.3.1).

This theme of an aberrant family to upbraid is amenable to a symbolic substitute for the church at large, which could be understood as Hermas's "family" to whom he must address his prophetic call to conversion. The sinful "children" could be not his own, but the members of that community—that is, one of the house-church groups then active in Rome.[28] Yet it is unclear in the text that Hermas occupies any position of authority in his faith community. Woman Church directs him to read what she dictates to the church with the presiding presbyters.[29] There is no indication that he is already one of them.

A second time, Hermas's family is raised as a problem, now accused of betrayal of their parents, yet with no details. This time his unnamed wife (συμβίος, *symbios*) is introduced, described as one who cannot control her tongue. Oddly, she is a problem talker who never talks in the story.[30] She is, however, according to the directive of Woman Church, about to become his sister, and is again referred to later as his sister, whom he must not neglect (Herm. Vis. 2.3.1). The change in title for his wife, from wife to sister, presumably reflects the ascetic practice, perhaps already referenced in 1 Corinthians 7:36–38, of living celibately as a couple. Hermas had protested that Rhoda was also loved as a sister, not as a

25. Given the usual ongoing relationship of freedmen/women to former owner, now patron, for support and labor, encountering her again after many years would lack contextual verisimilitude if she were the manumitter.

26. M. Leutzsch (*Die Wahrnehmung sozialer Wirklichkeit im "Hirten des Hermas"*, FRLANT 150 [Göttingen: Vandenhoeck & Ruprecht, 1989], 31–39) lists nine scenes of a mortal man surprising a bathing goddess, eighteen images of goddess statues being washed, and nine further erotic bathing scenes, besides biblical David and Bathsheba and Susanna and the elders.

27. This is another indication that at the time of writing, the author is free. While the enslaved could have wife and children, they would never have what is called a household. See Osiek, *Shepherd*, 49.

28. The interpretation of some, including S. Young, "Being a Man: The Pursuit of Manliness in *The Shepherd of Hermas*," *JECS* 2 (1994): 237–55.

29. If a dating of the late first to early second century is correct, the Roman church at this point was composed of several communities, some evolving from house-church settings into something larger, each led by a council of leaders with various titles, including presbyter and "presider" (προϊστaμένος, *proistamenos*; Osiek, *Shepherd*, 55, 59, and further references).

30. Grundeken, *Community*, 104.

potential sexual partner (Vis. 1.1.7).[31] Later, in the Mandates, Hermas will comment on practices of marriage and divorce. Here it is perhaps as taking on a prophetic identity, necessitating freedom from domestic constraints. At the same time, he is being encouraged to assert his patriarchal authority over those traditionally and legally in his power.

The third probably historical female character is Grapte, to whom a copy of his revelation is to be given so that she can admonish the widows and orphans (Herm. Vis. 2.4.3).[32] The name occurs with some frequency in Rome, mostly for enslaved and freedwomen.[33] Like Hermas, she is probably of freed status, like so many people with Greek names in Roman cities of the West. Her position in the church is uncertain. The tradition of women responsible for the religious instruction of women is a familiar role (e.g., Titus 2:3–5), in addition to other domestic instruction on crafts, weaving, cooking, and household management, according to the appropriate social status.[34] She may have been one of the presbyters or someone with diaconal status, though that title is not known for the church of Rome at this point.[35] That the widows and orphans are to get special instruction from Grapte does not suggest that they are excluded from the general community gathering but rather that they are recipients of special attention.

9.2 Mythological Female Characters

The mythological female figures in Shepherd of Hermas include Woman Church, seven women who support the tower in the Visions, dancing virtues in the Similitudes (Herm. Sim. 9.2; 9.10), and sets of good and bad virgins there (9.15).

While the Shepherd is the guiding figure in the Mandates and Similitudes, Woman Church holds that place in the Visions. She first appears unidentified in the second vision, as the presence of Rhoda recedes. She is elderly but radiant. She is revealed as the church at Visions 2.4.1, elderly because she is preexistent to the creation of the world. Throughout the rest of the next three Visions, she is teacher, guide, revealer, and consoler to Hermas. She is first elderly, but she becomes progressively younger as the visions continue and as the members become converted to changing their evil ways, especially that of social inequality and lack of sharing among members (Vis. 3.9). Finally, she appears as a παρθένος (virgin or young girl), fresh, young, and dressed like a bride at Visions 4.2.1. In that capacity, she is able to interpret for Hermas the disarming of the terrible beast that threatened him and to explain the meaning of the four colors that the beast sports (Vis. 4.2–3).

There are various ways to understand the significance of Woman Church. She is elderly but gets younger as she goes, so she is a symbol of the possibility of rejuvenation. On the other hand, she has an important place to play in the Visions, but disappears completely after that, in favor of the male Shepherd who announces himself in the fifth vision as Hermas's escort for life. She is called πρεσβῦτις, *presbytis*, and more frequently πρεσβυτέρα, *presbytera*, which could simply mean "elderly woman." Her roles as teacher and interpreter, however, can be seen as presbyteral, even as model for presbyteral leadership. There are

31. For the custom of *virgines subintroductae* (couples living together celibately), see Osiek and Balch, *Families*, 152–55.

32. On the significance of widows and orphans, see comment on Ignatius and Polycarp above (sec. 4). While dating from a century or more later, note Cornelius of Rome, as quoted by Eusebius, running an organization that cares for more than fifteen hundred widows and other needy people in the Roman church (*Hist. eccl.* 6.43.11–12).

33. See Osiek, *Shepherd*, 59n10.

34. See Osiek and Balch, *Families*, 167–73; Osiek, MacDonald, and Tulloch, *Woman's Place*, 90–92.

35. In later years, though more widely in the East, the order of female deacons will be established exactly for this purpose; see Madigan and Osiek, *Ordained Women*.

others in the Roman church who bear that title, in a context that surely means not just elderly people but church leaders (Herm. Vis. 2.4.3). Her position of authority is undercut by the description of her original old age as weak, and once rejuvenated, cast aside in favor of the male leadership of the Shepherd (Vis. 3.10).[36] Thus the most significant reduction of feminine elements is "the elimination of the feminine Church and the usurpation of the three dominant roles she held in the *Visions*: revealer-figure, ecclesiological symbol, and pre-created companion of God."[37]

In the course of the Visions, Woman Church reveals to Hermas a tower being built by six young men, later revealed to be angels (Herm. Vis. 3.2; 3.4), with help from unspecified thousands of others. The many stones of various shapes, either used or rejected, are an allegory of various kinds of community members with regard to their faith or lack thereof. In a further vision, Hermas is shown seven women (γυναίκας, *gynaikas*) who surround and uphold the tower. There is gender complementarity in this first vision of the tower: young men build it, and the seven women sustain it. Each of the women is a particular characteristic or virtue. The first is Faith. The second, daughter of Faith, is Restraint (ἐγκράτεια, *enkrateia*), who is girded and ἀνδριζομένη, *andrizomenē* ("acting like a man," or "courageously"). The others are daughters of one another: Simplicity, Knowledge, Innocence, Reverence, and Love. Whoever serves them is promised a place in the tower (Vis. 3.8.1–8).

The retelling of the building of the tower in Similitudes 9 is more complicated. No longer is the tower built on water, but on stone and level ground. While this development could be seen as strengthening the tower, it also abandons the imagery of water, often associated with fluidity, depth, and birth, and thus with the feminine.[38] However, entry into the seal of baptism in water is still the way of salvation, in which the faithful enter dead and emerge alive (Herm. Sim. 9.16). The seven women of the third vision have become twelve virgins, beautifully clad, with bare right shoulders in order to lift the stones, a masculine allusion, so they can actually be engaged in the building process. Six men, later identified as holy spirits (Sim. 9.13.2), now build the tower, with encouragement from the virgins. The virgins guard the four-sided gates of the tower in a manner that is ἀνδρείως, *andreiōs* ("manly"), as if they could uphold the whole sky (Sim. 9.2).

Meanwhile, there are another twelve women dressed in black, belted, with bare shoulders, who to Hermas look ἄγριαι, *agriai* ("wild"). Theirs is a cleansing role. Their job is to remove from the area of the tower those stones that will not be used in the building (Herm. Sim. 9.9). A little later, both groups of women are named (Sim. 9.15). The twelve virgins, in a folding back on Vision 3, are led by πίστις, *pistis* (Faith) and ἐγκράτεια (Restraint) (see Herm. Vis. 3.8). Three other names among the twelve match those of the seven in the Visions: ἁπλότης, *haplotēs*, ἀκακία, *akakia*, and ἀγάπη, *agapē* (Simplicity, Innocence, and Love). The other names differ; the next is Power, and the rest are of the kinds expected in a catalogue of virtues: Endurance, Purity, Joy, Truth, Understanding, and Harmony. Later, the Shepherd takes a night off, and Hermas spends the night with the virtues, "as a brother, not as a husband," and enjoys dancing and rejoicing with them. Like the admonition in the Visions that Hermas is to live with his wife "as a sister," this scene may be reflective of the practice of celibacy already growing in the early church (Sim. 9.11; see Vis. 2.2.3).

The other twelve, wild-looking women are also given names, all typical of a catalogue of

36. L. Walsh, "The Lady as Elder in the *Shepherd of Hermas*," *JECS* 27 (2019): 523–29.

37. L. Walsh, "Lost in Revision: Gender Symbolism in *Vision* 3 and *Similitude* 9 of the *Shepherd of Hermas*," *HTR* 112.4 (2019): 472; Young, "Being a Man," 251–52.

38. Walsh, "Lost in Revision," 471–72, 482–87.

vices. The list leads off with the opposites of the leading names among the virgins: ἀπιστία, *apistia* (Unbelief) and ἀκρασία, *akrasia* (Dissipation). The others are: Disobedience, Deceit, Sadness, Evil, Sensuality, Bad Temper, Untruth, Senselessness, Slander, and Hatred (Herm. Sim. 9.15.3). They entice the faithful into their way of disobedience, so that they will be rejected from the tower, unless they repent and return to the ways of the virgins (Sim. 9.13–14).

The seven women who were daughters of one another and upheld the tower in the Visions have proliferated into twelve virgins (or young women) and twelve negative and destructive women in the Similitudes. The seven have become twenty-four, twelve positively charged and their twelve opposites negatively. One way to interpret this increase in number is to see it as part of the additive nature of the whole work. Initial images and insights are developed in more detail and complexity, especially from Visions to Similitudes 9. The author seems to run with one image for a while, then later think of new ways to enhance it. The allegory of the various stones that fit (or do not fit) into the tower, along with who builds the tower with what and when, is augmented with newly developed applications. Personification of virtues and vices is typical in the literature and even civic symbolism and so is not surprising. It is augmented here by the increase in female figures. Woman Church is lost, but the women tower-builder-virtues have increased, along with their vice-counterparts.

On the other hand, now the male Shepherd has taken over the revelatory and tutelary role of Woman Church. Another elusive authority presence, male everywhere except Woman Church of the Visions, is otherwise called the great angel, the Lord of the tower, and the Son of God. The six women who upheld the tower on their own in the Visions now take orders from the seven male builders (Herm. Sim. 9.3.3–4), who employ the virgins to bring into the tower some of the stone that would otherwise not be acceptable (Sim. 9.4.7–8). The tower is now built to please the Lord of the tower, the Son of God, and to be joined to him as his household. The proliferation of women-virtues is joined by equal numbers of women-vices, so that the stereotypes of idealized women are countered by stereotypes of women as destructive.[39]

9.3 Comments on Marriage and Marital Fidelity

Amid instruction about living according to God come a few questions about marriage, remarriage, and adultery. The fourth Mandate begins with an exhortation to ἁγνεία, *hagneia* ("purity"), probably in this context marital chastity (Herm. Mand. 4.1.1). The exhortation is to guard against thoughts that would lead to πορνεία (see note 15). In the instruction later on good and bad desire, desire for wife or husband of another is a primary example of what to avoid (Herm. Mand. 12.2.1–5). Perhaps Hermas's ambiguous relationship with Rhoda at the beginning of the Visions is background, but if Hermas remembers his own wife, he will not sin, a charming appeal to fidelity, not breaking a law. If, however, the directive now to treat his wife as sister at Visions 2.2.3 is correctly understood as the embrace of celibacy, this directive would seem to stand in contradiction. Time sequencing in these narratives is not always cohesive.

The chapter goes on to discuss the male response to female adultery, the usual kind envisioned in ancient law and custom, where a married woman was adulterous with anyone other than her husband, but a man only with someone else's wife. The husband must divorce his adulterous wife, so far in line with Roman marriage law, but he should not

39. Walsh, "Lost in Revision," 476–82.

remarry because of the possibility that she might have a change of heart and want to return to him. In this case, he should take her back: this is in contradiction to Augustan marriage law, which forbids him to take her back.[40]

Three chapters later comes the question of remarriage in widowhood, already an issue in the Corinthian church of Paul's time (1 Cor 7:39–40). Like Paul, the Shepherd expresses no prohibition about remarriage in this case, and no question of sin. Yet the author seems to have the same reluctance about it as did Paul, adding that remaining single gives greater status and honor (Herm. Mand. 4.4). The reluctance toward second marriages already seen there will soon develop more widely, as already reflected, for example, in 1 Timothy 3:2.[41]

9.4 Be a Man!

The quality of ἀνδρεία (manliness) is not limited to men but refers to the kind of courage and assertiveness associated with conventional masculine stereotype. One of the seven women around the tower, ἐγκράτεια (Restraint), is girded and is ἀνδριζομένη, to be translated either as "courageous" or "manly" (Herm. Vis. 3.8.4). The twelve virgins standing around the later tower built on rock look sufficiently ἀνδρείως (manly, courageous) to hold up the whole sky (Herm. Sim. 9.2.5). Likewise, among the examples of courage proposed in 1 Clement are women empowered by God to perform many deeds of "manly" courage (πολλὰ ἀνδρεία, *polla andreia*, 1 Clem. 55.3). The immediate example there is Judith, who placed herself in danger for love of her threatened people. The same quality is attributed to the flesh of the Son of God in partnership with the Holy Spirit, acting ἰσχυρῶς, *ischyrōs* ("strongly") and ἀνδρείως, *andreiōs* ("manly, courageous," Herm. Sim. 5.6.6).[42] The language can be included in a general directive to take courage and be strengthened (1 Cor 16:13). In his explanation of the rejuvenation of Woman Church, from elderly to younger, the Shepherd compares the process to an old man who has given up all hope because of bodily diminishment, but then suddenly receives an inheritance and as a result, his behavior changes: he stands and ἀνδρίζεται, *andrizetai* ("acts like a man," Herm. Vis. 3.12.2). Similarly, eighty-six-year-old Polycarp, who had been in hiding, was then betrayed, arrested, and treated abusively, hears an encouraging heavenly voice, also heard by his community nearby, as he enters the amphitheater to meet his death there: ἴσχυε . . . καὶ ἀνδρίζου, *ischye . . . kai andrizou* ("be strong and act like a man," Mart. Pol. 9.1).

However, Hermas himself is addressed by Woman Church with the command, ἀνδρίζου ("be manly!"), as she departs from her first appearance to him (Herm. Vis. 1.4.3). This command to be courageous serves as an antidote for his terror at the heavenly revelation and realization that this message was heavy and would implicate him in future trouble. The former slave who, in his servile existence, was according to social stereotype not expected to act with anything akin to courage or virility, now a freedman, is commanded to do so. The un-man is commanded now to be a man.[43] The accusation of neglect of his household (Vis. 1.3) takes on further meaning. As *paterfamilias* (head of household), he is responsible for the property, behavior, and reputation of wife, children, and any household dependents, slaves or freedpersons.[44] The lack of asserted control of which he

40. For more, see Osiek, *Shepherd*, 109–12.

41. See further Osiek, *Shepherd*, 116.

42. The reference is part of one of the most difficult passages in the Shepherd with regard to Christology. It is not clear exactly what is the subject of the characterization.

43. M. B. Kartzow, *The Slave Metaphor and Gendered Enslavement in Early Christian Discourse: Double Trouble Embodied*, Routledge Studies in the Early Christian World (London: Routledge, 2018), 117.

44. Further, Osiek, *Shepherd*, 49.

is accused would be indeed a lack of ἀνδρεία, manliness, precisely what a free male in his situation is expected to do. The narrative plot here is that Hermas becomes what Woman Church says he should be. His crisis of manhood is also spiritual, consisting of overcoming doubts and learning to cast all his concern on God and so find joy.[45] Inasmuch as Woman Church is a metaphor for the church or community, Hermas exercises a leadership that he believes he is called to perform. What was his immediate reception by the members is unknown. Judging, however, from the later popularity of the writing, it may have been quite positive. At the end of the narrative, Hermas is once again encouraged, this time by the Shepherd, to carry on with this *ministerium* (= διακονία?) in a manner that is *viriliter* (= ἀνδρείως?), to proclaim this message to everyone so they can live the promised happy life (Herm. Sim. 10.4.1).[46]

Despite the rich and complex feminine imagery in the Shepherd of Hermas, ultimately the dominant figure of the Shepherd, the great angel, and the Son of God are male. However, the virgins accompany the Shepherd back to Hermas's house at the end, with the promise of abiding there (Herm. Sim. 10.3–4). The feminine presence, though now eclipsed by male authority figures, remains.

10. CONCLUSION

The Apostolic Fathers, with little convergence as a collection, present a variety of ways in which gender symbolism, metaphor, and male and female characters play out the narratives and questions that were being worked out in the postapostolic era. Passing references to female biblical and mythological figures exchange with probably real women who appear and quickly disappear. Gender stereotypes prevail yet are sometimes intriguingly counterbalanced by surprising exceptions. Masculine strength and courage are celebrated, whether on the part of men or women. Through it all runs the thread of mutual love and respect that characterized the message of early Christianity.

BIBLIOGRAPHY

Balch, D. L. "Violence in Pompeian/Roman Domestic Art as a Visual Context for the Pauline and Deutero-Pauline Letters." Pages 123–65 in *Early Christianity in Pompeian Light: People, Texts, Situations*. Edited by B. Longenecker. Minneapolis: Fortress, 2016.

Donfried, K. P. *The Setting of Second Clement in Early Christianity*. NovTSup 38. Leiden: Brill, 1974.

Glancy, J. A. "Slavery and Sexual Availability." Pages 627–44 in *The Oxford Handbook of New Testament, Gender, and Sexuality*. Edited by B. H. Dunning. Oxford: Oxford University Press, 2019.

Grundeken, M. *Community Building in the Shepherd of Hermas: A Critical Study of Some Key Aspects*. VC Supplements 131. Leiden: Brill, 2015.

Kartzow, M. B. *The Slave Metaphor and Gendered Enslavement in Early Christian Discourse: Double Trouble Embodied*. Routledge Studies in the Early Christian World. London: Routledge, 2018.

Lookadoo, J. *The Shepherd of Hermas: A Literary, Historical, and Theological Handbook*. London: T&T Clark, 2021.

Osiek, C. *The Shepherd of Hermas*. Hermeneia. Minneapolis: Augsburg Fortress, 1999.

Osiek, C., and M. Y. MacDonald, with J. H. Tulloch. *A Woman's Place: House Churches in Earliest Christianity*. Minneapolis: Augsburg Fortress, 2006.

Pratscher, W., ed. *The Apostolic Fathers: An Introduction*. Translated by E. G. Wolfe. Waco, TX: Baylor University Press, 2010.

Walsh, L. "Lost in Revision: Gender Symbolism in *Vision* 3 and *Similitude* 9 of the *Shepherd of Hermas*." *HTR* 112.4 (2019): 467–90.

Young, S. "Being a Man: Pursuit of Manliness in *The Shepherd of Hermas*." *JECS* 2.3 (1994): 237–55.

45. Young, "Being a Man," 239–40, 247–50.

46. Most of the ninth Similitude beyond Herm. Sim. 9.30 is preserved only in Latin.

CHAPTER 18

ETHICS AND EDUCATION IN THE APOSTOLIC FATHERS

TERESA MORGAN

1. INTRODUCTION

The study of ethics is concerned with how individuals or groups think about the way they live—what, for instance, they consider is good, right, appropriate, or necessary to think or do, and why—and how thought relates to action.[1] In any systematic, formally agreed, or theorized sense, there is no such thing as "the ethics of the Apostolic Fathers," any more than there is such a thing as "New Testament ethics" or "early Christian ethics."[2] The only text discussed in this volume that we might be tempted to define as primarily ethical is the Didache, and the Didache also includes liturgical and other material. All the Apostolic Fathers claim some kind of authority to speak, even to teach, and we see 1 Clement and the letters of Ignatius and Polycarp reaching out to claim authority over communities beyond their own, but in the period in which they are likely to have been writing, no one was in a position to define a set of ethical conventions for all churches.[3] The texts under discussion, moreover, were written for different purposes, and mostly for communities diverse in location and probably social composition, which were facing different challenges. We might therefore expect their ethical ideas to be varied and situationally specific, and ethics probably not to be equally central to every text and, up to a point, this is what we find. First Clement, for example, which addresses the rebellion of some Corinthians against their presbyters, has much to say about obedience, humility, love, and peace. The writer of the Shepherd of Hermas is concerned with how those who sin after baptism can be saved and develops a teaching about postbaptismal repentance and good behavior that he hopes can restore church members to righteousness.[4] In his letter to the Romans, Ignatius claims to be worried that the Romans, in their love for him, will try to prevent the martyrdom he

1. Ethical attitudes and actions are distinguishable, but early Christians share the common ancient assumption that ideally they go together (Rom 7:15–24 draws on a topos of ancient literature to describe Paul's distress when they do not).

2. I follow this volume's definition of the corpus of Apostolic Fathers, though I think it possible that only Ignatius's Letter to the Romans is authentic (following a view that goes back to E. Renan, *Histoire des origenes du christianisme 2: Les évangiles et la seconde generation chrétienne* [Paris: Lévy, 1877], 485–98).

3. As, for instance, the canons of later church councils often do.

4. This is a matter of concern for most, if not all early communities; in practice, almost all seem to accept postbaptismal repentance (though Heb 6:6 does not, and Acts 8:22 expresses uncertainty about it), but with various conditions. E.g., Gal 6:1; Jas 5:16; 1 Clem. 57.1; 2 Clem 6.9; Ign. *Phil.* 3.2; Pol. *Phil.* 11.4 allow it (sometimes with evident reluctance); 1 John 5:16–17 accepts it sometimes; Did. 14.1 allows it except when someone has misjudged a prophet (11.7); Herm. Mand. 4.1.8 allows it once, but elsewhere allows it more often.

desires (Ign. *Rom.* 1.2), but he has almost nothing to say about how the living should think or act.

All the Apostolic Fathers, however, make ethical claims of some kind, and, in broad terms, they have a good deal in common. They employ many of the same key concepts, including love, longsuffering, obedience, humility, peace, forgiveness, piety, purity, simplicity, truthfulness, continence, prudence, hospitality, and nonattachment to wealth.[5] They use much of the same evaluative language—good, evil, righteous, sinful. They appeal to a common range of authorities—God, Jesus Christ, the Scriptures, the apostles, church office-holders—and share the hope that ethical thinking and behavior will help community members to be saved.[6] The modern tendency in scholarship on the Apostolic Fathers is to treat the texts separately, but some of the most distinctive and significant aspects of their ethics are so widely shared that we will begin by looking at them as a group, and note differences between them as we encounter them.

2. GOD, GOOD, AND THE ORIGINS OF EVIL

Christian ethics are often treated as a pendant to theology, with a hint that, being concerned with human behavior and the regulation of communities, they are a relatively straightforward, literally and metaphorically down-to-earth subject.[7] This does less than justice to the role played by ethics in early—or later—Christian writings. The proclamation, which precedes our earliest surviving sources, that God, through Christ, makes possible the forgiveness of human sins and human beings' salvation, involves the ethical claims that God is good, humanity's situation before the Christ event is not good, and the situation needs to change. Many of the ways in which God's relationship with humanity is described—God is merciful, generous, loving, just—particularize the concept of divine goodness in different directions, and all the ways in which Christians are called to think and behave are defined by their relationship with a good God. Ethics are therefore intrinsic to Christian theology, Christology, pneumatology, ecclesiology, and eschatology.

The understanding of God as good is part of Christianity's Jewishness, and its familiarity from Jewish tradition is one reason why many early Christians take it for granted and it does not surprise modern commentators.[8] It is worth remembering, though, how much it may have surprised early gentile converts. Some Stoics and Middle Platonists in this period

---

5. There is no sign in these writings that faith, hope, and love are distinguished as "theological virtues," and it is worth noting that all good attitudes and actions are theological, for Christians as for Jews, in the sense that they are commanded by and seek to serve God. *Pistis*, and probably also *agapē*, are already recognized not only as goods but as the attitudes and actions which justify or save human beings.

6. "Scriptures" here and elsewhere refers to the Jewish Scriptures.

7. The relationship between early Christian theology and ethics has been explored especially in relation to NT texts: see notably V. P. Furnish, *Theology and Ethics in Paul* (Nashville: Abingdon, 1968); J. G. Lewis, *Looking for Life: The Role of "Theo-Ethical" Reasoning in Paul's Religion* (London: T&T Clark, 2005); M. Konradt, *Ethik im Neuen Testament* (Göttingen: Vandenhoeck & Ruprecht, 2022).

8. "Jewish" and "Judaism," of course, as concepts are both too general to be very helpful. There is not space here to discuss which strands of Jewish literature and tradition the Apostolic Fathers draw on in their ethical thinking—nor which earlier Christian writings they use most—but, in broad terms, they draw heavily on the Decalogue, the love command, and the golden rule, and sometimes on wisdom traditions which encourage domestic harmony, chastity, justice, and care for the poor. Josephus observes (*Ag. Ap.* 2.170–71) that Moses made virtue a department of piety, so Jewish ethics (unlike Greek) are part of worship. On the importance of "good" as a moral category in early Christianity see H. Löhr, "Good as a Moral Category in the Early Jesus Tradition," in *Early Christian Ethics in Interaction with Jewish and Greco-Roman Contexts*, ed. J. W. van Henten and J. Verheyden (Leiden: Brill, 2013), 205–22. Löhr argues (206–7) for distinguishing the "adverbially" good (which measures a degree of excellence) from the functionally and morally good, but where goodness is defined by God all three converge.

can speak of the ultimate divine—which is identified with the good and is the cause of all things—metaphorically as "he," "creator," "father," or "lawgiver."[9] The philosophical divine, however, is much less strongly anthropomorphized than is the God of Israel: it is not imagined, for instance, as responding to prayer, or as acting to save human beings from harm or sin. Most gentiles, anyway, were not philosophers, and none of the mainstream gods of the ancient Mediterranean and Near East is reliably as good, from a human perspective, as God and Christ are understood as being.[10] The whole thought-world of Christ-confession is ethical in a way that must have seemed remarkable to most gentiles, and may have been one of its attractions.

The Apostolic Fathers share the view of all Christians that the God of Israel is consistently good, and human ethics are defined in relation to divine goodness, but they describe evil in slightly different ways.[11] The Ignatian corpus sometimes refers to the devil or hostile powers in terms that suggest they are metaphysical powers (Ign. *Rom.* 5.3; *Smyrn.* 3.1). Introducing its teaching about the Two Ways, the Letter of Barnabas envisages God as opposed by Satan and his angels, who preside over the present time of misrule (Barn. 18.1). For the writer of the Didache, in contrast, the "way of life" (Did. 1.1) involves loving the God who made you, keeping God's commandments, and avoiding evil people (3.1), but there is no mention of a metaphysical evil power whom community members should reject, and the Didache's description of baptism (7.1–4) does not involve renouncing Satan.[12]

The Didache seems to imagine sin as arising in human beings. So does 1 Clement. Describing the beginning of the problems he is addressing in the Corinthian community, the author quotes Deuteronomy 32:15: "My beloved ate and drank, and he was puffed up, and fattened, and kicked." From this, says the writer, arose jealousy, envy, strife, conflict, persecution, and the rest (1 Clem. 3.1–2). People have followed their own wicked hearts and revived the unjust and impious envy by which "death came into the world" (3.4, quoting Wis 2:34), but there is no indication that an external power has influenced them.

The picture in the Shepherd of Hermas is more complex. The four apocalyptic visions that open the book show no signs of cosmic dualism. Evil begins when an evil desire arises in a human heart (Herm. Vis. 1.1.8), and evil thoughts lead to evil actions (2.2.2; 2.3.2; 3.6; 3.9.3). Human beings battle evil by listening to instruction (1.3.2), repenting of their sins (2.2.4), and practicing self-control, good behavior, and prayer (2.2.3–4; 2.3.2; 3.1.6; 3.9.5). In the Mandates that follow, however, Hermas can speak of the human heart as divided between good and evil and ruled by a good or evil spirit or a righteous or evil angel (Herm. Mand. 5.1–2; 6.2). Hermas's language here is that of metaphysical powers, but there is no clear indication that they exist outside the person. Most commentators think they are allegorical, describing a psychological dualism that individuals can overcome by faith and repentance (Mand. 8.1–12; 9.10–12).

---

9. J. M. Dillon, *The Middle Platonists: A Study of Platonism, 80 B.C. to A.D. 220*, rev. ed. (London: Duckworth, 1996), 88–89, 199–200, 366–72; R. Salles, ed., *God and Cosmos in Stoicism* (Oxford: Oxford University Press, 2009).

10. The classic study is H. Lloyd-Jones, *The Justice of Zeus*, 2nd ed. (Berkeley: University of California Press, 1983). Arguably, however, a tendency toward henotheism or monotheism through the principate went with an increasing tendency to see the one or the highest god as good or benevolent, perhaps under the influence of the philosophical schools; see, e.g., S. Mitchell and P. Van Nuffelen, eds., *One God: Pagan Monotheism in the Roman Empire* (Cambridge: Cambridge University Press, 2010).

11. See the discussion of J. Burke, "Satan and Demons in the Apostolic Fathers: A Minority Report," *SEÅ* 81 (2016): 127–68.

12. Unless otherwise noted, the translations of the Apostolic Fathers in this chapter are from B. D. Ehrman, *The Apostolic Fathers*, 2 vols., LCL (Cambridge: Harvard University Press, 2003).

The Apostolic Fathers share the absolute conviction of all early Christian writers that there is only one "true and living God" (cf. 1 Thess 1:9),[13] that Jesus Christ has a unique relationship and place with God (variously described), and that forgiveness and salvation come through God's action in Christ (also variously described). The fact that their view of the nature and source of evil varies is, in part, an inheritance from the range of Jewish views about evil, but it also suggests that ultimately, for these writers, theorizing about the nature of evil matters less than making one's commitment to God and Christ and doing as God and Christ command. It is also striking that even works like Barnabas, which envisage evil as a metaphysical entity, take for granted that human beings can combat it by practicing the "way of light." All these writings, apart from the Letter to Diognetus, appear to address community members who may already have been baptized, but none of them suggests that human beings, whether before or after baptism, lack free will to choose God and the good.[14] Rather, as 2 Clement describes it, Jesus Christ gave humanity "the light" and saved it when it was heading for destruction, and human beings' sight was cleared and they were able to "cast off the cloud which covered us" (2 Clem. 1.4–6).

3. THE LANGUAGE OF GOD AND EVIL

The vocabulary of ethics in the ancient world is quite varied, including good/bad, good/evil, lawful/unlawful, holy/unholy, pure/impure, pious/impious, blessed/cursed, righteous/unrighteous, righteous/sinful, spiritual/carnal, worthy/unworthy, necessary/unnecessary, useful/useless, honorable/dishonorable, proper/improper, sweet/sour, great/small, light/heavy, upright/crooked, beautiful/ugly, charming/charmless, precious/worthless, noble/slavish, normal/abnormal, native/foreign, decorous/indecorous, and appropriate/disgraceful or shameful.

Ethical ideas that use this language can be couched as statements or commands, and though modern moral philosophers argue that "is" does not imply "ought," ancient ethical writings, popular, philosophical, and religious, all tend to use both interchangeably. In mainstream, civic or popular moral thinking in the early empire, evaluative terms divide broadly into three kinds of appeals: appeals to God or the gods as ethical arbiters, appeals to society, and appeals to natural human preferences. For example, something "holy" or "pure" is typically something God, or a god, approves of. Something "useful" or "necessary" is something society approves of. Something "sweet" or "lovely" is something people find naturally appealing (such as love or home).[15]

The Didache, which is usually considered the most Jewish of all these writings, signals its continuity with Jewish tradition as strongly in its evaluative language as in the content of its ethics.[16] The two ways it describes are ways of life and death (cf., e.g., Deut. 30:15). The one who follows the way of life can hope to be perfect (τέλειος, *teleios*, Did. 1.4), while the one who gives to everyone who asks him is blessed (μακάριος, *makarios*) and innocent

---

13. Though to judge by the injunctions against use of gentile temples that punctuate Christian literature into late antiquity, not all community members followed suit.

14. God's grace is often invoked (e.g., 1 Clem. 7.4; 8.1; Ign. *Smyrn.* 6.2; 12.1; Ign. *Eph.* 11.1; Barn. 1.2), but without any suggestion that it is necessary to enable human beings to turn to God or to confess Christ (on the contrary, according to, e.g., Ign. *Magn.* 5.2; Diogn. 7.4; 10.4); see, e.g., M. Knell, *Sin, Grace and Free Will: The Apostolic Fathers to Augustine* (Cambridge: Clarke, 2017), 5–26.

15. T. Morgan, *Popular Morality in the Early Roman Empire* (Cambridge: Cambridge University Press, 2007), 191–206.

16. Though J. S. Kloppenborg, "The Transformation of Moral Exhortation in *Didache* 1–5," in *The Didache in Context: Essays on Its Text, History, and Transmission*, ed. C. N. Jefford (Leiden: Brill, 1994), 97–99, emphasizes that even the Didache's ethics have been decisively Christianized by reference to the teaching of Christ.

(ἀθῷος, *athōos*) (1.5). Being "perfect" is strongly associated, in the Septuagint and elsewhere in Greek Jewish writing, with keeping the law (e.g., Deut 18:13).[17] *Makarios* is fairly common in Greek of all kinds, while *athōos* is rare, but both are used in the Septuagint of those who love God. The Didache references the Decalogue from its opening verses, and in that spirit it uses the imperative throughout: community members must do everything they do because God commands it. The evil from which they must flee is consistently called πονηρός *ponēros* (Did. 2.6; 3.1; 4.14; 5.1, 2), which is another common term in the Septuagint, referring to absolute moral evil.

The ethics of 1 Clement also look traditionally Jewish, but its evaluative language is more varied. The letter begins with an attack on some members of the Corinthian community, referring to their "foul [μιαρός, *miaros*, literally, "blood-stained" or "polluted"] and unholy sedition, foreign [ἀλλότριος, *allotrios*] and alien [ξένος, *xenos*] to the chosen of God" (1 Clem. 1.1). The combination of language of cult pollution and political conflict underlines that some people's conduct is betraying God and God's people, and also the community on the human plane. The writer contrasts this situation with the Corinthians' "absolutely virtuous [πανάρετος, *panaretos*] and steadfast faith" in the past, the "magnificence [μεγαλοπρεπής, *megaloprepēs*] of your hospitality" and their "perfect and unfailing knowledge" (1.2). The adjective *panaretos* is resonant of Greek virtue, while *megaloprepēs*, though it occurs in the Septuagint, is more strongly associated with Greek civic values, so the writer is flattering the Corinthians here as both people of piety and cultural sophisticates. This combination of language, which invokes the piety and obedience that the Corinthians owe to God with the civic-style Greek (and Roman) virtues they owe to the community, runs throughout the letter.

The opening of 2 Clement taps into a slightly different mixture of Jewish, Greek, and distinctively Christian imagery in sketching the relationship between humanity and Jesus Christ, of whom the "brothers" must think as they think of God (2 Clem. 1.1). Christ has saved them, but if they do not look forward to the end time and eventual judgment, they will find themselves sinning again (1.2). "What return payment [ἀντιμισθία, *antimisthia*], therefore, shall we give him, or what fruit, worthy of what he has given us?" (1.3). Gentile gods sometimes save, but linking past salvation with future judgment is a Jewish theme; the idea of owing and giving firstfruits is common to Jews and gentiles, but the term *antimisthia* seems to have been coined by Paul (Rom 1:27, 2 Cor 6:13). The writer draws on language of Jewish and gentile obligation, and invokes the apostle Paul, to appeal to all parts of the Corinthian community.

These writers can also draw on a wide range of imagery to describe their ideas. Righteousness can act as armor against evil, especially the evil of money (Pol. *Phil.* 4.1). The Coptic text of the Didache (Did. 10.8) gives thanks to God for the "word with the sweet scent" that God has made known to humanity through Christ. (Among gentiles, as noted above, sweetness is a quality of natural goods, but the Didache is probably referring to the sweetness of divine wisdom in Jewish wisdom literature.[18]) The Didache can also see good behavior in functional, even economic terms, as "useful" or "profitable" (ὠφελέω, *ōpheleō*)

---

17. The writer may also be referencing the teaching of Jesus to be perfect, as P. J. Hartin argues in "Ethics in the Letter of James, the Gospel of Matthew, and the Didache: Their Place in Early Christian Literature," in *Mathew, James, and Didache: Three Related Documents in Their Jewish and Christian Setting*, ed. J. K. Zengenberg and H. W. M. van de Sandt (Atlanta: Society of Biblical Literature, 2008), 300–301.

18. D. A. Kurek-Chomycz, "The Sweet Scent of the Gospel in the *Didache* and in Second Corinthians: Some Comments on Two Recent Interpretations of the *Stinoufi* Prayer in the Coptic *Did.* 10.8," *VC* 63 (2009): 323–44.

for the soul (Did. 16.2). But the language and imagery that dominate all these writings are those of relationship. What is good, holy, righteous, and so on is what serves God or Christ (e.g., 1 Clem. 37.1; 2 Clem. 6.1; Ign. *Pol.* 8.1; Herm. Vis. 4.2.5), what pleases God (1 Clem. 41.1; 62.2, Ign. *Rom.* 2.1; Did. 4.12), what shows the love of community members for God and Christ (1 Clem. 21.8; Did. 1.1; Barn. 19.2; Mart. Pol. 2.2), or what is worthy of God or Christ (e.g., Ign. *Eph.* 2.2; Ign. *Rom.* salut.; Did. 15.1; Diogn. 11.1). In an influential article about Pauline ethics, Leander E. Keck distinguished between the ethical questions, "What must/ought/should/may I do?" and, "To whom am I accountable, and for what?" and argued for the primacy of the second in Paul.[19] The distinction is equally important for the Apostolic Fathers.[20] It highlights that the divine-human relationship is the focal point of all their thinking and also helps to explain how Christians, despite the many obvious overlaps between their ethics and those of (other) Jews and gentiles, can understand themselves as in a divine-human relationship that is, ethically as in other respects, unique.[21]

Whatever terms different writings favor, however, the ethical language of these texts is consistently binary. Everything that God and Christ command is good; what God and Christ command is all Christ-confessors need to be saved; nothing good lies outside God's authority; and anything commended by a power other than God or Christ is evil. This tendency is most starkly displayed in the Two Ways imagery of the Didache and the letter of Barnabas, and it contrasts markedly with contemporary philosophical ethics, according to which many of the things one can think or do are ethically neutral, and with popular morality, where the value of any attitude or action more often than not depends on circumstances.[22] In broad terms, this is another aspect of Christianity's Jewishness, but it is also worth noting that most of these texts are less nuanced than much Jewish ethical writing of a similar period. Among the Pharisees, for example, and in early rabbinic writing, though what the law commands may, at first sight, seem clear, there is also often room to debate better and worse ways of carrying it out, or to discuss ethical questions that it does not address directly.[23] There is little such extended debate or reflection in the Apostolic Fathers, partly perhaps because they belong to communities still in formation, but probably mainly because most of them have a strongly paraenetic agenda, so their aim is to give advice, not to debate what advice to give.

4. FOUNDATIONS OF ETHICS

The God to whom all these writings appeal is, first, the creator of the universe (1 Clem. 7.3; Did. 1.2; Barn. 19.2; Herm. Vis. 1.1.6; Herm. Mand. 1.1; Diogn. 3.2). These writers do

19. L. E. Keck, "Rethinking New Testament Ethics," *JBL* 115 (1996): 3–16.

20. Paul's influence on the Apostolic Fathers used to be seen only in 1 Clement, Ignatius's *To the Ephesians* and *To the Romans*, and Polycarp's, *To the Philippians*, where he is cited explicitly, but is now detected much more widely; see, e.g., J. Carleton Paget, "Paul and the *Epistle of Barnabas*," in *The Apostolic Fathers and Paul: Pauline and Patristic Scholars in Debate*, ed. T. D. Still and D. E. Wilhite (London: Bloomsbury, 2017), 79–100, J. E. Soyars, *The Shepherd of Hermas and the Pauline Legacy* (Leiden: Brill, 2019).

21. Keck's distinction is equally useful in the study of gentile ethics, where members of a given group often regard their ethics as distinctive to them, though to an outsider eye they look indistinguishable from those of their neighbors, because they are validated by their own founder figures or heroes; e.g., Spartan justice is Spartan because it was handed down by Lycurgus, Roman justice is Roman because it goes back to King Numa.

22. Morgan, *Popular Morality*, 179–83. James N. Rhodes, "The Two Ways Tradition in the *Epistle of Barnabas*: Revisiting an Old Question," *CBQ* 73 (2011): 797–816, shows how the idea of "two ways" informs not only the writer's ethics but his theology and vision of the church as a whole.

23. L. E. Newman, *Past Imperatives: Studies in the History and Theory of Jewish Ethics* (Albany, NY: State University of New York, 1998); Tzvi Novick, *What Is Good, and What God Demands: Normative Studies in Tannaitic Literature* (Leiden: Brill, 2010).

not raise the question that some ancient philosophers raise, whether God commands what is good because it is good, or whether what is good is good because God commands it, but they probably assume the latter. When 1 Clement (7.3), for example, calls the Corinthians to "see what is beautiful and pleasing and admissible before the face of the one who made us," he implies that God is the arbiter of the good.

More often than these texts refer to God as creator, however, they refer to God as Father of Jesus Christ, who, through the Christ event, has made possible human beings' release from sin and ultimate salvation (e.g., 1 Clem. 7.3; 2 Clem. 1.2–3; Ign. *Rom.* 6.1, 3; Pol. *Phil.* 2.2; Did. 4.6–7; Barn. 5.1–4; Herm. Sim. 9.7.3–4; Mart. Pol. 9.3; Diogn. 7.1–6). The Christ-event is the proximate and compelling reason for Christians to think and act ethically as they do.

Some of these texts appeal above all to God and God's commands as a basis for ethics. Others appeal more strongly to Christ, and some invoke God and Christ together. The Didache begins by invoking the biblical twofold commandment (Lev 19:18) to love God and love one's neighbor (Did. 1.2). The letter of Barnabas, in contrast, which in places seems to want to distance Christ-confessors from God's past relationship with Israel and mainstream Jewish interpretation of the law, begins by greeting "sons and daughters, in the name of the Lord, who loved us, in peace" (Barn. 1.1).[24] The past tense "loved" indicates that "the Lord" is Jesus Christ in his earthly life. Immediately afterward (1.2), the writer refers to God's ordinances, but as his introduction continues it is Christ whom he describes as pouring out the Spirit on community members, traveling with "me on the path of righteousness," speaking through the prophets, and teaching the hope of life, righteousness, and love of joy and gladness (1.3, 4, 7, 6). In the present evil days, moreover, it is Christ whose ordinances community members must follow (2.1).

The Ignatian corpus takes a middle road. Each letter introduces itself, and its ethical exhortations, with reference to both God and Christ, together or in close succession.[25] The Ephesians, for example, are beloved by God and deemed righteous through the faith and love that come through Christ Jesus (Ign. *Eph.* 1.1). They have shown their brotherly love for Ignatius by imitating God and sending Onesimus to visit him in prison on their behalf (1.1–2). In return, Ignatius begs them "according to Jesus Christ" to love Onesimus (1.3). All these writers would undoubtedly affirm the moral authority of both God and Christ, but several show a subtle preference for invoking one or the other.

Almost all the Apostolic Fathers, from time to time, hold the promise of salvation or the threat of damnation over their listeners, in a way that suggests they hope it will encourage good behavior (e.g., 1 Clem. 26.1; 2 Clem. 16.3; Ign. *Eph.* 11.1; Pol. *Phil.* 5.1–3; Barn. 21.6; Herm. Vis. 3.7.1–2; Diogn. 10.2). This could indicate an element of consequentialism in their thinking, according to which attitudes and actions are judged by their outcome. Consequentialism is common, especially in ancient popular and civic ethics, and for some community members the fear of not being saved may indeed have been an incentive to behave well.[26] The eschatology of these texts, however, is strongly dependent on their sense

24. On Barnabas as distancing itself from God's past relationship with Israel, see J. Carleton Paget, "Paul and the Epistle of Barnabas," *NovT* 38 (1996): 359–81, esp. 364–67.

25. Ignatius can also refer to Christ as "our God"; e.g., Ign. *Rom.* 3.3.

26. J. A. Kelhoffer, "Eschatology, Androgynous Thinking, Encratism, and the Question of Anti-Gnosticism in 2 Clement 12 (Part Two)," *VC* 72 (2018): 353–68, sees a hint of this in 2 Clement, but W. Pratscher, "The Motivations of Ethos in 2 Clement," in *Identity, Ethics, and Ethos in the New Testament*, ed. J. G. van der Watt (Berlin: de Gruyter, 2006), 597–610, esp. 597–601, argues convincingly that God's action through Christ is as important for the writer as eschatological hope.

of God's and Christ's grace and love ("O surpassing philanthropy and love of God!" as the letter to Diognetus puts it [Diogn. 9.2]), which call human beings to love God and Christ as creator and redeemer. Though what these writers hope for is a central part of their faith, and nobody aspires to be damned, we can assume they do not think future hope is Christians' main reason to behave ethically.

If future salvation is not the mainspring of Christian ethics, neither is human nature. In the early principate, some Stoics and Middle Platonists saw human goodness as a natural response to the goodness of the divine—an idea on which some later Christian writers would also draw.[27] In popular moral thinking too, some goods are understood as appealing naturally to human beings.[28] The Apostolic Fathers, as we have seen, can envisage human beings as possessing both good and evil impulses. Since human beings can respond to God and Christ, they are never helplessly in the grip of evil. But these writers all represent Christians' ethical attitudes and behavior as a voluntary response to God and Christ, rather than as something to which their human nature draws them.

New Testament scholars debate whether faith (which is sometimes, though not always, treated as a virtue) is a gift of the Holy Spirit, and at Galatians 5:22–23 Paul lists nine qualities, some or all of which are virtues, which he calls the "fruit of the Spirit." The Apostolic Fathers do not explicitly describe the Spirit as an ethical authority alongside God and Christ, but most of them affirm, and almost certainly they all believe, that those who confess Christ receive the Spirit (e.g., Barn. 1.2; cf. Did. 7.1, 3; 1 Clem. 2.2 suggests this does not necessarily happen at baptism). Christians live in the Spirit (e.g., Barn. 11.10), and the Spirit lives in them (Herm. Mand. 5.1.2; 5.2.5; 11.2), and the flesh must live well and cooperate with the Spirit to be worthy of it (Ign. *Pol.* 1.2; Herm. Sim. 6.5, 7). The Spirit prepares one for salvation (Barn. 19.7), and it is the rope that carries community members up to God (Ign. *Eph.* 9.1). If the Spirit is not explicitly a source or arbiter of good, therefore, we can assume that only an ethical life in obedience to God and Christ is compatible with life with and in the Spirit.

5. THE CONTENT OF ETHICS

Ethical ideas are woven throughout these texts, and they also appear in clusters in virtue and vice lists and household codes (both of which are probably borrowed from Hellenistic philosophy, directly or via Judaism, and appear in several earlier epistles).[29] The letter of Barnabas, for example, describing "the way of the Black One," lists "the things that destroy the soul" as "idolatry, over-boldness, high-handedness with power, hypocrisy, double-heartedness, adultery, murder, robbery, pride, transgression, treachery, evil-doing, arrogance, use of potions, magic-working, greed, lack of fear of God . . ." (Barn. 20.1). Lists like this, in works that we assume were written to instruct, are dramatic but rather indigestible. They may have been meant to intimidate the audience into obedience as much as inform it. Mixing what any audience would agree were evils (murder, treachery, hypocrisy) with more community-specific injunctions (against idolatry, boldness, or use of potions) may also have been a way of adding the weight (or possibly the agreeability) of convention to

27. E.g., Cicero, *Fin.* 2.46; Plutarch, *Mor.* 550d; Epictetus, *Diatr.* 2.8.3.

28. Babrius 57, 58, Phaedrus, prose paraphrase 274. Nature herself can also be invoked as a moral authority in popular moral thinking; see Morgan, *Popular Morality*, 211–13.

29. E.g., Plato, *Resp.* 6.490c; Aristotle, *Eth. eud.* 2.3.4; Cicero, *Tusc.* 4.5.9; Wis 8:7; 14:25–26; Jub. 21.21; 23.14; 1QS 4.2–14; Sib. Or. 2.254–83; 3.36–45. On the background to NT virtue and vice lists, see E. Kamlah, *Die Form der katalogischen Paränese im Neuen Testament* (Tübingen: Mohr Siebeck, 1964); J. T. Fitzgerald, "Virtue/Vice Lists," *ABD* 6:857–59.

some potentially more controversial, community-specific ethics. Household codes tend to be more structured and easier to digest. Polycarp's letter to the Philippians, for example, instructs male community members who are householders to teach their wives to remain in the faith they have been taught, to love their husbands and others in chastity, and to educate their children. Widows should be discreet, pray constantly, and abstain from bad behavior. The code then extends its range to advise deacons to be blameless in thought and action, young men to care above all for purity, presbyters to be compassionate and restrained, and everyone to be "zealous for good" (Pol. *Phil.* 4.2–6.3). The ethical content of household codes like this is conventional and widely shared by Jews and gentiles, but Polycarp's particular interest in widows, deacons, and presbyters signals this one as Christian.

The Decalogue, the twofold love command, and the golden rule (cf. Tob 4:15; Sir 31:15, Matt 7:12; Luke 6:31) are referenced throughout these texts.[30] They show, once more, these writings' Jewishness, but arguably the most striking thing about them is that they are accompanied by little in the way of practical problem-solving. Christians are exhorted to love one another, and when they fail (as, for instance, the Corinthians have according to 1 Clement), they are essentially exhorted to repent and return to loving one another. Where Jewish and gentile laws alike not only define how people should behave in community but put in place regulations and procedures for problem-solving when needed, most of these writings offer almost no mechanisms for resolving conflict beyond the authority of the writer (in the case of 1 Clement; e.g., 7.1; 55.1), the local bishop (Ign. *Pol.* 2.1), or individual conscience (1 Clem. 48.1). One explanation for this may be that these communities still look forward actively, if perhaps not quite so urgently as the first Christians, to the end time, and in that context creating the mechanisms that would help a community solve its problems and survive in the long-term is not a priority.[31] But it also attests to the ethical idealism of early churches, which may have been part of what attracted outsiders to them.

The big themes of the love command and the Decalogue can be broken down into numerous more specific injunctions that, in some cases, are particularly relevant to the situation of the audience. The commandment against adultery, for instance, can be elaborated to include prohibitions against dishonoring a respectable woman, engaging in extramarital sex, or giving in to lust (Pol. *Phil.* 5.3; Did. 1.4; Herm. Vis. 3.7.2; Diogn. 9.1). (Only 1 Clem. 38.2; and Ign. *Pol.* 5.2, however, seem to follow, e.g., 1 Cor 7:5–8 in encouraging celibacy, within or without marriage.) The value of (nonsexual) continence can be expressed as exhortations not to overeat or overdrink, or not to love money or power (2 Clem. 4.3; 6.1; Pol. *Phil.* 2.2; 5.2; Did. 15.1). The theme of love can be expressed through exhortations to peace and humility, and also injunctions against bearing malice, causing schism, speaking evil, getting angry, or being devious or hypocritical (1 Clem. 2.5; 2 Clem. 4.3; Pol. *Phil.* 2.2; Did. 2.3–6; Barn. 19.3–4, 7; Herm. Mand. 2.3). Within their broad theme of harmony within the household, household codes add different details to

30. K. D. Stanglin, "The Historical Connection Between the Golden Rule and the Second Greatest Love Command," *Journal of Religious Ethics* 33 (2005): 357–71, explores the relationship between the two and argues that the golden rule only makes sense with reference to the love command. J. A. Steenbuch, "How 'Trivial' Is the Golden Rule in Patristic Ethics?," *Danish Yearbook of Philosophy* 51 (2018): 3–23, helpfully discusses the various (positive and negative) versions of the golden rule in patristic texts and agrees with Stanglin that it is only useful in a larger ethical context—e.g., when related to the love command.

31. On the ethical idealism and lack of problem-solving mechanisms in Paul's letters, which probably acted as one model for later communities, and which have points in common with gentile visions of golden ages past or future, see T. Morgan, *Being "in Christ" in the Letters of Paul: Saved Through Christ and in His Hands* (Tübingen: Mohr Siebeck, 2020), 221–34.

the picture (a tendency already at work in the Pastoral Epistles).[32] First Clement 1.3, for instance, commends the Corinthians' former conduct, when they honored the elderly, encouraged the young in temperance, and instructed married women to have a blameless, seemly, and pure conscience, to give dutiful love to their husbands, and to take their domestic management seriously and wisely. Polycarp exhorts the wives in the Philippian community to remain in the faith given to them, to love their husbands and chastely love everyone else, and to educate their children in the fear of the Lord, while widows should be wise in faith, pray ceaselessly, and avoid slander, evil speech, false witness, love of money, and any other evil (Pol. *Phil.* 4.2–3).

Some of these ideas are clearly specific to the context of composition. First Clement begins by emphasizing that conflict and disloyalty to community leaders should be wholly foreign to those among God's elect (1 Clem. 1.1). It enlarges on the happiness of the Corinthians when they lived in peace and humility toward one another (2.1–7), and how jealousy, envy, sedition and strife have removed peace, righteousness, and faith from the community (3.2–4). The writer's solution centers on a return to peace, humility, and obedience (e.g., 14.1; 15.1; 16.1; 22.5; 37.1–2; 38.1). Ignatius's *To Polycarp*, much of which is about how to be a good bishop, draws on some of the same themes but treats them appropriately to its context. The writer urges Polycarp to work to preserve the unity of his community (Ign. *Pol.* 1.2) and "hold up" the whole community in love (1.2), to be "prudent as the serpent" as well as "pure as the dove" (2.2), to keep sober and work hard (1.3; 2.3; 3.1), and to look after different groups within the community as they require (4.1–3).[33] The letter to Diognetus, much of the aim of which is apologetic, casts Christian virtues in part as the opposite of the bad behaviors that are inflicted on them: Christians bless those who abuse them, honor those who insult them, and celebrate the attacks they suffer as if they give life (Diogn. 5.15–16).[34] Ignatius's letter to the Romans about his martyrdom, and the Martyrdom of Polycarp, meanwhile, both emphasize the importance of endurance, steadfastness, and imitation of Christ (Ign. *Rom.* 1.1; 4.2; 5.3; Mart. Pol. 1.2; 2.2, 4; 9.3).[35]

Around what we might call the "core" ideas that recur in multiple texts, we find a wide periphery of less common ideas, including injunctions against working magic (Did. 2.2; Barn. 20.1), bitterness (Herm. Mand. 10.2.2), and being double-minded, double-hearted, or double-tongued (which may refer to either doubt or duplicity; Pol. *Phil.* 5.2; Did. 2.4; Herm. Vis. 3.7.1; Mand. 10.2.2).[36] Other ancient ethical systems take a clear "core and periphery" shape, with some attitudes and actions that are (or claim to be) accepted by everyone, and some outliers which are cited more rarely or generate less agreement. If we

32. J. Lookadoo, "Categories, Relationships and Imitation in the Household Codes of 1 Clement, Ignatius and Polycarp: A Comparison with Household Codes in the Pauline Corpus," *Neot* 53 (2019): 31–52, shows how the Apostolic Fathers tend to expand earlier codes and add detail.

33. Did. 3.7–8, from the perspective of community members, links living quietly and meekly with treating the words one has heard—and presumably, by extension, the community leaders who usually deliver those words—with respect.

34. The contrast between the flesh and spirit or soul, however, seems to have involved more of an evolution out of biblical and later Jewish language; see, e.g., the discussions of J. Aitken, H. M. Patmoer, and I. Rosen-Zvi, "Introduction," and B. Wold, "'Fleshly Spirit' and 'Vessel of Flesh' in 4QInstruction and the Thanksgiving Hymns," in *The Evil Inclination in Early Judaism and Christianity*, ed. J. Aitken, H. M. Patmore, and I. Rosen-Zvi (Cambridge: Cambridge University Press, 2021), 49–64 and 1012. D. M. Reis explores the role of *psychē* in the formation of Christian identity, including in the letter to Diognetus ("Thinking with Soul: *Psychē* and *Psychikos* in the Construction of Early Christian Identities," *JECS* 17 [2009]: 563–603, esp. 569–77).

35. Though imitation of Christ is key here, a work like the Martyrdom of Polycarp might also seek to appeal to a gentile audience by invoking other models. L. S. Cobb, "Polycarp's Cup: *Imitatio* in the *Martyrdom of Polycarp*," *JRH* 38 (2013): 224–40, argues that the death of Socrates is a subsidiary model for Polycarp.

36. On the "core and periphery" model in ethics, see Morgan, *Popular Morality*, 183–84.

looked at a much larger group of Christian texts, we might be able to identify such a pattern with more certainty, but in such a small and diverse corpus as this we cannot draw too many conclusions from the fact that some ideas appear in only a minority of texts.

We should not, of course, assume that because certain attitudes and behaviors are commended, they are always practiced. The Apostolic Fathers are sometimes explicit that community members are failing in their ethical obligations, and many people will have made their own accommodations with what was preached and taught to them. A well-evidenced example is that of magic-working and potion-making, which are forbidden by the Didache and the letter of Barnabas, as under Jewish law. Papyri and other documents, however, preserve abundant evidence of spells that appeal to the God of Israel, angels, Moses, or Jesus Christ, or are decorated with Christian symbols.[37]

That said, there is no reason to doubt that these writers and their communities took their ethics seriously.[38] Some of the ideas they preached, moreover, were sufficiently unusual (in gentile and even, in one or two cases, in Jewish contexts), or were defined in such a way as to suggest that they were meant to distinguish Christians from others. A few of these ideas are worth discussing a little further: in particular, some accounts of the love command and the qualities of humility, care for the poor, and chastity.

It was important to early Christian leaders to impress on community members that being a Christ-confessor was a whole-life commitment. For both Jews and gentiles, those who confessed Christ as Lord were God's redefined people, in all aspects of their lives and hopes. Though the letter to Diognetus, moreover, is distinctive in the boldness with which it states that Christians are a "new race" (Diogn. 1), similar ideas can be found in texts from Paul's letters onward. For Jewish Christians, we can imagine that it was important to emphasize that Christ-confessors were now God's people in all the senses in which, by tradition, the people of Israel were. For gentiles, it was important to make clear that confessing Christ was not simply something one could add to one's portfolio of religious observance; it meant transferring one's trust, one's allegiance, and one's hopes wholly to the God of Israel and to Jesus Christ and becoming fully part of the reconfigured people of God.

Within this mindset, the love command has an important role to play. By invoking the giving of the law to Israel (Deut 6:5; Lev 19:18), it identifies Christians as God's people: those who love God. By referencing an existing summary of the law (cf. Jub. 36.7–8; T. Benj. 3.3; T. Jos. 11.1), it puts Christians in continuity with the law without committing them to the ritual aspects of it, which increasing numbers of Christians did not see as applicable to them. In communities in which Jesus was remembered as having taught that one should love God and one's neighbor (cf. Matt 5:44; 19:19; 22:36–9; Mark 12:29–33; Luke 10:25–28)—none of the Apostolic Fathers explicitly attributes this saying to Jesus, but all know a good deal of Matthaean, and some Lukan material—the love command identifies Christians as followers of Christ. Whether the command to love one's neighbor included noncommunity members, therefore, which is debated in relation to both Judaism and Christianity, it is regularly invoked by these writers to identify someone as a Christian.[39]

37. H. D. Betz, *The Greek Magical Papyri in Translation: Including the Demotic Spells* (Chicago: University of Chicago Press, 1986), gives some examples; e.g., pp. 144 (*PGM* 7.973–80), 182–88, 318–20, 322 (*PGM* 126a.1–21), 323 (*PGM* 128.1–11).

38. If Tertullian, *Apol.* 39.7 has any basis in fact, Christians' love for each other may have been remarked on by outsiders.

39. G. Lee-Miller, "Obligations to Outsiders in Select Texts of the Apostolic Fathers" (PhD diss., Fuller Theological Seminary, 2008), surveys the history of debate (pp. 25–34) and argues that the Didache and Letter of Barnabas can both be read as commending to Christians a general obligation to love outsiders and treat them as one would want to be treated, and also a number of specific obligations including helping the poor and vulnerable.

Invoking the love command, however, does not in itself distinguish a Christ-confessor from (other) Jews. Nor does taking care of the poor, since the idea that loving and worshiping God can be expressed by taking care of one's neighbors in need is widespread in Jewish Scripture and tradition.[40] It is the theological framework within which Christians love their neighbors and take care of the poor that makes them, in their own eyes, distinctive. The Didache looks forward to the "last days" (Did. 16.3), and the "way of life" is connected with the command to pray three times a day for the coming of God's kingdom (8.2–3) and the celebration of the Eucharist as symbol of the coming of the kingdom (9.4). The letter of Barnabas sees the present days as evil (2.1), but it affirms that the Lord has already given Christians the "firstfruits of the taste of things to come" (Barn. 1.7), and it is in this context that Christians are called to follow the "way of light" (18.1), which includes loving God and doing good to one's neighbor (19.1, 3). The call to love is fueled, for these writers, by their conviction that they have already been sanctified by God through Christ (e.g. 1 Clem. salut.) and that they are destined for glory (e.g. Ign. *Eph.* salut.); they are already living with one foot, as it were, in the kingdom of God, and can look forward to its fulfillment before too long.

The love command is also treated as distinctive of Christians when it is linked with the call to humility and/or to loving one's enemies and nonretaliation. The Didache follows up its invocation of the love command (Did. 1.2) with the interpretation, "The teaching of these words is this: bless those who curse you and pray for your enemies, and fast for those who persecute you" (Did. 1.3; cf. 3.8–9). For 1 Clement (1 Clem. 49.5), too, longsuffering is a characteristic of love. The letter to Diognetus describes the distinctiveness of Christians as being in part that they love all people, though they are persecuted by all (Diogn. 5.11), and that when they are abused, insulted, or hurt they respond with blessings, honor, and rejoicing (5.15–16). Polycarp's martyrdom is described as expressing both his love for God (Mart. Pol. 2.2) and his love for his neighbors, when he allows himself to be arrested partly in order to act as a model for them, and to foster their love of their neighbors in turn (1.2). Christians are those who love when they love in these particular ways, for these particular reasons.

The call to quietness of life and nonretaliation may have involved an element of self-preservation. It could also draw on remembered teachings of Jesus that the persecuted are blessed (Herm. Sim. 9.28.5 may reference Matt 5:11–12), and a wealth of testimony in apostolic writings that Christ-confessors can expect to be persecuted (Diogn. 5.8–15 references several Pauline passages to this effect), and/or that it is a blessing to suffer for God (cf. 1 Pet 4:14, which may also be referenced at Herm. Sim. 9.28.5). It could refer to the advice of Paul to the Thessalonians and Romans to lead a quiet life (1 Thess 4:11) and obey the political authorities (Rom 13:1). (This would also echo the commonsense advice regularly given to the weak and vulnerable in popular morality not to make trouble for those more powerful than themselves.) Additionally, it could, like the call to love and care for one's neighbors, root itself in the conviction that the final coming of Christ is, if not imminent, at least in view.

Above all, however, the love command and the call to quietness of life and nonretaliation together appeal to the example of Christ and the call to imitate Christ. In *To the Philippians*, Polycarp reminds listeners that "for our sakes, so that we might live through

40. E.g., Isa 1:17; Amos 5:24; Mic 6:6–8; cf. Exod 22:21–24; Isa 1:23; Jer 7:5–6; 22:3; 49:11. On care for the poor, see, e.g., Barn. 3.3–5; 20.2; Did. 5.2; Diogn. 10.5–6, with Barn. 3.3 invoking the exhortations of Isa 58:6–10.

[Christ], he bore everything" (Pol. *Phil.* 8.1). "Let us then be imitators of his endurance," he continues, "and if we suffer for his name's sake let us glorify him" (8.2). Polycarp describes what it was that Christ endured: he was betrayed, wrongly accused, and put to death, all of which he accepted for God's sake.[41] Imitating Christ's endurance can be expressed not only by nonretaliation but by loving those who hate you and (as Luke's Jesus does on the cross) blessing those who curse you. The story of Polycarp's martyrdom makes extensive use of this theme. Polycarp, implicitly but clearly, imitates Christ by not wanting to evade arrest (Mart. Pol. 5.1; 7.1), spending the time before he is arrested in prayer (5.2), and refusing to say anything at his trial that might exonerate him (9.2–3). After death, he is celebrated for his endurance (19.2). Not dissimilarly, Ignatius, writing to the Romans, sees his hoped-for martyrdom as a sacrifice, in imitation of Christ's sacrifice (Ign. *Rom.* 4.3; cf. 6.3), in which he is as humble as a slave (4.4). On the way to Rome, he endures the ill treatment of the soldiers who guard him, and even provokes worse treatment by treating them well (5.1). The example of Christ's humility, nonretaliation, and blessing of those who cursed him is the most compelling reason these texts offer for the prominence of these qualities, and they point to how, in ethics as in other aspects of their faith, the example of Christ in his suffering and death are central to Christians and fundamentally shape their conduct.

Much work has been done in recent decades on early Christian attitudes to wealth, which are complex and nuanced.[42] The Apostolic Fathers take slightly different approaches. They agree that love of money is a bad thing. Second Clement goes furthest, quoting the saying of Jesus that "no servant can serve two masters," God and mammon (2 Clem. 6.1; cf. Matt 16:26; Mark 8:36; Luke 9:25), and exhorting his listeners to say goodbye to all the things of this world, including money (2 Clem. 6.4–5). For the writer of the letter to Diognetus (Did. 10.4–6), sharing one's wealth with neighbors in need imitates God's own generosity toward humanity.[43] The Shepherd of Hermas takes the view that worldly wealth harms the rich specifically if they do not use it to help the poor (Vis. 3.6.5; 3.9.4). If the wealthy use their wealth to help those less fortunate, it seems (to this as to many later Christian writers) to be acceptable.[44] The Ignatian letter to Polycarp (Ign. *Pol.* 4.3) refers to some kind of "common fund" that was in existence for the benefit, presumably, of those in most need (though the writer says that Christian slaves cannot expect it to be used to

41. In discussing imitation of Christ, scholars of Christianity sometimes borrow the classical topos that imitation is of either a virtue (such as courage) or a specific action. Imitation of Christ, however, is better seen as neither of these (Christians are not encouraged, for instance, to seek to be crucified, and what is most important about Christ is not that he exemplifies generic virtues), but as imitation of Christ's acceptance of the consequences of his commitment to God; see T. Morgan, "Not the Whole Story? Moralizing Biography and *Imitatio Christi*," in *Fame and Infamy: Essays for Christopher Pelling on Characterization in Greek and Roman Biography and History*, ed. R. Ash, J. Mossman, and F. Titchmarsh (Oxford: Oxford University Press, 2015), 353–66.

42. E.g., G. de Ste. Croix, *Early Christian Attitudes to Property and Slavery* (Oxford: Blackwell, 1975); V. Neri, *I marginali nell'occidente tardoantico* (Bari: Edipuglia, 1998); S. Holman, *"The Hungry Are Dying": Beggars and Bishops in Roman Cappadocia* (Oxford: Oxford University Press, 2001); P. Brown, *Through the Eye of the Needle* (Princeton: Princeton University Press, 2012).

43. W. Horst and B. J. Robinson, "This Person Is an Imitator of God: *Philanthropia*, and the Addressee of *Ad Diognetum*," *JECS* 29 (2021): 309–39.

44. A. J. Malherbe, "Godliness, Self-Sufficiency, Greed, and the Enjoyment of Wealth: 1 Timothy 6:3–19. Part I," *NovT* 52 (2010): 376–405, and "Part II," *NovT* 53 (2011): 73–96, traces this view back to 1 Tim 6:3–19. D. J. Downs, "Almsgiving and Competing Soteriologies in Second-Century Christianity," *Religions* 9 (2018): 201–13, argues that for the writer of 2 Clement, Ignatius, and Polycarp generosity to the poor is linked with their expectation of physical resurrection, when God will judge the deeds done in the body. J. A. Draper, "The Moral Economy of the *Didache*," *HTS Theological Studies* 67.1 (2011): 1–10, argues that hints of patron-client language in the Didache suggest a similar idea is known to the writer, though he emphasizes more strongly the importance of sharing wealth.

set them free).[45] None of these writers, however, follows the vision of Acts 2:44–45 and encourages the faithful to pool all their resources.[46]

Perhaps the most unexpected teaching in these texts, as in early Christianity more widely, and certainly the one that causes the most debate among Christians today, concerns sexual ethics. We noted above that, unlike some later Christian writings, especially from the fourth century onward, these texts do not advocate virginity or celibacy. They do, however, widely advocate fidelity within marriage, especially for women (2 Clem. 4.3; Pol. *Phil.* 4.2; Ign. *Pol.* 5.1; Barn. 19.4),[47] and temperance among the young (1 Clem. 1.3; Pol. *Phil.* 5.3), and attack adultery (2 Clem. 4.3; Did. 2.2; Barn. 19.4; Herm. Mand. 4.1.9), lust, fornication (Ign. *Pol.* 5.2; Did. 1.4; Barn. 19.4; Herm. Vis. 1.2.4; 3.7.2; cf. 3.8.4), and sodomy (Did. 2.2; Barn. 19.4), together with abortion and infanticide (Did. 2.2). It seems likely, though it is never explicit, that these exhortations draw on a Jewish tradition that claimed to see gentile morality as riddled with impurity and self-indulgence.[48] It is worth noting, however, that although there is evidence that abortion and infanticide were practiced around the Mediterranean at this time, and some Greek and philhellene aristocratic groups practiced pederasty (in which the younger partner was probably in his late teens or early twenties), there is no good evidence that most gentiles were less "moral" in other ways, by their own or even Jewish standards, than Jews or early Christians.[49] Claiming that an individual or group one does not like is sexually depraved is a commonplace of ancient invective, and Jewish and Christian attacks on gentile morality are part of this tradition. We should probably see Christians in this period not as promoting any particularly unusual or extreme sexual ethics, but as commending chastity in traditional Jewish terms and borrowing a well-tried topic of invective to seek to discredit gentiles who sought to discredit them.

We have seen throughout this chapter that these writers' ethical thinking is strongly Jewish, with the important distinction that it looks to the authority of Jesus Christ as well as God the Father. We have also noted points of contact with upper-class gentile and civic morality in their more idealistic moods, and with popular morality, but we may imagine that part of the appeal of Christianity to gentiles was its vision of a divine-human community in which one could hope to find reliable justice, love, generosity, and trust. Most Greek philosophers, however, took a more optimistic view of the relationship between goodness and the divine than did mainstream society, and in some schools human virtue was seen as deriving from the divine and cultivable in relationship with the divine. Some modern scholars see Stoic ethics of the early principate, in particular, as having much in common

45. J. A. Harrill, "Ignatius, *Ad Polycarp.* 4.3 and the Corporate Manumission of Christian Slaves," *JECS* 1 (1993): 102–42, warns against taking this as evidence of a general opposition to manumitting slaves—though there is no evidence that any of the Apostolic Fathers favored manumission, in principle, either.

46. J. M. G. Barclay, "Early Christianity, Mission, and the Survival of the Poor in the Graeco-Roman World," *Teologisk tidsskrift* 8 (2019): 243–53, esp. 249–51, argues that Christians' practical support of each other, and perhaps also of some beyond their communities, may not only have strengthened communities but also worked as a tool of mission.

47. Female chastity within marriage is specified more often in these texts than male.

48. See the discussions of W. Loader, "'Not as the Gentiles': Sexual Issues at the Interface Between Judaism and Its Greco-Roman World," *Religions* 9 (2018): 258–79, and M. Blidstein, *Purity, Community, and Ritual in Early Christian Literature* (Oxford: Oxford University Press), 149–82.

49. For various perspectives on Greek and Roman sexualities, see, e.g., J. R. Clarke, *Looking at Lovemaking: Constructions of Sexuality in Roman Art, 100 BC–AD 250* (Berkeley: University of California Press, 1998); T. K. Hubbard, ed., *A Companion to Greek and Roman Sexualities* (Chichester: Wiley-Blackwell, 2014); M. Skinner, *Sexuality in Greek and Roman Culture*, 2nd ed. (Chichester: Wiley-Blackwell, 2014); R. Blondell and K. Ormand, eds., *Ancient Sex: New Essays* (Columbus: Ohio State University Press, 2015).

with Christian ethics. This case has been made in detail by Runar M. Thorsteinsson, who argues that for both Stoics and Christians, the divine is good and it is the concern of human beings to be good as the divine is good.[50] Both see living in a certain way as part of proper worship of the divine, and certain individuals (such as Socrates or Christ) as paradigms of right living. Both see ethics as having an intra-human as well as a divine-human aspect, and emphasize the importance of mutual love and care, and of nonretaliation and love of enemies. Thorsteinsson does not take the further step of arguing that Stoicism shaped early Christian ethics, but others do.[51]

Early Christians could undoubtedly have heard Stoics, along with other philosophers, poets, and rhetoricians perform publicly in cities around the Mediterranean, and some could have read philosophical inscriptions in public spaces, or even got hold of philosophical texts (though these would have been expensive), even if they were not sufficiently wealthy to study with a philosopher. But Christians could also have derived the topics that Thorsteinsson discusses from Jewish tradition, some of them also from mainstream gentile ethics, and some from their particular situations, and all these must be more likely sources of Christian thinking than the elite philosophy that, in any depth, was only available to a social and educational elite. We have also noted that many ethical ideas and practices are widely shared across the ancient Mediterranean and Near East, and what makes them distinctive to particular communities is often not their content but the local role models they invoke, the claim that they characterize, say, Spartanness or Romanness, or the divinity (if any) who is understood as their source. It need not surprise us that Christianity shares some ethical ideas with Stoicism and other philosophical schools and parts of contemporary society, but similarity need not imply influence unless, as in the case of Christianity's Jewishness, the influence is beyond question on multiple fronts.

It is often suggested that early Christian ethics owe much to the system of patronage in gentile society, which seeks to strengthen and articulate social relations by emphasizing, for instance, the importance of solidarity, friendship, and respect for authority, and the benefits that richer and poorer community members can provide for each other.[52] Again, one can see parallels between Christian and wider society, and patronage would have been a familiar concept to many Christians and quite likely (though not necessarily) part of their experience. Again, though, we should be wary of seeing influence wherever we find similarity. It is also worth bearing in mind that similarities between the patronage system and relationships among Christians are partly a matter of perspective. Scholars of early Christianity tend to describe patronage in structural terms, emphasizing the distance between the rich and poor and more and less powerful, and their need of each other. Ancient historians tend to see patronage in more dynamic terms: as a means to various ends and a mechanism of control, from which the poor get (usually) some material benefit, but the socioeconomically privileged get larger benefits of power and security. Everyone

---

50. R. M. Thorsteinsson, *Roman Christianity and Roman Stoicism: A Comparative Study of Ancient Morality* (Oxford: Oxford University Press, 2010).

51. E.g., T. Engberg-Pedersen, *Paul and the Stoics* (Edinburgh: T&T Clark, 2000); T. Rasimus, T. Engberg-Pedersen, and I. Dunderberg, eds., *Stoicism in Early Christianity* (Grand Rapids: Baker Academic, 2010). M. J. Edwards, however (I think rightly), sees philosophy as having little influence on Christianity before Justin, at the earliest ("Early Christianity and Philosophy," in *The Routledge Companion to Early Christian Thought*, ed. D. J. Bingham (London: Routledge, 2010), 44–45.

52. C. Eilers, *Roman Patrons of Greek Cities* (Oxford: Oxford University Press, 2002). E. Hemelrijk, "Patronage of Cities: The Role of Women," in *Roman Rule and Civic Life: Local and Regional Perspectives*, ed. L. de Ligt, E. Hemelrijk, and H. W. Singer (Leiden: Brill, 2003), 415–27; J. Nichols, *Civic Patronage in the Roman Empire* (Leiden: Brill, 2013).

is in a Greek or Roman patronage system for what they can get out of it, and recognition of that is never far from the surface of even its most idealized representations. No doubt leaders of early churches, for instance, also used ideas such as mutual love and care in part to secure their position and authority, but there is also no good reason to doubt they understood themselves as answerable to God for the working of their communities. The community's shape and functioning, therefore, was not only, or mainly, a matter of various interested parties getting something out of it on the human plane but of its ordering such that every member, eventually, could be saved. The structures of mainstream gentile and Christian communities may therefore have had points in common, but their dynamics were significantly different.

6. THE AIMS OF ETHICS

We cannot understand Christian ethics, or any group's ethics, without asking what they seek to achieve. Their most obvious aim, which these texts articulate regularly, is service to God and conformity with what God requires of humanity. First Clement, for example, upbraiding the Corinthians for their arguments and strife, describes their behavior as "foreign to God's elect" (1 Clem. 1.1). Christians, in response to God's goodness to them, should act in the fear of God (2.8), govern themselves in a way that is worthy of God (21.1), and be pleasing to God in their own rank of life (40.1). In the Ignatian letter to the Ephesians, obedience to the bishop, mutual love, concord, and good works create a chorus in God's own musical key, hearing which, God recognizes Christians as his own people and "members of his Son" (Ign. *Eph.* 4.1–2).

In an earlier section, we resisted the idea that Christian ethics are, in principle, functionalist or consequentialist: that Christians are called to behave as they do in order to achieve salvation (even if, in practice, for some, salvation was an incentive). For those who had put their trust in God and Christ, however, and were waiting in hope of being saved, ethical instruction may have been seen as helping them to stay on the right way. Polycarp seems to indicate this when he advises the Philippians that "abstaining from all unrighteousness" is the appropriate response to the lordship of the exalted Christ and to his teaching and also leads to resurrection to eternal life at the end-time (Pol. *Phil.* 2.1–3). Second Clement, similarly, affirms that keeping God's commands, with lips, heart, and mind, is both the appropriate response when one recognizes Christ's mercy toward human beings, and also leads ultimately to salvation (2 Clem. 3.1–4). For the Didache, the way of life is first a response to "the God who made you" (Did. 1.2) and gave you all your gifts (1.5), and those who do not follow it will be judged (1.5). It is not always clear in these writings whether salvation is imagined ultimately as of the individual or of the group, but since they all assume that individuals can choose whether to think and behave ethically or not, it is likely that it is the individual's salvation that is the focus of ethical exhortation.

What responds appropriately to God and Christ and leads to salvation also fosters community (for the present, even if community members do not know how long the future of this world will be). First Clement, in particular, emphasizes the dangers of bad behavior to the community. The behavior of some members has created *stasis* in the community (1 Clem. 1.1), a "trigger" word in Greek political thought, which evokes dangerous, potentially catastrophic discord, conflict, and social dissolution. This is in sharp contrast with the Corinthians' earlier humility toward each other (2.1), which made for "a deep and rich peace" for everyone (2.2; cf. 3.3). The letter to Diognetus, with a different agenda, praises Christians for their virtuous behavior: they not only keep the appointed laws of the heavenly constitution under which they live but exceed them (Diogn. 5.9–10). This demonstrates "the amazing and admittedly paradoxical nature of the constitution of their state" (5.4). Christian conduct is the proof of the superiority of God's polity over all others.[53]

The Shepherd of Hermas links ethics with community in a distinctive way. For the writer, as for other Apostolic Fathers, living ethically is essential if one wants to live in obedience to God the creator (Herm. Vis. 1.1.6) and to gain the life and all good things that are to come (1.1.8; cf. Herm. Sim. 5.7.1–2). But, in Hermas's third vision, a tower appears, which is interpreted as the church (Herm. Vis. 3.3.3) and which is built on a mixture of qualities—faith, continence, simplicity, understanding, goodness, holiness, and love (3.8.4–5)—all of which are either essentially ethical or have ethical dimensions.[54] Continence is said to be the daughter of faith (3.8.4); all the others are daughters of one another, and whoever performs the works of their mother will live (3.8.5). Here, it seems, the church as an institution is built on ethics, and failing in ethical behavior is damaging to the church in the sense not only of a particular community of individuals, as at Corinth, but in the sense of the universal church that encompasses and transcends all human communities.

7. WHO ARE THE ADDRESSEES OF ETHICAL EXHORTATIONS?

The ethics encoded in the law of Moses are what are sometimes called "householder ethics": they are addressed primarily to male heads of households, who are expected to govern their households in such a way that everyone follows their guidance and example. In the Apostolic Fathers, ethical injunctions, as we have seen, can be directed at all community members or be specific to officeholders, householders, wives, widows, orphans, children, young men, the more or less wealthy, or slaves. Of these, however, wives, widows, orphans, children, and youths are not addressed directly (unlike, for instance, in some of Paul's letters, or in stories of Jesus's interactions and teachings in the Gospels), and slaves are directly addressed only twice (Did. 4.11; Barn. 19.7).[55] Not only Jewish law, but also gentile popular ethics, tends to address either male individuals or male householders, so the focus of the Apostolic Fathers on male officeholders or householders would have been both familiar and uncontroversial (at least to those who were male, free, and married).[56]

The first part of the Didache (Did. 1–6) is sometimes taken to be addressed to catechumens. The only description of the envisaged addressee, however, comes at the beginning, where the book is said to be "the teaching of the Lord through the twelve apostles to the gentiles," suggesting it is aimed at socializing gentiles into a Jewish ethical milieu rather than being aimed at catechumens specifically.[57] Nor is there any sign of a change of addressee at the beginning of chapter 7, which concerns how to baptize people and is

53. Josephus, *Ag. Ap.* 2.170–78 makes a similar claim when he says that Jews, unlike gentiles, both know and follow all their laws, and this is one reason for the superiority of their polity.

54. "Faith" (*pistis*) here could be the attitude and act of trust that brings people into a relationship with God and Christ but, alongside continence and the rest, may be ethical faithfulness.

55. E.g. Ign. *Pol.* 4.1 refers to widows, 4.3 slaves, 5.1 wives; Barn. 19.5 to sons and daughters, 19.7 slaves and handmaids (probably male and female slaves); Pol. *Phil.* 4.2 to wives, 4.3 widows, 6.1 widows, orphans, and the poor (cf. Herm. Vis. 2.4.3, referring to exhortation to widows and orphans); Did. 4.9 to sons and daughters, 4.10 slaves and handmaids.

56. Greek ἀνδρεία, *andreia*, and Latin *virtus*, "courage," both literally mean "manliness," which is a Greek and Roman virtue in its own right. Traces of this idea may be visible at Mart. Pol. 9.1, where a voice from heaven exhorts Polycarp to "be strong and be a man," and occasionally in the Shepherd of Hermas (S. Young, "Being a Man: The Pursuit of Manliness in *The Shepherd of Hermas*," *JECS* 2 [1994]: 237–55).

57. The addressee is also addressed as "child" in, e.g., Did. 5.1, 6.1, but this could mean either a community member or a learner.

clearly not intended for catechumens. It is likely that the primary addressees, at least, of all these texts are community members.

There is a good deal of debate about whether the ethics advocated by the Apostolic Fathers are intended to be practiced only toward insiders, or also toward outsiders. The roots of this debate lie in the interpretation of commands such as the love command in Jewish writings, which some scholars argue refers only to one's Jewish neighbors, and others see as referring to gentiles too.[58] In practice, the command was likely read differently in different contexts by both Jews and Christians. The letter of Barnabas, for example, commands community members to love their neighbors (Barn. 19.5), but leaves it open to interpretation who their neighbors are. The Didache, in contrast, opens with the double command to love God and love one's neighbor (Did. 1.2) and immediately interprets it by saying that "the teaching of the words is this: bless those who curse you and pray for your enemies and fast on behalf of those who persecute you; for what kind of generosity is it, to love those who love you?" (1.3). This could refer to loving one's fellow community members even when tensions and disagreements arise, but the strength of the wording suggests it is applicable to hostile outsiders too.[59] The letter to Diognetus describes Christians as loving all people and being persecuted by all (Diogn. 5.11). "All" are later defined as Jews, who look on Christians as foreigners, and Greeks (5.17), indicating that the writer sees the love command as applicable to insiders and outsiders alike.[60] Since all the writings we are discussing, however (apart from the Letter to Diognetus), are directed at community members and mainly deal with community matters, when the love command and other ethics are invoked, the writer likely has the community in mind first.

8. IS THERE SUCH A THING AS CHRISTIAN EDUCATION?

First Clement 21.6, 8 makes the first explicit reference to "Christian education." The writer exhorts the Corinthians, "Let us teach the young the teaching [παιδεία, *paideia*] of the fear of God . . . let our children share the teaching [*paideia*] that is ours in Christ [ἐν Χριστῷ, *en Christō*]" (21.6, 8). The first use of *paideia* here could refer to the education whose content is the fear of God, or the education appropriate to those who fear God, but in context it probably means the first. The writer is telling the community how to be "citizens worthy of [God]" (21.1): among other things, by doing God's will, revering Christ, instructing the young, and regulating their wives for good (21.4, 6). This suggests that not only must the men, who are the primary addressees of the letter, be good Christians, but they must ensure their wives and children are too (cf. 1.3). Responsibility for Christian education, as for ethics, belongs to community leaders and male householders. The second reference to *paideia* probably also refers to the content of this education, which includes humility, love of God, and recognition that fear and love of God bring salvation (21.8). The reference to *paideia* as "in Christ" is notable its own right, since the meaning of this phrase is much debated. In the context of ethical instruction, its most likely meaning is instrumental: children are to learn the teaching that has come to humanity through Christ in his earthly ministry (cf. 1 Clem. 2.1; 49.1).[61]

---

58. K. Stendahl, in "Hate, Non-Retaliation, and Love: 1QS 10.17–20 and Rom 12.19–21," *HTR* 55 (1962): 343–55, esp. 345, notes that early Christian references to *echthroi*, "enemies," or those who are hostile, never refer to other Christians; in the Didache (Did. 5.2), those who persecute the good are on the way of death, so are not Christians.

59. This teaching may reflect a memory of Matt 7:12, Luke 6:31; it is ambiguous in these verses too toward whom the golden rule should be enacted, but in the context of Jesus's own life and death, both insiders and outsiders may be implied.

60. Mart. Pol. 7.3 and 19.1 suggest that Christians can, at least, impress outsiders by their behavior.

61. On 1 Clement's use of "in Christ" language, see Morgan, *Being "in Christ"*, 254–55.

Throughout these writings, the ultimate teacher is God, through God's commandments, through the Scriptures (including the example of characters in the Scriptures from Abraham to Rahab; e.g., 1 Clem. 10.12, 17–18), through inherited teachings derived from the Scriptures, such as the Two Ways, or through God's sending of Christ to earth (e.g., 1 Clem. 2.8; 2 Clem. 13.4; Pol. *Phil.* 2.2; Did. 1.2; Barn. 1.2; Herm. Vis. 1.3.4; cf. Diogn. 7.2–6).[62] In early Christian writings, it is extremely rare for the risen or exalted Christ to teach, but 1 Clement 22.1 may offer an example, when he tells the Corinthians that Christ speaks to them through his Holy Spirit, in the words of Psalm 34:11–17: "Come, children, listen to me: I will teach you the fear of the Lord."[63] The Apostolic Fathers, however, often refer to Jesus as teaching in his earthly ministry (1 Clem. 13.1–2; 2 Clem. 6.1; Ign. *Eph.* 9.2; Pol. *Phil.* 2.2–3; probably 1 Clem. 49.1; Barn. 5.7–8), and quote or refer to teachings by Jesus that appear in the Gospels as we have them (e.g., 1 Clem. 24.5; 2 Clem. 3.1; Ign. *Eph.* 14.2; Ign. *Rom.* 7.3; Pol. *Phil.* 5.2; Did. 11.7; Barn. 5.9; Herm. Vis. 4.2.6; Herm. Mand. 6.2.4; Herm. Sim. 6.3.6; 9.20.2; Diogn. 9.6). Alongside the law of Moses, Christ in his earthly life is their single most important source of teaching. Christ also teaches by example, by bearing his suffering with faithfulness and humility (1 Clem. 16.3–7; Ign. *Rom.* 6.3; Pol. *Phil.* 10.1; Mart. Pol. 1.2).[64]

After God and Christ, the authority most often invoked is that of the apostles, who appear everywhere, sometimes by name, but more often in quotations or allusions to their writings. The writer of the letter to Diognetus invokes the apostles as his own teachers: "Having become a disciple of the apostles, I am becoming a teacher of the nations" (Diogn. 11.1). He rejoices that, through Christ, what the apostles handed down to later generations is well guarded (11.6). Other writers also invoke the authority of the apostles in their own support, while emphasizing their inferiority to the apostolic generation. For example, Ignatius tells the Romans he cannot order them to pray on his behalf, as Peter and Paul could (Ign. *Rom.* 4.3), and he addresses the Ephesians as a fellow learner who is only beginning to be a disciple (Ign. *Eph.* 3.1).

That said, all these writers, by the act of writing, claim a degree of authority over their immediate addressees, and potentially later readers.[65] Hermas's claim to authority comes from his visions, and from the "ancient lady," the church, who tells him to write "two little books" and, as well as using them himself, to send them to Clement and to Grapte, in order to distribute them around to other cities (Herm. Vis. 2.4.3).[66] Grapte is instructed to teach widows and orphans, which suggests that some women officeholders taught women about

62. The relationship between divine and human agency in Christian education is explored by P. Gemeinhardt, "Teaching the Faith in Early Christianity: Divine and Human Agency," *VC* 74 (2020): 129–64.

63. The risen Christ does instruct the disciples at Matt 28:19 and teaches at Luke 24:25–28, 44–47; Acts 1:2–3; cf. John 21:15–17, while the exalted Christ teaches in some later writings. Alternatively, in 1 Clem. 22.1 the preexistent Christ may be envisaged as teaching, which would be even rarer.

64. At Ign. *Eph.* 1.1, the reference to imitating God is probably to Christ (cf. Ign. *Rom.* 3.3). Diogn. 10.4, however, can talk of Christians' imitating the goodness of God himself, on which see W. Horst, "The Secret Plan of God and the Imitation of God: Neglected Dimensions of Christian Differentiation in *Ad Diognetum*," *JECS* 27 (2019): 161–83.

65. J. C. H. Smith, in "The *Epistle of Barnabas* and the Two Ways of Teaching Authority," *VC* 68 (2014): 465–97, argues that one effect of the Two Ways language of the Didache and Barnabas is to magnetize the identity of its audience around the authority of the writer.

66. T. W. Proctor, "Books, Scribes, and Cultures of Reading in the Shepherd of Hermas," *JEH* 30 (2021): 1–19, shows the importance, for this writer, of books and reading in Christian education and the construction of authority, arguing that he is working in a strongly "reading culture" (p. 2). A. Tagliabue, "Learning from Allegorical Images in the *Book of Visions* of *The Shepherd of Hermas*," *Arethusa* 50 (2017): 221–55, points out that Hermas also validates visions as teaching.

their faith, separately from the education of men or boys.[67] The writer to Diognetus claims authority primarily from God, to whom he prays for the power of speech for himself and, for Diognetus, the power of hearing (Diogn. 1.1), but also attributes authority to Diognetus himself, who had apparently sought instruction from him (1.1).

The Ignatian letters are well-known for their concern for the authority of presbyters, deacons, and especially bishops (e.g. Ign. *Eph.* 4.1; *Magn.* 4.1; *Phld.* 1.1–2; *Smyrn.* 8.1). As a bishop, according to the letter to the Trallians, Ignatius speaks "with a great voice, the voice of God: 'Pay attention to the bishop and to the presbytery, and to the deacons!'" (Ign. *Trall.* 7.1). Writing to Polycarp as a bishop, Ignatius exhorts him to justify his position with all care of both the flesh and the spirit (Ign. *Pol.* 1.2). First Clement was prompted in part by a rebellion by some Corinthians against their presbyters (1 Clem. 44.5–6), and the writer urges them to obey their leaders as soldiers obey their generals (37.1–3; cf. 42.1–44.6).

Writing to the Romans, Ignatius has less interest in his authority as a bishop to give advice to the Romans, but aspires to become "a word of God" in himself by the example of his martyrdom (Ign. *Rom.* 2.1)—a theme that becomes endemic in later Christian martyrologies. For Polycarp and the writer to Diognetus, taking up a theme of Paul's letters, not only martyrs and community leaders but all community members can teach by example, instructing one another and outsiders by their faithfulness, righteousness, and endurance under persecution (Pol. *Phil.* 9.1–2; Diogn. 5.10–16; cf., e.g., 1 Thess 1:7).[68]

One of the duties of bishops and presbyters is to teach (Ign. *Pol.* 5.1), but there are also references to teachers of more uncertain status in these letters. The Didache envisages teachers (like Jesus himself and the apostles) sometimes arriving from elsewhere to teach, and it tells its community to receive them—but warily, testing them and recognizing that there are false teachers, as there are false prophets (Did. 11.1–2; cf. 6.1; 12.1). The writer of the letter to the Magnesians urges the Magnesians not to be led astray by false teachings, nor by "old fables which are now useless" (Ign. *Magn.* 8.10), while the letter to the Ephesians warns that teachers who corrupt households will not inherit the kingdom of God (Ign. *Eph.* 16.1). Potentially false teachers, together with false prophets, are evidently a concern for these communities, just as the Gospels and canonical epistles testify they were in the communities among which Jesus taught and in the earliest churches. In general (though not always), the authority of those who live in a community and are known to it is presented as much less problematic. The authority to teach, among other things, comes partly from an individual's being personally known—his or her character, past, family, and lifestyle.

The Didache envisages all community members as teaching each other by reproving each other where they see sin (e.g., Did. 4.3; 15.3). Male householders are sometimes explicitly told to teach their own households, especially their wives and children (Did. 4.9; Herm. Vis. 1.3.1). At the same time, all community members are learners, as the letter to the Ephesians emphasizes. As learners, they have a responsibility to pay attention to

---

67. The earliest references to female deacons and community leaders do not describe them as teaching women specifically, but in the later second-century apocryphal Acts of Paul and Thecla (10.15), Thecla is described as instructing women, some of whom become monastics.

68. C. L. de Wet, "No Small Counsel About Self-Control: *Enkrateia* and the Virtuous Body as Missional Performance in 2 Clement," in *Sensitivity Towards Outsiders*, ed. J. Kok, T. Nicklas, D. T. Roth, and C. M. Hays (Tübingen: Mohr Siebeck, 2014), 447–69, shows how for 2 Clement, Christian self-discipline is an example for outsiders; in the same volume P. Foster, "Mission and Ethics in the Writings of Ignatius of Antioch," 505–26, argues that for Ignatius, Christians' ethical behavior in general should be attractive to noncommunity members.

teachers, teachings, and examples; to consider and confess their transgressions (including before the Eucharist, according to Did. 14.1); and to imitate Christ and the longsuffering of fellow Christians, especially under persecution. Though male householders may take a lead in teaching their own households, the responsibilities of learners are probably assumed to be the same for men, women, children (though from what age, in these communities, we cannot be sure), slaves, and free people, because each person's salvation depends ultimately on their own affirmation and practice of faith.[69]

In this connection, it is worth noting that all these writings seem to take for granted that being a good Christian (both in the sense of a good *Christian*, and in the sense of a *good* Christian) involves both faith and works. The letter of Barnabas impresses on its community that they should keep the law of Moses spiritually rather than physically, and all these texts are more concerned with ethical than ritual aspects of the law, but none of them, for instance, cites Romans 3:28, 4:2–5, or Galatians 2:16 to argue that being a good Christian involves faith rather than "works" (in any sense of the term), nor do they cite James 2:14–26 to argue that "faith without works is dead." Passing over that debate, they take for granted what most Jews and gentiles take for granted—namely, that ethical attitudes and actions, good or bad, normally go hand in hand.

These glimpses of early Christian education suggest that it is firmly embedded in the organizing structures and practices of its communities. Teaching is a responsibility of officeholders—bishops, presbyters, and deacons—or of those who have a spiritual gift of teaching, but community members also teach each other, especially by example. Teachers can move between communities, but most are probably local. Their authority comes ultimately from God, from the Scriptures, from the teaching of Christ, especially in his earthly ministry, and from the teaching of the apostles, together with their own calling. Teaching is aimed primarily at male householders or future householders, who are expected to pass it on to their households, though sometimes women may be taught separately. There is no obvious distinction in these writings between what is taught to adults and to children, which is perhaps not surprising in communities in which most new members were probably adults: young in faith if not in years. It is unclear in what contexts teaching takes place, but just as it was a regular part of meetings in the synagogue—and teaching by Jesus and the apostles is also remembered as taking place in private houses and in the open air—we may imagine that Christian teaching, both before and after baptism, occurred both when the community gathered for prayer or the Eucharist, and in less formal, perhaps mainly household gatherings. The focus of this essay is ethics, but Christian education, after as well as before baptism, likely also encompasses the interpretation of Scriptures, the earthly teaching of Jesus Christ, and the nature of ultimate hope.[70]

There is—to those familiar with rabbinic Judaism, surprisingly—little evidence for Jewish education in the Hellenistic world, as opposed to the Greek education many Jews received, but it is plausible that this sketch of education in early Christian communities

---

69. J. N. Yuh, "Do as I Say, Not as They Do: Social Construction in the Epistle of Barnabas Through Canonical Interpretation and Ritual," *HTR* 112 (2019): 273–95, points to the responsibility of Barnabas's listeners to understand what they are taught by the "circumcision of hearing" (Barn. 9.1–3).

70. In these writings, baptism comes after hearing the kerygma preached and interpreted (1 Clem. [Latin version] 42.4; Herm. Vis. 3.7.3), and we can assume that the symbolism of baptism itself was explained to catechumens, but there is no strong indication that ethical teaching formed part of catechumens' instruction. In perhaps the early third century, the pseudo-Clementine *Recog.* 3.76–78 refers to catechumens being instructed in the "mysteries of the kingdom of heaven," but not specifically to ethics.

(part of which is derived from Judaism) is close to what took place in many Jewish communities and synagogues.[71] It also has points of contact with the gentile moral formation of children, which may have made it less foreign to some gentiles. There was, in particular, a Roman tradition that saw parents, especially fathers, as responsible for the moral formation of their offspring.[72]

If this sketch is plausible, however, Christian education at this time has rather less in common with the education that dominated the Hellenistic and Roman sociocultural landscape from the early Hellenistic period into late antiquity. *Enkyklios paideia*, the curriculum of "general education," included reading, writing, basic mathematics, ethics, grammar, and elementary rhetoric. It offered practical skills and acculturation into the upper levels of Greek and Roman society to children whose families could pay for it.[73] In wealthy households this teaching was carried by educated slaves; for everyone else, it was conducted by freelance teachers who convened "schools" in public places and whose only authority was a demonstrable knowledge of what they taught. These teachers did not always receive much honor—one Greek proverb says, "He's either dead or teaching letters"—but by the early principate they were a feature of every city neighborhood, town, and village.[74]

Like Christian education, early imperial *enkyklios paideia* introduces people (in this case, normally children) to a distinctive society: that of cultural Greeks or Romans. It is ahead of Christian education in making use of an established canon of Greek and, in the West, increasingly Latin literary texts. In the process of teaching children to read and write, it introduces learners to a good deal of ethical material via moralizing quotations from canonical Greek or Latin literature. But unlike what we have seen of Christian education, *enkyklios paideia* does not aspire to shape the lives of all the members of early imperial societies. Being conducted mainly by paid freelance teachers, it is not socially embedded to the same degree as Christian education seems to be in churches. Though ethical ideas are much in evidence in the texts used for teaching literacy, the teaching of ethics is not explicitly central to it. Crucially, though children read texts that involve the gods, *enkyklios paideia* has no particular connections with cult, nor any religious agenda except insofar as conventional piety is part of Greek and Roman culture. At the time when the Apostolic Fathers were writing, therefore, *enkyklios paideia*, in content, social context, and rationale, was very different from Christian education. It was only in the fourth century that Christians became extensively interested in the interaction, even integration of the two, with all the theological and ethical dilemmas such an exercise would generate.[75]

---

71. Less close, perhaps, to minority groups such as the Qumran community, on which see W. O. McCready, "Education in the *Sacrospace* of Qumran Judaism," in *Religions and Education in Antiquity: Studies in Honour of Michel Dejardins*, ed. Alex Damm (Leiden: Brill, 2018), 55–75.

72. The paradigm is Cato the Elder (Plu. *Cat. Maj.* 20); on the role of parents more broadly see J. McWilliam, "The Socialization of Roman Children," in *The Oxford Handbook of Childhood and Education in the Classical World*, ed. J. E. Grubbs and T. Parkin (Oxford: Oxford University Press, 2013), 269–74.

73. T. Morgan, *Literate Education in the Hellenistic and Roman Worlds* (Cambridge: Cambridge University Press, 1998), R. Cribiore, *Gymnastics of the Mind: Greek Education in Hellenistic and Roman Egypt* (Princeton: Princeton University Press, 2001). Perhaps 10 percent of men and rather fewer women had some degree of literate education under the principate.

74. From Zenobius's early imperial proverb collection (4.17). Other forms of education were also endemic, from apprenticeships to practical language learning (E. Dickey, *Learning Latin the Ancient Way: Latin Textbooks from the Ancient World* [Cambridge: Cambridge University Press, 2016]) and the teaching of philosophy and rhetoric to wealthy young men (cf. Suetonius, *De grammaticis*; Philostratus, *Vitae sophistarum*).

75. On the interaction of early Christian with mainstream education, see, e.g., S. Rappe, "The New Math: How to Add and Subtract Pagan Elements in Christian Education," in *Education in Greek and Roman Antiquity*, ed. Y. L. Too (Leiden: Brill, 2001), 405–32; N. McLynn, "Disciplines of Discipleship in Late Antique Education: Augustine and Gregory Nazianzen," in *Augustine and the Disciplines: From Cassiciacum to*

BIBLIOGRAPHY

Burke, J. "Satan and Demons in the Apostolic Fathers: A Minority Report." *SEÅ* 81 (2016): 127–68.

Downs, D. J. "Almsgiving and Competing Soteriologies in Second-Century Christianity." *Religions* 9 (2018): 201–13.

Gemeinhardt, P. "Teaching the Faith in Early Christianity: Divine and Human Agency." *VC* 74 (2020): 129–64.

Knell, M. *Sin, Grace and Free Will: The Apostolic Fathers to Augustine*. Cambridge: Clarke, 2017.

Konradt, M. *Ethik im Neuen Testament*. Göttingen: Vandenhoeck & Ruprecht, 2022.

Löhr, H. "Good as a Moral Category in the Early Jesus Tradition." Pages 205–22 in *Early Christian Ethics in Interaction with Jewish and Greco-Roman Contexts*. Edited by J. W. van Henten and J. Verheyden. Leiden: Brill, 2013.

Morgan, T. *Literate Education in the Hellenistic and Roman Worlds*. Cambridge: Cambridge University Press, 1998.

Morgan, T. *Popular Morality in the Early Roman Empire*. Cambridge: Cambridge University Press, 2007.

Novick, T. *What Is Good, and What God Demands: Normative Studies in Tannaitic Literature*. Leiden: Brill, 2010.

Proctor, T. W. "Books, Scribes, and Cultures of Reading in the Shepherd of Hermas." *JEH* 30 (2021): 1–19.

Steenbuch, J. A. "How 'Trivial' Is the Golden Rule in Patristic Ethics?" *Danish Yearbook of Philosophy* 51 (2018): 3–23.

Thorsteinsson, R. M. *Roman Christianity and Roman Stoicism: A Comparative Study of Ancient Morality*. Oxford: Oxford University Press, 2010.

Watt, J. G. van der, ed. *Identity, Ethics, and Ethos in the New Testament*. Berlin: de Gruyter, 2006.

Confessions, ed. K. Pollmann and M. Vessey (Oxford: Oxford University Press, 2007), 25–48, P. Gemeinhardt, "In Search of Christian *Paideia*: Education and Conversion in Early Christian Biography," *ZAC* 16 (2012): 88–98; C. Osiek, "The Education of Girls in Early Christian Ascetic Tradition," *Studies in Religion* 41 (2012): 401–7; C. Harrison, *The Art of Listening in the Early Church* (Oxford: Oxford University Press, 2013); M. R. Hauge and A. W. Pitts, *Ancient Education and Early Christianity* (London: Bloomsbury, 2016).

CHAPTER 19

MARTYRDOM IN THE APOSTOLIC FATHERS

PAUL HARTOG

1. INTRODUCTION

We cannot understand early Christianity apart from "the profound shaping of Christian life and faith" effected by the experience of and reflection upon Christian martyrdom.[1] Historians point out that the actual occurrence of martyrdom was probably less common than often assumed.[2] Nevertheless, the perceived danger is reflected across the literary genres of early Christianity.[3] More specifically, the vocabulary, conceptualization, and mindset of martyrdom appear throughout the diverse works comprising the Apostolic Fathers. As in early Christian literature in general, the Apostolic Fathers reflect diverse "theologies" of martyrdom, presented in a "layered and complex" fashion.[4]

Surveying the theme of martyrdom within the Apostolic Fathers is a daunting task. Beyond a narrow focus upon the μάρτυς *martys* / μαρτύριον *martyrion* / μαρτυρέω *martyreō* word group, one may also examine the conceptualization of martyrdom by studying the references to being killed for one's beliefs or dying for one's faith (without the exact terms μάρτυς / μαρτύριον / μαρτυρέω being used). One may also investigate the underlying martyrological mindset—the ordering of values prone to support and motivate the willingness to die for one's faith. Therefore, an examination of martyrdom in the Apostolic Fathers may investigate the vocabulary and the conceptualization, but also the supporting, axiological mindset. This "martyrological mindset" provided the foundation and rationale supporting martyrdom,[5] and it appears not only in the Ignatian correspondence and the Martyrdom of Polycarp, but also in texts like 1 Clement, Polycarp's *To the Philippians*, the Shepherd of Hermas, and Diognetus.

The unique character of this martyrological mindset was its contempt for death, which

1. M. E. Johnson, "Sharing 'the Cup of Christ': The Cessation of Martyrdom and Anaphoral Development," in *Studies on the Liturgies of the Christian East*, ed. S. Hawkes-Teeples, B. Groen, and S. Alexopolous, ECS 18 (Leuven: Peeters, 2013), 125. Thomas Heffernan even asserts that "Christianity is in its core a religion of martyrdom" (T. J. Heffernan, "Martyrdom, Charisma, and Imitation: Paths to Christian Sanctity," *Greek Orthodox Theological Review* 55 [2010]: 253).

2. R. MacMullen, "Ordinary Christians in the Later Persecutions," in *Changes in the Roman Empire: Essays in the Ordinary* (Princeton: Princeton University Press, 1990), 156.

3. See P. Hartog, "The Maltreatment of Early Christians: Refinement and Response," *The Southern Baptist Journal of Theology* 18 (2014): 49–79.

4. J. D. McLarty, "Early Christian Theologies of Martyrdom," in *The Wiley Blackwell Companion to Christian Martyrdom*, ed. P. Middleton, WBCR (Chichester: Wiley Blackwell, 2020), 132. See also C. R. Moss, *Ancient Christian Martyrdom: Diverse Practices, Theologies, and Traditions* (New Haven: Yale University Press, 2012).

5. D. W. Riddle, "From Apocalypse to Martyrology," *AThR* 9 (1927): 267.

reflected "a relativist approach to suffering, and indifference to pain."[6] As many scholars have emphasized, early Christian martyrdom was often portrayed as a heightened form of *imitatio Christi*.[7] "For a person to sacrifice his or her life for the faith is to practice the *imitatio Christi* in a very special sense."[8] But the martyrological mindset entailed renunciation as well as imitation.[9] The axiological perspectives that undergirded the choice and assessment of martyrdom downplayed various temporal values. Inherent in this axiological ordering was the willingness to renounce lesser values for the sake of higher ones. Such a mindset, with its axiological preferences, was to be inculcated as a means of transforming the volitional agent. Therefore, an examination of the axiological perspectives of a "martyrological mindset" further complicates our understanding of so-called voluntary martyrdom within early Christianity, a spectrum of phenomena "embedded within the rhetorical discourse" of early Christian texts.[10]

In recent scholarship, "voluntary martyrdom" comes off as a problematic label that may still retain some heuristic value.[11] "Voluntary martyrdom" has been described as "the bringing about of martyrdom either by presenting oneself to authorities or by the unsolicited disclosure of one's Christian identity."[12] The naming of such a "voluntary martyr" rests on the ability to assign responsibility for the distinct roles of initiation and response. Did the authority initiate the situation, and was the martyr gathered up in persecution? Or did the martyr initiate the encounter, and the authority responded? Nevertheless, if the would-be martyr was a preformed agent with preexisting dispositions, questions arise concerning where along the spectrum such "inclination" may morph into an "initiatory" predisposition or fervent penchant.

2. THE VOCABULARY OF Μάρτυς / Μαρτύριον / Μαρτυρέω IN THE MARTYRDOM OF POLYCARP

Early Christian views of martyrdom were rooted in preceding Jewish tradition,[13] but they were also influenced by Greco-Roman "noble death" traditions.[14] Of course, the distinction

6. J. M. Kozlowski, "Polycarp as a Christian Gymnosophist," StPatr 51 (2011): 16.

7. C. R. Moss, *The Other Christs: Imitating Jesus in Ancient Christian Ideologies of Martyrdom* (Oxford: Oxford University Press, 2010); M. Taveirne, "Das Martyrium als *imitatio Christi*: Die literarische Gestaltung der spätantiken Märtyrerakten und Passionen nach der Passion Christi," *ZAC* 18 (2014): 167–203.

8. D. Loades, "Introduction," in *Martyrs and Martyrologies*, ed. D. Wood, SCH 30 (Oxford: Blackwell, 1993), xv.

9. M. Haykin, "'Come to the Father': Ignatius of Antioch and His Calling to Be a Martyr," *Them* 32 (2007): 34–35. Haykin illustrates this "theme of renunciation" through a quotation from Ign. *Rom*. 7.8.

10. P. L. Tite, "Voluntary Martyrdom and Gnosticism," *JECS* 23 (2015): 27. Candida Moss notes that there was no specific, technical term for "voluntary martyrdom" in the ancient world—the category has grown out of modern scholarly discussions. See C. R. Moss, "The Discourse of Voluntary Martyrdom: Ancient and Modern," *Church History* 81 (2012): 531–51. "It is not possible to provide a single definition of what early Christians meant by voluntary martyrdom any more than it is possible to identify a single spirit of the martyrs" (O. Nicholson, "What Makes a Voluntary Martyr?," StPatr 65 [2013]: 161).

11. B. Doherty, "Competing for the Crown: Tertullian, Montanism and 'Voluntary Martyrdom' Revisited," *Phronema* 36 (2021): 5.

12. See Moss, "Discourse of Voluntary Martyrdom," 532. A "voluntary martyr" is also described as one "who proactively sought to provoke the Roman legal authorities by presenting himself or herself as a Christian, either during, or even in the absence of, a period of heightened persecution or harassment" (Doherty, "Competing for the Crown," 9).

13. W. H. C. Frend, *Martyrdom and Persecution in the Early Church* (Oxford: Basil Blackwell, 1965).

14. G. W. Bowersock, *Martyrdom and Rome* (Cambridge: Cambridge University Press, 1995); L. S. Cobb, "Martyrdom in Roman Context," in Middleton, *Wiley Blackwell Companion to Christian Martyrdom*, 92–95; R. G. Tanner, "Martyrdom in Saint Ignatius of Antioch and the Stoic View of Suicide," StPatr 16 (1985): 201–5.

between these influences is permeable.[15] The discussions and portrayals of martyrdom within the Apostolic Fathers were also informed by earlier Christian materials, such as Pauline perspectives.[16] In their theologies of martyrdom, the Apostolic Fathers were both receptors of earlier traditions but also innovators of new imageries.[17]

The Greek word μάρτυς ("witness") had a long pre-Christian history, where the meaning "gradually became increasingly restrictive to testimony in a legal setting."[18] Within early Christianity, one finds a shift toward the concept of a "blood witness" or "final witness."[19] Over time, the notion of μαρτύριον reflected two facets, the content of the testimony and the unto-death, terminal form in which it was delivered.[20] In short, as Jane McLarty quips, "The body's suffering was faith made visible."[21] Some have pointed to the confluence of pouring out one's blood and μάρτυς in Acts 22:20, although the latter term (in context) appears to denote "witness" in a more general sense.[22] A case can be made for the μάρτυς word group designating "witness to the point of death" within the book of Revelation (Rev 12:11; 20:4).[23] Thomas Heffernan considers the association of μάρτυς with a "blood witness" in Revelation 20:4 to be "unequivocal" and "unambiguous."[24] Others are not as confident.[25] First Clement seems to employ the vocabulary in an inconsistent but at times germane manner.[26] Among the Apostolic Fathers, the Martyrdom of Polycarp alone uses the μάρτυς word group repeatedly and unambiguously of "witness to the point of death."[27]

The Martyrdom of Polycarp employs the μάρτυς / μαρτύριον / μαρτυρέω word group

---

15. See A. J. Droge and J. D. Tabor, *A Noble Death: Suicide and Martyrdom Among Christians and Jews in Antiquity* (San Francisco: Harper, 1992); D. Boyarin, *Dying for God: Martyrdom and the Making of Christianity and Judaism*, Figurae: Reading Medieval Culture (Stanford: Stanford University Press, 1999).

16. W. Rebell, "Das Leidensverständnis bei Paulus und Ignatius von Antiochien," *NTS* 32 (1986): 457–65; A. T. Hanson, "The Theology of Suffering in the Pastoral Epistles and Ignatius of Antioch," StPatr 17 (1982): 694–96; C. B. Smith, "Ministry, Martyrdom, and Other Mysteries: Pauline Influence on Ignatius of Antioch," in *Paul and the Second Century*, ed. M. F. Bird and J. R. Dodson, LNTS 412 (London: T&T Clark, 2011), 37–56.

17. Smith, "Ministry, Martyrdom, and Other Mysteries," 55–56; W. R. Schoedel, *Polycarp, Martyrdom of Polycarp, Fragments of Papias*, vol. 5 of *The Apostolic Fathers: A New Translation and Commentary* (London: Thomas Nelson, 1967), 48.

18. Heffernan, "Martyrdom, Charisma, and Imitation," 257.

19. B. Dehandschutter, "Some Notes on 1 Clement 5,4–7," in *Fructus centesimus*, ed. A. A. R. Bastiaensen, A. Hilhorst, and C. H. Kneepkens, InstPatr 19 (Dordrecht: Kluwer, 1989), 85–86; for studies of the development of "martyr" language within early Christianity, see T. Baumeister, *Die Anfänge der Theologie des Martyriums*, MBT 45 (Münster: Aschendorff, 1980); B. Dehandschutter, "Martyr—Martyrium: Quelques observations à propos des actes d'un Christianisme sémantique," in *Polycarpiana: Studies on Martyrdom and Persecution in Early Christianity: Collected Essays*, ed. J. Leemans, BETL 205 (Leuven: Peeters, 2007), 105–11.

20. See Kozlowski, "Polycarp as Christian Gymnosophist," 16.

21. McLarty, "Early Christian Theologies of Martyrdom," 120.

22. Heffernan, "Martyrdom, Charisma, and Imitation," 260. Cf. Luke 21:12–13.

23. Dehandschutter, "Martyr—Martyrium," 110; S. Fuhrmann, "Traditions of Martyrdom in the Ignatian Letters," *In die Skriflig* 45 (2011): 694.

24. Heffernan, "Martyrdom, Charisma, and Imitation," 260–61.

25. B. Dehandschutter, "The Meaning of Witness in the Apocalypse," in Leemans, *Polycarpiana*, 181–87. See also R. Bergmeier, "Zeugnis und Martyrium," in *Die Johannesapokalypse: Kontexte—Konzepte—Rezeption*, ed. J. Frey, J. A. Kelhoffer, and F. Tóth (Tübingen: Mohr Siebeck, 2012), 619–47; Dehandschutter, "Some Notes on 1 Clement 5,4–7," 86; J. W. van Henten, "Early Jewish and Christian Martyrdom," in Middleton, *Wiley Blackwell Companion to Christian Martyrdom*, 74–75.

26. N. Brox, *Zeuge und Märtyrer: Untersuchungen zur frühchristlichen Zeugnis-Terminologie*, SANT 5 (Münich: Kösel, 1961), 211–37; Dehandschutter, "Some Notes on 1 Clement 5,4–7," 83–89; S. Giet, "Le témoignage de Clément de Rome: La cause des persecutions romaines," *Revue des sciences religieuses* 29 (1955): 333–54.

27. See B. Dehandschutter, "Le Martyre de Polycarpe et le développement de la conception du martyre au deuxième siècle," in Leemans, *Polycarpiana*, 93–104.

on twenty occasions.[28] The work self-identifies as a telling of "the story of the blessed Polycarp" (Mart. Pol. 19.1).[29] The first chapter introduces the "account of those who were martyred [μαρτυρήσαντας, *martyrēsantas*]," especially highlighting the role of Polycarp, "who put an end to the persecution [τὸν διωγμόν, *ton diōgmon*] as though he were setting his seal upon it by his martyrdom [μαρτυρίας, *martyrias*]." The text then introduces the theme of the work ("a martyrdom according to the gospel"): "For nearly all the preceding events happened in order that the Lord might show us once again a martyrdom that is in accord with the gospel [τὸ κατὰ τὸ εὐαγγέλιον μαρτύριον, *to kata to euangelion martyrion*]" (Mart. Pol. 1.1). Such a martyr waits to be betrayed and regards the welfare (and salvation) of others.[30]

> For [Polycarp] waited to be betrayed, just as the Lord did, in order that we too might be imitators [μιμηταί, *mimētai*] of him, looking not only to our own interests but to our neighbors' interests as well. For it is the mark of true and steadfast love to desire that not only oneself be saved but all the brothers and sisters as well. (Mart. Pol. 1.2)

While various scholars have maintained that "a martyrdom according to the gospel" is one that recapitulates particular events in Jesus's final sufferings, Michael Holmes argues that this view does not give "sufficient weight to the explicit definition" of such a martyrdom within the document itself, and "it confuses a literary feature of the narrative with the meaning of the narrative."[31] Moreover, the readers of the Martyrdom of Polycarp were exhorted to become "partners and fellow disciples" of the Christian martyrs, who were to be loved "as disciples and imitators of the Lord" (Mart. Pol. 17.3; cf. 22.1). But the readers could not have been expected necessarily to recapitulate such particulars as being apprehended on a Friday evening after hosting a final meal (Mart. Pol. 7.1–3), riding into town on a donkey (8.1), and being interrogated by an authority named "Herod" (8.2).[32] Imitating Christ was not so much recapitulating the exact details but the manner of his

---

28. The dating of the Martyrdom of Polycarp is greatly disputed. Michael Holmes argues for a mid-150s composition; see M. W. Holmes, "Dating the Martyrdom of Polycarp," *Early Christianity* 9 (2018): 181–200. Paul Hartog hesitantly lands on a composition within the third quarter of the second century; see P. Hartog, *Polycarp's Epistle to the Philippians and the Martyrdom of Polycarp*, OAF (Oxford: Oxford University Press, 2013), 76–86. J. Kozlowski maintains that the work was "most probably written in the 170s"; see Kozlowski, "Polycarp as a Christian Gymnosophist," 17. Candida Moss contends for a third-century composition; see C. R. Moss, "On the Dating of Polycarp: Rethinking the Place of the *Martyrdom of Polycarp* in the History of Christianity," *Early Christianity* 1 (2010): 539–74. The dating of the work's composition is an issue distinct from the dating of Polycarp's execution. See Hartog, *Polycarp's Epistle to the Philippians and the Martyrdom of Polycarp*, 182.

29. Unless otherwise noted, all translations of the Apostolic Fathers in this essay come from M. W. Holmes, *The Apostolic Fathers: Greek Texts and English Translations*, 3rd ed. (Grand Rapids: Baker Academic, 2007). Alternative, and at times quite disparate, retellings of Polycarp's story can be found in the Harris fragments, *Vita Polycarpi*, an Epitome of the Life and Death of Polycarp (*Bios kai martyrion*), and a Pseudo-Chrysostom homily on Polycarp; see B. Dehandschutter, "Polycarpiana: Notes on the Hagiographic 'Dossier' of a Saint," in Leemans, *Polycarpiana*, 259–70.

30. S. Rosell, "Loving God . . . unto Death: The Witness of the Early Christians," *HTS Theological Studies* 66 (2010): 5. Cf. Clement of Alexandria, *Strom.* 14.3.

31. M. W. Holmes, "The *Martyrdom of Polycarp* and the New Testament Passion Narratives," in *Trajectories Through the New Testament and the Apostolic Fathers*, ed. A. F. Gregory and C. M. Tuckett (Oxford: Oxford University Press, 2005), 419. Willem van Henten believes the phrase "means that Polycarp followed up Jesus' example in fulfilling his mission to the very end"; see van Henten, "Early Jewish and Christian Martyrdom," 80.

32. Hartog, *Polycarp's Epistle to the Philippians and the Martyrdom of Polycarp*, 208–9; P. Hartog, "The *Martyrdom of Polycarp* as Communal, Moral Formation," *Science et Esprit* 67 (2015): 443–44; P. Hartog, "The Christology of the *Martyrdom of Polycarp*: Martyrdom as Both Imitation of Christ and Election by Christ," *Perichoresis* 12 (2014): 140–41. For a further list of Gospel allusions, see L. S. Cobb, "Polycarp's Cup: *Imitatio* in the *Martyrdom of Polycarp*," *JRH* 38 (2014): 224.

suffering, for his sake and with others in mind.[33] In the Martyrdom of Polycarp, the notion of imitating Christ is "the encouragement to follow a demeanor rather than a reenactment of Christ's death."[34]

The opening of the Martyrdom of Polycarp explicates "a martyrdom according to the gospel" (Mart. Pol. 1.1–2.2). Holmes notes the following three characteristics.[35] First, such a martyrdom ("a martyrdom according to the gospel") is a matter of divine calling and thus involves submission to God's will and sovereignty.[36] It transpires "in accordance with the will of God," because "we must reverently assign to God the power over all things" (Mart. Pol. 2.1).[37] Later, Polycarp (echoing Jesus's entreaty in Gethsemane) prayed, "May God's will be done" (7.1). Second, a "martyrdom according to the gospel" exhibits a concern for the well-being and salvation of others (1.2).[38] Third, such a martyrdom exhibits endurance in the midst of suffering—and, one could add, an associated nobility as well.[39] The exemplary "martyrdoms [μαρτύρια]" were "blessed" and "noble [γενναῖα, *gennaia*]" deaths that embodied "nobility [γενναῖον, *gennaion*]," "patient endurance [ὑπομονητικόν, *hypomonētikon*]," and love of the Master (2.1–2). The "martyrs [μάρτυρες, *martyres*] of Christ" attained "such a level of nobility [γενναιότητος, *gennaiotētos*] that not one of them uttered a cry or a groan" (2.2).[40] They "endured so patiently [ὑπέμειναν, *hypemeinan*] that even the bystanders had pity and wept" (2.2). The martyrs thus embodied heroic courage in the face of adversity.[41]

The introduction of the Martyrdom of Polycarp is bookended by the narrative's conclusion in chapter 19: "Such is the story of the blessed Polycarp. Although he (together with those from Philadelphia) was the twelfth person martyred [μαρτυρήσας] in Smyrna, he alone is especially remembered by everyone, so that he is spoken of everywhere, even by pagans" (Mart. Pol. 19.1). The conclusion adds, "By his endurance [ὑπομονῆς] he defeated the unrighteous magistrate and so received the crown of immortality" (19.2). Through his martyrdom, Polycarp demonstrated his true character: "He proved to be not only a distinguished teacher but also an outstanding martyr [μάρτυς] whose martyrdom [μαρτύριον] all desire to imitate [μιμεῖσθαι] since it was in accord with the pattern of the gospel [κατὰ τὸ εὐαγγέλιον] of Christ" (19.1).

The addenda and epilogues to the Martyrdom of Polycarp continue the μάρτυς / μαρτύριον / μαρτυρέω vocabulary usage. Chapter 21 time-stamps the execution of

33. M. Franzmann, "*Imitatio Christi*: Copying the Death of the Founder and Gaining Paradise," in *A Wandering Galilean*, ed. Z. Rodgers, M. Daly-Denton, and A. Fitzpatrick-McKinley, JSRSup (Leiden: Brill, 2009), 381.

34. See Dehandschutter, "Le Martyre de Polycarpe," 94–99; H. H. Drake Williams, "'Imitate Me': Interpreting Imitation in 1 Corinthians in Relation to Ignatius of Antioch," *Perichoresis* 11 (2013): 82.

35. See Holmes, "*Martyrdom of Polycarp* and the New Testament Passion Narratives," 418–22. For early studies of these characteristics, see W. C. Weinrich, *Spirit and Martyrdom: A Study of the Work of the Holy Spirit in Contexts of Persecution and Martyrdom in the New Testament and Early Christian Literature* (Lanham, MD: University Press of America, 1981), 167–68; G. Buschmann, *Das Martyrium des Polykarp*, KAV 6 (Göttingen: Vandenhoeck & Ruprecht, 1998), 83. For later developments, see Cobb, "Polycarp's Cup," 224–40; P. Hartog, "Polycarp's Martyrdom 'According to the Gospel' and Paul's Philippians," StPatr 45 (2010): 391–96; Hartog, "*Martyrdom of Polycarp* as Communal, Moral Formation," 435–49; S. J. Wilhite, "'That We Too Might Be Imitators of Him': The *Martyrdom of Polycarp* as *Imitatio Christi*," *Churchman* 129 (2015): 319–36.

36. See A. Vincelette, "On the Frequency of Voluntary Martyrdom in the Patristic Era," *JTS* 70 (2019): 678–79.

37. Cf. Ign. *Eph.* salut.; Ign. *Smyrn.* 11.1.

38. Hartog, "Polycarp's Martyrdom 'According to the Gospel,'" 394.

39. Hartog, "Polycarp's Martyrdom 'According to the Gospel,'" 392; Hartog, "*Martyrdom of Polycarp* as Communal, Moral Formation," 446–47.

40. I have adapted Holmes's translation, by substituting "nobility" for "bravery."

41. Heffernan, "Martyrdom, Charisma, and Imitation," 253–54.

Polycarp: "Now the blessed Polycarp was martyred [μαρτυρεῖ] on the second day of the month Xanthicus, seven days before the calends of March, on a great sabbath, about two o'clock in the afternoon" (Mart. Pol. 21.1).[42] The following addition recaps the themes of the work: "We bid you farewell, brothers and sisters, as you walk by the word of Jesus Christ that is in accord with the gospel [κατὰ τὸ εὐαγγέλιον]; with whom be glory to God for the salvation of the holy elect; just as the blessed Polycarp was martyred [ἐμαρτύρησεν], in whose footsteps may we also be found in the kingdom of Jesus Christ" (22.1). The addenda include another reference to "the martyrdom [μαρτυρίου] of the bishop Polycarp" (Mart. Pol. Mosc. Ep. 2).[43] And the addenda cite "the very day and hour when Polycarp was martyred [ἐμαρτύρησεν] in Smyrna," claiming that Irenaeus concurrently heard a voice declare, "Polycarp has been martyred [ἐμαρτύρησεν]!" (Mart. Pol. Mosc. Ep. 2).

Throughout the body of the narrative, the Martyrdom of Polycarp praises the character of the martyr Polycarp, who "had been honored in every respect on account of his holy life even before his martyrdom [μαρτυρίας]" (Mart. Pol. 13.2). Chapter 16 eulogizes, "This man was certainly one of the elect, the most remarkable Polycarp, who proved to be an apostolic and prophetic teacher in our own time, bishop of the catholic church in Smyrna. For every word that came from his mouth was accomplished and will be accomplished" (16.2). Nevertheless, although adulated and revered, martyrs like Polycarp were not to be placed on the same level as Jesus Christ.[44] "For we worship this one, who is the Son of God, but the martyrs [μάρτυρας] we love as disciples and imitators of the Lord, as they deserve, on account of their matchless devotion to their own King and Teacher" (17.3).

In "blatant sacrificial" language, the narrative declares, "So they did not nail him, but tied him instead. Then, having placed his hands behind himself and having been bound, like a splendid ram chosen from a great flock for a sacrifice, a burnt offering prepared and acceptable to God, he looked up to heaven" (Mart. Pol. 14.1).[45] The imagery of this passage reminds various scholars of the Aqedah of Isaac in Genesis 22.[46]

At the time of execution, Polycarp raises a prayer to God, "I bless you because you have considered me worthy of this day and hour, so that I might receive a place among the number of the martyrs [μαρτύρων] in the cup of your Christ, to the resurrection to eternal life, both of soul and of body, in the incorruptibility of the Holy Spirit" (Mart. Pol. 14.2).[47] Interpreters have noted the similarities between Polycarp's prayer and eucharistic prayers.[48]

42. Cf. John 19:31. See D. W. Riddle, "A Literary Allusion in the Martyrdom of Polycarp," *AThR* 8 (1925): 136–42; J. M. Kozlowski, "*Pionius Polycarpi Imitator*: References to *Martyrium Polycarpi* in *Martyrium Pionii*," *Science et Esprit* 67 (2015): 420.

43. On the colophons, see J. Hoover, "False Lives, False Martyrs: 'Pseudo-Pionius' and the Redating of the *Martyrdom of Polycarp*," *VC* 67 (2013): 471–98.

44. According to the narrative, the opponents wondered whether the Smyrnaean Christians might "abandon the crucified one and begin to worship this man" (Mart. Pol. 17.2). The narrator responds, "They did not know that we will never be able either to abandon the Christ who suffered for the salvation of the whole world of those who are saved, the blameless on behalf of sinners, or to worship anyone else" (17.2).

45. A. K. Petersen, "Attaining Divine Perfection Through Different Forms of Imitation," *Numen* 60 (2013): 17.

46. See C. R. Moss, "Nailing Down and Tying Up: Lessons in Intertextual Impossibility from the *Martyrdom of Polycarp*," *VC* 67 (2013): 133.

47. See Cobb, "Polycarp's Cup," 224–40.

48. D. Tripp, "The Prayer of St. Polycarp and the Development of Anaphoral Prayer," *Ephemerides Liturgicae* 104 (1990): 97–132; Johnson, "Sharing 'the Cup of Christ,'" 109–26. See also F. G. Clancy, "Imitating the Mysteries That You Celebrate: Martyrdom and Eucharist in the Early Patristic Period," in *The Great Persecution*, ed. V. Twomey and M. Humphries (Dublin: Four Courts, 2009), 106–40; A. G. A. Horsting, "Transfiguration of Flesh: Literary and Theological Connections Between Martyrdom Accounts and Eucharistic Prayers," in *Issues in Eucharistic Praying in East and West: Essays in Liturgical and Theological Analysis*, ed. M. E. Johnson (Collegeville, MN: Liturgical Press, 2010), 307–25.

The fire subsequently envelops the martyr. "For the fire, taking the shape of an arch, like the sail of a ship filled by the wind, completely surrounded the body of the martyr [μάρτυρος], and it was there in the middle, not like flesh burning but like the bread baking or like gold and silver being refined in a furnace" (15.2). This passage prompts olfactory as well as visual imagery.[49] "For we also perceived a very fragrant aroma, as if it were the scent of incense or some other precious spice" (15.2).

When the fire did not consume Polycarp, an executioner stabbed him with a dagger (Mart. Pol. 16.1). After his death, his followers desired to honor his remains.[50] "And so later on we took up his bones, which are more valuable than precious stones and finer than refined gold, and deposited them in a suitable place" (18.2). The narrative expresses the intention that "the Lord will permit us to celebrate the birthday of his martyrdom [μαρτυρίου] in commemoration of those who have already fought in the contest and also for the training and preparation of those who will do so in the future" (18.3).

3. THE CONCEPTUALIZATION OF MARTYRDOM: PAPIAS, 1 CLEMENT, AND POLYCARP'S *TO THE PHILIPPIANS*

A standard distinction in logical reasoning is the differentiation between the term (word) and the concept (idea). One may discuss a conceptualization (or ideation) without ever using the exact term (or word). The Apostolic Fathers often discussed the notions of martyrdom or being a martyr without using the words μάρτυς or μαρτύριον or μαρτυρέω. The conceptualization surfaces through the language of being "killed" or being "put to death" for one's faithfulness, especially in contexts that incorporate other pertinent words, such as persecute/persecution, punish/punishment, and suffer/suffering. Specific methods of execution, such as being "thrown to wild beasts" and being cast into "the fire" are also referenced, without employment of the exact words "martyr" or "martyrdom."

For example, although the Papian materials that survive do not employ the μάρτυς / μαρτύριον / μαρτυρέω word group, Papias nevertheless directly discussed the executions of the apostles.[51] According to a fragment preserved in Philip of Side (5th c.), "Papias says in his second book that John the Theologian and James his brother were killed [ἀνηρέθησαν, *anērethēsan*] by Jews" (Papias, frag. 5.5). George the Sinner (9th c.) concurs: "For Papias, the bishop of Hierapolis, who had seen him [the apostle John] with his own eyes, claims in the second book of the *Sayings of the Lord* that John was killed [ἀνηρέθη] by Jews" (Papias, frag. 6.3).[52]

Within 1 Clement, the μαρτυρέω word group appears twelve times but is generally used of being "testified of" or "witnessed to" in the sense of being "renowned" or "illustrious." First Clement 17.2 states that Abraham was ἐμαρτυρήθη or "renowned."[53]

49. A. Lallemand, "Le parfum des martyrs dans les Actes des martyrs de Lyon et le Martyre de Polycarpe," StPatr 16 (1985): 186–92.

50. See W. Rordorf, "Aux origenes du culte des martyrs," *Irénikon* 45 (1972): 315–31; T. Baumeister, "Zur Entstehung der Märtyrerlegende," in *Christian Martyrdom in Late Antiquity (300–45 AD): History and Discourse, Tradition and Religious Identity*, ed. P. Gemeinhardt and J. Leemans (Berlin: de Gruyter, 2012), 35–48.

51. See M. Oberweis, "Das Papias-Zeugnis vom Tode des Johannes-Zebedäi," *NovT* 38 (1996): 277–95. Eusebius's framing of Papias's materials includes the following: "The same writer [Papias] utilized testimonies [μαρτυρίαις] from the first letter of John and, likewise, from that of Peter" (Papias, frag. 3.17; cf. Eusebius, *Hist. eccl.* 3.39.16).

52. In his framing of this fragment, George the Sinner himself avers that John "was honored with martyrdom [μαρτυρίου]" (Papias, frag. 6.2). He adds, "Origen also affirms in his interpretation of the Gospel according to Matthew that John was martyred [μεμαρτύρηκεν]" (Papias, frag. 6.6).

53. "Abraham was greatly renowned [ἐμαρτυρήθη] and was called 'the friend of God'" (1 Clem. 17.2).

First Clement 18.1 uses μεμαρτυρημένῳ ("illustrious") of David.[54] The next chapter similarly refers to "so many people of such great renown [μεμαρτυρημένων]" (1 Clem. 19.1). First Clement 38.2 exhorts, "The humble person should not testify [μαρτυρείτω] to his own humility, but leave it to someone else to testify [μαρτυρεῖσθαι] about him" (1 Clem. 38.2). First Clement 44.3 refers to church leaders who "for a long time have been well-spoken of [μεμαρτυρημένους] by all." First Clement 47.4 references the "highly reputed [μεμαρτυρημένοις] apostles."

The noun cognates in 1 Clement are similarly used in the broad sense of "testimony" or "witness." Clement exhorts, "Let the testimony [μαρτυρία] of our good deeds be given by others, as it was given to our fathers who were righteous" (1 Clem. 30.7). Both 1 Clement 43.2 and 43.5 refer to the tabernacle as "the tent of the testimony [τοῦ μαρτυρίου]." Finally, 1 Clement 63.3 describes "trustworthy and prudent" envoys "who from youth to old age have lived blameless lives among us, who will be witnesses [μάρτυρες] between you and us."

Only with chapter 5 does one find the μάρτυς / μαρτυρέω word group being closely tied with fatal suffering within 1 Clement. Chapter 5 refers to the "champions" and "noble examples [τὰ γενναῖα ὑποδείγματα, *ta gennaia hypodeigmata*]," who served as "the greatest and most righteous pillars" because they were "persecuted [ἐδιώχθησαν, *ediōchthēsan*] and fought to the death" (1 Clem. 5.1–2). Among these stood "the good apostles" Peter (5.4) and Paul (5.5–7). Peter went to "his appointed place of glory" after "having given his testimony [μαρτυρήσας]" (5.4).[55] Paul was "an outstanding example of patient endurance" who had also "given his testimony [μαρτυρήσας]" and then "went to his appointed place of glory" (5.7). Because of the more generic use of μαρτυρέω throughout his epistle, Clement probably means that Peter and Paul had simply "testified" or "borne witness," without a precise sense of being a "martyr."[56] Nevertheless, Clement closely affiliates Peter's "having given his testimony [μαρτυρήσας]" with going to "his appointed place of glory" (5.4), even as he closely affiliates Paul's "giving testimony [μαρτυρήσας] before the rulers" with his departing from "the world" and going to "the holy place" (5.7). "After [Paul] had been seven times in chains, had been driven into exile, had been stoned, and had preached in the east and in the west, he won the genuine glory for his faith" (5.6).[57]

The author of 1 Clement uses these examples to his paraenetic advantage. The faithful "champions" and "noble examples" were persecuted "because of jealousy and envy [διὰ ζῆλον καὶ φθόνον, *dia zēlon kai phthonon*]" (1 Clem. 5.1–2).[58] Peter endured many trials "because of unrighteous jealousy [διὰ ζῆλον ἄδικον, *dia zēlon adikon*]" (5.4). Paul suffered and was martyred "because of jealousy and strife [διὰ ζῆλον καὶ ἔριν, *dia zēlon kai erin*]" (5.5). All of this fits Clement's broader purpose of addressing the envy and strife that had entangled his Corinthian audience. The following chapter, although refraining from any use of the μάρτυς / μαρτύριον / μαρτυρέω word group, continues the theme. "To these men who lived holy lives [i.e., the "good apostles" as the "most righteous pillars" in ch. 5] there was joined a vast multitude of the elect who, having suffered many torments and

54. "And what shall we say about the illustrious [μεμαρτυρημένῳ] David" (1 Clem. 18.1).

55. See S. Giet, "Le témoignage de Clément de Rome sur la venue à Rome de saint Pierre," *Revue des sciences religieuses* 29 (1955): 123–36.

56. Dehandschutter, "Some Notes on 1 Clement 5,4–7," 83–89.

57. The clause τὸ γενναῖον τῆς πίστεως αὐτοῦ κλέος ἔλαβεν (1 Clem. 5.6) could be translated as "he received the noble reputation for his faith."

58. See S. Giet, "Le témoignage de Clément de Rome: La cause des persecutions romaines," *Revue des sciences religieuses* 29 (1955): 333–54.

tortures because of jealousy [διὰ ζῆλος, *dia zēlos*], set an illustrious example among us" (6.1). Because of such jealousy, women also were persecuted, "suffering in this way terrible and unholy tortures, but they safely reached the goal in the race of faith and received a noble reward, their physical weakness notwithstanding" (6.2).

Various scholars have noted the similarities between 1 Clement 5 and Polycarp, *To the Philippians* 9, which also focuses on the martyrdom of Paul (without using the μάρτυς / μαρτύριον / μαρτυρέω word group). "I urge all of you, therefore, to obey the teaching about righteousness and to exercise unlimited endurance, like that which you saw with your own eyes not only in the blessed Ignatius and Zosimus and Rufus but also in others from your congregation and in Paul himself and the rest of the apostles" (Pol. *Phil.* 9.1). Polycarp continues, "Be assured that all these did not run in vain but with faith and righteousness, and that they are now in the place due them with the Lord, with whom they also suffered" (9.2). Polycarp thus employs exemplary martyrs in a manner similar to 1 Clement (while adding "the blessed Ignatius" and local heroes like Zosimus and Rufus), and he uses similar terminology.

Unlike 1 Clement, Polycarp's letter employs the μάρτυς / μαρτύριον / μαρτυρέω word group on only one occasion ("the testimony [μαρτύριον] of the cross" in Pol. *Phil.* 7.1). Yet the material in Polycarp, *To the Philippians* 9 resembles 1 Clement 5 (which employs μαρτυρήσας twice). Key links between the two passages are the terms "endurance [ὑπομονή]" and "righteousness [δικαιοσύνη]," which also happen to be two central themes in Polycarp's *To the Philippians.* While Polycarp, *To the Philippians* 9.1 calls for "unlimited endurance [πᾶσαν ὑπομονήν]," 1 Clement 5.5–7 refers to Paul as "an outstanding example of patient endurance [ὑπομονῆς]" who "showed the way to the prize for patient endurance [ὑπομονῆς]." Peter had "endured [ὑπήνεγκεν] not one or two but many trials" (1 Clem. 5.4). Clement describes the apostolic leaders as "the greatest and most righteous [δικαιότατοι] pillars" (5.2). And Clement claims that Paul in particular "taught righteousness [δικαιοσύνην] to the whole world" (5.7).[59] According to Polycarp's letters, the apostolic and similar exemplars "did not run in vain but with faith and righteousness [δικαιοσύνῃ]" (Pol. *Phil.* 9.2). Like Clement, Polycarp contrasts such righteous endurance with an attachment to this world. "For they did not love the present world but the one who died on our behalf and was raised by God for our sakes" (Pol. *Phil.* 9.2). Therefore, Polycarp writes, "they are now in the place due them with the Lord, with whom they also suffered" (9.2).

Polycarp's epistolary opening praises the Philippians for their reception of "those confined by chains suitable for saints, which are the diadems of those who are truly chosen by God and our Lord" (Pol. *Phil.* 1.1). Throughout his epistle, Polycarp encourages a mindset of endurance [ὑπομονή]. He appends the Ignatian correspondence to his own letter, hoping that the Philippians would increase in "faith and patient endurance [ὑπομονήν] and every kind of spiritual growth that has to do with our Lord" (13.2). Similarly, the readers are to manifest "steadfastness and patient endurance,"[60] resulting in God's granting "a share and a place among his saints" (12.2). Polycarp entreats, "Let us, therefore, become imitators of his patient endurance [ὑπομονῆς], and if we should suffer for the sake of his name, let us glorify him" (8.2).

---

59. 1 Clem. 5 sets up an implicit contrast between the apostolic leaders as "most righteous [δικαιότατοι] pillars" and Paul's teaching on "righteousness [δικαιοσύνην]" on the one hand and the "unrighteous [ἄδικον] jealousy" of the opponents of Peter and Paul on the other (1 Clem. 5.2, 4, 7).

60. *In patientia et in longanimitate* (Pol. *Phil.* 12.2 is only extant in Latin).

4. THE AXIOLOGICAL MINDSET SUPPORTING MARTYRDOM: THE EPISTLE TO DIOGNETUS AND THE SHEPHERD OF HERMAS

The Epistle of Barnabas, the Shepherd of Hermas, and the Epistle to Diognetus also use the μάρτυς / μαρτύριον / μαρτυρέω word group, but only in the broader sense of "witness" or "testimony/testify" (Barn. 1.6; 8.3, 4; 9.3; 15.4; Herm. Sim. 5.2.6 [2x]; 5.7.1; Diogn. 4.4; 12.6). Within its parable of the vineyard, the Shepherd of Hermas declares, "And they congratulated the slave on the testimony [μαρτυρίᾳ] that his master gave him [ἐμαρτύρησεν]" (Herm. Sim. 5.2.6). The Shepherd later exhorted, "Keep this flesh of yours clean and undefiled, so that the spirit that lives in it may bear witness [μαρτυρήσῃ] to it, and your flesh may be justified" (5.7.1). In its polemical argumentation, the Epistle to Diognetus disparages the Jewish rite of circumcision: "And is it not also ridiculous to take pride in the mutilation of the flesh as a witness [μαρτύριον] to election, as though they were especially beloved by God because of this?" (Diogn. 4.4).[61] The Epistle to Diognetus later promotes "the true knowledge that is endorsed [μαρτυρουμένης] by life" (12.6).[62] These are the only uses of the μάρτυς / μαρτύριον / μαρτυρέω word group within the Shepherd of Hermas and the Epistle to Diognetus.

Nevertheless, an axiological framework supporting and motivating martyrdom is patent within both the Shepherd of Hermas and the Epistle to Diognetus. The Shepherd of Hermas distinguishes those who "suffered [παθόντες]" to the point of victorious death ("the ones who have wrestled with the devil and conquered him") from those who were "tried without suffering [θλιβέντες μὴ παθόντες]," while still not denying their commitments (Herm. Sim. 8.3.6–7).[63] A while later, the Shepherd of Hermas exalts "those who suffered [παθόντες] for the name of the Son of God, who suffered willingly [προθύμως ἔπαθον] with all their heart, and gave up their lives" (9.28.2). All those who "suffered [ἔπαθον] for the name of the Son of God" are "glorious in God's sight" (9.28.3). Hermas contrasts steadfast confessors (those who "were questioned with torture when brought before the authorities and did not deny, but suffered willingly [ἔπαθον προθύμως]") and hesitant confessors ("as many as were cowardly and hesitated, and debated in their hearts whether they should deny or confess, and yet suffered [ἔπαθον]") (9.28.4). Hermas writes:

> But you who suffered [πάσχοντες] for the sake of the name ought to glorify God, because God has considered you worthy that you should bear the name and that all your sins be healed. So consider yourselves blessed; indeed, realize that you have done a great work if any of you suffers [πάθῃ] for God's sake. (Herm. Sim. 9.28.5–6)

One of the themes of the Shepherd of Hermas is a strong disapproval of "double-mindedness [διψυχία]." The word appears over forty times within the work. It is not surprising, then, that Hermas interlaces the theme of "double-mindedness" with conceptualizations of "suffering" and "persecution" (usually θλῖψις rather than διωγμός). Because of their disordered values, "the double-minded [δίψυχοι], whenever they hear about a persecution [θλῖψιν], worship idols because of their cowardice and are ashamed of the name of their Lord" (Herm. Sim. 9.21.3).

The third vision of the Shepherd of Hermas relates that an "elderly woman" appeared

61. I have adapted Holmes's translation by changing "sign of election" to "witness to election," in order to draw attention to the noun μαρτύριον.

62. Translation is my own, to draw attention to the use of μαρτυρουμένης with the word "endorsed."

63. Translation is my own, to bring out the vocabulary point I have emphasized.

to Hermas (Herm. Vis. 3.1.2). The honor of sitting on her right side is reserved for those "who have already pleased God and have suffered [παθόντων] for the sake of the Name" (3.1.9). Hermas asks what they have "endured [ὑπήνεγκαν]," and she replies, "Scourgings, imprisonments, severe persecutions [θλίψεις μεγάλας], crosses, wild beasts, for the sake of the Name" (3.2.1). "This is why," she adds, "the right side of holiness belongs to them, and to anyone who suffers [πάθη] because of the Name" (3.2.1). "Indeed," promised the lady, "all those who are not double-minded [διψυχοῦντες] will be cleansed of all their sins to this day" (3.2.2).

A later episode within Hermas's visions reveals stones that are placed into a building. "They are those who have suffered [παθόντες] for the name of the Lord" (Herm. Vis. 3.5.2). Some white, round stones did not fit into the building. The lady explained, "These are the ones who have faith, but also have the riches of this world. Whenever persecution [θλῖψις] comes, they deny their Lord because of their riches and their business affairs" (3.6.5). When their riches are cut away, they will become useful to God and will be useful for the building. Until then, "those who are rich in this world cannot become useful to the Lord unless their riches are cut away" (3.6.6).[64] As in the third vision, the Shepherd of Hermas generally tends to use the language of "trial [θλῖψις]" rather than "persecution [διωγμός]."

The Epistle to Diognetus claims that Christians "all disregard the world and despise death" (Diogn. 1.1). Christians "endure [ὑπομένουσιν] everything as foreigners" (5.5). "They love everyone, and by everyone they are persecuted. They are known, yet they are condemned; they are put to death, yet they are brought to life" (5.11–12). "When they do good, they are punished [κολάζονται, *kolazontai*] as evildoers; when they are punished [κολαζόμενοι], they rejoice as though brought to life" (5.16). The author adds, "By Jews they are assaulted as foreigners, and by the Greeks they are persecuted, yet those who hate them are unable to give reason for their hostility" (5.17).

According to the Epistle to Diognetus, "the world hates the Christians, even though it has suffered no wrong, because they [the Christians] set themselves against its pleasures" (Diogn. 6.5). Christians "live as strangers amid perishable things, while waiting for the imperishable in heaven" (6.8). As a result, "Christians when punished [κολαζόμενοι] daily increase more and more" (6.9). The author queries, "Do you not see that as more of them are punished [κολάζονται], the more others increase?" (7.8). He claims that Christians "are thrown to wild beasts to make them deny the Lord, and yet they are not conquered" (7.7). "These things do not look like human works; they are the power of God, they are proofs of his presence" (7.9).

Diognetus 10 highlights "those who are punished [κολαζομένους] because they refuse to deny God" (Diogn. 10.7). They serve as reminders to "realize what is the true life in heaven, when you despise the apparent death here on earth, when you fear the real death, which is reserved for those who will be condemned to the eternal fire that will punish [κολάσει] to the very end those delivered to it" (10.7). The author reasons, "Then you will admire those who for righteousness' sake [ὑπὲρ δικαιοσύνης] endure [ὑπομένοντας] the transitory fire, and you will consider them blessed, when you comprehend that other fire" (10.8).

The larger context in this tenth chapter contrasts two opposing loves. On the one hand, those who are selfish, greedy, and authoritarian can never "imitate God in these matters"

64. The lady adds, "Learn first from yourself: when you were rich, you were useless, but now you are useful and beneficial to life" (Herm. Vis. 3.6.7).

(Diogn. 10.5). On the other hand, "those who have loved him [God]" will also "both love and admire those who are punished [κολαζομένους] because they refuse to deny God" (10.2, 7).[65] This second path is characterized by grace, because its followers are simply loving "the one who so loved you first" (10.3). "By loving him you will be an imitator [μιμητής, *mimētēs*] of his goodness," thus becoming "an imitator [μιμητής] of God" (10.4, 6). This way of grace is "motivated as well by a love for the things that have been revealed to us" (11.5–8). Ultimately, such lovers and imitators of God bear fruit as their reward. "You will know what God bestows on those who love him as they should, who become a paradise of delight, raising up in themselves a flourishing tree bearing all kinds of fruit, who are adorned with various fruits" (12.1).

Within the Shepherd of Hermas and the Epistle to Diognetus, a martyrological mindset (an ordering of values prone to depreciating temporal affairs in view of the afterlife reached through death) is opposed to double-mindedness and entanglement with the riches of the world. Instead, such a mindset disregards the world and despises death (Diogn. 1.1). It is firm in opposition to worldly pleasures, encouraging believers to "live as strangers amid perishable things" (6.8). And it despises temporal death, thus serving as a preparatory disposition in equipping for martyrdom. Such a fundamental ordering of values could have served as the "backstory" for approaches to martyrdom that seemed rather "spontaneous" from an outsider's perspective.[66] Such axiological perspectives served not as "theological flights of fancy" but as "a real source of strength."[67]

5. AN EXEMPLAR OF A MARTYROLOGICAL MINDSET: IGNATIUS OF ANTIOCH

According to those majority scholars who accept the authenticity of (the middle recension of) the Ignatian correspondence, Ignatius wrote his letters while on his way toward martyrdom in Rome.[68] He had served as "bishop" of Antioch before his arrest and was being transported to Rome under the watch of "ten leopards" (or armed guards) (Ign. *Rom.* 5.1).[69] He warns that these "wild beasts . . . only get worse when they are well treated" (5.1). While in transit, Ignatius wrote epistles to the Ephesian, Magnesian, Trallian, Philadelphian, and Smyrnaean churches of Asia Minor, as well as a personal letter to Polycarp of Smyrna. He is further credited with an epistle to the Christians in Rome, his expected destination.

Like 1 Clement, Ignatius uses the verb μαρτυρέω of being "witnessed to," "testified of," "renowned," "endorsed," or "approved." The Hebrew prophets were "saints worthy of love and admiration, approved [μεμαρτυρημένοι] by Jesus Christ and included in the gospel of our shared hope" (Ign. *Phld.* 5.2). He refers to the "deservedly blessed" Paul, "who was approved [μεμαρτυρημένου]" and in whose footsteps Ignatius desired to follow (Ign. *Eph.* 12.2).[70] Ignatius describes Philo, a deacon from Cilicia, as "a man with a good reputation [μεμαρτυρημένου]" (Ign. *Phld.* 11.1). Ignatius adds that both Philo and Rhaius Agathopus ("a chosen man who followed me from Syria") "speak well [μαρτυροῦσιν] of you" (11.1).

Similarly, Ignatius uses the noun μαρτύριον of a "testimony" or "witness." He beseeches

65. The immediate context affirms that God "loved humanity, for whose sake he made the world" (Diogn. 10.1).

66. See P. L. Buck, "Voluntary Martyrdom Revisited," *JTS* 63 (2012): 133.

67. Nicholson, "What Makes a Voluntary Martyr?," 162.

68. J. G. Bushur, "Ignatius of Antioch's Letter to the Romans: The Passionate Confession of Christian Identity," *Logia* 24 (2005): 15.

69. Some have conjectured that the soldiers came from the *cohort I Lepidiana*, perhaps nicknamed "the leopards." See A. R. Birley, "Voluntary Martyrs in the Early Christian Church: Heroes or Heretics?," *Cristianesimo nella Storia* 27 (2006): 106.

70. Polycarp also refers to the apostle Paul as "blessed" in Pol. *Phil.* 3.2; see also 11.3.

his Trallian recipients to heed his advice in love, "so that I may not by virtue of having written to you become a witness [μαρτύριον] against you" (Ign. *Trall.* 12.3). "Moreover," he entreats the Philadelphians, "I pray that all those to whom I spoke will not cause what I said to become a witness [μαρτύριον] against them" (Ign. *Phld.* 6.3). Most striking is the use of μάρτυς in Ignatius, *To the Philadelphians* 7.2: "But the one for whose sake I am in chains is my witness [μάρτυς]." Although Ignatius was in chains, the word μάρτυς in this passage is applied to Christ, not to himself.

Beyond the μάρτυς / μαρτύριον / μαρτυρέω word group, Ignatius addresses his Ephesian readers as "united and elect through genuine suffering [ἐν πάθει ἀληθινῷ, *en pathei alēthinō*] by the will of the Father and of Jesus Christ our God" (Ign. *Eph.* salut.). And he describes himself as "on my way from Syria in chains for the sake of our shared name and hope," adding that he hopes through their prayers "to succeed in fighting with wild beasts in Rome—in order that by so succeeding I might be able to be a disciple" (Ign. *Eph.* 1.2; cf. Ign. *Trall.* 12.3; Ign. *Rom.* 1.2; 8.3; Ign. *Phld.* 5.1). Ignatius's *To the Romans* speaks of being "an offering to God," "food for the wild beasts," and "a sacrifice to God" (Ign. *Rom.* 2.2; 4.1, 2).

Throughout his correspondence, Ignatius's favored way of describing his impending martyrdom was his goal of "reaching God."[71] Ultimately, Ignatius's path of martyrdom leads to God, and "it is a journey in which his own identity is changing in the most fundamental way."[72] Ignatius expresses his yearning to be found in the footsteps of the apostle Paul "when I reach [ἐπιτύχω, *epitychō*] God" (Ign. *Eph.* 12.2). He exhorts the Magnesians, "Remember me in your prayers, in order that I may reach [ἐπιτύχω] God" (Ign. *Magn.* 14.1; cf. 1.2). He carries around his chains for the sake of Jesus Christ, while praying that he might "reach [ἐπιτυχεῖν] God" (Ign. *Trall.* 12.2). He informs the Trallians, "My spirit is dedicated to you, not only now but also when I reach [ἐπιτύχω] God" (13.3). Ignatius cautions the Romans that "it is difficult for me to reach [ἐπιτυχεῖν] God, unless you spare me. . . . For I will never again have an opportunity such as this to reach [ἐπιτυχεῖν] God" (Ign. *Rom.* 1.2–2.1). He pleads, "Let me be food for the wild beasts, through whom I can reach [ἐπιτυχεῖν] God" (4.1). He desires "that I may reach [ἐπιτύχω] Jesus Christ . . . only let me reach [ἐπιτύχω] Jesus Christ!" (5.3). He declares, "But I have been granted the mercy to be someone, if I reach [ἐπιτύχω] God" (9.2). He beseeches the Smyrnaeans "that by your prayer I may reach [ἐπιτύχω] God" (Ign. *Smyrn.* 11.1; cf. 9.2). Ignatius calls upon Polycarp to be "God's athlete," remembering "the time" so as "to reach [ἐπιτυχεῖν] God" (Ign. *Pol.* 2.3).[73] And he informs Polycarp of his intense desire to "reach [ἐπιτύχω] God" through suffering, "so that I may prove to be a disciple by means of your prayer" (Ign. *Pol.* 7.1).

Elizabeth Castelli affirms, "Ignatius's letters are frequently used as one of the earliest sources for documenting both the historical experience of martyrdom and the emergent Christian theology of suffering and persecution."[74] Yet scholars have greatly debated his approach to martyrdom. As Michael Wilkins comments, Ignatius's "vivid, almost macabre eagerness" in anticipation of death "has repelled many readers" and "has unfailingly disturbed readers."[75] Ignatius has been accused of manifesting not only "fanaticism" but

71. See W. Willis, "Martyr Eschatology: Ignatius' Use of *Epitugchanō*," *ResQ* 10 (1967): 81–88.

72. Bushur, "Ignatius of Antioch's Letter to the Romans," 18.

73. For the influence of spectacle entertainment upon discourses of Christian martyrdom, see Cobb, "Martyrdom in Roman Context," 95–100.

74. E. A. Castelli, *Martyrdom and Memory: Early Christian Culture Making*, GTR (New York: Columbia University Press, 2004), 78.

75. M. J. Wilkins, "The Interplay of Ministry, Martyrdom, and Discipleship in Ignatius of Antioch," in *Worship, Theology and Ministry in the Early Church*, ed. M. J. Wilkins and T. Paige (Sheffield: JSOT Press, 1992), 298.

a "pathological yearning" and an "abnormal mentality," a "pathological," "psychopathic," "psychotic," or "disturbed" state of mind.[76] To some, Ignatius's "thirst for martyrdom" or "zeal for martyrdom" seems to manifest a "neurotic deathwish" or "abnormal mentality" or to be "symptomatic of a borderline personality."[77] He displays "a state of exaltation bordering on mania."[78] His language, as evaluated by some interpreters, "sometimes betrays an exuberance and wildness which could be interpreted as neurotic."[79] In a seeming case of morbid obsession, Ignatius declares, "For though I am still alive, I am passionately in love with death as I write to you" (Ign. *Rom.* 7.2).

Yet was Ignatius truly neurotic or delusional? Peter-Ben Smit encourages "a rediscovery of the logic of early Christian martyrdom, in which an embrace of suffering rendered the executioners powerless, given that what was intended as punishment was received as a reward."[80] According to Smit, this martyrological logic "has also led to the acknowledgment that there is indeed method to this Syrian bishop's apparent madness and that his desire to suffer is also a way of coping spiritually with the situation in which he finds himself."[81]

Ignatius desired to be devoured by the wild beasts, as "the total consumption of his body" would spare his fellow Christians the burden of burial.[82] But, as Smit argues, Ignatius's desire to be consumed did more, by "(a) functioning as a means of identification with his suffering; (b) offering proof of his faithful discipleship until the very end; (c) enabling Ignatius to disappear from this life to become completely and safely ensconced with Christ in Christ's realm."[83] Ignatius's own self-identity was intertwined with his suffering and imminent martyrdom.[84] He viewed himself as following in the footsteps of the original disciples, who "despised death" and "proved to be greater than death" (Ign. *Smyrn.* 3.2). He declared, "But I have been granted the mercy to be someone, if I reach God" (Ign. *Rom.* 9.2). "But if I suffer, I will be a freedman of Jesus Christ and will rise up free in him. In the meantime, as a prisoner, I am learning to desire nothing" (4.3). He further explained, "Though I am in chains for his sake, I am all the more afraid, because I am still imperfect. But your prayer to God will make me perfect, so that I may attain the fate by which I have received mercy" (Ign. *Phld.* 5.1; cf. Ign. *Eph.* 3.1).

Ignatius seems to have viewed martyrdom as personal vindication and thus as

---

76. See W. R. Schoedel, *Ignatius of Antioch*, Hermeneia (Philadelphia: Fortress, 1985), xii; G. E. M. de Ste. Croix, "Why Were the Early Christians Persecuted?," in *Christian Persecution, Martyrdom, and Orthodoxy*, ed. M. Whitby and J. Streeter (Oxford: Oxford University Press, 2006), 133; J. E. Lawyer, "Eucharist and Martyrdom in the Letters of Ignatius of Antioch," *AThR* 73 (1991): 295; Tanner, "Martyrdom in Saint Ignatius of Antioch," 201, 204; Wilkins, "Interplay of Ministry," 298; cf. Riddle, "From Apocalypse to Martyrology," 270–71.

77. See Lawyer, "Eucharist and Martyrdom," 295; K. R. Morris, "'Pure Wheat of God' or Neurotic Deathwish? A Historical and Theological Analysis of Ignatius of Antioch's Zeal for Martyrdom," *Fides et Historia* 26 (1994): 24–25, 41; Ste. Croix, "Why Were the Early Christians Persecuted?," 133. See the summary in J. Perkins, *The Suffering Self: Pain and Narrative Representation in the Early Christian Era* (London: Routledge, 1995), 33.

78. Frend, *Martyrdom and Persecution in the Early Church*, 197.

79. L. W. Barnard, "The Background of St. Ignatius of Antioch," *VC* 17 (1963): 193.

80. P.-B. Smit, "On Being Consumed: The Martyred Body as a Site of Divine-Human Encounter in Ignatius of Antioch," *Religions* 11 (2020): 3.

81. Smit, "On Being Consumed," 3. Madison Trammel also defends Ignatius against the charges of being "a chaser of suffering, akin in his mindset to the follower of a modern-day death cult" (M. Trammel, "A Defense of Ignatius of Antioch's Martyrdom and View of Redemption," *Midwestern Journal of Theology* 16 [2017]: 66).

82. Tanner, "Martyrdom in Saint Ignatius of Antioch," 204.

83. Smit, "On Being Consumed," 7.

84. A. Brent, *Ignatius of Antioch: A Martyr Bishop and the Origin of Episcopacy*, T&T Clark Theology (London: T&T Clark, 2007).

buttressing his own claims to authority.[85] He affirms that because of the "mistreatment" from his military escort, "I am becoming more of a disciple" (Ign. *Rom.* 5.1). Ignatius considers himself "elect through genuine suffering" (Ign. *Eph.* salut.) as he is being taken "in chains" to fight "wild beasts in Rome" (Ign. *Eph.* 1.2; cf. 21.2; Ign. *Rom.* 4.3–5.1; Ign. *Trall.* 5.2; 10.1). He is "a prisoner in Christ Jesus" (Ign. *Trall.* 1.1), and he speaks of bearing his "chains" for the sake of Jesus Christ (Ign. *Eph.* 3.1; Ign. *Phld.* 5.1; 7.2; cf. Ign. *Rom.* 1.1). In fact, they are "God-pleasing chains" (Ign. *Smyrn.* 11.1) and "spiritual pearls" (Ign. *Eph.* 3.2). Therefore, Ignatius was grateful when others did not "despise" his chains (Ign. *Smyrn.* 10.2; cf. 4.2).

Ignatius expressly rejoices that he has "been judged worthy to bear a most godly name, in these chains" (Ign. *Magn.* 1.2; cf. 12.1). Notwithstanding, with a note of questioning, he muses, "For while I strongly desire to suffer, I do not know whether I am worthy" (Ign. *Trall.* 4.2).[86] Therefore, he entreats the Trallians to pray for him, "so that I may be reckoned worthy of the fate that I am eager to obtain, lest I be found disqualified" (12.3). He believes he has been "judged worthy" only through grace, "in accordance with the divine will" (Ign. *Smyrn.* 11.1). The overall focus on worthiness is reflected in Ignatius's remarkable vocabulary of ἀξιο-, *axio-*, compounds: ἀξιομακάριστος (Ign. *Eph.* salut.; 12.2; Ign. *Rom.* salut.; 10.1); ἀξιονόμαστος (Ign. *Eph.* 4.1); ἀξιόθεος (Ign. *Magn.* 2.1; Ign. *Trall.* salut.; Ign. *Rom.* 1.1 [2x]; Ign. *Smyrn.* 12.2); ἀξιοπρεπής (Ign. *Magn.* 13.1); ἀξιόπλοκος (Ign. *Magn.* 13.1); ἀξιαγάπητος and ἀξιοθαύμαστος (Ign. *Phld.* 5.2); ἀξιόπιστος (Ign. *Phld.* 12.2; Ign. *Pol.* 3.1).[87] The salutation of Ignatius's *To the Romans* rapidly fires off ἀξιόθεος, ἀξιοπρεπής, ἀξιομακάριστος, ἀξιέπαινος, ἀξιοεπίτευκτος, and ἀξίαγνος.

Ignatius intertwines the concepts of imitation and discipleship.[88] In fact, he references the concepts of discipleship and imitation more than all the other Apostolic Fathers combined.[89] For some readers, "the most perplexing feature" of Ignatius's theology of discipleship is this association with martyrdom.[90] As Carl Smith notes, "Ignatius views suffering as a basic feature of faithful discipleship."[91] "For Ignatius," confirms Wilkins, "imitation of Christ, even in suffering, is not a special saintliness. Rather, it is the calling of Christians in general."[92] Therefore, in the Ignatian view, "martyrological endurance was a powerful argument for the validity of Christian truth claims."[93] It was important to Ignatius that Christ really suffered (and not in appearance only), or else his own sufferings would be in vain.

> For if these things were done by our Lord in appearance only, then I am in chains in appearance only. Why, moreover, have I surrendered myself to death, to fire, to sword, to beasts? But

85. R. F. Stoops Jr., "If I Suffer: Epistolary Authority in Ignatius of Antioch," *HTR* 80 (1987): 161–78. Fuhrmann, "Traditions of Martyrdom," 689–705.

86. Smit refers to this "somewhat paradoxical emphasis on suffering," in which Ignatius desires suffering as a means of reaching God but questions his worthiness of it (Smit, "On Being Consumed," 4).

87. See A. Brent, "Ignatius of Antioch in Second Century, Asia Minor," in *Intertextuality in the Second Century*, ed. D. J. Bingham and C. N. Jefford (Leiden: Brill, 2016), 64.

88. Williams, "'Imitate Me,'" 84; see also T. H. Hubert, "The Two-Fold Witness of St. Ignatius of Antioch," *Chicago Studies* 56 (2017): 43–44.

89. V. Corwin, *St. Ignatius and Christianity in Antioch*, Yale Publications in Religion 1 (New Haven: Yale University Press, 1960), 228n9; Wilkins, "Interplay of Ministry," 299.

90. Wilkins, "Interplay of Ministry," 302. See also D. Wade McClain, "Repurposing the Body: Sacramentality and the Poetics of Discipleship," *AThR* 96 (2014): 339–56.

91. Smith, "Ministry, Martyrdom, and Other Mysteries," 52.

92. Wilkins, "Interplay of Ministry," 308.

93. Morris, "'Pure Wheat of God,'" 41.

> in any case, "near the sword" means "near to God"; "with the beasts" means "with God." Only let it be in the name of Jesus Christ, so that I may suffer together with him! I endure everything because he himself, who is the perfect human being, empowers me. (Ign. *Smyrn.* 4.2)

In the Ignatian perspective, being found ultimately as a disciple requires patient endurance (Ign. *Magn.* 9.1).[94] Even apart from the explicit association with martyrdom, "endurance" remains an important virtue throughout the Ignatian correspondence (cf. Ign. *Eph.* 3.1; *Trall.* 1.1; *Rom.* 10.3; *Smyrn.* 12.2; *Pol.* 3.1; 6.2). This ὑπομονή is modeled after "the patient endurance of Jesus Christ" (Ign. *Rom.* 10.3). For Ignatius, as H. H. Drake Williams quips, "Proper imitation is an act of patient endurance through suffering."[95] Through imitation, the imitator is both assimilated into the exemplar and also becomes a representation of the exemplar.[96]

A specific mindset lies behind Ignatius's approach to (and even anticipation of) death.[97] Ignatius's underlying axiological mindset (ordering of values) becomes clear in *To the Magnesians* 5.2:

> For just as there are two coinages, the one of God and the other of the world, and each of them has its own stamp impressed upon it, so the unbelievers bear the stamp of this world, but the faithful in love bear the stamp of God the Father through Jesus Christ, whose life is not in us unless we voluntarily choose to die into his suffering." (Ign. *Magn.* 5.2)

The Ignatian correspondence draws a contrast between thinking in a merely "human" manner and thinking in a thoroughly "Christian" or "Christlike" manner. One should not live "in accordance with human standards but in accordance with Jesus Christ" (Ign. *Trall.* 2.1; cf. Ign. *Phld.* 3.2). Christian discipleship involves living "in accordance with Christ Jesus" or living "in accordance with Christianity" (Ign. *Magn.* 8.2; 10.1). Ignatius exhorts the Philadelphians, "Whatever you do, you do in accordance with God" (Ign. *Phld.* 4) and "in accordance with the teaching of Christ" (8.2). Even one's neighbors are not to be regarded "in merely human terms" (Ign. *Magn.* 6.2).

The largest concentration of martyrdom language within the Ignatian correspondence appears within his *To the Romans*, often framed by "rather extravagant" and "excessive metaphors."[98] Ignatius desires to be "an imitator of the suffering [πάθους] of [his] God" (Ign. *Rom.* 6.3). Ignatius informs the Romans, "I die for God of my own free will" (4.1).[99] Therefore, he did not want them interfering with his impending martyrdom. "I implore you: do not be unseasonably kind to me. Let me be food for the wild beasts, through whom I can reach God. I am God's wheat, and I am being ground by the teeth of the wild beasts, so that I may prove to be pure bread" (4.1).[100] Ignatius continues,

---

94. Wilkins, "Interplay of Ministry," 303.

95. Williams, "'Imitate Me,'" 79.

96. Smit, "On Being Consumed," 10.

97. Corwin, *St. Ignatius and Christianity in Antioch*, 227; Wilkins, "Interplay of Ministry," 299, 307. See S. Zañartu, "Les concepts de vie et de mort chez Ignace d'Antioche," *VC* 33 (1979): 324–41.

98. Petersen, "Attaining Divine Perfection," 18. See also Trammel, "Defense of Ignatius of Antioch's Martyrdom," 68; Haykin, "'Come to the Father,'" 28.

99. Tanner reasons that "though a voluntary death, his martyrdom was not strictly self-slaying" (Tanner, "Martyrdom in Saint Ignatius of Antioch," 204). The tension is further amplified by Greco-Roman traditions that sanctioned "principled suicide" (Heffernan, "Martyrdom, Charisma, and Imitation," 256–57).

100. On possible eucharistic implications, see Lawyer, "Eucharist and Martyrdom," 280–96.

> Better yet, coax the wild beasts, so that they may become my tomb and leave nothing of my body behind, lest I become a burden to anyone once I have fallen asleep. Then I will truly be a disciple of Jesus Christ, when the world will no longer see my body. Pray to the Lord on my behalf, so that through these instruments I may prove to be a sacrifice to God. (Ign. *Rom.* 4.2)[101]

Ignatius further desires to "be faithful" when "no longer visible to the world" (Ign. *Rom.* 3.2). With a "clever rhetorical turn," Ignatius insists that to truly "spare" him would actually entail allowing him to "reach God" through martyrdom (1.2).[102] Echoing Paul's reflections in Philippians 2:17, Ignatius entreats, "Grant me nothing more than to be poured out as an offering to God while there is still an altar ready, so that in love you may form a chorus and sing to the Father in Jesus Christ" (Ign. *Rom.* 2.2).[103]

In an extended passage, Ignatius declares,

> May I have the pleasure of the wild beasts that have been prepared for me; and I pray that they prove to be prompt with me. I will even coax them to devour me quickly, not as they have done with some, whom they were too timid to touch. And if when I am willing and ready they are not, I will force them. Bear with me—I know what is best for me. Now at last I am beginning to be a disciple. May nothing visible or invisible envy me, so that I may reach Jesus Christ. Fire and cross and battles with wild beasts, mutilation, mangling, wrenching of bones, the hacking of limbs, the crushing of my whole body, cruel tortures of the devil—let these come upon me, only let me reach Jesus Christ! (Ign. *Rom.* 5.2–3)[104]

By portraying himself as "voluntarily" choosing to die into Christ's suffering (Ign. *Magn.* 5.2) and dying of his "own free will [ἑκών, *hekōn*]" (Ign. *Rom.* 4.1), Ignatius is able to depict himself as the active agent of his own impending death.[105] As Henk Bakker explains, "He gives the impression that he alone is orchestrating [the] bizarre spectacle," thus divesting the executioners and the beasts of the initiative and retaining it for himself.[106] Moreover, he frames himself as the one who "stands to gain the most of the situation."[107] In this manner, he "also renegotiates and reinterprets a conflict, in the course of which the roles of victor and victim are completely reversed."[108] Nevertheless, this "reversal of agency," when wielded in the hands of others, could easily lead to more direct forms of so-called voluntary martyrdom (in which one initiated or even provoked martyrdom).[109]

---

101. Cf. Morris, "'Pure Wheat of God,'" 30–31.

102. The use of "sparing" may be an echo of the Aqedah account of Isaac (cf. Rom 8:32). See Bushur, "Ignatius of Antioch's Letter to the Romans," 16.

103. See McLarty, "Early Christian Theologies of Martyrdom," 127; D. L. Eastman, "Ignatius, Pseudo-Ignatius, and the Art of Pauline Reception," *Early Christianity* 7 (2016): 213–29. Cf. 2 Tim 4:6; J. W. Smith, "Martyrdom: Self-Denial or Self-Exaltation?: Motives for Self-Sacrifice from Homer to Polycarp: A Theological Reflection," *Modern Theology* 22 (2006): 181–82.

104. On the "cross" in Ignatius, see T. Nicklas, "Leid, Kreusz und Kreuzesnachfolge bei Ignatius von Antiochien," in *Gelitten—Gestorben—Auferstanden*, ed. T. Nicklas, A. Merkt, and J. Verheyden (Tübingen: Mohr Siebeck, 2010), 267–98.

105. See T. McDonnell, "Ignatius of Antioch: Death Wish or Last Request of a Condemned Man?," StPatr 45 (2010): 385–89.

106. H. A. Bakker, "Exemplar Domini: Ignatius of Antioch and His Martyrological Self-Concept" (PhD diss., Rijksuniversiteit Groningen, 2003), 172–73.

107. Smit, "On Being Consumed," 8. Cf. D. N. Saxon, "Martyrdom Represented as Care of the Self in the Texts of Clement, Ignatius, and Polycarp," in *The Care of the Self in Early Christian Texts*, The Bible and Cultural Studies (Cham: Palgrave Macmillan, 2017), 31–57.

108. Smit, "On Being Consumed," 8.

109. On the difficulties and complexities of the label "voluntary martyrdom," see Moss, "Discourse of

In sum, although Ignatius was "in chains," he was able to "comprehend heavenly things" (Ign. *Trall.* 5.2), leading to a subversion of the world's values. Ignatius declares, "I take no pleasure in corruptible food or the pleasure of this life" (Ign. *Rom.* 7.3). He adds, "I no longer want to live according to human standards" (8.1). He attests, "It is better for me to die for Jesus Christ than to rule over the ends of the earth" (6.1). Allen Brent describes this passage as "a self-conscious reversal of imperial values on the part of a bishop who is contrasting his individual purpose with that of the Roman Emperor."[110] He beseeched the Romans, "Pray for me, that I may reach the goal [of reaching God through martyrdom]. I write to you not according to human perspective but in accordance with the mind of God" (8.3). As a result of this mindset, the true disciple is ready to renounce this life (Ign. *Phld.* 11.1).

6. CIRCLING BACK TO THE MARTYRDOM OF POLYCARP

A life-in-this-world-renouncing axiology also undergirds the Martyrdom of Polycarp. The work begins by describing the church of Smyrna, the church of Philomelium, and even the universal church as "sojourning" (Mart. Pol. salut.), which implies that their true priorities lay elsewhere than in "this world" (cf. Eph 2:19; Heb 11:9–13; 1 Pet 1:17; 2:11; 1 Clem. salut.; Pol. *Phil.* salut.; *Mart. Lyons* 4.23).[111] Throughout the narrative, the temporary nature of suffering is contrasted with the eternal nature of reward. The work says of the martyrs:

> And turning their thoughts to the grace of Christ they despised the tortures of this world, purchasing at the cost of one hour an exemption from eternal punishment . . . for they set before their eyes the escape from that eternal fire which is never extinguished, while with the eyes of their heart they gazed upon the good things that are reserved for those who endure patiently, things that neither ear has heard nor eye has seen, nor has it entered into the human heart, but that were shown to them by the Lord. (Mart. Pol. 2.3; cf. 11.2)

The thoughts of these martyrs were framed by a definite axiological mindset.

Within the same chapter, the martyrs resisted the compulsion to apostatize, as they struggled with the devil.[112]

> Those who were condemned to the wild beasts endured terrible punishments—they were forced to lie on sharp shells and afflicted with various other forms of torture in order that he [the devil] might, if possible, by means of the unceasing punishment compel them to deny their faith—for the devil tried many things against them. (Mart. Pol. 2.4)[113]

Polycarp himself was divinely empowered to endure his sufferings: "Leave me as I am; for the one who enables me to endure the fire will also enable me to remain on the pyre

---

Voluntary Martyrdom," 531–51; Boyarin, *Dying for God*, 121. For more genealogical perspectives of "voluntary martyrdom," see G. E. M. de Ste. Croix, "Voluntary Martyrdom in the Early Church," in Whitby and Streeter, *Christian Persecution, Martyrdom, and Orthodoxy*, 153–200; Birley, "Voluntary Martyrs," 108–16.

110. A. Brent, "Ignatius of Antioch and the Imperial Cult," *VC* 52 (1998): 31.

111. See F. W. Weidmann, "'To Sojourn' or 'To Dwell'? Scripture and Identity in the *Martyrdom of Polycarp*," in *Reading in Christian Communities: Essays on Interpretation in the Early Church*, ed. C. A. Bobertz and D. Brakke (Notre Dame: University of Notre Dame Press, 2002), 29–40.

112. For early Christian martyrdom as a cosmic struggle, see P. Middleton, *Radical Martyrdom and Cosmic Conflict in Early Christianity*, LNTS 307 (London: T&T Clark, 2006).

113. On Satan's role in the narrative, see P. Hartog, "The Devil's in the Details: The Apocalyptic 'Adversary' in the *Martyrdom of Polycarp* and the *Martyrs of Lyons*," in *Studies on the Text of the New Testament and Early Christianity*, ed. D. Gurtner, J. Hernández, and P. Foster, NTTSD (Leiden: Brill, 2015), 432–52.

without moving, even without the sense of security that you get from the nails" (Mart. Pol. 13.3). Polycarp is portrayed as exhibiting an extraordinary suppression of painful suffering, "without flinching or without feeling it."[114] The depiction resembles the emphasis upon ἀπαθεία, *apatheia* ("undisturbed composure," "equanimity," or "imperturbability"), within the Greek philosophical tradition.[115]

Such resistance in the hour of trial was made possible through the formation of worthy character. In his dying prayer, Polycarp praises the Lord: "I bless you because you have considered me worthy of this day and hour, so that I might receive a place among the number of martyrs in the cup of your Christ, to the resurrection to eternal life, both of soul and of body, in the incorruptibility of the Holy Spirit" (Mart. Pol. 14.2). He adds, "May I be received among them in your presence today, as a rich and acceptable sacrifice, as you have prepared and revealed beforehand, and have now accomplished" (14.2). In this manner, "sharing the cup of Christ" (cf. Mark 10:38; 14:36; John 18:11) is equated with "receiving a place among the martyrs," which is paralleled with "being received as an acceptable sacrifice."[116] The text thus draws together a "relationship between the sacrifice of Christ, the sacrifice of the martyrs, and the sacrifice that Christians may be expected to offer as their cost of discipleship in the world."[117]

Martyrs were informed and formed by a mindset that valued divine approbation. This is not to say that martyrs and confessors did not receive any human praise in the here and now. Within the Martyrdom of Polycarp, the exhibition of "bravery" results in onlookers "marveling" at the "God-loving and God-fearing race of Christians" (Mart. Pol. 3.2). Polycarp himself is adulated as "blessed" and "holy" (1.1; 13.2; 17.1; 19.1; 21.1; 22.1, 2, 4), and even as "most admirable" (5.1). Moreover, he is depicted as being prophetically gifted (5.2; 12.3). "For every word that came from his mouth was accomplished and will be accomplished" (16.2). Even his captors "marveled at his age and his composure" (7.2). After he had prayed for two hours, they "were amazed, and many regretted that they had come after such a godly old man" (7.3).

With a defined, axiological mindset firmly in place, Christian martyrdom seems a rather "natural" result of the chosen framework of valuation. The martyrs "despised the tortures of this world," and they purchased "at the cost of one hour an exemption from eternal punishment," "for they set before their eyes the escape from that eternal fire which is never extinguished, while with the eyes of their heart they gazed upon the good things that are reserved for those who endure patiently" (Mart. Pol. 2.3). As Paul Middleton quips, "For early Christians, embracing death was rushing towards life."[118]

The axiology of the martyr's mindset, however, could reasonably motivate a problematic phenomenon. If martyrs win eternal reward for themselves through the price of temporary suffering, why not calculatedly and deliberately hand oneself over to the persecuting authorities?[119] This was the perspective of so-called voluntary martyrdom in early

114. Franzmann, "*Imitatio Christi*," 381.

115. Franzmann, "*Imitatio Christi*," 380. For Polycarp as a form of *imitatio Socratis*, see Moss, "Nailing Down and Tying Up," 129–31; Cobb, "Polycarp's Cup," 227–40; Cobb, "Martyrdom in Roman Context," 92–95.

116. Cobb, "Polycarp's Cup," 224–40.

117. Johnson, "Sharing 'the Cup of Christ,'" 126.

118. P. Middleton, "Early Christian Voluntary Martyrdom: A Statement for the Defence," *JTS* 64 (2013): 560.

119. The true Christian, according to Clement of Alexandria, "can readily give up his life because of his distaste for the body, and so avoids denying his faith and does not fear death because of the hope for earthly rewards. He will approach death with gladness and thankfulness, both to God who had predestined him for

Christianity. "In a world that offered nothing of value except the opportunity to leave it for a better one," explains Lorraine Buck, "surely voluntary martyrdom for the early Christians would have been, not self-destructive, but self-preserving."[120]

The Martyrdom of Polycarp implicitly addresses the perils by contrasting the characters of Germanicus and Quintus.[121] Like Polycarp himself, Germanicus is described as "noble" and possessing "patient endurance" (Mart. Pol. 3.1). He "fought with the wild beasts in an outstanding way" (3.1). "For when the proconsul wished to persuade him and asked him to consider his youthfulness, he forcibly dragged [προσβιασάμενος, *prosbiasamenos*] the wild beast toward himself, desiring to be released as quickly as possible from their unrighteous and lawless life" (3.1). Interestingly, although Germanicus "forcibly dragged [προσβιασάμενος] the wild beast toward himself," he retained his reputation (within the narrative) of being "noble" and "patient."[122]

By contrast, when Quintus the "Phrygian" saw the wild beasts, he "turned coward" (Mart. Pol. 4).[123] The irony is that "this was the man who had forced [παραβιασάμενος, *parabiasamenos*] himself and some others to come forward voluntarily [ἑκόντας, *hekontas*]" (Mart. Pol. 4).[124] "For this reason," the narrator reasons, "we do not praise those who hand themselves over, since the gospel does not so teach" (Mart. Pol. 4). The narrator draws a dividing line of acceptable practice. Once facing the wild beasts directly, the narrator seems to condone beckoning (and even forcing) them upon oneself. Nevertheless, to back up a step, one should not actively seek to be placed into that terminal position. A "martyrdom according to the gospel" waits to be betrayed, captured, and committed to the arena. But once in the throes of martyrdom, the "noble" Christian may actually beckon death. Not all interpreters are satisfied with such distinctions. Furthermore, if one backs up to the mindset preceding the actions, the volition-forming nature of axiological preparation for martyrdom further complicates an absolute polarity between initiation and response.

7. CONCLUSION

These investigations of the vocabulary, conceptualization, and axiological mindset of martyrdom nuance our understanding of martyrdom and identity formation. Recent scholars have emphasized how martyr accounts were intended to form general Christian identity.[125] By backing up to focus upon the mindset *behind* the phenomenon of martyrdom, one reveals a dual-direction transmission of formation. Exhortations toward the adoption of a properly ordered axiological mindset among the general Christian populace were meant to form the identity of would-be martyrs. Thus, Christian identity formed prospective martyrs, even as martyrs through martyr accounts formed Christian identity.

These investigations also reveal tensions concerning agency and the notion of

---

martyrdom, and the one who gave the opportunity for death" (Clement of Alexandria, *Strom.* 4.4; English translation from Middleton, "Early Christian Voluntary Martyrdom," 563).

120. P. L. Buck, "Voluntary Martyrdom Revisited," *JTS* 63 (2012): 132.

121. Eusebius's account differs slightly from the MS tradition. See F. W. Weidmann, "'Rushing Judgment'? Willfulness and Martyrdom in Early Christianity," *USQR* 53 (1999): 64.

122. See Buck, "Voluntary Martyrdom Revisited," 131; Nicholson, "What Makes a Voluntary Martyr?," 160.

123. Some scholars have argued that the Quintus episode in Mart. Pol. 4 is an interpolation. See, for example, H. F. von Campenhausen, *Bearbeitungen und Interpolationen des Polykarpmartyriums*, SHAW (Heidelberg: Winter, 1957).

124. See Nicholson, "What Makes a Voluntary Martyr?," 160.

125. See J. Leemans, ed., *More Than a Memory: The Discourse on Martyrdom and the Construction of Christian Identity in the History of Christianity*, Annua Nuntia Lovaniensia 51 (Leuven: Peeters, 2005); Castelli, *Martyrdom and Memory*; D. L. Eastman, "The Linguistic Turn and the Expanding Horizons of Early Christian Martyrdom," *Religion and Theology* 28 (2021): 26–40.

"voluntary" martyrdom. If one acknowledges a "martyrological mindset," an axiological ordering of values that supports and motivates a willingness to die in testimony of one's faith, then this mindset precedes the action and can even precede the relevant opportunities arising from times of persecution. Scholars of the past, borrowing from and building on evaluative assessments in various (especially later) patristic sources, discussed and often critiqued so-called voluntary martyrdom.[126] G. E. M. de Ste. Croix's "classic treatment of voluntary martyrdom" influenced an entire generation of scholarship.[127] More recently, scholars have deconstructed the notion of "voluntary martyrdom" or have stepped forward in its defense.[128] So-called voluntary martyrdom was both more common and more lauded than commonly believed.[129] It was not confined to heretics and schismatics alone.[130]

Daniel Boyarin posited that perhaps "provocative martyrdom" is a more suitable label than "voluntary martyrdom," since (in his words) "if martyrdom is not voluntary it is not martyrdom."[131] Buck expounds that "a willingness to die, however, which clearly *all* the martyrs displayed, was not necessarily an intentional bid for martyrdom."[132] Past interpreters have attempted to splice between the "initiative" taken in so-called voluntary martyrdom versus so-called normative martyrdom.[133] Our discussion of the underlying "martyrological mindset," however, further complicates the already complex mapping of the phenomena.[134] Such a mindset would have served as a precedent to the occasion of martyrdom—a predisposition firmly in place before any tangible threat of death.[135] And such a proactive mindset was to be voluntarily embraced—a proclivity solidified in one's character as a responsible (volitional and deliberating) agent.

---

126. See Clement of Alexandria, *Strom.* 4.4, 10; 7.11; Tertullian, *Ux.* 1.3; Origen, *Cels.* 8.65; Origen, *Comm. Jo.* 28.23; Cyprian, *Act. Procons.* 1.5; Cyprian, *Laps.* 8; Cyprian, *Epistle* 81 [82].1–2; *Acts of Cyprian* 1.5; 4.3–5. However, cf. Eusebius, *Hist. eccl.* 7.12.1.

127. Ste. Croix, "Voluntary Martyrdom in the Early Church," 153–200; cf. Tite, "Voluntary Martyrdom and Gnosticism," 32. Ste. Croix classified individuals as "voluntary martyrs," "quasi-volunteers," and "true martyrs." He defined a "voluntary martyr" as "a Christian who deliberately and unnecessarily provoked persecution and thus sought a death which he might have avoided without any sacrifice of Christian principles." See Ste. Croix, "Voluntary Martyrdom in the Early Church," 153. For pushback against Ste. Croix's schemata, see Vincelette, "On the Frequency of Voluntary Martyrdom," 652–79.

128. Middleton, "Early Christian Voluntary Martyrdom," 556–73. Middleton contends that voluntary martyrdom was "a valid mainstream Christian practice, which faced only isolated challenge in the first three centuries"; it "was unremarkable for many in the early Church, and certainly attracted little criticism" (556, 566). "From both Christian and pagan witnesses, we may conclude that Christian voluntary martyrdom was in fact a significant historical as well as literary phenomenon" (573).

129. Doherty, "Competing for the Crown," 4; Boyarin, *Dying for God*, 121.

130. Ste. Croix, "Why Were the Early Christians Persecuted?," 130. Buck, "Voluntary Martyrdom Revisited," 135; Middleton, "Early Christian Voluntary Martyrdom," 556–73.

131. Boyarin, *Dying for God*, 121. A similar point is made in A. Wypustek, "Magic, Montanism, Perpetua, and the Severan Persecution," *VC* 51 (1997): 281; Birley, "Voluntary Martyrs," 99; Doherty, "Competing for the Crown," 4.

132. Buck, "Voluntary Martyrdom Revisited," 127. Thomas Heffernan defines a Christian martyr generally as "one who dies *volitionally* under persecution professing Christ with the expectation that his or her death will benefit the community, and that by their death they will rise again with Christ" (Heffernan, "Martyrdom, Charisma, and Imitation," 259; italics added).

133. E. Ferguson, "Early Christian Martyrdom and Civil Disobedience," *JECS* 1 (1993): 81. Contrast Middleton, "Early Christian Voluntary Martyrdom," 568.

134. Weidmann, "'Rushing Judgment'?," 69.

135. See T. Baumeister, "Die Norm des evangeliumgemässen Blutzeugnisses: Das Martyrium Polycarpi als vorsichtige *exhortatio ad martyrium*," in *Stimuli: Exegese und ihre Hermeneutik in Antike und Christentum*, G. Schöllgen, C. Scholten, and E. Dassmann (Münster: Aschendorff, 1996), 122–28; O. Nicholson, "Preparation for Martyrdom in the Early Church," in *The Great Persecution*, ed. V. Twomey and M. Humphries (Dublin: Four Courts), 61–90; P. Hartog, "Themes and Intertextualities in Pre-Nicene Exhortations to Martyrdom," in Middleton, *Wiley Blackwell Companion to Christian Martyrdom*, 102–19.

In a broader view, Quintus's real fault was not the "voluntary" nature of his martyrdom per se. Ultimately, his depicted fault was not even the "initiatory" nature of his role, so much as the "impulsive" and even "impatient" character of his actions. Yes, he took the initiative in presenting himself to authorities, but he did so (or so it was believed) in an "impulsive" manner that was not well-founded upon a solid axiological ordering of values, including the loving, unselfish prioritization of others.[136] Such a lack betrayed a further flaw in his approach—he was "impatient" in allowing God's sovereign will to work its way through his situation. He chose to offer himself, but he was not among the elect martyrs chosen by God to be worthy of the role. Such evaluative judgments, however, were only wholly ascertained after the fact—after events had worked themselves out fully.[137]

The Ignatian correspondence already reflects a tension of agency, as Ignatius actively seeks "a death which is imposed but avoidable."[138] He tells the Magnesians, "We voluntarily choose to die into his suffering" (Ign. *Magn.* 5.2). And he informs the Romans, "I die for God of my own free will" (Ign. *Rom.* 4.1). He even declares of the wild beasts, "If when I am willing and ready they are not, I will force them" (5.2). According to early Christian tradition, Ignatius successfully fulfilled his intense longing to "reach God" as reflected in his epistles.[139] If he had failed in his mission, what would the tradition have made of his martyrological yearning?[140] Would he have been perceived as an impulsive zealot along the lines of Quintus?

Such theorization remains mere guesswork, of course, as the full evaluation of martyrs and would-be martyrs could only be accomplished *post facto*.[141] The differentiation between personal enthusiasm and divine call, and between human strength and divine power, could only be suitably ascertained through the unfolding of events.[142] Moreover, the *ex post facto* assessments of episodes along the spectrum of so-called voluntary martyrdom are enveloped within broader social-rhetorical frameworks of "acceptable" and "unacceptable" behavior, and thus within the constructions of social identities (including the "wider disputes, polemical techniques, and social boundary divisions" of competing communities).[143]

Prior to validation through the unfolding of events, leaders and authors could only hope to instill a proactive mindset that would survive the test. Such a preparatory mindset was intended to form dispositions and inclinations. In some cases, characters thus equipped were not only ready but eager to follow their volitional impulses. Some martyrs so imbibed the proactive mindset that they viewed the occasion of persecution as an opportunity to

---

136. See W. Tabbernee, "Early Montanism and Voluntary Martyrdom," *Colloquium* 17 (1985): 35, 40–41. See also W. Tabbernee, "Montanists and Voluntary Martyrdom," in *Fake Prophecy and Polluted Sacraments*, VCSup (Leiden: Brill, 2007), 201–42.

137. Cf. the praise of Saturus, "who for our sakes had handed himself over" (*Passio Perpetuae* 4.5). The Latin version of the martyrdom of Agathonicê attempts to "de-radicalize" the narrative, making it more palatable for those opposed to the excesses of "voluntary martyrdom." See Middleton, "Early Christian Voluntary Martyrdom," 568–69; Tite, "Voluntary Martyrdom and Gnosticism," 36; Moss, "Discourse of Voluntary Martyrdom," 545–46.

138. Tanner, "Martyrdom in Saint Ignatius of Antioch," 203.

139. See A. Bolhuis, "Die Acta Romana des Martyriums des Ignatius Antiochenus," *VC* 7 (1953): 143–53.

140. "His letter to the Roman church includes sentiments which make him sound like a voluntary martyr" (Birley, "Voluntary Martyrs," 104). See also Middleton, "Early Christian Voluntary Martyrdom," 558.

141. Middleton, "Early Christian Voluntary Martyrdom," 569.

142. Tite, "Voluntary Martyrdom and Gnosticism," 36, 40; Nicholson, "What Makes a Voluntary Martyr?," 159–64.

143. Tite, "Voluntary Martyrdom and Gnosticism," 37–38. See also Middleton, "Early Christian Voluntary Martyrdom," 572; Moss, "Discourse of Voluntary Martyrdom," 541–42, 551.

be embraced and welcomed. Those preformed in this manner were longing not for extinction but eternal reward.[144] Nevertheless, their lived experiences, and the discourses they engendered, reflected a varied spectrum of "voluntary" martyrdoms in which "proactive" preparation could further muddy the already murky waters swirling about tidy distinctions between the roles of initiation and response.

BIBLIOGRAPHY

Baumeister, T. *Die Anfänge der Theologie des Martyriums*. MBT 45. Münster: Aschendorff, 1980.

Bowersock, G. W. *Martyrdom and Rome*. Cambridge: Cambridge University Press, 1995.

Boyarin, D. *Dying for God: Martyrdom and the Making of Christianity and Judaism*. Stanford: Stanford University Press, 1999.

Brent, A. *Ignatius of Antioch: A Martyr Bishop and the Origin of Episcopacy*. T&T Clark Theology. London: T&T Clark, 2007.

Brox, N. *Zeuge und Märtyrer: Untersuchungen zur frühchristlichen Zeugnis-Terminologie*. SANT 5. Münich: Kösel, 1961.

Buschmann, G. *Das Martyrium des Polykarp*. KAV 6. Göttingen: Vandenhoeck & Ruprecht, 1998.

Castelli, E. A. *Martyrdom and Memory: Early Christian Culture Making*. New York: Columbia University Press, 2004.

Dehandschutter, B. *Polycarpiana: Studies on Martyrdom and Persecution in Early Christianity: Collected Essays*. Edited by J. Leemans. BETL 205. Leuven: Peeters, 2007.

Frend, W. H. C. *Martyrdom and Persecution in the Early Church: A Study of a Conflict from the Maccabees to Donatus*. Oxford: Blackwell, 1965.

Hartog, P. *Polycarp's Epistle to the Philippians and the Martyrdom of Polycarp*. OAF. Oxford: Oxford University Press, 2013.

Middleton, P. *The Wiley Blackwell Companion to Christian Martyrdom*. Chichester: Wiley Blackwell, 2019.

Moss, C. R. *Ancient Christian Martyrdom: Diverse Practices, Theologies, and Traditions*. New Haven: Yale University Press, 2012.

Moss, C. R. *The Other Christs: Imitating Jesus in Ancient Christian Ideologies of Martyrdom*. Oxford: Oxford University Press, 2010.

Schoedel, W. R. *Ignatius of Antioch*. Hermeneia. Philadelphia: Fortress, 1985.

Schoedel, W. R. *Polycarp, Martyrdom of Polycarp, Fragments of Papias*. Vol. 5 of *The Apostolic Fathers: A New Translation and Commentary*. London: Thomas Nelson, 1967.

144. See Buck, "Voluntary Martyrdom Revisited," 134; McLarty, "Early Christian Theologies of Martyrdom," 130.

CHAPTER 20

THE WRITINGS OF THE NEW TESTAMENT IN THE APOSTOLIC FATHERS

MICHAEL J. KRUGER

1. INTRODUCTION

When it comes to the transmission and reception of the New Testament writings within early Christianity, the end of the second century proves to be a pivotal moment.[1] It is at this time that patristic sources begin to speak more plainly about the books they are using—as seen particularly in Irenaeus,[2] the Muratorian fragment,[3] and Clement of Alexandria.[4] Moreover, the oldest New Testament papyri in our possession date to the late second or early third century, providing the earliest glimpse at the state of (some of) the text, at least as it appears in an actual manuscript.[5] While the end of the second century, at least in the

1. For an overview of text and canon in the second century, see L. W. Hurtado, "The New Testament in the Second Century: Texts, Collections, and Canon," in *Transmission and Reception: New Testament Text-Critical and Exegetical Studies*, ed. J. W. Childers and D. C. Parker (Piscataway, NJ: Gorgias, 2006), 3–27; Michael J. Kruger, *Christianity at the Crossroads: How the Second Century Shaped the Future of the Church* (Downers Grove, IL: IVP Academic, 2018), 202–26.

2. D. J. Bingham, "Senses of Scripture in the Second Century: Irenaeus, Scripture, and Noncanonical Christian Texts," *JR* 97 (2017): 26–55; M. C. Steenberg, "Irenaeus on Scripture, *Graphe*, and the Status of *Hermas*," *SVTQ* 53 (2009): 29–66; D. M. Farkasfalvy, "Theology of Scripture in St. Irenaeus," *Rev. Bénédictine* 76 (1968): 319–33.

3. The second-century date of the Muratorian fragment has been challenged: A. C. Sundberg, "Canon Muratori: A Fourth-Century List," *HTR* 66 (1973): 1–41; G. M. Hahneman, *The Muratorian Fragment and the Development of the Canon* (Oxford: Clarendon, 1992). Others have defended the earlier date: J. Verheyden, "The Canon Muratori: A Matter of Dispute," in *The Biblical Canons*, ed. J.-M. Auwers and H. J. de Jonge (Leuven: Leuven University Press, 2003), 487–556; P. Henne, "La datation du Canon de Muratori," *RB* 100 (1993): 54–75; C. E. Hill, "The Debate over the Muratorian Fragment and the Development of the Canon," *WTJ* 57 (1995): 437–52; and E. Ferguson, "Canon Muratori: Date and Provenance," StPatr 18 (1982): 677–83.

4. E. Osborn, "Clement and the Bible," in *Origeniana Sexta: Origène et La Bible/Origen and the Bible. actes du Colloquium Origenianum Sextum, Chantilly, 30 Août–3 Septembre 1993*, ed. G. Dorival and A. L. Boulluec (Leuven: Leuven University Press, 1995), 121–32; J. A. Brooks, "Clement of Alexandria as a Witness to the Development of the Canon," *SecCent* 9 (1992): 41–55.

5. Some of our earliest papyri include P52 (John), P66 (John), P90 (John), P98 (Revelation), P104 (Matthew), P129 (1 Corinthians), and P137 (Mark). However, doubts have been raised recently about the reliability of our dating methods: R. S. Bagnall, *Early Christian Books in Egypt* (Princeton: Princeton University Press, 2009), 1–24; B. Nongbri, "The Use and Abuse of P52: Papyrological Pitfalls in the Dating of the Fourth Gospel," *HTR* 98 (2005): 23–48; B. Nongbri, "The Limits of Palaeographic Dating of Literary Papyri: Some Observations on the Date and Provenance of P.Bodmer II (P66)," *MH* 71 (2014): 1–35; B. Nongbri, "Palaeographic Analysis of Codices from the Early Christian Period: A Point of Method," *JSNT* 42 (2019): 84–97. For a defense of the traditional dates, see L. W. Hurtado, "New Testament Scholarship and the Dating of New Testament Papyri," in *Texts and Artefacts: Selected Essays on Textual Criticism and Early Christian Manuscripts* (London: Bloomsbury T&T Clark, 2018), 48–63.

scope of two millennia, is still quite early to have such resources at our disposal, scholars are (understandably) left with more questions. What was the state of the text *before* the end of the second century? Which books were Christians reading and using in this earlier time?

In order to answer these questions, scholars have often turned to some of the only Christian writings (outside of the NT) that are available in this earlier period: the Apostolic Fathers.[6] The hope has been that citations and allusions to New Testament writings within the Apostolic Fathers can illumine our understanding of which texts were being read, and how faithfully they were being transmitted. In 1905 a group of scholars from the Oxford Society of Historical Theology took up just this task in a volume entitled *The New Testament in the Apostolic Fathers*.[7] While the study focused less on the state of the text and more on identifying which writings were being utilized, it demonstrated that identifying and extracting citations of the New Testament was more difficult than perhaps many had realized.[8] Ever since, the debate over how much the Apostolic Fathers contribute to our knowledge of the New Testament has continued unabated over the last century.[9]

The purpose of this chapter is to reopen this complex discussion by (a) briefly exploring the methodological challenges of utilizing the Apostolic Fathers to speak to both the state of the text and the canon of the New Testament in the second century; and (b) offering a limited survey of which New Testament writings might have been utilized by the Apostolic Fathers, and how that might illumine our understanding of the reception of these writings within early Christianity.

2. METHODOLOGICAL CONSIDERATIONS

2.1 The Apostolic Fathers and the New Testament Text

We begin with the question of whether the Apostolic Fathers can inform our understanding of the state of the New Testament text during the early to middle second century. While there is little doubt that later patristic sources (usually third century or later) play

6. Discussion of the dates of individual books in the Apostolic Fathers can be found in P. Foster, ed., *The Writings of the Apostolic Fathers* (London: T&T Clark, 2007). The other second-century source that has received substantial attention is Justin Martyr; e.g., J. Verheyden, "Assessing Gospel Quotations in Justin Martyr," in *New Testament Textual Criticism and Exegesis, Festschrift J. Delobel*, ed. A. Denaux (Leuven: Peeters, 2002), 361–78; G. N. Stanton, "Jesus Traditions and Gospels in Justin Martyr and Irenaeus," in *The Biblical Canons*, ed. J.-M. Auwers and H. J. de Jonge (Leuven: Leuven University Press, 2003), 353–70.

7. A Committee of the Oxford Society of Historical Theology, ed., *The New Testament in the Apostolic Fathers* (Oxford: Clarendon, 1905).

8. Earlier studies were more optimistic that the Apostolic Fathers depended on the canonical Gospels; e.g., W. Sanday, *The Gospels in the Second Century* (London: MacMillan, 1876), 58–87.

9. Most influential in the debate over the NT writings in the Apostolic Fathers is undoubtedly H. Koester, *Synoptische Überlieferung bei den apostolischen Vätern* (Berlin: Akademie, 1957), whose methodology stands in contrast to É. Massaux, *The Influence of the Gospel of Saint Matthew on Christian Literature Before Saint Irenaeus*, trans. N. J. Belval and S. Hecht, 3 vols. (Macon, GA: Mercer University Press, 1994; French original, 1950), and later W.-D. Köhler, *Die Rezeption des Matthäusevangeliums in der Zeit vor Irenäus* (Tübingen: Mohr Siebeck, 1987). Other studies include D. A. Hagner, *The Use of the Old and New Testaments in Clement of Rome* (Leiden: Brill, 1973); D. A. Hagner, "The Sayings of Jesus in the Apostolic Fathers and Justin Martyr," in *Gospel Perspectives: The Jesus Tradition Outside the Gospels*, ed. D. Wenham (Sheffield: JSOT Press, 1985), 233–68; C. M. Tuckett, "Synoptic Tradition in the *Didache*," in *The New Testament in Early Christianity = La réception des écrits néotestamentaires dans le christianisme primitif*, ed. J.-M. Sevrin (Leuven: Leuven University Press, 1989), 197–230; A. Gregory, *The Reception of Luke and Acts in the Period Before Irenaeus* (Tübingen: Mohr Siebeck, 2003); A. F. Gregory and C. M. Tuckett, eds., *The Reception of the New Testament in the Apostolic Fathers* (Oxford: Oxford University Press, 2005); A. F. Gregory and C. M. Tuckett, *Trajectories Through the New Testament and the Apostolic Fathers* (Oxford: Oxford University Press, 2005); P. Foster, "The Text of the New Testament in the Apostolic Fathers," in *The Early Text of the New Testament*, ed. C. E. Hill and M. J. Kruger (Oxford: Oxford University Press, 2012), 282–301; and S. E. Young, *Jesus Tradition in the Apostolic Fathers*, WUNT 2/311 (Tübingen: Mohr Siebeck, 2011).

a useful and necessary role in text-critical discussions,[10] the complexities and pitfalls of extracting citations even from those sources have long been recognized.[11] Even so, some scholars remain insistent that even earlier sources—like the Apostolic Fathers—can provide equally reliable text-critical information. Indeed, William Petersen argues there "is abundant Patristic evidence for the text of the New Testament, much of it very ancient," and expresses his frustration that such "evidence has been largely ignored, while the papyri . . . receive so much attention."[12] Such patristic data matters to Petersen because the deviations in the New Testament citations in the Apostolic Fathers (at least as compared to the text we find in the later manuscripts) provide the basis for his claim that the first 150 years of transmission were marked by "textual chaos."[13]

However, despite the optimism of Petersen, there are significant doubts about whether the Apostolic Fathers can tell us much about the state of the New Testament text during this time period. The following factors should be considered:

1. *Identifying citations.* A fundamental challenge in extracting a patristic citation is determining whether an author *intended* to cite his source, or whether he is simply offering an allusion, reminiscence (echo), or locution.[14] Exegetical (e.g., commentaries) or polemical patristic works—most of which arose around the time of Irenaeus or later—are more likely to provide actual citations.[15] This presents real challenges for the Apostolic Fathers, which generally lack these characteristics and are significantly earlier.
2. *Citation practices.* Even if we might conclude that an author intended to cite a source, there is still the question of the *manner* of citation. Charles Hill—surveying the traditions of Homer, Herodotus, Philo, Plutarch, Philo and others—has argued that "Christian writers inherited from Greco-Roman and from Jewish culture an

10. E.g., B. D. Ehrman, *Didymus the Blind and the Text of the Gospels*, New Testament in the Greek Fathers (Atlanta: Scholars Press, 1986), was the first in its series. Since that time, other volumes have appeared on Gregory of Nyssa, Origen, Basil of Caesarea, Epiphanius of Salamis, Cyril of Jerusalem, Athanasius, and Clement of Alexandria. For Pauline texts, see C. M. Kreinecker, "The Earliest Commentaries on Paul as Sources for the Biblical Text—A New Research Project at the Institute for Textual Scholarship and Electronic Editing at the University of Birmingham," *Early Christianity* 3 (2012): 411–15.

11. For more on analyzing patristic citations of the NT, see C. D. Osburn, "Methodology in Identifying Patristic Citations in New Testament Textual Criticism," *NovT* 47 (2005): 313–43; G. D. Fee, "The Use of the Greek Fathers for New Testament Textual Criticism," in *The Text of the New Testament in Contemporary Research: Essays on the Status Quaestionis* (Eugene, OR: Wipf & Stock, 2001), 191–207; G. D. Fee, "The Text of John in Origen and Cyril of Alexandria: A Contribution to Methodology in the Recovery and Analysis of Patristic Citations," *Bib* 52 (1971): 357–73; B. D. Ehrman, "The Use and Significance of Patristic Evidence for NT Textual Criticism," in *New Testament Text Criticism, Exegesis, and Early Church History: A Discussion of Methods*, ed. B. Aland and J. Delobel (Kampen, Netherlands: Kok Pharos, 1994), 118–35; B. M. Metzger, "Patristic Evidence and the Textual Criticism of the New Testament," in *New Testament Studies: Philological, Versional, and Patristic* (Leiden: Brill, 1980), 167–88; and M. J. Suggs, "The Use of Patristic Evidence in the Search for a Primitive New Testament Text," *NTS* 4 (1957–58): 139–47.

12. W. L. Petersen, "What Text Can New Testament Textual Criticism Ultimately Reach?," in Aland and Delobel, *New Testament Textual Criticism*, 136–52, at 139.

13. W. L. Petersen, "The Genesis of the Gospel," in Denaux, *New Testament Textual Criticism*, 33–65, at 63. For a similar view, see H. Koester, "The Text of the Synoptic Gospels in the Second Century," in *Gospel Traditions in the Second Century: Origins, Recensions, Text, and Transmission*, ed. W. L. Petersen (Notre Dame: University of Notre Dame Press, 1989), 19–37.

14. See discussion of these different categories in Osburn, "Patristic Citations," 318ff.

15. Metzger, "Patristic Evidence," 168. As an example of this principle, when Ehrman makes the case for the value of patristic citations for textual criticism, his primary example is Origen's commentary on the Gospel of John—a work that is not only explicitly exegetical but also polemical against Heracleon ("Use and Significance of Patristic Evidence," 124–26).

approach to literary borrowing which did not prize exact replication of the text."[16] In other words, Christian authors, even when citing a text, would often adapt, modify, conflate, or make other stylistic changes, in order to make that text more applicable to their particular context.[17] Moreover, Hill observes that such imprecise quotations have little to do with whether a text was considered sacred. Even for texts regarded as Scripture, adaption or paraphrase was not uncommon.[18] The principle here is fundamental: there is a difference between the way a patristic writer might cite a New Testament writing and the way a scribe would copy an actual manuscript of a New Testament writing. The difference, as Barbara Aland has observed, is "der größeren Freiheit des Zitierenden im Vergleich mit dem Kopisten eines Manuskripts."[19] If so, then it is difficult to see how the Apostolic Fathers could provide reliable data about the state of the text in this early period.

3. *Intermediate sources.* One of Petersen's primary arguments that second-century writers (including the Apostolic Fathers) were in fact citing directly and precisely from their sources (as opposed to paraphrasing or adapting) is because the "variant" readings in these citations would also appear in *other patristic texts*.[20] However, we should not forget that it was not uncommon for church fathers to either cite one another, or to cite a common source such as a testimonia book or collection of excerpts—which themselves may have been conflated or harmonized.[21] The use of such "intermediate" sources is evident in the way the fathers cited the Old Testament,[22] but also in the way they cited the New Testament.[23] Thus, such shared variant readings do not necessarily reflect the state of the New Testament text itself.
4. *Oral Tradition.* When it comes to citations of Jesus tradition in the Apostolic Fathers (the NT epistles are another matter), we cannot always be sure the author is actually drawing upon one of our canonical Gospels as opposed to oral tradition about Jesus, which continued to be utilized well into the second century and beyond.[24] Thus,

16. C. E. Hill, "'In These Very Words': Methods and Standards of Literary Borrowing in the Second Century," in Hill and Kruger, *Early Text of the New Testament*, 261–81, at 278. See also J. Whittaker, "The Value of Indirect Tradition in the Establishment of Greek Philosophical Texts or the Art of Misquotation," in *Editing Greek and Latin Texts: Papers Given at the Twenty-Third Annual Conference on Editorial Problems, University of Toronto 6–7 November 1987*, ed. J. Grant (New York: AMS, 1989), 63–95.

17. Of course, this is not a new observation—the fact that Christian writers often engaged in such "loose" citation practices has been long observed by scholars; e.g., C. D. Stanley, *Paul and the Language of Scripture: Citation Technique in the Pauline Epistles and Contemporary Literature* (Cambridge: Cambridge University Press, 1992); F. G. Downing, "Writers' Use or Abuse of Written Sources," in *New Studies in the Synoptic Problem: Oxford Conference, April 2008*, ed. P. Foster (Leuven: Peeters, 2011), 523–48.

18. Hill, "'In These Very Words,'" 273–77.

19. B. Aland, "Die Rezeption des neutestamentlichen Textes in den ersten Jahrhunderten," in Sevrin, *New Testament in Early Christianity*, 36.

20. For examples, see Petersen, "What Text," 140–47.

21. Metzger, "Patristic Evidence," 184–85.

22. M. C. Albl, *And Scripture Cannot Be Broken: The Form and Function of the Early Christian Testimonia Collections* (Leiden: Brill, 1999); T. H. Lim, *Holy Scripture in the Qumran Commentaries and Pauline Letters* (Clarendon: Oxford University Press, 1997), 55.

23. As just one example, Justin Martyr is thought to have drawn many of his Gospels quotes from a collection of Jesus sayings used for catechetical instruction; see A. J. Bellinzoni, *The Sayings of Jesus in the Writings of Justin Martyr* (Leiden: Brill, 1967); L. L. Kline, "Harmonized Sayings of Jesus in the Pseudo-Clementine Homilies and Justin Martyr," *ZNW* 66 (1975): 223–41; Verheyden, "Assessing Gospel Quotations in Justin Martyr," 361–78.

24. The recent focus on orality can be traced back to the groundbreaking work of W. Kelber, *The Oral and Written Gospel: The Hermeneutics of Speaking and Writing in the Synoptic Tradition, Mark, Paul, and Q* (Philadelphia: Fortress, 1983), who leaned heavily on the earlier work of Walter Ong, Eric Havelock, Albert Lord, and Milman Parry. Other notable works include (though not all agreeing with Kelber): S. Byrskog, *Story*

what appears to be a citation from one of the Gospels may in fact be an appeal to an oral version of the same story or saying. We will explore this further below, but for now it's worth noting that divergent citations of Jesus tradition in the Apostolic Fathers cannot prove that "textual chaos" marked the transmission of the Gospels if these citations are not from the Gospels in the first place.[25]

5. *Transmission of the Apostolic Fathers.* Perhaps most overlooked in discussions of the New Testament text in the Apostolic Fathers is whether the text of the Apostolic Fathers itself has been reliably transmitted. Metzger raised this issue years ago,[26] and it has been rightly raised again by Paul Foster: "None of the manuscripts that preserve the writings of the Apostolic Fathers comes from the second century. . . . The reality is that even the limited manuscript evidence that attests the transmission of these writings shows that the copying of these documents [the Apostolic Fathers] was at times extremely unstable."[27] In other words, when we find a textual variant in what appears to be a citation of a New Testament writing by the Apostolic Fathers, we cannot know whether that variant comes from the writing being cited or comes from a later scribe who copied the text of the Apostolic Fathers.

2.2 The Apostolic Fathers and the New Testament Writings

Having explored whether the Apostolic Fathers can provide substantive information about the state of the text in the early second century, we now turn to the second and corollary issue—namely, whether the Apostolic Fathers can provide any insights as to which *writings* were being used (and how they were being used) in this time period. While here we are on firmer ground, significant residual challenges remain. Most notable in this regard (as discussed above), is the ongoing presence of oral tradition (and even other written sources, like Q). The presence of these other sources means that even if a supposed citation is a word-for-word match with a known New Testament writing, we can never be absolutely sure it is coming from that writing. This problem is particularly acute in the Apostolic Fathers because they so rarely indicate the source of their citation.[28] When Jesus tradition is cited, it is usually with no introductory formula—and sometimes without any acknowledgment that the words are from Jesus.[29]

---

as History–History as Story: The Gospel Tradition in the Context of Ancient Oral History (Leiden: Brill, 2002); R. Bauckham, *Jesus and the Eyewitnesses: The Gospels as Eyewitness Testimony* (Grand Rapids: Eerdmans, 2017); J. D. G. Dunn, *Jesus Remembered* (Grand Rapids: Eerdmans, 2003); H. Wansbrough, ed., *Jesus and the Oral Gospel Tradition* (Edinburgh: T&T Clark, 2004); B. Gerhardsson, *Memory and Manuscript with Tradition and Transmission in Early Christianity*, rev. ed. (Grand Rapids: Eerdmans, 1998); K. E. Bailey, "Informal Controlled Oral Tradition and the Synoptic Gospels," *Them* 20 (1995): 4–11; J. M. Vansina, *Oral Tradition as History* (Madison: University of Wisconsin Press, 1985); R. A. Horsley, J. A. Draper, and J. M. Foley, eds., *Performing the Gospel: Orality, Memory, and Mark* (Minneapolis: Fortress, 2006); and W. Kelber and S. Byrskog, eds., *Jesus in Memory: Traditions in Oral and Scribal Perspectives* (Waco, TX: Baylor University Press, 2009). For a helpful overview of recent research on orality in early Christianity, see K. R. Iverson, "Orality and the Gospels: A Survey of Recent Research," *CBR* 8 (2009): 71–206; and Young, *Jesus Tradition*, 1–35.

25. See the excellent discussion of this problem with Petersen's method in M. W. Holmes, "Text and Transmission in the Second Century," in *The Reliability of the New Testament: Bart D. Ehrman and Daniel B. Wallace in Dialogue*, ed. R. B. Stewart (Minneapolis: Fortress, 2011), 61–79, at 69–73.

26. Metzger, "Patristic Evidence," 185–86.

27. Foster, "Text of the New Testament," 282–83.

28. See A. F. Gregory and C. M. Tuckett, "Reflections on Method: What Constitutes the Use of the Writings That Later Formed the New Testament in the Apostolic Fathers?," in Gregory and Tuckett, *Reception of the New Testament in the Apostolic Fathers*, 61–82, at 68.

29. E.g., Ign. *Smyrn.* 1.1.; Did. 1.3–5.

Such considerations have led some scholars to shift the burden of proof onto those who argue that the written Gospels lie behind the citations in the Apostolic Fathers. Koester is quite plain: "Unless it can be proved otherwise, it must be assumed that authors who referred to and quoted such materials [Jesus tradition] were dependent on these life situations of the church and did not quote from written documents."[30] In short, oral sources should be the default position.

However, while acknowledging the complexities and difficulties of identifying written sources, there are questions about whether Koester's default position is warranted. The following considerations suggest the burden of proof may not lie solely on one side of the debate:

1. *Orality and textuality.* While no one doubts the ongoing use of oral traditions in the second century, Koester's approach is beholden to a now-questionable model of form-criticism from the early twentieth century. More recent studies have pushed back against that model in fundamental ways,[31] particularly against the idea that early Christianity was an "oral culture" with an aversion (if not animosity) toward written texts.[32] Now scholars are realizing that (a) early Christianity was a culture of *textuality*, despite low literacy rates;[33] (b) orality and textuality were not mutually exclusive, but complemented one another;[34] and (c) oral performances were often based on written texts.[35] If so, then there are significant doubts about whether we are required to make oral sources in the Apostolic Fathers our default position.

---

30. H. Koester, "Written Gospels or Oral Tradition?," *JBL* 113 (1994): 293–97, at 297.

31. E.g., Bauckham, *Jesus and the Eyewitnesses*, 240–63; M. F. Bird, *The Gospel of the Lord: How the Early Church Wrote the Story of Jesus* (Grand Rapids: Eerdmans, 2014), 113–24; C. S. Keener, *The Historical Jesus of the Gospels* (Grand Rapids: Eerdmans, 2009), 139–64; C. M. Tuckett, "Form Criticism," in Kelber and Byrskog, *Jesus in Memory*, 21–38.

32. Form criticism is well-known for its claim that early Christians despised the written text: e.g., F. Overbeck, "Über die Anfänge der partristischen Literatur," *Historische Zeitschrift* 48 (1882): 417–72; M. Dibelius, *From Tradition to Gospel* (Cambridge: Clarke, 1971), 9; R. W. Funk, "The Once and Future New Testament," in *The Canon Debate*, ed. L. M. McDonald and J. A. Sanders (Peabody, MA: Hendrickson, 2002), 541–57, at 544.

33. M. M. Mitchell, "The Emergence of the Written Record," in *Origins to Constantine*, vol. 1 of *The Cambridge History of Christianity*, ed. M. M. Mitchell and F. M. Young (Cambridge: Cambridge University Press, 2006), 177–94; M. Beard, "Writing and Religion," in *Ancient Religions*, ed. S. Johnston (Cambridge: Belknap Press, 2007), 127–38, at 135; H. Gamble, "Literacy, Liturgy, and the Shaping of the New Testament Canon," in *The Earliest Gospels*, ed. C. Horton (London: T&T Clark, 2004), 27–39; M. J. Kruger, *The Question of Canon: Challenging the Status Quo in the New Testament Debate* (Downers Grove, IL: IVP Academic, 2013), 79–118; and most recently C. Keith, *The Gospel as Manuscript: An Early History of Jesus Tradition as Material Artifact* (Oxford: Oxford University Press, 2020), esp. 73–99.

34. H. Hearon, "Implications of Orality for the Study of the Biblical Text," in *Performing the Gospel: Orality, Memory and Mark*, ed. R. A. Horsley, J. A. Draper, and J. M. Foley (Minneapolis: Fortress, 2006), 9; B. Gerhardsson, *The Reliability of Gospel Tradition* (Peabody, MA: Hendrickson, 2001), 110–23; J. F. McGrath, "Written Islands in an Oral Stream: Gospel and Oral Traditions," in *Jesus and Paul: Global Perspectives in Honor of James D. G. Dunn* (London: T&T Clark, 2009), 3–12; A. Kirk, "Memory, Scribal Media, and the Synoptic Problem," in Foster, *New Studies in the Synoptic Problem*, 459–82; and J. M. Foley, *Homer's Traditional Art* (University Park: Pennsylvania State University Press, 1999), 9.

35. L. Alexander, "Memory and Tradition in the Hellenistic Schools," in Kelber and Byrskog, *Jesus in Memory*, 113–53; S. Talmon, "Oral Tradition and Written Transmission, or the Heard and the Seen Word in Judaism of the Second Temple Period," in *Jesus and the Oral Gospel Tradition*, ed. H. Wansbrough (Sheffield: Sheffield Academic, 1991), 121–58; T. C. Mournet, "The Jesus Tradition as Oral Tradition," in Kelber and Byrskog, *Jesus in Memory*, 39–61; and A. Kirk, "Manuscript Tradition as a Tertium Quid: Orality and Memory in Scribal Practices," in *Jesus, the Voice, and the Text: Beyond the Oral and Written Gospel*, ed. T. Thatcher (Waco, TX: Baylor University Press, 2008), 215–34.

2. *Access to written sources.* An overlooked factor in this discussion is whether there are good reasons to think the Apostolic Fathers would have been aware of (or had access to) the New Testament writings.[36] Put differently, does the social-literary context of these authors suggest they tended to interact with other Christian leaders and other Christian texts? Several factors speak in favor of that possibility: (a) in general, Christians in this time were highly networked across the empire, with an extensive and impressive amount of literary traffic;[37] Christian communities were not isolated with "inward-looking parochialism," but had an outward facing spirit of interaction and cooperation.[38] (b) The Apostolic Fathers themselves were engaged in extensive literary exchanges with other Christians/churches as can be seen in the Shepherd of Hermas,[39] Ignatius's multi-letter correspondence,[40] and the fact that Polycarp both retained copies of Ignatius's letters and distributed them to the Philippian church upon request (along with his own cover letter).[41] (c) Even in the first century, authors were drawing on the canonical Gospels in *written* form, as can be seen by the fact that nearly all solutions to the Synoptic problem involve some sort of literary borrowing between Gospels.[42] Beyond this, Kelhoffer has argued that the long ending of Mark was dependent on the *written* Gospels in the early second century.[43] If such literary borrowing was happening already in the first century, and early second century, why so hard to imagine it happening among the Apostolic Fathers? (d) We have evidence that some of the Apostolic Fathers would have known the immediate followers of the apostles, and even the apostle John directly; for example, Polycarp was a disciple of the apostle John[44] (and later teacher of Irenaeus),[45] and Papias knew at

---

36. Gregory and Tuckett never really address this issue but simply state, "We make no assumption about whether each of the Apostolic Fathers was familiar with any of the writings later canonized as part of the New Testament" ("Reflections on Method," 65). Granted, one cannot assume the very thing that is in dispute—namely, whether each of these authors knew/used the NT writings. But is it not worth asking whether the larger socio-literary context of these authors provides broad reasons to think this likely or unlikely? After all, historical study is about probabilities, not just possibilities (or certainties).

37. H. Y. Gamble, *Books and Readers in the Early Church* (New Haven: Yale University Press, 1995), argues that there was a "busy, almost hectic traffic of messengers and letters between churches" (112). See also M. B. Thompson, "The Holy Internet: Communication Between Churches in the First Christian Generation," in *The Gospel for All Christians: Rethinking the Gospel Audiences*, ed. R. Bauckham (Grand Rapids: Eerdmans, 1998), 113–45; E. J. Epp, "New Testament Papyrus Manuscripts and Letter Carrying in Greco-Roman Times," in *The Future of Early Christianity: Essays in Honor of Helmut Koester* (Minneapolis: Fortress, 1991), 35–56; and L. W. Hurtado, "Interactive Diversity: A Proposed Model for Christian Origins," *JTS* 64 (2013): 445–62.

38. R. Bauckham, "For Whom Were Gospels Written?," in Bauckham, *Gospels for All Christians*, 9–48, at 31.

39. E.g., Herm. Vis. 8. Gamble referred to Clement's role in this passage as an "ecclesiastical publisher, a standing provision in the Roman church for duplicating and distributing texts to Christian communities elsewhere" (Gamble, *Books and Readers*, 109). See further discussion in M. J. Kruger, "Manuscripts, Scribes, and Book Production Within Early Christianity," in *Christian Origins and Classical Culture: Social and Literary Contexts for the New Testament*, ed. S. E. Porter and A. W. Pitts (Leiden: Brill, 2010), 15–40, at 34–35.

40. P. Foster, "The Epistles of Ignatius of Antioch," in Foster, *Writings of the Apostolic Fathers*, 81–107.

41. Pol. *Phil.* 13.1–2; discussion in Kruger, "Manuscripts, Scribes, and Book Production," 35–36.

42. Even if one argues that oral tradition should play a significant role in solving the Synoptic problem (e.g., J. D. G. Dunn, "Altering the Default Setting: Re-Envisaging the Early Transmission of the Jesus Tradition," *NTS* 49 [2003]: 139–75), most agree that *some* literary borrowing took place; see A. Gregory, "What Is Literary Dependence?," in Foster, *New Studies in the Synoptic Problem*, 87–114.

43. J. A. Kelhoffer, "'How Soon a Book' Revisited: EUAGGELION as a Reference to 'Gospel' Materials in the First Half of the Second Century," *ZNW* 95 (2004): 1–34.

44. Eusebius, *Hist. eccl.* 5.20.4–7; 5.33.4.

45. Eusebius, *Hist. eccl.* 5.20.6–7.

least some of the immediate followers of the apostles,[46] and maybe John himself.[47] At a minimum, this suggests a plausible historical context for knowing some of the New Testament writings. (e) Perhaps most importantly, at numerous points the Apostolic Fathers actually state that they have knowledge of New Testament texts: Polycarp, Ignatius, and 1 Clement all express knowledge of Paul's letters, and presume such knowledge is shared by their audiences;[48] Papias expressly names two New Testament writings—namely, Matthew and Mark; and numerous passages in the Apostolic Fathers use the term "Gospel" (and other terms like "Scripture," "ordinances," and "decrees") in such a manner that suggests written gospels are in view—for example, the Epistle to Diognetus,[49] 2 Clement,[50] Ignatius,[51] and the Didache.[52] While this does not necessarily demonstrate usage of our canonical Gospels, it does suggest oral tradition was not the dominant source that so many suppose. Given all these considerations and given that just a few years later Irenaeus (who was taught by Polycarp) appears to have an extensive and well-established collection of New Testament writings,[53] it seems unlikely that the Apostolic Fathers would have remained entirely unaware of such texts.

3. *Author consciousness.* One of the primary reasons for the default position toward oral tradition in the Apostolic Fathers is that the source or author of citations is rarely identified. In the minds of some, this means that the Apostolic Fathers are merely drawing on "anonymous" tradition, rather than written texts. However, there may be other explanations for this phenomenon. Larry Hurtado argues for a shift in citation practices after the middle of the second century, but not in the way some think. Rather than a shift toward written texts (and away from oral sources), it was a shift toward "an emergent *author-consciousness*."[54] He argues, "I suggest that what changes in the post-150 CE period is a greater tendency to see texts as the *works of authors* and so to cite them as such, rather than simply appropriating the contents of texts."[55] Moreover, we should not forget that *later* patristic sources would still cite Jesus tradition without identifying the source, even though we know with certainty that the author was familiar with the canonical Gospels.[56]

---

46. Eusebius, *Hist. eccl.* 3.39.3–4. Some helpful discussions of Papias can be found in Bauckham, *Jesus and the Eyewitness*, 202–39; Byrskog, *Story as History*, 272–92; and R. H. Gundry, *Matthew: A Commentary on His Handbook for a Mixed Church Under Persecution* (Grand Rapids: Eerdmans, 1994), 609–22.

47. Eusebius, *Hist. eccl.* 5.33.4. It should be noted that Papias is also described as a friend of Polycarp—so if the latter knew John, it is at least not unthinkable that Papias might have also.

48. 1 Clem. 47.1–3; Ign. *Eph.* 12.2; Pol. *Phil.* 3.2.

49. Diogn. 11.6.

50. 2 Clem. 2.4; 8.5.

51. Ign. *Magn.* 13.1; Ign. *Trall.* 7.1; Ign. *Phld.* 8.2. For discussion of these texts, see C. E. Hill, "Ignatius, 'The Gospel,' and the Gospels," in Gregory and Tuckett, *Trajectories Through the New Testament and the Apostolic Fathers*, 267–85; and C. E. Hill, "Ignatius and the Apostolate," StPatr 36 (2001): 226–48.

52. Did. 8.2; 11.3–4; 15.3–4. See discussion in Kelhoffer, "'How Soon a Book,'" 16–29.

53. Most notable in this regard is Irenaeus's remarkable confidence in the fourfold Gospel collection: "It is not possible that the gospels can be either more or fewer than the number they are. For since there are four zones of the world in which we live and four principal winds . . . [and] the cherubim, too, were four-faced" (*Haer.* 3.11.8).

54. Hurtado, "New Testament in the Second Century," 27 (emphasis his).

55. Hurtado, "New Testament in the Second Century," 27 (emphasis his).

56. E.g., Irenaeus often cites Gospel material as just "words of the Lord," even though he knew all four Gospels and cited from them frequently; see W. R. Farmer and D. M. Farkasfalvy, *The Formation of the New Testament Canon* (New York: Paulist, 1976), 50.

4. *Certain vs. probable results.* It is not always recognized that different assessments of these citations in the Apostolic Fathers may be due to a different *philosophical* starting point. Some scholars believe that "a small sample of quite secure evidence may be of more value than a large sample of less secure evidence."[57] Consequently, their methodology for determining what counts as a citation from New Testament writing is often so restrictive and rigorous that one is left with only very limited results.[58] The conclusion is determined by the method.[59] While there is nothing objectionable about such an approach per se, it must be acknowledged that there is no *historical* reason why it is better than the alternative. Rather than a method that produces more certain results, what if one preferred a method that led to results that were *probable*? No doubt, this is why some scholars, when looking for the source of a citation, prefer *known* sources rather than conjectural ones.[60] If a citation can be explained by, say, the Gospel of Matthew, why should we be required to default to a source that is merely hypothetical?

In sum, the above factors suggest Koester's insistence that oral tradition must be the default explanation, unless proven otherwise, simply does not hold. Rather, the burden of proof should lie equally on both sides of the argument. On this score, we can agree with Kelhoffer's approach: "The burden of proof for ascertaining literary dependence should not necessarily rest with those who tend to argue either in favor or against literary dependence . . . [witnesses] must be considered on a case-by-case basis."[61]

3. THE USE OF THE NEW TESTAMENT WRITINGS IN THE APOSTOLIC FATHERS: A BRIEF SURVEY

If the above considerations suggest that we should be open to the possibility that the Apostolic Fathers utilized New Testament writings (and not just oral tradition), we now turn our attention to briefly exploring some of the key passages in greater detail. Given that some of the Apostolic Fathers demonstrate little or no awareness of New Testament writings, we can restrict ourselves to the writings with the most potential: the Didache, 1 Clement, the letters of Ignatius, Polycarp's *To the Philippians*, Epistle of Barnabas, and 2 Clement.[62] This is not to suggest that the authors of the other writings—Martyrdom of Polycarp, Epistle to Diognetus, Papias, Quadratus, and the Shepherd of Hermas—were unaware of the New Testament books. On the contrary, and as already noted, several of

57. Gregory, *Reception of Luke and Acts*, 13.

58. In the original 1905 Oxford study of the Apostolic Fathers, eighty-five possible citations were examined, and only six received an "A" rating (meaning that the apostolic father certainly knew it).

59. Young, *Jesus Tradition*, 26, complains against those who find more NT writings in the Apostolic Fathers on the grounds that their "method largely predetermined the outcome." Agreed. But the same could be said of Young's more minimalist approach.

60. Massaux, *Influence of the Gospel of Saint Matthew*, 2:32.

61. Kelhoffer, "'How Soon a Book,'" 9–10.

62. The selection and order of books in this chapter is the same as that used in Gregory and Tuckett, *Reception of the New Testament in the Apostolic Fathers*, with the exception of the Shepherd of Hermas. The latter is not covered here because it has decidedly less potential NT material than the other writings. As Verheyden observes, the Shepherd is "widely regarded as the least rewarding for the question that concerns us here . . . [whether] the author of the *Shepherd* knew and made use of one or another of the writings that will afterwards be included in the New Testament" (J. Verheyden, "The *Shepherd of Hermas* and the Writings That Later Formed the New Testament," in Gregory and Tuckett, *Reception of the New Testament in the Apostolic Fathers*, 293–329, at 293). The order of these books roughly approximates their respective dates, but dating issues continue to be debated; for more, see the collection of essays in Foster, *Writings of the Apostolic Fathers*.

these books seem to indicate they are aware of written texts, and Papias even mentions two such texts by name, Matthew and Mark.[63] But we are concerned here not just with the mention of books, but the *usage* or *citation* of books, and these texts (for the most part) offer comparatively less in that regard.[64]

3.1 Didache

The Didache—or the "Teaching of the Twelve Apostles"—is a manual of early Christian instruction on morality (the "Two Ways") and church life (baptism, Lord's Supper, church leaders).[65] It has featured heavily in discussions about the use of New Testament writings because of its purported early date and possible connections to the Synoptic Gospels.[66] While many passages in the Didache bear only loose similarities to the Synoptics, there are others with more substantial verbal overlap.

Didache 1.3–2.1 significantly overlaps with material from Matthew 5 (Sermon on the Mount), as well as some portions of parallel material in Luke 6, even (at times) seeming to hop back and forth.[67] Particularly noteworthy are the following connections: Did. 1.3// Luke 6:27; Did. 1.4//Matt 5:39; Did. 1.5a//Luke 6:30; and Did. 1.5b//Matt 5:26. The patchwork nature of these allusions has led some to doubt dependence on the canonical Gospels here.[68] However, at numerous points the wording is nearly an exact match,[69] and at other points a connection with redactional material from either Matthew or Luke is evident, suggesting familiarity with the finished versions of these Gospels.[70] Such connections have even led Koester, who is generally skeptical of the usage of the Synoptics in the Didache, to concede that Matthew and Luke are the likely sources here.[71]

---

63. Eusebius, *Hist. eccl.* 3.39.15–16.

64. Though it should be observed that Diognetus probably exhibits more Pauline influence than typically acknowledged; see M. F. Bird, "The Reception of Paul in the *Epistle to Diognetus*," in *Paul and the Second Century*, ed. M. F. Bird and Joseph R. Dodson, LNTS 412 (London: T&T Clark, 2011), 70–90.

65. For an introduction, see J. A. Draper, "The *Didache*," in Foster, *Writings of the Apostolic Fathers*, 13–20; and H. van de Sandt and D. Flusser, *The Didache: Its Jewish Sources and Its Place in Early Judaism and Christianity* (Minneapolis: Fortress, 2002).

66. General works on the Synoptics and the Didache include C. M. Tuckett, "The *Didache* and the Writings That Later Formed the New Testament," in Gregory and Tuckett, *Reception of the New Testament in the Apostolic Fathers*, 83–127; J. S. Kloppenborg, "The Use of the Synoptics or Q in *Did.* 1.3b–2.1," in *The Didache and Matthew: Two Documents from the Same Jewish-Christian Milieu?*, ed. H. van de Sandt (Minneapolis: Fortress, 2005), 105–29; A. Milavec, "Synoptic Tradition in the *Didache* Revisited," *JECS* 11 (2003): 443–80; C. N. Jefford, *The Sayings of Jesus in the Teaching of the Twelve Apostles* (Leiden: Brill, 1989); and R. Glover, "The *Didache's* Quotations and the Synoptic Gospels," *NTS* 5 (1958): 12–29.

67. We will not attempt to resolve the debate about whether the "Two Ways" material is due to a later expansion or interpolation. For more on the compositional history of the Didache, see B. Layton, "The Sources, Date, and Transmission of *Didache* 1.3b–2.1," *HTR* 61 (1968): 343–83; and Sandt and Flusser, *Didache*, 55–190.

68. Young, *Jesus Tradition*, 212–13.

69. As just one example:

> Did. 1.4: ἐάν τίς σοι δῷ ῥάπισμα εἰς τὴν δεξιὰν σιαγόνα, στρέψον αὐτῷ καὶ τὴν ἄλλην / "If anyone slaps your right cheek, turn the other to him as well"
>
> Matt 5:39: ἀλλ᾽ ὅστις σε ῥαπίζει εἰς τὴν δεξιὰν σιαγόνα, στρέψον αὐτῷ καὶ τὴν ἄλλην / "If anyone strikes you on the right cheek, turn to him the other also"

Unless otherwise noted, English translations of the Apostolic Fathers are drawn from B. D. Ehrman, *The Apostolic Fathers*, 2 vols., LCL (Cambridge: Harvard University Press, 2003); and English translations of the New Testament are RSV.

70. Examples of Matthean and Lukan redaction found in Did. 1.3–2.1 can be found in Tuckett, "*Didache*," 119–25. For a rebuttal to Tuckett's analysis, see Young, *Jesus Tradition*, 207–18; Milavec, "Synoptic Tradition," 461–65.

71. Koester, *Synoptische Überlieferung*, 217–39. Similar conclusions are reached by Layton, "Sources, Date and Transmission," 369–72.

Another notable passage is Didache 8.2: "As the Lord commanded in his gospel, you should pray as follows, 'Our Father in heaven . . .'" The text that follows is a version of the Lord's prayer that is "extremely close"[72] to that of Matthew's Gospel. Given that the Lord's Prayer would have been a well-known block of material in early Christianity, some scholars have rightly argued that Matthew is not the only possible source.[73] But this just brings us back to the philosophical question of whether we should prefer unknown sources when we have known sources that can explain a citation. Perhaps the impasse could be broken here by observing that Didache 8.2 introduces this material as (a) a citation, (b) a citation of "the Lord," and (c) a citation of the Lord from a "gospel" (εὐαγγέλιον, *euangelion*). As observed above, Kelhoffer has made a substantive argument that the term εὐαγγέλιον in the Didache (cf. 11.3–4; 15.4) refers to a written gospel.[74] Given that Matthew is the only known written Gospel that provides a close verbal match to this citation, that may make it the preferable option.

A final example is Didache 9.5, "For also the Lord has said about this, 'Do not give what is holy to the dogs.'" The saying itself is an exact match with the Greek text of Matthew 7:6:[75]

Did. 9.5: Μὴ δῶτε τὸ ἅγιον τοῖς κυσί
Matt 7:6: Μὴ δῶτε τὸ ἅγιον τοῖς κυσίν

Once again, even an exact match does not prove the use of Matthew's Gospel, especially given the proverbial nature of this saying.[76] However, the Didache explicitly attributes it to what "the Lord has said," which elsewhere the author indicates can be found in an εὐαγγέλιον (Did. 8.2; 11.3–4; 15.4). Thus, we should at least be open to the possibility that Didache 9.5 is another instance where the author is drawing on Matthew's Gospel.

In sum, there are good reasons to think the author of the Didache drew on Matthew and Luke, but it does not rise to the level of certainty—other explanations are still possible. If he did use these writings, it seems evident that he referenced them using the term "gospel" and understood them to contain the authoritative commands of Jesus.

3.2 First Clement

Written from Rome at the very end of the first century (ca. 96 CE), 1 Clement is a lengthy letter to the Corinthian church addressing the various problems that had arisen there.[77] The author—whose identity is uncertain—calls the Corinthians to look to the

72. Tuckett, "*Didache*," 104. For further textual comparisons, though with a different conclusion, see Koester, *Synoptische Überlieferung*, 203–9.

73. H. Koester, *Ancient Christian Gospels: Their History and Development* (London: SCM, 1990), 16; Glover, "*Didache's* Quotations," 19; Young, *Jesus Tradition*, 219–20.

74. Kelhoffer, "'How Soon a Book,'" 16–29. Didache 15.4 is particularly suggestive of a written text: "But say your prayers, give to charity, and engage in all your activities as you have learned in the gospel of our Lord [ἐν τῷ εὐαγγελίῳ τοῦ κυρίου ἡμῶν]."

75. See also parallels in Gos. Thom. 90; and Epiphanius, *Pan*. 24.5.2.

76. K. Lake, "Didache," in *New Testament in the Apostolic Fathers*, 27. In addition, Glover, "*Didache*'s Quotations," 19, and Milavec, "Synoptic Tradition," 456–57, both argue against Matthean dependence on the basis that the author has changed the context of the saying in Did. 9.5. But it is unclear why sayings cannot be applied to new settings or contexts as Matthew and Luke sometimes do in their own utilization of Mark.

77. For a general overview, see A. F. Gregory, "*1 Clement*: An Introduction," in Foster, *Writings of the Apostolic Fathers*, 21–31.

"apostles,"[78] to whom he ascribes significant authority and honor,[79] and two of whom he mentions by name—Peter and Paul.[80] The author does not call his audience merely to remember the oral teachings of the apostles, but points to *written texts*. The author writes: "Take up [Ἀναλάβετε, *analabete*] the epistle of that blessed apostle, Paul. . . . To be sure, he sent you a letter in the Spirit [πνευματικῶς, *pneumatikōs*] concerning himself and Cephas and Apollos."[81] Most scholars agree that this is a clear reference to the letter of 1 Corinthians, a conclusion supported by additional connections that our author makes elsewhere: 1 Clem. 24.1//1 Cor 15:20; 1 Clem. 37.5//1 Cor 12:12–14; 1 Clem. 49.5//1 Cor 13:4–7.[82] In addition, the author states that 1 Corinthians was written "in the Spirit" (πνευματικῶς), language that is used elsewhere for the inspiration of scriptural writings,[83] though it is sometimes used for noncanonical works as well.[84] The exhortation to "take up" (Ἀναλάβετε) Paul's letter forms a striking parallel with 1 Esdras 9:45 where Ezra "takes up" (ἀναλαβών) the law of God to read it to the assembled people, leading Martin Hengel to argue that it refers to the public reading of Paul's letter as Scripture.[85]

But the author's Pauline letter collection included more than 1 Corinthians. There is widespread agreement that Romans was also a key source, as exemplified in 1 Clem. 35.5–6//Rom 1:29–32.[86] Both passages share the same lengthy list of vices, followed by the same dramatic conclusion:

	Greek	English
1 Clem. 35.6	οὐ μόνον δὲ οἱ πράσσοντες αὐτά, ἀλλὰ καὶ οἱ συνευδοκοῦντες αὐτοῖς	"not only those who do them, but also those who approve of them"
Rom 1:32	οὐ μόνον αὐτὰ ποιοῦσιν ἀλλὰ καὶ συνευδοκοῦσιν τοῖς πράσσουσιν	"they not only do them but approve those who practice them"

The "coincidences between these two lists are remarkable,"[87] making it "practically certain"[88] that Romans was the source of 1 Clement here.[89] As for the other Pauline letters, the evidence is less certain, but Metzger argues for "definite allusions" also to Galatians, Ephesians, and Philippians.[90] Hagner goes even further, suggesting that the author of 1 Clement had access to a complete Pauline letter collection, minus only 1 and 2 Thessalonians and Philemon.[91] Beyond this, if the author of 1 Clement regarded the book of Hebrews as

78. 1 Clem. 5.3; 42.1–4; 44.1; 47.1.
79. 1 Clem. 5.2; 42.1–2.
80. 1 Clem. 5.4–5; 47.1–3.
81. 1 Clem. 47.1–3.
82. A. Lindemann, *Paulus im ältesten Christentum: Das Bild des Apostels und die Rezeption der Paulinischen Theologie in der frühchristlichen Literatur bis Marcion* (Tübingen: Mohr Siebeck, 1979), 190–91; A. F. Gregory, "*1 Clement* and the Writings That Later Formed the New Testament," in Gregory and Tuckett, *Reception of the New Testament in the Apostolic Fathers*, 129–57; Hagner, *Clement of Rome*, 196–97.
83. E.g., 1 Clem. 8.1; Barn. 14.2; Ign. *Magn.* 9.2; see also Ezek 37:1; Matt 22:43; Rev 1:10.
84. E.g., 1 Clem. 63.2.
85. M. Hengel, *The Four Gospels and the One Gospel of Jesus Christ* (Harrisburg, PA: Trinity Press International, 2000), 128. For more on the public reading of Scripture in early Christianity, see Keith, *Gospel as Manuscript*, 163–200.
86. See also 1 Clem. 33.1//Rom 6:1; 1 Clem. 32.2//Rom 9:5.
87. A. E. Barnett, *Paul Becomes a Literary Influence* (Chicago: University of Chicago Press, 1941), 95.
88. A. J. Carlyle, "Clement of Rome," in *New Testament in the Apostolic Fathers*, 37–62, at 38.
89. For further discussion, see Massaux, *Influence of the Gospel of Saint Matthew*, 1:42–43.
90. Metzger, *Canon of the New Testament*, 42.
91. Hagner, *Clement of Rome*, 237.

Pauline,[92] then his letter collection would be even bigger since "there can be practically no doubt"[93] that 1 Clement drew upon the book of Hebrews.[94] Most notable is 1 Clem. 36.2–5// Heb 1:3–5, 7, 13 where the verbal overlap extends over many verses, even including the same three Old Testament citations (Pss 104:4; 2:7; 110:1),[95] and the version of Psalm 104:4 in 1 Clement even matches the version in Hebrews 1:7 over and against the Septuagint.[96]

While it is apparent that 1 Clement utilized some sort of Pauline letter collection—the extent of which is uncertain—much less can be said about the remaining books of the New Testament.[97] However, there are some intriguing parallels with the Synoptic Gospels,[98] particularly the collection of phrases in 1 Clement 13.2 that overlaps at various points with material from Matthew 5–7 and Luke 6.[99] At times this overlap is considerable:

	Greek	English
1 Clem. 13.2a	ὡς δίδοτε, οὕτως δοθήσεται ὑμῖν	"As you give, so it will be given to you."
Luke 6:38a	δίδοτε, καὶ δοθήσεται ὑμῖν	"Give, and it will be given to you."

1 Clem. 13.2b	ὡς κρίνετε, οὕτως κριθήσεσθε	"as you judge, so you will be judged"
Matt 7:1[100]	Μὴ κρίνετε, ἵνα μὴ κριθῆτε	"judge not, that you be not judged"

1 Clem. 13.2c	ᾧ μέτρῳ μετρεῖτε, ἐν αὐτῷ μετρηθήσεται ὑμῖν	"With what measure you measure, with the same shall it be measured to you"[101]
Matt 7:2[102]	ᾧ μέτρῳ μετρεῖτε μετρηθήσεται ὑμῖν	"the measure you measure with will be measured to you"[103]

Even so, most scholars have argued that dependence on the Synoptic Gospels cannot be proven here—especially since there is no indication that 1 Clement is aware of Matthean

92. For an overview of the canonical history of Hebrews, see W. H. P. Hatch, "The Position of Hebrews in the Canon of the New Testament," *HTR* 29 (1936): 133–51.

93. Carlyle, "Clement of Rome," 46.

94. See also arguments in Gregory, "*1 Clement* and the Writings That Later Formed the New Testament," 152–53. Others argue that the letters are independent of one another but draw on a common liturgical tradition; e.g., G. Theissen, *Untersuchungen zum Hebräerbrief* (Gütersloh: Mohn, 1969), 34–37; P. Ellingsworth, "Hebrews and *1 Clement*: Literary Dependence or Common Tradition?," *BZ* 23 (1979): 262–69. A rebuttal to Theissen can be found in G. L. Cockerill, "Heb 1:1–14, *1 Clem.* 36.1–6 and the High Priest Title," *JBL* 97 (1978): 437–40.

95. Though it should be noted that the OT citations are in a different order in 1 Clement than in Hebrews.

96. 1 Clem. 36.3//Heb 1:7 both have πυρὸς φλόγα, as opposed to πῦρ φλέγον in Ps 104:4 (103:4 LXX). Other overlapping passages include: 1 Clem. 17.5//Heb 3:2; 1 Clem. 36.1//Heb 2:18; 3:1; 1 Clem. 17.1// Heb 11:37, 39.

97. However, there appear to be a number of curious connections to 1 Peter (the author mentions the apostle Peter in 1 Clem. 5.4). See discussion in Hagner, *Clement of Rome*, 239–46; and C. Bigg, *A Critical and Exegetical Commentary on the Epistles of St. Peter and St. Jude*, ICC (Edinburgh: T&T Clark, 1978), 8, who points out the following links: 1 Clem. 7.4//1 Pet 1:19; 1 Clem. 9.4//1 Pet 3:20; 1 Clem. 36.2//1 Pet 2:9; 1 Clem. 30.2//1 Pet 5:5; 1 Clem. 49.5//1 Pet 4:8.

98. E.g., 1 Clem. 46.7–8//Matt 26:24; Mark 14:21; Luke 22:22; 1 Clem. 15.2//Matt 15:7–8; Mark 7:6 (Isa 29:13).

99. Carlyle, "Clement of Rome," 58–62.

100. See also the parallel in Pol. *Phil.* 2.3.

101. English translation from *The Apostolic Fathers*, vol. 1 of *The Fathers of the Church*, trans. F. X. Glimm, J. M.-F. Marique, and G. G. Walsh (Washington, DC: Catholic University of America Press, 1947), 20.

102. Cf. Mark 4:24 and Luke 6:38; as well as Pol. *Phil.* 2.3.

103. English translation my own.

or Lukan redaction—preferring instead to posit oral or catechetical tradition as the likely source.[104]

3.3 Ignatius

In the early second century, Ignatius, the influential bishop of Antioch, wrote seven letters en route to his martyrdom in Rome.[105] Like the author of 1 Clement, Ignatius is not merely dependent on oral tradition but explicitly refers to a Pauline letter collection. Writing to the church at Ephesus, he points to some of these letters: "You are fellow initiates with Paul, the holy one who received a testimony and proved worthy of all fortune. When I attain to God, may I be found in his footsteps, this one *who mentions you in every epistle* in Christ Jesus."[106] If Ignatius is referring to the Pauline letters that expressly mention the Ephesian church, then his collection would have consisted of at least Ephesians, 1 Corinthians, and 1 and 2 Timothy.[107]

While some scholars have dismissed this language as a "polite exaggeration"[108] of sorts, Ignatius's knowledge of these four letters is confirmed by other allusions to them throughout his letters. The connections to 1 Corinthians are considerable,[109] leading W. Inge to suggest that "Ignatius must have known this epistle almost by heart."[110] Particularly notable is the following parallel:

	Greek	English
Ign. *Eph.* 18.1	τοῦ σταυροῦ, ὅ ἐστιν σκάνδαλον τοῖς ἀπιστοῦσιν, ἡμῖν δὲ σωτηρία καὶ ζωὴ αἰώνιος. ποῦ σοφός; ποῦ συζητητής;	". . . the cross, which is a scandal to those who do not believe but salvation and eternal life to us. Where is the one who is wise? Where is the debater?"
1 Cor 1:18, 20	Ὁ λόγος γὰρ ὁ τοῦ σταυροῦ τοῖς μὲν ἀπολλυμένοις μωρία ἐστίν, τοῖς δὲ σῳζομένοις ἡμῖν δύναμις θεοῦ ἐστιν . . . ποῦ σοφός . . . ποῦ συζητητής	"For the word of the cross is folly to those who are perishing, but to us who are being saved it is the power of God . . . Where is the wise man? . . . Where is the debater?"

Remarkably, Ignatius combines a reference to the "scandal" (σκάνδαλον, *skandalon*) of the "cross" (σταυροῦ, *staurou*), which brings "salvation" (σωτηρία, *sōtēria*; σῳζομένοις, *sōzomenois*), with an overt challenge to the "wise" one (σοφός, *sophos*) and "debater" (συζητητής, *syzētētēs*) of this age—all of which are found in 1 Corinthians 1, particularly verses 18 and 20.[111]

104. Note particularly the extensive argumentation in Hagner, *Clement of Rome*, 140–51; Young, *Jesus Tradition*, 150. In agreement is Koester, *Synoptische Überlieferung*, 12–16. However, H. B. Green, "Matthew, Clement and Luke: Their Sequence and Their Relationship," *JTS* 40 (1989): 1–25, makes a lengthy argument that the author of 1 Clement knew all three Synoptics.

105. For an introduction to Ignatius and his writings, see P. Foster, "The Epistles of Ignatius of Antioch," in Foster, *Writings of the Apostolic Fathers*, 81–107; and W. R. Schoedel, *Ignatius of Antioch*, Hermeneia (Philadelphia: Fortress, 1985).

106. Ign. *Eph.* 12.2 (emphasis mine).

107. Eph 1:1; 1 Cor 15:32; 16:8; 1 Tim 1:3; 2 Tim 1:18; 4:12. See discussion in P. Foster, "The Epistles of Ignatius of Antioch and the Writings That Later Formed the New Testament," in Gregory and Tuckett, *Reception of the New Testament in the Apostolic Fathers*, 172.

108. D. Hoffman, "The Authority of Scripture and Apostolic Doctrine in Ignatius of Antioch," *JETS* 28 (1985): 75.

109. E.g., Ign. *Eph.* 16.1//1 Cor 6:9–10; Ign. *Magn.* 10.2//1 Cor 5:7–8; Ign. *Rom.* 5.1//1 Cor 4:4; Ign. *Rom.* 9.2//1 Cor 15:8–10.

110. W. R. Inge, "Ignatius," in *New Testament and the Apostolic Fathers*, 67.

111. Cf. σκάνδαλον in 1 Cor 1:23.

While not as clear as the connections to 1 Corinthians, it is "almost certain"[112] that Ignatius used the book of Ephesians due to the cumulative effect of many words and phrases that overlap: Ign. *Eph.* inscript//Eph 1:3–14; Ign. *Eph.* 20.1//Eph 2:15; 4:24; Ign. *Smyrn.* 1.2//Eph 2:16; Ign. *Pol.* 1.2//Eph 4:2. The following parallel is illustrative:

	Greek	English
Ign. *Pol.* 5.1	ἀγαπᾶν τὰς συμβίους ὡς ὁ κύριος τὴν ἐκκλησίαν	"love their wives as the Lord loves the church"
Eph 5:25	ἀγαπᾶτε τὰς γυναῖκας, καθὼς καὶ ὁ Χριστὸς ἠγάπησεν τὴν ἐκκλησίαν	"love your wives, as Christ loved the church"

While Ignatius uses some different terminology (e.g., συμβίους, *symbious*, in place of γυναῖκας, *gynaikas*; κύριος, *kyrios*, in place of Χριστός, *Christos*)—a typical feature when citing from memory as he is known to do[113]—the thrust of the two passages is fundamentally the same: husbands are to love their wives as Christ loves the church.

There is also a "high likelihood of dependence"[114] on 1 and 2 Timothy, especially as seen in Ign. *Pol.* 4.3//1 Tim 6:2; Ign. *Rom.* 9.2//1 Tim 1:13; Ign. *Eph.* 2.1//2 Tim 1:16; Ign. *Pol.* 6.2//2 Tim 2:3. Most notable is the resemblance between Ign. *Eph.* 14.1; 20.1; Ign. *Magn.* 8.1 and 1 Tim 1:3–4, which Inge regards as "very close."[115]

Beyond this likely knowledge of 1 Corinthians, Ephesians, and 1 and 2 Timothy, some scholars have suggested Ignatius's Pauline letter collection may have been even more extensive, including also Romans, Philippians, and Galatians.[116] As for other apostolic writings, we should observe that Ignatius refers to other apostles,[117] regards these apostles has having a distinct and higher authority than himself,[118] and exhorts his readers to follow the "decrees" (δόγμασιν, *dogmasin*)[119] and "ordinances" (διαταγμάτων, *diatagmatōn*)[120] of the apostles—terminology that often refers to written texts.[121]

Given Ignatius's high regard for apostolic writings, we should not be surprised that Ignatius also appears to know the Gospels of Matthew and John.[122] While there are a number of connections between Ignatius and Matthew,[123] most significant is the following:

112. Inge, "Ignatius," 69.

113. Foster, "Epistles of Ignatius of Antioch," 161.

114. Foster, "Epistles of Ignatius of Antioch," 171.

115. Inge, "Ignatius," 72.

116. Schoedel, *Ignatius*, 73; Metzger, *Canon of the New Testament*, 49. Ignatius's potential knowledge of a wider Pauline corpus is supported by the extensive *theological* overlap between the two writers; see C. B. Smith, "Ministry, Martyrdom, and Other Mysteries: Pauline Influence on Ignatius of Antioch," in Bird and Dodson, *Paul and the Second Century*, 37–56; and D. M. Reis, "Following in Paul's Footsteps: *Mimēsis* and Power in Ignatius of Antioch," in Gregory and Tuckett, *Trajectories Through the New Testament and the Apostolic Fathers*, 287–305.

117. Ign. *Rom.* 4.4.

118. Ign. *Trall.* 3.3. See also Hill, "Ignatius and the Apostolate," 226–48.

119. Ign. *Magn.* 13.1.

120. Ign. *Trall.* 7.1.

121. Hill, "Ignatius and the Apostolate," 235–39.

122. R. M. Grant, "Scripture and Tradition in St. Ignatius of Antioch," *CBQ* 25 (1963): 325–27. There is also evidence that Ignatius may have known Luke: Ign. *Smyrn.* 3.2//Luke 24:39.

123. Some key examples: Ign. *Trall.* 11.1; Ign. *Phld.* 3.1//Matt 15:13; Ign. *Pol.* 2.2//Matt 10:16; Ign. *Smyrn.* 6.1//Matt 19:12. Fuller discussion can be found in Massaux, *Influence of the Gospel of Saint Matthew*, 1:85–122; and C. Trevett, "Approaching Matthew from the Second Century: The Under-Used Ignatian Correspondence," *JSNT* 20 (1984): 59–67.

	Greek	English
Ign. *Smyrn.* 1.1	ἵνα πληρωθῇ πᾶσα δικαιοσύνη ὑπ' αὐτοῦ	"that all righteousness might be fulfilled by him"
Matt 3:15	οὕτως γὰρ πρέπον ἐστὶν ἡμῖν πληρῶσαι πᾶσαν δικαιοσύνην	"for thus it is fitting for us to fulfill all righteousness"

In addition to the obvious verbal overlap and the fact that both writings place the saying within the same context (John's baptism), this passage in Matthew is widely regarded as a Matthean redaction.[124] Thus, we have evidence here that Ignatius is aware of the finished form of Matthew—one of Koester's key criteria for establishing literary dependence.[125]

As for John, Inge argues that it is "highly probable"[126] that Ignatius used the Fourth Gospel, relying on a number of points of contact between the two writings.[127] Most notable are Ign. *Rom.* 7.2–3//John 4:10; 6:33 where we see shared Johannine language of "living water" (ὕδωρ ζῶν, *hydōr zōn*) and "bread of God" (ἄρτον θεοῦ, *arton theou*), and Ign. *Phld.* 7.1//John 3:8 where both passages refer to the Spirit and "where it comes from and where it goes" (πόθεν ἔρχεται καὶ ποῦ ὑπάγει, *pothen erchetai kai pou hypagei*). Such considerations have led Hill to declare that "Ignatius' knowledge of John can be taken as proved,"[128] while other scholars like Schoedel remain unpersuaded, leaving the question open.[129]

3.4 Polycarp

As someone who knew the apostle John personally,[130] as well as being a companion to Papias[131] and teacher of Irenaeus,[132] Polycarp is well-situated to provide information about the (possible) use of New Testament writings. Writing about 110 CE, Polycarp also moves beyond oral tradition and refers to written apostolic texts, particularly encouraging his audience to read the "letters"[133] of the "blessed and glorious" Paul so that they can be "built up in the faith."[134] He mentions these letters with the assumption that "the Philippians had a collection of Paul's letters that was the same as his own."[135] While he does not enumerate the precise content of this collection, there is widespread agreement that it would

124. W. D. Davies and D. C. Allison, *The Gospel According to Saint Matthew*, 3 vols., ICC (Edinburgh: T&T Clark, 1997), 1:324–25.

125. Koester, *Synoptische Überlieferung*, 3. Despite his own criteria, Koester refuses to acknowledge direct literary dependence in this case (57–59), leading Foster to rightly argue that it makes his work, at least at this point, "appear somewhat arbitrary and agenda-driven" (Foster, "Epistles of Ignatius of Antioch," 180).

126. Inge, "Ignatius," 83.

127. Inge, "Ignatius," 81–83.

128. C. E. Hill, *The Johannine Corpus in the Early Church* (Oxford: Oxford University Press, 2004), 442. In agreement is Massaux, who argues that "the resemblance is much too close to be purely accidental" (*Influence of the Gospel of Saint Matthew*, 1:104).

129. Schoedel, *Ignatius*, 206.

130. Eusebius, *Hist. eccl.* 5.20.4–7; 5.24.16.

131. Irenaeus, *Haer.* 5.33.4.

132. Eusebius, *Hist. eccl.* 5.20.6–7.

133. The plural "letters" (Pol. *Phil.* 3.2) here has raised questions, given that Paul is only known to have sent a single letter to the Philippians. However, a natural solution is that Polycarp understood all of Paul's letters to be applicable to any church, despite their original destinations. For more, see A. Lindemann, "Paul in the Writings of the Apostolic Fathers," in *Paul and the Legacies of Paul*, ed. W. S. Babcock (Dallas: Southern Methodist University Press, 1990), 41–42.

134. Pol. *Phil.* 3.2.

135. K. Berding, *Polycarp and Paul: An Analysis of Their Literary and Theological Relationship in Light of Polycarp's Use of Biblical and Extra-Biblical Literature* (Leiden: Brill, 2002), 188.

have certainly included 1 Corinthians, Ephesians, and 1 and 2 Timothy, and probably also Romans, Galatians, and Philippians.[136]

In terms of the authority Polycarp attributes to these letters, we should observe not only the high regard for the apostolic office,[137] but the manner in which Polycarp often juxtaposes these "apostles" with the Old Testament "prophets" as dual authorities for the teachings of the church.[138] Moreover, in one passage Polycarp appears to refer to one of Paul's letters as Scripture: "As it is written in these Scriptures, 'Be angry and do not sin and do not let the sun go down on your anger.'"[139] While the first half could conceivably derive from Psalm 4:4, the two parts together are found in Ephesians 4:26, leading Benecke to conclude that "the collocation of the two passages is almost certainly due to Ephesians."[140] Even so, some scholars remain hesitant about Ephesians being labeled "Scripture," suggesting only the first half of the citation is Scripture,[141] or that Polycarp mistakenly thought the entire citation was from the Old Testament.[142] But there is no positive evidence for either of these suggestions.[143] The fact that this portion of Polycarp is in Latin has understandably led some to be more cautious in their conclusions, but there is nothing about the Latin text that would make us doubt the dependency on Ephesians 4:26 here.[144] If so, then it seems we do have an instance where a text from the Apostolic Fathers refers to a New Testament writing as "Scripture." Indeed, Nielsen regards this passage as evidence that by the early second century "a sacred Christian Scripture was emerging with the Pauline corpus as its foundation."[145]

In regard to other apostolic writings, 1 Peter is "almost certainly presupposed by Polycarp."[146] Most notable in this regard is Pol. *Phil.* 1.3//1 Pet 1:8, particularly the overlapping phrase χαρᾷ ἀνεκλαλήτῳ καὶ δεδοξασμένῃ, *chara aneklalētō kai dedoxasmenē* ("an inexpressible and glorious joy"). There is also an impressive overlap at Pol. *Phil.* 8.1–2//1 Pet 2:21–24, where Polycarp shows familiarity with 1 Peter's text of Isaiah 53 over and against the Septuagint's version.[147] Similarly, Polycarp contains an unmistakable echo of 1 John 4:2–3 (cf. 2 John 7): "For anyone who does not confess that Jesus Christ has come in the flesh is an antichrist."[148] Indeed, outside of the Johannine epistles, the term ἀντιχριστός, *antichristos*, is found only here in all of early Christian literature.[149] Polycarp's

136. M. W. Holmes, "Polycarp's *Letter to the Philippians* and the Writings That Later Formed the New Testament," in Gregory and Tuckett, *Reception of the New Testament in the Apostolic Fathers*, 226; Berding, *Polycarp and Paul*, 187; P. Hartog, *Polycarp and the New Testament: The Occasion, Rhetoric, Theme, and Unity of the Epistle to the Philippians and Its Allusions to New Testament Literature* (Tübingen: Mohr Siebeck, 2001), 195; P. V. M. Benecke, "The Epistle of Polycarp," in *New Testament in the Apostolic Fathers*, 84–104.

137. Pol. *Phil.* 3.2.

138. Pol. *Phil.* 6.3. See discussion in M. J. Kruger, "2 Peter 3:2, the Apostolate, and a Bi-Covenantal Canon," in *Studies on the Intersection of Text, Paratext, and Reception: A Festschrift in Honor of Charles E. Hill*, ed. G. R. Lanier and J. N. Reid (Leiden: Brill, 2021), 201–31.

139. Pol. *Phil.* 12.1. Latin: *Modo, ut his scripturis dictum est, irascimini et nolite peccare, et sol non occidat super iracundiam vestram.*

140. Benecke, "Polycarp," 93.

141. L. M. White, *From Jesus to Christianity* (San Francisco: Harper, 2004), 354.

142. Koester, *Synoptische Überlieferung*, 113.

143. The plural *scripturis* ("Scriptures") suggests that both halves of the citation were regarded as such; see Berding, *Polycarp and Paul*, 118. B. Dehandschutter, "Polycarp's Epistle to the Philippians: An Early Example of 'Reception,'" in Sevrin, *New Testament in Early Christianity*, 275–91, argues that some may be uncomfortable with this passage in Polycarp simply because of "the implications for the history of the canon" (282).

144. Holmes, "Polycarp's *Letter to the Philippians*," 210n99.

145. C. M. Nielsen, "Polycarp, Paul, and the Scriptures," *AThR* 47 (1965): 216.

146. Benecke, "Polycarp," 86.

147. Holmes, "Polycarp's *Letter to the Philippians*," 221.

148. Pol. *Phil.* 7.1. See discussion in Hill, *Johannine Corpus*, 418–19.

149. Holmes, "Polycarp's *Letter to the Philippians*," 224.

knowledge of the Johannine letters, not to mention his personal relationship with John, certainly provide good circumstantial reasons to think he would have known John's Gospel, but the evidence from his letter is inconclusive.[150]

Evidence that Polycarp knew the Synoptics is stronger, though we will consider just one example here.[151] Polycarp cites what appears to be a portion of the Lord's Prayer:

	Greek	English
Pol. *Phil.* 7.2	μὴ εἰσενεγκεῖν ἡμᾶς εἰς πειρασμόν	"to lead us not into temptation"[152]
Matt 6:13	μὴ εἰσενέγκῃς ἡμᾶς εἰς πειρασμόν	"lead us not into temptation"

Then, in the very next clause, Polycarp introduces a citation with, "just as the Lord said":

Pol. *Phil.* 7.2	καθὼς εἶπεν ὁ κύριος· Τὸ μὲν πνεῦμα πρόθυμον, ἡ δὲ σὰρξ ἀσθενής	"just as the Lord said, 'For the spirit is willing but the flesh is weak'"
Matt 26:41 (Mark 14:38)	τὸ μὲν πνεῦμα πρόθυμον ἡ δὲ σὰρξ ἀσθενής	"the spirit is indeed willing, but the flesh is weak"

Several observations are worth noting: (a) both citations are nearly an exact verbal match with Matthew; (b) in the second citation Polycarp indicates he is actually quoting Jesus; (c) only Matthew's Gospel contains both sayings (Matt 6:13 and 26:41); and (d) though the second saying is often said to be a free-floating "proverb,"[153] Polycarp clearly places it firmly in the context of the Gethsemane scene when he prefaces it with the exhortation to be "alert in prayer,"[154] a clear parallel to Jesus's "watch and pray" (Matt 26:41a). Of course, this does not prove this material could only have come from Matthew, but it is sufficient for Berding to declare it "almost certain" that Polycarp is citing Matthew here.[155] Even Koester concedes that the Synoptics are in use in this passage,[156] though other scholars remain unconvinced.[157]

3.5 Epistle of Barnabas

Written in the early second century (ca. 130 CE), the Epistle of Barnabas was a popular theological treatise that argued Christians (not Jews) were the rightful heirs of the Old Testament.[158] In terms of knowledge of New Testament writings, a number of contacts with Matthew's Gospel are worth noting.[159] Most significant is Barnabas 4.14 where the Greek overlap with Matthew 22:14 is considerable:

150. Cf. Pol. *Phil.* 5.2//John 5:21; 6:44; Pol. *Phil.* 7.1//John 8:44 (cf. 1 John 3:8).

151. See also Pol. *Phil.* 2.3a//Matt 5:7; 6:14; 7:1–2//Luke 6:37–38 (cf. 1 Clem. 13.2); Pol. *Phil.* 2.3b//Matt 5:3, 10//Luke 6:20; and Pol. *Phil.* 6.2//Matt 6:12//Luke 11:4.

152. English translation from K. Lake, *The Apostolic Fathers*, 2 vols., LCL (London: Heinemann, 1919).

153. Young, *Jesus Tradition*, 236.

154. Pol. *Phil.* 7.2.

155. Berding, *Polycarp and Paul*, 94.

156. Koester, *Synoptische Überlieferung*, 114–15.

157. Young, *Jesus Tradition*, 235.

158. For a broad overview, see J. Carleton Paget, *The Epistle of Barnabas: Outlook and Background* (Tübingen: Mohr Siebeck, 1994).

159. In addition to the examples below, see Barn. 5.12//Matt 26:31 (cf. Zech 13:7); Barn. 7.3–5//Matt 27:34, 48.

	Greek	English
Barn. 4.14	ὡς γέγραπται, πολλοὶ κλητοί, ὀλίγοι δὲ ἐκλεκτοὶ εὑρεθῶμεν	"As it is written, 'Many of us were found called, but few chosen'"
Matt 22:14	πολλοὶ γάρ εἰσιν κλητοί, ὀλίγοι δὲ ἐκλεκτοί	"For many are called, but few are chosen"

Given that Matthew 22:14 is the only known parallel to Barnabas 4.14, along with the fact that the author indicates he is citing a *written* text (ὡς γέγραπται, *hōs gegraptai*), a number of scholars have argued the source here is almost certainly Matthew.[160] This conclusion is bolstered by two additional considerations: (a) both citations share the same theological setting—namely, a polemic against Israel's unbelief;[161] and (b) Matthew 22:14 is likely an instance of Matthean redaction, showing that Barnabas knew the finished Gospel.[162]

Despite these considerations, some have insisted that the parallel can be explained in other ways. Young, for example, argues that Barnabas may actually be drawing on 4 Ezra 8.3: "Many are created but few are saved."[163] However, while such an option is certainly possible, it is difficult to see how it proves to be a *better* parallel than Matthew 22:14. Indeed, it is more likely that Matthew 22:14 is itself an extrapolation of an earlier Jewish source—whether 4 Ezra 8.3 or something else—which was later cited by Barnabas.[164] Carleton Paget suggests such resistance to Matthew as a source may be "partly motivated by a desire to avoid the implications of the *formula citandi* ['it is written'] which introduces the relevant words: namely, that the author of *Barnabas* regarded Matthew as scriptural."[165]

Another notable parallel can be found in Barnabas 5.9 where, again, the Greek is nearly identical with the version in Matthew:

	Greek	English
Barn. 5.9	ὅτι οὐκ ἦλθεν καλέσαι δικαίους, ἀλλὰ ἁμαρτωλούς	"That he came not to call the righteous but sinners"[166]
Matt 9:13	οὐ γὰρ ἦλθον καλέσαι δικαίους ἀλλ' ἁμαρτωλούς	"For I came not to call the righteous, but sinners"

Of course, this same saying can be found in Mark 2:17 and may have also been available through oral tradition. So, it is not possible to determine the source with any certainty.

160. Köhler, *Die Rezeption des Matthäusevangeliums*, 113; J. Carleton Paget, "The *Epistle of Barnabas* and the Writings That Later Formed the New Testament," in Gregory and Tuckett, *Reception of the New Testament in the Apostolic Fathers*, 232–33. J. V. Bartlet, "The Epistle of Barnabas," in *The New Testament in the Apostolic Fathers*, 1–23, argues that Barnabas and Matthew drew on a common source, largely because the saying appears as a textual variant in Matt 20:16, and consequently Bartlet regards it as having a "proverbial character" (18). However, this textual variant does not necessarily indicate a free-floating proverb but is more likely due to the scribe attempting a harmonization with Matt 22:14; see B. M. Metzger, *A Textual Commentary on the Greek New Testament*, 2nd ed. (Stuttgart: German Bible Society, 1994), 41.

161. P. F. Beatrice, "Une citation de l'Évangile de Matthieu dans l'Épître de Barnabé," in Sevrin, *New Testament in Early Christianity*, 231–45.

162. Gundry, *Matthew*, 169–70; J. Jeremias, *The Parables of Jesus* (New York: Scribner, 1955), 38; B. B. Scott, *Hear Then the Parable: A Commentary on the Parables of Jesus* (Minneapolis: Fortress, 1989), 162.

163. Young, *Jesus Tradition*, 27. See parallels in Barn. 44.15 and Plato, *Phaed.* 69c.

164. For more on this point, see D. C. Olson, "Matthew 22:1–14 as Midrash," *CBQ* 67 (2005): 435–53; and B. F. Meyer, "Many (=All) Are Called, But Few (=Not All) Are Chosen," *NTS* 36 (1990): 89–97.

165. Carleton Paget, "*Epistle of Barnabas*," 233.

166. English translation from Lake, *Apostolic Fathers*.

However, if we are correct above about the connections to Matthew in Barnabas 4.14, then we already know the author was familiar with Matthew's Gospel, making that the preferable option here.[167]

As for the Pauline letters, a number of curious connections are worth exploring. In Barnabas 13:7, our author cites Genesis 15:6 regarding Abraham's faith, but then curiously adds a description of Abraham as one who did "believe . . . while uncircumcised" (τῶν πιστευόντων δι' ἀκροβυστίας, *tōn pisteuontōn di' akrobystias*). This exact phrase appears in Romans 4:10, soon after Paul also cites Genesis 15:6 in Romans 4:3. This unusual and distinctive Pauline echo led Bartlet to suggest that Romans is the source and that it "can hardly be explained otherwise."[168] Another example can be found in Barnabas 2.6 where we learn of the "law of the Lord Jesus Christ" (νόμος τοῦ κυρίου ἡμῶν Ἰησοῦ Χριστοῦ, *nomos tou kyriou hēmōn Iēsou Christou*), a curious parallel to the Pauline expression, "law of Christ" (τὸν νόμον τοῦ Χριστοῦ, *ton nomon tou Christou*) as found in Galatians 6:2 and 1 Corinthians 9:21. But this was likely a common phrase within the early Christian movement and is not necessarily indicative that our author knew these letters. As a final example, Barnabas 6.15 describes believers as a "holy temple" (ναὸς ἅγιος, *naos hagios*), which is the "dwelling place" (κατοικητήριον, *katoikētērion*) of the Lord, an intriguing parallel to Ephesians 2:21 where believers are also called a "holy temple" (ναὸν ἅγιον) and a "dwelling place" (κατοικητήριον) for the Spirit. Indeed, in the New Testament the word κατοικητήριον occurs only in Ephesians, and in the Apostolic Fathers it occurs only in Barnabas.[169] For Bartlet, this is sufficient to conclude the author knew "the Pauline writings themselves."[170]

As for other New Testament writings, the connections are quite sparse, though Barnabas does show possible awareness of the book of Hebrews. For example, in Barnabas 5.6 we are told that Jesus suffered to "destroy death" (καταργήσῃ τὸν θάνατον, *katargēsē ton thanaton*), whereas in Hebrews 2:14 Jesus suffered that he might "destroy him who has the power of death" (καταργήσῃ τὸν τὸ κράτος ἔχοντα τοῦ θανάτου, *katargēsē ton to kratos echonta tou thanatou*). In a similar fashion, Barnabas 5.1 refers to the "blood of sprinkling" (αἵματι τοῦ ῥαντίσματος, *haimati tou rhantismatos*), while Hebrews 12:24 refers also to the "blood of sprinkling" (αἵματι ῥαντισμοῦ, *haimati rhantismou*). While these connections are curious, they are too limited to be definitive.[171] However, the two writings share a number of theological or conceptual links, largely pertaining to how the Old Testament cultic system was inadequate to provide spiritual purification.[172] Bartlet is convinced that "Hebrews influenced Barnabas' thinking and language,"[173] whereas Carleton Paget suggests the evidence only points to a "similar milieu."[174]

3.6 Second Clement

The writing known as 2 Clement appears to come from a different author than 1 Clement and is also dated considerably later, about 140–150 CE.[175] In fact, this work is

167. Massaux, *Influence of the Gospel of Saint Matthew*, 1:67.

168. Bartlet, "Epistle of Barnabas," 4.

169. Carleton Paget, "*Epistle of Barnabas*," 244n54.

170. Bartlet, "Epistle of Barnabas," 6.

171. Other connections include Barn. 6.17–19//Heb 2:5–9; Barn. 7.4//Heb 9:12, 19; 10:4.

172. For a discussion of the theological links between the two writings, see Carleton Paget, *Epistle of Barnabas*, 214–25.

173. Bartlet, "Epistle of Barnabas," 11.

174. Carleton Paget, "*Epistle of Barnabas*," 248.

175. For an overview and introduction, see P. Parvis, "*2 Clement* and the Meaning of the Christian Homily," in Foster, *Writings of the Apostolic Fathers*, 32–41.

not really a letter at all, but likely an early Christian homily. Regardless, the two writings were often linked together by early Christians and even appear together at the end of the fifth-century Codex Alexandrinus.[176]

Certain passages in 2 Clement appear to echo ideas and themes in the Pauline epistles,[177] and even in the book of Hebrews,[178] raising questions about whether the author knew these writings. This possibility finds support in the author's declaration that he is relying on two primary authorities: "the books [τὰ βιβλία, *ta biblia*] and the apostles [οἱ ἀπόστολοι, *hoi apostoloi*]."[179] Since the former is almost certainly a reference to written texts (the OT), the latter may be as well, suggesting our author may have access to written apostolic sources. However, most scholars do not regard the linguistic connections between Paul (and Hebrews) and 2 Clement to be substantial enough to say for certain that the author knew or used these writings.[180]

In contrast, there are significant connections between 2 Clement and the Synoptic Gospels, particularly Matthew and Luke. Therefore, we will devote our attention to a few key examples. We begin with 2 Clement 2.4, which cites a Jesus saying as Scripture that is nearly an exact match with Matthew 9:13 (cf. Mark 2:17):

	Greek	English
2 Clem. 2.4	καὶ ἑτέρα δὲ γραφὴ λέγει, ὅτι οὐκ ἦλθον καλέσαι δικαίους, ἀλλὰ ἁμαρτωλούς	"And another Scripture also says, 'I came not to call righteous but sinners'"[181]
Matt 9:13	οὐ γὰρ ἦλθον καλέσαι δικαίους ἀλλ' ἁμαρτωλούς	"For I came not to call the righteous, but sinners"

Given that this same phrase (in some form or another) has circulated in other early sources,[182] some have argued that 2 Clement 2.4 may be dependent merely on free-floating oral tradition.[183] However, the author's introductory phrase, "And also another Scripture says," clearly indicates a *written* source, and one that would have borne scriptural authority.[184] While this does not prove Matthew is the source (as opposed to some unknown gospel),[185] the early popularity of Matthew suggests it is the most likely candidate.[186]

There are also passages where 2 Clement appears to be familiar with redactional

176. However, Eusebius raises questions about the authenticity of 2 Clement as compared to 1 Clement (*Hist. eccl.* 3.38.4).

177. E.g., 2 Clem. 8.2//Rom 9:21; 2 Clem. 1.8//Rom 4:17; 2 Clem. 7.1//1 Cor 9:24–25; 2 Clem. 9.3//1 Cor 3:16; 6:19; 2 Clem. 2.1//Gal 4:27; 2 Clem. 14.2//Eph 1:22; 5:23.

178. E.g., 2 Clem. 11.6//Heb 10:23; 2 Clem. 1.6//Heb 12:1; 2 Clem. 16.4//Heb 13:18.

179. 2 Clem. 14.2.

180. A. F. Gregory and C. M. Tuckett, "*2 Clement* and the Writings That Later Formed the New Testament," in Gregory and Tuckett, *Reception of the New Testament in the Apostolic Fathers*, 251–92.

181. English translation from Lake, *Apostolic Fathers*.

182. E.g., Luke 5:32; Barn. 5.9 (see discussion above); Justin, *1 Apol.* 15.8.

183. K. P. Donfried, *The Setting of Second Clement in Early Christianity* (Leiden: Brill, 1974), 59–60.

184. Gregory and Tuckett, "*2 Clement*," 255. It should also be noted that both 2 Clem. 2.4 and Matt 9:13 offer this saying immediately after quoting an OT passage (Isa 54:1 and Hos 6:6, respectively).

185. Young, *Jesus Tradition*, 241–42.

186. Of course, Mark could still be a possibility, but Mark was used much less frequently in this time period than Matthew. See discussion in Koester, *Synoptische Überlieferung*, 71. Foster, "Text of the New Testament," 292, argues that Mark (not Matthew) is in view because the author uses Mark's οὐκ ἦλθον rather than Matthew's οὐ ἦλθον. Donfried, however, suggests Matthew's οὐ is merely due to his use of the connective γὰρ (*Setting of Second Clement*, 57).

portions of Matthew, making the use of Matthew's finished Gospel more certain. For instance, 2 Clement 3.2 reads: "And even he [Christ] himself also says, 'I will acknowledge before my Father the one who acknowledges me before others.'"[187] While this passage demonstrates obvious overlap with Matthew 10:32//Luke 12:8, Gregory and Tuckett observe that it is not only closer to Matthew but "agrees with Matthew at just those points where Matthew has redacted the tradition."[188] Similarly, 2 Clement 4.2 is quite similar to Matthew 7:21 (cf. Luke 6:46): "For he [Christ] says, 'Not everyone who says to me Lord, Lord, will be saved, but only the one who practices righteousness.'" It is particularly noteworthy that 2 Clement 4.2 shares the same overall structure of Matthew 7:21—the combination of "not everyone who says . . . but only the one"—which is considered by most scholars to be the result of Matthew's redaction of his Q source (now preserved in Luke 6:46).[189] Thus, again, the author seems to know the final version of Matthew's Gospel.

The author of 2 Clement also appears to demonstrate an awareness of Luke, but usually as mediated through a "harmonized" source of Jesus sayings that reflect knowledge of both Matthew and Luke's finished Gospels.[190] For example, 2 Clement 4.5 has clear links to Matthew 7:23//Luke 13:27: "Leave me! I do not know where you are from, you who do what is lawless."[191] While this passage is a mix of both Matthean and Lukan material, scholars have argued that the "where you are from" (πόθεν ἐστέ, *pothen este*) language is distinctively Luke's (cf. Luke 13:25).[192] Thus, even if the author used a harmonized sayings source, it appears to be one that itself drew on the final version of Luke's Gospel. Likewise, 2 Clement 9.11 reflects a mix of Matthew 12:50 and Luke 8:21: "For the Lord also said, 'My brothers are these who do the will of my Father.'" Second Clement includes precisely those portions where Matthew and Luke have redacted their source—namely, Mark 3:35. Thus, the "will of my Father" (τὸ θέλημα τοῦ πατρός μου, *to thelēma tou patros mou*) comes from Matthew, and the "my brothers are these" (ἀδελφοί μου οὗτοί εἰσιν, *adelphoi mou houtoi eisin*) comes from Luke. Whatever source 2 Clement is using, that source itself appears to know both Matthew and Luke's Gospel.[193]

4. CONCLUSION

The above survey has sought to answer the question of whether the Apostolic Fathers utilized New Testament writings and what that can tell us about the way these texts might

187. Ehrman's English translation switches the order of the clauses as they appear in Greek. In contrast, Lake translates the sentence: "Whosoever confessed me before men, I will confess him before my Father" (Lake, *Apostolic Fathers*, 133).

188. Gregory and Tuckett, "*2 Clement*," 258; Koester, *Ancient Christian Gospels*, 350. Young, *Jesus Tradition*, pushes back against dependence on Matthew here, arguing that Rev 3:5 "is closer to the wording of Matthew than 2 Clement," thus making it likely this saying "circulated independently" of the canonical Gospels (243). The problem, however, is that the saying in 2 Clement has two halves, and Rev 3:5 is missing the first half entirely: "the one who acknowledges me before others." Matthew and 2 Clement have both halves (plus the redactional parts of Matthew). So it is not altogether clear that Rev 3:5 is actually "closer" to 2 Clement than Matthew.

189. Davies and Allison, *Matthew*, 1:711–12; J. M. Robinson, P. Hoffmann, and J. S. Kloppenborg, eds., *The Critical Edition of Q* (Minneapolis: Fortress, 2000), 94. In contrast, Donfried argues that Matthew (not Luke) reflects the Q source (*Setting of Second Clement*, 62).

190. Koester, *Ancient Christian Gospels*, 151. As mentioned above in note 23, Justin Martyr was also known to use a harmonized source for Jesus sayings.

191. It should be noted that the portion that precedes this saying has no known source: "If you have gathered with me in my bosom and you do not do my commandments" (2 Clem. 4.5a). For this reason (among others), Gregory, *Reception of Luke and Acts*, 142, thinks it doubtful that Luke is the source.

192. Robinson, Hoffmann, and Kloppenborg, *Critical Edition of Q*, 412–13; Gregory and Tuckett, "*2 Clement*," 262.

193. Koester, *Synoptische Überlieferung*, 79; Gregory, *Reception of Luke and Acts*, 148. There are also curious parallels here to apocryphal gospels: Gos. Thom. 99 and Gos. Eb. (as cited in Epiphanius, *Pan.* 30.14).

have functioned within the early Christian movement. While citation practices in this early period were not as explicit as they would later become—and often frustratingly imprecise—we can still see the murky outlines of what would later become a full-orbed New Testament:

1. There is considerable evidence for the use of Gospel writings—most often Matthew and Luke (and possibly Mark)—in the Didache, Ignatius, Polycarp, Barnabas, and 2 Clement. While there is still ongoing scholarly disagreement about whether such citations can be explained solely by oral tradition, the regular appearance of redactional portions of Matthew and Luke, often combined with substantive textual overlap, suggests at least these finished Gospels are being used. While the evidence for John is much less clear, it does appear to be known and used by Ignatius.[194] As for the status of these Gospels, they apparently bear some level of authority as a repository for the words of Jesus. At one point, Barnabas and 2 Clement even cite a Gospel writing as Scripture.[195]
2. There is also considerable evidence of some sort of Pauline letter collection during this time period, particularly in the writings of 1 Clement, Ignatius, Polycarp, and Barnabas. As for the status of these writings, there is little doubt they functioned as an authoritative guide to the early Christian communities as demonstrated by the way these authors affirm the distinctive authority of Paul's apostolic office, with Polycarp even calling Paul's letters "Scripture."[196]
3. There are also indications that other New Testament books were being used occasionally, including 1 Peter, 1 John, and Hebrews, but the evidence for these books is much more limited.

In sum, it seems that oral tradition was not the only influence on the Apostolic Fathers. Written documents that would be part of a future New Testament were also being used, some of which were even regarded as Scripture.

BIBLIOGRAPHY

Committee of the Oxford Society of Historical Theology, ed. *The New Testament in the Apostolic Fathers.* Oxford: Clarendon, 1905.

Foster, P. "The Text of the New Testament in the Apostolic Fathers." Pages 282–301 in *The Early Text of the New Testament.* Edited by C. E. Hill and M. J. Kruger. Oxford: Oxford University Press, 2012.

Gregory, A., and C. M. Tuckett, eds. *The Reception of the New Testament in the Apostolic Fathers.* Oxford: Oxford University Press, 2005.

Gregory, A., and C. M. Tuckett, eds. *Trajectories Through the New Testament and the Apostolic Fathers.* Oxford: Oxford University Press, 2005.

Hill, C. E. "'In These Very Words': Methods and Standards of Literary Borrowing in the Second Century." Pages 261–81 in *The Early Text of the New Testament.* Edited by C. E. Hill and M. J. Kruger. Oxford: Oxford University Press, 2012.

Koester, H. *Synoptische Überlieferung bei den apostolischen Vätern.* Berlin: Akademie, 1957.

Köhler, W.-D. *Die Rezeption des Matthäusevangeliums in der Zeit vor Irenäus.* Tübingen: Mohr Siebeck, 1987.

Kruger, M. J. *The Question of Canon: Challenging the Status Quo in the New Testament Debate.* Downers Grove, IL: IVP Academic, 2013.

Massaux, É. *The Influence of the Gospel of Saint Matthew on Christian Literature Before Saint Irenaeus.* Translated by N. J. Belval and S. Hecht. 3 vols. Macon, GA: Mercer University Press, 1994.

Young, S. E. *Jesus Tradition in the Apostolic Fathers.* WUNT 2/311. Tübingen: Mohr Siebeck, 2011.

---

194. Inge, "Ignatius," 81–83.

195. Barn. 4.14; 2 Clem. 2.4.

196. Pol. *Phil.* 12.1.

BIBLIOGRAPHY

1. TEXTS AND EDITIONS OF THE APOSTOLIC FATHERS

Anger, R., and G. Dindofius, eds. *Hermae Pastor: Graece*. Leipzig: Weigel, 1856.

Bihlmeyer, K., ed. *Die apostolischen Väter: Neubearbeitung der Funkschen Ausgabe, I: Didache, Barnabas, Klemens I und II, Ignatius, Polykarp, Papias, Quadratus, Diognetbrief.* SAQ 2.1.1. Tübingen: Mohr Siebeck, 1924.

Brannan, R., ed. *The Apostolic Fathers: A New Translation*. Bellingham, WA: Lexham, 2017.

Bryennios, P. (ed.). *Διδαχὴ τῶν δώδεκα ἀποστόλων ἐκ τοῦ ἱεροσολυμιτικοῦ χειρογράφου νῦν πρῶτον ἐκδιδομένη μετὰ προλεγομένων καὶ σημειώσεων ἐν οἷς καὶ τῆς Συνόψεως τῆς Π.Δ., τῆς Ἰωανν. τοῦ Χρυσοστόμου αὐτοῦ χειρογράφου.* Constantinople: Voutyra, 1883.

Carlson, S. C., ed. *Papias of Hierapolis Exposition of Dominical Oracles: The Fragments, Testimonia, and Reception of a Second-Century Commentator*. OECT. Oxford: Oxford University Press, 2021.

Cotelier, J.-B. *SS. Patrum qui temporibus apostolicis floruerunt; Barnabae, Clementis, Hermae, Ignatii, Polycarpi; Opera, edita et inedita, vera et suppositicia. Una cum Clementis, Ignatii, Polycarpi Actis atque Martyriis*. Paris: Petri le Petit, 1672.

d'Étaples, J. L., ed. *Theologia vivificans, Dionysii coelestis hierarchia, Ss. Ignatii XV epistolae, Polycarpi epistolai.* Paris, 1498.

Ehrman, B. D., ed. *The Apostolic Fathers*. 2 vols. LCL. Cambridge: Harvard University Press, 2003.

Frey, J. L. *Epistolae Sanctorum Patrum Apostolicorum Clementis, Ignatii et Polycarpi atque Duorum Posteriorum Martyria: Omnia Graece et Latine cum Variorum Annotationibus et Praefatione*. Basel: J. K. von Mechel Witwe, 1742.

Frid, H., ed. *Του μακαριου ιερομαρτυρος Ιγνατιου, Beati Ignatii opuscula omnia*. Dilligen: Sebaldus Mair, 1557.

Funk, F. X., ed. *Die apostolischen Väter*. SAQ 2.1. Tübingen: Mohr Siebeck, 1901.

Gebhardt, O. von, A. von Harnack, and T. Zahn, eds. *Patrum Apostolicorum Opera: Textum ad fidem codicum Graecorum et Latinorum adhibitis praestantissimus editionibus*. 3 vols. Leipzig, 1875–1877.

Halloix, P., ed. *Illustrium ecclesiae orientalis scriptorum vitae et documenta*. Douai: Bogard, 1633.

Harris, J. R., ed. *The Teaching of the Apostles: Newly Edited with a Facsimile Text and a Commentary*. Baltimore: Johns Hopkins University, 1887.

Hefele, C. J., ed. Patrum Apostolicorum Opera: Textum ex Editionibus Praestantissimus Repetitum Recognovit, Annotationibus Illustravit, Versionem Latinam Emendatiorem, Prolegomena et Indices. Tübingen: Henrici Laupp, 1839.

Hitchcock, R. D., and F. Brown, eds. *Teaching of the Twelve Apostles: Recently Discovered and Published by Philotheos Bryennios, Metropolitan of Nicomedia*. New York: Scribner, 1884.

Holmes, M. W., ed. *The Apostolic Fathers: Greek Texts and English Translations*. 3rd ed. Grand Rapids: Baker Academic, 2007.

Ittig, T., ed. *Bibliotheca Patrum Apostolicorum Græco-Latina, Qua Continentur I. S. Clementis Romani Prior & Posterior ad Corinthios Epistola, II. S. Ignatii Epistolæ Septem Genuinæ, Qvibus ejusdem Interpolatæ & Spuriæ Epistolæ, Nec Non Acta Ignatiani Martyrii Accedunt, III. S. Polycarpi Epistola ad Philippenses, Cui Præter Fragmenta Polycarpi Ecclesiæ Smyrnensis de Polycarpi Martyrio Epistola Integra Adjungitur Præmissa Est Dissertatio de Patribus Apostolicis, Seu Scriptoribus Ecclesiasticis, Qvi Apostolorum Comites & Discipuli Fuisse Perhibentur*. Leipzig: Lipsiae Lanckisch Lipsiae Richter, 1699;

Lake, K., ed. *The Apostolic Fathers*. 2 vols. LCL. Cambridge: Harvard University Press, 1912, 1913.

Lightfoot, J. B., ed. *The Apostolic Fathers: Clement, Ignatius, and Polycarp: Revised Texts with Introductions, Notes, Dissertations, and Translations*. 2nd ed. 2 vols. in 5 parts. London: Macmillan, 1889–1891.

Lightfoot, J. B., ed. *The Apostolic Fathers: Revised Texts with Short Introductions and English Translations*. Edited and completed by J. R. Harmer. London: Macmillan, 1891.

Lindemann, A., and H. Paulsen, eds. *Die apostolischen Väter: Griechisch-deutsche Parallelausgabe*. Tübingen: Mohr Siebeck, 1992.

Russel, R., ed. *SS. Patrum Apostolicorum Barnabae: Hermae, Clementis, Ignatii, Polycarpi, Opera Genuina; Una cum Ignatii & Polycarpi Martyriis: Versionibus Antiquis ac Recentioribus, Variantibus Lectionibus, Selectisque Variorum Notis Illustrata: Accesserunt S. Ignatii Epistolae, tum Interpolatae, tum Supposititiae, I–II*. London: Apud Gulielmum Russel, sub Horatii Capite, extra Portam Temple-Bar, 1746.

Ussher, J., ed. *Polycarpi et Ignatii Epistolae*. Oxford: Leonardus Lichfield Academiae Typographus, and Henry Hall, 1644.

Varner, W. C. *The Apostolic Fathers: Introduction and Translation*. London: T&T Clark, 2023.

Voss, I., ed. *Epistolæ Genuinæ s. Ignatii, ex Bibl. Florentina. Adduntur s. Ignatii Epistolæ, Quales Vulgo Circumferuntur. Adhæc s. Barnabæ Epistola*. Amsterdam: Ioannem Blaev, 1646.

Wake, W., ed. *The Genuine Epistles of the Apostolical Fathers; St. Clement, St. Polycarp, St. Ignatius, St. Barnabas, the Pastor of Hermas; and an Account of the Martyrdoms of St. Ignatius and St. Polycarp Written by Those Who Were Present at Their Sufferings: Being, Together with the Holy Scriptures of the New Testament, A Complete Collection of the Most Primitive Antiquity, for About a Hundred and Fifty Years After Christ*. London, 1693.

Whittaker, M., ed. *Die Hirt des Hermas*. 2nd ed. Die grieschische christliche Schriftsteller 48. Berlin: Akademie, 1967.

Young, P., ed. *Clementis ad Corinthios Epistola Prior*. Oxford: Iohannes Lichfield, 1633.

Young, P., ed. *Clementis ad Corinthios Epistola Prior*. 2nd ed. Oxford: Iohannes Lichfield, 1637.

2. SCHOLARLY STUDIES AND ARTICLES

Albl, M. C. *And Scripture Cannot Be Broken: The Form and Function of the Early Christian Testimonia Collections*. Leiden: Brill, 1999.

Andriessen, P. "The Authorship of the *Epistula ad Diognetum*." *VC* 1 (1947): 129–36.

Arnold, B. J. *Justification in the Second Century*. Waco, TX: Baylor University Press, 2018.

Ayali-Darshan, N. "The Origin and Meaning of the Crimson Thread in the Mishnaic Scapegoat Ritual in Light of an Ancient Syro-Anatolian Custom." *JSJ* 44 (2013): 530–52.

Back, S.-O. "The Eucharist and the Letters of Ignatius of Antioch." Pages 113–28 in *Institutions in the Emerging Church*. Edited by S.-O. Back and E. Koskenniemi. London: Bloomsbury T&T Clark, 2016.

Backhaus, K., "Das Bundesmotiv in der frühkirchlichen Schwellenzeit: Hebräerbrief, Barnabasbrief, Dialogus cum Tryphone." Page 155–73 in *Der sprechende Gott: Gesammelte Studien zum Hebräerbrief*. Edited by K. Backhaus. WUNT 240. Tübingen: Mohr Siebeck, 2009.

Backhouse, J. H. *The Editio Princeps of the Epistle of Barnabas by Archbishop Ussher, as Printed at Oxford A.D. 1642, and Preserved in an Imperfect Form in the Bodleian Library*. Oxford: Clarendon, 1883.

Bagnall, R. S. *Early Christian Books in Egypt*. Princeton: Princeton University Press, 2009.

Bakke, O. M. *"Concord and Peace": A Rhetorical Analysis of the Language of the First Letter of Clement with an Emphasis on the Language of Unity and Sedition*. WUNT 2/143. Tübingen: Mohr Siebeck, 2001.

Balabanski, V. *Eschatology in the Making: Mark, Matthew, and the Didache*. SNTSMS 97. Cambridge: Cambridge University Press, 1997.

Balch, D. L. "Greek Tragedy, Pompeian Amphitheater Art, and Christian Martyrs in Nero's Gardens (1 Clem. 6.2 and Tacitus, *Ann.* 15.44)" Pages 225–255 in *The Social Worlds of Ancient Jews and Christians: Essays in Honor of L. Michael White*. Edited by J. Gunderson, G. A. Keddie, and D. Boin. NovTSup 189. Leiden: Brill, 2022.

Balch, D. L. "Violence in Pompeian/Roman Domestic Art as a Visual Context for the Pauline and Deutero-Pauline Letters." Pages 123–65 in *Early Christianity in Pompeian Light: People, Texts, Situations*. Edited by B. Longenecker. Minneapolis: Fortress, 2016.

Barclay, J. M. G. *Paul and the Gift*. Grand Rapids: Eerdmans, 2015.

Barnard, L. W. "The Background of St. Ignatius of Antioch." *VC* 17 (1963): 193–206.

Barnard, L. W. "The Enigma of the Epistle to Diognetus." Pages 165–71 in *Studies in the Apostolic Fathers and Their Backgrounds*. By L. W. Bernard. Oxford: Oxford University Press, 1966.

Barnes, T. D. "The Date of Ignatius." *ExpTim* 120 (2008): 119–30.

Barrett, C. K. "Jews and Judaizers in the Epistles of Ignatius." Pages 220–44 in *Jews, Greeks and Christians: Religious Cultures in Late Antiquity: Essays in Honor of William David Davies*. Edited by R. Hamerton-Kelly and R. Scroggs. Studies in Judaism in Late Antiquity 21. Leiden: Brill, 1976.

Bartlet, V. "Papias's 'Exposition': Its Date and Contents." Pages 15–44 in *Amicitiae Corolla: A Volume of Essays Presented to James Rendel Harris, D.Litt. on the Occasion of His Eightieth Birthday*. Edited by H. G. Wood. London: University of London Press, 1933.

Bartsch, H.-W. *Gnostisches Gut und Gemeindetradition bei Ignatius von Antiochien*. BFCT 2.44. Gütersloh: Bertelsmann, 1940.

Batovici, D. "Apostolic by Proxy: Corpora, *editiones minores*, and Networks of Texts." *Ephemerides Theologicae Lovanienses* 98 (2022): 503–24.

Batovici, D. "Contrasting Ecclesiastical Functions in the Second Century: 'Diakonia,' 'Diakonoi,' 'Episkopoi,' and 'Presbyteroi' in the *Shepherd of Hermas* and Ignatius of Antioch's *Letters*." *Augustinianum* 51 (2011): 303–14.

Batovici, D. "Four New Syriac Witnesses to the Middle Recension of the Ignatian Corpus." Pages 122–37 in *Caught in Translation: Studies on Versions of Late-Antique Christian Literature*. Edited by M. Toca and D. Batovici. Texts and Studies in Eastern Christianity 17. Leiden: Brill, 2020.

Batovici, D., and J. Verheyden. "Digitizing the Ancient Versions of the Apostolic Fathers: Preliminary Considerations." Pages 103–23 in *Digital Humanities and Christianity: An Introduction*. Edited by T. Hutchings and C. Clivaz. Introductions to Digital Humanities—Religion 4. Berlin: de Gruyter, 2021.

Bauckham, R. B. "Did Papias Write History or Exegesis?" *JTS* 65 (2014): 463–88. Republished on pages 143–64 in *The Christian World Around the New Testament*. Grand Rapids: Baker Academic, 2017.

Bauckham, R. B. "Papias on the Eyewitnesses." Pages 12–38 in *Jesus and the Eyewitnesses: The Gospels as Eyewitness Testimony*. 2nd ed. Grand Rapids: Eerdmans, 2017.

Bauckham, R. B. "Sabbath and Sunday in the Post-Apostolic Church." Pages 251–98 in *From Sabbath to Lord's Day: A Biblical, Historical, and Theological Investigation*. Edited by D. A. Carson. Grand Rapids: Zondervan, 1982.

Bauer, J. B. *Die Polykarpbriefe*. KAV 5. Göttingen: Vandenhoeck & Ruprecht, 1995.

Bauer, T. J. "Ignatios—alter Paulus? Die Präskripte und Postskripte des Ignatianen." Pages 93–129 in *Die Briefe des Ignatius von Antiochien: Motive, Strategien, und Kontexte*. Edited by T. J. Bauer and P. von Möllendorff. Berlin: de Gruyter, 2018.

Bauer, T. J. "Ignatius von Antiochia und Polykarp von Smyrna: Aporien bei der Analyse und Interpretation frühchristlicher Briefe." *Cristianesimo nella storia* 42 (2021): 357–96.

Bauer, T. J. "'Von Syrien bis Rom kämpfe ich mit wilden Tieren . . .' (IgnRom 5,1): Die ignatianischen Briefe als literarische Fiktion aufs Neue verteidigt." Pages 169–98 in *Epistolary Fiction in Ancient Greek Literature*. Edited by É. Marquis. Philologus: Supplementary Volumes 19. Berlin: de Gruyter, 2023.

Bauer, W. *Die Briefe des Ignatius von Antiochia und der Brief des Polykarp von Smyrna*. HNT Ergänzungsband, Die Apostolischen Väter 2. Tubingen: Möhr Siebeck, 1920.

Baumeister, T. *Die Anfänge der Theologie des Martyriums*. MBT 45. Münster: Aschendorff, 1980.

Baur, F. C. *The Church History of the First Three Centuries*. Translated by A. Menzies. 3rd ed. 2 vols. Theological Translation Fund Library. London: Williams and Norgate, 1878–1879.

Beare, F. W. *A Commentary on the Epistle to the Philippians*. BNTC. London: A&C Black, 1959.

Beatrice, P. F. "Une citation de l'Évangile de Matthieu dans l'Épître de Barnabé." Pages 231–45 in *The New Testament in Early Christianity = La réception des écrits néotestamentaires dans le christianisme primitive*. Edited by J.-M. Sevrin. BETL 86. Leuven: Leuven University Press, 1989.

Becker A. H., and A. Y. Reed. *The Ways That Never Parted: Jews and Christians in Late Antiquity and the Early Middle Ages*. Tübingen: Mohr Siebeck, 2003.

Bellinzoni, A. J. *The Sayings of Jesus in the Writings of Justin Martyr*. Leiden: Brill, 1967.

Ben Ezra, D. S. "Fasting with Jews, Thinking with Scapegoats: Some Remarks on Yom Kippur in Early Judaism and Christianity, in Particular 4Q541, *Barnabas* 7, Matthew 27 and Acts 27." Pages 165–87 in *The Day of Atonement: Its Interpretations in Early Jewish and Christian Traditions*. Edited by T. Hieke and T. Nicklas. Themes in Biblical Narrative 15. Leiden: Brill, 2012.

Berding, K. *Polycarp and Paul: An Analysis of Their Literary and Theological Relationship in Light of Polycarp's Use of Biblical and Extrabiblical Literature*. VCSup 62. Leiden: Brill, 2002.

Berglund, C. J. *Origen's References to Heracleon: A Quotation-Analytical Study of the Earliest Known Commentary on John*. WUNT 450. Tübingen: Mohr Siebeck, 2020.

Bergmeier, R. "Zeugnis und Martyrium." Pages 619–47 in *Die Johannesapokalypse: Kontexte—Konzepte—Rezeption*. Edited by J. Frey, J. A. Kelhoffer, and F. Tóth. Tübingen: Mohr Siebeck, 2012.

Betz, H. D. *The Greek Magical Papyri in Translation: Including the Demotic Spells*. Chicago: University of Chicago Press, 1986.

Bingham, D. J. "Senses of Scripture in the Second Century: Irenaeus, Scripture, and Noncanonical Christian Texts." *JR* 97 (2017): 26–55.

Bingham, D. J., ed. *The Routledge Companion to Early Christian Thought*. London: Routledge 2010.

Bigg, C. *A Critical and Exegetical Commentary on the Epistles of St. Peter and St. Jude*. ICC. Edinburgh: T&T Clark, 1901.

Bird, M. F. *The Gospel of the Lord: How the Early Church Wrote the Story of Jesus*. Grand Rapids: Eerdmans, 2014.

Bird, M. F. "The Reception of Paul in the *Epistle to Diognetus*." Pages 70–90 in *Paul in the Second Century*. Edited by M. F. Bird and J. R. Dodson. LNTS 412. London: T&T Clark, 2011.

Bird, M. F., and K. MacKerras. "The Epistle to Diognetus and the Fragment of Quadratus." Pages 39–331 in *The Cambridge Companion to the Apostolic Fathers*. Edited by M. Bird and S. Harrower. Cambridge: Cambridge University Press, 2021.

Blomkvist, V. "The Teaching on Baptism in the Shepherd of Hermas." Pages 849–70 in vol. 2 of *Ablution, Initiation, and Baptism: Late Antiquity, Early Judaism, and Early Christianity = Waschungen, Initiation und Taufe: Spätantike, Frühes Judentum und Frühes Christentum*. Edited by D. Hellholm, T. Vegge, Ø. Norderval, and C. Hellholm. 3 vols. BZNW 176.1–3. Berlin: de Gruyter, 2011.

Blondell, R., and K. Ormand, eds. *Ancient Sex: New Essays*. Columbus: Ohio State University Press, 2015.

Bockmuehl, M. *Jewish Law in Gentiles Churches: Halakhah and the Beginning of Christian Public Ethics*. Edinburgh: T&T Clark, 2000.

Bockmuehl, M. "New Testament *Wirkungsgeschichte* and the Early Christian Appeal to Living Memory." Pages 341–68 in *Memory in the Bible and Antiquity*. Edited by S. C. Barton, L. T. Stuckenbruck, and B. G. Wold. WUNT 212. Tübingen: Mohr Siebeck, 2007.

Boer, E. A. de. "Tertullian on 'Barnabas' Letter to the Hebrews' in De pudicitia 20.1–5." *VC* 68 (2014): 243–63.

Bolhuis, A. "Die Acta Romana des Martyriums des Ignatius Antiochenus." *VC* 7 (1953): 143–53.

Boswell, J. *The Kindness of Strangers: The Abandonment of Children in Western Europe from Late Antiquity to the Renaissance*. New York: Pantheon, 1988.

Bovon-Thurneysen, A. "Ethik und Eschatologie im Philipperbrief des Polykarp von Smyrna." *TZ* 29 (1973): 241–56.

Bowe, B. E. *A Church in Crisis: Ecclesiology and Paranesis in Clement of Rome*. Minneapolis: Fortress, 1988.

Bower, R. A. "The Meaning of ΕΠΙΤΥΓΧΑΝΩ in the Epistles of St. Ignatius of Antioch." *VC* 28 (1974): 1–14.

Bowersock, G. W. *Martyrdom and Rome*. Cambridge: Cambridge University Press, 1995.

Boyarin, D. *Dying for God: Martyrdom and the Making of Christianity and Judaism*. Figurae: Reading Medieval Culture. Stanford: Stanford University Press, 1999.

Brändle, R. "*Ad Diognetum*: Eine Wiederaufnahme paulinischer und johanneischer Theologie am Ausgang des zweiten Jahrhunderts." Pages 40–52 in *A Diognète*. Edited by G. Aragione, E. Norelli, and F. G. Nuvolone. CahGSEP 1. Prahins: Éditions du Zèbre, 2012.

Bremmer, J. N. "*Ioudaismos, Christianismos* and the Parting of the Ways." Pages 57–88 in *Jews and Christians—The Parting of the Ways in the First Two Centuries CE? Reflections on the Gains and Losses of a Model*. Edited by J. Schröter, B. A. Edsall, and J. Verheyden. BZNW 253. Berlin: de Gruyter, 2021.

Bremmer, J. N. "The Place, Date and Author of the *Ignatian Letters*: An Onomastic Approach." Pages 405–33 in *Die Datierung neutestamentlicher Pseudepigraphen: Herausforderungen und neuere Lösungsansätze*. Edited by W. Grünstäudl and K. M. Schmidt. WUNT 470. Tübingen: Mohr Siebeck, 2021.

Brennecke, H. C. "*Die recensio longior* des Corpus Ignatianum." Pages 249–69 in *Die Briefe des Ignatius von Antiochien: Motive, Strategien, und Kontexte*. Edited by T. J. Bauer and P. von Möllendorff. Mil-S 72. Berlin: de Gruyter, 2018.

Brent, A. "Can There Be Degrees of Docetism?" Pages 5–26 in *Docetism in the Early Church: The Quest for an Elusive Phenomenon*. Edited by J. Verheyden, R. Bieringer, J. Schröter, and I. Jäger. WUNT 402. Tübingen: Mohr Siebeck, 2018.

Brent, A. *Cultural Episcopacy and Ecumenism: Representative Ministry in Church History from the Age of Ignatius of Antioch to the Reformation with Special Reference to Contemporary Ecumenism*. Studies in Mission 6. Leiden: Brill, 1992.

Brent, A. "The Enigma of Ignatius of Antioch." *JEH* 57 (2006): 429–56.

Brent, A. "History and Eschatological Mysticism in Ignatius of Antioch." *ETL* 65 (1989): 309–29.

Brent, A. "The Ignatian Epistles and the Threefold Ecclesiastical Order." *JRH* 17 (1992): 18–32.

Brent, A. "Ignatius and Polycarp: The Transformation of New Testament Traditions in the Context of Mystery Cults." Pages 325–49 in *Trajectories Through the New Testament and the Apostolic Fathers*. Edited by A. F. Gregory and C. M. Tuckett. Oxford: Oxford University Press, 2005.

Brent, A. *Ignatius of Antioch: A Martyr Bishop and the Origin of Episcopacy*. London: T&T Clark, 2007.

Brent, A. "Ignatius of Antioch and the Imperial Cult." *VC* 52 (1998): 30–58.

Brent, A. *Ignatius of Antioch and the Second Sophistic: A Study of Early Christian Transformation of Pagan Culture*. Studies and Texts in Antiquity and Christianity 36. Tübingen: Mohr Siebeck, 2006.

Brent, A. "Ignatius of Antioch in Second Century, Asia Minor." Pages 62–86 in *Intertextuality in the Second Century*. Edited by D. J. Bingham and C. N. Jefford. The Bible in Ancient Christianity 11. Leiden: Brill, 2016.

Brent, A. "Ignatius' Pagan Background in Second Century Asia Minor." *ZAC* 10 (2006): 207–32.

Breytenbach, C., and L. Welborn, eds. *Encounters with Hellenism: Studies on the First Letter of Clement*. AGJU 53. Leiden: Brill, 2003.

Brooks, J. A. "Clement of Alexandria as a Witness to the Development of the Canon." *SecCent* 9 (1992): 41–55.

Brown, C. T. *The Gospel and Ignatius of Antioch*. StBibLit 12. New York: Lang, 2000.

Brown, M. P. *The Authentic Writings of Ignatius: A Study of Linguistic Criteria*. Duke Studies in Religion 2. Durham: Duke University Press, 1963.

Brox, N. *Der Hirt des Hermas*. KAV 7. Göttingen: Vandenhoeck & Ruprecht, 1991.

Brox, N. "Pseudo-Paulus und Pseudo-Ignatius: Einige Topoi altchristlicher Pseudepigraphie." *VC* 30 (1976): 181–88.

Brox, N. *Zeuge und Märtyrer: Untersuchungen zur frühchristlichen Zeugnis-Terminologie*. SANT 5. Münich: Kösel, 1961.

Bruce, F. F. "St. John at Ephesus." *BJRL* 60 (1978): 339–61.

Buck, P. L. "Justin Martyr's Apologies: Their Number, Destination and Form." *JTS* 54 (2003): 45–59.

Buck, P. L. "Voluntary Martyrdom Revisited." *JTS* 63 (2012): 125–35.

Bucur, B. G. "The Son of God and the Angelomorphic Holy Spirit: A Rereading of the Shepherd's Christology." *ZNW* 98 (2007): 120–42.

Buell, D. K. *Why This New Race? Ethnic Reasoning in Early Christianity*. New York: Columbia University Press, 2005.
Bultmann, R. "Ignatius and Paul." Pages 267–77 in *Existence and Faith: Shorter Writings of Rudolf Bultmann*. Edited by S. M. Ogden. New York: Meridian, 1960.
Burgess, R. "The Dates and Editions of Eusebius' *Chronici Canones* and *Historia Ecclesiastica*." *JTS* 48.2 (1997): 471–504.
Burke, J. "Satan and Demons in the Apostolic Fathers: A Minority Report." *SEÅ* 81 (2016): 127–68.
Buschmann, G. *Das Martyrium des Polykarp*. KAV 6. Göttingen: Vandenhoeck & Ruprecht, 1998.
Byers, A. J. "Johannine Bishops? The Fourth Evangelist, John the Elder, and the Episcopal Ecclesiology of Ignatius of Antioch." *NovT* 60 (2018): 121–39.
Byrskog, S. *Story as History—History as Story: The Gospel Tradition in the Context of Ancient Oral History*. Leiden: Brill, 2002.
Callon, C. "A Re-Examination of Ignatius' Use of the Term 'Leopards.'" *JTS* 66 (2015): 585–95.
Camelot, P.-T. *Ignace d'Antioche–Polycarpe de Smyrne: Lettres. Martyre de Polycarpe*. 2nd ed. SC 10 bis. Paris: Éditions du Cerf, 1998.
Cameron, A. *The Last Pagans of Rome*. Oxford: Oxford University Press, 2011.
Campenhausen, H. F. von. *Bearbeitungen und Interpolationen des Polykarpmartyriums*. SHAW. Heidelberg: Winter, 1957.
Carleton Paget, J. "Barnabas 9:4: A Peculiar Verse on Circumcision." *VC* 45 (1991): 242–54.
Carleton Paget, J. "Barnabas and the Outsiders: Jews and Their World in the *Epistle of Barnabas*." Pages 177–202 in *Early Christian Communities Between Ideal and Reality*. Edited by M. Grundeken and J. Verheyden. WUNT 342. Tübingen: Mohr Siebeck, 2015.
Carleton Paget, J. *The Epistle of Barnabas: Outlook and Background*. WUNT 2/64. Tübingen: Mohr Siebeck, 1994.
Carleton Paget, J. "The *Epistle of Barnabas* and the Writings That Later Formed the New Testament." Pages 229–49 in *The Reception of the New Testament in the Apostolic Fathers*. Edited by A. F. Gregory and C. M. Tuckett. Oxford: Oxford University Press, 2005.
Carleton Paget, J. "The Epistle of Barnabas, Jews and Christians." Pages 217–47 in *Jews and Christians—Parting Ways in the First Two Centuries CE? Reflections on the Gains and Losses of a Model*. Edited by J. Schröter, B. Edsall, and J. Verheyden. BZNW 253. Berlin: de Gruyter, 2021.
Carleton Paget, J. "Paul and the *Epistle of Barnabas*." Pages 79–100 in *The Apostolic Fathers and Paul*. Edited by T. D. Still and D. E. Wilhite. Pauline and Patristic Scholars in Debate 2. London: Bloomsbury T&T Clark, 2017.
Carlini, A. "Amicus Plato . . .: A proposito di PSI XI 1200, Gorg. 447B ss." Pages 41–45 in *Miscellanea Papyrologica*. Edited by R. Pintaudi. Florence: Edizioni Gonnelli, 1980.
Carriker, A. J. *The Library of Eusebius of Caesarea*. VCSup 67. Leiden: Brill, 2003.
Carson, D. A., ed. *From Sabbath to Lord's Day: A Biblical, Historical and Theological Investigation*. Grand Rapids: Zondervan, 1982.
Castelli, E. A. *Martyrdom and Memory: Early Christian Culture Making*. GTR. New York: Columbia University Press, 2004.
Chadwick, H. "The Silence of Bishops in Ignatius." *HTR* 43 (1950): 169–72.
Chester, A. "The Parting of the Ways: Eschatology and Messianic Hope." Pages 239–313 in *Jews and Christians: The Parting of the Ways A.D. 70–135*. Edited by J. D. G. Dunn. WUNT 66. Tübingen: Mohr Siebeck, 1992.
Clancy, F. G. "Imitating the Mysteries That You Celebrate: Martyrdom and Eucharist in the Early Patristic Period." Pages 106–40 in *The Great Persecution*. Edited by V. Twomey and M. Humphries. Dublin: Four Courts, 2009.
Clarke, J. R. *Looking at Lovemaking: Constructions of Sexuality in Roman Art, 100 BC–AD 250*. Berkeley: University of California Press, 1998.
Cobb, L. S. "Martyrdom in Roman Context." Pages 92–95 in *The Wiley Blackwell Companion to Christian Martyrdom*. Edited by P. Middleton. WBCR. Chichester: Wiley Blackwell, 2020.
Cobb, L. S. "Neither 'Pure Evangelical Manna' nor 'Tainted Scraps': Reflections on the Study of Pseudo-Ignatius." Pages 181–202 in *The Apostolic Fathers and Paul*. Edited by T. D. Still and D. E. Wilhite. Pauline and Patristic Scholars in Debate 2. London: Bloomsbury T&T Clark, 2017.
Cobb, L. S. "Polycarp's Cup: *Imitatio* in the *Martyrdom of Polycarp*." *JRH* 38 (2013): 224–40.
Cohen, S. J. D. "Dancing, Clapping, Meditating: Jewish and Christian Observance of the Sabbath in Pseudo-Ignatius." Pages 29–53 in *Judaea-Palaestina, Babylon and Rome: Jews in Antiquity*. Edited by B. Isaac and Y. Shahar. TSAJ 147. Tübingen: Mohr Siebeck, 2012.
Cohen, S. J. D. "Judaism Without Circumcision and 'Judaism' Without 'Circumcision' in Ignatius." *HTR* 95 (2002): 395–415.
Coleman, E. M. "Fatal Charades: Roman Executions Staged as Mythological Enactments." *JRS* 80 (1990): 44–73.

Corke-Webster, J. *Eusebius and Empire: Constructing Church and Rome in the Ecclesiastical History*. Cambridge: Cambridge University Press, 2019.

Corwin, V. *St. Ignatius and Christianity in Antioch*. New Haven: Yale University Press, 1960.

Cotterill, J. M. "The Epistle of Polycarp to the Philippians and the Homilies of Antiochus Palaestinensis." *Journal of Philology* 19 (1891): 241–85.

Cribiore, R. *Gymnastics of the Mind: Greek Education in Hellenistic and Roman Egypt*. Princeton: Princeton University Press, 2001.

Crowe, B. D. "Oh Sweet Exchange! The Soteriological Significance of the Incarnation in the Epistle to Diognetus." *ZNW* 102 (2011): 96–109.

Cullmann, O. *The Christology of the New Testament*. London: SCM, 1959.

Cureton, W. *The Ancient Syriac Version of the Epistles of Saint Ignatius to St. Polycarp, the Ephesians, and the Romans*. London: Rivingtons, 1845.

Cureton, W. *Corpus Ignatianum: A Complete Collection of the Ignatian Epistles, Genuine, Interpolated, and Spurious*. London: Rivingtons, 1849.

Cureton, W. *Vindiciae Ignatianae, or The Genuine Writings of St. Ignatius as Exhibited in the Antient Syriac Version, Vindicated from the Charge of Heresy*. London: Rivingtons, 1846.

Daley, B. E. *The Hope of the Early Church*. Cambridge: Cambridge University Press, 1991.

Daniélou, J. *From Shadows to Reality, or Sacramentum Futuri: Studies in the Biblical Typology of the Fathers*. London: Burns & Oates, 1960.

Daube, D. "Τρία μυστήρια κραυγῆς: Ignatius, *Ephesians*, XIX, 1." *JTS* 16 (1965): 128–29.

Davies, S. L. "The Predicament of Ignatius of Antioch." *VC* 30 (1976): 175–80.

Dehandschutter, B. "L'authenticité des épîtres d'Ignace d'Antioche." StPatr 18 (1989): 103–10.

Dehandschutter, B. "The Epistle of Polycarp." Pages 117–33 in *The Apostolic Fathers: An Introduction*. Edited by W. Pratscher. Waco, TX: Baylor University Press, 2010.

Dehandschutter, B. "Leben und/oder Sterben für Gott bei Ignatius und Polykarp." Pages 191–202 in *Martyriumsvorstellungen in Antike und Mittelalter: Leben oder sterben für Gott?* Edited by S. Fuhrmann and R. Grundmann. AJEC 80. Leiden: Brill, 2012.

Dehandschutter, B. *Polycarpiana: Studies on Martyrdom and Persecution in Early Christianity: Collected Essays*. Edited by J. Leemans. BETL 205. Leuven: Peeters, 2007.

Dehandschutter, B. "Some Notes on 1 Clement 5,4–7." Pages 85–86 in *Fructus centesimus*. Edited by A. A. R. Bastiaensen, A. Hilhorst, and C. H. Kneepkens. InstPatr 19. Dordrecht: Kluwer, 1989.

De Quehen, H. "Politics and Scholarship in the Ignatian Controversy." *Seventeenth Century* 13 (1998): 69–84.

Del Verme, M. *Didache and Judaism: Jewish Roots of an Ancient Christian-Jewish Work*. London: T&T Clark, 2004.

Dickey, E. *Learning Latin the Ancient Way: Latin Textbooks from the Ancient World*. Cambridge: Cambridge University Press, 2016.

Dibelius, M. *Der Hirt des Hermas*. HNT Ergänzungsband, Die Apostolischen Väter 4. Tubingen: Möhr Siebeck, 1923.

Dillon, J. M. *The Middle Platonists: A Study of Platonism, 80 B.C. to A.D. 220*. Rev. ed. London: Duckworth, 1996.

Doherty, B. "Competing for the Crown: Tertullian, Montanism and 'Voluntary Martyrdom' Revisited." *Phronema* 36 (2021): 1–32.

Donfried, K. P. *The Setting of Second Clement in Early Christianity*. NovTSup 38. Leiden: Brill, 1974.

Donfried, K. P. "The Theology of Second Clement." *HTR* 66 (1973): 487–501.

Downs, D. J. *Alms: Charity, Reward, and Atonement in Early Christianity*. Waco, TX: Baylor University Press, 2016.

Downs, D. J. "Almsgiving and Competing Soteriologies in Second-Century Christianity." *Religions* 9 (2018): 201–13.

Downs, D. J. "The Pauline Concept of Union with Christ in Ignatius of Antioch." Pages 143–61 in *The Apostolic Fathers and Paul*. Edited by T. D. Still and D. E. Wilhite. Pauline and Patristic Scholars in Debate 2. London: Bloomsbury T&T Clark, 2017.

Drake, H. A. *A Century of Miracles: Christians, Pagans, Jews and the Supernatural, 312–410*. Oxford: Oxford University Press, 2017.

Draper, J. A. "A Continuing Enigma: The 'Yoke of the Lord' in Didache 6.2–3 and Early Jewish-Christian Relations." Pages 106–23 in *The Image of the Judaeo-Christians in Ancient Jewish and Christian Literature*. Edited by P. J. Tomson and D. Lambers-Petry. WUNT 158. Tübingen: Mohr Siebeck, 2003.

Draper, J. A. "The Didache." Pages 7–26 in *The Apostolic Fathers: An Introduction*. Edited by W. Pratscher. Waco, TX: Baylor University Press, 2010.

Draper, J. A. "The *Didache*." Pages 13–20 in *The Writings of the Apostolic Fathers*. Edited by P. Foster. London: T&T Clark, 2007.

Draper, J. A. "Eschatology in the Didache." Pages 567–82 in *Eschatology of the New Testament and Some Related Documents*. Edited by J. G. van der Watt. WUNT 2/315. Tübingen: Mohr Siebeck, 2011.

Draper, J. A. "The Jesus Tradition in the Didache." Pages 269–87 in *The Jesus Tradition Outside the Gospels*. Edited by D. Wenham. Sheffield: JSOT Press, 1984.

Draper, J. A., ed. *The Didache in Modern Research*. AGJU 37. Leiden: Brill, 1996.

Draper, J. A., and C. N. Jefford, eds. *The Didache: A Missing Piece of the Puzzle in Early Christianity*. ECL 14. Atlanta: SBL, 2015.

Drimbe, A. *The Church of Antioch and the Eucharistic Traditions (ca. 35–130 CE)*. WUNT 2/529. Tübingen: Mohr Siebeck, 2020.

Droge, A. J., and J. D. Tabor. *A Noble Death: Suicide and Martyrdom Among Christians and Jews in Antiquity*. San Francisco: Harper, 1992.

Dunn, J. D. G. "Altering the Default Setting: Re-Envisaging the Early Transmission of the Jesus Tradition." *NTS* 49 (2003): 139–75.

Dunn, J. D. G. *Christology in the Making: A New Testament Inquiry into the Origins of the Doctrine of the Incarnation*. 2nd ed. Grand Rapids: Eerdmans, 1989.

Dunn, J. D. G. *Jesus Remembered*. Grand Rapids: Eerdmans, 2003.

Dus, J. A. "Papers or Principles? Ignatius of Antioch on the Authority of the Old Testament." Pages 151–63 in *The Process of Authority: The Dynamics in Transmission and Reception of Canonical Texts*. Edited by J. Dušek and J. Roskovec. DCLS 27. Berlin: de Gruyter, 2016.

Eastman, D. L. "Ignatius, Pseudo-Ignatius, and the Art of Pauline Reception." *Early Christianity* 7 (2016): 213–29.

Eastman, D. L. "The Linguistic Turn and the Expanding Horizons of Early Christian Martyrdom." *Religion and Theology* 28 (2021): 26–40.

Edwards, J. C. *The Gospel According to the Epistle of Barnabas*. WUNT 2/503. Tübingen: Mohr Siebeck, 2019.

Edwards, J. R. *From Christ to Christianity: How the Jesus Movement Became the Church in Less Than a Century*. Grand Rapids: Baker Academic, 2021.

Edwards, M. J. "Ignatius and the Second Century: A Response to R. Hübner." *ZAC* 2 (1998): 214–26.

Eggenberger, C. *Die Quellen der poilitischen Ethik des I. Klemensbriefs*. Zurich: Zwingli, 1951.

Eijk, T. H. C. van. *La résurrection des morts chez les Pères apostoliques*. ThH 25. Paris: Beauchesne, 1974.

Eilers, C. *Roman Patrons of Greek Cities*. Oxford: Oxford University Press, 2002.

Engberg-Pedersen, T. *Paul and the Stoics*. Edinburgh: T&T Clark, 2000.

Ehrman, B. D. *Didymus the Blind and the Text of the Gospels*. Atlanta: Scholar, 1986.

Ehrman, B. D. "The Use and Significance of Patristic Evidence for NT Textual Criticism." Pages 118–35 in *New Testament Text Criticism, Exegesis, and Early Church History*. Edited by B. Aland and J. Delobel. Kampen, Netherlands: Kok Pharos, 1994.

Erho, T. "A Fourth Ethiopic Witness to the Shepherd of Hermas." Pages 241–66 in *Caught in Translation: Studies on Versions of Late-Antique Christian Literature*. Edited by M. Toca and D. Batovici. Texts and Studies in Eastern Christianity 17. Leiden: Brill, 2020.

Evans, D. "Christian Identity Formation in the Second Century: The Two Quadratuses of Athens." *Early Christianity* 10 (2019): 184–200.

Farkasfalvy, D. M. "Theology of Scripture in St. Irenaeus." *Rev. Bénédictine* 76 (1968): 319–33.

Farmer, W. R., and D. M. Farkasfalvy. *The Formation of the New Testament Canon*. New York: Paulist, 1976.

Fee, G. D. "The Use of the Greek Fathers for New Testament Textual Criticism." Pages 191–207 in *The Text of the New Testament in Contemporary Research: Essays on the Status Quaestionis*. Edited by G. D. Fee. Eugene, OR: Wipf & Stock, 2001.

Ferguson, E. "Canon Muratori: Date and Provenance." StPatr 17 (1982): 677–83.

Ferguson, E. "Was Barnabas a Chiliast? An Example of Hellenistic Number Symbolism in Barnabas and Clement of Alexandria." Pages 200–212 in *Catechesis, Baptism, Eschatology, and Martyrdom*. Vol. 2 of *The Early Church at Work and Worship*. Cambridge: Clarke, 2014.

Foster, P. "The Apology of Quadratus." Pages 52–62 in *The Writings of the Apostolic Fathers*. Edited by P. Foster. London: T&T Clark, 2007.

Foster, P. "Christ and the Apostles in the Epistles of Ignatius of Antioch." Pages 109–26 in *Early Christians Between Ideal and Reality*. Edited by M. Grundeken and J. Verheyden. WUNT 342. Tübingen: Mohr Siebeck, 2015.

Foster, P. "Deacons (Διάκονοι) and Διακονία in the Writings of Justin and Irenaeus." Pages 215–26 in *Deacons and Diakonia in Early Christianity: The First Two Centuries*. Edited by B. J. Koet, E. Murphy, and E. Ryökäs. WUNT 2/479. Tübingen: Mohr Siebeck, 2018.

Foster, P. "The Epistle to Diognetus." Pages 147–56 in *The Writings of the Apostolic Fathers*. Edited by P. Foster. London: T&T Clark, 2007.

Foster, P. "The Epistle of Ignatius of Antioch." Pages 81–107 in *The Writings of the Apostolic Fathers*. Edited by P. Foster. London: T&T Clark, 2007.

Foster, P. "The Epistles of Ignatius and the Writings That Later Formed the New Testament." Pages 159–86 in *The Reception of the New Testament and the Apostolic Fathers*. Edited by A. F. Gregory and C. M. Tuckett. Oxford: Oxford University Press, 2005.

Foster, P. "The Ignatian Problem: The Recensions of a Letter Corpus as a Reflection of Theological Concerns and Developments." Pages 5–50 in *Texts in Context: Essays on Dating and Contextualising Christian Writings from the Second and Early Third Centuries*. Edited by J. Verheyden, J. Schroter, and T. Nicklas. BETL 319. Leuven: Peeters, 2021.

Foster, P. "Ignatius and the Gospels." Pages 81–106 in *Gospels and Gospel Traditions in the Second Century: Experiments in Reception*. Edited by J. Schröter, T. Nicklas, and J. Verheyden. BZNW 235. Berlin: de Gruyter, 2019.

Foster, P. "Ignatius of Antioch's Reception of the Gospel of Matthew." Pages 249–88 in *The Gospel of Matthew: Studies on Its Composition, Theology, and Early Reception*. Edited by J. Verheyden, J. Schröter, and D. C. Sim. WUNT 477. Tübingen: Mohr Siebeck, 2022.

Foster, P. "Mission and Ethics in the Writings of Ignatius of Antioch." Pages 505–26 in *Sensitivity Towards Outsiders: Exploring the Dynamic Relationship Between Mission and Ethics in the New Testament and Early Christianity*. Edited by J. Kok, T. Nicklas, D. T. Roth, and C. M. Hays. WUNT 2/364. Tübingen: Mohr Siebeck, 2014.

Foster, P. "Polycarp in the Writings of Ignatius." Pages 411–31 in *Studies on the Text of the New Testament and Early Christianity: Essays in Honor of Michael W. Holmes on the Occasion of His 65th Birthday*. Edited by D. M. Gurtner, J. Hernández, and P. Foster. NTTSD 50. Leiden: Brill, 2015.

Foster, P. "Polycarp's Teaching: The Reception and Development of Theology." Pages 279–313 in *Studies on the Intersection of Text, Paratext, and Reception: A Festschrift in Honor of Charles E. Hill*. Edited by G. R. Lanier and J. N. Reid. TENTS 15. Leiden: Brill, 2021.

Foster, P. "The Story of Christ in the Writings of Ignatius." Pages 263–80 in *Christ of the Sacred Stories*. Edited by in P. Dragutinović, T. Nicklas, K. Rodenbiker, and V. Tatalović. WUNT 2/453. Tübingen: Mohr Siebeck, 2017.

Foster, P. "The Text of the New Testament in the Apostolic Fathers." Pages 92–118 in *The Cambridge Companion to the Apostolic Fathers*. Edited by M. F. Bird and S. Harrower. Cambridge: Cambridge University Press, 2021.

Foster, P. "The Text of the New Testament in the Apostolic Fathers." Pages 282–301 in *The Early Text of the New Testament*. Edited by C. E. Hill and M. J. Kruger. Oxford: Oxford University Press, 2012.

Foster, P., ed. *The Writings of the Apostolic Fathers*. London: T&T Clark, 2007.

Franzmann, M. "*Imitatio Christi*: Copying the Death of the Founder and Gaining Paradise." Pages 367–84 in *A Wandering Galilean: Essay in Honour of Sean Freyne*. Edited by Z. Rodgers, M. Daly-Denton, and A. Fitzpatrick-McKinley. JSJSup 132. Leiden: Brill, 2009.

Frend, W. H. C. *Martyrdom and Persecution in the Early Church*. Oxford: Basil Blackwell, 1965.

Fudge, E. "The Eschatology of Ignatius of Antioch: Christocentric and Historical." *JETS* 15 (1972): 231–37.

Fuhrmann, S. "Traditions of Martyrdom in the Ignatian Letters." *In die Skriflig* 45 (2011): 689–705.

Fullenbach, J. *Ecclesiastical Office and the Primacy of Rome: An Evaluation of Recent Theological Discussion of First Clement*. Washington, DC: Catholic University of America Press, 1980.

Funk, F. X. *Die Echtheit der ignatianischen Briefe aufs Neue Vertheidigt*. Tübingen: Laupp, 1883.

Furnish, V. P. *Theology and Ethics in Paul*. Nashville: Abingdon, 1968.

Gallagher, E. L., and J. D. Meade. *The Biblical Canon Lists from Early Christianity: Texts and Analysis*. Oxford: Oxford University Press, 2017.

Garrow, A. J. P. *The Gospel of Matthew's Dependence on the Didache*. LNTS 254. London: T&T Clark, 2004.

Gathercole, S. J. *The Composition of the Gospel of Thomas: Original Language and Influences*. SNTSMS 151. Cambridge: Cambridge University Press, 2012.

Gemeinhardt, P. "In Search of Christian *Paideia*: Education and Conversion in Early Christian Biography." *ZAC* 16 (2012): 88–98.

Gemeinhardt, P. "Teaching the Faith in Early Christianity: Divine and Human Agency." *VC* 74 (2020): 129–64.

Gerhardsson, B. *Memory and Manuscript with Tradition and Transmission in Early Christianity*. Rev. ed. Grand Rapids: Eerdmans, 1998.

Gibbard, S. M. "The Eucharist in the Ignatian Epistles." StPatr 8 (1966): 214–18.

Giet, S. "Le témoignage de Clément de Rome: La cause des persecutions romaines." *Revue des sciences religieuses* 29 (1955): 333–54.

Gilliam, P. R. *Ignatius of Antioch and the Arian Controversy*. VCSup 140. Leiden: Brill, 2017.

Given, J. G. "How Coherent Is the Ignatian Middle Recension? The View from the Coptic Versions of the Letters of Ignatius." *ETL* 98 (2022): 481–502.

Glancy, J. A. "Slavery and Sexual Availability." Pages 627–44 in *The Oxford Handbook of New Testament, Gender, and Sexuality*. Edited by B. H. Dunning. Oxford: Oxford University Press, 2019.

Glaser, T. "The Letters of Ignatius of Antioch: An Epistolary Novel on a Martyr Bishop and the Quest for Christian Identity." Pages 385–404 in *Die Datierung neutestamentlicher Pseudepigraphen: Herausforderungen und neuere Lösungsansätze*. Edited by W. Grünstäudl and K. M. Schmidt. WUNT 470. Tübingen: Mohr Siebeck, 2021.

Goldhahn-Müller, I. *Die Grenze der Gemeinde: Studien zum Problem der Zweiten Buße im Neuen Testament unter Berücksichtigung der Entwicklung im 2. Jh. bis Tertullian*. GTA 39. Göttingen: Vandenhoeck & Ruprecht, 1989.

Goodspeed, E. "The Didache, Barnabas, and the Doctrina." *AThR* 27 (1945): 228–47.

Goulder, M. D. "Ignatius' 'Docetists.'" *VC* 53 (1999): 16–30.

Grant, R. M. *Eusebius as Church Historian*. Oxford: Clarendon, 1980.

Grant, R. M. *Greek Apologists of the Second Century*. Philadelphia: Westminster, 1988.

Grant, R. M. *Ignatius of Antioch*. Vol. 4 of *The Apostolic Fathers: A New Translation and Commentary*. New York: Thomas Nelson, 1966.

Grant, R. M. *An Introduction*. Vol. 1 of *The Apostolic Fathers: A New Translation and Commentary*. New York: Thomas Nelson, 1965.

Grant, R. M. "Quadratus, the First Christian Apologist." Pages 177–83 in *A Tribute to Arthur Vööbus: Studies in Early Christian Literature and Its Environment, Primarily in the Syrian East*. Edited by R. H. Fischer. Chicago: Lutheran School of Theology at Chicago, 1977.

Grant, R. M. "Scripture and Tradition in St. Ignatius of Antioch." *CBQ* 25 (1963): 322–35.

Grant, R. M., and H. H. Graham. *First and Second Clement*. Vol. 2 of *The Apostolic Fathers: A New Translation and Commentary*. New York: Thomas Nelson, 1965.

Green, H. B. "Matthew, Clement and Luke: Their Sequence and Their Relationship." *JTS* 40 (1989): 1–25.

Gregory, A. F. "1 Clement and the Writings That Later Formed the New Testament." Pages 129–57 in *The Reception of the New Testament in the Apostolic Fathers*. Edited by A. F. Gregory and C. M. Tuckett. Oxford: Oxford University Press, 2005.

Gregory, A. F. "1 Clement: An Introduction." Pages 21–31 in *The Writings of the Apostolic Fathers*. Edited by P. Foster. London: T&T Clark, 2007.

Gregory, A. F. "Among the Apologists? Reading Acts with Justin Martyr." Pages 169–86 in *Engaging Early Christian History: Reading Acts in the Second Century*. Edited by R. R. Dupertuis and T. Penner. BibleWorld. Durham: Acumen, 2013.

Gregory, A. F. "Disturbing Trajectories: *1 Clement*, the *Shepherd of Hermas* and the Development of Early Roman Christianity." Pages 142–66 in *Rome in the Bible and the Early Church*. Edited by P. Oakes. Carlisle: Paternoster, 2002.

Gregory, A. F., ed. *The Gospel According to the Hebrews and the Gospel of the Ebionites*. OECGT. Oxford: Oxford University Press, 2017.

Gregory, A. F., and C. M. Tuckett, eds. *The Reception of the New Testament in the Apostolic Fathers*. Oxford: Oxford University Press, 2005.

Gregory, A. F., and C. M. Tuckett, eds. *Trajectories Through the New Testament and the Apostolic Fathers*. Oxford: Oxford University Press, 2005.

Grosvenor, E. A. "An Interview with Bishop Bryennios—The Discovery of the Teaching." *Andover Review* 2 (1884): 515–16.

Grundeken, M. *Community Building in the Shepherd of Hermas: A Critical Study of Some Key Aspects*. VCSup 131. Leiden: Brill, 2015.

Gundry, R. H. *Mark: A Commentary on His Apology for the Cross*. Grand Rapids: Eerdmans, 1999.

Gundry, R. H. *Matthew: A Commentary on His Handbook for a Mixed Church Under Persecution*. 2nd ed. Grand Rapids: Eerdmans, 1991.

Guth, C. "The Relationship of Faith and Works in the Soteriologies of the Apostolic Fathers." PhD diss., University of Aberdeen, 1994.

Hagner, D. A. *The Use of the Old and New Testaments in Clement of Rome*. NovTSup 34. Leiden: Brill, 1973.

Hahn, F. *The Titles of Jesus in Christology*. London: Lutterworth, 1969.

Hahneman, G. M. *The Muratorian Fragment and the Development of the Canon*. Oxford: Clarendon, 1992.

Hammond Bammel, C. P. "Ignatian Problems." *JTS* 33 (1982): 62–97.

Hannah, J. W. "The Long Recension of the Ignatian Epistles: By the Redactors of Paul and John." *Proceedings of the Eastern Great Lakes Biblical Society* 3 (1983): 108–21.

Hannah, J. W. "The Setting of the Ignatian Long Recension." *JBL* 79 (1960): 221–38.

Hanson, A. T. "The Theology of Suffering in the Pastoral Epistles and Ignatius of Antioch." StPatr 17 (1982): 694–96.

Harland, P. A. "Christ-Bearers and Fellow-Initiates: Local Cultural Life and Christian Identity in Ignatius' Letters." *JECS* 11 (2003): 481–99.

Harnack, A. von. *History of Dogma*. Vol. 1. Translated by N. Buchanan. Boston: Little, Brown, and Company, 1901.

Harrill, J. A. "Ignatius, *Ad Polycarp*. 4.3 and the Corporate Manumission of Christian Slaves." *JECS* 1 (1993): 107–42.

Harrison, C. *The Art of Listening in the Early Church*. Oxford: Oxford University Press, 2013.

Harrison, P. N. *Polycarp's Two Epistles to the Philippians*. Cambridge: Cambridge University Press, 1936.

Hartin, P. J. "Ethics in the Letter of James, the Gospel of Matthew, and the Didache: Their Place in Early

Christian Literature." Pages 289–314 in *Matthew, James, and Didache: Three Related Documents in Their Jewish and Christian Setting*. Edited by J. K. Zengenberg and H. W. M. van de Sandt. Atlanta: Society of Biblical Literature, 2008.

Hartmann, N. "Bones Ground by Wild Beast's Teeth: Late Ancient Imaginations of the Death of Ignatius of Antioch." Pages 155–75 in *Desiring Martyrs: Locating Martyrs in Space and Time*. Edited by H. O. Maier and K. Waldner. Berlin: de Gruyter, 2021.

Hartog, P. "The Christology of the *Martyrdom of Polycarp*: Martyrdom as Both Imitation of Christ and Election by Christ." *Perichoresis* 12 (2014): 137–52.

Hartog, P. "The *Martyrdom of Polycarp* as Communal, Moral Formation." *Science et Esprit* 67 (2015): 435–49.

Hartog, P. "The Devil's in the Details: The Apocalyptic 'Adversary' in the *Martyrdom of Polycarp* and the *Martyrs of Lyons*." Pages 432–52 in *Studies on the Text of the New Testament and Early Christianity: Essays in Honor of Michael W. Holmes*. Edited by D. Gurtner, J. Hernández, and P. Foster. NTTSD 50. Leiden: Brill, 2015.

Hartog, P. "The Good News in Old Texts? The 'Gospel' and the 'Archives' in Ign. *Phld.* 8.2." StPatr 93 (2017): 105–21.

Hartog, P. "The Impact of the Christological Controversies: Comparing the Ignatian Kerygma and Romans 1." Pages 175–95 in *Docetism in the Early Church: The Quest for an Elusive Phenomenon*. Edited by J. Verheyden, R. Bieringer, J. Schröter, and I. Jäger. WUNT 402. Tübingen: Mohr Siebeck, 2018.

Hartog, P. "Polycarp's Epistle to the Philippians and the Martyrdom of Polycarp." Pages 226–47 in *The Cambridge Companion to the Apostolic Fathers*. Edited by M. F. Bird and S. Harrower. Cambridge: Cambridge University Press, 2021.

Hartog, P. *Polycarp's Epistle to the Philippians and the Martyrdom of Polycarp: Introduction, Text, and Commentary*. OAF. Oxford: Oxford University Press, 2013.

Hartog, P. "Polycarp's Martyrdom 'According to the Gospel' and Paul's Philippians." StPatr 45 (2010): 391–96.

Hartog, P. "Themes and Intertextualities in Pre-Nicene Exhortations to Martyrdom." Pages 102–19 in *The Wiley Blackwell Companion to Christian Martyrdom*. Edited by P. Middleton. WBCR. Chichester: Wiley Blackwell, 2020.

Hauge, M. R., and A. W. Pitts. *Ancient Education and Early Christianity*. London: Bloomsbury, 2016.

Haykin, M. "'Come to the Father': Ignatius of Antioch and His Calling to Be a Martyr." *Them* 32 (2007): 26–39.

Heffernan, T. J. "Martyrdom, Charisma, and Imitation: Paths to Christian Sanctity." *Greek Orthodox Theological Review* 55 (2010): 251–67.

Heffernan, T. J. *The Passion of Perpetua and Felicity*. Oxford: Oxford University Press, 2012.

Heintz, M. "Μιμητὴς θεοῦ in the Epistle to Diognetus." *JECS* 12 (2004): 107–19.

Hellholm, D., T. Vegge, Ø. Norderval, and C. Hellholm, eds. *Ablution, Initiation, and Baptism: Late Antiquity, Early Judaism, and Early Christianity = Waschungen, Initiation und Taufe: Spätantike, Frühes Judentum und Frühes Christentum*. 3 vols. BZNW 176.1–3. Berlin: de Gruyter, 2011.

Hemelrijk, E. "Patronage of Cities: The Role of Women." Pages 415–27 in *Roman Rule and Civic Life: Local and Regional Perspectives*. Edited by L. de Ligt, E. Hemelrijk, and H. W. Singer. Leiden: Brill, 2003.

Henten, J. W. van. "Early Jewish and Christian Martyrdom." Pages 72–87 in *The Wiley Blackwell Companion to Christian Martyrdom*. Edited by P. Middleton. WBCR. Chichester: Wiley Blackwell, 2020.

Hermanns, A. "Le Pseudo-Barnabé: Est-il millénariste?" *ETL* 35 (1959): 848–76.

Henderson, I. H. "Didache and Orality in Synoptic Comparison." *JBL* 111 (1992): 283–306.

Hengel, M. *The Johannine Question*. Translated by J. Bowden. London, SCM, 1989.

Henne, P. *La christologie chez Clément de Rome et dans le Pasteur d'Hermas*. Paradosis 33. Fribourg: Éditions Universitaires, 1992.

Hill, C. E. "The Debate Over the Muratorian Fragment and the Development of the Canon." *WTJ* 57 (1995): 437–52.

Hill, C. E. *From the Lost Teaching of Polycarp: Identifying Irenaeus' Apostolic Presbyter and the Author of Ad Diognetum*. WUNT 186. Tübingen: Mohr Siebeck, 2006.

Hill, C. E. "Ignatius, the 'Gospel,' and the Gospels." Pages 267–85 in *Trajectories Through the New Testament and the Apostolic Fathers*. Edited by A. F. Gregory and C. M. Tuckett. Oxford: Oxford University Press, 2005.

Hill, C. E. "'In These Very Words': Methods and Standards of Literary Borrowing in the Second Century." Pages 261–81 in *The Early Text of the New Testament*. Edited by C. E. Hill and M. J. Kruger. Oxford: Oxford University Press, 2012.

Hill, C. E. *Johannine Corpus in the Early Church*. Oxford: Oxford University Press, 2006.

Hill, C. E. "Papias of Hierapolis." Pages 42–51 in *The Writings of the Apostolic Fathers*. Edited by P. Foster. London: T&T Clark, 2007.

Hill, C. E. *Regnum Caelorum: Patterns of Future Hope in Early Christianity*. OECS. Oxford: Clarendon, 1992.

Hoffman, R. J. *Marcion: On the Restitution of Christianity: An Essay on the Development of Radical Paulinist Theology in the Second Century*. American Academy of Religion Academy Series 46. Chico, CA: Scholars Press, 1984.

Hollander, A. T. "Hagiography Unbound: A Theory of Making and Using Holy Media." *JAAR* 89.1 (2021): 72–102.
Holmes, M. W. "Dating the Martyrdom of Polycarp." *Early Christianity* 9 (2018): 181–200.
Holmes, M. W. "The *Martyrdom of Polycarp* and the New Testament Passion Narratives." Pages 407–32 in *Trajectories Through the New Testament and the Apostolic Fathers*. Edited by A. F. Gregory and C. M. Tuckett. Oxford: Oxford University Press, 2005.
Hoover, J. "False Lives, False Martyrs: 'Pseudo-Pionius' and the Redating of the *Martyrdom of Polycarp*." *VC* 67 (2013): 471–98.
Horbury, W. "Jewish-Christian Relations in Barnabas and Justin Martyr." Pages 127–61 in *Jews and Christians in Contact and Controversy*. Edinburgh: T&T Clark, 1998.
Horbury, W. *Jewish War Under Trajan and Hadrian*. By W. Horbury. Cambridge: Cambridge University Press, 2014.
Horst, W. "The Secret Plan of God and the Imitation of God: Neglected Dimensions of Christian Differentiation in *Ad Diognetum*." *JECS* 27 (2019): 161–83.
Horsting, A. G. A. "Transfiguration of Flesh: Literary and Theological Connections Between Martyrdom Accounts and Eucharistic Prayers." Pages 307–25 in *Issues in Eucharistic Praying in East and West: Essays in Liturgical and Theological Analysis*. Edited by M. E. Johnson. Collegeville, MN: Liturgical Press, 2010.
Hubbard, T. K., ed. *A Companion to Greek and Roman Sexualities*. Chichester: Wiley-Blackwell, 2014.
Hübner, R. "Thesen zur Echtheit und Datierung der sieben Briefe des Ignatius von Antiochien." *ZAC* 1 (1997): 44–72.
Hurtado, L. W. *How on Earth Did Jesus Become a God? Historical Questions about Earliest Devotion to Jesus*. Grand Rapids: Eerdmans, 2005.
Hurtado, L. W. *Lord Jesus Christ: Devotion to Jesus in Earliest Christianity*. Eerdmans: Grand Rapids, 2003.
Hurtado, L. W. "The New Testament in the Second Century: Texts, Collections, and Canon." Pages 3–27 in *Transmission and Reception: New Testament Text-Critical and Exegetical Studies*. Edited by J. W. Childers and D. C. Parker. Piscataway, NJ: Gorgias, 2006.
Hurtado, L. W. "New Testament Scholarship and the Dating of New Testament Papyri." Pages 48–63 in *Texts and Artefacts: Selected Essays on Textual Criticism and Early Christian Manuscripts*. By L. W. Hurtado. London: Bloomsbury T&T Clark, 2018.
Hvalvik, R. "Barnabas 9:7–9 and the Author's Supposed Use of Gematria." *NTS* 33 (1987): 276–82.
Hvalvik, R. *The Struggle for Scripture and Covenant: The Purpose of the Epistle of Barnabas and Jewish-Christian Competition in the Second Century*. WUNT 2/82. Tübingen: Mohr Siebeck, 1996.
Inge, W. R. "Ignatius." Pages 63–83 in *The Reception of the New Testament and the Apostolic Fathers*. Edited by Committee of the Oxford Society of Historical Theology. Oxford: Clarendon, 1905.
Inowlocki, S. *Eusebius and the Jewish Authors: His Citation Technique in an Apologetic Context*. AJEC 64. Leiden: Brill, 2006.
Isacson, M. "Follow Your Bishop! Rhetorical Strategies in the Letters of Ignatius of Antioch." Pages 317–40 in *The Formation of the Early Church*. Edited by J. Ådna. WUNT 183. Tübingen: Mohr Siebeck, 2005.
Isacson, M. *To Each Their Own Letter: Structure, Themes, and Rhetorical Strategies in the Letters of Ignatius of Antioch*. ConBNT 42. Stockholm: Almqvist & Wiksell, 2004.
Jaubert, A. *Clément de Rome: Épitre aux Corenthiens*. SC 167 bis. Paris: Éditions du Cerf, 1971.
Jeffers, J. S. *Conflict at Rome: Social Order and Hierarchy in Early Christianity*. Minneapolis: Fortress, 1991.
Jefford, C. N. *The Apostolic Fathers and the New Testament*. Peabody, MA: Hendrickson, 2006.
Jefford, C. N. "*Didache*." Pages 248–67 in *The Cambridge Companion to the Apostolic Fathers*. Edited by M. F. Bird and S. Harrower. Cambridge: Cambridge University Press, 2021.
Jefford, C. N. *Didache: The Teaching of the Twelve Apostles*. ECA 5. Salem, OR: Polebridge, 2013.
Jefford, C. N. *The Epistle to Diognetus (with the Fragment of Quadratus): Introduction, Text, and Commentary*. OAF. Oxford: Oxford University Press, 2013.
Jefford, C. N. "Ignatius and the Apostolic Fathers." Pages 108–20 in *The Routledge Companion to Early Christian Thought*. Edited by D. J. Bingham. London: Routledge, 2010.
Jefford, C. N. *Reading the Apostolic Fathers: A Student's Introduction*. 2nd ed. Grand Rapids: Baker Academic, 2012.
Jefford, C. N. *The Sayings of Jesus in the Teaching of the Twelve Apostles*. VCSup 11. Leiden: Brill, 1989.
Jefford, C. N., ed. *The Didache in Context: Essays on Its Text, History, and Transmission*. NovTSup 77. Leiden: Brill, 1995.
Johnson, A. P. *Eusebius*. Understanding Classics. London: I. B. Tauris, 2014.
Johnson, M. E. "Sharing 'the Cup of Christ': The Cessation of Martyrdom and Anaphoral Development." Pages 109–26 in *Studies on the Liturgies of the Christian East*. Edited by S. Hawkes-Teeples, B. Groen, and S. Alexopolous. ECS 18. Leuven: Peeters, 2013.
Joly, R. *Le dossier d'Ignace d'Antioche*. Université libre Bruxelles, Faculté de philosophie et lettres 69. Brussels: Éditions de l'Université de Bruxelles, 1979.
Joly, R. *Le Pasteur*. SC 53 bis. 2nd ed. Paris: Éditions du Cerf, 1968.

Jones, C. P. *Between Pagan and Christian*. Cambridge: Harvard University Press, 2014.

Kartzow, M. B. *The Slave Metaphor and Gendered Enslavement in Early Christian Discourse: Double Trouble Embodied*. Routledge Studies in the Early Christian World. London: Routledge, 2018.

Keck, L. E. "Rethinking New Testament Ethics." *JBL* 115 (1996): 3–16.

Keener, C. S. *Galatians: A Commentary*. Grand Rapids: Baker Academic, 2019.

Kelber, W. *The Oral and Written Gospel: The Hermeneutics of Speaking and Writing in the Synoptic Tradition, Mark, Paul, and Q*. Philadelphia: Fortress, 1983.

Kelhoffer, J. A. "Eschatology, Androgynous Thinking, Encratism, and the Question of Anti-Gnosticism in 2 Clement 12 (part two)." *VC* 72 (2018): 353–68.

Kelhoffer, J. A. "'How Soon a Book' Revisited: *Euaggelion* as a Reference to 'Gospel' Materials in the First Half of the Second Century." *ZNW* 95 (2004): 1–34.

Kelhoffer, J. A. "If Second Clement Really Were a 'Sermon,' How Would We Know, and Why Would We Care? Prolegomena to Analyses of the Writing's Genre and Community." Pages 83–108 in *Early Christian Communities Between Ideal and Reality*. Edited by M. Grundeken and J. Verheyden. Tübingen: Mohr Siebeck, 2015.

Kelhoffer, J. A. "Passing the Audition: Mode and Harmony in Ignatius of Antioch's Chorus (*Eph*. 4.2; *Rom*. 2.2)." Pages 175–201 in *Why We Sing: Music, Word, and Liturgy in Early Christianity: Essays in Honour of Anders Ekenberg's 75th Birthday*. Edited by C. J. Berglund, B. Crostini, and J. A. Kelhoffer. VCSup 177. Leiden: Brill, 2023.

Kelly, J. N. D. *Early Christian Doctrines*. 5th ed. London: Continuum, 2000.

Keresztes, P. "The Imperial Roman Government and the Christian Church I. From Nero to the Severi." *ANRW* 23.1:247–315. Part 2, *Principat*, 23.1. Edited by H. Temporini and W. Haase. Berlin: de Gruyter, 1979.

Khomych, T. "Conflicting Choreographies: Dance as Doctrinal Expression in Ignatius' *Ephesians* 19 and *Acts of John* 94–96." Pages 217–29 in *Docetism in the Early Church: The Quest for an Elusive Phenomenon*. Edited by J. Verheyden, R. Bieringer, J. Schröter, and I. Jäger. WUNT 402. Tübingen: Mohr Siebeck, 2018.

Kirk, A. "Ignatius' Statements of Self-Sacrifice: Imitations of an Atoning Death or Expressions of Exemplary Suffering?" *JTS* 64 (2013): 66–88.

Kline, L. L. "Harmonized Sayings of Jesus in the Pseudo-Clementine Homilies and Justin Martyr." *ZNW* 66 (1975): 223–41.

Kloppenborg, J. S. "Didache 16 6–8 and Special Matthean Tradition." *ZNW* 70 (1979): 54–67.

Kloppenborg, J. S. "The Transformation of Moral Exhortation in *Didache* 1–5." Pages 88–109 in *The Didache in Context: Essays on Its Text, History, and Transmission*. Edited by C. N. Jefford. Leiden: Brill, 1994.

Knell, M. *Sin, Grace and Free Will: The Apostolic Fathers to Augustine*. Cambridge: Clarke, 2017.

Knoch, O. *Eigenart und Bedeutung der Eschatologie im theologischen Aufriss des ersten Clemensbriefes: Eine auslegungsgeschichtliche Untersuchung*. Theophaneia 17. Bonn: Hanstein, 1964.

Knopf, R. *Die Lehre der zwölf Apostel: Die zwei Clemensbriefe*. HNT Ergänzungsband, Die Apostolischen Väter 1. Tubingen: Möhr Siebeck, 1920.

Koch, D.-A. "Taufinterpretationen bei Ignatius und im Barnabasbrief: Christologische und soteriologische Deutungen." Pages 817–48 in vol. 2 of *Ablution, Initiation, and Baptism: Late Antiquity, Early Judaism, and Early Christianity = Waschungen, Initiation und Taufe: Spätantike, Frühes Judentum und Frühes Christentum*. Edited by D. Hellholm, T. Vegge, Ø. Norderval, and C. Hellholm. 3 vols. BZNW 176.1–3. Berlin: de Gruyter, 2011.

Koester, H. *Ancient Christian Gospels: Their History and Development*. London: SCM, 1990.

Koester, H. "Der Barnabasbrief." Pages 124–58 in *Synoptische Überlieferung bei den apostolischen Vätern*. By H. Koester. Berlin: Akademie, 1957.

Koester, H. *Synoptische Überlieferung bei den apostolischen Vätern*. Berlin: Akademie, 1957.

Köhler, W.-D. *Die Rezeption des Mattäusevangeliums in der Zeit vor Irenäus*. WUNT 2/24. Tübingen: Mohr Siebeck, 1987.

Kozlowski, J. M. "The Participle κολαφιζόμενοι in *Martyrium Polycarpi* 2.4 and 2 Cor 12:1–10." *VC* 72 (2018): 506–12.

Kozlowski, J. M. "*Pionius Polycarpi Imitator*: References to *Martyrium Polycarpi* in *Martyrium Pionii*." *Science et Esprit* 67 (2015): 417–34.

Kozlowski, J. M. "Polycarp as a Christian Gymnosophist." StPatr 51 (2011): 15–24.

Kraft, R. A. *The Didache and Barnabas*. Vol. 3 of *The Apostolic Fathers: A New Translation and Commentary*. New York: Thomas Nelson, 1965.

Kraft, R. A., and P. Prigent. *Épitre de Barnabé*. SC 172. Paris: Éditions du Cerf, 1971.

Krauss, S. *The Jewish-Christian Controversy from the Earliest Times to 1789, Volume 1: History*. Edited by W. Horbury. TSAJ 56. Tübingen: Mohr Siebeck, 1996.

Kreinecker, C. M. "The Earliest Commentaries on Paul as Sources for the Biblical Text—A New Research Project at the Institute for Textual Scholarship and Electronic Editing at the University of Birmingham." *Early Christianity* 3 (2012): 411–15.

Kruger, M. J. *Christianity at the Crossroads: How the Second Century Shaped the Future of the Church*. Downers Grove, IL: IVP Academic, 2018.

Kruger, M. J. "Manuscripts, Scribes, and Book Production Within Early Christianity." Pages 15–40 in *Christian Origins and Classical Culture: Social and Literary Contexts for the New Testament*. Edited by S. E. Porter and A. W. Pitts. Leiden: Brill, 2010.

Kruger, M. J. *The Question of Canon: Challenging the Status Quo in the New Testament Debate*. Downers Grove, IL: IVP Academic, 2013.

Külzer, A. *Disputationes graecae contra Iudaeos: Untersuchungen zur byzantinischen antijüdischen Dialogliteratur und ihrem Judenbild*. Byzantinisches Archiv 19. Leipzig: Teubner, 1999.

Kurek-Chomycz, D. A. "The Sweet Scent of the Gospel in the *Didache* and in Second Corinthians: Some Comments on Two Recent Interpretations of the *Stinoufi* Prayer in the Coptic *Did.* 10.8." *VC* 63 (2009): 323–44.

Lake, K. *Landmarks in the History of Early Christianity*. London: Macmillan, 1920.

Lallemand, A. "Le parfum des martyrs dans les Actes des martyrs de Lyon et le Martyre de Polycarpe." StPatr 16 (1985): 186–92.

Lampe, P. *Christians at Rome in the First Two Centuries: From Paul to Valentinus*. London: Continuum, 2006.

Lang, T. J. *Mystery and Making of a Christian Historical Consciousness: From Paul to the Second Century*. BZNW 219. Berlin: de Gruyter, 2017.

Lawlor, H. J., and I. E. L. Oulton, trans. and eds. *Eusebius, Bishop of Caesarea, the Ecclesiastical History and the Martyrs of Palestine*. 2 vols. London: SPCK, 1927.

Layton, B. "The Sources, Dates and Transmission of Didache 1:3b–2:1." *HTR* 61 (1968): 343–83.

Leavenworth, J. B. "Suffering for Our Sakes: The Soteriological Thought Process of Ignatius of Antioch." PhD diss., University of Edinburgh, 2022.

Lechner, T. "Ignatios von Antiochia und die Zweite Sophistik." Pages 19–69 in *Die Briefe des Ignatius von Antiochien: Motive, Strategien, und Kontexte*. Edited by T. J. Bauer and P. von Möllendorff. Mil-S 72. Berlin: de Gruyter, 2018.

Lechner, T. *Ignatius adversus Valentinianos? Chronologische und theologiegeschichtliche Studien zu den Briefen des Ignatius von Antiochien*. VCSup 47. Leiden: Brill, 1999.

Lee-Miller, G. "Obligations to Outsiders in Select Texts of the Apostolic Fathers." PhD diss., Fuller Theological Seminary, 2008.

Leemans, J., ed. *More Than a Memory: The Discourse on Martyrdom and the Construction of Christian Identity in the History of Christianity*. AnnNuntLov 51. Leuven: Peeters, 2005.

Leutzsch, M. "Hirt des Hermas." Pages 105–497 in *Papiasfragmente, Hirt des Hermas*. Edited by U. H. J. Körtner and M. Leutzsch. Schriften des Urchristentums 3. Darmstadt: Wissenschaftliche Buchgesellschaft, 1998.

Lewis, J. G. *Looking for Life: The Role of "Theo-Ethical" Reasoning in Paul's Religion*. London: T&T Clark, 2005.

Lim, T. H. *Holy Scripture in the Qumran Commentaries and Pauline Letters*. Oxford: Clarendon, 1997.

Limor, O., and G. G. Stroumsa, ed. *Contra Iudaeos: Ancient and Medieval Polemics Between Christians and Jews*. TSMEMJ 10. Tübingen: Mohr Siebeck, 1996.

Lincicum, D. "Against the Law: The *Epistle of Barnabas* and Torah Polemic in Early Christianity." Pages 105–21 in *Law and Lawlessness in Early Judaism and Early Christianity*. Edited by D. Lincicum, R. Sheridan, and C. M. Stang. WUNT 420. Tübingen: Mohr Siebeck, 2020.

Lincicum, D. "The Paratextual Invention of the Term 'Apostolic Fathers.'" *JTS* 66 (2015): 139–48.

Lindemann, A. "The First Epistle of Clement." Pages 47–69 in *The Apostolic Fathers: An Introduction*. Edited by W. Pratscher. Waco, TX: Baylor University Press, 2010.

Lindemann, A. *Paulus im ältesten Christentum: Das Bild des Apostels und die Rezeption der paulinischen Theologie in der frühchristlichen Literatur bis Marcion*. BHT 58. Tübingen: Mohr Siebeck, 1979.

Lloyd-Jones, H. *The Justice of Zeus*. 2nd ed. Berkeley: University of California Press, 1983.

Loader, W. R. G. "'Not as the Gentiles': Sexual Issues at the Interface Between Judaism and Its Greco-Roman World." *Religions* 9 (2018): 258–79.

Lohmann, H. *Drohung und Verheißung: Exegetische Untersuchungen zur Eschatologie bei den apostolischen Vätern*. BZNW 55. Berlin: de Gruyter, 1989.

Löhr, H. "The Epistles of Ignatius of Antioch." Pages 91–115 in *The Apostolic Fathers: An Introduction*. Edited by W. Pratscher. Waco, TX: Baylor University Press, 2010.

Löhr, H. "Good as a Moral Category in the Early Jesus Tradition." Pages 205–22 in *Early Christian Ethics in Interaction with Jewish and Greco-Roman Contexts*. Edited by J. W. van Henten and J. Verheyden. Leiden: Brill, 2013.

Lona, H. E. *An Diognet: Übersetzt und erklärt*. Kommentar zu frühchristlichen Apologeten 8. Freiburg: Herder, 2001.

Lona, H. E. *Die Clemensbriefe*. HNT 17. Tübingen: Möhr Siebeck, 1992.

Lona, H. E. *Der erste Clemensbrief*. KAV 2. Göttingen: Vandenhoeck & Ruprecht, 1998.

Lona, H. E. "The First Epistle of Clement." Pages 47–69 in *The Apostolic Fathers: An Introduction*. Edited by W. Pratscher. Waco, TX: Baylor University Press, 2010.

Lookadoo, J. "Christocentric Letters: Christology in the Greetings of Ignatius's *Romans*." *Journal of Biblical and Theological Studies* 3 (2018): 249–59.

Lookadoo, J. *The Christology of Ignatius of Antioch*. Studies in Early Christology. Eugene, OR: Cascade, 2023.

Lookadoo, J. "The Date and Authenticity of the Ignatian Letters: An Outline of Recent Discussions." *CBR* 19 (2020): 88–114.

Lookadoo, J. *The Epistle of Barnabas: A Commentary*. AFCS. Eugene, OR: Cascade, 2022.

Lookadoo, J. "Expanding the Narrative: The Reception of Ignatius of Antioch in Britain, ca. 1200–1700." *Church History* 89 (2020): 1–23.

Lookadoo, J. *The High Priest and the Temple: Metaphorical Depictions of Jesus in the Letters of Ignatius of Antioch*. WUNT 2/473. Tübingen: Mohr Siebeck, 2018.

Lookadoo, J. "The Letters of Ignatius." Pages 208–25 in *The Cambridge Companion to the Apostolic Fathers*. Edited by M. F. Bird and S. Harrower. Cambridge: Cambridge University Press, 2021.

Lookadoo, J. "Paul and Gender in Early Pauline Readers: Categories, Relationships, and Imitation in the Household Codes of *1 Clement*, Ignatius, and Polycarp." *Neot* 53 (2019): 31–52.

Lookadoo, J. "The Reception of the Gospel of John in the Long Recension of Ignatius's Letters." *JSNT* 42 (2020): 496–520.

Lookadoo, J. *The Shepherd of Hermas: A Literary, Historical, and Theological Handbook*. London: Bloomsbury T&T Clark, 2021.

Lotz, J.-P. *Ignatius and Concord: The Background and Use of the Language of Concord in the Letters of Ignatius of Antioch*. Patristic Studies 8. New York: Lang, 2007.

MacDiarmid, F. *The Memory of Ignatius of Antioch: The Martyr as a Locus of Christian Identity, Remembering and Remembered*. WUNT 2/581. Tübingen: Mohr Siebeck, 2022.

MacDonald, M. Y. *The Power of Children: The Construction of Christian Families in the Greco-Roman World*. Waco, TX: Baylor University Press, 2014.

MacMullen, R. "Ordinary Christians in the Later Persecutions." Pages 156–61 in *Changes in the Roman Empire: Essays in the Ordinary*. By R. MacMullen. Princeton: Princeton University Press, 1990.

Maier, H. O. "The Charismatic Authority of Ignatius of Antioch: A Sociological Analysis." *SR* 18.2 (1989): 185–99.

Maier, H. O. "Hermas' *The Shepherd*." Pages 867–70 in vol. 11 of *Encyclopedia of the Bible and Its Reception*. Edited by D. C. Allison et al. Berlin: de Gruyter, 2015.

Maier, H. O. "The Politics and Rhetoric of Discord and Concord in Paul and Ignatius." Pages 307–24 in *Trajectories Through the New Testament and the Apostolic Fathers*. Edited by A. F. Gregory and C. M. Tuckett. Oxford: Oxford University Press, 2005.

Maier, H. O. "Purity and Danger in Polycarp's Epistle to the Philippians: The Sin of Valens in Social Perspective." *JECS* 1 (1993): 229–43.

Maier, H. O. *The Social Setting of the Ministry as Reflected in the Writings of Hermas, Clement, and Ignatius*. Studies in Religion 1. Waterloo: Wilfrid Laurier University Press, 1991.

Maier, H. O. "Space, Body and Church in Ignatius of Antioch: Towards a Spatial Treatment." Pages 517–36 in *Studies on the Text of the New Testament and Early Christianity: Essays in Honor of Michael W. Holmes on the Occasion of His 65th Birthday*. Edited by D. M. Gurtner, J. Hernández, and P. Foster. NTTSD 50. Leiden: Brill, 2015.

Malherbe, A. J. "Godliness, Self-Sufficiency, Greed, and the Enjoyment of Wealth: 1 Timothy 6:3–19. Part 1." *NovT* 52 (2010): 376–405.

Malherbe, A. J. "Godliness, Self-Sufficiency, Greed, and the Enjoyment of Wealth: 1 Timothy 6:3–19. Part 2." *NovT* 53 (2011): 73–96.

Marrou, H.-I. *À Diognète*. 2nd ed. SC 33 bis. Paris: Éditions du Cerf, 1965.

Marshall, I. H. *The Gospel of Luke: A Commentary on the Greek Text*. NIGTC. Grand Rapids: Eerdmans, 1978.

Marshall, J. W. "The Objects of Ignatius' Wrath and Jewish Angelic Mediators." *JEH* 56 (2005): 1–23.

Massaux, É., *The Influence of the Gospel of Saint Matthew on Christian Literature Before Saint Irenaeus*. Translated by N. J. Belval and S. Hecht. 3 vols. Macon: Mercer University Press, 1994. French original, 1950.

McCready, W. O. "Education in the *Sacrospace* of Qumran Judaism." Pages 55–75 in *Religions and Education in Antiquity: Studies in Honour of Michel Dejardins*. Edited by A. Damm. Leiden: Brill, 2018.

McLarty, J. D. "Early Christian Theologies of Martyrdom." Pages 120–34 in *The Wiley Blackwell Companion to Christian Martyrdom*. Edited by P. Middleton. WBCR. Chichester: Wiley Blackwell, 2020.

McLynn, N. "Disciplines of Discipleship in Late Antique Education: Augustine and Gregory Nazianzen." Pages 25–48 in *Augustine and the Disciplines: From Cassiciacum to Confessions*. Edited by K. Pollmann and M. Vessey. Oxford: Oxford University Press, 2007.

McWilliam, J. "The Socialization of Roman Children." Pages 264–85 in *The Oxford Handbook of Childhood and Education in the Classical World*. Edited by J. E. Grubbs and T. Parkin. Oxford: Oxford University Press, 2013.

Meecham, H. G. *The Epistle to Diognetus*. Manchester: Manchester University Press, 1949.

Meeks, W. A. "The Image of the Androgyne: Some Uses of a Symbol in Early Christianity." Pages 3–54 in *In Search of the Early Christians: Selected Essays*. Edited by A. R. Hilton and H. G. Snyder. New Haven: Yale University Press, 2002.

Menken, M. J. J. "Old Testament Quotations in the *Epistle of Barnabas* with Parallels in the New Testament." Pages 295–321 in *Textual History and the Reception of Scripture in Early Christianity*. Edited by J. de Vries and M. Karrer. Atlanta: Society of Biblical Literature, 2013.

Metzger, B. M. "Patristic Evidence and the Textual Criticism of the New Testament." Pages 167–88 in *New Testament Studies: Philological, Versional, and Patristic*. Leiden: Brill, 1980.

Middleton, P. "Early Christian Voluntary Martyrdom: A Statement for the Defence." *JTS* 64 (2013): 556–73.

Milavec, A. *The Didache: Faith, Hope, and Life of the Earliest Christian Communities, 50–70 C.E.* New York: Newman, 2003.

Milavec, A. "Synoptic Tradition in the Didache Revisited." *JECS* 11 (2003): 443–480. With a reply by C. M. Tuckett and a rejoinder by Milavec in *JECS* 13 (2005): 509–18 and 519–23.

Minns, D. "The *Rescript* of Hadrian." Pages 38–49 in *Justin Martyr and His Worlds*. Edited by S. Parvis and P. Foster. Minneapolis: Fortress, 2007.

Mitchell, M. W. "In the Footsteps of Paul: Scriptural and Apostolic Authority in Ignatius." *JECS* 14 (2006): 27–45.

Mitchell, S., and P. Van Nuffelen, eds. *One God: Pagan Monotheism in the Roman Empire*. Cambridge: Cambridge University Press, 2010.

Molland, E. "The Heretics Combatted by Ignatius of Antioch." *JEH* 5 (1954): 1–6.

Morgan, T. *Being "in Christ" in the Letters of Paul: Saved Through Christ and in His Hands*. Tübingen: Mohr Siebeck, 2020.

Morgan, T. *Literate Education in the Hellenistic and Roman Worlds*. Cambridge: Cambridge University Press, 1998.

Morgan, T. "Not the Whole Story? Moralizing Biography and *Imitatio Christi*." Pages 353–66 in *Fame and Infamy: Essays for Christopher Pelling on Characterization in Greek and Roman Biography and History*. Edited by R. Ash, J. Mossman, and F. Titchmarsh. Oxford: Oxford University Press, 2015.

Morgan, T. *Popular Morality in the Early Roman Empire*. Cambridge: Cambridge University Press, 2007.

Moriarty, W. "1 Clement's View of Ministerial Appointments in the Early Church." *VC* 66 (2012): 115–38.

Morlet, S., O. Munnich, and B. Pouderon, eds. *Les dialogues adversus Iudaeos: Permanences et mutations d'une tradition polémique*. Collection des Études Augustiniennes, Série Antiquité 196. Paris: Institut d'Études Augustiniennes, 2013.

Moss, C. R. *Ancient Christian Martyrdom: Diverse Practices, Theologies, and Traditions*. New Haven: Yale University Press, 2012.

Moss, C. R. "Current Trends in the Study of Early Christian Martyrdom." *Bulletin for the Study of Religion* 41.3 (2012): 22–29.

Moss, C. R. "The Discourse of Voluntary Martyrdom: Ancient and Modern." *Church History* 81 (2012): 531–51.

Moss, C. R. "Nailing Down and Tying Up: Lessons in Intertextual Impossibility from the Martyrdom of Polycarp." *VC* 67 (2013): 117–36.

Moss, C. R. "On the Dating of Polycarp: Rethinking the Place of the *Martyrdom of Polycarp* in the History of Christianity." *Early Christianity* 1 (2010): 539–74.

Moss, C. R. *The Other Christs: Imitating Jesus in Ancient Christian Ideologies of Martyrdom*. Oxford: Oxford University Press, 2010.

Moss, Y. "'From Syria All the Way to Rome': Ignatius of Antioch's Pauline Journey to Christianity." Pages 409–21 in *Journeys in the Roman East: Imagined and Real*. Edited by M. R. Niehoff. Culture, Religion, and Politics in the Greco-Roman World 1. Tübingen: Mohr Siebeck, 2017.

Moxnes, H. "God and His Angel in the Shepherd of Hermas." *ST* 28 (1974): 49–56.

Muddiman, J. "The Church in Ephesians, 2 Clement, and the Shepherd of Hermas." Pages 107–21 in *Trajectories Through the New Testament and the Apostolic Fathers*. Edited by A. F. Gregory and C. M. Tuckett. Oxford: Oxford University Press, 2005.

Munier, C. "Où en est la question d'Ignace d'Antioche? Bilan d'un siècle de recherches 1870–1988." *ANRW* 27.1.359–484. Part 2, *Principat*, 27.1. Edited by H. Temporini and W. Haase. Berlin: de Gruyter, 1992.

Newman, L. E. *Past Imperatives: Studies in the History and Theory of Jewish Ethics*. Albany: State University of New York, 1998.

Nichols, J. *Civic Patronage in the Roman Empire*. Leiden: Brill, 2013.

Nicholson, O. "What Makes a Voluntary Martyr?" StPatr 65 (2013): 159–64.

Nicklas, T. "*Epistula ad Diognetum* (Diognetus): The Christian 'New Genos' and Its Construction of the Others." Pages 490–504 in *Sensitivity Towards Outsiders: Exploring the Dynamic Relationship Between Mission and Ethics in the New Testament and Early Christianity*. Edited by J. Kok, T. Nicklas, D. T. Roth, and C. M. Hays. WUNT 2/364. Tübingen: Mohr Siebeck, 2014.

Nicklas, T. "Living as a 'Christian': Christian Ethos According to the Writings of Ignatius of Antioch." Pages 537–54 in *Studies on the Text of the New Testament and Early Christianity: Essays in Honor of Michael W. Holmes on the Occasion of His 65th Birthday*. Edited by D. M. Gurtner, J. Hernández, and P. Foster. NTTSD 50. Leiden: Brill, 2015.

Niederwimmer, K. *Die Didache*. KAV 1. Göttingen: Vandenhoeck & Ruprecht, 1989.

Niederwimmer, K. *The Didache: A Commentary*. Translated by L. M. Maloney. Hermeneia. Minneapolis: Augsburg Fortress, 1998.

Nielsen, C. M. "Polycarp, Paul, and the Scriptures." *AThR* 47 (1965): 199–216.

Nock, A. D. *Early Gentile Christianity and Its Hellenistic Background*. New York: Harper & Row, 1964.

Nock, A. D. "Soter and Euergetes." Pages 720–35 in vol. 2 of *Essays on Religion and the Ancient World*. Edited by Z. Stewart. 2 vols. Oxford: Oxford University Press, 1972.

Nongbri, B. "The Limits of Palaeographic Dating of Literary Papyri: Some Observations on the Date and Provenance of P.Bodmer II (P66)." *MH* 71 (2014): 1–35.

Nongbri, B. "Palaeographic Analysis of Codices from the Early Christian Period: A Point of Method." *JSNT* 42 (2019): 84–97.

Nongbri, B. "The Use and Abuse of P52: Papyrological Pitfalls in the Dating of the Fourth Gospel." *HTR* 98 (2005): 23–48.

Noormann, R. "Himmelsbürger auf Erden: Anmerkungen zum Weltverhältnis und zum 'Paulinismus' des Auctor ad Diognetum." Pages 199–230 in *Die Weltlichkeit des Glaubens in der Alten Kirche*. FS U. Wickert. Edited by B. Aland, C. Schäublin, D. Wyrwa. BZNW 85. Berlin: de Gruyter, 1997.

Norelli, E. *Papia di Hierapolis, Esposizione degli Oracoli del Signore: I frammenti*. Letture cristiane del primo millennio 36. Milan: Paoline, 2005.

Norelli, E. "Ramener l'*A Diognète* en Asie Mineure? Une discussion de la these de Charles E. Hill." Pages 91–117 in *A Diognète*. Edited by G. Aragione, E. Norelli, and F. G. Nuvolone. CahGSEP 1. Prahins: Éditions du Zèbre, 2012.

Norris, R. A. "The Apologists." Pages 36–44 in *The Cambridge History of Early Christian Literature*. Edited by F. Young, L. Ayres, and A. Louth. Cambridge: Cambridge University Press, 2004.

Novick, T. *What Is Good, and What God Demands: Normative Studies in Tannaitic Literature*. Leiden: Brill, 2010.

Oberweis, M. "Das Papias-Zeugnis vom Tode des Johannes-Zebedäi." *NovT* 38 (1996): 277–95.

O'Hagan, A. P. *Material Re-Creation in the Apostolic Fathers*. TUGAL 100. Berlin: Akademie, 1968.

O'Loughlin, T. *The Didache: A Window on the Earliest Christians*. Grand Rapids: Baker Academic, 2010.

Osburn, C. D. "Methodology in Identifying Patristic Citations in New Testament Textual Criticism." *NovT* 47 (2005): 313–43.

Osiek, C. "Apostolic Fathers." Pages 529–46 in *The Early Christian World*. Edited by P. F. Esler. Rev. ed. London: Routledge, 2017.

Osiek, C. "The Bride of Christ (Ephesians 5:22–33): A Problematic Wedding." *BTB* 32.1 (2002): 29–39. Reprinted on pages 371–92 in *Sacred Marriages: The Divine-Human Sexual Metaphor from Sumer to Early Christianity*. Edited by M. Nissinen and R. Uro. Winona Lake, IN: Eisenbrauns, 2008.

Osiek, C. "The Education of Girls in Early Christian Ascetic Tradition." *Studies in Religion* 41 (2012): 401–7.

Osiek, C. *Shepherd of Hermas: A Commentary*. Hermeneia. Minneapolis: Augsburg Fortress, 1999.

Osiek, C., and D. L. Balch. *Families in the New Testament World: Households and House Churches*. Louisville: Westminster John Knox, 1997.

Osiek, C., and M. Y. MacDonald, with J. H. Tulloch. *A Woman's Place: House Churches in Earliest Christianity*. Minneapolis: Augsburg Fortress, 2006.

Ounsworth, R. *Joshua Typology in the New Testament*. WUNT 2/328. Tübingen: Mohr Siebeck, 2012.

Paramelle, J., and P. Adnès. "Hermas." Pages 316–34 in vol. 7.1 of *Dictionnaire de spiritualité, ascétique et mystique,* doctrine et histoire. Paris: Beauchesne, 1969.

Pardee, N. *The Genre and Development of the Didache*. WUNT 2/339. Tübingen: Mohr Siebeck, 2012.

Parvis, P. "Polycarp, *To the Philippians*." Pages 59–72 in *From Thomas to Tertullian: Christian Literary Receptions of Jesus in the Second and Third Centuries CE*. Vol. 2 of *The Reception of Jesus in the First Three Centuries*. Edited by C. Keith, H. K. Bond, C. Jacobi, and J. Schröter. London: Bloomsbury T&T Clark, 2020.

Parvis, S. "The Martyrdom of Polycarp." Pages 126–46 in *The Writings of the Apostolic Fathers*. Edited by P. Foster. London: T&T Clark, 2007.

Paulsen, H. *Die Briefe des Ignatius von Antiochia und der Brief des Polykarp von Smyrna*. 2nd ed. HNT 18. Tübingen: Möhr Siebeck, 1985.

Paulsen, H. *Studien zur Theologie des Ignatius von Antiochien*. Forschungen zur Kirchen- und Dogmengeschichte 29. Göttingen: Vandenhoeck & Ruprecht, 1978.

Pelikan, J. *Development of Christian Doctrine: Some Historical Prolegomena*. New Haven: Yale University, 1969.

Pendergraft, M. "'Thou Shalt Not Eat the Hyena': A Note on 'Barnabas' Epistle 10.7." *VC* 46 (1992): 75–79.

Perler, O. "Pseudo-Ignatius und Eusebius von Emesa." *Historisches Jahrbuch* 77 (1958): 73–82.

Pernveden, L. *The Concept of the Church in the Shepherd of Hermas*. Studia Theologica Lundensia 27. Lund: Gleerup, 1966.

Petersen, A. K. "Attaining Divine Perfection Through Different Forms of Imitation." *Numen* 60 (2013): 7–38.

Poschmann, B. *Paenitentia secunda: Die kirchliche Buße im ältesten Christentum bis Cyprian und Origenes: Eine dogmengeschichtliche Untersuchung*. Theophaneia 1. Bonn: Hanstein, 1940.

Pratscher, W. "The Motivations of Ethos in 2 Clement." Pages 597–610 in *Identity, Ethics, and Ethos in the New Testament*. Edited by J. G. van der Watt. Berlin: de Gruyter, 2006.

Pratscher, W. "Quadratus." Pages 181–95 in *The Apostolic Fathers: An Introduction*. Edited by W. Pratscher. Waco, TX: Baylor University Press, 2010.

Pratscher, W. *Der zweite Clemensbrief*. KAV 3. Göttingen: Vandenhoeck & Ruprecht, 2007.

Pratscher, W., ed. *The Apostolic Fathers: An Introduction*. Waco, TX: Baylor University Press, 2010.

Prigent, P. *Les Testimonia dans le christianisme primitif: L'Epître de Barnabé 1–16 et ses sources*. Paris: Gabalda, 1961.

Proctor, T. W. "Books, Scribes, and Cultures of Reading in the Shepherd of Hermas." *JEH* 30 (2021): 1–19.

Prostmeier, F. R. "Antijudaismus im Rahmen christlicher Hermeneutik: zum Streit über christliche Identität in der Alten Kirche. Notizen zum Barnabasbrief." *ZAC* 6 (2002): 38–58.

Prostmeier, F. R. *Der Barnabasbrief*. KAV 8. Göttingen: Vandenhoeck & Ruprecht, 1999.

Prostmeier, F. R. "The Epistle of Barnabas." Pages 27–45 in *The Apostolic Fathers: An Introduction*. Edited by W. Pratscher. Waco, TX: Baylor University Press, 2010.

Prostmeier, F. R. "Zur handschriftlichen Überlieferung des Polykarp- und des Barnabasbriefes: Zwei nicht beachtete Deszendenten des Cod. Vat. Gr. 859." *VC* 48 (1994): 48–64.

Quantin, J.-L. "L'orthodoxie, la censure et la gloire: La difficile édition princeps de l'Épître de Barnabé, de Rome à Amsterdam (1549–1646)." Pages 103–62 in *"Editiones Principes" delle Opere dei Padri Greci e Latini*. Edited by M. Cortesi. Florence: Edizioni del Galluzzo, 2006.

Rahner, K. "The Penitential Teaching of the Shepherd of Hermas." *Theological Investigations* 15 (1982): 57–113.

Rappe, S. "The New Math: How to Add and Subtract Pagan Elements in Christian Education." Pages 405–32 in *Education in Greek and Roman Antiquity*. Edited by Y. L. Too. Leiden: Brill, 2001.

Rawson, B. *Children and Childhood in Roman Italy*. Oxford: Oxford University Press, 2003.

Rebell, W. "Das Leidensverständnis bei Paulus und Ignatius von Antiochien." *NTS* 32 (1986): 457–65.

Rebillard, É. *Greek and Latin Narratives About the Ancient Martyrs*. Oxford: Oxford University Press, 2017.

Reis, D. M. "Following in Paul's Footsteps: *Mimēsis* and Power in Ignatius." Pages 287–305 in *Trajectories Through the New Testament and Apostolic Fathers*. Edited by A. F. Gregory and C. M. Tuckett. Oxford: Oxford University Press, 2005.

Remus, H. *Pagan-Christian Conflict Over Miracle in the Second Century*. PMS 10. Cambridge, MA: Philadelphia Patristic Foundation, 1983.

Renan, E. *Histoire des origenes du christianisme 2: Les évangiles et la seconde generation chrétienne*. Paris: Lévy, 1877.

Resch, A. *Agrapha: Aussercanonische Schriftfragmente gesammelt und untersucht*. 2nd ed. Leipzig: Hinrichs, 1906.

Rhee, H. "Wealth, Poverty, and Eschatology: Pre-Constantine Christian Social Thought and the Hope for the World to Come." Pages 64–84 in *Reading Patristic Texts on Social Ethics: Issues and Challenges for Twenty-First Century Christian Social Thought*. Edited by J. Leemans, B. J. Matz, and J. Verstraeten. CUA Studies in Early Christianity. Washington, DC: Catholic University of America Press, 2011.

Rhodes, J. N. "'Barnabas' 4.6b: The Exegetical Implications of a Textual Problem." *VC* 58.4 (2004): 365–92.

Rhodes, J. N. *The Epistle of Barnabas and the Deuteronomic Tradition: Polemics, Paraenesis, and the Legacy of the Golden-Calf Incident*. WUNT 2/188. Tübingen: Mohr Siebeck, 2004.

Rhodes, J. N. "The Two Ways Tradition in the Epistle of Barnabas: Revisiting an Old Question." *CBQ* 73 (2011): 797–816.

Riddle, D. W. "From Apocalypse to Martyrology." *AThR* 9 (1927): 260–280.

Riddle, D. W. "A Literary Allusion in the Martyrdom of Polycarp." *AThR* 8 (1925): 136–42.

Rius-Camps, J. *The Four Authentic Letters of Ignatius, the Martyr: A Critical Study Based in Anomalies Contained in the Textus Receptus*. Orientalia Christiana Analecta 213. Rome: Pontificium Institutum Orientalium Studiorum, 1980.

Rizzi, M., ed. *Hadrian and the Christians*. Millenium Studies 30. Berlin: de Gruyter, 2010.

Robinson, J. A. T. *Redating the New Testament*. London: SCM, 1976.

Robinson, T. A. *Ignatius of Antioch and the Parting of the Ways: Early Jewish-Christian Relations*. Peabody, MA: Hendrickson, 2009.

Rordorf, W. "Aux origenes du culte des martyrs." *Irénikon* 45 (1972): 315–31.

Rordorf, W. "Does the Didache Contain Jesus Tradition Independently of the Synoptic Gospels?" Pages 394–423 in *Jesus and the Oral Gospel Tradition*. Edited by H. Wansborough. JSNTSup 64. Sheffield: Sheffield Academic, 1991.

Rordorf, W., and A. Tuilier. *La Doctrine des douze apôtres (Didachè)*. 2nd ed. SC 248 bis. Paris: Éditions du Cerf, 1998.

Rosell, S. "Loving God unto Death: The Witness of the Early Christians." *HTS Theological Studies* 66 (2010): 1–9.

Rothschild, C. K. "Down the Rabbit Hole with Barnabas: Rewriting Moses in Barnabas 10." *NTS* 64 (2018): 410–34.

Rothschild, C. K. "Ethiopianising the Devil: ὁ μέλας in Barnabas 4." *NTS* 65 (2019): 223–45.

Rothschild, C. K. "*Horror vacui*: Welborn's 'Retrospect on a Challenge to the Consensus on the Date of 1 Clement.'" *BR* 65 (2020): 104–13.

Rothschild, C. K. *New Essays on the Apostolic Fathers*. WUNT 375. Tübingen: Mohr Siebeck, 2017.

Rothschild, C. K. "Soteriology and the Allegorical Construction of Opponents in the Epistle of Barnabas." Pages 561–76 in *Sōtēria: Salvation in Early Christianity and Antiquity*. Edited by D. S. du Toit, C. Gerber, and C. Zimmermann. NovTSup 175. Leiden: Brill, 2019.

Sailors, T. B. Review of *The Apostolic Fathers: Greek Texts and English Translations*, 3rd ed. by Michael W. Holmes. *Bryn Mawr Classical Review* (2009).

Salles, R., ed. *God and Cosmos in Stoicism*. Oxford: Oxford University Press, 2009.

Sanday, W. *The Gospels in the Second Century*. London: MacMillan, 1876.

Sanders, E. P. *Paul and Palestinian Judaism: A Comparison of Patterns of Religion*. Philadelphia: Fortress, 1977.

Sandt, H. van de. "Matthew and the Didache." Pages 123–38 in *Matthew and His Christian Contemporaries*. Edited by D. C. Sim and B. Repschinski. LNTS 133. London: T&T Clark, 2008.

Sandt, H. van de, ed. *Matthew and the Didache: Two Documents from the Same Jewish-Christian Milieu?* Minneapolis: Fortress, 2005.

Sandt, H. van de, and D. Flusser. *The Didache: Its Jewish Sources and Its Place in Early Judaism and Christianity*. CRINT III/5. Assen: Van Gorcum; Minneapolis: Fortress, 2002.

Sandt, H. van de, and J. K. Zangenberg, eds. *Matthew, James, and Didache: Three Related Documents in Their Jewish and Christian Settings*. SBLSymS 45. Atlanta: SBL, 2008.

Sargent, B. "Neither Jew nor Greek: Ignatius of Antioch's Use of Scripture and the 'Parting(s) of the Ways.'" *NovT* 65 (2023): 240–55.

Schmithals, W. "Zu Ignatius von Antiochien." *ZAC* 13 (2009): 181–203.

Schneider, A. *"Propter sanctam ecclesiam suam": Die Kirche als Geschöpf, Frau und Bau im Bußunterricht des Pastor Hermae*. SEAug 67. Rome: Institutum Patristicum Augustinianum, 1999.

Schneider, G. *Clemens von Rom, Epistola ad Corinthios / Brief an die Korinther*. Fontes Christiani 15. Freiburg: Herder, 1994.

Schoedel, W. R. "Ignatius and the Archives." *HTR* 71 (1978): 97–106.

Schoedel, W. R. *Ignatius of Antioch: A Commentary*. Hermeneia. Philadelphia: Fortress, 1985.

Schoedel, W. R. "Papias." *ABD* 5:140–42.

Schoedel, W. R. *Polycarp, Martyrdom of Polycarp, Fragments of Papias*. Vol. 5 of *The Apostolic Fathers: A New Translation and Commentary*. New York: Thomas Nelson, 1967.

Schoedel, W. R. "Polycarp of Smyrna and Ignatius of Antioch." *ANRW* 27.1:272–358. Part 2, *Principat*, 27.1. Edited by H. Temporini and W. Haase. Berlin: de Gruyter, 1992.

Schöllgen, G. "The Didache as Church Order: An Examination of the Purpose for the Composition of the Didache and Its Consequences for Interpretation." Pages 43–71 in *The Didache in Modern Research*. Edited by J. A. Draper. AGJU 37. Leiden: Brill, 1996.

Schöllgen, G. "Die Ignatianen als pseudepigraphisches Briefcorpus." *ZAC* 2 (1998): 16–25.

Schreckenberg, H. *Die christlichen Adversus-Judaeos-Texte und ihr literarisches und historisches Umfeld*. 3 vols. Frankfurt am Main: Lang, 1982–1994.

Schröter, J. "Jesus Tradition in Matthew, James, and the Didache: Searching for Characteristic Emphases." Pages 233–55 in *Matthew, James, and Didache: Three Related Documents in Their Jewish and Christian Settings*. Edited by H. van de Sandt and J. K. Zangenberg. SBLSymS 45. Atlanta: SBL, 2008.

Schwiebert, J. *Knowledge and the Coming Kingdom: The Didache's Meal Ritual and Its Place in Early Christianity*. LNTS 373. London: T&T Clark, 2008.

Scullard, H. H. "Minicius Fundanus, Gaius." In *Oxford Classical Dictionary*. Edited by S. Hornblower, A. Spawforth, and E. Eidinow. 4th ed. Oxford: Oxford University Press, 2012.

Setzer, C. *Resurrection of the Body in Early Judaism and Early Christianity: Doctrine, Community, and Self-Definition*. Leiden: Brill, 2004.

Sieben, H. J. "Die Ignatianen als Briefe: Einige formkritische Bemerkungen." *VC* 32 (1978): 1–18.

Simon, M. *Verus Israel: A Study of the Relations Between Christians and Jews in the Roman Empire AD 135–425*. Translated by H. McKeating. Littman Library of Jewish Civilization. London: Littman, 1986 [orig. 1964].

Skarsaune, O. *The Proof from Prophecy: A Study in Justin Martyr's Proof-Text Tradition: Text-Type, Provenance, Theological Profile*. NovTSup 56. Leiden: Brill, 1987.

Skinner, M. *Sexuality in Greek and Roman Culture*. 2nd ed. Chichester: Wiley-Blackwell, 2014.

Sly, D. I. *Philo's Perception of Women*. Providence, RI: Brown Judaic Studies, 2020.
Smit, P.-B. "On Being Consumed: The Martyred Body as a Site of Divine-Human Encounter in Ignatius of Antioch." *Religions* 11 (2020:) 1–13.
Smith, C. B. "Ministry, Martyrdom, and Other Mysteries: Pauline Influence on Ignatius of Antioch." Pages 37–56 in *Paul and the Second Century*. Edited by M. F. Bird and J. R. Dodson. LNTS 412. London: T&T Clark, 2011.
Smith, J. C. H. "The *Epistle of Barnabas* and the Two Ways of Teaching Authority." *VC* 68 (2014): 465–97.
Snyder, G. F. *Hermas*. Vol. 6 of *The Apostolic Fathers: A New Translation and Commentary*. New York: Thomas Nelson, 1968.
Snyder, G. F. "The Historical Jesus in the Letters of Ignatius of Antioch." *BR* 8 (1963): 3–12.
Soon, I. T. "Satan and Circumcision: The Devil as the ἄγγελος πονηρός in Barn 9:4." *VC* 76 (2022): 60–72.
Soyars, J. E. *The Shepherd of Hermas and the Pauline Legacy*. NovTSup 176. Leiden: Brill, 2019.
Stanglin, K. D. "The Historical Connection Between the Golden Rule and the Second Greatest Love Command." *Journal of Religious Ethics* 33 (2005): 357–71.
Stanley, C. D. *Paul and the Language of Scripture: Citation Technique in the Pauline Epistles and Contemporary Literature*. SNTSMS 74. Cambridge: Cambridge University Press, 1992.
Ste. Croix, G. de. *Early Christian Attitudes to Property and Slavery*. Oxford: Blackwell, 1975.
Ste. Croix, G. de. "Why Were the Early Christians Persecuted?" *Past & Present* 26 (1963): 6–38.
Steenbuch, J. A. "How 'Trivial' Is the Golden Rule in Patristic Ethics?" *Danish Yearbook of Philosophy* 51 (2018): 3–23.
Steenberg, M. C. "Irenaeus on Scripture, *Graphe*, and the Status of *Hermas*." *SVTQ* 53 (2009): 29–66.
Stewart-Sykes, A., ed. *On the Two Ways: Life or Death, Light or Darkness: Foundational Texts in the Tradition*. Popular Patristics Series 41. Yonkers, NY: St Vladimir's Seminary Press, 2011.
Still, T. D. "Ignatius and Paul on Suffering and Death: A Short Comparative Study." Pages 136–42 in *The Apostolic Fathers and Paul*. Edited by T. D. Still and D. E. Wilhite. Pauline and Patristic Scholars in Debate 2. London: Bloomsbury T&T Clark, 2017.
Stoops, R. F., Jr. "If I Suffer: Epistolary Authority in Ignatius of Antioch." *HTR* 80 (1987): 161–78.
Sundberg, A. C. "Canon Muratori: A Fourth-Century List." *HTR* 66 (1973): 1–41.
Svigel, M. J., and C. P. Buie. *The Shepherd of Hermas: A New Translation and Commentary*. AFCS. Eugene: Cascade, 2023.
Syreeni, K. "The Sermon on the Mount and the Two Ways Teaching of the Didache." Pages 87–103 in *Matthew, James, and Didache: Three Related Documents in Their Jewish and Christian Settings*. Edited by H. van de Sandt and J. K. Zangenberg. SBLSymS 45. Atlanta: SBL, 2008.
Tabbernee, W. "Early Montanism and Voluntary Martyrdom." *Colloquium* 17 (1985): 33–44.
Tabbernee, W. "Montanists and Voluntary Martyrdom." Pages 201–42 in *Fake Prophecy and Polluted Sacraments*. Edited by W. Tabbernee. VCSup 84. Leiden: Brill, 2007.
Tagliabue, A. "Learning from Allegorical Images in the *Book of Visions* of *The Shepherd of Hermas*." *Arethusa* 50 (2017): 221–55.
Tanner, R. G. "Martyrdom in Saint Ignatius of Antioch and the Stoic View of Suicide." StPatr 16 (1985): 201–5.
Taveirne, M. "Das Martyrium als *imitatio Christi*: Die literarische Gestaltung der spätantiken Märtyrerakten und Passionen nach der Passion Christi." *ZAC* 18 (2014): 167–203.
Taylor, M. S. *Anti-Judaism and Early Christian Identity: A Critique of the Scholarly Consensus*. Leiden: Brill, 1995.
Thiselton, A. C. *The First Epistle to the Corinthians*. NIGTC. Grand Rapids: Eerdmans, 2000.
Thomas, M. J. *Paul's "Works of the Law" in the Perspective of Second-Century Reception*. Downers Grove, IL: InterVarsity Press, 2020.
Thorsteinsson, R. M. *Roman Christianity and Roman Stoicism: A Comparative Study of Ancient Morality*. Oxford: Oxford University Press, 2010.
Tite, P. L. "Voluntary Martyrdom and Gnosticism." *JECS* 23 (2015): 27–54.
Tolley, H. "The Jewish-Christian Dialogue *Jason and Papiscus* in Light of the Sinaiticus Fragment." *HTR* 114 (2021): 1–26.
Tornau, C., and P. Cecconi, eds. *The Shepherd of Hermas in Latin: Critical Edition of the Oldest Translation Vulgata*. TUGAL 173. Berlin: de Gruyter, 2014.
Torrance, T. F. *The Doctrine of Grace in the Apostolic Fathers*. London: Oliver and Boyd, 1948.
Trebilco, P. "Christian Communities in Western Asia Minor into the Early Second Century: Ignatius and Others as Witnesses Against Bauer." *JETS* 49 (2006): 17–44.
Trebilco, P. *The Early Christians in Ephesus from Paul to Ignatius*. WUNT 166. Tübingen: Mohr Siebeck, 2004.
Trevett, C. *Christian Women and the Time of the Apostolic Fathers (AD c. 80–160): Corinth, Rome and Asia Minor*. Cardiff: University of Wales Press, 2006.
Trevett, C. *A Study of Ignatius of Antioch in Syria and Asia*. Studies in the Bible and Early Christianity 29. Lewiston: Edwin Mellen, 1992.

Tripp, D. "The Prayer of St. Polycarp and the Development of Anaphoral Prayer." *Ephemerides Liturgicae* 104 (1990): 97–132.

Tuckett, C. M. *2 Clement: Introduction, Text, and Commentary*. OAF. Oxford: Oxford University Press, 2012.

Tuckett, C. M. *Christology and the New Testament: Jesus and His Earliest Followers*. Edinburgh: Edinburgh University Press, 2001.

Tuckett, C. M. "The Didache and the Writings That Later Formed the New Testament." Pages 83–127 in *The Reception of the New Testament in the Apostolic Fathers*. Edited by A. F. Gregory and C. M. Tuckett. Oxford: Oxford University Press, 2005.

Tuckett, C. M. "Synoptic Tradition in the Didache." Pages 92–128 in *The Didache in Modern Research*. Edited by J. A. Draper. AGJU 37. Leiden: Brill, 1996.

Tuckett, C. M. "Synoptic Tradition in the Didache." Pages 197–230 in *The New Testament in Early Christianity = La réception des écrits néotestamentaires dans le christianisme primitive*. Edited by J.-M. Sevrin. BETL 86. Leuven: Leuven University Press, 1989.

Ulrich, J. "The Apostolic Fathers Yesterday and Today." Pages 255–60 in *The Apostolic Fathers: An Introduction*. Edited by W. Pratscher. Waco, TX: Baylor University Press, 2010.

Unnik, W. C. van. "Is 1 Clement 20 Purely Stoic?" *VC* 4 (1950): 181–89.

Unnik, W. C. van. "Zur Bedeutung von Ταπεινοῦν τὴν ψυχήν bei den apostolischen Vätern." *ZNW* 44 (1952–1953): 250–55.

Vall, G. "Attaining God: The Spiritual Theology of Ignatius of Antioch." Pages 91–108 in *Patristic Spirituality: Classical Perspectives on Ascent in the Journey to God*. Edited by D. W. Springer and K. M. Clarke. Studies in Theology and Religion 30. Leiden: Brill, 2022.

Vall, G. *Learning Christ: Ignatius of Antioch and the Mystery of Redemption*. Washington, DC: Catholic University of America Press, 2013.

Varner, W. C. "The Didache 'Apocalypse' and Matthew 24." *BSac* 165 (2008): 309–22.

Varner, W. C. *Second Clement: An Introductory Commentary*. AFCS. Eugene: Cascade Books, 2021.

Varner, W. C. *The Way of the Didache: The First Christian Handbook*. New York: University Press of America, 2007.

Verheyden, J. "The Canon Muratori: A Matter of Dispute." Pages 487–556 in *The Biblical Canons*. Edited by J.-M. Auwers and H. J. de Jonge. Leuven: Leuven University Press, 2003.

Verheyden, J. "Didache." Pages 337–62 in *From Paul to Josephus: Literary Receptions of Jesus in the First Century CE*. Vol. 1 of *The Reception of Jesus in the First Three Centuries*. Edited by C. Keith, H. K. Bond, C. Jacobi, and J. Schröter. London: Bloomsbury T&T Clark, 2020.

Verheyden, J. "Dreams, Visions and the World-to-Come According to the Shepherd of Hermas." Pages 215–34 in *Dreams, Visions, Imaginations: Jewish, Christian and Gnostic Views of the World to Come*. Edited by J. Schröter, T. Nicklas, and A. Puig i Tàrrech. BZNW 247. Berlin: de Gruyter, 2021.

Verheyden, J. "Eschatology in the Didache and the Gospel of Matthew." Pages 193–215 in *Matthew and the Didache: Two Documents from the Same Jewish-Christian Milieu?* Edited by H. van de Sandt. Minneapolis: Fortress, 2005.

Verheyden, J. "The Shepherd of Hermas and the Writings That Later Formed the New Testament." Pages 293–329 in *The Reception of the New Testament in the Apostolic Fathers*. Edited by A. F. Gregory & C. M. Tuckett. Oxford: Oxford University Press, 2005.

Vezzoni, A., ed. *Il Pastore di Erma: Versione Palatina*. Il Nuovo Melograno 13. Florence: Le Lettere, 1994.

Vincelette, A. "On the Frequency of Voluntary Martyrdom in the Patristic Era." *JTS* 70 (2019): 652–79.

Vinzent, M. "Ertragen und Ausharren: Die Lebenslehre des Barnabasbriefes." *ZNW* 86 (1995): 74–93.

Vinzent, M. *Writing the History of Early Christianity: From Reception to Retrospection*. Cambridge: Cambridge University Press, 2019.

Walls, A. F. "Papias and Oral Tradition." *VC* 21 (1967): 137–40.

Walsh, L. "Ecclesia Reconsidered: Two Premodern Encounters with the Feminine Church." *Journal of Feminist Studies in Religion* 33 (2017): 73–91.

Walsh, L. "The Lady as Elder in the *Shepherd of Hermas*." *JECS* 27 (2019): 517–47.

Walsh, L. "Lost in Revision: Gender Symbolism in *Vision* 3 and *Similitude* 9 of the *Shepherd of Hermas*." *HTR* 112 (2019): 467–90.

Wansborough, H., ed. *Jesus and the Oral Gospel Tradition*. Edinburgh: T&T Clark, 2004.

Watt, J. G. van der, ed. *Identity, Ethics, and Ethos in the New Testament*. Berlin: de Gruyter, 2006.

Weinandy, T. G. "The Apostolic Christology of Ignatius of Antioch: The Road to Chalcedon." Pages 71–84 in *Trajectories Through the New Testament and the Apostolic Fathers*. Edited by A. F. Gregory and C. M. Tuckett. Oxford: Oxford University Press, 2005.

Weinrich, W. C. *Spirit and Martyrdom: A Study of the Work of the Holy Spirit in Contexts of Persecution and Martyrdom in the New Testament and Early Christian Literature*. Lanham, MD: University Press of America, 1981.

Welborn, L. L. "1 Clement." *ABD* 1:1055–60.

Welborn, L. L. "On the Date of 1 Clement." *BR* 29 (1984): 35–54. Reprinted on pages 197–216 in *Encounters with Hellenism: Studies on the 1 Letter of Clement*. Edited by C. Breytenbach and L. L. Welborn. Leiden: Brill, 2003.

Welborn, L. L. "Retrospect on a Challenge to the Consensus on the Date of 1 Clement." *BR* 65 (2020): 95–103.

Welborn, L. L. *The Young and the Old: Generational Conflict in First Clement*. Lanham, MD: Fortress, 2018.

Wengst, K. *Didache (Apostellehre), Barnabasbrief, Zweiter Klemensbrief, Schrift an Diognet*. Munich: Kösel, 1984.

Wengst, K. *Tradition und Theologie des Barnabasbriefes*. Arbeiten zur Kirchengeschichte 42. Berlin: de Gruyter, 1971.

Wet, C. L de. "No Small Counsel About Self-Control: *Enkrateia* and the Virtuous Body as Missional Performance in 2 Clement." Pages 447–69 in *Sensitivity Towards Outsiders*. Edited by J. Kok, T. Nicklas, D. T. Roth, and C. M. Hays. Tübingen: Mohr Siebeck, 2014.

White, B. L. *Remembering Paul: Ancient and Modern Contests over the Image of the Apostle*. Oxford: Oxford University Press, 2014.

White, L. M. *From Jesus to Christianity*. San Francisco: Harper, 2004.

Wilhite, S. J. *The Didache: An Introductory Commentary*. AFCS. Eugene: Cascade, 2019.

Wilhite, S. J. *"One of Life and One of Death": Apocalypticism and the Didache's Two Ways*. Gorgias Studies in Early Christianity and Patristics 70. Piscataway, NJ: Gorgias, 2019.

Wilhite, S. J. "'That We Too Might Be Imitators of Him': The *Martyrdom of Polycarp* as *Imitatio Christi*." *Churchman* 129 (2015): 319–36.

Williams, A. L. "The Date of the Epistle of Barnabas." *JTS* 34 (1933): 337–46.

Williams, A. L. *Adversus Judaeos: A Bird's-Eye View of Christian Apologiae Until the Renaissance*. Cambridge Library Collection. Cambridge: Cambridge University Press, 1935.

Williams, D. H. *Defending and Defining the Faith: An Introduction to Early Christian Apologetic Literature*. Oxford: Oxford University Press, 2020.

Willis, W. "Martyr Eschatology: Ignatius' Use of *Epitugchanō*." *ResQ* 10 (1967): 81–88.

Windisch, H. *Der Barnabasbrief*. HNT Ergänzungsband, Die Apostolischen Väter 3. Tübingen: Möhr Siebeck, 1920.

Yarbrough, R. W. "The Date of Papias: A Reassessment." *JETS* 26 (1983): 181–91.

Young, F. M. "Greek Apologists of the Second Century." Pages 81–104 in *Apologetics in the Roman Empire: Pagans, Jews and Christians*. Edited by M. Edwards, M. Goodman, and S. Price, with C. Rowland. Oxford: Oxford University Press, 1999.

Young, S. "Being a Man: Pursuit of Manliness in *The Shepherd of Hermas*." *JECS* 2 (1994): 237–55.

Yuh, J. N. "Do as I Say, Not as They Do: Social Construction in the Epistle of Barnabas Through Canonical Interpretation and Ritual." *HTR* 112 (2019): 273–95.

Zahn, T. *Ignatius von Antiochien*. Gotha: Perthes, 1873.

Zelyck, L. "Irenaeus and the Authorship of the Fourth Gospel." Pages 239–58 in *The Origins of John's Gospel*. Edited by S. E. Porter and H. T. Ong. Leiden: Brill, 2016.

Zetterholm, M. *The Formation of Christianity in Antioch: A Social-Scientific Approach to the Separation Between Judaism and Christianity*. London: Routledge, 2003.

Zimbalist, B. "Comparative Hagiology and/as Manuscript Studies: Method and Materiality." *Religions* 10 (2019): 2–6.

Zizioulos, J. D. *Eucharist, Bishop, Church: The Unity of the Church in the Divine Eucharist and the Bishop During the First Three Centuries*. Translated by E. Theokritoff. Brookline, MA: Holy Cross Orthodox Press, 2001.

Zuiddam, B. A. "Other Letters of a Martyr? The Vossian Recension of Ignatius Reconsidered." *Ekklesiastikos Pharos* 92 (2010): 181–93.

SCRIPTURE AND OTHER ANCIENT LITERATURE INDEX

Romans

1 Corinthians

2 Corinthians

Galatians

2 Timothy

Titus

Philemon

Hebrews

James

1 Peter

2 Clement

Didache

Barnabas

To the Philadelphians

To Polycarp

To the Romans

Martyrdom of Polycarp

Polycarp

To the Philippians

Shepherd of Hermas

Mandates

Similitudes

Visions

ARTIFACTS, INSCRIPTIONS, PAPYRI

SUBJECT INDEX

AUTHOR INDEX